WILEY

IAS
2000

Interpretation and Application of
**INTERNATIONAL
ACCOUNTING STANDARDS
2000**

SUBSCRIPTION NOTICE

This Wiley product is updated on an annual basis to reflect important changes in the subject matter. If you purchased this product directly from John Wiley & Sons, Inc., we have already recorded your subscription for this annual service.

If, however, you purchased this product from a bookstore and wish to receive revised volumes billed separately with a 30-day examination review, please send your name, company name (if applicable), address, and the title of the product to:

Supplement Department
John Wiley & Sons, Inc.
One Wiley Drive
Somerset, NJ 08875
1-800-225-5945

For customers outside the United States, please contact the Wiley office nearest you:

Professional & Reference Division
John Wiley & Sons Canada, Ltd.
22 Worcester Road
Rexdale, Ontario M9W 1L1
CANADA
(416) 675-3580
1-800-567-4797
FAX (416) 675-6599

John Wiley & Sons Australia, Ltd.
PRT Division
P.O. Box 174
North Ryde, NSW 2113
AUSTRALIA
(02) 805-1100
FAX (02) 805-1597

John Wiley & Sons Ltd.
Baffins Lane
Chichester
West Sussex, PO19 1UD
UNITED KINGDOM
(44) (243) 779777

John Wiley & Sons (SEA) Pte. Ltd.
37 Jalan Pemimpin
Block B # 05-04
Union Industrial Building
SINGAPORE 2057
(65) 258-1157

WILEY

IAS
2000

Interpretation and Application of
**INTERNATIONAL
ACCOUNTING STANDARDS
2000**

Barry J. Epstein
Abbas Ali Mirza
Forewords by Aki Fujinuma and Sir Bryan Carsberg

JOHN WILEY & SONS, INC.
New York • Chichester • Weinheim • Brisbane • Singapore • Toronto

CONTENTS

FOREWORD 2000

It is astonishing to learn that International Accounting Standards (IAS) have now been widely recognized and accepted in many countries all over the world. For instance, a special television program was recently broadcast in Japan covering the new accounting rules which were developed based on IAS and their impact on corporate financial reporting in Japan. It is almost incredible that a topic such as IAS would even be covered in such a Japanese television program.

This means that the need for transparent, internationally comparable financial reporting has been recognized in society along with the globalization of the world economy. The globalized business community requires comprehensive and transparent accounting practices consistent across borders.

The primary purpose of implementing IAS is to provide benchmark accounting standards to the users and preparers of financial statements.

The first benefit is that comparable and transparent financial information helps in the making of informed decisions which, in turn, means reduced risk for investors. This will benefit everyone who participates in the market.

The second benefit is that transitional and emerging economies regard IAS as an efficient way of conforming to global norms, because they can avoid creating burdensome national standard-setting bodies of their own.

Other benefits brought about by the widespread acceptance of IAS include relieving the preparers of financial statements of the task of preparing multiple sets of statements to meet differing standards.

Accounting is in the spotlight at the moment, but auditing and uniform auditing standards are also important because they relate to the very heart of our profession, the reliability and credibility of a set of financial statements.

Audits are to be performed based on International Standards on Auditing (ISA) developed by the IFAC. The relationship between "accounting" and "auditing" is as close as "bread and butter"--the two are inseparable.

IAS 2000 by Barry Epstein and Abbas Ali Mirza first came to my attention during the Global Accounting Standards Forum held in the autumn of 1998 in Mumbai and Dubai where I met its coauthor, Abbas Ali Mirza.

It is "reader friendly" in that it is easy to use as a textbook or reference book on IAS. The reader may be able to expand his or her understanding of US GAAP as well. Accordingly, this book will be read not only by professional accountants but also by corporate accountants, financial analysts, regulators, students, and many others.

The fourth edition of *IAS 2000* includes the entire "core set of standards" which IASC agreed with IOSCO to be completed by 1998. Considering the expected endorsement of IAS by IOSCO in the near future, the publication of this book is most timely.

I congratulate the authors for their contributions and wish them every success.

Tsuguoki Fujinama
Deputy President
International Federation of Accountants

September 22, 1999

FOREWORD TO THE 1997 EDITION

The International Accounting Standards Committee (IASC) has been working for 23 years to develop a set of accounting standards which can be used to bring about uniformity in financial reporting around the world. Uniform accounting will reduce the costs of preparing financial statements for multinational companies and, perhaps more importantly, facilitate the jobs of investment analysts, investors, and other users in assessing business results.

This has always been recognized as a good idea, but it has been surprisingly long in yielding fruit. Only in the last few years have the benefits of global uniformity become sufficiently important to override domestic concerns. The last year or two has seen remarkable changes in the world for cross-border exchange listings, but there are three very important exceptions: the stock exchanges of Canada, Japan, and the United States. An agreement made with IOSCO, the international organization of the securities regulators, in July 1995 will lead to completion of the core set of International Accounting Standards which we plan by 1998. IOSCO has said that this will clear the way for their endorsement of International Accounting Standards, after which we hope that the standards will be accepted universally for the purposes of cross-border listings. The SEC in the United States has said that it supports our objectives and will work with IOSCO to help achieve this goal.

Similar good progress has been seen in Europe. The European Commission now regards International Accounting Standards as the way to harmonize accounting in the European Union. France is moving ahead in a dramatic way by introducing a new law which will provide for the recognition of International Accounting Standards for domestic use in France as well as overseas by French companies. IASC must play its part by completing good quality standards on a timely basis.

As a standard-setting body makes progress towards widespread acceptance and use of its standards in practice, so interest increases in understanding those standards, acquiring expertise in using them, and conducting research into their merits and effects. Textbooks are needed, conferences must be held, and university teachers must undertake research projects. All of these beneficial developments are well underway for International Accounting Standards. This book by Barry Jay Epstein and Abbas Ali Mirza is one of the pioneers in the textbook field. I wish it success. The need for it is great.

> Sir Bryan Carsberg
> Secretary General
> International Accounting Standards
> Committee (IASC)
>
> September 18, 1996

ACKNOWLEDGEMENTS

The authors are indebted to the many individuals who have inspired us to undertake this project and who have assisted us in bringing it to completion. This project had its inception in a series of conferences held in the Middle East in 1994 and 1995, which were cosponsored by a major public accounting firm, Talal Abu-Ghazaleh & Co. (TAGCO), with substantial support from the International Accounting Standards Committee. The authors express their gratitude particularly to Mr. Talal Abu-Ghazaleh and to Sir Bryan Carsberg, currently the secretary general of the IASC, for their ongoing support. We also appreciate the assistance of Qusay Abu-Ghazaleh and Hazem Farah, both of TAGCO, and of IASC board member Rolf Rundfelt of KPMG in Stockholm, Sweden. Mr. Abbas Ali Mirza expresses thanks to Graham Martins (PKF, United Arab Emirates), his father Ali Mirza, and his brother Dr. Hume Mirza for editorial assistance; to Bahadur Chacha for inspiration and moral support, and to his mother. Dr. Barry Epstein acknowledges the substantial copy editing contributions to the first edition of this book by his daughter, Brett Jocelyn Epstein, whose career intentions also include professional writing. Of course, the authors are very grateful to the production staff at John Wiley's DeKalb, Illinois, facility for their careful and timely efforts, and to the John Wiley editors in New York.

ABOUT THE AUTHORS

Barry J. Epstein, PhD, CPA, has been affiliated with several regional and national CPA firms over the past 25 years. He is currently a partner in the Chicago-based firm Gleeson, Sklar, Sawyers & Cumpata, LLP, where he specializes in accounting and auditing technical consultation and litigation consulting services. His work in the litigation field involves accountants' malpractice defense, contractual dispute resolution, and other matters in which the application of professional standards plays a significant role. Previously, Dr. Epstein had been director of quality control for several firms over a span of 15 years, and has been substantially engaged in administrative matters. Earlier, he taught at the university level and also served as a financial executive at a Fortune 250 corporation. Dr. Epstein has authored or coauthored six books and several professional articles, and previously wrote a regular business column for a major newspaper. He has served on numerous state and local professional and technical committees, was a member of the AICPA Board of Examiners for 5 years, has lectured throughout the US, as well as in Canada and the Middle East, and has been regularly involved in technical training for his firms and other professionals. Dr. Epstein holds a PhD from the University of Pittsburgh, an MBA from the University of Chicago, and a BSC from DePaul University. He is a member of the American Institute of CPAs, Illinois CPA Society, and the American Accounting Association.

Abbas Ali Mirza, ACA, AICWA, CPA, has had a distinguished career in the fields of auditing, finance, and taxation, and has worked for major international accounting firms around the globe including the United States of America and the Middle East. His diversified international auditing experience encompasses many industries and businesses. Currently, he is a director with a major international firm of chartered accountants, Pannell Kerr Forster, PKF, locally Ratan Mama & Co., with responsibilities for the Middle East (United Arab Emirates and Sultanate of Oman) and India. Through his previous Middle Eastern accounting and auditing experience as Director for Professional Development of a major Middle Eastern CPA firm, where he was responsible for quality assurance and technical support on complex accounting and auditing issues to the firm's 35 offices in 22 countries, he pioneered the practical application of International Accounting Standards. While in the United States of America, he worked for well-known CPA firms in Chicago and New York. He is a frequent principal speaker and a workshop leader at global conferences on International Accounting Standards and "US GAAP." He has traveled worldwide to address and/or attend major international conferences where he shared the forum with world-class speakers including standard setters from as far afield as Europe, Asia, and Australia. He is widely published in international accounting journals and is well-known in the Middle East as a columnist for a leading English newspaper. He is in the forefront of the international accounting movement in the Middle East. Recently he was co-opted on the Technical Standards Committee of the official Accountants and Auditors Association of the United Arab Emirates.

1 INTRODUCTION TO INTERNATIONAL ACCOUNTING STANDARDS

NEED FOR ACCOUNTING STANDARDS

Development of accounting and financial reporting. Accounting was created as a tool to aid in measuring economic activity. Renaissance-era monk Fra Luca Pacioli is normally credited with the invention of double entry bookkeeping, designed for trading accounts in Italian city-states of the fourteenth and fifteenth centuries. From these origins, double entry bookkeeping can be traced to Germany and France, and then to Britain, where it proliferated due to the dominant world commercial position held by the British Empire during the seventeenth and eighteenth centuries. British investments into the insurance and railroad industries of North America and Commonwealth countries brought about the accounting influence evident even today. Similarly, during this same era, Dutch accounting followed the discoveries and settlements made in Indonesia and South Africa. Other patterns of influence can be traced from their European origins throughout the world, as from Spain to Latin American nations. Later, with its economic ascendancy, the United States became the prime developer of accounting theory and exported its financial reporting model around the globe.

The evolution of accounting in various countries has inevitably led to different practices and regulations. As the economic systems and trading conditions vary from one country to another, so do the accounting models and methods. Factors influencing these variations include the degree of centralization in the economy, ranging from state control to unfettered free enterprise; the nature of economic activity, from simple agrarian societies to the most sophisticated and complex business enterprises; the stage of economic development, from emerging economies to fully matured postindustrial ones; the pattern and rate of economic growth, ranging from stagnation to the explosive growth of certain Asian economies; and the stability of the local currency, which connotes the inflationary experience of the local economy.

In addition to the economic system differences, disparate legal systems have had a profound effect on the approach to accounting and financial reporting. These are addressed in the following section.

Accounting and reporting models. Whatever the economic and legal system, in virtually every country in the free world there is some degree of regulation of the accounting profession by either government regulatory bodies or professional societies, or by both. The overall result is a complex agglomeration of laws, rules, and standards. In understanding the evolution of accounting principles, and the present and projected future state of those systems of reporting requirements, it is useful to review the factors that have led to the different approaches to accounting and reporting theory and regulations.

It is not the objective of this book to present a detailed comparison of accounting practices among the nations of the world. Rather, the focus will be on the rapidly evolving area of international accounting standards, which have the potential to eclipse the national standards of most of the world's developed and developing countries, eventually even those of the United States and the United Kingdom. (However, it must be appreciated that the international standards issued to date have been heavily based on US and UK standards.) The following abbreviated discussion, then, is intended merely to set the stage for the body of this book, which is a detailed consideration of the international standards.

Among the more developed countries of the world, there are two distinct types of regulatory environments, which in turn have fostered two different paths of evolution of accounting theory and practice. While there is a vast range of differences even within these groupings, it seems that a key distinction has been between those countries that have had a **common law** custom versus those that have followed a **code law** tradition. Those nations that have codified many rules of behavior have tended to formally prescribe accounting and financial reporting matters as well, and most often the role of financial reporting has been made subservient to the taxing system of the country. The Napoleonic Code is the universally referenced model of code law, and indeed most of the nations that were dominated by France during the reign of Napoleon subscribe to this approach.

The polar opposite to the code law approach and the analogous process of setting financial reporting standards by governmental actions is the common law tradition exemplified by England and those nations, including the United States, which were influenced by Great Britain. Whereas code law countries tend to prescribe what must be done, common law nations tend to be permissive until rulings are made regarding actions that cannot be taken, such as those proscribing fraudulent financial reporting. Common law countries tend not to define financial reporting requirements in their national laws, and the rules that have developed are largely those of the private sector, having over time been established by practitioners working through their professional societies, as well as by the labors of academicians. In common law countries, the goals of financial reporting are often at variance with those of national tax policy.

In addition to the code law versus common law dichotomy, there are other factors that have played roles in the manner in which the accounting professions and accounting and financial reporting rules have developed in various nations. Among these are the tradition of free enterprise versus centrally planned economies, the respective nations' experiences with price instability, and the extent to which the respective economies have developed and have fostered the growth of large-scale, complex business organizations.

A nation's tradition of free enterprise has historically been important to the development of accounting rules and of the profession of accounting. Nations that had thriving trading cultures hundreds of years ago, such as England and the Netherlands, not surprisingly had early needs for meaningful financial reporting. It is arguable whether the trading culture encouraged the development of accounting or whether the evolution of financial reporting encouraged the growth of business enterprises (both are probably true to a great extent), but clearly the profession flourished first in these environments. At the opposite extreme, nations that at one time had a Communist economic system had far less reason to focus on the development of financial reporting models, since production quotas, not enterprise economic performance, were of greater concern to central planners.

Experience with changing prices has also significantly influenced the development of accounting and financial reporting. The virtues of historical cost-based financial reporting (objectivity, reliability) have been most impressive in the context of price stability, but when prices are rapidly changing, these traits become less important than the characteristics exhibited by inflation-adjusted reporting (greater decision relevance, understandability, comparability). Nations that have had long histories of price instability (notably, Latin American countries) have been more supportive of departures from historical cost financial reporting, although none of the assorted approaches to financial reporting adjusted on the basis of general price level and specific price (current replacement cost) have been entirely satisfactory, and many even believe that the very fact that reported financial results are often adjusted contributes to these nations' inability to achieve a stable price regime. It is interesting to note that even those nations which traditionally have experienced relative price stability (e.g., the United States and the United Kingdom), have witnessed sporadic episodes of double-digit inflation (such as occurred during the 1920s and 1970s) accompanied by calls for and experiments with inflation-adjusted financial reporting, but as soon as price stability was reestablished, this interest waned dramatically.

Finally, those nations that have witnessed the growth of large and complex business organizations, particularly when accompanied by absentee ownership, have also seen the rise of the accounting profession and the development of more comprehensive theories of financial reporting. Large multinational companies tend to be headquartered in nations that have skilled labor forces, including professional accountants, and are subject to accounting rules established in those jurisdictions. Besides the United States and the United Kingdom, the countries of western Europe and Japan have the highest concentration of these characteristics.

Taking the foregoing factors together, one can conclude that there is a basic dichotomy between historically code law nations having governmentally sanctioned accounting and reporting rules heavily oriented toward tax compliance, and common law nations having accounting rules developed essentially in the private sector and not contrived to serve the government's fiscal objectives. This is further modified by other factors that, to greater or lesser degrees, encourage the development of comprehensive models of financial reporting that may or may not address the lack of price stability in the economy. This leads to a classification scheme that places the United States and the United Kingdom in one category; the nations of western, continental Europe (possibly including Japan) in another; the formerly communist nations of eastern Europe, including the former USSR, in yet another; and developing (third world) nations in a final category.

Setting accounting standards. The standard-setting process has proceeded by varying routes in the major nations of the developed world. To illustrate this thesis briefly, consider the United States, the United Kingdom, Germany, France, Japan, and several Latin American nations. The United States and the United Kingdom have been influenced by the same traditions of common law, capitalism, highly educated and professional work forces, large and sophisticated companies that raise equity capital in the public markets, and a belief in the responsibility of managements to report on their stewardship to the owners of the respective businesses. The early development of accounting theory, and the first flowering of the public accounting profession, took place in the United Kingdom, with most of the earliest US firms being offshoots of British ones.

The principle of full disclosure is very important in both the United States and the United Kingdom. Financial statements are expected to be transparent, so that the users, generally assumed to be investors and creditors, are able to understand fully the nature of the reporting enterprise's operations and finances. Rules are largely established by the profession itself (even when, as in the United States, the government has some statutory authority to establish accounting principles), and tax reporting is a distinct and separate matter, which does not drive financial reporting.

Accounting principles in the United Kingdom are established largely in the private sector, with enabling provisions being contained in the UK Companies Act of 1989. The present standard-setting structure actually dates only from 1990, replacing an earlier structure that was in place for 20 years. While there is due process, there is less openness to the opinions of interested parties outside the accountancy profession, and there is no British equivalent to the American Securities and Exchange Commission having a statutory oversight role. However, the Financial Reporting Review Panel (FRRP) in the UK does examine financial statements in order to determine whether there has been a failure to provide a "true and fair view" as a result of a departure from an accounting standard. When such a departure from an accounting standard is identified, the FRRP can seek a revision of the financial statements. If the company does not agree to a revision recommended by the FRRP, it is empowered to apply to a court of law to seek an order compelling revision of the financial statements. The court, in ordering the revision, could also order the directors of the company to personally bear not only the legal costs but even the cost of revising the financial statements. This threat of personal liability is perhaps unique, and could serve as a strong deterrent for directors of a company from non-compliance with the directions of the FRRP.

The main distinction between UK and US accounting is that there are many legal and institutional regulations that apply only to public companies in the UK (in the United States, the only accounting rules that are limited to public companies under current generally accepted accounting principles [GAAP] are those related to segment reporting and earnings per share). This is said to be a reflection of the historical development of accounting as a mechanism to protect shareholders, which still drives much of the standard-setting process in the United Kingdom.

Apart from the foregoing distinctions and the fact that the Companies Act dictates the formats in which financial statements may be presented, the British accounting model is very similar to that of the United States. This is not unexpected, given that both derived from almost identical traditions.

Standard setting in the United States is also in the private sector, although the public markets regulator, the Securities and Exchange Commission (the SEC) has statutory authority to establish GAAP for public companies, which it has virtually never exercised, although supplementary disclosures have been required and other interpretive guidance has been issued from time to time. For the past 25 years the Financial Accounting Standards Board (the FASB) has been the primary US accounting standard setter, with a lesser role still being played by the American Institute of Certified Public Accountants (the AICPA). The FASB was created as a full-time body to remedy the perceived inadequacies of its predecessor, the part-time Accounting Principles Board (the APB), which also suffered a diminished credibility by being a creature of the AICPA, which is the body representing the auditing profession. Since the advent of the FASB, the responsibility for setting accounting standards has been divorced from the process of making auditing rules.

US GAAP contains by far the largest number of specific rules, currently comprising several accounting research bulletins, 31 APB opinions, 137 FASB statements, and scores of interpretations and technical bulletins, statements of position, and accounting guides issued by the AICPA, as well as other relevant professional literature. The International Accounting Standards Committee (the IASC) has stated that it has no intention of trying to duplicate this body of guidance, and indeed, subscribes to a philosophy of providing general guidance rather than detailed standards addressing every nuance of business practice. There are many who believe that the troubles experienced by accountants in recent years, particularly the explosion of litigation against them, can be traced to the attempt (doomed to fail, some would argue) to establish specific guidance for a vast array of transactions and events. The IASC has determined not to follow that course of action.

General purpose financial reporting in the United States, as in the United Kingdom, is intended to serve the needs of investors, lenders, and other interested parties, that can also include regulatory authorities. However, there is no pretense that GAAP will measure taxable income, and indeed the reason for deferred income tax accounting is that tax reporting will almost always differ from financial reporting prepared in conformity with GAAP.

As compared with the United States and the United Kingdom, countries in Europe, plus Japan, have capitalist economic systems that rely far less on public equity markets and much more on bank financing. The relationships between the borrowers and lenders are much closer than those that generally exist between companies and their equity investors, as there are typically far fewer lenders than stockholders, and each lender has a much greater stake in the outcome of events than do passive investors. Thus, there is greater ability to obtain information informally: that is, key lenders can demand information from their borrowers at will, and are not limited by what disclosures are mandated by accounting standards, or by the frequency with which financial reporting is made to shareholders. The implication is that accounting rules are of less importance in these environments.

Both France and Germany have code law traditions, and in both nations the private sector accounting profession has limited influence on the development of accounting and financial reporting requirements. Financial reporting is dictated by law, which makes some distinctions between large or publicly held companies and small or privately held ones. The French system is very similar to the German, in fact, having been substantially influenced by the German during the World War II occupation. Furthermore, most of the basic underlying concepts, such as accrual basis accounting and the going concern assumption, are identical with those recognized by US and UK GAAP.

As an illustration of the sharp differences between UK and US accounting on the one hand, and French and German reporting on the other, consider the topic of interperiod tax allocation. Although the concepts of deferred income taxes are recognized in both France and Germany, there are few instances in which material amounts of deferred taxes appear on balance sheets, since most tax deductions are conditioned on the item being expensed currently for financial reporting purposes. To the limited extent that deferred taxes are provided, the deferred method is more commonly employed in France, while the liability approach is required in Germany.

As another example, consider the provision of **reserves**. In both of these nations, regulations exist to require that a defined percentage of earnings (currently 5%) be appropriated to a legal reserve account, until that account (shown in stockholders' equity) equals a defined amount (10% of share capital in France, 10% of the par value of share capital in Germany, in general). While these are allocations from earnings, and not charges against profits, per se, they do communicate that some fraction of earnings is, in a sense, not available currently to shareholders. Furthermore, especially in Germany, where accrual (by charges against earnings) of contingencies is governed by the concept of prudence, it is well known that earnings tend to be very conservatively stated even before the reserve appropriation is made. Thus, while it may be said that general contingency reserves, long prohibited in the US and many other nations, are also not permitted in France and Germany, nonetheless the overall effect of the conservative, prudent accounting which is subscribed to in both nations, plus the impact of providing so-called legal reserves, does tend to imply a greater tolerance for some degree of income smoothing. The goal of creditor protection, while possibly a worthy one, particularly given the historical dependence on debt financing in both France and Germany, leads to an understatement, in many cases, of net equity available to shareholders.

Japanese financial reporting rules were originally modeled after German accounting, as a result of the close association between those two nations in the first half of this century, although more recently they have been influenced by US standards. The overriding concern is with creditor protection, since most financing is provided by large commercial banks, not by individual shareholders. Japanese society is structured to be focused far more on the collective good, and this value system has also affected financial accounting. For example, accounting procedures to achieve income smoothing are tolerated if they can be shown to contribute to the success of the business enterprise over the long term, as that would tend to benefit society at large.

Despite the postwar influence of the United States, which dictated the structure of its public accounting profession, Japanese accounting and financial reporting continues to follow the European model closely. Thus statutory reserves are provided, thereby reducing reported profits from what would be acknowledged under US or UK GAAP. Prudence (i.e., conservatism) is the most significant concept underlying Japanese accounting principles. There is a high degree of correlation between tax reporting and financial accounting, and thus deferred tax accounting is not typically an issue.

Although the nations of Central and South America which were colonized and culturally influenced by Spain or Portugal employ financial reporting very similar to those of European nations, a major distinction is that the historical cost model is held in less reverence. This is the obvious result of many decades' experience with high levels of price inflation in most Latin American nations. Argentina, Bolivia, Brazil, and Chile require that financial statements be restated comprehensively to compensate for changes in the general price level. Certain Latin American nations require periodic revaluations of plant assets, which other countries permit on an elective basis.

Frequent currency devaluations, coupled with wage and other contractual agreements that call for automatic adjustments for the impact of changes in the general level of prices, have perhaps desensitized the public to the ravages of inflation and thus contributed to the rampant inflation experienced by many of these nations throughout the post-World War II era. Ill-advised government fiscal and monetary policies have contributed to the pervasiveness of this problem. The intractability of inflation has even led to acceptance of revaluations of plant assets as a basis for computing tax depreciation in a few Latin American nations, including Bolivia and Brazil. In general, tax policies are given the greatest consideration in the setting of financial reporting requirements, and the needs of government economic planners are viewed as more important than those of either stockholders or creditors.

Need for International Accounting Standards

While differing national traditions and experiences led to the development of alternative financial reporting models, the pressures for intensified development in the global environment have been evident as the needs of the ever-changing economy demand international harmonization. Major changes in business practices following World War II have led to demands for the internationalization of accounting and auditing practices. These changes are found principally in the evolution of multinational enterprises and, more recently, international capital markets. From these flow numerous professional practice issues.

Multinational companies (MNC) have grown dramatically and over the past 25 years have assumed a dominant role in many market segments, affecting almost every country, every government, and every person. From an accounting perspective, the complexity of conducting international business operations across national borders, each with a different set of business regulations and often different accounting methods, presents a daunting challenge for accountants and the professional bodies that establish accounting and auditing rules. Some of the significant complexities confronting international accountants are caused by the nature of the huge multinational enterprises themselves. The diversity of applicable accounting, auditing, and tax rules may affect the enterprise's ability to prepare reliable financial information necessary for a careful analysis of investment opportunities. As the number of countries of activity increases, so does the complexity.

There are some national differences in accounting and reporting approaches that should be addressed. A prime example is the complaint of many US companies about the competitive disadvantage that results from the US rules regarding accounting for goodwill. Entities complying with accounting standards of most European countries, including the United Kingdom, do not need to amortize goodwill, because it can be charged directly against shareholders' equity at the date of the business acquisition. Other international accounting and reporting matters, such as inflation accounting adjustments, deferred tax accounting, and translation of foreign subsidiaries' financial statements, also create disadvantages for some companies, and the persistence of these differences puts pressure on standard setters to work harder to achieve a "level playing field."

The globalization of capital markets has also contributed to the need to address harmonization of financial reporting requirements. Capital needs were once supplied almost exclusively from domestic sources, especially in the pre-World War II era. However, since that time, and especially as a result of major international economic assistance programs after the war, there has been a significant growth and development of international capital markets. There are now highly developed Eurodollar, Eurocurrency, and Asia-dollar capital markets in the developed world economies, especially those in the United States, the United Kingdom, Japan, and parts of Europe. That the financial marketplace is now global is abundantly evident from the October 1987 stock market crash, in which all major markets plunged by similar magnitudes.

This vast global capital market needs, but does not yet have, a common accounting "language" for the communication of financial information. Recognition of this need is another significant influence and a major force in the development of, and progress toward, internationalized accounting and auditing standards. Without this "common language" there is some doubt that given diverse national standards, a truly efficient international market will develop, and this may impair the ability of capital-seeking corporations to compete effectively for the capital otherwise available in the world markets.

National securities regulators, as well as the International Organization of Securities Commissioners (IOSCO), an organization of securities regulators promoting international coordination, have recently given increased support to the need for improved international accounting standards, and therefore to the IASC's harmonization proposal. As discussed elsewhere in this chapter, the IASC-IOSCO agreement promises greatly increased support for harmonization once the endorsement by the IOSCO of the IASC's comprehensive core set of standards, completed in 1998, is received. Given the obvious need for global harmonization of financial reporting practices, if not outright uniformity of generally accepted accounting principles, the importance of the IASC's efforts can readily be appreciated.

The International Accounting Standards Committee

The International Accounting Standards Committee was founded in 1973 by representatives of professional bodies in Australia, Canada, France, Germany, Japan, Mexico, the Netherlands, the United Kingdom, Ireland, and the United States, and presently includes representatives from 91 countries. Since 1983, the IASC's members have included all the professional accountancy bodies that are members of the International Federation of Accountants (IFAC) which, as of January 1999, comprised 142 member bodies in 103 countries, representing over 2 million accountants.

Since its formation, the IASC has engaged in a standard-setting program that has now gained worldwide recognition. IASC has issued 39 international accounting standards (IAS), of which 34 remain in force (five standards having been superseded by later pronouncements). A number of these standards are now in their second iteration, as a major project undertaken to revise the standards, principally to eliminate some previously acceptable alternative treatments and to update certain of the standards (most notably, to substitute cash flow reporting for funds flow statements), was largely completed in 1994. Also issued to date have been a conceptual release on the *Framework for the Preparation and Presentation of Financial Statements* and a number of exposure drafts (at least one of which preceded the final issuance of each standard). Two exposure drafts are outstanding as of late 1999, dealing with agriculture and with investment properties (these are addressed in the relevant chapters of this book).

The *Framework*, which was issued in 1989, was intended to be the IASC's conceptual foundation upon which later accounting standards would be built, and it has largely served this purpose. This document identifies the expected beneficiaries of financial reporting, the objective of the reporting process, the key underlying assumptions (going concern and accrual basis), the qualitative characteristics of financial statements (the primary ones being understandability, relevance, reliability, and comparability; there are a number of secondary ones as well), and the elements of the financial statements (assets, liabilities, equity, income, and expenses). It also sets forth the twin criteria for recognition of an item in the financial statements (the probability that the economic benefits associated with it will flow to or from the entity, and the reliability of measurement of the item).

Objectives and approach to standard setting (the IASC's "due process"). The objectives of IASC, as set forth in its constitution, are twofold. The first is to formulate and publish in the public interest accounting standards to be observed in the presentation of financial statements and to promote their worldwide acceptance and observance. The second is to work generally for the improvement and harmonization of regulations, accounting standards, and procedures relating to the presentation of financial statements.

Recognizing that differing accounting principles on a given subject exist in different countries, and that there are many accounting subjects which have not even been addressed in some jurisdictions, the IASC decided on a multipronged approach designed to serve the largest possible audience. The IASC has employed a range of strategies, including

1. Urging member bodies to invite IASC to participate whenever two or more countries that do not share common legislation are proposing to hold discussions on accounting standards;
2. Encouraging countries that have not previously established national accounting standards to adopt International Accounting Standards (IAS) as the country's own standards;
3. Inviting other countries, which may have some national standards but none on particular topics, to adapt IAS as a basis for a national standard on a particular subject, guaranteeing a certain level of quality and compatibility

for the particular standard, and reducing both the time and the development costs required to produce a national standard;

4. Suggesting that where national standards already exist, countries compare them with IAS and seek to eliminate any material differences; and

5. Endeavoring to demonstrate for those countries where the framework of accounting practice is contained in law the benefits of harmonization with IAS.

To accommodate such diverse approaches, the IASC has strived to deal mostly with broad principles and to avoid excessive details. The result is that the IAS seem avant-garde in some countries (primarily those without their own extensive national standards) but elementary in others (particularly the United States and the United Kingdom, which have fully developed systems of generally accepted accounting principles). The goal is, however, to filter out unsound practices over a period of time, recognizing the evolutionary nature of the task and the challenges that are to be faced in the process. Recently, there has been a trend toward including more detailed guidance in the IAS, largely in response to IOSCO demands (which in turn are heavily influenced by the US standard setter, the FASB, and the US securities regulator, the SEC) for a comprehensive "core set of standards" with consistent interpretation and application. While the attempt to accommodate IOSCO's wishes has forced the IASC to deviate somewhat from its historical practice and stated philosophy, achieving IOSCO endorsement of the IAS is of such importance that this has been done with few recriminations or regrets.

The IASC follows a program of due process for all of its projects. After a project is placed on the work program by the IASC Board, there typically will be the appointment of a steering committee (chaired by a board member, but staffed by representatives of accountancy bodies or other organizations involved in the standard-setting process), which will oversee the project. A "point outline" will be developed by the steering committee for Board consideration; this often will be a compendium of the various practices found worldwide for dealing with the subject of the project. Based on this outline, a "draft statement of principles" or other "discussion document" will be developed and circulated for public comment during the exposure period, usually around 3 months, after which a final statement of principles will be adopted. This final statement, while not published but available to the public on request, guides the steering committee as it develops the exposure draft of its proposed standard. If the exposure draft receives a favorable reception by the IASC (a two-thirds positive vote is required), then it is exposed for public comment during an exposure period from 1 to 3 months. After any comments are fully deliberated by both the steering committee and the Board, there may be a revised exposure draft issued, or the final standard will be prepared based on the comments received. Ratification of a new standard requires favorable votes by three-fourths of the Board.

Stages of Development in the International Accounting Standard-Setting Process

Reviewing the history of the IASC, it is possible to identify three stages through which it has passed in its development as a standard-setting body. These are, respectively, the early years of attempting to demonstrate attention to all the major accounting issues; the middle period of consolidation, when allowable alternative treatments were reduced as part of the effort to improve comparability; and the current era, when the core set of standards necessary to obtain the support of the international capital markets is being completed.

The stages through which the international standard-setting process has progressed are indicated by the history of the standards that have been issued to date. The first phase represented an attempt to establish a common body of standards on major topics, such as accounting for inventory, for leases, and for long-lived assets. Essentially (although the IASC might not care to admit to this) the strategy was to endorse virtually all the mainstream methods used in any of the major nations of the world. This "lowest common denominator" approach resulted in the promulgation of a number of standards that permitted the application of diverse accounting principles to similar fact situations, without necessarily setting forth any clear conceptual basis for allowing these alternative treatments. However, despite the limited achievement this represented, it did serve to establish the IASC's legitimacy as a transnational standard-setting body, albeit one without any enforcement mechanism.

The second phase in the IASC's evolution was marked by the Comparability/ Improvements Project which began with the release of Exposure Draft 32, *Comparability of Financial Statements*, in 1989, and concluded with the promulgation of 10 revised standards that took effect in 1995. The objective of this project was to narrow the range of the acceptable accounting treatments that could be brought to bear upon given fact situations. The project was a qualified success, as indeed the number of acceptable alternatives was reduced, although perhaps too many alternatives still remained available even when the project had been completed.

This experience reveals the very difficult task faced by the IASC, as a body whose only tool has been moral suasion. For example, in taking up the question of inventory accounting, which had been dealt with by IAS 2, which had granted financial statement preparers free choice among the FIFO, weighted-average, LIFO, and base stock costing methods, the IASC determined that the LIFO and base stock methods should be prohibited. However, in a number of countries, LIFO is both a popular method and one that depends on conformity between financial reporting and tax reporting (i.e., tax advantages are available only if published financial statements conform to the method used in the tax returns). As a result, the IASC found it necessary to accept the continued existence of LIFO, which was demoted to **allowed alternative** status, with FIFO and weighted-average cost flow assumptions becoming the **benchmarks**.

As a practical matter, there is no distinction between benchmark and alternative treatments, since reporting enterprises are not penalized for availing themselves of the alternatives. A proposal made by the IASC at the time the 10 revised standards were being developed--to require presentation of a reconciliation of net income to amounts that would have been produced by application of the benchmark standard-- was dropped. It should be noted, however, that in some cases, though this is extremely rare, an IASC standard may require disclosure of figures based on the benchmark treatment when the allowed treatment is used. For instance, under IAS 16, when items of property, plant, and equipment are stated at revalued amounts using the "allowed alternative treatment," the carrying amount of each class of property, plant and equipment that would have been included in the financial state- ments had the assets been carried under the "benchmark treatment" is required to be disclosed as well.

Notwithstanding the fact that the range of alternatives was not narrowed as much as might have been hoped, the Comparability/Improvements Project had its achievements. These accomplishments are summarized as follows:

IAS 2 Inventories

The base stock method was dropped and the LIFO method was relegated to allowed alternative status.

IAS 8 Net Profit or Loss for the Period, Fundamental Errors and Changes in Accounting Policies

The original standard addressed the reporting of unusual items, prior period items, and changes in accounting policies and accounting estimates. In the revised standard, benchmark and allowed alternative treatments are prescribed for correc- tion of what are called "fundamental" errors, with the benchmark involving adjust- ment of retained earnings and restatement of comparative prior periods, and the al- ternative being inclusion of the effect of the correction in current period income. The new standard also requires that extraordinary items be set forth separately on the face of the income statement, and the expanded disclosure of certain unusual items that are included in ordinary income (e.g., write-downs of inventories to net realizable values) and of discontinued operations. The effect of this revised stan- dard was to bring the international accounting standard into closer conformity with the US standard and to streamline financial statement disclosures.

IAS 9 Research and Development Costs

The original standard required expensing research costs but permitted either capitalization or expensing of defined development costs. The revised IAS 9 con- tinues to require expensing of all research costs but sets standards for capitalization of certain development costs. If certain conditions are met, the costs must be capi- talized and amortized; if not, they must be expensed at once. Thus, this revision did fully achieve the goal of eliminating alternative treatments. As part of its core set of standards project, the IASC has promulgated IAS 38, *Intangible Assets*, which has superseded IAS 9 and substantially requires the same accounting treatment as the erstwhile IAS 9.

IAS 11 Construction Contracts

The original standard permitted a free choice between percentage-of-completion and completed-contract methods of accounting, while the revised standard allows percentage-of-completion only. Once again, the goal of narrowing alternatives was fully achieved.

IAS 16 Property, Plant, and Equipment

The original standard permitted either historical cost or revalued amounts as the basis for reporting property, plant, and equipment; these remain in the revised standard, but historical cost is now designated as the benchmark treatment, with revalued amounts being relegated to the allowed alternative category. A number of other changes were also made, including incorporating the formerly separate guidance of IAS 4, *Depreciation Accounting,* and requiring that any revaluations be to fair value and that these be updated regularly (e.g., every 3 years). Although this revised standard offers guidance superior to its predecessor, it nonetheless still permits diverse accounting methods.

IAS 18 Revenue Recognition

Whereas the original standard permitted either percentage-of-completion or completed-contract accounting for recognition of revenue related to the rendering of services, in the revision only the percentage-of-completion method is allowed, if specified conditions are met.

IAS 19 Retirement Benefit Costs

Accounting for retirement benefits by employers was, and remains, a very complicated topic. In the original standard, the guidance was very general, essentially only demanding that costs be rationally allocated to the periods of benefit. This revised standard, on the other hand, is far more detailed but nonetheless still permits a range of methods, most notably defining the accrued benefit valuation method as the benchmark and the projected benefit method as the allowed alternative (contrasted to the US standard, SFAS 87, which mandates exclusive use of the projected benefit method alone). The revised standard also requires that actuarial valuations regarding projected salaries, past service costs, experience adjustments, and the effects of changes in actuarial assumptions be allocated to income on a systematic basis. It should be noted that yet another revision to this standard was undertaken by the IASC as part of the core set of standards project, under which program the revised standard was made more comprehensive and now deals with accounting treatment of not just retirement costs but other employee benefits as well. (The requirements of the latest revised standard, which eliminates the allowed alternative treatment of benefit costs, are discussed in detail in a later chapter.)

IAS 21 Effects of Changes in Foreign Exchange Rates

The revisions to this standard were rather modest in scope; certain choices relative to the deferral and amortization of exchange differences on long-term monetary items, on translation of income statements of foreign entities at the closing rate, and on translation of financial statements of foreign entities that report in the currency of a hyperinflationary economy without prior restatement, all were narrowed. Additional disclosures were also mandated by the revised standard. The revised standard largely duplicates the corresponding US standard, SFAS 52.

IAS 22 Accounting for Business Combinations

The revision more clearly defined which combinations (known as **acquisitions**) are to be accounted for using the purchase method and which (**unitings of interests**) must be accounted for by the pooling of interests method. The criteria for unitings are quite restrictive but are simpler than those in the parallel US standard, APB 16 (the latter defines 12 criteria that must all be met, while the former sets forth only 3). Furthermore, the revised IAS 22 prohibits the immediate write-off of goodwill against stockholders' equity that was allowed previously. On the other hand, the revised standard sets forth benchmark and allowed alternatives with regard to the measurement of minority interest and for the accounting for negative goodwill. Thus, alternative accounting for essentially identical events has not been eliminated completely.

IAS 23 Borrowing Costs

The original standard permitted either capitalization or expensing of borrowing costs incurred in connection with construction of assets, while the revision slightly alters this by defining expensing as the benchmark treatment and capitalization as the allowed alternative. This change is only a modest achievement, given that enterprises are under no real burden to conform to the benchmark treatment.

The IASC entered its third distinct phase of existence in 1995, when it embarked on its mission to complete what has been defined as the "comprehensive core set of standards." In a historic agreement with IOSCO, the IASC undertook to complete revisions of the set of standards which were deemed essential to IOSCO's willingness to consider endorsing the IAS for purposes of cross-border securities registrations by mid-1999 (later further accelerated to early 1998, and actually completed at the end of 1998).

Following are the terms of the IASC/IOSCO agreement:

> *The (IASC) Board has developed a work plan that the Technical Committee agrees will result, upon successful completion, in IAS comprising a comprehensive core set of standards. Completion of comprehensive core standards that are acceptable to the (IOSCO) Technical Committee will allow the Technical Committee to recommend endorsement of IAS for cross-border capital raising and listing purposes in all global markets. IOSCO has already endorsed IAS 7,* **Cash Flow Statements**, *and has indicated to the IASC that 14 of the existing international accounting standards do not require additional improvement, providing that the other core standards are successfully completed.*

The actual agreement between IASC and IOSCO had involved the formal acceptance of a work plan that set forth a number of projects to be completed on a targeted schedule. The standards that were addressed as part of this project included accounting for income taxes (which has since been achieved by revised IAS 12, issued in late 1996); financial instruments (which was divided into two projects: one on "disclosure and presentation," completed with the issuance of IAS 32 in 1995, and the second on "recognition and measurement," completed with the promulgation of IAS 39 at the end of 1998); earnings per share reporting (completed with the issuance of IAS 33 in mid-1997); segment reporting (revised IAS 14, issued in mid-1997); financial statement presentation (revised IAS 1, superseding IAS 1, 5, and 13, issued in mid-1997); accounting for intangibles, research and development, and goodwill (two Exposure Drafts, E50 and E60, which preceded the standard, IAS 38, that was finally issued mid-1998); employee benefits (Exposure Draft E54, issued late 1996 and IAS 19 [revised], issued in 1998); interim financial reporting (Exposure Draft E57, published mid-1997 and IAS 34, issued in 1998); reporting of discontinuing operations (Exposure Draft E59, published mid-1997 and IAS 37, issued in mid-1998); and impairment of assets (Exposure Draft E55, issued in mid-1997 and IAS 36, issued in mid-1998). Although these standards were completed over a period of three and a half years, the expectation is that the IOSCO will endorse them collectively for use in cross-border securities registrations, having earlier rejected a perhaps more logical approach, namely endorsing the standard-setting process itself, rather than the particular standards.

Since this endorsement is absolutely key to the ultimate legitimization of the international accounting standards, it was both prudent and necessary that the IASC agreed to the aforementioned time schedule. As the core set of standards project has now been successfully completed within the deadline, several things have become more or less apparent. First, the IASC has in fact accomplished a great deal, notwithstanding its limited resources (e.g., its funding is less than 10% of that for the US standard-setting body) and the logistical nightmare of conducting meetings around the globe.

Second, despite widespread skepticism about its self-imposed deadline to complete the core set of standards project, the IASC was able to benefit from all the research which had already been conducted and deliberations which had already taken place by national standard setters, and it successfully completed the project shortly after its self-imposed time limit.

Finally, it appears that some of the other major standard setters have begun to fear the possible emerging primacy of international accounting standards, and have begun to place their own survival into the political equation, with the result that support for the international harmonization program is wavering somewhat.

In light of the IASC's achievements to date, and the political issues which remain to be successfully traversed if the IOSCO endorsement is to be made as promised, the next year or so will be very critical. Since the core set of standards is now completed, the next step will be for IOSCO to review the standards to determine if they do in fact represent a cohesive, comprehensive set of high-quality standards. If IOSCO does vote to endorse these for cross-border securities registrations, there will be tremendous momentum which should lead to acceptance by major national securities regulators, including the SEC. This would mark a major milestone in the true global harmonization of financial reporting.

There is the possibility of complications arising from the IOSCO's likely endorsement, however. Since entities seeking cross-border listings of their securities in other countries will be able to submit financial statements prepared in conformity with IAS, some pressure will probably also develop to conform national standards with IAS. Otherwise, domestic registrants will be (from one perspective, at least) at a disadvantage in terms of types of disclosures and similar factors. This would be particularly true in countries such as the United States, where national accounting standards are more demanding than IAS in terms of financial statement disclosure. Although it is clearly too early to anticipate the outcome, it is very likely that the completion of the core set project, and the honoring of IOSCO's promised quid pro quo, will prove to be a watershed event in the history of IASC.

Other breakthroughs for IASC. In late 1995, the announcement by the European Commission's (EC) Single Market Commissioner that the European Union had abandoned its long-cherished goal of developing unique European standards of accounting gave a clear boost to the IASC's efforts. By effectively deferring to international accounting standards (IAS), the EC has removed the specter of yet another layer of national and supranational accounting standards and contributed to a quantum leap toward true internationalization of financial reporting and harmonization of accounting principles.

The EC statement of policy (1995), "Accounting Harmonization: A New Strategy vis-à-vis International Harmonization," clearly supports the efforts of the IASC. It states that, "Rather than amend existing Directives, the proposal is to improve the present situation by associating the EU with the efforts undertaken by IASC and IOSCO towards a broader international harmonization of accounting standards." This allegiance of support was reaffirmed in 1998 and 1999.

In fact, the EC's gesture of support has apparently had an impact, as the pace of adoptions of IAS has accelerated worldwide. A growing list of important nations has either adopted IAS outright or has crafted national standards around a core of IAS principles; in some cases nominally national standards are no more than thinly veiled international standards, without any substantive departures save the titles. Among the more important converts to or protagonists of IAS are Germany, Belgium, France, Australia, and Italy. Other adopters include Hong Kong, Malta, Korea, Barbados, Zimbabwe, Lebanon, Turkey, Trinidad and Tobago, Uganda, and Mongolia.

Many leading stock exchanges around the world have begun accepting listings based on financial statements prepared in accordance with international accounting standards. Included in this long list of IAS-friendly stock exchanges are the prominent ones in London, Zurich, Rome, Luxembourg, Australia, Amsterdam, Cyprus, Hong Kong, Stockholm, Copenhagen, Thailand, and others. A new pan-European securities market (known as EASDAQ) now permits the use of international accounting standards by its registrants. Furthermore, the Federation of Euro-Asian Stock Exchanges (FEAS), with 20 member exchanges in 18 nations in Europe (outside the EU and EFTA), Central and South Asia, and the Middle East, has recommended that its members should require the use of international accounting standards. In May 1998, a joint declaration was issued by the Arab Society of Certified Accountants and IASC, calling for all Arab nations to adopt IAS no later than year end 1998.

To summarize, the international accounting standard-setting process has evolved through three stages and is now poised on the brink of achieving widespread legitimacy, which may result, over time, in the IASC's becoming the premier accounting standard setter. If IASCO endorses the core set of IASC standards, the turn of the century may witness the true globalization of accounting standards.

Other Recent developments. In September 1996, the IASC approved the creation of the Standing Interpretations Committee (SIC). Apart from the obvious wisdom of taking this step, it was also done to accommodate the wishes of IOSCO and in particular the US regulatory community, which was concerned that absent a mechanism to ensure that IAS were uniformly interpreted and applied, there was no assurance that current diversity of practice would really be narrowed as intended. This group held its organizational meeting in April 1997 and has already met several times and finalized interpretations on controversial accounting issues. These are listed at the end of this chapter and discussed in this book in the sections to which they pertain.

In operation, the SIC receives recommendations from its constituencies concerning topics which are thought to contain ambiguities, and also may by other means identify issues which may need to be addressed. Typically these will be either narrow interpretation matters or applications to particular industries or types of operations. The SIC has indicated that it will deal with those suggested matters which involve interpretations of existing IAS (i.e., its role is not to break new ground), which have practical and widespread relevance, which relate to a specific fact pattern, and on which there is substantial divergence of practice. The IASC has published a suggested structure for the submission of suggested topics to the SIC.

The SIC is a team of accounting experts from 13 nations. If the committee is able to reach a consensus, a draft interpretation is first published and, after comments are received and considered, a final interpretation is adopted. In other cases, the SIC may urge the IASC itself to take up a project, if a need for new accounting standards is indicated which is beyond the scope of the SIC's efforts.

In 1996 the IASC also set up a "Strategy Working Party" to review the structure and future strategy of the IASC after the completion of the IASC's core set of standards program. The role of this group is to consider the need for restructuring the IASC itself.

In December 1998, the IASC published a discussion paper issued for comment by its Strategy Working Party, entitled "Shaping IASC for the Future." The main recommendations emerging from this document focused upon issues of restructuring the IASC by expanding the IASC Board and setting up a new committee, to be known as the Standards Development Committee (SDC) which would primarily be responsible for developing the IAS in future. The SDC in this role will be supported by the already-existing Standing Interpretations Committee, the new Standards Development Advisory Committee (SDAC) and the IASC Consultative Group. Appointments to the IASC Board, the SDC and the SIC would be made by "trustees" who will replace the existing IASC Advisory Council.

Alas, this "bicameral" concept was ultimately doomed by the adamant opposition of a number of national standard-setting bodies likely to have been key members of the "standards development committee," and by similar opposition from a few other important organizations, including the US SEC and the European Commission (whose objections were dissimilar, however). In response to overwhelming antagonism to this approach, the IASC has most recently withdrawn the idea and substituted a new proposal for a "unicameral" body comprised of both full-time and part-time members, probably 15 of the former plus 10 from the latter category. (An alternative also being discussed would have the body composed of 10 full-time and 7 part-time members.) It is likely that current or former national standard setters would largely comprise the full-time membership contingent. The part-time members could well come from the ranks of other represented groups, such as the European Commission and IOSCO.

Reportedly, this newly formulated approach would set a threshold of 15 votes to pass a standard (the smaller alternative would require 10 votes to pass). The full-time members would have voting control of the Board, were they to vote as a bloc. Most importantly, a unicameral approach (as under the present structure) would ensure that the standards would be enacted by the same body which had developed them, without any sort of "second look" and veto power being granted to another entity.

Whatever form the reconstituted Board takes, it appears necessary to take steps to reduce the level of suspicion and even animosity among groups such as G4 + 1 (the major English-speaking standard-setting bodies) and the EC and other non-English speakers. There is also a looming concern that the part-time members would lack the requisite level of independence which certain standard setters, such as the FASB, believe to be a necessary condition for the accounting standard-setting process.

Another issue being tackled by the IASC pertains to the providing of expanded implementation guidance. Currently, the IAS are very concise, conceptual documents, with little in the way of practical guidelines or examples (hence the need for books like this). Many users of the international standards have requested that the IAS be made more like the US or UK standards, which typically contain substantially more detailed guidance. To date, the IASC has been sensitive to the fact that developing nations and smaller enterprises constitute a large fraction of its current constituency, and from a cost/benefit perspective it is not clear that imposing thousands of pages of detailed rules on such entities would be justified. On the other hand, however, gaining support from the major standard-setting bodies and regulatory agencies for the hoped-for IOSCO endorsement of the core set of standards may necessitate some gesture toward providing this type of expanded implementation assistance.

As if these controversies noted above were not enough, shortly after the above-mentioned discussion document was published by the Strategy Working Party, the US FASB published its views on international standard setting, in the paper titled "International Accounting Standard Setting: A Vision for the Future." The FASB envisions the development and promulgation of IAS by a yet-to-be-constituted International Standard Setter (ISS), which according to it might be established in one of the following ways:

- By structurally changing the IASC itself;
- Through a successor organization to the IASC, possibly based on G4 + 1 (the organization of English-speaking national standard setters), which would build upon what the IASC has already accomplished; or
- By changing the US FASB itself in order to become more acceptable internationally.

In a way, the FASB has reiterated its objections with respect to the IASC's standard-setting process and the IAS themselves, recapitulating them succinctly through this vision statement. These matters were raised in public debates by senior members of the FASB on several occasions with rejoinders from the IASC--views of both the sides having been published extensively in the media. The FASB's long-standing contention that the IASC's core set of standards are not high-quality accounting standards, since the speed with which certain topics were handled in the IASC/IOSCO Work Program was unacceptable, has been reflected in this vision statement. Instead, some say that FASB's real goal (or hidden agenda) is that, through this vision statement, it wants to project itself as the ISS of the future (since the prerequisites or qualities of an ISS as envisaged by this vision statement closely match the structure and setup of the US FASB itself).

The foregoing are only some of the more important activities and developments currently occupying the IASC and impacting the course of future developments. These serve to underline the great significance of the years ahead in determining the ultimate success of global harmonization of accounting standards.

Benefits From Global Harmonization of Accounting Principles

From the standpoint of the users of financial statements (e.g., bankers and investors), it is rather difficult to make relative evaluations of companies that use diverse accounting standards. This tends to restrict the market for the shares of these companies and therefore greatly affects their rankings and attributed value. Today, for most businesses, the biggest opportunities lie in international markets: They have economic activities that extend far beyond domestic markets, they seek investment capital in foreign countries, and they conduct their operations through facilities in foreign lands. It is also fairly evident that in the share market arena, global fighters are emerging as winners, since investors seem to be ignoring domestic competitors and clearly casting their ballots in favor of international champions. Thus, harmonization of accounting standards worldwide will greatly help the users of accounting and financial information in making informed economic decisions about these companies.

From the standpoint of preparers of financial statements, the burden of financial reporting would be greatly lessened with increased harmonization, which would simplify the process of preparing individual as well as group financial statements. It is a well-known fact that multinational groups that have nondomestic subsidiaries have huge added costs of preparation of financial statements. To elaborate the point, consider an example of a company which has a subsidiary that is operating out of Saudi Arabia, with its parent company based in the United Kingdom, and whose shares are listed on the New York Stock Exchange. This company will have to prepare three sets of financial statements.

1. Financial statements to comply with the Saudi standards, to meet the requirements of the Saudi Arabian company
2. Financial statements to comply with the consolidation requirements in the United Kingdom
3. Financial statements to meet the registration and filing requirements in the United States

This means that enormous additional financial costs have to be incurred not only in the preparation of such financial statements but also in getting them audited. Imagine if this company were a multinational corporation (MNC) operating out of 50 countries, most of which had local licensing regulations that required financial reporting to be tailored according to their national standards. The company's accounting travails would then be extremely unpleasant, to say the least. Thus it is obvious that enormous benefits will emanate from harmonization of accounting standards worldwide.

Impediments to Harmonization

Based on an authoritative study on the subject of harmonization of international accounting standards, a paper was prepared by the International Federation of Accountants and distributed by the International Capital Markets Group. According to this study, the major barrier to harmonization seems to be the "manifestation of national sovereignty." A second very important factor is the "varying attitudes of standard setters around the world to the purpose of the financial statements." When the purpose is perceived as **creditor protection**, the tendency is to understate profits (and thereby require retention of profits) compared with countries where **shareholder protection** is the dominant feature. Further, countries where creditor protection is a high priority also tend to be more tax driven in their financial reporting, which means that in such countries recognition of expenses is influenced by the provisions of the tax code more than by the principles of commercial accounting.

Reporting Anomalies Resulting From Diversity in Accounting Standards Worldwide

Significant diversity in accounting standards of different countries not only poses the problem of additional cost to be incurred for financial reporting but could cause other difficulties for multinational companies. For instance, it is quite possible for a transaction to give rise to a profit under the accounting standards of one country, whereas it would require a deferral under the standards of another country. When a multinational company has to report under the standards of both countries, one is amazed to see some extremely odd financial results which could sometimes also be embarrassing. The case of lopsided financial reporting that instantly comes to mind is that of German industrial giant Daimler-Benz AG, which sought listing of its shares in the United States in 1993 and ended up reporting a massive loss of $1 billion under US GAAP, when in fact it had reported a profit of $370 million under its own national (German) GAAP.

Major Differences in National Accounting Standards

The following analysis is by no means an authoritative study of differences in accounting standards worldwide but is being attempted with the limited purpose of highlighting some of the well-known major differences in accounting standards. Four countries have been chosen for this comparison: the United Kingdom, the United States, France, and Japan.

1. **Measurement subsequent to initial recognition of fixed assets (historical cost vs. revaluations).** Revaluation is more of a choice than a requirement or stipulation. Even those standards that permit revaluations offer it as an alternative to the historical cost. It is prohibited in countries such as the United States and Japan, and if used would be considered a departure from GAAP. In the United Kingdom and France revaluation of assets is permitted, but not all assets are allowed to be carried at revalued amounts. In the United Kingdom the items that are permitted to be revalued are property, plant, equipment, and investments. In France, revaluations are rare, except when prescribed by law.

2. **Timing of recognition vs. deferrals.** Recognition of profits and losses causes major differences in financial reporting. Sometimes the method used in recognizing profits or losses could cause differences, and sometimes the number of years over which amortization is spread could cause disparities in the reporting of financial results. Two examples illustrating the foregoing causes of differences follow.

   a. **Accounting for goodwill.** There is great disparity among standards with regard to the accounting treatment of goodwill. Some countries have traditionally given a free choice of either writing it off to reserves on acquisition or capitalizing and recognizing it on the balance sheet. The other controversy is with regard to the number of years over which goodwill is to be amortized. The following summarizes these differences:

      (1) *United States and France.* Both treat goodwill as an asset and amortize it over its useful life. (Under US GAAP the amortization period is 40 years, while in France no set limit is prescribed but shorter periods are used.)

      (2) *United Kingdom.* Traditionally, alternatives are allowed: Goodwill could either be written off on acquisition by a charge to reserves (**not** to the income statement) **or** capitalized and amortized over its useful life. However, recent amendments (FRS10) have modified this approach.

      (3) *Japan.* Goodwill is capitalized and written off over 5 years, but this can be extended if a longer life can be justified.

   b. **Accounting for long-term contracts.** Long-term contracts could be accounted for under either the percentage-of-completion method or the completed contract method. Profit recognition under the methods is vastly different. While the completed contract method postpones the recognition of profits until the contact is completed, the percentage-of-completion method recognizes profits during the life of the contract. Following are the methods prescribed under the various standards:

(1) *United States, France, and Japan.* Both methods are permitted.

(2) *United Kingdom.* Only the percentage-of-completion method is permitted.

3. **Recognition of substance over form in accounting for leases: capital vs. operating**

   a. *United Kingdom and United States.* Certain categories of leases (called **finance leases** in the United Kingdom and **capital leases** in the United States) have to be capitalized (capital value of asset leased is recorded as an asset and future lease payments recorded as liability).

   b. *France.* Capitalizing is prohibited, except for consolidated accounts, for which it is optional.

   c. *Japan.* Although this treatment is not specifically prohibited, there are no accounting rules on this subject.

4. **Financial statement disclosures**

   a. **Related-party transactions**

      (1) *United States and France.* There are significant disclosure requirements on related-party transactions.

      (2) *United Kingdom.* Traditionally, only details of certain transactions with directors (and other specified personnel) were required to be disclosed. However, with the promulgation of a new standard (FRS 8), the related-party disclosure requirements have been broadened.

      (3) *Japan.* All material transactions with related parties must be disclosed under a footnote captioned "Conditions of Business Group."

   b. **Segmental information**

      (1) *United States.* Applicable only to publicly held (listed) companies.

      (2) *France and United Kingdom.* Applicable in case of all companies.

      (3) *Japan.* Applicable in case of listed companies and should be reported by the parent company for the group; to be disclosed in a footnote captioned "Conditions of Business Group."

Relevance of IAS to the Developing Countries of the World

Many developing nations do not have their own national accounting standards. The generally accepted accounting principles (GAAP) that they follow are either the UK, US, or international standards. In certain countries, governments and central banks have made the IAS mandatory. Rather than reinventing the wheel, the adoption of IAS, which are high-quality standards, developed after a truly international "due process," seems to be a step in the right direction, as it will help the process of uniformity in international financial reporting.

APPENDIX

CURRENT INTERNATIONAL ACCOUNTING STANDARDS

IAS 1   Presentation of Financial Statements (revised July 1997; effective for periods beginning on or after July 1, 1998)

IAS 2   Inventories

IAS 4   Depreciation Accounting

IAS 7   Cash Flow Statements

IAS 8   Net Profit or Loss for the Period, Fundamental Errors and Changes in Accounting Policies (Note that paragraphs 19-22 of IAS 8 have been superseded by IAS 35)

IAS 10   Events After the Balance Sheet Date (Revised May 1999: effective for periods beginning on or after January 1, 2000)

IAS 11   Construction Contracts

IAS 12   Accounting for Taxes on Income (replaced by IAS 12 [revised 1996], Income Taxes, effective for periods beginning on or after January 1, 1998)

IAS 14   Reporting Financial Information by Segment (replaced by IAS 14 [revised 1997], Segment Reporting, effective for periods beginning on or after July 1, 1998)

IAS 15   Information Reflecting the Effects of Changing Prices

IAS 16   Property, Plant, and Equipment (revised 1998 by issuance of IAS 36)

IAS 17   Accounting for Leases (replaced by IAS 17 [revised 1997], Leases, effective for periods beginning on or after January 1, 1999)

IAS 18   Revenue

IAS 19   Retirement Benefit Costs (replaced by IAS 19 [revised 1998], Employee Benefits, effective periods beginning on or after January 1, 1999)

IAS 20   Accounting for Government Grants and Disclosure of Government Assistance

IAS 21   The Effects of Changes in Foreign Exchange Rates

IAS 22   Business Combinations

IAS 23   Borrowing Costs

IAS 24   Related-Party Disclosures

IAS 25   Accounting for Investments

IAS 26   Accounting and Reporting by Retirement Benefit Plans

IAS 27   Consolidated Financial Statements and Accounting for Investments in Subsidiaries

IAS 28   Accounting for Investments in Associates (revised 1998 by issuance of IAS 36)

IAS 29   Financial Reporting in Hyperinflationary Economies

IAS 30   Disclosures in the Financial Statements of Banks and Similar Financial Institutions

IAS 31   Financial Reporting of Interests in Joint Ventures (revised 1998 by issuance of IAS 36)

IAS 32   Financial Instruments: Disclosures and Presentation

IAS 33   Earnings per Share (issued February 1997; effective for periods beginning on or after January 1, 1998)

IAS 34   Interim Financial Reporting (issued February 1998; effective for periods beginning on or after January 1, 1999)

IAS 35   Discontinuing Operations (issued mid-1998; effective for periods beginning on or after January 1, 1999)

IAS 36   Impairments of Assets (issued mid-1998; effective for periods beginning on or after July 1, 1999)

IAS 37   Provisions, Contingent Liabilities and Contingent Assets (issued mid-1998; effective for periods beginning on or after July 1, 1999)

IAS 38   Intangible Assets (issued mid-1998; effective for periods beginning on or after July 1, 1999)

IAS 39   Financial Instruments: Recognition and Measurement (issued December 1998; effective January 1, 2001)

SIC 1   Consistency--Different Cost Formulas for Inventories (IAS 2)

SIC 2   Consistency--Capitalization of Borrowing Costs (IAS 23)

SIC 3   Elimination of Unrealized Profits and Losses on Transactions With Associates (IAS 28)

SIC 5   Classification of Financial Instruments--Contingent Settlement Provisions (IAS 32)

SIC 6   Costs of Modifying Existing Software (IASC's Framework)

SIC 7   Introduction of the Euro (IAS 21)

SIC 8   First-Time Application of IAS as the Primary Basis of Accounting (IAS 1)

SIC 9   Business Combinations--Classification Either as Acquisitions or Unitings of Interests (IAS 22)

SIC 10   Government Assistance--No Specific Relation to Operating Activities (IAS 20)

SIC 11   Foreign Exchange--Capitalization of Losses Resulting From Severe Currency Devaluations (IAS 21)

SIC 12   Consolidation--Special Purpose Entities (IAS 27)

SIC 13   Jointly Controlled Entities--Nonmonetary Contributions by Ventures (IAS 31)

SIC 14   Property, Plant, and Equipment--Compensation for the Impairment or Loss of Items (IAS 16)

SIC 15   Operating Leases--Incentives (IAS 17)

SIC 16   Share Capital--Reacquired Own Equity Instruments (Treasury Shares) (IAS 32)

2 BALANCE SHEET

PERSPECTIVE AND ISSUES

The objective of presenting financial statements in a manner consistent with that outlined by the IASC in its *Framework for the Preparation and Presentation of Financial Statements* is to provide information regarding an enterprise's financial position, performance, and changes in financial position to a broad spectrum of users, to enable them to make rational and informed economic decisions. According to the IASC's *Framework*, the financial statements are meant to report on the "results of stewardship of the management, or the accountability of management for the resources entrusted to it."

These provisions of the *Framework* are consistent with the long debated, recently issued IAS 1 (revised), *Presentation of Financial Statements*. The revised standard, while eloquently referring to financial statements as "a structured financial representation of the financial position of and the transactions undertaken by an enterprise," elaborates further upon their purpose or objective. According to this standard, the objective of the "general-purpose financial statements" is to provide information about an enterprise's "financial position," its "performance," and its "cash flows," which information is then utilized by a wide spectrum of end-users in making economic decisions. This information is presented through a complete set of financial statements which, according to IAS 1 (revised 1997), para 7, comprises the following components:

1. The balance sheet
2. An income statement
3. Another statement showing either

    a. All changes in equity, or
    b. Changes in equity other than those arising from capital transactions with owners and distributions to owners

4. A cash flow statement
5. Accounting policies and other explanatory notes

The fact that revised IAS 1 provides a somewhat ambiguous definition of the financial statement which will summarize some or all changes in equity during the reporting period is particularly interesting. It will be remembered that this statement's immediate predecessor, Exposure Draft E53, required that an enterprise present a basic financial statement to be captioned as the "statement of nonowner movement in equity." In the interim, while comments on E53 were being received and considered, the US accounting standard setter imposed a somewhat similar requirement, for the presentation of a new "statement of comprehensive income," on US companies complying with GAAP (while this statement can be combined with the income statement or incorporated into a statement of changes in stockholders' equity, the same essential requirements have to be fulfilled in any event). Furthermore, the UK GAAP requirements had earlier been revised to mandate the presentation of a somewhat similar financial statement, the "statement of total recognized gains and losses." Thus, the easing of the requirements which were signaled by E53 is somewhat puzzling, although it appears at this early date that the practical differences between what was to have been imposed and what has now been codified might be minor.

A balance sheet, which is a major component of the financial statements, is a statement of financial position that presents assets, liabilities, and shareholders' equity (net worth) at a given point in time. The balance sheet reflects the financial status of an enterprise in conformity with the accounting principles on which the financial statements have been prepared; for instance, the international accounting standards. Alone among the traditional financial statements, it reports the aggregate effect of transactions at a point in time, whereas the other components of the financial statements, that is, the income statement, the newly prescribed statement showing either "all changes in equity" or "changes in equity other than those arising from capital transactions with owners and distributions to owners," and the statement of cash flows, summarize the totality of transactions over a period of time.

Whereas the early history of financial reporting was one of almost universal emphasis on the balance sheet (in fact, there was a time when only the balance sheet was presented for review by those outside an organization), for an extended period beginning in the 1960s, users of financial statements placed greater emphasis on the income statement than on the balance sheet. During this period, enterprise desirability was measured largely by earnings growth, as investors became more interested in short-run maximization of earnings per share. However, the cycles of worldwide inflation and recession that began during the 1970s, replete with "credit crunches" that precipitated the demise of many once-high-flying entities, brought about a renewed emphasis on the balance sheet. By the mid- to late 1980s a more balanced view became dominant, with both balance sheet and income statement (the cash flow statement did not achieve prominence until the very late 1980s and early 1990s) receiving close scrutiny.

This shift of emphasis back toward the balance sheet has signaled a departure from the traditional transaction-based concept of income toward a capital maintenance concept. This has historically been more favored by economists than by accountants, consistent with the former group's concern with real, not merely nominal, wealth creation. Under the capital maintenance approach to income measurement, the amount of beginning net assets (ideally measured by real economic value, not by accounting book values) would be compared to the amount of ending net assets, and the difference would be adjusted for dividends and capital transactions. Only to the extent that an entity maintained its net assets (after adjusting for capital transactions) would income be deemed to have been earned. By using a capital maintenance concept, it is argued, investors can better predict the overall profit potential of the firm. Notwithstanding the recognition of this, however, financial reporting almost universally continues to be grounded in historical costs, except in those economies where experience with hyperinflation has made such financial reporting obviously meaningless.

Financial statements should provide information that helps users make rational investment, credit, or economic decisions. The balance sheet must be studied to assess a firm's liquidity, its financial flexibility, and its ability to generate profits, pay its debts as they become due, and pay dividends. **Liquidity** refers to an entity's present cash and near-cash position as well as to the timing of its future cash flows which are anticipated to occur in the normal course of business. Liquidity thus refers to the enterprise's ability to meet its obligations as they fall due.

The concept of financial flexibility is broader than the concept of liquidity. **Financial flexibility** is the ability to take effective actions to alter the amounts and timings of cash flows so that it can respond to unexpected needs and opportunities. Financial flexibility includes the ability to raise new capital or tap into unused lines of credit.

Another important objective of financial reporting is to provide information that is useful in assessing the amounts, timing, and uncertainty of future cash flows. There have been two pertinent suggestions to make the balance sheet more useful in assessing a firm's liquidity. The first is to make alterations to the balance sheet's format. The second is to provide expanded information about liquidity in the notes to the balance sheet.

For most businesses, balance sheets are more meaningful if they are classified into categories. Assets are classified as **current assets** if they are used in the enterprise's operating activities and are reasonably expected to be converted into cash, sold, or consumed either within 12 months of the reporting date or in the normal course of one operating cycle, whichever is longer. Assets are also classified as current assets when they are held primarily for trading or short-term investment purposes and are expected to be realized within 12 months of the reporting date. Liabilities are classified as **current liabilities** if they are expected to be liquidated through the use of current assets or the creation of other current liabilities. The excess of current assets over current liabilities is known universally as **net working capital**.

For some other businesses, however, the concept of **working capital** has little or no relevance and the balance sheet is accordingly not classified. Such businesses include banks, similar financial institutions, and insurance enterprises. Personal financial statements are unclassified for the same reason.

Ultimately, each reporting entity must decide whether a classified balance sheet would be meaningful to users. IAS 1 (revised 1997) makes it incumbent upon each enterprise to make a determination, based on the nature of its operations, whether or not to present current and noncurrent assets and current and noncurrent liabilities as separate classifications on the face of the balance sheet. Even the predecessor to this standard, IAS 13, left it up to the reporting entity to resolve this matter; thus this position is not a new one in the context of the international accounting standards.

Additionally, the revised standard IAS 1 makes it incumbent upon enterprises, whether they choose to present a classified balance sheet or not, to disclose, for each asset and liability item, the amounts expected to be recovered or settled after more than 12 months. In imposing this new requirement, the revised standard on the presentation of financial statements recognizes that information about the maturity dates of financial assets and financial liabilities is now required by IAS 32, *Financial Instruments: Disclosure and Presentation*. IAS 1 (revised) thus builds upon this foundation, and emphasizes that additional information concerning the expected dates of recovery and settlement of nonmonetary assets and liabilities, like inventories or provisions, is also useful (whether or not an enterprise presents a classified balance sheet).

Consistency has always been a valued feature of financial reporting practices. A draft SIC (D18) addresses the concerns that arise from the fact that IAS often provide for "allowed alternatives" in the application of accounting principles. If adopted, this will provide that when more than one alternative accounting policies are available under the IAS, the reporting entity should choose one of the alternatives and then apply it consistently to balances or transactions having similar characteristics. Furthermore, once selected, the alternative should be changed only when the criteria set forth in IAS 8 are met. As IAS continue to be refined over time, however, it is anticipated that lack of consistency will become less of an issue, since the range of available alternatives is being rather steadily reduced.

Sources of IAS

IAS 1 (revised 1997), 5 (repealed by IAS 1), 7, 10 (revised 1999), 13 (repealed by IAS 1), 24, 30, 32, 38

IASC's Framework for the Preparation and Presentation of Financial Statements

DEFINITIONS OF TERMS

The IASC's *Framework* defines elements of the financial statements of business enterprises and several related concepts. Elements are the basic categories that appear on financial statements. To be included in financial statements, an item must meet the definitional requirements, recognition requirements, and measurement requirements. Although there may be other elements of financial statements, the IASC's *Framework* defines only those elements that relate to the status and performance of a business and which are therefore relevant to decisions that would require the commitment of resources to the business. Three of the ten elements (assets, liabilities, and equity) are related to the status of an entity at a particular point in time. The other elements, such as comprehensive income and expenses, are related to the performance of an entity over a period of time. The two categories of elements articulate. That is, a change in one category will affect the other.

Elements of balance sheets.

> *Assets--Probable future economic benefits obtained or controlled by a particular entity as a result of past transactions or events.*

The following three characteristics must be present for an item to qualify as an asset:

1. The asset must provide probable future economic benefit which enables it to provide future net cash inflows.
2. The entity is able to receive the benefit and restrict other entities' access to that benefit.
3. The event that provides the entity with the right to the benefit has occurred.

Assets remain an economic resource of an enterprise as long as they continue to meet the three requirements identified above. Transactions and operations act to change an entity's assets.

A valuation account is neither an asset nor a liability. Rather, it alters the carrying value of an asset and is not independent of that related asset.

Assets have features that help identify them in that they are exchangeable, legally enforceable, and have future economic benefit (service potential). It is that potential that eventually brings in cash to the entity and that underlies the concept of an asset.

> *Liabilities--Probable future sacrifices of economic benefits arising from present obligations of a particular entity to transfer assets or provide services to other entities in the future as a result of past transactions or events.*

The following three characteristics must be present for an item to qualify as a liability:

1. A liability requires that the entity settle a present obligation by the probable future transfer of an asset on demand when a specified event occurs or at a particular date.
2. The obligation cannot be avoided.
3. The event that obligates the entity has occurred.

Liabilities usually result from transactions that enable entities to obtain resources. Other liabilities may arise from nonreciprocal transfers, such as the declaration of dividends to the owners of the entity or the pledge of assets to charitable organizations.

An entity may involuntarily incur a liability. A liability may be imposed on the entity by government or by the court system in the form of taxes, fines, or levies. A liability may arise from price changes or interest rate changes. Liabilities may be legally enforceable or they may be equitable obligations that arise from social, ethical, or moral requirements. Liabilities continue in existence until the entity is no longer responsible for discharging them. A valuation account is not an independent item. It alters the carrying value of a liability and is directly related to that liability.

Most liabilities stem from financial instruments, contracts, and laws, which are legal concepts invented by a sophisticated economy. Enterprises incur liabilities primarily as part of their ongoing economic activities, in exchange for economic resources and services required to operate the business. The end result of a liability is that it takes the use of an asset or the creation of another liability to liquidate it. Liabilities are imposed by agreement, by law, by court, by equitable or constructive obligation, and by business ethics and custom.

The diagram that follows, which is taken from a document that formed part of the conceptual framework project by the US standard-setting body, the Financial Accounting Standards Board, identifies the three classes of events that affect an entity.

> *Equity*--*The residual interest in the assets that remains after deducting its liabilities. In a business enterprise, the equity is the ownership interest.*

Equity arises from the ownership relation and is the basis for distributions of earnings to the owners. Distributions of enterprise assets to owners are voluntary. Equity is increased by owners' investments and comprehensive income and is reduced by distributions to owners. In practice, the distinction between equity and liabilities may be difficult to ascertain. Securities such as convertible debt and certain types of preferred stock may have characteristics of both equity (residual ownership interest) and liabilities (nondiscretionary future sacrifices).

The other elements that change assets, liabilities, and equities are identified and defined in Chapter 3.

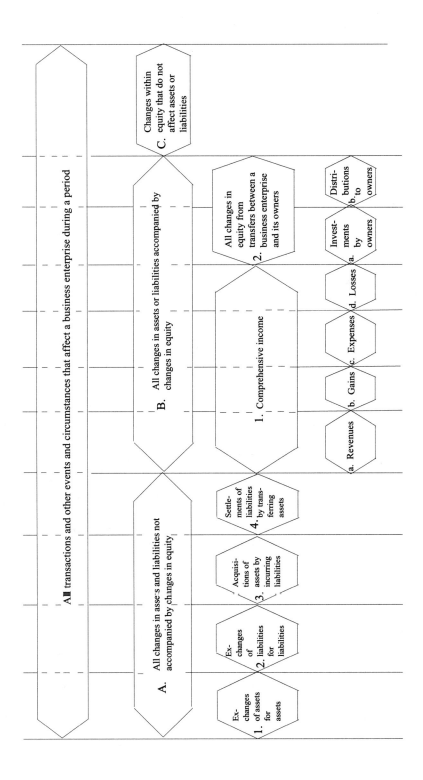

CONCEPTS, RULES, AND EXAMPLES

General Concepts

Under international accounting standards, assets and liabilities are recorded in financial statements under the historical cost principle, although in selected cases subsequent changes in values can be recognized. Historical exchange prices are used because they are objective and capable of being verified independently. When a balance sheet is presented, most assets are reported at cost. One very important limitation is that historical cost does not always (or even typically) reflect current value, and thus the balance sheet will not generally be indicative of the economic value of an enterprise.

Generally accepted accounting principles allow or require certain exceptions to the historical cost principle. For example, inventories and marketable equity securities may be reported at lower of cost or market, and certain long-term investments may be reported under the equity method, but neither of these exceptions is intended to result in a balance sheet that reflects current economic value. Depreciation, depletion, and amortization of long-term assets are acceptable practices, but appreciation of assets is not generally recorded. Appreciation of assets is usually recorded only when realized through an arm's-length transaction (sale), although international accounting standards do provide the option of revaluation for plant assets and for certain other investment assets, as described in more detail in Chapters 8, 9, and 10.

Many accountants, of course, believe that the balance sheet would be more useful if all assets were restated in terms of current values, and a number of strategies to accomplish this have been proposed or tried over the years. In general, these current values could be market-related (i.e., based on changes in specific prices) or could simply be historical costs adjusted for the changing value of the dollar (i.e., based on changes in the general price level). For a range of reasons, none of these approaches have been widely accepted in practice, and thus the historical cost approach continues as the most widely employed measurement model for financial reporting. However, under current generally accepted accounting principles, although assets are usually stated at historical cost, if market information indicates a permanent and material decline in value, recognition of the economic loss is immediate.

Another limitation of historical cost-based balance sheets is a consequence of the fact that estimates are used to determine the carrying, or book, values of many of the assets. Estimates are used in determining the collectibility of receivables, salability of inventory, and useful life of long-term assets, among other things. Estimates are necessary in order to divide and separate economic events occurring between two distinct accounting periods. However, such estimates require informed judgments for which there is perhaps not enough guidance in accounting literature.

An additional failing of the balance sheet is that it ignores items that are of financial value to the firm but the worth of which cannot be determined objectively. For example, internally generated goodwill, human resources, and secret processes are of financial value, but since these values are not measurable under current accounting principles and practices, they are not recorded on the balance sheet. Only assets obtained in a market transaction are incorporated into the financial statements of an entity. As the service economy becomes ever more dominant, the importance of assets that are not reflected in the traditional balance sheet (particularly those relating to human capital) will become a more critical issue which the accounting professions will eventually have to address.

A final constraint on the usefulness of the balance sheet is that it largely ignores the time value of its elements. Although certain receivables and payables may be discounted, most items are stated at face value regardless of the timing of the cash flows that they will generate. This tends to exacerbate the divergence between net worth as reported in balance sheets and the value of the enterprise in real economic terms.

The net result of the foregoing is that the balance sheet contains a mixture of historical costs and current values that may restrict its utility to users. It is true that, in the case of some assets and liabilities, cost is a reasonably close approximation of current value. Monetary assets such as cash, short-term investments, and receivables closely approximate current value. Current liabilities are payable within a short period, and the amounts reported thus also closely approximate current values. If these values were discounted, any discrepancy would be immaterial because of the short time period before payment. Current liabilities are not classified strictly on the basis of maturity value but on the concept that a current liability is one that requires either a current asset or another current liability to liquidate, and should be shown on the balance sheet at face value. Productive assets such as property, plant, and equipment, and intangibles are reported at cost less any reduction due to depreciation, depletion, or amortization. Long-term liabilities are recorded as the discounted value of future payments to be made under contract, since, on the date of issuance, the discount rate equals the market rate. However, as time passes and the market rate fluctuates, the recorded cost will not necessarily approximate the current value.

The rights of the common shareholders of a firm and the rights of other capital-supplying parties (bondholders and other lenders, and preferred stockholders) of a firm are many and varied. Both sources of capital are concerned with two basic rights: the right to share in the cash or property disbursements (interest and dividends) and the right to share in the assets in the event of liquidation. The disclosure of these rights is an important objective in the presentation of financial statements.

Form of Balance Sheet

The titles commonly given to the primary financial statement that presents an entity's financial position are balance sheet, statement of financial position, or statement of financial condition. Use of any of these terms implies that the statement was prepared in conformity with generally accepted accounting principles. If some other comprehensive basis of accounting, such as income tax or cash, is adhered to instead, the title of the financial statement should be adjusted to reflect this departure. Thus, a title such as "Statements of Assets and Liabilities" would be necessary to differentiate the financial statement being presented from a balance sheet.

The three elements that are displayed in the heading of a balance sheet are

1. The entity whose financial position is being presented
2. The title of the statement
3. The date of the statement

The entity's name should appear exactly as written in the legal document that created it (e.g., the certificate of incorporation, partnership agreement, etc.). The title should also clearly reflect the legal status of the enterprise as a corporation, partnership, sole proprietorship, or division of some other entity. Where the entity's name does not disclose its legal status, supplemental information should be added to the title to clarify that status. A few examples are

ABC Company
(A partnership)

ABC Company
(A limited partnership)

ABC Company
(A sole proprietorship)

ABC Company
(A division of DEF, Inc.)

The title of the financial statement should generally be "Balance Sheet" unless another name is indicative of the terminology used in the industry. For example, in the securities industry, the title "Statement of Financial Condition" is more widely used.

Finally, the last day of the month should be used as the statement date unless the entity uses a fiscal reporting period always ending on a particular day of the week, such as a Friday or Sunday (e.g., the last Friday in December, or the Sunday falling closest to December 31). In these cases, the balance sheet can appropriately be dated accordingly (i.e., December 26, October 1, etc.). In all cases, the implication is that the balance sheet captures the pertinent amounts as of the close of business on the date noted.

Balance sheets should generally be uniform in appearance from one period to the next, as indeed should all of the entity's financial statements. The form, terminology, captions, and pattern of combining insignificant items should be consistent. The goal is to enhance usefulness by maintaining a consistent manner of presentation unless there are good reasons to change these and the changes are duly reported.

Classification of Assets

Assets, liabilities, and stockholders' equity are separated in the balance sheet so that important relationships can be shown and so that attention can be focused on significant subtotals.

Current assets. According to IAS 1 (revised 1997), an asset should be classified as a current asset when it

1. Is expected to be realized in, or is held for sale or consumption in, the normal course of the enterprise's operating cycle; or
2. Is held primarily for trading purposes or for the short term, and is expected to be realized within 12 months of the balance sheet date; or
3. Is cash or a cash equivalent asset which is not restricted in its use.

All other assets should be classified as noncurrent assets, if a classified balance sheet is to be presented in the financial statements.

Thus, current assets include cash, cash equivalents and other assets which can be expected to be realized in cash or sold or consumed during one normal operating cycle of the business. The operating cycle of an enterprise is the time between the acquisition of materials entering into a process and its realization in cash or an instrument that is readily convertible into cash. The default assumption is that the operating cycle is a period of 12 months, and thus the current assets are expected to be realized within the period of 12 months. IAS 1 (revised 1997) makes an exception in the case of inventories and trade receivables and specifically states that even if these assets are not expected to be realized within 12 months from the balance sheet date they should still be classified as current assets in a classified balance sheet. However, marketable securities could only be classified as current assets if they are expected to be realized within 12 months of the balance sheet date, even though most would deem marketable securities to be more liquid than inventories and possibly even than receivables. The following items would be classified as current assets:

1. **Cash** and cash equivalents include cash on hand, consisting of coins, currency, and undeposited checks; money orders and drafts; and deposits in banks. Anything accepted by a bank for deposit would be considered as cash. Cash must be available for a demand withdrawal: Assets such as cer-

tificates of deposit would not be considered cash because of the time restrictions on withdrawal. Also, to be classified as a current asset, cash must be available for current use. According to IAS 1 (revised 1997), cash that is restricted in use and whose restrictions will not expire within the operating cycle, or cash restricted for a noncurrent use, would not be included in current assets. According to IAS 7 (revised 1992), cash equivalents include short-term, highly liquid investments that (1) are readily convertible to known amounts of cash, and (2) are so near their maturity (original maturities of 3 months or less) that they present negligible risk of changes in value because of changes in interest rates. Treasury bills, commercial paper, and money market funds are all examples of cash equivalents.

2. **Short-term investments** are readily marketable securities which are normally acquired through the use of temporarily idle cash. The basis of reporting of these items need not be reported on the face of the balance sheet provided that the different reporting classifications are reconciled in the notes. The balance sheet presentation would be as follows:

Marketable securities	$xxx

3. **Receivables** include accounts and notes receivable, receivables from affiliate companies, and officer and employee receivables. The term **accounts receivable** represents amounts due from customers arising from transactions in the ordinary course of business. Allowances due to lack of collectibility and any amounts discounted or pledged should be stated clearly. The allowances may be based on a relationship to sales or based on direct analysis of the receivables. If material, the receivables should be analyzed into their component parts. The receivables section may be presented as follows:

Receivables:			
Accounts	$xxx		
Notes	xxx	$xxxx	
Less allowance for doubtful accounts		(xxx)	$xxxx
Associated companies			xxx
Officers and employees			xxx
Total			$xxxx

4. **Inventories** are assets held, either for sale in the ordinary course of business or in the process of production for such sale, or in the form of materials or supplies to be consumed in the production process or in the rendering of services (IAS 2). The basis of valuation and the method of pricing should be disclosed.

Inventories--at the lower of cost (FIFO) or net realizable value	$xxx

In the case of a manufacturing concern, raw materials, work in process, and finished goods should be disclosed separately on the balance sheet or in the footnotes.

Inventories:		
Finished goods	$xxx	
Work in process	xxx	
Raw materials	xxx	$xxx

5. **Prepaid expenses** are assets created by the prepayment of cash or incurrence of a liability. They expire and become expenses with the passage of time, use, or events (e.g., prepaid rent, prepaid insurance, and deferred taxes).

Noncurrent assets. IAS 1 (revised 1997) uses the term "noncurrent" to include tangible, intangible, operating, and financial assets of a long-term nature. It does not prohibit the use of alternative descriptions, as long as the meaning is clear. Noncurrent assets include long-term investments, property and equipment, intangible assets and miscellaneous other assets, as described in the following paragraphs.

Long-term investments. Investments that are intended to be held for an extended period of time (longer than one operating cycle) would be classified as long-term investments. The following are the three major types of long-term investments:

1. **Debt and equity securities** are stocks, bonds, and long-term notes. The basis of reporting of these items is not reported on the face of the balance sheet but should be reported in the notes.

Long-term investments:			
Investments in A company stock	$xxx		
Notes receivable	xxx		
Less discount on notes receivable	(xxx)	xxx	
Investment in B company bonds		xxx	$xxx

2. **Tangible assets** not currently used in operations, such as surplus machinery being held on a standby basis.
3. **Investments held in special funds** (e.g., sinking funds, pension funds, amounts held for plant expansion, and cash surrender values of life insurance policies).

Property, plant, and equipment. Tangible assets that are held by an enterprise for use in the production or supply of goods or services, or for rental to others, or for administrative purposes and which are expected to be used during more than one period. Included are such items as land, buildings, machinery and equipment, furniture and fixtures, motor vehicles and equipment. These should be disclosed, with the related accumulated depreciation, as follows:

Machinery and equipment	$xxx	
Less accumulated depreciation	(xxx)	$xxx

or
Machinery and equipment (net of $xxx
   accumulated depreciation) $xxx

Accumulated depreciation should be shown by major classes of depreciable assets. In addition to showing this amount on the balance sheet, the notes to the financial statements should contain balances of major classes of depreciable assets, by nature or function, at the balance sheet date, along with a general description of the method or methods used in computing depreciation with respect to major classes of depreciable assets (IAS 16).

Intangible assets. Noncurrent, nonmaterialistic assets of a business, the possession of which provides anticipative benefits to the owner. Included in this category are such items as goodwill, trademarks, patents, copyrights, and organizational costs. These are defined by IAS 38, as identifiable, nonmonetary assets without physical substance that are held for use in the production or supply of goods or services, for rental to others, or for administrative purposes.

Generally, the amortization of an intangible asset is credited directly to the asset account, although it is acceptable to use an accumulated amortization account. The tradition of reporting tangible assets on a gross basis, with accumulated depreciation shown separately, developed from the goal of providing the reader with enough information to make a rough calculation of the age of plant assets used by the enterprise, partly to enable an assessment of the amount and timing of capital needed for the replacement of those assets. Intangible assets are not as regularly subject to replacement, however, and are often written down in carrying value for reasons other than the simple passage of time, and therefore amortization is typically, but not necessarily, credited directly to the asset account.

Other assets. An all-inclusive heading for accounts that do not fit neatly into any of the other asset categories (e.g., long-term prepaid expenses, deferred taxes, deferred bond issue costs, noncurrent receivables, and restricted cash).

Classification of Liabilities

The liabilities are normally displayed on the balance sheet in the order of payment.

Current liabilities. According to IAS 1 (revised 1997), a liability should be classified as a current liability when it

1. Is expected to be settled in the normal course of the enterprise's operating cycle; or
2. Is due to be settled within 12 months of the balance sheet date.

All other liabilities should be classified as noncurrent liabilities.

In other words, current liabilities are obligations the liquidation of which is reasonably expected to require the use of existing resources properly classifiable as current assets, or the creation of other current obligations. Obligations which are due on demand or which are callable at any time by the lender are classified as current regardless of the present intent of the entity or of the lender concerning early demand for repayment.

1. Obligations arising from the acquisition of goods and services entering the operating cycle (e.g., accounts payable, short-term notes payable, wages payable, taxes payable, and other miscellaneous payables).
2. Collections of money in advance for the future delivery of goods or performance of services, such as rent received in advance and unearned subscription revenues.
3. Other obligations maturing within the current operating cycle to be met through the use of current assets, such as the current maturity of bonds and long-term notes.

Per IAS 1 (revised 1997), certain liabilities, such as trade payables and accruals for operating costs, which form part of the working capital used in the normal operating cycle of the business, are to be classified as current liabilities even if they are due to be settled after more than 12 months from the balance sheet date.

Other current liabilities which are not settled as part of the operating cycle, but which are due for settlement within 12 months of the balance sheet date, such as dividends payable and the current portion of long-term debt, should also be classified as current liabilities. However, interest-bearing liabilities that provide the financing for working capital on a long-term basis, and which are not scheduled for settlement within 12 months, should not be classified as current liabilities.

IAS 1 (revised 1997) provides another exception to the general rule that a liability due to be repaid within 12 months of the balance sheet date should be classified as a current liability. If the original term was for a period longer than 12 months, and the enterprise intended to refinance the obligation on a long-term basis prior to the balance sheet date, and that intention is supported by an agreement to refinance, or to reschedule payments, which agreement is completed before the financial statements are approved, then the debt is to be reclassified as noncurrent as of the balance sheet date.

In two cases, obligations to be paid within one period should not be classified as current liabilities. Debt expected to be refinanced through another long-term issue, and debt that will be retired through the use of noncurrent assets, such as from the amount accumulated in a bond sinking fund, are treated as noncurrent liabilities because the liquidation does not require the use of current assets or the creation of other current liabilities.

The distinction between current and noncurrent liquid assets generally rests upon both the ability of the entity and the intent of the entity to liquidate or not to liquidate within the traditional 1-year concept. Intent is not of similar significance with regard to the classification of liabilities, however, because the creditor has the legal right to demand satisfaction of a currently due obligation, and even an expression of intent not to exercise that right does not diminish the entity's burden should there be a change in that intention. Thus, whereas an entity can control its use of current assets, it cannot be the master of its own fate with regard to current liabilities, and accordingly, accounting for current liabilities (with the two exceptions noted above) is based on legal terms, not expressions of intent.

Noncurrent liabilities. Obligations that are not expected to be liquidated within the current operating cycle, including

1. Obligations arising through the acquisition of assets, such as the issuance of bonds, long-term notes, and lease obligations;
2. Obligations arising out of the normal course of operations, such as pension obligations; and
3. Contingent obligations involving uncertainty as to possible losses. These are resolved by the occurrence or nonoccurrence of one or more future events that confirm the amount payable, the payee, and/or the date payable, such as product warranties (see the contingency section).

For all long-term liabilities, the maturity date, nature of obligation, rate of interest, and description of any security pledged to support the agreement should be clearly shown. Also, in the case of bonds and long-term notes, any premium or discount should be reported separately as an addition to or subtraction from the par (or face) value of the bond or note. Long-term obligations which contain certain covenants that must be adhered to are classified as current liabilities if any of those covenants have been violated and the lender has the right to demand payment. Unless the lender expressly waives that right or the conditions causing the default are corrected, the obligation is current.

Other liabilities. Items that do not meet the definition of a liability, such as deferred income taxes or deferred investment tax credits, where measured by the deferred method. Often these items will be included in current or noncurrent liabilities even though technically, they are not similar.

Offsetting assets and liabilities. In general, assets and liabilities should not be offset against each other. The reduction of accounts receivable by the allowance for doubtful accounts, or of property, plant, and equipment by the accumulated depreciation, are acts that reduce these assets by the appropriate valuation accounts. These are not equivalent to offsetting assets and liabilities, however.

The right of setoff must exist for the offsetting in the financial statements to be a proper presentation. This right of setoff exists only when all the following conditions are met:

1. Each of the two parties owes the other determinable amounts (although they may be in different currencies and bear different rates of interest).
2. The entity has the right to set off against the amount owed by the other party.
3. The entity intends to offset.
4. The right of setoff is legally enforceable.

In particular cases, laws of certain countries, including some bankruptcy laws, may impose restrictions or prohibitions against the right of setoff. Furthermore, when maturities differ, only the party with the nearest maturity can offset because the party with the longer maturity must settle in the manner determined by the earlier maturity party.

In the context of the presentation of current assets and current liabilities in financial statements, IAS 1 (revised 1997) clearly states that unless a legal right of setoff exists and offsetting represents the expectation as to the realization of the asset or settlement of the liability, amounts should not be offset against each other.

IAS 30 establishes disclosure requirements for banks and similar financial institutions. It prohibits offsetting of assets or liabilities on similar grounds. The offsetting of cash or other assets against a tax liability or other amounts due to governmental bodies is also not acceptable except under limited circumstances. The only exception is when it is clear that the purchase of securities is in substance an advance payment of taxes payable in the near future and that the securities are acceptable for the payment of taxes. This occurs primarily as an accommodation to governmental bodies.

For forwards, interest rate swaps, currency swaps, options, and other conditional or exchange contracts, the conditions for the right of offset must exist or the fair value of contracts in a loss position cannot be offset against the fair value of contracts in a gain position. Neither can accrued receivable amounts be offset against accrued payable amounts. If, however, there is a master netting arrangement, fair value amounts recognized for forwards, interest or currency swaps, options, or other such contracts may be offset without respect to the conditions specified previously.

Classification of Stockholders' Equity

Stockholders' equity represents the interest of the stockholders in the assets of a corporation. It shows the cumulative net results of past transactions and other events.

Share capital. This consists of the par or stated value of preferred and common shares. The number of shares authorized, the number issued, and the number outstanding should be clearly shown. For preferred share capital, the preference features must also be stated as follows:

6% cumulative preference shares, $100 par value, callable at $115, 10,000 shares authorized and outstanding	$xxx
Equity shares, $10 par value per share, 2,000,000 shares authorized, 1,500,000 shares issued and outstanding	$xxx

Preference share capital that is redeemable at the option of the holder is not considered to be part of equity but is usually shown in a separate caption between liabilities and equity. However, IAS 32 makes it clear that substance prevails over form in the case of compound financial instruments, including equity instruments such as mandatorily redeemable preference shares, which accordingly should be shown in the liability section of the balance sheet.

Additional paid-in capital. There are two major categories of additional paid-in capital.

1. Paid-in capital in excess of par or stated value, which is the difference between the actual issue price and par or stated value. Amounts in excess should be disclosed separately for equity shares and each issue of preferred shares as follows:

Additional paid-in capital--6% preference shares	$xxx
Additional paid-in capital--equity shares	$xxx

2. Paid-in capital from other transactions, which includes treasury stock, retirement of stock, stock dividends recorded at market, proceeds from the lapse of stock purchase warrants, proceeds from the conversion of convertible bonds in excess of the par value of the stock, and any other additional capital arising from the company's own stock transactions.

Donated capital. Donations of a noncash variety from either stockholders or outside parties, such as land, securities, buildings, and equipment. The most typical scenario giving rise to donated capital is when a governmental agency makes a contribution to induce a business to locate in the community, in the belief that the resulting job creation will boost the local economy.

Retained earnings. Accumulated earnings that have not been distributed to the shareholders.

1. **Appropriated**--A certain amount of retained earnings that are not to be distributed to stockholders as dividends.
2. **Unappropriated**--Earnings available to be distributed as dividends.

A balance sheet disclosure should reveal the pertinent provisions, source of restriction, amount subject to restriction, and restrictions on other items, such as working capital and additional borrowings. If a company appropriated retained earnings to satisfy bond indebtedness, the presentation would be as follows:

Retained earnings		
Appropriated for bond indebtedness	$xxx	
Free and unappropriated	xxx	$xxx

Many corporations do not record the restrictions in appropriated and unappropriated accounts but merely explain the restrictions in the footnotes, because financial statement users often believe the appropriation is held as cash.

Also included in the equity section of the balance sheet is treasury stock representing issued shares reacquired by the issuer. These are generally stated at their cost of acquisition and as a reduction of shareholders' equity.

Finally, net unrealized losses on noncurrent portfolios of marketable equity securities, the excess of minimum pension liability over unrecognized prior service cost, and unrealized gains (losses) on foreign currency translations will also be shown as adjustments of equity.

Classification of Partners' Capital

In partnership entities, the balance sheet is the same as for all other entities, except for the net worth section. In a partnership, this section is usually referred to as partners' capital. In partnership accounting, the net worth section of the balance sheet includes the equity interests of the partners. Although each individual partner's capital need not be displayed, the totals for each class of partner, general or limited, should be shown.

Loans to or from partners should be displayed as assets and liabilities of the partnership and not as reductions or additions to partners' capital, although a separate line item on the balance sheet may be combined with net worth in a separately defined subtotal on the balance sheet. Payments to partners of interest on loans are properly classified as expenses on the income statement. Payments of interest on capital or salaries to partners are considered an allocation of profits and are usually not expensed on the income statement. However, in an attempt to emulate corporate financial reporting, some partnerships, with adequate disclosure, do display part or all of such payments as expenses.

Relationship of the Balance Sheet to the Income Statement

The balance sheet and income statement are interrelated through the changes that take place in each as a result of business transactions. Choosing a method of valuing inventory determines the method of calculating cost of goods sold. This articulation enables the users of financial information to use the statements as predictive indicators of future cash flows.

In assessing information about overall firm performance, users are interested in bringing together information in the income statement and the balance sheet. The balance sheet can also be used as a guide to give an indication of a firm's continuing ability to earn income and pay dividends. By combining the two statements, investors can develop some important financial ratios. For example, users may wish to express income as a rate of return on net operating assets.

Supplemental Disclosures

In addition to the measurement accounting principles that guide the values placed on the elements included in the balance sheet, there are disclosure accounting principles which are necessary to make the financial statements not misleading because of their omission. The following are five techniques of disclosure:

1. Parenthetical explanations
2. Footnotes
3. Supporting schedules

4. Cross-references
5. Valuation accounts

Parenthetical explanations. Supplemental information is disclosed by means of parenthetical explanations following the appropriate balance sheet items. For example

Equity share capital ($10 par value, 200,000 shares authorized, 150,000 issued)	$1,500,000

Parenthetical explanations have an advantage over both footnotes and supporting schedules. Parenthetical explanations place the disclosure in the body of the statement. The supplemental information tends to be overlooked when it is placed in a footnote.

Footnotes. If the additional information cannot be disclosed in a relatively short and concise parenthetical explanation, a footnote should be used. For example

Inventories (see Note 1)	$2,550,000

The notes to the financial statements would then contain the following:

Note 1: Inventories are stated at the lower of cost or market. Cost is determined by the first-in, first-out method, and market is determined on the basis of estimated net realizable value. As of the balance sheet date, the market value of the inventory is $2,720,000.

Supporting schedules. To present adequate detail regarding certain balance sheet items, a supporting schedule may be used. Current receivables may be a single line item on the balance sheet, as follows:

Current receivables (see Schedule 2)	$2,500,000

A separate schedule for current receivables would then be presented as follows:

Schedule 2
Current Receivables

Customers' accounts and notes	$2,000,000
Associated companies	300,000
Nonconsolidated affiliates	322,000
Other	18,000
	2,640,000
Less allowance for doubtful accounts	(140,000)
	$2,500,000

Cross-references. Cross-referencing is used when there is a direct relationship between two accounts on the balance sheet. For example, among the current assets, the following might be shown if $1,500,000 of accounts receivable were required to be pledged as collateral for a $1,200,000 bank loan:

Accounts receivable pledged to bank	$1,500,000

Included in the current liabilities would be the following:

Bank loan payable--secured by accounts receivable	$1,200,000

Valuation accounts. Valuation accounts are used to reduce or increase the carrying amount of some assets and liabilities in financial statements. Accumulated depreciation reduces the book value for property, plant, and equipment, and a bond premium (discount) increases (decreases) the face value of a bond payable as shown in the following illustrations:

Equipment	$18,000,000	
Less accumulated depreciation	(1,625,000)	$16,375,000
Bonds payable	$20,000,000	
Less discount on bonds payable	(1,300,000)	$18,700,000
Bonds payable	$20,000,000	
Add premium on bonds payable	1,300,000	$21,300,000

Accounting policies. There are many different methods of valuing assets and assigning costs. IAS 1 (revised 1997) requires financial statements to include clear and concise disclosure of all significant accounting policies that have been used in the preparation of those financial statements. Financial statement users must be aware of the accounting policies used by enterprises so that sound economic decisions can be made. The disclosures should identify and describe the accounting principles followed by the entity and methods of applying those principles that materially affect the determination of financial position, changes in cash flows, or results of operations. The accounting policies should encompass those accounting principles and methods that involve the following:

1. Selection from acceptable alternatives
2. Principles and methods peculiar to the industry
3. Unique applications of IAS

Fairness exception under IAS 1 (revised). In what has become a somewhat controversial move, the IASC inserted what may be called a "fairness exception" in IAS 1 (revised), which was not included in the exposure draft which preceded that standard. This acknowledges that, while the use of IAS will result **in virtually all circumstances** in financial statements which achieve a fair presentation, in some instances this may not be the case. In such eventualities, IAS 1 (revised) permits departure from the standards to achieve the greater good of fair presentation, provided, however, that the enterprise discloses the following:

1. That management has concluded that the financial statements fairly present the entity's financial position, financial performance and cash flows;
2. That the entity has complied in all material respects with applicable IAS except that it departed from a standard to achieve a fair presentation; and
3. The standard from which the entity has departed; the nature of the departure, including the accounting treatment which the standard would have required; the reason why that treatment would have been misleading in the circumstances; the alternative treatment which was in fact applied; and the

financial impact of the departure on profit or loss, assets, liabilities, equity, and cash flows for each period presented.

It might be noted that in the US, while there is no similar exception under the accounting standards, under US auditing standards there is a provision that an unqualified opinion may be rendered even when there has been a GAAP departure, if the auditor concludes that it provides a fairer presentation than would have resulted had GAAP been strictly adhered to. Under IAS, this logic is built into the accounting standards themselves, and thus is not dependent upon the level of service, if any, being rendered by an independent accountant, but rather makes it a management responsibility, including the need to disclose the logic and the financial statement impact.

IAS 1 (revised 1997) requires that disclosure of these policies be an integral part of the financial statements. It recommends that these policies be disclosed in one location rather than being scattered throughout the footnotes. Though it makes it mandatory on enterprises to disclose all significant accounting policies, IAS 1 also recognizes that disclosure cannot rectify an incorrect or inappropriate treatment. Three considerations that govern the selection and application of the appropriate accounting policies are

1. Prudence
2. Substance over form
3. Materiality

The IASC not only encourages enterprises to present financial statements in conformity with the standards but also requires enterprises to disclose whether they have complied with or departed from the requirements of the standards (IAS 1 [revised 1997]; and the IASC's *Framework*).

Related-parties disclosures. According to IAS 24, *Related-Party Disclosures*, financial statements should include disclosure of material related-party transactions which are defined by the standard as "transfer of resources or obligations between related parties, regardless of whether a price is charged."

A **related party** is essentially any party that controls or can significantly influence the financial or operating decisions of the company to the extent that the company may be prevented from fully pursuing its own interests. Such groups would include associates, investees accounted for by the equity method, trusts for the benefit of employees, principal owners, key management personnel, and immediate family members of owners or management.

Disclosures should take place even if there is no accounting recognition made for such transactions (e.g., a service is performed without payment). Disclosures should generally not imply that such related-party transactions were on terms essentially equivalent to arm's-length dealings. Additionally, when one or more companies are under common control such that the financial statements might vary from those that would have been obtained if the companies were autonomous, the nature of the control relationship should be disclosed even if there are no transactions between the companies.

The disclosures generally should include

1. Nature of relationship
2. Description of transactions and effects of such transactions on the financial statements for each period for which an income statement is presented
3. Dollar amount of transactions for each period for which an income statement is presented and effects of any change in establishing the terms of such transactions different from that used in prior periods
4. Amounts due to and from such related parties as of the date of each balance sheet presented together with the terms and manner of settlement

Reporting comparative amounts for the preceding period. IAS 1 (revised 1997) requires that financial statements should show corresponding figures for the preceding period. To increase the usefulness of financial statements, many companies include in their annual reports 5- or 10-year summaries of condensed financial information. These comparative statements allow investment analysts and other interested readers to perform comparative analysis of pertinent information. The presentation of comparative financial statements in annual reports enhances the usefulness of such reports and brings out more clearly the nature and trends of current changes affecting the enterprise. Such presentation emphasizes the fact that the statements for a series of periods are far more significant than those for a single period and that the accounts for one period are but an installment of what is essentially a continuous history.

When comparative financial statements are presented (as they normally will be), the related footnote disclosures must also be presented on a comparative basis, except for items of disclosure that would be not meaningful, or might even be confusing, if set forth in such a manner. Although there is no official guidance on this issue, certain details, such as schedules of debt maturities as of the year earlier balance sheet date, would be of little interest to users of the current statements and would be largely redundant with information provided for the more recent year end. Accordingly, such details are often omitted from comparative financial statements. Another example of superfluous comparative data is the amount of undrawn borrowing capacity at the earlier year end. Most other disclosures, however, continue to be meaningful and should be presented for all years for which basic financial statements are displayed.

Subsequent events. The balance sheet is dated as of the last day of the fiscal period, but a period of time may elapse before the financial statements are actually prepared and issued. During this period, significant events or transactions may have occurred that materially affect the company's financial position. These events and transactions are usually referred to as **subsequent events**. IAS 10, which has recently been revised, refers to them as "events after the balance sheet date." If not disclosed, significant events occurring between the balance sheet date and issue date could make the financial statements misleading.

There are two types of subsequent events described by IAS 10 as revised in 1999. The first type consists of events that provide additional evidence with respect to conditions that existed at the date of the balance sheet and which affect the estimates inherent in the process of preparing financial statements. The second type consists of events that provide evidence with respect to conditions that did not exist at the date of the balance sheet being reported on but arose subsequent to that date (and prior to the actual issuance of the financial statements). Such post-balance-sheet events require either adjusting the financial statements or only disclosing them, depending on the character and timing of the event in question. The characterization of these events as being either adjusting or non-adjusting events is not unique to the international accounting standards. In fact, this terminology is found in other (i.e., national) accounting standards, like UK GAAP.

Examples of post-balance-sheet date events

1. A loss on an uncollectible trade account receivable as a result of a customer's deteriorating financial condition leading to bankruptcy subsequent to the balance sheet date would usually (but not always) be indicative of conditions existing at the balance sheet date, thereby calling for adjustment of the financial statements before their issuance. On the other hand, a loss on an uncollectible trade account receivable resulting from a customer's major casualty, such as a fire or flood subsequent to the balance sheet date, would not be indicative of conditions existing at the balance sheet date, and adjustment of the financial statements would not be appropriate. However, if the amount is material, disclosure would be required.

2. A loss arising from the recognition after the balance sheet date that an asset such as plant and equipment had suffered a material decline in value arising out of reduced marketability for the product or service it can produce. Such a reduction would be considered an economic event in process at the balance sheet date and would require adjustment and recognition of the loss.

3. Nonadjusting events, which are those not existing at the balance sheet date, require disclosure but not adjustment. These could include

    a. Sale of a bond or share capital issue after the balance sheet date, even if planned before that date.
    b. Purchase of a business, if the transaction is consummated after year end.
    c. Settlement of litigation when the event giving rise to the claim took place subsequent to the balance sheet date. The settlement is an economic event that would be accounted for in the period of occurrence. (However, if the event occurred before the balance sheet date, IAS 37 would require that the estimated amount of the contingency be accrued, in most instances, as discussed further in the next section of this chapter.)
    d. Loss of plant or inventories as a result of fire or flood.

e.   Losses on receivables resulting from conditions (such as a customer's major casualty) arising subsequent to the balance sheet date.

f.   Gains or losses on certain marketable securities.

Contingencies. Contingencies, formerly addressed by IAS 10, are now defined and described by IAS 37, issued in late 1998. While the former standard largely mirrored the corresponding US standard, and therefore required accrual of contingent losses deemed to be probable, IAS 37 has created in its stead a more complex typology comprised of provisions and contingencies. Under this new standard, the term provisions is used in the sense that contingent liabilities was earlier employed, to denote those contingencies which are deemed probable of occurrence--and which strictly speaking are no longer to be considered as being contingent at all, but rather merely uncertain as to timing and/or amount.

Under IAS 37, the term contingencies is reserved to those potential obligations which are not to be accrued and formally reported in the balance sheet. In other words, contingencies which under the predecessor standard were deemed to be either reasonably possible or remote are now the only categories being denoted as contingencies. Under the requirements of IAS 37 (which are not substantively at variance with IAS 10 in this regard), remote contingencies need not be disclosed, while those which are not remote (i.e., those which under the earlier standard would have been denoted as being reasonably possible) must be disclosed in the notes.

Apart from the terminological changes (which admittedly do have the potential to confuse), the actual accounting requirements are essentially unchanged. Provisions are to be accrued by a charge to income and the recording of a liability if

1.   The enterprise has a present obligation as a result of past events;

2.   It is probable that an outflow of the enterprise's resources will be required; and

3.   A reliable estimate can be made of the amount.

The above described conditions largely parallel those that were defined under IAS 10 (prior to its revision in 1999) for probable contingencies. As with practice under the former IAS 10, if an estimate could be made for the obligation with a reasonable degree of certitude, accrual was not prescribed, but rather disclosure in the notes to the financial statements would be needed.

For obligations which do not rise to the level of probable as used above, but which are more than remote in terms of likelihood of occurrence, disclosure in the notes was mandated. These items are now denoted as being contingencies, as indeed they were under the former IAS 10. In general, unless the obligation is deemed more than remote, disclosure is not required. However, it should be noted that common practice has long been to disclose certain categories of remote contingencies; an example is disclosure of the guarantee of the indebtedness of another party, even if it is not anticipated presently that the enterprise will be asked to honor that guarantee following a failure to perform by the primary obligor.

No disclosure is required for unasserted claims or assessments when no act by the potential claimant has transpired to suggest that there is an intent to make a claim. Also, general or unspecific business risks (e.g., the inherent possibility that foreign operations could be affected by changes in government) are neither accrued for nor disclosed.

Examples of loss contingencies

1. Collectibility of receivables
2. Obligations related to product warranties and product defects
3. Risk of loss or damage of enterprise property by fire, explosion, or other hazards
4. Threat of expropriation of assets
5. Pending or threatened litigation
6. Actual or possible claims and assessments
7. Risk of loss from catastrophes assumed by property and casualty insurance companies including reinsurance companies
8. Guarantees of indebtedness of other entities
9. Obligations of commercial banks under standby letters of credit
10. Agreements to repurchase receivables (or to repurchase the related property) that have been sold

Accrual and disclosure of loss contingencies should be based on an evaluation of the facts in each particular case. Accrual is not a substitute for disclosure, and disclosure is not a substitute for accrual.

An estimated gain from a gain contingency usually is not reflected in the accounts since to do so might be to recognize revenue prior to its realization. Adequate disclosure of the gain contingency shall be made, but care must be taken to avoid misleading implications as to the likelihood of realization.

Contracts and negotiations. All significant contractual agreements and negotiations should be disclosed in the footnotes to the financial statements. For example, lease contract provisions, pension obligations, requirements contracts, bond indenture covenants, and stock option plans should be clearly disclosed in the footnotes.

Other disclosures required by IAS 1 (revised). IAS 1 (revised) has added several new, required disclosure items. If not otherwise disclosed within the financial statements, these items should be reported in the footnotes.

1. The domicile and legal form of the entity, its country of incorporation, and the address of the registered office (or principal place of business, if different);
2. A description of the nature of the enterprise's operations and its principal activities;
3. The name of the parent entity and the ultimate parent of the group; and
4. The number of employees either at the end of the period or an average during the period being reported upon.

These disclosures (which may have been modeled on those already imposed under UK GAAP) are particularly of interest given the multinational character of many enterprises reporting in conformity with IAS.

Balance Sheet Format

The format of a balance sheet is not presently specified by International Accounting Standards but has become established as a matter of tradition and, in some circumstances, as a result of specific industry practices. IAS 5 categorically states that "this Standard does not propose a particular format for the presentation of financial statements." However, the appendix to IAS 1 (revised 1997) gives an example of a balance sheet format but also clarifies that it be considered as an example of the way in which the requirements of the proposed standard might be put into practice.

In general, the two types of formats are the report form and the account form. In the **report form** the balance sheet continues line by line from top to bottom as follows:

Assets	$xxx
Liabilities	$xxx
Stockholders' equity	xxx
Total liabilities and stockholders' equity	$xxx

In the **account form** the balance sheet appears in a balancing concept with assets on the left and liabilities and equity amounts on the right as follows:

Assets	$ xxx	Liabilities	$ xxx
		Stockholders' equity	xxx
Total assets	$ xxx	Total liabilities and stockholders' equity	$ xxx

The balance sheet format presented in Schedule 4 to the UK Companies Act of 1985, wherein a **net** asset total is presented (as a total of assets minus liabilities) as being equal to equity plus reserves, may be seen as a third variation, and is known as the UK GAAP format. This in fact is a report format, as illustrated above, with merely a minor alteration made to explicitly reveal the equality between net assets and net worth.

Example of balance sheet classification and presentation

The system of balance sheet classification and presentations is illustrated by the following comprehensive balance sheet:

ABC Corporation
Balance Sheet
December 31, 2000

Assets
Current assets:
  Cash and bank deposits

Restricted to current bond maturity	$xxx	
Unrestricted	xxx	$xxx

Short-term investments			
Marketable equity securities		xxx	
Marketable debt securities		xxx	
Refundable income taxes		xxx	
Receivables from associates		xxx	
Accounts receivable	xxx		
Less allowance for doubtful accounts	(xxx)	xxx	
Notes receivable due in 2001	xxx		
Less notes receivable discounted	(xxx)	xxx	
Dishonored notes receivable		xxx	
Installment notes due in 2001		xxx	
Interest receivable		xxx	
Creditors' accounts with debit balances		xxx	
Advances to employees		xxx	
Inventories (carried at lower of cost or market by FIFO):			
Finished goods	xxx		
Work in process	xxx		
Raw materials	xxx	xxx	
Prepaid expenses:			
Prepaid rent	xxx		
Prepaid insurance	xxx	xxx	
Total current assets			$xxx
Long-term investments:			
Investments in equity securities		xxx	
Investments in bonds		xxx	
Investments in equity securities (at cost, plus equity in un-			
distributed net earnings since acquisition)		xxx	
Investments in unused land and facilities		xxx	
Cash surrender value of officers' life insurance policies		xxx	
Sinking fund for bond retirement		xxx	
Plant expansion fund		xxx	
Total long-term investments			$xxx
Property, plant, and equipment:			
Land		$xxx	
Buildings		xxx	
Machinery and equipment		xxx	
Furniture and fixtures		xxx	
Leasehold improvements		xxx	
Less accumulated depreciation and amortization		(xxx)	
Total property, plant, and equipment			xxx
Intangible assets, net of amortization:			
Excess of cost over net assets of acquired businesses (goodwill)		$xxx	
Patents		xxx	
Trademarks		xxx	
Organization costs		xxx	
Total intangible assets, net			xxx
Other assets:			
Installment notes due after 2001		$xxx	
Unamortized bond issue costs		xxx	
Total other noncurrent assets			xxx
Total assets			$xxx

Liabilities and Stockholders' Equity

Current liabilities:

Commercial paper and other short-term notes	$xxx		
Accounts payable	xxx		
Salaries, wages, and commissions	xxx		
Taxes withheld from employees	xxx		
Income taxes payable	xxx		
Dividends payable	xxx		
Rent revenue collected in advance	xxx		
Other advances from customers	xxx		
Current portion of long-term debt	xxx		
Current obligations under capital leases	xxx		
Deferred tax liability	xxx		
Short-term portion of accrued warranty	xxx		
Other accrued liabilities	<u>xxx</u>		
Total current liabilities			$xxx

Noncurrent liabilities:

Notes payable due after 2001	$xxx		
Plus unamortized note premium	<u>xxx</u>	$xxx	
Long-term bonds:			
10% debentures due 2016	xxx		
9-1/2% collateralized obligations maturing serially to 2002	xxx		
8% convertible subordinated debentures due 2016	xxx		
Less unamortized discounts net of premiums	(<u>xxx</u>)	xxx	
Accrued pension cost		xxx	
Obligations under capital leases		xxx	
Deferred tax liability		xxx	
Long-term portion of accrued warranty		<u>xxx</u>	
Total noncurrent liabilities			<u>xxx</u>
Total liabilities			$<u>xxx</u>

Share capital:

$12.50 convertible preference shares stock, $100 stated value, 200,000 shares authorized, 175,000 outstanding	$xxx		
12% cumulative preferrence shares, $100 stated value, callable at $115, 100,000 shares authorized and outstanding	xxx		
Equity shares, $10 stated value, 500,000 shares authorized, 450,000 issued, 15,000 held in treasury	xxx		
Equity shares subscribed 10,000 shares	xxx		
Less: Subscriptions receivable	(<u>xxx</u>)	$xxx	

Additional paid-in capital:

From 12% cumulative preferrence	xxx		
From equity shares	xxx		
From treasury stock transactions	xxx		
From stock dividends	xxx		
From expiration of stock options	xxx		
Warrants outstanding	<u>xxx</u>	xxx	

Retained earnings:

Appropriated for bond indebtedness	xxx		
Free and unappropriated	<u>xxx</u>	<u>xxx</u>	
		xxx	

Less: Treasury stock at cost	(xxx)		
Net unrealized loss on available-for-sale securities	(xxx)		
Unrealized loss from foreign currency translation	(xxx)		
Excess of minimum pension liability over unrecognized prior service cost	(xxx)	(xxx)	
Total stockholders' equity			$xxx
Total liabilities and stockholders' equity			$xxx

The format of the balance sheet as illustrated by the appendix to IAS 1 (revised 1997) is the following:

**XYZ Limited
Consolidated Balance Sheet
as at 31 December 2000
(in thousands of currency units)**

	2000	*2000*	*1999*	*1999*
Assets				
Noncurrent assets	x		x	
Property, plant and equipment	x		x	
Goodwill	x		x	
Investments in associates	x		x	
Other financial assets	x	xx	x	xx
Current assets				
Inventories	x		x	
Trade and other receivables	x		x	
Prepayments	x		x	
Cash and cash equivalents	x	xx	x	xx
Total assets		xx		xx
Equity and Liabilities				
Capital and reserves				
Issued capital (Note__)	x		x	
Reserves (Note__)	x		x	
Accumulated profit (losses)	x	xx	x	xx
Minority interest		xx		xx
Noncurrent liabilities				
Interest-bearing borrowings	x		x	
Deferred taxes	x		x	
Retirement benefit obligations	x	xx	x	xx
Current liabilities				
Trade and other payables	x		x	
Short-term borrowings	x		x	
Current portion of interest-bearing borrowings	x		x	
Warranty provisions	x	xx	x	xx
Total equity and liabilities		xx		xx

3 INCOME STATEMENT, STATEMENT OF CHANGES IN EQUITY, AND STATEMENT OF RECOGNIZED GAINS AND LOSSES

PERSPECTIVE AND ISSUES

In discussing the concept of performance, the IASC's *Framework for the Preparation and Presentation of Financial Statements* states that profit is frequently used as a measure of performance. Historically, under all sets of extant accounting standards, the income statement has provided this vital piece of information about what is sometimes referred to as the "bottom line" for the enterprise, the ultimate measure of entity economic performance. However, under both IAS and various national GAAP standards, over the years a number of sources of changes in owner net worth, excluding investments by or distributions to the owners themselves, have become excluded from this "bottom line" measure, for various reasons. For example, revaluations of plant assets, which are sanctioned by IAS 16, are not considered to be culminations of the normal earnings process (inasmuch as commercial enterprises are not typically organized to speculate on the changing values of their productive assets), and thus such items have been relegated to equity accounts such as revaluation surplus. As a consequence, the income statement cannot and does not purport to reveal the totality of economic changes in the enterprise for the period.

To deal with the fact that the income statement has diverged increasingly from being a complete picture of the economic changes affecting the reporting entity over the course of the period, accounting standard setters in the US and the UK, as well as the IASC, have of late been deliberating the need either for an expanded income statement (one which would include the various changes which have, under the respective sets of standards, been consigned to assorted "contra equity" or "additional equity" accounts) or for a new financial statement which would summarize these changes in some other fashion. E53 did propose to require such a new statement, the statement of nonowner movements in equity, which would have included all these various nonincome statement changes in net worth, excluding owner transactions, plus net income. The US standard setter, the FASB, in fact has recently mandated just such a statement, the statement of comprehensive income.

A good deal of opposition was voiced to the IASC's proposal in E53, however, and the final standard, recently issued as IAS 1 (revised), has retreated somewhat from the earlier recommendation. However, to comply with IAS 1 (revised 1997) it will in fact be necessary to add one of two possible new financial statements, with expanded footnote disclosures needed under certain conditions. These are explored later in this chapter.

The traditional income statement is known by many titles. The international accounting standards, such as IAS 1 (revised 1997), *Presentation of Financial Statements,* and IAS 8, *Net Profit or Loss for the Period, Fundamental Errors and Changes in Accounting Polices,* refer to this statement as the income statement, but internationally it has a number of other common appellations. For instance, in the United Kingdom and certain developing countries it is also referred to as the profit and loss account; and in the United States other names, such as the statement of income, statement of earnings, or statement of operations, are sometimes used. By whatever name, this statement is a major component of an entity's periodic financial reporting and captures most of the changes in the entity's economic position over the course of the reporting period, which is most often 1 year.

Since the late 1960s or early 1970s, the income statement has been widely perceived by investors, creditors, management, and other interested parties as the single most important of an enterprise's basic financial statements. Investors consider the past income of a business as the most useful predictor of future earnings and performance, which in turn is widely deemed to be the best indicator of future dividends and market stock price performance. In fact, the reason that many other changes in net worth, such as that resulting from changes in fair values of plant assets or investments, are excluded from the income statement is that these are **not** considered to be useful as predictors of future economic performance.

Creditors look principally to the income statement for insight into the borrower's ability to generate the future cash flows needed to repay the obligations (while the cash flow statement would appear more logically to be the source for these insights, that statement is a relatively late development and not universally understood yet; thus, traditionally, financial statement users have been more comfortable drawing these inferences from the income statement). Management, then, must be concerned with the income statement by virtue of the importance placed on it by investors and creditors. Additionally, management uses the income statement as a gauge of its effectiveness and efficiency in combining the factors of production into the goods and/or services that it creates and sells.

The information provided by the income statement, relating to individual items of income and expense and to different combinations of these items (such as the amounts reported as gross margin or profit before interest and taxes), facilitates the process of financial analysis, especially that relating to the entity's profitability. Further, the manner of presentation of certain items of income and expense on the face of the income statement can provide relevant information for proper economic decision making.

For one example of this last matter, it is normal practice to distinguish between those items of income and expense that arise from ordinary activities and those that do not. IAS 8 requires that income and expenses (and profit or loss) from ordinary activities be disclosed separately on the face of the income statement, distinguishing them from any extraordinary items, which must be identified clearly and disclosed separately. The standard also requires that individual items of income and expense within profit or loss from ordinary activities, if due to materiality considerations or because of their nature or incidence, need disclosure to assist the user of the financial statements in understanding the performance of the enterprise, these must be given separate disclosure. The paramount concern is that financial statement users be able to assess the ability of the enterprise to replicate the item and thus to generate earnings and ultimately cash and cash equivalents in the future.

Much of current accounting theory is concerned with the measurement of income. Even with the renewed interest in the balance sheet, the income statement remains of great importance to the majority of financial statement users. This chapter focuses on key income measurement issues and on matters of income statement presentation and disclosure. It also explains and illustrates the presentation of the new component of financial statements prescribed by IAS 1 (revised 1997), **statement of changes in equity** (or, alternatively, the **statement of recognized gains and losses** together with the required footnote disclosure).

IAS 1 (revised 1997) has added, in a somewhat controversial move, what may be deemed a "fairness exception" to compliance with IAS. If management concludes that application of a particular provision of a standard would cause the financial statements to be misleading, it may choose to depart from that provision in order to achieve a fair presentation. In such circumstances, however, the fact of the departure, the nature of it, the treatment which IAS would have required, and why it was deemed to be misleading, must all be included in the notes to the financial statements.

Sources of IAS

IAS 1 (revised 1997), 8, 14 (revised 1997), 16, 18, 21, 25, 30, 35, 36, 37
IASC's Framework for the Preparation and Presentation of Financial Statements

---

DEFINITIONS OF TERMS

Elements of Financial Statements

Comprehensive income. The change in equity of an entity during a period from transactions and other events and circumstances from nonowner sources. It includes all changes in equity during a period, except those resulting from investments by owners and distributions to owners.

Expenses. Decreases in economic benefits during the accounting period in the form of outflows or depletions of assets or incurrences of liabilities that result in decreases in equity, other than those relating to distributions to equity participants. The term **expenses** is broad enough to include **losses** as well as normal categories of expenses; thus, the international standard differs from its US counterpart, which deems losses to be a separate and distinct element to be accounted for, denoting decreases in equity from peripheral or incidental transactions.

Income. Increases in economic benefits during the accounting period in the form of inflows or enhancements of assets that result in increases in equity, other than those relating to contributions from equity participants. The IASC's *Framework* clarifies that this definition of income encompasses both revenue and gains. Again, the corresponding US accounting standard holds that revenues and gains constitute two separate elements of financial reporting, with gains denoting increases in equity from peripheral or incidental transactions.

Statement of changes in equity. As prescribed by IAS 1 (revised 1997), *Presentation of Financial Statements*, an enterprise should present, as a separate component of financial statements, along with the traditional financial statements, a statement showing

1. The net profit or loss for the period;
2. Items of income (including gain) and expense (including loss) which are recognized in equity, as required by this standard, and the total of these items;
3. The cumulative effect of changes in accounting policy and the correction of fundamental errors (when the benchmark treatment, retrospective application and adjustment of beginning retained earnings, respectively, is elected under IAS 8);
4. Capital transactions and distributions with/to owners of the enterprise;
5. The balance of accumulated profit or loss at the beginning of the period and at the balance sheet date, and the movements for the period; and
6. A reconciliation between the carrying amounts of each class of equity capital, share premium and each reserve at the beginning and the end of the period, separately disclosing each movement.

Statement of recognized gains and losses. As an alternative to a statement of changes in equity (above), as prescribed by the IAS 1 (revised 1997), *Presentation of Financial Statements,* an enterprise may present, along with the traditional financial statements, a statement of recognized gains and losses. This statement highlights items of income and expense that are not recognized in the income statement, and it reports all changes in equity, including net income, other than those resulting from investments by and distributions to owners (items 1-3 shown under the foregoing, should be presented in this statement). When an enterprise chooses to present the statement of recognized gains and losses, it should, additionally, present in footnotes to the financial statements, items 4 to 6 shown under the discussion of the statement of changes in equity, above.

Other Terminology

Discontinuing operations. IAS 35 defines a "discontinuing operation" as a component of an enterprise

1. That the enterprise, pursuant to a single plan, is disposing of substantially in its entirety, such as by selling the component in a single transaction, by de-merger or spin-off of ownership of the component to the enterprise's share-holders; is disposing of piecemeal, such as by selling off the component's assets and settling its liabilities individually; or is terminating through abandonment;
2. That represents a separate major line of business or geographical area of operations; and
3. Than can be distinguished operationally and for financial reporting pur-poses.

Extraordinary item. Events and transactions that are clearly distinct from the ordinary activities of the enterprise and are distinguished by the infrequency of their occurrence.

Initial disclosure event. For the purposes of IAS 35, with respect to discon-tinuing operations, the "initial disclosure event" is the occurrence of one of the fol-lowing, whichever occurs earlier:

1. The enterprise has entered into a binding sale agreement for substantially all of the assets attributable to the discontinuing operation; or
2. The enterprise's board of directors or similar governing body has both ap-proved a detailed, formal plan for the discontinuance, and made an an-nouncement of the plan.

Major line of business. In the context of discontinued operations, IAS 8 defines a major line of business as a separate line of business of an enterprise that is "distinguishable from other business activities," such as a segment, as determined in accordance with IAS 14.

Ordinary activities. Activities that are undertaken by the enterprise as part of its normal business and include related activities that are incidental to or are pursued in furtherance of regular business.

Realization. The process of converting noncash resources and rights into money or, more precisely, the sale of an asset for cash or claims to cash.

Recognition. The process of formally recording or incorporating in the financial statements of an entity items that meet the definition of an element and satisfy the criteria for recognition.

Segment of a business. A distinguishable component of an enterprise which is engaged in providing products or services which are subject to risks and returns different from other "business segments" or "geographical segments." A segment may be in the form of a subsidiary, a division, a department, a joint venture or other nonsubsidiary investee. Its assets, results of operations, and activities can be clearly distinguished (physically and operationally, and for financial reporting purposes) from the other assets, results of operations, and activities of the entity. Business segments are distinguishable components of an enterprise engaged in providing different products or services, or a different group of related products or services, primarily to customers outside an enterprise. Geographical segments are distinguishable components of an enterprise engaged in operations in different countries or group of countries within particular geographical areas as may be determined to be appropriate in an enterprise's particular circumstances.

CONCEPTS, RULES, AND EXAMPLES

Concepts of Income

Economists have generally adopted a wealth maintenance concept of income. Under this concept, income is the maximum amount that can be consumed during a period and still leave the enterprise with the same amount of wealth at the end of the period as existed at the beginning. Wealth is determined with reference to the current market values of the net productive assets at the beginning and end of the period. Therefore, the economists' definition of income would fully incorporate market value changes (both increases and decreases in wealth) in the determination of periodic income.

Accountants, on the other hand, have generally defined income by reference to specific events that give rise to recognizable elements of revenue and expense during a reporting period. The events that produce reportable items of revenue and expense comprise a subset of economic events that determine economic income. Many changes in the market values of wealth components are deliberately excluded from the measurement of accounting income but are included in the measurement of economic income.

The discrepancy between the accounting and economic measures of income are the result of a preference on the part of accountants and financial statement users for information that is reliable. Since many fluctuations in the market values of assets are matters of conjecture, accountants have retained the historical cost model, which generally precludes the recognition of market value changes until realized by a transaction. Similarly, both accountants and economists understand that the earnings process occurs throughout the various stages of production, sales, and final delivery of the product. However, the difficulty in measuring the precise rate at which this earnings process is taking place has led accountants to conclude that income should normally be recognized only when it is fully realized. Realization generally implies that the enterprise producing the item has completed all of its obligations relating to the product and that collection of the resulting receivable is assured beyond reasonable doubt. For very sound reasons, accountants have developed a reliable system of income recognition that is based on generally accepted accounting principles applied consistently from period to period. The interplay between recognition and realization generally means that values on the balance sheet are recognized only when realized through an income statement transaction.

A separate but equally important reason for the disparity between the accounting and economic measures of income relates to the need for periodic reporting. The economic measure of income would be relatively simple to apply on a life cycle basis. Economic income would be measured by the difference between its wealth at the termination point and its wealth at the origination date, plus withdrawals or other distributions and minus additional investments over the course of its life. However, applying the same measurement strategy to discrete fiscal periods, as accountants apply, is much more difficult. The continual earnings process, in which the earnings of a business occur throughout the various stages of production and delivery of a product, is conceptually straightforward. Allocating those earnings to individual years, quarters, or months is substantially more difficult, requiring both estimates and judgment. Consequently, accountants have concluded that there must be unambiguous guidelines for revenue recognition. These have required recognition only at the completion of the earnings cycle.

The appropriate measurement of income is partially dependent on the vantage point of the party doing the measuring. From the perspective of outside investors taken as a whole, income might be defined as earnings before any payments to those investors, including bondholders and preferred stockholders, as well as common shareholders. On the other hand, from the viewpoint of the common shareholders, income might better be defined as earnings after payments to other investors, including creditors and preferred shareholders. Currently, net income is defined as earnings available for the preferred and common stockholders. However, in various statistics and special reports, a variety of these concepts are employed.

Recognition and Measurement

Recognition involves the depiction of an item in words and by a monetary amount, and the inclusion of that amount in the balance sheet or the income statement. For recognition of an item on financial statements, it should meet the definition of an element as prescribed by the IASC's *Framework* and satisfy the criteria for recognition as set out in that document. The criteria are needed to assist accountants in determining which economic events are in the domain of items included in the measurement of income. The IASC's *Framework* has identified the following recognition criteria, which have not been altered by the issuance of IAS 1 (revised):

1. **Item must meet the definition of an element.** To be recognized, an item must meet one of the definitions of an element of the financial statements. For instance, a resource must meet the definition of an asset, an obligation must meet the definition of a liability, and so on. It is interesting to note that sometimes the interrelationship between the elements requires that an item that meets the definition and recognition criteria for a particular element, for instance, an asset, automatically requires the recognition of another element, for example, income or a liability.

2. **Assessment of degree of uncertainty regarding future economic benefits.** This refers to the degree of uncertainty that the future economic benefits associated with an item will flow to or from the enterprise. The assessment of this uncertainty is made on the basis of evidence available at the time of preparation of the financial statements. This concept can be illustrated through the following example: At year end while valuing inventory, if it is uncertain whether or not the full cost of the inventory could be recovered in the future, say, when part of the inventory is damaged, recognition is given to this uncertainty and the inventory is written down to its net realizable value.

3. **Item's cost or value can be measured with reliability.** An item must possess a relevant attribute, such as cost or value, which can be quantified in monetary units with sufficient reliability. Measurability must be considered in terms of both relevance and reliability, the two primary qualitative characteristics of accounting information.

4. **Relevance.** An item is relevant if the information about it has the capacity to make a difference in investors', creditors', or other users' decisions. The relevance of information is affected by its nature and materiality.

5. **Reliability.** An item is reliable if the information about it is representationally faithful, free of material errors, and is neutral or free from bias. Further, to possess the quality of reliability, two more features should be present.

    a. The transactions and other events the information purports to represent should be accounted for and presented in accordance with their *substance* and economic reality and *not merely their legal form.*

    b. The preparers of financial statements, while dealing with and recognizing uncertainties, should exercise judgment or a degree of caution: in other words, *prudence.*

To be given accounting recognition, an asset, liability, or item of income or expense would have to meet the above-mentioned five criteria.

Income. According to the IASC's *Framework*

> ***Income*** *is increases in economic benefits during the accounting period in the form of inflows or enhancements of assets or decreases of*

liabilities that result in increases in equity, other than those relating to contributions from equity participants.   The definition of income encompasses both revenue and gains, and revenue arises in the course of ordinary activities of an enterprise and is referred to by different names, such as sales, fees, interest, dividends, royalties, and rent.

IAS 18 is the standard that deals with the accounting for revenue. It sets forth the following characteristics of the term **revenue**:

1. Inflows of economic benefits arise in the course of ordinary activities of an enterprise.
2. Inflows are to be reported gross.
3. Inflows result in increases in equity, other than increases relating to contributions from equity participants.

The measurement concept requires that revenue be measured at the fair value of the consideration received or receivable. **Fair value** is defined as

the amount for which an asset could be exchanged, or a liability settled, between knowledgeable, willing parties in an arm's-length transaction.

The realization concept stipulates that revenue is recognized only when the following occur:

1. The earnings process is complete or virtually complete.
2. Revenue is evidenced by the existence of an exchange transaction that has taken place.

The existence of an exchange transaction is critical to the accounting recognition of revenue. Generally, it means that a sale to an outside party has occurred, resulting in the receipt of cash or the obligation by the purchaser to make future payment for the item received. However, an exchange transaction is viewed in a broader sense than the legal concept of a sale. Whenever an exchange of rights and privileges takes place, an exchange transaction is deemed to have occurred. For example, interest revenue and interest expense are earned or incurred ratably over a period without a discrete transaction taking place. Accruals are recorded periodically to reflect the interest realized by the passage of time. Similarly, the percentage-of-completion method recognizes revenue based on the measure of progress on a long-term construction project. The earnings process is considered to occur simultaneously with the measure of progress (e.g., the incurrence of costs).

The conditions for the timing of revenue recognition would also be varied if the production of certain commodities takes place in environments in which the ultimate realization of revenue is so assured that it can be recognized upon the completion of the production process. At the opposite extreme is the situation in which the exchange transaction has taken place but significant uncertainty exists as to the ultimate collectibility of the amount. For example, in certain sales of real estate, where the down payment percentage is extremely small and the security for the buyer's notes is minimal, revenue is often not recognized until collections are actually received.

Expenses. According to the IASC's *Framework*

> ***Expenses*** *are decreases in economic benefits during an accounting period in the form of outflows or depletions of assets or incurrences of liabilities that result in decreases in equity, other than those relating to distributions to equity participants.   Thus the characteristics of expenses include the following:*
>
> 1.   *Sacrifices involved in carrying out the earnings process*
> 2.   *Actual or expected cash outflows resulting from ordinary activities*
> 3.   *Outflows reported gross*

Expenses are expired costs, or items that were assets but are no longer assets because they have no future value.   The matching principle requires that all expenses incurred in the generating of revenue be recognized in the same accounting period as the revenues are recognized. The matching principle is broken down into three pervasive measurement principles: associating cause and effect, systematic and rational allocation, and immediate recognition.

Costs such as materials and direct labor consumed in the manufacturing process are relatively easy to identify with the related revenue elements.   These cost elements are included in inventory and expensed as cost of sales when the product is sold and revenue from the sale is recognized. This is associating cause and effect.

Some costs are more closely associated with specific accounting periods.   In the absence of a cause and effect relationship, the asset's cost should be allocated to benefiting accounting periods in a systematic and rational manner.   This form of expense recognition involves assumptions about the expected length of benefit and the relationship between benefit and cost of each period.   Depreciation of fixed assets, amortization of intangibles, and allocation of rent and insurance are examples of costs that would be recognized by the use of a systematic and rational method.

All other costs are normally expensed in the period in which they are incurred. This would include those costs for which no clear-cut future benefits can be identified, costs that were recorded as assets in prior periods but for which no remaining future benefits can be identified, and those other elements of administrative or general expense for which no rational allocation scheme can be devised.   The general approach is first to attempt to match costs with the related revenues. Next, a method of systematic and rational allocation should be attempted. If neither of these measurement principles is beneficial, the cost should be immediately expensed.

As stated in the IASC's *Framework*, the term **expenses** is broad enough to include losses as well. Expenses that arise in the course of the ordinary activities of an enterprise include such items as cost of sales, wages, and depreciation. They usually take the form of an outflow of cash or depletion of other assets.

Losses also represent decreases in economic benefits and are similar in nature to expenses. However, there is a subtle difference between the two concepts: losses may or may not arise in the course of ordinary activities, whereas expenses arise from ordinary activities. Thus, a loss from an extraordinary item such as a natural disaster would also qualify as a loss according to this definition. It is to be noted that even unrealized losses are covered here. For example, losses arising from the effects of increases or decreases in the exchange rates for a foreign currency in respect of the borrowings of an enterprise in that currency, which are unrealized losses, are also contemplated by this definition.

It is interesting to note that in the United States, the FASB's conceptual framework project defined expenses as "outflows or other using up of assets or incurrences of liabilities (or a combination of the two) resulting from delivery of goods, rendering of services, or other activities constituting the enterprise's major or central operations." This definition, although crisp and concise, is quite comprehensive; it seems to cover all conceivable ways of incurring expenses. For instance, the expression "a combination of the two" probably was intended to be a catch-all clause but for some reason has not been included in the definition given in IASC's *Framework*.

Gains and losses. According to the IASC's *Framework*

> *Gains (losses) represent items that meet the definition of income (expenses) and may or may not arise in the course of ordinary activities of an enterprise. Gains (losses) represent increases (decreases) in economic benefits and as such are no different in nature from revenue (expenses). Hence they are not regarded as separate elements in IASC's Framework. Characteristics of gains and losses include the following:*
>
> 1. *Result from peripheral transactions and circumstances that may be beyond entity's control*
> 2. *May be classified according to sources or as operating and nonoperating*

The recognition of gains and losses should follow the principles stated below.

1. Gains often result from transactions and other events that involve no earnings process; therefore, in terms of recognition, it is more significant that the gain be realized than earned.
2. Losses are recognized when it becomes evident that future economic benefits of a previously recognized asset have been reduced or eliminated, or that a liability has been incurred without associated economic benefits. The main difference between expenses and losses is that expenses result from

continuing operations, whereas losses result from peripheral transactions that may be beyond the entity's control.

Statement of changes in equity and statement of recognized gains and losses. IAS 1 (revised 1997) prescribes a new component of financial statements (to be presented along with the traditional financial statements). While the IASC had earlier been intending to mandate a new prescribed financial statement, the statement of nonowner movements in equity, opposition to its proposal in E53 has resulted in a somewhat modified final standard. Although different in some particulars and offering more options in terms of format, this will nonetheless reveal to financial statement users the full scope of changes in economic position, whether due to traditional items of income and expense, or to such other phenomena as revaluations of plan assets and investments, or the translations of foreign subsidiaries' and affiliates' balance sheets.

IAS 1 (revised) offers preparers two principal mechanisms for reporting the changes in enterprise equity for a period. The first of these would have the reporting entity present a new financial statement, to be captioned the **statement of changes in equity**. This statement should present

1. An enterprise's total recognized gains or losses for the period, including those that are recognized directly in equity (giving details of each item of income, expense, gain, or loss which are required by other IAS to be shown directly in equity, along with the total of these items, plus net profit or loss for the period and cumulative effect of changes in accounting policy and of correction of fundamental errors if accounted for by the benchmark treatments prescribed by IAS 8); and, in addition,
2. Also present, other changes in the equity accounts, along with a reconciliations of beginning and ending balances in each of the components of equity (giving details by each class of equity capital) and balances of accumulated profit or loss (giving details of the movements for the period).

An example of the statement of changes in equity is presented in the following section of this chapter.

Under the second of the two permitted approaches, the enterprise would present a **statement of recognized gains and losses** for the period, which would only include the **net** effect of income, expense, gain or loss reported in the income statement for the period. That is, net income or loss, including if applicable the cumulative effect of changes in accounting policy and of the correction of any fundamental errors accounted for by the benchmark treatments prescribed by IAS 8, would be added to the other items of income, expense, gain or loss which are carried directly to equity, with the total of these being presented as the final amount in the statement of recognized gains and losses.

If the second approach is utilized, the changes in other capital accounts resulting from transactions with owners, as well as the changes in retained earnings (referred to in IAS 1 as accumulated profit or loss), must be presented elsewhere in the notes to the financial statements. An example of this second approach is also shown in the following section of this chapter.

IAS 1 (revised 1997) explains that it is important to take into consideration all income, expenses, gains, and losses (including those not recognized in the income statement) in assessing the overall financial performance of an enterprise. Thus, the revised standard on presentation of financial statements has prescribed this new component of financial statements, to capture those items of gains or losses that are not included in the determination of net income or loss for the period. This standard further justifies the need for the presentation of this new component of financial statements, by setting forth the following reasoning for its prescription:

1. Since IAS 8 requires that all items of income and expense in a period be included in the determination of net profit or loss for the period, unless an international accounting standard requires or permits otherwise; and also

2. Since other standards, such as IAS 16, IAS 25, and IAS 21, require that specified gains and losses, such as revaluation surpluses or deficits and foreign currency translation differences, be recognized directly as changes in equity along with capital transactions with and distributions to the enterprise's owners; thus,

3. In order to capture all gains or losses that have a bearing on the enterprise's financial position, it is important that a separate component of financial statements be presented along with the traditional components of financial statement.

While the new standard refers to this as "a separate component of the financial statements," what, in fact, is required is a new financial statement, per se, which (depending in which alternative version is adopted) may also require additional footnote materials. This "separate component" will have to be presented as an integral part of all complete sets of financial statements, and accordingly, once IAS 1 (revised) becomes operative, any set of financial statements would be considered incomplete without this new statement.

It is to be noted that the IASC's action is in line with the current thinking in the UK and US. In the US, recently promulgated SFAS 129 prescribes a similar statement to be presented as a separate component of the financial statements, based on the FASB's concept of "comprehensive income." In the UK, which was the first to take this step, the treatment is very similar to that embraced by IAS 1 (revised), and the new component of financial statement prescribed under FRS 3 of the UK GAAP is captioned the "statement of total recognized gains and losses," which is similar to that suggested by IAS 1 when the second suggested approach is utilized.

Examples of the new statements alternatively required by IAS 1 (revised 1997).

Example 1: If the statement of changes in equity is to be employed

XYZ Malta Inc.
Statement of Changes in Equity
For the Year Ended December 31, 2000
(in thousands of US dollars)

	Share capital	*Share premium*	*Revaluation reserve*	*Currency translation*	*Accumulated profits*	*Total*
Balance at Dec. 31, 1998	$1,000	$100	$200	$200	$100	$1,600
Changes in accounting policy	--	--	--	--	50	50
Opening balances, as restated	1,000	100	200	200	150	1,650
Currency translation difference	--	--	--	(50)	--	(50)
Surplus from revaluation of buildings	--	--	100	--	--	100
Net gains and losses not recognized in income statement	--	--	100	(50)	--	50
Net profit for the period	--	--	--	--	100	100
Issuance of share capital	100	10	--	--	--	110
Balance at Dec. 31, 1999	1,100	110	300	150	250	1,910
Currency translation difference	--	--	--	150	--	150
Deficit on revaluation of investments	--	--	--	--	(50)	(50)
Net gains and losses not recognized in income statement	--	--	--	150	(50)	100
Net profit for the period	--	--	--	--	200	200
Dividends	--	--	--	--	(50)	(50)
Balance at Dec. 31, 2000	$1,100	$110	$300	$300	$350	$2,160

Example 2: If the statement of recognized gains and losses is to be presented (see note below)

ABC Barbados Co. Ltd.
Statement of Recognized Gains and Losses
For the Year Ended December 31, 2000
(in thousands of US dollars)

	2000	*1999*
Surplus on revaluation of buildings	$ 500	$ --
Surplus (deficit) on revaluation of investments	1,000	(1,000)
Exchange differences on translation of the financial statements of a foreign subsidiary	2,000	(2,000)
Net gains (losses) not recognized in the income statement	3,500	(3,000)
Net profit for the year	5,000	2,800
Total recognized gains and losses	8,500	(200)
Effect of changes in accounting policy	$ --	$ 500

NOTE: If this approach is used, then a reconciliation of the opening and closing balances of share capital, reserves, and retained earnings (accumulated profits) as illustrated in the first example, above, should be presented in the footnotes to the financial statements.

Impact of Legal Form on Financial Reporting

Revenues and expenses of a corporation are easily identified and separated from the revenues and expenses of the shareholders. In both the sole proprietorship and partnership form of entity, the identification process can be more difficult. Items such as interest or salaries paid to partners or owners may be thought of as distributions of profits rather than expenses. However, many entities adopt the philosophy that income reporting should be the same regardless of legal form (economic substance takes precedence over legal form). Under the corporate form of business, interest on stockholder loans and salaries paid to stockholders are clearly classified as expenses and not as distributions. Accordingly, under this theory, these items may be treated as expenses for both partnerships and sole proprietorships. However, full disclosure and consistency of financial reporting treatment would be required. Circumstances may involve treating certain payments, such as guaranteed salaries, as expenses while classifying other "salaries" as profit distributions.

Income Statement Classification and Presentation

Statement title. Income statements measure economic performance for a period of time and, except for this variation, follow the same basic rule for headings and titles as do balance sheets. For instance, the legal name of the entity must be used to identify the financial statements and the title "Income Statement" used to distinguish the statement from other information presented in the annual report. This is important also so that users can identify the information that is presented in accordance with international accounting standards from other information which may not be the subject of accounting requirements.

If another comprehensive basis of accounting is used, as is explicitly contemplated under US GAAP, such as the "cash basis" or "income tax basis," the title of the financial statement should be modified accordingly. "Statement of Revenue and Expenses--Income Tax Basis" or "Statement of Revenue and Expense--Modified Cash Basis" are examples of such titles. However, it should be noted that international accounting standards neither refer to nor contain guidance relating to these so-called other comprehensive bases of accounting. One could interpret this omission to mean that current international accounting standards (i.e., the IASC's *Framework*, IAS 1 (revised 1997), *Presentation of Financial Statements)* recognize only the accrual basis of accounting.

Reporting period. The period covered by the income statement must clearly be identified, such as "year ending (ended) December 31, 2000." Such dating informs the user of the financial statements not only about the length of the period covered by the income statement, but also the starting and ending dates. Dating such as "the period ending March 31, 2000" or "through March 31, 2000" would represent a violation of accounting principles because of the lack of precise definition in these titles. Income statements are normally presented annually (i.e., for a period of 12 months or a year). However, in exceptional circumstances, income statements could be presented for periods in excess of 1 year or for shorter periods as well, say for 5 months or a quarter of a year. IAS 1 (revised 1997) requires that when financial statements are presented for periods other than a year, the following additional disclosures should be made:

1. The reason for presenting the income statement (and other financial statements, such as the cash flow statement, statement of changes in equity and notes) for a period other than 1 year; and,
2. The fact that the comparative information presented (in the income statement, changes in equity, cash flow statement and notes) is not truly comparable.

Entities whose operations form a natural cycle may have a reporting period end on a specific day (e.g., the last Friday of the month). Certain enterprises (typically retail enterprises) prepare income statements for a fiscal period of 52 or 53 weeks instead of a year (thus, to always end on a day, such as Sunday, on which no business is transacted, so that inventory may be taken). These entities should clearly state that the income statement has been presented, for instance, "for the 52-week period ended March 28, 2000." The new standard on presentation of financial statements specifically addresses enterprises that prefer to report consistently for a 52- or 53-week period, and states categorically that it does not preclude this practice since it is unlikely that the financial statements thus presented would be materially different from those that are presented for 1 full year.

In order that the presentation and classification of items in the income statement be consistent from period to period, items of income and expenses should be uniform both with respect to appearance and categories from one time period through the next. That is, if a decision is made to change classification schemes, the comparative prior period financials should be restated to conform and thus to maintain comparability between the two periods being presented together. Disclosure must, of course, be made of this reclassification, since the earlier period financial statements being presented currently will differ in appearance from those nominally same statements presented in the earlier year.

Aggregating items. Aggregation of items should not serve to conceal significant information, such as netting revenues against expenses or combining elements of interest to readers, such as bad debts and depreciation. The categories "other" or "miscellaneous expense" should contain, at maximum, an immaterial total amount of aggregated insignificant elements. Once this total approaches, say, 10% of total expenses (or any other materiality threshold), some other aggregations with explanatory titles should be selected.

Information is **material** if its omission or misstatement or nondisclosure could influence the economic decisions of users taken on the basis of the financial statements. Materiality depends on the size of the item judged in the particular circumstances of its omission (IASC's *Framework*, para 30). But it is often forgotten that materiality is also linked with understandability and the level of precision in which the financial statements are to be presented. For instance, the financial statements are often rendered more understandable by rounding information to the nearest thousand currency units (i.e., US dollars). This obviates the necessity of loading the financial statements with unnecessary detail. However, it should be borne in mind that the use of the level of precision that makes presentation possible in the nearest thousands of currency units is acceptable only as long as the threshold of materiality is not surpassed.

Offsetting items of revenue and expense. Materiality also plays a role in the matter of allowing or disallowing offsetting of the items of income and expense. The new standard IAS 1 (revised 1997) addresses this issue and prescribes rules in this area. According to this standard, items of income and expense should be offset when, and only when

1. An international accounting standard requires or permits it. For example, IAS 30 permits banks and similar financial institutions to offset income and expense items relating to hedging; or
2. Gains, losses, and related expenses arising from the same or similar transactions and events are not material. Such amounts should be aggregated in such cases.

The standard also states that immaterial amounts should be aggregated with amounts of similar nature or function and need not be presented separately. However, when such gains or losses are individually material, then they should not be offset, but instead should be presented on a gross basis. For example, gain on the sale of a building is $5 million and loss on the sale of land during the same accounting period is $10 million. If both of these amounts are individually material, they should not be offset but be shown on a gross basis.

Usually, losses and gains on disposal of noncurrent assets are seen reported on a net basis, which may be due to the fact that they are not material individually (compared to other items on the income statement). However, if they were material individually, as in the example above, it goes without saying that they would need to be disclosed separately according to the requirements of IAS 1 (revised 1997). It is the authors' opinion that even under the existing international accounting standards, they would not be required to be offset and shown on a net basis. For instance, IAS 16 stipulates that "gains or losses arising from the retirement or disposal of an item of property, plant, and equipment...should be recognized as income or expense in the income statement." Read in the light of the guidelines contained in the IASC's *Framework*, which categorically states that "when gains (losses) are recognized in the income statement, they are usually displayed separately because knowledge of them is useful for the purpose of making economic decisions," it would be unreasonable to interpret that IAS 16 does not require disclosure of gains or losses arising from the retirement or disposal of property, plant, and equipment.

Further, based on the discussion above, it seems unreasonable to read between the lines of IAS 16 in an attempt to reach a conclusion, as some have done, that it does **not** require the disclosure of gains or losses arising from the retirement or disposal of property, plant, and equipment, and therefore that such gains or losses may be included as an undisclosed net amount within broad expense categories such as "general and administrative expenses." In the authors' opinion, although gains or losses arising from retirement or disposal of property, plant, and equipment are not mentioned in the disclosure section of IAS 16, they are specifically dealt with in an earlier paragraph of that IAS. Thus, reading all the provisions of IAS 16, together with the IASC's *Framework* (as explained earlier), it would not be unreasonable to interpret that such gains or losses should be disclosed separately in the income statement, if material.

IAS 1 (revised 1997) further clarifies that when items of income or expense are offset, the enterprise should nevertheless consider, based on materiality, the need to disclose the gross amounts in the notes to the financial statements. This new standard gives the following examples of transactions that are incidental to the main revenue generating activities of an enterprise and whose results when presented by offsetting or reporting on a net basis, such as netting any gains with related expenses, reflect the substance of the transaction:

1. Gains or losses on the disposal of noncurrent assets, including investments and operating assets, are reported by deducting from the proceeds on disposal the carrying amounts of the asset and related selling expenses.
2. Extraordinary items are presented net of related taxation and minority interest.
3. Expenditure that is reimbursed under a contractual arrangement with a third party may be netted against the related reimbursement.

For example, an enterprise based on a time-share arrangement processes computerized accounting data electronically for its own accounting department as well as for certain other companies in the area and incurs a total expenditure of $5 million for an accounting period. The expenditure it incurs on this data-processing activity should be presented after netting the related reimbursable expenditure, which amounts to $3 million. Thus, the income statement presentation would display the net figure (expense) of $2 million (instead of a gross basis presentation of a $5 million expense and a $3 million income). This financial statement presentation reflects the substance of the transaction. (It should be noted, however, that a disclosure of the gross amounts, if they are material, may need to be made in the notes to the financial statements; this is also a requirement of IAS 1 [revised 1997] and was explained earlier in this chapter.)

Major components of the income statement. IAS 1 (revised) stipulates that, at the minimum, the income statement must include line items which present the following items (if they are pertinent to the entity's operations for the period in question):

1. Revenue
2. Results of operating activities
3. Finance costs
4. Share of profits and losses of associates and joint ventures accounted for by the equity method
5. Tax expense
6. Profit or loss from ordinary activities
7. Extraordinary items
8. Minority interest
9. Net profit for the period

The foregoing items represent the barest minimum: Other line items can be included as deemed useful or necessary to fairly communicate the results of the enterprise's operations. It should be carefully noted that this requirement must be satisfied by presentation on the face of the income statement; it cannot be dealt with by incorporating the items into the notes to the financial statements.

While the objectives of the line items are uniform across all reporting entities, the manner of presentation may differ. Specifically, IAS 1 (revised) offers preparers two different manners of classifying operating and other expenses: the so-called natural scheme, or the functional one. While entities are encouraged to apply one or the other of these on the face of the income statement, it would be permissible to relegate this information to the notes.

The natural expense classification scheme identifies costs and expenses in terms of their character, such as salaries and wages, raw materials consumed, and depreciation of plant assets. On the other hand, the functional classification scheme (also referred to as the "cost of sales" method) reports on the purpose of the expenditure, such as for manufacturing, distribution, and administration. Note that the minimum line item disclosures mandated by the standard must be met in any case; thus, finance costs must be so identified regardless of which classification scheme is employed.

The IASC has recently completed a new standard, IAS 35, governing the presentation and disclosures pertaining to discontinuing operations. This is discussed later in this chapter. Measurement matters relating to discontinuing operation are not covered by this standard; rather, other guidance, particularly IAS 36 dealing with impairment of assets, must be consulted.

IAS 1 (revised) furthermore stipulates that if a reporting entity adopts the functional classification scheme, it must also provide information on the nature of its expenses, including depreciation and amortization and staff costs (salaries and wages). The standard does not provide detailed guidance on this requirement, however. Presumably the traditional disclosures (e.g., depreciation expense as defined in IAS 16, etc.) would be sufficient to satisfy this rule.

As a practical matter, most traditionally structured income statements employ a combination of functional and natural classifications, or are effectively supplemented by disclosures made in other financial statements or in the footnotes. For example, even when depreciation is not set forth as a line item on the income statement, it will appear on the cash flow statement (if the popular indirect method is employed). As noted, finance costs must be separately stated on the income statement, whichever classification scheme is primarily used.

Finally, IAS 1 (revised) requires that dividends, on a per share basis, be disclosed either on the face of the income statement or in the notes thereto. Dividends include both those paid and those declared but unpaid at year end.

While IAS does not require the inclusion of subsidiary schedules to support major captions in the income statement, it is commonly found that, for example, detailed schedules of costs of goods manufactured and/or sold are included in full sets of financial statements. These will be illustrated in the following section to provide a more expansive discussion of the meaning of certain major sections of the income statement.

Income from ordinary activities. This section of the income statement will serve to summarize the revenues and expenses of the company's central operations.

1. **Sales or other operating revenues** are charges to customers for the goods and/or services provided to them during the period. This section of the income statement should include information about discounts, allowances, and returns, to determine net sales or net revenues.

2. **Cost of goods sold** is the cost of the inventory items sold during the period. In the case of a merchandising firm, net purchases (purchases less discounts, returns, and allowances plus freight-in) are added to beginning inventory to obtain the cost of goods available for sale. From the cost of goods available for sale amount, the ending inventory is deducted to compute cost of goods sold.

Example of schedule of cost of goods sold

ABC Merchandising Company
Schedule of Cost of Goods Sold
For the Year Ended December 31, 2000

Beginning inventory			$xxx
Add: Purchases		$xxx	
Freight-in		xxx	
Cost of purchases		xxx	
Less: Purchase discounts	$xx		
Purchase R&A	xx	(xxx)	
Net purchases			xxx
Cost of goods available for sale			xxx
Less: Ending inventory			(xxx)
Cost of goods sold			$xxx

A manufacturing enterprise computes the cost of goods sold in a slightly different way. Cost of goods manufactured would be added to the beginning inventory to arrive at cost of goods available for sale. The ending inventory is then deducted from the cost of goods available for sale to determine the cost of goods sold. Cost of goods manufactured is computed by adding to raw (direct) materials on hand at the beginning of the period the raw materials purchases during the period and all other costs of production, such as labor and direct overhead, thereby yielding the cost of goods placed in production during the period. When adjusted for changes in work in process during the period and for raw materials on hand at the end of the period, this results in the calculation of goods produced.

Example of schedules of cost of goods manufactured and sold

XYZ Manufacturing Company
Schedule of Cost of Goods Manufactured
For the Year Ended December 31, 2000

Direct materials inventory 1/1/00	$xxx	
Purchases of materials (including freight-in and deducting purchase discounts)	xxx	
Total direct materials available	$xxx	
Direct materials inventory 12/31/00	(xxx)	
Direct materials used		$xxx
Direct labor		xxx
Factory overhead:		
Depreciation of factory equipment	$xxx	
Utilities	xxx	
Indirect factory labor	xxx	
Indirect materials	xxx	
Other overhead items	xxx	xxx
Manufacturing cost incurred in 2000		$xxx
Add: Work in process 1/1/00		xxx
Less: Work in process 12/31/00		(xxx)
Cost of goods manufactured		$xxx

XYZ Manufacturing Company
Schedule of Cost of Goods Sold
For the Year Ended December 31, 2000

Finished goods inventory 1/1/00	$xxx
Add: Cost of goods manufactured	xxx
Cost of goods available for sale	$xxx
Less: Finished goods inventory 12/31/00	(xxx)
Cost of goods sold	$xxx

3. **Operating expenses** are primary recurring costs associated with central operations, other than cost of goods sold, that are incurred to generate sales. Operating expenses are normally classified into the following two categories:

   a. Selling expenses

    b. General and administrative expenses

        Selling expenses are those expenses related directly to the company's efforts to generate sales (e.g., sales salaries, commissions, advertising, delivery expenses, depreciation of store furniture and equipment, and store supplies). General and administrative expenses are expenses related to the general administration of the company's operations (e.g., officers and office salaries, office supplies, depreciation of office furniture and fixtures, telephone, postage, accounting and legal services, and business licenses and fees).

4. **Gains and losses** stem from the peripheral transactions of the entity. These items are shown with the normal recurring revenues and expenses. If they are *material,* they should be disclosed separately and shown above income (loss) from continuing operations before income taxes. Examples are write-downs of inventories and receivables, effects of a strike, and gains and losses from exchange or translation of foreign currencies.

5. **Other revenues and expenses** are revenues and expenses not related to the central operations of the company (e.g., gains and losses on the disposal of equipment, interest revenues and expenses, and dividend revenues).

6. **Separate disclosure items** are items that are within the profit or loss from the ordinary activities but are of such size, nature, or incidence that their disclosure becomes important in order to explain the performance of the enterprise for the period. They should be reported as a separate component of income from continuing operations. Examples of items that require such disclosure are as follows:

    a. Write-down of inventories to net realizable value, or of property, plant, and equipment to recoverable amounts, and subsequent reversals of such write-downs

    b. Costs of restructuring the activities of an enterprise and any subsequent reversals of such provisions

    c. Gains or losses resulting from disposals of items of property, plant, and equipment

    d. Gains or losses from disposals of long-term investments

    e. Results of discontinued operations

    f. Costs of litigation settlements

    g. Other reversals of provisions

7. **Discontinuing operations.** In IAS 35, *Discontinuing Operations,* which supersedes paragraphs 19-22 of IAS 8 (that originally dealt with "discontinued operations"), and which is effective for periods beginning on or after January 1, 1999, the requirement is set forth that what are now referred to as "discontinuing operations" must be reported in those circumstances when an enterprise, pursuant to a single plan, sells, either in its entirety or piece-

meal, or terminates through abandonment, a separate major line of business or geographical area of operations, such as a **segment** (as that term is defined by revised IAS 14), which can be distinguished operationally and for financial reporting purposes.

Per IAS 35, a "discontinuing operation" is a component of a business which, pursuant to a single plan, is either to be disposed of substantially in its entirety or to be terminated through abandonment or piecemeal sale of assets and settlement of liabilities. In order to qualify as a "discontinuing operation," the operation would need to comprise either a **separate major line of business**, geographical area of operations, or class of customer, and furthermore be organized such that it could be so distinguished both operationally and for financial reporting purposes.

In other words, while a "discontinuing operation" would **not** have to meet the test of being a segment as that term is defined in IAS 14 (revised), clearly it would have to be a substantial operation and be readily identifiable both in terms of its actual physical operations (e.g., by having separate factory facilities, etc.) as well as from a financial reporting perspective (e.g., by having divisional financial statements prepared for management use, etc.). The standard points out that even a major part of a segment could qualify as a discontinuing operation, but the question of how significant a part this would have to be to potentially comprise an operation which could be segregated as described in IAS 35 once a decision to discontinue had been made is not addressed in the standard. Thus, this will remain in the domain of individual judgements until such time, if ever, when the IASC provides further guidance.

The standard notes that major product lines and portions of segments would often qualify as discontinuing operations, provided that certain conditions were met. If operating assets and liabilities, and income, could be attributed to the component, and at least a majority of its operating expenses could be attributed to it, then it would likely be valid under the new standard to define this operation (if it were being sold or abandoned) as a discontinuing operation.

Furthermore, to qualify as a "discontinuing operation," the act of discontinuing the operation would have to involve a significant management event, such as the sale or abandonment of the entire operation or an organized, even if piecemeal, effort to sell off the assets and settle the obligations of the operation. This limitation suggests that any discontinuation decision will be of sufficient import that it will be clear that it indeed involves a major portion of the enterprise's operations, even if not an entire segment as defined by IAS 14.

It should be noted that under the new standard the term "discontinuing" is used in place of the formerly employed term "discontinued." This change has been made largely to acknowledge that the disclosures are being made while the act of discontinuation is in process, and not merely once it has been fully achieved. Notwithstanding this change, the meaning is intended to be essentially that which was earlier ascribed to the previously employed terminology.

IAS 35, paragraph 27, prescribes the following disclosures for a discontinuing operation in the financial statements beginning with the period in which the **initial disclosure event** occurs:

a. A description of the discontinuing operation;
b. The business or geographical segment(s) in which it is reported in accordance with IAS 14;
c. The date and nature of the initial disclosure event;
d. The date or period in which the discontinuance is expected to be completed if known or determinable;
e. The carrying amounts, as of the balance sheet date, of the total assets and the total liabilities to be disposed of;
f. The amount of revenue, expenses, and pretax profit or loss from ordinary activities attributable to the discontinuing operation during the current financial reporting period, and the income tax expense relating thereto as required by paragraph 81(h) of IAS 12; and
g. The net cash flows attributable to the operating, investing, and financing activities of the discontinuing operation during the current financial reporting period.

The reason that the carrying amount (i.e., book value) of discontinuing operations has been defined to be the reportable amount is that IAS 35 does not address measurement matters as such; rather, it presumes that other IAS deal with these concerns, and that the carrying values of assets (whether to be disposed of or not) have already been adjusted for any impairment (the subject of IAS 36, discussed in Chapter 8). Thus, if the carrying amounts of assets needed to be adjusted upon being declared to be part of a discontinuing operation, this would imply that accounting standards had not previously been complied with. If all existing impairments had been properly recognized, then logically the mere act of declaring an operational segment a discontinuing operation would not, in and of itself, have any further impact on carrying value.

Also since IAS 35 sets forth only disclosure requirements (and not recognition or measurement requirements), the standard is able to take a somewhat different than normal position regarding the relevance of the reporting entity's fiscal year end. The decision to segregate the results of the discontinuing operation need not be made by the actual year end in order to present the income statement as required under the standard. Rather, if it is known at the date on which the financial statements are authorized for issue by the board of directors (or similar governing body) that an initial disclosure event has occurred after the end of the enterprise's financial reporting period, the above-noted disclosures, should be presented.

The standard categorically states that income and expenses relating to a discontinuing operation should **not** be presented as extraordinary items. The reason for proscribing extraordinary treatment is as follows: extraordinary items as defined in IAS 8 (discussed in detail below) are events that are clearly distinct from ordinary activities of the enterprise and as contemplated by IAS 8, based on the two examples of extraordinary items given in IAS 8, are events which are not within the control of the management of the enterprise. By contrast, a discontinuing operation, per IAS 35, is a component of the enterprise which is either being disposed of or terminated through abandonment, based on a plan by an enterprise's management. Being thus based on a "plan by an enterprise's management," a discontinuing operation could hardly be considered an event "not within the control of management," and hence income and expenses relating to a discontinuing operation should not be presented as extraordinary items. The results of discontinuing operations should be included in the profit or loss from ordinary activities.

Under the provisions of IAS 35, an initial disclosure event is that which first causes the enterprise to disclose, in the financial statements, initial information about a planned discontinuance. This event is defined by the earlier of two occurrences: the reporting entity's entering into a binding sale agreement, or **both** the approval by its governing board (or equivalent) of a detailed, formal plan for the discontinuance, and the announcement thereof to the public. According to IAS 37 (discussed in Chapter 12) offers instructive examples to help in distinguishing situations in which an initial disclosure event has occurred from those in which the event has not occurred. For example, a pre-year-end decision to close a division, which has yet to be communicated to any affected parties (workers, customers, etc.) would not trigger disclosure of a discontinuing operation under IAS 35.

IAS 35, paragraph 39, allows such a disclosure to be made **either** in the notes to the financial statements or on the face of the financial statements. It should be noted, however, that disclosure of the amount of pretax gain or loss recognized on the disposal of assets or settlement of liabilities attributable to the discontinuing operation should be made on the face of the income statement. Also, paragraph 40 of the standard recommends (encourages) presentation on the face of the statements of income and of cash flows disclosures relating to revenues, expenses, pretax profits or losses, income tax expense, and cash flows attributable to discontinuing operations.

Under the provisions of IAS 35, in reporting periods after that in which the initial disclosure event has occurred, the entity would need to incorporate updated disclosures in the financial statements, until such time as the planned discontinuance has been completed. A discontinuance effected by the sale of, say, a division would be completed once the transaction had taken place; it would not require that payments from the buyer(s) to the seller have been fully collected. If the plan to discontinue is abandoned, this event would also terminate the need to present information about the discontinuing operation.

Example of disclosure of discontinuing operations under IAS 35:

Alternative I - Columnar presentation

Taj Mahal Enterprises
Statement of Income
For the years ended December 31, 2000 and 1999
(In 1,000 UAE Dirhams)

	Continuing Operations (Segments X & Y)		Discontinuing Operation (Segment Z)		Enterprise as a Whole	
	2000	1999	2000	1999	2000	1999
Revenue	10,000	5,000	3,000	2,000	13,000	7,000
Operating expenses	(7,000)	(3,500)	(1,800)	(1,400)	(8,800)	(4,900)
Impairment loss	--	--	(500)	(400)	(500)	(400)
Provision for employee end-of-service benefits	--	--	(900)	--	(900)	--
Pre-tax profit (loss) from operating activities	3,000	1,500	(200)	200	2,800	1,700
Interest expenses	(300)	(200)	(100)	(100)	(400)	(300)
Profit (loss) before tax	2,700	1,300	(300)	100	2,400	1,400
Income tax expense (@ 20%)	(540)	(260)	60	(20)	(480)	(280)
Profit (loss) from operating activities after tax	2,160	1,040	(240)	80	1,920	1,120

Alternative II - Tabular presentation

Taj Mahal Enterprises
Statement of Income
For the years ended December 31, 2000 and 1999
(In UAE Dirhams)

	2000	1999
Continuing Operations (Segments X & Y):		
Revenue	10,000	5,000
Operating expenses	(7,000)	(3,500)
Pretax profit from operating activities	3,000	1,500
Interest expense	(300)	(200)
Profit before tax	2,700	1,300
Income tax expense	(540)	(260)
Profit after taxes (@ 20%)	2,160	1,040

Discontinuing operation (Segment Z):

Revenue	3,000		2,000	
Operating expenses	(1,800)		(1,400)	
Impairment loss	(500)		(400)	
Provision for employee end-of-service benefits	(900)		--	
Pretax profit (loss) from operating activities	(200)		200	
Interest expense	(100)		(100)	
Profit (loss) before tax	(300)		100	
Income tax expense (@ 20%)	60		(20)	
Profit (loss) after taxes		(240)		80

Total enterprise:

Profit (loss) from ordinary activities		1,920		1,120

Alternative III - Not presented in the body of the income statement

As an alternative to the foregoing income statement presentations, disclosure by means of footnotes is allowed. A range of methods are potentially useful, from full pro forma presentation in the notes to a narration of the nature of the operations which are being discontinued, including relevant amounts.

8. **Income tax expense related to ordinary activities** is that portion of the total income tax expense applicable to continuing operations.

9. **Extraordinary items** are income or expenses that arise from events or transactions that are clearly distinct from ordinary activities of an enterprise.

Only on rare occasions does an event or a transaction give rise to an extraordinary item. The nature of the event in relation to the business ordinarily carried out by the enterprise determines whether or not an event is clearly distinct from the ordinary activities of the enterprise and hence should be classified as an extraordinary event. Thus an event may be extraordinary for one enterprise but may not be extraordinary for another enterprise. For instance, losses sustained from a hurricane would be an extraordinary event for most enterprises but claims resulting from such a natural disaster by an insurance company do not qualify for such treatment (since such claims are part of the ordinary activities of an insurance company's business).

Examples of events or transactions that generally qualify as extraordinary items, as included in IAS 8, are the following:

a. Losses resulting from the expropriation of assets
b. Losses sustained from natural disasters such as an earthquake

The nature and the amount of each extraordinary item should be disclosed separately. Disclosures may be made either on the face of the income statement or in footnotes to the financial statements.

Example of presentation of extraordinary item

XYX Malta, Ltd.
Income Statement
For the year ended December 31, 2000

	2000	*1999*
Sales	$1,000,000	$ 800,000
Cost of sales	(700,000)	(600,000)
Gross profit	300,000	200,000
Distribution costs	(50,000)	(40,000)
Administrative expenses	(30,000)	(40,000)
Net financing costs	(20,000)	(20,000)
Loss from sale of scooter division (Note 1)	(50,000)	--
Profit from ordinary activities, before taxes	150,000	100,000
Income tax expense	(60,000)	(40,000)
Extraordinary item		
Loss on expropriation of Suzukiyo moped		
manufacturing operations in India		
(net of income taxes of $30,000) (Note 2)	--	(30,000)
Net profit for the year	$ 90,000	$ 30,000

Note 1: On September 1, 2000, the company sold its scooter division. The results of this operation had previously been reported in the scooter industry segment and the domestic geographic segment. The loss on the sale was computed based on the sale proceeds and the net carrying amounts of assets and liabilities of the operation at the date of the sale. The revenues recognized relating to this operation from January 1, 2000, until the date of sale, September 1, 2000, were $100,000 (the comparable 1999 amount was $150,000), and the profits before income taxes were $30,000 ($40,000 in 1999).

Note 2: On July 1, 1999, the company's Suzukiyo moped manufacturing operations were expropriated in India, without compensation, by government decree. The results of this operation had previously been reported in the moped industry segment and the Far East geographic segment. The extraordinary loss from this operation was computed using the carrying amounts of assets and liabilities at the date of expropriation. The revenues recognized relating to this operation from January 1, 1999, to July 1, 1999, were $50,000, and the profits before tax were $22,000.

Development Stage Enterprises

A recurring concern among newly established enterprises is that, given what is often a multiyear process of achieving a normal level of operations and absorbing the typically heavy start-up costs needed to achieve this, the income statements prepared and presented under generally accepted accounting principles may be insufficient to provide the user with meaningful insights into the operations and potential of the entity. In years gone by, a commonly employed solution was to defer many costs that normally are deemed to be period costs, and then to amortize these over what was often an arbitrary period, say, 5 years. The logic was that these costs were incurred to benefit operations after the entity began to operate in a normal fashion, and to expense these upon incurrence would result, most commonly, in reportable losses which would imply that future successful operations would not be achieved.

The obvious flaw in the deferral of start-up costs, from a financial reporting perspective, is that these deferred costs would necessarily be presented as assets on the enterprise's balance sheet, when in fact these sunk costs would have no demonstrable value for the future, particularly if the entity's strategies proved unsuccessful. Thus, there is an inherent conflict among some of accounting's most fundamental concepts: the going concern assumption, realization, and conservatism. Ultimately, the US and other accounting standard setters had to rule that costs must be accounted for by development stage enterprises no differently than by operating enterprises: If the cost represents an asset, it is accounted for as such, but if a sunk cost does not meet the definition of an asset, it must be expensed when incurred.

In recognition of the not unreasonable argument that strict application of the foregoing rule would result in income statements for development stage enterprises which might not be as meaningful as would be hoped, the salient US accounting standard provides that **cumulative** statements of income be presented for development stage enterprises, so that users can better understand the full scope of the activities undertaken to achieve normal operations. Although there is currently no corresponding standard under IAS, there is also no prohibition against the presentation of such statements (at least on a supplementary basis). The following discussion is offered to those who may choose to report on this basis.

Development stage enterprises defined. Under the applicable US GAAP standard, SFAS 7, a development stage enterprise is defined as one that is devoting substantially all of its efforts to establishing a new business, and **either** of the following conditions exists:

1. Planned principal operations have not begun.
2. Planned principal operations have begun but there has been no significant revenue.

SFAS 7 indicates that these enterprises should prepare their financial statements in accordance with the same GAAP applicable to established operating entities. SFAS 7 indicated that specialized accounting practices are unacceptable and that development stage enterprises were to follow the same generally accepted accounting principles as those that applied to an established operating entity. SFAS 7 also provided that a development stage enterprise should disclose certain additional information that would alert readers to the fact that the company is in the development stage. Disclosure requirements include

1. All disclosures applicable to operating entities
2. Identification of the statements as those of a development stage enterprise
3. Disclosure of the nature of development stage activities

4. A balance sheet that includes the cumulative net losses since inception in the equity section

5. An income statement showing current period revenue and expense as well as the cumulative amount from the inception of the entity

6. A statement of cash flows showing cash flows for the period as well as those from inception

7. A statement of stockholders' equity showing the following from the enterprise's inception:

   a. For each issuance, the date and number of equity securities issued for cash or other consideration

   b. For each issuance, the dollar amounts per share assigned to the consideration received for equity securities

   c. For each issuance involving noncash consideration, the nature of the consideration and the basis used in assigning the valuation

8. For the first period in which an enterprise is no longer a development stage enterprise, it shall be disclosed that in prior periods the entity was a development stage enterprise. If comparative statements are presented, the foregoing disclosure presentations (2 through 7) need not be shown.

Given the absence of guidance under IAS regarding the possible utility of presenting cumulative operating statements for enterprises which have yet to begin normal scale operations, the insights offered by the relevant US standard could be employed by those seeking expanded financial statement disclosures to accomplish a similar goal.

4 CASH FLOW STATEMENTS

PERSPECTIVE AND ISSUES

The IASC issued revised IAS 7, *Cash Flow Statements*, in 1992, superseding the original standard, also denoted as IAS 7, which had been issued in 1977 and which required enterprises to prepare the statement of changes in financial position (commonly referred to as the **funds flow statement**) as an integral part of the financial reporting process. This revised standard, which established the currently applicable rules for cash flow reporting, became operative for financial statements of periods beginning on or after January 1, 1994.

The primary purpose of the statement of cash flows is to provide information about the cash receipts and cash payments of an entity during a period. A secondary purpose is to provide insight into the investing and financing activities of the entity. More specifically, the statement of cash flows should help investors and creditors assess

1. The ability to generate future positive cash flows
2. The ability to meet obligations and pay dividends
3. Reasons for differences between income and cash receipts and payments
4. Both cash and noncash aspects of entities' investing and financing transactions

The adoption of a requirement for cash flow reporting by the IASC completes what has been virtually a universal movement away from the formerly popular funds flow mode of reporting to cash reporting. In the United States, the move was completed with the issuance of SFAS 95 (which became effective in 1988). A similar change in the United Kingdom occurred with the issuance of FRS 1 in 1991. (However, the UK rules were substantially revised in October 1996, so that financial reporting of cash flow information in the UK now differs significantly from practice under both US and International standards, as noted in greater detail below.) The purpose of this shift was to provide external users of financial statements with a better tool to project future cash flows, which is now deemed to be the ultimate concern of investors and creditors. While the formerly popular concept of funds did permit this assessment to be made, albeit with difficulty on the part of the users of the statements, cash flow reporting is now seen as being a central objective of the financial reporting process. The requirements of IAS 7 are generally similar to the requirements of both SFAS 95 and the **original** UK FRS 1, as it stood before its overhaul in 1996, although IAS 7 does contain a few peculiarities, which are highlighted in the following discussion.

Sources of IAS
IAS 7

DEFINITIONS OF TERMS

Cash. Cash on hand and demand deposits with banks or other financial institutions.

Cash equivalents. Short-term highly liquid investments that are (1) readily convertible to known amounts of cash, and (2) so near their maturity (original maturity of 3 months or less) that they present negligible risk of changes in value because of changes in interest rates. Treasury bills, commercial paper, and money market funds are all examples of cash equivalents.

Direct method. A method that derives the net cash provided by or used in operating activities from major components of operating cash receipts and payments.

Financing activities. The transactions that cause changes in the size and composition of an enterprise's capital and borrowings.

Indirect (reconciliation) method. A method that derives the net cash provided by or used in operating activities by adjusting net income (loss) for the effects of transactions of a noncash nature, any deferrals or accruals of past or future operating cash receipts or payments, and items of income or expense associated with investing or financing activities.

Investing activities. The acquisition and disposal of long-term assets and other investments not included in cash equivalents.

Operating activities. The transactions not classified as financing or investing activities, generally involving producing and delivering goods or providing services.

CONCEPTS, RULES, AND EXAMPLES

Benefits of Cash Flow Statements

The concepts underlying the balance sheet and the income statement have long been established in financial reporting; they are, respectively, the stock measure or a snapshot at a point in time of an entity's resources and obligations, and a summary of the entity's economic performance over a period of time. The third major financial statement, the cash flow statement, is a more recent innovation but has evolved substantially since introduced. What has ultimately developed into the cash flow statement began life as a flow statement which reconciled changes in enterprise resources over a period of time but in a fundamentally different manner than did the income statement.

Most of the basic progress on this financial statement occurred in the United States, where during the 1950s and early 1960s a variety of formats and concepts were experimented with. By the mid-1960s the most common approach in the United States was that of reporting the sources and applications (or uses) of funds, although such reporting did not become mandatory until 1971, and even then, **funds** could be defined by the reporting entity in at least four different ways, including as cash and as net working capital (current assets minus current liabilities).

One reason why the financial statement preparer community did not more quickly embrace a cash flow concept is that the accounting profession had long had a significant aversion to the cash basis measurement of enterprise operating performance. This was largely the result of its commitment to accrual basis accounting, which recognizes revenues when earned and expenses when incurred, and which views cash flow reporting as a back door approach to cash basis accounting. By focusing instead on **funds**, which most typically was defined as net working capital, items such as receivables and payables were included, thereby preserving the essential accrual basis characteristic of the flow measurement. On the other hand, this failed to give statement users meaningful insight into the entities' sources and uses of cash per se.

By the 1970s there was widespread recognition of the myriad problems associated with funds flow reporting, including the required use of the **all financial resources** approach, under which all major, noncash (and nonfund) transactions, such as exchanges of stock or debt for plant assets, were included in the funds flow statement. This ultimately led to a renewed call for cash flow reporting. Most significantly, the FASB's conceptual framework project of the late 1970s to mid-1980s identified usefulness in predicting future cash flows as a central purpose of the financial reporting process. This presaged the nearly universal move away from funds flows to cash flows as a third standard measurement to be incorporated in financial reports.

Cash flow statements thus became required in the late 1980s in the United States, with the United Kingdom following along soon thereafter, with an approach that largely mirrored the US standard; albeit with a somewhat refined classification scheme, which solves some of the problems inherent in the US model (as described in greater detail below) and which, in the 1996 revision of FRS 1, has embraced an even more extensive classification scheme, as described below. The international accounting standard, which was adopted a year after that of the United Kingdom (both of these were revisions to earlier requirements that had mandated the use of funds flow statements), embraces the somewhat simpler US approach but offers greater flexibility, thus effectively incorporating the UK view without adding to the structural complexity of the cash flow statement itself.

Today, the clear consensus of national and international accounting standard setters is that the statement of cash flows is a necessary component of complete financial reporting. The perceived benefits of presenting the statement of cash flows in conjunction with the statement of financial position (balance sheet) and the statement of income (or operations) have been highlighted by IAS 7 to be as follows:

1. It provides an insight into the financial structure of the enterprise (including its liquidity and solvency) and its ability to affect the amounts and timing of cash flows in order to adapt to changing circumstances and opportunities.

The statement of cash flows discloses important information about the cash flows from operating, investing, and financing activities, information that is not available or as clearly discernible in either the balance sheet or the income statement. The additional disclosures which are either recommended by IAS 7 (such as those relating to undrawn borrowing facilities or cash flows that represent increases in operating capacity) or required to be disclosed by the standard (such as that about cash held by the enterprise but not available for use) provide a wealth of information for the informed user of financial statements. Taken together, the statement of cash flows coupled with these required or recommended disclosures provide the user with vastly more insight into the entity's performance and position, and its probable future results, than would the balance sheet and income statement alone.

2. It provides additional information to the users of financial statements for evaluating changes in assets, liabilities, and equity of an enterprise.

When comparative balance sheets are presented, users are given information about the enterprise's assets and liabilities at the end of each of the years. Were the statement of cash flows not presented as an integral part of the financial statements, it would be necessary for users of comparative financial statements either to wonder how and why certain amounts reported on the balance sheet changed from one period to another, or to compute (at least for the latest year presented) approximations of these items for themselves. At best, however, such a do-it-yourself approach would derive the net changes (the increase or decrease) in the individual assets and liabilities and attribute these to normally related income statement accounts. (For example, the net change in accounts receivable from the beginning to the end of the year would be used to convert reported sales to cash basis sales or cash collected from customers.) More complex combinations of events (such as the acquisition of another entity, along with its accounts receivables, which would be an increase in that asset which was not related to sales to customers by the reporting entity during the period) would not immediately be comprehensible and might lead to incorrect interpretations of the data unless an actual cash flow statement were presented.

3. It enhances the comparability of reporting of operating performance by different enterprises because it eliminates the effects of using different accounting treatments for the same transactions and events.

There was considerable debate even as early as the 1960s and 1970s over accounting standardization, which led to the emergence of cash flow accounting. The principal argument in support of cash flow accounting by its earliest proponents was that it avoids the arbitrary allocations inherent in accrual accounting. For example, cash flows provided by or used in operating activities are derived, under the indirect method, by adjusting net income (or loss) for items such as depreciation and amortization, which might have been computed by different entities using different accounting methods. Thus, accounting standardization will be achieved by converting the accrual basis net income to cash basis income, and the resultant figures will become comparable across enterprises.

4. It serves as an indicator of the amount, timing, and certainty of future cash flows. Furthermore, if an enterprise has a system in place to project its future cash flows, the statement of cash flows could be used as a touchstone to evaluate the accuracy of past projections of those future cash flows. This benefit is elucidated by the standard as follows:

   a. The statement of cash flows is useful in comparing past assessments of future cash flows against current year's cash flow information, and
   b. It is of value in appraising the relationship between profitability and net cash flows, and in assessing the impact of changing prices.

Exclusion of Noncash Transactions

The statement of cash flows includes only inflows and outflows of cash and cash equivalents. On the other hand, it excludes all transactions that do not directly affect cash receipts and payments. However, IAS 7 does require that the effects of transactions not resulting in receipts or payments of cash be disclosed elsewhere in the financial statements. The reason for not including noncash transactions in the statement of cash flows and placing them elsewhere in the financial statements (e.g., the footnotes) is that it preserves the statement's primary focus on cash flows from operating, investing, and financing activities.

Components of Cash and Cash Equivalents

The statement of cash flows, under the various national and international standards, may or may not include transactions in cash equivalents as well as cash. Under US standards, for example, preparers may choose to define cash as "cash and cash equivalents," as long as the same definition is used in the balance sheet as in the cash flow statement (i.e., the cash flow statement must tie to a single caption on the balance sheet). With the recent dramatic revision to the UK standard on cash flow reporting, on the other hand, the **revised** UK FRS 1 now defines cash flows to include movements only in "cash." IAS 7, on the other hand, rather clearly required that the changes in both cash and cash equivalents be explained by the cash flow statement. Thus, the three major standards (US, UK, and International) have taken three different roads (optionally including cash equivalents; mandatorily excluding cash equivalents; and including cash equivalents) to the presentation of the statement of cash flows.

Cash and cash equivalents include unrestricted cash (meaning cash actually on hand, or bank balances whose immediate use is determined by the management), other demand deposits, and short-term investments whose maturities at the date of acquisition by the enterprise were 3 months or less. **Equity investments** do not qualify as cash equivalents unless they fit the definition above of short-term maturities of 3 months or less. **Redeemable preference shares**, if acquired within 3 months of their predetermined redemption date, would meet the criteria above since they are, in substance, cash equivalents. These are very infrequently encountered circumstances, however.

Bank borrowings are normally considered as financing activities. However, in some countries, bank overdrafts play an integral part in the enterprise's cash management, and as such, overdrafts are to be included as a component of cash equivalents if the following conditions are met:

1. The bank overdraft is repayable on demand, and
2. The bank balance often fluctuates from positive to negative (overdraft).

Postdated checks (cheques), commonly referred to as **PDC**, are used a great deal in business transactions in certain countries. In such situations, vendors usually insist upon PDC to back up the credit extended by them in the normal course of business. Banks will then offer to discount these postdated checks (on a recourse basis, normally) if the discounting party's credit is strong, and thus vendors may end up collecting their receivables before the due date. Under such circumstances, where vendors use PDC as an integral component of their cash management strategy, it could very well be argued that PDC should be considered cash equivalents. However, if it is not certain at the balance sheet date whether or not the PDC are to be discounted, a case could be made to at least consider those PDC that mature within 3 months after the balance sheet date as cash equivalents (while those having original maturities longer than 3 months would be precluded from being so treated).

The customer who issued those PDC, however, has no control over them once they are issued and would not be able to use them as an integral part of its cash management; thus, in the debtors' financial statements PDC are simply accounts payable and are not cash transactions until the dates of the PDC occur.

Statutory deposits by banks (i.e., those held with the central bank for regulatory compliance purposes) are often included in the same balance sheet caption as cash. There is difference of opinion and even some controversy in certain countries, which is fairly evident from scrutiny of published financial statements of banks, as to whether these deposits should be considered a cash equivalent or an operating asset. If the latter, changes in amount would be presented in the operating activities section of the cash flow statement, and the item could not then be combined with cash in the balance sheet. Since the appendix to IAS 7, which illustrates the application of the standard to cash flow statements of financial institutions, does not include statutory deposits with the central bank as a cash equivalent, the authors have concluded that there is little logic to support the alternative presentation of this item as a cash equivalent. Given the fact that deposits with central banks are more or less permanent (and in fact would be more likely to increase over time than to be diminished, given a going concern assumption about the reporting financial institution) the presumption must be that these are not cash equivalents in normal practice.

Classifications in the Statement of Cash Flows

The statement of cash flows prepared in accordance with international accounting standards (and also in accordance with US GAAP) requires classification into these three categories:

1. **Investing activities** include the acquisition and disposition of property, plant and equipment and other long-term assets and debt and equity instruments of other enterprises that are not considered cash equivalents or held for dealing or trading purposes. Investing activities include cash advances and collections on loans made to other parties (other than advances and loans of a financial institution).
2. **Financing activities** include obtaining resources from and returning resources to the owners. Also included is obtaining resources through borrowings (short-term or long-term) and repayments of the amounts borrowed.
3. **Operating activities** include all transactions that are not investing and financing activities. In general, cash flows that relate to, or are the corollary of, items reported in the income statement are operating cash flows. Operating activities are principal revenue-producing activities of an enterprise and include delivering or producing goods for sale and providing services.

While both US and international accounting standards define these three components of cash flows, the international standards offer somewhat more flexibility in how certain types of cash flows are categorized. For example, under US GAAP, interest paid must be included in operating activities, but under the provisions of

IAS 7 this may consistently be included in either operating or financing activities. (These and other discrepancies among the standards will be discussed further throughout this chapter.) This is a reflection of the fact that although interest expense is operating in the sense of being an item that is reported in the income statement, it also clearly relates to the entity's financing activities.

The **original** UK standard on cash flow reporting, FRS 1, tried to solve this dilemma by defining **five**, not merely three, categories for the cash flow statement. In addition to the three standard classifications discussed above, it added two others: "returns on investments and servicing of finance," and "taxation." The first of these added categories was used to report all dividends and interest paid or received, leaving the traditional financing section to report only principal transactions, and averting the issue of whether dividends and interest are operating, investing, or financing in nature. The segregation of taxation into a category of its own avoids a very similar debate, since taxation can be the result of normal operating activities as well as of investing or financing events.

The recently **revised** UK standard on cash flow reporting, which is also denoted as FRS 1, now requires classification into the following **eight** categories:

1. Operating activities
2. Returns on investments and servicing of finance
3. Taxation
4. Capital expenditure and financial investment
5. Acquisitions and disposals
6. Equity dividends paid
7. Management of liquid resources
8. Financing

As a result of this new classification scheme, financial statements prepared in conformity with UK GAAP will differ rather notably from those prepared under either US GAAP or IAS. With the growing world-wide interest in the standardization of financial reporting in general, and in the international accounting standards in particular, it remains to be seen how well this unorthodox approach will be accepted. In any event, it is deemed to be extremely unlikely that the IAS will be modified to acknowledge the UK approach.

The following are examples of the statement of cash flows classification under the provisions of IAS 7:

	Operating	*Investing*	*Financing*
Cash inflows	• Receipts from sale of goods or services	• Principal collections from loans and sales of other entities' debt instruments	• Proceeds from issuing share capital
	• Sale of loans, debt, or equity instruments carried in trading portfolio	• Sale of equity instruments of other enterprises and from returns of investment in those instruments	• Proceeds from issuing debt (short-term or long-term)
	• Returns on loans (interest)	• Sale of plant and equipment	• Not-for-profits' donor restricted cash that is limited to long-term purposes
	• Returns on equity securities (dividends)		
Cash outflows	• Payments to suppliers for goods and other services	• Loans made and acquisition of other entities' debt instruments	• Payment of dividends
	• Payments to or on behalf of employees	• Purchase of equity instruments* of other enterprises	• Repurchase of company's shares
	• Payments of taxes	• Purchase of plant and equipment	• Repayment of debt principal, including capital lease obligations
	• Payments of interest		
	• Purchase of loans, debt, or equity instruments carried in trading portfolio		

Unless held for trading purposes or considered to be cash equivalents.

Noncash investing and financing activities should, according to IAS 7, be disclosed in the footnotes to financial statements ("elsewhere" is how the standard actually identifies this), but apparently are not intended to be included in the cash flow statement itself. This contrasts somewhat with the US standard, SFAS 95, which encourages inclusion of this supplemental information on the face of the statement of cash flows, although it can, under that standard, be relegated to a footnote as well. (The UK standard on cash flow reporting, FRS 1, revised in 1996, also requires that major noncash transactions be disclosed in a note to the cash flow statement.) Examples of significant noncash financing and investing activities might include

1. Acquiring an asset through a finance lease
2. Conversion of debt to equity
3. Exchange of noncash assets or liabilities for other noncash assets or liabilities
4. Issuance of stock to acquire assets

Basic example of a classified statement of cash flows

Liquid Corporation
Statement of Cash Flows
For the Year Ended December 31, 1999

Net cash flows from operating activities		$ xxx
Cash flows from investing activities:		
Purchase of property, plant, and equipment	$(xxx)	
Sale of equipment	xx	
Collection of notes receivable	xx	
Net cash **used** in investing activities		(xx)
Cash flows from financing activities:		
Proceeds from issuance of share capital	xxx	
Repayment of long-term debt	(xx)	
Reduction of notes payable	(xx)	
Net cash **provided** by financing activities		xx
Effect of exchange rate changes on cash		xx
Net increase in cash and cash equivalents		$ xxx
Cash and cash equivalents at beginning of year		xxx
Cash and cash equivalents at end of year		$xxxx

Footnote Disclosure of Noncash Investing and Financing Activities

Note 4: **Supplemental Cash Flow Statement Information**

Significant noncash investing and financing transactions:

Conversion of bonds into common stock	$ xxx
Property acquired under finance leases	xxx
	$ xxx

Reporting Cash Flows From Operating Activities

Direct vs. indirect method. The operating activities section of the statement of cash flows can be presented under the direct or the indirect method. However, the IASC has expressed a preference for the direct method of presenting net cash from operating activities. In this regard the IASC was probably following in the well-worn path of the FASB in the United States, which similarly urged that the direct method of reporting be adhered to. Under UK GAAP, however, though the UK Accounting Standards Board considered the advantages of the direct method in developing FRS 1, it was noted that it did not believe that in all cases the benefits to users outweighed the costs to the reporting entity of providing that mode of reporting. The UK Board remains of this view, and the revised FRS 1 continues to encourage the direct method only where the potential benefits to users outweigh the costs of providing it. For their part, preparers of financial statements in the other parts of the world, like those in the US, have chosen overwhelmingly to ignore the recommendation of the IASC, preferring by a very large margin to use the indirect method in lieu of the recommended direct method.

The **direct method** shows the items that affected cash flow and the magnitude of those cash flows. Cash received from, and cash paid to, specific sources (such as customers and suppliers) are presented, as opposed to the indirect method's converting accrual basis net income (loss) to cash flow information by means of a series of add-backs and deductions. Entities using the direct method are required by IAS 7 to report the following major classes of gross cash receipts and gross cash payments:

1. Cash collected from customers
2. Interest and dividends received[*]
3. Cash paid to employees and other suppliers
4. Interest paid[**]
5. Income taxes paid
6. Other operating cash receipts and payments

Given the availability of alternative modes of presentation of interest and dividends received, and of interest paid, it is particularly critical that the policy adopted be followed consistently. Since the face of the statement of cash flows will in almost all cases make it clear what approach has been elected, it is not usually necessary to spell this out in the accounting policy note to the financial statements, although this certainly can be done if it would be useful to do so.

An important advantage of the direct method is that it permits the user to better comprehend the relationships between the company's net income (loss) and its cash flows. For example, payments of expenses are shown as cash disbursements and are deducted from cash receipts. In this way the user is able to recognize the cash receipts and cash payments for the period. Formulas for conversion of various income statement amounts for the direct method presentation from the accrual basis to the cash basis are summarized below.

Accrual basis	*Additions*	*Deductions*	*Cash basis*
Net sales	+ Beginning AR	– Ending AR AR written off	= Cash received from customers

Cost of goods sold	+ Ending inventory
	    Beginning AP
		– Depreciation and amortization‡
		    Beginning inventory
		    Ending AP
			= Cash paid to suppliers

Operating expenses	+ Ending prepaid expenses
	    Beginning accrued
	        expenses
		– Depreciation and amortization
		    Beginning prepaid expenses
		    Ending accrued expenses payable
		    Bad debts expense
			= Cash paid for operating
			    expenses

‡*Applies to a manufacturing entity only*

---

[*] *Alternatively, interest and dividends received may be classified as investing cash flows rather than as operating cash flows because they are returns on investments. In this important regard, the IAS differs from the corresponding US rule, which does not permit this elective treatment, making the operating cash flow presentation mandatory.*

[**] *Alternatively, also, IAS 7 permits interest paid to be classified as a financing cash flow, because this is the cost of obtaining financing. As with the foregoing, the availability of alternative treatments differs from the US approach, which makes the operating cash flow presentation the only choice.*

From the foregoing it can be appreciated that the amounts to be included in the operating section of the statement of cash flows, when the direct approach is utilized, are derived amounts that must be computed (although the computations are not onerous); they are not, generally, amounts that exist as account balances simply to be looked up and then placed in the statement. The extra effort needed to prepare the direct method operating cash flow data may be a contributing cause of why this method has been distinctly unpopular with preparers. (There is an extra reason why the direct method is unpopular with entities that report in conformity with US GAAP: SFAS 95 requires that when the direct method is used, a supplementary schedule be prepared reconciling net income to net cash flows from operating activities, which effectively means that **both** the direct and indirect methods must be employed. This rule does not apply under international accounting standards, however.)

The **indirect method** (sometimes referred to as the reconciliation method) is the most widely used means of presentation of cash from operating activities, primarily because it is easier to prepare. It focuses on the differences between net operating results and cash flows. The indirect format begins with net income (or loss), which can be obtained directly from the income statement. Revenue and expense items not affecting cash are added or deducted to arrive at net cash provided by operating activities. For example, depreciation and amortization would be added back because these expenses reduce net income without affecting cash.

The statement of cash flows prepared using the indirect method emphasizes changes in the components of most current asset and current liability accounts. Changes in inventory, accounts receivable, and other current accounts are used to determine the cash flow from operating activities. Although most of these adjustments are obvious (most preparers simply relate each current asset or current liability on the balance sheet to a single caption in the income statement), some changes require more careful analysis. For example, it is important to compute cash collected from sales by relating sales revenue to both the change in accounts receivable and the change in the related bad debt allowance account.

As another example of possible complexity in computing the cash from operating activities, the change in short-term borrowings resulting from the purchase of equipment would not be included, since it is not related to operating activities. Instead, these short-term borrowings would be classified as a financing activity. Other adjustments under the indirect method include changes in the account balances of deferred income taxes, minority interest, unrealized foreign currency gains or losses and the income (loss) from investments under the equity method.

IAS 7 offers yet another alternative way of presenting the cash flows from operating activities. This could be referred to as the **modified indirect method**. Under this variant of the indirect method, the starting point is not net income but rather revenues and expenses as reported in the income statement. In essence, this approach is virtually the same as the regular indirect method, with two more details: revenues and expenses for the period. There is no equivalent rule under US GAAP.

The following summary, actually simply an expanded balance sheet equation, may facilitate understanding of the adjustments to net income necessary for converting accrual-basis net income to cash-basis net income when using the indirect method.

	Current assets*	_	Fixed assets	=	Current liabilities	+	Long-term liabilities	+	Income	Accrual income adjustment to convert to cash flow
1.	Increase			=					Increase	Decrease
2.	Decrease			=					Decrease	Increase
3.				=	Increase				Decrease	Increase
4.				=	Decrease				Increase	Decrease

*Other than cash and cash equivalents

For example, using row 1 in the above chart, a credit sale would increase accounts receivable and accrual-basis income but would not affect cash. Therefore, its effect must be removed from the accrual income to convert to cash income. The last column indicates that the increase in a current asset balance must be deducted from income to obtain cash flow.

Similarly, an increase in a current liability, row 3, must be added to income to obtain cash flows (e.g., accrued wages are on the income statement as an expense, but they do not require cash; the increase in wages payable must be added back to remove this noncash flow expense from accrual-basis income).

Under the US GAAP, when the indirect method is employed, the amount of interest and income taxes paid must be included in the related disclosures (supplemental schedule). However, under international accounting standards, as illustrated by the appendix to IAS 7, instead of disclosing them in the supplemental schedules, they are shown as part of the operating activities under both the direct and indirect methods. (Examples presented later in the chapter illustrate this.)

The major drawback to the indirect method involves the user's difficulty in comprehending the information presented. This method does not show from where the cash was received or to where the cash was paid. Only adjustments to accrual basis net income are shown. In some cases the adjustments can be confusing. For instance, the sale of equipment resulting in an accrual basis loss would require that the loss be added to net income to arrive at net cash from operating activities. (The loss was deducted in the computation of net income, but because the sale will be shown as an investing activity, the loss must be added back to net income.)

Although the indirect method is more commonly used in practice, the IASC and the FASB both encourage enterprises to use the direct method. As pointed out by IAS 7, a distinct advantage of the direct method is that it provides information that may be useful in estimating or projecting future cash flows, a benefit that is clearly not achieved when the indirect method is utilized instead. Both the direct and indirect methods are presented below.

Direct method

Cash flows from operating activities:		
Cash received from sale of goods	$xxx	
Cash dividends received*	<u>xxx</u>	
Cash provided by operating activities		$xxx
Cash paid to suppliers	(xxx)	
Cash paid for operating expenses	(xxx)	
Cash paid for income taxes**	<u>(xxx)</u>	
Cash disbursed for operating activities		(<u>$xxx</u>)
Net cash flows from operating activities		$<u>xxx</u>

   * *Alternatively, could be classified as investing cash flow.*
  ** *Taxes paid are usually classified as operating activities. However, when it is practical to identify the tax cash flow with an individual transaction that gives rise to cash flows that are classified as investing or financing activities, then the tax cash flow is classified as an investing or financing activity as appropriate.*

Indirect method

Cash flows from operating activities:	
Net income before income taxes	$ xx
Adjustments for:	
Depreciation	xx
Unrealized loss on foreign exchange	xx
Interest expense	<u>xx</u>
Operating profit before working capital changes***	xx
Increase in accounts receivable	(xx)
Decrease in inventories	xx
Increase in accounts payable	<u>xx</u>
Cash generated from operations	xx
Interest paid	(xx)
Income taxes paid (see note**above)	<u>(xx)</u>
Net cash flows from operating activities	$<u>xxx</u>

 *** *The appendix to IAS 7 uses the term "working capital changes," but the authors believe that "changes in operating assets and liabilities" is preferable since the emphasis has clearly shifted from working capital changes, and the related concept of fund flows, to cash flows by the supplanting of the erstwhile IAS 7, which dealt with the now obsolete "statement of changes in financial position."*

Other Requirements

Gross vs. net basis. The emphasis in the statement of cash flows is on gross cash receipts and cash payments. For instance, reporting the net change in bonds payable would obscure the financing activities of the entity by not disclosing separately cash inflows from issuing bonds and cash outflows from retiring bonds.

IAS 7 (paragraph 22) specifies two exceptions where netting of cash flows is allowed. Items with quick turnovers, large amounts, and short maturities may be presented as net cash flows. Cash receipts and payments on behalf of customers when the cash flows reflect the activities of the customers rather than those of the enterprise may also be reported on a net rather than a gross basis.

Foreign currency cash flows. Foreign operations must prepare a separate statement of cash flows and translate the statement to the reporting currency using the exchange rate in effect at the time of the cash flow (a weighted-average exchange rate may be used if the result is substantially the same). This translated statement is then used in the preparation of the consolidated statement of cash flows. Noncash exchange gains and losses recognized on the income statement should be reported as a separate item when reconciling net income and operating activities. For a more detailed discussion about the exchange rate effects on the statement of cash flows, see Chapter 20.

Cash flow per share. There is presently no requirement either under the international accounting standards or under US GAAP to disclose such information in the financial statements of an enterprise, unlike the requirement to report earnings per share (EPS). In fact, cash flow per share is a somewhat disreputable concept, since it was sometimes touted, in an earlier era, as being indicative of an entity's "real" performance, when of course it is not a meaningful alternative to earnings per share; because, for example, enterprises that are self-liquidating by selling productive assets can generate very positive total cash flows, and hence cash flows per share, while decimating the potential for future earnings. Since, unlike a comprehensive cash flow statement, cash flow per share cannot reveal the components of cash flow (operating, investing, and financing), its usage could be misleading.

Exemption From Presentation of a Statement of Cash Flows Under US GAAP and IAS

Under US GAAP, as set forth in SFAS 102, a statement of cash flows is not required for a defined benefit pension plan that presents financial information consistent with the guidelines of SFAS 35. Other employee benefit plans are exempted provided that the financial information presented is similar to the requirements of SFAS 35. Investment enterprises or a common trust fund held for the collective investment and reinvestment of moneys are not required to provide a statement of cash flows if the following conditions are met:

1. Substantially all of the entity's investments are highly liquid
2. Entity's investments are carried at market value
3. Entity had little or no debt, based on average debt outstanding during the period in relation to average total assets
4. Entity provides a statement of changes in net assets

However, with the issuance of SFAS 117, the requirements for presentation of statements of cash flows have been made almost universal except in the case of investment companies and employee benefit plans, which are still exempted. IAS 7, on the other hand, categorically states that all enterprises regardless of the nature of their activities should present a statement of cash flows as an integral part of their financial reports. No exceptions have been identified to this requirement.

Net Reporting by Financial Institutions

IAS 7 permits financial institutions to report cash flows arising from certain activities on a net basis. These activities, and the related conditions under which net reporting would be acceptable, are as follows:

1. Cash receipts and payments on behalf of customers, when the cash flows reflect the activities of the customers rather than those of the bank. For example, the acceptance and repayment of demand deposits
2. Cash flows relating to deposits with fixed maturity dates
3. Placements and withdrawals of deposits from other financial institutions
4. Cash advances and loans to banks customers and repayments thereon

US GAAP has similar requirements. According to SFAS 104, banks, savings institutions, and credit unions are allowed to report net cash receipts and payments for the following:

1. Deposits placed with other financial institutions
2. Withdrawals of deposits
3. Time deposits accepted
4. Repayments of deposits
5. Loans made to customers
6. Principal collections of loans

Reporting Futures, Forward Contracts, Options, and Swaps

IAS 7 stipulates that cash payments for and cash receipts from futures contracts, forward contracts, option contracts, and swap contracts are normally classified as investing activities, except

1. When such contracts are held for dealing or trading purposes and thus represent operating activities
2. When the payments or receipts are considered by the enterprise as financing activities and are reported accordingly

Further, when a contract is accounted for as a hedge of an identifiable position, the cash flows of the contract are classified in the same manner as the cash flows of the position being hedged. In this matter, US GAAP establishes similar requirements (by SFAS 104).

Reporting Extraordinary Items in the Cash Flow Statement

The cash flows associated with extraordinary items should be disclosed separately as arising from operating, investing, or financing activities in the statement of cash flows, as appropriate. By way of contrast, US GAAP permits, but does not require, separate disclosure of cash flows related to extraordinary items. If an entity reporting under US GAAP chooses to make this disclosure, however, it is expected to do so consistently in all periods.

Reconciliation of Cash and Cash Equivalents

An enterprise should disclose the components of cash and cash equivalents and should present a reconciliation of the difference, if any, between the amounts reported in the statement of cash flows and equivalent items reported in the balance sheet. By contrast, under the US GAAP the definition must tie to a specific caption on the balance sheet. For example, if short-term investments are shown as a separate caption in the balance sheet, the definition of cash for the purposes of the statement of cash flows must include "cash" alone (and not also include short-term investments). On the other hand, if "cash and cash equivalents" is the adopted definition in the statement of cash flows, a single caption in the balance sheet must include both "cash" and "short-term investments."

Acquisitions and Disposals of Subsidiaries and Other Business Units

IAS 7 requires that the aggregate cash flows from acquisitions and from disposals of subsidiaries or other business units should be presented separately as part of the investing activities section of the statement of cash flows. The following disclosures have also been prescribed by IAS 7 in respect to both acquisitions and disposals:

1. The total consideration included
2. The portion thereof discharged by cash and cash equivalents
3. The amount of cash and cash equivalents in the subsidiary or business unit acquired or disposed
4. The amount of assets and liabilities (other than cash and cash equivalents) acquired or disposed, summarized by major category

Other Disclosures Required or Recommended by IAS 7

Certain additional information may be relevant to the users of financial statements in gaining an insight into the liquidity or solvency of an enterprise. With this objective in mind, IAS 7 sets forth other disclosures that are required or in some cases, recommended.

1. **Required disclosure**--Amount of significant cash and cash equivalent balances held by an enterprise that are not available for use by the group should be disclosed along with a commentary by management.
2. **Recommended disclosures**--The disclosures that are encouraged are the following:

   a. Amount of undrawn borrowing facilities, indicating restrictions on their use, if any

b. In case of investments in joint ventures, which are accounted for using proportionate consolidation, the aggregate amount of cash flows from operating, investing and financing activities that are attributable to the investment in the joint venture

c. Aggregate amount of cash flows that are attributable to the increase in operating capacity separately from those cash flows that are required to maintain operating capacity

d. Amount of cash flows segregated by reported industry and geographical segments

The disclosures above recommended by the IAS 7, although difficult to present, are unique since such disclosures are not required even under the US GAAP. They are useful in enabling the users of financial statements to understand the enterprise's financial position better.

Basic example of the preparation of the cash flow statement under IAS 7 using a worksheet approach

Using the following financial information for ABC (Middle East) Ltd., preparation and presentation of the cash flow statement according to the requirements of IAS 7 are illustrated. (Note that all figures in this example are in thousands of US dollars.)

ABC (Middle East) Ltd.
Balance Sheets
As at December 31, 2000 and 1999

Assets	*2000*	*1999*
Cash and cash equivalents	$ 3,000	$ 1,000
Debtors	5,000	2,500
Inventories	2,000	1,500
Preoperative expenses	1,000	1,500
Due from associates	19,000	19,000
Property, plant, and equipment cost	12,000	22,500
Accumulated depreciation	(5,000)	(6,000)
Property, plant, and equipment, net	7,000	16,500
Total assets	$37,000	$42,000
Liabilities		
Accounts payable	$ 5,000	$12,500
Income taxes payable	2,000	1,000
Deferred taxes payable	3,000	2,000
Total liabilities	10,000	15,500
Shareholders' equity		
Share capital	6,500	6,500
Retained earnings	20,500	20,000
Total shareholders' equity	27,000	26,500
Total liabilities and shareholders' equity	$37,000	$42,000

ABC (Middle East) Ltd.
Statement of Income
For the Year Ended December 31, 2000

Sales	$ 30,000
Cost of sales	(10,000)
Gross operating income	20,000
Administrative and selling expenses	(2,000)
Interest expenses	(2,000)
Depreciation of property, plant and equipment	(2,000)
Amortization of preoperative expenses	(500)
Investment income	2,000
Net income before taxation and extraordinary item	15,500
Extraordinary item--proceeds from settlement	
with government for expropriation of business	1,000
Net income after extraordinary item	16,500
Taxes on income	(4,000)
Net income	$ 12,500

The following additional information is relevant to the preparation of the statement of cash flows:

1. Equipment with a net book value of $7,500 and original cost of $10,500 was sold for $7,500.
2. All sales made by the company are credit sales.
3. The company received cash dividends (from investments) amounting to $2,000, recorded as income in the income statement for the year ended December 31, 2000.
4. The company received $1,000 in settlement from government for the expropriation of business, which is accounted for as an extraordinary item.
5. The company declared and paid dividends of $12,000 to its shareholders.
6. Interest expense for the year 2000 was $2,000, which was fully paid during the year. All administration and selling expenses incurred were paid during the year.
7. Income tax expense for the year 2000 was provided at $4,000, out of which the company paid $2,000 during 2000 as an estimate.

A worksheet can be prepared to ease the development of the cash flow statement, as follows:

Cash Flow Worksheet

	2000	1999	Change	Operating	Investing	Financing	Cash and equivalents
Cash and equivalents	3,000	1,000	2,000				2,000
Debtors	5,000	2,500	2,500	(2,500)			
Inventories	2,000	1,500	500	(500)			
Preoperative expenses	1,000	1,500	(500)	500			
Due from associates	19,000	19,000	0				
Property, plant, and equipment	7,000	16,500	(9,500)	2,000	7,500		
Accounts payable	5,000	12,500	7,500	(7,500)			
Income taxes payable	2,000	1,000	1,000	1,000			
Deferred taxes payable	3,000	2,000	1,000	1,000			
Share capital	6,500	6,500	0				
Retained earnings	20,500	20,000	500	10,500	2,000	(12,000)	--
				4,500	9,500	(12,000)	2,000

ABC (Middle East) Ltd.
Statement of Cash Flows
For the Year Ended December 31, 2000
(Direct method)

Cash flows from operating activities

Cash receipts from customers	$ 27,500	
Cash paid to suppliers and employees	(20,000)	
Cash generated from operations	7,500	
Interest paid	(2,000)	
Income taxes paid	(2,000)	
Cash flow before extraordinary item	3,500	
Proceeds from settlement with government		
for appropriation of business*	1,000	
Net cash flows from operating activities		$ 4,500

Cash flows from investing activities

Proceeds from the sale of equipment	7,500	
Dividends received	2,000	
Net cash flows from investing activities		9,500

Cash flows from financing activities

Dividends paid	(12,000)	
Net cash flows used in financing activities		(12,000)
Net increase in cash and cash equivalents		2,000
Cash and cash equivalents, beginning of year		1,000
Cash and cash equivalents, end of year		$ 3,000

* *Cash flows associated with extraordinary items should be classified as arising from operating, investing, or financing activities as appropriate and disclosed separately. Thus, part of the proceeds (i.e., those pertaining to property, plant and equipment) could be presented as cash flows from investing activities, if information needed to do so is available.*

Details of the computations of amounts shown in the statement of cash flows are as follows:

Cash received from customers during the year

Credit sales	30,000	
Plus: Accounts receivable, beginning of year	2,500	
Less: Accounts receivable, end of year	(5,000)	
Cash received from customers during the year		$27,500

Cash paid to suppliers and employees

Cost of sales	10,000	
Less: Inventory, beginning of year	(1,500)	
Plus: Inventory, end of year	2,000	
Plus: Accounts payable, beginning of year	12,500	
Less: Accounts payable, end of year	(5,000)	
Plus: Administrative and selling expenses paid	2,000	
Cash paid to suppliers and employees during the year		$20,000
Interest paid equals interest expense charged to the income statement		
(per additional information)		$ 2,000

Income taxes paid during the year

Tax expense during the year (comprising current and deferred portions)		4,000	
Plus:	Beginning income taxes payable	1,000	
Plus:	Beginning deferred taxes payable	2,000	
Less:	Ending income taxes payable	(2,000)	
Less:	Ending deferred taxes payable	(3,000)	
Cash paid toward income taxes			$ 2,000
Proceeds from settlement with government--expropriation of business (per additional information)			$ 1,000
Proceeds from sale of equipment (per additional information)			$ 7,500
Dividends received during 2000 (per additional information)			$ 2,000
Dividends paid during 2000 (per additional information)			$12,000

ABC (Middle East) Ltd.
Statement of Cash Flows
For the Year Ended December 31, 2000
(Indirect method)*

Cash flows from operating activities		
Net income before taxation and extraordinary item	$ 15,500	
Adjustments for:		
Depreciation of property, plant and equipment	2,000	
Amortization of preoperative expenses	500	
Investment income	(2,000)	
Interest expense	2,000	
Operating income before working capital changes*	18,000	
Increase in accounts receivable	(2,500)	
Increase in inventories	(500)	
Decrease in accounts payable	(7,500)	
Cash generated from operations	7,500	
Interest paid	(2,000)	
Income taxes paid	(2,000)	
Cash flow before extraordinary item	3,500	
Proceeds from government settlement--expropriation of business**	1,000	
Net cash from operating activities		4,500
Cash flows from investing activities		
Proceeds from sale of equipment	7,500	
Dividends received	2,000	
Net cash from investing activities		9,500
Cash flows from financing activities		
Dividends paid	(12,000)	
Net cash used in financing activities		(12,000)
Net increase in cash and cash equivalents		2,000
Cash and cash equivalents, beginning of year		1,000
Cash and cash equivalents, end of year		$ 3,000

* *The format of the statement of cash flows presented under the indirect method is in accordance with the presentation in the appendix of IAS 7; thus the wording "working capital changes" has been used instead of "changes in operating assets and liabilities," as recommended by the authors. For a detailed discussion on this subject, refer to the earlier section of this chapter.*

** *Cash flows associated with extraordinary items should be classified as arising from operating, investing, or financing activities as appropriate and disclosed separately. Thus, part of the proceeds (i.e., those pertaining to property, plant and equipment) could be presented as cash flows from investing activities, if information needed to do so is available.*

A Comprehensive Example of the Preparation of the Cash Flow Statement Using the T-Account Approach

Under a cash and cash equivalents basis, the changes in the cash account and any cash equivalent account is the bottom line figure of the statement of cash flows. Using the 1999 and 2000 balance sheets shown below, an increase of $17,000 can be computed. This is the difference between the totals for cash and treasury bills between 1999 and 2000 ($33,000 – $16,000).

When preparing the statement of cash flows using the direct method, gross cash inflows from revenues and gross cash outflows to suppliers and for expenses are presented in the operating activities section.

In preparing the reconciliation of net income to net cash flow from operating activities (indirect method), changes in all accounts other than cash and cash equivalents that are related to operations are additions to or deductions from net income to arrive at net cash provided by operating activities.

A T-account analysis may be helpful when preparing the statement of cash flows. A T-account is set up for each account, and beginning (1999) and ending (2000) balances are taken from the appropriate balance sheet. Additionally, a T-account for cash and cash equivalents from operating activities and a master or summary T-account of cash and cash equivalents should be used.

Example of preparing a statement of cash flows

The financial statements will be used to prepare the statement of cash flows.

Johnson Company
Balance Sheets
December 31, 2000 and 1999

	2000	*1999*
Assets		
Current assets		
Cash	$ 29,000	$ 10,000
Treasury bills	4,000	6,000
Accounts receivable--net	9,000	11,000
Inventory	14,000	9,000
Prepaid expenses	10,000	13,000
Total current assets	$ 66,000	$ 49,000
Noncurrent assets		
Investment in XYZ (35%)	16,000	14,000
Patent	5,000	6,000
Leased asset	5,000	-0-
Property, plant, and equipment	39,000	37,000
Less accumulated depreciation	(7,000)	(3,000)
Total assets	$124,000	$103,000

Liabilities
Current liabilities

Accounts payable	$ 2,000	$ 12,000
Notes payable--current	9,000	-0-
Interest payable	3,000	2,000
Dividends payable	5,000	2,000
Income taxes payable	2,000	1,000
Lease obligation	700	-0-
Total current liabilities	21,700	17,000

Noncurrent liabilities

Deferred tax liability	9,000	6,000
Bonds payable	10,000	25,000
Lease obligation	4,300	-0-
Total liabilities	$ 45,000	$ 48,000

Stockholders' equity

Common stock, $10 par value	$ 33,000	$ 26,000
Additional paid-in capital	16,000	3,000
Retained earnings	30,000	26,000
Total stockholders' equity	$ 79,000	$ 55,000
Total liabilities and stockholders' equity	$124,000	$103,000

Johnson Company
Statement of Earnings
For the Year Ended December 31, 2000

Sales	$100,000
Other income	8,000
	$108,000
Cost of goods sold, excluding depreciation	60,000
Selling, general, and administrative expenses	12,000
Depreciation	8,000
Amortization of patents	1,000
Interest expense	2,000
	$ 83,000
Income before taxes	$ 25,000
Income taxes (36%)	9,000
Net income	$ 16,000

Additional information (relating to 2000)

1. Equipment costing $6,000 with a book value of $2,000 was sold for $5,000.
2. The company received a $3,000 dividend from its investment in XYZ, accounted for under the equity method and recorded income from the investment of $5,000, which is included in other income.
3. The company issued 200 shares of common stock for $5,000.
4. The company signed a note payable for $9,000.
5. Equipment was purchased for $8,000.
6. The company converted $15,000 bonds payable into 500 shares of common stock. The book value method was used to record the transaction.
7. A dividend of $12,000 was declared.
8. Equipment was leased on December 31, 2000. The principal portion of the first payment due December 31, 2001, is $700.

Summary of Cash and Cash Equivalents			
Inflows		**Outflows**	
(d)	5,000	8,000	(g)
(h)	5,000	9,000	(i)
(n)	9,000		
(s)	15,000		
	34,000	17,000	
		17,000	Net increase in cash
	34,000	34,000	

Cash and Cash Equivalents--Oper. Act.			
(a)	16,000		
(b)	8,000		
(c)	1,000	3,000	(d)
(e)	3,000	5,000	(f)
(f)	3,000		
(j)	2,000	5,000	(k)
(l)	3,000	10,000	(m)
(o)	1,000		
(p)	1,000		
	38,000	23,000	
		15,000	(s)
	38,000	38,000	

Accounts Receivable (Net)			
	11,000		
		2,000	(j)
	9,000		

Inventory			
	9,000		
(k)	5,000		
	14,000		

Prepaid Expenses			
	13,000		
		3,000	(l)
	10,000		

Investment in XYZ			
	14,000		
(f)	5,000	3,000	(f)
	16,000		

Patent			
	6,000		
		1,000	(c)
	5,000		

Leased Equipment			
(r)	5,000		
	5,000		

Prop., Plant, & Equip.			
	37,000		
		6,000	(d)
(g)	8,000		
	39,000		

Accumulated Depr.			
		3,000	
		8,000	(b)
(d)	4,000		
		7,000	

Accounts Payable			
		12,000	
(m)	10,000		
		2,000	

Notes Payable			
		9,000	(n)
		9,000	

Interest Payable			
		2,000	
(o)	1,000	2,000	(o)
		3,000	

Dividends Payable			
		2,000	
(i)	9,000	12,000	(i)
		5,000	

Income Taxes Payable			
		1,000	
(p)	5,000	6,000	(p)
		2,000	

Deferred Tax Liability			
		6,000	
		3,000	(e)
		9,000	

Bonds Payable			
		25,000	
(q)	15,000		
		10,000	

Lease Obligation			
		5,000	(r)
		5,000	

Common Stock		
	26,000	
	2,000	(h)
	5,000	(q)
	33,000	

Addl. Paid-in Capital		
	3,000	
	3,000	(h)
	10,000	(q)
	16,000	

Retained Earnings			
		26,000	
		16,000	(a)
(i)	12,000		
		30,000	

Explanation of entries

a. Cash and Cash Equivalents--Operating activities is debited for $16,000, and credited to Retained Earnings. This represents the net income figure.

b. Depreciation is not a cash flow; however, depreciation expense was deducted to arrive at net income. Therefore, Accumulated Depreciation is credited and Cash and Cash Equivalents--Operating activities is debited.

c. Amortization of patents is another expense not requiring cash; therefore, Cash and Cash Equivalents--Operating activities is debited and Patent is credited.

d. The sale of equipment (additional information, item 1) resulted in a $3,000 gain. The gain is computed by comparing the book value of $2,000 with the sales price of $5,000. Cash proceeds of $5,000 are an inflow of cash. Since the gain was included in net income, it must be deducted from net income to determine cash provided by operating activities. This is necessary to avoid counting the $3,000 gain both in cash provided by operating activities and in investing activities. The following entry would have been made on the date of sale:

Cash	5,000	
Accumulated depreciation (6,000 – 2,000)	4,000	
Property, plant, and equipment		6,000
Gain on sale of equipment (5,000 – 2,000)		3,000

Adjust the T-accounts as follows: debit Summary of Cash and Cash Equivalents for $5,000, debit Accumulated Depreciation for $4,000, credit Property, Plant, and Equipment for $6,000, and credit Cash and Cash Equivalents--Operating activities for $3,000.

e. The $3,000 increase in Deferred Income Taxes must be added to income from operations. Although the $3,000 was deducted as part of income tax expense in determining net income, it did not require an outflow of cash. Therefore, debit Cash and Cash Equivalents--Operating activities and credit Deferred Taxes.

f. Item 2 under the additional information indicates that the investment in XYZ is accounted for under the equity method. The investment in XYZ had a net increase of $2,000 during the year after considering the receipt of a $3,000 dividend. Dividends received (an inflow of cash) would reduce the investment in XYZ, while the equity in the income of XYZ would increase the investment without affecting cash. In order for the T-account to balance, a debit of $5,000 must have been made, indicating earnings of that amount. The journal entries would have been

Cash (dividend received)	3,000	
Investment in XYZ		3,000
Investment in XYZ	5,000	
Equity in earnings of XYZ		5,000

The dividend received ($3,000) is an inflow of cash, while the equity earnings are not. Debit Investment in XYZ for $5,000, credit Cash and Cash Equivalents--Operating activities for $5,000, debit Cash and Cash Equivalents--Operating activities for $3,000, and credit Investment in XYZ for $3,000.

g. The Property, Plant, and Equipment account increased because of the purchase of $8,000 (additional information, item 5). The purchase of assets is an outflow of cash. Debit Property, Plant, and Equipment for $8,000 and credit Summary of Cash and Cash Equivalents.

h. The company sold 200 shares of common stock during the year (additional information, item 3). The entry for the sale of stock was

Cash	5,000	
Common stock (200 shares x $10)		2,000
Additional paid-in capital		3,000

This transaction resulted in an inflow of cash. Debit Summary of Cash and Cash Equivalents $5,000, credit Common Stock $2,000, and credit Additional Paid-in Capital $3,000.

i. Dividends of $12,000 were declared (additional information, item 7). Only $9,000 was actually paid in cash resulting in an ending balance of $9,000 in the Dividends Payable account. Therefore, the following entries were made during the year:

Retained Earnings	12,000	
Dividends Payable		12,000
Dividends Payable	9,000	
Cash		9,000

These transactions result in an outflow of cash. Debit Retained Earnings $12,000 and credit Dividends Payable $12,000. Additionally, debit Dividends Payable $9,000 and credit Summary of Cash and Cash Equivalents $9,000 to indicate the cash dividends paid during the year.

j. Accounts Receivable (net) decreased by $2,000. This is added as an adjustment to net income in the computation of cash provided by operating activities. The decrease of $2,000 means that an additional $2,000 cash was collected on account above and beyond the sales reported in the income statement. Debit Cash and Cash Equivalents--Operating activities and credit Accounts Receivable for $2,000.

k. Inventories increased by $5,000. This is subtracted as an adjustment to net income in the computation of cash provided by operating activities. Although $5,000 additional cash was spent to increase inventories, this expenditure is not reflected in accrual-basis cost of goods sold. Debit Inventory and credit Cash and Cash Equivalents--Operating activities for $5,000.

l. Prepaid Expenses decreased by $3,000. This is added back to net income in the computation of cash provided by operating activities. The decrease means that no cash was spent when incurring the related expense. The cash was spent when the prepaid assets were purchased, not when they were expended on the income statement. Debit Cash and Cash Equivalents--Operating activities and credit Prepaid Expenses for $3,000.

m. Accounts Payable decreased by $10,000. This is subtracted as an adjustment to net income. The decrease of $10,000 means that an additional $10,000 of purchases were paid for in cash; therefore, income was not affected but cash was decreased. Debit Accounts Payable and credit Cash and Cash Equivalents--Operating activities for $10,000.

n. Notes Payable increased by $9,000 (additional information, item 4). This is an inflow of cash and would be included in the financing activities. Debit Summary of Cash and Cash Equivalents and credit Notes Payable for $9,000.

o. Interest Payable increased by $1,000, but interest expense from the income statement was $2,000. Therefore, although $2,000 was expensed, only $1,000 cash was paid ($2,000 expense – $1,000 increase in interest payable). Debit Cash and Cash Equivalents--Operating activities for $1,000, debit Interest Payable for $1,000, and credit Interest Payable for $2,000.

p. The following entry was made to record the incurrence of the tax liability:

Income tax expense	9,000	
Income taxes payable		6,000
Deferred tax liability		3,000

Therefore, $9,000 was deducted in arriving at net income. The $3,000 credit to Deferred Income Taxes was accounted for in entry (e) above. The $6,000 credit to Taxes Payable does not, however, indicate that $6,000 cash was paid for taxes. Since Taxes Payable increased $1,000, only $5,000 must have been paid and $1,000 remains unpaid. Debit Cash and Cash Equivalents--Operating activities for $1,000, debit Income Taxes Payable for $5,000, and credit Income Taxes Payable for $6,000.

q. Item 6 under the additional information indicates that $15,000 of bonds payable were converted to common stock. This is a **noncash** financing activity and should be reported in a separate schedule. The following entry was made to record the transaction:

Bonds payable	15,000	
Common stock (500 shares x $10 par)		5,000
Additional paid-in capital		10,000

Adjust the T-accounts with a debit to Bonds Payable, $15,000; a credit to Common Stock, $5,000; and a credit to Additional Paid-in Capital, $10,000.

r. Item 8 under the additional information indicates that leased equipment was acquired on the last day of 2000. This is also a noncash financing activity and should be reported in a separate schedule. The following entry was made to record the lease transaction:

Leased asset	5,000	
Lease obligation		5,000

s. The cash and cash equivalents from operations ($15,000) is transferred to the Summary of Cash and Cash Equivalents.

Since all of the changes in the noncash accounts have been accounted for and the balance in the Summary of Cash and Cash Equivalents account of $17,000 is the amount of the year-to-year increase in cash and cash equivalents, the formal statement may now be prepared. The following classified SCF is prepared under the direct method and includes the reconciliation of net income to net cash provided by operating activities. The T-account, Cash and Cash Equivalents--Operating activities, is used in the preparation of this reconciliation. The calculations for gross receipts and gross payments needed for the direct method are shown below.

Johnson Company
Statement of Cash Flows
For the Year Ended December 31, 2000

Cash flows from operating activities

Cash received from customers	$102,000	(a)	
Dividends received	3,000		
Cash provided by operating activities			$105,000
Cash paid to suppliers	$ 75,000	(b)	
Cash paid for expenses	9,000	(c)	
Interest paid	1,000	(d)	
Taxes paid	5,000	(e)	
Cash paid for operating activities			(90,000)
Net cash provided by operating activities			$ 15,000

Cash flows from investing activities

Sale of equipment	5,000	
Purchase of property, plant, and equipment	(8,000)	
Net cash used in investing activities		(3,000)

Cash flows from financing activities

Sale of common stock	$ 5,000	
Increase in notes payable	9,000	
Dividends paid	(9,000)	
Net cash provided by financing activities		5,000
Net increase in cash and cash equivalents		$ 17,000
Cash and cash equivalents at beginning of year		16,000
Cash and cash equivalents at end of year		$ 33,000

Calculation of amounts for operating activities section of Johnson Co.'s statement of cash flows

(a)   Net sales + Beginning AR – Ending AR = Cash received from customers

  $100,000 + $11,000 – $9,000 = $102,000

(b)   Cost of goods sold + Beginning AP – Ending AP + Ending inventory – Beginning inventory
  = Cash paid to suppliers

  $60,000 + $12,000 – $2,000 + $14,000 – $9,000 = $75,000

(c)   Operating expenses + Ending prepaid expenses – Beginning prepaid expenses –
  Depreciation expense (and other noncash operating expenses) = Cash paid for operating
  expenses

  $12,000 + $10,000 – $13,000 = $9,000

(d)   Interest expense + Beginning interest payable – Ending interest payable = Interest paid

  $2,000 + $2,000 – $3,000 = $1,000

(e)   Income taxes + Beginning income taxes payable – Ending income taxes payable +
  Beginning deferred income taxes – Ending deferred income taxes = Taxes paid

  $9,000 + $1,000 – $2,000 + $6,000 – $9,000 = $5,000

Reconciliation of net income to net cash provided by operating activities

Net income	$16,000	
Add (deduct) items not using (providing) cash:		
Depreciation	8,000	
Amortization	1,000	
Gain on sale of equipment	(3,000)	
Increase in deferred taxes	3,000	
Equity in XYZ	(2,000)	
Decrease in accounts receivable	2,000	
Increase in inventory	(5,000)	
Decrease in prepaid expenses	3,000	
Decrease in accounts payable	(10,000)	
Increase in interest payable	1,000	
Increase in income taxes payable	1,000	
Net cash provided by operating activities		$15,000

(The reconciliation above is required by US GAAP when the direct method is used, but there is no equivalent requirement under the international accounting standards. The reconciliation above illustrates the presentation of the operating section of the cash flow statement when the indirect method is used. The remaining sections [i.e., the investing and financing sections] of the statement of cash flows are common to both methods, hence have not been presented above.)

Schedule of noncash transactions (to be reported in the footnotes)

Conversion of bonds into common stock	$15,000
Acquisition of leased equipment	$ 5,000

Disclosure of accounting policy
For purposes of the statement of cash flows, the company considers all highly liquid debt instruments purchased with original maturities of 3 months or less to be cash equivalents.

Statement of Cash Flows for Consolidated Entities

A consolidated statement of cash flows must be presented when a complete set of consolidated financial statements is issued. The consolidated statement of cash flows would be the last statement to be prepared, as the information to prepare it will come from the other consolidated statements (consolidated balance sheet, income statement, and statement of retained earnings). The preparation of these other consolidated statements is discussed in Chapter 10.

The preparation of a consolidated statement of cash flows involves the same analysis and procedures as the statement for an individual entity, with a few additional items. The direct or indirect method of presentation may be used. When the indirect method is used, the additional noncash transactions relating to the business combination, such as the differential amortization, must also be reversed. Furthermore, all transfers to affiliates must be eliminated, as they do not represent a cash inflow or outflow of the consolidated entity.

All unrealized intercompany profits should have been eliminated in preparation of the other statements; thus, no additional entry of this sort should be required. Any income allocated to noncontrolling parties would need to be added back, as it would have been eliminated in computing consolidated net income but does not represent a true cash outflow. Finally, any dividend payments should be recorded as cash outflows in the financing activities section.

In preparing the operating activities section of the statement by the indirect method following a purchase business combination, the changes in assets and liabilities related to operations since acquisition should be derived by comparing the consolidated balance sheet as of the date of acquisition with the year-end consolidated balance sheet. These changes will be combined with those for the acquiring company up to the date of acquisition as adjustments to net income. The effects due to the acquisition of these assets and liabilities are reported under investing activities. Under the pooling-of-interests method the combination is treated as having occurred at the beginning of the year. Thus, the changes in assets and liabilities related to operations should be those derived by comparing the beginning of the year balance sheet amounts on a consolidated basis with the end of the year consolidated balance sheet amounts.

5 CASH, RECEIVABLES, AND FINANCIAL INSTRUMENTS

PERSPECTIVE AND ISSUES

The accounting for cash and for receivables has been fairly well settled for many years, but since the international accounting standards are not explicit regarding these matters, financial statements preparers have had to look to national GAAP (such as US or UK GAAP) for guidance. In effect, while certain reporting procedures may be said to be advisable based on the preponderance of practice, there are few if any strictures which could be said to apply to those adhering to IAS. This chapter will present detailed examples on a range of topics involving cash and receivables (e.g., accounting for factored receivables) which are derived from the most widespread and venerable practices in these areas.

The accounting for financial instruments, on the other hand, has received a great deal of attention by the IASC. The original intent, to address all matters of recognition, measurement, derecognition, presentation and disclosure in a single, comprehensive standard, proved to be unworkable (as was also the case under US GAAP), and thus the first standard, IAS 32, issued in 1995 and first effective in 1996, addressed only the less complex issues of presentation and disclosure. The more intractable problems of recognition, measurement, and derecognition have more recently been dealt with by the issuance of IAS 39, which is not mandatorily effective until 2001. IAS 39 is viewed as being only an interim standard, since it failed to comprehensively embrace fair value accounting for all financial assets and liabilities, which is predicted to be the ultimate financial reporting goal, to which the IASC is committed (and toward which a new standard is presently being developed).

IAS 39 establishes extensive new requirements for the recognition, measurement, and derecognition of financial assets and liabilities and also addresses special hedging accounting (which of course would not be necessary if all financial assets and liabilities were simply carried at fair value). It also supersedes certain of the disclosure requirements set forth by IAS 32. IAS 39 effectively supersedes most of IAS 25, but since the older rules can still be applied until the reporting entity's first year beginning after January 2001, these remain of importance.

Accounting for investments under both IAS 25 and IAS 39 will be addressed in detail in Chapter 10. In this chapter, however, the overall requirements of IAS 32 and 39 will be set forth. It is important to understand that, should IAS 39 not be adopted early, the presentation and disclosure requirements of IAS 32 continue to be effective, while the requirements contained in IAS 25 will guide the recognition and measurement of various financial instruments held as investments. If IAS 39 is adopted early, it is the relevant guidance for most questions of recognition, measurement, presentation and disclosure, supplemented by the sections of IAS 32 which have not been superseded.

Sources of IAS
IAS 32, 39

DEFINITIONS OF TERMS

Accounting loss. Loss that may have to be recognized due to credit and market risk as a direct result of the rights and obligations of a financial instrument.

Accounts receivable. Amounts due from customers for goods or services provided in the normal course of business operations.

Aging the accounts. Procedure for the computation of the adjustment for uncollectible accounts receivable based on the length of time the end-of-period outstanding accounts have been unpaid.

Amortized cost of financial asset or financial liability. The amount at which the asset or liability was measured at original recognition, minus principal repayments, plus or minus the cumulative amortization of any premium or discount, and minus any write-down for impairment or uncollectibility.

Assignment. Formal procedure for collateralization of borrowings through the use of accounts receivable. It normally does not involve debtor notification.

Available-for-sale financial assets. Those financial assets which are not held for trading or held to maturity, and are not loans and receivables originated by the entity.

Carrying amount (value). Amount at which marketable equity securities are being carried, net of allowances. This amount is fair value.

Cash. Coins and currency on hand and balances in checking accounts available for immediate withdrawal.

Cash equivalents. Short-term, highly liquid investments that are readily convertible to known amounts of cash. Examples include treasury bills, commercial paper, and money market funds.

Control. The power to obtain the future economic benefits that flow from an asset.

Cost (of a security). Original purchase price plus all costs incidental to the acquisition (e.g., brokerage fees and taxes) unless a new cost basis is assigned as a result of a decline in market value which is other than temporary.

Credit risk. Possibility that a loss may occur from the failure of another party to perform according to the terms of a contract.

Current assets. Assets that are reasonably expected to be realized in cash or sold or consumed within a year or within the normal operating cycle of the entity.

Derecognize. Remove a financial asset or liability, or a portion thereof, from the entity's balance sheet.

Derivative. A financial instrument (1) whose value changes in response to changes in a specified interest rate, security price, commodity price, foreign exchange rate, index of prices or rates, a credit rating or credit index, or similar variable (which is known as the underlying), (2) that requires no initial net investment or little initial net investment relative to other types of contracts that have a similar response to changes in market conditions, and (3) that is settled at a future date.

Effective interest method. The means of computing amortization using the effective interest rate of a financial asset or liability. The effective interest rate is the rate that exactly discounts the expected stream of future cash payments through maturity or the next market-based repricing date to the current net carrying amount of the asset or liability. The computation includes all fees and points paid or received between parties to the contract.

Equity instrument. Any contract that evidences a residual interest in the assets of an enterprise after deducting all its liabilities.

Factoring. Outright sale of accounts receivable to a third-party financing entity. The sale may be with or without recourse.

Fair value. Amount for which an asset could be exchanged, or a liability settled, between knowledgeable willing parties in an arm's-length transaction.

Financial asset. Any asset that is

1. Cash
2. A contractual right to receive cash or another financial asset from another enterprise
3. A contractual right to exchange financial instruments with another enterprise under conditions that are potentially favorable
4. An equity instrument of another enterprise

Financial asset or liability held for trading. One which is acquired or incurred principally for the purpose of generating a profit from short-term fluctuations in price or dealer's margin. Regardless of why acquired, a financial asset should be denoted as held-for-trading if there is a pattern of short-term profit-taking by the entity. Derivative financial assets and liabilities are always deemed held-for-trading unless designated and effective as hedging instruments.

Financial instrument. Any contract that gives rise to both a financial asset of one enterprise and a financial liability or equity instrument of another enterprise.

Financial instrument with off-balance-sheet risk. Financial instrument that has a risk of accounting loss if the risk to the entity may exceed the amount recognized as an asset, if any, or if the ultimate obligation may exceed the amount that is recognized as a liability in the statement of financial position.

Financial liability. Any liability that is a contractual obligation (1) to deliver cash or another financial asset to another enterprise, or (2) the obligation to exchange financial instruments with another enterprise under conditions that are potentially unfavorable.

Firm commitment. A binding agreement for the exchange of a specified quantity of resources at a specified price on a specified future date or dates.

Hedge effectiveness. The degree to which offsetting changes in fair values or cash flows attributable to the hedged risk are achieved by the hedging instrument.

Hedged item. An asset, liability, firm commitment, or forecasted future transaction that (1) exposes the entity to risk of changes in fair value or changes in future cash flows, and that (2) for hedge accounting purposes is designated as being hedged.

Hedging. Designating one or more hedging instruments such that the change in fair value is an offset, in whole or in part, to the change in the fair value or the cash flows of a hedged item.

Hedging instrument. For hedge accounting purposes, a designated derivative or (in limited instances) another financial asset or liability whose fair value or cash flows are expected to offset changes in the fair value or cash flows of a designated hedged item. Nonderivative financial assets or liabilities may be designated as hedging instruments for hedge accounting purposes only if they hedge the risk of changes in foreign currency exchange rates.

Held-to-maturity investments. Financial assets with fixed or determinable payments and fixed maturities, that entity has positive intent and ability to hold to maturity, except for loans and receivables originated by the entity.

Loans and receivables originated by the entity. Financial assets created by the enterprise by providing money, goods, or services directly to a debtor, other than those that are originated with the intent to be sold immediately or in the short term, which should instead be classified as held for trading. Loans and receivables originated by the entity are not included in the held-to-maturity category, but are classified separately.

Market risk. Possibility that future changes in market prices may make a financial instrument less valuable.

Market value. Amount obtainable from a sale, or payable on acquisition, of a financial instrument in an active market.

Marketable equity securities. Instruments representing actual ownership interest, or the rights to buy or sell such interests, which are actively traded or listed on a national securities exchange.

Monetary financial assets and financial liabilities. Financial assets and financial liabilities to be received or paid in fixed or determinable amounts of money.

Net realizable value. Amount of cash anticipated to be produced in the normal course of business from an asset, net of any direct costs of the conversion into cash.

Operating cycle. Average time between the acquisition of materials or services and the final cash realization from the sale of products or services.

Other than temporary decline. Downward movement in the value of a marketable equity security for which there are known causes. The decline indicates the remote likelihood of a price recovery.

Percentage-of-sales method. Procedure for computing the adjustment for uncollectible accounts receivable based on the historical relationship between bad debts and gross credit sales.

Pledging. Process of using an asset as collateral for borrowings. It generally refers to borrowings secured by accounts receivable.

Realized gain (loss). Difference between the cost or adjusted cost of a marketable security and the net selling price realized by the seller, which is to be included in the determination of net income in the period of the sale.

Recourse. Right of the transferee (factor) of accounts receivable to seek recovery for an uncollectible account from the transferor. It is often limited to specific conditions.

Repurchase agreement. An agreement to transfer a financial asset to another party in exchange for cash or other considerations, with a concurrent obligation to reacquire the asset at a future date for an amount equal to the cash or other consideration plus interest.

Risk of accounting loss. Includes (1) the possibility that a loss may occur from the failure of another party to perform according to the terms of a contract (credit risk), (2) the possibility that future changes in market prices may make a financial instrument less valuable (market risk), and (3) the risk of theft or physical loss.

Securitization. The process whereby financial assets are transformed into securities.

Short-term investments. Securities or other assets acquired with excess cash, having ready marketability and intended by management to be liquidated, if necessary, within the current operating cycle.

Temporary decline. Downward fluctuation in the value of a marketable equity security that has no known cause which suggests that the decline is of a permanent nature.

Tranasaction costs. Incremental costs directly attributable to the acquisition or disposal of a financial asset or liability.

CONCEPTS, RULES, AND EXAMPLES

Cash

The promulgated international accounting standards for cash are, at present, rather minimal. While the yet-to-be-developed standard on financial instruments recognition and measurement will doubtless address cash (which does meet the definition of a financial instrument according to IAS 32), at the present time the only real guidance is that offered in IAS 1 (revised 1997), *Presentation of Financial Statements*.

Common practice is to define cash as including cash on hand as well as current and other accounts maintained with banks. Cash which is not immediately available for use is normally given separate disclosure to avoid misleading the users of the financial statements. IAS 1, as revised, while stating that restricted cash is not to be included in current assets, does not require presentation of a classified balance sheet, nor does it mandate that restricted and unrestricted cash be shown in separate balance sheet captions in the absence of the current/noncurrent distinction. Thus, the question remains open as to whether mere footnote disclosure of restrictions would suffice under some circumstances.

IAS 1 (revised 1997) states that cash and cash equivalents which are not restricted as to use should always be included in current assets, if indeed the reporting enterprise chooses to present a classified balance sheet. Since this standard also states that unless this criterion is satisfied, all assets are to be included in the noncurrent category, presumably cash subject to any restrictions, even if these are set to expire within 1 year, would be excluded from current assets

Given the limited guidance offered by the standard, it is the authors' belief that to be included as cash in the balance sheet, funds must be represented by actual coins and currency on hand or demand deposits available without restriction. It must furthermore be management's intention that the cash be available for current purposes. For example, cash in a demand deposit account, which is being held for the retirement of long-term debts not maturing currently, should be excluded from current assets and shown as a noncurrent investment. This would apply only if management's intention was clear; it would not otherwise be necessary to segregate from the general cash account the funds that presumably will be needed for a scheduled debt retirement, as those funds could presumably be obtained from alternative sources, including new borrowings.

With the increased availability to, and popularity with, corporate investors of such short-term, safe earning assets as NOW accounts and money market funds, it has become more common to see the caption "cash and cash equivalents" in the balance sheet. This term includes other forms of near-cash as well as demand deposits and liquid, short-term securities. To justify inclusion, cash equivalents must be available upon demand.

IAS 7 defines these as short-term, highly liquid investments readily convertible into a known amount of cash which are subject to an insignificant risk of changes in value. The reasonable, if arbitrary, limit of 3 months is placed on the maturity dates of any instruments acquired to be part of cash equivalents. (This is, not coincidentally, the same limit applied by the US standard on cash flow statements, SFAS 95, the promulgation of which preceded the revision of IAS 7 by some years.)

Compensating balances are cash balances which are not immediately accessible by the owner. Pursuant to borrowing arrangements with lenders, an entity will often be required to maintain a minimum amount of cash on deposit (compensating balance). The purpose of this balance is to increase the yield on the loan to the lender. Since most organizations will need to maintain a certain working balance in their cash accounts simply to handle routine transactions and to cushion against unforeseen fluctuations in the demand for cash, borrowers will often not find compensating balance arrangements objectionable and may well have sufficient liquidity to maintain these with little hardship being incurred. They may even be viewed as comprising "rotating" normal cash balances which are flowing into and out of the bank on a regular basis. Notwithstanding how these are viewed by the debtor, however, the fact is that compensating balances are not available for unrestricted use, and penalties will result if they are used rather than being left intact, as called for. Therefore, the portion of an entity's cash account that is a compensating balance must be segregated and shown as a noncurrent asset if the related borrowings are noncurrent liabilities. If the borrowings are current liabilities, it is acceptable to show the compensating balance as a separately captioned current asset, but under no circumstances should these be included in the caption "cash."

In some jurisdictions, certain cash deposits, such as savings accounts or corporate time deposits, are held by banks subject to terms and conditions that give the banks the right, which is not always exercised, to delay honoring withdrawal requests for a stated period of time, such as 7 days or 30 days. The reason for such rules is to discourage panic withdrawals and to give the depository institution adequate time to liquidate investments in an orderly fashion. Cash in savings accounts subject to a statutory notification requirement and cash in certificates of deposit maturing during the current operating cycle or within 1 year may be included as current assets, but as with compensating balances, should be separately captioned in the balance sheet to avoid the misleading implication that these funds are available immediately upon demand. Typically, such items will be included in the short-term investments caption, but these could also be labeled as time deposits or restricted cash deposits.

Petty cash and other imprest cash accounts are usually presented in financial statements with other cash accounts. Due to materiality considerations, these need not be set forth in a separate caption, although that may be done if desired.

Receivables

Receivables include trade receivables, which are amounts due from customers for goods sold or services performed in the normal course of business, as well as such other categories of receivables as notes receivable, trade acceptances, third-party instruments, and amounts due from officers, stockholders, employees, or affiliated companies.

Notes receivable are formalized obligations evidenced by written promissory notes. The latter categories of receivables generally arise from cash advances but could develop from sales of merchandise or the provision of services. The basic nature of amounts due from trade customers is often different from that of balances receivable from related parties, such as employees or stockholders. Thus, the general practice is to insist that the various classes of receivables be identified separately either on the face of the balance sheet or in the notes. Former standard IAS 5 did require that trade receivables, amounts due from officers, amounts due from related parties, and other distinct categories of receivables be separately presented in the balance sheet, but superseding standard IAS 1 (revised 1997) fails to address this. However, the authors believe that distinguishing among categories of receivables is an important financial reporting objective, and that the formerly prescribed guidelines should continue to be observed.

International accounting standards do not address explicitly the recognition or measurement of receivables as a discrete topic, although presumably the forthcoming financial instruments' recognition and measurement standard will do so. However, a number of international standards do allude to the accounting for receivables. For example, IAS 18, *Revenue Recognition*, addresses the timing of revenue recognition, and hence also the matter of when the existence of receivables may be acknowledged. None of these address the key measurement issues.

For several reasons, receivables should be presented at net realizable amounts (i.e., amounts realistically anticipated to be collectible). First, the matching concept suggests that all costs of generating revenue be accrued and reported in the same period as the related revenue. By accruing an estimate of the amount of receivables due at the balance sheet date that are not likely to be collected, the matching objective will be largely achieved relative to the associated income statement. Second, the general concept of conservatism, which underlies much of financial reporting, demands that assets which are presented as representing claims to cash not be reported at amounts in excess of that which will ultimately be collected.

If the gross amount of receivables includes unearned interest or finance charges, these should be deducted in arriving at the net amount to be presented in the balance sheet. Deductions should be taken for amounts estimated to be uncollectible and also for the estimated returns, allowances, and other discounts to be taken by customers prior to or at the time of payment. In practice, the deductions that would be made for estimated returns, allowances, and trade discounts are usually deemed to be immaterial, and such adjustments are rarely made. However, if it is known that sales are often recorded for merchandise that is shipped on approval and available data suggests that a sizable proportion of such sales are returned by the customers, these estimated future returns must be accrued. Similarly, material amounts of anticipated discounts and allowances should be recorded in the period of sale.

The foregoing comments apply where revenues are recorded at the gross amount of the sale and subsequent sales discounts are recorded as debits (contra revenues). An alternative manner of recording revenue, which does away with any need to estimate future discounts, is to record the initial sale at the net amount; that is, at the amount that will be remitted if customers take advantage of the available discount terms. If customers pay the gross amount later (they fail to take the discounts), this additional revenue is recorded as income when it is remitted. The net method of recording sales, however, is rarely encountered in practice.

Bad Debts Expense

Whereas accrual of anticipated sales returns, allowances, and discounts is usually not required because of materiality, the recording of anticipated uncollectible amounts is almost always necessary. The direct write-off method, in which a receivable is charged off only when it is clear that it cannot be collected, is unsatisfactory since it results in a significant mismatching of revenues and expenses. Proper matching can be achieved only if bad debts expense is recorded in the same fiscal period as the revenues to which they are related. Since this expense is not known with certainty, an estimate must be made.

There are two popular estimation techniques. The percentage-of-sales method is principally oriented toward achieving the best possible matching of revenues and expenses. Aging the accounts is more oriented toward the presentation of the correct net realizable value of the trade receivables in the balance sheet. Both methods are acceptable and widely employed.

Percentage-of-sales method of estimating bad debts. Historical data are analyzed to ascertain the relationship between credit sales and bad debts. The derived percentage is then applied to the current period's sales revenues to arrive at the appropriate debit to bad debts expense for the year. The offsetting credit is made to allowance for uncollectibles. When specific customer accounts are subsequently identified as uncollectible, they are written off against this allowance.

Example of percentage-of-sales method

Total credit sales for year:	$7,500,000
Bad debt ratio from prior years or other data source:	1.75% of sales
Computed year-end adjustment for bad debts expense:	$ 131,250 ($7,500,000 x .0175)

The entry required is

Bad debts expense	131,250	
Allowance for uncollectibles		131,250

Note that the foregoing entry assumes that no bad debts expense has yet been recognized with respect to the year's credit sales. If some such expense has already been recognized, as a consequence of interim accruals, for example, the final adjusting entry would be suitably reduced.

Aging method of estimating bad debts. An analysis is prepared of the customer receivables at the balance sheet date. These accounts are categorized by the number of days or months they have remained outstanding. Based on the entity's past experience or on other available statistics, historical bad debts percentages are applied to each of these aggregate amounts, with larger percentages being applicable to the older accounts. The end result of this process is a computed total dollar amount that is the proper balance in the allowance for uncollectibles at the balance sheet date. As a result of the difference between the previous years' adjustments to the allowance for uncollectibles and the actual write-offs made to the account, there will usually be a balance in this account. Thus, the adjustment needed will be an amount other than that computed by the aging.

Example of the aging method

	Under 30 days	*Age of accounts* 30-90 days	Over 90 days	Total
Gross receivables	$1,100,000	$425,000	$360,000	
Bad debt percentage	0.5%	2.5%	15%	
Provision required	$5,500	$10,625	$54,000	$70,125

The credit balance required in the allowance account is $70,125. Assuming that a debit balance of $58,250 already exists in the allowance account (from charge-offs during the year), the necessary entry is

Bad debts expense	128,375	
Allowance for uncollectibles		128,375

Both of the estimation techniques should produce approximately the same result. This will be true especially over the course of a number of years. Nonetheless, it must be recognized that these adjustments are based on estimates and will never be totally accurate. When facts subsequently become available to indicate that the amount provided as an allowance for uncollectible accounts was incorrect, an adjustment classified as a change in estimate is made. According to IAS 8, adjustments of this nature are never considered fundamental errors subject to subsequent correction or restatement. Only if an actual clerical or mechanical error occurred in the recording of allowance for uncollectibles would correction as a fundamental error be warranted.

Pledging, Assigning, and Factoring Receivables

An organization can alter the timing of cash flows resulting from sales to its customers by using its accounts receivable as collateral for borrowings or by selling the receivables outright. A wide variety of arrangements can be structured by the borrower and lender, but the most common are pledging, assignment, and factoring. The IAS do not offer specific accounting guidance on these assorted types of arrangements, although the derecognition rules of newly promulgated IAS 39 can be said to generally apply to these as well as other financial instruments which are assets of the reporting entity.

Pledging of receivables. Pledging is an agreement whereby accounts receivable are used as collateral for loans. Generally, the lender has limited rights to inspect the borrower's records to achieve assurance that the receivables do exist. The customers whose accounts have been pledged are not aware of this event, and their payments are still remitted to the original obligee. The pledged accounts merely serve as security to the lender, giving comfort that sufficient assets exist that will generate cash flows adequate in amount and timing to repay the debt. However, the debt is paid by the borrower whether or not the pledged receivables are collected and whether or not the pattern of such collections matches the payments due on the debt.

The only accounting issue relating to pledging is that of adequate disclosure. The accounts receivable, which remain assets of the borrowing entity, continue to be shown as current assets in its financial statements but must be identified as having been pledged. This identification can be accomplished either parenthetically or by footnote disclosures. Similarly, the related debt should be identified as having been secured by the receivables.

Example of proper disclosure for pledged receivables

Current assets:
Accounts receivable, net of allowance for doubtful
  accounts of $600,000 ($3,500,000 of which has been
  pledged as collateral for bank loans) 	8,450,000

Current liabilities:
Bank loans payable (secured by pledged accounts
  receivable) 	2,700,000

A more common practice is to include the disclosure in the notes to the financial statements.

Assignment of receivables. The assignment of accounts receivable is a more formalized transfer of the asset to the lending institution. The lender will make an investigation of the specific receivables that are being proposed for assignment and will approve those that are deemed to be worthy as collateral. Customers are not usually aware that their accounts have been assigned and they continue to forward their payments to the original obligee. In some cases, the assignment agreement requires that collection proceeds be delivered to the lender immediately. The borrower is, however, the primary obligor and is required to make timely payment on the debt whether or not the receivables are collected as anticipated. The borrowing is with recourse, and the general credit of the borrower is pledged to the payment of the debt.

Since the lender knows that not all the receivables will be collected on a timely basis by the borrower, only a fraction of the face value of the receivables will be advanced as a loan to the borrower. Typically, this amount ranges from 70 to 90%, depending on the credit history and collection experience of the borrower.

Assigned accounts receivable remain the assets of the borrower and continue to be presented in its financial statements, with appropriate disclosure of the assignment similar to that illustrated for pledging. Prepaid finance charges would be debited to a prepaid expense account and amortized to expense over the period to which the charges apply.

Factoring of receivables. This category of financing is the most significant in terms of accounting implications. Factoring traditionally has involved the outright sale of receivables to a financing institution known as a factor. These arrangements involved (1) notification to the customer to forward future payments to the factor, and (2) the transfer of receivables without recourse. The factor assumes the risk of an inability to collect. Thus, once a factoring arrangement was completed, the entity had no further involvement with the accounts except for a return of merchandise.

The classical variety of factoring provides two financial services to the business: (1) it permits the entity to obtain cash earlier, and (2) the risk of bad debts is transferred to the factor. The factor is compensated for each of the services. Interest is charged based on the anticipated length of time between the date the factoring is consummated and the expected collection date of the receivables sold, and a fee is charged based on the factor's anticipated bad debt losses.

Some companies continue to factor receivables as a means of transferring the risk of bad debts but leave the cash on deposit with the factor until the weighted-average due date of the receivables, thereby avoiding interest charges. This arrangement is still referred to as factoring, since the customer receivables have been sold. However, the borrowing entity does not receive cash but instead has created a new receivable, usually captioned "due from factor." In contrast to the original customer receivables, this receivable is essentially riskless and will be presented in the balance sheet without a deduction for estimated uncollectibles.

Another variation is known as factoring with recourse. Some entities had such a poor history of uncollectible accounts that factors were willing to purchase their accounts only if a substantial fee were collected to compensate for the risk. When the company believed that the receivables were of better quality, a way to avoid excessive factoring fees was to sell these receivables with recourse. This variation of factoring was really an assignment of receivables with notification to the customers. Factoring does transfer title. Where there is a no recourse provision, the removal of these receivables from the borrower's balance sheet is clearly warranted.

Merchandise returns will normally be the responsibility of the original vendor, who must then make the appropriate settlement with the factor. To protect against the possibility of merchandise returns that diminish the total of receivables to be collected, very often a factoring arrangement will not advance the full amount of the factored receivables (less any interest and factoring fee deductions). Rather, the factor will retain a certain fraction of the total proceeds relating to the portion of sales that are anticipated to be returned by customers. This sum is known as the factor's **holdback**. When merchandise is returned to the borrower, an entry is made offsetting the receivable from the factor. At the end of the return privilege period, any remaining holdback will become due and payable to the borrower.

Examples of journal entries to be made by the borrower in a factoring situation

1. Thirsty Corp. on July 1, 2000, enters into an agreement with Rich Company to sell a group of its receivables without recourse. A total face value of $200,000 accounts receivable (against which a 5% allowance had been recorded) are involved. The factor will charge 20% interest computed on the (weighted) average time to maturity of the receivables of 36 days plus a 3% fee. A 5% holdback will also be retained.
2. Thirsty's customers return for credit $4,800 of merchandise.
3. The customer return privilege period expires and the remaining holdback is paid to the transferor.

The entries required are as follows:

1. Cash	180,055	
Allowance for bad debts (200,000 x .05)	10,000	
Interest expense (or prepaid) (200,000 x .20 x 36/365)	3,945	
Factoring fee (200,000 x .03)	6,000	
Factor's holdback receivable (200,000 x .05)	10,000	
Bad debts expense		10,000
Accounts receivable		200,000

(Alternatively, the interest and factor's fee can be combined into a $9,945 charge to loss on sale of receivables.)

2. Sales returns and allowances	4,800	
Factor's holdback receivable		4,800
3. Cash	5,200	
Factor's holdback receivable		5,200

Transfers of Receivables With Recourse

In recent years, a newer variant on factoring has become popular. This variation has been called factoring with recourse, the terms of which suggest somewhat of a compromise between true factoring and the assignment of receivables. Accounting practice has varied considerably because of the hybrid nature of these transactions, and a strong argument can be made, in fact, that factoring with recourse is nothing more than the assignment of receivables and that the proper accounting (as discussed above) is to present this as a secured borrowing, not as a sale of the receivables. Under the requirements of recently promulgated IAS 39, a financial asset (such as receivables) can be derecognized (i.e., treated as having been sold or transferred to another entity) only when the enterprise loses control of the contractual rights that comprise the asset. As discussed more fully later in this chapter, the fact that the transferee has been given a "put" option (the right to force the transferor to take back the transferred asset under defined conditions) does not negate the fact that the asset was transferred and that derecognition is warranted--it merely means that the transferor has assumed a liability, which is to be measured at fair value (if it can be assessed). Thus it would appear that "factoring with recourse" qualifies for derecognition by the transferor under the terms of IAS 39.

FINANCIAL INSTRUMENTS

Accounting for Financial Instruments: Evolution of the Current Standards

Financial instruments, as they have grown in complexity and variation, have provided accounting standard-setting bodies worldwide with some of their greatest challenges. While even nonderivative instruments have become bewilderingly convoluted, the most formidable hurdles have been the need to comprehend and set reporting and disclosure rules for derivatives. The fact that many derivative-based transactions do not involve initial cash outlays, or involve outlays which are trivial in comparison to the amounts which are placed at risk, has caused accountants to first question and ultimately largely abandon the venerable historical cost concept, which has been the basis for most transaction reporting.

Standard setters have long since dealt with such mundane instruments as corporate stocks and bonds, although even in this context the financial reporting standards (such as IAS 25) have exhibited evolutionary development and, until IAS 39, offered perhaps excessive flexibility, which has impeded comparability among different entities' financial statements.

The more intractible problems, however, have arisen as a result of the explosive expansion in the use of financial derivatives. While some accounting guidance has previously been available pertaining to the more prosaic of these derivatives, such as warrants and futures contracts, this has been minimal and has not been sufficiently robust to address recognition, measurement, and disclosure issues, matters involving such exotic, yet now commonplace, instruments as interest rate swaps, options, and complex hedges of interest rates or foreign currencies. Derivatives found commonly in today's business environment include option contracts, interest rate caps, interest rate floors, fixed-rate loan commitments, note issuance facilities, letters of credit, forward contracts, forward interest rate agreements, interest rate collars, futures, swaps, mortgage-backed securities, interest-only obligations, principal-only obligations, indexed debt, and other optional characteristics which are directly incorporated within receivables and payables such as convertible bond conversion or call terms (embedded derivatives).

The basic business purpose of derivative financial instruments is to manage some category of risk, such as stock price movements, interest rate variations, currency fluctuations and commodity price volatility. The parties involved tend to be brokerage firms, financial institutions, insurance companies, and large corporations, although any two or more entities of any size can hold or issue derivatives. The derivatives are contracts that are supposed to protect or hedge one or more of the parties from adverse movement in the underlying base. Previous accounting rules (both the various national standards and IAS) had not coped well with these innovative instruments, but with the recent promulgation of IAS 39 (and the similar US standard, SFAS 133), there are now clear-cut requirements which should prove to be universally suitable, whatever the future developments from the so-called "financial engineers."

Beginning in 1989, the IASC attempted to develop a comprehensive standard which would address recognition, derecognition, measurement, presentation and disclosure issues pertaining to financial instruments. One intention was to establish uniform standards which would be applicable to both financial assets and financial liabilities--a goal which has not to date been achieved. Two successive exposure drafts--E40, issued in 1991, and E48, issued in 1994--were widely debated and ultimately shown to be perhaps too ambitious, given the level of concern and opposition by certain constituent groups, and the limited progress made by other national standard-setting bodies in their similar efforts. Thus the IASC concluded, as did the US's FASB, that it would not be feasible to promulgate a single standard which would definitively resolve all the issues; nor could a new standard impose uniform requirements on both assets and liabilities, regardless of the logic of doing so.

Accordingly, the IASC's efforts were bifurcated, with IAS 32 (issued in 1995) setting presentation and disclosure requirements, while the more troublesome matters of recognition, derecognition and measurement were given further deliberation. The result of those extended efforts was the exposure draft E62, in mid-1998, followed by IAS 39, published late in 1998, which represents the final component of the IASC's "core set of standards" program. However, the necessary compromises made to meet the IOSCO-IASC deadline (which was somewhat delayed from the original March 1998 target, in fact) has necessitated labeling this standard as only an "interim" one. Further work has been promised, intended to yield, within another few years, a successor to this standard--this time a truly comprehensive one. The objective remains to ultimately have a universal standard which would govern accounting and reporting for all financial assets and liabilities, but this will remain a difficult goal to achieve.

While IAS 32 set requirements for the classification by issuers of financial instruments as either liabilities or equity, and for offsetting of financial assets and liabilities, as well as for the disclosure of related information in the financial statements, the recent IAS 39 has tackled the somewhat more substantive questions of recognition, derecognition, measurement, and hedge accounting. Fair value reporting has been embraced, with limited exceptions, for financial assets, while historical cost-based reporting has been largely preserved for financial liabilities. Special hedge accounting has been endorsed for those situations in which a strict set of criteria are met, with the objectives of achieving good "matching" and of ensuring that all derivative financial instruments receive formal financial statement recognition. Of course, had the IASC fully endorsed fair value accounting for all financial assets **and** liabilities, special hedge accounting rules would have been unnecessary. Thus, if the IASC is successful in completing the next phase of the financial instruments project, the final rules could well be significantly more straightforward than are those embodied in IAS 32 and 39, since the convoluted hedge accounting requirements would be rendered unnecessary.

In the remainder of this chapter, the general requirements of IAS 32 and IAS 39 will be set forth and illustrated. While the mandatory implementation deadline for IAS 39 is not until years beginning after 2000, early application is encouraged. IAS 39 supersedes the disclosure requirements of IAS 32, but until IAS 39 is adopted by reporting entities, the disclosures mandated by IAS 32 remain in effect. Accordingly, the disclosure requirements of both of these standards will be set forth in the following discussion.

Reporting and Disclosure of Financial Instruments Under IAS 32

While some were disappointed that the standard issued in 1995 failed to comprehensively address the range of issues posed by financial assets and liabilities, IAS 32 was an important achievement for several reasons. IAS 32 represented a commitment to a strict "substance over form" approach. The most signal accomplishment, however, was the requirement for separate presentation of disparate elements of compound financial instruments, an approach which had been discussed in detail by the FASB in the early 1990s but which had not been incorporated into the corresponding US standards at that time.

Under IAS 32, adopting the definitions first advanced by E40 and carried forward by E48, financial assets and liabilities are defined as follows:

1. **Financial asset**: Any asset that is

    a. Cash
    b. A contractual right to receive cash or another financial asset from another enterprise
    c. A contractual right to exchange financial instruments with another enterprise under conditions that are potentially favorable
    d. An equity instrument of another enterprise

2. **Financial liability**: Any liability that is a contractual obligation

    a. To deliver cash or another financial asset to another enterprise; or
    b. To exchange financial instruments with another enterprise under conditions that are potentially unfavorable.

According to the foregoing definition, financial instruments encompass a broad domain within the balance sheet. Included are both primary instruments, such as stocks and bonds, and derivative instruments, such as options, forwards, and swaps. Physical assets, such as inventories or plant assets, and such long-lived intangible assets as patents and goodwill, are excluded from the definition; although control of such assets may create opportunities to generate future cash inflows, it does not grant to the holder a present right to receive cash or other financial assets. Similarly, liabilities that are not contractual in nature, such as income taxes payable (which are statutory, but not contractual, obligations), are not financial instruments either.

Some contractual rights and obligations do not involve the transfer of financial assets. For example, a commitment to deliver commodities such as agricultural products or precious metals is not a financial instrument, although in practice these contracts are often used for hedging purposes by enterprises and are often settled in cash (technically, the contracts are closed out by entering into offsetting transactions before their mandatory settlement dates). The fact that the contracts call for delivery of physical product, unless canceled by a closing market transaction prior to the maturity date, prevents these from being included within the definition of financial instruments.

Presentation Issues Addressed by IAS 32

Distinguishing liabilities from equity. In practice, it is commonly observed that financial instruments of a given issuer may have attributes of both liabilities and equity. From a financial reporting perspective, the central issue is whether to account for these "compound" instruments in toto as **either** liabilities or equity, or to disaggregate them into both liabilities and equity instruments. While the notion of disaggregation has long been discussed (conceptually, of course, this issue should not have been difficult to resolve, since the time-honored accounting tradition of substance over form should have provided clear guidance on this matter) it had not been effectively dealt with prior to IAS 32. The reluctance to resolve this derived from a variety of causes, including the concern that a strict doctrine of substance over form could trigger serious legal complications.

One example of the foregoing problem pertains to mandatorily redeemable preferred stock, which has historically been considered part of an entity's equity base despite having important characteristics of debt. Requiring that such quasi-equity issuances be recategorized as debt might have resulted in many entities being deemed to be in violation of existing debt covenants and other contractual commitments. At a minimum, their balance sheets would imply a greater amount of leverage than previously, with possibly negative implications for lenders. Concerns such as this caused the FASB to demur from adopting a strict "substance over form" approach in its financial instruments standards, despite having stated in its 1991 discussion memorandum that all debt-like instruments should be classified as debt, not equity. The IASC, however, has resolutely dealt with this matter, to its great credit.

Under the provisions of IAS 32, the issuer of a financial instrument must classify it, or its component parts, if a compound instrument (defined and discussed below), in accordance with the substance of the respective contractual arrangement.

Thus it is quite clear that under international accounting standards, when the instrument gives rise to an obligation on the part of the issuer to deliver cash or another financial asset or to exchange financial instruments on potentially unfavorable terms, it is to be classified as a liability, not as equity. Mandatorily redeemable preferred stock and preferred stock issued with put options (options that can be exercised by the holder, potentially requiring the issuer to redeem the shares at agreed-upon prices) must, under this definition, be presented as liabilities.

The presentation of common stock subject to a buyout agreement with the entity's shareholders is less clear. Closely held enterprises frequently structure so-called **buy-sell agreements** with each shareholder, which require that upon the occurrence of defined events, such as a shareholder's retirement or death, the entity will be required to redeem the former shareholder's ownership interest at a defined or determinable price, such as fair or book value. The practical effect of buy-sell agreements is that all but the final shareholder will eventually become creditors; the last to retire or die will be, by default, the residual owner of the business, since the entity will be unable to redeem that holder's shares unless a new investor enters the picture. IAS 32 does not address this type of situation explicitly, although circumstances of this sort are clearly alluded to by the standard, which notes that "if a financial instrument labeled as a share gives the holder an option to require redemption upon the occurrence of a future event that is highly likely to occur, classification as a financial liability on initial recognition reflects the substance of the instrument." Notwithstanding this guidance, enterprises can be expected to be quite reluctant to reclassify the majority of stockholders' equity as debt in cases such as that described above.

IAS 32 goes beyond the formal terms of a financial instrument in seeking to determine whether it might be a liability. It also looks to the implied establishment of an obligation to redeem. For example, when preferred stock is issued that has a contractually increasing dividend requirement coupled with a call provision (giving the issuer the right, but not the obligation, to redeem the shares), the practical effect is that the issuer will be compelled, at some point, to call the shares for redemption. For this reason, the instrument is to be classified and accounted for as a liability upon its original issuance.

Classification of compound instruments. IAS 32 also addresses the difficult question of how compound instruments are to be categorized. Consistent with the substance over form stance taken regarding simple debt or equity instruments, the IASC has mandated that at inception compound instruments be analyzed into their constituent elements and accounted for accordingly.

Compound instruments may be comprised of one or more liabilities and/or equities, which need to be evaluated as separate instruments. Since IAS 32 does not address recognition or measurement matters, no single method of valuation is prescribed. However, the standard does suggest two possible approaches.

1. Assign to the least easily measured components the residual amounts, after assigning values to the more easily measured components of the compound instrument.
2. Measure the values of each component directly, and then, if necessary, adjust each on a pro rata basis if the total amounts exceed the proceeds from the issuance of the compound instrument.

Example of value allocation using the suggested value allocation approaches

To illustrate the allocation of proceeds in a compound instrument situation, assume these facts.

1. 5,000 convertible bonds are sold January 1, 2000, due December 31, 2003.
2. Issuance price is par ($1,000 per bond); total issuance proceeds are $5,000,000.
3. Interest is due in arrears, semiannually, at a nominal rate of 5%.
4. Each bond is convertible into 150 shares of common stock of the issuer.
5. At issuance date, similar, nonconvertible, debt must yield 8%.
6. At issuance date, common shares are trading at $5, and expected dividends over the next 4 years are $.20 per share per year.
7. The relevant risk-free rate on 4-year obligations is 4%.
8. The historical variability of the stock price is indicated by a standard deviation of annual returns of 25%.

Residual value method. The residual value of the equity component of the compound instrument is computed as follows:

1. Use the reference discount rate, 8%, to compute the market value of straight debt carrying a 5% yield:

PV of $5,000,000 due in 4 years	$3,653,451
PV of semiannual payments of $125,000 for 8 periods	841,593
Total	$4,495,044

2. Compute the amount allocable to the conversion feature

Total proceeds from issuance of compound instrument	$5,000,000
Value allocable to debt	4,495,044
Residual value allocable to equity component	$ 504,956

Alternative approach using options pricing model. This approach values the conversion feature directly, using the Black-Scholes option pricing model (or an equivalent technique).

1. Compute the standard deviation of proportionate changes in the fair value of the asset underlying the option multiplied by the square root of the time to expiration of the option

$$.25 \text{ x } \sqrt{4} = .25 \text{ x } 2 = .50$$

2. Compute the ratio of the fair value of the asset underlying the option to the present value of the option exercise price

    a. Since expected dividend per share is $.20 per year, the present value of this stream over 4 years would (at the risk-free rate) be $.726.

   b.   The shares are trading at $5.00.

   c.   Therefore, the value of the underlying optioned asset, stripped of the stream of dividends which a holder of an unexercised option would forfeit, is

$$\$5.00 - .726 = \$4.274 \text{ per share.}$$

   d.   The implicit exercise price is $\$1,000 \div 150$ shares $= \$6.667$ per share. This must be discounted at the risk-free rate, 5%, over 4 years, assuming that conversion takes place at the expiration of the conversion period, as follows:

$$\$6.667 \div 1.05^4 = 6.667 \div 1.2155 = \$5.485$$

   e.   Therefore, the ratio of the underlying asset, $4.274, to the exercise price, $5.485, is .7792.

3.   Reference must now be made to a call option valuation table to assign a fair value to these two computed amounts (the standard deviation of proportionate changes in the fair value of the asset underlying the option multiplied by the square root of the time to expiration of the option, .50, and the ratio of the fair value of the asset underlying the option to the present value of the option exercise price, .7792). For this example, assume that the table value is 13.44% (meaning that the fair value of the option is 13.44%) of the fair value of the underlying asset.

4.   The dollar valuation of the conversion option, then, is given as

$$.1344 \text{ x } \$4.274 \text{ per share x } 150 \text{ shares/bond x } 5,000 \text{ bonds} = \$430,819$$

5.   Since the fair value of the straight debt (computed above, $4,495,044) plus the fair value of the options ($430,819) does not equal the proceeds, $5,000,000, both amounts should be adjusted pro rata (resulting in recording the debt at $4,562,697 and the options at $437,303).

     Reporting interest, dividends, losses and gains. IAS 32 establishes that income earned while holding financial instruments, and gains or losses from disposing of financial instruments should be reported in the income statement. Dividends paid on equity instruments issued should be charged directly to equity. (These will be reported in the statement of changes in equity.) The balance sheet classification of the instrument drives the income statement classification of the related interest or dividends. For example, if mandatorily redeemable preferred shares have been categorized as debt on the issuer's balance sheet, dividend payments on those shares must be reported in the income statement in the same manner as interest expense. Gains or losses on redemptions or refinancings of financial instruments classed as liabilities would be reported similarly in the income statement, while gains or losses on equity are credited or charged to equity directly.

     Offsetting financial assets and liabilities. Under the provisions of IAS 32, offsetting financial assets and liabilities is permitted only when the enterprise **both** (1) has the legally enforceable right to set off the recognized amounts, and (2) intends to settle the asset and liability on a net basis, or to realize the asset and settle the liability simultaneously. Of great significance is the fact that offsetting does not give rise to gain or loss recognition, which distinguishes it from the derecognition of an instrument (which is not addressed by IAS 32, but is one of the subjects dealt with by IAS 39).

Simultaneous settlement of a financial asset and a financial liability can be presumed only under defined circumstances. The most typical of such cases is when both instruments will be settled through a clearinghouse functioning for an organized exchange. Other situations may superficially appear to warrant the same accounting treatment but in fact do not give rise to legitimate offsetting. For example, if the entity will exchange checks with a single counterparty for the settlement of both instruments, it becomes exposed to credit risk for a time, however brief, when it has paid the other party for the amount of the obligation owed to it but has yet to receive the counterparty's funds to settle the amount it is owed by the counterparty. Offsetting would not be warranted in such a context.

The standard sets forth a number of other circumstances in which offsetting would **not** be justified. These include

1. When several different instruments are used to synthesize the features of another type of instrument (which typically would involve a number of different counterparties, thus violating a basic principle of offsetting).
2. When financial assets and financial liabilities arise from instruments having the same primary risk exposure (such as when both are forward contracts) but with different counterparties.
3. When financial assets are pledged as collateral for nonrecourse financial liabilities (as the intention is not typically to effect offsetting, but rather, to settle the obligation and gain release of the collateral).
4. When financial assets are set aside in a trust for the purpose of discharging a financial obligation but the assets have not been formally accepted by the creditor (as when a sinking fund is established, or when in-substance defeasance of debt is arranged).
5. When obligations incurred as a consequence of events giving rise to losses are expected to be recovered from a third party by virtue of an insurance claim (again, different counterparties means that the entity is exposed to credit risk, however slight).

Even the existence of a master netting agreement does not automatically justify the offsetting of financial assets and financial liabilities. Only if both the stipulated conditions (both the right to offset and the intention to do so) are met can this accounting treatment be employed.

Disclosure Issues Addressed by IAS 32

IAS 39 has superseded the disclosure requirements set forth in IAS 32. However, since the mandatory effective date of IAS 39 is not until years beginning after calendar year 2000, the disclosure rules of IAS 32 are still pertinent for many preparers of financial statements. Accordingly, in the following paragraphs, these requirements will be set forth and discussed.

Primacy of risk considerations. The major objective of the disclosure requirements established by IAS 32 is to give financial statement users the ability to assess on- and off-balance-sheet risks, which prominently includes risks relating to future cash flows associated with the financial instruments. The standard presents the following typology of risk:

1. **Price risk**, which implies not merely the risk of loss but also the potential for gain, and which is in turn comprised of

   a. **Currency risk**--The risk that the value of an instrument will vary due to changes in currency exchange rates.
   b. **Interest-rate risk**--The risk that the value of the instrument will fluctuate due to changes in market interest rates.
   c. **Market risk**--A broader concept that subsumes interest rate risk, this is, the risk that prices will fluctuate due to factors specific to the financial instrument or due to factors that are generally affecting other securities trading in the same markets.

2. **Credit risk** is related to the failure of one party to perform as it is required to contractually.
3. **Liquidity risk** (also known as **funding risk**) is a function of the possible difficulty to be encountered in raising funds to meet commitments; it may result from an inability to sell a financial asset at its fair value.
4. **Cash flow risk** is the risk that the future cash flows associated with a monetary financial instrument will fluctuate in amount, as when a debt instrument carries a floating interest rate, potentially causing a change in cash flows while fair values will remain constant (absent a coincidentally occurring change in creditworthiness).

The standard does address the means by which interest rate and credit risk factors are to be addressed in the financial statements, while cash flow and liquidity risk are discussed in general terms only. These matters are elaborated upon in the following paragraphs.

Interest-rate risk in greater detail. Interest-rate risk is the risk associated with holding fixed-rate instruments in a changing interest-rate environment. As market rates rise, the price of fixed-interest-rate instruments will decline, and vice versa. This relationship holds in all cases, irrespective of other specific factors, such as changes in perceived creditworthiness of the borrower. However, with certain complex instruments such as mortgage-backed bonds (a popular form of derivative instrument), where the behavior of the underlying debtors can be expected to be altered by changes in the interest-rate environment (i.e., as market interest rates decline, prepayments by mortgagors increase in frequency, raising reinvestment rate risk to the bondholders and accordingly tempering the otherwise expected upward movement of the bond prices), the inverse relationship will become distorted.

IAS 32 requires that for each class of financial asset and financial liability, both those that are recognized (i.e., on-balance-sheet) and those that are not recognized (off-balance-sheet), the reporting entity should disclose information which will illuminate its exposure to interest-rate risk. This includes disclosure of contractual repricing dates or maturity dates, whichever are earlier, as well as effective interest rates, if applicable.

These data provide the user of the financial statements with an ability to predict cash flows, since fixed-rate instruments will generate cash inflows (if assets) or outflows (if liabilities) at a given rate until the maturity date or the earlier repricing date, although other features, such as optional call dates or serial retirements, can complicate this further. The combination of information on contractual (or coupon) rates, maturity dates, and changing market conditions (not provided by the financial statements, but presumably available to anyone with access to the financial press) also provides insight into the price risk of the underlying debt instruments, while for debt having floating rates of interest, knowledge of market conditions provides insight into cash flow risk.

The standard also suggests, but does not require, that when **expected** repricings are to occur at dates that differ significantly from contractual dates, such information be provided as well. An example is when the enterprise is an investor in fixed-rate mortgage loans and when prepayments can be reliably estimated; as the funds thereby generated will need to be reinvested at then-current market rates, altering the patterns and amounts of future cash flows from what a simple reading of the balance sheet might otherwise suggest. Information based on management expectations should be clearly distinguished from that which is based on contractual provisions.

IAS 32 suggests that a meaningful way to present this information is to group financial assets and financial liabilities into categories as follows:

1. Those debt instruments that have fixed rates and thus expose the reporting entity to interest-rate (price) risk
2. Those debt instruments that have floating rates and thus expose the entity to cash-flow risk
3. Those instruments, typically equity, which are not interest-rate sensitive

Effective interest rates, as used in this standard, means the internal rate of return, which is the discount rate that equates the present value of all future cash flows associated with the instrument with its current market price. Put another way, this is the measure of the time value of money as it relates to the financial instrument in question. Effective interest rates cannot be determined for derivative financial instruments such as swaps, forwards and options, although these are often affected by changes in interest rates, and the effective rate disclosures prescribed by

IAS 32 do not apply in such cases. In any event, the risk characteristics of such instruments must be discussed in the footnote disclosures.

The nature of the reporting enterprise's business and the extent to which it holds financial assets or is obligated by financial liabilities will affect the manner in which such disclosures are presented, and no single method of making such disclosures will be suitable for every entity. The standard suggests that in many cases a tabular disclosure of amounts of financial instruments exposed to interest-rate risk will be useful, with the instruments grouped according to repricing or maturity dates (e.g., within 1 year, from 1 to 5 years, and over 5 years from the balance sheet date). In other cases (for financial institutions, for example), finer distinctions of maturities might be warranted. Similar tabular presentations of data on floating-rate instruments (which create cash-flow risk rather than interest-rate [price] risk) should also be presented, when pertinent. When other risk factors are also present, such as credit risk (discussed in the following section), a series of tabular presentations, segregating instruments into risk classes and then categorizing each in terms of maturities, and so on may be necessary to convey the risk dimensions adequately to readers.

Sensitivity analysis has been alluded to in a number of accounting standards over the years. Since it has always been presented as an optional feature, it has rarely been employed in actual disclosures, despite having great potential for being useful to readers. In the context of financial instruments, sensitivity analysis would imply a discussion of the effect on portfolio value of a hypothetical change (say, a 1% change, plus or minus) in interest rates. There are at least two reasons why such information, unless accompanied by an adequate discussion of the particular characteristics of the financial instruments in question, might be misleading to financial statement readers.

First, because of the phenomenon known as convexity, the value change of each successive 1% interest change in rates is not a constant, but rather, a function of current market rates. For example, if the market rate at the balance sheet date is 8%, a move to 9% might cause a $20,000 decline in value in a given bond portfolio, but a further 1% change in the market rate, from 9% to 10%, would not have a further $20,000 effect. Instead, the effect would be an amount greater or lesser depending on the coupon (contractual) rate of interest of the underlying financial instruments. A reader, however, would rarely appreciate this fact and would probably extrapolate the sensitivity data in a linear manner, which could be materially misleading in the absence of further narrative information.

Second, sensitivity data most often are presented in a manner that suggests that they apply symmetrically. Thus, in the foregoing example, the presumption is that a 1% market rate decline would boost the portfolio value by $20,000 and that a 1% rate increase would depress it by a similar amount. However, some instruments, most notably those with embedded options (mortgage-backed bonds, having prepayment options, are the most common example cited, although exotic derivatives can be far more difficult to analyze) will not exhibit symmetrical price behavior, and the asymmetries will become exaggerated as hypothetical market rates stray further from the current rates. As a practical matter, the only way to convey these subtleties in a meaningful fashion would be to incorporate extensive tables of information into the footnotes, which many users would find to be impossibly confusing.

For these and possibly other reasons, although recommended by IAS 32, it is not anticipated that sensitivity data will be provided widely in the near term. If provided, however, any assumptions and the methodologies employed should be explained adequately, along with any needed caveats concerning the validity of extrapolation over greater ranges of market rate changes and over time.

Credit risk in greater detail. IAS 32 also demands that for each class of financial asset, both recognized (i.e., on-balance-sheet) and unrecognized (off-balance-sheet), information be provided as to exposure to credit risk. Specifically, the maximum amount of credit risk exposure as of the balance sheet date, without considering possible recoveries from any collateral that may have been provided, should be stated and any significant concentrations of credit risk should be discussed.

Credit risk is defined as the maximum amount of accounting loss that might be incurred by the reporting enterprise should the counterparty fail to perform. In many cases, this is simply the carrying value of such instruments; for example, accounts receivable net of any allowance for uncollectibles already provided would be the measure of credit risk associated with trade receivables. In other cases, the maximum loss would be an amount less than that which is revealed on the balance sheet, as when a legal right of offset exists but the financial asset was not presented on a net basis on the balance sheet because one of the required conditions set forth in IAS 32 (intention to settle on a net basis) was not met. In yet other circumstances, the maximum accounting loss that could be incurred would be greater, as when the asset is unrecognized in the balance sheet although otherwise disclosed in the footnotes as, for example, when the entity has guaranteed collection of receivables that have been sold to another party (often called factoring with recourse, discussed earlier).

There are a large number of potential combinations of factors that could affect maximum credit risk exposure, and in other than the most basic circumstances it is likely that extended narratives will be needed to convey the risks fully in the most meaningful way to users of the financial statements. For example, when an entity has financial assets owed from and financial liabilities owed to the same counterparty, with the right of offset but without having an intent to settle on a net basis, the maximum amount subject to credit risk may be lower than the carrying value of the asset. However, if past behavior suggests that the enterprise would probably respond to the debtor's difficulties by extending the maturity of the financial asset beyond the maturity of the related liability, it will voluntarily expose itself to greater risk since it will presumably settle its obligation and thus forfeit the opportunity to offset these related instruments.

When the maximum credit risk associated with a particular financial asset or group of assets is the same as the amount presented on the face of the balance sheet, it is not necessary to reiterate this fact in the footnotes. The presumption is that there will be disclosures made for all material items for which this fact does not hold, however.

In addition to disclosure of maximum credit risk, IAS 32 requires disclosure of concentrations of credit risk when these are not otherwise apparent from the financial statements. Common examples of this involve trade accounts receivable that are due from debtors within one geographic region or operating within one industry segment, as when a large fraction of receivables are due from, say, housing construction contractors in the Netherlands, many of whom might find themselves in financial difficulty if economic conditions deteriorated in that narrowly defined market. In addition to geographic locale and industry, other factors to consider would include the creditworthiness of the debtors (e.g., if the reporting entity targets a market such as college students not having steady employment, or third-world governments) and the nature of the activities undertaken by the counterparties. The disclosures should provide a clear indication of the characteristics shared by the debtors.

Examples of disclosures of credit risk

Note 5: Interest Rate Swap Agreements

The differential to be paid or received is accrued as interest rates change and is recognized over the life of the agreements.

Note 8: Foreign Exchange Contracts

The corporation enters into foreign exchange contracts as a hedge against accounts payable denominated in foreign currencies. Market value gains and losses are recognized, and the resulting credit or debit offsets foreign exchange losses or gains on those payables.

Note 13: Financial Instruments With Off-Balance-Sheet Risk

In the normal course of business, the corporation enters into or is a party to various financial instruments and contractual obligations that, under certain conditions, could give rise to or involve elements of market or credit risk in excess of that shown in the statement of financial condition. These financial instruments and contractual obligations include interest rate swaps, forward foreign exchange contracts, financial guarantees, and commitments to extend credit. The corporation monitors and limits its exposure to market risk through management policies designed to identify and reduce excess risk. The corporation limits its credit risk through monitoring of client credit exposure, reviews, and conservative estimates of allowances for bad debt and through the prudent use of collateral for large amounts of credit. The corporation monitors collateral values on a daily basis and requires additional collateral when deemed necessary.

Note 6: Interest Rate Swaps and Forward Exchange Contracts

The corporation enters into a variety of interest rate swaps and forward foreign exchange contracts. The primary use of these financial instruments is to reduce interest rate fluctuations and to stabilize costs or to hedge foreign currency liabilities or assets. Interest rate swap transactions involve the exchange of floating-rate and fixed-rate interest payment of obligations without the exchange of underlying notional amounts. The company is exposed to credit risk in the unlikely event of nonperformance by the counterparty. The differential to be received or paid is accrued as interest rates change and is recognized over the life of the agreement. Forward foreign exchange contracts represent commitments to exchange currencies at a specified future date. Gains (losses) on these contracts serve primarily to stabilize costs. Foreign currency exposure for the corporation will result in the unlikely event that the other party fails to perform under the contract.

Note 3: Financial Guarantees

Financial guarantees are conditional commitments to guarantee performance to third parties. These guarantees are primarily issued to guarantee borrowing arrangements. The corporation's credit risk exposure on these guarantees is not material.

Note 8: Commitment to Extend Credit

Loan commitments are agreements to extend credit under agreed-upon terms. The corporation's commitment to extend credit assists customers to meet their liquidity needs. These commitments generally have fixed expiration or other termination clauses. The corporation anticipates that not all of these commitments will be utilized. The amount of unused commitment does not necessarily represent future funding requirements.

Note 9: Summary of Off-Balance-Sheet Financial Instruments

The off-balance-sheet financial instruments are summarized as follows (in thousands):

Financial instruments whose notional or contract amounts exceed the amount of credit risk:

	Contract or Notional amount
Interest rate swap agreements	$8,765,400
Forward foreign exchange contracts	7,654,300

Financial instruments whose contract amount represents credit risk:

	Contract or Notional amount
Financial guarantees	$6,543,200
Commitments to extend credit	5,432,100

Concentration of credit risk for certain entities. For certain corporations, industry or regional concentrations of credit risk may be disclosed adequately by a description of the business. Some examples of such disclosure language are

1. Credit risk for these off-balance-sheet financial instruments is concentrated in Asia and in the trucking industry.
2. All financial instruments entered into by the corporation relate to Japanese Government, international, and domestic commercial airline customers.

Example of disclosure of concentration of credit risk

Note 5: Significant Group Concentrations of Credit Risk

The corporation grants credit to customers throughout Europe and the Middle East. As of December 31, 2000, the five areas where the corporation had the greatest amount of credit risk were as follows:

United Kingdom	$8,765,400
Germany	7,654,300
United Arab Emirates	6,543,200
Turkey	5,432,100
France	4,321,000

Disclosure of fair values. IAS 32 further requires that for each class of financial asset and financial liability, the reporting enterprise should disclose information about fair value. An escape valve is provided in the case when it is not deemed practicable within the constraints of timeliness or cost to determine fair value with sufficient reliability. However, when an entity avails itself of this option, it must disclose that fact, coupled with a summary of pertinent characteristics of the instrument, such that readers can make their own assessments of fair value should they so choose.

Stockholders and others have every reason to expect that management understands the values of the assets it acquires for the business or of the obligations it incurs. Therefore, a confession in the financial statements to the effect that fair values could not be determined, if made more than infrequently, would appear either disingenuous or an admission of managerial malfeasance. For this reason, a good-faith attempt to determine the fair value data requested by IAS 32, coupled with disclosures that set forth whatever caveats are deemed necessary to make the information not misleading, is probably the best course to follow.

Beyond the basic concern of computing fair values, there is the further issue of what this information is intended to imply. This question arises most commonly in the context of financial obligations, which represent contractual commitments to repay fixed sums at fixed points in time, which are not subject to adjustment for market-driven changes in value per se.

For example, assume that an entity owes a bank loan carrying fixed 9.5% interest, with the principal due as a $300,000 balloon payment 3 years hence. If current rates are 7%, the fair value of this obligation is something greater than its face value (in fact, the computed present value of future cash flows, discounted at 7%, is $342,060, which will be the surrogate for fair value), yet the contractual obligation is unchanged at the original $300,000. What, then, is the purpose of communicating to financial statement users that the fair value is the higher, $342,060, amount?

The explanation of this disclosure is that the economic burden being borne by the entity is heavier than would have been the case had a floating market rate of interest been attached to the debt. The spread between the disclosed fair value, $342,060, and the face amount of the debt, $300,000, is the present value of the additional interest to be paid in the future under the fixed-rate agreement over the amount that would be payable at the current market rate. Thus, fair value disclosure does not measure future cash flows, per se, but rather is an indication of economic burden or benefit in the assumed absence of any restructuring or other alteration of the debt.

Fair value is the exchange price in a current transaction (other than in a forced or liquidation sale) between willing parties. If a quoted market price is available, it should be used, after adjustment for transaction costs that would normally be incurred in a real transaction of this type. If there is more than one market price, the one used should be the one from the most active market. The possible effects on market price from the sale of large holdings and/or from thinly traded issues should generally be disregarded for purposes of this determination, since it would tend to introduce too much subjectivity into this measurement process.

If quoted market prices are unavailable, management's best estimate of fair value can be used. A number of standardized techniques, which attempt to tie the prices of various financial instruments to those having readily determinable fair values, are widely employed for this purpose. Some bases from which an estimate may be made include

1. Matrix pricing models
2. Option pricing models
3. Financial instruments with similar characteristics adjusted for risks involved
4. Financial instruments with similar valuation techniques (i.e. present value) adjusted for risks involved

IAS 32 notes that in some instances when the instruments are not traded in active markets (or perhaps when bid-ask prices are widely spread, as with thinly traded or unlisted securities), rather than presenting a single fair value estimate, which might convey a sense of precision that is not warranted under the circumstances, a range of fair values should be displayed. Actually, in a number of earlier proposals and discussions among academics, standards setters, users, and others, the idea of matrix reporting, showing alternative valuations relating to defined conditions, this approach has been proposed, but it has rarely been seen as an attractive option. The opposition generally derives from the fear that offering readers alternative valuations will serve to cause confusion. Furthermore, it could devalue the financial reporting process by alluding to an inability to ascertain a single correct answer. It is the authors' expectation that few preparers will avail themselves of this suggestion and more likely will present a single fair value amount to be associated with each class of financial asset and financial liability, with appropriate caveats expressed, as needed, in the accompanying narrative disclosures.

Example

Note X: Financial Instruments Disclosures of Fair Value

The estimates of fair value of financial instruments are summarized as follows (in thousands):

Instruments for which carrying amounts approximate fair values:

	Carrying amount
Cash	$987.6
Cash equivalents	876.5
Trade receivables	765.4
Trade payables	(654.3)

Fair values approximate carrying values because of the short time until realization or liquidation.

Instruments for which fair values exceed carrying amounts:

	Carrying amount	*Fair value*
Short-term securities	$876.5	$987.6
Long-term investments	765.4	876.5
Forward foreign exchange contracts	654.3	765.4

Estimated fair values are based on available quoted market prices, present value calculations, and option pricing models.

Instruments for which carrying amounts exceed fair values:

	Carrying amount	*Fair value*
Long-term debt	($543.2)	($432.1)

Estimated fair values are based on quoted market prices, present value calculations, and the prices of the same or similar instruments after considering risk, current interest rates, and remaining maturities.

Unrecognized financial instruments:

	Carrying amount	*Fair value*
Interest rate swap agreements		
Net receivable	$7,012.3	$7,865.4
Net payable	(1,753.1)	(1,543.2)
Commitments to extend credit	(5,432.1)	(4,321.0)
Financial guarantees	(6,543.2)	(7,654.3)

Estimated fair values after considering risk, current interest rates and remaining maturities were based on the following:

1. **Interest rate swaps**--Amounts to be received or paid to terminate swap agreements at reporting date.
2. **Credit commitments**--Value of the same or similar instruments after considering credit ratings of counterparties.

3.   **Financial guarantees**--Cost to settle or terminate obligations with counterparties at reporting date.

Fair value not estimated:

	Carrying amount	*Fair value*
Long-term investment	$1,234.5	--

Fair value could not be estimated without incurring excessive costs. Investment is carried at original cost and represents an 8% investment in the common stock of a privately held untraded company that supplies the corporation. Management considers the risk of loss to be negligible.

Financial assets carried at amounts in excess of fair value.   Prior to the implementation of IAS 39, there were certain circumstances in which an entity might have carried one or several financial assets at amounts that exceeded fair value, notwithstanding the general rule under accounting theory that such declines should be formally recognized in most instances. Normally, failure to recognize such declines would have been justified only when the decline is deemed to be temporary in nature.

IAS 32 requires that when one or more financial assets are reported at amounts that exceed fair value, disclosure should be made of both carrying amount and fair value, either individually or grouped in an appropriate manner, and the reasons for not reducing the carrying value to fair value should be set forth, including the nature of the evidence that provides the basis for management's belief that the carrying value will be recovered. The purpose is to alert the financial statement readers to the risk that carrying amounts might later be reduced if a change in circumstances causes management to reassess the likelihood of recovery.

For example, before IAS 39 is adopted, a fixed-rate loan held as an investment may be carried at amortized cost, which may exceed fair value due to a temporary increase in the market rates of interest. In the absence of any evidence of increased risk of default by the borrower, and assuming an intention to hold the loan to maturity, there would not be a need to write this investment down to fair value in such a circumstance, under the provisions of IAS 25 (see discussion in Chapter 10; note that these provisions of IAS 25 will be superseded by IAS 39). On the other hand, if the reporting entity intends to sell its investment prior to maturity, or if a value decline that is other than temporary is expected to occur as a corollary to the changes in market rates (e.g., the increased costs of its other borrowings place a strain on the borrower that is expected to affect credit risk as well), a write-down is necessitated under pertinent accounting standards.

(IAS 39 will supersede IAS 25 and there will no longer be the option to maintain investments at cost when this exceeds fair value, with the sole exception of those investments in debt instruments held to maturity. See the discussion of IAS 39 in the following section of this chapter for a complete explanation of these provisions.)

Hedges of anticipated transactions. As noted earlier, the entire subject of hedging accounting is controversial, complex, and prior to the issuance of IAS 39 was largely unresolved. Conceptually, the accounting for hedging positions should be coordinated with that for the underlying position being hedged, so that, for example, if gains or losses on the "cash" position are being deferred, so will be the (hopefully offsetting) losses or gains on the hedge position. A special difficulty arises in the case of anticipated transactions, however, because the reporting entity does not have a hedged position on its balance sheet. It is permitted, under current rules, to defer gain or loss recognition on hedging positions related to anticipated transactions under certain circumstances.

IAS 32 requires that if the entity hedges anticipated transactions (e.g., by entering into currency forward transactions to hedge movements in exchange rates that may occur while purchases or sales of goods that will be settled in foreign currencies are being processed), disclosure be made of the nature of the anticipated transactions, including the period of time that will elapse until actual occurrence; the nature of the hedging transactions and instruments used; and the amount of any deferred or unrecognized gain or loss and the expected timing of ultimate recognition as income or expense.

Other disclosure requirements under IAS 32. IAS 32 encourages financial statement preparers to make other disclosures as warranted to enhance the readers' understanding of the financial statements and hence, of the operations of the enterprise being reported on. It suggests that these further disclosures could include such matters as

1. The total amount of change in the fair value of financial assets and financial liabilities that has been recognized in income for the period
2. The total amount of deferred or unrecognized gain or loss on hedging instruments other than those relating to anticipated transactions (which is already a disclosure issue, as noted above)
3. The average aggregate carrying amount during the year being reported on of recognized financial assets and financial liabilities; the average aggregate principal, stated, notional, or similar amounts of unrecognized financial assets and financial liabilities; and the average aggregate fair value of all financial assets and financial liabilities, all of which information is particularly useful when the amounts on hand at the balance sheet dates are not representative of the levels of activity during the period

IAS 39: Financial Instruments--Recognition and Measurement

Evolution of the standard. Since the IASC's original efforts to develop a comprehensive standard on accounting and reporting for financial instruments failed to bear fruit and the program had to be bifurcated (with the first part resulting in the issuance of IAS 32 in 1995), substantial attention has been directed to the development of a standard on recognition and measurement. The two major challenges were (1) to decide whether to impose uniform measurement and reporting standards on financial assets and financial liabilities, and (2) to determine whether special hedge accounting would be necessary and acceptable. The IASC's experience was similar to that of national standard-setting bodies regarding both of these; strong opposition, coupled with some perceived practical difficulties, precluded the imposition of uniform asset and liability requirements, and special hedge accounting was therefore made a necessity.

To an extent, the IASC's failure to develop, at this time, a comprehensive and uniform set of standards for all financial assets and liabilities can be excused because it, unlike national standard setters, was faced with a deadline for completion of the so-called core set of standards by the terms of its agreement with IOSCO. While the ultimate outcome of IOSCO's consideration of an endorsement of IAS for cross-border registrations cannot be predicted, it was necessary for IASC to meet its part of the bargain regarding completion of the set of agreed-upon standards. Although IOSCO may be tempted to criticize IAS 39's failure to apply fair value accounting to all financial liabilities, IAS 39 goes as far as (and in certain areas even further than) any of the currently extant national standards with regard to this matter. Therefore, it would seem that IASC's claim to have completed the core set of standards would have to be accepted as an accurate assessment of its progress as of year end 1998.

The IASC has stated that it intends to continue work on the financial instruments project and will produce, perhaps as early as 2001, a comprehensive standard dealing with all financial assets and financial liabilities. A joint working party has been formed to cooperate with major national standard-setting bodies in achieving such a result.

The major changes wrought by IAS 39 are to greatly expand the use of fair values for measuring and reporting financial instruments (replacing most of the provisions of IAS 25, which permitted a wide range of measurement options for various categories of investments), and to address the important issue of financial derivatives, requiring that these be formally recognized and measured at fair value in most cases. IAS 39 is very similar to the recently imposed US standard, SFAS 133, although without the vast and detailed guidance offered by that standard, as is typical of US financial reporting rules.

Financial instrument recognition and measurement. With the recent issuance of IAS 39, *Financial Instruments: Recognition and Measurement*, the IASC has produced what it represents to be the final and, some would argue, most important element in the core set of standards project, making possible endorsement of the international standards for use in cross-border securities registrations. IAS 39 also completes the unfinished business of E48, which was only half-consummated when the IASC issued IAS 32, dealing with presentation and disclosure issues and leaving the more controversial and complicated topics unresolved. IAS 39 is not a perfect document, and was agreed to only after the IASC staff attempted the somewhat quixotic gambit of urging the committee to endorse (for interim purposes only, in order to complete the core set of standards project within the self-imposed time deadline) the full body of US GAAP on financial instruments. That ill-advised effort offended the political sensibilities of non-US standard setters and was quickly abandoned, leaving it to the IASC to produce IAS 39 late in 1998, a few months after the nominal deadline for the core set of standards had passed.

Both the US and international standard setters are clearly gravitating toward a pure fair value model for all financial instruments, perhaps with changes in value included in current period earnings in all cases. For a range of reasons, this solution has not been universally greeted with enthusiasm, and as a consequence both the US standard, SFAS 133, and the recently promulgated international standard, IAS 39, have endorsed mixed attribute models, although the IASC has candidly labeled its new standard an interim solution. Special accounting has been adopted for hedging situations, which among other things necessitates that hedging be defined and that measures be established to evaluate the effectiveness of those hedges, to determine whether the special accounting is warranted in any given circumstance. A pure fair value reporting model for financial assets and liabilities would have obviated the need for these specially designed treatments, of course.

As contemplated in E62, the new standard would possibly have departed from past IASC practice by being applicable only to enterprises which have equity or debt securities which are publicly traded and to enterprises that are in the process of issuing equity or debt securities in public securities markets. This was being considered in order to exempt, temporarily, smaller entities which might have had a more difficult time applying this standard. Upon deliberation, however, the IASC apparently decided to extend applicability of the standard, as finalized, to all reporting entities purporting to comply with the IAS, thereby avoiding entering into the "Big GAAP/Little GAAP" debate which various national standard setters have made previous unsuccessful attempts to navigate.

Applicability. IAS 39 is applicable to all financial instruments except interests in subsidiaries, associates and joint ventures that are accounted for in accordance with IAS 27, IAS 28, and IAS 31, respectively; rights and obligations under operating leases, to which IAS 17 applies; most rights and obligations under insurance contracts; employers' assets and liabilities under employee benefit plans and employee equity compensation plans, to which IAS 19 applies; and equity instruments issued by the reporting enterprise. It is also inapplicable (and unnececessary) in the case of entities operating in industries that have established an industry practice of measuring substantially all financial assets at fair value with adjustments to fair value recorded in net profit or loss, such as mutual funds, unit trusts, securities brokers and dealers, and insurance companies.

IAS 39 is not applicable to financial guarantee contracts, such as letters of credit, when these call for payments which would have to be made only if the primary debtor fails to perform. Accounting for these types of arrangements is specified by IAS 37. On the other hand, if the guarantor will have to make payments when a defined change in credit rating, commodity prices, interest rates, security price, foreign exchange rate, an index of rates or prices, or other underlying indicator occurs, then the provisions of IAS 39 do apply. Also, if a guarantee arises from an event leading to the derecognition of a financial instrument, the guarantee must be recognized as set forth in this standard.

IAS 39 does not apply to contingent consideration arrangements pursuant to a business combination. Also, the standard does not apply to contracts which require payments dependent upon climatic, geological, or other physical factors or events, although if other types of derivatives are embedded therein, IAS 39 would set the requirements for recognition, measurement, disclosure and derecognition.

IAS 39 must be applied to commodity-based contracts that give the enterprise the right to settle by cash or some other financial instrument, with the exception of commodity contracts that were entered into and continue to meet the enterprise's expected purchase, sale, or usage requirements and were designated for that purpose at their inception. With regard to embedded derivatives, if their economic characteristics and risks are not closely related to the economic characteristics and risks of the host contract, and if a separate instrument with the same terms as the embedded derivative would meet the definition of a derivative, they are to be separated from the host contract and accounted for as a derivative in accordance with the standard.

Recognition and derecognition criteria. Criteria for both recognition and derecognition are set forth in IAS 39, and these are consistent with existing and evolving practice under US and other national rules, as well as under international standards. An entity is now required to recognize a financial asset or financial liability on its balance sheet when it becomes a party to the contractual provisions of the instrument. The entity will derecognize a financial asset or a portion of a financial asset when it realizes the rights to benefits specified in the contract, the rights expire, or the enterprise surrenders or otherwise loses control of the contractual rights that comprise the financial asset (or a portion of the financial asset).

If an entity transfers a part of a financial asset to others while retaining a portion of the asset or assumes a related liability, the carrying amount of the financial asset should be allocated between the part retained and the part sold or amount of liability retained, based on their relative fair values on the date of sale. Gain or loss should be recognized based only on the proceeds for the portion sold. If the fair value of the part of the asset retained cannot be measured reliably, then a "cost recovery" approach should be used to measure profit (that is, allocate all the cost of the portion sold). If a related liability is retained and cannot be valued, no gain should be recognized on the transfer, and the liability should be measured at the difference between the proceeds and the carrying amount of the part of the financial asset that was sold, with a loss recognized equal to the difference between the proceeds and the sum of the amount recognized for the liability and the previous carrying amount of the financial asset transferred.

Examples of allocation between asset sold and asset or liability retained

Assume that an investment in mortgages, carried at a fair value of $14.5 million, is being sold, but the enterprise is retaining the "servicing rights" to these mortgages. Servicing rights entail making monthly collections of principal and interest and forwarding these to the holders of the mortgages; it also involves other activities such as taking legal action to compel payment by delinquent debtors, and so forth. For such efforts, the servicing party is compensated; in this example, the present value of future servicing income can be estimated at $1.2 million, while the mortgage portfolio, without servicing, is sold for $13.6 million. Since values of both components (the portion sold and the portion retained) can be reliably valued, gain or loss is determined by first allocating the carrying value pro rata to the two portions, as follows:

	Selling price or fair value	*Percentage of total*	*Allocated amount*
Mortgages without servicing rights	$ 13.6 M	91.89%	$ 13.32 M
Servicing rights	1.2	8.11	1.18
Total	$ 14.8 M	100.00%	$ 14.50 M

The sale of the portfolio, *sans* servicing rights, will result in a gain of $13.6 M - 13.32 M = $280,000. The servicing rights will be recorded as an asset in the amount $1.18 million.

Under other circumstances, transactions such as the foregoing will necessitate loss recognition. Assume the same facts as above, **except** that the selling price of the mortgage portfolio with servicing is only $13.1 million. In this case, the allocation of fair values and loss recognition will be as follows:

	Selling price or fair value	*Percentage of total*	*Allocated amount*
Mortgages without servicing rights	$ 13.1 M	91.61%	$ 13.28 M
Servicing rights	1.2	8.39	1.22
Total	$ 14.3 M	100.00%	$ 14.50 M

A loss on the sale of the mortgages amounting to $13.28 M - 13.1 M = $180,000 will be recognized. The servicing rights will be recorded as an asset in the amount $1.22 million.

Finally, consider a sale as above, but the obligation to continue servicing the portfolio, rather than representing an asset to the seller, is a liabilility, since the estimate of future costs to be incurred in carrying out these duties exceeds the future revenues to be derived therefrom. Assume this net **liability** has a present fair value of $1.1 million and that the selling price of the mortgages is $14.6 million. The allocation process and resulting gain or loss recognition is as follows:

	Selling price or fair value	*Percentage of total*	*Allocated amount*
Mortgages without servicing rights	$ 14.6 M	108.15%	$ 15.68 M
Servicing rights	(1.1)	(8.15)	(1.18)
Total	$ 14.8 M	100.00%	$ 14.50 M

A loss on the sale of the mortgages amounting to $15.68 M - 14.6 M = $1,080,000 will be recognized. The servicing rights will be recorded as a liability in the amount $1.1 million.

It should be added that, for the foregoing examples in which a net asset is retained, the servicing asset is deemed to be an intangible and accordingly will be accounted for under the provisions of IAS 38, *Intangible Assets*. Normally, this asset would be reported at amortized cost, unless an impairment occurs which would necessitate a downward adjustment in carrying value. The net servicing liability would be considered similar to other liabilities and accounted for at its amortized amount.

Transfers of financial liabilities, with part of the obligation retained or with a new obligation created pursuant to the transfer, should be accounted for in a manner analogous to the foregoing examples. Using fair values and transaction prices, the carrying amount of the obligation should be allocated so that gain or loss can be computed and the liability retained or created can be appropriately recorded.

According to IAS 39, in those circumstances in which the asset retained cannot be valued, it should be recorded at zero (i.e., no portion of the carrying amount of the asset sold should be allocated to the asset retained). When the retained asset is valued at zero, the gain to be recognized from the transaction will be less than would have otherwise been the case, and any loss recognized will be greater than otherwise would have been true. Thus, this is a conservative procedure to follow under these circumstances.

On the other hand, if a new financial liability is assumed but cannot be measured reliably, assigning a zero carrying amount would obviously not achieve the same conservative financial reporting objective that assigning zero value to a retained asset would. Therefore, in such a situation the initial carrying amount of the retained liability should be a large enough amount such that no gain is recognized on the transaction. Furthermore, if application of IAS 37, *Provisions, Contingent Liabilities, and Contingent Assets*, requires recognition of a larger provision, a loss should be recognized on the transaction.

IAS 39 holds that a financial liability (or a part of a financial liability) should be removed from the balance sheet only when it is extinguished, that is, when the obligation specified in the contract is discharged, canceled, or expires, or when the primary responsibility for the liability (or a part thereof) is transferred to another party. Among other implications, this means that in-substance defeasance (which involves segregation of assets to be used for the future retirement of specific obligations of the interprise) may no longer be given accounting recognition, since this does not entail actual discharge of the liability.

Initial recognition of financial assets at cost. Initial recognition of financial assets is to be at cost, which is assumed to be equal to fair value for assets acquired in arm's-length transactions. In E62, it had been proposed that transaction costs be included in the initial measurement of a held-to-maturity investment but be excluded from the initial measurement of financial assets and liabilities which are to be remeasured at fair value subsequent to acquisition. The logic was that, unless this were done, there would be an almost immediate need for a write-down in those assets' carrying values inasmuch as the addition of transaction costs would have caused the total amount recorded to exceed fair value.

After initial recognition, financial assets would be measured at fair value excluding transaction costs, except for the held-to-maturity investments and any financial asset whose fair value cannot be reliably measured. Held-to-maturity investments would be reported at amortized cost; other financial assets which have indeterminate fair values but fixed maturities would be measured at amortized cost using the effective interest rate method, while those that do not have fixed maturities would be measured at cost. The use of the held-to-maturity classification would be strictly limited to situations in which **both** intent plus ability to hold are present, and past behavior would be used to evaluate whether the expression of intent is sincere. A formerly held-to-maturity security reclassified to another category would be remeasured at fair value, with gain or loss recognition for any difference from amortized cost, either included in net income or in stockholders' equity, as discussed below.

As promulgated, however, IAS 39 does require that transaction costs be included in the recognized amount of all financial assets and liabilities. When subsequently remeasured at fair values, financial assets (if those values have not changed since acquisition) will have to be written down, effectively causing loss recognition for the transaction costs at that time. If the values have increased, however, some or all of this loss recognition will be averted. The standard notes that when applying the fair value measure, the transaction costs which would have to be incurred if there were to be a sale of the asset are not recognized (i.e., fair value is **not** net of selling costs), and that accordingly the fair value for reporting purposes is without the impact of transaction costs on either acquisition or assumed disposition.

Example

Consider the following example of the acquisition of a financial asset. Assume an investment security is acquired as follows: 2,000 shares of Ravinia Corp. common stock, par value $5 per share, are purchased on the open market on October 15 for $76 per share, plus total commissions and fees of $1,775. At December 31, the shares are quoted at 76^1/_2$, and a sale at that date would entail the payment of commissions and fees of $1,550. The investment is recorded on October 15 at a total of [($76 x 2,000 shares) + $1,775 =] $153,775. When the time comes to prepare the year-end balance sheet, this investment will be presented at 76^1/_2$ x 2,000 shares = $153,000, which will necessitate a write-down of $775. Thus, part but not all of the original commissions and fees will be reclassified to a loss account at that time. On the other hand, the potential cost of a sale, which would make the net realizable amount [$153,000 - 1,550 = $151,450] lower than fair value, as defined by IAS 39, is to be ignored in all such remeasurements.

In rare instances, when the value of consideration given or received cannot be observed directly or indirectly by means of other market values, then IAS 39 directs that value be ascribed by means of computing the present value of all future cash payments or receipts, using the prevailing market rate of similar types of instruments as the discount rate.

Trade date vs. settlement date accounting. Normal (regular way) purchases of securities may be accounted for either as of the trade date or as of the slightly later settlement date. (In most markets, settlement date will be 3 to 5 days after trade date for regular way transactions.) The reporting entity must adopt a consistently applied approach for each of the four categories of financial assets defined by IAS 39 (trading, available-for-sale, held-to-maturity, and loans and receivables originated by the entity and not held for trading purposes). Under trade date accounting, the transaction is recorded when it is executed, while settlement date accounting does not reflect the transaction until the date payment is due and delivery is promised. However, even when settlement date accounting is utilized, changes in the fair value of the underlying security during the interval from trade date to settlement date must be given accounting recognition, to the extent that changes in fair value would otherwise have been accounted for consistent with the nature of the investment. Thus, for held-to-maturity investments, fair value changes between trade and settlement dates are not reported, since these investments are accounted for at amortized historical cost, not at fair values (unless a permanent impairment occurs). In the case of trading securities, changes in fair value between the trade and settlement dates would be taken into income. For available-for-sale investments, the changes in fair value during the time interval from trade date to settlement date would be reported in stockholders' equity or in earnings, depending on which of these options had been elected by the enterprise (see discussion below).

The choice of trade date or settlement date accounting only applies to the purchase of investments. Sales of investments are to be accounted for on the settlement date in all instances.

Subsequent remeasurement issues. Under the previously applicable guidance, IAS 25, financial instruments qualifying as investments were to be presented on one of a wide variety of bases in subsequently prepared financial statements. The available options varied with the nature of the investments (e.g., stocks versus bonds), but included amortized cost, lower of cost or market, and fair value. IAS 39 supersedes IAS 25 (except for nonfinancial instrument investments, such as land) and establishes that subsequent remeasurement of financial assets at fair value excluding transaction costs is to be universally applied, except for loans and receivables originated by the entity and not held for trading purposes, held-to-maturity investments, and any financial asset whose fair value cannot be reliably measured. Held-to-maturity investments and loans and receivables originated by the entity are to be reported at amortized cost; other financial assets which have indeterminate fair values but fixed maturities will be measured at amortized cost using the effective interest rate method, while those that do not have fixed maturities are to be measured at cost; in all cases, periodic review for possible impairment is needed, and if impairment exists, a loss would have to be recognized. Derivative financial instruments which are assets must be valued at fair value.

Financial assets which are hedged must be accounted for at fair value, with the hedging instrument likewise accounted for at fair value, as discussed later in this chapter. Financial assets which have values less than zero are to be accounted for as financial liabilities--that is, at fair value if held for trading or if a derivative instrument, otherwise at amortized cost in most cases.

Changes in the value of held-to-maturity investments are generally not recognized. However, the use of the held-to-maturity classification is strictly limited to situations in which both intent and ability to hold are present, and past behavior is to be used to evaluate whether the expression of intent is indeed sincere. Intent to hold for an indefinite period would not be a basis for classification as held-to-maturity, nor would a willingness to dispose of the investment if certain changes in interest rates or market risks were to occur, or if improved yields on alternative investments or other factors were to develop.

If the issuer of the instrument which the enterprise holds as a financial asset has the right to settle it at an amount materially below amortized cost, the use of the held-to-maturity classification is not permitted, but a normal call feature will not preclude this. If the entity holding the investment has a put option (giving it the right to demand early redemption, but not the obligation to do so), classification as held-to-maturity remains possible, if the enterprise has the intent and ability to hold to maturity, coupled with a positive intent to not exercise the option.

As a practical matter, the held-to-maturity category will be reserved to debt securities held as investments, since equity securities have indefinite life (thus rendering untestable the holder's representation of its intent to hold to maturity) or else have indeterminable returns to the holder (as with warrants and options). Notwithstanding the nature of the investment, use of the held-to-maturity classification is prohibited if the reporting entity has, during the current reporting year or 2 prior years, sold, transferred, or exercised the put option on a significant amount of held-to-maturity investments before maturity. However, IAS 39 provides certain exceptions to the foregoing rule: sales close to maturity or an exercised call date such that market rate changes would not affect the asset's fair value; a sale after substantially all of the original principal had been recovered; and sales due to isolated events beyond the enterprise's control, which are nonrecurring and which could not have been reasonably anticipated by it (e.g., a significant decline in the issuer's creditworthiness, changes in tax laws, or other changes in the legal or regulatory environment. To the extent that any of these conditions exist, sales from the held-to-maturity portfolio will not taint the remaining assets.

Reclassifications from and to held-to-maturity. Under the provisions of IAS 39, the determination that there is both intent and ability to hold financial assets to maturity must be made not merely at acquisition, but also at each subsequent balance sheet date. If at one of these later determination dates it is concluded that the criteria are no longer met, then the investment should be remeasured at fair value at that time. In general, the investment would be reclassified to the available-for-sale category under such circumstances, and accordingly the adjustment to fair value would be recognized in stockholders' equity directly or else in earnings, depending on which method was elected by the reporting enterprise (see discussion below regarding this one-time election). It is also possible, if not likely, that formerly held-to-maturity securities would be reclassified to the "trading" category, in which case the adjustment to fair value would be taken to current earnings.

It is far less conceivable that securities could be reclassified to the held-to-maturity category after being first held in another portfolio. However, IAS 39 notes that a change in intent may occur under some circumstances. Furthermore, securities acquired for the held-to-maturity portfolio may have been recently valued at fair value because the entity violated the conditions with regard to other held-to-maturity investments (i.e., selling before maturity, etc., without having any of the exception conditions satisfied). When the 2 year period during which fair value accounting was mandatorily applied expires, the enterprise would be free to resume amortized cost accounting with regard to the other, remaining held-to-maturity securities. In such instances, the then-current fair value would become the new amortized cost basis. Any earlier gain or loss from fair value adjustments, if recognized in stockholders' equity, would be amortized over the remaining term to maturity, in the manner of premium and discount. In the very rare case when the investment in question does not have a fixed maturity date, the earlier gain or loss held in equity will be maintained there until the asset is ultimately disposed of.

Remeasurement of trading and available-for-sale financial assets. Changes in the value of trading securities are reported currently in earnings. IAS 39 defines derivative financial instruments as being, ipso facto, trading securities, unless held for designated hedging purposes. Regarding other investments which are neither held-to-maturity nor trading (i.e., which are available for sale), IAS 39 offers reporting entities a choice of reporting methods, election of which is limited to initial application of the standard. An entity may elect to report these gains and losses either in income, or directly in stockholders' equity--being reported in the statement of changes in equity as set forth in IAS 1 (and discussed in Chapter 3 of this book).

This position is in contrast, for example, with the requirement under the corresponding US standard (SFAS 133), which does **not** provide the option of reporting gains or losses from fair value changes on available-for-sale securities in current earnings. It is likely that a preponderance of entities reporting under IAS 39 will similarly choose to avoid impacting the current year's operating results and will instead logically conclude that since over time many of these market-based value fluctuations will reverse and offset, recordation within equity would be preferable.

As noted, the selection of the method to be used to account for changes in the fair value of available-for-sale investments is to be made when IAS 39 is first applied. A subsequent change in method would have to be justified under the provisions of IAS 8; the IASC has stated that it is deemed to be highly unlikely that a change from current earnings recognition to accumulation directly in equity could be supported.

Notwithstanding the option to accumulate the effects of changes in the fair values of available for sale financial assets in equity, IAS 39 does mandate that permanent impairments in value have to be recognized in earnings. This is described below.

Impairments of Investments Held for Trading or Available for Sale

An impairment in value of equity securities classified as available-for-sale must be reflected in earnings. By impairment, the implication is that there has been an other than temporary, or permanent, decline in the value of the investment, from which a recovery is expected to be extremely unlikely to occur. Specifically, this is meant to be the result of other than the normal fluctuations in value characteristic of all investments, due to general movements in the underlying markets, etc. In the absence of an ability to demonstrate that a decline is temporary, the conclusion must be that the loss in value is other than temporary, in which case it must be recognized in income. Declines are measured at the individual security level and thus, losses in one security's value cannot be offset by gains in another's value.

While temporary declines in value of available-for-sale investments are reported either in earnings or directly in stockholders' equity (as discussed later in this chapter, this is an election to be made by the reporting entity upon adoption of IAS 39), impairments **must** be included in earnings. Once an impairment is recognized, the reduced carrying amount becomes the new cost basis from which other increases or decreases in value are measured. In general, later increases or decreases in value which are temporary are recognized either in the statement of changes in equity and then included in stockholders' equity, or in earnings, again depending upon which of the methodologies had been elected by the reporting entity; further impairments in value are recognized in earnings. However, recoveries in the value of available-for-sale securities which have previously suffered a decline which was judged to be an impairment (if the recovery can be objectively attributed to events occurring after the impairment recognition) should always be reported in earnings.

Transfers Between Available-for-Sale and Trading Investments

Under IAS 39, transfers among portfolios are accounted for at fair value as of the date of the transfer. For investments in the trading category being transferred to available-for-sale, there will generally not be an issue of further recognition of gain or loss at this point, as the investments have been marked to fair value already. The only exception to this general case is that, if the investment accounts have not been updated for fair value changes since the latest balance sheet date, any changes since that time will need to be recognized at the date the transfer occurs. The fair value at the date of transfer becomes the new cost of the equity security to the available-for-sale portfolio.

Accounting for Investments in Debt Securities

Under IAS 25 (which is in effect until the reporting entity adopts IAS 39) the accounting for debt securities held as investments was driven by its classification as a current or a noncurrent asset; within each of these categories, diverse accounting methods were acceptable. Thus, for noncurrent investments, either the amortized historical cost method or revaluation was allowed.

Under IAS 39, however, no optional methods are offered, and fair value is required for debt securities held for trading or available for sale, while amortized cost is prescribed for those in the held-to-maturity portfolio, as that is narrowly defined by the standard. The held-to-maturity category is the most restrictive of the three; debt instruments can be so classified only if the reporting entity has the positive intent and the ability to hold the securities for that length of time. A mere intent to hold an investment for an indefinite period is not adequate to permit such a classification. On the other hand, a variety of isolated causes may necessitate transferring an investment in a debt security from the held-for-investment category without calling into question the investor's general intention to hold other similarly classified investments to maturity. Among these are declines in the creditworthiness of a particular investment's issuer or a change in tax law or regulatory rules. On the other hand, sales of investments which were classified as held-to-maturity for other reasons will call into question the entity's assertions, both in the past and in the future, about its intentions regarding these and other similarly categorized securities. For this reason, transfers from or sales of held-to-maturity securities will be very rare, indeed.

If it cannot be established that a particular debt security held as an investment will be held for trading or held to maturity, it must be classed as available-for-sale. Whatever the original classification of the investment, however, transfers among the three portfolios will be made as intentions change.

Accounting for debt securities which are held for trading and those which are available for sale is based on fair value. For balance sheet purposes, increases or decreases in value are reflected by adjustments to the asset account; such adjustments are to be determined on an individual security basis. Changes in the values of debt securities in the trading portfolio are recognized in earnings immediately, while changes in the values of debt securities in the available-for-sale category are reported either in earnings or in stockholders' equity, based on an election made when IAS 39 is first adopted.

Transfers of Debt Securities Among Portfolios

IAS 39 says very little regarding the reclassifications of investments. Nonetheless, from the basic principles espoused by the standard, it is clear that transfers of any given security between classifications should be accounted for at fair market value. IAS 39 states that transfers from the trading category should not take place, because classification as a trading security is based on the original intent in acquiring it. The standard also says that transfers to the trading category would be unusual, but not prohibited per se. In the case of a transfer to the trading portfolio, any previously unrecognized unrealized gain or loss is recognized immediately (that is, if from the available-for-sale portfolio and the fair value adjustments were being made to equity, not to earnings, and also if the transfer is from the held-to-maturity category).

If a debt security is being transferred from held-to-maturity to the available-for-sale portfolio, and if fair value adjustments to items in the available-for-sale portfolio are being accounted for as changes in stockholders' equity without being reported in earnings, then the unrealized gain or loss, not previously reflected in the investment account, must be added to the appropriate equity account at the date of transfer and reported in the statement of changes in equity at that time. On the other hand, if fair value adjustments are reported in earnings, then transfers from the held-to-maturity portfolio to the available-for-sale portfolio will trigger income or loss recognition in most cases.

If a security is being transferred from available-for-sale to held-to-maturity, there will similarly be alternative accounting ramifications depending on how the fair value adjustments had been dealt with when the security was considered to be available-for-sale. If those adjustments were taken to income, as permitted by IAS 39, then no further adjustment is necessary (assuming the records are up-to-date as of the date of the transfer). However, if the fair value adjustments were made directly to equity, then logic suggests that the unrealized holding gain or loss previously accumulated in equity should be maintained in the equity account, and should prospectively be amortized to income over the remaining term to maturity as an adjustment of yield, using the effective interest method.

Impairments in value of held-to-maturity investments. IAS 39 establishes a need for earnings recognition when impairments in value occur which affect investments included in the held-to-maturity portfolio. Evaluation of whether there is objective evidence of impairment is to be made at each balance sheet date; if this exists, the recoverable amount of the financial asset should be ascertained. Evidence of impairment could be provided by information about the financial difficulties of the issuer, an actual breach or default by the obligor, a debt restructuring by the issuer, a delisting of the issuer's securities or a high probability that this will occur in the near term, and similar developments. On the other hand, IAS 39 cautions that a change in status to not being publicly traded does not constitute evidence of a security's impairment, nor does a downward credit rating revision, taken alone, although in combination with other factors these could have significance.

For held-to-maturity securities, the standard provides that when it becomes probable that the holder will not be able to collect all amounts which are due contractually (including both interest and principal), an impairment loss is to be recognized. Similarly, when loans or receivables originated by the entity and not held for trading have such an impairment, a bad debt loss is to be recognized currently. In determining the amount of such loss, the carrying amount (typically, amortized cost) is compared to its recoverable amount, defined as the present value of projected future cash flows, discounted using the instrument's original effective interest rate (**not** the current market interest rate). A write-down to this recoverable amount is indicated when impairment has been found to have occurred. Use of the current market rate of interest is prohibited because to use this rate would be to indirectly impose a fair value measure, which of course is contrary to the concept of accounting for held-to-maturity financial assets, and loans and receivables originated by the entity, at amortized historical cost.

When in a later period there is a reversal of the impairment recognized earlier with regard to held-to-maturity financial assets or loans and receivables originated by the entity, this recovery should be appropriately reported in earnings. However, the reversal cannot result in carrying the asset at an amount in excess of that which it would have been reported at on that date, considering intervening periods' amortization if pertinent.

When the carrying value of a held-to-maturity financial asset is reduced due to findings of impairment, future interest income must be computed on the basis used to reduce the asset to its recoverable amount. That is, the **effective** rate of the original investment (including the impact of any premium or discount amortization) will be used, not its contractual rate.

Having once been reduced in carrying value due to a finding of impairment, there often will be a heightened need to monitor further impairments in later periods. If such evidence is objectively determinable, yet another computation of recoverable amount (and possibly a further adjustment to the financial asset's carrying amount) will be required.

In the case of available-for-sale securities for which adjustments due to changes in fair value have been accumulated in stockholders' equity (for enterprises which had elected that optional reporting methodology), the discovery that there has been a permanent impairment in value will also necessitate accounting recognition. The appropriate amount of the accumulated fair value adjustment must be removed from equity and reported in earnings at the time a permanent impairment is determined to exist. The difference between acquisition cost and either current fair value (for equity-type instruments) or recoverable amount (for debt instruments) is the usual measure of impairment.

Recoverable amount, as used in the context of available-for-sale financial assets, differs from the identically named concept applied to held-to-maturity assets. In the latter case, as noted above, projected future cash flows are to be discounted at the instrument's original effective rate, to avoid confounding the impairment measure by reference to current fair values, which would be inappropriate if applied to this class of investment. In the setting of available-for-sale instruments, however, fair value is both quite appropriate and required. Thus, if debt instruments are in the available-for-sale category and are being evaluated for impairment, future cash flows must be discounted at the **current** market rate of interest applicable to such instruments.

Remeasurement of financial liabilities. The remeasurement of financial liabilities is discussed and illustrated in Chapter 12.

As under the similar US standard, IAS 39 provides for special hedge accounting under defined circumstances. The standard defines three types of hedging relationships: fair value hedges, cash flow hedges, and hedges of net investment in a foreign entity. These are described in IAS 39 as follows:

- **Fair value hedges.** A hedge, using a derivative or other financial instrument, of the exposure to changes in the fair value of a recognized asset or liability, or an identified portion of such an asset or liability, that is attributable to a particular risk and will affect reported net income.
- **Cash flow hedges.** A hedge, using a derivative or other financial instrument, of the exposure to variability in cash flows that is attributable to a particular risk associated with a recognized asset or liability (such as all or a portion of future interest payments on variable rate debt) or forecasted transaction (such as an anticipated purchase or sale) that will affect reported income or loss. A hedge of an unrecognized firm commitment to buy an asset at a fixed price is treated as a cash flow hedge, although actually a fair value hedge.
- **Hedges of a net investment in a foreign entity** (as defined in IAS 21, *The Effects of Changes in Foreign Exchange Rates*) using a derivative or other financial instrument.

The most contentious issue regarding hedging has been the decision to apply special hedge accounting to such transactions. Obviously, if all financial instruments were marked to market (fair) values, there would be no need for special accounting. However, given that fair value accounting has yet to be fully accepted for financial instruments held as assets, and is even less widely accepted for financial instruments classed as liabilities, the topic of hedge accounting must be addressed. Under the provisions of IAS 39, a hedging relationship will qualify for special hedge accounting presentation if all of the following conditions are met:

1. At the inception of the hedge there is formal documentation of the hedging relationship and the enterprise's risk management objective and strategy for undertaking the hedge. That documentation should include identification of the hedging instrument, the related hedged item or transaction, the nature of the risk being hedged, and how the enterprise will assess the hedging instrument's effectiveness if offsetting the exposure to changes in the hedged item's fair value or the hedged transaction's cash flows that is attributable to the hedged risk.
2. The hedge is expected to be highly effective in achieving offsetting changes in fair value or cash flows attributable to the hedged risk, consistent with

the originally documented risk management strategy for that particular hedging relationship.

3. For cash flow hedges, a forecasted transaction that is the subject of the hedge must be probable and present an exposure to price risk that could produce variation in cash flows that will affect reported income.

4. The effectiveness of the hedge can be reliably measured, that is, the fair value or cash flows of the hedged item and the fair value of the hedging instrument can be reliably measured.

5. The hedge was assessed and determined actually to have been effective throughout the financial reporting period.

Under IAS 39, a hedging relationship could be designated for a hedging instrument taken as a whole, or for a component of a hedging instrument, provided that the fair value of each component can be measured reliably over its life. Thus, an enterprise could designate the change in the intrinsic value of an option as the hedge, while the remaining component of the option (its time value) is excluded.

As noted, to qualify for hedge accounting, the effectiveness of a hedge would have to be subject to effectiveness testing. The method an enterprise adopts for this would depend on its risk management strategy, and this could vary for different types of hedges. If the principal terms of the hedging instrument and of the entire hedged asset or liability or hedged forecasted transaction are the same, the changes in fair value and cash flows attributable to the risk being hedged offset fully, both when the hedge is entered into and thereafter until completion. An interest rate swap is likely to be an effective hedge if the notional and principal amounts, term, repricing dates, dates of interest or principal receipts and payments, and basis for measuring interest rates are the same for the hedging instrument and the hedged item.

Also, to qualify for special hedge accounting under IAS 39's provisions, the hedge would have to relate to a specific identified and designated risk, and not merely to overall enterprise business risks, and must ultimately affect the enterprise's net profit or loss, not just its equity.

The standard provides that a hedge can be judged to be highly effective if, both at inception and throughout its life, the reporting entity can expect that changes in the fair value or cash flows (depending on the type of hedge) of the hedged item will be virtually fully offset by changes in the fair value or cash flows of the underlying or hedged item, and that actual results are within a range of 80% to 125% of full offset. While there is flexibility in terms of how an entity measures and monitors effectiveness (and this may even vary within an entity regarding different types of hedges) the fact that IAS 39 provides quantified upper and lower effectiveness thresholds underlines the importance of making such a determination. The documentation of the enterprise's hedging strategy must stipulate how this will be achieved, and hedging effectiveness must be assessed at least as often as financial reports are prepared.

With specific regard to fair value hedges, IAS 39 prescribes the following special hedge accounting:

1. The gain or loss from remeasuring the hedging instrument at fair value is to be recognized currently in net profit or loss; and,
2. The gain or loss on the hedged item attributable to the hedged risk should adjust the carrying amount of the hedged item and be recognized currently in net profit or loss.

These requirements apply even if a hedged item is otherwise measured at fair value with changes in fair value recognized directly in equity (i.e., financial instruments not held for trading purposes, for which recordation in equity had been elected by the reporting entity). Hedge accounting must be discontinued, however, when the hedging instrument expires or is sold, terminated, or exercised, or when the hedge no longer meets the criteria for qualification for hedge accounting.

When there has been an adjustment made to the carrying amount of a hedged, interest-bearing instrument, it should be amortized to earnings, beginning no later than when it ceases to be adjusted for changes in fair value attributable to the risk being hedged.

Cash flow hedges. Gain or loss relating to the portion of a cash flow hedge which is determined to be effective is to be recognized directly in stockholders' equity, through the statement of changes in equity. The ineffective portion, if any, must be recognized currently in earnings if the hedging instrument is a derivative or if it pertains to a trading instrument. If it relates to an available-for-sale instrument and in the (highly unusual) event the hedging instrument is not a derivative, then the ineffective portion may be either included in income or in equity, depending on which method the entity has elected for reporting fair value changes for such instruments.

Per IAS 39, the separate component of equity associated with the hedged item is to be adjusted to the lesser of two amounts: (1) the cumulative gain or loss on the hedging instrument needed to offset the cumulative change in expected future cash flows on the hedged item from inception of the hedge, less the portion associated with the ineffective component, or (2) the fair value of the cumulative change in expected future cash flows on the hedged item from inception of the hedge. Any remaining gain or loss (the ineffective portion) is either taken to earnings or equity as described above.

If the hedge relates to a firm commitment or forecasted transaction, and this in turn results in the recognition of an asset or liability, then when the asset or liability is first recognized the related gains or losses previously taken directly to equity should be removed from equity and added to or deducted from the basis of the asset or liability. When the asset or liability later affects earnings (e.g., when the asset is amortized or depreciated), the gain or loss will likewise impact operating results. However, the standard on impairment (and other IAS) are fully applicable, so that, for example, if deferred hedging losses are added to the cost of an asset, and it later fails an impairment test, some or all of that deferred loss will have to be immediately recognized.

In the case of other cash flow hedges (i.e., those not resulting in recognition of assets or liabilities), amounts reflected in equity will be recognized in earnings in the period or periods when the hedged firm commitment or forecasted transaction also affects earnings.

Hedge accounting is to be discontinued when the hedging instrument is sold, expires, is terminated or exercised. If the gain or loss was accumulated in equity, it should remain there until such time as the forecasted transaction occurs, when it is added to the asset or liability recorded or is taken into earnings when the transaction impacts earnings. Hedge accounting is also discontinued prospectively when the hedge ceases meeting the criteria for qualification of hedge accounting. The accumulated gain or loss remains in equity until the committed or forecasted transaction occurs, whereupon it will be handled as discussed above.

Finally, if the forecasted or committed transaction is no longer expected to occur, hedge accounting is prospectively discontinued. In this case, the accumulated gain or loss included in equity must be immediately taken into earnings.

Hedges of a net investment in a foreign entity. Hedges of a net investment in a foreign entity are accounted for similarly to those of cash flows. To the extent it is determined to be effective, accumulated gains or losses are reflected in equity via the statement of changes in equity. The ineffective portion is generally reported in earnings, but to the limited extent the hedging instrument is not a derivative, the gain or loss is accounted for consistent with IAS 21, which states that exchange differences arising on a foreign currency liability accounted for as a hedge of a net investment in a foreign entity should be classified as equity until the investment is disposed of, at which time it should be recognized in earnings.

In terms of financial reporting, the gain or loss on the effective portion of these hedges should be classified in the same manner as the foreign currency translation gain or loss. According to IAS 21, translation gains and losses are not reported in earnings but instead are reported directly in equity, with allocation being made to minority interest when the foreign entity is not wholly owned by the reporting entity. Likewise, any hedging gain or loss would be reported in equity. When the foreign entity is disposed of, the accumulated translation gain or loss would be reported in earnings, as would any related deferred hedging gain or loss.

When a hedge does not qualify for special hedge accounting (due to failure to properly document, ineffectiveness, etc.), any gains or losses are to be accounted for based on the nature of the hedging instrument. If a derivative financial instrument, the gains or losses must be reported in earnings. Similarly, if the item is held for trading, immediate recognition in earnings is mandatory. If it is not a derivative, and is an available-for-sale instrument, then the provision of IAS 39 which offers a choice of reporting methods comes into play. Thus, either immediate earnings recognition or recognition in equity can be elected when IAS 39 is first applied. Consistent application of the chosen methodology will be required thereafter.

Assessing hedge effectiveness. Under the provisions of IAS 39, assuming other conditions are also met, hedge accounting may be applied as long as, and to the extent that, the hedge is effective. By effective, the standard is alluding to the degree to which offsetting changes in fair values or cash flows attributable to the hedged risk are achieved by the hedging instrument. A hedge is generally deemed effective if, at inception and throughout the period of the hedge, the ratio of changes in value of the underlying to changes in value of the hedging instrument are in a range of 80 to 125%.

Hedge effectiveness will be heavily impacted by the nature of the instruments used for hedging. For example, interest rate swaps will be almost completely effective if the notional and principal amounts match, and the terms, repricing dates, interest and principal payment dates, and basis for measurement are the same. On the other hand, if the hedged and hedging instruments are denominated in different currencies, effectiveness will not be 100% in most instances. Also, if the rate change is partially due to changes in perceived credit risk, there will be a lack of perfect correlation as well.

Hedges must be defined in terms of specific identified and designated risks. Overall (enterprise) risk cannot be the basis for hedging. Also, it must be possible to precisely measure the risk being hedged; thus, threat of expropriation (which may be an insurable risk) is not a risk which can be hedged, as that term is used in IAS 39. Similarly, investments accounted for by the equity method cannot be hedged, since these are not measured at fair value. In contrast, a net investment in a foreign subsidiary can be hedged, since this is a function of currency exchange rates alone.

If a hedge does not qualify for special hedge accounting because it is not effective, any gains or losses arising from changes in the fair value of a hedged item measured at fair value, subsequent to initial recognition, are reported as otherwise prescribed by IAS 39. That is, if an item is held for trading, changes in value are reported in earnings; if available for sale, the changes are reported in earnings or in equity, consistent with the onetime election made by the reporting entity.

IAS 39: Financial Instruments--Disclosures

IAS 39 mandates continuation of the disclosures imposed by IAS 32, with the obvious caveat that supplemental fair value disclosures would not be needed for assets or liabilities already being carried at fair value. The disclosures of the enterprise's accounting policies should note the methods and significant assumptions applied in estimating fair values for significant classes of financial assets and financial liabilities that are carried at fair value, and should indicate whether gains and losses arising from changes in fair values of those financial assets and liabilities, other than those held for trading purposes, are included in net profit or loss for the period or are recognized directly in equity until the financial asset is disposed of or the liability is extinguished.

IAS 39 defines four categories of financial assets and liabilities.

1. Held for trading;
2. Available for sale;
3. Held-to-maturity; and
4. Loans and receivables originated by the entity and not held for trading.

When relevant, the financial statements must disclose, for each of these four categories of instruments, whether regular way purchases of securities are accounted for at trade date or settlement date.

Also to be disclosed are a description of the reporting entity's financial risk management objectives and policies, including its policy for each major type of forecasted transaction (for example, in the case of hedges of risks relating to future sales, that description should indicate the nature of the risks being hedged, approximately how many months or years of future sales have been hedged, and the approximate percentage of sales in those future months or years); whether gain or loss on financial assets and liabilities measured at fair value subsequent to initial recognition, other than those relating to hedges, has been recognized directly in equity, and if so, the cumulative amount recognized as of the balance sheet date; and, when fair value cannot be reliably measured for a group of financial assets or financial liabilities that would otherwise have to be carried at fair value, that fact should be disclosed together with a description of the financial instruments, their carrying amount, and an explanation of why fair value cannot be reliably measured.

For designated fair value hedges, cash flow hedges, and hedges of net investment in a foreign entity, there is to be separate descriptions of the hedges, the financial instruments designated as hedging instruments together with fair values at the balance sheet date, the nature of the risks being hedged, and--for forecasted transactions--the periods in which the forecasted transactions are expected to occur, when they are expected to enter into the determination of net profit or loss (e.g., a forecasted acquisition of property may affect earnings over the asset's depreciable lifetime), plus a description of any forecasted transaction for which hedge accounting was previously employed but which is no longer expected to occur.

When there has been a gain or loss on derivative and nonderivative financial assets or liabilities designated as hedging instruments in cash flow hedges which has been recognized directly in equity, disclosure is to be made of the amount so recognized during the current reporting period, the amount removed from equity and included in earnings for the period, and the amount removed from equity and included in the initial measurement of acquisition cost or carrying amount of the asset or liability in a hedged forecasted transaction during the current period.

The financial statements must also disclose the following with regard to financial instruments: the amount of any gains or losses resulting from remeasuring available-for-sale instruments at fair value, included directly in equity in the current period, and the amount removed from equity and reported in current operating results; a description of any held-for-trading or available-for-sale financial assets for which fair value cannot be determined, together with (when possible) the range of possible fair values thereof; the carrying amount and gain or loss on sale of any financial assets whose fair value was not previously determinable; significant items of income, expense, gain and loss resulting from financial assets or liabilities, whether included in earnings or in equity, with separate (gross) reporting of interest income and interest expense, and with separate reporting of realized and unrealized gains and losses resulting from available-for-sale financial assets. It is not necessary to distinguish realized and unrealized gains and losses resulting from held-for-trading financial assets, however.

If there are impaired loans, the amount of interest accrued but not received in cash must be disclosed.

If the entity has participated in securitizations or repurchase agreements, these must be described, and the nature of any collateral and key assumptions made in computing retained or new interests are to be discussed. There must be disclosure of whether the financial assets have been derecognized.

Any reclassifications of financial assets from categories reported at fair value to those reported at amortized historical cost (either because now deemed held-to-maturity, or because fair values are no longer obtainable) are to be explained.

Finally, any impairments or reversals of impairments are to be disclosed, separately for each class (held-to-maturity, etc.) of investment.

6 INVENTORY

PERSPECTIVE AND ISSUES

The accounting for inventories is a major consideration for many entities because of its significance on both the income statement (cost of goods sold) and the balance sheet. Inventories are defined by IAS 2 as items that are

> ...held for sale in the ordinary course of business; in the process of production for such sale; or in the form of materials or supplies to be consumed in the production process or in the rendering of services.

The complexity of accounting for inventories arises from several factors.

1. The high volume of activity (or turnover) in the account
2. The various cost flow alternatives that are acceptable
3. The classification of inventories

There are two types of entities for which we must consider the accounting for inventories. The merchandising entity (generally, a retailer or wholesaler) has a single inventory account that is usually titled **merchandise inventory**. These are the goods on hand that are purchased for resale. The other type of entity is the manufacturer. The manufacturer generally has three types of inventory: (1) raw materials, (2) work in process, and (3) finished goods. **Raw materials inventory** represents the goods purchased that will act as inputs in the production process leading to the finished product. **Work in process** (WIP) consists of the goods entered into production but not yet completed. **Finished goods inventory** is the completed product that is on hand awaiting sale.

In the case of either type of entity we are concerned with satisfying the same basic questions.

1. At what point in time should the items be included in inventory (ownership)?
2. What costs incurred should be included in the valuation of inventories?
3. What cost flow assumption should be used?
4. At what value should inventories be reported (net realizable value)?

The promulgated GAAP that addresses these questions is IAS 2. This standard discusses the definition, valuation, and classification of inventory. The extant standard is a modest revision of an earlier standard, the principal difference being that the base stock method formerly permitted is now prohibited. International standards are somewhat less detailed than national standards issued by certain jurisdictions, and in this chapter the requirements of IAS 2 are supplemented with guidance from other sources, where pertinent.

Under the provisions of IAS 2 as revised, the first-in, first-out and weighted-average cost methods are defined as benchmark treatments, with the last-in, first-out method relegated to allowable alternative treatment. Since the international standards went to some length to avoid naming certain methods as being preferred or recommended (hence the term "benchmark," which was deemed to be more neutral), it is fair to consider all three methods as being acceptable under the IAS. An interpretation (SIC 1) by the newly constituted Standing Interpretations Committee (SIC) of the IASC states that entities should use the same cost formula for all inventories having similar nature and use. It furthermore states that differences in geographic location would not, *ipso facto*, justify the use of different cost formulas. In reaching this conclusion, the SIC analogized from the guidance on consolidations provided in IAS 27, and that on property, plant, and equipment assets in IAS 16.

Sources of IAS	
IAS 2	*SIC* 1

DEFINITIONS OF TERMS

Absorption (full) costing. Inclusion of all manufacturing costs (fixed and variable) in the cost of finished goods inventory, in accordance with GAAP.

Base stock. Based on the theory that a minimal level of inventory is a permanent investment, this amount is carried on the books at its historical cost.

By-products. Goods that result as an ancillary product from the production of a primary good; often having minor value when compared to the value of the principal product(s).

Ceiling. In lower of cost or market computations, market is limited to net realizable value. Market (replacement cost) cannot be higher than the ceiling (net realizable value). Net realizable value is selling price less selling costs and costs to complete.

Consignments. Marketing method in which the consignor ships goods to the consignee, who acts as an agent for the consignor in selling the goods. The inventory remains the property of the consignor until sold by the consignee.

Direct (variable) costing. Inclusion of only variable manufacturing costs in the cost of ending finished goods inventory. This method is not acceptable for financial reporting purposes.

Dollar-value LIFO. Variation of conventional LIFO in which layers of inventory are priced in dollars adjusted by price indexes instead of layers of inventory priced at unit prices.

Double-extension. Method used to compute the conversion price index. The index indicates the relationship between the base year and current prices in terms of a percentage.

Finished goods. Completed but unsold products produced by a manufacturing firm.

First-in, first-out (FIFO). Cost flow assumption; the first goods purchased or produced are assumed to be the first goods sold.

Floor. In lower of cost or market computations, market is limited to net realizable value less a normal profit, called the floor. Market (replacement cost) cannot be below the floor.

Goods in transit. Goods being shipped from seller to buyer at year end.

Gross profit method. Method used to estimate the amount of ending inventory based on the cost of goods available for sale, sales, and the gross profit percentage.

Inventory. Assets held for sale in the normal course of business, or which are in the process of production for such sale, or are in the form of materials or supplies to be consumed in the production process or in the rendering of services.

Inventory layer. Under the LIFO method, an increase in inventory quantity during a period.

Joint products. Two or more products produced jointly, where neither is viewed as being more important; in some cases additional production steps are applied to one or more joint products after a split off point.

Last-in, first-out (LIFO). Cost flow assumption; the last goods purchased are assumed to be the first goods sold.

LIFO liquidation. Liquidation of the LIFO base or old inventory layers when inventory quantities decrease. This can distort income since old costs are matched against current revenues.

LIFO retail. Inventory costing method that combines the LIFO cost flow assumption and the retail inventory method.

Link-chain. Method of applying dollar-value LIFO by developing a single cumulative index. This method may be used instead of double-extension only when there are substantial changes in product lines over the years.

Lower of cost or market. Inventories must be valued at lower of cost or market (replacement cost). Market cannot exceed the ceiling (net realizable value) or be less than the floor (net realizable value less a normal markup).

Markdown. Decrease below original retail price. A markdown cancelation is an increase (not above original retail price) in retail price after a markdown.

Markup. Increase above original retail price. A markup cancelation is a decrease (not below original retail price) in retail price after a markup.

Moving average. Inventory costing method used in conjunction with a perpetual inventory system. A weighted-average cost per unit is recomputed after every purchase. Goods sold are costed at the most recent moving average cost.

Net realizable value. Estimated selling price in the ordinary course of business less the estimated costs of completion and the estimated costs necessary to make the sale.

Periodic. Inventory system where quantities are determined only periodically by physical count.

Perpetual. Inventory system where up-to-date records of inventory quantities are kept.

Product financing arrangements. Arrangements whereby an entity buys inventory for another firm that agrees to purchase the inventory over a certain period at specified prices which include handling and financing costs; alternatively, an entity can buy inventory from another firm with the understanding that the seller will repurchase the goods at the original price plus defined storage and financing costs.

Purchase commitments. Noncancelable commitment to purchase goods. Losses on such commitments are recognized in the accounts.

Raw materials. For a manufacturing firm, materials on hand awaiting entry into the production process.

Replacement cost. Cost to reproduce an inventory item by purchase or manufacture. In lower of cost or market computations, the term **market** means replacement cost, subject to the ceiling and floor limitations.

Retail method. Inventory costing method that uses a cost ratio to reduce ending inventory (valued at retail) to cost.

Specific identification. Inventory system where the seller identifies which specific items are sold and which remain in ending inventory.

Standard costs. Predetermined unit costs, which are acceptable for financial reporting purposes if adjusted periodically to reflect current conditions.

Weighted-average. Periodic inventory costing method where ending inventory and cost of goods sold are priced at the weighted-average cost of all items available for sale.

Work in process. For a manufacturing firm, the inventory of partially completed products.

CONCEPTS, RULES, AND EXAMPLES

Basic Concept of Inventory Costing

International accounting standards (IAS 2, revised effective 1995) establish cost, not to exceed net realizable value, as the basis for valuation of inventories. In contrast to the standard for plant assets, there is no option for revaluing inventories to current replacement cost or fair value, presumably due to the far shorter period of time over which such assets are held, thereby limiting the cumulative impact of inflation on reported amounts. Furthermore, the benchmark treatment prescribes the relatively more conservative FIFO or weighted-average cost methods as the means of measuring historical cost of inventories, although the allowed alternative method, LIFO, may result in a somewhat more meaningful measure of earnings in periods of rising prices. These methods are discussed fully later in this chapter.

Ownership of Goods

From the accounting perspective, concern with the ownership of inventories is to assist in the determination of the actual physical quantity of inventory on hand. In general, an enterprise should record purchases and sales of inventory when legal title passes. Although strict adherence to this rule may not be important in daily transactions, a proper inventory cutoff at the end of an accounting period is crucial. Thus, for accounting purposes, to obtain an accurate measurement of inventory quantity and corresponding monetary representation of inventory and cost of goods sold in the financial statements, it is necessary to determine when title has passed.

The most common error made in this regard is to assume that title is synonymous with possession of goods on hand. This may be incorrect in two ways: (1) the goods on hand may not be owned, and (2) goods that are not on hand may be owned. There are four matters that may create a question as to proper ownership: (1) goods in transit, (2) consignment sales, (3) product financing arrangements, and (4) sales made with the buyer holding the right of return.

At year end, any **goods in transit** from seller to buyer may properly be includable in one, and only one, of those parties' inventories, based on the conditions of the sale. Under traditional legal and accounting interpretation, such goods are included in the inventory of the firm financially responsible for transportation costs. This responsibility may be indicated by shipping terms such as FOB, which is used in overland shipping contracts, and by FAS, CIF, C&F, and ex-ship, which are used in maritime contracts.

The term **FOB** stands for "free on board." If goods are shipped FOB destination, transportation costs are paid by the seller and title does not pass until the carrier delivers the goods to the buyer; thus these goods are part of the seller's inventory while in transit. If goods are shipped FOB shipping point, transportation costs are paid by the buyer and title passes when the carrier takes possession; thus these goods are part of the buyer's inventory while in transit. The terms **FOB destina-**

tion and **FOB shipping point** often indicate a specific location at which title to the goods is transferred, such as FOB Milan. This means that the seller retains title and risk of loss until the goods are delivered to a common carrier in Milan who will act as an agent for the buyer.

A seller who ships **FAS** (free alongside) must bear all expense and risk involved in delivering the goods to the dock next to (alongside) the vessel on which they are to be shipped. The buyer bears the cost of loading and of shipment; thus title passes when the carrier takes possession of the goods.

In a **CIF** (cost, insurance, and freight) contract the buyer agrees to pay in a lump sum the cost of the goods, insurance costs, and freight charges. In a C&F contract, the buyer promises to pay a lump sum that includes the cost of the goods and all freight charges. In either case, the seller must deliver the goods to the carrier and pay the costs of loading; thus both title and risk of loss pass to the buyer upon delivery of the goods to the carrier.

A seller who delivers goods **ex-ship** bears all expense and risk until the goods are unloaded, at which time both title and risk of loss pass to the buyer.

The foregoing is meant only to define normal terms and usage; actual contractual arrangements between a given buyer and a given seller can vary widely. The accounting treatment should in all cases strive to mirror the substance of the legal terms established between the parties.

In **consignments**, the consignor (seller) ships goods to the consignee (buyer), who acts as the agent of the consignor in trying to sell the goods. In some consignments, the consignee receives a commission; in other arrangements, the consignee "purchases" the goods simultaneously with the sale of the goods to the customer. Goods out on consignment are included in the inventory of the consignor and excluded from the inventory of the consignee.

A **product financing arrangement** is a transaction in which an entity sells and agrees to repurchase inventory with the repurchase price equal to the original sales price plus the carrying and financing costs. The purpose of this transaction is to allow the seller (sponsor) to arrange financing of its original purchase of the inventory. The substance of the transaction is illustrated by the diagram below.

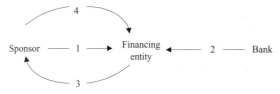

1. In the initial transaction the sponsor "sells" inventoriable items to the financing entity in return for the remittance of the sales price and at the same time agrees to repurchase the inventory at a specified price (usually the sales price plus carrying and financing costs) over a specified period of time.

2. The financing entity procures the funds remitted to the sponsor by borrowing from a bank (or other financial institution) using the newly purchased inventory as collateral.
3. The financing entity actually remits the funds to the sponsor and the sponsor presumably uses these funds to pay off the debt incurred as a result of the original purchase of the inventoriable debt.
4. The sponsor then repurchases the inventory for the specified price plus costs from the financing entity at a later time when the funds are available.

In a variant of this transaction, an entity can acquire goods from a manufacturer or dealer, with the contractual understanding that they will be resold to another entity at the same price, plus handling, storage, and financing costs.

The purpose of either variation of product financing arrangement is to enable the sponsor to acquire or control inventory without incurring additional reportable debt. Under international accounting standards, transactions of this type are not directly addressed, and thus it would appear that, if a "form over substance" approach is subscribed to, these transactions may successfully result in financing that is not reported in the balance sheet. It would therefore be instructive to look to the standard imposed in the United States by the FASB, which ruled that the substance of this type of transaction is that of a borrowing.

Under the pertinent US standard (SFAS 49, *Accounting for Product Financing Arrangements*), such transactions are, in substance, no different from those where a sponsor obtains third-party financing to purchase its inventory. As a result, the FASB ruled that when an entity sells inventory with a related arrangement to repurchase it, proper accounting is to record a liability when the funds are received for the initial transfer of the inventory in the amount of the selling price. The sponsor is then to accrue carrying and financing costs in accordance with its normal accounting policies. These accruals are eliminated and the liability satisfied when the sponsor repurchases the inventory. The inventory is not to be taken off the balance sheet of the sponsor and a sale is not to be recorded. Thus, although legal title has passed to the financing entity, for purposes of measuring and valuing inventory, the inventory is considered to be owned by the sponsor. Although the other variation on this financing arrangement, with a nominee entity acquiring the goods for the ultimate purchaser, is not addressed in SFAS 49, logic suggests that an analogous accounting treatment be prescribed.

A final issue that requires special consideration is the situation that exists when the buyer holds the right of return. Again, while international accounting standards do not address this topic directly, logical guidance is suggested by the US accounting standards. SFAS 48, *Revenue Recognition When Right of Return Exists*, addresses the propriety of recognizing revenue at the point of sale under these circumstances. Generally speaking, the sale is to be recorded if the future amount of the returns can reasonably be estimated. If the ability to make a reasonable estimate is precluded, the sale is not to be recorded until the returns are unlikely. In this situation, although legal title has passed to the buyer, the seller must continue to include the goods in its measurement and valuation of inventory. Absent a standard to the contrary under international GAAP, the "substance over form" dictum would seemingly support the guidelines suggested by SFAS 48.

Accounting for Inventories

Introduction. The major objectives of accounting for inventories is the matching of appropriate costs against revenues in order to arrive at the proper determination of periodic income, and accurate representation of inventories on hand as assets of the enterprise as of the balance sheet date. As it happens, these two goals are in conflict and, under any system of accounting in which the financial statements are fully articulated (i.e., where the balance sheet and income statement are linked together mechanically), it will be virtually impossible to achieve both fully.

The accounting for inventories is done under either a periodic or a perpetual system. In a **periodic inventory system**, the inventory quantity is determined periodically by a physical count. The quantity so determined is then priced in accordance with the cost method used. Cost of goods sold is computed by adding beginning inventory and net purchases (or cost of goods manufactured) and subtracting ending inventory.

Alternatively, a **perpetual inventory system** keeps a running total of the quantity (and possibly the cost) of inventory on hand by recording all sales and purchases as they occur. When inventory is purchased, the inventory account (rather than purchases) is debited. When inventory is sold, the cost of goods sold and reduction of inventory are recorded. Periodic physical counts are necessary only to verify the perpetual records and to satisfy the tax regulations (tax regulations require that a physical inventory be taken, at least annually).

Valuation of Inventories

According to IAS 2, the primary basis of accounting for inventories is cost. **Cost** is defined as the sum of all costs of purchase, costs of conversion, and other costs incurred in bringing the inventories to their present location and condition. This definition allows for significant interpretation of the costs to be included in inventory.

For raw materials and merchandise inventory that are purchased outright and not intended for further conversion, the identification of cost is relatively straightforward. The cost of these purchased inventories will include all expenditures incurred in bringing the goods to the point of sale and putting them in a salable condition. These costs include the purchase price, transportation costs, insurance, and handling costs. Trade discounts, rebates, and other such items are to be deducted in determining inventory costs; failure to do so would result in carrying inventory at amounts in excess of true historical costs.

The impact of interest costs as they relate to the valuation of inventoriable items (IAS 23) is discussed in Chapter 8. In general, even when the allowed alternative treatment prescribed by IAS 23 is employed, borrowing costs will not be capitalized in connection with inventory acquisitions, since the period required to ready the goods for sale will not be significant. However, where a lengthy production process is required to prepare the goods for sale, the provisions of IAS 23 would be applicable and a portion of borrowing costs would become part of the cost of inventory.

Conversion costs for manufactured goods should include all costs that are directly associated with the units produced, such as labor and overhead. The allocation of overhead costs, however, must be systematic and rational, and in the case of fixed overhead costs (i.e., those which do not vary directly with level of production) the allocation process should be based on normal production levels. In periods of unusually low levels of production, a portion of fixed overhead costs must accordingly be charged directly to operations, and not taken into inventory.

Costs other than material and conversion costs are inventoriable only to the extent they are necessary to bring the goods to their present condition and location. Examples might include certain design costs and other types of preproduction expenditures if intended to benefit specific classes of customers. On the other hand, all research costs and most development costs (per IAS 9, as discussed in Chapter 8) would typically **not** become part of inventory costs. Also generally excluded from inventory would be such costs as administrative and selling expenses, which must be treated as period costs; the cost of wasted materials, labor, or other production expenditures; and most storage costs. Included in overhead, and thus allocable to inventory, would be such categories as repairs, maintenance, utilities, rent, indirect labor, production supervisory wages, indirect materials and supplies, quality control and inspection, and the cost of small tools not capitalized.

Joint products and by-products. In some production processes, more than one product is produced simultaneously. Typically, if each product has significant value, they are referred to as **joint products**; if only one has substantial value, the others are known as **by-products**. Under IAS 2, when the costs of each jointly produced good cannot be clearly determined, a rational allocation among them is required. Generally, such allocation is made by reference to the relative values of the jointly produced goods, as measured by ultimate selling prices. Often, after a period of joint production the goods are split off, separately incurring additional costs before being completed and ready for sale. The allocation of joint costs should take into account the additional individual product costs yet to be incurred after the point at which joint production ceases.

By-products by definition are products that have limited value when measured with reference to the primary good being produced. IAS 2 suggests that by-products be valued at net realizable value, with the costs allocated to by-products thereby being deducted from the cost pool, being otherwise allocated to the sole or several principal products.

For example, products A and B have the same processes performed on them up to the split-off point. The total cost incurred to this point is $80,000. This cost can be assigned to products A and B using their relative sales value at the split-off point. If A could be sold for $60,000 and B for $40,000, the total sales value is $100,000. The cost would be assigned on the basis of each product's relative sales value. Thus, A would be assigned a cost of $48,000 (60,000/100,000 x 80,000) and B a cost of $32,000 (400,000/100,000 x 80,000).

If inventory is exchanged with another entity for similar goods, the earnings process is generally not culminated. Accordingly, the acquired items are recorded at the recorded, or book, value of the items given up.

In some jurisdictions, the categories of costs that are includable in inventory for tax purposes may differ from those that are permitted for financial reporting purposes under international accounting standards. To the extent that differential tax and financial reporting is possible (i.e., that there is no statutory requirement that the taxation rules constrain financial reporting) this situation will result in interperiod tax allocation. This is discussed more fully in Chapter 15.

Direct costing. The method of allocating fixed overhead to both ending inventory and cost of goods sold is commonly known as (full) absorption costing. IAS 2 requires that absorption costing be employed. However, often for managerial decision making purposes an alternative to absorption costing, variable or direct costing, is utilized. Direct costing requires classifying only direct materials, direct labor, and variable overhead related to production as inventory costs. All fixed costs are accounted for as period costs. The virtue of direct costing is that under this accounting strategy there will be a predictable, linear effect on marginal contribution from each unit of sales revenue, which can be useful in planning and controlling the business operation. However, such a costing method does not result in inventory which includes all costs of production, and therefore this is deemed not to be in accordance with GAAP under international standards. If an entity uses direct costing for internal budgeting or other purposes, adjustments must be made to develop alternative information for financial reporting purposes.

BENCHMARK METHODS OF INVENTORY COSTING

Specific Identification

The theoretical basis for valuing inventories and cost of goods sold requires assigning the production and/or acquisition costs to the specific goods to which they relate. For example, the cost of ending inventory for an entity in its first year, during which it produced 10 items (say, exclusive single family homes), might be the actual production cost of the first, sixth, and eighth unit produced if those are the actual units still on hand at the balance sheet date. This method of inventory valuation is usually referred to as **specific identification**.

Specific identification is generally not a practical technique, as the product will generally lose its separate identity as it passes through the production and sales process. Exceptions to this would arise in situations involving small inventory quantities with high unit value and low turnover rate. Under IAS 2, specific identification must be employed to cost inventories that are not ordinarily interchangeable, and goods and services produced and segregated for specific projects. For inventories meeting either of these criteria, the specific identification method is mandatory and the other benchmark methods cannot be used.

Because of the limited applicability of specific identification, it is more likely to be the case that certain assumptions regarding the cost flows associated with inventory will need to be made. One of accounting's peculiarities is that these cost flows may or may not reflect the physical flow of inventory. Over the years, much attention has been given to both the flow of physical goods and the assumed flow of costs associated with those goods. In most jurisdictions, it has long been recognized that the flow of costs need not mirror the actual flow of the goods with which those costs are associated. For example, a key provision in an early US accounting standard stated that

> *...cost for inventory purposes shall be determined under any one of several assumptions as to the flow of cost factors; the major objective in selecting a method should be to choose the one which, under the circumstances, most clearly reflects periodic income.*

Under international accounting standards, there are two benchmark cost flow assumptions, and one additional method, which is an allowed alternative treatment. The most common cost flow assumptions used are: (1) first-in, first-out (FIFO), (2) weighted-average, and (3) last-in, first-out (LIFO). Additionally, there are variations of each of these assumptions which have commonly been used in practice. In certain jurisdictions, other costing procedures, such as the base stock method, have also been permitted.

First-In, First-Out (FIFO)

The FIFO method of inventory valuation assumes that the first goods purchased are the first goods used or sold, regardless of the actual physical flow. This method is thought to parallel most closely the physical flow of the units for most industries having moderate to rapid turnover of goods. The strength of this cost flow assumption lies in the inventory amount reported on the balance sheet. Because the earliest goods purchased are the first ones removed from the inventory account, the remaining balance is composed of items acquired at more recent costs. This yields results similar to those obtained under current cost accounting on the balance sheet. However, the FIFO method does not necessarily reflect the most accurate income figure when viewed from the perspective of underlying economic performance, as older historical costs are being matched against current revenues. Depending on the rate of inventory turnover and the speed with which general and specific prices are changing, this mismatching could potentially have a material distorting effect on reported income. At the extreme, if reported earnings are fully distributed to owners as dividends, the enterprise could be left without sufficient resources to replenish its inventory stocks due to changing prices.

The following example illustrates the basic principles involved in the application of FIFO:

	Units available	Units sold	Actual unit cost	Actual total cost
Beginning inventory	100	--	$2.10	$210
Sale	--	75	--	--
Purchase	150	--	2.80	420
Sale	--	100	--	--
Purchase	50	--	3.00	150
Total	300	175		$780

Given these data, the cost of goods sold and the ending inventory balance are determined as follows:

	Units	Unit cost	Total cost
Cost of goods sold	100	$2.10	$210
	75	2.80	210
	175		$420
Ending inventory	50	3.00	$150
	75	2.80	210
	125		$360

Notice that the total of the units in cost of goods sold and ending inventory, as well as the sum of their total costs, is equal to the goods available for sale and their respective total costs.

The unique characteristic of the FIFO method is that it provides the same results under either the periodic or perpetual system. This will not be the case for any other costing method.

Weighted-Average

The other benchmark method of inventory valuation under IAS 2 involves averaging and is commonly referred to as the weighted-average method. The cost of goods available for sale (beginning inventory and net purchases) is divided by the units available for sale to obtain a weighted-average unit cost. Ending inventory and cost of goods sold are then priced at this average cost. For example, assume the following data:

	Units available	Units sold	Actual unit cost	Actual total cost
Beginning inventory	100	--	$2.10	$210
Sale	--	75	--	--
Purchase	150	--	2.80	420
Sale	--	100	--	--
Purchase	50	--	3.00	150
Total	300	175		$780

The weighted-average cost is $780/300, or $2.60. Ending inventory is 125 units at $2.60, or $325; cost of goods sold is 175 units at $2.60, or $455.

When the weighted-average assumption is applied to a perpetual inventory system, the average cost is recomputed after each purchase. This process is referred to as a moving average. Sales are costed at the most recent average. This combination is called the moving average method and is applied below to the same data used in the weighted-average example above.

	Units on hand	Purchases in dollars	Sales in dollars	Total cost	Inventory unit cost
Beginning inventory	100	$ --	$ --	$210.00	$2.10
Sale (75 units @ $2.10)	25	--	157.50	52.50	2.10
Purchase (150 units, $420)	175	420.00	--	472.50	2.70
Sale (100 units @ $2.70)	75	--	270.00	202.50	2.70
Purchase (50 units, $150)	125	150.00	--	352.50	2.82

Cost of goods sold is 75 units at $2.10 and 100 units at $2.70, or a total of $427.50.

Last-In, First-Out (LIFO)

The LIFO method of inventory valuation costs the ending inventory as if the last goods purchased were the first goods used or sold. This allows the matching of current costs with current revenue and as proponents of the method argue, provides the best measure of periodic income, which is a major objective for periodic financial reporting. However, unless costs remain relatively unchanged, the LIFO method will usually distort the ending inventory balance for balance sheet purposes because inventory usually consists of costs from earlier periods. Critics of the method also point out that LIFO does not usually follow the physical flow of merchandise or materials. However, this last argument should not affect the selection of a cost flow assumption, because the matching of physical flow is not considered to be an objective of accounting for inventories.

Despite the arguable logic of using a LIFO cost flow assumption during periods of changing prices, to achieve a more meaningful measure of income, the method actually is not truly derived from a promulgated accounting principle. Rather, the basis for LIFO is found in various tax codes enacted in certain jurisdictions from time to time. Since rising general price levels have been almost the rule during the past half century, LIFO has been enacted as a form of tax relief by a number of important tax jurisdictions and was widely embraced for financial reporting purposes principally in those instances in which use for tax reporting purposes was linked to financial reporting. Other requirements of LIFO, largely dependent on local tax regulations, have included restrictions on abandoning the LIFO after first adopting it, and limitations on supplementary disclosures of income determined by alternative costing stategies. Given LIFO's genesis as an offspring of tax rules, the precise methods of applying LIFO that are permitted in different nations will vary widely; the following discussion sets forth many of the computational techniques that may validly be employed, but does not represent which, if any, may be permitted in any particular circumstance. (IAS 2 does not describe how LIFO is to be operational-ized.)

The actual implementation of LIFO requires valuation of the quantity of ending inventory at prices in effect earlier. The quantity of ending inventory on hand in the year when the method is first applied is termed the **base layer**. This inventory is valued at actual (full absorption) cost, and unit cost is determined by dividing total cost by the quantity on hand. In subsequent periods, increases in the quantity of inventory on hand are referred to as **increments**, or **LIFO layers**. These incre-ments are valued individually by applying one of several possible costs to the quan-tity of inventory representing a layer.

1.   The actual cost of the goods most recently purchased or produced
2.   The actual cost of the goods purchased or produced in order of acquisition
3.   An average unit cost of all goods purchased or produced during the current year
4.   A hybrid method that will more clearly reflect income

Thus, after using the LIFO method for 5 years, it is possible that an enterprise could have ending inventory consisting of the base layer and five additional layers (or increments) provided that the quantity of ending inventory increased every year.

Example of the single goods (unit) LIFO approach

Fenetre Co. is in its first year of operation and elects to use the periodic LIFO method of inventory valuation. The company sells only one product. Fenetre will apply the LIFO method using the order of current year acquisition cost. The following data are given for years 1 through 3:

Year 1	Units	Unit cost	Total cost
Purchase	200	$2.00	$400
Sale	100	--	--
Purchase	200	3.00	600
Sale	150	--	--
Year 2			
Purchase	300	$3.20	$960
Sale	200	--	--
Purchase	100	3.30	330

Year 3	Units	Unit cost	Total cost
Purchase	100	$3.50	$350
Sale	200	--	--
Sale	100	--	--

In year 1 the following occurred:

1. The total goods available for sale were 400 units.
2. The total sales were 250 units.
3. Therefore, the ending inventory was 150 units.

The ending inventory is valued at the earliest current year acquisition cost of $2.00 per unit. Thus, ending inventory is valued at $300 (150 x $2.00).

Another way to look at this is to analyze both cost of goods sold and ending inventory.

	Units	Unit cost	Total cost
Cost of goods sold	200	$3.00	$600
	50	2.00	100
	250		$700
Ending inventory	150	$2.00	$300

Note that the base-year cost is $2.00 and that the base-year level is 150 units. Therefore, if ending inventory in the subsequent period exceeds 150 units, a new layer will be created.

Year 2	Units	Unit cost	Total cost
Cost of goods sold	100	$3.30	$330
	100	3.20	320
	200		$650
Ending inventory	150	$2.00	$300
	200	3.20	640
	350		$940

Now, if ending inventory exceeds 350 units in the next period, a new layer will be created.

Year 3	Units	Unit cost	Total cost
Cost of goods sold	100	$3.50	$350
	200	3.20	640
	300		$990
Ending inventory base year	150	$2.00	$300

Notice how the decrement of 200 units in year 3 eliminated the entire year 2 increment. Thus, any year 4 increase in the quantity of inventory would result in a new increment that would be valued at year 4 prices.

In situations where the ending inventory decreases from the level established at the close of the preceding year, the enterprise experiences a decrement or **LIFO liquidation**. Decrements will reduce or eliminate previously established LIFO layers. Once any part of a layer has been eliminated, it cannot be reinstated. For example, if in its first year after the election of LIFO an enterprise establishes a layer (increment) of 10 units, in the next year inventory decreases by 4 units, leaving the first layer at 6 units, the enterprise cannot reestablish the first layer (back up to 10 units) in the year that inventory next increases. Rather, it will be forced to create a new layer for the increase. The effect of LIFO liquidations in periods of rising prices is to release costs, which are significantly below the current cost being paid, into cost of goods sold from ending inventory. Thus, the resultant effect of a LIFO liquidation is to increase income, typically for both accounting and tax purposes (since most jurisdictions demand conformity between financial reporting and tax reporting). Because of this, LIFO is most commonly used by industries in which inventories are maintained or increased over time.

LIFO liquidations can take two forms, voluntary or involuntary. A **voluntary liquidation** exists when an enterprise decides, for one reason or another, to let inventory levels drop. Such a liquidation occurs because current prices may be too high, less inventory is needed for efficient production, or because of a transition in the product lines. **Involuntary LIFO liquidations** stem from reasons beyond the control of the enterprise, such as a strike, shortages, or shipping delay. Regardless of the reason, all liquidations result in a corresponding increase in income (assuming a trend of rising costs).

To compute the effect of the liquidation, the company must compute the difference between actual cost of sales and what cost of sales would have been had the inventory been reinstated. The Internal Revenue Service has ruled that this hypothetical reinstatement must be computed under the company's normal pricing procedures for valuing its LIFO increments. In the example above the effect of the year 3 LIFO liquidation would be computed as follows:

Inventory reinstatement:

$$200 \text{ units @ } \$3.50 - \$3.20 = \$60$$

Because the 200 units liquidated would have been stated at the year 3 price of $3.50 if there had been an increment, the difference between $3.50 and the actual amount charged to cost of sales for these units ($3.20) measures the effect of the liquidation.

An inordinate amount of recordkeeping is required in applying the unit LIFO method. Remember that the illustration above involved only one product. The recordkeeping burden becomes much greater as the number of products increases. For this reason a **pooling** approach is generally applied to LIFO inventories.

Pooling is the process of grouping items which are naturally related and then treating this group as a single unit in determining the LIFO cost. Because the quantity of ending inventory includes many more items, decreases in one item can be made up for by increases in others, whereas under the single goods unit approach a decrease in any one item results in a liquidation of LIFO layers.

The problem in applying the pooling method emanates from the tax regulations, not the practical side of application. In applying LIFO, the tax regulations state that each type of good in the opening inventory must be compared with a similar type in the closing inventory. These items must be similar as to character, quality, and price. This qualification has generally been interpreted to mean identical. The effect of this statement is to require a separate pool for each item under the unit LIFO method. The need for a simpler, more practical approach to using the LIFO concept and allowing for a greater use of the pooling concept was met by dollar-value LIFO.

Dollar-Value LIFO

Dollar-value LIFO may be employed in those jurisdictions where it is permitted by the tax or other regulatory authorities. The dollar-value LIFO method of inventory valuation determines the cost of inventories by expressing base-year costs in terms of total dollars rather than specific prices of specific units. As discussed later, the dollar-value method also gives rise to an expanded interpretation of the use of pools. Increments and liquidations are treated the same but are reflected only in terms of a net liquidation or increment for the entire pool.

Creating pools. Essentially three alternatives exist for determining pools under dollar-value LIFO: (1) the natural business unit, (2) multiple pools, and (3) pools for wholesalers, retailers, jobbers, and so on.

The natural business unit is defined by the existence of separate and distinct processing facilities and operations and the maintenance of separate income (loss) records. The concept of the natural business unit is generally dependent on the type of product, not the various stages of production for that project. Thus, the pool can (and will) contain raw materials, WIP, and finished goods. The three examples below, taken from treasury regulations, illustrate the application of the natural business unit concept.

Example 1

A corporation manufactures, in one division, automatic clothes washers and dryers of both commercial and domestic grade as well as electric ranges, mangles, and dishwashers. The corporation manufactures, in another division, radios and television sets. The manufacturing facilities and processes used in manufacturing radios and television sets are distinct from those used in manufacturing automatic clothes washers, for example. Under these circumstances, the enterprise would consist of two business units and two pools would be appropriate: one consisting of all of the LIFO inventories involved with the manufacture of clothes washers and dryers, electric ranges, mangles, and dishwashers, and the other consisting of all the LIFO inventories involved with the production of radios and television sets.

Example 2

An enterprise produces plastics in one of its plants. Substantial amounts of the production are sold as plastics. The remainder of the production is shipped to a second plant of the enterprise for the production of plastic toys which are sold to customers. The company operates its plastics plant and toy plant as separate divisions. Because of the different product lines and the separate divisions, the enterprise has two natural business units.

Example 3

A company is engaged in the manufacture of paper. At one stage of processing, uncoated paper is produced. Substantial amounts of uncoated paper are sold at this stage of processing. The remainder of the uncoated paper is transferred to the company's finishing mill, where coated paper is produced and sold. This company has only one natural business unit since coated and uncoated paper are within the same product line.

The multiple-pooling method is the grouping of substantially similar items. In determining substantially similar items, consideration should be given to the processing applied, the interchangeability, the similarity of use, and the customary practice of the industry. While the election of multiple pools will necessitate additional recordkeeping, it may result in a better estimation of periodic income. Depending on local tax regulations, diverse inventory types, such as inventory items of wholesalers, retailers, jobbers, and distributors, might be required to be placed into pools by major lines, types, or classes of goods.

All three methods of pooling allow for a change in the components of inventory. New items that properly fall within the pool may be added, and old items may disappear from the pool, but neither will necessarily effect a change in the total dollar value of the pool.

Computing dollar-value LIFO. The purpose of the dollar-value LIFO method of valuing inventory is to convert inventory that is priced at end-of-year prices to that same inventory priced at base-year (or applicable LIFO layer) prices. The dollar-value method achieves this result through the use of a conversion price index. The inventory at current year cost is divided by the appropriate index to arrive at the base-year cost. Thus, the main focus is on the determination of the conversion price index. There are three basic methods that can be used in computation of the LIFO value of a dollar-value pool: (1) double-extension, (2) link-chain, and (3) the index method. Each of these is discussed below with examples provided where appropriate.

Double-extension method. This was the method originally developed to compute the conversion price index. It involves extending the entire quantity of ending inventory for the current year at both base-year prices and end-of-year prices to arrive at a total dollar value for each, hence the title of double extension. The end-of-year dollar total is then divided by the base-year dollar total to arrive at the index, usually referred to as the **conversion price index**. This index indicates the relationship between the base-year and current prices in terms of a percentage. Each layer (or increment) is valued at its own percentage. Although a representative sample is allowed (meaning that not all of the items need be double extended; this is discussed in more detail under indexing), the recordkeeping under this method is very burdensome. The base-year price must be kept for each inventory item. Depending on the number of different items included in the inventory of the company, the necessary records may be too detailed to keep past the first year.

The following example illustrates the double-extension method of computing the LIFO value of inventory. The example presented is relatively simple and does not attempt to incorporate all of the complexities of inventory accounting.

Example of the double-extension LIFO method

Van de Voort, Inc. uses the dollar-value method of LIFO inventory valuation and computes its price index using the double-extension method. Van de Voort has a single pool that contains two inventory items, A and B. Year 1 is the company's initial year of operations. The following information is given for years 1 through 4:

	Ending inventory	*Ending quantity (units) and current price*			
	current prices	*A*		*B*	
Year					
1	$100,000	5,000	$6.00	7,000	$10.00
2	120,300	6,000	6.30	7,500	11.00
3	122,220	5,800	6.40	7,400	11.50
4	133,900	6,200	6.50	7,800	12.00

In year 1 there is no computation of an index; the index is 100%. The LIFO cost is the same as the actual current year cost. This is our base year.

In year 2 the first step is to double extend the quantity of ending inventory at base-year and current year costs. This is illustrated below.

		Base-year		*Current year*	
Item	*Quantity*	*cost/unit*	*Extended*	*cost/unit*	*Extended*
A	6,000	$ 6.00	$ 36,000	$ 6.30	$ 37,800
B	7,500	10.00	75,000	11.00	82,500
			$111,000		$120,300*

** When using the double-extension method and extending **all** the inventory items to arrive at the index, this number must equal the ending inventory at current prices. If a sampling method is used (as discussed under indexing), this number **divided by** your ending inventory at current prices will give you the percentage sampled.*

Now we can compute the conversion price index which is

$$\frac{\text{Ending inventory at current year prices}}{\text{Ending inventory at base-year prices}}$$

In this case $\dfrac{120,300}{111,000} = 108.4\%$ (rounded)

Next, the year 2 layer at the base-year cost is computed by taking the current year ending inventory at base-year prices (if only a sample of the inventory is extended, this number is arrived at by dividing the ending inventory at current year prices by the conversion price index) of $111,000 and subtracting the base-year cost of $100,000. In year 2 there is an increment (layer) of $11,000 at base-year costs.

The year 2 layer of $11,000 at base-year cost must be converted so that the layer is valued at the prices in effect when it came into existence (i.e., at year 2 prices). This is done by multiplying the increment at base-year cost ($11,000) by the conversion price index (1.08). The result is the year 2 layer at LIFO prices.

			$100,000
Base-year cost			$100,000
Year 2 layer ($11,000 x 1.084)			11,924
			$111,924

In year 3 the same basic procedure is followed.

Item	*Quantity*	*Base-year cost/unit*	*Extended*	*Current year cost/unit*	*Extended*
A	5,800	$ 6.00	$ 34,800	$ 6.40	$ 37,120
B	7,400	10.00	74,000	11.50	85,100
			$108,800		$122,200

There has been a decrease in the base-year cost of the ending inventory, which is referred to as a **decrement**. A decrement results in the decrease (or elimination) of layers provided previously. In this situation, computation of the index is not necessary, as there is no LIFO layer that requires valuation. If a sampling approach has been used, the index is needed to arrive at the ending inventory at base-year cost and thus to determine if there has been an increment or a decrement.

Now the ending inventory at base-year cost is $108,800. The base-year cost is still $100,000, so the total increment is $8,800. Since this is less than the $11,000 increment of year 2, no additional increment is established in year 3. The LIFO cost of the inventory is as shown below.

Base-year cost	$100,000
Year 2 layer ($8,800 x 1.084)	9,539
	$109,539

The fourth year then follows the same steps.

Item	*Quantity*	*Base-year cost/unit*	*Extended*	*Current year cost/unit*	*Extended*
A	6,200	$ 6.00	$ 37,200	$ 6.50	$ 40,300
B	7,800	10.00	78,000	12.00	93,600
			$115,200		$133,900

The conversion price index is 116.2% (133,900/115,200).

A current year increment exists because the ending inventory at base-year prices in year 4 of $115,200 exceeds the year 3 number of $108,800. The current year increment of $6,400 must be valued at year 4 prices. Thus the LIFO cost of the year 4 inventory is

Base-year cost	$100,000
Year 2 layer ($8,800 x 1.084)	9,539
Year 4 layer ($6,400 x 1.162)	7,437
	$116,976

It is important to point out that once a layer is reduced or eliminated, it is never replaced (as with the year 2 increment).

Link-chain method. As shown in this example, the computations for application of the double-extension method become arduous even if only a few items exist in the inventory. Also, consider the problems that arise when there is a constant change in the inventory mix or in situations in which the breadth of the inventory is large. The link-chain method of applying dollar-value LIFO was developed to combat these problems.

Another purpose served by the link-chain method is to eliminate the problem created by a significant turnover in the components of inventory. Under the double-extension or indexing method, it is presumed that any new products added to the inventory will be costed at base-year prices. If these are not available, the earliest cost available after the base year is used. If the item was not in existence in the base year, the reporting entity will attempt to reconstruct the base cost, using a reasonable method to determine what the cost would have been if the item had been in existence in the base year. Although this might not appear to be a problem upon first consideration, imagine identifying a cost from a base period 25 to 50 years past. Should that be impossible, a more recent cost would have to be identified to serve as the base-year cost value, which would eliminate some of the LIFO benefit.

Also imagine a situation faced by a high-tech industry where inventory is continually being replaced by newer, more advanced products. The effect of this rapid change under the double-extension method (because the new products did not exist in the base period) is to use current prices as base-year costs. Thus, when inventory has such a rapid turnover, the LIFO advantage is nonexistent, as current and base-year costs are sometimes synonymous. This is the major reason for the development of the link-chain method.

The link-chain method is the process of developing a single cumulative index that is applied to the ending inventory amount priced at the beginning-of-the-year costs. A separate cumulative index is used for each pool regardless of the variations in the components of these pools over the years. Technological change is allowed for by the method used to calculate each current year index. The index is derived by double extending a representative sample (between 50% and 75% of the dollar value of the pool is generally thought to be appropriate) at both beginning-of-year prices and end-of-year prices. This annual index is then applied (multiplied) to the previous period's cumulative index to arrive at the new current year cumulative index.

Example of the link-chain method

Notice that the end-of-year costs and inventory quantity used are the same as those used in the double-extension example. Assume the following inventory data for years 1 to 4. Year 1 is assumed to be the initial year of operation for the company. The LIFO method is elected on the first tax return. Assume that A and B constitute a single pool.

Product	Ending inventory quantity	Cost per unit Beg. of yr.	Cost per unit End of yr.	Extension Beginning	Extension End
Year 1:					
A	5,000	N/A	$ 6.00	N/A	30,000
B	7,000	N/A	10.00	N/A	70,000
Year 2:					
A	6,000	$ 6.00	6.30	36,000	37,800
B	7,500	10.00	11.00	75,000	82,500

Product	Ending inventory quantity	Cost per unit Beg. of yr.	Cost per unit End of yr.	Extension Beginning	Extension End
Year 3:					
A	5,800	6.30	6.40	36,540	37,120
B	7,400	11.00	11.50	81,400	85,100
Year 4:					
A	6,200	6.40	6.50	39,680	40,300
B	7,800	11.50	12.00	89,700	93,600

The initial year (base year) does not require the computation of an index under any LIFO method. The base-year index will always be 1.00.

Thus, the base-year inventory layer is $100,000 (the end-of-year inventory restated at base-year cost).

The second year requires the first index computation. Notice that in year 2 our extended totals are

	Beginning-of-year prices	End-of-year prices
A	$ 36,000	$ 37,800
B	75,000	82,500
	$111,000	$120,300

The year 2 index is 1.084 (120,300/111,000). This is the same as computed under the double-extension method because the beginning-of-the-year prices reflect the base-year price. This will not always be the case, as new items may sometimes be added to the pool, causing a change in the index.

Thus, the cumulative index is the 1.084 current year index multiplied by the preceding year index of 1.00 to arrive at a link-chain index of 1.084.

This index is then used to restate the inventory to base-year cost by dividing the inventory at end-of-year dollars by the cumulative index: $120,300/1.084 = $111,000. The determination of the LIFO increment or decrement is then basically the same as the double-extension method. In year 2 the increment (layer) at base-year cost is $11,000 ($111,000 – 100,000). This layer must be valued at the prices effective when the layer was created, or extended at the cumulative index for that year. This results in an ending inventory at LIFO cost of

	Base-year cost	Index	LIFO cost
Base year	$100,000	1.00	$100,000
Year 2 layer	11,000	1.084	11,924
	$111,000		$111,924

The index for year 3 is computed as follows:

	Beginning-of-year prices	End-of-year prices
A	$ 36,540	$ 37,120
B	81,400	85,100
	$117,940	$122,220

$$122,220/117,940 = 1.036$$

The next step is to determine the cumulative index, which is the product of the preceding year's cumulative index and the current year index, or 1.123 (1.084 x 1.036). The new cumulative index is used to restate the inventory at end-of-year dollars to base-year cost. This is accomplished by dividing the end-of-year inventory by the new cumulative index. Thus, current inventory at base-year cost is $108,833. In this instance we have experienced a decrement (a decrease from the prior year's $111,000). The determination of ending inventory is

	Base-year cost	*Index*	*LIFO cost*
Base year	$100,000	1.00	$100,000
Year 2 layer	8,833	1.084	9,575
Year 3 layer	--	1.123	--
	$108,833		$109,575

Finally, perform the same steps for the year 4 computation. The current year index is 1.035 (133,900/129,380). The new cumulative index is 1.162 (1.035 x 1.123). The base-year cost of the current inventory is $115,232 (133,900/1.162). Thus, LIFO inventory at the end of year 4 is

	Base-year cost	*Index*	*LIFO cost*
Base year	$100,000	1.00	$100,000
Year 2 layer	8,833	1.084	9,575
Year 3 layer	--	1.123	--
Year 4 layer	6,399	1.162	7,435
	$115,232		$117,010

Notice how even though the numbers used were the same as those used in the double-extension example, the results were different (year 4 inventory under double extension was $116,976); however, not by a significant amount. It is much easier to keep track of beginning-of-the-year prices than it is to keep base-year prices, but perhaps more important, it is easier to establish beginning-of-the-year prices for **new items** than to establish their base-year price. The latter reason is why the link-chain method is so much more desirable than the double-extension method. However, before electing or applying this method, a company must be able to establish a sufficient need as defined in the treasury regulations.

Finally, it should be noted that the link-chain method was originally developed for those enterprises that wanted to use LIFO but because of substantial changes in product lines over time were unable to recreate or keep the historical records necessary to make accurate use of the double-extension method. It is important to note that the double-extension and link-chain methods are not intended to be selective alternatives for the same situation. The link-chain election requires that substantial change in product line be evident over the years, and it is not meant to be used solely because of its ease of application. The double-extension method, which is more accurate, should be demonstrated to be impractical before the link-chain method is invoked as an alternative.

Indexing. The last major alternative available for computing the dollar-value LIFO inventory is indexing. These indexing methods can basically be broken down into two types: (1) an internal index, and (2) an external index.

The **internal index** is merely a variation of the double-extension method. A representative sample (or some other statistical method) of the inventory will be double extended; the representative index computed from the sample is then used to restate the inventory to base-year cost and to value the new layer.

The **external index** method involves using indices published by governmental or private sources and applying the index chosen to the inventory figures. Because of this method's complexity and limited applicability, and due to the fact that local taxing authorities or other official agencies would have to endorse one or more indices for such use, this application is not discussed further.

The methods described for the application of LIFO, as noted above, have been based on tax rules rather than on financial accounting pronouncements. GAAP has tended to permit the use of LIFO, when it has, because it had earlier been endorsed by the taxing or other relevant authorities, not because of the theoretical validity of the technique, although it can be argued that LIFO does more accurately measure periodic income. In recognition of the lack of authoritative accounting guidelines in the implementation of LIFO in the United States, for example, the AICPA prepared an issues paper on this topic. This paper, *Identification and Discussion of Certain Financial Accounting and Reporting Issues Concerning LIFO Inventories*, described numerous accounting problems in the use of LIFO and includes advisory conclusions for these problems. Because of the possible applicability of the guidance in this paper to those entities that choose to use the available alternative method under IAS 2, selected sections of it are detailed in the appendix to this chapter.

Interim Treatment of LIFO

Interim financial reporting has not received formal attention from the international GAAP standard setters, although the topic is on the IASC draft work plan, with a projected date of mid-1997 for a discussion document. Under US GAAP, however, it is well established that interim periods are not equivalent to full fiscal periods, but rather, should be viewed as integral parts of the full period of which they will form a part. Thus, it is not expected that inventories will be taken at the end of each interim period, and estimation techniques such as the gross profit method can be used instead.

While for most issues of revenue or expense it is largely academic whether the interim period is treated as a stand-alone period or as a part of the fiscal year to which it belongs (as accrual accounting principles will dictate the same result in either case), entities using the LIFO inventory method will almost always be affected. The most commonly encountered issue is that of temporary liquidations of inventories; while these must be dealt with as permanent declines if occurring at year end, at interim dates these may be accounted for as temporary (assuming that this is supportable by the relevant facts and circumstances), with a "reserve" established for replenishment, thereby avoiding absorbing old, lower costs into cost of sales.

Although there are other measurement issues under GAAP that necessitate an annual perspective (such as the need to provide income taxes based on the entity's expected effective tax rate over the full year), inventory costing, particularly under LIFO, is probably the most notable interim reporting problem. The reason for permitting the use of a "reserve" is that LIFO was conceived of as an annual measurement strategy. US and other tax laws, where they permit LIFO inventory accounting, are strictly annual measures. Were companies permitted to treat LIFO measures as applicable to shorter reporting periods, depending on each company's possibly unique decisions regarding frequency of reporting, the results would not conform to the annual tax computations. This emphasizes the fact that LIFO has little conceptual validity and probably would not exist under GAAP were it not a popular tax strategy.

Comparison of Cost Assumptions

Of the three basic cost flow assumptions, LIFO and FIFO produce the most extreme results, with results using the weighted-average method generally falling somewhere in between. The selection of one of these methods involves a detailed analysis, including a determination of the organization's objectives and the current and future economic state.

As mentioned above, in periods of rising prices the LIFO method is generally thought best to fulfill the objective of providing the clearest measure of periodic income. It does not provide an accurate estimate of the inventory value in an inflationary environment; however, this can usually be overcome by the issuance of supplementary fair value data. In periods of rising prices, a prudent business should use the LIFO method because it will result in a decrease in the current tax liability when compared to other alternatives, for those jurisdictions where the use of LIFO is acceptable. Yet in a deflationary period, the opposite is true.

FIFO is a balance-sheet-oriented costing method, as it gives the most accurate estimate of the current value of the inventory account during periods of changing prices. In periods of rising prices, the FIFO method will result in higher taxes than the other alternatives, while in a deflationary period FIFO provides for a reduced tax burden. However, a major advantage of the FIFO method is that it is not subject to all the regulations and requirements of the tax codes as LIFO typically is.

The average methods do not provide an estimate of current cost information on either the balance sheet or income statement. The average method will not serve to minimize the tax burden, nor will it result in the highest burden among the various alternatives.

Although price trends and underlying objectives are important in the selection of a cost flow assumption, other considerations, such as the risk of LIFO liquidations, cash flow, and capital maintenance, are also important but were not mentioned above.

Net Realizable Value

As stated in IAS 2

Net realizable value is the estimated selling price in the ordinary course of business less the estimated costs of completion and the estimated costs necessary to make the sale.

The utility of an item of inventory is limited to the amount to be realized from its ultimate sale; where the item's recorded cost exceeds this amount, GAAP requires that a loss be recognized for the difference. The logic for this requirement is twofold: first, assets (in particular, current assets such as inventory) should not be reported at amounts that exceed net realizable value; and second, any decline in value in a period should be reported in that period's results of operations in order to achieve proper matching with current period's revenues. Were the inventory to be carried forward at an amount in excess of net realizable value, the loss would be recognized on the ultimate sale in a subsequent period. This would mean that a loss incurred in one period, when the value decline occurred, would have been deferred to a different period, which would clearly be inconsistent with several key accounting concepts, including conservatism.

IAS 2 states that estimates of net realizable value should be applied on an item-by-item basis in most instances, although it makes an exception for those situations where there are groups of related products or similar items that can be properly valued in the aggregate. As a general principle, item-by-item comparisons of cost to net realizable value are required, lest unrealized "gains" on some items (i.e., where the net realizable values exceed historical costs) offset the unrealized losses on other items, thereby reducing the net loss to be recognized. Since recognition of unrealized gains in earnings is generally proscribed under GAAP, evaluation of inventory declines on a grouped basis would be an indirect or "back door" mechanism to recognize gains that should not be given such recognition. Accordingly, the basic requirement is to apply the net realizable value tests on an individual item basis.

In many jurisdictions, the term **lower of cost or market** is used, as contrasted to IAS 2's **lower of cost or net realizable value**. As a practical matter, this difference in terminology will have little or no impact, since **market** is usually defined operationally as being replacement cost or net realizable value. However, one important distinction is that **market** is usually defined as a conditional term that contemplates a range of values, based not only on the costs to complete and sell an item, but also, in some circumstances, on the expected or normal profit to be earned on the sale. Since IAS 2 provides only general guidance concerning the determination of net realizable value, it will be useful to look to other existing standards for insight into how these measures are to be developed in a practical situation.

Measuring the decline to net realizable value. The IAS 2 definition of net realizable value makes explicit reference only to "costs of completion and costs incurred in order to make the sale." However, as illustrated below, if expected or normal profit margins on sales of inventory items are not taken into account, excessive profits or losses might be recognized in future periods, due to an incomplete application of the net realizable value concept.

The application of these principles is illustrated in the following example. In this example, replacement cost will be used as the primary operational definition of inventory value when that amount is lower than carrying value determined by historical cost. Replacement cost is a valid measure of the future utility of the inventory item since increases or decreases in the purchase price generally foreshadow related increases or decreases in the selling price. Assume the following information for products A, B, C, D, and E:

Item	Cost	Replacement cost	Est. selling price	Cost to complete	Normal profit percentage
A	$2.00	$1.80	$ 2.50	$0.50	24%
B	4.00	1.60	4.00	0.80	24%
C	6.00	6.60	10.00	1.00	18%
D	5.00	4.75	6.00	2.00	20%
E	1.00	1.05	1.20	0.25	12.5%

Consider item A: The net realizable value defined in accordance with IAS 2 is $2.50 – 0.50 = $2.00 (estimated selling price less costs to complete and sell). As it happens, this is exactly equal to historical cost, suggesting that there would be no adjustment required. However, if no adjustment is recorded, the profit realized upon the sale next period will be $2.50 – 2.00 – 0.50 = $0, which would be an unnaturally low net margin given the historical experience of a 24% margin. To preserve the normal margin, which would amount to $0.60 ($2.50 x 24%), the inventory would have to be written down to $1.40 ($2.50 – 0.50 – 0.60). However, the actual cost to replace the item in inventory is known to be $1.80, which suggests that the normal margin of 24% cannot be replicated under current conditions.

The foregoing explains why some standards setters and accounting theoreticians (but it should be stressed, not the IASC) have concluded that inventory should be reported at the lower of cost or market, where **market** is defined as replacement cost subject to ceiling and floor values; where **ceiling** is defined as net realizable value (NRV), and **floor** as the NRV minus the normal profit margin. Using this approach (which is the standard in the United States, Belgium, Canada, Germany, Italy, the Netherlands, and Spain, among other jurisdictions), the amount of profit to be recognized in the period of later sale, absent other changes in the marketplace after the reporting date, will not be abnormally high or low.

To continue with this example, the data in the foregoing table are used to compute market values consistent with the definition set forth earlier. Note that the primary measure in all cases is replacement cost; if this falls between the ceiling and the floor, it becomes the measure of market, which is then compared to historical cost; the lower of cost or market is then used to actually value the inventory item. If the replacement cost exceeds the ceiling value (as for items D and E), the ceiling value becomes the market next to be compared to historical cost. On the other hand, if replacement cost is lower than the floor (as for items B and C), the floor is used as the market value to be compared next to the historical cost.

Determination of Net Realizable Value

Item	Cost	Replacement cost	NRV (ceiling)	NRV less profit (floor)	Market	LCM
A	$2.00	$1.80	$2.00	$1.40	$1.80	$1.80
B	4.00	1.60	3.20	2.24	2.24	2.24
C	6.00	6.60	9.00	7.20	7.20	6.00
D	5.00	4.75	4.00	2.80	4.00	4.00
E	1.00	1.05	0.95	0.80	0.95	0.95

Note that, under a strict reading of IAS 2, NRV would be compared directly to historical cost; the other values in the above table would not be given any consideration. However, it is the authors' opinion that there is sufficient flexibility in IAS 2 to permit some application of the principle of lower of cost or market as discussed above. If a strict application of the net realizable value rule were insisted upon, in contrast, item A would be valued at $2.00 instead of $1.80, resulting in a zero profit upon sale; and item B would be valued at $3.20 instead of $2.24, also resulting in a zero profit upon ultimate disposition. In general, the impact of using net realizable value, rather than market, would be to preclude preservation of some (if not a normal amount of) profit upon later sale of the item.

Recoveries of previously recognized losses. IAS 2 stipulates that a new assessment of net realizable value should be made in each subsequent period; when the reason for a previous write-down no longer exists (i.e., when net realizable value has improved), it should be reversed. Since the write-down was taken into income, the reversal should also be reflected in earnings.

Other Valuation Methods

There are instances in which an accountant must estimate the value of inventories. Whether for interim financial statements or as a check against perpetual records, the need for an inventory valuation without an actual physical count is required. Some of the methods used, which are discussed below, are the retail method, the LIFO retail method, and the gross profit method.

Retail method. IAS 2 notes that the retail method may be used by certain industry groups but does not provide details on how to employ this method, nor does it address the many variations of the technique. The conventional retail method is used by retailers as a method to estimate the cost of their ending inventory. The retailer can either take a physical inventory at retail prices or estimate ending retail inventory and then use the cost-to-retail ratio derived under this method to convert the ending inventory at retail to its estimated cost. This eliminates the process of going back to original invoices or other documents to determine the original cost for each inventoriable item. The retail method can be used under any of the three cost flow assumptions discussed earlier: FIFO, LIFO, or average cost. As with ordinary FIFO or average cost, the LCM rule can also be applied to the retail method when either one of these two cost assumptions is used.

The key to applying the retail method is determining the cost-to-retail ratio. The calculation of this number varies depending on the cost flow assumption selected. Essentially, the cost-to-retail ratio provides a relationship between the cost of goods available for sale and the retail price of these goods. This ratio is used to convert the ending retail inventory back to cost. Computation of the cost-to-retail ratio for each of the available methods is described below. The use of the LIFO cost flow assumption with this method is discussed in the next section and, therefore, is not addressed in this listing.

1. **FIFO cost**--The concept of FIFO indicates that the ending inventory is made up of the latest purchases; therefore, beginning inventory is excluded from computation of the cost-to-retail ratio, and the computation becomes net purchases divided by their retail value adjusted for both net markups and net markdowns.

2. **FIFO (using a lower of cost or market approach)**--The computation is basically the same as FIFO cost except that markdowns are excluded from the computation of the cost-to-retail ratio.

3. **Average cost**--Average cost assumes that ending inventory consists of all goods available for sale. Therefore, the cost-to-retail ratio is computed by dividing the cost of goods available for sale (Beginning inventory + Net purchases) by the retail value of these goods adjusted for both net markups and net markdowns.

4. **Average cost (using a lower of cost or market approach)**--This is computed in the same manner as average cost except that markdowns are excluded for the calculation of the cost-to-retail ratio.

A simple example illustrates the computation of the cost-to-retail ratio under both the FIFO cost and average cost methods in a situation where no markups or markdowns exist.

| | *FIFO cost* | | *Average cost* | |
	Cost	*Retail*	*Cost*	*Retail*
Beginning inventory	$100,000	$ 200,000	$100,000	$ 200,000
Net purchases	500,000	800,000	500,000	800,000
Total goods available for sale	$600,000	1,000,000	$600,000	1,000,000
Sales at retail		(800,000)		(800,000)
Ending inventory at retail		$ 200,000		$ 200,000
Cost-to-retail ratio	$\frac{500,000}{800,000} =$ 62.5%		$\frac{600,000}{1,000,000} =$ 60%	
Ending inventory at cost				
200,000 x 0.625		$ 125,000		
200,000 x 0.60				$ 120,000

Note that the only difference in the two examples is the numbers used to calculate the cost-to-retail ratio.

As shown above, the lower of cost or market aspect of the retail method is a result of the treatment of net markups and net markdowns. **Net markups** (markups less markup cancellations) are net increases above the original retail price, which are generally caused by changes in supply and demand. **Net markdowns** (markdowns less markdown cancellations) are net decreases below the original retail price. An approximation of lower of cost or market is achieved by including net markups but excluding net markdowns from the cost-to-retail ratio.

To understand this approximation, assume that a toy is purchased for $6 and the retail price is set at $10. It is later marked down to $8. A cost-to-retail ratio including markdowns would be $6 divided by $8 or 75%, and ending inventory would be valued at $8 times 75%, or $6 (original cost). A cost-to-retail ratio excluding markdowns would be $6 divided by $10 or 60%, and ending inventory would be valued at $8 times 60%, or $4.80 (on a lower of cost or market basis). The write-down to $4.80 reflects the loss in utility that is evidenced by the reduced retail price.

The application of the lower of cost or market rule is illustrated for both the FIFO and average cost methods in the example below. Remember, if the markups and markdowns below had been included in the preceding example, **both** would have been included in the cost-to-retail ratio.

	FIFO cost (LCM)		*Average cost (LCM)*	
	Cost	*Retail*	*Cost*	*Retail*
Beginning inventory	$100,000	$ 200,000	$100,000	$ 200,000
Net purchases	500,000	800,000	500,000	800,000
Net markups	--	250,000	--	250,000
Total goods available for sale	$600,000	1,250,000	$600,000	1,250,000
Net markdowns		(50,000)		(50,000)
Sales at retail		(800,000)		(800,000)
Ending inventory at retail		$ 400,000		$ 400,000
Cost-to-retail ratio	$\frac{500,000}{1,050,000} =$	47.6%	$\frac{600,000}{1,250,000} =$	48%

Ending inventory at cost

400,000 x 0.476	$ 190,400	
400,000 x 0.48		$ 192,000

Notice that under the FIFO (LCM) method all of the markups are considered attributable to the current period purchases. Although this is not necessarily accurate, it provides the most conservative estimate of the ending inventory.

There are a number of additional inventory topics and issues that affect the computation of the cost-to-retail ratio and, therefore, deserve some discussion. Purchase discounts and freight affect only the cost column in this computation. The sales figure that is subtracted from the adjusted cost of goods available for sale in the retail column must be gross sales after adjustment for sales returns. If sales are recorded at gross, deduct the gross sales figure. If sales are recorded at net, both the recorded sales and sales discount must be deducted to give the same effect as deducting gross sales (i.e., sales discounts are not included in the computation). Normal spoilage is generally allowed for in the firm's pricing policies, and for this reason it is deducted from the retail column after calculation of the cost-to-retail ratio. Abnormal spoilage, on the other hand, should be deducted from **both** the cost and retail columns **before** the cost-to-retail calculation, as it could distort the ratio. It is then generally reported as a loss separate from the cost of goods sold section. Abnormal spoilage is generally considered to arise from a major theft or casualty, while normal spoilage is usually due to shrinkage or breakage. These determinations and their treatments will vary depending on the firm's policies.

When applying the retail method, separate computations should be made for any departments that experience significantly higher or lower profit margins. Distortions arise in the retail method when a department sells goods with varying margins in a proportion different from that purchased, in which case the cost-to-retail percentage would not be representative of the mix of goods in ending inventory. Also, manipulations of income are possible by planning the timing of markups and markdowns.

The retail method is an acceptable method of valuing inventories for tax purposes in some, but not all, jurisdictions. The foregoing examples are not meant to imply that the method would be usable in any given jurisdiction; readers should ascertain whether or not it can be used.

LIFO retail method. As with other LIFO concepts, tax regulations are the governing force behind the LIFO retail method. Readers must ascertain whether regulations in their local jurisdictions permit application of this or any similar method.

The steps used in computing the value of ending inventory under the LIFO retail method are listed below and then applied to an example for illustrative purposes.

1. Calculate (or select) the current year conversion price index. Recall that in the base year this index will be 1.00.
2. Calculate the value of the ending inventory at both cost and retail. Remember, as with other LIFO methods, tax regulations do not permit the use of LCM, so both markups and markdowns are included in computation of the cost-to-retail ratio. However, the beginning inventory is excluded from goods available for sale at cost and at retail.
3. Restate the ending inventory at retail to base-year retail. This is accomplished by dividing the current ending inventory at retail by the current year index determined in step 1.
4. Layers are then treated in the same fashion as they were for the dollar-value LIFO example presented earlier. If the ending inventory restated to base-year retail exceeds the previous year's amount at base-year retail, a new layer is established.

5. The computation of LIFO cost is the last step and requires multiplying each layer at base-year retail by the appropriate price index and multiplying this product by the cost-to-retail ratio in order to arrive at the LIFO cost for each layer.

The following example illustrates a 2-year period to which the LIFO retail method is applied. The first period represents the first year of operations for the organization and, thus, is its base year.

Year 1

Step 1 -- Because this is the base year, there is no need to compute an index, as it will always be 1.00.

Step 2 --

	Cost	Retail
Beginning inventory	$ --	$ --
Purchases	582,400	988,600
Markups	--	164,400
Markdowns	--	(113,000)
Subtotal	$582,400	$1,040,000
Total goods available for sale		$1,040,000
Sales at retail		840,000
Ending year 1 inventory at retail		$ 200,000

Cost-to-retail index 582,400/1,040,000 = 56%
Ending inventory at cost
$200,000 x 0.56 $112,000

Step 3 -- Because this is the base year, the restatement to base-year cost is not necessary; however, the computation would be

$200,000/1.00 = $200,000.

Steps 4

and 5 -- The determination of layers is again unnecessary in the base year; however, the computation would take the following format.

	Ending inventory at base-year retail	*Conversion price index*	*Cost-to-retail ratio*	*LIFO cost*
Base year ($200,000/1.00)	$200,000	1.00	0.56	$112,000

Year 2

Step 1 -- The assumption is made that the computation of an internal index yields a result of 1.12 (obtained by double extending a representative sample).

Step 2 --

	Cost	Retail
Beginning inventory	$112,000	$ 200,000
Purchases	716,300	1,168,500
Markups	--	87,500
Markdowns	--	(21,000)
Subtotal	$716,300	$1,235,000

Total goods available for sale	$1,435,000
Sales at retail	1,171,800
Ending year 2 inventory at retail	$ 263,200

Cost-to-retail index   716,300/1,235,000 = 58%

Step 3 -- The restatement of ending inventory at current year retail to base-year retail is done using the index computed in step 1. In this case it is $263,200/1.12 = $235,000.

Steps 4
and 5 -- We know that there is a LIFO layer in year 2 because the $235,000 inventory at base-year retail exceeds the year 1 amount of $200,000.

The computation of the LIFO cost for each layer is shown below.

	Ending inventory at base-year retail	*Conversion price index*	*Cost-to-retail ratio*	*LIFO cost*
Base year				
($200,000/1.00)	$200,000	1.00	0.56	$112,000
Year 2 layer	35,000	1.12	0.58	22,736
	$235,000			
Ending year 2 inventory at LIFO cost				$134,736

The treatment of subsequent increments and decrements is the same for this method as it is for the regular dollar-value method.

Gross profit method. The gross profit method is used to estimate ending inventory when a physical count is not possible or feasible. It can also be used to evaluate the reasonableness of a given inventory amount. The cost of goods available for sale is compared with the estimated cost of goods sold. For example, assume the following data:

Beginning inventory	$125,000
Net purchases	450,000
Sales	600,000
Estimated gross profit	32%

Ending inventory is then estimated as follows:

Beginning inventory	$125,000
Net purchases	450,000
Cost of goods available for sale	575,000
Cost of goods sold [$600,000 – (32% x $600,000)] or (68% x $600,000)	408,000
Estimated ending inventory	$167,000

The gross profit method is used for interim reporting estimates, analyses by auditors, and estimates of inventory lost in fires or other catastrophes. The method is generally not acceptable for either tax or annual financial reporting purposes (and is not in conformity with IAS 2). Thus, its major purposes are for internal and interim reporting.

Other Cost Topics

Base stock. The base stock method assumes that a certain level of inventory investment is necessary for normal business activities and is, therefore, permanent. The base stock inventory is carried at historical cost. Decreases in the base stock are considered temporary and are charged to cost of goods sold at replacement cost. Increases are carried at current year costs. The base stock approach is seldom used in practice and it is not allowed for tax purposes in many jurisdictions, and the LIFO method, which is more commonly permitted, gives similar results. Although the original IAS 2 permitted the base stock method, it has been proscribed by the revised IAS 2, which became effective for periods beginning in 1995.

Standard costs. Standard costs are predetermined unit costs used by many manufacturing firms for planning and control purposes. Standard costs are often incorporated into the accounts, and materials, work in process, and finished goods inventories are all carried on this basis of accounting. The use of standard costs in financial reporting is acceptable if adjustments are made periodically to reflect current conditions and if its use approximates one of the recognized cost flow assumptions.

Purchase commitments. Purchase commitments generally are not recorded in the accounts because they are executory in nature. However, footnote disclosure is required for firm purchase commitments that are material in amount in accordance with IAS 37, which recently superseded the portion of IAS 10 that dealt with contingencies.

Furthermore, and in conformity with the same standard, if losses have been incurred in connection with firm purchase commitments, the losses must be accrued if probable and reasonably estimable. Note that this results in recognition of loss before the asset is recognized on the books. Contingencies are discussed in detail in Chapter 12.

Inventories valued at selling price. In exceptional cases, inventories may be reported at sales price less disposal costs. Such treatment is justified when cost is difficult to determine, quoted market prices are available, marketability is assured, and units are interchangeable. IAS 2 stipulates that producers' inventories of livestock, agricultural and forest products, and mineral ores, to the extent that they are measured at net realizable value in accordance with well established practices, are to be valued in this manner. When inventory is valued above cost, revenue is recognized before the point of sale; full disclosure in the financial statements would, of course, be required.

Use of more than one cost method. IAS 2 did not address the question of whether a single reporting entity would be justified in using a multiplicity of costing methods for different components of its inventory. In practice, many reporting enterprises have used different methods; for example, the uses of LIFO for raw materials and FIFO for work in process and finished goods inventories are fairly common. In other cases, conglomerate entities have certain operations or divisions which use one method, and others which employ alternative costing formulae.

While the issue was not raised, logic suggests that if a variety of costing methods were employed for essentially similar inventories by a single entity, it would make meaningful interpretation of the resulting financial statements more difficult for users. Accordingly, the newly constituted Standing Interpretations Committee (SIC) of the IASC has, as its maiden effort, addressed this matter. In reaching its conclusion that similar inventories must be costed by the same method, it weighed the guidance already contained in IAS 27 (on consolidated financial reporting) and IAS 16 (on property, plant, and equipment).

The existing standard on consolidations provides that uniform accounting policies are to be used for like transactions and other events in similar circumstances, The logic is to avoid adding apples and oranges to develop consolidated financial statements which are unintelligible as a consequence. The IASC's *Framework for the Preparation and Presentation of Financial Statements* similarly expresses the notion that measurement of like transactions and other events should be carried out in a consistent manner throughout an entity and over the time of its ongoing existence, for purposes of both separate and consolidated financial reporting.

IAS 16 permits the use of different methods of measurement for different classes of property and equipment. Thus, for example, buildings might be depreciated by the straight line method, and equipment may be depreciated using an accelerated method, it can be justified based on patterns of usage and other factors, such as likely incidence of repair and maintenance costs. However, the use of different methods for similar assets in similar modes of use would not be consistent with IAS.

Taking these matters into account, the logical conclusion would be that inventories used in similar fashion by a given entity, even differently sited or managed operations of a given enterprise, should be costed by the same formula or method. The first interpretative release by the IASC's Standing Interpretations Committee has endorsed this position. In SIC 1, it has held that, regarding the possible use of different cost formulae (e.g., LIFO versus FIFO) for different types of inventories, for inventories having different natures and uses, differing cost formulae could be justified. It was noted, however, that differences in geographical locations are not sufficient to warrant using different costing methods. Inventories having the same characteristics should, on the other hand, be valued by means of the same cost formulae. Disclosure should be made of the accounting methods used in any event.

Disclosure Requirements

IAS 2 sets forth certain disclosure requirements relative to inventory accounting methods employed by the entity preparing the financial statements. According to this standard, the following must be disclosed:

1. The accounting policies adopted in measuring inventories, including the costing methods (e.g., FIFO, weighted-average, or LIFO) employed
2. The total carrying amount of inventories and the carrying amount in classifications appropriate to the enterprise

3. The carrying amount of inventories carried at net realizable value
4. The amount of any reversal of any previous write-down that is recognized in earnings for the period
5. The circumstances or events that led to the reversal of a write-down of inventories to net realizable value
6. The carrying amount of inventories pledged as security for liabilities

The type of information to be provided concerning inventories held in different classifications is somewhat flexible, but traditional classifications, such as raw materials, work in progress, finished goods, and supplies, should normally be employed. In the case of service providers, inventories (which are really akin to unbilled receivables) can be described as work in progress.

When the cost of inventories is determined in accordance with the LIFO method, which is an available alternative under IAS 2, the financial statements must disclose the difference between the amount of inventories shown on the balance sheet and either (1) the cost determined in accordance with either the FIFO or weighted-average costing methods, subject to the net realizable value rule, or (2) the lower of current (i.e., replacement) cost as of the balance sheet date or net realizable value.

In addition to the foregoing, the financial statements should disclose either the cost of inventories recognized as an expense during the period (i.e., reported as cost of sales or included in other expense categories), or the operating costs, applicable to revenues, recognized as an expense during the period, categorized by their respective natures.

Costs of inventories recognized as expense includes, in addition to the costs inventoried previously and attaching to goods sold currently, the excess overhead costs charged to expense for the period because, under the standard, they could not be deferred to future periods.

7 REVENUE RECOGNITION, INCLUDING CONSTRUCTION CONTRACT ACCOUNTING

REVENUE RECOGNITION

PERSPECTIVE AND ISSUES

IAS 18, *Revenue*, sets forth the principles which govern the recognition of revenue. The principal issue in revenue accounting is the determination of the point in time at which revenue is to be formally recognized. According to the IASC's *Framework*, revenue is to be recognized when **both** of the following conditions are met:

- When it is probable that future economic benefits will flow to the enterprise; and
- When such benefits can be measured reliably.

IAS 18 addresses the recognition of revenue from the sale of goods, from the rendering of services, and from the use by others of the enterprise's assets. In addition to setting forth criteria for the measurement of revenue, the standard, through examples contained in its appendix, provides practical guidance on the application of these criteria.

IAS 18, *Revenue Recognition*, the predecessor standard to the current IAS 18, was approved in 1982. It was among the standards to be revised in 1993 as part of the Comparability and Improvements Project. A very important revision to the earlier standard was the elimination of the ability to elect the "completed contract method" for the recognition of revenue from the rendering of services. This revision was consistent with a concurrent change made to IAS 11, which applies only to construction contracts. The current version of IAS 18 became operative for periods beginning on or after January 1, 1995.

Sources of IAS
IASC's *Framework for Preparation and Presentation of Financial Statements*
IAS 18 (revised 1993), *Revenue*

DEFINITIONS OF TERMS

Fair value. An amount for which an asset could be exchanged, or a liability settled, between knowledgeable, willing parties in an arm's-length transaction.

Ordinary activities. Those activities of an enterprise which it undertakes as part of its business and such related activities in which the enterprise engages in furtherance of, incidental to, or arising from those activities.

Revenue. Gross inflow of economic benefits resulting from an enterprise's ordinary activities is considered "revenue," provided those inflows result in increases in equity, other than increases relating to contributions from owners or equity participants. Revenue refers to the gross amount (of revenue) and excludes amounts collected on behalf of third parties.

CONCEPTS, RULES, AND EXAMPLES

Revenue. The IASC's *Framework* defines "income" to include both revenue and gains. IAS 18 deals only with revenue. Revenue is defined as income arising from the ordinary activities of an enterprise and may be referred to by a variety of names including sales, fees, interest, dividends and royalties. Revenue encompasses only the gross inflow of economic benefits received or receivable by the enterprise, on its own account. This implies that amounts collected on behalf of others--such as in the case of sales tax or value added tax, which also flow to the enterprise along with the revenue from sales--do not qualify as revenue. Thus, these other collections should not be included in an entity's reported revenue. Put another way, gross revenue from sales should be shown net of amounts collected on behalf of third parties.

Similarly, in an agency relationship the amounts collected on behalf of the principal is not regarded as revenue for the agent. Instead, the commission earned on such collections qualifies as revenue of the agent. For example, in the case of a travel agency, the collections from ticket sales do not qualify as revenue or income from its ordinary activities. Instead, it will be the commission on the tickets sold by the travel agency that will constitute that entity's gross revenue.

Scope of the standard. This standard applies to the accounting for revenue arising from

- The sale of goods;
- The rendering of services; and
- The use of the enterprise's assets by others, yielding (for the enterprise) interest, dividends and royalties.

A sale of goods encompasses **both** goods produced by the enterprise for sale to others and goods purchased for resale by the enterprise. The rendering of services involves the performance by the enterprise of an agreed-upon task, based on a contract, over a contractually agreed period of time.

The use of the enterprise's assets by others gives rise to revenue for the enterprise in the form of

- **Interest** which is a charge for the use of cash and cash equivalent or amounts due to the enterprise;
- **Royalties** which are charges for the use of long-term assets of the enterprise such as patents or trademarks owned by the enterprise; and
- **Dividends** which are distributions of profit to the holders of equity investments in the share capital of other enterprises.

The standard **does not** apply to revenue arising from

- Lease agreements which are covered by IAS 17;
- Dividends arising from investments in associates which are accounted for using the equity method, which are dealt with in IAS 28;
- Insurance contracts of insurance enterprises, a topic presently not covered by any IAS although this is on the IASC's agenda for development of a standard in future;
- Changes in fair values of financial instruments, which is addressed by IAS 39;
- Natural increases in herds, agriculture and forest products, a subject currently in exposure draft stage and soon to be promulgated as a standard;
- The extraction of mineral ores, presently not covered by any IAS but which is also on the agenda of the IASC for development of a standard in the future; and
- Changes in the value of other current assets.

Measurement of revenue. The quantum of revenue to be recognized is usually dependent upon the terms of the contract between the enterprise and the buyer of goods, the recipient of the services, or the users of the assets of the enterprise.

Revenue should be measured at the fair value of the consideration received or receivable, net of any trade discounts and volume rebates allowed by the enterprise.

When the inflow of the consideration, which is usually in the form of cash or cash equivalents, is deferred, the fair value of the consideration will be an amount lower than the nominal value of the consideration. The difference between the fair value and the nominal value of the consideration, which represents the time value of money, is recognized as interest revenue.

When the enterprise offers interest-free extended credit to the buyer or accepts a promissory note from the buyer (as consideration) which bears either no interest or a below-market interest rate, such an arrangement would be construed as a financing transaction. In such a case the fair value of the consideration is ascertained by discounting the future inflows using an imputed rate of interest. The imputed rate of interest is either "the prevailing rate of interest for a similar instrument of an issuer with a similar credit rating, or a rate of interest that discounts the nominal amount of the instrument to the current cash sales price of the goods or services." (IAS 18, Paragraph 11)

To illustrate this point, let us consider the following example:

> *Hero International is a car dealership that is known to offer excellent packages for all new models of Japanese cars. Currently, it is advertising on the television that there is a special offer for all Year 2000 models of a certain make. The offer is valid for all purchases made on or before September 30, 1999. The special offer deal is either a cash payment in full of $20,000 or a zero down payment with extended credit terms of 2 years--24 monthly installments of $1,000 each. Thus, anyone opting for the extended credit terms would pay $24,000 in total.*
>
> *Since there is a difference of $4,000 between the cash price of $20,000 and the total amount payable if the car is paid for in 24 installments of $ 1,000 each, this arrangement is effectively a financing transaction (and of course a sale transaction as well). The cash price of $20,000 would be regarded as the amount of consideration attributable to the sale of the car. The difference between the cash price and the aggregate amount payable in monthly installments is interest revenue and is to be recognized over the period of 2 years on a time proportion basis (using the effective interest method).*

Exchanges of similar and dissimilar goods and services. When goods or services are exchanged or swapped for **similar** goods or services, the earning process is not considered to be complete. Thus the exchange is not regarded as a transaction that generates revenue. Such exchanges are common in certain commodity industries, such as oil or milk industries, where suppliers usually swap inventories in various locations in order to meet geographically diverse demand on a timely basis.

When goods or services of a **dissimilar** nature are swapped, the earning process is considered to be complete, and thus the exchange is regarded as a transaction that generates revenue. The revenue thus generated is measured at the fair value of the goods or services received or receivable. If in this process cash or cash equivalents are also transferred, then the fair value should be adjusted by the amount of cash or cash equivalents (commonly referred to as "boot") transferred. In certain cases, the fair value of the goods or services received cannot be measured reliably. Under such circumstances, fair value of goods or services given up, adjusted by the amount of boot transferred, is the measure of revenue to be recognized. Barter arrangements are examples of such exchanges involving goods that are dissimilar in nature.

Identification of the transaction. While setting out clearly the criteria for the recognition of revenue under three categories--sale of goods, rendering of services and use of the enterprise's assets by others--the standard clarifies that these should be applied separately to each transaction. In other words, the recognition criteria should be applied to the separately identifiable components of a single transaction consistent with the principle of "substance over form."

For example, a washing machine is sold with an after-sale service warranty. The selling price includes a separately identifiable portion attributable to the after-sale service warranty. In such a case, the standard requires that the selling price of the washing machine should be apportioned between the two separately identifiable components and each one recognized according to an appropriate recognition criterion. Thus, the portion of the selling price attributable to the after-sales warranty should be deferred and recognized over the period during which the service is performed. The remaining selling price should be recognized immediately if the recognition criteria for revenue from sale of goods (explained below) are satisfied.

Similarly, the recognition criteria are to be applied to two or more separate transactions together when they are connected or linked in such a way that the commercial effect (or "substance over form") cannot be understood without considering the series of transactions as a whole. For example, company X sells a ship to company Y and later enters into a separate contract with company Y to repurchase the same ship from it. In this case the two transactions need to be considered together in order to ascertain whether or not revenue is to be recognized.

Revenue recognition criteria. According to the IASC's *Framework*, revenue is to be recognized when it is probable that future economic benefits will flow to the enterprise and reliable measurement of the quantum of revenue is possible. Based on these fundamental tenets of revenue recognition laid down in the IASC's *Framework*, IAS 18 establishes criteria for recognition of revenue from three categories of transactions--the sale of goods, the rendering of services, and the use by others of the enterprise's assets. In the case of the first two categories of transactions producing revenue, the standard prescribes certain additional criteria for recognition of revenue. In the case of revenue from the use by others of the enterprise's assets, the standard does not overtly prescribe additional criteria, but it does provide guidance on the bases to be adopted in revenue recognition from this source. This may, in a way, be construed as an additional criterion for revenue recognition from this source of revenue.

Revenue recognition from the sale of goods. Revenue from the sale of goods should be recognized if the **all** of the five conditions mentioned below are met.

- The enterprise has transferred significant risks and rewards of ownership of the goods to the buyer;
- The enterprise does not retain **either** continuing managerial involvement (akin to that usually associated with ownership) **or** effective control over the goods sold;
- The quantum of revenue to be recognized can be measured reliably;
- The probability that economic benefits related to the transaction will flow to the enterprise exists; and
- The costs incurred or to be incurred in respect of the transaction can be measured reliably.

The determination of the point in time when an enterprise is considered to have transferred the significant risks and rewards of ownership in goods to the buyer is critical to the recognition of revenue from the sale of goods. If upon examination of the circumstances of the transfer of risks and rewards of ownership by the enterprise it is determined that the enterprise could still be considered as having retained significant risks and rewards of ownership, the transaction could not be regarded as a sale.

Some examples of situations illustrated by the standard in which an enterprise may be considered to have retained significant risks and rewards of ownership, and thus revenue is not recognized, are set out below.

- A contract for the sale of an oil refinery stipulates that installation of the refinery is an integral and a significant part of the contract. Therefore, until the refinery is completely installed by the enterprise that sold it, the sale would not be regarded as complete. In other words, until the completion of the installation, the enterprise that sold the refinery would still be regarded as the effective owner of the refinery even if the refinery has already been delivered to the buyer. Accordingly, revenue will not be recognized by the enterprise until it completes the installation of the refinery.
- Goods are sold on approval, whereby the buyer has negotiated a limited right of return. Since there is a possibility that the buyer may return the goods, revenue is not recognized until the shipment has been formally accepted by the buyer, or the goods have been delivered as per the terms of the contract, and the time stipulated in the contract for rejection has expired.
- In the case of "layaway sales," under terms of which the goods are delivered only when the buyer makes the final payment in a series of installments, revenue is not recognized until the last and final payment is received by the enterprise. Upon receipt of the final installment, the goods are delivered to the buyer and revenue is recognized. However, based upon experience, if it can reasonably be presumed that most such sales are consummated, revenue

may be recognized when a significant deposit is received from the buyer and goods are on hand, identified and ready for delivery to the buyer.

If the enterprise retains only an insignificant risk of ownership, the transaction is considered a sale and revenue is recognized. For example, a department store has a policy to offer refunds if a customer is not satisfied. Since the enterprise is only retaining an insignificant risk of ownership, revenue from sale of goods is recognized. However, since the enterprise's refund policy is publicly announced and thus would have created a valid expectation on the part of the customers that the store will honor its policy of refunds, a provision is also recognized for the best estimate of the costs of refunds, as explained in IAS 37.

Another important condition for recognition of revenue from the sale of goods is the existence of the probability that the economic benefits will flow to the enterprise. For example, an enterprise for several years has been exporting goods to a foreign country. In the current year, due to sudden restrictions by the foreign government on remittances of currency outside the country, collections from these sales were not made by the enterprise. As long as it is uncertain if these restrictions will be removed, revenue should not be recognized from these exports, since it may not be probable that economic benefits will flow to the enterprise. Once the restrictions are withdrawn and uncertainty is removed, revenue may be recognized.

Yet another important condition for recognition of revenue from the sale of goods relates to the reliability of measuring costs associated with the sale of goods. Thus, if expenses such as those relating to warranties or other postshipment costs cannot be measured reliably, then revenue from the sale of such goods should also not be recognized. This rule is based on the principle of matching of revenues and expenses.

Revenue recognition from the rendering of services. When the outcome of the transaction involving the rendering of services can be estimated reliably, revenue relating to that transaction should be recognized. The recognition of revenue should be with reference to the stage of completion of the transaction at the balance sheet date. The outcome of a transaction can be estimated reliably when each of the four conditions set out below are met.

- The amount of revenue can be measured reliably;
- The probability that the economic benefits related to this transaction will flow to the enterprise exists;
- The stage of completion of the transaction at the balance sheet date can be measured reliably; and
- The costs incurred for the transaction and the costs to complete the transaction can be measured reliably.

This manner of recognition of revenue, based on the stage of completion, is often referred to as the "percentage-of-completion" method. IAS 11, *Construction Contracts,* also mandates recognition of revenue on this basis. Revenue is recognized only when it is probable that the economic benefits related to the transaction will flow to the enterprise. However, if there is uncertainty with regard to the collectability of an amount already included in revenue, the uncollectable amount should be recognized as an expense instead of adjusting it against the amount of revenue originally recognized.

In order to be able to make reliable estimates, an enterprise should agree with the other party to the following:

- Each other's enforceable rights with respect to the services provided;
- The consideration to be exchanged; and
- The manner and terms of settlement.

It is important that the enterprise has in place an effective internal financial budgeting and reporting system. This ensures that the enterprise can promptly review and revise the estimates of revenue as the service is performed. It should however be noted that because there is a need for revisions it does not by itself make the estimate of the outcome of the transaction unreliable.

Progress payments and advances received from customers are not a measure of the stage of completion. The stage of completion of a transaction may be determined in a number of ways. Depending on the nature of the transaction, the method used may include

- Surveys of work performed;
- Services performed to date as a percentage of total services to be performed; or
- The proportion that costs incurred to date bear to the estimated total costs of the transaction. (Only costs that reflect services performed or to be performed are included in costs incurred to date or estimated total costs.)

In certain cases services are performed by an indeterminable number of acts over a specified period of time. Revenue in such a case should be recognized on a straight-line basis unless it is possible to estimate the stage of completion by some other method more reliably. Similarly when in a series of acts to be performed in rendering a service, a specific act is much more significant than other acts, the recognition is postponed until the significant act is performed.

During the early stages of the transaction it may not be possible to estimate the outcome of the transaction reliably. In all such cases, where the outcome of the transaction involving the rendering of services cannot be estimated reliably, revenue should be recognized only to the extent of the expenses recognized that are recoverable. However, in a later period when the uncertainty that precluded the reliable estimation of the outcome no longer exists, revenue is recognized as usual.

NOTE: The "percentage-of-completion" method is discussed in detail in the second part of this chapter. For numerical examples illustrating the method please refer to the second part of this chapter relating to "Construction Contracts."

Revenue recognition from interest, royalties, and dividends. Revenue arising from the use by others of the enterprise's assets yielding interest, royalties and dividends should be recognized when both of the following two conditions are met:

1. It is probable that the economic benefits relating to the transaction will flow to the enterprise; and
2. The amount of the revenue can be measured reliably.

The bases prescribed for the recognition of the revenue are the following:

a. In the case of interest--the time proportion basis that takes into account the effective yield on the assets;
b. In the case of royalties--the accrual basis in accordance with the substance of the relevant agreement; and
c. In the case of dividends--when the shareholder's right to receive payment is established.

According to IAS 18, para 31, "the effective yield on an asset is the rate of interest used to discount the stream of future cash receipts expected over the life of the asset to equate to the initial carrying amount of asset." Interest revenue includes the amount of amortization of any discount, premium or other difference between the initial carrying amount of a debt security and its amount at maturity.

When unpaid interest has accrued before an interest-bearing investment is purchased by the enterprise, the subsequent receipt of interest is to be allocated between preacquisition and postacquisition periods. Only the portion of interest that accrued subsequent to the acquisition by the enterprise is recognized as income. The remaining portion of interest which is attributable to the preacquisition period is treated as a reduction of the cost of the investment, as explained by IAS 25. Similarly, dividends on equity securities declared from preacquisition profits are treated as reduction of the cost of investment. If it is difficult to make such an allocation except on an arbitrary basis, dividends are recognized as revenue unless they clearly represent a recovery of part of the cost of the equity securities (IAS 18, para 32).

Disclosures. An enterprise should disclose the following:

- The accounting policies adopted for the recognition of revenue including the methods adopted to determine the stage of completion of transactions involving the rendering of services;
- The amount of each significant category of revenue recognized during the period including revenue arising from

  - The sale of goods;
  - The rendering of services; and
  - Interest, royalties, and dividends.

- The amounts revenue arising from exchanges of goods or services included in each significant category of revenue.

CONSTRUCTION CONTRACT ACCOUNTING

PERSPECTIVE AND ISSUES

Accounting for construction contracts involves questions as to when revenue should be recognized and how to measure the revenue to be recorded. The basic international accounting standard underlying these questions is covered in IAS 11 (revised 1993), *Construction Contracts*. This standard, which became effective January 1, 1995, superseded the original International Accounting Standard (IAS 11), *Accounting for Construction Contracts*, which was approved in 1978.

This standard uses the recognition criteria established by the IASC's *Framework for the Preparation and Presentation of Financial Statements* as the basis for the guidance it offers on accounting for construction contracts. This area of accounting is complicated by the need to rely on estimates of revenues, costs, and progress toward completion, and by the principle of recognition of losses when apparent.

Sources of IAS
IAS 10, 11, 23, 37

DEFINITIONS OF TERMS

Additional asset stipulation. A special provision in a construction contract which either gives the option to the customer to require construction of an additional asset or permits amendment to the construction contract so as to include an additional asset not envisioned by the original contract should be construed as a separate construction contract when

1. The additional asset differs significantly (in design, function, or technology) from the asset(s) covered by the original contract; or
2. The extra contract price fixed for the construction of the additional asset is negotiated without regard to the original contract price.

Back charges. Billings for work performed or costs incurred by one party that, in accordance with the agreement, should have been performed or incurred by the party billed.

Billings on long-term contracts. Accumulated billings sent to the purchaser at intervals as various milestones in the project are reached.

Change orders. Modifications of an original contract that effectively change the provisions of the contract without adding new provisions; synonymous with **variations**.

Claims. Amounts in excess of the agreed-on contract price that a contractor seeks to collect from a customer (or another party) for customer-caused delays, errors in specifications and designs, disputed variations in contract work, or other oc-currences that are alleged to be the causes of unanticipated costs.

Combining (grouping) contracts. Grouping two or more contracts, whether with a single customer or with several customers, into a single profit center for ac-counting purposes, provided that

1. The group of contracts is negotiated as a single package;
2. The contracts combined are so closely interrelated that, in essence, they could be considered as a single contract negotiated with an overall profit margin; and
3. The contracts combined are either executed concurrently or in a sequence.

Construction contract. Contract specifically entered into for the construction of an asset or a combination of assets that are closely interrelated or interdependent in terms of their design, technology, and function or their end use or purpose.

Construction-in-progress (CIP). Inventory account used to accumulate the construction costs of the contract project. For the percentage-of-completion method, the CIP account also includes the gross profit earned to date.

Contract costs. Comprised of costs directly related to a specific contract, costs that are attributable to the contract activity in general and can be allocated to the contract, and other costs that are specifically chargeable to the customer under the terms of the contract.

Contract revenue. Comprised of initial amount of revenue stipulated by the contract plus any variations in contract work, claims, and incentive payments, pro-vided that these extra amounts of revenue meet the recognition criteria set by the IASC's *Framework* (i.e., regarding the probability of future economic benefits flowing to the contractor and reliability of measurement).

Cost-plus contract. Construction contract in which the contractor is reim-bursed for allowable costs plus either a percentage of these costs or a fixed fee.

Cost-to-cost method. Percentage-of-completion method used to determine the extent of progress toward completion on a contract. The ratio of costs incurred through the end of the current year divided by the total estimated costs of the project is used to recognize income.

Estimated cost to complete. Anticipated additional cost of materials, labor, subcontracting costs, and indirect costs (overhead) required to complete a project at a scheduled time.

Fixed-price contract. Construction contract wherein the contract revenue is fixed either in absolute terms or is fixed in terms of unit rate of output; in certain cases both fixed prices being subject to any cost escalation clauses, if allowed by the contract.

Incentive payments. Any additional amounts payable to the contractor if specified performance standards are either met or surpassed.

Percentage-of-completion method. Method of accounting that recognizes income on a contract as work progresses by matching contract revenue with contract costs incurred, based on the proportion of work completed. However, any expected loss, which is the excess of total incurred and expected contract costs over the total contract revenue, is recognized immediately, irrespective of the stage of completion of the contract.

Precontract costs. Costs that are related directly to a contract and are incurred in securing a contract (e.g., architectural designs, purchase of special equipment, engineering fees, and start-up costs).They are included as part of contract costs if they can be identified separately and measured reliably and it is probable that the contract will be obtained.

Profit center. Unit for the accumulation of revenues and cost for the measurement of income.

Segmenting contracts. Dividing a single contract, which covers the construction of a number of assets, into two or more profit centers for accounting purposes, provided that

1. Separate proposals were submitted for each of the assets that are the subject matter of the single contract
2. The construction of each asset was the subject of separate negotiation wherein both the contractor and the customer were in a position to either accept or reject part of the contract pertaining to a single asset (out of numerous assets contemplated by the contract)
3. The costs and revenues pertaining to each individual asset can be separately identified

Stage of completion. Proportion of the contract work completed, which may be determined using one of several methods that reliably measures it, including

1. Percentage-of-completion method
2. Surveys of work performed
3. Physical proportion of contract work completed

Subcontractor. Second-level contractor who enters into a contract with a prime contractor to perform a specific part or phase of a construction project.

Substantial completion. Point at which the major work on a contract is completed and only insignificant costs and potential risks remain.

Variation. Instruction by the customer for a change in the scope of the work envisioned by the construction contract.

CONCEPTS, RULES, AND EXAMPLES

Construction contract revenue may be recognized during construction rather than at the completion of the contract. This "as earned" approach to revenue recognition is justified because under most long-term construction contracts, both the buyer and the seller (contractor) obtain enforceable rights. The buyer has the legal right to require specific performance from the contractor and, in effect, has an ownership claim to the contractor's work in progress. The contractor, under most long-term contracts, has the right to require the buyer to make progress payments during the construction period. The substance of this business activity is that a continuous sale occurs as the work progresses.

IAS 11, as revised in 1993, recognizes the percentage-of-completion method as the only valid method of accounting for construction contracts. Prior to the revision of IAS 11, the international accounting standards recognized both the percentage-of-completion method and the completed-contract method as being acceptable alternative methods of accounting for long-term construction activities.

The thinking worldwide on this issue is equivocal and rather confusing. Many countries still recognize both the foregoing methods as being in accordance with generally accepted accounting principles (GAAP), although they may not be viewed as equally acceptable under given circumstances. The United States, Canada, and Japan are usually noted as protagonists of both GAAP methods on this subject. There is another set of countries whose GAAP is in line with the current IAS on the subject. The national accounting standards of the United Kingdom, Australia, China, and New Zealand recognize only the percentage-of-completion method. Germany, on the other hand, seems to have taken the extreme viewpoint as a supporter of only the completed-contract method. Although it may seem that the world is completely divided on this matter, a closer look into this contentious issue offers a better insight into the diversity in approaches.

Although Germany seems to be alone in the contest of alternative methods of accounting for long-term contracts, its position is more explicable when it is recalled that this country has traditionally been known for its conservative approach and its emphasis on creditor protection. Thus, it seems to have been guided primarily by the prudence concept in developing this accounting principle.

For countries that support both the methods, it is well-known that some also express a clear preference for the percentage-of-completion method. US GAAP, for instance, exemplifies this position. It recommends the percentage-of-completion method as preferable when estimates are reasonably dependable and the following conditions exist:

1. Contracts executed by the parties normally include provisions that clearly specify the enforceable rights regarding goods or services to be provided and received by the parties, the consideration to be exchanged, and the manner and terms of settlement.
2. The buyer can be expected to satisfy his/her obligations under the contract.
3. The contractor can be expected to perform its contractual obligations.

The Accounting Standards Division of the AICPA believes that these two methods should not be used as acceptable alternatives for the same set of circumstances. US GAAP states that in general, when estimates of costs to complete and extent of progress toward completion of long-term contracts are reasonably depend-able, the percentage-of-completion method is preferable. When lack of dependable estimates or inherent hazards cause forecasts to be doubtful, the completed-contract method is preferable.

Percentage-of-Completion Method in Detail

A number of controversial issues are encountered when the percentage-of-completion method is used in practice. In the following paragraphs, the authors address a number of these, offering proposed approaches to follow for those matters that have not been authoritatively resolved, or, in many instances, even discussed by the international accounting standards.

Revised IAS 11 defines the percentage-of-completion method as follows:

> *The percentage of completion method recognizes income as work on a contract (or group of closely related contracts) progresses. The recognition of revenues and expenses is generally based on the stage of completion of the contract(s), except when a loss is expected, in which case immediate recognition of the loss is called (irrespective of the stage of completion). Under this method contract revenue is matched with the contract costs incurred in reaching the stage of completion, resulting in the reporting of contract revenue, contract costs and profit based on proportion of work completed.*

Under the percentage-of-completion method, the construction-in-progress (CIP) account is used to accumulate costs and recognized income. When the CIP exceeds billings, the difference is reported as a current asset. If billings exceed CIP, the difference is reported as a current liability. Where more than one contract exists, the excess cost or liability should be determined on a project-by-project basis, with the accumulated costs and liabilities being stated separately on the balance sheet. Assets and liabilities should not be offset unless a right of offset exists. Thus, the net debit balances for certain contracts should not ordinarily be offset against net credit balances for other contracts. An exception may exist if the balances relate to contracts that meet the criteria for combining.

Under the percentage-of-completion method, income should not be based on advances (cash collections) or progress (interim) billings. Cash collections and interim billings are based on contract terms that do not necessarily measure contract performance.

Costs and estimated earnings in excess of billings should be classified as an asset. If billings exceed costs and estimated earnings, the difference should be classified as a liability.

Contract costs. Contract costs comprise costs that are identifiable with a specific contract, plus those that are attributable to contracting activity in general and can be allocated to the contract and those that are contractually chargeable to a customer. Generally, contract costs would include all direct costs, such as direct materials, direct labor, and direct expenses and any construction overhead that could specifically be allocated to specific contracts.

Direct costs or costs that are identifiable with a specific contract include

1. Costs of materials consumed in the specific construction contract
2. Wages and other labor costs for site labor and site supervisors
3. Depreciation charges of plant and equipment used in the contract
4. Lease rentals of hired plant and equipment specifically for the contract
5. Cost incurred in shifting of plant, equipment, and materials to and from the construction site
6. Cost of design and technical assistance directly identifiable with a specific contract
7. Estimated costs of any work undertaken under a warranty or guarantee
8. Claims from third parties

With regard to claims from third parties, these should be accrued if they rise to the level of "provisions" as defined by recently promulgated standard IAS 37 (which corresponds to "probable" contingencies under former standard IAS 10). This requires that an obligation exists at the balance sheet date which is subject to reasonable measurement. However, if either of the above-mentioned conditions is not met (and the possibility of the loss is not remote), this contingency will only be disclosed. Contingent losses are specifically required to be disclosed under IAS 11.

Contract costs may be reduced by incidental income if such income is not included in contract revenue. For instance, sale proceeds (net of any selling expenses) from the disposal of any surplus materials or from the sale of plant and equipment at the end of the contract may be credited or offset against these expenses. Drawing an analogy from this principle, it could be argued that if advances received from customers are invested by the contractor temporarily (instead of being allowed to lie idle in a current account), any interest earned on such investments could be treated as incidental income and used in reducing contract costs, which may or may not include borrowing costs (depending on how the contractor is financed, whether self-financed or leveraged). On the other hand, it may also be argued that instead of being subtracted from contract costs, such interest income should be added to contract revenue.

In the authors' opinion, the latter argument may be valid if the contract is structured in such a manner that the contractor receives lump-sum advances at the beginning of the contract (or for that matter, even during the term of the contract, such that the advances at any point in time exceed the amounts due the contractor from the customer). In these cases, such interest income should in fact be treated as contract revenue and not offset against contract costs. The reasoning underlying treating this differently from the earlier instance (where idle funds resulting from advances are invested temporarily) is that such advances were envisioned by the terms of the contract and as such were probably fully considered in the negotiation process that preceded fixing contract revenue. Thus, since negotiated as part of the total contract price, this belongs in contract revenues. (It should be borne in mind that the different treatments for interest income will in fact have a bearing on the determination of the percentage or stage of completion of a construction contract.)

Indirect costs or overhead expenses should be included in contract costs provided that they are attributable to the contracting activity in general and could be allocated to specific contracts. Such costs include construction overhead, cost of insurance, cost of design, and technical assistance that is not related directly to specific contracts. They should be allocated using methods that are systematic and rational and are applied in a consistent manner to costs having similar features or characteristics. The allocation should be based on the normal level of construction activity, not on theoretical maximum capacity.

Example of contract costs

A construction company incurs $700,000 in annual rental expense for the office space occupied by a group of engineers and architects and their support staff. The company utilizes this group to act as the quality assurance team that overlooks all contracts undertaken by the company. The company also incurs in the aggregate another $300,000 as the annual expenditure toward electricity, water, and maintenance of this office space occupied by the group. Since the group is responsible for quality assurance for all contracts on hand, its work, by nature, cannot be considered as being directed toward any specific contract but is in support of the entire contracting activity. Thus, the company should allocate the rent expense and the cost of utilities in accordance with a systematic and rational basis of allocation, which should be applied consistently to both types of expenditure (since they have similar characteristics).

Although the bases of allocation of this construction overhead could be many (such as the amounts of contract revenue, contract costs, and labor hours utilized in each contract) the basis of allocation that seems most rational is contract revenue. Further, since both expenses are similar in nature, allocating both the costs on the basis of the amount of contract revenue generated by each construction contract would also satisfy the consistency criteria.

Other examples of construction overhead or costs that should be allocated to contract costs are

1. Costs of preparing and processing payroll of employees engaged in construction activity
2. Borrowing costs that are capitalized under IAS 23 in conformity with the allowed alternative treatment

Certain costs are specifically excluded from allocation to the construction contract, as the standard considers them as not attributable to the construction activity. Such costs may include

1. General and administrative costs that are not contractually reimbursable
2. Costs incurred in marketing or selling
3. Research and development costs that are not contractually reimbursable

4. Depreciation of plant and equipment that is lying idle and not used in any particular contract

Types of contract costs. Contract costs can be broken down into two categories: costs incurred to date and estimated costs to complete. The **costs incurred to date** include precontract costs and costs incurred after contract acceptance. **Precontract costs** are costs incurred before a contract has been entered into, with the expectation that the contract will be accepted and these costs will thereby be recoverable through billings. The criteria for recognition of such costs are

1. They are capable of being identified separately.
2. They can be measured reliably.
3. It is probable that the contract will be obtained.

Precontract costs include costs of architectural designs, costs of learning a new process, cost of securing the contract, and any other costs that are expected to be recovered if the contract is accepted. Contract costs incurred after the acceptance of the contract are costs incurred toward the completion of the project and are also capitalized in the construction-in-progress (CIP) account. The contract does not have to be identified before the capitalization decision is made; it is only necessary that there be an expectation of the recovery of the costs. Once the contract has been accepted, the precontract costs become contract costs incurred to date. However, if the precontract costs are already recognized as an expense in the period in which they are incurred, they are not included in contract costs when the contract is obtained in a subsequent period.

Estimated costs to complete. These are the anticipated costs required to complete a project at a scheduled time. They would be comprised of the same elements as the original total estimated contract costs and would be based on prices expected to be in effect when the costs are incurred. The latest estimates should be used to determine the progress toward completion.

Although IAS 11 does not specifically provide instructions for estimating costs to complete, practical guidance can be gleaned from other international accounting standards, as follows: The first rule is that systematic and consistent procedures should be used. These procedures should be correlated with the cost accounting system and should be able to provide a comparison between actual and estimated costs. Additionally, the determination of estimated total contract costs should identify the significant cost elements.

A second important point is that the estimation of the costs to complete should include the same elements of costs included in accumulated costs. Additionally, the estimated costs should reflect any expected price increases. These expected price increases should not be blanket provisions for all contract costs, but rather, specific provisions for each type of cost. Expected increases in each of the cost elements such as wages, materials, and overhead items should be taken into consideration separately.

Finally, estimates of costs to complete should be reviewed periodically to reflect new information. Estimates of costs should be examined for price fluctuations and should also be reviewed for possible future problems, such as labor strikes or direct material delays.

Accounting for contract costs is similar to accounting for inventory. Costs necessary to ready the asset for sale would be recorded in the construction-in-progress account, as incurred. CIP would include both direct and indirect costs but would usually not include general and administrative expenses or selling expenses since they are not normally identifiable with a particular contract and should therefore be expensed.

Subcontractor costs. Since a contractor may not be able to do all facets of a construction project, a subcontractor may be engaged. The amount billed to the contractor for work done by the subcontractor should be included in contract costs. The amount billed is directly traceable to the project and would be included in the CIP account, similar to direct materials and direct labor.

Back charges. Contract costs may have to be adjusted for back charges. Back charges are billings for costs incurred which the contract stipulated should have been performed by another party. These charges are often disputed by the parties involved.

Example of a back charge situation

The contract states that the subcontractor was to raze the building and have the land ready for construction; however, the contractor/seller had to clear away debris in order to begin construction. The contractor wants to be reimbursed for the work; therefore, the contractor back charges the subcontractor for the cost of the debris removal.

The contractor should treat the back charge as a receivable from the subcontractor and should reduce contract costs by the amount recoverable. If the subcontractor disputes the back charge, the cost becomes a **claim**. Claims are an amount in excess of the agreed contract price or amounts not included in the original contract price that the contractor seeks to collect. Claims should be recorded as additional contract revenue only if the requirements set forth in IAS 11 are met.

The subcontractor should record the back charge as a payable and as additional contract costs if it is probable that the amount will be paid. If the amount or validity of the liability is disputed, the subcontractor would have to consider the probable outcome in order to determine the proper accounting treatment.

Fixed-Price and Cost-Plus Contracts

IAS 11 recognizes two types of construction contracts which are distinguished based on their pricing arrangements: (1) fixed-price contracts and (2) cost-plus contracts.

Fixed-price contracts are contracts for which the price is not usually subject to adjustment because of costs incurred by the contractor. The contractor agrees to a fixed contract price or a fixed rate per unit of output. These amounts are sometimes subject to escalation clauses.

There are two types of **cost-plus contracts**.

1. **Cost-without-fee contract**--Contractor is reimbursed for allowable or otherwise defined costs with no provision for a fee. However, a percentage is added that is based on the foregoing costs.
2. **Cost-plus-fixed-fee contract**--Contractor is reimbursed for costs plus a provision for a fee. The contract price on a cost-type contract is determined by the sum of the reimbursable expenditures and a fee. The fee is the profit margin (revenue less direct expenses) to be earned on the contract. All reimbursable expenditures should be included in the accumulated contract costs account.

There are a number of possible variations of contracts which are based on a cost-plus-fee arrangement. These could include cost-plus-fixed-fee, under which the fee is a fixed monetary amount; cost-plus-award, under which an incentive payment is provided to the contractor, typically based on the project's timely or on-budget completion; and cost-plus-a-percentage-fee, under which a variable bonus payment will be added to the contractor's ultimate payment based on stated criteria.

Some contracts may have features of both a fixed-price contract and a cost-plus contract. A cost-plus contract with an agreed maximum price is an example of such a contract.

Recognition of Contract Revenue and Expenses

Percentage-of-completion accounting cannot be employed if the quality of information will not support a reasonable level of accuracy in the financial reporting process. Generally, only when the outcome of a construction contract can be estimated reliably, should the contract revenue and contract costs be recognized by reference to the stage of completion at the balance sheet date.

Different criteria have been prescribed by the standard for assessing whether the outcome can be estimated reliably for a contract, depending on whether it is a fixed-price contract or a cost-plus contract. The following are the criteria in each case:

1. If it is a fixed-price contract *(NOTE: **All** conditions should be satisfied)*

   a. It meets the recognition criteria set by the IASC's *Framework*; that is

      (1) Total contract revenue can be measured reliably.
      (2) It is probable that economic benefits flow to the enterprise.

   b. Both the contract cost to complete and the stage of completion can be measured reliably.

    c.   Contract costs attributable to the contract can be identified properly and measured reliably so that comparison of actual contract costs with estimates can be done.

2.   If it is a cost-plus contract (*NOTE: **All** conditions should be satisfied*)

    a.   It is probable that the economic benefits will flow to the enterprise.
    b.   The contract costs attributable to the contract, whether or not reimbursable, can be identified and measured reliably.

When Outcome of a Contract Cannot Be Estimated Reliably

As stated above, unless the outcome of a contract can be estimated reliably, contract revenue and costs should not be recognized by reference to the stage of completion. IAS 11 establishes the following rules for revenue recognition in cases where the outcome of a contract cannot be estimated reliably:

1.   Revenue should be recognized only to the extent of the contract costs incurred that are probable of being recoverable.
2.   Contract costs should be recognized as an expense in the period in which they are incurred.

Any expected losses should, however, be recognized immediately.

It is not unusual that during the early stages of a contract, outcome cannot be estimated reliably. This would be particularly likely to be true if the contract represents a type of project with which the contractor has had limited experience in the past.

Contract Costs Not Recoverable Due to Uncertainties

Recoverability of contract costs may be considered doubtful in the case of contracts that have any of the following characteristics:

1.   The contract is not fully enforceable.
2.   Completion of the contract is dependent on the outcome of pending litigation or legislation.
3.   The contract relates to properties that are likely to be expropriated or condemned.
4.   The contract is with a customer who is unable to perform its obligations, perhaps because of financial difficulties.
5.   The contractor is unable to complete the contract or otherwise meet its obligation under the terms of the contract, as when, for example, the contractor has been experiencing recurring losses and is unable to get financial support from creditors and bankers and may be ready to declare bankruptcy.

In all such cases, contract costs should be expensed immediately. Although the implication is unambiguous, the determination that one or more of the foregoing conditions holds will be subject to some imprecision. Thus, each such situation needs to be assessed carefully on a case-by-case basis.

If and when these uncertainties are resolved, revenue and expenses should again be recognized on the same basis as other construction-type contracts (i.e., by the percentage-of-completion method). However, it is not permitted to restore costs already expensed in prior periods, since the accounting was not in error, given the facts that existed at the time the earlier financial statements were prepared.

Revenue Measurement--Determining the Stage of Completion

The standard recognizes that the stage of completion of a contract may be determined in many ways and that an enterprise uses the method that measures reliably the work performed. The standard further stipulates that depending on the nature of the contract, one of the following methods may be chosen:

1. The proportion that contract costs incurred bear to estimated total contract cost (also referred to as the cost-to-cost method)
2. Survey of work performed method
3. Completion of a physical proportion of contract work (also called units-of-work-performed) method.

    NOTE: Progress payments and advances received from customers often do not reflect the work performed.

Each of these methods of measuring progress on a contract can be identified as being either an input or an output measure. The **input measures** attempt to identify progress in a contract in terms of the efforts devoted to it. The cost-to-cost method is an example of an input measure. Under the cost-to-cost method, the percentage of completion would be estimated by comparing total costs incurred to date to total costs expected for the entire job. **Output measures** are made in terms of results by attempting to identify progress toward completion by physical measures. The units-of-work-performed method is an example of an output measure. Under this method, an estimate of completion is made in terms of achievements to date. Output measures are usually not considered to be as reliable as input measures.

When the stage of completion is determined by reference to the contract costs incurred to date, the standard specifically refers to certain costs that are to be excluded from contract costs. Examples of such costs are

1. Contract costs that relate to future activity (e.g., construction materials supplied to the site but not yet consumed during construction)
2. Payments made in advance to subcontractors prior to performance of the work by the subcontractor

Example of the percentage-of-completion method

The percentage-of-completion method works under the principle that "recognized income (should) be that percentage of estimated total income…that incurred costs to date bear to estimated total costs." The cost-to-cost method has become one of the most popular measures used to determine the extent of progress toward completion.

Under the cost-to-cost method, the percentage of revenue to recognize can be determined by the following formula:

$$\frac{\text{Cost to date}}{\begin{array}{c}\text{Cumulative costs incurred}\\ \text{+ Estimated costs}\\ \text{to complete}\end{array}} \quad \text{x} \quad \begin{array}{c}\text{Contract}\\ \text{price}\end{array} \quad - \quad \begin{array}{c}\text{Revenue}\\ \text{previously}\\ \text{recognized}\end{array} \quad = \quad \begin{array}{c}\text{Current}\\ \text{revenue}\\ \text{recognized}\end{array}$$

By slightly modifying this formula, current gross profit can also be determined.

$$\frac{\text{Cost to date}}{\begin{array}{c}\text{Cumulative costs incurred}\\ \text{+ Estimated costs}\\ \text{to complete}\end{array}} \quad \text{x} \quad \begin{array}{c}\text{Expected}\\ \text{total gross}\\ \text{profit}\end{array} \quad - \quad \begin{array}{c}\text{Gross profit}\\ \text{previously}\\ \text{recognized}\end{array} \quad = \quad \begin{array}{c}\text{Current}\\ \text{gross}\\ \text{profit}\end{array}$$

Example of the percentage-of-completion (cost-to-cost) and completed-contract methods with profitable contract

Assume a $500,000 contract that requires 3 years to complete and incurs a total cost of $405,000. The following data pertain to the construction period:

	Year 1	Year 2	Year 3
Cumulative costs incurred to date	$150,000	$360,000	$405,000
Estimated costs yet to be incurred at year end	300,000	40,000	--
Progress billings made during year	100,000	370,000	30,000
Collections of billings	75,000	300,000	125,000

Completed-Contract and Percentage-of-Completion Methods

	Year 1		Year 2		Year 3	
Construction in progress	150,000		210,000		45,000	
Cash, payables, etc.		150,000		210,000		45,000
Contract receivables	100,000		370,000		30,000	
Billings on contracts		100,000		370,000		30,000
Cash	75,000		300,000		125,000	
Contract receivables		75,000		300,000		125,000

Completed-Contract Method Only

Billings on contracts			500,000	
Cost of revenues earned			405,000	
Contracts revenues earned				500,000
Construction in progress				405,000

Percentage-of-Completion Method Only

Construction in progress	16,667		73,333		5,000	
Cost of revenues earned	150,000		210,000		45,000	
Contract revenues earned		166,667		283,333		50,000
Billings on contracts					500,000	
Construction in progress						500,000

Income Statement Presentation

	Year 1	Year 2	Year 3	Total
Percentage-of-completion:				
Contract revenues earned	$166,667*	$283,333**	$ 50,000***	$ 500,000
Cost of revenues earned	(150,000)	(210,000)	(45,000)	(405,000)
Gross profit	$ 16,667	$ 73,333	$ 5,000	$ 95,000
Completed-contract:				
Contract revenues earned	--	--	$ 500,000	$ 500,000
Cost of contracts completed	--	--	(405,000)	(405,000)
Gross profit	--	--	$ 95,000	$ 95,000

* $\dfrac{\$150,000}{450,000} \quad x \quad 500,000 \quad = \quad \$166,667$

** $\dfrac{\$360,000}{400,000} \quad x \quad 500,000 \quad - \quad 166,667 \quad = \quad \$283,333$

*** $\dfrac{\$405,000}{405,000} \quad x \quad 500,000 \quad - \quad 166,667 \quad - \quad 283,333 \quad = \quad \$50,000$

Balance Sheet Presentation

	Year 1	Year 2	Year 3
Percentage-of-completion:			
Current assets:			
Contract receivables		$ 25,000	$ 95,000	*
Costs and estimated earn-			
ings in excess of billings			
on uncompleted contracts			
Construction in progress	166,667**		
Less billings on long-			
term contracts	(100,000)	$ 66,667	
Current liabilities:			
Billings in excess of costs			
and estimated earnings on			
uncompleted contracts, year 2		$ 20,000	
($470,000*** 450,000****)			
Completed-contract:			
Current assets:			
Contract receivables		$ 25,000	$ 95,000	*
Costs in excess of billings			
on uncompleted contracts			
Construction in progress	150,000		
Less billings on long-			
term contracts	(100,000)	$ 50,000	
Current liabilities:			
Billings in excess of costs			
on uncompleted contracts,			
year 2		$110,000	
($470,000 – 360,000)			

*   *Since the contract was completed and title was transferred in year 3, there are no balance sheet amounts. However, if the project is complete but transfer of title has not taken place, there would be a balance sheet presentation at the end of the third year because the entry closing out the Construction-in-progress account and the Billings account would not have been made yet.*

**   *$150,000 (Costs) + 16,667 (Gross profit)*

***   *$100,000 (Year 1 Billings) + 370,000 (Year 2 Billings)*

****   *$360,000 (Costs) + 16,667 (Gross profit) + 73,333 (Gross profit)*

Recognition of Expected Contract Losses

When the current estimate of total contract cost exceeds the current estimate of total contract revenue, a provision for the entire loss on the entire contract should be made. Provisions for losses should be made in the period in which they become evident under either the percentage-of-completion method or the completed-contract method. In other words, when it is probable that total contract costs will exceed total contract revenue, the expected loss should be recognized as an expense immediately. The loss provision should be computed on the basis of the total estimated costs to complete the contract, which would include the contract costs incurred to date plus estimated costs (use the same elements as contract costs incurred) to complete. The provision should be shown separately as a current liability on the balance sheet.

In any year when a percentage-of-completion contract has an expected loss, the amount of the loss reported in that year can be computed as follows:

Reported loss = Total expected loss + All profit previously recognized

Example of the percentage-of-completion and completed-contract methods with loss contract

Using the previous information, if the costs yet to be incurred at the end of year 2 were $148,000, the total expected loss is $8,000 [$500,000 − (360,000 + 148,000)], and the total loss reported in year 2 would be $24,667 ($8,000 + 16,667). Under the completed-contract method, the loss recognized is simply the total expected loss, $8,000.

Journal entry at end of year 2	*Percentage-of-completion*	*Completed-contract*
Loss on uncompleted long-term contract	24,667	8,000
Construction in progress (or estimated loss on uncompleted contact)	24,667	8,000

Profit or Loss Recognized on Contract (Percentage-of-Completion Method)

	Year 1	Year 2	Year 3
Contract price	$500,000	$500,000	$500,000
Estimated total costs:			
Costs incurred to date	$150,000	$360,000	$506,000*
Estimated cost yet to be incurred	300,000	148,000	--
Estimated total costs for the 3-year period, actual for year 3	$450,000	$508,000	$506,000
Estimated income (loss), actual for year 3	$ 16,667	$ (8,000)	$ (6,000)
Less income (loss) previously recognized	--	16,667	(8,000)
Amount of estimated income (loss) recognized in the current period, actual for year 3	$ 16,667	$ (24,667)	$ 2,000

*Assumed

Profit or Loss Recognized on Contract
(Completed-Contract Method)

	Year 1	Year 2	Year 3
Contract price	$500,000	$500,000	$500,000
Estimated total costs:			
Costs incurred to date	$150,000	$360,000	$506,000*
Estimated costs yet to be incurred	300,000	148,000	--
Estimated total costs for the 3-year			
period, actual for year 3	$ 50,000	$ (8,000)	$ (6,000)
Loss previously recognized	--	--	(8,000)
Amount of estimated income (loss) recognized in the current period, actual for year 3	$ --	$ (8,000)	$ 2,000

*Assumed

Upon completion of the project during year 3, it can be seen that the actual loss was only $6,000 ($500,000 – 506,000); therefore, the estimated loss provision was overstated by $2,000. However, since this is a change of an estimate, the $2,000 difference must be handled prospectively; consequently, $2,000 of income should be recognized in year 3 ($8,000 previously recognized – $6,000 actual loss).

Combining and Segmenting Contracts

The profit center for accounting purposes is usually a single contract, but under some circumstances the profit center may be a combination of two or more contracts, a segment of a contract, or a group of combined contracts. Conformity with explicit criteria set forth in IAS 11 is necessary to combine separate contracts, or segment a single contract; otherwise, each individual contract is presumed to be the profit center.

For accounting purposes, a group of contracts may be combined if they are so closely related that they are, in substance, parts of a single project with an overall profit margin. A group of contracts, whether with a single customer or with several customers, should be combined and treated as a single contract if the group of contracts

1. Are negotiated as a single package
2. Require such closely interrelated construction activities that they are, in effect, part of a single project with an overall profit margin
3. Are performed concurrently or in a continuous sequence

Segmenting a contract is a process of breaking up a larger unit into smaller units for accounting purposes. If the project is segmented, revenues can be assigned to the different elements or phases to achieve different rates of profitability based on the relative value of each element or phase to the estimated total contract revenue. According to IAS 11, a contract may cover a number of assets. The construction of each asset should be treated as a separate construction contract when

1. The contractor has submitted separate proposals on the separate components of the project
2. Each asset has been subject to separate negotiation and the contractor and customer had the right to accept or reject part of the proposal relating to a single asset
3. The cost and revenues of each asset can be separately identified

Contractual Stipulation for Additional Asset--Separate Contract

The contractual stipulation for an additional asset is a special provision in the international accounting standard. IAS 11 provides that a contract may stipulate the construction of an additional asset at the option of the customer, or the contract may be amended to include the construction of an additional asset. The construction of the additional asset should be treated as a separate construction contract if

1. The additional asset significantly differs (in design, technology or function) from the asset or assets covered by the original contract
2. The price for the additional asset is negotiated without regard to the original contract price

Changes in Estimate

Since the percentage-of-completion method uses current estimates of contract revenue and expenses, it is normal to encounter changes in estimates of contract revenue and costs frequently. Such changes in estimate of the contract's outcome are treated on a par with changes in accounting estimate as defined by IAS 8, *Net Profit or Loss for the Period, Fundamental Errors and Changes in Accounting Policies.*

Disclosure Requirements Under IAS 11

A number of disclosures are prescribed by IAS 11; some of them are for all the contracts and others are only for contracts in progress at the balance sheet date. These are summarized below.

1. Disclosures relating to all contracts

    a. Aggregate amount of contract revenue recognized in the period
    b. Methods used in determination of contract revenue recognized in the period

2. Disclosures relating to contracts in progress

    a. Methods used in determination of stage of completion (of contracts in progress)
    b. Aggregate amount of costs incurred and recognized profits (net of recognized losses) to date
    c. Amounts of advances received (at balance sheet date)
    d. Amount of retentions (at balance sheet date)

Financial Statement Presentation Requirements Under IAS 11

Gross amounts due from customers should be reported as an asset. This amount is the net of

1. Costs incurred plus recognized profits, less
2. The aggregate of recognized losses and progress billings.

This represents, in the case of contracts in progress, excess of contract costs incurred plus recognized profits, net of recognized losses, over progress billings.

Gross amounts due to customers should be reported as a liability. This amount is the net of

1. Costs incurred plus recognized profits, less
2. The aggregate of the recognized losses and progress billings.

This represents, in the case of contract work in progress, excess of progress billings over contract costs incurred plus recognized profits, net of recognized losses.

APPENDIX A

ACCOUNTING UNDER SPECIAL SITUATIONS-- GUIDANCE FROM US GAAP

A number of specialized situations that are fairly common in long-term construction contracting are not addressed by international accounting standards. To provide guidance on certain of these matters, the following interpretations are offered, based on existing practice under US GAAP.

Joint Ventures and Shared Contracts

Many contracts obtained by long-term construction companies are shared by more than one contractor. When the owner of the contract puts it up for bids, many contractors form syndicates or joint ventures to bid on and obtain a contract under which each contractor could not perform individually.

When this transpires, a separate set of books is maintained for the joint venture. If the percentages of interest for each venture are identical in more than one contract, the joint venture might keep its records almost like another construction company. Usually, the joint venture is for a single contract and ends on completion of that contract.

A joint venture is a form of a partnership, although a partnership for a limited purpose. An agreement of the parties and the terms of the contract successfully bid on will determine the nature of the accounting records. Income statements are usually cumulative statements showing all totals from the date of contract determination until the reporting date. Each venturer records its share of the amount from the venture's income statement less its previously recorded portion of the venture's income as a single line item similar to the equity method for investments. Similarly, balance sheets of the venture give rise to a single line asset balance of investment and advances in joint ventures. In most cases, footnote disclosure is similar to the equity method in displaying condensed financial statements of material joint ventures.

Accounting for Change Orders

Change orders are modifications of specifications or provisions of an original contract. Contract revenue and costs should be adjusted to reflect change orders that are approved by the contractor and customer. According to US GAAP, the accounting for the change order depends on the scope and price of the change. If the scope and price have both been agreed on by the customer and contractor, contract revenue and cost should be adjusted to reflect the change order.

According to US GAAP, accounting for unpriced change orders depends on their characteristics and the circumstances in which they occur. Under the completed-contract method, costs attributable to unpriced change orders should be deferred as contract costs if it is probable that total contract costs, including costs attributable to the change orders, will be recovered from contract revenues. Recovery should be deemed probable if the future event or events are likely to occur.

According to US GAAP, the following guidelines should be followed when accounting for unpriced change orders under the percentage-of-completion method:

1. Costs attributable to unpriced change orders should be treated as costs of contract performance in the period in which the costs are incurred if it is not probable that the costs will be recovered through a change in the contract price.

2. If it is probable that the costs will be recovered through a change in the contract price, the costs should be deferred (excluded from the cost of contract performance) until the parties have agreed on the change in contract price, or alternatively, they should be treated as costs of contract performance in the period in which they are incurred, and contract revenue should be recognized to the extent of the costs incurred.

3. If an adjustment to the contract price will be made in an amount which will exceed the costs attributable to the change order, this may be given recognition under certain circumstances. Specifically, if the amount of the excess can be reliably estimated, and if realization is probable, then the original contract price should be so adjusted. However, since the substantiation of the amount of future revenue is difficult, revenue in excess of the costs attributable to unpriced change orders should only be recorded in circumstances in which realization is assured beyond a reasonable doubt, such as circumstances in which an entity's historical experience provides such assurance or in which an entity has received a bona fide pricing offer from a customer and records only the amount of the offer as revenue.

Accounting for Contract Options

According to US GAAP, an addition or option to an existing contract should be treated as a separate contract if any of the following circumstances exist:

1. The product or service to be provided differs significantly from the product or service provided under the original contract.

2. The price of the new product or service is negotiated without regard to the original contract and involves different economic judgments.

3. The products or services to be provided under the exercised option or amendment are similar to those under the original contract, but the contract price and anticipated contract cost relationship are significantly different.

If the addition or option does not meet the foregoing circumstances, the contracts should be combined. However, if the addition or option does not meet the criteria for combining, they should be treated as change orders.

Accounting for Claims

These represent amounts in excess of the agreed contract price that a contractor seeks to collect from customers for unanticipated additional costs. The recognition of additional contract revenue relating to claims is appropriate if it is probable that the claim will result in additional revenue and if the amount can be estimated reliably. US GAAP specifies that all of the following conditions must exist for the probable and estimable requirements to be satisfied:

1. The contract or other evidence provides a legal basis for the claim; or a legal opinion has been obtained, stating that under the circumstances there is a reasonable basis to support the claim.
2. Additional costs are caused by circumstances that were unforeseen at the contract date and are not the result of deficiencies in the contractor's performance.
3. Costs associated with the claim are identifiable or otherwise determinable and are reasonable in view of the work performed.
4. The evidence supporting the claim is objective and verifiable, not based on management's "feel" for the situation or on unsupported representations.

When the foregoing requirements are met, revenue from a claim should be recorded only to the extent that contract costs relating to the claim have been incurred. When the foregoing requirements are not met, a contingent asset should be disclosed in accordance with US GAAP governing contingencies.

8 PROPERTY, PLANT, AND EQUIPMENT

PERSPECTIVE AND ISSUES

Long-lived tangible and intangible assets (which include plant, property and equipment as well as development costs, intellectual property intangibles, and goodwill) provide economic benefits to an enterprise for a period greater than that covered by the current year's financial statements. Accordingly, these assets must be capitalized and their costs must be allocated over the periods of benefit to the reporting enterprise. Generally accepted accounting principles for long-lived assets address matters such as the determination of the amount at which to initially record the acquisition, the amount at which to present the asset at subsequent reporting dates, and the appropriate method(s) by which to allocate their costs to future periods. Under current international accounting standards, while historical cost is identified as the benchmark treatment, it is also acceptable to periodically revalue long-lived assets if certain defined conditions are met.

Long-lived assets are primarily operational in character, and they may be classified into two basic types: tangible and intangible. **Tangible assets,** which are the subject of the present chapter, have physical substance and can be further categorized as follows:

1. Depreciable assets
2. Depletable assets
3. Other tangible assets

Intangible assets, on the other hand, have no physical substance. The value of an intangible asset is a function of the rights or privileges that its ownership conveys to the business enterprise. Intangible assets, which are explored at length in the following chapter of this book, can be further categorized as being either

1. Identifiable, or
2. Unidentifiable (i.e., goodwill).

Property (such as factory buildings) is often constructed by an enterprise over an extended period of time, and during this interval, when the property has yet to be placed in productive service, the enterprise may incur interest cost on funds borrowed to finance the construction. IAS 23 provides, as an allowed alternative treatment, that such cost be added to the carrying value of the asset under construction. However, the benchmark treatment is to expense such costs as period costs, as they are incurred. A recently issued IASC interpretation has stipulated that, once an enterprise adopts the allowed alternative as its accounting policy, interest costs should be added to the carrying value of all qualifying assets.

It has long been accepted that an enterprise's balance sheet should not present assets at amounts in excess of some threshold level, often described as net realizable value or fair value, even if its (amortized) cost exceeds that amount. Until recently, however, there was no specific guidance under international accounting principles directing preparers of financial statements in how to measure long-lived assets' fair values, or how to account for any diminution in value which may have occurred during the reporting period. Recently issued standard IAS 36, *Impairment of Assets*, has significantly altered the accounting landscape by providing thorough coverage of this subject. IAS 36 is equally applicable to tangible and intangible long-lived assets, and will be accordingly addressed in both this and the immediately succeeding chapters.

Long-lived assets are sometimes acquired in nonmonetary transactions, either in exchanges of assets between the entity and another business, or when assets are contributed by shareholders to the enterprise. Although there are no specific standards on the accounting for these transactions under existing international accounting standards, the accounting that may logically be applied to these commonly encountered transactions is also considered in this chapter.

Sources of IAS
IAS 16, 23, 36   *SIC* 2, 14

DEFINITIONS OF TERMS

Amortization. In general, the allocation of the cost of a long-term asset over its useful life; the term is also used specifically to define the allocation process for intangible assets.

Boot. A term commonly applied to monetary consideration given or received as a net settle-up in what is otherwise an asset exchange situation.

Carrying amount. The amount at which an asset is presented on the balance sheet, which is its cost (or other allowable basis, such as fair value), net of any accumulated depreciation and accumulated impairment losses thereon.

Cash generating unit. The smallest identifiable group of assets that generates cash inflows from continuing use, largely independent of the cash inflows associated with other assets or groups of assets.

Corporate assets. Assets, excluding goodwill, that contribute to future cash flows of both the cash generating unit under review for impairment and other cash generating units.

Cost. Amount of cash or cash equivalent paid or the fair value of other consideration given to acquire or construct an asset.

Costs of disposal. The incremental costs directly associated with the disposal of an asset; these do not include financing costs or related income tax effects.

Depreciable amount. Cost of an asset or the other amount that has been substituted for cost, less the residual value of the asset.

Depreciation. Systematic and rational allocation of the depreciable amount of an asset over its economic life.

Exchange. Reciprocal transfer between an enterprise and another entity that results in the acquisition of assets or services, or the satisfaction of liabilities through a transfer of other assets, services, or other obligations.

Fair value. Amount that would be obtained for an asset in an arm's-length exchange transaction between knowledgeable, willing parties.

Fixed assets. Assets used in a productive capacity that have physical substance, are relatively long-lived, and provide future benefit that is readily measurable. Also referred to as **property, plant, and equipment.**

Impairment loss. The excess of the carrying amount of an asset over its recoverable amount.

Intangible assets. Nonmonetary assets, without physical substance, held for use in the production or supply of goods or services or for rental to others, or for administrative purposes, which are identifiable and are controlled by the enterprise as a result of past events, and from which future economic benefits are expected to flow.

Monetary assets. Assets whose amounts are fixed in terms of units of currency. Examples are cash, accounts receivable, and notes receivable.

Net selling price. The amount which could be realized from the sale of an asset by means of an arm's-length transaction, less costs of disposal.

Nonmonetary assets. Assets other than monetary assets. Examples are inventories; investments in common stock; and property, plant, and equipment.

Nonmonetary transactions. Exchanges and nonreciprocal transfers that involve little or no monetary assets or liabilities.

Nonreciprocal transfer. Transfer of assets or services in one direction, either from an enterprise to its owners or another entity, or from owners or another entity to the enterprise. An enterprise's reacquisition of its outstanding stock is a nonreciprocal transfer.

Property, plant, and equipment. Tangible assets with an expected useful life of more than 1 year, that are held for use in the process of producing goods or services for sale, that are held for rental to others, or that are held for administrative purposes; also referred to commonly as **fixed assets**.

Recoverable amount. The greater of an asset's net selling price or its value in use.

Residual value. Estimated net amount expected to be obtained on ultimate disposition of the asset after its useful life has ended, net of estimated costs of disposal.

Similar productive assets. Productive assets that are of the same general type, that perform the same function, or that are employed in the same line of business.

Useful life. Period over which an asset will be employed in a productive capacity, as measured either by the time over which it is expected to be used, or the number of production units expected to be obtained from the asset by the enterprise.

CONCEPTS, RULES, AND EXAMPLES

Property, Plant, and Equipment

Property, plant, and equipment (also variously referred to as plant assets, or fixed assets, or as PP&E) is the term most often used to denote tangible property to be used in a productive capacity that will benefit the enterprise for a period of greater than 1 year. This term is meant to distinguish these assets from intangibles, which are long-term, generally identifiable, assets that do not have physical substance, or whose value is not fully indicated by their physical existence.

There are four concerns to be addressed in accounting for fixed assets.

1. The amount at which the assets should be recorded initially on acquisition;
2. How value changes subsequent to acquisition should be reflected in the accounts, including questions of both value increases and possible decreases due to impairments;
3. The rate at which the amount the assets are recorded should be allocated to future periods; and
4. The recording of the subsequent disposal of the assets.

Initial measurement. All costs required to bring an asset into working condition should be recorded as part of the cost of the asset. Examples of such costs include sales or other nonrefundable taxes or duties, finders' fees, freight costs, site preparation and other installation costs, and setup costs. Thus, any reasonable cost incurred prior to using the asset in actual production involved in bringing the asset to the buyer is capitalized. These costs are not to be expensed in the period in which they are incurred, as they are deemed to add value to the asset and indeed were necessary expenditures to obtain the asset, provided that this does not lead to recording the asset at an amount greater than fair value.

Under IAS 16, prior to the amendments made in 1998, the estimated costs of dismantling, removing or restoring property, if subject to determination and if representing a legal or constructive commitment by the reporting entity, were to be recognized over the life of the asset by one of two acceptable means. First, these could have been estimated and offset against the estimated residual value of the asset, which had the effect of increasing periodic depreciation charges. Alternatively, the estimated costs could have been accrued periodically, by a charge to current operations and a credit to a provision for an estimated liability. With the issuance of the revised IAS 37, *Provisions, Contingent Liabilities, and Contingent Assets,* IAS 16 has been amended with regard to the accounting for these estimated costs.

Under the newly revised standard, the elements of cost to be incorporated in the initial recognition of an asset are to include the estimated cost of dismantlement and the asset, and hence increase periodic depreciation, which is no different in ultimate effect than the methods previously endorsed. This recognition will be mandated only if the criteria of IAS 37 are met. These criteria are that a provision will be recognized when (1) the reporting entity has a present obligation, whether legal or only constructive, as a result of a past event; (2) it is probable that an outflow of resources embodying economic benefits will be required to settle the obligation; and (3) a reliable estimate can be made of the amount of the obligation.

For example, if it were necessary to obtain a government license in order to construct a particular asset, such as a power generating plant, and a condition of said license is that at the end of the expected life of the property the owner would be required to dismantle it, remove any debris, and then restore the land to its previous condition, this would qualify as a present obligation resulting from a past event (the plant construction) probable to result in a future outflow of resources. An estimation of the cost of this, while perhaps challenging due to the long time horizon involved and the possible evolution of technology over that period, can normally be made. Per IAS 37, a best estimate is to be made of the future cost, and then discounted to present value. The cost of dismantlement and similar legal or constructive obligations do not extend to operating costs to be incurred in the future, since those would not qualify as "present obligations." The precise mechanism for making these computations is addressed in Chapter 12.

If estimated costs of dismantlement, removal and restoration are in fact provided for as part of the cost of the plant asset, because making a provision is required under IAS 37, the effect will be to allocate this cost over the life of the asset through the depreciation process. While not explicitly addressed by either IAS 37 or the revisions to IAS 16, logic suggests that, if originally recorded at discounted present value, each period the provision (i.e., the estimate liability) should be accreted, so that at the expected date on which the expenditure is to be incurred it will be appropriately stated. The offset to this accretion should be to interest expense, and should not be added to the cost of the asset to which the estimated dismantlement costs related.

In certain cases, other costs will be incurred during the initial break-in period; these may, alternatively, be referred to as start-up or preproduction costs. Under the provisions of IAS 16, these costs are **not** to be added to the amount recorded for the asset unless they are absolutely necessary to bring the asset to a workable condition. Notwithstanding this rule, this remains an area of subjective judgment; under many circumstances there will be justification for adding certain costs, such as those associated with materials used in testing or adjusting the machinery or equipment in order to place it into actual production. If these amounts are significant and incurrence of the costs is a necessary precedent to using the asset, they should be added to the carrying amount of the asset. On the other hand, losses incurred in the early stages of actually employing the asset in its intended use clearly cannot be capitalized, but instead must be charged to expense as incurred, as these are not assets (i.e., these do not represent economic benefits that will later be received by the entity).

While interest costs incurred during the construction of certain assets may be added to the cost of the asset (as described below), if an asset is purchased on deferred payment terms, the interest cost, whether made explicit or imputed, is **not** part of the cost of the asset. Accordingly, such costs should be expensed currently as interest charges. If the purchase price for the asset incorporates a deferred payment scheme, only the cash equivalent price should be capitalized as the initial carrying amount of the asset. If the cash equivalent price is not explicitly stated, the deferred payment amount should be reduced to present value by the application of an appropriate discount rate. This would normally be best approximated by use of the enterprise's incremental borrowing cost for debt having a maturity similar to the deferred payment term.

Administrative costs, as well as other categories of overhead, are not normally allocated to fixed asset acquisitions, despite the fact that some such costs, such as the salaries of the personnel who evaluate assets for proposed acquisitions, are in fact incurred as part of the acquisition process. As a general principle, administrative costs are expensed in the period incurred. On the other hand, truly incremental costs, such as a consulting fee or commission paid to an agent hired specifically to assist in the acquisition, may be treated as part of the initial amount to be recognized.

Initial recognition of self-constructed assets. Essentially the same principles that have been established for recognition of the cost of purchased assets also apply to self-constructed assets. All costs that must be incurred to complete the construction of the asset can be added to the amount to be recognized initially, subject only to the constraint that if these costs exceed the recoverable amount (as discussed fully later in this chapter), the excess must be expensed currently. This rule is necessary to avoid the "gold-plated hammer syndrome," whereby a misguided or unfortunate asset construction project incurs excessive costs that then find their way onto the balance sheet, consequently overstating the entity's current net worth and distorting future periods' earnings. Of course, internal (intracompany) profits cannot be allocated to construction costs.

Self-constructed assets may include, in addition to the range of costs discussed earlier, the cost of borrowed funds used during the period of construction. Capitalization of borrowing costs, as set forth by IAS 23, is discussed in a later section of this chapter.

The other issue that arises most commonly in connection with self-constructed fixed assets relates to overhead allocations. While capitalization of all direct costs (labor, materials, and variable overhead) is a well settled matter in accounting thought, a controversy exists regarding the proper treatment of fixed overhead. Two alternative views of how to treat fixed overhead are to

1. Charge the asset with its fair share of fixed overhead (i.e., use the same basis of allocation used for inventory); or
2. Charge the fixed asset account with only the identifiable incremental amount of fixed overhead.

While international standards do not address this concern, it may be instructive to consider nonbinding guidance included in US GAAP. AICPA Accounting Research Monograph 1 has suggested that

> . . . *in the absence of compelling evidence to the contrary, overhead costs considered to have 'discernible future benefits' for the purposes of determining the cost of inventory should be presumed to have 'discernible future benefits' for the purpose of determining the cost of a self-constructed depreciable asset.*

The implication of this statement is that a logic similar to what was applied to determining which acquisition costs may be included in inventory might reasonably also be applied to the costing of fixed assets. Also, consistent with the standards applicable to inventories, if the costs of fixed assets exceed realizable values, any excess costs should be written off to expense and not deferred to future periods.

Costs incurred subsequent to purchase or self-construction. Costs that are incurred subsequent to the purchase, such as those for repairs, maintenance, or betterments, are treated in one of the following ways:

1. Expensed;
2. Capitalized; or
3. Recognized by a reduction of accumulated depreciation.

Costs can be added to the carrying value of the related asset only when it is probable that future economic benefits, beyond those originally anticipated for the asset, will be received by the entity. For example, modifications to the asset made to extend its useful life (measured either in years or in units of potential production) or to increase its capacity (e.g., as measured by units per hour) would be capitalized. Similarly, if the expenditure results in an improved quality of output, or permits a reduction in other cost inputs (e.g., would result in labor savings), it is a candidate for capitalization. As with self-constructed assets, if the costs incurred exceed the defined threshold, they must be expensed currently.

It can usually be assumed that ordinary maintenance and repair expenditures will occur on a ratable basis over the life of the asset and should be charged to expense as incurred. Thus, if the purpose of the expenditure is either to maintain the productive capacity anticipated when the asset was acquired or constructed, or to restore it to that level, the costs are not subject to capitalization.

A partial exception is encountered if an asset is acquired in a condition that necessitates that certain expenditures be incurred in order to put it into the appropriate state for its intended use. For example, a deteriorated building may be purchased with the intention that it be restored and then utilized as, say, a factory or office facility. In such cases, costs that otherwise would be categorized as ordinary maintenance items might be subject to capitalization, subject, of course, to the constraint that the asset not be presented at a value that exceeds its recoverable amount. Once the restoration is completed, further expenditures of similar type would be viewed as being ordinary repairs or maintenance, and thus expensed as incurred.

Extraordinary repairs. In contrast to normal maintenance costs, extraordinary repairs or maintenance increase the value (utility) of the asset or increase the estimated useful life of the asset. IAS 16 does not stipulate whether such expenditures should be added to the gross carrying value of the asset or should be used to reduce the previously accumulated depreciation. However, there is a logical basis for increasing the asset account for those repairs that increase the value of the asset while decreasing the accumulated depreciation account for those repairs that extend the useful life of the asset. In effect, those that extend the life of the asset have recovered some of the depreciation recorded previously, and the asset will be depreciated again over its new, lengthier, lifetime. The chart on the following page summarizes the treatment of expenditures subsequent to acquisition consistent with the foregoing discussion.

Depreciation of fixed assets. In accordance with one of the more important basic accounting concepts, the matching principle, the costs of fixed assets are allocated to the periods benefited through depreciation. Whatever the method of depreciation chosen, it must result in the systematic and rational allocation of the cost of the asset (less its residual value) over the asset's expected useful life. The determination of the useful life must take a number of factors into consideration. These factors include technological change, normal deterioration, actual physical use, and legal or other limitations on the ability to use the property. The method of depreciation is based on whether the useful life is determined as a function of time (e.g., technological change or normal deterioration) or as a function of actual physical usage.

Since depreciation accounting is intended as a strategy for cost allocation, it does not necessarily reflect changes in the value of the asset being amortized. Thus, with the exception of land, which has infinite life, all tangible fixed assets must be

Costs Subsequent to Acquisition of Property, Plant, and Equipment

Type of expenditure	Characteristics	Expense when incurred	Normal accounting treatment — Capitalize — Charge to asset	Normal accounting treatment — Capitalize — Charge to accum. deprec.	Other
1. Additions	Extensions, enlargements, or expansions made to an existing asset		x		
2. Repairs and maintenance					
a. Ordinary	Recurring, relatively small expenditures 1. Maintain normal operating condition 2. **Do not** add materially to use value 3. **Do not** extend useful life	x x x			
b. Extraordinary (major)	Not recurring, relatively large expenditures 1. Primarily increase the use value 2. Primarily extend the useful life		x	x	
3. Replacements and betterments	Major component of asset is removed and replaced with the same type of component with comparable performance capabilities (replacement) or a different type of component having superior performance capabilities (betterment)				
a. Book value of old component is known					• Remove old asset cost and accum. deprec. • Recognize any loss (or gain) on old asset • Charge asset for replacement component
b. Book value of old component is not known			x	x	
4. Reinstallations and rearrangements	Provide greater efficiency in production or reduce production costs 1. Material costs incurred; benefits extend into future accounting periods 2. No measurable future benefit	x	x		

depreciated, even if (as sometimes occurs, particularly in periods of general price inflation) their nominal or real values increase.

Furthermore, if the recorded amount of the asset is allocated over a period of time (as opposed to units of production), it should be the expected period of usefulness to the entity, not the physical life of the property itself, that governs. Thus, such concerns as technological obsolescence, as well as normal wear and tear, must be addressed in the initial determination of the period over which to allocate the asset cost. The reporting entity's strategy for repairs and maintenance will also affect this computation, since the same physical asset might have a longer or shorter economic useful life in the hands of differing owners, depending on the care with which it is intended to be maintained.

Similarly, the same asset may have a longer or shorter economic life, depending on its intended use. A particular building, for example, may have a 50-year expected life as a facility for storing goods or for use in light manufacturing, but as a showroom would have a shorter period of usefulness, due to the anticipated disinclination of customers to shop at enterprises housed in older premises. Again, it is not physical life, but useful economic life, that should govern.

Compound assets, such as buildings containing such disparate components as heating plant, roofs, and other structural elements, are most commonly recorded in several separate accounts, to facilitate the process of amortizing the different elements over varying periods. Thus, a heating plant may have an expected useful life of 20 years, the roof a life of 15 years, and the basic structure itself a life of 40 years. Recordation in separate accounts eases the calculation of periodic depreciation in such situations, although for financial reporting purposes certain of these categories might be combined, based on materiality or other considerations.

IAS 16 has superseded IAS 4 concerning guidance on depreciation of property, plant, and equipment. The remaining guidance in IAS 4 has more recently been obsoleted by the new standard on intangibles, IAS 38, which is discussed in the following chapter.

Depreciation methods based on time.

1. Straight-line--Depreciation expense is incurred evenly over the life of the asset. The periodic charge for depreciation is given as

$$\frac{\text{Cost or amount substituted for cost, less residual value}}{\text{Estimated useful life of asset}}$$

2. Accelerated methods--Depreciation expense is higher in the early years of the asset's useful life and lower in the later years. IAS 16 only mentions one accelerated method, the diminishing balance method, but other methods have been employed in various countries under earlier or other contemporary accounting standards.

a. Diminishing balance--A multiple of the straight-line rate times the net carrying value at the beginning of the year.

$$\text{Straight-line rate} = \frac{1}{\text{Estimated useful life}}$$

Example

Double-declining balance depreciation (if salvage value is to be recognized, stop when book value = estimated salvage value)

Depreciation = 2 x Straight-line rate x Book value at beginning of year

Another method to accomplish a diminishing charge for depreciation is the sum-of-the-years' digits method, that is commonly employed in the United States and certain other venues.

b. Sum-of-the-years' digits (SYD) depreciation =

(Cost less salvage value) x Applicable fraction

where applicable fraction = $\dfrac{\text{number of years of estimated life remaining as of the beginning of the year}}{\text{SYD}}$

and SYD $= \dfrac{n(n+1)}{2}$ and n = estimated useful life

Example

An asset having a useful economic life of 5 years and no salvage value would have 5/15 (= 1/3) of its cost allocated to year 1, 4/15 to year 2, and so on.

3. Present value methods--A characteristic of this method of depreciation is that expense will be lower in the early years and higher in the later years. The effect of this pattern results in having the rate of return on the investment remain constant over the life of the asset. Time value of money formulas are used to effect this method of depreciation.

a. Sinking fund method--Uses the future value of an annuity formula.
b. Annuity fund method--Uses the present value of an annuity formula.

The present value approach is rarely encountered in practice, due to computational complexity, despite what many consider to be its theoretical validity. IAS 16 is silent regarding these methods, and the fact that the standard refers only to straight-line, diminishing balance, and sum-of-the-units methods may suggest that increasing charge methods would not be acceptable. However, the statement in IAS 16 that a "variety of depreciation methods can be used to allocate the depreciable amount of an asset on a systematic and rational basis over its useful life" would at the same time seemingly support other unnamed methods, albeit that they are not explicitly discussed in that standard. Clearly, it would be incumbent upon those choosing to employ such methods to demonstrate why these better represented the actual economic depreciation of the assets in question.

Partial-year depreciation. Although IAS 16 is silent on the matter, when an asset is either acquired or disposed of during the year, the full year depreciation calculation should be prorated between the accounting periods involved. This is necessary to achieve proper matching. However, if individual assets in a relatively homogeneous group are regularly acquired and disposed of, one of several conventions can be adopted, as follows:

1. Record a full year's depreciation in the year of acquisition and none in the year of disposal.
2. Record one-half year's depreciation in the year of acquisition and one-half year's depreciation in the year of disposal.

Example of partial-year depreciation

Assume the following:

Taj Mahal Milling Co., a calendar-year entity, acquired a machine on June 1, 2000, that cost $40,000 with an estimated useful life of 4 years and a $2,500 salvage value. The depreciation expense for each full year of the asset's life is calculated as follows:

	Straight-line	*Double-declining balance*			*Sum-of-years' digits*		
Year 1	37,500* ÷ 4 = 9,375	50% x	40,000	= 20,000	4/10 x	37,500*	= 15,000
Year 2	9,375	50% x	20,000	= 10,000	3/10 x	37,500	= 11,250
Year 3	9,375	50% x	10,000	= 5,000	2/10 x	37,500	= 7,500
Year 4	9,375	50% x	5,000	= 2,500	1/10 x	37,500	= 3,750

\$40,000 – \$2,500.

Because the first full year of the asset's life does not coincide with the company's year, the amounts shown above must be prorated as follows:

	Straight-line	*Double-declining balance*			*Sum-of-years' digits*		
2000	7/12 x 9,375 = 5,469	7/12 x	20,000	= 11,667	7/12 x	15,000	= 8,750
2001	9,375	5/12 x	20,000	= 8,333	5/12 x	15,000	= 6,250
		7/12 x	10,000	= 5,833	7/12 x	11,250	= 6,563
				14,166			12,813
2002	9,375	5/12 x	10,000	= 4,167	5/12 x	11,250	= 4,687
		7/12 x	5,000	= 2,917	7/12 x	7,500	= 4,375
				7,084			9,062
2003	9,375	5/12 x	5,000	= 2,083	5/12 x	7,500	= 3,125
		7/12 x	2,500	= 1,458	7/12 x	3,750	= 2,188
				3,541			5,313
2004	5/12 x 9,375 = 3,906	5/12 x	2,500	= 1,042	5/12 x	3,750	= 1,562

Depreciation method based on actual physical use--Sum-of-the-units (or units of production) method. Depreciation may also be based on the number of units produced by the asset in a given year. IAS 16 identifies this as the sum-of-the-units method, but it is also commonly known as the units of production approach. It is best suited to those assets, such as machinery, that have an expected life that is most rationally defined in terms of productive output; in periods of reduced production (such as economic recession) the machinery is used less, thus extending its life when measured in units of time. It would not be rational to charge the same depreciation expense to such periods, as would be the case if straight-line or diminishing balance depreciation were used. Furthermore, if the depreciation finds its way into inventory, the unit cost in periods of reduced production would be exaggerated and could even exceed net realizable value unless a units of production approach to depreciation were taken.

$$\text{Depreciation rate} = \frac{\text{Cost less residual value}}{\substack{\text{Estimated number of units to be} \\ \text{produced by the asset over} \\ \text{its estimated useful life}}}$$

$$\substack{\text{Units of} \\ \text{production} \\ \text{depreciation}} = \text{Depreciation rate} \quad \text{x} \quad \substack{\text{Number of units} \\ \text{produced during} \\ \text{the period}}$$

Other depreciation methods. Although IAS 16 does not discuss other methods of depreciation (nor even all the variations noted in the foregoing paragraphs), at different times and in various jurisdictions other methods have been used. Some of these are summarized as follows:

1. **Retirement method**--Cost of asset is expensed in period in which it is retired.
2. **Replacement method**--Original cost is carried in accounts and cost of replacement is expensed in the period of replacement.
3. **Group (or composite) method**--Averages the service lives of a number of assets using a weighted-average of the units and depreciates the group or composite as if it were a single unit. A group consists of similar assets, while a composite is made up of dissimilar assets.

$$\text{Depreciation rate} = \frac{\substack{\text{Sum of the straight-line} \\ \text{depreciation of individual assets}}}{\text{Total asset cost}}$$

$$\text{Depreciation expense} = \text{Depreciation rate x Total group (composite) cost}$$

A peculiarity of the composite approach is that gains and losses are not recognized on the disposal of an asset, but rather, are netted into accumulated depreciation. This is because it is a presumption of this method that although dispositions of individual assets may yield proceeds greater than or less than their respective book values, the ultimate gross proceeds from a group of assets will not differ materially from the aggregate book value thereof, and accordingly, recognition of those individual gains or losses should be deferred and effectively netted out.

Residual value. Most depreciation methods discussed above require that a factor be applied to the net depreciable cost of the asset, where net depreciable cost is the historical cost or amount substituted therefor (i.e., fair value) less the estimated residual value of the asset. Although residual value is often not material and in practice is frequently ignored, the concept should nonetheless be understood, particularly since it is defined differently in the context of the benchmark and allowed alternative methods described by IAS 16.

If the benchmark method (historical cost) is used, residual value is defined as the expected worth of the asset, in present dollars (i.e., without any consideration of the impact of future inflation), at the end of its useful life. Residual value should, however, be net of any expected costs of disposition. In some cases, assets will have a negative residual value, as for example when the entity must incur out-of-pocket costs to dispose of the asset, or to return the property to an earlier condition, as in the case of certain operations, such as strip mines, that are subject to environmental protection or other laws. In such instances, periodic depreciation should total more than the asset's original cost, such that at the expected disposal date, an estimated liability has been accrued equal to the negative residual value.

If the alternative (revaluation) method is elected, residual value takes on a rather different meaning. Under this scenario, residual value must be assessed anew at the date of each revaluation of the asset. This is accomplished by using data on realizable values for similar assets, ending their respective useful lives at the time of the revaluation, after having been used for purposes similar to the asset being valued. Again, no consideration can be paid to anticipated inflation, and expected future values are not to be discounted to present values to give recognition to the time value of money. As with historical cost based accounting for plant assets, if a negative residual value is anticipated, this should be effectively recognized over the useful life of the asset by charging extra depreciation, such that the estimated liability will have been accrued by the disposal date.

Choice of depreciation method. While a number of different methods have been officially endorsed by international accounting standards, and others might be rationally supportable as well, in theory one method will be best in any given fact situation at reporting on the expiration of the service potential of the asset. Thus, straight-line presumes that the same economic value is obtained from use of the asset each period, while such accelerated approaches as the diminishing balance method are intended to combine decreasing periodic charges for depreciation with presumably increasing costs for repairs and maintenance as the asset ages, for an approximately level total cost of use across the years.

In practice, the amount of real support marshaled for the particular depreciation method employed will vary significantly, and it is very unusual for certifying (i.e., outside) accountants to dispute any entity's choice of method, as long as it is among those deemed to be GAAP. It is presumed that full disclosure of the methods used will permit the financial statement reader to interpret the financial statements meaningfully, in any event.

IAS 16 requires that the method of depreciation be critically reviewed periodically. If the expected pattern of utility of the asset has changed from when the method used was decided on, a different and more appropriate method should be selected. This change would be accounted for as a change in an accounting estimate and would affect financial reporting only on a prospective basis.

Useful lives. Irrespective of the method of depreciation used, the estimate of useful life must be revisited periodically. Useful life is defined in terms of expected utility to the enterprise, and as such may differ from both the physical life and economic life of the asset. Useful life is affected by such things as the entity's practices regarding repairs and maintenance of its assets, as well as the pace of technological change and the market demand for goods produced and sold by the entity using the assets as productive inputs. If it is determined that the estimated life is greater or less than previously believed, the change is handled as a change in accounting estimate, not as a correction of fundamental error. Accordingly, no restatement is made to previously reported depreciation; rather, the change is accounted for strictly on a prospective basis, being reflected in the period of change and all subsequent periods.

Example of estimating the useful life

To illustrate this concept, consider an asset costing $100,000 and originally estimated to have a productive life of 10 years. The straight-line method is used, and there was no residual value anticipated. After 2 years, management revises its estimate of useful life to a total of 6 years. Since the net carrying value of the asset is $80,000 after 2 years ($100,000 x 8/10), and the remaining expected life is 4 years (2 of the 6 revised total years having already elapsed), depreciation in years 3 through 6 will be $20,000 ($80,000/4) each.

Tax methods. The methods of computing depreciation discussed in the foregoing sections relate only to financial reporting under international accounting standards. Tax laws in different nations of the world vary widely in terms of the acceptability of depreciation methods, and it is not possible for a general treatise such as this to address those in any detail. However, to the extent that depreciation allowable for income tax reporting purposes differs from that required or permitted for financial statement purposes, deferred income taxes might have to be presented. Interperiod income tax allocation is discussed more fully in Chapter 15.

Revaluation of Fixed Assets

IAS 16 establishes two alternative approaches to accounting for fixed assets. The first of these is the benchmark (normal) treatment, under which acquisition or construction cost is used for initial recognition, subject to depreciation over the expected economic life and to possible write-down in the event of a permanent impairment in value. The allowed alternative treatment is to recognize upward revaluations.

The logic of recognizing revaluations relates to both the balance sheet and the measure of periodic performance provided by the income statement. Due to the effects of inflation (which even if quite moderate when measured on an annual basis can compound dramatically during the lengthy period over which fixed assets remain in use) the balance sheet can become a virtually meaningless agglomeration of dissimilar costs.

Furthermore, if income is determined by reference to historical costs of assets acquired in earlier periods, the replacement of those assets in the normal course of events may well require more resources than are provided by depreciation. Under these circumstances, even a nominally profitable enterprise might find that it has self-liquidated and is unable to continue in existence, at least, not with the same level of productive capacity, without new debt or equity infusions. In fact, a number of enterprises in many capital intensive industries have suffered just such a fate over the past generation.

At varying times the securities regulatory and other authorities and private sector standard setters in different nations have proposed or even required a range of alternative price level adjusted or current cost methods of accounting to address this problem. Notwithstanding these efforts, no uniform approach has ever gained the wide acceptance that would create a de facto standard. In certain jurisdictions, less complex and less useful methods have been tried to crudely compensate for the effects of inflation; accelerated depreciation methods (including 100% write-offs in the year of acquisition, in some cases) and LIFO inventory costing are the most prominent of these. Of course, these are not true substitutes for a comprehensive system of inflation-adjusted financial reporting.

Fair value. As a practical, yet reasonably effective alternative, IAS 16 promotes the concept of asset revaluation. The standard stipulates that fair value (defined as the amount for which the asset could be exchanged between knowledgeable, willing parties in an arm's-length transaction) be used in any such revaluations. Furthermore, the standard requires that, once an entity undertakes revaluations, they must continue to be made with sufficient regularity that the carrying amounts in any subsequent balance sheet are not materially at variance with then-current fair values. In other words, if the reporting entity adopts the allowed alternative treatment, it cannot report balance sheets that contain obsolete fair values, since that would not only obviate the purpose of the allowed treatment, but would actually make it impossible for the user to meaningfully interpret the financial statements.

Fair value is defined in IAS 16 as generally being the market value of assets such as land and buildings, as determined by appraisers employing normal commercial valuation techniques. Market values can also be used for machinery and equipment, but since such items often do not have readily determinable market values, particularly if intended for specialized applications, they may instead be valued at depreciated replacement cost.

As originally promulgated, IAS 16 stipulated that an estimate of the fair value of any given asset was to be made in the context of the same type of service for which the asset had been deployed. Thus, under the previous wording of this standard, it would not have been appropriate to assume an alternative use of the asset (e.g., a factory building which could potentially be redeveloped as residential units).

The explanation of how fair value is to be applied has now been restated. The definition of fair value is IAS 16 conforms to that in IAS 22: It is the amount at which the property would be exchanged between parties in an arm's-length transaction. Since this does not restrict the hypothetical buyer to utilize the asset in the same way as the present owner of the property, the operative definition of fair value is not restricted as it was previously. Fair value should be understood now to denote the amount at which the property could be exchanged, whether or not this implicitly means the usage would conform to that currently in effect. Fair values of land and buildings are still to be determined, in most instances, by reference to appraisals made by qualified personnel.

Alternative concepts of current value. A number of different concepts have been proposed over the years to achieve inflation accounting. Methods that address changes in specific prices, in contrast to those that attempt to adjust for general purchasing power changes, have measured reproduction cost, replacement cost, sound value, exit value, entry value, and net present value.

In brief, **reproduction cost** refers to the actual current cost of exactly reproducing the asset, essentially ignoring changes in technology in favor of a strict bricks-and-mortar concept. Since the same service potential could be obtained currently, in many cases, without a literal reproduction of the asset, this method fails to fully address the economic reality that accounting should ideally attempt to measure.

Replacement cost, in contrast, deals with the service potential of the asset, which is, after all, what truly represents value for its owner. An obvious example can be found in the realm of computers. While the cost to reproduce a particular mainframe machine exactly might be the same or somewhat lower today versus its original purchase price, the computing capacity of the machine might easily be replaced by one or a small group of microcomputers that could be obtained for a fraction of the cost of the larger machine. To gross up the balance sheet by reference to reproduction cost would be distorting, at the very least. Instead, the replacement cost of the service potential of the owned asset should be used to accomplish the revaluation contemplated by IAS 16.

Furthermore, even replacement cost, if reported on a gross basis, would be an exaggeration of the value implicit in the reporting entity's asset holdings, since the asset in question has already had some fraction of its service life expire. The concept of sound value addresses this concern. Sound value is the equivalent of the cost of replacement of the service potential of the asset, adjusted to reflect the relative loss in its utility due to the passage of time or the fraction of total productive capacity that has already been utilized.

Example of depreciated replacement cost (sound value)

An asset acquired January 1, 1997, at a cost of $40,000 was expected to have a useful economic life of 10 years. On January 1, 2000, it is appraised as having a gross replacement cost of $50,000. The sound value, or depreciated replacement cost, would be 7/10 x $50,000, or $35,000. This compares with a book, or carrying, value of $28,000 at that same date. Mechanically, to accomplish a revaluation at January 1, 2000, the asset should be written up by $10,000 (i.e., from $40,000 to $50,000 gross cost) and the accumulated depreciation should be proportionally written up by $3,000 (from $12,000 to $15,000). Under IAS 16, the net amount of the revaluation adjustment, $7,000, would be credited to revaluation surplus, an additional equity account.

An alternative accounting procedure is also permitted by the standard, under which the accumulated depreciation at the date of the revaluation is written off against the gross carrying value of the asset. In the foregoing example, this would mean that the $12,000 of accumulated depreciation at January 1, 2000, immediately prior to the revaluation, would be credited to the gross asset amount, $40,000, thereby reducing it to $28,000. Then the asset account would be adjusted to reflect the valuation of $35,000 by increasing the asset account by $7,000 ($35,000 − $28,000), with the offset again in stockholders' equity. In terms of total assets reported in the balance sheet, this has exactly the same effect as the first method.

However, many users of financial statements, including credit grantors and prospective investors, pay heed to the ratio of net property and equipment as a fraction of the related gross amounts. This is done to assess the relative age of the enterprise's productive assets and, indirectly, to estimate the timing and amounts of cash needs for asset replacements. There is a significant diminution of information under the second method. Accordingly, the first approach described above, preserving the relationship between gross and net asset amounts after the revaluation, is recommended as being the preferable alternative if the goal is meaningful financial reporting.

Application of revaluation to all assets in class. IAS 16 prudently requires that if any assets are revalued, all other assets in those groupings or categories also be revalued. This is necessary to avert the presentation of a balance sheet that contains an unintelligible mixture of historical costs and current values. Coupled with the requirement that revaluations take place with sufficient frequency to approximate fair values as of each balance sheet date, this preserves the integrity of the financial reporting process. In fact, given that a balance sheet prepared under the benchmark method of historical cost will, in fact, contain different historical costs (due to assets being acquired at varying times using dollars having different general and specific purchasing powers) the allowable alternative approach has the promise of providing even more consistent financial reporting. Offsetting this potential improvement somewhat, of course, is the greater subjectivity applied in determining fair values, vs. actual historical costs.

Although the requirement of IAS 16 is to revalue all assets in a given class, the standard recognizes that it may be more practical to accomplish this on a rolling, or cycle, basis. This would be done by, say, revaluing one-third of the assets in a given asset category, such as machinery, in each year, so that as of any balance sheet date one-third of the group is valued at current fair value, another one-third is valued at amounts that are 1 year obsolete, and another one-third are valued at amounts that are 2 years obsolete. Unless values are changing rapidly, it is likely that the balance sheet would not be materially distorted, and therefore this approach would in all likelihood be a reasonable means to facilitate the revaluation process.

Revaluation adjustments taken into income. While in general revaluation adjustments are to be shown directly in stockholders' equity as revaluation surplus, if a downward adjustment had previously been made to the asset and was recognized as an expense, the later upward revaluation would also be reported as income. Any revaluation receiving this treatment would be limited to the amount of expense recognized previously. As a practical matter, this should be a rare occurrence, since if the asset was revalued downward, the reference for that measurement would have been the estimated recoverable amount, and given what was judged to be a permanent impairment at an earlier date, it is very unlikely that there could be a later upward revaluation that could recover more than a minor portion of that impairment. However, in these unusual situations, a gain would be taken through the income statement.

The converse of the foregoing is also true: If an asset's carrying amount is decreased by recognition of a permanent impairment, but the asset had previously been revalued upward by crediting revaluation surplus, the decline should be reported as a reduction of that surplus account rather than being reported as income. Any decline in value in excess of the amount previously recognized as an upward revaluation should be reported in earnings currently.

Under the provisions of IAS 16, the amount credited to revaluation surplus can either be amortized to retained earnings (but **not** through the income statement!) as the asset is being depreciated, or it can be held in the surplus account until such time as the asset is disposed of or retired from service. In the example below, periodic amortization is utilized.

Example of revaluation and later downward adjustment

Consider the following example to illustrate the foregoing:

An asset was acquired January 1, 1998, for $10,000 and is expected to have a 5-year life. Straight-line depreciation will be used. At January 1, 2000, the asset is appraised as having a sound value (depreciated replacement cost) of $9,000. On January 1, 2002, the asset is appraised at a sound value of $1,500. The entries to reflect these events are as follows:

1/1/98	Asset		10,000	
	Cash, etc.			10,000
12/31/98	Depreciation expense		2,000	
	Accumulated depreciation			2,000
12/31/99	Depreciation expense		2,000	
	Accumulated depreciation			2,000
1/1/00	Asset		5,000	
	Accumulated depreciation			2,000
	Revaluation surplus			3,000
12/31/00	Depreciation expense		3,000	
	Accumulated depreciation			3,000
	Revaluation surplus		1,000	
	Retained earnings			1,000
12/31/01	Depreciation expense		3,000	
	Accumulated depreciation			3,000
	Revaluation surplus		1,000	
	Retained earnings			1,000
1/1/02	Accumulated depreciation		6,000	
	Revaluation surplus		1,000	
	Loss from asset impairment		500	
	Asset			7,500

Certain of the entries in the foregoing example may need elaboration. The entries at 1998 and 1999 year ends are to record depreciation based on original cost, since there had been no revaluations through that point in time. On January 1, 2000, the revaluation is recorded; the appraisal of sound value ($9,000) suggests a 50% increase in value over depreciated historical cost ($6,000), which in turn means that the gross asset should be written up to $15,000 (a 50% increase over the historical cost, $10,000) and the accumulated depreciation should be written up proportionately (from $4,000 to $6,000). Had the appraisal revealed that the useful life of the equipment had also changed from its originally estimated amount, that would have been dealt with prospectively, as prescribed by IAS 8 (see Chapter 21 for a discussion of this matter).

In 2000 and 2001, depreciation must be provided on the new, higher value recorded at the beginning of 2000 (assuming that no additional appraisal is obtained in 2001). Since the asset has been written up by 50%, the periodic charge for depreciation must reflect the higher cost of doing business. However, while the income statements in each year must absorb greater depreciation expense, within the equity section of the balance sheet there will be an offsetting adjustment to transfer revaluation surplus to retained earnings, in the amount of the extra depreciation recognized each year.

As of January 1, 2002, the book value of the equipment is $3,000, which reflects the fact that the asset, having a gross replacement cost when last appraised of $15,000, is now 80% used up. A new appraisal reveals that the fair value is only $1,500 at this time. However, rather than charging the $1,500 decline in value

($3,000 – $1,500) to income, the portion of the decline that represents a retracing of the value increase previously recognized should be accounted for as a reversal of the revaluation surplus, not as a realized loss.

To effect the foregoing, the gross asset and related accumulated depreciation should be written down from amounts based on the 2000 appraisal (updated, in the case of accumulated depreciation, to the current balance) to original cost. Thus, the asset should be written down from $15,000 to $10,000, and the accumulated depreciation adjusted downward from $12,000 to $8,000. The further reduction in book value (from $2,000 to $1,500, as indicated by the latest appraisal) will be taken into income as a realized loss. The offset will be to accumulated depreciation, since the decline in value effectively means that the amount recognized as depreciation in prior periods had been understated; assuming no change in useful life, the depreciation charge for the final year (2002) will be $1,500, reducing the book value to zero at year end.

Exchanges of assets. IAS 16 discusses the accounting to be applied to those situations in which assets are exchanged for other similar or dissimilar assets, with or without the additional consideration of monetary assets. This topic is addressed later in this chapter, under the heading "Nonmonetary (Exchange) Transactions."

Revisions to estimated residual value. Under the benchmark treatment prescribed by IAS 16, the amount estimated for residual value is made at the date of acquisition (or date a self-constructed asset is placed in service) and is not revised subsequently. In this regard the international standard departs from what has been the common practice of treating changes in estimated residual or salvage value as a change in an accounting estimate, and accounting for it prospectively by altering the annual depreciation charge for later years.

If the allowable alternative treatment is elected, at the date of each revaluation of the asset the expected residual amount should also be reassessed. The standard suggests that reference be made to actual residual values of similar assets reaching the end of their useful economic lives about the time the reevaluation is being conducted.

Impairment of Tangible Long-Lived Assets

Until the recent promulgation of IAS 36, *Impairment of Assets*, there was very limited guidance available under international accounting standards to deal with the possible diminution in value that might be associated with long-lived assets. It had long been established under various national accounting standards that permanent impairments (sometimes called "other than temporary" impairments) in long-lived assets necessitated write-downs in carrying values, but in general the two critical questions--when to test for impairment and how to measure it--were left unaddressed. IAS 16 did state, of course, that property, plant, and equipment items should be periodically reviewed for possible impairment, defined as having occurred when an asset's recoverable amount fell below its carrying value. While some reporting enterprises undoubtedly did apply the spirit, as well as the letter, of IAS 16, particularly when a significant event had occurred which made economic viability of major assets an obvious issue, in general the lack of specific guidance more likely was an impediment to application of the impairment requirements of that standard. Now, however, with the issuance of this comprehensive new standard, the process of considering impairments will be greatly facilitated.

Principal requirements of IAS 36. The newly enacted standard on impairment requires that the recoverable amount of tangible (and intangible--discussed in the following chapter) long-lived assets be estimated, for purpose of identifying and measuring impairments, whenever there are indications that such a circumstance might exist. There is no fixed requirement to make this determination on a regular schedule (as there is for certain intangible assets), but a fairly extensive set of criteria are included in IAS 36 to assist entities in making the determination of when such a review might be warranted. If an asset--or a group of assets which comprise what is now called a "cash generating unit"--is found to be impaired, which means that the carrying amount exceeds the net recoverable amount as determined by reference to net selling prices and value in use, a write-down is required. Thus, IAS 36 responds to the two key questions which, because they were heretofore left unanswered, made it difficult to formally address impairment concerns.

Impairment is defined as the excess of carrying value over recoverable amount; recoverable amount is the greater of net selling price or value in use. Net selling price is essentially fair value less costs of disposal (i.e., what would be netted by the entity in an arm's-length transaction, or what is sometimes referred to as "exit value") and value in use is most commonly defined as the net present value of future cash flows associated with the asset or group of assets. Under different circumstances, it may be more or less difficult to obtain these data, but IAS 36 offers sufficient guidance to deal with most situations likely to be encountered in practice.

When it is determined that an asset (or cash generating unit) has indeed been impaired, IAS 36 requires that its carrying value be reduced. Any decline in value is recognized currently in income, for assets accounted for by the benchmark (amortized historical cost) method as set forth in IAS 16. Declines affecting assets accounted for by the allowed alternative (revaluation) method are recognized in the revaluation (stockholders' equity) account. Recoveries in value, not to exceed pre-impairment carrying value, are also given recognition, consistent with the accounting applied to the decline in value.

Identifying impairments. According to IAS 36, at each financial reporting date the reporting entity should determine whether there are conditions which would indicate that impairments may have occurred. Note that this is **not** a requirement that possible impairments be calculated for all assets at each balance sheet date, which would be a formidable undertaking for most enterprises. Rather, it is the existence of conditions which might be suggestive of a heightened risk of impairment which must be evaluated. However, if such indicators are present, then further analysis will be necessary.

The standard provides a set of indicators of potential impairment and suggests that these represent a minimum array of factors to be given consideration. Other, presumably more industry- or entity-specific gauges can and should be devised and employed by the reporting enterprise, particularly when the more general indicators are found over time to be less sensitive than is deemed to be desirable. As experience with IAS 36 is gained, it is likely that more tailored indicators will evolve for some industries.

At a minimum, the following external and internal signs of possible impairment are to be given consideration on an annual basis:

- Market value declines for specific assets or cash generating units, beyond the declines expected as a function of asset aging and use;
- Significant changes in the technological, market, economic or legal environments in which the enterprise operates, or the specific market to which the asset is dedicated;
- Increases in the market interest rate or other market-oriented rate of return such that increases in the discount rate to be employed in determining value in use can be anticipated, with a resultant enhanced likelihood that impairments will emerge;
- Declines in the (publicly owned) entity's market capitalization suggest that the aggregate carrying value of assets exceeds the perceived value of the enterprise taken as a whole;
- There is specific evidence of obsolescence or of physical damage to an asset or group of assets;
- There have been significant internal changes to the organization or its operations, such as product discontinuation decisions or restructurings, so that the expected remaining useful life or utility of the asset has seemingly been reduced; and
- Internal reporting data suggest that the economic performance of the asset or group of assets is, or will become, worse than previously anticipated.

The indicators which are derived from information internally generated by the reporting entity are the more difficult to interpret, and also the ones which, should it be so inclined to do so, may be subject to greater obfuscation by the entity. Information such as the cash flows being generated by an asset or group of assets, or the future cash needs to operate or maintain the asset, for example, may be rather subjective and not immediately apparent. Some of the information is likely to only be accessible "off-line" (i.e., from budgets and forecasts, rather than from the entity's actual accounting system) and thus may lack the credibility of historical data. Finally, the financial performance of individual assets will almost never be ascertainable even from historical accounting records, and the minimum level of aggregation of bookkeeping information will almost always be higher than the level required by IAS 36 (discussed below). Thus, in practical terms, there will be many instances in which there are at best only vague intimations of impairment, and whether further corroborating or disconfirming data is sought out will be a matter of judgment.

The mere fact that one or more of the foregoing indicators suggests that there might be cause for concern about possible asset impairment does not necessarily imply that formal impairment testing must proceed. For example, as noted in IAS 36, an increase in the market rate of interest would not trigger a formal impairment evaluation if either (1) the relevant discount rate to be applied in the determination of the value in use of an asset (via the present value of future net cash flows) would not be expected to track the general changes in market rates of interest, or (2) the effects of changes in the discount rate, tracking changes in market rates of interest, would tend to be offset by other changes in future cash flow, as when an entity has a history of adjusting revenues (and thus cash inflows) to compensate for interest rate rises. However, in the absence of a plausible explanation of why the signals of possible impairment should not be further considered, the implication is that the presence of one or more of these would necessitate some follow-up investigation.

Computing recoverable amounts--General concepts. IAS 36 defines impairment as the excess of carrying value over recoverable amount, and goes on to define recoverable amount as the greater of two alternative measures, net selling price and value in use. The objective is to recognize an impairment only when the economic value of an asset (or cash generating unit consisting of a group of assets) is truly below its book (carrying) value. In theory, and, for the most part, in practice also, an entity making rational choices would sell an asset if its net selling price (fair value less costs of disposal) were greater than the asset's value in use, and would continue to employ the asset if value in use exceeded salvage value. Thus, the economic value of an asset is most meaningfully measured with reference to the greater of these two amounts, since the entity will retain or dispose of the asset consistent with what appears to be its highest and best use. Once recoverable amount has been determined, this is to be compared to carrying value; if recoverable amount is lower, the asset has been impaired, and under the new rules this impairment must be given accounting recognition.

Determining net selling prices. While the concept of recoverable amount has a clear meaning, the actual determination of both the net selling price and the value in use of the asset being evaluated will typically present some difficulties. For actively traded assets, of course, net selling price can be ascertained by reference to publicly available information (e.g., from price lists or dealer quotations), and costs of disposal will either be implicitly factored into those amounts (such as when a dealer quote includes pick-up, shipping, etc.) or can be readily estimated. Most productive, tangible assets, such as machinery and equipment, will not be easily priced in active markets, however. While IAS 36 offers only limited guidance for such situations, it is clear that it will often be necessary to reason by analogy (i.e., to draw inferences from recent transactions in similar assets), making adjustments for age, condition, productive capacity, and other variables. In many industries, trade publications and other data sources can provide a great deal of insight into the market value of key assets, and if there is a sincere effort to tap into these resources, much could be accomplished. On the other hand, some work will be required and it is not difficult to imagine that there may be reluctance to undertake this, although an entity's ability to claim compliance with IAS will encourage it to do so.

Despite the concerns noted above, the difficulties in identifying net selling prices should not be overstated. Experience with SFAS 121, the US GAAP requirement for determining, measuring, and reporting on asset impairments, suggests that there is a wealth of information to be used; in this era of Internet access and vast amounts of published industry data, from both governmental and private sources, estimating net selling prices for a wide range of productive assets should be quite feasible. Furthermore, in many nations for which persistent inflation has been a problem for decades, some form of inflation-adjusted financial reporting may have been practiced, as indeed it was for a period in both the US and the UK, and that experience taught many corporate and public accountants how to develop similar information. Finally, in many (perhaps most) cases, there will either be no signs of possible impairment, in which case no effort to compute recoverable amounts will be needed, or despite one or more indicators of possible impairment the asset's value in use will clearly exceed carrying amount, thus dispensing with any need to measure impairment.

Computing value in use. The second component of recoverable amount is value in use, and when there are indicators of impairment and no clear evidence that either net selling price or value in use exceed carrying value, then value in use will often need to be estimated. The computation of value in use involves a two-step process: first, future cash flows must be estimated; and second, the present value of these cash flows must be calculated by application of an appropriate discount rate. These will be discussed in turn, in the following paragraphs.

Projection of future cash flows must be based on reasonable assumptions; exaggerated revenue growth rates, significant anticipated cost reductions, or unreasonable useful lives for plant assets must be avoided. In general, recent past experience is a fair guide to the near-term future, but a recent growth spurt should not be extrapolated to more than the near-term future. Industry patterns, as well as the experiences of the entity itself, usually must be considered, since no single company, no matter how well managed or fortunate, can long escape from the implications of industry or economy-wide trends. For one example, an entity producing a product line which is being made, or is forecast to become, obsolete, even if currently very astute and profitable, can expect to continually generate healthy cash flows from machinery and equipment dedicated to that product line.

Typically, extrapolation to future periods cannot exceed the amount of "base period" data upon which the projection is built. Thus, a 5-year projection, to be mathematically sound, must be based on at least 5 years of actual historical performance data. Also, since no business can exponentially grow forever, even if, for example, a 5-year historical analysis suggests a 20% annual (inflation adjusted) growth rate, beyond a horizon of 2 years, a moderation of that growth must be hypothesized. This is even more true for a single asset or small cash generating unit, since physical constraints and the ironclad law of diminishing marginal returns-makes it virtually inevitable that a plateau will be reached, beyond which further growth will be tightly constrained. If exceptional returns are being reaped from the assets used to produce a product line, competitors will enter the market and ultimately this too will restrict future cash flows.

For purposes of determining value in use, cash flow projections must represent management's best estimate, not its most optimistic view of the future. Externally sourced data is considered to be more valid than purely internal information. To the extent that internal sources, such as budgets and forecasts, are employed, these will have greater probative value if they have been reviewed and approved by upper levels of management, and if similar budgets and forecasts used in prior periods have been shown to be accurate. More modest assumptions should be made when projecting beyond the periods covered in the formally prepared and reviewed budgets, since not only are estimates about the future inherently less reliable as the horizon is extended, but also the absence of a formal budgeting process regarding the so-called "out years" reduces the credibility of any such projections.

IAS 36 stipulates that steady or declining growth rates must be utilized for periods beyond those covered by the most recent budgets and forecasts. It further states that, barring an ability to demonstrate why a higher rate is appropriate, the growth rate should not exceed the long-term growth rate of the industry in which the entity participates.

Finally, with regard to cash flow projections, it is clear that projections for a period longer than the asset's remaining depreciable life would not be credible. Since the cost of tangible long-lived assets should be rationally allocated over their useful lives, it is implicitly management's representation that no cash flows will occur after the estimated lives are completed. On the other hand, an insistence that there will be work produced by the asset after its nominal terminal date would imply that IAS governing depreciation accounting was not conformed with.

With reference to cash flow projections, the guidance offered by IAS 36 suggests that only normal, recurring cash inflows from the continuing use of the asset being evaluated should be considered, plus the estimated salvage value at the end of its useful life, if any. Cash outflows needed to generate the cash inflows must also be included in the analysis, including any cash outflows needed to prepare the asset for its intended, productive use. Noncash costs, such as depreciation of the asset, obviously must be excluded, inasmuch as these do not affect cash flows, and in the case of depreciation, this would in effect "double count" the very thing being measured. Projections should always exclude cash flows related to financing the asset, for example, interest and principal repayments on any debt incurred in acquiring the asset, since operating decisions (e.g., keeping or disposing of an asset) are separate from financing decisions (borrowing, leasing, buying with equity capital funds). Also, cash flow projections must pertain to the asset that exists and is in use, not to hypothetical future assets or assets currently in use but to be value enhanced by later overhauls or redesigns. Income tax effects are also to be disregarded (i.e., the entire analysis should be on a pretax basis).

The need to identify specific cash flows is the reason why an asset-by-asset approach will most often be ineffective or impossible to perform, since few individual assets have identifiable cash flows. For example, a factory which employs dozens of drill presses, lathes, grinding machines, and other related types of equipment to produce, say, precision components for the automobile industry cannot possibly identify the contribution to cash flow made by, say, a given drill press. For this reason, IAS 36 has developed the concept of the "cash generating unit."

Cash generating units. Under IAS 36, when cash flows cannot be identified with individual assets, these may need to be grouped in order to conduct an impairment test. The requirement is that this grouping be performed at the lowest level possible, which would be the smallest aggregation of assets for which discrete cash flows can be identified, and which are independent of other groups of assets. In practice, this may be a department, a product line, or a factory, for which the output of product and the input of raw materials, labor, and overhead can be identified. While the precise contribution to overall cash flow made by a given drill press may be impossible to surmise, the cash inflows and outflows of a department which produces and sells a discrete product line to an identified group of customers can be readily determined.

An obvious temptation would be to essentially aggregate the entire enterprise into a single cash generating unit, arguing perhaps that it represents an integrated operation. While in some instances this may be correct, in most cases it will not. The risk in too-generously aggregating long-lived assets into cash generating units is that many possible impairments will be concealed, as the subunits having recoverable amounts in excess of carrying amounts will offset those having the opposite circumstance. In this, the effect is identical to applying lower of cost or market to the aggregate inventory of an entity, rather than to component groups or to each inventory item taken by itself. Thus IAS 36 is clear that care must be exercised to be sure that all aggregation is conducted at the lowest feasible level.

Some expansion of the aggregation process will become necessary when an entity's operations are vertically integrated. IAS 36 provides one such example of a mining enterprise which has a private railway to haul its ore; since the railway has no external customers and thus no independent cash inflows, impairment can only be assessed by grouping the mine and the railway into a single cash generating unit. Another such example is a bus line which is a contract provider to a municipality; evaluation of subunits, such as individual bus routes, is not feasible since the contractual arrangement precludes taking individual decisions, such as discontinuing service, regarding any single route. IAS 36 requires that cash generating units be defined consistently from period to period.

Discount rate. The other part of the challenge in computing value in use comes from identifying the appropriate discount rate to apply to projected future cash flows. There are actually two key issues to address. The first is to determine an appropriate rate, ignoring inflation effects. IAS 36 stipulates that a risk rate must be used which is pertinent to the type of asset being valued. Thus, arguably at least, the discount rate to be applied to projected cash flows relating to a steel mill might be somewhat lower than that used to compute the present value of cash flows arising from the use of a piece of high-technology equipment, since the latter may be subject to far greater risk of sudden, unanticipated obsolescence than the former. This concept is supported by market data, which prices debt offerings by entities in riskier industries at higher yields than those in more stable industries.

IAS 36 suggests that identifying the appropriate risk-adjusted cost of capital to employ as a discount rate can be accomplished by reference to the implicit rates in current market transactions (e.g., leasing transactions), or from the weighted-average cost of capital of publicly traded enterprises in the same industry grouping. There are such statistics available in many markets, and the entity's own recent transactions, typically in leasing or borrowing to buy other long-lived assets, will be highly salient information.

When risk-adjusted rates are not available, however, it will become necessary to develop a rate from surrogate data. The two aspects of this are to (1) identify the pure time value of money for the requisite time horizon over which the asset will be utilized--short term almost always carrying a lower rate than intermediate- or long-term; and (2) to add an appropriate risk premium to the pure interest factor, which is related to the variability of future cash flows, with greater variability (the technical definition of risk) being associated with higher risk premiums. Of these two tasks, the latter is likely to prove the more difficult in practice. IAS 36 provides a fairly extended discussion of the methodology to utilize, however, addressing such factors as country risk, currency risk, cash flow risk, and pricing risk. As with all aspects of the impairment analysis, this must be done on a pretax basis and is independent of any considerations regarding how the asset was financed.

The second aspect of determining an appropriate discount rate is somewhat more subtle than that discussed above. The rate used must either be inflation-adjusted or inflation-unadjusted, consistent with how the future cash flows were determined. If the future cash flows were developed in so-called nominal currency units, and if (as has often been true, although for much of the developed world less so now than for any time over the past generation) there is an expectation that prices will inflate over time, future cash inflows and outflows will be projected to grow even if input and output factors will remain constant. If nominal currency units are used, thus inflating the gross amounts and net cash flows increasingly over the years due to the compounding effect of annual inflation assumptions, the discount rate must be similarly increased.

On the other hand, if future cash inflows and outflows are projected in real currency units, the appropriate discount rate will be a lower, inflation-unadjusted rate. If consistent assumptions are used for cash flows and the discount rate, the net result, that is, the present value of future cash flows, will be identical, and thus either approach, if properly applied, is acceptable. The practical risk is that in performing the analyses inconsistent assumptions will be made, thus making the results of little worth.

The interest rate to apply must reflect current market conditions as of the balance sheet date. This means that, during periods of changing rates (as, for example, the mid- to late-1990s have seen secularly declining rates in many industrial nations) the computed value in use of assets will change, perhaps markedly, even if projected cash flows before discounting are stable. This reflects economic reality; however, as rates decline, holdings of productive assets become more valuable, holding all other considerations constant; and as rates rise, such holdings lose value as alternative, market-priced investments (such as fixed-income securities) become more attractive. The accounting implication is that long-lived assets which were unimpaired 1 year earlier may fail an impairment test in the current period if rates have risen during the interim. Since accountants tend not to contemplate such economic matters, however, the risk is that impairments may be overlooked when they are due only to market rate changes, as contrasted to those which result from more attention-getting events such as technological obsolescence or macroeconomic trends such as recessions.

Corporate assets. Another issue which is prone to being ignored has to do with corporate assets, such as headquarters buildings and other long-lived tangible assets such as data processing equipment, which do not generate identifiable cash flows. It should be clear that all such assets need to be tested for impairment, and it should be equally clear that these cannot be tested in the abstract, since there are no cash inflows to weigh against the cash outflows and the net result of any stand-alone test would be to indicate severe impairment.

To cope with the foregoing matter, IAS 36 requires that corporate assets be allocated among or assigned to cash generating units with which they are most closely associated. For a large and diversified enterprise, this probably implies that corporate assets will be allocated among all the cash generating units, perhaps in proportion to annual turnover (revenue). Failure to do this will not only ignore the possible impairment of the corporate assets, per se, but also will distort the impairment testing for the operating assets, since in effect they will be held accountable for shouldering too light a burden, as in reality the cash generating units in the aggregate must cover not only their own costs, but the corporate overhead as well. (The issue of impairment of corporate assets is similar to the matter of impairment of goodwill, which is discussed later in this chapter.)

Accounting for impairments. After computing net selling price and value in use, and then comparing the greater of these to carrying value of an asset or cash generating unit, and assuming an impairment is indicated, this must be reflected in the financial statements. The mechanism for recording an impairment depends upon whether the entity adheres to the benchmark or the allowed alternative treatment prescribed by IAS 16. The benchmark treatment is amortized historical cost, and any impairments computed under this scenario will be reported as a charge against current period earnings, either included with depreciation or set forth separately in the income statement.

For assets for which impairment was determined on a stand-alone basis, the write-down in carrying value is accomplished directly. However, for assets grouped into cash generating units, it will not be determinable which specific assets have suffered the impairment loss, and thus a formulaic approach is prescribed by IAS 36. If goodwill (discussed later in this chapter) was allocated to the cash generating unit, any impairment should be allocated fully to that intangible asset until its carrying value has been reduced to zero. Any further impairment would be allocated proportionately to all the other assets in the cash generating unit. While IAS 36 is silent on this point, presumably the pro rata allocation would also include any corporate assets which had been assigned to that cash generating unit. The standard also does not provide guidance regarding whether the impairment should be credited to the asset account or to the accumulated depreciation (contra asset) account; in either event, the net result would be the same, although for certain analytical purposes (such as computing return on gross investment in the operations of the business) some prefer to leave the gross asset balances intact.

The charge arising from a recognition of an impairment will be reflected either in earnings or directly in stockholders' equity, depending on whether the reporting entity applies the benchmark or the allowable alternative method of accounting for its long-lived assets. If the benchmark method (amortized historical cost) is used, then impairments must be recognized as current period expenses and charged against earnings. Logically, it would seem that the charge could be merged with depreciation expense, since the impairment does represent part of the process of cost allocation to operations over the period of the asset's use. Presumably a separate caption could also be presented, if it is desired that the charge for impairments be made distinct from that for depreciation. It would **not** be appropriate, however, to imply that impairment losses are not part of recurring operations costs (i.e., to suggest that these expenses are somehow extraordinary or unusual in nature). Whether part of depreciation or a separate charge, therefore, impairment costs should be included in income from operations.

If the entity has applied the allowed alternative method of revaluation of long-lived assets, the impairment adjustment will be accounted for as the partial reversal of a previous upward revaluation. Thus, the charge will be made against the revaluation account in stockholders' equity, and not shown in the current period's income statement. However, if the entire revaluation account is eliminated due to recognition of an impairment, any excess impairment should be charged to expense. In other words, the revaluation account cannot contain a net debit balance.

Example of accounting for impairment

Xebob Corp. has one (of its many) departments which performs machining operations on parts which are sold to contractors. A group of machines have an aggregate book value at the latest balance sheet date (December 31, 2000) totaling $123,000. It has been determined that this group of machinery constitutes a cash generating unit for purposes of applying IAS 36.

Upon analysis, the following facts about future expected cash inflows and outflows become apparent, based on the diminishing productivity expected of the machinery as it ages, and the increasing costs which will be incurred to generate output from the machines:

Year	Revenues	Costs, **excluding** depreciation
2001	$75,000	$ 28,000
2002	80,000	42,000
2003	65,000	55,000
2004	20,000	15,000
Totals	$240,000	$140,000

The net selling price of the machinery in this cash generating unit is determined by reference to used machinery quotation sheets obtained from a prominent dealer. After deducting estimated disposition costs, the net selling price is calculated as $84,500.

Value in use is determined with reference to the above-noted expected cash inflows and outflows, discounted at a risk rate of 5%. This yields a present value of about $91,981, as shown below:

Year	Cash flows	PV factors	Net PV of cash flows
2001	47,000	.95238	$44,761.91
2002	38,000	.90703	34,467.12
2003	10,000	.86384	8,638.38
2004	5,000	.82270	4,113.51
Total			$91,980.91

Since value in use exceeds net selling price, value in use is selected to represent the recoverable amount of this cash generating unit. This is lower than the carrying value of the group of assets, however, and thus an impairment must be recognized as of the end of 2000, in the amount of $123,000 – 91,981 = $31,019. This will be included in operating expenses (either depreciation or a separate caption in the income statement) for 2000.

Reversals of previously recognized impairments--Benchmark method used for long-lived assets. Recoveries in value of previously impaired assets are also to be given recognition, provided that criteria established by IAS 36 are met. In order to recognize what is ostensibly a recovery of a previously recognized impairment, a process similar to that which led to the original loss recognition must be followed. This begins with a consideration, as of each balance sheet date, of whether there are indicators of possible impairment recoveries, utilizing external and internal sources of information, including that pertaining to material market value increases; changes in the technological, market, economic or legal environment or the market in which the asset is employed; and the occurrence of a favorable change in interest rates or required rates of return on assets which would imply changes in the discount rate used to compute value in use. Also to be given consideration are data about any changes in the manner in which the asset is employed, as well as evidence that the economic performance of the asset has exceeded expectations and/or is expected to do so in the future. If one or more of these indicators is present, it will be necessary to compute the recoverable amount of the asset in question or, if appropriate, the cash generating unit containing that asset, to determine if the current recoverable amount exceeds the carrying amount of the asset, which had been reduced for the impairment.

If the current recoverable amount exceeds the carrying amount of the asset or cash generating unit, a recovery can be recognized. The amount of recovery to be given accounting recognition is limited to the difference between the carrying value and the amount which would have been the current carrying value had the earlier impairment not been given recognition. Note that this means that restoration of the full amount at which the asset was carried at the time of the earlier impairment cannot be made, since time has elapsed between these two events and further depreciation of the asset would have been recognized in the interim.

Example of impairment recovery--Benchmark method

To illustrate, assume an asset had a carrying value of $40,000 at December 31, 1999, based on its original cost of $50,000, less accumulated depreciation representing the one-fifth, or 2 years, of its projected useful life of 10 years which already has elapsed. The carrying value of $40,000 is after depreciation for 1999 has been computed, but before impairment has been addressed. At that date, a determination was made that the asset's recoverable amount was only $32,000 (assume this was properly computed and that recognition of the impairment was warranted), so that an $8,000 adjustment must be made. For simplicity, assume this was added to accumulated depreciation, so that at December 31, 1999, the asset cost remains $50,000 and accumulated depreciation is stated as $18,000.

At December 31, 2000, before any adjustments are posted, the carrying value of this asset is $32,000. Depreciation for 2000 would be $4,000 ($32,000 book value ÷ 8 years remaining life), which would leave a net book value, after current period depreciation, of $28,000. However, a determination is made that the asset's recoverable amount at this date is $37,000. Before making an adjustment to reverse some or all of the impairment loss previously recognized, the carrying value at December 31, 2000, as it would have existed had the impairment not been recognized in 1999 must be computed.

December 31, 1999 preimpairment carrying value	$40,000
1999 depreciation based on above	5,000
Indicated December 31, 2000 carrying value	$35,000

The December 31, 2000 carrying value would have been $40,000 – 5,000 = $35,000; this is the maximum carrying value which can be reflected on the December 31, 2000 balance sheet. Thus, the full recovery cannot be recognized; instead, the 2000 income statement will reflect (net) a **negative** depreciation charge of $35,000 – 32,000 = $3,000, which can be thought of (or recorded) as follows:

Actual December 31, 1999 carrying value	$32,000
2000 depreciation based on above	4,000 (a)
Indicated December 31, 2000 carrying value	$28,000
Indicated December 31, 2000 carrying value	$28,000
Actual December 31, 2000 carrying value	35,000
Recovery of previously recognized impairment	$ 7,000 (b)

Thus, the net effect on the 2000 income statement is (a) – (b) = $(3,000). The asset cannot be restored to its indicated recoverable amount at December 31, 2000, amounting to $37,000, as this exceeds the carrying amount that would have existed at this date had the impairment in 1999 never been recognized.

Reversals of previously recognized impairments--Allowed alternative method used for long-lived assets. Reversals of impairments are accounted for differently if the reporting entity used the allowed alternative method of accounting for long-lived assets. Under this approach, assets are periodically adjusted to reflect current fair values, with the write-up being recorded in the asset accounts and the corresponding credit reported directly in stockholders' equity and not included in earnings. Impairments are viewed as being downward adjustments of fair value in this scenario, and accordingly are reported as reversals of previous revaluations, not reported in income unless the entire remaining, undepreciated portion of the revaluation is eliminated as a consequence of the impairment; any further impairment is reported in earnings in such case.

When an asset (or cash generating group of assets) was first revalued upward, then written down to reflect an impairment, and then later adjusted to convey a recovery of the impairment, the procedure is to report the recovery as a reversal of the impairment, as with the historical cost (benchmark) method. Since, in most instances, impairments were accounted for as reversals of upward revaluations, a still-later reversal of the impairment will be seen as yet another upward revaluation and accounted for as an addition to an equity account, not reported through earnings. In the event that the impairment had eliminated the entire revaluation capital account, and the excess loss was reported in earnings, the later recovery will be reported in earnings to the extent the earlier write-down had been so reported, with the balance taken to stockholders' equity.

Example of impairment recovery--Allowed alternative method

To illustrate, assume an asset was acquired January 1, 1998, and it had a net carrying value of $45,000 at December 31, 1999, based on its original cost of $50,000, less accumulated depreciation representing the one-fifth, or 2 years, of its projected useful life of 10 years, which has already elapsed, plus a revaluation write-up of $5,000, net. The increase in carrying value was recorded a year earlier, based on an appraisal showing the asset's then fair value was $56,250.

At December 31, 2000, an impairment is detected, and the recoverable amount at that date is determined to be $34,000. Had this not occurred, depreciation for 2000 would have been $45,000 ÷ 8 years remaining life = $5,625; book value after recording 2000 depreciation would have been $45,000 – $5,625 = $39,375. Thus the impairment loss recognized in 2000 is $39,375 – $34,000 = $5,375. Of this loss amount, $4,375 represents a reversal of the net amount of the previously recognized valuation increase remaining (i.e., undepreciated) at the end of 2000, as shown below.

Gross amount of revaluation at December 31, 1998	$6,250
Portion of the above allocable to accumulated depreciation	625
Net revaluation increase at December 31, 1998	5,625
Depreciation taken on appreciation for 1999	625
Net revaluation increase at December 31, 1999	5,000
Depreciation taken on appreciation for 2000	625
Net revaluation increase at December 31, 2000 before recognition of impairment	4,375
Impairment recognized as reversal of earlier revaluation	4,375
Net revaluation increase at December 31, 2000	$ 0

The remaining $1,000 impairment recognized at December 31, 2000, is reported as a current period expense, since it exceeds the available amount of revaluation surplus.

In 2001 there is a recovery of value which pertains to this asset; at December 31, 2001, it is valued at $36,500. This represents a $2,500 increase in carrying amount from the year-earlier balance, net of accumulated depreciation. The first $1,000 of this recovery in value is credited to income, since this is the amount of previously recognized impairment which was charged against earnings; the remaining $1,500 of recovery is accounted for as revaluation, and thus is to be credited to a stockholders' equity (revaluation surplus) account.

Deferred tax effects. Recognition of an impairment for financial reporting purposes is most likely to not be accompanied by a deduction for current tax purposes. As a consequence of the nondeductibility of most impairments, the book value and tax basis of the impaired assets will diverge, with the difference thus created to gradually be eliminated over the remaining life of the asset, as depreciation for tax purposes varies from that which is recognized for financial reporting. Following the dictates of IAS 12 (revised), deferred taxes must be recognized for this new discrepancy. The accounting for deferred taxes is discussed at great length in Chapter 14 and will not be addressed here.

Impairments which will be mitigated by recoveries or compensation from third parties. Impairments of tangible long-lived assets may result from natural or other damages, such as from floods or windstorms; in some such instances, there will be the possibility that payments from third parties (typically commercial insurers) will mitigate the gross loss incurred. A reasonable question in such circumstances is whether the gross impairment must be recognized, or whether it may be offset by the actual or estimated amount of the recovery to be received by the reporting entity.

An interpretation from the Standing Interpretations Committee of the IASC (SIC 14) holds that when property is damaged or lost, impairments and claims for reimbursements should be accounted for separately. Impairments are to be accounted for per IAS 36, as discussed above; disposals (of damaged or otherwise impaired assets) should be accounted for consistent with guidance in IAS 16. Compensation from third parties should be recognized as income when the funds become receivable. The cost of replacement items or of restored items is determined in accordance with IAS 16.

Disclosure requirements. IAS 36 has set forth an array of new disclosure requirements pertaining to impairments. For each class of long-lived asset, the amount of impairment losses recognized in earnings for each period being reported upon must be stated, with indication of where in the income statement it is included (i.e., depreciation or other charges). For each class of asset, the amount of any reversals of previously recognized impairment must also be stipulated, again with an identification of where in the income statement this is included. If any impairment losses were recognized in stockholders' equity directly (i.e., as a reversal of previously recognized upward revaluation), this must be disclosed. Finally, any reversals of impairment losses which were recognized in equity must be stated.

If the reporting entity applies IAS 14 (revised), the amounts of impairments, and the amounts of reversals of impairments, recognized in income and in stockholders' equity during the year must be stipulated also. Note that the segment disclosures pertaining to impairments need not be categorized by asset class, and the income statement location of the charge or credit need not be stated (but will be understood from the disclosures relating to the primary financial statements themselves, of course).

IAS 36 further provides that if an impairment loss for an individual asset or group of assets categorized as a cash generating unit is either recognized or reversed during the period, in an amount which is material to the financial statements taken as a whole, disclosures should be made of the following:

- The events or circumstances that caused the loss or recovery of loss;
- The amount of the impairment loss recognized or reversed;
- If for an individual asset, the nature of the asset and the reportable segment to which it belongs, using the primary format as defined under IAS 14 (revised);
- If for a cash generating unit, a description of that unit (e.g., defined as a product line, a plant, geographical area, etc.), the amount of impairment recognized or reversed by class of asset and by reportable segment based on the primary format, and, if the unit's composition has changed since the previous estimate of the unit's recoverable amount, a description of the reasons for such changes;
- Whether net selling price or value in use was employed to compute the recoverable amount;
- If recoverable amount is net selling price, the basis used to determine it (e.g., whether by reference to active market prices or otherwise); and
- If recoverable amount is value in use, the discount rate(s) used in the current and prior period's estimate.

Furthermore, when impairments recognized or reversed in the current period are material in the aggregate, the reporting entity should provide a description of the main classes of assets affected by impairment losses or reversals of losses, as well as the main events and circumstances that caused recognition of losses or reversals.

This information is not required to the extent that the disclosures above are given for individual assets or cash generating units.

Adopting the new impairment standard. IAS 36 is effective for periods beginning on or after July 1, 1999, with earlier application encouraged. However, it must be applied prospectively, with impairments first recognized as a result of applying the standard initially included in current period results of operations (except as to revalued assets, which would be reported in equity). Retroactive application is not permitted, and neither the benchmark treatment nor the allowed alternative treatment prescribed under IAS 8 (retrospective application, with cumulative effects included in retained earnings or current earnings, respectively) is to be applied.

Retirements and Other Dispositions

In general, when an asset is no longer employed by an entity, it is removed from the balance sheet. In the case of fixed assets, both the asset and the related contra asset, accumulated depreciation, should be eliminated. The difference between the net carrying amount and any proceeds received will be given immediate recognition as a gain or loss on the disposition.

If the allowed alternative treatment has been employed, the asset and the related accumulated depreciation account have been adjusted upward, and the asset is subsequently disposed of before the asset is fully depreciated, note that the gain or loss computed will be identical to what would have been determined had the benchmark treatment been used. That is because, at any point in time, the net amount of the revaluation (the step-up in gross asset amount less the present balance in the step-up in accumulated depreciation) will be offset exactly by the remaining balance in the revaluation surplus account. Elimination of the asset, contra asset, and equity accounts will balance precisely, and there will be no gain or loss on this part of the disposition transaction. The gain or loss will be determined by the discrepancy between the net book value, based on historical cost, and the proceeds from the disposition.

Examples of accounting for asset disposition

On January 1, 2000, Zara Corp. acquired a machine at a cost of $12,000; it had an estimated life of 6 years, no residual value, and was expected to provide a level pattern of utility to the enterprise. Thus, straight-line depreciation in the amount of $2,000 was charged to operations. At the end of 4 years, the asset was sold for $5,000. Accounting in conformity with the IAS 16 benchmark approach was elected. The entries to record depreciation and to report the ultimate disposition on January 1, 2004, are as follows:

1/1/00	Machinery	12,000	
	Cash, etc.		12,000
12/31/00	Depreciation expense	2,000	
	Accumulated depreciation		2,000
12/31/01	Depreciation expense	2,000	
	Accumulated depreciation		2,000
12/31/02	Depreciation expense	2,000	
	Accumulated depreciation		2,000
12/31/03	Depreciation expense	2,000	
	Accumulated depreciation		2,000
1/1/04	Cash	5,000	
	Accumulated depreciation	8,000	
	Machinery		12,000
	Gain on asset disposition		1,000

Now assume the same facts as above, but that the allowed alternative method is used. At the beginning of year 4 (2003) the asset is revalued at a gross replacement cost of $15,000. A year later it is sold for $5,000. The entries are as follows (note in particular that the gain on the sale is identical to that reported under the benchmark approach):

1/1/00	Machinery	12,000	
	Cash, etc.		12,000
12/31/00	Depreciation expense	2,000	
	Accumulated depreciation		2,000
12/31/01	Depreciation expense	2,000	
	Accumulated depreciation		2,000
12/31/02	Depreciation expense	2,000	
	Accumulated depreciation		2,000
1/1/03	Machinery	3,000	
	Accumulated depreciation		1,500
	Revaluation surplus		1,500
12/31/03	Depreciation expense	2,500	
	Accumulated depreciation		2,500
	Revaluation surplus	500	
	Retained earnings		500
1/1/04	Cash	5,000	
	Accumulated depreciation	10,000	
	Revaluation surplus	1,000	
	Machinery		15,000
	Gain on asset disposition		1,000

Depletion

IAS 16 specifically excludes forests and other regenerative natural resources, as well as mineral rights and other nonregenerative resources, from applicability. No other international accounting standard addresses these matters, either. However, given the long-lived nature of those assets, the allocation of cost to periods benefited by a process similar to depreciation is an obvious necessity.

For example, under US GAAP, depletion is the annual charge for the use of natural resources. The depletion base includes all development costs, such as exploring, drilling, excavating, and other preparatory costs. The amount of the depletion base charged to income is determined by the following formula:

$$\frac{1}{\text{Total expected recoverable units}} \times \text{Depletion base} \times \text{Units sold}$$

The unit depletion rate is revised frequently due to the uncertainties surrounding the recovery of natural resources. The revision is made prospectively; the remaining undepleted cost is allocated over the remaining recoverable units.

Given the absence of an international standard on the matter of depletion, and given the need for rational allocation of the cost of long-lived mineral and other natural resource assets to the periods to be benefited, it is reasonable to follow the guidelines set forth above, which are based on US GAAP. For natural resource assets, which are typically harvested, mined, or otherwise placed into production or sold in patterns that are not stable over time (demand for commodities typically being far more volatile than demand for manufactured goods), the units of production method of depletion is almost always superior to straight-line methods.

Example of computing depletion costs

Assume that the rights to extract oil from a field are obtained for an initial payment of $2 million at the start of 2000, plus a commitment to restore the topography of the land, for an estimated cost of $1 million, after the extraction process has run its course. Geological surveys have suggested that the field contains 1,000,000 recoverable barrels of crude oil. Actual recoveries are 300,000 barrels in 2000 and 400,000 barrels in 2001. At the end of 2001, the estimated remaining recoverable crude oil was thought to be 400,000 barrels, and the cost to restore the condition of the land was now believed to be $900,000. Recovery in 2002 is 140,000 barrels, after which the field is abandoned and agreed-upon restoration is performed at a cost of $850,000 in early 2003. The entries to record these events are as follows:

1/1/00	Drilling rights	2,000,000	
	Cash		2,000,000
12/31/00	Depletion expense	900,000	
	Accumulated depletion		900,000
12/31/01	Depletion expense	1,200,000	
	Accumulated depletion		1,100,000
	Land restoration liability		100,000
12/31/02	Depletion expense	280,000	
	Land restoration liability		280,000
2/15/03	Land restoration liability	380,000	
	Depletion expense	470,000	
	Cash		850,000

The annual depletion costs in 2000 and 2001 are based on estimates of recoverable oil of 1,000,000 barrels and total costs of $3 million, including estimated land restoration (which is effectively negative salvage value). Depletion in 2002 is based on remaining accruable cost of $800,000 (the newly estimated land recovery cost of $900,000, less the already accrued $100,000) and revised recoverable oil of 400,000 barrels. When the facts ultimately become known in 2003 (that the recoverable oil was less than forecast and the restoration costs differ somewhat from the estimate made in 2002) the adjustment is really a change in an accounting estimate and thus must be reflected as an operating cost in 2003.

Disclosure Requirements: Tangible Long-Lived Assets

The disclosures required under IAS 16, for property, plant, and equipment, and under IAS 38, for intangibles, are similar. Furthermore, IAS 36 requires extensive disclosures when assets are impaired or when formerly recognized impairments are being reversed. The requirements that pertain to property, plant, and equipment are as follows:

For each class of tangible asset, disclosure is required of

1. The measurement basis used (benchmark or alternative approaches)
2. The depreciation method(s) used
3. Useful lives or depreciation rates used
4. The gross carrying amount and accumulated depreciation at both the beginning and end of the period
5. A reconciliation of the carrying amount at the beginning and end of the period, showing additions, dispositions, acquisitions by means of business combinations, increases or decreases resulting from revaluations, reductions to recognize impairments, amounts written back to recognize recoveries of prior impairments, depreciation, the net effect of translation of foreign entities' financial statements, and any other material items. (An example of such a reconciliation is presented below.) This reconciliation is to be provided for only the current period, if comparative financial statements are being presented.

In addition, the statements should also disclose the following facts:

1. Any restrictions on titles and any assets pledged as security for debt.
2. The accounting policy regarding restoration costs for items of property, plant, and equipment.
3. The expenditures made for property, plant, and equipment, including any construction in progress.
4. The amount of outstanding commitments for property, plant, and equipment acquisitions.

In addition, the statements should also disclose the following facts:

1. Whether, in determining recoverable amounts, future projected cash flows have been discounted to present values.
2. Any restrictions on titles and any assets pledged as security for debt.
3. The amount of outstanding commitments for property, plant, and equipment acquisitions.

Example of reconciliation of asset carrying amounts

Date	*Gross cost*	*Accumulated depreciation*	*Net book value*
1/1/00	$4,500,000	$2,000,000	$2,500,000
Acquisitions	3,000,000		3,000,000
Disposals	(400,000)	(340,000)	(60,000)
Impairment		600,000	(600,000)
Depreciation		200,000	(200,000)
12/31/00	$7,100,000	$2,460,000	$4,640,000

Nonmonetary (Exchange) Transactions

Under US GAAP there exist very detailed rules (APB Opinion 29) governing accounting for nonmonetary transactions. By contrast, under international standards, this topic is dealt with only superficially. Both IAS 16 and the new standard for intangibles, IAS 38, note the accounting implications of exchanges of one item of property, plant, or equipment, or one intangible, for another of similar nature. The rules are simply that

1. The value is to be ascertained by reference to the asset received in the exchange, adjusted for any cash or equivalents paid or received.
2. If the exchange involves similar assets, to be used by the enterprise in essentially the same manner and for the same purpose as the item given up in the exchange, the exchange is not deemed to be the culmination of an earnings process, and accordingly, no gain or loss is recognized; the new asset will be recorded as the carrying amount of the asset given up, adjusted for any cash or equivalent given or received.
3. If dissimilar assets are exchanged, the cost of the item received is measured by reference to its fair value, which is generally the fair value of the asset given up, adjusted for any cash or cash equivalent received or given.

Dissimilar assets. An exchange is deemed to be the culmination of the earnings process when dissimilar assets are exchanged. The general rule is to value the transaction at the **fair market value** of the asset given received (unless the fair value of the asset given up is more clearly evident) and to recognize the gain or loss. If there is a settle-up paid or received in cash or cash equivalent, this is often referred to as **boot**.

Example of an exchange involving dissimilar assets and no boot

Assume the following:

1. Jamok, Inc. exchanges an automobile with a carrying value of $2,500 with Springsteen & Co. for a tooling machine with a fair market value of $3,200.
2. No boot is exchanged in the transaction.
3. The fair value of the automobile is not readily determinable.

In this case, Jamok, Inc. has recognized a gain of $700 ($3,200 – $2,500) on the exchange. Because the exchange involves dissimilar assets, the earnings process has culminated and the gain should be included in the determination of net income. The entry to record the transaction would be as follows:

Machine	3,200	
Automobile		2,500
Gain on exchange of automobile		700

Similar assets. Similar assets are those that are used for the same general purpose, are of the same general type, and are employed in the same line of business. Thus, it is not necessary to exchange identical assets. The treatment described applies to those assets that are exchanged as a result of technological advancement as well as to those that are exchanged as a result of wearing out. The general rule involving the exchange of similar assets involving a gain is to value the transaction at the book value of the asset given up. In this situation, the gain is effectively deferred over the life of the new asset by causing a lesser amount of annual depreciation to be charged to operations.

If cash or an equivalent is also included in the transaction, this suggests that the nonmonetary assets exchanged did not have equivalent values. If there is evidence that the asset given up was impaired as to value, as might be suggested if cash was needed to even up the trade, the impairment must be recognized. To fail to do this would result in an overstatement of the carrying amount of the new asset and excessive periodic depreciation charges over the term of its use.

Example of an exchange involving similar assets and boot

Assume the following:

1. Metronome exchanged a casting machine for a technologically newer model. The cost of the old machine was $75,000, and the accumulated depreciation was $5,000.
2. The fair value of the machine received was $90,000.
3. Boot was paid in the amount of $40,000.

A loss in the amount of $20,000 is recognized in connection with this transaction. This amount is the difference between the fair value of the asset received less the boot paid ($90,000 – $40,000 = $50,000) and the carrying value of the asset surrendered ($70,000). The entry required to record the transaction is as described below.

Loss on trade of machine	20,000	
New machine	90,000	
Accumulated depreciation	5,000	
Old machine		75,000
Cash		40,000

International accounting standards do not presently address the accounting for other types of nonmonetary exchanges that are nonreciprocal in nature. Under US GAAP, nonreciprocal transfers with owners and with nonowners are dealt with as described below.

Nonreciprocal transfers. Examples of nonreciprocal transfers with owners include dividends-in-kind, nonmonetary assets exchanged for common stock, split-ups, and spin-offs. An example of a nonreciprocal transaction with other than the owners is a donation of property either by or to the enterprise.

The valuation of most nonreciprocal transfers should be based on the fair market value of the asset given (or received, if the fair value of the nonmonetary asset is both objectively measurable and would be clearly recognizable). However, nonmonetary assets distributed to owners of an enterprise in a spin-off or other form of reorganization or liquidation should be based on the recorded amount. Where there is no asset given, the valuation of the transaction should be based on the fair value of the asset received.

Example of accounting for a nonreciprocal transfer

Assume the following:

1. XYZ donated property with a book value of $10,000 to a charity during the current year.
2. The property had a fair market value of $17,000 at the date of the transfer.

According to the US GAAP requirements, the transaction is to be valued at the fair market value of the property transferred, and any gain or loss on the transaction is to be recognized. Thus, XYZ should recognize a gain of $7,000 ($17,000 – $10,000) in the determination of the current period's net income. The entry to record the transaction would be as follows:

Charitable donations	17,000	
Property		10,000
Gain on transfer of property		7,000

Capitalization of Borrowing Costs

Logic, as well as promulgated GAAP, suggests that the cost of an asset should include all the costs necessary to get the asset set up and functioning properly for its intended use. For some years there has been a question of whether such costs should be included in the definition of all costs necessary or whether such costs should continue to be treated as purely a period expense. A corollary issue is whether an imputed cost of capital for equity financing should similarly be treated as a cost to be capitalized: The implicit argument being that the cost of a self-constructed asset, for example, should not differ between two entities simply because one finances it internally while another finances the asset with externally supplied (debt) capital.

This question was resolved in the United States with the promulgation of FASB Statement 34, which established US GAAP concerning the capitalization of interest. Borrowing costs, under defined conditions, are added to the cost of fixed assets (and inventory, in very limited circumstances), but the cost of equity capital may not be imputed.

The principal purposes to be accomplished by the capitalization of interest costs are as follows:

1. To obtain a more accurate original asset investment cost
2. To achieve a better matching of costs deferred to future periods with revenues of those future periods

International accounting standards differ from US GAAP in that both benchmark and allowed alternative treatments have been prescribed; the alternative treatment is very similar to that which is mandatory in the United States.

Benchmark treatment. The IAS 23 benchmark remains the method formerly universally followed in the United States and elsewhere. All borrowing costs are treated as period costs and expensed as incurred.

Alternative treatment. Interest actually incurred on borrowed funds used to finance the acquisition, construction, or production of a qualifying asset (defined below) is added to the carrying value of the asset. The amount of interest so accounted for depends on whether funds were borrowed specifically for the project in question or whether a pool of borrowed funds was deployed for a variety of projects, some of which may be subject to the interest capitalization rules.

Qualifying assets are those that normally take an extended period of time to prepare for their intended uses. While IAS 23 does not give further insight into the limitations of this definition, over 15 years of experience with FASB Statement 34 yields certain insights that may be germane to this matter. In general, interest capitalization has been applied to those asset acquisition and construction situations in which

1. Assets are being constructed for an entity's own use or for which deposit or progress payments are made.
2. Assets are produced as discrete projects that are intended for lease or sale.
3. Investments are being made that are accounted for by the equity method, where the investee is using funds to acquire qualifying assets for its principal operations which have not yet begun.

Generally, inventories and land that are not undergoing preparation for intended use are not qualifying assets. When land is in the process of being developed, it is a qualifying asset. If land is being developed for lots, the capitalized interest cost is added to the cost of the land. The related borrowing costs are then matched against revenues when the lots are sold. If, on the other hand, the land is being developed for a building, the capitalized interest cost should instead be added to the cost of the building. The interest is then matched against revenues as the building is depreciated.

The capitalization of interest costs would probably not apply to the following situations:

1. The routine production of inventories in large quantities on a repetitive basis
2. For any asset acquisition or self-construction, when the effects of capitalization would not be material, compared to the effect of expensing interest
3. When qualifying assets are already in use or ready for use
4. When qualifying assets are not being used and are not awaiting activities to get them ready for use
5. When qualifying assets are not included in a consolidated balance sheet
6. When principal operations of an investee accounted for under the equity method have already begun
7. When regulated investees capitalize both the cost of debt and equity capital
8. When assets are acquired with grants and gifts restricted by the donor to the extent that funds are available from those grants and gifts

If funds are borrowed specifically for the purpose of obtaining a qualified asset, the interest costs incurred thereon should be deemed eligible for capitalization, net of any interest earned from the temporary investment of idle funds. It is likely that there will not be a perfect match between funds borrowed and funds actually applied to the asset production process, at any given time, although in some construction projects funds are drawn from the lender's credit facility only as vendors' invoices, and other costs, are actually paid. Only the interest incurred on the project should be included as a cost of the project, however.

In other situations, a variety of credit facilities may be used to generate a pool of funds, a portion of which is applied to the asset construction or acquisition program. In those instances, the amount of interest to be capitalized will be determined by applying an average borrowing cost to the amount of funds committed to the project. Interest cost could include the following:

1. Interest on debt having explicit interest rates
2. Interest related to finance leases
3. Amortization of any related discount or premium on borrowings, or of other ancillary borrowing costs, such as commitment fees

The amount of interest to be capitalized is that portion that could have been avoided if the qualifying asset had not been acquired. Thus, the capitalized amount is the incremental amount of interest cost incurred by the entity to finance the acquired asset. A weighted-average of the rates of the borrowings of the entity should be used. The selection of borrowings to be used in the calculation of the weighted-average of rates requires judgment. In resolving this problem, particularly in the case of consolidated statements, the best criterion to use is the identification and determination of that portion of interest that could have been avoided if the qualifying assets had not been acquired.

The base (which should be used to multiply the rate by) is the average amount of accumulated net capital expenditures incurred for qualifying assets during the relevant time frame. Capitalized costs and expenditures are not the same terms. Theoretically, a capitalized cost financed by a trade payable for which no interest is recognized is not a capital expenditure to which the capitalization rate should be applied. Reasonable approximations of net capital expenditures are acceptable, however, and capitalized costs are generally used in place of capital expenditures unless there is a material difference.

If the average capitalized expenditures exceed the specific new borrowings for the time frame involved, the **excess** expenditures amount should be multiplied by the weighted-average of rates and not by the rate associated with the specific debt. This requirement more accurately reflects the interest cost incurred by the entity to bring the fixed asset to a properly functioning position.

The interest being paid on the debt may be simple or compound. Simple interest is computed on the principal alone, whereas compound interest is computed on principal and on any interest that has not been paid. Compounding may be yearly, monthly, or daily. Most fixed assets will be acquired with debt having interest compounded, and that feature should be considered when computing the amount of interest to be capitalized.

The total amount of interest actually incurred by the entity during the relevant time frame is the ceiling for the amount of interest cost capitalized. Thus, the amount capitalized cannot exceed the amount actually incurred during the period involved. On a consolidated basis, the ceiling is defined as the total of the parent's interest cost plus that of the consolidated subsidiaries. If financial statements are issued separately, the interest cost capitalized should be limited to the amount that the separate entity has incurred, and that amount should include interest on intercompany borrowings. The interest incurred is a gross amount and is not netted against interest earned except in rare cases, such as when there are externally restricted tax-exempt borrowings in certain jurisdictions.

IAS 11, while offering a choice between immediate expensing and capitalization of qualifying borrowing costs, did not indicate whether a given enterprise could use both procedures, for different qualifying properties. In SIC 2, the Standing Interpretations Committee has responded to this previously unanswered question. The consensus stipulates that if capitalization (the allowed alternative treatment under the standard) is elected, it should be used for all qualifying assets and for all periods. It also states that if interest is capitalized, the asset must not be reflected at an amount in excess of recoverable amount--any excess is an impairment to be recognized immediately.

Example of accounting for capitalized interest costs

Assume the following:

1. On January 1, 2000, Gemini Corp. contracted with Leo Company to construct a building for $2,000,000 on land that Gemini had purchased years earlier.
2. Gemini Corp. was to make 5 payments in 2000, with the last payment scheduled for the date of completion.
3. The building was completed December 31, 2000.
4. Gemini Corp. made the following payments during 2000:

January 1, 2000	$ 2,000,000
March 31, 2000	4,000,000
June 30, 2000	6,100,000
September 30, 2000	4,400,000
December 31, 2000	3,500,000
	$20,000,000

5. Gemini Corp. had the following debt outstanding at December 31, 2000:

    a. A 12%, 4-year note dated 1/1/00 with interest compounded quarterly. Both principal and interest due 12/31/03 (relates specifically to building project) $8,500,000
    b. A 10%, 10-year note dated 12/31/96 with simple interest and interest payable annually on December 31 $6,000,000
    c. A 12%, 5-year note dated 12/31/98 with simple interest and interest payable annually on December 31 $7,000,000

The amount of interest to be capitalized during 2000 is computed as follows:

Average Accumulated Expenditures

Date	Expenditure	Capitalization period*	Average accumulated expenditures
1/1/00	$ 2,000,000	12/12	$2,000,000
3/31/00	4,000,000	9/12	3,000,000
6/30/00	6,100,000	6/12	3,050,000
9/30/00	4,400,000	3/12	1,100,000
12/31/00	3,500,000	0/12	--
	$20,000,000		$9,150,000

The number of months between the date when expenditures were made and the date on which interest capitalization stops (December 31, 2000).

Potential Interest Cost to be Capitalized

($8,500,000 x 1.12551)*	− $850,000	=	$1,066,840
650,000 x 0.1108**		=	72,020
$9,150,000			$1,138,860

*   *The principal, $8,500,000, is multiplied by the factor for the future amount of $1 for 4 periods at 3% to determine the amount of principal and interest due in 2000.*
** *Weighted-average interest rate*

	Principal	Interest
10%, 10-year note	$ 6,000,000	$ 600,000
12%, 5-year note	7,000,000	840,000
	$13,000,000	$1,440,000

$$\frac{\text{Total interest}}{\text{Total principal}} = \frac{\$ 1,440,000}{\$13,000,000} = 11.08\%$$

The actual interest is

12%, 4-year note [($8,500,000 x 1.12551) – $8,500,000]	=	$1,066,840
10%, 10-year note ($6,000,000 x 10%)	=	600,000
12%, 5-year note ($7,000,000 x 12%)	=	840,000
Total interest		$2,506,840

The interest cost to be capitalized is the lesser of $1,138,860 (avoidable interest) or $2,506,840 (actual interest). The remaining $1,367,980 ($2,506,840 – $1,138,860) would be expensed.

Determining the time period for interest capitalization. Three conditions must be met before the capitalization period should begin.

1. Expenditures for the asset are being incurred
2. Borrowing costs are being incurred
3. Activities that are necessary to prepare the asset for its intended use are in progress

As long as these conditions continue, interest costs can be capitalized.

Necessary activities are interpreted in a very broad manner. They start with the planning process and continue until the qualifying asset is substantially complete and ready to function as intended. These may include technical and administrative work prior to actual commencement of physical work, such as obtaining permits and approvals, and may continue after physical work has ceased. Brief, normal interruptions do not stop the capitalization of interest costs. However, if the entity intentionally suspends or delays the activities for some reason, interest costs should not be capitalized from the point of suspension or delay until substantial activities in regard to the asset resume.

If the asset is completed in a piecemeal fashion, the capitalization of interest costs stops for each part as it becomes ready to function as intended. An asset that must be entirely complete before the parts can be used as intended can continue to capitalize interest costs until the total asset becomes ready to function.

Suspension and cessation of capitalization. If there is an extended period during which there is no activity to prepare the asset for its intended use, capitalization of borrowing costs should be suspended. As a practical matter, unless the break in activity is significant, it is usually ignored. Also, if delays are normal and expected given the nature of the construction project (such as a suspension of building construction during the winter months), this would have been anticipated as a cost and would not warrant even a temporary cessation of borrowing cost capitalization.

Capitalization would cease when the project has been substantially completed. This would occur when the asset is ready for its intended use or for sale to a customer. The fact that routine, minor administrative matters still need to be attended to would not mean that the project had **not** been completed, however. The measure should be substantially complete, in other words, not absolutely finished.

Costs in excess of recoverable amounts. If the capitalization of borrowing costs causes the carrying value of the asset to exceed its recoverable value (if property, plant, or equipment) or its net realizable value (if an item held for resale), it will be necessary to record an adjustment to write the asset carrying value down. In the case of plant, property, and equipment, a later write-up may occur due to use of the allowed alternative (i.e., revaluation) treatment, recognizing fair value increases, in which case, as described earlier, recovery of a previously recognized loss will be reported in earnings.

Consistency of application. IAS 23 did not address the question of whether an entity would be justified in capitalizing interest costs (i.e., using the allowed alternative treatment) for some qualifying assets, while expensing currently (i.e., applying the benchmark treatment) interest incurred in the acquisition, construction, or production of other qualifying assets. While the issue was not raised at the time, logic suggested that if both methods were employed for qualifying assets by a single entity, it would make meaningful interpretation of the resulting financial statements more difficult for users. Subsequently, the IASC's Standing Interpretations Committee (SIC) addressed this matter. It concluded that if the allowed alternative method (i.e., capitalizing borrowing costs) is used for some qualifying assets, the method should be used for all such assets.

In reaching this conclusion, the committee weighed the guidance already contained in IAS 27 (on consolidated financial reporting) and the *Framework for the Preparation and Presentation of Financial Statements*. The existing standard on consolidations provides that uniform accounting policies are to be used for like transactions and other events in similar circumstances. The logic is to avoid having consolidated financial statements which are the summation of dissimilar measurements of like transactions or other economic phenomena. The IASC's *Framework for the Preparation and Presentation of Financial Statements* similarly expresses the notion that measurement of like transactions and other events should be carried out in a consistent manner throughout an entity and over the time of its ongoing existence, for purposes of both separate and consolidated financial reporting. Finally, as IAS 23 stipulates only one alternative methodology, capitalization of interest costs, the SIC was led to conclude that the intention was to not leave financial statement preparers with any further discretion. Accordingly, the Committee's finding was that it would not be appropriate to apply capitalization to some, but not all, qualifying assets.

Disclosure requirements. With respect to an entity's accounting for borrowing costs, the financial statements must disclose which policy (benchmark or allowed alternative) is being utilized, as well as the actual borrowing costs capitalized during the period and the rate used to determine the amount of such costs eligible for capitalization. As noted above, this rate will be the weighted-average of rates on all borrowings included in an allocation pool or the actual rate on specific debt identified with a given asset acquisition or construction project.

9 INTANGIBLE ASSETS

PERSPECTIVE AND ISSUES

Long-lived assets are those that will provide economic benefits to an enterprise for a number of future periods. Accounting standards regarding long-lived assets involve determination of the appropriate cost at which to record the assets initially, the amount at which to present the assets at subsequent reporting dates, and the appropriate method(s) to be used to allocate the cost or other recorded values over the periods being benefited. Under international accounting standards, while historical cost is the defined benchmark treatment, revalued amounts may also be used for presenting long-lived assets in the statement of financial position if certain conditions are met.

Long-lived assets are primarily operational in character, and they may be classified into two basic types: tangible and intangible. Tangible assets have physical substance, while intangible assets either have no physical substance, or have a value which is not conveyed by what physical substance they do have (e.g., the value of computer software is not reasonably measured with reference to the cost of the diskettes on which these are contained).

The value of an intangible asset is a function of the rights or privileges that its ownership conveys to the business enterprise. Intangible assets can be further categorized as being either

1. Identifiable, or
2. Unidentifiable (i.e., goodwill).

Identifiable intangibles include patents, copyrights, brand names, customer lists, trade names, and other specific rights that, typically, can be conveyed by an owner without necessarily also transferring related physical assets. **Goodwill**, on the other hand, cannot be meaningfully transferred to a new owner without also selling the other assets and/or the operations of the business.

Research and development costs are also addressed in this chapter. Formerly the subject of a separate international standard (IAS 9), but more recently guided by the new standard covering all intangibles (IAS 38), research costs must be expensed as incurred, whereas development costs, as defined and subject to certain limitations, are to be classified as assets and amortized over the period to be benefited.

The recently promulgated international accounting standard on impairment of assets (IAS 36) pertains to both tangible and intangible long-lived assets. This chapter will consider the implications of this new standard for the accounting for intangible assets. The matter of goodwill, an unidentifiable intangible asset deemed to be the residual cost of a business combination accounted for as an acquisition, has been addressed by IAS 22 (revised 1998) and is covered in Chapter 11; accounting for all other intangibles, addressed in IAS 38, is discussed in this chapter.

Sources of IAS	
IAS 36, 38	*SIC* 6

DEFINITIONS OF TERMS

Amortization. In general, the systematic allocation of the cost of a long-term asset over its useful economic life; the term is also used specifically to define the allocation process for intangible assets.

Carrying amount. The amount at which an asset is presented on the balance sheet, which is its cost (or other allowable basis), net of any accumulated depreciation and impairment losses.

Cash generating unit. The smallest identifiable group of assets that generates cash inflows from continuing use, largely independent of the cash inflows associated with other assets or groups of assets.

Corporate assets. Assets, excluding goodwill, that contribute to future cash flows of both the cash generating unit under review for impairment and other cash generating units.

Cost. Amount of cash or cash equivalent paid or the fair value of other consideration given to acquire or construct an asset.

Depreciable amount. Cost of an asset or the other amount that has been substituted for cost, less the residual value of the asset.

Depreciation. Systematic and rational allocation of the depreciable amount of an asset over its economic life.

Development. The application of research findings or other knowledge to a plan or design for the production of new or substantially improved materials, devices, products, processes, systems, or services prior to commencement of commercial production or use. This should be contrasted to **research**.

Fair value. Amount that would be obtained for an asset in an arm's-length exchange transaction between knowledgeable willing parties.

Goodwill. The excess of the cost of a business combination accounted for as an acquisition over the fair value of the net assets thereof, to be amortized over its useful economic life which, as a rebuttable presumption, is no greater than 20 years.

Impairment loss. The excess of the carrying amount of an asset over its recoverable amount.

Intangible assets. Nonmonetary assets, without physical substance, held for use in the production or supply of goods or services or for rental to others, or for administrative purposes, which are identifiable and are controlled by the enterprise as a result of past events, and from which future economic benefits are expected to flow.

Monetary assets. Assets whose amounts are fixed in terms of units of currency. Examples are cash, accounts receivable, and notes receivable.

Net selling price. The amount which could be realized from the sale of an asset by means of an arm's-length transaction, less costs of disposal.

Nonmonetary transactions. Exchanges and nonreciprocal transfers that involve little or no monetary assets or liabilities.

Nonreciprocal transfer. Transfer of assets or services in one direction, either from an enterprise to its owners or another entity, or from owners or another entity to the enterprise. An enterprise's reacquisition of its outstanding stock is a nonreciprocal transfer.

Recoverable amount. The greater of an asset's net selling price or its value in use.

Research. The original and planned investigation undertaken with the prospect of gaining new scientific or technical knowledge and understanding. This should be contrasted to **development**.

Residual value. Estimated amount expected to be obtained on ultimate disposition of the asset after its useful life has ended, net of estimated costs of disposal.

Useful life. Period over which an asset will be employed in a productive capacity, as measured either by the time over which it is expected to be used, or the number of production units expected to be obtained from the asset by the enterprise.

CONCEPTS, RULES, AND EXAMPLES

Background

Historically, there has been a dearth of guidance on the topic of intangible assets under international accounting standards, while the need for a standard dealing with all aspects of the subject has been large and growing. To appreciate the practical importance of this subject in countries which do not yet have their own national accounting standards, but which instead rely on IAS for guidance, consider the following two scenarios:

- In many countries, it has been common practice to defer recognition of certain types of expenditures; examples of expenses which are commonly deferred include advertising costs, set-up costs, and so forth. Protagonists of such a practice argue that such expenses result in benefits that will flow to an enterprise in future years as well. As a result of this widespread and therefore allegedly acceptable "best practice," many enterprises, particularly in developing countries, defer expenses to future periods and thereby present better current operating results than their counterparts in developed countries. This issue has now been comprehensively dealt with in the new IAS on intangible assets.
- Enterprises in some countries follow the practice of capitalizing "brand names" and "internally generated goodwill," and vehemently argue that the useful lives of such assets, especially in case of established companies, are infinite or indefinite, and on these grounds do not provide any amortization of these capitalized costs. The new standard on intangible assets has mandated amortization of intangible assets if they are put to use, and has also limited (as a rebuttable presumption) the amortization period to 20 years.

The subject of intangible assets was first addressed by the IASC in its Exposure Draft, E50, captioned *Intangible Assets*, published in June 1995. This draft was subsequently revised extensively by the IASC, and the revised draft, E60, was issued in 1997. Recently, and after long debate, the IASC has approved the standard on the topic intangible assets (IAS 38), which is applicable to financial statements covering annual periods beginning on or after July 1, 1999. Since IAS 38 offers comprehensive guidance on accounting for all intangible assets, including those resulting from research and development expenditures, the extant International Accounting Standard on research and development costs, IAS 9, has been withdrawn.

The new standard sets forth recognition criteria, measurement bases, and disclosure requirements for intangible assets. It also prescribes impairment testing for intangible assets to be undertaken on a regular basis. This is to ensure that only assets having a recoverable value are capitalized and carried forward to future periods. It is interesting to note that in prescribing the amortization period the standard has ruled out the concept of intangible assets having infinite lives. Also, by simultaneously withdrawing the existing standard on research and development costs (IAS 9) and by the revising the standard on business combinations, the IASC has considerably streamlined and rationalized the accounting standards relating to this subject.

Scope of the standard. The standard applies to all enterprises. It prescribes the accounting treatment for intangible assets, including development costs. However, it does not apply to intangible assets covered by other IAS; for instance, deferred tax assets covered under IAS 12, leases that fall within the purview of IAS 17, goodwill arising on a business combination and dealt with by IAS 22, assets arising from employee benefits that are covered by IAS 19, and financial assets as defined by IAS 32 and as also covered by IAS 25, 27, 28, and 31. This standard also does not apply to intangible assets arising in insurance companies from contracts with policyholders and mineral rights and the costs of exploration for, or development and extraction of, minerals, oil, natural gas and similar nonregenerative resources; however, it does apply to intangible assets that are used to develop or maintain these activities.

Identifiable intangible assets include patents, copyrights, licenses, customer lists, brand names, import quotas, computer software, leasehold improvements, marketing rights, and specialized know-how. These items have in common the fact that there is little or no tangible substance to them (there may be tangible evidence of an asset's existence, such as a certificate indicating that a patent had been granted, but this does constitute the asset itself), they have an economic life of greater than 1 year, and they have a decline in utility over that period which can be measured or reasonably assumed. In many but not all cases, the asset is separable; that is, it could be sold or otherwise disposed of without simultaneously disposing of or diminishing the value of other assets held.

Intangible assets are, by definition, assets that have no physical substance. However, there may be instances where intangibles also have some physical form. For example

- There may be tangible evidence of an asset's existence, such as a certificate indicating that a patent had been granted, but this does constitute the asset itself;
- Some intangible assets may be contained in or on a physical substance such as a compact disc (in case of computer software); and
- Identifiable assets that result from research and development activities are intangible assets because the tangible prototype or model is secondary to the knowledge that is the primary outcome of those activities.

Recognition Criteria

Identifiable intangible assets have much similarity to tangible long-lived assets (property, plant, and equipment), and the accounting for them is accordingly also very similar. The key criteria for determining whether intangible assets are to be recognized are

1. Whether the intangible asset has an identity separate from other aspects of the business enterprise;
2. Whether the use of the intangible asset is controlled by the enterprise as a result of its past actions and events;
3. Whether future economic benefits can be expected to flow to the enterprise; and
4. Whether the cost of the asset can be measured reliably.

Identifiability. As to the first issue, the principal concern is to distinguish these intangibles from goodwill arising from a business combination , the accounting for which is addressed by IAS 22. Goodwill is the residual cost of a business acquisition that cannot be assigned either to tangible assets, net of any liabilities assumed, or to identifiable intangibles. Unlike identifiable intangibles, goodwill cannot be separated from the assets (the physical as well as the identifiable intangible) it was acquired with. Since goodwill cannot be severed and sold, its real value is often questioned and the period over which it can be amortized is accordingly often made as brief as possible.

To capitalize the cost of an intangible asset other than goodwill, it must have an independently observable existence and a cost that can be assigned to it. Independent observable independence can be established if the enterprise could rent, sell, exchange, or distribute the future economic benefits from the assets without also disposing of other assets; that is, that an owner can convey them without necessarily also transferring related physical assets. Goodwill, on the other hand, cannot be meaningfully transferred to a new owner without also selling other assets and hence, will not meet the recognition criteria for intangible assets as defined by IAS 38.

Control. The provisions of IAS 38 require that an enterprise should be in a position to control the use of the intangible asset. Control implies the power to both obtain future economic benefits from the asset as well as restrict the access of others to those benefits. Normally enterprises register patents, copyrights, etc. to ensure its control over an intangible asset. A patent gives the holder the exclusive right to use the underlying product or process without any interference or infringement from others. Intangible assets arising from technical knowledge of staff, customer loyalty, long-term training benefits, etc., will have difficulty meeting this recognition criteria in spite of expected future economic benefits from them. This is due to the fact that the enterprise would find it impossible to fully control these resources or to prevent others from controlling them.

Future economic benefits. Under IAS 38, it is mandated that an intangible asset be recognized only if future economic benefits specifically associated therewith will flow to the reporting entity. It must be demonstrated that the intangible asset will enhance the expected inflow of benefits to the enterprise, that it in fact will be able to perform effectively in that role, and that the entity intends to use the intangible in the manner represented. Furthermore, the enterprise must be able to show that it has the other resources necessary to exploit the intangible asset's utility so as to reap the benefits that it possesses.

Measurement of Cost of Intangibles

The conditions under which the intangible asset has been acquired will determine the measurement of cost.

The cost of an intangible asset acquired separately is determined in the same manner used for tangible assets as described in Chapter 8. Cost comprises the purchase price itself and any directly attributable costs of preparing the asset for its intended use.

In some situations, identifiable intangibles are acquired as part of a **business combination** or other bulk purchase transaction. According to the provisions of IAS 38, the cost of an intangible asset acquired as part of a business combination is its fair value as at the date of acquisition. If the intangible asset can be freely traded in an active market, then the quoted market price is the best measurement of cost. If the intangible asset has no active market, then cost is determined based on the amount that the enterprise would have paid for the asset in an arm's length transaction, at the date of acquisition. If the cost of an intangible asset acquired as part of a business combination cannot be measured reliably, then that asset is not recognized, but rather is included in goodwill.

Under US GAAP, the aggregate purchase cost is to be allocated to assets acquired and liabilities assumed. If one or more of the assets are intangibles, the extent of judgment required in the allocation process becomes somewhat greater than would otherwise be the case; in extreme situations it may be impossible to determine how much, if any, of the aggregate cost should be allocated to intangibles. It is most likely to be determinable when the intangibles were actually negotiated for in the transaction rather than being thrown in to the deal. Furthermore, if the allocation of the purchase price to individual assets is accomplished by applying discounted present value measures to future revenue streams, unless this same process is usable with regard to the intangibles, it is likely that any unallocated purchase price will have to be assigned to goodwill.

Internally generated goodwill is not recognized as an intangible asset, because it fails to meet the recognition criteria of

- Reliable measurement at cost,
- Lack of an identity separate from other resources, and
- Control by the reporting enterprise.

In practice, accountants are usually confronted with the desire to recognize internally generated goodwill based on the premise that at a certain point in time the market value of an enterprise exceeds the carrying value of its identifiable net assets. However, as IAS 38 categorically points out, such differences cannot be considered to represent the cost of intangible assets **controlled by the enterprise** and, hence, would not meet the criteria for recognition (i.e., capitalization) of such an asset on the books of the enterprise.

Intangibles acquired by means of government grants. If the intangible is acquired free of charge or by payment of nominal consideration, as by means of a government grant (say, when the government grants the right to operate a radio station) or similar program, and assuming the benchmark accounting treatment (historical cost) is employed, obviously there will be little or no amount reflected as an asset. If the asset is important to the reporting entity's operations, however, it must be adequately disclosed in the notes to the financial statements. If the allowed alternative (fair value) method is used, the fair value should be determined by reference to an active market. However, given the probable lack of an active market, since government grants are generally not transferable, it is unlikely that this situation will be encountered. If an active market does not exist for this type of an intangible asset, the enterprise must recognize the asset at cost. Cost would include those that are directly attributable to preparing the asset for its intended use.

Intangibles Acquired Through an Exchange of Assets

If an intangible asset is acquired in exchange or partial exchange for a **dissimilar** intangible or other asset, then the cost of the asset is measured at its fair value. This amount is to be ascertained by reference to the fair value of the asset received, which is equivalent to the fair value of the asset given up in the exchange, adjusted for any cash or cash equivalents transferred.

If the exchange involves **similar** assets, to be used by the enterprise in essentially the same manner and for the same purpose as the item given up in the exchange, the exchange is not deemed to be the culmination of an earnings process and, accordingly, no gain or loss is recognized. The new asset will be recorded at the carrying amount of the asset given up, adjusted for any cash or cash equivalent (often called "boot") given or received.

Internally Generated Intangibles Other Than Goodwill

In the event that intangibles are internally generated (e.g., when patents are obtained following a period of research and development, or customer lists are developed), it may be possible to identify the relevant costs and thus to justify capitalization. Similar to what had been prescribed by IAS 9, *Research and Development Costs*, the provisions of the new standard identify projects into research phase and development phase. The provisions of IAS 38 are similar to the provisions of the erstwhile IAS 9, in that

1. Costs incurred in the **research** phase are expensed immediately; and
2. If costs incurred in the **development** phase meet the recognition criteria for an intangible asset, such costs should be capitalized. However once costs have been expensed during the development phase, they cannot later be capitalized.

For example, certain expenditures may be made to enhance brand names, such as image-advertising campaigns, but these costs will also have ancillary benefits, such as promoting specific products that are being sold currently, and possibly even enhancing employee morale and performance. As a practical matter, it will be difficult to determine what portion of the expenditures relate to which achievement, and thus to ascertain how much, if any, of the cost may be capitalized as part of brand names. Thus, it is considered to be unlikely that threshold criteria for recognition can be met in such a case. For this reason the standard has specifically disallowed the capitalization of internally generated assets like brands, mastheads, publishing titles, customer lists, and items similar to these in substance.

Along with the issuance of a standard on intangible assets, IAS 38, it was imperative that the IASC simultaneously withdraw the existing standard on research and development costs, IAS 9. The reason this was so important was because, if both the standards were operative in the same year, then the accounting for certain internally generated assets, which would meet the criteria of both standards, would cause confusion. For example, software programs developed in-house as a result of research and development activities would be covered under IAS 9, while patented software programs developed in-house would meet the recognition criteria of intangible assets as well. In order to avoid confusion caused by differences in accounting treatments prescribed by the two standards, the IASC rightly decided to combine the provisions of the two standards into one.

When an internally generated intangible asset meets the recognition criteria, the cost is determined using the same principles as for an acquired asset. Thus, cost comprises all costs directly attributable to creating, producing and preparing the asset for its intended use. IAS 38 closely follows IAS 16 with regard to elements of cost that may be considered as part of the asset, and the need to recognize the cash equivalent price when the acquisition transaction provides for deferred payment terms. As with self-constructed tangible assets, elements of profit must be eliminated from amounts capitalized, but incremental administrative and other overhead costs can be allocated to the intangible and included in the asset's cost. Initial operating losses, on the other hand, **cannot** be deferred by being added to the cost of the intangible, but must be expensed as incurred.

As noted above, the standard presents the concepts of the research phase and the development phase of a research and development project. The standard mandates that the expenditure incurred during the research phase of an internal project should be recognized as an expense when incurred (as opposed to recognizing it as an intangible asset). The standard takes this view based on the premise that an enterprise cannot demonstrate that the expenditure incurred in the research phase will generate probable future economic benefits and consequently that an intangible asset exists (thus, such expenditure should be expensed). Examples of research activities include: activities aimed at obtaining new knowledge; the search for, evaluation, and final selection of applications of research findings; and the search for and formulation of alternatives for new and improved systems, etc.

The standard recognizes that the development stage is further advanced than the research stage, and that an enterprise can possibly, in certain cases, identify an intangible asset and demonstrate that this asset will probably generate future economic benefits for the organization. Thus, the standard allows recognition of an intangible asset during the development phase, provided the enterprise can demonstrate **all** the following:

- Technical feasibility of completing the intangible asset so that it will be available for use or sale;
- Its intention to complete the intangible asset and either use it or sell it;
- Its ability to use or sell the intangible asset;
- The mechanism by which the intangible will generate probable future economic benefits;
- The availability of adequate technical, financial and other resources to complete the development and to use or sell the intangible asset; and
- The entity's ability to reliably measure the expenditure attributable to the intangible asset during its development.

Examples of development activities include: the design and testing of preproduction models; design of tools, jigs, molds, and dies; design of a pilot plant which is not otherwise commercially feasible; design and testing of a preferred alternative for new and improved systems, etc.

Recognition of the cost of internally generated computer software costs. The recognition of computer software costs poses several questions.

1. Should the costs incurred in developing the software, in the case of a company developing software programs for sale, be expensed or should the costs be capitalized and amortized?
2. Is the treatment for developing software programs different if the program is to be used for in-house applications only?
3. In the case of purchased software, should the cost of the software be capitalized as a tangible asset or as an intangible asset, or should it be expensed fully and immediately?

In view of the new IAS on intangible assets, the position can be clarified as follows:

1. In the case of a software developing company, the costs incurred in the development of software programs are research and development costs. Accordingly, all expenses incurred in the research phase would be expensed. Thus all expenses incurred until **technological feasibility** for the product has been established should be expensed. The enterprise would have to demonstrate technical feasibility and probability of its commercial success. Technological feasibility would be established if the enterprise has completed a detailed program design or working model. The enterprise should have completed the planning, designing, coding, and testing activities and established that the product can be successfully produced. Apart from being capable of production, the enterprise should demonstrate that it has the intention and ability to use or sell the program. Action taken to obtain control over the program in the form of copyrights or patents would support capitalization of these costs. At this stage the software program would be

able to meet the criteria of identifiability, control, and future economic benefits and can thus be capitalized and amortized as an intangible asset.

2. In the case of software internally developed for in-house use, for example a payroll program developed by the reporting enterprise itself, the accounting approach would be different. While the program developed may have some utility to the enterprise itself, it would be difficult to demonstrate how the program would generate future economic benefits to the enterprise. Also, in the absence of any legal rights to control the program or to prevent others from using it, the recognition criteria would not be met. Further, the cost proposed to be capitalized should be recoverable. In view of the impairment test prescribed by the standard, the carrying amount of the asset may not be recoverable and would accordingly have to be adjusted. Considering the above facts, such costs may need to be expensed.

3. In the case of purchased software, the treatment would differ on a case-to-case basis. Software purchased for sale would be treated as inventory. However, software held for licensing or rental to others should be recognized as an intangible asset. On the other hand, cost of software purchased by an enterprise for its own use and which is integral to the hardware (because without that software the equipment cannot operate), would be treated as part of cost of the hardware and capitalized as property, plant, or equipment. Thus, the cost of an operating system purchased for an in-house computer (or cost of software purchased for computer-controlled machine tool) are treated as part of the related hardware.

    Cost of other software programs should be treated as intangible assets (as opposed to being capitalized along with the related hardware), as they are not an integral part of the hardware. For example, the cost of payroll or inventory software (purchased) may be treated as an intangible asset provided it meets the capitalization criteria under IAS 38 (in practice, the conservative approach, would be to expense such costs as they are incurred, since their ability to generate future economic benefits is always questionable).

Costs Not Satisfying the IAS 38 Recognition Criteria

The standard has specifically provided that expenditures incurred for nonmonetary intangible assets should be recognized as an expense unless either

1. It relates to an intangible asset dealt with in another IAS;
2. The cost forms part of the cost of an intangible asset that meets the recognition criteria prescribed by IAS 38; or
3. It is acquired in a business combination and cannot be recognized as an identifiable intangible asset. In this case, this expenditure should form part of the amount attributable to goodwill as at the date of acquisition.

As a consequence of applying the above criteria, the following costs are expensed as they are incurred:

- Research costs;
- Preopening costs to open a new facility or business, and plant start-up costs incurred during a period prior to full scale production or operation, unless these costs are capitalized as part of the cost of an item of property, plant, and equipment;
- Organization costs such as legal and secretarial costs, which are typically incurred in establishing a legal entity;
- Training costs involved in operating a business or a product line;
- Advertising and related costs;
- Relocation, restructuring and other costs involved in organizing a business or product line;
- Customer lists, brands, mastheads and publishing titles that are internally generated.

Thus, the IASC has finally resolved the controversy regarding the potential deferral of costs like "preoperating expenses." In the past, many enterprises have been known to defer setup costs and preoperating costs on the premise that benefits from them flow to the enterprise over future periods as well. Due to the unequivocal stand taken by the IASC on this contentious issue, enterprises can no longer defer such costs. Further, by adding the provision relating to annual impairment testing of all internally generated intangible assets being amortized (over a period exceeding 20 years), the IASC has ensured that all such costs capitalized in the past would need to be adjusted for impairment.

The criteria for recognition of intangible assets, as provided in IAS 38, are rather stringent, and many enterprises will find that expenditures either to acquire or to develop intangible assets will fail the test for capitalization. In such instances, all these costs must be expensed currently as incurred. Furthermore, once expensed, these costs cannot in a later period be resurrected and capitalized, even if the conditions for such treatment are later met (it is interesting to note, that this is not meant, however, to preclude correction of an error made in an earlier period, if the conditions for capitalization were met but interpreted incorrectly by the reporting entity at that time).

Subsequently Incurred Costs

With the promulgation of IAS 38, the IASC has made capitalization of any subsequent costs incurred on intangible assets difficult to justify. This is because the nature of an intangible asset is such that, in many cases, it is not possible to determine whether subsequent costs are likely to enhance the specific economic benefits that will flow to the enterprise from those assets. Thus, subsequent costs incurred on an intangible asset should be recognized as an expense when they are incurred unless

1. It is probable that those costs will enable the asset to generate specifically attributable future economic benefits in **excess** of its originally assessed standard of performance; and
2. Those costs can be **measured reliably** and attributed to the asset reliably.

Thus, if the above two criteria are met, any subsequent expenditure on an intangible after its purchase or its completion should be capitalized along with its cost. The following example should help to illustrate this point better.

Example

An enterprise is developing a new product. Costs incurred by the R&D department in 2000 on the "research phase" amounted to $200,000. In 2001, technical and commercial feasibility of the product was established. Costs incurred in 2001 were $20,000 personnel costs and $15,000 legal fees to register the patent. In 2002, the enterprise incurred $30,000 to successfully defend a legal suit to protect the patent. The enterprise would account for these costs as follows:

- Research and development costs incurred in 2000, amounting to $200,000, should be expensed, as they do not meet the recognition criteria for intangible assets. The costs do not result in an identifiable asset capable of generating future economic benefits.
- Personnel and legal costs incurred in 2001, amounting to $35,000, would be capitalized as patents. The company has established technical and commercial feasibility of the product, as well as obtained control over the use of the asset. The standard specifically prohibits the reinstatement of costs previously recognized as an expense. Thus $200,000, recognized as an expense in the previous financial statements, cannot be reinstated and capitalized.
- Legal costs of $30,000 incurred in 2002 to defend the enterprise in a patent law suit should be expensed. Under US GAAP, legal fees and other costs incurred in successfully defending a patent law suit can be capitalized in the patents account, to the extent that value is evident, because such costs are incurred to establish the legal rights of the owner of the patent. However, in view of the stringent conditions imposed by IAS 38 concerning the recognition of subsequent costs, the IASC seems to be in favor of the conservative approach of expensing such costs Only such subsequent costs should be capitalized which would enable the asset to generate future economic benefits **in excess of the originally assessed standards of performance**. This represents, in most instances, a very high, possibly insurmountable, hurdle. Thus, legal costs incurred in connection with defending the patent which could be considered as expenses incurred to maintain the asset at its originally assessed standard of performance, would not meet the recognition criteria under IAS 38.
- Alternatively, if the enterprise were to lose the patent law suit, then the useful life and the recoverable amount of the intangible asset would be in question. The enterprise would be required to provide for any impairment loss and, in all

probability, even to fully write off the intangible asset. What is required must be determined by the facts of the specific situation.

Measurement Subsequent to Initial Recognition

Benchmark treatment. After initial recognition, an intangible asset should be carried at its cost less any accumulated amortization and any accumulated impairment losses.

Allowed alternative treatment--Revaluation. As with tangible assets under IAS 16, the new standard for intangibles permits revaluation subsequent to original acquisition, with the asset being written up to fair value. Inasmuch as most of the particulars of IAS 38 follow IAS 16 to the letter, and were described in detail in Chapter 8, these will not be repeated here. The unique features of IAS 38 are as follows:

1. If the intangibles were not initially recognized (i.e., they were expensed rather than capitalized) it will not be possible to later recognize them at fair value.
2. Deriving fair value by applying a present value concept to projected cash flows (a technique that can be used in the case of tangible assets under IAS 16) is deemed to be too unreliable in the realm of intangibles, primarily because it would tend to commingle the impact of identifiable assets and goodwill. Accordingly, fair value of an intangible asset should **only** be determined by reference to an active market in that type of intangible asset. Active markets providing meaningful data are not expected to exist for such unique assets as patents and trademarks, and thus it is presumed that revaluation will not be applied to these types of assets in the normal course of business. As a consequence, the IASC has effectively restricted revaluation of intangible assets to only freely tradable intangible assets.

As with the rules pertaining to plant, property, and equipment under IAS 16, if some intangible assets in a given class are subjected to revaluation, all the assets in that class should be consistently accounted for, unless fair value information is not, or ceases to be, available. Also in common with the requirements for tangible fixed assets, IAS 38 requires that revaluations be taken directly to equity through the use of a revaluation surplus account, except to the extent that previous impairments had been recognized by a charge against income.

Example of revaluation of intangible assets

A patent right is acquired July 1, 2000, for $250,000; while it has a legal life of 15 years, due to rapidly changing technology, management estimates a useful life of only 5 years. Straight-line amortization will be used. At January 1, 2001, management is uncertain that the process can actually be made economically feasible, and decides to write down the patent to an estimated market value of $75,000. Amortization will be taken over 3 years from that point. On January 1, 2003, having perfected the related production process, the asset is now appraised at a sound value of $300,000. Furthermore, the estimated useful life is now believed to be 6 more years. The entries to reflect these events are as follows:

7/1/00	Patent	250,000	
	Cash, etc.		250,000
12/31/00	Amortization expense	25,000	
	Patent		25,000
1/1/01	Loss from asset impairment	150,000	
	Patent		150,000
12/31/01	Amortization expense	25,000	
	Patent		25,000
12/31/02	Amortization expense	25,000	
	Patent		25,000
1/1/03	Patent	275,000	
	Gain on asset value recovery		100,000
	Revaluation surplus		175,000

Certain of the entries in the foregoing example will be explained further. The entry at year-end 2000 is to record amortization based on original cost, since there had been no revaluations through that time; only a half-year amortization is provided [($250,000/5) x ½]. On January 1, 2001, the impairment is recorded by writing down the asset to the estimated value of $75,000, which necessitates a $150,000 charge to income (carrying value, $225,000, less fair value, $75,000).

In 2001 and 2002, amortization must be provided on the new lower value recorded at the beginning of 2001; furthermore, since the new estimated life was 3 years from January 2001, annual amortization will be $25,000.

As of January 1, 2003, the carrying value of the patent is $25,000; had the January 2001 revaluation not been made, the carrying value would have been $125,000 ($250,000 original cost, less 2.5 years amortization versus an original estimated life of 5 years). The new appraised value is $300,000, which will fully recover the earlier write-down and add even more asset value than the originally recognized cost. Under the guidance of IAS 38, the recovery of $100,000 that had been charged to expense should be taken into income; the excess will be credited to stockholders' equity.

Development costs pose a special problem in terms of the application of the allowed alternative method under IAS 38. The utilization of the allowed alternative method of accounting for long-lived intangibles is only permissible when stringent conditions are met concerning the availability of fair value information. In general, it will **not** be possible to obtain fair value data from active markets, as is required by IAS 38, and this is particularly true with regard to development costs. Accordingly, the expectation is that the benchmark (historical cost) method will be almost universally applied for development costs. The use of the available alternative method for development costs, while theoretically valid, is expected to be very unusual in practice.

Example of development cost capitalization

Assume that Creative, Incorporated incurs substantial research and development costs for the invention of new products, many of which are brought to market successfully. In particular, Creative has incurred costs during 2000 amounting to $750,000 relative to a new manufacturing process. Of these costs, $600,000 were incurred prior to December 1, 2000. As of December 31, the viability of the new process was still not known, although testing had been conducted on December 1. In fact, results were not conclusively known until February 15, 2001, after another $75,000 in costs were incurred post-January 1. Creative, Incorporated's financial statements for 2000 were issued February 10, 2001, and the full $750,000 in research and development costs were expensed, since it was not yet known whether a portion of these qualified as development costs under IAS 38. When it is learned that feasibility had in fact been shown as of December 1, Creative management asks to restore the $150,000 of post-December 1 costs as a development asset. Under IAS 38 this is prohibited. However, the 2001 costs ($75,000 thus far) would qualify for capitalization, in all likelihood, based on the facts known.

If, however, it is determined that fair value information derived from active markets is indeed available, and the enterprise desires to apply the allowed alternative (revaluation) method of accounting to development costs, then it will be necessary to perform revaluations on a regular basis, such that at any reporting date the carrying amounts are not materially different from the current fair values. From a mechanical perspective, the adjustment to fair value can be accomplished either by "grossing up" the cost and the accumulated amortization accounts proportionally, or by netting the accumulated amortization, prerevaluation, against the asset account and then restating the asset to the net fair value as of the revaluation date. In either case, the net effect of the upward revaluation will be recorded in stockholders' equity as revaluation surplus; the only exception would be when an upward revaluation is in effect a reversal of a previously recognized impairment which was reported as a charge against earnings or a revaluation decrease (reversal or a yet earlier upward adjustment) which was reflected in earnings.

The accounting for revaluations is illustrated as follows:

Example of accounting for revaluation of development cost

Assume Breakthrough, Inc. has accumulated development costs which meet the criteria for capitalization at December 31, 2000, amounting to $39,000. It is estimated that the useful life of this intangible asset will be 6 years; accordingly amortization of $6,500 per year is anticipated. Breakthrough uses the allowed alternative method of accounting for its long-lived tangible and intangible assets. At December 31, 2002, it obtains market information regarding the then-current fair value of this intangible asset, which suggests a current fair value of these development costs is $40,000; the estimated useful life, however, has not changed. There are two ways to apply IAS 38: the asset and accumulated amortization can be "grossed up" to reflect the new fair value information, or the asset can be restated on a "net" basis. These are both illustrated below.

For both illustrations, the book value (amortized cost) immediately prior to the revaluation is [$39,000 – (2 x $6,500) =] $26,000. The net upward revaluation is given by the difference between fair value and book value, or ($40,000 – 26,000 =) $14,000.

If the "gross up" method is used: Since the fair value after 2 years of the 6 year useful life have already elapsed is found to be $40,000, the gross fair value must be (6/4 x $40,000 =) $60,000. The entries to record this would be as follows:

Development cost (asset)	21,000	
Accumulated amortization - development cost		7,000
Revaluation surplus (stockholders' equity)		14,000

If the "netting" method is used: Under this variant, the accumulated amortization as of the date of the revaluation is eliminated against the asset account, which is then adjusted to reflect the net fair value.

Accumulated amortization - development cost	13,000	
Development cost (asset)		13,000
Development cost (asset)	14,000	
Revaluation surplus (stockholders' equity)		14,000

Amortization Period

As with tangible assets subject to depreciation or depletion, the cost (or revalued carrying amount) of intangible assets is subject to rational and systematic amortization. Given that the useful economic life of many intangibles would be difficult to assess, the rule is that a maximum 20-year life is permissible, with amortization being over a shorter useful life if known. The only exceptions would occur in those instances where the legal right has a life of greater than 20 years **and** either of the following conditions exist:

1. The intangible has an existence that is not separable from a **specific** tangible asset, the useful life of which can be reliably determined to exceed 20 years, **or**
2. There is an active secondary market for the intangible.

The thrust of these requirements is to make the 20-year life an upper limit for most intangibles.

If there is persuasive evidence that the useful life of an intangible asset is longer than 20 years, then the 20-year presumption is rebutted and the enterprise must

- Amortize the intangible asset over that longer period;
- Estimate the recoverable amount of the intangible asset at least annually in order to identify any impairment loss; and
- Disclose the reasons why the presumption has been rebutted.

Note that IAS 38 provides for amortization of **all** intangible assets; it does not subscribe to the view that any intangible asset can possess an infinite life. The thrust of these requirements is to make the 20-year life an upper limit for most intangibles.

If control over the future economic benefits from an intangible asset is achieved through legal rights for a finite period, then the useful life of the intangible asset should not exceed the period of legal rights, unless the legal rights are renewable and the renewal is a virtual certainty. Thus, as a practical matter, the shorter legal life will set the upper limit for an amortization period in most cases.

The amortization method used should reflect the pattern in which the economic benefits of the asset are consumed by the enterprise. Amortization should commence when the asset is available for use and the amortization charge for each period should be recognized as an expense unless it is included in the carrying amount of another asset (e.g., inventory). Intangible assets may be amortized by the same systematic and rational methods that are used to depreciate tangible fixed assets. Thus, IAS 38 would seemingly permit straight-line, diminishing balance, and units of production methods. If a method other than straight-line is used, it must accurately mirror the expiration of the asset's economic service potential.

Residual Value

Tangible assets often have a positive residual value, before considering the disposal costs, because tangible assets can generally be sold for scrap or possibly be transferred to another user that has less need for, or ability to afford, new assets of that type. Intangibles, on the other hand, lacking the physical attributes that would make scrap value a meaningful concept, often have little or no residual worth. Accordingly, IAS 38 requires that a zero residual value be presumed unless an accurate measure of residual is possible. Thus, the residual value is presumed to be zero **unless**

- There is a commitment by a third party to purchase the asset at the end of its useful life; or
- There is an active market for that type of intangible asset, and residual value can be measured reliably by reference to that market and it is probable that such a market will exist at the end of the useful life.

Periodic review of useful life assumptions and amortization methods employed. As for fixed assets accounted for in conformity with IAS 16, the new standard on intangibles suggests that the amortization period be reconsidered at the end of each reporting period, and that the method of amortization also be reviewed at similar intervals. There is the expectation that due to their nature, intangibles are more likely to require revisions to one or both of these judgments. In either case, a change would be accounted for as a change in estimate, affecting current and future periods' reported earnings but not requiring restatement of previously reported periods.

Impairment Losses

IAS 38 has provided that

- Amortization of an asset should commence when the asset is available for use; and
- The amortization period should not exceed 20 years, although this presumption is rebuttable.

In view of the above, some enterprises may be tempted to

- Capitalize intangible assets and defer amortization for long periods on the grounds that the assets are not available for use; and/or
- Rebut the presumption of 20-year life and amortize assets over a longer period.

To combat the risk that either of these strategies might be employed, the standard provides that in addition to the universal provisions of IAS 36 (which require that the recoverable amount of an asset should be estimated when certain indications of impairment exist, as described in detail in Chapter 8), IAS 38 requires that an enterprise should estimate the recoverable amount of the following intangible assets at least at each financial year end even if there is no indication of impairment:

1. Intangible assets that are not yet ready for use; and
2. Other intangible assets that are amortized over a period exceeding 20 years from the date when the asset becomes available for use.

Apart from the special case of assets not yet in use, or being amortized over greater than 20 years, the major complication arises in the context of goodwill. Unlike other intangible assets, which are individually identifiable, goodwill is amorphous and cannot exist, from a financial reporting perspective, apart from the tangible and identifiable intangible assets with which it was acquired. Thus, a direct evaluation of the recoverable amount of goodwill is not actually feasible; accordingly, the standard requires that goodwill be combined with other assets which together define a cash generating unit, and that an evaluation of any potential impairment (if warranted by the facts and circumstances) be conducted on an aggregate basis. A more detailed consideration of goodwill is presented in Chapter 11, *Business Combinations and Consolidated Financial Statements*.

The impairment of intangible assets other than goodwill (such as patents, copyrights, trade names, customer lists, and franchise rights) should be considered in precisely the same way that long-lived tangible assets are dealt with. Carrying amounts must be compared to the greater of net selling price or value in use when there are indications that an impairment may have been suffered. Reversals of impairment losses, under defined conditions, are also recognized. The effects of impairment recognitions and reversals will be reflected in current period operating results, if the intangible assets in question are being accounted for in accordance with the benchmark method set forth in IAS 38 (i.e., at historical cost). On the other hand, if the allowed alternative method (presenting intangible assets at revalued amounts) is followed, impairments will normally be charged to stockholders' equity to the extent that revaluation surplus exists, and only to the extent that the loss exceeds previously recognized valuation surplus will the impairment loss be reported as a charge against earnings. Recoveries are handled consistent with the method by which impairments were reported, in a manner entirely analogous to the explanation earlier in this chapter, dealing with impairments of plant, property, and equipment.

Disposals of Intangible Assets

With regard to questions of accounting for the disposition of assets, the guidance of IAS 38 virtually mirrors that of IAS 16. Gain or loss recognition will be for the difference between carrying amount (net, if applicable, of any remaining revaluation surplus) and the net proceeds from the sale.

Year 2000 computer software revisions. One of the most talked-about issues over the past year has been the enormity of the task facing organizations in dealing with the so-called Year 2000 (or "Y2K" in computer jargon) problem. Older computers and software were designed to recognize only the last two digits of the year, and this means that many programs will, disastrously, attempt to treat the year 2000 as 1900. Huge costs are being incurred to address the problem, which predictions say will cause worldwide havoc (and maybe economic depression) unless successfully dealt with. The accounting issue relating to this is whether costs to repair, modify, and upgrade software can be capitalized (as development costs or other intangible assets), or must be expensed as incurred.

The Standing Interpretations Committee has ruled in SIC 6 that costs incurred to maintain or restore benefits originally intended when software systems were installed must be expensed as incurred. This guidance is not limited to Y2K matters, but rather extends to any costs incurred to restore software to its original value, and thus would also apply to software modifications necessitated by the upcoming introduction of the Euro currency, among other reasons. Logically, if these modification costs were to be capitalized, the recorded amount of the asset would be exaggerated--effectively double counting at least a portion of the cost of the economic benefits actually represented by the asset in question. Thus it has been interpreted that these costs must be expensed in all instances.

A related question is whether the cost of upgrading or repairing the software should be accrued in anticipation of having to engage in this effort. It appears that accrual in anticipation of these expenses is not warranted, however, since a legal or constructive obligation to incur such costs does not exist in advance.

Disclosure Requirements

The disclosure rules set forth in IAS 16 for property, plant, and equipment, and those set forth in IAS 38 for intangible assets, are largely identical, and both demand a large amount of detail in the financial statement notes.

For each class of intangible asset (distinguishing between internally generated and other intangible assets), disclosure is required of

1. The amortization method(s) used;
2. Useful lives or amortization rates used;
3. The gross carrying amount and accumulated amortization (including accumulated impairment losses) at both the beginning and end of the period;
4. A reconciliation of the carrying amount at the beginning and end of the period showing additions, retirements, disposals, acquisitions by means of business combinations, increases or decreases resulting from revaluations, reductions to recognize impairments, amounts written back to recognize recoveries of prior impairments, amortization during the period, the net effect of translation of foreign entities' financial statements, and any other material items; and
5. The line item of the income statement in which the amortization charge of intangible assets is included.

Note that presentation of comparative information is not required (this is in line with similar amendments made to IAS 16, *Property, Plant, and Equipment*).

In addition, the statements should also disclose the following facts:

1. If the amortization period for any intangibles exceeds 20 years, the justification therefor;
2. The nature, carrying amount, and remaining amortization period of any individual intangible asset that is material to the financial statements of the enterprise as a whole;
3. For intangible assets acquired by way of a government grant and initially recognized at fair value, the fair value initially recognized, their carrying amount, and whether they are carried under the benchmark or allowed alternative treatment for subsequent measurement;
4. Any restrictions on titles and any assets pledged as security for debt; and
5. The amount of outstanding commitments for the acquisition of intangible assets.

In addition, the financial statements should disclose the aggregate amount of research and development expenditure recognized as an expense during the period.

Transitional Provisions

The provisions of this standard are applicable to **annual** financial statements covering periods beginning on or after July 1, 1999. Upon first application, IAS 38 includes transitional provisions that require retrospective application in order to

1. Eliminate an item that no longer qualifies for recognition under IAS 38; or
2. Correct the previous measurement of an intangible asset in contradiction to principles set out in IAS 38.

These requirements are as follows:

Circumstances	Requirements
1. Elimination of an item no longer meeting the recognition criteria	
a. The item was acquired in a business combination	Reallocate the amount to goodwill resulting from the same acquisition and adjust the goodwill retrospectively, as if the item had always been included in the goodwill.
b. The item was purchased or internally generated	Eliminate the item from the balance sheet
2. Correction of previous measurement	
a. The asset was initially recognized at an amount other than cost	Reestimate the carrying amount of the asset at cost less accumulated amortization, as determined under this standard. If cost cannot be determined, then the asset should be eliminated from the balance sheet.
b. The item was previously not recognized as an asset (it was expensed):	
• The asset was acquired in a business combination and formed part of goodwill	Measure the carrying amount of the asset at cost less accumulated amortization, as determined under this standard, and adjust the goodwill retrospectively, as if the item had always been included in the goodwill.
• The asset was purchased or internally generated	The intangible asset should not be recognized.
c. The asset was not previously amortized	Restate the carrying amount of the asset as if the accumulated amortization had always been determined under this standard.
d. The asset was amortized for a different amortization period or by a different amortization method	Amortize any carrying amount of the asset over its remaining useful life (change is treated as a change in accounting estimate and applied prospectively).
e. Revalued amount was not determined by reference to an active market:	
• There is an active market for the asset	The asset should be revalued by reference to this active market.
• There is no active market for the asset	Eliminate the effect of any revaluation and measure the carrying amount of the asset at cost less accumulated amortization.

Adjustments resulting from the above reallocations or reestimations, should be recognized in accordance with the provisions of IAS 8, *Net Profit or Loss for the*

Period, Fundamental Errors and Changes in Accounting Policies. The enterprise may follow the benchmark treatment, whereby the opening balance of retained earnings is adjusted, or the alternative treatment, where the current period's net profit or loss is adjusted. Thus, the new provisions of IAS 38 are of great importance as they are to be applied retrospectively to correct or eliminate policies not in line with the standard.

10 INVESTMENTS

PERSPECTIVE AND ISSUES

Several important international accounting standards address a number of related aspects of accounting for investments. IAS 25 (until it was superseded by recently promulgated, but not yet fully effective, IAS 39) deals with the generic topic of investments in the debt and equity securities of other enterprises, for those situations where the investor is passive and does not exert significant influence over the investee. Under still-extant standard IAS 25, such investments may be accounted for by a variety of permissible methods, depending on whether the investments are deemed to be current or long-term in nature. The existence of alternative measurement and reporting strategies means that financial statements of different entities might not be fully comparable, but at the time of its development, an inability to gain a consensus made it impossible to narrow the range of options permitted by IAS 25. Among the methods that are acceptable are historical cost, lower of cost or market, and pure market value--not all of which are appropriate in every circumstance, however.

IAS 39, which will supersede most of IAS 25 (excluding the portions dealing with nonfinancial investments--which will eventually be replaced by the standard which evolves from currently outstanding exposure draft E64, *Investment Properties*), eliminates the various alternative methods of accounting permitted by the older standard, and imposes a fair value model for most, but not all, financial investments. IAS 39 becomes effective in 2001, unless earlier adoption is elected by reporting entities. Given that, in 2000, there will be enterprises applying both

IAS 25 and 39, these are both detailed in this chapter. (The general requirements of IAS 39 were addressed in Chapter 5 and will not be repeated in this chapter.)

E64 sets forth the proposed standards for accounting for nonfinancial instrument investments, intended to supersede the requirements currently presented in IAS 25. Since this is widely expected to be enacted by the IASC in late 1999, this is detailed in this chapter. Until adopted, however, accounting and reporting for such investments remains as set forth in IAS 25, which is also detailed in the following pages.

IAS 28, which addresses investments in associates, is pertinent where the investor can be shown to possess significant influence over the investee. Whether significant influence in any given situation truly exists is a question of fact, but the standard does provide a mechanical rule to be employed in most circumstances. Under this standard, when an investor has more than 20% of the voting power, it generally will account for its investment by the equity method, whereby the proportional share of the investee's operating results will be reflected in the investor's financial statements. The equity method is sometimes described as being **one-line consolidation** since the same net effect on the investor's income and net assets will result as when consolidated financial statements are prepared, but without grossing up the income statement and balance sheet for all the investee's revenues, expenses, assets, and liabilities.

Finally, IAS 31 concerns the accounting by an investor for its interest in a joint venture arrangement. A **joint venture**, in which two or more entities have control jointly over the operations and/or assets of another enterprise, is a specialized type of investment situation, conceptually falling between significant influence and control. As with investments in general, there are several acceptable alternative accounting treatments for accounting for joint venture investments. However, one method, proportional consolidation, is designated as being preferred in this scenario, while the other defined technique, the equity method, is permitted as an allowed alternative.

Sources of IAS		
IAS 25, 28, 31, 39	*SIC* 3	E64

DEFINITIONS OF TERMS

Associate. An enterprise over which an investor has significant influence but which is neither a subsidiary nor a joint venture of the investor company.

Available-for-sale financial assets. Those financial assets which are not held for trading or held to maturity, and are not loans and receivables originated by the entity.

Control. The power to obtain the future economic benefits that flow from an asset.

Cost method. A method of accounting for investment whereby the investment is recorded at cost; the income statement reflects income from the investment only to the extent that the investor receives distributions from the investee's accumulated net profits arising after the date of acquisition.

Current investment. An investment that is, by its nature, readily realizable and is intended to be held for not more than 1 year.

Derecognize. Remove a financial asset or liability, or a portion thereof, from the entity's balance sheet.

Derivative. A financial instrument (1) whose value changes in response to changes in a specified interest rate, security price, commodity price, foreign exchange rate, index of prices or rates, a credit rating or credit index, or similar variable (which is known as the "underlying"), (2) that requires no initial net investment or little initial net investment relative to other types of contracts that have a similar response to changes in market conditions, and (3) that is settled at a future date.

Differential. The difference between the carrying value of common stock investment and the book value of underlying net assets of the investee; this should be allocated between excess (or deficiency) of fair value over (or under) book value of net assets and goodwill (a negative goodwill) and amortized appropriately against earnings from investee.

Equity method. A method of accounting whereby the investment is initially recorded at cost and subsequently adjusted for the postacquisition change in the investor's share of net assets of the investee. The investor's income statement reflects the investor's share of the investee's results of operations.

Fair value. The amount for which an asset could be exchanged between a knowledgeable, willing buyer and seller in an arm's-length transaction.

Goodwill. The excess of the cost of the acquired enterprise over the sum of the amounts assigned to identifiable assets acquired net of any liabilities assumed.

Hedge effectiveness. The degree to which offsetting changes in fair values or cash flows attributable to the hedged risk are achieved by the hedging instrument.

Hedged item. An asset, liability, firm commitment, or forecasted future transaction that (1) exposes the entity to risk of changes in fair value or changes in future cash flows, and that (2) for hedge accounting purposes is designated as being hedged.

Hedging. Designating one or more hedging instruments such that the change in fair value is an offset, in whole or part, to the change in the fair value or the cash flows of a hedged item.

Hedging instrument. For hedge accounting purposes, a designated derivative or (in limited instances) another financial asset or liability whose fair value or cash flows are expected to offset changes in the fair value or cash flows of a designated hedged item. Nonderivative financial assets or liabilities may be designated as hedging instruments for hedge accounting purposes only if they hedge the risk of changes in foreign currency exchange rates.

Held-for-trading. A financial asset which is acquired principally for the purpose of generating a profit from short-term fluctuations in price or dealer's margin. Regardless of why acquired, a financial asset should be denoted as held-for-trading if there is a pattern of short-term profit taking by the entity. Derivative financial assets are always deemed held-for-trading unless designated and effective as hedging instruments.

Held-to-maturity investments. Financial assets with fixed or determinable payments and fixed maturities, that entity has positive intent and ability to hold to maturity, except for loans and receivables originated by the entity.

Investee. An enterprise that issued voting stock that is held by an investor.

Investee capital transaction. The purchase or sale by the investee of its own common shares, which alters the investor's ownership interest and is accounted for by the investor as if the investee were a consolidated subsidiary.

Investment. An asset held by an enterprise for purposes of accretion of wealth through distributions of interest, royalties, dividends, and rentals, or for capital appreciation or other benefits to be obtained.

Investment property. Investment in land and/or building that are not occupied substantially for use by, or in the operations of, the investor or an affiliate of the investor.

Investor. A business enterprise that holds an investment in the voting stock of another enterprise.

Joint control. The contractually agreed-on joint sharing of control over the operations and/or assets of an economic activity.

Joint venture. A contractual arrangement whereby two or more parties undertake an economic activity subject to their joint control.

Long-term investment. An investment other than a current investment.

Market value. The amount obtainable from the sale of an investment in an active market.

Marketable. Assets for which there are active markets and from which market values, or other indicators that permit determination thereof, are available.

Significant influence. The power of the investor to participate in the financial and operating policy decisions of the investee; however, this is less than the ability to control those policies.

Subsidiary. An enterprise that is controlled by another enterprise (its parent).

Undistributed investee earnings. The investor's share of investee earnings in excess of dividends paid.

CONCEPTS, RULES, AND EXAMPLES

General Considerations--IAS 39 to Supersede IAS 25 in 2001

The current standard which governs the accounting for investments other than those covered by IAS 28 (equity method accounting) or 31 (joint venture accounting) is IAS 25. This single standard addresses both financial investments (e.g.,stocks and bonds) and nonfinancial investments (e.g., land and buildings not held for the entity's own use as productive assets). Under the oft-criticized IAS 25, there is a side range of alternative measurement strategies which can be applied to the same fact situation; for example, the current portfolio of investments in stocks and bonds can either be valued on a "pure" market value basis, or by employing the well-known "lower of cost or market" (LCM) method. Furthermore, those choosing the LCM approach can elect either to apply this to the entire portfolio, to categories of the portfolio, or to individual securities in the portfolio. This huge set of acceptable alternatives has been rightly attackeds making comparisons across enterprises almost impossible to perform.

While the lack of consensus at the time of IAS 25's development made it impractical to narrow the range of measurement methodologies at that time, the accounting profession has since come to the general realization that fair value is probably the most direct and most relevant measurement mode for all financial assets (and for financial liabilities as well). Most national standard setters, as well as the IASC, have been moving toward a universal application of the fair value model, although opposition by certain industries (banking in particular) has impeded progress on this. Nonetheless, the recently promulgated IAS 39 does impose a far more uniform set of requirements, eliminates almost all alternatives, and paves the way for the ultimate development of a simple, universal fair value model.

IAS 39 will become mandatorily effective in 2001, although earlier application is possible. For those enterprises which do not elect early application of IAS 39, the accounting for investments in financial assets will continue to be governed by IAS 25. Because in 2000 there will be enterprises using both sets of rules, the current edition of this book will include coverage of both IAS 25 and IAS 39. The general requirements of IAS 39 have been addressed in Chapter 5; specific illustrations of how IAS 39 is to be applied are given later in this chapter.

In the following presentation, the current IAS 25-based rules are discussed first, followed by a discourse on the new IAS 39-derived requirements.

Accounting for Investments in Marketable Equity Securities

General background. Except if an enterprise chooses early adoption of the requirements of IAS 39, the currently relevant international standard pertaining to accounting for investments is IAS 25, *Accounting for Investments*. This standard was reformatted in 1994 but has not otherwise been altered materially since it became effective in 1987. This standard applies to both debt and equity securities, whether being held as long-term or short-term investments, subject to certain defined limitations. It does not, however, apply to investments in subsidiaries (which are addressed by IAS 27, discussed later in this chapter), or to investments in associates (IAS 28, covered later in this chapter), or investments in joint ventures (IAS 31, also covered later in this chapter). Furthermore, it does not address other categories of assets, such as patents or trademarks, finance leases, or retirement or other benefit plans.

Criticisms of IAS 25 centered on two of its characteristics: the range of acceptable accounting alternatives permitted for identical fact situations, and the dependence of accounting on management's classification of the investments as being either current or noncurrent. While in recent years there has been a worldwide trend away from imposing on accounting for investments requirements that are conditioned on the balance sheet classification of these assets, the IAS 25 requirement have remained as first promulgated. In the view of many, this offers management the opportunity, and even the incentive, to manipulate the accounting results by declaring its intentions regarding specific investments, which adversely impacts the quality and reliability of the financial reporting process. IAS 39 eliminates both of these major perceived weaknesses of IAS 25.

IAS 13 sets forth certain criteria to be applied when a reporting entity chooses to distinguish between current and noncurrent assets in its balance sheet. However, there is no requirement under generally accepted accounting principles that the balance sheet be presented on a classified basis, and in fact the discussion in IAS 13 offers compelling arguments why classification may be misleading in many circumstances. Furthermore, in certain industries it is traditional not to present classified balance sheets, either because regulatory authorities do not permit or encourage it, or because the distinction is not meaningful, given the nature of the entity's operations.

An interesting aspect of IAS 25 is that the accounting implications of the current vs. noncurrent classification are operative even if the reporting entity does not present a classified balance sheet. Thus, a determination must be made for each investment as to whether or not it meets the criteria for being a current investment. If it does, the measurement strategies available for current investments are the available options, even though the investment will not be characterized as a current asset in the enterprise's balance sheet. Similarly, those investments that meet the criteria as being long-term investments will be measured according to one of the options prescribed for long-term investments, although they will not be described as noncurrent in the enterprise's balance sheet.

Current investments are deemed to be those that by their nature are readily realizable (i.e., marketable) and which are intended to be held for only a short time. Note that **both** criteria must be satisfied since many marketable investments will not be held with the intention of a sale in the near term and would accordingly not be candidates for accounting as current investments. Under the provisions of IAS 25, the reporting entity has a choice of using either pure market value or the lower of cost or market to account for current investments. These alternative accounting methods are offered as equally acceptable strategies, being denoted as neither the benchmark nor the available alternative.

Long-term equity investments may be accounted for in accordance with one of a number of alternative measurement strategies: historical cost, revalued amounts, or the lower of cost or market. Again, neither of these is denoted as being the benchmark treatment, and thus all are equally acceptable. Regardless of the valuation method utilized, however, permanent declines in value must be recognized.

The specific methodologies identified above will be explored in greater detail on the following pages.

Determining the cost of equity investments. The cost of any investment should include all associated acquisition charges, such as brokerage fees, duties, or other costs that must be incurred to obtain the investment asset in the condition and location desired. This basic principle applies to all assets that are acquired by an entity, of course, and is hardly unique to investments.

In some instances, an equity investment may be acquired in exchange for shares of stock in the investor entity. In such cases the measure of acquisition cost is given by the fair value of the shares surrendered, not by their nominal, par, or stated value, if any. In rare cases, the fair value of the equity shares acquired might be more objectively determinable than the value of the equity or other securities given up, and in such instances this alternative measurement tactic should be pursued.

In other situations, the equity investment will be acquired in exchange for other assets owned by the investor. Essentially the same rules apply as noted in the preceding discussion: The primary evidence of value will be the fair value of the assets given up; absent reliable data on this, the fair value of the assets acquired should be assessed directly.

In general, the historical cost of investments will not be modified having once been determined. Exceptions arise only in instances of permanent impairments (discussed later in this chapter) and liquidating dividends or returns of capital. Returns of capital occur when an investee makes distributions to investors from earnings that were accumulated prior to the date of the investment. In such instances the amounts received by the investor rightfully should not be deemed to be a return **on** the investment but must be recognized as being a partial return **of** the investment. As a practical matter, since a passive investor cannot know with certainty the investee's intention in making a distribution or whether the distribution is being made from preacquisition date earnings, and since that date will differ for each investor, the convention to be adopted is to treat distributions in excess of current earnings as returns of capital.

For example, if during the initial year an investment is held, earnings per share amount to $3.50 but dividends of $5.00 per share are paid, it would be reasonable to conclude that dividends in the amount of $1.50 per share are a return of capital. However, it is not necessary for dividends to exceed current earnings for there to be a return of capital, since it is common that only a fraction of annual earnings are paid out as dividends to stockholders. Thus, even distributions from earlier periods' earnings might not make the current total dividend exceed current earnings. In these instances, lacking specific knowledge that the intent was to pay out prior periods' earnings, it would be reasonable to account for these as normal distributions rather than returns of the funds invested.

Carrying amounts for current investments. IAS 25 offers financial statement preparers the option of using a pure market value approach or the more traditional lower of cost or market measurement scheme. Historically, lower of cost or market (LCM) has been viewed as an appropriate strategy because it adheres to the time-honored accounting concepts of conservatism and realization. Conservatism demands that all losses be provided for at the earliest date of occurrence; while the realization concept stipulates that gains not be recognized until actually realized by the enterprise. LCM preserves the integrity of the historical cost based system of accounting except when economic losses have been incurred; in those instances, the losses are recognized and carrying value is reduced below historical cost. Under LCM, unrealized gains are not recognized under any circumstances.

The market value method, which is an equally acceptable accounting method under IAS 25, reflects the trend in recent years to move to a mark-to-market approach for some or all financial instruments. Although the international standards have not kept pace, to date, with the changes made under US GAAP, the trend is evident nonetheless. The belief is that for assets that are readily marketable, the most objective and meaningful measure is current fair value. This observation is particularly astute in the case of current investments in equity securities, since any temporary increase or decline in market value is less likely to be reversed prior to the disposition of the asset than would be true if the investment were to be held for the long term. Thus, a pure mark-to-market measurement approach to current investments can readily be endorsed from a theoretical perspective.

Accounting for changes in value. If current investments in equity securities are carried at LCM, declines in value are to be reflected currently in income. Later recoveries in value, not to exceed original cost, are also reported in current earnings.

On the other hand, if the investments are being accounted for purely on a market value basis, the reporting entity must elect an accounting policy (which, once chosen, may only be revised in accordance with the criteria established by IAS 8). The unrealized gains and losses resulting from recognition of market values may either be taken into income currently, or alternatively, the approach prescribed for long-term investments can be employed.

Under the latter strategy, increases in market value are credited to owners' equity, not income, and subsequent declines (but not in excess of unrealized gains recognized earlier) are offset against the revaluation surplus account. Any losses in excess of unrealized gains must be taken into earnings. If these losses are later reversed, the gains are also reflected in income. Put another way, under the alternative approach any **net** unrealized losses are reported in income (and thus eventually in retained earnings), while any **net** unrealized gains are reported in an additional equity account known as revaluation surplus.

Accounting for Investments Under IAS 25

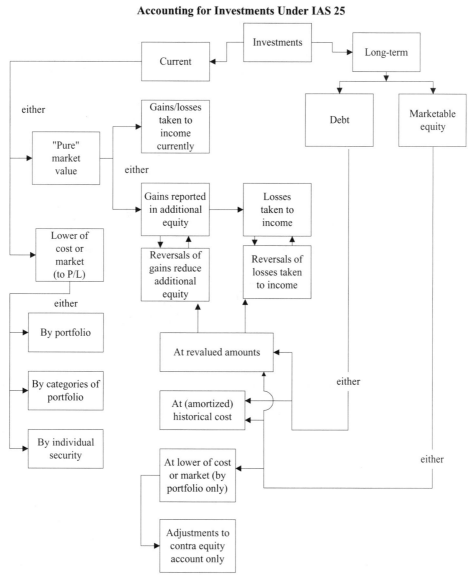

NOTE: *The foregoing chart does not address other than temporary declines in value.*

Examples of accounting for investments under the lower of cost or market approach

Assume that Nirvana Corporation acquires the following investments on January 2, 2000:

1,000 shares Dubayy Trading Corp. common	$140,000
2,000 shares Kazakh Oil Drilling Co. common	320,000
Total cost	$460,000

Under the provisions of IAS 25, if the lower of cost or market method is utilized, the provision for market decline, if any, can be applied on the basis of individual securities, by categories of investments, or on a portfolio-wide basis. In the following sections, the individual investment and portfolio-wide approaches are illustrated, both with and without also reflecting the tax effects as prescribed by IAS 12 (for simplicity, an effective rate of 40% is presumed, and the distinctions between the deferral and liability approaches to interperiod income tax allocation will be ignored; these are fully described and illustrated in Chapter 14). In all the following, assume that the securities are valued at year end (December 31, 2000) as follows:

1,000 shares Dubayy Trading Corp. common	$128,000
2,000 shares Kazakh Oil Drilling Co. common	325,000
Total market value	$453,000

Also assume that the decline in value of the Dubayy Trading common stock does not represent an other than temporary loss in market worth.

Example of computing the LCM adjustment on a portfolio-wide basis--Ignoring tax effects

The overall portfolio decline is $7,000 in this example; under IAS 25's rules, this should be credited not to any particular investment but to a valuation allowance (also known as a reserve or contra asset account). This is for two reasons. First, conceptually, if the portfolio is being valued s whole, the intent is not to adjust any particular securities' carrying values, as the expectation is that the overall portfolio will regain its value, even if a given security does not recover. Second, neither security declined in value by $7,000, but rather, one declined by more than this amount while another actually gained in value; however, LCM does not accept that any security will be written up to an amount in excess of historical cost.

The entry to record this adjustment would be as follows:

Loss on current investment portfolio	7,000	
Allowance for decline in market value of current investments		7,000

Including tax effects. In many jurisdictions, market value declines cannot be claimed as losses for tax purposes. Instead, the entity will be able to claim a loss only when the security is sold (i.e., when the loss is actually realized in an arm's-length transaction). However, under the provisions of IAS 12, tax effects are to be provided in the period the related gain or loss is reported in the income statement, under the concept of matching all costs associated with reported revenue in the same reporting period. In the present case, it is assumed that the effective tax rate is 40%; the entry to record the tax provision is

Deferred tax benefit	2,800	
Income tax expense (credit)		2,800

Example of computing the LCM adjustment on an individual security basis--Ignoring tax effects

While IAS 25 shows a clear preference for reporting the decline to LCM on a portfolio-wide or investment category basis, it does permit reporting LCM on an individual security basis. In fact, many believe that the portfolio-wide approach is a departure from the concept of LCM, since implicitly gains are being recognized on those components that had a value increase, thereby offsetting the declines which otherwise would have been recognized on those portfolio securities that did, in fact, decrease in value. In the present case, the Dubayy shares declined in value by $12,000, but this was offset by the $5,000 increase in value of the Kazakh shares. If the individual item approach were instead used, the full $12,000 decline would be recognized, while none of the $5,000 increase would be acknowledged. The entry to adjust to LCM at year end would be

Loss on current investment portfolio	12,000	
Investment in Dubayy Trading Corp.		12,000

Note that a contra asset or valuation account is not used in this case, since the loss can be directly associated with a particular investment security.

Including tax effects. As with the earlier illustration, tax effects are provided at 40%. The entry to record the tax provision is

Deferred tax benefit	4,800	
Income tax expense (credit)		4,800

Recoveries in value of investments accounted for at the lower of cost or market.

As shown in the foregoing examples, downward adjustments to reflect the lower of cost or market must be taken directly to the income statement; these declines are not hidden in a contra account in the equity section of the balance sheet as is done in the case of certain long-term investments suffering declines in value. To be consistent, any later recoveries in value, but not to exceed the original carrying value, must also be reflected in income (and the deferred tax provision relating thereto will be reversed to tax expense, as well).

Examples of accounting for investments under the market value approach

Ignoring tax effects. IAS 25 also permits a pure market value approach to be applied to determine the financial statement presentation of current investments. The difference between LCM and market value is that under the former (subject to the observation that if applied on a portfolio-wide basis or on the basis of investment categories, some unrealized gains may implicitly be given recognition to the extent they offset unrealized losses), only declines in value and recoveries thereof can be reported, while under the latter both unrealized gains and losses are given recognition, without limitation.

IAS 25 provides a further complication if the market value method is elected: The reporting entity can adopt and consistently apply either of two rather distinct approaches to pure market value reporting. The first of these is to mark all the securities to market value, with all gains or losses reported in income currently. The second approach is to use the technique prescribed for long-term investments accounted for on the basis of revaluations (described below). Under this application, unrealized gains are reported in an additional equity account, and reversals of unrealized gains (but not in excess of previously reported increases) are adjusted to that account, with further declines reported in income. Also, if this technique is utilized, unrealized losses are reported as charges against earnings, and later recoveries (but not in excess of unrealized losses recognized previously) are also taken into income, with any further increases credited to an additional equity account.

To illustrate the accounting for current investments in securities, on the market value basis, using the method also prescribed for long-term investments (i.e., not taking all gains and losses immediately into income) as set forth in the preceding paragraph, consider these facts.

Assume that Utopia Corporation acquires the following investments on January 2, 2000:

1,000 shares Pan-Europe Trading Corp. common	$540,000
2,000 shares Transcontinental Co. common	230,000
Total cost	$770,000

At year end 2000, these investments have the following values:

1,000 shares Pan-Europe Trading Corp. common	$520,000
2,000 shares Transcontinental Co. common	310,000
Total cost	$830,000

At year end 2001, these investments have the following values:

1,000 shares Pan-Europe Trading Corp. common	$510,000
2,000 shares Transcontinental Co. common	165,000
Total cost	$675,000

IAS 25 stipulates that if the market value method is used, the adjustments should be made based on changes in values of specific, individual securities, not on a portfolio basis. Given that directive, it will be noted that the overall portfolio increase of $60,000 in 2000 actually is comprised of an unrealized loss of $20,000 on the Pan-European stock and an unrealized gain of $80,000 on the Transcontinental shares. The former must be reported in income, while the latter will be reported as an additional equity account, using the method chosen, and applied consistently, by Utopia Corporation. The entry in 2000 is as follows:

Loss on investment in Pan-Europe stock	20,000	
Investment in Transcontinental stock	80,000	
Investment in Pan-Europe stock		20,000
Unrealized gain on investment in		
Transcontinental stock (equity)		80,000

The decline in value of Pan-Europe shares continues in 2001, and further losses must be recognized as a charge against earnings. On the other hand, the Transcontinental shares also decline, fully reversing the gain of 2000 and ending 2001 below the original purchase cost. To the extent that the decline reverses the gain reported in an additional equity account, that account is reduced or eliminated; to the extent that the decline in value exceeds the previously recognized gain, the additional loss is reported in income. The entry for 2001 is therefore as follows:

Loss on investment in Pan-Europe stock	10,000	
Unrealized gain on investment in		
Transcontinental stock (equity)	80,000	
Loss on investment in Transcontinental stock	65,000	
Investment in Pan-Europe stock		10,000
Investment in Transcontinental stock		145,000

Including tax effects. The foregoing entries in 2000 and 2001 do not reflect the tax effects of the unrealized gains and losses recognized relative to the investments in Pan-

Europe Trading Co. and Transcontinental Corp. shares. Again assuming that the local tax laws do not tax unrealized gains nor permit deductions for unrealized losses, the related tax entries in 2000 and 2001 would be as follows:

Deferred tax benefit	8,000	
Unrealized gain on investment in		
Transcontinental stock (equity)	32,000	
Income tax expense (credit)		8,000
Deferred tax liability		32,000

Note that the offset for the deferred tax liability recognized in connection with the unrealized gain on the Transcontinental stock is charged to the additional equity account, not to the tax provision in the income statement, since the gain was not reported in the income statement.

The entry in 2001 is as follows:

Deferred tax benefit	30,000	
Deferred tax liability	32,000	
Unrealized gain on investment in		
Transcontinental stock (equity)		32,000
Income tax expense (credit)		30,000

The charge to the deferred tax benefit account is made up of a $4,000 debit associated with the further $10,000 decline in value of Pan-Europe shares, that was taken as a charge to income, and a $26,000 charge relating to the $65,000 decline in value of Transcontinental **beyond** the reversal of the gain reported in the prior year. This excess loss was reported in income, and thus the tax effect must also be shown in the income statement. The tax effect of the $80,000 reversal of the earlier value increase is adjusted against the additional equity account.

Carrying amounts for long-term equity investments. Investments classified as long-term, or that would be categorized as noncurrent assets in a classified balance sheet, may be carried in the balance sheet under one of three available valuation approaches: original cost, revalued amounts, or lower of cost or market. The latter method is available only for investments in equity securities, and if utilized, must be applied on a portfolio basis.

IAS 25 states that long-term investments are usually carried at cost, absent a decline that is other than temporary in nature. The concept other than temporary represents a lower threshold than the term permanent would have, since there must be positive evidence to support a conclusion that a decline is only temporary in nature; absent that evidence, it would be presumed that any decline observed would be other than temporary. On the other hand, had the term "permanent" been invoked, this would have presented a rather higher threshold, which often could not be surmounted, leading to the conclusion that any given decline was other than permanent or temporary in nature. Thus, while neither term is unambiguous, it should be presumed that there must be positive evidence that a decline is indeed temporary to apply the accounting discussed below.

Reporting changes in value of long-term equity investments when the revaluation method is used. If the investment is being accounted for in accordance with the revaluation method, increases in value of long-term equity investments are reported in stockholders' (owners') equity as an additional equity account and are not first reflected in income. If later losses on the same investment are recognized, not in excess of the earlier gains, these are to be recognized by reducing the additional equity account, again without first passing through the income statement. Any further losses, however, must be reported as charges against earnings as incurred.

On the other hand, if losses are first recognized, these must be taken to the income statement. If market values later reverse, so that unrealized gains on the same investment are to be reported, these are also reflected in income, but only to the extent of previously recognized losses. Any further gains are taken to the additional equity account, not to income.

If this method is elected, revaluations should be made to fair value at regular intervals. The reporting entity would be required under these circumstances to adopt a firm policy regarding the frequency of revaluation, to prevent a capricious and possibly distorting use of this technique, such as to invoke fair value only during times of favorable changes in market prices. In addition to regularly timed revaluations, IAS 25 demands that all long-term investments be revalued essentially simultaneously, or that, at the minimum, entire categories be revalued together. The standard does not make clear its use of the term categories, but logically this might denote different risk classes and types of investments, such as corporate debt, government debt, and equity holdings. It might also imply that equity investments be further categorized (e.g., investments in public utilities, in blue chip industrial companies, in speculative high-technology companies, etc.).

The examples presented above under the discussion of accounting for current investments on the pure market value method, are identical to the effects of accounting for long-term investments in equity securities on the revaluation method. Deferred taxes should, similarly, be provided for as demonstrated above, assuming that the tax laws do not permit tax recognition of unrealized gains or losses.

Accounting for long-term investments at cost. If this method is selected, no adjustments are made for later value changes, as long as these can be supported as being temporary in nature. If the changes are deemed to be other than temporary, the declines must be charged against earnings immediately, and the written-down amount becomes the new cost basis, from which upward adjustments for later value increases cannot be made.

Accounting for long-term investments at the lower of cost or market. Under the third available alternative for accounting for long-term investments which is, however, applicable only in the case of equity investments, a lower of cost or market approach is applied. IAS 25 mandates that a portfolio-wide LCM methodology be used in the case of long-term investments, which is a more restrictive prescription than that given for current investments which are subject to evaluation on individual, category-wide, or full portfolio bases (although the portfolio approach is officially favored).

This requirement seemingly is intended to make downward adjustments in the portfolio carrying value less likely to occur, since unrealized gains on some investments in the portfolio will offset unrealized losses on other investments, so that the net effect of any declines will be moderated. Lower of cost or market cannot be applied to debt securities, even if readily marketable, or to nonmarketable equity investments.

Reductions to LCM are reported in a contra equity account rather than being reflected in income. Recoveries of previously recognized declines would reduce or eliminate this contra equity account. Under no circumstances could this account have a net credit balance, however.

Accounting for Debt Securities Under IAS 25

Determining the cost of debt investments. As with investments in equity securities, the cost of any given investment in debt instruments should include any associated acquisition charges, such as brokerage fees, duties, or other costs. The essential difference between investments in debt and equity securities is that in the case of the former any variance between face or par value and the cost of acquisition, whether due to market forces or the fact that additional fees and costs were incurred, will affect the computed premium or discount on the investment. Depending on the method of accounting employed, as illustrated below, this premium or discount may need to be amortized over the expected holding period of the asset.

As with equity investments, investments in debt instruments may be acquired in exchange for shares of stock in the investor entity. The measure of acquisition cost is given by the fair value of the shares surrendered, not the face or par value of the debt. If the fair value of the debt acquired is more objectively determinable than the value of the equity or other securities given up, which is not expected to be the predominant situation, it should be used to record the transaction.

In other situations, the investment in debt securities will be acquired in exchange for other assets, such as land or equity in other investees. Again, primary evidence of value will be the fair value of the assets given up; in the absence of reliable data about this, the fair value of the debt instruments acquired should be determined directly.

With investments in debt, returns of capital will occur only when interest has been accrued, but unpaid, at the date of acquisition of the investment. When the interest due is paid later, it will not represent income to the investor, but merely return of a portion of the funds invested. Since normal accounting procedures are to record accrued interest as an asset distinct from the investment itself at the time the purchase is made, there will usually be little judgment required in properly accounting for the later collection of the amount owed.

Carrying amounts for current investments. The methods of accounting offered by IAS 25 for current equity investments apply equally to investments in debt. Either a lower of cost or market approach or a pure market value approach are fully acceptable. The standard does not directly address the meaning of cost in the context of current investments, but presumably there would be little virtue in amortizing any premium or discount on acquisition of such investments since by definitionthe intent is to dispose of these in the near term. Thus, it is concluded that cost means original acquisition cost in this context.

If market value is defined as the exit value (i.e., the price that the investor would receive on a sale of the investment), it is likely that market would be lower than cost immediately on acquisition. The amount of this discrepancy would be equal to the spread between bid and ask prices, or would otherwise reflect normal transaction costs. However, notwithstanding this fact, it is unlikely that this difference would be a material amount, and therefore an immediate write-down to LCM would not be anticipated. Later price changes might necessitate such an adjustment, though.

The market value method is an equally acceptable accounting method under IAS 25 and reflects the trend in recent years to move to a mark-to-market approach for some, or all, financial instruments. Many accounting theoreticians, in fact, have argued that for all assets that are readily marketable and indeed, for debt obligations as well, the most objective and meaningful measure is current fair value. Investment in debt securities often have more objectively determinable fair market values, since there is an inverse mathematical relationship between market interest rates and prices for the securities in question, assuming that there are not also changes in other factors, such as the perceived credit risk of the debtor.

Changes in value of current investments in debt securities. If current investments in debt securities are carried at LCM, declines in value are to be reflected currently in income. Later recoveries in value, but not to exceed original cost, are also reported in current earnings.

If the debt investments are being accounted for on the basis of market value, the reporting entity will choose either to report unrealized gains and losses in income currently or to employ the approach prescribed for long-term investments. Under the latter strategy, increases in market value are credited to owners' equity, not income, and later declines (but not in excess of unrealized gains recognized earlier) are offset against the revaluation surplus account. Losses in excess of unrealized gains, however, must be taken into earnings. If these losses are later reversed, the gains are also reflected in income. Put another way, under the alternative approach any net unrealized losses are reported in income (and thus eventually in retained earnings), while any net unrealized gains are reported in the additional equity account, revaluation surplus.

Examples of accounting for current investments in debt securities

In the following illustrations, assume that Zanibar Mfg. Corp. has acquired, on January 2, 2000, $100,000 of Tralog Corp. bonds, bearing 8% coupons, for a price of 104 (bonds are quoted at percent of par or face value). The bonds are due to mature on December 31, 2003, but Zanibar does not intend to hold them to that date; rather, it is the expectation that these will be liquidated to generate the cash needed to begin construction on a new factory building. The project is delayed, however, and 3 years pass without the investment being sold. The bonds are quoted on the market at 104.25 at December 31, 2000; 102 at December 31, 2001; and 100.5 at December 31, 2002.

Example of accounting for debt investments under the lower of cost or market approach

In 2000 the market value of the bonds increases; under the LCM approach, no unrealized gains are recognized, and therefore the investment is maintained at cost this year. In later years, market values decline, and these declines are fully reported in earnings under the LCM method. Note that with the due date approaching, it is only normal that the market value of bonds sold at a premium decline to par at maturity date, but this underlying reason makes no difference to the accounting to be applied. Since these bonds are classified as current, amortization of the premium (or of a discount, had there been any) is not affected. (Any deferred tax effects are ignored in this example.)

The entry at January 2, 2000, is as follows:

Current investment in bonds	104,000	
Cash		104,000

There is no entry at December 31, 2000.
The entry at December 31, 2001, is as follows:

Loss on decline in current investment in bonds	2,000	
Current investment in bonds		2,000

The entry at December 31, 2002, is as follows:

Loss on decline in current investmentin bonds	1,500	
Current investment in bonds		1,500

Note that the offset to the loss is directly to the investment account, since the write-down is on the individual security. If the adjustment was for a decline in the entire portfolio, a valuation account would have been used instead.

Example of accounting for investments under the market value approach

The entry at January 2, 2000, is as follows:

Current investment in bonds	104,000	
Cash		104,000

The entry at December 31, 2000, is as follows:

Current investment in bonds	250	
Gain on increase in current investment in bonds		250

The entry at December 31, 2001, is as follows:

Loss on decline in current investment in bonds	2,250	
Current investment in bonds		2,250

The entry at December 31, 2002, is as follows:

Loss on decline in current investment in bonds	1,500	
Current investment in bonds		1,500

Note that on a pure market value basis, the gain in value in 2000 is taken into income and the losses in 2000 and 2001 are reflected in earnings.

Carrying amounts for long-term investments in debt securities. Debt investments classified as long-term, or which would be categorized as noncurrent assets in a classified balance sheet, may be carried in the balance sheet at either original cost or revalued amounts. The third method permitted by IAS 25 for equity investments, the lower of cost or market, is **not** available for investments in debt securities.

The standard states that long-term investments are usually carried at cost, absent a decline that is other than temporary in nature. The use of the term other than temporary rather than the simpler term permanent is intentional: The latter would imply a stricter standard of evidence to support an adjustment to the cost basis of the investment, since it would be necessary to support strongly the notion that the decline was permanent in nature. Under the other-than-temporary standard, there is, instead, a presumption that any material decline is not temporary, unless evidence (such as past market fluctuations) can be marshaled to suggest that a recovery is likely.

As applied to investments in debt securities, the term cost actually means amortized cost, since any premium or discount on acquisition must be charged or credited to interest income on a rational and systematic basis over the expected holding period. In most instances, there is no expectation that the investment will be liquidated before maturity, and therefore the premium or discount will be amortized to the maturity date (or, in the case of a premium, to an earlier call date).

Changes in value of long-term investments in debt securities. Increases in value of long-term debt investments are reported in stockholders' (owners') equity as an additional equity account and are not first reflected in income. If later losses on the same investment, not in excess of the earlier gains are incurred, these are to be recognized by reducing the additional equity account, again without first passing through the income statement. Any further losses in excess of earlier unrealized gains, however, must be reported as charges against earnings.

On the other hand, if losses are first incurred, these must be reported in the income statement. If market values later reverse, so that unrealized gains on the same investment are to be reported, these should also be reflected in income, but only to the extent of previously recognized losses. Any further gains are taken to the additional equity account, not to income.

Examples of accounting for long-term investments at revalued amounts

In the following illustrations, assume that Trafalgar Co. has acquired on January 2, 2000, $100,000 of Supercompute Corp. bonds, bearing 8% coupons, for a price of 104. The bonds are due to mature on December 31, 2006, and Trafalgar does intend to hold them to that date. Also on January 2, 2000, Trafalgar acquires $150,000 face value of Xenobe PLC 6% bonds due December 31, 2006, at a price of 89.5. The intention is also to hold these to maturity. The Supercompute bonds are quoted on the market at 104.25 at December 31, 2000; 102 at December 31, 2001; and 100.5 at December 31, 2002. The

Xenobe bonds are quoted on the market at 89 at December 31, 2000; 94 at December 31, 2001; and 93 at December 31, 2002.

Ignoring tax effects. Under IAS 25, long-term investments are deemed to be individually important, and the unrealized gains or losses will be computed individually.

The entry at January 2, 2000, is as follows:

Investment in Supercompute bonds	104,000	
Investment in Xenobe bonds	134,250	
Cash		238,250

The entries at December 31, 2000, are as follows:

Investment in Supercompute bonds	250	
Additional equity from increase in value of Supercompute bonds		250
Loss on decline in Xenobe bonds	750	
Investment in Xenobe bonds		750

Note that the decline in value of Xenobe bonds is taken as a charge against earnings, while the increase in value of Supercompute bonds is credited to an additional equity account.

The entries at December 31, 2001, are as follows:

Additional equity from increase in value of Supercompute bonds	250	
Loss on decline in Supercompute bonds	2,000	
Investment in Supercompute bonds		2,250
Investment in Xenobe bonds	7,500	
Additional equity from increase in value of Xenobe bonds		6,750
Gain on recovery in Xenobe bonds		750

In the foregoing entries, the previously recognized unrealized gain of $250 in Supercompute bonds has been reversed, and a further decline in value amounting to $2,000 is now recognized as a charge against earnings. At the same time, a previously recognized loss in the value of Xenobe bonds, reported as charge against earnings in 1999, is reversed by a credit to income in 2001; a further gain in value, amounting to $6,750, is reported in an additional equity account.

The entries at December 31, 2002, are as follows:

Loss on decline in Supercompute bonds	1,500	
Investment in Supercompute bonds		1,500
Additional equity from increase in value of Xenobe bonds	1,500	
Investment in Xenobe bonds		1,500

In 2002 there is a further decline in Supercompute bonds' value, which is reported in earnings. There is also a decline in the value of Xenobe bonds, which represents a partial reversal of the unrealized gain reported in 2001 as a credit to additional equity and thus does not affect earnings.

Including tax effects. Assume the same facts as in the foregoing example, but now also assume that Trafalgar is taxed at a marginal rate of 40% and that unrealized gains or losses on long-term investments are not taxable or deductible. In addition to the entries shown above, the following entries relating to the deferred tax impact of the changes in the values of these investments are needed.

The entries at December 31, 2000, are as follows:

Additional equity from increase in		
value of Supercompute bonds	100	
Deferred tax liability		100
Deferred tax benefit	300	
Provision for income taxes--deferred		300

Note that the tax effect of the decline in value of Xenobe bonds is taken as a credit to earnings, since the loss in value was reported in the income statement, while the tax effect of the increase in value of Supercompute bonds is charged against the same additional equity account to which the gross value increase was credited.

The tax entries at December 31, 2001, are as follows:

Deferred tax liability	100	
Deferred tax benefit	800	
Additional equity from increase in		
value of Supercompute bonds		100
Provision for income taxes--deferred		800
Provision for income taxes--deferred	300	
Additional equity from increase in		
value of Xenobe bonds	2,700	
Deferred tax benefit		300
Deferred tax liability		2,700

In the foregoing entries, the $100 tax effect of the previously recognized unrealized gain in Supercompute bonds has been reversed, and the tax effect of a further decline in value, amounting to $800, is now recognized as a credit to earnings. Also, a previously recognized loss in the value of Xenobe bonds is reversed, necessitating a charge against income in 2001; the tax effect of the further gain in value, amounting to $2,700, is reported as a debit to additional equity account.

The entries at December 31, 2002, are as follows:

Deferred tax benefit	600	
Provision for income taxes--deferred		600
Deferred tax liability	600	
Provision for income taxes--deferred		600

In 2002 there is a further decline in Supercompute bonds' value, which is reported in earnings. The tax effect of this currently nondeductible loss is debited to deferred tax benefit and credited to tax expense. There is also a (coincidentally similar) decline in the value of Xenobe bonds, which represents a partial reversal of the unrealized gain reported in 2001; the tax effect of this is charged to the deferred tax liability provided previously.

Example of accounting for long-term investment at cost

If the historical cost method of accounting for long-term investments in debt securities is elected, the premium or discount should be amortized to interest income by the effective yield (constant return) method. If straight-line amortization produces results that are not materially different from the more precise effective yield method, it may be used (although, with wide use of computers, the formerly pragmatic decision to use a straight-line approximation is much less likely to serve as an excuse). In the present example, using the same facts as the foregoing illustration of the revaluation method, and ignoring tax effects, straight-line amortization will be employed.

The Supercompute bonds were purchased at a price of 104 when there were 4 years to maturity; absent an earlier call date, these will be amortized at a rate of $1,000 per year. The entries will be (each year)

Interest income	1,000	
Investment in Supercompute bonds		1,000

The Xenobe bonds were acquired at a discount of 10.5 points, which, given the 7 years to the maturity date, requires amortization of $2,250 per year (inasmuch as $150,000 face value were purchased). The entries will be

Investment in Xenobe bonds	2,250	
Interest income		2,250

Accounting for Dispositions of Investments Under IAS 25

Current investments. Current investments may, under the provisions of IAS 25, be carried at either market value or lower of cost or market (LCM). If carried at market, of course, in theory the selling price will be equal to the latest market price, which is already reflected in the carrying value, and thus there will be no further gain or loss on the actual sale transaction. As a practical matter, however, the accounting records will contain the market value as of the latest date on which the records were updated, or marked to market, which probably was the date the last interim or annual financial statement was prepared. Thus, the change in market value from that date until the actual transaction date would not yet have been reflected, and this amount would therefore be first recognized at the time of sale. The net result is the same in either case, of course.

If the investments to be disposed of had instead been accounted for under the LCM method, the impact on currently reported earnings of the sale will depend on whether LCM had been applied on an individual investment or portfolio basis. If the individual investment approach (which is the less preferred, per IAS 25) had been used, any gain or loss, determined as the difference between the carrying value of that individual investment and the proceeds realized on its disposition, would be reflected currently in earnings.

On the other hand, if the aggregate portfolio (or relevant portion of the portfolio) had been adjusted to LCM, that implicitly permitted some or all of the portfolio's unrealized gains to offset its unrealized losses, the gain or loss on the disposition of part of the portfolio should be determined with reference to the **cost** of the asset sold. That is, reference should be made to original cost, regardless of the unrealized gain or loss that subsequent to acquisition had been implicitly recognized as a part of the net LCM adjustments. The logic for this position is that accounting for these investments should be driven by the value of the entire portfolio (or a subpart of the portfolio if LCM is applied to categories of investments), and an occasional sale of one or another of the components of the portfolio would not immediately affect valuation of the entire portfolio. However, given the need to reassess the allowance for market decline at the time when the next balance sheet is being prepared, there will still be a partial reckoning of the real gain or loss on the transaction. Depending on how much unrealized gain had implicitly offset unrealized loss in the portfolio, the amount reported as a gain or loss on the trade, including the impact of any later reassessment of the LCM reserve, may still differ from the real gain or loss on the transaction itself.

Example of disposition of current investment, carried at lower of cost or market value

Assume that the company acquires the following investment portfolio during 1999 at the costs noted, and that the fair values are as shown as of year end:

Security description	Acquisition cost	Year-end value
1,000 shares Ball Steel common	$ 34,500	$ 37,000
2,000 shares Whammer Pfd. A	125,000	109,500
1,000 shares Hilltopper common	74,250	84,750
Total for portfolio	$233,750	$231,225

Using the lower of cost or market method, a valuation reserve of $2,525 is provided at year end 2000. Individual investments, however, are not adjusted; the net reserve effectively credits the unrealized gain on the investments in Ball Steel and Hilltopper as offsets against the decline in Whammer.

Now, assume that the investment in Whammer is sold in 2001 for $106,000, for an indicated loss of $3,500 versus its most recently measured market value ($109,500 at the end of 2000). However, under IAS 25, this is not used to measure the loss for financial reporting purposes. Rather, the comparison is made to cost, which in this case yields an indicated loss of $19,000. The transaction is reflected in the following journal entry:

Loss on sale of investment	19,000	
Cash	106,000	
Current investment in marketable securities		125,000

It is also necessary to reassess the allowance for the decline in the value of the portfolio when the composition of the portfolio changes. In the present example, assume that the value of the other components of the portfolio continue at their December 2000 amounts; in that case, the entire allowance ($2,525) needs to be reversed to income, since the remaining portfolio has a market value greater than cost, which, under the LCM method, will not be given recognition. Thus, the net loss recognized in the period of sale will be $19,000 – $2,525 = $16,475.

Long-term investments. Under the provisions of IAS 25, long-term investments may be carried at cost, at revalued amounts (market values), or (for marketable equity securities only) at LCM. The recognition of gain or loss on the disposition of a long-term investment depends on the method of accounting used.

If the investment had been accounted for at cost (or amortized cost, in the case of investments in debt securities), the gain or loss on disposition would simply be determined by reference to the difference between original (or amortized) cost and the selling price.

If the investment had been adjusted to a market value that was in excess of historical cost, and the revaluation was reflected in a revaluation surplus account, the question that arises on disposition of the investment is how to eliminate any remaining balance in this account. Under the provisions of IAS 25, the reporting entity is to adopt a policy of either transferring this balance to income, or else transferring directly to retained earnings. Of these options, logically the former, recognizing the now realized (but previously unrealized) gain in income, would undeniably seem to be the more appropriate. From an accounting perspective, the only difference is whether this component of the realized gain is credited to current income or directly to retained earnings; the tax effect would need to be charged to tax expense or to retained earnings, for proper matching against the gain to which it relates.

If long-term investments in equity securities had been accounted for at the lower of cost or market, on a portfolio basis, gain or loss recognition on the sale of individual investments should follow the same general approach as outlined above, in the discussion of LCM applied to current investments. Accordingly, determination of gain or loss will be based on historical cost, not on carrying value. Any allowance for market decline (a contra asset account) would have to be reassessed at that time, with any adjustment thereto being made to the contra equity account.

Accounting for Debt and Equity Investments Under IAS 39

IAS 39, which may be adopted early in 1999 but which is not mandatorily effective until years beginning after 2000, provides an entirely different strategy for the recognition and measurement of financial instruments such as debt and equity securities held as investment assets. While IAS 39 also addresses accounting for financial liabilities, and the matter of hedging using financial derivatives and other instruments, those topics are dealt with elsewhere in this book (in Chapters 12 and 5, respectively).

Under the provisions of IAS 39, the formerly important distinction between current and noncurrent investments is eliminated completely. Instead, the issue of "management intent" is manifested in the tripartite distinction of investments into those held for trading, those available for sale albeit not held for trading purposes, and those intended to be held to maturity. The accounting for debt and equity securities held as investments is dependent upon which of these categories they are placed in, as described in detail in Chapter 5. In the following sections of this chapter, illustrations of the accounting for such investments will be presented, in a manner similar to the foregoing presentation of accounting under the provisions of IAS 25, in order to demonstrate the (relatively few) similarities and the (many) distinctions between these two sets of requirements.

For convenience, some of the key provisions of IAS 39 are repeated in the following discussion, but these are less extensive than the presentation in Chapter 5, which should be referred to by the reader.

Determining the cost of debt and equity investments. Debt and equity securities held as investment assets are recorded at cost, including transactions costs, as of the date when the investor entity becomes a party to the contractual provisions of the instrument. In general this date is readily determinable and unambiguous. For securities purchased "regular way" when settlement date follows the trade date by several days), however, recognition may be on either the trade or the settlement date. Any change in fair value between these dates must be recognized (strictly speaking, regular-way trades involve a forward contract, which is a derivative financial instrument, but IAS 39 does not require that these be actually accounted for as derivatives).

Carrying amount for investments. Debt and equity securities held as investments are to be accounted for at fair value, if held for trading or if otherwise available for sale. Transaction costs are excluded from the fair value determinations, and thus, unless there has been an increase in value since acquisition date, there will often be a loss recognized in the first holding period, due to the fact that when originally recorded, transaction costs were included.

In the case of investments held for trading purposes, changes in fair value from period to period are included in operating results, or recognized directly in equity--through the statement of changes in equity--but each reporting entity must make a onetime election of which of these alternatives it will conform to thereafter. While apparently a change from reporting in equity to inclusion in current operating results would be tolerated, IAS 39 makes it quite clear that the converse could not be justified under the terms of IAS 8. In other words, it is implicit that inclusion of these gains and losses in earnings is deemed a preferable method of financial reporting.

Debt securities to be held to maturity (assuming that the conditions for this as set forth by IAS 39 are met--namely, that management has demonstrated both the intent and the ability to hold the securities until the maturity date) are maintained at amortized historical cost, unless evidence of a permanent impairment exists. The transaction costs included in the originally recorded basis are not eliminated, but are typically amortized as part of any premium or discount.

In addition to debt securities being held to maturity, any financial asset that does not have a quoted market price in an active market, and the fair value of which cannot be reliably measured, will of necessity also be maintained at historical cost, again absent any evidence of impairment in value. Furthermore, loans or receivables which are originated by the reporting entity, and which are **not** held for trading purposes, are also to be maintained at historical cost, per IAS 39. Loans or receivables which are acquired from others, however, are accounted for in the same manner as other debt securities (i.e., they must be classified as held-for-trading, available-for-sale, or held-to-maturity, and accounted for accordingly).

Example of accounting for investments in equity securities

Assume that Raphael Corporation purchases the following equity securities for investment purposes during 2000:

Security description	Acquisition cost	Fair value at year end
1,000 shares Belarus Steel common stock	$ 34,500	$ 37,000
2,000 shares Wimbledon pfd. "A" stock	125,000	109,500
1,000 shares Hillcrest common stock	74,250	88,750

Assume that, at the respective dates of acquisition, management of Raphael Corporation designated the Belarus Steel and Hillcrest common stock investments as being for trading purposes, while the Wimbledon preferred shares were designated as having been purchased for long term-investment purposes (and will thus be categorized as available-for-sale rather than trading). Accordingly, the entries to record the purchases were as follows:

Investment in equity securities--held-for-trading	108,750	
Cash		108,750
Investment in equity securities--available-for-sale	125,000	
Cash		125,000

At year end, both portfolios are adjusted to fair market value; the decline in Wimbledon preferred stock, series A, is judged to be a temporary market fluctuation rather than a permanent decline. Raphael Corporation makes a onetime election to report these changes in fair value in equity, rather than in earnings. The entries to adjust the investment accounts at December 31, 2000, are

Investment in equity securities--held-for-trading	17,000	
Gain on holding equity securities		17,000
Unrealized loss on securities--available-for-sale		
(an equity account)	15,500	
Investment in equity securities--available-for-sale		15,500

Thus, the change in value of the portfolio of trading securities is recognized in earnings, whereas the change in the value of the available-for-sale securities is reflected directly in stockholders' equity, after being reported in equity, via the statement of changes in equity.

Accounting for changes in value. Changes in the value of held-for-trading securities are taken into income currently. Changes in the value of available-for-sale securities are reflected either in earnings or directly in equity, depending on which method had been initially elected by the reporting entity. Changes in value of held-to-maturity securities, unless deemed to be impairments, are ignored. Values are normally determined with reference to market prices, but in some circumstances other approaches will need to be used, such as discounted cash flow analysis, using the discount rate appropos to the instrument's risk characteristics, term to maturity, and so forth.

Accounting for changes in classification. There is a limited ability to revise the classification of certain investments in financial instruments under IAS 39. Those which are first denoted as being held for trading, however, can almost never be later defined as being held to maturity or as being available for sale, since it has been held by the IASC that an initial categorization as held-for-trading must be based on the original objective for the investment's acquisition. Investments denoted as available-for-sale may be reclassified to trading only if there is sufficient evidence of a recent actual pattern of short-term-profit taking to warrant this change.

Investments are also very unlikely to be reclassified to held-to-maturity after acquisition, since here, too, the original intent will be of great importance. Furthermore, investments classified as held-to-maturity may be manditorily reclassified to available-for-sale if the entity, during the current year or the two prior years, has sold, transferred, or exercised a put option on more than an insignificant amount of similarly classified securities before maturity date. However, sales very close to the maturity dates (or exercised call dates) will not "taint" the classification of other held-to-maturity securities, nor will sales occurring after substantially all of the asset's principal has been collected (e.g., in the case of serial bonds or mortgage securities), or when made in response to isolated events beyond the entity's control (e.g., the debtor's impending financial collapse) when nonrecurring in nature and not subject to having been forecast by the entity.

Transfers to held-to-maturity category. Under IAS 39's provisions, intent and ability to hold to maturity should be assessed at each balance sheet date. While normally investments to be held to maturity are acquired with that intention specifically in mind, it is not impossible that investments first classified as available-for-sale would later be reclassified as held-to-maturity. If so, the then fair value becomes the cost basis of the investment, which thereafter is reported at amortized cost. For example, if bonds with a face value of $100,000 were acquired as an available-for-sale investment at a cost of $82,000 and have since risen in value to $87,500 are recategorized as held-to-maturity, the $87,500 will be the new cost basis. The $12,500 "discount" from face value will be amortized, using the effective interest method, to the projected maturity date.

The accounting for the $5,500 difference between the original acquisition cost and the fair value at the date of transfer to the held-to-maturity portfolio depends upon whether the entity had elected to report fair value changes on available-for-sale securities in earnings or in equity. If the former, the $5,500 gain had already been recognized in results of operations, and this will not be revised on a retrospective basis. However, if the gain had been reported in shareholders' equity (after being included in a statement of changes in equity), it will be accounted for by amortizing it to earnings over the remaining holding period. In the present case, assuming recognition in equity had been chosen, the effective discount on the bonds will be $18,000, all of which will be amortized to earnings over the term to maturity, so as to produce a constant return on the increasing book value of the investment.

Transfers between available-for-sale and trading investment categories. Under the provisions of IAS 39, investments held first for trading purposes cannot later be reclassified to available-for-sale; conversely, transfers to the trading portfolio are expected to be infrequent, occurring only when there is evidence of trading behavior by the enterprise which strongly suggests that the investment in question will indeed be traded in the short-term.

To illustrate, consider Raphael Corporation's investment in Hillcrest common stock, which was assigned to the trading portfolio and at December 31, 2000, was marked to fair value of $88,750. If in April 2001 management were to determine that this investment will not be traded, but rather will continue to be held indefinitely, it would be constrained by IAS 39 from altering the accounting for the investment. Thus, it would have to be maintained as a trading investment, continually marked to fair value, with value changes reflected in current operating results, notwithstanding the intent to not trade it.

On the other hand, transfers to the trading portfolio are permissible. However, there must be sufficient evidence of actual trading behavior to support this reclassification. For securities being transferred into the trading category, any unrealized gain or loss which had been recorded in equity (as illustrated above) is deemed to be realized at the date of the transfer. Also, any fair value changes since the date of the most recent balance sheet may need to be recognized at this time. To illustrate, consider the investment in Wimbledon preferred stock, which was held in the available-for-sale portfolio, and which in March 2001 was adjusted to a fair value of $112,000 (as illustrated above). The increase from adjusted cost ($109,500, after an impairment in value had been recognized) was reflected in changes in equity, rather than in earnings, consistent with the entity's elected accounting method, and given that the security was not at the time being held for trading. Now assume that, in June 2001, a decision is made to try to sell the investment in the short term. This means that the holding of Wimbledon stock will be treated as being in the trading portfolio. Further, the value of the shares held, at the date of this decision, is $114,700. The entry to record the transfer from available-for-sale to trading, and the "realization" of the increased value at that date, is as follows:

Investment in equity securities--held-for-trading	114,700	
Unrealized gain on securities--available-for-sale (an equity account)	2,500	
Investment in equity securities--available-for-sale		112,000
Gain on holding equity securities (an income statement account)		5,200

The recognized gain at the time of transfer, in this case, is the sum of the previously unrecognized gain which had been recorded in the equity account ($2,500) plus the further gain not yet given any recognition in the investor's financial statements ($2,700). Note that the elimination of the equity representing the previously reported unrealized gain will be included in the statement of changes in equity in the current period as a debit, since the equity account is being reversed at this time.

Had there been a decline in fair value since the date of the last balance sheet, the gain to be recognized at the date of this transfer would have been the net of the previous, unrecognized gain, and the later loss; if the loss exceeded the earlier gain, a net loss would be recognized at this point. Any further gains or losses after the transfer to the trading portfolio will be handled as earlier described (i.e., recognized in income currently).

Transfers among portfolios, to the extent permitted, are to be made at fair value as of the date of transfer.

Example of accounting for debt securities

Marseilles Corporation purchases the following debt securities as investments in 2000:

Issue	Face value	Price paid*
DeLacroix Chemical 8% due 2004	$ 200,000	$ 190,000
Forsythe Pharmaceutical 9.90% due 2016	500,000	575,000
Luckystrike Mining 6% due 2001	100,000	65,000

Accrued interest is ignored in these amounts; the normal entries for interest accrual and receipt are assumed.

Management has stated that Marseilles's objectives differed among the various investments. Thus, the DeLacroix bonds are considered to be suitable as a long-term investment, with the intention that they will be held until maturity. The Luckystrike bonds are a speculation; the significant discount from par value was seen as very attractive, despite the low coupon rate. Management believes the bonds were depressed because mining stocks and bonds have been out of favor, but believes the economic recovery will lead to a surge in market value, at which point the bonds will be sold for a quick profit. The Forsythe Pharmaceutical bonds are deemed a good investment, but with a maturity date 16 years in the future, management is unable to commit to holding these to maturity.

Based on the foregoing, the appropriate accounting for the three investments in bonds would be as follows:

DeLacroix Chemical 8% due 2004

These should be accounted for as held-to-maturity; maintain at historical cost, with discount ($10,000) to be amortized over term to maturity (assumed to be 4 years, for an amortization of $2,500 per year, using straight-line in this case to approximate the effective interest method, which is required to be used).

Forsythe Pharmaceutical 9.90% due 2016

Account for these as available-for-sale, since neither the held-for-trading nor held-to-maturity criteria apply. These should be reported at fair market value at each balance sheet date, with any unrealized gain or loss included in the equity account (consistent with the entity's normal accounting practice), unless an impairment occurs.

Luckystrike Mining 6% due 2001

As an admitted speculation, these should be accounted for as part of the trading portfolio, and also reported at fair market value on the balance sheet. All adjustments to carrying value will be included in earnings each year, whether the fair value fluctuations are temporary or permanent in nature.

Accounting for Transfers Between Portfolios

Transfers between portfolio categories are to be accounted for at fair market value at the date of the transfer, as described above. Consider the following events.

1. Marseilles management decides in 2001, when the Forsythe bonds have a market (fair) value of $604,500, that the bonds will be disposed of in the short-term, hopefully when the price hits $605,000. The bonds are presently carried on the books at $580,000, which was the fair value at the time the year-end 2000 financial statements were being prepared. Based on this description of the decision, the bonds should be transferred to the trading portfolio at a "cost" of $604,500. The entry to record this would be the following:

Investment in debt securities--held-for-trading	604,500	
Unrealized gain on holding debt securities as investment	5,000	
Investment in debt securities--available-for-sale		580,000
Gain on holding debt securities		29,500

Transfers to the trading portfolio are permissible under IAS 39, although these are not expected to occur often. The previously unrealized gain (reflected in the write-up of the investment from original cost, $575,000, to the fair market value at year end 2000, $580,000) is now realized for financial reporting purposes, as is the further rise in value from $580,000 to $604,500 at the time the portfolio transfer takes place.

2. Assume that at year end 2000 the investment in the Forsythe bonds is still held, and the fair value has declined to $602,000. Management's intentions regarding this holding have not changed since the decision to transfer to held-for-trading. The year-end adjustment will be

Loss on holding debt securities	2,500	
Investment in debt securities--held-for-trading		2,500

The market decline is reflected in earnings in 2001, since the bonds are in the held-for-trading portfolio.

3. In 2001 Marseilles management also made a decision about its investment in De-Lacroix Chemical bonds. These bonds, which were originally designated as held-to-maturity, were accounted for at amortized historical cost. Assume the amortization in 2000 was $2,000 (because the bonds were not held for a full year), so that the book value of the investment at year end 2000 was $192,000. In 2001, at a time when the value of these bonds was $198,000, management concluded that it was no longer certain that they would be held to maturity, and therefore transferred this holding to the available-for-sale portfolio. The entry to record this would be

Investment in debt securities--available-for-sale	198,000	
Unrealized gain on holding debt securities as investment		6,000
Investment in debt securities--held-to-maturity		192,000

The transfer is at fair market value, but since the bonds are being transferred into the available-for-sale category (for which unrealized gains and losses are recorded directly in equity, per company policy), the gain at this date, $6,000, is not recognized in earnings, but rather will be reported in the statement of changes in equity.

4. In 2002, management reverses its prior decision regarding the DeLacroix Chemical bond holding. It now professes an intention to hold these until their maturity, in 2004. At the date this decision is made, the DeLacroix bonds are quoted at $195,000. Assume that the fair market value at year end 2001 was $198,000, so no adjustment was needed at that time to the carrying value of the investment. Again the transfer will be recorded at fair market value.

Investment in debt securities--held-to-maturity	195,000	
Unrealized gain on holding debt securities as investment	3,000	
Investment in debt securities--available-for-sale		198,000

The unrealized gain previously recognized in an equity account is partially eliminated, since fair value at the date of this transfer is less than the previously recorded amount. The change in this equity account must be reported in the statement of changes in equity for the period in which this portfolio reclassification occurs. The remaining balance in the equity account (whether a net debit or credit) is accounted for as additional premium or discount, and is amortized over the remaining term to maturity. IAS 39 mandates that the effective yield method be used, but for this example, assume that the discount will be amortized over the remaining 2 years on the straight-line basis (if this difference from the effective yield method is not material, it is an acceptable practice). Thus, the actual discount as measured by the spread between the new carrying value, $195,000, and face value to be received at maturity, $200,000, plus the additional discount measured by the unrealized gain being reported currently in the equity section of $3,000, giving a total discount amounting to $8,000 to be amortized over the remaining 2 years. This $8,000, when added to the $2,000 discount amortized in 1999 (when the bonds were in the original held-to-maturity portfolio), equals $10,000, which is the discount between the face value, $200,000 and the price paid by Marseilles Corporation ($190,000).

Accounting for impairments in value. A financial asset will be deemed to have become impaired whenever the carrying amount exceeds the recoverable amount. This is to be assessed at each balance sheet date, making reference, for example, to any significant financial difficulties of the issuer, a contractual breach by the issuer, the probability of a bankruptcy or financial reorganization, or the disappearance of an active market for the issuer's securities (although an enterprise which has "gone private" does not create the presumption of impairment).

In general, trading securities will be carried at fair value and any impairment will have been recognized as it was developing, with immediate recognition in the operating results of the investor. Available-for-sale securities will similarly have been adjusted to fair value, with any loss given recognition in earnings, even if the reporting enterprise had elected to report normal value changes (i.e., those not due to permanent impairments) in equity. In this latter instance, the amount of value decline previously reported in equity must also be removed from equity and reported in current operations.

For securities being reported at amortized historical cost (those held to maturity, plus loans or receivables originated by the enterprise) the amount of the impairment to be recognized will be the difference between the carrying amount and the present value of expected future cash flows, discounted using the instrument's original discount rate. The current market discount rate is not to be used, since to do so would introduce an element of fair value accounting, which is not pertinent to such investments. Any write-down for impairment, which may be made directly or via an allowance account, must be reported in current operating results. If later events, such as a revision in the obligor's credit rating, result in a lessened measure of impairment, the previously recognized impairment may be partially or fully reversed, also through reported earnings.

Securities which are not carried at fair value because of the absence of fair value information are nonetheless subject to review for possible impairments. These are measured as the difference between carrying amount and the present value of expected future cash flows, discounted using the current market interest rate for similar instruments. Note that current rates, not the original effective rate, are the relevant reference, since these investments were being maintained at cost by default (i.e., due to the absence of reliable fair value data), not because they qualified for amortized historical cost due to being held to maturity. Accordingly, the application of fair value accounting, or a reasonable surrogate for it, is valid in such instances.

Once an asset is deemed impaired and written down to its estimated recoverable amount, future interest is accreted using the same discount rate used to compute the impaired value. Thus, for held-to-maturity investments, after being adjusted to recoverable amount, the interest accruals will continue to be consistent with the original effective rate. For securities not carried at fair value due to lack of sufficient information, however, future interest income, if any, will be accrued using the current rate employed to determine the recoverable amount to which the asset's carrying value was adjusted.

Example of impairment of investments

Given the foregoing, assume now, with reference again to the Raphael Corporation example first presented earlier in this chapter, that in January 2001 new information comes to Raphael Corporation management regarding the viability of Wimbledon Corp. Based on this information, it is determined that the decline in Wimbledon preferred stock is probably not a temporary one, but rather is an impairment of the asset as that term is used in IAS 39. The standard prescribes that such a decline be reflected in earnings, and the written down value be treated as the new cost basis. The stock's fair value has remained at the amount last reported, $109,500, but this value is no longer viewed as being only a market fluctuation. Accordingly, the entry to recognize the fact of the investment's permanent impairment is as follows:

Loss on holding equity securities	15,500	
Unrealized loss on securities--available-for-sale (an equity account)		15,500

Any recovery in this value would be recognized in earnings if it can be objectively demonstrated that the recovery was based on subsequent developments. Otherwise, later market fluctuations will be reported in either equity or earnings, based on the accounting method the entity elected for reporting normal changes in the fair value of available-for-sale investments.

To illustrate this point, assume that in March 2001 further information comes to management's attention, which now suggests that the decline in Wimbledon preferred had indeed been only a temporary decline; in fact, the value of Wimbledon now rises to $112,000. There is no evidence of any specific event after the date of the impairment which is responsible for this recovery in value. Since the carrying value after the recognition of the impairment was $109,500, which is treated as the cost basis for purposes of measuring further declines or recoveries, the increase to $112,000 will be accounted for as an increase to be reflected either in earnings or in stockholders' equity, based on the election made originally by the entity. Assume that Rafael management had determined to report fair value changes in the available-for-sale portfolio in equity, not earnings. Accordingly, the entry now required is

Investment in equity securities--available-for-sale	2,500	
Unrealized gain on securities--available-for-sale (an equity account)		2,500

Note that this increase in value is not taken into earnings, since the investment is still considered to be available-for-sale, rather than a part of the trading portfolio. Even though the previous decline in Wimbledon stock was realized in current earnings, because judged at the time to be a permanent impairment in value, the recovery is not (given management's accounting policy) recognized in earnings. Rather, the change in value will be included in the statement of changes in equity, and then displayed in an additional equity account.

Accounting for sales of investments in financial instruments. In general, sales of investments are accounted for by eliminating the carrying value and recognizing a gain or loss for the difference between carrying amount and sales proceeds. Derecognition will occur only when the entity loses control over the contractual rights which comprise the financial asset, or a portion thereof. IAS 39 sets forth certain conditions to define loss of control. Thus, for example, in most cases if the transferor has the right to reacquire the transferred asset, derecognition will not be warranted, unless the asset is readily obtainable in the market or reacquisition is to be at then-fair value. Arrangements which are essentially repurchase (repo) arrangements are similarly not sales and do not result in derecognition. In general, the transferee must obtain the benefits of the transferred asset in order to warrant derecognition by the transferor.

In some instances, the asset will be sold as part of a compound transaction in which the transferor either retains part of the asset, obtains another financial instrument, or incurs a financial liability. If the fair values of all components of the transaction (asset retained, new asset acquired, etc.) are known, computing the gain or loss will be no problem. However, if one or more elements are not subject to an objective assessment, special requirement apply. In the unlikely event that the fair value of the component retained cannot be determined, it should be recorded at zero, thereby conservatively measuring the gain (or loss) on the transaction. Similarly, if a new financial asset is obtained and it cannot be objectively valued, it must be recorded at zero value.

On the other hand, if a financial liability is assumed (e.g., a guarantee) and it cannot be measured at fair value, then the initial carrying amount should be such (i.e., large enough) that no gain is recognized on the transaction. If necessitated by IAS 39's provisions, a loss should be recognized on the transaction. For example, if an asset carried at $4,000 is sold for $4,200 in cash, with the transferor assuming a guarantee obligation which cannot be valued (admittedly, this is unlikely to occur in the context of a truly "arm's-length" transaction), no gain would be recognized and the financial liability would accordingly be initially recorded at $200. On the other hand, if the selling price were instead only $3,800, a loss of $200 would be immediately recognized, and the guarantee obligation would be given no value (but would be disclosed).

Sales made "regular way" are to be recognized on the settlement, not the trade, date. This is in contrast to purchases, for which either trade date or settlement date accounting may be elected under the terms of IAS 39.

If a nominal sale is actually determined to be only a collateralized borrowing, the transferor/debtor does not derecognize the financial asset. The asset should, however, be segregated from other investments in its balance sheet. In general, the transferee/creditor will recognize the collateral as an asset, as well as the related obligation, in its financial statements, unless it is constrained from selling or pledging the collateral.

Presentation and Disclosure Issues

Income statement presentation. For enterprises that engage in transactions in investments, periodic results of operations should include income arising from interest, royalties, dividends, and rentals on long-term and current investments, as well as profits or losses on the disposal of such investments. Depending on the policy adopted by the entity, unrealized gains and losses on current investments that are carried at market value may also be included in current income (the alternative would be to include these in an additional equity account). If the LCM method is used for current investments, any reductions to market value, and any reversals of such reductions, should be included in income. If other than temporary declines in the value of long-term investments have been given recognition, and if any of these declines have later been reversed, these should be explained to financial statement users. Finally, profits and losses on disposals of investments should be included in earnings.

Disclosures required. IAS 25 requires certain disclosures to be made in the income statement and in the balance sheet, if investments are held by the reporting entity or had been held and were sold during the reporting period.

Accounting policies, as defined in IAS 8, are to be disclosed. These should address the method of determining the carrying amounts of investments, recognition afforded to changes in the market value of current investments that are carried at market value, and the treatment of revaluation surplus in the event that a revalued investment is sold.

Disclosure is also required of significant amounts included in income for interest, royalties, dividends, and rentals on current and long-term investments; profits or losses on the disposal of current investments; and the changes in value of such investments.

If investments are not carried at market values, the market values must be shown in the footnote disclosures (or parenthetically in the balance sheet, if preferred). For other long-term investments, if the properties are not reported at fair value as permitted under the standard, the fair values are also to be disclosed.

If there are any material restrictions on the ability to realize the investments (i.e., to dispose of them freely and to obtain the proceeds therefrom), these matters need to be disclosed to readers of the financial statements. Any restrictions on the ability to collect income distributions on the investments must also be disclosed.

For long-term investments accounted for at revalued amounts, disclosure of the reporting entity's policy regarding the frequency of revaluation is required, as is the date of the most recent revaluation, the basis for the revaluation, and whether an external valuation expert's services were employed.

A reconciliation of the amount of the revaluation surplus account from the beginning to the end of the reporting period should be provided. Finally, for those enterprises for which the holding of investments is the primary business, an analysis of the investment portfolio is a required disclosure.

Optional disclosures. In addition to the disclosures enumerated above, IAS 25 identifies a number of useful, if not required, items of information that could assist in understanding the investments held by a reporting entity. These include an analysis of long-term investments by category, management's assessment of the fair values of nonmarketable investments, the methods used to value nonmarketable investments, the amount of revaluation surplus associated with assets disposed of during the period and converted to share capital (retained earnings), and information about any individually significant investments.

Specialized industry accounting practices. IAS 25 notes that in some countries investment companies are prohibited from distributing profits accumulated from the disposal of investments. For these entities, the distinction between interest and dividends, on the one hand, and gains or losses, on the other hand, is of great importance. Such enterprises are permitted to exclude from income realized and unrealized investment gains if investments are carried at fair value. Expanded disclosures of changes in investment values are required under these circumstances.

Accounting for Hedging Activities

Hedging accounting under IAS 39. When there is a hedging relationship between a hedging instrument and another item (the underlying), and certain conditions are met, then special "hedging accounting" will be applied. The purpose is to relate the value changes in the hedging instrument and the underlying so that these affect earnings in the same period. Hedging instruments are often so-called financial derivatives, such as options or futures, but this is not a necessary condition. Hedging may be engaged in to protect against changes in fair values, changes in expected cash flows, or changes in the value of an investment in a foreign operation, such as a subsidiary, due to currency rate movements. There is no requirement that enterprises engage in hedging, but the principles of good management will often dictate that this be done.

For a simplistic example of the need for, and means of, hedging, consider an entity which holds US Treasury bonds as an investment. The bonds have a maturity some 10 years in the future, but the entity actually intends to dispose of these in the intermediate term, for example, within 4 years to partially finance a plant expansion currently being planned. Obviously, an unexpected increase in general interest rates during the projected 4-year holding period would be an unwelcome development, since it would cause a decline in the market value of the bonds and could accordingly result in an unanticipated loss of principal. One means of guarding against this would be to purchase a put option on these bonds, permitting the enterprise to sell them at an agreed-upon price, which would be most valuable should there be a price decline. If interest rates do indeed rise, the increasing value of the "put" will (if properly structured) offset the declining value of the bonds themselves, thus providing an effective fair value hedge. (Other hedging strategies are also available, including selling short Treasury bond futures, and the entity of course could have reduced or eliminated the need to hedge entirely by having invested in Treasury bonds having a maturity more closely matched to its anticipated cash need.)

Special hedge accounting is necessitated by the fact that fair value changes in not all financial instruments are reported in current earnings. Thus, if the entity in the foregoing example holding the Treasuries has elected to report changes in available-for-sale investments (which would include the Treasury bonds in this instance) directly in equity, but the changes in the hedging instrument's fair value were to be reported in current operations, there would be a fundamental mismatching which would distort the real hedging relationship which had been established. To avoid this result, special hedge accounting is prescribed by IAS 39, as was discussed in some detail in Chapter 5.

Accounting for gains and losses from fair value hedges. The accounting for qualifying gains and losses on fair value hedges is as follows:

1. On the hedging instrument, they are recognized in earnings.
2. On the hedged item, they are recognized in earnings even if the gains or losses would normally have been included in other comprehensive income if not hedged.

The foregoing rule applies even in the case of investments (classified as available-for-sale) for which unrealized gains and losses are being accumulated directly in equity, if that method was appropriately elected by the reporting enterprise, as permitted by IAS 39. In all instances, to the extent that there are differences between the amounts of gain or loss on hedging and hedged items, these will be due either to amounts excluded from assessment effectiveness, or to hedge ineffectiveness; in either event, these are recognized currently in earnings.

As an example, consider an available-for-sale security, the carrying amount of which is adjusted by the amount of gain or loss resulting from the hedged risk, a fair value hedge. It is assumed that the entire investment was hedged, but it is also possible to hedge merely a portion of the investment. The facts are as follows:

Hedged Item:	Available-for-sale security
Hedging Instrument:	Put option
Underlying:	Price of the security
Notional amount:	100 shares of the security

Example 1

On July 1, 1999, Gardiner Company purchased 100 shares of Disney Co. common stock at a cost of $15 per share and classified it as an available-for-sale security. On October 1, Gardiner Company purchased an at-the-money put on Disney with an exercise price of $25 and an expiration date of April 2002. This put purchase locks in a profit of $650, if the price stays at $15 or goes lower, but allows continued profitability if the price of the Disney stock continues to go up. (In other words, the put cost a premium of $350, which if deducted from the locked in gain [$2,500 market value less $1,500 cost] leaves a net gain of $650 to be realized.)

The premium paid for an at-the-money option (i.e., where the exercise price is current market value of the underlying) is the price paid for the right to have the entire remaining option period in which to exercise the option. In the present example, Gardiner Company specifies that only the intrinsic value of the option is to be used to measure effectiveness. Thus, the time value decreases of the put will be charged against the income of the period, and not offset against the change in value of the underlying, hedged item. Gardiner Company then documents the hedge's strategy, objectives, hedging relationships, and method of measuring effectiveness. The following table shows the fair value of the hedged item and the hedging instrument.

Case One

	10/1/99	12/31/99	3/31/00	4/17/00
Hedged item:				
Disney share price	$ 25	$ 22	$ 20	$ 20
Number of shares	100	100	100	100
Total value of shares	$2,500	$2,200	$2,000	$2,000
Hedging instrument:				
Put option (100 shares)				
Intrinsic value	$ 0	$ 300	$ 500	$ 500
Time value	350	215	53	0
Total	$ 350	$ 515	$ 553	$ 500
Intrinsic value				
Gain (loss) on put from last				
measurement date	$ 0	$ 300	$ 200	$ 0

Entries to record the foregoing changes in value, ignoring tax effects and transaction costs, are as follows:

7/1/99	Purchase:	Available-for-sale securities	1,500	
		Cash		1,500
9/30/99	End of quarter:	Valuation allowance--available-for-sale securities	1,000	
		Shareholders' equity		1,000
10/1/99	Put purchase:	Put option	350	
		Cash		350
12/31/99	End of year:	Put option	300	
		Hedge gain/loss (intrinsic value gain)		300
		Hedge gain/loss	135	
		Put option (time value loss)		135
		Hedge gain/loss	300	
		Available-for-sale securities (market value loss)		300
3/31/00	End of quarter:	Put option	200	
		Hedge gain/loss (intrinsic value changes)		200
		Hedge gain/loss	162	
		Put option (time value loss)		162
		Hedge gain/loss	200	
		Available-for-sale securities (market value loss)		200
4/17/00	Put expires:	Put option	0	
		Hedge gain/loss (intrinsic value changes)		0
		Hedge gain/loss	53	
		Put option (time value changes)		53
		Hedge gain/loss	0	
		Available-for-sale securities (market value changes)		0

An option is said to be "in-the-money" if the exercise price is above the market value (for a put option) or below the market value (for a call option). At or before expiration, an in-the-money put should be sold or exercised (to let it simply expire would be to effectively discard a valuable asset). It should be stressed that this applies to so-called "American options," which may be exercised at any time prior to expiration; so-called "European options" can only be exercised at the expiration date. Assuming that the put option is sold immediately before its expiration date, the entry would be

4/17/00	Put sold:	Cash	500	
		Put option		500

On the other hand, if the put is exercised (i.e., the underlying security is delivered to the counterparty, which is obligated to pay $25 per share for the stock), the entry would be

Cash	2,500	
Shareholders' equity	1,000	
Valuation allowance--available-for-sale securities		1,000
Valuation allowance		1,000
Put option		500
Gain on sale of securities		1,000

The cumulative effect on retained earnings of the hedge and sale is a net gain of $650 ($1,000 – $350).

Example 2

To further illustrate fair value hedge accounting, the facts in the preceding example will now be slightly modified. Now, the share price increases after the put option is purchased, thus making the put worthless, since the shares could be sold for a more advantageous price on the open market

Case Two

	10/1/99	12/31/99	3/31/00	4/17/00
Hedged item:				
Disney share price	$ 25	$ 28	$ 30	$ 31
Number of shares	100	100	100	100
Total value of shares	$2,500	$2,800	$3,000	$3,100
Hedging instrument:				
Put option (100 shares)				
Intrinsic value	$ 0	$ 0	$ 0	$ 0
Time value	350	100	25	0
Total	$ 350	$ 100	$ 25	$ 0
Intrinsic value				
Gain (loss) on put from last measurement date	$ 0	$ 0	$ 0	$ 0

Entries to record the foregoing changes in value, ignoring tax effects and transaction costs, are as follows:

7/1/99	Purchase:	Available-for-sale securities	1,500	
		Cash		1,500
9/30/99	End of quarter:	Valuation allowance--available-for-sale security	1,000	
		Shareholders' equity		1,000
10/1/99	Put purchase:	Put option	350	
		Cash		350
12/31/99	End of year:	Put option	300	
		Hedge gain/loss (intrinsic value gain)		300
		Hedge gain/loss	135	
		Put option (time value loss)		135
		Available-for-sale security	300	
		Hedge gain/loss (market value gain)		300

3/31/00	End of quarter:	Put option	0	
		Hedge gain/loss (intrinsic value change)		0
		Hedge gain/loss	75	
		Put option (time value loss)		75
		Available-for-sale securities	300	
		Hedge gain/loss (market value gain)		300
4/17/X2	Put expires:	Put option	0	
		Hedge gain/loss (intrinsic value change)		0
		Hedge gain/loss	25	
		Put option (time value change)		25
		Available-for-sale securities	100	
		Hedge gain/loss (market value change)		100

The put expired unexercised and Gardiner Company must decide whether to sell the security. If it continues to hold, normal IAS 39 accounting would apply. In this example, since it was hypothesized that Gardiner had elected to record the effects of value changes (apart from those which were hedging related) directly in shareholders' equity, it would continue to apply this accounting after the expiration of the put option. Assuming, however, that the security is instead sold, the entry would be

Cash	3,100	
Shareholders' equity	1,000	
Available-for-sale securities		2,100
Valuation allowance--available-for-sale securities		1,000
Gain on sale of securities		1,000

Accounting for gains and losses from cash flow hedges. Cash flow hedges generally involve forecasted transactions or events. The intention is to defer the recognition of gains or losses arising from the hedging activity itself until the forecasted transaction takes place, and then to have the formerly deferred gain or loss affect earnings when the forecasted transaction affects earnings. While overwhelmingly it will be derivative financial instruments which are used to hedge cash flows relating to forecasted transactions, IAS 39 contemplates the use of non-derivatives for this purpose as well. Forecasted transactions may include future cash flows arising from presently existing, recognized assets or liabilities--for example, future interest rate payments to be made on debt carrying floating interest rates are subject to cash flow hedging.

The accounting for qualifying gains and losses on cash flow hedges is as follows:

1. On the hedging instrument, the portion of the gain or loss that is determined to be an effective hedge will be recognized directly in equity.
2. Also on the hedging instrument, the ineffective portion should be reported in earnings, if the instrument is a derivative; otherwise, it should be reported in a manner consistent with the accounting for other financial assets or liabilities as set forth in IAS 39. Thus, if an available-for-sale security has been used as the hedging instrument in a particular cash flow hedging situation, and the enterprise has elected to report value changes in equity,

then any ineffective portion of the hedge should continue to be recorded in equity.

According to IAS 39, the separate component of equity associated with the hedged item should be adjusted to the lesser (in absolute terms) of either the cumulative gain or loss on the hedging instrument necessary to offset the cumulative change in expected future cash flows on the hedged item from hedge inception, excluding the ineffective portion, **or** the fair value of the cumulative change in expected future cash flows on the hedged item from inception of the hedge. Furthermore, any remaining gain or loss on the hedging instrument (i.e., the ineffective portion) must be recognized currently in earnings or directly in equity, as dictated by the nature of the instrument and entity's accounting policy (for available-for-sale instruments, where there is a choice of reporting directly in equity or in earnings). If the entity's policy regarding the hedge is to exclude a portion from the measure of hedge effectiveness (e.g., time value of options in the preceding example in this section of Chapter 10), then any related gain or loss must be incorporated into either earnings or equity based on the nature of the item and the elected policy.

Example of "plain vanilla" interest rate swap

On July 1, 1999, Abbott Corp. borrows $5 million with a fixed maturity (no prepayment option) of June 30, 2003, carrying interest at the US prime interest rate + 1/2%. Interest payments are due semiannually; the entire principal is due at maturity. At the same date, Abbott Corp. enters into a so-called "plain-vanilla-type" swap arrangement, calling for fixed payments at 8% and the receipt of prime + 1/2%, on a notional amount of $5 million. At that date prime is 7.5%, and there is no premium due on the swap arrangement since the fixed and variable payments are equal. (Note that swaps are privately negotiated and, accordingly, a wide range of terms will be encountered in practice; this is simply intended as an example, albeit a very typical one.)

The foregoing swap qualifies as a cash flow hedge under IAS 39. Given the nature of this swap, it is reasonable to assume no ineffectiveness, but in real world situations this must be carefully evaluated with reference to the specific circumstances of each case; IAS 39 does not provide a listing of characteristics which might suggest greater or lesser degrees of effectiveness (which contrasts with the corresponding US GAAP standard). IAS 39 defines effectiveness in terms of results: if at inception and throughout the life of the hedge, the enterprise can expect an almost complete offset of cash flow variations, and in fact (retrospectively) actual results are within a range of 80 to 125%, the hedge will be judged highly effective.

In the present example, assume that in fact the hedge proves to be highly effective. Also, assume that the prime rate over the 4-year term of the loan, as of each interest payment date, is as follows, along with the fair value of the remaining term of the interest swap at those dates:

Date	Prime rate (%)	Fair value of swap*
December 31, 1999	6.5	$(150,051)
June 30, 2000	6.0	(196,580)
December 31, 2000	6.5	(111,296)
June 30, 2001	7.0	(45,374)
December 31, 2001	7.5	0
June 30, 2002	8.0	23,576
December 31, 2002	8.5	24,038
June 30, 2003	8.0	0

* *Fair values are determined as the present values of future cash flows resulting from expected interest rate differentials, based on current prime rate, discounted at 8%.*

Regarding the fair values presented in the foregoing table, it should be assumed that the market (fair) values of the swap contract are precisely equal to the present value, at each valuation date (assumed to be the interest payment dates), of the differential future cash flows resulting from utilization of the swap. Future variable interest rates (prime + 1/2%) are assumed to be the same as the existing rates at each valuation date (i.e., there is no basis for any expectation of rate changes, and therefore the best estimate at any given moment is that the current rate will persist over time). The discount rate, 8%, is assumed to be constant over time.

Thus, for example, the fair value of the swap at December 31, 1999, would be the present value of an annuity of seven payments (the number of remaining semiannual interest payments due) of $25,000 each (pay 8%, receive 7%, based on then-existing prime rate of 6.5%) to be made to the swap counterparty, discounted at an annual rate of 8%. (In a slight simplification, 4% is used for the semiannual discounting, rather than the rate which would compound to 8% annually.) The present value of a stream of seven $25,000 payments to the swap counterparty amounts to $150,051 at December 31, 1999, which is the swap liability to be reported by Abbott Corp. at that date. The offset is a debit to other comprehensive income, since the hedge is continually judged to be 100% effective in this case.

The semiannual accounting entries will be as follows:

December 31, 1999

Interest expense	175,000	
Accrued interest (or cash)		175,000

To accrue or pay interest on the debt at the variable rate of prime + 1/2% (7.0%)

Interest expense	25,000	
Accrued interest (or cash)		25,000

To record net settle-up on swap arrangement [8.0 - 7.0%]

Shareholders' equity	150,051	
Obligation under swap contract		150,051

To record the fair value of the swap contract as of this date (a net liability because fixed rate payable is below expected variable rate based on current prime rate)

June 30, 2000

Interest expense	162,500	
Accrued interest (or cash)		162,500

To accrue or pay interest on the debt at the variable rate of prime + 1/2% (6.5%)

Interest expense	37,500	
Accrued interest (or cash)		37,500

To record net settle-up on swap arrangement [8.0 - 6.5%]

Shareholders' equity	46,529	
Obligation under swap contract		46,529

To record the fair value of the swap contract as of this date (increase in obligation because of further decline in prime rate)

December 31, 2000

Interest expense	175,000	
Accrued interest (or cash)		175,000

To accrue or pay interest on the debt at the variable rate of prime + 1/2% (7.0%)

Interest expense	25,000	
Accrued interest (or cash)		25,000

To record net settle-up on swap arrangement [8.0 - 7.0%]

Obligation under swap contract	85,284	
Shareholders' equity		85,284

To record the fair value of the swap contract as of this date (decrease in obligation due to increase in prime rate)

June 30, 2001

Interest expense	187,500	
Accrued interest (or cash)		187,500

To accrue or pay interest on the debt at the variable rate of prime + 1/2% (7.5%)

Interest expense	12,500	
Accrued interest (or cash)		12,500

To record net settle-up on swap arrangement [8.0 - 7.5%]

Obligation under swap contract	65,922	
Shareholders' equity		65,922

To record the fair value of the swap contract as of this date (further increase in prime rate reduces fair value of derivative)

December 31, 2001

Interest expense	200,000	
Accrued interest (or cash)		200,000

To accrue or pay interest on the debt at the variable rate of prime + 1/2% (8.0%)

Interest expense	0	
Accrued interest (or cash)		0

To record net settle-up on swap arrangement [8.0 - 8.0%]

Obligation under swap contract	45,374	
Shareholders' equity		45,374

To record the fair value of the swap contract as of this date (further increase in prime rate eliminates fair value of the derivative)

June 30, 2002

Interest expense	212,500	
Accrued interest (or cash)		212,500

To accrue or pay interest on the debt at the variable rate of prime + 1/2% (8.5%)

Accrued interest (or cash)	12,500	
Interest expense		12,500

To record net settle-up on swap arrangement [8.0 - 8.5%]

Receivable under swap contract	23,576	
Shareholders' equity		23,576

To record the fair value of the swap contract as of this date (increase in prime rate creates net asset position for derivative)

December 31, 2002

Interest expense	225,000	
Accrued interest (or cash)		225,000

To accrue or pay interest on the debt at the variable rate of prime + 1/2% (9.0%)

Accrued interest (or cash)	25,000	
Interest expense		25,000

To record net settle-up on swap arrangement [8.0 - 9.0%]

Receivable under swap contract	462	
Shareholders' equity		462

To record the fair value of the swap contract as of this date (increase in asset value due to further rise in prime rate)

June 30, 2003

Interest expense	212,500	
Accrued interest (or cash)		212,500

To accrue or pay interest on the debt at the variable rate of prime + 1/2% (8.5%)

Accrued interest (or cash)	12,500	
Interest expense		12,500

To record net settle-up on swap arrangement [8.0 - 8.5%]

Shareholders' equity	24,038	
Receivable under swap contract		24,038

To record the fair value of the swap contract as of this date (value declines to zero as expiration date approaches)

Example of option on an interest rate swap

The facts of this example are a further variation on the previous one (the "plain vanilla" swap). Abbott Corp. anticipates, as of June 30, 1999, that as of June 30, 2001, it will become a borrower of $5 million with a fixed maturity 4 years hence (i.e., at June 30, 2005). Based on its current credit rating, it will be able to borrow at the US prime interest rate + 1/2%. As of June 30, 1999, it is able to purchase a so-called "swaption" (an option on an interest rate swap, calling for fixed pay at 8% and variable receipt at prime + 1/2%, on a notional amount of $5 million, for a term of 4 years) for a single payment of $25,000. The option will expire in 2 years. At June 30, 1999, the prime is 7.5%. (Note: The interest rate behavior in this example differs somewhat from the prior example, to better illustrate the "one-sideness" of options, versus the obligation under a plain vanilla swap arrangement or of other futures and forwards.) It will be assumed that the time value of the swaption expires ratably over the 2 years.

This swaption qualifies as a cash flow hedge under IAS 39. However, while the change in fair value of the contract is an effective hedge of the cash flow variability of the prospective debt issuance, the premium paid is a reflection of the time value of money and would not be an effective part of the hedge. Accordingly, it is to be expensed as incurred, rather than being deferred.

The table below gives the prime rate at semiannual intervals including the 2-year period prior to the debt issuance, plus the 4 years during which the debt (and the swap, if the option is exercised) will be outstanding, as well as the fair value of the swaption (and later, the swap itself) at these points in time.

Date	Prime rate (%)	Fair value of swaption/swap*
December 31, 1999	7.5	$ 0
June 30, 2000	8.0	77,925
December 31, 2000	6.5	0
June 30, 2001	7.0	(84,159)
December 31, 2001	7.5	0
June 30, 2002	8.0	65,527
December 31, 2002	8.5	111,296
June 30, 2003	8.0	45,374
December 31, 2003	8.0	34,689
June 30, 2004	7.5	0
December 31, 2004	7.5	0
June 30, 2005	7.0	0

* *Fair value is determined as the present value of future expected interest rate differentials, based on current prime rate, discounted at 8%. An "out-of-the-money" swaption is valued at zero, since the option does not have to be exercised. Since the option is exercised on June 30, 2001, the value at that date is recorded, although negative.*

The value of the swaption contract is only recorded (unless and until exercised, of course, at which point it becomes a contractually binding swap) if it is positive, since if "out-of-the-money," the holder would forego exercise in most instances and thus there is no liability by the holder to be reported. This illustrates the asymmetrical nature of options, where the most that can be lost by the option holder is the premium paid, since exercise by the holder is never required, unlike the case with futures and forwards, in which both parties are obligated to perform.

The present example is an illustration of counter-intuitive (but not really illogical) behavior by the holder of an out-of-the-money option. Despite having a negative value, the option holder determines that exercise is advisable, presumably because it expects that over the term of the debt unfavorable movements in interest rates will occur.

At June 30, 2000, the swaption is an asset, since the reference variable rate (prime + 1/2%) is greater than the fixed swap rate, and thus the expectation is that the option will be exercised at expiration. This would (if present rates hold steady, which is the naïve assumption) result in a series of eight semiannual payments from the swap counterparty in the amount of $12,500. Discounting this at a nominal 8%, the present value as of the debt origination date (to be June 30, 2001) would be $84,159, which, when further discounted to June 30, 2000, yields a fair value of $74,925.

Note that the following period (at December 31, 2000) prime drops to such an extent that the value of the swaption evaporates entirely. Actually, the value becomes negative, which will not be reported since the holder is under no obligation to exercise the option under unfavorable conditions; the carrying value is therefore eliminated as of that date.

At the expiration of the swaption contract, the holder does (for this example) exercise, notwithstanding a negative fair value, and from that point forward the fair value of the swap will be reported, whether positive (an asset) or negative (a liability). Once exercised, the swap represents a series of forward contracts, the fair value of which must be fully recognized under IAS 39. (Note that, in the real world, the holder would have likely had another choice: to let the unfavorable swaption expire unexercised, but to negotiate a new interest rate swap, presumably at more favorable terms given that prime is only 7% at that date; for example, a swap of 7.5% fixed versus prime + 1/2% would likely be available at little or no cost.)

As noted above, assume that, at the option expiration date, despite the fact that prime + 1/2% is below the fixed pay rate on the swap, the management is convinced that rates will climb over the 4-year term of the loan, and thus it does exercise the swaption at that date. Given this, the accounting journal entries over the entire 6 years are as follows:

June 30, 1999

Swaption contract	25,000	
Cash		25,000

To record purchase premium on swaption contract

December 31, 1999

Gain/loss on hedging arrangement	6,250	
Swaption contract		6,250

To record change in time value of swaption contract--charge premium to income since this represents payment for time value of money, which expires ratably over 2-year term

June 30, 2000

Swaption contract	77,925	
Shareholders' equity		77,925

To record the fair value of the swaption contract as of this date

Gain/loss on hedging arrangement	6,250	
Swaption contract		6,250

To record change in time value of swaption contract--charge premium to income since this represents payment for time value of money, which expires ratably over 2-year term

December 31, 2000

Shareholders' equity	77,925	
Swaption contract		77,925

To record the change in fair value of the swaption contract as of this date; since contract is out-of-the-money, it is not written down below zero (i.e., a net liability is not reported)

Gain/loss on hedging arrangement	6,250	
Swaption contract		6,250

To record change in time value of swaption contract--charge premium to income since this represents payment for time value of money, which expires ratably over 2-year term

June 30, 2001

Shareholders' equity	84,159	
Swaption contract		84,159

To record the fair value of the swaption contract as of this date--a net liability is reported since swap option was exercised

Gain/loss on hedging arrangement	6,250	
Swaption contract		6,250

To record change in time value of swaption contract--charge premium to income since this represents payment for time value of money, which expires ratably over 2-year term

December 31, 2001

Interest expense	200,000	
Accrued interest (or cash)		200,000

To accrue or pay interest on the debt at the variable rate of prime + 1/2% (8.0%)

Interest expense	0	
Accrued interest (or cash)		0

To record net settle-up on swap arrangement [8.0 - 8.0%]

Swap contract	84,159	
Shareholders' equity		84,159

To record the change in the fair value of the swap contract as of this date

June 30, 2002

Interest expense	212,500	
Accrued interest (or cash)		212,500

To accrue or pay interest on the debt at the variable rate of prime + 1/2% (8.5%)

Accrued interest (or cash)	12,500	
Interest expense		12,500

To record net settle-up on swap arrangement [8.0 - 8.5%]

Swap contract	65,527	
Shareholders' equity		65,527

To record the fair value of the swap contract as of this date

December 31, 2002

Interest expense	225,000	
Accrued interest (or cash)		225,000

To accrue or pay interest on the debt at the variable rate of prime + 1/2% (9.0%)

Accrued interest (or cash)	25,000	
Interest expense		25,000

To record net settle-up on swap arrangement [8.0 - 9.0%]

Swap contract	45,769	
Shareholders' equity		45,769

To record the fair value of the swap contract as of this date

June 30, 2003

Interest expense	212,500	
Accrued interest (or cash)		212,500

To accrue or pay interest on the debt at the variable rate of prime + 1/2% (8.5%)

Accrued interest (cash)	12,500	
Interest expense		12,500

To record net settle-up on swap arrangement [8.0 - 8.5%]

Shareholders' equity	65,922	
Swap contract		65,922

To record the change in the fair value of the swap contract as of this date (declining prime rate causes swap to lose value)

December 31, 2003

Interest expense	212,500	
Accrued interest (or cash)		212,000

To accrue or pay interest on the debt at the variable rate of prime + 1/2% (8.5%)

Accrued interest (or cash)	12,500	
Interest expense		12,500

To record net settle-up on swap arrangement [8.0 - 8.5%]

Shareholders' equity	10,685	
Swap contract		10,685

To record the fair value of the swap contract as of this date (decline is due to passage of time, as the prime rate expectations have not changed from the earlier period)

June 30, 2004

Interest expense	200,000	
Accrued interest (or cash)		200,000

To accrue or pay interest on the debt at the variable rate of prime + 1/2% (8.0%)

Accrued interest (or cash)	0	
Interest expense		0

To record net settle-up on swap arrangement [8.0 - 8.5%]

| Shareholders' equity | 34,689 | |
| Swap contract | | 34,689 |

To record the fair value of the swap contract as of this date

December 31, 2004

| Interest expense | 200,000 | |
| Accrued interest (or cash) | | 200,000 |

To accrue or pay interest on the debt at the variable rate of prime + 1/2% (8.0%)

| Accrued interest (or cash) | 0 | |
| Interest expense | | 0 |

To record net settle-up on swap arrangement [8.0 - 8.0%]

| Swap contract | 0 | |
| Shareholders' equity | | 0 |

No change to the fair value of the swap contract as of this date

June 30, 2005

| Interest expense | 187,500 | |
| Accrued interest (or cash) | | 187,500 |

To accrue or pay interest on the debt at the variable rate of prime + 1/2% (7.5%)

| Interest expense | 12,500 | |
| Accrued interest (or cash) | | 12,500 |

To record net settle-up on swap arrangement [8.0 - 7.5%]

| Shareholders' equity | 0 | |
| Swap contract | | 0 |

No change to the fair value of the swap contract, which expires as of this date

Example of using options to hedge a future purchase of inventory

Friendly Chemicals Corp. uses petroleum as a feedstock from which it produces a range of chemicals for sale to producers of synthetic fabrics and other consumer goods. It is concerned about the rising price of oil and decides to hedge a major purchase it plans to make in mid-2000. Oil futures and options are traded on the New York Mercantile Exchange and in other markets; Friendly decides to use options rather than futures because it is only interested in protecting itself from a price increase; if prices decline, it wishes to reap that benefit rather than suffer the loss which would result from holding a futures contract in a declining market environment.

At December 31, 1999, Friendly projects a need for 10 million barrels of crude oil of a defined grade to be purchased by mid-2000; this will suffice for production through mid-2001. The current world price for this grade of crude is $14.50 per barrel, but prices have been rising recently. Management desires to limit its crude oil costs to no higher than $15.75 per barrel, and accordingly purchases, at a cost of $2 million, an option to purchase up to 10 million barrels at a cost of $15.55 per barrel, at any time through December 2000. When the option premium is added to this $15.55 per barrel cost, it would make the total cost $15.75 per barrel if the full 10 million barrels are acquired.

Management has studied the behavior of option prices and has concluded that changes in option prices which relate to time value are not correlated to price changes and hence are ineffective in hedging price changes. On the other hand, changes in option prices which pertain to pricing changes (so-called "intrinsic value changes") are highly effective as hedging vehicles. The table below reports the value of these options, analyzed in terms of time value and intrinsic value, over the period from December 1999 through December 2000.

Date	Price of oil/barrel	Fair value of option relating to	
		Time value*	Intrinsic value
December 31, 1999	$14.50	$2,000,000	$ 0
January 31, 2000	14.90	1,900,000	0
February 28, 2000	15.30	1,800,000	0
March 31, 2000	15.80	1,700,000	2,500,000
April 30, 2000	16.00	1,600,000	4,500,000
May 31, 2000	15.85	1,500,000	3,000,000
June 30, 2000**	16.00	700,000	2,250,000
July 31, 2000	15.60	650,000	250,000
August 31, 2000	15.50	600,000	0
September 30, 2000	15.75	550,000	1,000,000
October 31, 2000	15.80	500,000	1,250,000
November 30, 2000	15.85	450,000	1,500,000
December 31, 2000~	15.90	400,000	1,750,000

* *This example does not address how the time value of options would be computed in practice.*

** *Options for 5 million barrels exercised; remainder held until end of December, then sold.*

~ *Values cited are immediately prior to sale of remaining options.*

At the end of June 2000, Friendly Chemicals exercises options for 5 million barrels, paying $15.55 per barrel for oil which is then selling on world markets for $16.00 each. It holds the remaining options until December, when it sells these for an aggregate price of $2.1 million, a slight discount to the nominal fair value at that date.

The inventory acquired in mid-2000 is processed and included in goods available for sale. Sales of these goods, in terms of the 5 million barrels of crude oil which were consumed in their production, are as follows:

Date	Equivalent barrels sold in month	Equivalent barrels on hand at month end
June 30, 2000	300,000	4,700,000
July 31, 2000	250,000	4,450,000
August 31, 2000	400,000	4,050,000
September 30, 2000	350,000	3,700,000
October 31, 2000	550,000	3,150,000
November 30, 2000	500,000	2,650,000
December 31, 2000	650,000	2,000,000

Based on the foregoing facts, the journal entries prepared on a **monthly** basis (for illustrative purposes) for the period December 1999 through December 2000 are as follows:

December 31, 1999

Option contract	2,000,000	
Cash		2,000,000

To record purchase premium on option contract for up to 10 million barrels of oil at price of $15.55 per barrel

January 31, 2000

Gain/loss on hedging transaction	100,000	
Option contract		100,000

To record change in time value of option contract--charge premium to income since this represents payment for time value of money, which expires ratably over 2-year term and does not qualify for hedge accounting treatment

Option contract	0	
Shareholders' equity		0

To reflect change in intrinsic value of option contracts (no value at this date)

February 28, 2000

Gain/loss on hedging transaction	100,000	
Option contract		100,000

To record change in time value of option contract--charge premium to income since this represents payment for time value of money, which expires ratably over 2-year term and does not qualify for hedge accounting treatment

Option contract	0	
Shareholders' equity		0

To reflect change in intrinsic value of option contracts (no value at this date)

March 31, 2000

Gain/loss on hedging transaction	100,000	
Option contract		100,000

To record change in time value of option contract--charge premium to income since this represents payment for time value of money, which expires ratably over 2-year term and does not qualify for hedge accounting treatment

Option contract	2,500,000	
Shareholders' equity		2,500,000

To reflect change in intrinsic value of option contracts

April 30, 2000

Gain/loss on hedging transaction	100,000	
Option contract		100,000

To record change in time value of option contract--charge premium to income since this represents payment for time value of money, which expires ratably over 2-year term and does not qualify for hedge accounting treatment

Option contract	2,000,000	
Shareholders' equity		2,000,000

To reflect change in intrinsic value of option contracts (further increase in value)

May 31, 2000

Gain/loss on hedging transaction	100,000	
Option contract		100,000

To record change in time value of option contract--charge premium to income since this represents payment for time value of money, which expires ratably over 2-year term and does not qualify for hedge accounting treatment

Shareholders' equity	1,500,000	
Option contract		1,500,000

To reflect change in intrinsic value of option contracts (decline in value)

June 30, 2000

Gain/loss on hedging transaction	800,000	
Option contract		800,000

To record change in time value of option contract--charge premium to income since this represents payment for time value of money, which expires ratably over 2-year term and does not qualify for hedge accounting treatment; since one-half the options were exercised in June, the remaining unexpensed time value of that portion is also entirely written off at this time

Option contracts	1,500,000	
Shareholders' equity		1,500,000

To reflect change in intrinsic value of option contracts (further increase in value) before accounting for exercise of options on 5 million barrels

June 30 value of options before exercise	4,500,000
Allocation to oil purchased at $15.55	2,250,000
Remaining option valuation adjustment	2,250,000

The allocation to exercised options will be maintained in shareholders' equity until transferred to cost of goods sold as a contra cost, as the 5 million barrels are sold, at the rate of 45¢ per equivalent barrel.

Inventory	77,750,000	
Cash		77,750,000

To record purchase of 5 million barrels of oil at option price of $15.55/barrel

Inventory	2,250,000	
Option contract		2,250,000

To increase the recorded value of the inventory to include the fair value of options given up in acquiring the oil (taken together, the cash purchase price and the fair value of options surrendered add to $16 per barrel, the world market price at date of purchase)

Cost of goods sold	4,800,000	
Inventory		4,800,000

To record cost of goods sold (300,000 barrels at $16) before amortizing deferred hedging gain in shareholders' equity

Shareholders' equity	135,000	
Cost of goods sold		135,000

To amortize deferred hedging gain at rate of 45¢ per barrel sold

July 31, 2000

Gain/loss on hedging transaction	50,000	
Option contract		50,000

To record change in time value of option contract--charge premium to income since this represents payment for time value of money, which expires ratably over 2-year term, and does not qualify for hedge accounting treatment

Shareholders' equity	2,000,000	
Option contract		2,000,000

To reflect change in intrinsic value of remaining option contracts (decline in value)

Cost of goods sold	4,000,000	
Inventory		4,000,000

To record cost of goods sold (250,000 barrels at $16) before amortizing deferred hedging gain in shareholders' equity

Shareholders' equity	112,500	
Cost of goods sold		112,500

To amortize deferred hedging gain at rate of 45¢ per barrel sold

August 31, 2000

Loss on hedging transaction	50,000	
Option contract		50,000

To record change in time value of option contract--charge premium to income since this represents payment for time value of money, which expires ratably over 2-year term, and does not qualify for hedge accounting treatment

Shareholders' equity	250,000	
Option contract		250,000

To reflect change in intrinsic value of remaining option contracts (decline in value)

Cost of goods sold	6,400,000	
Inventory		6,400,000

To record cost of goods sold (400,000 barrels at $16) before amortizing deferred hedging gain in shareholders' equity

Shareholders' equity	180,000	
Cost of goods sold		180,000

To amortize deferred hedging gain at rate of 45¢ per barrel sold

September 30, 2000

Gain/loss on hedging transaction	50,000	
Option contract		50,000

To record change in time value of option contract--charge premium to income since this represents payment for time value of money, which expires ratably over 2-year term, and does not qualify for hedge accounting treatment

Option contract	1,000,000	
Shareholdres' equity		1,000,000

To reflect change in intrinsic value of remaining option contracts (increase in value)

Cost of goods sold	5,600,000	
Inventory		5,600,000

To record cost of goods sold (350,000 barrels at $16) before amortizing deferred hedging gain in shareholders' equity

Shareholders' equity	157,500	
Cost of goods sold		157,500

To amortize deferred hedging gain at rate of 45¢ per barrel sold

October 31, 2000

Gain/loss on hedging transaction	50,000	
Option contract		50,000

To record change in time value of option contract--charge premium to income since this represents payment for time value of money, which expires ratably over 2-year term, and does not qualify for hedge accounting treatment

Option contract	250,000	
Shareholders' equity		250,000

To reflect change in intrinsic value of remaining option contracts (further increase in value)

Cost of goods sold	8,800,000	
Inventory		8,800,000

To record cost of goods sold (550,000 barrels at $16) before amortizing deferred hedging gain in shareholders' equity

Shareholders' equity	247,500	
Cost of goods sold		247,500

To amortize deferred hedging gain at rate of 45¢ per barrel sold

November 30, 2000

Gain/loss on hedging transaction	50,000	
Option contract		50,000

To record change in time value of option contract--charge premium to income since this represents payment for time value of money, which expires ratably over 2-year term, and does not qualify for hedge accounting treatment

Option contract	250,000	
Shareholders' equity		250,000

To reflect change in intrinsic value of remaining option contracts (further increase in value)

Cost of goods sold	8,000,000	
Inventory		8,000,000

To record cost of goods sold (500,000 barrels at $16) before amortizing deferred hedging gain in shareholders' equity

Shareholders'equity	225,000	
Cost of goods sold		225,000

To amortize deferred hedging gain at rate of 45¢ per barrel sold

December 31, 2000

Gain/loss on hedging transaction	50,000	
Option contract		50,000

To record change in time value of option contract--charge premium to income since this represents payment for time value of money, which expires ratably over 2-year term, and does not qualify for hedge accounting treatment

Option contract	250,000	
Shareholders' equity		250,000

To reflect change in intrinsic value of remaining option contracts (further increase in value) before sale of options

Cost of goods sold	10,400,000	
Inventory		10,400,000

To record cost of goods sold (650,000 barrels at $16) before amortizing deferred hedging gain in shareholders' equity

Shareholders' equity	292,500	
Cost of goods sold		292,500

To amortize deferred hedging gain at rate of 45¢ per barrel sold

Cash	2,100,000	
Loss on sale of options	50,000	
Option contract		2,150,000
Shareholders' equity	1,750,000	
Gain on sale of options		1,750,000

To record sale of remaining option contracts; the cash price was $50,000 lower than carrying value of asset sold (options having unexpired time value of $400,000 plus intrinsic value of $1,750,000), but transfer of shareholders' equity to income recognizes formerly deferred gain; since no further inventory purchases are planned in connection with this hedging activity, the unrealized gain is taken into income

Note that at December 31, 2000, shareholders' equity has a remaining credit balance of $900,000, which represents the deferred gain pertaining to the 2 million equivalent barrels of oil in inventory. As this is sold, the shareholders' equity will be transferred to cost of goods sold as a reduction of cost of sales.

Equity Method of Accounting for Investments

In previous sections of this chapter the focus was on investments that are essentially passive in nature, where the investor has a small minority ownership interest (or, in the case of debt, no actual ownership interest at all) and accordingly, cannot control or materially influence decisions by management of the investee. In other situations an investor will have actual control over the actions taken by the management of the investee, or have joint control (discussed in a subsequent part of this chapter) over those decisions along with its co-investors. The third logical possibility is that the investor will have something less than control but will clearly also not be a passive investor. This is the issue of significant influence over an investee.

As GAAP has evolved over the past 30 years or so, it has become evident that investors having significant influence should not account for such investments on a cost basis, since to do so would permit deliberate manipulation of the financial reporting process and, more important, would not reflect economic reality. For example, if an investee has substantial income but the investor uses its influence to defer declaration of dividends, the cost method of accounting would result in the investor not reporting its share of the operating results, even though it had been in a position to cause a distribution of dividends, had it chosen to do so.

To respond to this set of real and potential reporting problems, GAAP has developed a number of proposed solutions. These include the equity method, the expanded equity method, and proportionate consolidation. International accounting standards and the various national standard-setting bodies have given differing levels of attention to these alternatives over the years, with the simple equity method being the one receiving the closest to a consensus of support.

The equity method, which has been referred to as one-line consolidation, permits an entity (the investor) owning a percentage of the common stock of another entity (the investee) to incorporate its pro rata share of the investee's operating results into its earnings. However, rather than include its share of each component of the investee's revenues, expenses, assets and liabilities into its financial statements, the investor should only include its share of the investee's **net** income as a separate line item in its income. The bottom-line impact on the investor's financial statements is **identical** whether the equity method or full consolidation is employed; only the amount of detail presented within the statements will differ.

Expanded equity method. Less commonly discussed are the expanded equity method and the proportionate consolidation method, which are effectively successive points along a continuum ranging from a pure cost basis to full consolidation.

In contrast to the one-line consolidation approach of the simple equity method, the expanded equity method is an attempt to provide a bit more meaningful detail about the various assets and liabilities, and revenues and expenses in which the investor has an interest. Thus, the investor's interest in the investee's aggregate current assets would be presented, as a single number, in the current asset section of the investor's balance sheet. Similarly, the investor's share of the investee's noncurrent assets, current liabilities, and noncurrent liabilities would be captioned separately. On the income statement, the investor's share of significant items of revenue, expense, gains, and losses would be set forth separately. This would not extend to every item of the income statement, but would highlight the major ones.

A major advantage of this method is that the investor's financial statements will provide a more meaningful insight into the true economic scope of its operations, including indications of the volume of business being transacted. Furthermore, financial position will not be distorted by, for example, effectively merging the investee's current assets with the investor's noncurrent assets, which would be the result of placing equity in investee in the noncurrent asset section. As the amount of detail expands, this method edges into proportionate consolidation, however.

The expanded equity method has not been endorsed officially, although the equity method as defined by US standards setters (in Accounting Principles Board

Opinion 18) does incorporate elements of this approach. Specifically, APB 18 mandates one-line consolidation for the balance sheet, but requires that certain elements of the investee's income statement (such as extraordinary items) retain their character when incorporated into the investor's income statement.

Proportionate consolidation. This is a more completely developed version of the expanded equity method, whereby the investor's share of each element of the investee's balance sheet and income statement is reported in the investor's statements. Although there is nonauthoritative GAAP in the United States supporting this method of accounting for investments in joint ventures, and under international accounting standards (as discussed later in the chapter) this method is prescribed optionally for joint ventures, it has not been widely advocated for investments in which the investor does not exercise, at a minimum, joint control.

Equity method as prescribed by IAS 28. The equity method is generally **not** a substitute for consolidation; it is employed where the investor has significant influence over the operations of the investee but lacks control. In general, significant influence is inferred when the investor owns between 20% and 50% of the investee's voting common stock. Any ownership percentage over 50% presumably gives the investor actual control, making full consolidation of financial statements necessary (or, if precisely 50% is owned in a joint venture, proportionate consolidation may be employed). The 20% threshold stipulated in IAS 28 is not absolute; circumstances may suggest that significant influence exists even though the investor's level of ownership is less than 20%, or that it is absent despite a level of ownership above 20%. The 20% lower threshold is identical to that prescribed under US GAAP.

In considering whether significant influence exists, IAS 28 identifies the following factors as evidence that such influence is present: (1) investor representation on the board of directors or its equivalent, (2) participation in policy-making processes, (3) material transactions between the investor and investee, (4) interchange of managerial personnel, and (5) provision of essential technical information. There may be other factors present that suggest a lack of significant influence, such as organized opposition by the other shareholders, majority ownership by a small group of shareholders not inclusive of the investor, and inability to achieve representation on the board or to obtain information on the operations of the investee. Whether sufficient contrary evidence exists to negate the presumption of significant influence is a matter of judgment and requires a careful evaluation of all pertinent facts and circumstances, over an extended period of time in some cases.

When equity method is required. IAS 28 stipulates that the equity method should be employed by the investor for all investments in associates, unless the investment is acquired and held exclusively with a view to its disposal in the near term, or if it operates under severe long-term restrictions that would preclude making distributions to investors. In the latter cases, accounting by the cost method is preferred.

The standard does make something of a distinction between the accounting for investments in associates in consolidated financials versus that in separate financials of the investor. Most important, in separate financial statements of the investor, the investment may be carried at cost or at revalued amounts as prescribed by IAS 25 (discussed earlier in the chapter), as an alternative to the equity method. This mandate seemingly results from a view of separate statements of a parent entity, without consolidation of subsidiaries and without applying equity method accounting to associated entities, as reporting the financial position and results of operations of the enterprise on its own. This also is a consequence of the fact that the international standard-setting process is somewhat of a compromise approach, incorporating most, if not all, of the methods advocated by national standard-setting bodies worldwide. Thus, since different bodies have taken varying positions on such matters as consolidation and equity method accounting, this result has obtained.

In practice, many parent-only financial statements apply equity method accounting to subsidiaries and significant influence investees alike. This probably does provide the most meaningful reporting, avoiding detailed inclusion of any assets, liabilities, revenues, or expenses other than the parent company's own in its financial statements, while not distorting the bottom line measure of economic performance.

If the investment in the associate is presented in accordance with IAS 25 in these separate financial statements of the parent/investor, IAS 28 does require that there be disclosure of what would have been the effect had the equity method been applied.

Complications in applying equity method accounting. Complexities in the use of the equity method arise in two areas. First, the cost of the investment to the investor might not be equal to the fair value of the investor's share of investee net assets; this is analogous to the existence of goodwill in a purchase business combination. Or the fair value of the investor's share of the investee's net assets may not be equal to the book value thereof; this situation is analogous to the purchase cost allocation problem in consolidations. Since the ultimate income statement result from the use of equity method accounting must generally be the same as full consolidation, an adjustment must be made for each of these differentials.

The second major complexity relates to interperiod income tax allocation. The equity method causes the investor to reflect current earnings based on the investee's operating results; however, for income tax purposes the investor reports only dividends received and gains or losses on disposal of the investment. Thus, temporary differences result, and IAS 12 provides guidance as to the appropriate method of computing the deferred tax effects of these differences.

In the absence of these complicating factors, use of the equity method by the investor is straightforward: The original cost of the investment is increased by the investor's share of the investee's earnings and is decreased by its share of investee losses and by dividends received. The basic procedure is illustrated below.

Example of a simple case ignoring deferred taxes

Assume the following information:

On January 2, 2000, Regency Corporation (the investor) acquired 40% of Elixir Company's (the investee) voting common stock on the open market for $100,000. Unless demonstrated otherwise, it is assumed that Regency Corporation can exercise significant influence over Elixir Company's operating and financing policies. On January 2, Elixir's stockholders' equity is comprised of the following accounts:

Common stock, par $1, 100,000 shares authorized,	
50,000 shares issued and outstanding	$ 50,000
Additional paid-in capital	150,000
Retained earnings	50,000
Total stockholders' equity	$250,000

Note that the cost of Elixir Company common stock was equal to 40% of the book value of Elixir's net assets. Assume also that there is no difference between the book value and the fair value of Elixir Company's assets and liabilities. Accordingly, the balance in the investment account in Regency's records represents exactly 40% of Elixir's stockholders' equity (net assets). Assume further that Elixir Company reported a 2000 net income of $30,000 and paid cash dividends of $10,000. Its stockholders' equity at year end would be as follows:

Common stock, par $1, 100,000 shares authorized,	
50,000 shares issued and outstanding	$ 50,000
Additional paid-in capital	150,000
Retained earnings	70,000
Total stockholders' equity	$270,000

Regency Corporation would record its share of the increase in Elixir Company's net assets during 2000 as follows:

Investment in Elixir Company	12,000	
Equity in Elixir income ($30,000 x 40%)		12,000
Cash	4,000	
Investment in Elixir Company ($10,000 x 40%)		4,000

When Regency's balance sheet is prepared at December 31, 2000, the balance reported in the investment account would be $108,000 ($100,000 + $12,000 – $4,000). This amount represents 40% of the book value of Elixir's net assets at the end of the year (40% x $270,000). Note also that the equity in Elixir income is reported as one amount on Regency's income statement under the caption "Other income and expense."

IAS 12 established the requirement that deferred income taxes be provided for the tax effects of timing differences. Under this standard, which is discussed in detail in Chapter 15, a choice between two very different approaches to deferred tax accounting is permitted: the deferral method, which computes the tax effect when the timing difference is originated and does not later adjust the provision until the difference reverses; and the liability method, under which the provision is adjusted at each balance sheet date to reflect the current expectations regarding ultimate settlement amount.

Under either deferred tax accounting approach permitted under IAS 12, in computing the deferred tax effects of income recognized by the equity method, the investor must make an assumption regarding the means by which the undistributed earnings of the investee will be realized by the investor. The earnings can be realized either through later dividend receipts or by disposition of the investment at a gain, which, depending on tax jurisdiction, may result in differing tax implications. For example, in many jurisdictions the former assumption would result in taxes at the investor's marginal tax rate on ordinary income (net of any dividends received deduction or exclusion permitted by the local taxing authorities). The latter option would commonly be treated as a capital gain, which may be taxed at a different rate, or not at all.

Example of a simple case including deferred taxes

Assume the same information as in the example above. In addition, assume that Regency Corporation has a combined (federal, state, and local) marginal tax rate of 34% on ordinary income and that it anticipates realization of Elixir Company earnings through future dividend receipts. In Regency's tax jurisdiction, there is an 80% deduction for dividends received from nonsubsidiary investees, meaning that only 20% of the income is subject to ordinary tax. Regency Corporation's entries at year end 2000 will be as follows:

1. Investment in Elixir Company   12,000
      Equity in Elixir income   12,000
2. Income tax expense   816
      Deferred taxes   816
   (Taxable portion of investee earnings to be received in the future as dividends times marginal tax rate: $12,000 x 20% x 34% = $816)

3. Cash   4,000
      Investment in Elixir Company   4,000
4. Deferred taxes   272
      Taxes payable--current   272
   [Fraction of investee earnings currently taxed ($4,000/12,000) x 816 = $272]

If the liability method permitted under IAS 12 has been elected, the tax provision should be based on the projected tax effect of the temporary difference reversal, and this will be subsequently adjusted for a variety of reasons, including changed tax rates and altered management expectations (see Chapter 15 for a complete discussion). Notwithstanding this requirement, the actual tax effect of the temporary difference reversal may still differ from the deferred tax provided. This difference may occur because the actual tax effect is a function of the entity's other current items of income and expense in the year of reversal. It may also result from a realization of the investee's earnings in a manner other than anticipated (assuming that tax rates on ordinary income differ from those on capital gains).

To illustrate this last point, assume that in 2001, before any further earnings or dividends are reported by the investee, the investor sells the entire investment for $115,000. The tax impact is

Selling price	$115,000
Less cost	100,000
Gain	$ 15,000
Capital gain rate (marginal corporate rate)	x 34%
Tax liability	$ 5,100

The entries to record the sale, the tax thereon, and the amortization of deferred taxes provided previously on the undistributed 2000 earnings are as follows:

1.	Cash	115,000	
	Investment in Elixir Company		108,000
	Gain on sale of investment		7,000
2.	Income tax expense	4,556	
	Deferred tax liability		544
	Taxes payable--current		5,100

The income tax expense of $4,556 is the sum of two factors: (1) the capital gains rate of 34% applied to the actual book gain realized ($115,000 selling price less $108,000 carrying value), for a tax of $2,380, and (2) the difference between the capital gains tax rate (34%) and the effective rate on dividend income (20% x 34% = 6.8%) on the undistributed 2000 earnings of Elixir Company previously recognized as ordinary income by Regency Corporation [$8,000 x (34% – 6.8%) = $2,176].

Note that if the realization through a sale of the investment had been anticipated at the time the 2000 balance sheet was being prepared, the deferred tax liability account would have been adjusted (possibly to the entire $5,100 amount of the ultimate obligation), with the offsetting entry applied to 2000's ordinary tax expense. This approach, mandated by the liability approach under IAS 12, is radically different than that required by the deferral method under that same standard. The example above explicitly assumes that sale of the investment was not anticipated prior to 2001.

Accounting for a differential between cost and book value. The simple examples presented thus far avoided the major complexity of equity method accounting, the allocation of the differential between the cost to the investor and the investor's share in the net equity (net assets at book value) of the investee. Since the net impact of equity method accounting must equal that of full consolidation accounting, this differential must be analyzed into the following components and accounted for accordingly:

1. The difference between the book and fair values of the investee's net assets at the date the investment is made.
2. The remaining difference between the fair value of the net assets and the cost of the investment, that is generally attributable to goodwill.

According to IAS 28, any difference between the cost of the investment and the investor's share of the fair values of the net identifiable assets of the associate should be identified and accounted for in accordance with IAS 22 (as detailed in Chapter 11). Thus, the differential should be allocated to specific asset categories, and these differences will then be amortized to the income from investee account as appropriate, for example, over the economic lives of fixed assets whose fair values exceeded book values. The difference between fair value and cost will be treated like goodwill and, in accordance with the provisions of IAS 22, amortized over a period generally not to exceed 5 years, but potentially as long as 20 years.

Example of a complex case ignoring deferred taxes

Assume again that Regency Corporation acquired 40% of Elixir Company's shares on January 2, 2000, but that the price paid was $140,000. Elixir Company's assets and liabilities at that date had the following book and fair values:

	Book value	Fair value
Cash	$ 10,000	$ 10,000
Accounts receivable (net)	40,000	40,000
Inventories (FIFO cost)	80,000	90,000
Land	50,000	40,000
Plant and equipment (net of accumulated depreciation)	140,000	220,000
Total assets	$320,000	$400,000
Liabilities	(70,000)	(70,000)
Net assets (stockholders' equity)	$250,000	$330,000

The first order of business is the calculation of the differential, as follows:

Regency's cost for 40% of Elixir's common stock	$140,000
Book value of 40% of Elixir's net assets ($250,000 x 40%)	(100,000)
Total differential	$ 40,000

Next, the $40,000 is allocated to those individual assets and liabilities for which fair value differs from book value. In the example, the differential is allocated to inventories, land, and plant and equipment, as follows:

Item	Book value	Fair value	Difference debit (credit)	40% of difference debit (credit)
Inventories	$ 80,000	$ 90,000	$ 10,000	$ 4,000
Land	50,000	40,000	(10,000)	(4,000)
Plant and equipment	140,000	220,000	80,000	32,000
Differential allocated				$32,000

The difference between the allocated differential of $32,000 and the total differential of $40,000 is goodwill of $8,000. As shown by the following computation, goodwill represents the excess of the cost of the investment over the fair value of the net assets acquired

Regency's cost for 40% of Elixir's common stock	$140,000
40% of Elixir's net assets ($330,000 x 40%)	(132,000)
Excess of cost over fair value (goodwill)	$ 8,000

At this point it is important to note that the allocation of the differential is not recorded formally by either Regency Corporation or Elixir Company. Furthermore, Regency does not remove the differential from the investment account and allocate it to the respective assets, since the use of the equity method (one-line consolidation) does not involve the recording of individual assets and liabilities. Regency leaves the differential of $40,000 in the investment account, as part of the balance of $140,000 at January 2, 2000.

Accordingly, information pertaining to the allocation of the differential is maintained by the investor, but this information is outside the formal accounting system, which is comprised of journal entries and account balances.

After the differential has been allocated, the amortization pattern is developed. To develop the pattern in this example, assume that Elixir's plant and equipment have 10 years of useful life remaining and that Elixir depreciates its fixed assets on a straight-line basis. Furthermore, assume that Regency amortizes goodwill over a 20-year period. Regency would prepare the following amortization schedule:

	Differential	Useful	Amortization		
Item	*debit (credit)*	*life*	*2000*	*2001*	*2002*
Inventories (FIFO)	$ 4,000	Sold in 1997	$4,000	$ --	$ --
Land	(4,000)	Indefinite	--	--	--
Plant and equipment (net)	32,000	10 years	3,200	3,200	3,200
Goodwill	8,000	20 years	400	400	400
Totals	$40,000		$7,600	$3,600	$3,600

Note that the entire differential allocated to inventories is amortized in 2000 because the cost flow assumption used by Elixir is FIFO. If Elixir had been using LIFO instead of FIFO, no amortization would take place until Elixir sold some of the inventory that existed at January 2, 2000. Since this sale could be delayed for many years under LIFO, the differential allocated to LIFO inventories would not be amortized until Elixir sold more inventory than it manufactured/purchased. Note also that the differential allocated to Elixir's land is not amortized, because land is not a depreciable asset.

The amortization of the differential is recorded formally in the accounting system of Regency Corporation. Recording the amortization adjusts the equity in Elixir's income that Regency recorded based on Elixir's income statement. Elixir's income must be adjusted because it is based on Elixir's book values, not on the cost that Regency incurred to acquire Elixir. Regency would make the following entries in 2000, assuming that Elixir reported net income of $30,000 and paid cash dividends of $10,000:

1.	Investment in Elixir	12,000	
	Equity in Elixir income ($30,000 x 40%)		12,000
2.	Equity in Elixir income (amortization of differential)	7,600	
	Investment in Elixir		7,600
3.	Cash	4,000	
	Investment in Elixir ($10,000 x 40%)		4,000

The balance in the investment account on Regency's records at the end of 2000 is $140,400 [$140,000 + $12,000 – ($7,600 + $4,000)], and Elixir's stockholders' equity, as shown previously, is $270,000. The investment account balance of $140,000 is not equal to 40% of $270,000. However, this difference can easily be explained, as follows:

Balance in investment account at December 31, 2000		$140,400
40% of Elixir's net assets at December 31, 2000		108,000
Difference at December 31, 2000		$ 32,400
Differential at January 2, 2000	$40,000	
Differential amortized during 2000	(7,600)	
Unamortized differential at December 31, 2000		$ 32,400

As the years go by, the balance in the investment account will come closer and closer to representing 40% of the book value of Elixir's net assets. After 20 years, the remaining difference between these two amounts would be attributed solely to the original differential allocated to land (a $4,000 credit). This $4,000 difference would remain until Elixir sold the property.

To illustrate how the sale of land would affect equity method procedures, assume that Elixir sold the land in the year 2020 for $80,000. Since Elixir's cost for the land was $50,000, it would report a gain of $30,000, of which $12,000 ($30,000 x 40%) would be recorded by Regency, when it records its 40% share of Elixir's reported net income, ignoring income taxes. However, from Regency's viewpoint, the gain on sale of land should have been $40,000 ($80,000 – $40,000) because the cost of the land from Regency's perspective was $40,000 at January 2, 2000. Therefore, besides the $12,000 share of the gain recorded above, Regency should record an additional $4,000 gain [($40,000 – $30,000) x 40%] by debiting the investment account and crediting the equity in Elixir income account. This $4,000 debit to the investment account will negate the $4,000 differential allocated to land on January 2, 2000, since the original differential was a credit (the fair market value of the land was $10,000 less than its book value).

Example of a complex case including deferred taxes

The impact of interperiod income tax allocation in the foregoing example is similar to that demonstrated earlier in the simplified example. However, a complication arises with regard to the portion of the differential allocated to goodwill, since in some jurisdictions amounts representing goodwill are not amortizable for tax purposes and, therefore, are a permanent (not a timing) difference that does not give rise to deferred taxes. The other components of the differential in this example are all generally defined as being timing differences.

The entries recorded by Regency Corporation in 2000 would be

1.	Investment in Elixir	12,000	
	Equity in Elixir income		12,000
2.	Income tax expense	816	
	Deferred tax liability ($12,000 x 20% x 34%)		816
3.	Cash	4,000	
	Investment in Elixir		4,000
4.	Deferred tax liability	272	
	Taxes payable--current ($4,000/12,000 x 816)		272
5.	Equity in Elixir income	7,600	
	Investment in Elixir		7,600
6.	Deferred tax liability	490	
	Income tax expense ($7,200 x 20% x 34%)		490

Note that the tax effect of the amortization of the differential is based on $7,200, not $7,600, since the $400 goodwill amortization would not have been tax deductible.

Reporting disparate elements of the investee's income statement. As suggested earlier in this section, the expanded equity method would require that the major captions in the investee's income statement maintain their character when reported, pro rata, by the investor. IAS 28 does not mandate use of the expanded equity method, although it notes in its disclosure requirements that the investor's share of extraordinary and prior period items should be noted. Although the standard is silent on separate reporting on the face of the financial statements themselves, the authors are of the opinion that, to the extent that certain items would be a material part of the investor's income statement and thus have the potential to mislead users of those financial statements, it would be prudent and fully consistent with the spirit of IAS 28 to report these separately. For example, if the investee reports a correction of a fundamental error according to IAS 8, or an extraordinary gain or loss, it would be distortive to include the investor's share of these in equity in earnings of investee without signaling that these are not normal, recurring items of income or loss.

The solution, of course, is to include the investor's share of these items with similar items in the investor's financial statements. That is, the expanded equity method concept should be applied, judiciously, to the investor's income statement. This would not extend, however, to separate reporting of any items of operating income or expense (gross sales, salaries, depreciation, etc.)

Example of accounting for separately reportable items

Assume that both an extraordinary item and a prior period adjustment reported in an investee's income and retained earnings statements are individually considered material from the investor's viewpoint.

Investee's income statement:

Income before extraordinary item	$ 80,000
Extraordinary loss from earthquake (net of taxes of $12,000)	(18,000)
Net income	$ 62,000

Investee's retained earnings statement:

Retained earnings at January 1, 2000as originally reported	$250,000
Add prior period adjustment--correction of an error made in 1999 (net of taxes of $10,000)	20,000
Retained earnings at January 1, 2000, as restated	$270,000

If an investor owned 30% of the voting common stock of this investee, the investor would make the following journal entries in 2000:

1.	Investment in investee company	24,000	
	Equity in investee income before extraordinary item		24,000
	($80,000 x 30%)		
2.	Equity in investee extraordinary loss	5,400	
	Investment in investee company		5,400
	($18,000 x 30%)		
3.	Investment in investee company	6,000	
	Equity in investee prior period adjustment		6,000
	($20,000 x 30%)		

The equity in the investee's prior period adjustment should be reported on the investor's retained earnings statement, and the equity in the extraordinary loss should be reported separately in the appropriate section on the investor's income statement.

Intercompany transactions between investor and investee. Transactions between the investor and the investee may require that the investor make certain adjustments when it records its share of the investee earnings. According to the realization concept, profits can be recognized by an entity only when realized through a sale to outside (unrelated) parties in arm's-length transactions (sales and purchases) between the investor and investee. Similar problems can arise when sales of fixed assets between the parties occur. In all cases, there is no need for any adjustment when the transfers are made at book value (i.e., without either party recognizing a profit or loss in its separate accounting records).

In preparing consolidated financial statements, all intercompany (parent-subsidiary) transactions are eliminated. However, when the equity method is used to account for investments, only the **profit component** of intercompany (investor-investee) transactions is eliminated. This is because the equity method does not result in the combining of all income statement accounts (such as sales and cost of sales) and therefore will not cause the financial statements to contain redundancies. In contrast, consolidated statements would include redundancies if the gross amounts of all intercompany transactions were not eliminated.

IAS 28 was not explicit regarding the percentage of unrealized profits on investor-investee transactions which were to be eliminated. Logical arguments can be made either to eliminate 100% of intercompany profits not realized through a subsequent transaction with unrelated third parties, which would follow the model of consolidated financial statements, or to eliminate only the percentage held by the investor. In SIC 3, the Standing Interpretations Committee has held that when applying the equity method, unrealized profits should be eliminated for both "upstream" and "downstream" transactions (i.e., sales from investee to investor, and from investor to investee) to the extent of the investor's interest in the investee. This proportional method is set forth in IAS 31, dealing with joint ventures, which does address this issue. The logic is that in an investor-investee situation, the investor does not have control (as would be the case with a subsidiary), and thus the nonowned percentage is effectively realized through an arm's-length transaction. For joint ventures, IAS 31 prescribes proportionate consolidation, which implies likewise that profits on intercompany transactions be eliminated only to the extent of the investor's interest in the venture. However, to the extent that losses are indicative of impairment in the value of the investment, the rule that profit elimination be limited to the investor's ownership percentage would not apply.

Example of accounting for intercompany transactions

Continue with the same information from the previous example and also assume that Elixir Company sold inventory to Regency Corporation in 2001 for $2,000 above Elixir's cost. Thirty percent of this inventory remains unsold by Regency at the end of 2001. Elixir's net income for 1999, including the gross profit on the inventory sold to Regency, is $20,000; Elixir's income tax rate is 34%. Regency should make the following journal entries for 2001 (ignoring deferred taxes):

1.	Investment in Elixir	8,000	
	Equity in Elixir income ($20,000 x 40%)		8,000
2.	Equity in Elixir income (amortization of differential)	3,600	
	Investment in Elixir		3,600
3.	Equity in Elixir income	158	
	Investment in Elixir ($2,000 x 30% x 66% x 40%)		158

The amount in the last entry needs further elaboration. Since 30% of the inventory remains unsold, only $600 of the intercompany profit is unrealized at year end. This profit, net of income taxes, is $396. Regency's share of this profit ($158) is included in the first ($8,000) entry recorded. Accordingly, the third entry is needed to adjust or correct the equity in the reported net income of the investee.

Eliminating entries for intercompany profits in fixed assets are similar to those in the examples above. However, intercompany profit is realized only as the assets are depreciated by the purchasing entity. In other words, if an investor buys or sells fixed assets from or to an investee at a price above book value, the gain would only be realized piecemeal over the asset's remaining depreciable life. Accordingly, in the year of sale the pro rata share (based on the investor's percentage ownership interest in the investee, regardless of whether the sale is upstream or downstream) of the unrealized portion of the intercompany profit would have to be eliminated. In each subsequent year during the asset's life, the pro rata share of the gain realized in the period would be added to income from the investee.

Example of eliminating intercompany profit on fixed assets

Assume that Radnor Co., that owns 25% of Empanada Co., sold to Empanada a fixed asset having a 5-year remaining life, at a gain of $100,000. Radnor Co. is in the 34% marginal tax bracket. The sale occurred at the end of 2000; Empanada Co. will use straight-line depreciation to amortize the asset over the years 2001 through 2005.

The entries related to the foregoing are

2000:

1.	Gain on sale of fixed asset	25,000	
	Deferred gain		25,000
	(To defer the unrealized portion of the gain)		
2.	Deferred tax benefit	8,500	
	Income tax expense		8,500
	(Tax effect of gain deferral)		

Alternatively, the 2000 events could have been reported by this single entry.

Equity in Empanada income	16,500	
Investment in Empanada Co.		16,500

2001 through 2005 (each year):

1.	Deferred gain	5,000	
	Gain on sale of fixed assets		5,000
	(To amortize deferred gain)		

2.	Income tax expense	1,700	
	Deferred tax benefit		1,700
	(Tax effect of gain realization)		

The alternative treatment would be

| | Investment in Empanada Co. | 3,300 | |
| | Equity in Empanada income | | 3,300 |

In the example above, the tax currently paid by Radnor Co. (34% x $25,000 taxable gain on the transaction) is recorded as a deferred tax benefit in 2000 since taxes will not be due on the book gain recognized in the years 2001 through 2005. Under provisions of IAS 12, deferred tax benefits should be recorded to reflect the tax effects of all deductible timing differences. Unless Radnor Co. could demonstrate that future taxable amounts arising from existing temporary differences exist, this deferred tax benefit might be offset by an equivalent valuation allowance in Radnor Co.'s balance sheet at year end 2000, because of the doubt that it will ever be realized. Thus, the deferred tax benefit might not be recognizable, net of the valuation allowance, for financial reporting purposes unless other temporary differences not specified in the example provided future taxable amounts to offset the net deductible effect of the deferred gain.

NOTE: The deferred tax impact of an item of income for book purposes in excess of tax is the same as a deduction for tax purposes in excess of book.

This is discussed more fully in Chapter 15.

Accounting for a partial sale or additional purchase of the equity investment. This section covers the accounting issues that arise when the investor either sells some or all of its equity or acquires additional equity in the investee. The consequence of these actions could involve discontinuation of the equity method of accounting, or resumption of the use of that method.

Example of accounting for a discontinuance of the equity method

Assume that Plato Corp. owns 10,000 shares (30%) of Xenia Co. common stock for which it paid $250,000 10 years ago. On July 1, 2000, Plato sells 5,000 Xenia shares for $375,000. The balance in the Investment in Xenia Co. account at January 1, 2000, was $600,000. Assume that all the original differential between cost and book value has been amortized. To calculate the gain (loss) on this sale of 5,000 shares, it is necessary first to adjust the investment account so that it is current as of the date of sale. Assuming that the investee had net income of $100,000 for the 6 months ended June 30, 2000, the investor should record the following entries:

1.	Investment in Xenia Co.	30,000	
	Equity in Xenia income($100,000 x 30%)		30,000
2.	Income tax expense	2,040	
	Deferred tax liability ($30,000 x 20% x 34%)		2,040

The gain on sale can now be computed, as follows:

Proceeds on sale of 5,000 shares	$375,000
Book value of the 5,000 shares ($630,000 x 50%)	315,000
Gain from sale of Xenia common	$ 60,000

Two entries will be needed to reflect the sale: one to record the proceeds, the reduction in the investment account, and the gain (or loss); the other to record the tax effects thereof. Recall that the investor must have computed the deferred tax effect of the undistributed earnings of the investee that it had recorded each year, on the basis that those earnings either would eventually be paid as dividends or would be realized as capital gains. When those dividends are ultimately received or when the investment is disposed of, the deferred tax liability recorded previously must be amortized.

To illustrate, assume that the investor in this example, Plato Corp., provided deferred taxes at an effective rate for dividends (considering the assumed 80% exclusion of intercorporate dividends) of 6.8%. The realized capital gain will be taxed at an assumed 34%. For tax purposes, this gain is computed as $375,000 – $125,000 = $250,000, giving a tax effect of $85,000. For accounting purposes, the deferred taxes already provided are 6.8% x ($315,000 – $125,000), or $12,920. Accordingly, an additional tax expense of $72,080 is incurred on the sale, due to the fact that an additional gain was realized for book purposes ($375,000 – $315,000 = $60,000; tax at 34% = $20,400) **and** that the tax previously provided for at dividend income rates was lower than the real capital gains rate [$190,000 x (34% – 6.8%) = $51,680 extra tax due]. The entries are as follows:

1.	Cash	375,000	
	Investment in Xenia Co.		315,000
	Gain on sale of Xenia Co. stock		60,000
2.	Deferred tax liability	12,920	
	Income tax expense	72,080	
	Taxes payable--current		85,000

The gains (losses) from sales of investee stock are reported on the investor's income statement in the other income and expense section, assuming that a multistep income statement is presented.

According to IAS 28, an investor should discontinue use of the equity method when (1) it ceases to have significant influence in an associate while retaining some or all of its investment, or (2) the use of the equity method is no longer deemed to be appropriate because the associate is operating under severe and long-lasting restrictions that will limit its ability to transfer funds to the investor entity.

In the foregoing example, the sale of investee stock reduced the percentage owned by the investor to 15%. In such a situation, the investor should probably discontinue use of the equity method. The balance in the investment account on the date the equity method is suspended ($315,000 in the example) remains as an asset, subject to the applicable international accounting rules (i.e., historical cost, revalued amounts, or lower of cost or market, per IAS 25). This accounting principle change does not require computation of a cumulative effect or any retroactive disclosures in the investor's financial statements. In periods subsequent to this principles change, the investor records cash dividends received from the investment as dividend revenue. Any dividends received in excess of the investor's share of postdisposal earnings of the investee should be credited to the investment account rather than to income, as they would represent a return of capital.

If an entity has an investment in another enterprise's common stock that is below the level that would create a presumption of significant influence, and later increases that investment so that the threshold for application of the equity method is exceeded, the guidance of IAS 28 would suggest that at that time the difference between the carrying value of the investment and the fair value of the underlying net identifiable assets must be computed, as described earlier in the chapter. The carrying value of the investment will depend on which of the available alternative methods set forth in IAS 25 had been employed. Thus, if the investment had been carried at original cost, the variance between carrying value and underlying fair value will probably have changed by the time the threshold for applying the equity method will have been exceeded. On the other hand, if the investment had been adjusted to fair value on a regular basis, this variance will probably be somewhat less or even nonexistent.

Example of accounting for a return to the equity method of accounting

Continuing the same example, Xenia Co. reported earnings for the second half of 2000 and all of 2001, respectively, of $150,000 and $350,000; Xenia paid dividends of $100,000 and $150,000 in December of those years. During the period July 2000 through December 2001, Plato Corp. accounted for its investment in Xenia Co. as a long-term investment in marketable securities, using the revaluation method, with increases in carrying value being credited to an additional equity account. At December 31, 2000, the fair value of Plato's holding of Xenia's stock is assessed at $335,000; at December 31, 2001, the fair value is $365,000.

In January 2002, the Plato Corp. purchased 10,000 Xenia shares for $700,000, increasing its ownership to 45% and thereby necessitating a return for equity method accounting. The fair value of the underlying identifiable assets of Xenia at this date is $1,000,000. The relevant entries are as follows:

1.	Cash	15,000	
	Income from Xenia dividends		15,000
	(To report dividends paid in 2000)		
2.	Investment in Xenia Corp.	20,000	
	Revaluation surplus		20,000
	(To reflect increased value of investment)		
3.	Income tax expense	1,020	
	Revaluation surplus	6,800	
	Taxes payable--current		1,020
	Taxes payable--deferred		6,800
	(To record taxes on dividends at current effective tax rate [$15,000 x .068] and deferred taxes on value increase [$20,000 x .34] in 2000)		
4.	Cash	22,500	
	Income from Xenia dividends		22,500
	(To report dividends paid in 2001)		

5.	Investment in Xenia Corp.	30,000	
	Revaluation surplus		30,000
	(To reflect increased value of investment)		

6.	Income tax expense	1,530	
	Revaluation surplus	10,200	
	Taxes payable--current		1,530
	Taxes payable--deferred		10,200
	(To record taxes on dividends at current effective tax rate		
	[$22,500 x .068] and deferred taxes on value increase		
	[$30,000 x .34] in 2001)		

7.	Investment in Xenia Co.	700,000	
	Cash		700,000
	(To record additional investment in Xenia)		

8.	Revaluation surplus	33,000	
	Retained earnings		33,000
	(See explanation below)		

The last entry above is further explained as follows. IAS 28 does not suggest that a return to the equity method should result in a restatement of the investment account and the revaluation surplus and retained earnings accounts to catch up to what the balances would have been had the equity method not been discontinued earlier. Accordingly, the authors believe that the new cost basis of the investment at the time the equity method is reestablished should be the adjusted carrying amount immediately prior thereto. In the present example, the carrying amount was as follows:

Balance 6/30/00	$ 315,000
Adjust to fair value 12/00	20,000
Adjust to fair value 12/01	30,000
Balance, 12/01	$ 365,000
Additional investment, 1/02	700,000
Carrying value, 1/02	$1,065,000

The difference between the cost of $1,065,000 and Plato's equity in Xenia's net identifiable assets, $65,000, would be treated similar to goodwill and amortized over a maximum of 5 years (in limited circumstances, a maximum of 20 years), as illustrated earlier in the chapter.

The amount reflected in the revaluation surplus account, $33,000, would not be appropriate to carry forward, since the investment is no longer to be accounted for under IAS 25. Accordingly, this should be transferred to retained earnings, since it effectively has been realized by adoption or readoption of the equity method. Note that the $33,000 balance is the net of the $50,000 upward revaluation recognized, cumulatively, in 2000 and 2001, and the $17,000 tax provision, at capital gain rates (assumed in this example to be 34%), which was expected to affect the ultimate realization of this value increase. If the effective tax rate is expected to differ from the amount provided earlier, due to the effect of the significant influence over the investee's dividend decisions, then if the liability method under IAS 12 has been elected, there would also be an adjustment to the deferred tax provision.

To illustrate the latter point, assume that Plato now expects to realize all its income from Xenia in the form of dividends, to be taxed at an effective rate of 6.8%. The entry to adjust the deferred tax liability would be

Taxes payable--deferred	13,600	
Tax expense		13,600
(To record adjustment to deferred taxes)		

Note that the offset to the deferred tax adjustment is to current period (i.e., 2002) tax expense, under the rules of IAS 12, as described more fully in Chapter 15.

While the illustration above adjusts the revaluation surplus account directly to retained earnings, a good argument could be made that this should be reported in earnings instead, on the basis that this is an economic event occurring in 2002 and thus reportable in that period. Since IAS 28 is silent on this issue (as well as many others), the authors have elected to treat this in a manner analogous to a prior period adjustment (which is approximately equivalent to the treatment prescribed under US GAAP, which has been used as a benchmark), but with the understanding that adequate disclosure would have to be given in the financial statements to avoid any misunderstandings. The alternative treatment, reporting the adjustment in income, would also be acceptable, again with adequate explanations for financial statement users.

Investor accounting for investee capital transactions. IAS 28 does not address how the investor should reflect the impact of investee capital transactions that affect the worth of the investor's investment. However, given that the ultimate effects of equity method accounting are to be identical to full consolidation, it is logical that investee transactions of a capital nature that affect the investor's share of the investee's stockholders' equity should be accounted for as if the investee were a consolidated subsidiary. These transactions principally include situations where the investee purchases treasury stock from, or sells unissued shares or shares held in the treasury to, outside shareholders. (If the investor participates in these transactions on a pro rata basis, its percentage ownership will not change and no special accounting will be necessary.) Similar results will be obtained when holders of outstanding options or convertible securities acquire investee common shares.

When the investee engages in one of the foregoing capital transactions, the investor's ownership percentage is changed. This gives rise to a gain or loss, depending on whether the price paid (for treasury shares acquired) or received (for shares issued) is greater or lesser than the per share carrying value of the investor's interest in the investee. However, since no gain or loss can be recognized on capital transactions, these purchases or sales will affect paid-in capital and/or retained earnings directly, without being reflected in the investor's income statement. This method is consistent with the treatment that would be accorded to a consolidated subsidiary's capital transaction.

Example of accounting for an investee capital transaction

Assume that Roger Corp. purchases, on 1/2/00, 25% (2,000 shares) of Energetic Corp.'s outstanding shares for $80,000. The cost is equal to both the book and fair values of Roger's interest in Energetic's underlying net assets (i.e., there is no differential to be accounted for). One week later, Energetic Corp. buys 1,000 shares of its stock from other shareholders for $50,000. Since the price paid ($50/share) exceeded Roger Corp.'s per share carrying value of its interest, $40, Roger Corp. has in fact suffered an economic loss by the transaction. Also, its percentage ownership of Energetic Corp. has increased as the number of shares held by third parties has been reduced.

Roger Corp.'s new interest in Energetic's net assets is

$$\frac{2{,}000 \text{ shares held by Roger Corp.}}{7{,}000 \text{ shares outstanding in total}} \quad \text{x} \quad \text{Energetic Corp. net assets}$$

$$.2857 \text{ x } (\$320{,}000 - \$50{,}000) = \$77{,}143$$

The interest held by Roger Corp. has thus been diminished by $80,000 – $77,143 = $2,857. Therefore, Roger Corp. should make the following entry:

Paid-in capital (or retained earnings)	2,857	
Investment in Energetic Corp.		2,857

Roger Corp. should charge the loss against paid-in capital if paid-in capital from past transactions of a similar nature exists; otherwise, the debit is to retained earnings. Had the transaction given rise to a gain, it would have been credited to paid-in capital only (never to retained earnings) following the GAAP principle that transactions in one's own shares cannot produce earnings.

Note that the amount of the charge to paid-in capital (or retained earnings) in the entry above can be verified as follows: Roger Corp.'s share of the posttransaction net equity (2/7) times the excess price paid ($50 – $40 = $10) times the number of shares purchased = 2/7 x $10 x 1,000 = $2,857.

Other than temporary impairment in value of equity method investments. IAS 28 provides that if there is a decline in value of an investment accounted for by the equity method which is determined to be other than temporary in nature, the carrying value of the investment should be adjusted downward. Other than temporary is used in the same sense as in IAS 25, described earlier in this chapter. This criterion must be applied on an individual investment basis.

Other disclosures required by IAS 28. The standard requires that there be disclosure of the percentage of ownership that is held by the investor in each investment and, if it differs, the percentage of voting rights that are controlled. The method of accounting that is being applied to each significant investment should also be identified.

In addition, there may have been certain assumptions or adjustments made in developing information so that the equity method was applied. For example, the investee may have used different accounting principles than the investor, for which the investor made allowances in determining its share of the investee's operating results. The reported results of an investee that used LIFO inventory accounting, for instance, may have been adjusted by the investor to conform to its FIFO costing method. Also, the investee's fiscal year may have differed from the investor's, and the investor may have converted this to its fiscal year by adding and subtracting stub period data. In any such case, if the impact is material, the fact of having made these adjustments should be disclosed, although it would be unusual to report the actual amount of such adjustments to users of the investor's financial statements.

If an associate has outstanding cumulative preferred stock, held by interests other than the investor, the investor should compute its equity interest in the investee's earnings after deducting dividends due to the preferred shareholders, whether or not declared. If material, this should be explained in the investor's financial statements.

Finally, if cumulative losses have been incurred by the investee such that under equity method accounting, the carrying value has been reduced to zero, normally no further share of the investee's losses will be reported. (The major exception to this rule: If the investor has guaranteed debt of the investee or otherwise indicated that it will stand behind the investee, it should record further losses and accordingly let the investment account go negative to reflect a liability on the investor's part.) However, disclosure should be made of the unrecorded negative equity, since this is a measure of the amount of future investee earnings that will have to be realized **before** any further income will be recognized by the investor.

Accounting for Investments in Joint Ventures

International accounting standards address accounting for interests in joint ventures as a topic separate from accounting for other investments. Joint ventures share many characteristics with investments that are accounted for by the equity method: The investor clearly has significant influence over the investee but does not have absolute control, and hence full consolidation is typically unwarranted. According to the provisions of IAS 31, two different methods of accounting are possible, although not as true alternatives for the same fact situations: the proportional consolidation method and the equity method.

Joint ventures can take many forms and structures. Joint ventures may be created as partnerships, as corporations, or as unincorporated associations. The standard identifies three distinct types, referred to as jointly controlled operations, jointly controlled assets, and jointly controlled entities. Notwithstanding the formal structure, all joint ventures are characterized by certain features: having two or more venturers that are bound by a contractual arrangement, and by the fact that the contractual agreement establishes joint control of the enterprise.

The contractual provision(s) establishing joint control most clearly differentiates joint ventures from other investment scenarios in which the investor has significant influence over the investee. In fact, in the absence of such a contractual provision, joint venture accounting would not be appropriate, even in a situation in which two parties each have 50% ownership interests in an investee. The actual existence of such a contractual provision can be evidenced in a number of ways, although most typically it is in writing and often addresses such matters as the nature, term of existence, and reporting obligations of the joint venture; the governing mechanisms for the venture; the capital contributions by the respective venturers; and the intended division of output, income, expenses, or net results of the venture.

The contractual arrangement also establishes joint control over the venture. The thrust of such a provision is to ensure that no venturer can control the venture unilaterally. Certain decision areas will be stipulated as requiring consent by all the venturers, while other decision areas may be defined as needing the consent of only a majority of the venturers. There is no specific set of decisions that must fall into either grouping, however.

Typically, one venturer will be designated as the manager or operator of the venture. This does not imply the absolute power to govern; however, if such power exists, the venture would be a subsidiary, subject to the requirements of IAS 27 and not accounted for properly under IAS 31.

Specific accounting guidance is dependent on whether the enterprise represents jointly controlled operations, jointly controlled assets, or a jointly controlled entity.

Jointly controlled operations. The first of three types of joint ventures, this is characterized by the assigned use of certain assets or other resources, in contrast to an establishment of a new entity, be it a corporation or partnership. Thus, from a formal or legal perspective, this variety of joint venture may not have an existence separate from its sponsors; from an economic point of view, however, the joint venture can still be said to exist, which means that it may exist as an accounting entity. Typically, this form of operation will utilize assets owned by the venture partners, often including plant and equipment as well as inventories, and the partners will sometimes incur debt on behalf of the operation. Actual operations may be conducted on an integrated basis with the partners' own, separate operations, with certain employees, for example, devoting a part of their efforts to the jointly controlled operation. The European Consortium Airbus may be a prototype of this type of enterprise.

IAS 31 is concerned not with the accounting by the entity conducting the jointly controlled operations, but by the venturers having an interest in the enterprise. Each venturer should recognize in its separate financial statements all assets of the venture that it controls, all liabilities that it incurs, all expenses that it incurs, and its share of any revenues produced by the venture. Often, since the assets are already owned by the venturers, they would be included in their respective financial statements in any event; similarly, any debt incurred will be reported by the partner even absent this special rule. Perhaps the only real challenge, from a measurement and disclosure perspective, would be the revenues attributable to each venturer's efforts, which will be determined by reference to the joint venture agreement and other documents.

Jointly controlled assets. In certain industries, such as oil and gas exploration and transmission and mineral extraction, jointly controlled assets are frequently employed. For example, oil pipelines may be controlled jointly by a number of oil producers, each of which uses the facilities and shares in its costs of operation. Certain informal real estate partnerships may also function in this fashion.

IAS 31 stipulates that in the case of jointly controlled assets, each venturer must report in its own financial statements its share of all jointly controlled assets, appropriately classified according to their natures. It must also report any liabilities that it has incurred on behalf of these jointly controlled assets, as well as its share of any jointly incurred liabilities. Each venturer will report any income earned from the use its share of the jointly controlled assets, along with the pro rata expenses and any other expenses it has incurred directly.

Jointly controlled entities. The major type of joint venture is the jointly controlled enterprise, which is really a form of partnership (although it may well be structured legally as a corporation) in which each partner has a form of control, rather than only significant influence. The classic example is an equal partnership of two partners; obviously, neither has a majority and either can block any important action, so the two partners must effectively agree on each key decision. Although this may be the model for a jointly controlled entity, it may in practice have more than two venturers and, depending on the partnership or shareholders' agreement, even minority owners may have joint control. For example, a partnership whose partners have 30%, 30%, 30%, and 10% interests, respectively, may have entered into a contractual agreement that stipulates that investment or financing actions may be taken only if there is unanimity among the partners.

Jointly controlled entities control the assets of the joint venture and may incur liabilities and expenses on its behalf. As a legal entity, it may enter into contracts and borrow funds, among other activities. In general, each venturer will share the net results in proportion to its ownership interest. As an entity with a distinct and separate legal and economic identity, the jointly controlled entity will normally produce its own financial statements and other tax and legal reports.

IAS 31 provides alternative accounting treatments that may be applied by the venture partners to reflect the operations and financial position of the venture. The objective is to report economic substance, rather than mere form, but there is not universal agreement on how this may best be achieved.

The benchmark treatment under the standard is the use of proportionate consolidation, which requires that the venture partner reflect its share of all assets, liabilities, revenues, and expenses on its financial statements as if these were incurred or held directly. In fact, this technique is very effective at conveying the true scope of an entity's operations, when those operations include interests in one or more jointly controlled entities. In this regard, the international accounting standards are more advanced than US, UK, or other national standards, which at best permit proportionate consolidation but do not mandate this accounting treatment.

If the venturer employs the proportionate consolidation method, it will have a choice between two presentation formats that are equally acceptable. First, the venture partner may include its share of the assets, liabilities, revenues, and expenses of the jointly controlled entity with similar items under its sole control. Thus, under this method, its share of the venture's receivables would be added to its own accounts receivable and presented as a single total on its balance sheet. Alternatively, the items that are undivided interests in the venture's assets, and so on, may be shown on separate lines of the venturer's financial statements, although still placed within the correct grouping. For example, the venture's receivables might be shown immediately below the partner's individually owned accounts receivable. In either case, the same category totals (aggregate current assets, etc.) will be presented; the only distinction is whether the venture-owned items are given separate recognition. Even if presented on a combined basis, however, the appropriate detail can still be shown in the financial statement footnotes, and indeed to achieve a fair presentation, this might be needed.

The proportionate consolidation method should be discontinued when the partner no longer has the ability to control the entity jointly. This may occur when the interest formerly held is disposed of, or when external restrictions are placed on the ability to exercise control. In some cases a partner will waive its right to control the entity, possibly in exchange for other economic advantages, such as a larger interest in the operating results.

Under the provisions of IAS 31, a second accounting method, the equity method, is also considered to be acceptable, although its designation as an allowed alternative signals that this is not the preferred treatment. The equity method in this context is as described in IAS 28 and as explained in the preceding section. As with the proportionate consolidation method, use of the equity method must be discontinued when the venturer no longer has joint control or significant influence over the jointly controlled entity.

Accounting for jointly controlled entities as passive investments. Although the expectation is that investments in jointly controlled entities will be accounted for by the proportionate consolidation or equity method (the benchmark and allowed alternative treatments, respectively), in certain circumstances the venturer should account for its interest following the guidelines of IAS 25, that is, as a passive investment. This would be the prescription when the investment has been acquired and is being held with a view toward disposition in the short term, or when the investee is operating under severe long-term restrictions that severely impair its ability to transfer funds to its venturer owners.

If the investment is seen as being strictly temporary, effectively it is being held for trading purposes in the same manner as a temporary investment in marketable securities would be. In such a situation it would not be logical to apply either the proportionate consolidation or equity method, since it would not be the venturer's share of the operating results of the venture that provided value to the venturer, but rather, the change in market value.

Similarly, if the venture were operating under such severe restrictions, expected to persist beyond a short time horizon, that transfers of funds from the jointly controlled entity to its venture parents were precluded, it would be misleading and conceptually invalid to treat the venture's operating results as bearing directly on the venture parents' earnings results. In such a case, an inability to transfer funds would mean that the venture partners would be unable to obtain any benefit, in the short run at least, from their investment in the jointly controlled entity.

Change from joint control to full control status. If one of the venturers' interest in the jointly controlled entity is increased, whether by an acquisition of some or all of another of the venturers' interest, or by action of a contractual provision of the venture agreement (resulting from a failure to perform by another venturer, etc.), the proportionate consolidation method of accounting ceases to be appropriate and full consolidation will become necessary. Guidance on preparation of consolidated financial statements is provided by IAS 27 and is discussed fully in Chapter 11.

Accounting for Transactions Between Venture Partner and Jointly Controlled Entity

Transfers at a gain to the transferor. A general, underlying principle of financial reporting is that earnings are to be realized only by engaging in transactions with outside parties. Thus, gains cannot be recognized by transferring assets (be they productive assets or goods held for sale in the normal course of the business) to a subsidiary, affiliate, or joint venture, to the extent this really would represent a transaction by an entity with itself. Were this not the rule, enterprises would establish a range of related entities to sell goods to, thereby permitting the reporting of profits well before any sale to real, unrelated customers ever took place. The potential for abuse of the financial reporting process in such a scenario is too obvious to need elaboration.

IAS 31 stipulates that when a venturer sells or transfers assets to a jointly controlled entity, it may recognize profit only to the extent that the venture is owned by the other venture partners, and then only to the extent that the risks and rewards of ownership have indeed been transferred to the jointly controlled entity. The logic is that a portion of the profit has in fact been realized, to the extent that the purchase was agreed on by unrelated parties that jointly control the entity making the acquisition. For example, if venturers A, B, and C jointly control venture D (each having a 1/3 interest), and A sells equipment having a book value of $40,000 to the venture for $100,000, only 2/3 of the apparent gain of $60,000, or $40,000, may be realized. In its balance sheet immediately after this transaction, A would report its share of the asset reflected in the balance sheet of D, 1/3 x $100,000 = $33,333, minus the unrealized gain of $20,000, for a net of $13,333. This is identical to A's remaining 1/3 interest in the pretransaction basis of the asset (1/3 x $40,000 = $13,333). Thus, there is no step up in the carrying value of the proportionate share of the asset reflected in the transferor's balance sheet.

If the asset is subject to depreciation, the deferred gain on the transfer (1/3 x $60,000 = $20,000) would be amortized in proportion to the depreciation reflected by the venture, such that the depreciated balance of the asset reported by A is the same as would have been reported had the transfer not taken place. For example, assume that the asset has a useful economic life of 5 years after the date of transfer to D. The deferred gain ($20,000) would be amortized to income at a rate of $4,000 per year. At the end of the first posttransfer year, D would report a net carrying value of $100,000 – $20,000 = $80,000; A's proportionate interest is 1/3 x $80,000 = $26,667. The unamortized balance of the deferred gain is $20,000 – $4,000 = $16,000. Thus the net reported amount of A's share of the jointly controlled entity's asset is $26,667 – $16,000 = $10,667. This amount is precisely what A would have reported the remaining share of its asset at on this date: 1/3 x ($40,000 – $8,000) = $10,667.

Of course, A has also reported a gain of $40,000 as of the date of the transfer of its asset to joint venture D, but this represents the gain that has been realized by the sale of 2/3 of the asset to unrelated parties B and C, the coventurers in D. In short, two-thirds of the asset has been sold at a gain, while one-third has been retained and is continuing to be used and depreciated over its remaining economic life and is reported on the cost basis in A's financial statements.

The matters described above have been further emphasized by the Standing Interpretation Committee's draft interpretation, D13, which holds that gains or losses will result from contributions of nonmonetary assets to a jointly controlled enterprise **only** when significant risks and rewards of ownership have been transferred and the gain or loss can be reliably measured. However, no gain or loss would be recognized when the asset is contributed in exchange for an equity interest in the jointly controlled enterprise when the asset is similar to assets contributed by the other venturers. Any unrealized gain or loss should be netted against the related assets, and not presented as deferred gain or loss in the venturer's consolidated financial statements.

Transfers of assets at a loss. The foregoing illustration was predicated on a transfer to the jointly controlled entity at a nominal gain to the transferor, of which a portion was realized for financial reporting purposes. The situation when a transfer is at an amount below the transferor's carrying value is not analogous; rather, such a transfer is deemed to be confirmation of a permanent decline in value, which must be recognized by the transferor immediately rather than being deferred. This reflects the conservative bias in accounting: Unrealized losses are often recognized, while unrealized gains are deferred.

Assume that venturer C (a 1/3 owner of D, as described above) transfers an asset it had been carrying at $150,000 to jointly controlled entity D at a price of $120,000. If the decline is deemed to be other than temporary in nature (that presumptively it is, since C would not normally have been willing to engage in this transaction if the decline were expected to be reversed in the near term), C must recognize the full $30,000 at the time of the transfer. Subsequently, C will pick up its 1/3 interest in the asset held by D (1/3 x $120,000 = $40,000) as its own asset in its balance sheet, before considering any depreciation, and so on.

Accounting for Assets Purchased From a Jointly Controlled Entity

Transfers at a gain to the transferor. A similar situation arises when a venture partner acquires an asset from a jointly controlled entity: The venturer cannot reflect the gain recognized by the joint venture, to the extent that this represents its share in the results of the venture's operations. For example, again assuming that A, B, and C jointly own D, an asset having a book value of $200,000 is transferred by D to B for a price of $275,000. Since B has a 1/3 interest in D, it would (unless an adjustment were made to its accounting) report $25,000 of D's gain as its own, which would violate the realization concept under GAAP.

To avoid this result, B will record the asset at its cost, $275,000, less the deferred gain, $25,000, for a net carrying value of $250,000, which represents the transferor's basis, $200,000, plus the increase in value realized by unrelated parties (A and C) in the amount of $50,000.

As the asset is depreciated, the deferred gain will be amortized apace. For example, assume that the useful life of the asset in B's hands is 10 years. At the end of the first year, the carrying value of the asset is $275,000 - $27,500 = $247,500; the unamortized balance of the deferred gain is $25,000 - $2,500 = $22,500. Thus the net carrying value, after offsetting the remaining deferred gain, will be $247,500 - $22,500 = $225,000. This corresponds to the remaining life of the asset (9/10 of its estimated life) times its original net carrying amount, $250,000. The amortization of the deferred gain should be credited to depreciation expense to offset the depreciation charged on the nominal acquisition price and thereby to reduce it to a cost basis as required by GAAP.

Transfers at a loss to the transferor. If the asset was acquired by B at a loss to D, on the other hand, and the decline was deemed to be indicative of an other than temporary diminution in value, B should recognize its share of this decline. This contrasts with the gain scenario discussed immediately above, and as such is entirely consistent with the accounting treatment for transfers from the venture partner to the jointly controlled venture.

For example, if D sells an asset carried at $50,000 to B for $44,000, and the reason for this discount is an other than temporary decline in the value of said asset, the venture, D, records a loss of $6,000 and each venture partner will in turn recognize a $2,000 loss. B would report the asset at its acquisition cost of $44,000 and will also report its share of the loss, $2,000. This loss will not be deferred and will not be added to the carrying value of the asset in B's hands (as would have been the case if B treated only the $4,000 loss realized by unrelated parties A and C as being recognizable).

Disclosure Requirements

A venture partner is required to disclose in the notes to the financial statements its ownership interests in all significant joint ventures, including its ownership percentage and other relevant data. If the venturer uses proportionate consolidation and merges its share of the assets, liabilities, revenues, and expenses of the jointly controlled entity with its own assets, liabilities, revenues, and expenses, or if the venturer uses the equity method, the notes should disclose the amounts of the current and long-term assets, current and long-term liabilities, revenues, and expenses related to its interests in jointly controlled ventures.

Furthermore, the joint venture partner should disclose any contingencies that the venturer has incurred in relation to its interests in any joint ventures, noting any share of contingencies jointly incurred with other joint venturers. In addition, the venturer's share of any contingencies of the joint venture (as distinct from contingencies incurred in connection with its investment in the venture) for which it may be contingently liable must be reported. Finally, those contingencies that arise because the venturer is contingently liable for the liabilities of the other partners in the jointly controlled entity must be set forth. These disclosures are a logical application of the rules set forth in IAS 10, which is discussed in Chapter 12 of this book.

A venture partner should also disclose in the notes to her/his financial statements information about any commitments s/he has outstanding in respect to interests s/he has in joint ventures. These include any capital commitments s/he has and her/his share of any joint commitments s/he may have incurred with other venture partners, as well as her/his share of the capital commitments of the joint ventures themselves, if any.

Accounting for Other Investment Property

The accounting for investments in assets other than financial instruments was addressed by IAS 25, which remains as the extant guidance for investments in land and buildings, for example, following the effective date of IAS 39. However, the IASC is developing new requirements for these types of investments, and has recently exposed E64 which sets forth its conclusions on this topic. While cautioning readers that the final standard, when adopted, may differ from E64, that proposal is summarized in the following paragraphs.

Under IAS 25, investments in properties, such as land or buildings, other than those being held for use, may be accounted for either as property per se, in accordance with the applicable international accounting standards (as described in Chapter 8), or as investments. If the latter method is selected, depreciation will not be recorded, but instead the investment will be marked to fair value in a manner consistent with the guidelines of IAS 25. Changes in market value should be reflected in income or in equity in the same manner as are changes in value of other long-term investments, as described in the earlier sections of this chapter.

The objective of the new standard which will replace the remaining effective portions of IAS 25 is to deal with so-called investment property, which is property other than property and equipment employed in the business (which is governed by IAS 16) or held for sale in the ordinary course of the business (the accounting for which is specified by IAS 2). Investment property is held for long-term capital appreciation or to generate cash flows in a passive manner. Property held by the enterprise and leased out under operating leases qualifies as investment property, as does a vacant--but ultimately to be leased out--building. Intangible assets are addressed by IAS 38 and would never be accounted for under the provisions of the standard which evolves from E64. The standard will guide accounting by lessees of property under financing leases, as well as by lessors under operating leases, although this standard will not change any of the provisions set forth in IAS 17.

The basic principle of E64 is that investment property should be reported at fair value, and that changes in fair value should be included in the results of operations as they occur. There is a rebuttable presumption that, if an entity acquires or constructs property which will qualify as investment property under this standard, it will be able to assess fair value on an ongoing basis.

Recognition and measurement. Investment property will be recognized when it becomes probable that the enterprise will enjoy the future economic benefits which are attributable to it, and when the cost or fair value can be reliably measured. In general, this will occur when first acquired or constructed by the reporting entity. In only unusual circumstances would it be concluded that the owner's likelihood of receipt of the economic benefits would be less than probable.

Initial measurement will be at cost, which is equivalent to fair value, assuming that the acquisition was the result of an arm's-length exchange transaction. Included in the purchase cost will be such expenditures as legal fees and transfer taxes, if incurred in the transaction. If the asset is self-constructed, cost will include not only direct expenditures on product or services consumed, but also overhead charges which can be allocated on a reasonable and consistent basis, in the same manner as these are allocated to inventories under the guidelines of IAS 2. To the extent that the acquisition cost includes an interest charge, if the payment is deferred, the amount to be recognized as an investment asset should not include the interest charges.

In some instances there may be further expenditures made on the property after the date of initial recognition. Consistent with similar situations pertaining to plant, property and equipment, if it can be demonstrated that the further expenditures will enhance the generation of future economic benefits to the entity, then those costs may be added to the asset's carrying value. As an example, if an asset (e.g., an office building) is acquired for investment purposes in a condition which makes the undertaking of significant renovations necessary, those renovation costs will be added to the property carrying value when later incurred.

Subsequent value changes. E64 stipulates that investment property is to be reported at fair value. Thus, as of each financial reporting date, the carrying amount must be adjusted to then-current fair value, with the adjustment being reported in current income. Ideally, an independent appraisal will be performed, but the standard will not make this an absolute requirement, in consideration of the likely cost of doing this on an annual or more frequent basis.

Fair value will be defined as the most probable price reasonably obtainable in the marketplace as of the valuation date. Factors which could distort the value, such as the incorporation of particularly favorable or unfavorable financing terms, the inclusion of sale and leaseback arrangements, or any other concession by either buyer or seller, are not to be given any consideration in the valuation process. However, the actual conditions in the marketplace at the valuation date, even if these represent somewhat atypical climatic factors, will govern the valuation process. For example, if the economy is in the midst of a recession and rental properties' prices are depressed, no attempt should be made to normalize fair value, since that would add a subjective element and depart from the concept of fair value as of the balance sheet date.

Transfers from (or to) investment property to (or from) plant and equipment. In some instances, property which at first is appropriately classified as investment property under E64 may later become plant, property and equipment as defined under IAS 16. For example, a building is obtained and leased to unrelated parties, but at a later date the entity expands its own operations to the extent that it now chooses to utilize the building formerly held as a passive investment for its own purposes, such as for the corporate executive offices. The amount reflected in the accounts as the fair value of the property as of the date of change in status would become the cost basis for subsequent accounting purposes. Previously recognized changes in value, if any, would not be reversed.

Similarly, if property first included as plant and equipment is later redeployed as investment property, it is to be measured at fair value at the date of the change in its usage. If the value is lower than the carrying amount (i.e., if there is a previously unrecognized decline in fair value) then this will be reflected in earnings in the period of redeployment as an investment property. On the other hand, if there has been an unrecognized increase in value, the accounting will depend on whether this is a reversal of a previously recognized value impairment. If the increase is a reversal of a decline in value, the increase should be recognized currently in earnings; the amount so reported, however, should not exceed the amount needed to restore the carrying amount to what it would have been, net of depreciation, had the earlier impairment loss not occurred.

If, on the other hand, there was no previously recognized impairment which the current value increase is effectively reversing (or, to the extent that the current increase exceeds the earlier decline) then the increase should be reported directly in equity, by means of the statement of changes in equity. If the investment property is later disposed of, any resultant gain or loss computation should not include the effect of the amount reported directly in equity.

Transfers from inventory to investment property. It may also happen that property originally classified as inventory, that is, originally held for sale in the normal course of the business, is later redeployed as investment property. When reclassified, the initial carrying amount should be fair value as of that date. Any gain or loss resulting from this reclassification would be reported in current period's earnings.

E64 does not contemplate reclassification from investment property to inventory, however. When the enterprise determines that property held as investment property is to be disposed of, that property should be retained as investment property until actually sold. It should not be derecognized or transferred to an inventory classification.

Disclosure requirements. It is anticipated that in many cases investment property will be property which is owned by the reporting entity and leased to others under operating-type lease arrangements. The disclosure requirements set forth in IAS 17 (and discussed in Chapter 14) continue unaltered by E64. However, a number of new disclosure requirements will be imposed by the standard.

An entity holding investment property will need to set forth the criteria used to distinguish investment property from owner-occupied property (which is accounted for under IAS 16) or which is treated as inventory (per IAS 2). Brief descriptions should be offered of each of the types of property which are included in the investment property caption in the balance sheet. The methods and any significant assumptions which were used in ascertaining the fair values of the properties are to be stipulated also.

The standard will require that a reconciliation be presented of the carrying amounts of the investment property, from the beginning to the end of the reporting period. The reconciliation will separately identify additions resulting from acquisitions, those resulting from business combinations, and those deriving from capitalized expenditures subsequent to the property's initial recognition. It will also identify disposals, gains or losses from revaluations, the net exchange differences, if any, arising from the translation of the financial statements of a foreign subsidiary, and any other reconciling items. It will not be required that comparative reconciliation data be presented for prior periods.

The amount of property under construction at year end must be identified as well, and separately set forth in the balance sheet to distinguish it from properties which are already productively deployed. When physical construction is substantially complete, property should be transferred to the regular investment property category.

If investment property has been revalued by an independent party having credentials or formal qualifications, and who has recent experience with properties having similar characteristics of location and type, that should be disclosed in the notes to the financial statements.

Also to be disclosed are the amount of rental income derived from investment property which is included in the income statement of the period being presented; the carrying value of any unleased or vacant investment properties; any restrictions which may potentially affect the realizability of investment property or of the income and proceeds from disposal to be received; and any material contractual obligations to purchase or build investment property or for repairs, maintenance or improvements thereto.

11 BUSINESS COMBINATIONS AND CONSOLIDATED FINANCIAL STATEMENTS

PERSPECTIVE AND ISSUES

Regardless of its legal form, a business combination will be accounted for as either a uniting of interests or as an acquisition of one business by another, depending on the facts of the specific case. A uniting of interests presumes that the ownership interests of the combining entities continue essentially unchanged in the new combined enterprise. A series of restrictive criteria must be satisfied for a combination to be accounted for as a uniting of interests. Acquisition accounting is applicable when one entity acquires the assets, operations, or ownership interest from another enterprise or from its former owners. Most combinations are accounted for as acquisitions.

When a combination is to be accounted for as an acquisition, the assets acquired and liabilities assumed are recorded at their fair values, using purchase accounting. If the assets and liabilities total an amount other than the total acquisition price, the excess (or deficiency) is generally referred to as goodwill (negative goodwill). Goodwill can arise only in the context of a business combination that is an acquisition. In a uniting of interests, the assets and liabilities of the combining entities are carried forward at precombination book values, using the pooling method of accounting. This treatment is consistent with the theory that since a pooling does not result in the acquisition of one business entity by another, a new basis of accountability cannot be established.

When the acquired entity is **merged** into the acquiring entity or when both entities are **consolidated** into a new (third) entity, all assets and liabilities are recorded directly on the books of the surviving organization. Depending on whether the conditions stipulated by IAS 22 are met, the transaction will be treated as either a uniting of interests or an acquisition. However, when the acquirer obtains a majority (or all) of the common stock of the acquired entity (which maintains a separate legal existence), the assets and liabilities of the company acquired will not be recorded on the acquirer's books. In this case, GAAP normally requires that consolidated financial statements be prepared (i.e., that an accounting consolidation be effected, and either pooling or purchase accounting used, depending on the circumstances). In certain cases combined financial statements of entities under common control, neither of which is owned by the other, are also prepared. This process is very similar to an accounting consolidation using pooling accounting, except that the equity accounts of the combining entities are carried forward intact.

The major accounting issues in business combinations and consolidated or combined financial statement preparation are as follows:

1. The proper accounting basis for the assets and liabilities of the combining entities
2. The decision to treat a combination as a uniting of interests or as an acquisition
3. The elimination of intercompany balances and transactions in the preparation of consolidated or combined statements

Sources of IAS	
IAS 22 (revised 1998), 27, 37, 38	*SIC* 9, 12

DEFINITIONS OF TERMS

Accounting consolidation. The process of combining the financial statements of a parent company and one or more legally separate and distinct subsidiaries.

Acquisition. A business combination in that one entity (the acquirer) obtains control over the net assets and operations of another (the acquiree) in exchange for the transfer of assets, incurrence of liability, or issuance of equity.

Business combination. The bringing together of separate enterprises into one economic entity as a result of one enterprise uniting with or obtaining control over the net assets and operations of another.

Combination. Any transaction whereby one enterprise obtains control over the assets and properties of another enterprise, regardless of the resulting form of the enterprise emerging from the combination transaction.

Combined financial statements. Financial statements presenting the financial position and/or results of operations of legally separate entities, related by common ownership, as if they were a single entity.

Consolidated financial statements. The financial statements of a group presented as those of a single enterprise.

Consolidation. A new enterprise is formed to acquire two or more other enterprises through an exchange of voting stock. The acquired enterprises then cease to exist as separate legal entities.

Control. The power to govern the financial and operating policies of an enterprise so as to obtain benefits from its activities.

Date of acquisition. The date on which control of the net assets and operations of the acquiree is effectively transferred to the acquirer.

Fair value. The amount for which an asset could be exchanged or a liability settled between knowledgeable, willing parties in an arm's-length transaction.

Goodwill. The excess of the cost of a business acquisition accounted for by the purchase method over the fair value of the net assets thereof; it must be amortized over a useful life of up to 20 years (available under defined circumstances only; the normal life is up to 5 years).

Group. A parent and all its subsidiaries.

Merger. One enterprise acquires all of the net assets of one or more other enterprises through an exchange of stock, payment of cash or other property, or the issue of debt instruments.

Minority interest. That part of the net results of operations and net assets of a subsidiary attributable to interests that are not owned, directly or indirectly through subsidiaries, by the parent.

Negative goodwill. This amount represents the net excess of fair value of the net assets of a business acquisition accounted for as a purchase, either determined after offsetting the maximum amount against the fair value of all nonmonetary assets acquired (the benchmark treatment) or without so offsetting (the alternative treatment).

Parent. An enterprise that has one or more subsidiaries.

Pooling-of-interests method. An accounting method used for a business combination that is predicated on a mutual exchange and continuation of ownership interests in the combining entities. It does not result in the establishing of a new basis of accountability. The pooling method is to be used for unitings of interests.

Purchase method. An accounting method used for a business combination that recognizes that one combining entity was acquired by another. It establishes a new basis of accountability for the acquiree. The purchase method is to be used for acquisitions.

Purchased preacquisition earnings. An account used to report the earnings of a subsidiary attributable to percentage ownership acquired at the interim date in the current reporting period.

Subsidiary. An enterprise that is controlled, directly or indirectly, by another enterprise.

Uniting of interests. A business combination in which the shareholders of the combining enterprises combine control over the whole, or effectively the whole, of their respective net assets and operations to achieve a continuing mutual sharing in the risks and benefits attaching to the combined entity such that neither party can be identified as the acquirer.

Unrealized intercompany profit. The excess of the transaction price over the carrying value of an item (usually inventory or plant assets) transferred from (or to) a parent to (or from) the subsidiary (or among subsidiaries) and not sold to an outside entity. For purposes of consolidated financial statements, recognition must be deferred until subsequent realization through a transaction with an unrelated party.

CONCEPTS, RULES, AND EXAMPLES

Introduction to Business Combinations

Business combinations occur under two different scenarios. By far, the most common type of combination is referred to as an acquisition, which is sometimes also known as a purchase or as a purchase business combination. The other business combinations, which represent a very small minority of cases, are effected in a manner known as a uniting of interests, which is also referred to as a pooling of interests or as a merger.

The aforenoted typology is independent of the legal form of the business combination. Thus, two entities may consolidate to create a new, third enterprise. Alternatively, one entity may purchase, for cash or for stock, the stock of another enterprise, which may or may not be followed by a formal merging of the acquired entity into the acquirer. In yet other cases, one entity may simply purchase the assets of another, with or without assuming the debts of that enterprise. The form of the combination does not define whether it will be viewed as an acquisition or a uniting of interests, however. Rather, it is the substance of the transaction, which will be explored in great detail in the following paragraphs, which will serve to define it. The accounting for acquisitions differs markedly from that prescribed for unitings of interests.

Uniting of Interests

In many countries it has long been accepted that some business combinations may be accounted for as unitings of interests. The practice actually precedes the naming of the accounting methodology used. For example, in the United States the pooling method has been used since at least the early 1930s, although the term was not applied until the mid-1940s. The earliest examples of transactions accounted for as poolings or unitings of interests generally involved affiliated entities (such as parents and subsidiaries), where the use of this method clearly made sense, since the mere act of formally joining previously affiliated entities would not seem to warrant establishing a new basis of accountability. Broader application of the method really began in the 1940s; initially, pooling treatment was accepted only for those mergers where the combining entities had roughly the same economic substance (so that it was difficult to discern which party was actually the acquirer). However, as time passed, pooling was accepted for a broad range of business combinations among economic unequals.

Official support for the method, in the form of a professional standard issued by the standard setters in the United States, first occurred in 1950. That standard permitted pooling accounting when the shareholders of each of the combining entities continued forward as participating owners of the new or surviving business. This criterion remains one of the clearest tests of whether a combination should be accorded pooling treatment. That standard also established comparable size and management continuity as criteria, but these terms were not quantitatively defined, and a wide range of combinations continued to be accounted for as poolings of interests.

Other US accounting standards addressing pooling accounting were promulgated during the following decade, with the eventual effect that pooling treatment became acceptable even when the size disparity among the combining entities was as great as 19:1. As a result, accounting for business combinations as poolings became extremely popular in the early and mid-1960s. The major reason was (and continues to be) that the true cost (as would be measured by the market value of the consideration, usually stock or debt instruments issued by the acquirer) of the acquisition was concealed, with the result that a lower basis of assets acquired would be carried forward, in turn, producing lower amortization expense and higher reportable earnings in future periods. Also, the acquirer could incorporate the acquired entity's retained earnings (subject to some limitations) into its financial statements, thereby enhancing the appearance of the financial strength of the ongoing enterprise.

By the end of the decade of the 1960s, abuse of pooling-of-interests accounting in the United States had received so much attention that the standard setters imposed a new standard on accounting for business.

Recent evolution of uniting (pooling) of interests rules. Many standard-setting bodies now explicitly permit certain consolidations to be accounted for as poolings or unitings of interests. These independent national accounting standards vary substantially in terms of the criteria that must be satisfied in order to employ this methodology. A minority of national accounting standard-setting bodies prohibit pooling accounting altogether, however, with France and Spain being two of the more important industrialized nations in this group.

In the United States, standard setters established perhaps the most complex criteria yet devised for determining if a business combination could be accounted for as a pooling of interests. The US Accounting Principles Board, in its Opinion 16, established 12 tests, all of which must be met for any given combination to be so treated. Some of these tests are indeed difficult to apply, and the overall effect is virtually to eliminate pooling treatment for any combination other than a pure stock swap between parties having roughly equal bargaining power; although, perhaps surprisingly, parity of size is not one of the 12 criteria.

Among the 12 criteria imposed in the United States are several that relate to the characteristics of the combining entities (being independent of each other as well as of any other enterprise, etc.), others that relate to the nature of exchange transactions (primarily a swap of voting common stock, effected in a single transaction, with continuity of interests by the combining parties in essentially the same proportions as prior to the merger, etc.), and yet another set that precludes planned-for postcombination transactions that would alter the relative ownerships of the combining groups.

International accounting standard for pooling. The international accounting standard, IAS 22, provides a rather more direct set of criteria for determining the appropriateness of pooling accounting treatment. Three tests must all be met, as follows:

1. The shareholders of the combining enterprises must achieve a continuing mutual sharing of the risks and benefits attaching to the combined enterprise.
2. The basis of the transaction must be principally an exchange of voting common shares of the enterprises involved.
3. The whole, or effectively the whole, of the net assets and operations of the combining enterprises are combined into one entity.

The first of these criteria relates to the continual sharing of risks and benefits by the combining shareholder groups. To achieve this, according to IAS 22, the following must occur:

1. The substantial majority, if not all, of the voting common shares of the combining enterprises are exchanged or pooled.
2. The fair value of one enterprise is not significantly different from that of the other enterprise.
3. The shareholders of each enterprise maintain substantially the same voting rights and interest in the combined entity, relative to each other, after the combination as before.

Thus, the international standards have effectively defined the essential characteristics of a true uniting of interests and have established tests that address these. In describing a uniting of interests, IAS 22 states that "...the shareholders of the combining enterprises join in a *substantially equal arrangement* to share control over the whole, or effectively the whole, of their net assets and operations." Furthermore, it states that to achieve such a mutual sharing of risks and benefits, "the fair value of one enterprise [cannot be] significantly different from that of the other." Although these words are perhaps suggestive of the notion that unitings cannot be said to occur unless the combining entities are virtually identical in size, the precise meaning is not made clear. Thus, it would appear that under these criteria the mergers of entities of at least somewhat differing sizes can continue to be accounted for as poolings if the other terms stated are met.

In addressing the "substantially equal arrangement" the IAS 22 approach is clearly not as ambiguous as the US standard, APB 16, which makes no reference to the relative sizes of the combining entities or their relative net worths. However, neither is it as restrictive as the recently proposed UK standard (FRED 6), which demands approximately equal size under what is virtually a "marriage of equals" doctrine.

While IAS 22 goes on to state that a "mutual sharing...is usually not possible without a substantially equal exchange of voting common shares..." this can be read to mean that the **relative** interests of the combining parties cannot be altered by the transaction. For example, if one combining entity has a fair value of two-thirds of that of the other entity, this would imply that after the combination the former shareholders of the smaller enterprise should control about 40% [= 2/3 ÷ (2/3 + 3/3)] of the new, combined entity. If this condition were not to be met, these shareholders would have either gained or lost **relative** voting power in the transaction, which would be strongly suggestive of an acquisition of one enterprise by the other. In practice, there will be many borderline circumstances in which judgment must be applied to ascertain if the terms of IAS 22 have indeed been met.

Indicators that a uniting has not occurred. The presence of certain attributes are presumptive evidence that a uniting of interests characterization would be inappropriate. These include

1. The relative equality in fair values of the combining enterprises is reduced and the percentage of voting common shares exchanged decreases.
2. The financial arrangements provide a relative advantage to one group of shareholders over the other shareholders; such arrangements may take effect either prior to or after the business combination occurs.
3. One party's share of the equity in the combined entity depends on how the business that it previously controlled performs subsequent to the business combination.

The Standing Interpretations Committee has recently offered a further set of observations which supports the notion that true unitings of interests rarely occur in practice. In SIC 9, it is noted that business combinations must be accounted for as either acquisitions or unitings of interests (no hybrid treatments are to be allowed), and that most such transactions are expected to be acquisitions, with only those for which an acquirer cannot be identified qualifying for unitings of interests accounting. The determination of whether there in fact is an acquirer, and whether control exists, should be based on an overall evaluation of all the relevant facts and circumstances. While the criteria in IAS 22 cannot be seen as an absolute checklist, the failure to meet any one of the following would require acquisition accounting treatment to be followed:

1. There is an exchange or pooling of the substantial majority of the voting common shares of the combining entities
2. There is a relative equality in the fair values of the combining enterprises
3. There is a continuation of substantially the same relative percentage in voting rights and interest of the former shareholders of each combining entity in the new combined entity

While the failure to meet these criteria will absolutely necessitate acquisition accounting, the converse is not true. Even if all the foregoing are met, if an acquirer can be identified, the combination will have to be accounted for as an acquisition.

Accounting procedures in respect to unitings of interests. The pooling-of-interests method of accounting should be used to account for unitings of interest. Financial statements of the combining enterprises, for the period of the combination and for any comparative (i.e., earlier) periods shown, should include the assets, liabilities, revenues, and expenses of the combining enterprises as if they had always been combined in fact. No new basis of accounting is established; the bases of all assets and liabilities remains as before the uniting. These rules are essential to the concept of a uniting of interests, which represents that formerly separate entities have merely come together to do in the future as one enterprise what they did separately in the past, without either having acquired or been acquired by the other.

No goodwill or negative goodwill can be created in a uniting of interests. Goodwill is the excess of purchase price over the fair value of net identifiable assets acquired; absent an acquisition, there can be no new basis of accounting established and thus no goodwill. The same applies to negative goodwill, which is merely the excess of the fair value of the net identifiable assets acquired over the purchase price. Once again, no acquisition means no negative goodwill.

Although it is easiest to explain the accounting for a uniting of interests as resulting simply in the combining of all recorded assets, liabilities, and equities, in fact the equity sections of the combining enterprises' balance sheets may require certain adjustments. The reason is that, depending on the legal form of the uniting (e.g., one entity issuing shares for the shares of the other, or a new third entity acquiring the shares of the combining parties) and the par or stated values of the shares of the combining entities, it may be necessary to capitalize some or all of the retained earnings of one or both of the combining companies. In no event, however, can a uniting of interests result in the creation of retained earnings: The immediate postuniting combined balance of retained earnings will be equal to **or less than** the sum of the constituents' retained earnings. Put another way, any difference between the recorded capital accounts plus any additional consideration, and the recorded share capital acquired, should be adjusted against equity.

Any expenses incurred in consummating a uniting of interests should be recognized as expenses when incurred; they cannot be capitalized or adjusted against equity.

Basic example of uniting of interests

To illustrate the essential elements of the pooling-of-interests method of accounting, consider the following balance sheets of the combining entities:

Condensed Balance Sheets as of Date of Merger

	Company A	Company B	Company C
Assets	$30,000,000	$4,500,000	$6,000,000
Liabilities	$18,000,000	$1,000,000	$1,500,000
Common stock:			
$100 par	6,000,000	--	--
$10 par	--	3,000,000	--
$1 par	--	--	1,000,000
Additional paid-in capital	2,000,000	--	500,000
Retained earnings	4,000,000	500,000	3,000,000
Liabilities and stockholders' equity	$30,000,000	$4,500,000	$6,000,000

Company A will issue its shares for those of companies B and C, and both B and C will tender 100% of their common shares. A will give one of its shares for each 15 shares of B stock and one of its shares for each 25 shares of C stock. Thus, A will issue 20,000 shares to acquire B and 40,000 shares to acquire C.

In a uniting of interests, the historical basis of the assets and liabilities of the combining entities is continued. No new basis of accountability is established. The assets of the combined (postcombination) company A will total $40,500,000; total liabilities will be $20,500,000. Total equity (net assets) will, therefore, equal $20,000,000.

While the total stockholders' equity of the postcombination entity will equal the sum of the combining entities' individual equity accounts, the allocation between paid-in capital and retained earnings can vary. Total (postcombination) retained earnings can be equal to or less than the sum of the constituent entities' retained earnings but cannot be more than that amount. Consider the cases of companies B and C.

In the present example, company A issues 20,000 shares of its stock, or an aggregate par value of $2,000,000, to substitute for company B's $3,000,000 aggregate paid-in capital in effecting the merger with company B. Therefore, the combined (postacquisition) balance sheet will include $2,000,000 of par value capital stock, plus $1,000,000 of additional paid-in capital. Even though only $2,000,000 of stock was issued to replace company B's $3,000,000 of aggregate par, there can be no increase in retained earnings and no decrease in contributed capital as a consequence of the uniting.

The Company C merger presents the opposite situation: An aggregate of $4,000,000 of Company A stock is to be issued to supersede $1,000,000 of aggregate par and $500,000 of additional paid-in capital. To accomplish this, $2,500,000 of Company C retained earnings is capitalized, leaving only $500,000 of Company C retained earnings to be carried as retained earnings into the postacquisition balance sheet. In reality, such a situation would not exist. If the pooling of interests took place simultaneously, APB 16 requires only that the combined contributed capital of all entities not be reduced. Therefore, the issuance of 60,000 shares would create an entry on A's books as follows:

Net assets	8,000,000	
Additional paid-in capital	1,500,000	
Common stock		6,000,000
Retained earnings		3,500,000

Note that the additional paid-in capital on the books of Company A is reduced by an amount sufficient to make the total increase in contributed capital of A ($4,500,000), which equals the total contributed capital of both B ($3,000,000) and C ($1,500,000). In this way, all the retained earnings of B and C are transferred to A. This accounting would hold even if A, B, and C simultaneously transferred their net assets to a new entity, D (a consolidation). The opening entry on the books of D would look the same as the consolidated balance sheet of A after the merger, as presented below.

The balance sheet of Company A after the mergers are completed is as follows:

Assets	$40,500,000
Liabilities	$20,500,000
Common stock, $100 par	12,000,000
Additional paid-in capital	500,000
Retained earnings	7,500,000
Liabilities and stockholders' equity	$40,500,000

The historical basis of assets and liabilities is normally continued, but this rule has an exception: Where different accounting principles were employed by the combining entities, these principles should be conformed, where possible, by retroactive adjustment. Prior period financial statements, when reissued on a pooled basis, should be restated for these changes.

If any combining entity has a deficit in its retained earnings, that deficit is continued in the combined entity (and may even be increased as a consequence of the par value changeover, as illustrated above for a nondeficit situation). It cannot be reduced or eliminated as a consequence of the combination.

Any expenses relating to a business combination accounted for as a pooling of interests (e.g., stock registration costs, finders' fees, and costs of preparing stockholders' prospectuses) must be charged against income in the period in which the combination is effected. No new assets can arise from a pooling.

Conforming accounting principles employed by the combining entities. The historical basis of assets and liabilities is normally continued, but this rule has an exception: Where different accounting principles were employed by the combining entities, these principles should be conformed, where possible, by retroactive adjustment. Prior period financial statements, when reissued on a pooled basis, should be restated for these changes.

Reporting on the combined entity. When the pooling-of-interests method is used, it is necessary to report all periods presented on a combined basis. Thus, if only a single year is presented, the effect will be as if the combination occurred at the beginning of that year. If comparative statements are presented, the effect will be as if the combination occurred at the beginning of the earliest year being reported on. This is consistent with the concept of a pooling not being a discrete economic event, but rather as a combining of common interests, such that the most meaningful reporting, **after the date of the combination**, is to present the financial position and results of operations of those entities as if they had always been combined.

The combining entities may have had transactions with each other prior to the combination and may have had amounts due to or from each other at the end of earlier fiscal periods. To present combined statements of financial position and results of operations, all intercompany balances and transactions should be eliminated, to the extent that this is practical to accomplish.

Detailed example of uniting of interests using pooling method

To explain further the applicability of the criteria for applying uniting of interests accounting set forth earlier, a comprehensive example will be developed here and continued in the subsequent discussion of acquisition accounting.

Ahmadi Corporation (whose balance sheet is presented as Exhibit I) is about to merge with or acquire four other entities: Belfast (Exhibit II), Cairo (Exhibit III), Delhi (Exhibit IV), and Eyre (Exhibit V). Some of these business combinations may qualify for uniting of interests accounting; others will have to be treated as acquisitions.

1. The acquisitions will take place as follows:

    a. Belfast is acquired by exchanging one Ahmadi common share for each 15 of Belfast common shares.

    b. Cairo is acquired by exchanging one Ahmadi common share for each 75 of Cairo common shares.

    c. Delhi is acquired by paying $12,750,000 in 90-day demand notes to retire the $13.5 million bank loan, and by exchanging one Ahmadi share for each 20 of Delhi common shares (except as noted in 8. below).

    d. Eyre is acquired by exchanging a new issue of $100 par, 7% preferred stock subject to a mandatory retirement plan (ending in 2000), plus common shares, for all Eyre common stock. Shareholders of Eyre will receive .35 share of Ahmadi preferred for each Eyre common share (total of 175,000 preferred shares), and one share of Ahmadi common for each four Eyre common shares (total of 125,000 common shares). Based on the dividend yield, the preferred stock has been appraised as having a fair market value of about $105.70 per share, or a total of $18,500,000.

2. The appraised value of each acquired firm is given as follows (amounts in thousands):

	Assets acquired	Liabilities assumed	Net asset value (FMV)
Belfast Corporation	$ 78,500	$ 2,500	$ 76,000
Cairo Company, Inc.	42,500	6,500	36,000
Delhi Corporation	111,000	7,500	103,500
Eyre, Inc.	168,000	78,000	90,000

In each case, current assets are appraised to be worth book values according to the acquired firms' balance sheets. Thus, any excess fair value vs. the respective book values is due to values of the entities' plant assets.

3. Eyre originally issued 8% debentures on 1/1/00 at par value. Ahmadi purchased $20.0 million (face value) of these debentures on 1/1/03 at the market

price of $97.60. The discount has been regularly amortized to earnings on a straight-line basis.

4. Investments by Belfast and Cairo in the common shares of Ahmadi Corporation were recorded at cost.

5. Each of the five corporations in question has been in business for at least 5 years, and none has ever been a subsidiary of each other or of any other entity.

6. The acquisition agreement with Cairo provides that if earnings of the acquired subsidiary exceed certain amounts in each or any of the following 5 years, additional shares of Ahmadi will be distributed to former Cairo shareholders. Specifically, for each 50% earnings advance over 2000 levels ($2,800,000 net), an additional 10% of shares are to be issued.

7. The agreement with Eyre provides that the purchase price of $80,000,000 (based on the market value of Ahmadi common shares received, plus the fair value of preferred stock received) is protected against market declines for 2 years subsequent to the merger (i.e., if the value of securities distributed to Eyre shareholders is below $80 million as of 12/31/02, additional Ahmadi Corporation common shares will be issued at that time, in an amount sufficient to bring the total value to the sum stipulated).

8. Holders of 5,000 shares of Delhi stock angrily dissented to the merger plan, and Ahmadi agreed to pay them $75 for each share tendered instead of issuing common stock.

9. Common stocks of the various firms were traded on stock exchanges or were quoted in the over-the-counter market in 1999 at these prices:

	High		Low		Average		Ending	
Ahmadi Corporation	$512		$388		$495		$492	
Belfast Corporation	51	7/8	28	1/2	35	1/4	35	3/4
Cairo Company, Inc.	8	3/4	7	1/2	8		8	1/8
Delhi Corporation	12	1/2	83	1/8	90	3/8	94	1/2
Eyre, Inc.	80	1/2	61		70	1/2	76	

10. Key management personnel of each of the merging entities, except for the directors and officers of Cairo Company, Inc., will continue in important management roles in the new, combined enterprise. The Cairo owners and managers have indicated their plans to retire and, henceforth, to be no more than passive investors in Ahmadi Corporation.

Exhibit I
Ahmadi Corporation
Condensed Balance Sheet
December 31, 2000

Sundry current assets		$ 75,000,000
Plant and equipment, net	$80,000,000	
Investment in Eyre 8% debentures	4,900,000	84,900,000
Total assets		$159,900,000
Sundry liabilities		$ 87,000,000
Common stock, $100 par	$22,500,000	
Additional paid-in capital	12,200,000	
Retained earnings	38,200,000	72,900,000
Total liabilities and stockholders' equity		$159,900,000

Exhibit II
Belfast Corporation
Condensed Balance Sheet
December 31, 2000

Sundry current assets		$ 3,900,000
Plant and equipment, net	$38,500,000	
Investment in Ahmadi common stock (11,250 shares)	9,800,000	48,300,000
Total assets		$52,200,000
Sundry liabilities		$ 2,500,000
Common stock, $10 par	$20,000,000	
Paid-in surplus	14,700,000	
Retained earnings	15,000,000	49,700,000
Total liabilities and stockholders' equity		$52,200,000

Exhibit III
Cairo Company, Inc.
Condensed Balance Sheet
December 31, 2000

Sundry current assets		$ 4,000,000
Plant and equipment, net	$17,400,000	
Investment in Acquisitive common stock (4,500 shares)	3,100,000	20,500,000
Total assets		$24,500,000
Sundry liabilities		$ 6,500,000
Common stock (no par), 3 million shares outstanding	$14,500,000	
Retained earnings	3,500,000	18,000,000
Total liabilities and stockholders' equity		$24,500,000

Exhibit IV
Delhi Corporation
Condensed Balance Sheet
December 31, 2000

Sundry current assets		$12,000,000
Plant and equipment, net		72,000,000
Total assets		$84,000,000
Sundry liabilities		$ 7,500,000
Bank term loan due 2003 (6%)		13,500,000
Common stock, $1 par	$ 1,000,000	
Premium on common stock	3,500,000	
Retained earnings	58,500,000	63,000,000
Total liabilities and stockholders' equity		$84,000,000

Exhibit V
Eyre, Inc.
Condensed Balance Sheet
December 31, 2000

Sundry current assets		$ 50,000,000
Plant and equipment, net		88,000,000
Total assets		$138,000,000
Sundry liabilities		$ 28,000,000
8% debentures due 1/1/2011		50,000,000
Common stock, $10 par	$ 5,000,000	
Paid-in capital	6,200,000	
Retained earnings	48,800,000	60,000,000
Total liabilities and stockholders' equity		$138,000,000

All the foregoing balance sheets are before recording the business combinations.

The first task is to determine which, if any, of the four business combinations qualify for uniting-of-interests treatment. The first company to be acquired, Belfast Corporation, is to be obtained in exchange for only the issuing corporation's shares (which suggests a uniting). Prior to the merger, Belfast does own some of Ahmadi Corporation's shares, but there is no requirement in IAS 22 that prevents some cross-ownership prior to an acquisition or a uniting of interests. In the present instance, Belfast owned 5% of Ahmadi's common stock prior to the transaction, which is not deemed to be a deterrent to pooling accounting.

Of more importance under IAS 22 are such matters as continuity of interests, sharing of risks and rewards, and relative size of the combining parties. In the case of the Ahmadi–Belfast merger, book values are discrepant but not dramatically so ($72.9 million vs. $49.7 million); market values based on recent stock prices are also similar, but a bit less so than book values would suggest ($111 million vs. $72 million). On the other hand, the book value of Ahmadi is very similar to Belfast's fair value ($72.9 million vs. $76 million), which provides some support for the notion that these entities do not have significantly different values. Although this area remains one to which a good deal of judgment must be applied, it would appear that in this instance the relative values are close enough to warrant consideration of the pooling method of accounting. Since Belfast management will remain in place and the transaction is essentially a common stock exchange (with Belfast owners having about 35% of the total shares after the swap, before considering the effects of the other mergers), the conclusion in this case will be to permit designation of this transaction as a uniting of interests.

The Cairo Company, Inc. case is somewhat easier to resolve. In terms of relative market values, there is great disparity between the participants to this transaction ($111 million vs. $24 million), and even if the assessed fair value of Cairo's assets ($36 million) is considered, the gulf is probably too wide to bridge, in terms of satisfying IAS 22 criteria. More obviously, the fact that none of the Cairo owners and managers will continue in active roles belies the notion that there will be true coming together of the constituent parties' interests. Thus, notwithstanding that the former Cairo shareholders will continue as passive investors in Ahmadi, their perspective on the investment will almost certainly differ from that of active participants in the daily affairs of the company.

The Cairo transaction also includes an element of contingent consideration, with former Cairo stockholders eligible to receive additional Ahmadi shares if future earnings are greater than forecast. This does suggest a disparity of risks and rewards as between the two groups of owners, which would make it questionable to use pooling accounting even if the other problems noted did not exist. For all of the foregoing reasons, the conclusion will be that this transaction must be accounted for as an acquisition, not a uniting of interests.

The Delhi Corporation merger involves both cash and stock, raising a possible red flag since unitings of interest are, generally, purely stock swaps among the parties to the combination. However, the "only-stock" rule relates only to that which is issued by the acquirer for the acquired entity's **voting** stock; cash or other means of payment may be given in exchange for other securities (nonvoting equity or debt) of the entity acquired. In this case, Ahmadi gives an interest-bearing note for preexisting debt of Delhi, which does not affect the uniting of interests criteria. Also, the fact that a small minority of Delhi shareholders (owning 0.5% of its shares) are bought out for cash does not have any negative consequences, since this normally occurs in many business combinations of this type. The relative sizes of the combining entities (in terms of market value of stock, $111 million vs. $95 million) are extremely favorable to uniting treatment. Finally, continuity of management makes this combination clearly eligible for uniting-of-interests treatment.

Finally, consider the Eyre, Inc. merger. Common shares of Eyre are being obtained in exchange for a package of preferred and common Ahmadi shares, and additional common shares may be issued in the future if the market value of the shares originally given falls below a specified threshold.

The issuance of preferred stock that is nonvoting is a clear violation of the concept of an exchange of voting interests among the parties to the transaction. Effectively, about one-fourth of the purchase is being made for preferred stock, with the remaining three-fourths being paid for with common stock (based on relative market values of the preferred and common shares). Whether this tainting is sufficient to preclude the use of uniting of interests accounting is a matter of professional judgment, however.

More significantly, the Eyre shareholders are to be given a form of price protection in this transaction. The arrangement is for a remeasurement of the value of the consideration paid (Ahmadi's preferred and common stock) to be made in 2 years, with additional payments owed if there has been a market decline. This effectively means that the Eyre shareholders are not facing the same set of risks and rewards as are the Ahmadi shareholders, and this discrepancy means that this transaction is probably an acquisition, not a uniting of interests.

Furthermore, the market value of Eyre ($38 million) is vastly lower than that of Ahmadi, meaning that these transacting parties are not equals in terms of economic power and will not be equals in future operations of the combined operations. All told, therefore, it is clear that this transaction must be accounted for as an acquisition.

The necessary entries to record the Belfast and Delhi mergers as poolings on Ahmadi's books are as follows:

1.	Sundry current assets	3,900,000	
	Plant and equipment (net)	38,500,000	
	Treasury stock	9,800,000	
	Sundry liabilities		2,500,000
	Common stock, $100 par		13,333,300
	Additional paid-in capital		21,366,700
	Retained earnings		15,000,000
	(To record Belfast acquisition by pooling)		

2.	Paid-in capital	475,000	
	Sundry current assets	12,000,000	
	Plant and equipment (net)	72,000,000	
	Sundry current assets (cash)		375,000
	Sundry liabilities		7,500,000
	Demand note payable		12,750,000
	Gain on retirement of debt		750,000
	Common stock, $100 par		4,975,000
	Retained earnings		58,125,000
	(To record Delhi acquisition by pooling)		

If, instead of a merger, the combination (acquisition) form is utilized, whereby Ahmadi shares are exchanged directly for Belfast and Delhi shares held by the respective stockholders of those companies, Belfast and Delhi will continue their separate existence (albeit as wholly-owned subsidiaries of Ahmadi Corporation). The entries to record the transactions assuming a pooling are as follows:

1.	Investment in Belfast common	49,700,000	
	Common stock, $100 par		13,333,300
	Additional paid-in capital		21,366,700
	Retained earnings		15,000,000
	(To record acquisition of Belfast shares)		

2.	Investment in Delhi common	63,000,000	
	Due from Delhi	13,500,000	
	Paid-in capital	475,000	
	Notes payable		12,750,000
	Cash		375,000
	Gain on retirement of debt		750,000
	Common stock, $100 par		4,975,000
	Retained earnings		58,125,000
	(To record acquisition of Delhi stock, payment of bank loan and retirement of minority shares for cash)		

The purchase accounting entries will be presented in the following section, after the basic elements of this method of accounting for business combinations are discussed. Disclosure requirements for both acquisitions and unitings are set forth later in this chapter.

Acquisition Accounting

In most business combinations, one enterprise gains control over another, and the identity of the acquirer can readily be determined. Generally, the combining enterprise that obtains more than one-half of the voting rights of the other combining enterprises is the acquirer. In exceptional cases, the party that is the acquirer does not obtain over one half of the voting rights; but the identity of the acquirer will be the party that obtains power

1. Over more than one half of the voting rights of the other enterprise by virtue of agreement with the other investors (e.g., voting trust arrangements or other contractual provisions)

2. To govern the financial and operating policies of the other enterprise, under a statute or agreement
3. To appoint and remove the majority of the board of directors or equivalent governing body of the other enterprise
4. To cast the majority of votes at meetings of the board of directors or equivalent body

Other indicators of which party was the acquirer in any given business combination are as follows (these are **suggestive** only, not conclusive):

1. The fair value of one entity is significantly greater than that of the other combining enterprises; in such a case, the larger entity would be deemed the acquirer.
2. The combination is effected by an exchange of voting stock for cash; the entity paying the cash would be deemed to be the acquirer.
3. Management of one enterprise is able to dominate selection of management of the combined entity; the dominant entity would be deemed to be the acquirer.

The major accounting issue in business acquisitons pertains to the allocation of the purchase price to the individual assets obtained and liabilities assumed. In this regard, IAS 22 (revised 1998) has made some modifications to the requirements set forth in the original standard. While previously fair value of acquired assets was to be determined with reference to the intended use by the acquirer (as assets can obviously have alternative values based on intended use. As has traditionally been the case, if the fair value of net assets (i.e., assets acquired less liabilities assumed) is less than the aggregate purchase cost, the excess will be deemed to represent goodwill. If the fair value of net assets acquired is greater than the cost, this difference will be negative goodwill, to be accounted for as specified by IAS 22. In the case of positive goodwill, the recently revised IAS 22 has deleted the former 20-year limit on amortizable life; in its place (to conform with the rules for all other intangible assets, as set forth in recently promulgated IAS 38) is the rebuttable presumption of a life of no longer than 20 years, but the possibility that a longer life (but not an indefinitely long one) can be justified. As for negative goodwill, the former benchmark and alternative treatments have been scrapped, replaced by an entirely new prescription. These matters are dealt with in detail later in this chapter.

Another major change in accounting for business acquisitions mandated by IAS 22 (revised 1998) relates to recognition of certain liabilities which arise as a consequence of the acquisition transaction. Under these new rules, liabilities which relate to the acquiree's business and which arise directly as a consequence of the acquisition transaction, are recorded and will affect the allocation of the purchase price to assets acquired and liabilities assumed, when the acquirer has done all the following:

1. It has, at or before the date of acquisition, essentially developed a plan which involves certain specified resource outflows, such as compensation to terminated employees of the acquiree entity
2. It has raised an expectation among those affected by the plan as a consequence of public announcements or similar overt actions
3. It has developed the plan into a formal detailed plan which meets the criteria of IAS 37 pertaining to restructurings by the earlier of 3 months after the date of acquisition, or the date when financial statements are approved

When the foregoing criteria are met, accrual of certain obligations of the acquiree is required by the acquirer as an integral part of the purchase price allocation process.

If the acquisition form of combination is used, the acquired entity maintains a separate legal and accounting existence and all assets and liabilities remain at their premerger book values. However, when an accounting consolidation is performed (i.e., when consolidated financial statements are prepared), exactly the same results are obtained as those outlined above (i.e., assets and liabilities are adjusted to fair values, and goodwill is recorded). When less than 100% of the stock of the acquired entity is owned by the acquirer, a complication arises in the preparation of consolidated statements, and a minority interest (discussed below) must be computed.

The other major distinguishing characteristic of the purchase accounting method is that none of the equity accounts of the acquired entity (including its retained earnings) will appear on the acquirer's books or on consolidated financial statements. In other words, ownership interests of the acquired entity's shareholders are **not** continued after the merger, consolidation, or combination (acquisition) takes place.

Reverse acquisitions. IAS 22 establishes the notion of reverse acquisitions. These are characterized by an entity issuing shares in exchange for shares in its target acquiree, such that control passes to the acquiree due to the number of additional shares issued by the acquirer. In such cases, notwithstanding the nominal or legal identification of the acquirer and acquiree, for accounting purposes, the enterprise whose shareholders now control the combined entity is the acquirer.

Accounting for acquisitions. The purchase method is to be used to report acquisitions; the transaction is to be recorded in a manner similar to that applied to other purchases of assets. That is, the purchase price must be allocated among the various assets that are obtained, net of any liabilities assumed in the transaction, commensurate with the fair values of those assets. If the price equals the fair value of the net assets, the allocation process will be straightforward, with each asset being recorded at fair value. If the price exceeds the fair value of the net identifiable assets, a goodwill issue must be addressed, as discussed below, since the individual identifiable assets cannot be recorded at amounts greater than their respective fair values. Similarly, if the fair values of the net identifiable assets acquired exceeds the price paid, negative goodwill exists; this is also discussed later in this chapter.

The acquisition should be recognized as of the date it is effected, since this form of business combination is a discrete transaction occurring at a point in time, caused by a change in ownership and resulting in changes in the bases of accountability. The standard suggests that the critical date is that when control of the net assets and operations of the acquired entity is effectively transferred to the acquirer. One important consequence of this rule is that results of operations of the acquiree are included only from the date of the transaction. Financial statements for earlier periods are not restated to reflect the combination (although pro forma results for earlier periods can, of course, be presented for purposes of supplementary analysis).

Acquisitions should be accounted for at the cost paid or incurred. Cost is the amount of cash paid or the fair value of other consideration given to the shareholders of the acquired entity. It includes transaction costs such as legal and accounting fees, investment banking charges, and so on. Depending on the terms of the acquisition agreement, it may include certain contingent consideration as well (discussed below).

Individual assets and liabilities should be recognized separately at the date acquired, if it is both probable that any associated economic benefits will flow to the enterprise, and a reliable measure of cost or fair value to the acquirer is available. In the case of most acquisitions, these conditions will readily be met, since in an arm's-length transaction the parties normally will have knowledge of the price paid and the acquirer would not have consummated the purchase unless all the attendant benefits would flow to it in subsequent periods.

If the fair value of the identifiable net assets acquired is lower than the price paid, the excess cost should be allocated to goodwill (excess of cost over fair value of net assets acquired). If the fair value of the identifiable net assets acquired is greater than the price paid, the excess value should be allocated to negative goodwill (excess of fair value of net assets acquired over cost).

Determining purchase price. In some acquisitions, a package consisting of different forms of consideration may be given. As is often stipulated in accounting rules, the primary measure should be the fair value of any assets given up in the transaction; these may include, in addition to cash, promissory notes, shares of stock, and even operating assets of the acquirer. Except when actual cash is exchanged, fair values may differ from book values. Thus, promissory notes may carry a rate of interest other than a market rate, in which case a premium or discount will be ascribed to the obligation. (For example, if a $10 million, 5% interest-bearing 2-year note is proffered in a business acquisition, in an environment where the buyer would normally pay 8% on borrowed funds, the actual purchase price will be computed as being somewhat lower than the nominal $10 million.)

Similarly, the acquirer's common stock will virtually always have a market value different from par or stated amounts. If there is an active market for the shares, reference should be made to the price quoted, although a small discount might be imputed to reflect the fact that a large offering of new shares would, in a perfect market, have a depressing effect on price. If the market price on any given day is not deemed to be a reliable indicator, the prices over a period of days before and after the announcement of the terms of the acquisition transaction should be considered. If the stock is thinly traded, or not traded at all, or if shares in a listed company are offered with restrictions (not salable for a fixed period of time, etc.), it would be necessary to ascertain a reasonable value, possibly in consultation with investment bankers or other experts. In extreme cases, the fair value of the proportionate interest in the acquired entity's net assets, or the fair value of the fraction of the acquirer's net assets represented by the shares issued would be used as a measure, whichever is more objectively determinable. If dissenting minority shareholders of the acquiree are paid in cash, the price paid may also serve as a reliable indicator of the value of the transaction. Of course, the parties to the transaction, being at arm's length, should also be able to place an objective value on the stock being exchanged, inasmuch as they had negotiated for this price.

If the acquirer exchanges certain of its assets, either operating assets that had been subject to depreciation, or investment securities or other investments assets, such as idle land, for the stock of the acquired entity, again an assessment of fair value must be made. Book value, even if the assets had been adjusted to fair value under the alternative treatment permitted by IAS 16, could not be taken as being fair value for purposes of accounting for the business combination, unless corroborated by other evidence.

If the acquisition is to be paid for on a deferred basis, the cost to be reflected will be the present value of the future payments, discounted at the acquiring entity's normal borrowing cost, given the terms of the arrangement.

Step acquisitions.   In many instances, control over another entity is not achieved in a single transaction, but rather, after a series of such transactions. For example, one enterprise may acquire a 25% interest in another entity, followed by another 20% some time later, and then followed by another 10% at yet a later date. The last step gives the acquirer a 55% interest and, thus, control. The accounting concern is at what point in time the business combination took place and how to measure the cost of the acquisition.

IAS 22 stipulates that the cost of the acquisition is measured with reference to the cost and fair value data as of **each** exchange transaction. In the foregoing example, therefore, it would be necessary to look to the consideration paid for each of the three separate purchases of stock; if noncash, these would have to be valued as described earlier in this section. To the extent that the value of the consideration given differed from the fair value of the underlying net assets, measured at the date of the respective exchange, goodwill or negative goodwill would have to be recognized. Conceivably, successive purchases could be at premiums over and discounts from fair values.

In the example above, the first acquisition results in a 25% holding in the investee, which is over the threshold where significant influence is assumed to be exerted by the investor. Thus, the equity method should be employed beginning at the time of the first exchange and continuing through the second exchange (when a 45%

ownership interest is achieved). Application of the equity method is explained in Chapter 10; one important aspect, however, is that the difference between cost and the fair value of the underlying interest in the net assets of the investee is to be treated as goodwill or negative goodwill and accounted for consistent with the provisions of IAS 22. Accordingly, this needs to be computed and then amortized as discussed in this chapter. The amount of unamortized goodwill (or negative goodwill) at the date of the next exchange transaction should not be merged into the next computation of goodwill, lest the amortization period for the first component be inadvertently extended beyond the limitations of the standard. In other words, each step in the transaction sequence should be accounted for as a separate acquisition.

The only exception to the foregoing requirements would occur if, as permitted under IAS 25, the entire investment is revalued to fair value at the dates of subsequent share purchases. Under this scenario, each revaluation must be accounted for as such, with the appropriate disclosures being made in the financial statements.

When control (majority ownership) is finally achieved (the third step acquisition in the example above), if an accounting consolidation is performed to produce consolidated financial statements, the fair values to be presented for the acquired entity's assets would be an appropriate blending of the fair values as of the various steps in the acquisition. In the present case, for example, using the benchmark treatment specified in IAS 22 (discussed in detail below), 25% of each asset would be reported at the fair value as of the date of the first exchange, another 20% at the fair value as of the date of the second exchange, and the final 10% at the fair value as of the date of the third exchange, with the remaining 45% of the asset stated at cost, that is, at the predecessor entity's carrying value.

Recording the Assets Acquired and Liabilities Assumed

The assets acquired and liabilities assumed in the business combination should be recorded at fair values. If the acquirer obtained a 100% interest in the acquired entity, or if a legal merger were effected, this process is straightforward. As suggested above, if the cost exceeds the fair value of the net assets acquired, the excess is deemed to be goodwill, and capitalized as an intangible asset, subject to amortization. If the fair value of net assets exceeds total cost, the difference is referred to as negative goodwill and is subjected to one of two treatments: either offset against nonmonetary assets, or credited to a liability account and later amortized (these are discussed in detail below).

Determining fair market values. The purchase method requires a determination of the fair market value for each of the acquired company's identifiable tangible and intangible assets and for each of its liabilities at the date of combination. The determination of these fair market values is crucial for proper application of the purchase method. The list below indicates how this is done for various assets and liabilities.

1. **Marketable securities**--Current market values.
2. **Nonmarketable securities**--Estimated fair values, determined on a basis consistent with relevant price-earnings ratios, dividend yields, and expected growth rates of comparable securities of entities having similar characteristics.
3. **Receivables**--Present values of amounts to be received determined by using current interest rates, less allowances for uncollectible accounts.
4. **Inventories**

   a. Finished goods and merchandise inventories--Estimated selling prices less the sum of the costs of disposal and a reasonable profit.
   b. Work-in-process inventories--Estimated selling prices of finished goods less the sum of the costs of completion, costs of disposal, and a reasonable profit.
   c. Raw material inventories--Current replacement costs.

5. **Plant and equipment**--At market value as determined by appraisal; in the absence of market values, use depreciated replacement cost. Land and building are to be valued at market value.
6. **Identifiable intangible assets** (such as patents and licenses)--Fair values determined primarily with reference to active markets as per IAS 38; in the absence of market data, use the best available information, with discounted cash flows being useful only when information about cash flows which are directly attributable to the asset, and which are largely independent of cash flows from other assets, can be developed.
7. **Net employee benefit assets or obligations for defined benefit plans**-- The actuarial present value of promised benefits, net of the fair value of related assets. (Note that an asset can be recognized only to the extent that it would be available to the enterprise as refunds or reductions in future contributions.)
8. **Tax assets and liabilities**--The amount of tax benefit arising from tax losses or the taxes payable in respect to net earnings or loss, assessed from the perspective of the combined entity or group resulting from the acquisition. The amount to be recorded is net of the tax effect of restating other identifiable assets and liabilities at fair values.
9. **Liabilities** (such as notes and accounts payable, long-term debt, warranties, claims payable)--Present value of amounts to be paid determined at appropriate current interest rates.
10. **Onerous contract obligations**--At the present value of the amounts to be disbursed, including any amounts (e.g., plant closures) arising incidental to the acquisition.

IAS 22 explicitly requires that in certain cases, such as for monetary liabilities, fair value be determined by the use of discounting. In other instances, such as for intangible assets, discounting is not explicitly prescribed. However, the standard permits the use of discounting in determining fair values of any identifiable assets and liabilities.

Since aggregate purchase cost is allocated to the identifiable assets (and liabilities) according to their respective fair values to the acquirer, assets having no value are assigned no cost. For example, facilities of the acquired entity that duplicate those of the acquirer and are to be disposed of should be assigned a cost equal to estimated net salvage value, or zero if no salvage is anticipated. In rare instances, however, a **negative** cost equal to the estimated costs of disposal is assigned. It could also be reasonably argued that holding costs should be allocated to assets to be disposed of when debt from the business acquisition is to be paid down from the proceeds of such asset sales. In effect, the value assigned to such assets to be sold would be the present value of the estimated selling price; interest incurred on debt used to finance these assets would then be charged to the asset rather than to interest expense until the disposition actually occurs. On the other hand, if facilities of the acquired entity duplicate and are superior to facilities of the purchaser, with the intention that the latter will be disposed of, fair value must be allocated to the former. Eventual disposition of the redundant facilities of the **acquirer** may later result in a recognized gain or loss. This would fall into the general category of indirect costs of acquisition, which are not capitalizable or allocable to assets acquired in the purchase business combination.

Allocation of Cost of Acquisition When the Acquirer Obtains Less Than 100% of the Acquiree's Voting Interest

When an acquirer obtains a majority interest, but not 100% ownership, in another entity, the process of recording the transaction will be more complicated. The portion of the acquired operation not owned by the acquirer, but claimed (in an economic sense) by outside interests, is referred to as **minority interest**. The accounting issue is whether, in a situation in which goodwill or negative goodwill will be reported, to value it with reference only to the price paid by the new (majority) owner, or whether to gross up the balance sheet for the minority's share as well. In general, an actual arm's-length transaction must take place before a new value can be placed on existing assets and operations (although under IAS 16 revaluations of plant assets can be made). Since the minority did not partake of the acquisition transaction, it can be argued that there is no basis on which to posit any recognition of goodwill for its share of the acquired entity.

The counterargument usually posed is that the majority change in ownership in such a situation is the most objective recent evidence of the value of the acquired enterprise. Furthermore, not to reflect the minority's interest at current market value would be to create a balance sheet having an amalgamation of dissimilar costs, some new, some old. In fact, in some countries the concept of push-down accounting (also known as new-basis accounting) had gained currency, and some regulatory authorities, including the US Securities and Exchange Commission (SEC), demand the application of this form of accounting within very narrowly defined circumstances. Due to the strength of arguments on both sides of this debate, the international accounting standards setters have decided to permit both approaches, as described further in the following paragraphs.

Benchmark treatment. Assets and liabilities recognized are measured at the aggregate of the fair value of the identifiable assets and liabilities acquired as of the date of the exchange transaction, to the extent of the acquirer's interest obtained in the transaction; plus the minority's proportion of the preacquisition carrying amounts of the assets and liabilities of the subsidiary (acquiree). This means that there will be no step up of the minority interest to reflect the valuation indirectly being placed on the enterprise being acquired by the new majority owner.

Under this benchmark approach, the minority interest shown in a consolidated balance sheet will be the minority percentage times the net assets of the subsidiary as reported in the subsidiary's stand-alone balance sheet. Goodwill will be reported to reflect only the excess paid by the majority owner in excess of the fair value of the net identifiable assets acquired. This is illustrated in an example later in the chapter.

The logic of this approach is its adherence to the cost principle. Since the new parent/majority owner has effectively acquired only a fraction of the acquired entity's assets and liabilities, only that fraction should logically be revalued to reflect the purchase price. The remaining fraction, representing the minority shareholders' interests, has not been acquired and therefore should not, under a cost concept approach, be revalued. This method of accounting treats business acquisitions like any other type of asset acquisition.

Allowed alternative treatment. All identifiable (i.e., excluding goodwill) assets and liabilities are recognized at their respective fair values, including those corresponding to the minority's ownership interest. This means that there is a step up in value to equal the valuation being placed on the enterprise indirectly by the new majority owner.

Under this approach, the minority interest shown in a consolidated balance sheet will be the minority percentage times the net assets of the subsidiary as reported in the parent's consolidated balance sheet. Goodwill will be reported, as under the benchmark treatment, to reflect only the excess paid by the majority owner in excess of the fair value of the net identifiable assets acquired. This, too, is illustrated in a later example.

This approach uses the purchase price for the majority interest as an indicator of the value of the entire acquired entity. The strength of this approach is that the acquired entity's assets and liabilities are valued on a consistent basis, presumably using the most recent, objectively determined valuation data. Since international accounting standards recognize the validity of revaluations of certain assets (see the discussion of IAS 16 in Chapter 8 and of IAS 25 in Chapter 10), this approach is not really a conceptual departure from accepted practice.

Example of accounting for a purchase

Continuing the Ahmadi Corporation example begun in the uniting of interests discussion earlier in this chapter, the journal entries to record the purchase of the Cairo Company, Inc. and Eyre, Inc. shares will be presented. Tax effects are ignored in these examples.

Using the fair market value information given earlier and assuming that a legal merger (or consolidation) form is used, Ahmadi makes these entries:

1.	Sundry current assets	4,000,000	
	Plant and equipment	19,080,000	
	Treasury stock	3,100,000	
	Sundry liabilities		6,500,000
	Common stock, $100 par		4,000,000
	Additional paid-in capital		15,680,000
	(To record purchase of net assets of Cairo)		
2.	Sundry current assets	50,000,000	
	Plant and equipment	108,000,000	
	Sundry liabilities		28,000,000
	8% debentures		50,000,000
	Preferred stock, $100 par		17,500,000
	Premium on preferred		1,000,000
	Common stock, $100 par		12,500,000
	Additional paid-in capital		49,000,000
	(To record purchase of net assets of Eyre)		

The value of the Cairo purchase was determined by reference to the latest market value of the Ahmadi shares given ($492 per share). Notice that although the price paid (based on the market value of Ahmadi shares given up) was slightly greater than Cairo's net **book** value ($19.68 million vs. $18 million), it was considerably less than estimated fair value ($36 million, net). In other words, there was an excess of fair value over cost that, in accordance with the procedures specified by IAS 22, was allocated against plant and equipment (the only nonmonetary asset). Had this deficiency been large enough to reduce plant and equipment to zero, any remaining amount would have been recorded as a deferred credit (excess of fair value of net assets acquired over cost) and amortized systematically, like goodwill, over not more than 20 years, unless a longer life could be justified. Implicitly, of course, by offsetting the negative goodwill against nonmonetary assets, it will be amortized over the depreciable lives of these assets.

The total value of the Eyre purchase was $80 million ($61.5 million of common shares, measured at the market value of $492 each multiplied by the 125,000 shares given, plus 175,000 shares of preferred having an approximate value of $105.70 each). The total price exceeded the net book value of Eyre's identifiable assets, although it was still lower than the fair value thereof, so here again there is an excess of fair value over cost (i.e., negative goodwill), and the noncurrent assets are recorded at less than their fair values.

If the shares are to be held by the parent as an investment instead (i.e., the companies are not to be legally combined), the entries by the parent company would be as follows:

1.	Investment in Cairo common	19,680,000	
	Common stock, $100 par		4,000,000
	Additional paid-in capital		15,680,000
2.	Investment in Eyre common	80,000,000	
	Preferred stock, $100 par		17,500,000
	Premium on preferred		1,000,000
	Common stock, $100 par		12,500,000
	Additional paid-in capital		49,000,000

Goodwill and Negative Goodwill

Goodwill. Goodwill represents the excess purchase price paid in a business acquisition over the fair value of the identifiable net assets obtained. Presumably, when an acquiring enterprise pays this premium price, it sees value that transcends the worth of the tangible assets and the identifiable intangibles, or else the deal would not have been consummated on such terms. Goodwill arising from acquisitions must be recognized as an asset and then amortized over a useful life not exceeding 20 years, unless a longer life can be demonstrated. A longer life can sometimes be justified by reference to factors such as the foreseeable life of the business or industry; the effects of physical obsolescence, changes in demand, and other economic factors; the service life expectations of key individuals or groups of workers; any expected actions by competitors or potential competitors; and legal, regulatory, or contractual provisions affecting the useful life. In general, goodwill would have to be related closely to such identifiable assets as a patent or specific productive plant assets such as buildings, if a life longer than 20 years is to be supported.

Under previous IAS, goodwill was absolutely limited to a life of no longer than 20 years, but to conform the treatment of all intangible assets with that prescribed by recently promulgated IAS 38, the new standard imposed by IAS 22 (revised) sets 20 years as the rebuttable presumption of the useful life limit rather than the absolute maximum. The range of factors to be considered in determining the useful life of goodwill has also been expanded to include public information on estimates of useful life of goodwill in similar businesses or industries, as well as the level of maintenance expenditure or funding required to glean the benefits from the business to which the goodwill relates, and the acquirer's ability and intent to achieve that level. While cautioning against placing undue emphasis on these undeniably more subjective factors, IAS 22 (revised) also suggests that when goodwill is closely related to an asset or group of assets having longer lives (e.g., a broadcast license), a longer life may indeed be justified. If a life of greater than 20 years is elected, however, annual evaluations for impairment, consistent with provisions of IAS 37, must be undertaken, and the reasons why the 20-year limitation presumption was overcome must be disclosed.

The amortization of recorded goodwill should be accomplished using the straight-line method in most cases, since it would be unusual, although not inconceivable, to be able to demonstrate a different pattern of expiration of value. Furthermore, the balance in the goodwill account should be reviewed at each balance sheet date to determine whether the asset had suffered any impairment. If goodwill is no longer deemed probable of being fully recovered through the profitable operations of the acquired business, it should be partially written down or fully written off. Any write-off of goodwill must be charged to expense just as normal amortization is. Once written down, goodwill cannot later be restored as an asset, again reflecting the concern that the measurement of goodwill is difficult and proof of its existence almost impossible to develop.

It should be noted that goodwill is recorded, in the case of acquisitions of less than 100%, only for the price paid by the new parent company in excess of the fair values of the net identifiable assets of the subsidiary. That is, no goodwill is imputed to the minority interests based on the price paid by the majority. While under the allowed alternative (see below) the net identifiable assets attributable to the minority may be written up to the values implied by the majority's purchase decision, goodwill will not be imputed for the minority share.

Impairment of goodwill. Assume that an entity acquires another enterprise in a transaction accounted for as a purchase, and that after allocation of the purchase price to all identifiable assets and liabilities an unallocated excess cost of $500,000 remains. Also assume that, when it later becomes necessary to consider impairment of assets, it is determined that the acquired business comprises seven discrete cash generating units. The goodwill recorded on the acquisition (originally $500,000), net of any accumulated amortization, must be evaluated for possible impairment which will require that it be allocated to those of the seven cash generating units which can be identified with the goodwill. For example, it may be that the goodwill is associated with only one or a few of the seven cash generating units, in which case, the goodwill recognized in the balance sheet should be allocated to those assets or groups of assets. IAS 36 describes what are referred to as "bottom up" and "top down" tests, to be applied in such circumstances.

The so-called "bottom up" test compares the recoverable amount of a cash generating unit, including allocated goodwill, to the aggregate carrying amount of those assets. If all goodwill is allocated to operating assets and cash generating units, this "bottom up" test will be adequate to accomplish the goal of testing for impairment.

In some instances, it may not be possible to allocate all goodwill to assets or groups of assets with which cash inflows and outflows can be identified. In such instances, the standard prescribes a so-called "top down" test to be administered. In this testing mode, it is necessary to identify the smallest cash generating unit which contains the unit being evaluated, to which the goodwill can be reasonably and consistently allocated. Having done this, the recoverable amount of the larger unit (containing the unit being evaluated) is evaluated by comparing the recoverable amount to the corresponding carrying amount. If an impairment is detected in this evaluation process, the goodwill will be written down as described in the following paragraphs.

The purpose of prescribing the "top down" test is to ensure that all goodwill presented on the balance sheet gets tested for impairment (if conditions warrant), and that an inability to assign goodwill to a group of operating assets not be a terminal impediment to achieving impairment testing. At some level of aggregation (the extreme case would be to aggregate the enterprise as a whole) it will be possible to compare recoverable amounts with carrying values. A failure to follow this procedure would create the risk that goodwill could be retained on the balance sheet even if it had no further value to the enterprise, thus departing from generally accepted accounting principles in the larger sense, and from IAS 36 in particular. By applying first the "bottom up" and then the "top down" test, if there is no impairment identified during the first phase, it becomes clear that an impairment found during the subsequent testing must be associated with goodwill.

When an impairment is computed for a cash generating asset that includes goodwill, whether as a result of "bottom up" or "top down" analyses, an adjustment will be required. Under the rules established by IAS 36, an impairment loss is first absorbed by goodwill, and only when this has been eliminated entirely are further impairment losses credited to other assets in the group. This is perhaps somewhat arbitrary, but it is also logical, since the excess earnings power represented by goodwill must be deemed to have been lost if the recoverable amount of the cash generating unit is less than its carrying amount. It is also a conservative approach, and will diminish or eliminate the display of that often misunderstood and always suspiciously viewed asset, goodwill, before the carrying values of identifiable intangible and tangible assets are adjusted.

Reversal of previously recognized impairment of goodwill. Regarding the reversal of an impairment pertaining to a cash generating unit that included goodwill, which was recognized in an earlier period, due to the special character of goodwill, IAS has imposed a requirement that, in general, reversals not be recognized for previous write-downs in goodwill. Thus, with limited exceptions, a later recovery in value of the cash generating unit will be allocated to the identifiable assets only. (Of course, the adjustments to those assets cannot be for amounts greater than would be needed to restore them to the carrying amounts at which they would be currently stated had the earlier impairment not been recognized.)

The only exception provided by IAS 36 regarding the restoration of goodwill previously written down or written off due to impairment occurs when the impairment had been the result of a discrete, externally derived event of exceptional nature, which is not anticipated to recur, coupled with the occurrence of a subsequent externally sourced event which reverses the earlier impairment. The standard notes that IAS 38 prohibits the recognition of internally generated goodwill, and further observes that most later recoveries in impaired goodwill will be the result of internally generated goodwill, in effect, replacing the externally acquired goodwill which had previously been written off. Thus, it is very unlikely that goodwill, once impaired, can be restored, since what would otherwise be characterized as a recovery of previously lost goodwill is instead more likely to be newly created, internal goodwill which cannot be recognized under the standards.

Notwithstanding the foregoing, IAS 36 does allow that externally sourced events beyond the control of the reporting entity can occur. Examples of such truly exceptional events would be the imposition of new regulations that significantly curtail the entity's operations, or decrease its profitability. If such regulations were first imposed, then later lifted, it is conceivable that an impairment which resulted in a downward adjustment to goodwill, or its elimination, could later be reversed.

Negative goodwill from business acquisitions. Although the term **negative goodwill** sounds oxymoronic, since goodwill must be a positive good, in many business combinations there is an element of bargain purchase that gives rise to what has become popularly, and now officially, known as negative goodwill. This represents the shortfall of the purchase price paid in a business acquisition vs. the fair value of the net identifiable assets so obtained. It may be indicative of certain future costs that will have to be borne by the buyer to restore the profitability of the acquired operations, or may simply mean that the acquirer has achieved a favorable deal. In any event, this difference between cost and fair value must be accounted for in a manner analogous to (positive) goodwill.

Under the provisions of the original IAS 22 standard, three alternative treatments for negative goodwill were permitted. These included immediately writing off negative goodwill to equity (which would increase stockholders' equity), offsetting negative goodwill against the recorded amount of the nonmonetary assets acquired in the business combination, and amortizing negative goodwill in a manner akin to positive goodwill.

The logic of immediate write-off of negative goodwill is essentially the same as the immediate expensing of positive goodwill. Since the liability is as difficult to explain, if not more so, as the asset goodwill, many accountants and others in the business community believed it would be a more conservative approach to eliminate this item from the balance sheet. However, while immediate expensing of goodwill is conservative in the sense that it minimizes the reported net worth of the acquirer, immediate write-off of negative goodwill increases net worth, and thus can hardly be justified as a conservative accounting procedure.

A more intellectually appealing argument in support of immediately writing off negative goodwill was the capital from consolidation thesis. This held that since the acquiring entity had negotiated a bargain purchase, the financial reporting impact of that action should be reflected at once. The counterargument, however, is more impressive: Entities do not generate earnings or net worth by purchasing assets, but rather, by using those assets in a productive manner. Thus, if negative goodwill indeed represents the result of a bargain acquisition, it should be taken into earnings over the useful period of the acquired assets.

It was the latter argument that led directly to the second proposed method of accounting for negative goodwill--offsetting it against certain assets acquired in the business combination transaction. By reducing the carrying value of such assets, future periods would be relieved of some (or all) of the depreciation charges with which they would otherwise have been burdened. This conforms more closely to the matching concept, which is a basic underlying postulate of accrual basis accounting, as required under the international accounting standards. As originally promulgated, IAS 22 permitted negative goodwill to be offset against nonmonetary assets acquired in the business combination (other standards apply a slight variation to this: under US GAAP, the offset is against noncurrent assets); this continues under the revised standard.

The third alternative treatment is also easily understood, and essentially accomplishes the same matching goal as the second method, above. Just as positive goodwill is recorded as an asset, subject to amortization, negative goodwill is placed on the balance sheet and amortized. The difference is that negative goodwill, having a credit balance, must be grouped with the liabilities, when in fact this does not represent a real obligation at all. Analogies to deferred revenue can be made, and have been, but these have limited appeal, since other deferred revenues represent collections in advance from customers along with the concomitant obligation to perform future services for them or to deliver goods to them in the future. Notwithstanding this conceptual limitation, reporting negative goodwill as a liability and amortizing it over the useful period of the related identifiable assets does accomplish the goal of matching future revenues with related costs. It does so, however, at the price of having "grossed up" the balance sheet, which the previously noted approach has the virtue of avoiding.

The achievement of the 1993 revision of IAS 22 was that the first-named method, immediately crediting negative goodwill to shareholders' interests (equity), was eliminated. The other two methods, recording negative goodwill as a liability and amortizing it over a period of no more than 5 years, (or 20 years if convincing evidence can be accumulated to support that), or offsetting against nonmonetary assets obtained in the acquisition (with any excess recorded as a liability and amortized), remained allowable.

The benchmark treatment under IAS 22 (revised 1993) was to reduce the carrying value of all nonmonetary assets acquired on a pro rata basis. Thus, it was not acceptable to select particular assets to absorb the negative goodwill: Assets that have a short life, such as inventories, had to be credited with proportionately the same amount of negative goodwill as long-lived assets such as building and land. If the nonmonetary assets fully absorb the negative goodwill, any remaining balances in the assets were to be accounted for normally. Thus, inventories would flow into cost of sales as the goods were disposed of, most plant assets would be depreciated over their respective useful economic lives, and some others, such as land, would be carried without modification (unless revaluation accounting is employed, as described in Chapter 8) until the asset was disposed of.

If the aggregate amount of nonmonetary assets, before absorbing negative goodwill, was less than the computed amount of negative goodwill from the business acquisition, these assets were to be reduced to zero, and the remaining, unabsorbed negative goodwill was to be accounted for as deferred income and amortized in the same manner as goodwill (see above).

IAS 22 (1993) also provided for an allowed alternative treatment, under which the negative goodwill was not offset against nonmonetary assets but was reported gross as deferred income. Negative goodwill was to be amortized as discussed above: generally on a straight-line basis, over no more than 5 years, unless a reason can be demonstrated to extend this to as long as 20 years. (Since amortization of negative goodwill **increases** reported earnings, there were typically few reporting entities seeking support for a longer amortization period.)

In the most recent revision to IAS 22 (1998), the accounting for negative goodwill has been substantially altered, combining some features of both the benchmark and alternative treatments found under the preceding (1993) version of this standard. Only a single method is permitted under this recently promulgated requirement. When negative goodwill can be associated with expectations of future losses or expenses identified in the acquirer's plans, and can be reliably measured, but these items do not constitute present obligations to be recorded as liabilities, then the "matching concept" should be applied such that the negative goodwill is amortized to income as these future expenses are incurred. If these costs and losses do not occur as anticipated, or when no such expenses had been anticipated, then negative goodwill should be amortized to income over the useful life of acquired identifiable nonmonetary assets, subject to the limitation that the amount of negative goodwill recorded cannot exceed the allocated cost (fair value) of those assets. Any excess negative goodwill should not be deferred, but rather should be taken into income immediately--which is somewhat of a throwback to the method of crediting stockholders' equity, which was outlawed by the 1993 revision of IAS 22.

An example of the process of crediting negative goodwill to earnings as future planned expenses are incurred could involve a so-called "bargain purchase" of an entity having substantial amounts of inventories. The initial inventory will be recorded at fair value, which is greater than actual cost, and the offset will be credited to negative goodwill. As this inventory is sold, proportional amounts of negative goodwill should be credited to income; the net effect will be to report actual earnings from the sale of the initial inventory consistent with the real bargain cost.

Perhaps the most unexpected change in the rules governing accounting for negative goodwill arises from IAS 22's (revised 1998) requirement that negative goodwill be presented as a negative asset on the balance sheet. While the logic of excluding this from the liability section of the balance sheet is fairly clear, negative goodwill represents no obligation to outside entities to transfer economic resources out from the enterprise, presentation as a deduction from assets will probably cause some level of consternation. However, it is possible to understand negative goodwill as a "contra account" which serves to reduce the assets to actual cost.

One final (and last-minute) amendment to IAS 22 (1998) limits the amount of identifiable intangible assets to be recognized, under certain circumstances. Based on a desire to avoid creating negative goodwill, unless clearly warranted by the fair value amounts being charged to the assets acquired in the business combination, the new standard has decreed that no amount of identifiable intangible can be recorded, if the effect would be to increase the amount credited to negative goodwill, unless the value of the identifiable intangible is supported by an active market. The practical effect of this limit will be to have the recognized amounts of certain intangible assets either reduced or eliminated in bargain purchase situations (e.g., when the acquiree has certain trade names, customer lists, and other real but not actively traded identifiable intangible assets, and it is acquired as a going concern for a price below aggregate fair value).

Contingent Consideration

In some business combinations, the purchase price is not fixed at the time of the exchange, but is instead dependent on future events. There are two major types of future events that can be used to affect the purchase price: the performance of the acquired entity, and the market value of the consideration given for the acquisition.

If the amount of the contingent consideration is likely to be incurred and can be measured reliably at the date of the acquisition, it should be included in the cost of the acquisition. If the contingent consideration is not paid later, adjustments to certain amounts recorded need to be made: The usual effects are to adjust goodwill or negative goodwill, but other assets may need adjustment if negative goodwill was offset against nonmonetary assets according to the benchmark treatment. In other cases, resolution of an uncertainty after the date of the acquisition will necessitate recording contingent consideration, which should be recognized when probable and subject to reliable estimation.

The accounting for subsequent payment of the added consideration, if the effects had not been accrued at the date of the business combination as described above, depends on whether the contingency was related to the earnings of the acquired entity or to the market value of the original consideration package given by the acquirer.

In the former instance (exemplified by the purchase of Cairo Corp. in the example presented earlier), a later payment of added cash, stock, or any other valuable consideration will require revaluation of the purchase price. This revaluation could alter the amounts allocable to noncurrent assets (where cost in the original purchase transaction was less than fair value acquired and the difference was offset against those assets), or could result in an increased amount of goodwill being recognized. The effects of a revaluation are handled prospectively: The additional amortization of goodwill and/or fixed assets is allocated to the remaining economic lives of those items, without adjustment of any postacquisition periods' results already reported.

In the latter case (exemplified by the Eyre Co. merger in the earlier illustration), the event triggering the issuance of additional shares is a decline in market value of the original purchase package. The total value of the purchase ($80,000,000 in the Epsilon case) would not be changed and thus no alteration of allocated amounts would be needed. However, the issuance of extra shares of common stock will require that the allocation between the common stock and the additional paid-in capital accounts be adjusted. Had part of the original price been bonds or other debt, the reallocation could have affected the premium or discount on the debt, which would have an impact on future earnings as these accounts are subsequently amortized.

Consolidated Financial Statements

Requirements for consolidated financial statements. IAS 27 prescribes the requirements for the presentation of consolidated financial statements. Essentially, if one entity controls another enterprise, consolidated financial statements are required, unless certain, rarely met conditions are satisfied. Control is deemed to exist when the parent owns, directly or indirectly through subsidiaries, more than one half of the voting power over an enterprise. It may also exist even absent this level of ownership if the parent has more than one half of the voting power as a result of a voting trust or similar arrangement; the power to govern the financial and operating policies of the enterprise by operation of law or by means of an agreement, the power to appoint or remove the majority of the directors or equivalent governing persons, or the power to cast a majority of votes at the meetings of the directors or its equivalent.

In limited circumstances, a majority owner may not have operating control over an enterprise, and consolidated financial reporting would not be deemed appropriate in such cases. This would be true when control is intended to be temporary, because the subsidiary was acquired with the definite intention to dispose of it in the near future. It would also be valid if the subsidiary operates under severe, long-term restrictions which limit its ability to remit funds to its parent entity. In either of these types of situations, the parent should account for its interest in the subsidiary as set forth in IAS 25 (discussed in Chapter 10).

It had previously been common to exclude subsidiaries from consolidated financial statements on the basis of nonhomogeneity of operations. For example, an integrated manufacturer might have excluded a financing subsidiary from its consolidated financial statements, since (it was argued) the operations were so dissimilar any resulting consolidated statements would have been impossible to interpret. IAS 27 makes it clear that such reasons are no longer acceptable; if the consolidated statements need further explanation for them to be meaningful, supplementary consolidating statements, showing details for each constituent entity, or detailed footnote schedules can be used to satisfy this need.

Intercompany transactions and balances. In preparing consolidated financial statements, any transactions among members of the group must be eliminated. For example, a parent may sell merchandise to its subsidiary, at cost or with a profit margin added, before the subsidiary ultimately sells the merchandise to unrelated parties in arm's-length transactions. Furthermore, any balances due to or from members of the consolidated group at the date of the balance sheet must also be eliminated. The reason for this requirement: to avoid grossing up the financial statements for transactions or balances that do not represent economic events with outside parties. Were this rule not in effect, a consolidated group could deliberately give the appearance of being a much larger enterprise than it is in truth, merely by engaging in multiple transactions with itself.

If assets have been transferred among the entities in the controlled group at amounts in excess of the transferor's cost, and they have not yet been further transferred to outside parties (e.g., inventories) or not yet consumed (e.g., plant assets subject to depreciation) by the date of the balance sheet, the amount of profit not yet realized through an arm's-length transaction must be eliminated. This is illustrated in the following examples.

Different fiscal periods of parent and subsidiary. A practical consideration in preparing consolidated financial statements is to have information on all constituent entities current as of the parent's year end. If the subsidiaries have different fiscal years, they may prepare updated information as of the parent's year end, to be used for preparing consolidated statements. Failing this, IAS 27 permits combining information as of different dates, as long as this discrepancy does not exceed 3 months. Of course, if this option is elected, the process of eliminating intercompany transactions and balances may become a bit more complicated, since reciprocal accounts (e.g., sales and cost of sales) will be out of balance for any events occurring after the earlier fiscal year end but before the later one.

Consistency of accounting policies. There is a presumption that all the members of the consolidated group should use the same accounting principles to account for similar events and transactions. However, in many cases this will not occur, as, for example, when a subsidiary is acquired that uses FIFO costing for its inventories while the parent has long employed the LIFO method. IAS 27 does not demand that one or the other entity change its method of accounting; rather, it merely requires that there be adequate disclosure of the accounting principles employed.

If a subsidiary was acquired during the period or was disposed of during the period, under the acquisition method of accounting, the results of the operations of the subsidiary should be included in consolidated financial statements only for the period it was owned. Since this may cause comparability with earlier periods presented to be impaired, there must be adequate disclosure in the accompanying footnotes to make it possible to interpret the information properly.

Example of consolidation workpaper (date of acquisition, 100% ownership)

The worksheet for the preparation of a consolidated balance sheet for Ahmadi Corp. and its four wholly owned subsidiaries at the date of the acquisitions is shown below. Remember that it is presumed that Ahmadi (the parent) acquired the common stock of each subsidiary; had it acquired the net assets directly (through a legal merger or a consolidation), this **accounting consolidation** would not be necessary.

Except for Eyre, the entries are straightforward and need no further explanation, as they are necessary to eliminate the investment accounts of the parent and the equity accounts of the subsidiaries. Note that there are upward adjustments to the plant and equipment relative to the **acquisitions** of Cairo and Eyre. The **unitings** of Belfast and Delhi result in their book values being carried forward.

The elimination of the investment in Eyre debentures needs explanation. The parent paid $4,880,000 for debentures having a $5 million par on January 1, 2000. The discount has been properly amortized in 2000 and 2001, so that the carrying value at the date of acquisition of Eyre is $4,900,000. Therefore, on a consolidated basis, debt of $5 million has been extinguished at a cost of $4.9 million, for a gain on retirement of $100,000. Since the workpapers shown are only for the preparation of a consolidated balance sheet, the gain has been credited to retained earnings. This gain could also be recorded on the books of the parent, Ahmadi Corp., that would make its retained earnings equal to consolidated retained earnings.

Ahmadi Corporation and Subsidiaries
Workpapers for Consolidated Balance Sheet
As of December 31, 2000

	Ahmadi Corp.	Belfast Corp.	Cairo Co., Inc.	Delhi Corp.	Eyre, Inc.	Elimination entries	Consolidated balance sheet
Current assets	$ 74,625,000	$ 3,900,000	$ 4,000,000	$12,000,000	$ 50,000,000	$ --	$144,525,000
Plant and equipment	80,000,000	38,500,000	17,400,000	72,000,000	88,000,000	1,680,000 [c] 5,000,000 [f]	317,580,000
Investments:							
Eyre 8% debentures	4,900,000					(4,900,000) [g]	
Ahmadi stock		9,800,000	3,100,000			(9,800,000) [b] (3,100,000) [d]	
Belfast Corp.	49,700,000					(49,700,000) [a]	
Cairo Co., Inc.	19,680,000					(19,680,000) [c]	
Delhi Corp.	76,500,000					(25,500,000) [e]	
Eyre, Inc.	80,000,000					(20,000,000) [f]	
	$385,405,000	$52,200,000	$24,500,000	$84,000,000	$138,000,000		$462,105,000
Current liabilities	$ 99,750,000	$ 2,500,000	$ 6,500,000	$21,000,000	$ 28,000,000	$(13,500,000) [e]	$144,250,000
8% debentures					50,000,000	(5,000,000) [g]	45,000,000
Preferred stock, $100 par	17,500,000						17,500,000
Premium on pfd. stock	1,000,000						1,000,000
Common stock:							
$100 par	57,308,300						57,308,300
$10 par		20,000,000				(20,000,000) [a]	
No par			14,500,000			(14,500,000) [c]	
$1 par				1,000,000		(1,000,000) [e]	
$10 par					5,000,000	(5,000,000) [f]	
Additional paid-in capital, etc.	97,771,700	14,700,000		3,500,000	6,200,000	(14,700,000) [a] (3,500,000) [e] (6,200,000) [f]	97,771,700
Retained earnings	112,075,000	15,000,000	3,500,000	58,500,000	48,800,000	(15,000,000) [a] (3,500,000) [c] (58,500,000) [e] (48,800,000) [f] 100,000 [g]	112,175,000
	$385,405,000	$52,200,000	$24,500,000	$84,000,000	$34,500,000		
Treasury stock (at cost)						(9,800,000) [b] (3,100,000) [d]	(12,900,000)
							$462,105,000

Consolidated Statements in Subsequent Periods With Minority Interests

When a company acquires some, but not all, of the voting stock of another entity, the shares held by third parties represent a **minority interest** in the acquired company. This occurs when the acquisition form is employed. A legal merger or consolidation would give the acquirer a 100% interest in whatever assets it obtained from the selling entity. Under international accounting standards, if a parent company owns more than half of another entity, the two should be consolidated for financial statement purposes (unless to do so would mislead the statement users because control is temporary or the businesses are heterogeneous, etc.). The minority interest in the assets and earnings of the consolidated entity must also be accounted for.

When consolidated statements are prepared, the full amount of assets and liabilities (in the balance sheet) and income and expenses (in the income statement) of the subsidiary are generally presented. Accordingly, a contra must be shown for the portion of these items that does not belong to the parent company. In the balance sheet this contra is normally a credit item shown between total liabilities and stockholders' equity, representing the minority interest in consolidated net assets equal to the minority's percentage ownership in the net assets of the subsidiary entity. Although less likely, a debit balance in minority interest could result when the subsidiary has a deficit in its stockholders' equity and when there is reason to believe that the minority owners will make additional capital contributions to erase that deficit. This situation sometimes occurs where the entities are closely held and the minority owners are related parties having other business relationships with the parent company and/or its stockholders. In other circumstances, a debit in minority interest would be charged against parent company retained earnings under the concept that the loss will be borne by that company.

IAS 27 stipulates that minority interest be presented in the consolidated balance sheet separately from both liabilities and stockholders' equity. Accordingly, it will be shown in a separate caption after liabilities, but ahead of equity.

In the income statement, the minority interest in the income (or loss) of a consolidated subsidiary is shown as a deduction from (or addition to) the consolidated net income account. As above, if the minority interest in the net assets of the subsidiary has already been reduced to zero, and if a net debit minority interest will not be recorded (the usual case), the minority's interest in any further losses should not be recorded. (However, this must be explained in the footnotes.) Furthermore, if past minority losses have not been recorded, the minority's interest in current profits will not be recognized until the aggregate of such profits equals the aggregate unrecognized losses. This closely parallels the rule for equity method accounting recognition of profits and losses.

IAS 27 states that income attributable to minority interest be separately presented in the statement of earnings or operations. Generally, this is accomplished by presenting net income before minority interest, followed by the allocation to the minority, and then followed by net income.

Example of consolidation process involving a minority interest

Assume the following:

Alto Company and Bass Company
Balance Sheets at January 1, 2000
(before combination)

	Alto Company	Bass Company
Assets		
Cash	$ 30,900	$ 37,400
Accounts receivable (net)	34,200	9,100
Inventories	22,900	16,100
Equipment	200,000	50,000
Less accumulated depreciation	(21,000)	(10,000)
Patents	--	10,000
Total assets	$267,000	$112,600
Liabilities and stockholders' equity		
Accounts payable	$ 4,000	$ 6,600
Bonds payable, 10%	100,000	--
Common stock, $10 par	100,000	50,000
Additional paid-in capital	15,000	15,000
Retained earnings	48,000	41,000
Total liabilities and stockholders' equity	$267,000	$112,600

Note that in the foregoing, the net assets of Bass Company may be computed by one of two methods.

Method 1: Subtract the book value of the liability from the book values of the assets:

$$\$112,600 - \$6,600 = \$106,000$$

Method 2: Add the book value of the components of Bass Company's stockholders' equity:

$$\$50,000 + \$15,000 + \$41,000 = \$106,000$$

At the date of the combination, the fair value of all the assets and liabilities were determined by appraisal, as follows:

Bass Company Item	Book value (BV)	Fair market value (FMV)	Difference between BV and FMV
Cash	$ 37,400	$ 37,400	$ --
Accounts receivable (net)	9,100	9,100	--
Inventories	16,100	17,100	1,000
Equipment (net)	40,000	48,000	8,000
Patents	10,000	13,000	3,000
Accounts payable	(6,600)	(6,600)	--
Totals	$106,000	$118,000	$12,000

When a minority interest exists, as in this example, the concept employed will determine whether the consolidated balance sheet reflects the full excess of fair market values over book values of the subsidiary's identifiable net assets, or only the parent company's percentage share thereof. Under the provisions of IAS 22, both approaches are acceptable. The benchmark treatment is to recognize a "step up" for only the share of the subsidiary's assets that have effectively been purchased by the parent; thus the subsidiary's assets as included in the parent's consolidated balance sheet will be comprised of a mixture of cost bases: the parent's cost for its share of identifiable assets, and the minority interest's predecessor cost basis for its share of the assets.

The allowed alternative treatment is to record all the assets and liabilities at their fair values as of the date of the acquisition, including the portion represented by the minority interest's ownership share. There will be no mixture of costs for the net identifiable assets acquired in the business combination on the consolidated balance sheet; all items will be presented at fair values as of the acquisition date. Goodwill, however, will be presented only to the extent that the acquirer paid more than the fair values of the net identifiable assets; there will not be any goodwill attributable to the minority interest.

In the present example, Bass's identifiable (i.e., before goodwill) net assets will be reported in the Alto consolidated balance sheet at either $116,800 or at $118,000, depending on whether the benchmark treatment or the allowed alternative treatment is used under IAS 22. These amounts are computed as follows:

Benchmark treatment

Bass Company net assets, at FMV	$118,000	
90% thereof (majority interest)		$106,200
Bass Company net assets, at cost	106,000	
10% thereof (minority interest)		10,600
Total identifiable net assets		$116,800

Allowed alternative treatment

Bass Company net assets, at FMV	$118,000	
90% thereof (majority interest)		$106,200
Bass Company net assets, at FMV	118,000	
10% thereof (minority interest)		11,800
Total identifiable net assets		$118,000

The benchmark treatment will be utilized in the following discussion.

Assume that on January 1, 2000, Alto acquired 90% of Bass in exchange for 5,400 shares of $10 par common stock having a market value of $120,600. The purchase method is used to account for this transaction; any goodwill will be written off over 10 years.

Workpapers for the consolidated balance sheet as of the date of the transaction will be as shown below.

**Alto Company and Bass Company Consolidated Working Papers
For Date of Combination--1/1/00**

*Purchase accounting
90% interest*

	Alto Company	Bass Company	Adjustments and eliminations Debit	Adjustments and eliminations Credit	Minority interest	Consolidated balances
Balance sheet, 1/1/00						
Cash	$ 30,900	$ 37,400				$ 68,300
Accounts receivable	34,200	9,100				43,300
Inventories	22,900	16,100	$ 900b			39,900
Equipment	200,000	50,000	9,000b			259,000
Accumulated depreciation	(21,000)	(10,000)		$ 1,800b		(32,800)
Investment in stock of						
Bass Company	120,600			120,600a		
Difference between cost and						
book value			25,200a	25,200b		
Excess of cost over fair value						
(goodwill)			14,400b			14,400
Patents		10,000	2,700b			12,700
Total assets	$387,600	$112,600				$404,800
Accounts payable	$ 4,000	$ 6,600				$ 10,600
Bonds payable	100,000					100,000
Capital stock	154,000	50,000	45,000a		$ 5,000	154,000
Additional paid-in capital	81,600	15,000	13,500a		1,500	81,600
Retained earnings	48,000	41,000	36,900a		4,100	48,000
Minority interest					$10,600	10,600 MI
Total liabilities and equity	$387,600	$112,600	$147,600	$147,600		$404,800

Based on the foregoing, the consolidated balance sheet as of the date of acquisition will be as follows:

**Alto Company and Bass Company
Consolidated Balance Sheet at January 1, 2000**
(immediately after combination)

Assets	
Cash	$ 68,300
Accounts receivable, net	43,300
Inventories	39,900
Equipment	259,000
Less accumulated depreciation	(32,800)
Goodwill	14,400
Patents	12,700
Total assets	$404,800
Liabilities and stockholders' equity	
Accounts payable	$ 10,600
Bonds payable, 10%	100,000
Minority interest in Bass	10,600
Common stock, $10 par	154,000
Additional paid-in capital	81,600
Retained earnings	48,000
Total liabilities and stockholders'equity	$404,800

1. Investment on Alto Company's books

   The entry to record the 90% purchase-acquisition on Alto Company's books was

Investment in stock of Bass Company	120,600	
Capital stock		54,000
Additional paid-in capital		66,600

   (To record the issuance of 5,400 shares of $10 par stock to acquire a 90% interest in Bass Company)

   Although common stock is used for the consideration in our example, Alto Company could have used debentures, cash, or any other form of consideration acceptable to Bass Company's stockholders to make the purchase combination.

2. Difference between investment cost and book value

   The difference between the investment cost and the parent company's equity in the net assets of the subsidiary is computed as follows:

Investment cost		$120,600
Less book value % at date of combination		
Bass Company's		
Capital stock	$ 50,000	
Additional paid-in capital	15,000	
Retained earnings	41,000	
Total	$106,000	
Parent's share of ownership	x 90%	
Parent's share of book value		95,400
Excess of cost over book value		$ 25,200

   This difference is due to several undervalued assets and to unrecorded goodwill. The allocation procedure is similar to that for a 100% purchase; however, in this case, the parent company obtained a 90% interest and thus will recognize 90% of the difference between the fair market values and book values of the subsidiary's assets, not 100%. The allocation of the cost differential was determined as follows:

	Difference between BV and FMV	x 90%
Cash	$ --	$ --
Accounts receivable	--	--
Inventories	1,000	900
Equipment, net	8,000	7,200
Patents	3,000	2,700
Accounts payable	--	--
Totals	$12,000	$10,800
Less differential between investment cost ($120,600) and 90% of Bass' book value ($106,000)		25,200
Net purchase cost allocated to goodwill		$14,400

   The equipment has a book value of $40,000 ($50,000 less 20% depreciation of $10,000). An appraisal concluded that the equipment's replacement cost was $60,000 less 20% accumulated depreciation of $12,000, resulting in a net fair value of $48,000.

3. Elimination entries on workpaper

   The basic reciprocal accounts are the investment in subsidiary account on the parent's books and the subsidiary's stockholder equity accounts. Only the parent's share of the subsidiary's accounts may be eliminated as reciprocal accounts. The remaining 10% portion is allocated to the minority interest. The entries below include documentation showing the company source for the information. The workpaper entry to eliminate the basic reciprocal accounts is as follows:

Capital stock--Bass Co.	45,000	
Additional paid-in capital--Bass Co.	13,500	
Retained earnings--Bass Co.	36,900*	
Differential	25,200	
Investment in stock of Bass Co.--Alto Co.		120,600

$41,000 x 90% = $36,900

Note that only 90% of Bass Company's stockholders' equity accounts are eliminated. Also, an account called differential is debited in the workpaper entry. The differential account is a temporary account to record the difference between the cost of the investment in Bass Company from the parent's books and the book value of the parent's interest (90% in our case) from the subsidiary's books.

The next step is to allocate the differential to the specific accounts by making the following workpaper entry:

Inventory	900	
Equipment	9,000	
Patents	2,700	
Goodwill	14,400	
Accumulated depreciation		1,800
Differential		25,200

This entry reflects the allocations prepared in step 2 above and recognizes the parent's share of the asset revaluations.

The minority interest column is the 10% interest of Bass Company's net assets owned by outside third parties. Minority interest must be disclosed because 100% of the book values of Bass Company are included in the consolidated statements, although Alto Company controls only 90% of the net assets. An alternative method to prove minority interest is to multiply the net assets of the subsidiary by the minority interest share, as follows:

Stockholders' equity of Bass Company	x	Minority interest %	=	Minority interest
$106,000	x	10%	=	$10,600

The $10,600 would be reported on the credit side of the consolidated balance sheet between liabilities and stockholders' equity.

The benchmark treatment prescribed by IAS 22 was used above to prepare the consolidated balance sheet. If the allowed alternative treatment had been employed, minority interest would have been as follows:

Total fair market value of identifiable net assets of Bass Company	x	Minority percentage	=	Minority interest
$118,000	x	10%	=	$11,800

The example does not include any other intercompany accounts as of the date of combination. If any existed, they would be eliminated to present the consolidated entity fairly. Several examples of other reciprocal accounts will be shown later for the preparation of consolidated financial statements subsequent to the date of acquisition.

If the preceding example were accounted for on a push-down basis, Bass would record the following entry on its books:

Inventories	1,000	
Equipment	10,000	
Patents	3,000	
Accumulated depreciation		2,000
Paid-in capital		12,000

As a result, Alto would have an investment of $120,600 in a company whose net equity was $118,000. Then 90% x $118,000 or $106,200 contrasted with the cost of $120,600 would mean that the only number unaccounted for by Alto would be goodwill of $14,400. The elimination entry on the worksheet would change only with respect to the paid-in capital of Bass as follows:

Capital stock	45,000	
Paid-in capital	24,300	
Retained earnings	36,900	
Goodwill	14,400	
Investment		120,600

This would leave $5,000 of capital stock, $2,700 of paid-in capital, and $4,100 of retained earnings as minority interest or the same $11,800 as under the entity concept.

Example of consolidation for uniting involving minority interest

The foregoing entries are based on the combination being accounted for as an acquisition, using the purchase method of accounting. The same example will now be used to demonstrate the uniting of interests method, using the pooling method, applied to a minority interest situation. Assume the following:

1. On January 1, 2000, Alto Company acquired a 90% interest in Bass Company in exchange for 5,400 shares of $10 par value stock of Alto Company.
2. All criteria for a pooling have been met, and the combination is treated as a pooling of interests.

The workpaper for a consolidated balance sheet at the date of combination is presented below. Note that the first two columns are trial balances of Alto Company and Bass Company immediately after the combination was recorded by Alto Company.

1. Investment entry recorded on Alto Company's books
   The following entry was made by Alto Company to record its 90% acquisition-pooling of Bass Company:

Investment in stock of Bass Co.	95,400	
Capital stock, $10 par		54,000
Additional paid-in capital		4,500
Retained earnings		36,900

Alto Company and Bass Company Consolidated Working Papers
For Date of Combination--1/1/00

Purchase accounting
90% interest

	Alto Company	Bass Company	Adjustments and eliminations Debit	Adjustments and eliminations Credit	Minority interest	Consolidated balances
Balance sheet, 1/1/00						
Cash	$ 30,900	$ 37,400				$ 68,300
Accounts receivable	34,200	9,100				43,300
Inventories	22,900	16,100				39,000
Equipment	200,000	50,000				250,000
Accumulated deprecia-tion	(21,000)	(10,000)				(32,800)
Investment in stock of Bass Company	95,400			95,400a		
Patents		10,000				10,000
Total assets	$362,400	$112,600				$379,600
Accounts payable	$ 4,000	$ 6,600				$ 10,600
Bonds payable	100,000					100,000
Capital stock	154,000	50,000	45,000a		$ 5,000	154,000
Additional paid-in capital	19,500	15,000	13,500a		1,500	19,500
Retained earnings	84,000 a	41,000	36,900a		4,100	84,900
Minority interest					$10,600	10,600 MI
Total liabilities and equity	$362,400	$112,600	$95,400	$95,400		$362,400

The investment entry reflects the capital mix for a pooling of less than a 100% investment. The following schedule shows the mix for our 90% combination accomplished by the issuance of 5,400 shares of Alto Company's $10 par stock:

	Bass Company	Alto Company's percentage share	Alto's share of Bass's equity
Capital stock	$ 50,000	90%	$45,000
Additional paid-in capital	15,000	90%	13,500
Retained earnings	41,000	90%	36,900
	$106,000		$95,400

The $54,000 (5,400 shares x $10 par) in new capital issued by Alto Company represents $45,000 from Bass Company's capital stock and $9,000 of the $13,500 Bass Company's additional paid-in capital. Note that the remaining $4,500 of capital and $36,900 of Bass Company's retained earnings are carried over to Alto Company's books in the combination date entry. The $10,600 of Bass's capital that is not carried over to Alto will eventually be shown as minority interest on the consolidated balance sheet.

2. Elimination entry on workpaper
    Pooling accounting uses book values as a basis of valuation; therefore, no differential will ever occur in a pooling. The reciprocal accounts in a pooling consolidated balance sheet are in the investment in stock of Bass Company account from the parent's books and the stockholders' equity accounts from the subsidiary's books. Again, note that only 90% of the equity of Bass Company is being eliminated; the 10% remainder will be recognized as minority interest. The workpaper elimination entry is

Capital stock--Bass Co.	45,000	
Additional paid-in capital--Bass Co.	13,500	
Retained earnings--Bass Co.	36,900*	
Investment in stock of Bass Co.--Alto Co.		95,400

$41,000 x 90% = $36,900

Consolidation process in periods subsequent to acquisition. Given the foregoing, the following additional information is available in the first year after the acquisition (2000):

1. Alto Company uses the partial equity method to record changes in the value of the investment account. The partial equity method means that the parent reports its share of earnings, and so on, of the subsidiary on its books using the equity method, but any differential between acquisition cost and underlying fair value of net assets, and so on, is not addressed on an ongoing basis; rather, these matters await the typical year-end accounting adjustment process.
2. During 2000, Alto Company sold merchandise to Bass Company that originally cost Alto Company $15,000, and the sale was made for $20,000. On December 31, 2000, Bass Company's inventory included merchandise purchased from Alto Company at a cost to Bass Company of $12,000.
3. Also during 2000, Alto Company acquired $18,000 of merchandise from Bass Company. Bass Company uses a normal markup of 25% above its cost. Alto Company's ending inventory includes $10,000 of the merchandise acquired from Bass Company.
4. Bass Company reduced its intercompany account payable to Alto Company to a balance of $4,000 as of December 31, 2000, by making a payment of $1,000 on December 30. This $1,000 payment was still in transit on December 31, 2000.
5. On January 2, 2000, Bass Company acquired equipment from Alto Company for $7,000. The equipment was originally purchased by Alto Company for $5,000 and had a book value of $4,000 at the date of sale to Bass Company. The equipment had an estimated remaining life of 4 years as of January 2, 2000.
6. On December 31, 2000, Bass Company purchased for $44,000, 50% of the outstanding bonds issued by Alto Company. The bonds mature on December 31, 2003, and were originally issued at par. The bonds pay interest annually on December 31 of each year, and the interest was paid to the prior investor immediately before Bass Company's purchase of the bonds.

The worksheet for the preparation of consolidated financial statements as of December 31, 2000, is presented on the following pages, on the assumption that purchase accounting is used for the business combination.

The investment account balance at the statement date should be reconciled to ensure that the parent company made the proper entries under the method of accounting used to account for the investment. Since the partial equity method is used by Alto, the amortization of the excess of cost over book value will be recognized only on the worksheets.

An analysis of the investment account at December 31, 2000, is as presented below.

	Investment in Stock of Bass Company		
Original cost	120,600		
% of Bass Co.'s income			% of Bass Co.'s dividends
($9,400 x 90%)	8,460	3,600	declared ($4,000 x 90%)
Balance, 12/31/00	125,460		

Any errors will require correcting entries before the consolidation process is continued. Correcting entries will be posted to the books of the appropriate company; eliminating entries are not posted to either company's books.

The difference between the investment cost and the book value of the net assets acquired was determined and allocated in the preparation of the date of combination consolidated statements presented earlier. The same computations are used in preparing financial statements for as long as the investment is owned.

The following adjusting and eliminating entries will be required to prepare consolidated financials as of December 31, 2000. Note that a consolidated income statement is required, and therefore, the nominal (i.e., income and expense) accounts are still open. The number or letter in parentheses to the left of the entry corresponds to the key used on the worksheets presented after the following discussion.

Step 1 -- Complete the transaction for any intercompany items in transit at the end of the year.

(a)	Cash	1,000	
	Accounts receivable		1,000

This adjusting entry will now properly present the financial positions of both companies, and the consolidation process may be continued.

Step 2 -- Prepare the eliminating entries.

(a)	Sales	38,000	
	Cost of goods sold		38,000

Total intercompany sales of $38,000 include $20,000 in a downstream transaction from Alto Company to Bass Company and $18,000 in an upstream transaction from Bass Company to Alto Company.

(b)	Cost of goods sold	5,000	
	Inventory		5,000

The ending inventories are overstated because of the unrealized profit from the intercompany sales. The debit to cost of goods sold is required because a decrease in ending inventory will increase cost of goods sold to be deducted on the income statement. Supporting computations for the entry are as follows:

	In ending inventory of	
	Alto Company	*Bass Company*
Intercompany sales not resold, at selling price	$10,000	$12,000
Cost basis of remaining intercompany merchandise		
From Bass to Alto (÷ 125%)	(8,000)	
From Alto to Bass (÷ 133 1/3%)		(9,000)
Unrealized profit	$ 2,000	$ 3,000

Note: When preparing consolidated workpapers for 2001 (the next fiscal period), an additional eliminating entry will be required if the goods in 2000's ending inventory are sold to outsiders during 2001. The additional entry will recognize the profit for 2001 that was eliminated as unrealized in 2000. This entry is necessary since the entry at the end of 2000 was made only on the worksheet. The 2001 entry will be as follows:

Retained earnings--Bass Co., 1/1/01	2,000	
Retained earnings--Alto Co., 1/1/01	3,000	
Cost of goods sold, 2000		5,000

(c)

Accounts payable	4,000	
Accounts receivable		4,000

This entry eliminates the remaining intercompany receivable/payable owed by Bass Company to Alto Company. This eliminating entry is necessary to avoid overstating the consolidated entity's balance sheet. The receivable/payable is not extinguished, and Bass Company must still transfer $4,000 to Alto Company in the future.

(d)

Gain on sale of equipment	3,000	
Equipment		2,000
Accumulated depreciation		250
Depreciation expense		750

This entry eliminates the gain on the intercompany sale of the equipment, eliminates the overstatement of equipment, and removes the excess depreciation taken on the gain. Supporting computations for the entry are as follows:

	Cost	*At date of intercompany sale accum. depr.*	*2000 depr. ex.*	*End-of-period accum. depr.*
Original basis (to seller, Alto Co.)	$5,000	($1,000)	$ 1,000	($2,000)
New basis (to buyer, Bass Co.)	7,000	--	1,750	(1,750)
Difference	($2,000)		($ 750)	$ 250

If the intercompany sale had not occurred, Alto Company would have depreciated the remaining book value of $4,000 over the estimated remaining life of 4 years. However, since Bass Company's acquisition price ($7,000) was more than Alto Company's basis in the asset ($4,000), the depreciation recorded on the books of Bass Company will include part of the intercompany unrealized profit. The equipment must be reflected on the consolidated statements at the original cost to the consolidated entity. Therefore, the write-up of $2,000 in the equipment, the excess depreciation of $750, and the gain of $3,000 must be eliminated. The ending balance of accumulated depreciation must be shown at what it would have been if the intercompany equipment transaction had not occurred. In future periods, a retained earnings account will be used instead of the gain account; however, the other concepts will be extended to include the additional periods.

(e)	Bonds payable	50,000	
	Investment in bonds		
	of Alto Company		44,000
	Gain on extinguishment		
	of debt		6,000

This entry eliminates the book value of Alto Company's debt against the bond investment account of Bass Company. To the consolidated entity, this transaction must be shown as a retirement of debt even though Alto Company has the outstanding intercompany debt to Bass Company. SFAS 4 specifies that gains or losses on debt extinguishment, if material, should be shown as an extraordinary item. In future periods, Bass Company will amortize the discount, thereby bringing the investment account up to par value. A retained earnings account will be used in the eliminating entry instead of the gain account.

(f)	Equity in subsidiary's		
	income--Alto Co.	8,460	
	Dividends declared--Bass Co.		3,600
	Investment in stock of Alto Co.		4,860

This elimination entry adjusts the investment account back to its balance at the beginning of the period and also eliminates the subsidiary income account.

(g)	Capital stock--Bass Co.	45,000	
	Additional paid-in capital-- Bass Co.	13,500	
	Retained earnings--Bass Co.	36,900	
	Differential	25,200	
	Investment in stock of Bass Company--Alto Co.		120,600

This entry eliminates 90% of Bass Company's stockholders' equity at the beginning of the year, 1/1/00. Note that the changes during the year were eliminated in entry (f). The differential account reflects the excess of investment cost over the book value of the assets acquired.

(h) Inventory   900
     Equipment   9,000
     Patents   2,700
     Goodwill   14,400
        Accumulated depr.   1,800
        Differential   25,200

This entry allocates the differential (excess of investment cost over the book values of the assets acquired). Note that this entry is the same as the allocation entry made to prepare consolidated financial statements for January 1, 2000, the date of acquisition.

(i) Cost of goods sold   900
     Depreciation expense   1,800
     Other operating expenses--
       patent amortization   270
     Other operating expenses--
       goodwill amortization   1,440
        Inventory   900
        Accumulated depr.   1,800
        Patents   270
        Goodwill   1,440

The elimination entry amortizes the revaluations to fair market value made in entry (h). The inventory has been sold and therefore becomes part of cost of goods sold. The remaining revaluations will be amortized as follows:

	Revaluation	Amortization period	Annual amortization
Equipment (net)	$7,200	4 years	$1,800
Patents	2,700	10 years	270
Goodwill	14,400	10 years	1,440

The amortizations will continue to be made on future worksheets. For example, at the end of the next year (2001), the amortization entry (i) would be as follows:

Differential   4,410
Depreciation expense   1,800
Other operating expenses--patent amortization   270
Other operating expenses--goodwill amortization   1,440
   Inventory   900
   Accumulated depreciation   3,600
   Patents   540
   Goodwill   2,880

The initial debit of $4,410 to differential is an aggregation of the prior period's charges to income statement accounts ($900 + $1,800 + $270 + $1,440). During subsequent years, some accountants prefer reducing the allocated amounts in entry (h) for prior period's charges. In this case the amortization entry in future periods would reflect just that period's amortizations.

All the foregoing entries were based on the assumption that the acquisition was accounted for as a purchase. Had the pooling-of-interests method been used, however, book value rather than fair value would have been the basis for recording the accounting consolidation entries. Thus, entry (g) would be different, while entries (h) and (i) would not be made for a pooling. All other eliminating entries would be the same. The basic elimination entry (g) for a pooling, using the equity method of accounting for the investment, would be as follows:

Capital stock--Bass Co.	45,000	
Additional paid-in capital--Bass Co.	13,500	
Retained earnings--Bass Co.	36,900	
Investment in stock of Bass Co.		95,400

In adjusting for the minority interest in the consolidated entity's equity and earnings, the following guidelines should be observed:

1. Only the parent's share of the subsidiary's shareholders' equity is eliminated in the basic eliminating entry. The minority interest's share is presented separately.
2. The entire amount of intercompany reciprocal items is eliminated. For example, all receivables/payables and sales/cost of sales with a 90% subsidiary are eliminated.
3. For intercompany transactions in inventory and fixed assets, the possible effect on minority interest depends on whether the original transaction affected the subsidiary's income statement. Minority interest is adjusted only if the subsidiary is the selling entity. In this case, the minority interest is adjusted for its percentage ownership of the common stock of the subsidiary. The minority interest is not adjusted for unrealized profits on downstream sales. The effects of downstream transactions are confined solely to the parent's (i.e., controlling) ownership interests.

The minority interest's share of the subsidiary's income is shown as a deduction on the consolidated income statement since 100% of the sub's revenues and expenses are combined, even though the parent company owns less than a 100% interest. For our example, the minority interest deduction on the income statement is computed as follows:

Bass Company's reported income	$9,400
Less unrealized profit on an upstream inventory sale	(2,000)
Bass Company's income for consolidated financial purposes	$7,400
Minority interest share	x 10%
Minority interest on income statement	$ 740

The minority interest's share of the net assets of Bass Company is shown on the consolidated balance sheet between liabilities and controlling interest's equity. The computation for the minority interest shown in the balance sheet for our example is as follows:

Bass Company's capital stock, 12/31/00	$50,000	
Minority interest share	x 10%	$ 5,000
Bass Company's additional paid-in capital, 12/31/00	$15,000	
Minority interest share	x 10%	1,500
Bass Company's retained earnings, 1/1/00	$41,000	
Minority interest share	x 10%	4,100
Bass Company's 2000 income for consolidated purposes	$ 7,400	
Minority interest share	x 10%	740
Bass Company's dividends during 2000	$ 4,000	
Minority interest share	x 10%	(400)
Total minority interest, 12/31/00		$10,940

Alto Company and Bass Company Consolidated Working Papers
Year Ended December 31, 2000

Purchase Accounting
90% Owned Subsidiary
Subsequent Year, Partial Equity Method

	Alto Company	Bass Company	Adjustments and eliminations Debit	Credit	Minority interest	Consolidated balances
Income statements for year ended 12/31/00						
Sales	$750,000	$420,000	$ 38,000[a]			$1,132,000
Cost of sales	581,000	266,000	5,000[b] 900[i]	$ 38,000[a]		814,900
Gross margin	169,000	154,000				317,100
Depreciation and interest expense	28,400	16,200	1,800[i]	750[d]		45,650
Other operating expenses	117,000	128,400	1,710[i]			247,110
Net income from operations	23,600	9,400				24,340
Gain on sale of equipment	3,000		3,000[d]			
Gain on bonds				6,000[e]		6,000
Equity in subsidiary's income	8,460		8,460[f]			
Minority income ($7,400 x .10)					$ 740	(740)
Net income	$ 35,060	$ 9,400	$ 58,870	$ 44,750	$ 740	$ 29,600
Statement of retained earnings for year ended 12/31/00						
1/1/00 retained earnings						
Alto Company	$ 48,000					$ 48,000
Bass Company		$ 41,000	$ 36,900[g]		$ 4,100	
Add net income (from above)	35,060	9,400	58,870	$ 44,750	740	29,600
Total	83,060	50,400			4,840	77,600
Deduct dividends	15,000	4,000		3,600[f]	400	15,000
Balance, 12/31/00	$ 68,060	$ 46,400	$ 95,770	$ 48,350	$ 4,440	$ 62,600

	Alto Company	Bass Company	Adjustments and eliminations Debit	Adjustments and eliminations Credit	Minority interest	Consolidated balances
Cash	$ 45,300	$ 6,400	$ 1,000[l]			$ 52,700
Accounts receivable (net)	43,700	12,100		$ 1,000[l] 4,000[c]		50,800
Inventories	38,300	20,750	900[h]	5,000[b] 900[i]		54,050
Equipment	195,000	57,000	9,000[h]	2,000[d]		259,000
Accumulated depreciation	(35,200)	(18,900)		250[d] 1,800[h] 1,800[i]		(57,950)
Investment in stock of Bass Company	125,460			4,860[f] 120,600[g]		
Differential			25,200[g]	25,200[h]		
Goodwill			14,400[h]	1,440[i]		12,960
Investment in bonds of Alto Company		44,000		44,000[e]		
Patents		9,000	2,700[h]	270[i]		11,430
	$412,560	$130,350				$382,990
Accounts payable	$ 8,900	$ 18,950	4,000[c]			$ 23,850
Bonds payable	100,000		50,000[e]			50,000
Capital stock	154,000	50,000	45,000[g]		$ 5,000	154,000
Additional paid-in capital	81,600	15,000	13,500[g]		1,500	81,600
Retained earnings (from above)	68,060	46,400	95,770	48,350	4,440	62,600
Minority interest					$10,940	10,940
	$412,560	$130,350 $261,470		$261,470		$382,990

The remainder of the consolidation process consists of the following worksheet techniques:

1. Take all income items across horizontally, and foot the adjustments, minority interest, and consolidated columns down to the net income line.
2. Take the amounts on the net income line (on income statement) in the adjustments, minority interest, and consolidated balances columns down to retained earnings items across the consolidated balances column. Foot and crossfoot the retained earnings statement.
3. Take the amounts of ending retained earnings in each of the four columns down to the ending retained earnings line in the balance sheet. Foot the minority interest column and place its total in the consolidated balances column. Take all the balance sheet items across to consolidated balances column.

Other Accounting Issues Arising in Business Combinations

Depending on the tax jurisdiction, an acquirer may or may not succeed to the available tax loss carryforward benefits of an acquired entity. International accounting standards (IAS 12, revised, addressed in detail in Chapter 15) now require that a liability approach be used in accounting for the tax effects of temporary differences, which includes the tax effects of tax loss carryforwards. If an acquirer is permitted to use the predecessor's tax benefits, the amount to be reflected in its balance sheet will be measured in accordance with IAS 12, which is the amount of the benefits expected to be realized. As expectations change over time, this amount will be amended, with any such adjustments being taken into tax expense of the period in which expectations change. If the acquirer can only utilize the benefits to offset taxes on earnings of the operations acquired (i.e., it cannot shelter other sources of earnings), it will be necessary to project profitable operations to support recording this benefit as an asset.

Subsequent identification of, or changes in value of, assets and liabilities acquired. IAS 22 stipulates that individual assets and liabilities should be recorded in an acquisition to the extent that it is probable that any associated future economic benefits will flow to the acquirer and a reliable measure is available of the cost or fair values. In some cases, due to one or both of these criteria not being met at the date of the transaction, some assets or liabilities may not be recognized (which would normally have the ramification that goodwill or negative goodwill would be adjusted accordingly).

If new information becomes available after the date of the acquisition regarding the existence or the fair value of acquired assets or the amount of liabilities, it will be necessary to make an adjustment to some of the recorded amounts. IAS 22 sets as a time limit, however, the end of the first annual accounting period after the acquisition for any reallocation from goodwill or negative goodwill to other assets or liabilities. If such information becomes available after that date, the adjustment must be made to current period income or expense. The reason for this requirement is to avoid having changes made to goodwill or negative goodwill over an unlimited time horizon.

Changes in majority interest. The parent's ownership interest can change as a result of purchases or sales of the subsidiary's common shares by the parent or as a consequence of capital transactions of the subsidiary. The latter circumstance is generally handled precisely as demonstrated in the equity method discussion in Chapter 10. If the parent's relative book value interest in the subsidiary has changed, gains or losses are treated as incurred in an entity's own treasury stock transactions. Gains are credited to paid-in capital; losses are charged to any paid-in capital or to retained earnings created previously.

When the parent's share of ownership increases through a purchase of additional stock, simply debit investment and credit cash for the cost. A problem occurs with consolidated income statements when the change in ownership takes place in midperiod. Consolidated statements should be prepared based on the ending ownership level.

Example of a consolidation with a change in the majority interest

Assume that Alto Company increased its ownership of Bass Company from 90% to 95% on October 1, 2000. The investment was acquired at book value of $5,452.50 and is determined as follows:

Retained earnings at 10/1/00		$50,000
Additional paid-in capital, 10/1/00		15,000
Retained earnings at 10/1/00		
Balance, 1/1/00	$41,000	
Net income for 9 months ($9,400 x .75)	7,050*	
Preacquisition dividends	(4,000)	44,050
		$ 109,050
		x 5%
Book value acquired		$5,452.50

* Assumes income was earned evenly over the year.

The consolidated net income should reflect a net of

90%	x	$9,400	x	12/12	=	$8,460.00
5%	x	$9,400	x	3/12	=	117.50
95%						$8,577.50

The interim stock purchase will result in a new account being shown on the consolidated income statement. The account is **purchased preacquisition earnings**, which represents the percentage of the subsidiary's income earned, in this case, on the 5% stock interest from January 1, 2000, to October 1, 2000. The basic eliminating entries would be based on the 95% ownership as follows:

Equity in subsidiary's income--Alto Co.	8,577.50	
Dividends declared--Bass Co.		3,600.00
Investment in stock of Bass Co.		4,977.50
Capital stock--Bass Co.	47,500.00	
Additional paid-in capital--Bass Co.	14,250.00	
Retained earnings--Bass Co.	38,750.00**	
Purchased preacquisition earnings	352.50***	
Differential	25,200.00	
Investment in stock of Bass Co.--Alto Co.		126,052.50

** 95% x $41,000 beginning 1999 balance	$38,950
Less preacquisition dividend of 5% x $4,000	(200)
Retained earnings available, as adjusted	$38,750
*** 5% x $9,400 x 9/12 = $352.50*	

Purchased preacquisition earnings is shown as a deduction, along with minority interest, to arrive at consolidated net income. Purchased preacquisition earnings are used only with interim acquisition under the purchase accounting method; all poolings are assumed to take place at the beginning of the period regardless of when, during the period, the acquisition was actually made.

Combined Financial Statements

When a group of entities is under common ownership, control, or management, it is often useful to present combined (or combining, showing the separate as well as the combined entities) financial statements. In this situation, the economic substance of the nominally independent entities' operations may be more important to statement users than is the legal form of those enterprises. When consolidated statements are not presented, combined statements may be used to show the financial position, or operating results, of a group of companies that are each subsidiaries of a common parent.

The process of preparing combined statements is virtually the same as consolidations employing the pooling-of-interests method. The major exception is that the equity section of the combined balance sheet will incorporate the paid-in capital accounts of each of the combining entities. However, only a single combined retained earnings account need be presented.

Example of a combined financial statement

Adams Corporation and Benbow Company, Inc.
Combined Balance Sheet
December 31, 2000

Stockholders' equity
  Capital stock:

Preferred, $100 par, authorized 90,000 shares, issued 5,000 shares	$ 500,000
Common, $50 par, authorized 100,000 shares, issued 60,000 shares	3,000,000
Common, $10 par, authorized 250,000 shares, issued 100,000 shares	1,000,000
Additional paid-in capital	650,000
Retained earnings	3,825,000
	$8,975,000

Combinations of Entities Under Common Control

IAS 22 explicitly does **not** apply to entities under common control (e.g., brother-sister corporations). However, logic suggests that mergers among such affiliated entities must be accounted for "as if" poolings. This treatment is consistent with the concept of poolings as combinations of common shareholder interests. A question arises, however, when a parent (Company P) transfers ownership in one of its subsidiaries (Company B) to another of its subsidiaries (Company A) in exchange for additional shares of Company A. In such an instance, A's carrying value for the investment in B should be P's basis, not B's book value. Furthermore, if A subsequently retires the interests of minority owners of B, the transaction should be accounted for as a purchase, whether it is effected through a stock issuance by A or by a cash payment to the selling shareholders.

Furthermore, when a purchase transaction is closely followed by a sale of the parent's subsidiary to the newly acquired (target) entity, these two transactions should be viewed as a single transaction. Accordingly, the parent should recognize gain or loss on the sale of its subsidiary to the target company, to the extent of minority interest in the target entity. As a result, there will be a new basis (step up) not only for the target company's assets and liabilities, but also for the subsidiary company's net assets. Basis is stepped up to the extent of minority participation in the target entity to which the subsidiary company was transferred.

A related issue having to do with entities under common control arises when one enterprise has been created solely or largely for the purpose of accommodating the other's need for financing or for obtaining capital assets. The objective may be to effect a lease, conduct research and development activities, or to securitize financial assets, among others. Entities created for reasons such as these are known as "special purpose entities," and they have often been used to escape from lease capitalization or other financial reporting requirements which the sponsoring enterprise wishes to evade. While there are often legitimate (i.e., not financial reporting driven) reasons for the use of special purpose entities (SPE), at least a side effect, if not the main one, is that the sponsoring entity's apparent financial strength (e.g., leverage) will be distorted.

In many instances an adroitly structured SPE will not be owned, or majority owned, by the true sponsor. Were ownership the only criterion for determining whether entities need to be consolidated for financial reporting purposes, this factor could result in a "form over substance" decision to not consolidate the SPE with its sponsor. However, under the provisions of SIC 12, ownership is not the critical element in determining the need for consolidation, rather, "beneficial interest" is used. Beneficial interest can take various forms, including ownership of debt instruments, or even a lease relationship.

SIC 12 states that consolidation of an SPE should be effected if the substance of its relationship with another entity indicates that it is effectively controlled by the other entity. Control can derive from the nature of the predetermined activities of the SPE (what the interpretation refers to as being on "autopilot"), and emphatically can exist even when the sponsor has less than a majority interest in the SPE. SIC 12 specifically notes that the following conditions would suggest that the sponsor controls the SPE:

1. The activities of the SPE are conducted so as to provide the sponsor with the benefits thereof;
2. The sponsor in substance has decision making powers to obtain most of the benefits of the SPE, or else an autopilot mechanism has been established such that the decision making powers have been delegated;
3. The sponsor has the right to obtain the majority of the benefits of the SPE and consequently is exposed to risks inherent in the SPE's activities; or
4. The sponsor retains the majority of the residual or ownership risks of the SPE or its assets, in order to obtain the benefits of the SPE's activities.

SIC 12 is particularly concerned that so-called autopilot arrangements may have been put into place specifically to confuse the control issue. It cautions that although difficult to assess in some situations, control is to be attributed to the enterprise having the principal beneficial interest. The entity which arranged the autopilot mechanism would generally have had, and continue to have, control. Consolidation with the sponsor for financial reporting purposes would accordingly be indicated. SIC 12 offers a number of examples of conditions which would be strongly indicative of control and thus of a need to consolidate the SPE's financial statements with those of its sponsor.

Accounting for Leveraged Buyouts

Possibly one of the most complex accounting issues to have arisen over the past decade has been the appropriate accounting for leveraged buyouts (LBO). At the center of this issue is the question of whether a new basis of accountability has been created by the LBO transaction. If so, a step up in the reported value of assets and/or liabilities is warranted. If not, the carryforward bases of the predecessor entity should continue to be reported in the company's financial statements.

International accounting standards do not address this issue directly. However, guidance can be obtained from the decisions made by the standard setters in the United States, which have dealt with this question. Although this guidance is not definitive, it is instructive.

The conclusion was that partial or complete new-basis accounting is appropriate only when the transaction is characterized by a change in control of voting interest. A series of mechanical tests were developed by which this change in interest is to be measured. The EITF identified three groups of interests: shareholders in the newly created company, management, and shareholders in the old company (who may or may not also have an interest in the new company). Depending on the relative interests of these groups in the old entity (OLDCO) and in the new enterprise (NEWCO), there will be either (1) a finding that the transaction was a purchase (new-basis accounting applies), or (2) that it was a recapitalization or a restructuring (carryforward basis accounting applies).

Among the tests decreed to determine proper accounting for any given LBO transaction is the **monetary test**. This test requires that at least 80% of the net consideration paid to acquire OLDCO interests must be monetary. In this context, monetary means cash, debt, and the fair value of any equity securities given by NEWCO to selling shareholders of OLDCO. Loan proceeds provided by OLDCO to assist in the acquisition of NEWCO shares by NEWCO shareholders are excluded from this definition. If the portion of the purchase that is effected through monetary consideration is less than 80%, but other criteria are satisfied, there will be a step up. This step up will be limited to the percentage of the transaction represented by monetary consideration.

US GAAP guidance also presents an extensive series of examples illustrating the circumstances that would and would not meet the purchase accounting criteria to be employed in LBO. These examples should be consulted as needed when addressing an actual LBO transaction accounting issue.

Spin-Offs

Occasionally, an entity disposes of a wholly or partially owned subsidiary or of an investee by transferring it unilaterally to the entity's shareholders. The proper accounting for such a transaction, generally known as a spin-off, depends on the percentage of the company that is owned.

If the ownership percentage is relatively minor, 25% for example, the transfer to stockholders would be viewed as a **dividend in kind** and would be accounted for at the fair value of the property (i.e., shares in the investee) transferred.

However, when the entity whose shares are distributed is majority or wholly owned, the effect is not merely to transfer a passive investment, but to remove the operations from the former parent and to vest them with the parent's shareholders. This transaction is a true spin-off transaction, not merely a property dividend. Although international accounting standards have not addressed this matter, as a point of reference, US GAAP requires that spin-offs and similar nonreciprocal transfers to owners be accounted for at the recorded book values of the assets and liabilities transferred.

If the operations (or subsidiary) being spun off are distributed during a fiscal period, it may be necessary to estimate the results of operations for the elapsed period prior to spin-off to ascertain the net book value as of the date of the transfer. Stated another way, the operating results of the subsidiary to be disposed of should be included in the reported results of the parent through the actual date of the spin-off.

In most instances, the subsidiary being spun off will have a positive net book value. This net worth represents the cost of the nonreciprocal transfer to the owners, and like a dividend, will be reflected as a charge against the parent's retained earnings at the date of spin-off. In other situations, the operations (or subsidiary) will have a net deficit (negative net book value). Since it is unacceptable to recognize a credit to the parent's retained earnings for other than a culmination of an earnings process, the spin-off should be recorded as a credit to the parent's paid-in capital. In effect, the stockholders (the recipients of the spun-off subsidiary) have made a capital contribution to the parent company by accepting the operations having a negative book value. As with other capital transactions, this would **not** be presented in the income statement, only in the statement of changes in stockholders' equity (and in the statement of cash flows).

Push-Down Accounting

Push-down accounting is an unresolved issue in accounting for an entity that has had a substantial change in the ownership of its outstanding voting shares. This technique reflects the revaluation of the assets and/or liabilities of the acquired company (on its books) based on the price paid for some or all of its shares by the acquirer. Push-down accounting has no impact on the presentation of consolidated financial statements or on the separate financial statements of the parent (investor) company. These financial statements are based on the price paid for the acquisition, not on the acquired entity's book value. However, the use of this accounting technique represents a departure in the way separate financial statements of the acquired entity are presented.

Advocates of push-down accounting point out that in a purchase business combination, a new basis of accounting is established. They believe that the new basis should be pushed down to the acquired entity and should be used when presenting its own separate financial statements.

While the push-down treatment has been used by a number of entities whose shares have been purchased by others, the entire area of push-down accounting remains controversial and without clear authoritative guidance. Although push-down makes some sense in the case where a major block of the investee's shares is acquired in a single free-market transaction, a series of step transactions would require continual adjustment of the investee's carrying values for assets and liabilities. Furthermore, the price paid for a fractional share of ownership of an investee may not always be meaningfully extrapolated to a value for the investee company as a whole.

Non-Sub Subsidiaries

An issue that has recently concerned accountants is the sudden popularity of what have been called **non-sub subsidiaries**. This situation arises when an entity plays a major role in the creation and financing of what is often a start-up or experimental operation but does not take an equity position at the outset. For example, the parent might finance the entity by means of convertible debt or debt with warrants for the later purchase of common shares. The original equity partner in such arrangements most often will be the creative or managerial talent, that generally exchanges its talents for a stock interest. If the operation prospers, the parent will exercise its rights to a majority voting stock position; if it fails, the parent presumably avoids reflecting the losses in its statements.

Although this strategy may seem to avoid the requirements of equity accounting or consolidation, the economic substance clearly suggests that the operating results of the subsidiary should be reflected in the financial statements of the real parent, even absent stock ownership. Until formal requirements are established in this area, an approach akin to the preparation of combined statements would seem reasonable.

Disclosure Requirements

Business combinations. For all business combinations, the following disclosures are required in the financial statements for the year in which the transaction occurs:

1. The name and descriptions of combining enterprises
2. The methods of accounting for the combinations
3. The effective date of the combinations, for accounting purposes
4. The identity of any operations resulting from the combination that are intended for disposition

For business combinations accounted for as acquisitions, the following disclosures are required:

1. The percentage of voting interests acquired
2. The cost of the acquisitions, and a description of consideration paid or contingently payable
3. The nature and amount of provisions for any restructuring or plant closure expenses arising as a result of any acquisitions, and recognized as of the date of the acquisitions

Furthermore, the financial statements should disclose the following:

1. The accounting treatment for goodwill and negative goodwill, including amortization periods
2. Justification for amortization periods greater than 5 years, if applicable
3. Description of and justification for amortization of goodwill or negative goodwill by other than the straight-line method
4. A reconciliation, with respect to both goodwill and negative goodwill, at the beginning and the end of the period, showing:

    a. The gross amount and accumulated amortization at the beginning of the period
    b. Any additional goodwill or negative goodwill recorded during the period
    c. Amortization recorded during the period
    d. Any adjustments resulting from the subsequent identification or changes in value of assets and liabilities
    e. Any other write-offs during the period
    f. The gross amount and accumulated amortization at year end

If the allocation of the purchase price to assets and liabilities is only made on a provisional basis, this fact must be disclosed, with the reasons therefor noted. When these matters are later resolved, this should also be disclosed.

For business combinations that are unitings of interests, the following disclosures are required in the period in which the event occurs:

1. A description of the shares issued, together with the percentages of each combining entity's voting shares exchanged to effect the uniting of interests
2. The amounts of assets and liabilities contributed by each constituent enterprise
3. Sales revenue, other operating revenues, extraordinary items, and net profit or loss of each enterprise prior to the date of the combination, which are included in the combined financial statements

If a business combination is effected **after** the balance sheet date, the foregoing disclosures should be made if practical, but the transaction should not be accounted for as if it had occurred prior to year end.

Consolidated financial statements. IAS 27 requires that for consolidated financial reporting, the names, countries of incorporation or residence, proportion of ownership interests, and if different, voting interests held be disclosed for all significant subsidiaries.

If any subsidiary is not included in the consolidated financial statements, the reasons must be set forth. If an entity over which the parent does not have majority voting control is included in the consolidated financial statements, the reasons for this must also be explained.

If a subsidiary was acquired or disposed of during the period, the effect of the event on the consolidated financial statements should be discussed. If parent-only financial statements are being presented (which is permitted, but not as a substitute for consolidated financial reporting), the method of accounting for interests in subsidiaries should be stated.

12 CURRENT LIABILITIES, PROVISIONS, CONTINGENCIES, AND EVENTS AFTER THE BALANCE SHEET DATE

PERSPECTIVE AND ISSUES

The division of assets and liabilities into current and noncurrent allows working capital (current assets minus current liabilities) to be calculated. Working capital, which is the relatively liquid portion of total enterprise capital, can be used to determine the ability of an enterprise to repay obligations. Working capital assumes a going-concern concept. If the enterprise is to be liquidated in the near future, classification of assets and liabilities is inappropriate.

Current liabilities are those enterprise obligations whose liquidation is reasonably expected to require the use of existing resources properly classifiable as current assets or the creation of other current liabilities. This definition excludes from the current liability classification any currently maturing obligations that will be satisfied by using long-term assets and currently maturing obligations expected to be refinanced.

Offsetting of assets and liabilities is improper except where a right of setoff exists. A right of setoff is a debtor's legal right to discharge debt owed to another party by applying against the debt an amount the other party owes to the debtor.

The subject of contingencies (assets or liabilities whose ultimate outcome will be determined by future events) was initially dealt with by IAS 10, which also addresses post-balance-sheet events. The portion of that standard relating to contingencies has recently been superseded by a comprehensive new standard, IAS 37, which pertains to provisions, contingent liabilities and contingent assets. The new standard is effective for annual financial statements covering periods beginning on or after July 1, 1999. The remaining portion of IAS 10 has been superseded by IAS 10 (revised 1999), which prescribes rules for accounting and disclosure of "events after the balance sheet date." IAS 10 (revised 1999) is effective for annual financial statements covering periods beginning on or after January 1, 2000.

While IAS 10 largely mirrored the corresponding standard under US GAAP, with accrual of contingent losses mandated when the obligation was deemed to be probable, the replacement standard has created a more complex typology of provisions and contingencies. Under IAS 37, the term "provisions" largely replaces "contingent liabilities" for those which meet the threshold test for recognition which remains at the level of probable. Provisions are real liabilities (i.e., their existence is not contingent on future events) but have amounts or timings which are uncertain; these have heretofore been referred to most commonly as estimated liabilities. IAS 37 reserves the term "contingent liability" for those potential obligations which are **not** to be given recognition--although those which meet a lower threshold (i.e., involving a more than remote possibility of an outflow of resources) must be disclosed. The new standard offers detailed practical guidance regarding several types of provisions, most importantly restructurings.

IAS 37 also addresses the matter of contingent assets (which are presented in this chapter to unify the discussion of contingencies in a single location) which would be disclosed where an inflow of economic benefits is deemed to be probable. However, when the realization of income is virtually certain, then the related asset is not considered to be a contingent asset, and recognition is appropriate.

IAS 10 (revised 1999) prescribes rules for accounting and disclosure of events, both favorable and unfavorable, that occur between the balance sheet date and the date when the financial statements are authorized for issue. Such post-balance-sheet events require either adjusting the financial statements or only disclosing them, depending on the character and timing of the event in question. The characterization of these events as being either "adjusting" or "nonadjusting" events is not unique to the international accounting standards. In fact, this terminology is found in other (i.e., national) accounting standards, like UK GAAP.

The revised standard recognizes that the process involved in authorizing the financial statements for issue will vary from case to case and is dependent upon the enterprise's management structure, statutory requirements, and the procedures followed in preparing and finalizing the financial statements. Thus, the revised standard illustrates in detail the principles governing the determination of the authorization date of the financial statements which, as required by the revised standard, needs to be disclosed. This is yet another unique feature of revised IAS 10.

Sources of IAS

IAS 1 (revised), 10 (revised 1999), 37, 39

DEFINITIONS OF TERMS

Adjusting events after the balance sheet date. Those post-balance-sheet events that provide evidence of conditions that existed at the balance sheet date and require that the financial statements be adjusted.

Authorization date. The date when the financial statements would be considered legally authorized for issue.

Constructive obligation. An obligation resulting from an enterprise's actions such that the enterprise

- By an established pattern of past practice, published policies or a sufficiently specific current statement, has indicated to third parties that it will accept certain responsibilities; and
- As a result, has created a valid expectation in the minds of third parties that it will discharge those responsibilities.

Contingent asset. A possible asset that arises from past events and whose existence will be confirmed only by the occurrence or nonoccurrence of one or more uncertain future events not wholly within the control of the reporting enterprise.

Contingent liability. An obligation which is either

- A possible obligation arising from past events, the outcome of which will be confirmed only on the occurrence or nonoccurrence of one or more uncertain future events which are not wholly within the control of the reporting enterprise; or
- A present obligation arising from past events which is not recognized either because it is not probable that an outflow of resources will be required to settle an obligation, or where the amount of the obligation cannot be measured with sufficient reliability.

Current liabilities. Enterprise obligations whose liquidation is reasonably expected to require the use of existing resources properly classified as current assets or the creation of other current liabilities. Obligations that are due on demand or will be due on demand within 1 year or the operating cycle, if longer, are current liabilities.

Estimated liability. An obligation that is known to exist, although the obligee may not be known, and the amount and timing of payment is subject to uncertainty. Now referred to as provisions.

Events after the balance sheet date. Events that occur after an enterprise's accounting year end (also referred to as the balance sheet date) and the date they are authorized for issue that would necessitate either adjusting the financial statements or disclosure. The concept is comprehensive enough to cover both favorable and unfavorable post-balance-sheet date events.

Guarantee. A commitment to honor an obligation of another party in the event certain defined conditions are not met.

Indirect guarantee of indebtedness of others. A guarantee under an agreement that obligates one enterprise to transfer funds to a second enterprise upon the occurrence of specified events under conditions whereby (1) the funds are legally available to the creditors of the second enterprise, and (2) those creditors may enforce the second enterprise's claims against the first enterprise.

Legal obligation. An obligation that derives from the explicit or implicit terms of a contract, or from legislation or other operation of law.

Liability. A present obligation of the reporting enterprise arising from past events, the settlement of which is expected to result in an outflow from the enterprise of resources embodying economic benefits.

Nonadjusting events after the balance sheet date. Those post-balance-sheet events that are indicative of conditions that arose after the balance sheet date and which thus would not necessitate adjusting financial statements. Instead, if significant, these would require disclosure.

Obligating event. An event that creates a legal or constructive obligation which results in an enterprise having no realistic alternative but to settle that obligation.

Onerous contract. A contract in which the unavoidable costs of meeting the obligations under the contract exceed the economic benefits expected to be received therefrom.

Operating cycle. The average length of time necessary for an enterprise to convert inventory to receivables to cash.

Possible loss. A contingent loss based on the occurrence of a future event or events whose likelihood of occurring is more than remote but less than likely.

Probable loss. A contingent loss based on the occurrence of a future event or events that are likely to occur.

Provision. Liabilities having uncertain timing or amount.

Remote loss. A contingent loss based on the occurrence of a future event or events whose likelihood of occurring is slight.

Restructuring. A program which is planned and controlled by management and which materially changes either the scope of business undertaken by the enterprise or the manner in which it is conducted.

CONCEPTS, RULES, AND EXAMPLES

Current Liabilities

Classification of balance sheets. Although balance sheets most often will present both assets and liabilities classified into current and noncurrent categories, there is no requirement under international accounting standards, nor indeed under national standards in various countries, that this be done. The salient international standard, IAS 1 (revised 1997), notes that "when an enterprise supplies goods or services within a clearly identifiable operating cycle, separate classification of current and noncurrent assets and liabilities on the face of the balance sheet provides useful information by distinguishing the net assets that are continuously circulating as working capital from those used in the enterprise's long-term operations. It also highlights assets that are expected to be realized within the current operating cycle, and liabilities that are due for settlement within the same period."

IAS 1 (revised) continues IAS 13's optional use of balance sheet classification into current and noncurrent, while clearly supporting such a presentation scheme. In practice, most manufacturing and distributing enterprises do present classified balance sheets, while financial institutions and certain other businesses engaging in long-term projects, such as construction companies, typically do not.

The presentation of a classified balance sheet reveals important information about liquidity, or the debt-paying ability of the enterprise. IAS 1 (revised) places substantial weight on this goal, as revealed by the requirement it imposes on entities which choose not to present classified balance sheets. Those enterprises must list assets and liabilities "broadly in order of their liquidity." Furthermore, the standard requires that there must be disclosure of assets expected to be recovered, and liabilities expected to be liquidated, more than 12 months after the date of the balance sheet. This does not necessarily require that these be placed in separate captions in the balance sheet, per se, although that can be done; rather, footnote disclosures can be used to accomplish this objective.

IAS 1 (revised) also makes explicit reference to the requirements imposed by IAS 32 concerning financial assets and liabilities. Since such common balance sheet items as trade and other receivables and payables are within the definition of financial instruments, information about maturity dates is already required under IAS. While most trade payables and accrued liabilities will be due within 30 to 90 days, and thus are understood by all financial statement readers to be current, this requirement would necessitate additional disclosure, either on the face of the balance sheet or in the footnotes thereto, when this assumption is not warranted.

The other purpose of presenting a classified balance sheet is to highlight those assets and obligations that are "continuously circulating" in the phraseology of IAS 1 (revised). That is, the goal is to identify specifically resources and commitments that are consumed or settled in the normal course of operating the business. In some types of businesses, such as certain construction enterprises, the normal operating cycle may exceed 1 year. Thus, some assets or liabilities might fail to be incorporated into a definition based on the first goal of reporting, providing insight into liquidity, but be included in one that meets the second goal.

As a compromise, if a classified balance sheet is indeed being presented, the convention for financial reporting purposes is to consider assets and liabilities current if they will be realized and liquidated within 1 year or one operating cycle, whichever is longer. Since this may vary in practice from one reporting entity to another, however, it is important for users to read the accounting policies set forth in notes to the financial statements. The classification criterion should be set forth there, particularly if it is other than the rule most commonly employed: 1-year threshold.

Nature of current liabilities. Current liabilities are generally perceived to be those that are due within a brief time span. Convention is to use 1 year from the balance sheet date as the threshold for categorization as current, although for enterprises that have operating cycles longer than 1 year (e.g., certain types of construction projects), the longer period is often advocated as a more meaningful demarcation line. IAS 1 (revised 1997) states that liabilities are to be considered current when they are expected to be settled in the normal course of the entity's operating cycle or are due to be settled within 12 months from the balance sheet date, whichever is longer. Examples of liabilities which are not expected to be settled in the normal course of the operating cycle but which, if due within 12 months would be deemed current, are current portions of long-term debt and bank overdrafts, dividends declared and payable, and various nontrade payables.

Current liabilities would almost always include not only obligations that are due on demand (typically including bank lines of credit, other demand notes payable, and certain overdue obligations for which forbearance has been granted on a day-to-day basis), but also the currently scheduled payments on longer-term obligations, such as installment notes. Also included in this group would be trade credit and accrued expenses, and deferred revenues and advances from customers for which services are to be provided or product delivered within 1 year. If certain conditions are met (described below), short-term obligations that are intended to be refinanced may be excluded from current liabilities.

Like all liabilities, current liabilities may be known with certainty as to amount, due date, and payee, or one or more of these elements may be unknown or subject to estimation. Under the principles of accrual accounting, however, the lack of specific information on, say, the amount owed, will not serve to justify a failure to record and report on such obligations. The formerly common term "estimated liabilities" has been superseded per IAS 37 by the term "provisions." Provisions and contingent liabilities are discussed in detail later in this chapter.

Offsetting current assets against related current liabilities. IAS 1 (revised) provides that current liabilities not be reduced by the deduction of a current asset (or vice versa) unless required or permitted by another IAS. In practice, there are few circumstances that would meet this requirement; certain financial institution transactions are the most commonly encountered exceptions.

Types of liabilities. Current obligations can be divided into those where

1. Both the amount and the payee are known;
2. The payee is known but the amount may have to be estimated;
3. The payee is unknown and the amount may have to be estimated; and
4. The liability has been incurred due to a loss contingency.

These types of liabilities are discussed in the following sections.

Amount and Payee Known

Accounts payable arise primarily from the acquisition of materials and supplies to be used in the production of goods or in conjunction with providing services. Payables that arise from transactions with suppliers in the normal course of business, which customarily are due in no more than 1 year, may be stated at their face amount rather than at the present value of the required future cash flows.

Notes payable are more formalized obligations that may arise from the acquisition of materials and supplies used in operations or from the use of short-term credit to purchase capital assets. Although international accounting standards do not explicitly address the matter, it is widely agreed that monetary obligations, other than those due currently, should be presented at the present value of the amount owed, thus giving explicit recognition to the time value of money. However, most would agree that this exercise would not be needed to present current obligations fairly. (Of course, if the obligations are interest-bearing at a reasonable rate determined at inception, this is not an issue.)

Dividends payable become a liability of the enterprise when the board of directors declares a cash dividend. Since declared dividends are usually paid within a short period of time after the declaration date, they are classified as current liabilities.

Unearned revenues or advances result from customer prepayments for either performance of services or delivery of product. They may be required by the selling enterprise as a condition of the sale or may be made by the buyer as a means of guaranteeing that the seller will perform the desired service or deliver the product. Unearned revenues and advances should be classified as current liabilities at the balance sheet date if the services are to be performed or the products are to be delivered within 1 year or the operating cycle, whichever is longer.

Returnable deposits may be received to cover possible future damage to property. Many utility companies require security deposits. A deposit may be required for the use of a reusable container. Refundable deposits are classified as current liabilities if the firm expects to refund them during the current operating cycle or within 1 year, whichever is longer.

Accrued liabilities have their origin in the end-of-period adjustment process required by accrual accounting. They represent economic obligations, even when the legal or contractual commitment to pay has not yet been triggered, and as such must be given recognition if the matching concept is to be adhered to. Commonly accrued liabilities include wages and salaries payable, interest payable, rent payable, and taxes payable.

Agency liabilities result from the legal obligation of the enterprise to act as the collection agent for employee or customer taxes owed to various federal, state, or local government units. Examples of agency liabilities include sales taxes, income taxes withheld from employee paychecks, and employee social security contributions, where mandated by law. In addition to agency liabilities, an employer may have a current obligation for unemployment taxes. Payroll taxes typically are not legal liabilities until the associated payroll is actually paid, but in keeping with the concept of accrual accounting, if the payroll has been accrued, the associated payroll taxes should be as well.

Current maturing portion of long-term debt is shown as a current liability if the obligation is to be liquidated by using assets classified as current. However, if the currently maturing debt is to be liquidated by using other than current assets (i.e., by using a sinking fund that is properly classified as an investment), these obligations should be classified as long-term liabilities.

Obligations that, by their terms, are due on demand or will be due on demand within 1 year (or operating cycle, if longer) from the balance sheet date, even if liquidation is not expected to occur within that period, are classified as current liabilities. Although the international standards are not explicit on this point, it is also widely agreed that long-term obligations that contain call provisions are to be classified as current liabilities if, as of the balance sheet date, one of the following occurs:

1. The debtor is in violation of the agreement, and this violation makes the obligation callable; or
2. The debtor is in violation of the agreement, and such violation, unless cured within the grace period specified in the agreement, makes the obligation callable.

Note, however, that if circumstances arise that effectively negate the creditor's right to call the obligation, the obligation may be classified as long-term. Examples are

1. The creditor has waived the right to call the obligation caused by the debtor's violation, or the creditor has subsequently lost the right to demand repayment for more than 1 year (or operating cycle, if longer) from the balance sheet date.
2. Obligations contain a grace period for remedying the violation, and it is probable that the violation will be cured within the grace period. In these situations, the circumstances must be disclosed.

Short-term obligations expected to be refinanced may be classified as noncurrent liabilities if certain conditions are met. If an enterprise intends to refinance the currently maturing portion of long-term debt or intends to refinance callable obligations by replacing them with either new long-term debt or with equity securities, IAS 1 (revised) must be followed. IAS 1 (revised) states that an enterprise should reclassify currently maturing portions of long-term debt as long-term provided that the enterprise intends to refinance the obligation on a long-term basis and its intent is supported by any of the following:

1. **Original term greater than 12 months.** If the debt was originally scheduled for repayment within 1 year, a later agreement to extend it cannot,

under new standard IAS 1 (revised), be reclassified as noncurrent, although once it is extended or refinanced, the new or replacement debt will be classified according to its terms, and not be limited by the terms of the predecessor debt.

2. **The enterprise intends to refinance the debt on a long-term basis.** This intention must be present as of the balance sheet date in order to be useful in justifying a reclassification of the debt to noncurrent status.

3. **The intention to refinance is supported by an agreement to refinance, or to reschedule payments, which is completed before the financial statements are issued.** Absent an actual consummation of this agreement before the statements are issued, there can be no assurance that it will be successfully completed, and it would be foolish to permit reclassifying short-term obligations as being long-term under such a scenario. Given that there is often a lag between the date of the financial statements and the issuance thereof, an intention that existed as of the former should be consummated with an actual refinancing by the latter date. In some cases, release of the financial statements will be delayed until the refinancing is put into place, for the very reason that there is a strong desire to report the reclassified debt on the balance sheet.

Logic suggests that if short-term debt is classified as long-term due to the existence of a post-balance-sheet-date refinancing or a lender or investor commitment, the replacement debt should not be callable unless there is a violation of a provision of the agreement with which compliance is objectively determinable or measurable. As of the balance sheet date, the reporting enterprise should not be in violation of the terms of the agreement.

Furthermore, the amount of currently maturing debt to be reclassified should not exceed the amount raised by the actual refinancing, nor can it exceed the amount specified in the refinancing agreement. If the amount specified in the refinancing agreement can fluctuate, the maximum amount of debt that would be reclassified is equal to a reasonable estimate of the minimum amount expected to be available on any date from the maturing date of the maturing obligation to the end of the fiscal year. If no estimate can be made of the minimum amount available under the financing agreement, none of the maturing debt should be reclassified as long-term.

Finally, although again not stipulated overtly in IAS 1 (revised), a reasonable interpretation would be that if an enterprise uses current assets after the balance sheet date to liquidate a current obligation, and replaces those current assets by issuing either equity securities or long-term debt before the issuance of the balance sheet, the current obligation must still be classified as a current liability in the balance sheet. Without such a provision, it could be argued successfully that many current liabilities in fact are noncurrent, since these are paid off and then reinstated on a regular, sometimes monthly, cycle.

Long-term debt subject to demand for repayment. What may be thought of as the polar opposite of short-term debt to be refinanced long-term is the situation in which an enterprise is obligated under a long-term (noncurrent) debt arrangement where the lender has either the right to demand immediate or significantly accelerated repayment, or such acceleration rights vest with the lender upon the occurrence of certain events. For example, long-term (and even many short-term) debt agreements typically contain so-called covenants, which effectively are restrictions on the borrower as to undertaking further borrowings, paying dividends, maintaining specified levels of working capital, and so forth. If the covenants are breached by the borrower, the lender will have the right to call the debt or otherwise accelerate repayment.

In other cases, the lender will have certain "subjective acceleration clauses" inserted into the loan agreement, giving it the right to demand repayment if it perceives that its risk position has deteriorated as a result of changes in the borrower's business operations, liquidity, or other vaguely defined factors. Obviously, this gives the lender great power and subjects the borrower to the real possibility that the nominally long-term debt will, in fact, be short-term.

IAS 1 (revised) addresses the matter of breach of loan covenants, but does not address the less common phenomenon of subjective acceleration clauses in loan agreements. As to the former, it provides that continued classification of the debt as noncurrent, when one or more of the stipulated default circumstances has occurred, is contingent upon meeting two conditions: First, the lender has agreed, prior to approval of the financial statements, not to demand payment as a consequence of the breach (this is known as a debt compliance waiver); and second, that it is considered not probable that further breaches will occur within 12 months of the balance sheet date. If one or both of these cannot be met, the debt must be reclassified to current status if a classified balance sheet is presented.

Logic suggests that the existence of subjective acceleration clauses convert nominally long-term debt into currently payable debt. US GAAP, in fact, formally recognizes this reality. The authors therefore suggest that in the presence of such provisions, it would be misleading to categorize debt as noncurrent, regardless of the actual maturity date, since continued forbearance by the lender would be required, and this cannot be controlled by the enterprise reporting the debt. Such debt should be shown as current, with sufficient disclosure to inform the reader that the debt could effectively be "rolled over" until the nominal maturity date, at the sole discretion of the lender.

Payee Known but Amount May Have to Be Estimated

Provisions. Under the recently promulgated standard, IAS 37, *Provisions, Contingent Liabilities, and Contingent Assets*, those liabilities for which amount or timing of expenditure is uncertain are deemed to be provisions. While this term has been widely used informally (sometimes also being applied to contra asset accounts such as accumulated depreciation or allowance for uncollectible accounts receivable), it now has been given this precise definition (which explicitly excludes contra asset accounts).

IAS 37 provides a comprehensive definition of the term provision. It mandates, in a clear-cut manner, that a provision should be recognized **only** if

- The enterprise has a present obligation (legal or constructive) as a result of a past event;
- It is probable that an outflow of resources embodying economic benefits will be required to settle the obligation; and
- A reliable estimate can be made of the amount of the obligation.

In addition, the standard offers in-depth guidance on the topic of provisions. Each of the key words in the definition of the term provision is explained in detail by the standard. Explanations and clarifications offered by the standard for above key words are summarized below.

- **Present obligation.** The standard opines that in almost all cases it will be clear that a past event has given rise to a present obligation. However, in exceptional cases, for example: in case of a lawsuit when it is not clear whether a present obligation has arisen, an enterprise should determine whether a present obligation exists at the balance sheet date by taking into account all available evidence including, for example, opinion of an expert (legal counsel).
- **Past event.** Not all past events lead to a present obligation. Only an "obligating event" which, according to the standard, is an event that leaves the enterprise with no realistic option but to settle the obligation, leads to a present obligation. Thus, past events which are obligating events alone need to be provided for (i.e., recognized as provisions). For example, past events, like unlawful environmental damage by an enterprise, would be considered obligating events which would then necessitate the recognition of a provision for costs like cleanup costs or penalties and fines. Similarly, recognition of a provision for (future) decommissioning costs (e.g., of an oil installation or a nuclear power station), to the extent that the enterprise is obliged to rectify damage already caused, is essential. In contrast, however, when it is deemed possible that an enterprise can avoid future expenditure by its future action, no provision is to be recognized for the anticipated future expenditure.
- **Probable outflow of resources embodying economic benefits.** For a provision to qualify for recognition it is essential that it is not only a present obligation of the reporting enterprise but also it should be probable that an outflow of resources embodying benefits to settle the obligation will in fact result. For the purposes of this standard, a unique definition of the term probable has been propounded: by way of a footnote to IAS 37, Para-

graph 23, this definition is made applicable only to this standard. The footnote states that this interpretation of the term probable, which for the purposes of IAS 37 has been defined to mean "more likely than not," does not necessarily apply to other IAS. Put differently, this means, that the probability of the event occurring should be greater than the probability of its nonoccurrence. In contrast, where it is not probable that a present obligation exists, an enterprise need only disclose (as opposed to recognizing a provision) a contingent liability, unless the possibility is remote.

• **Reliable estimate of the obligation.** The standard recognizes that except in extremely rare cases, an enterprise will usually be able to make an estimate of the obligation that is sufficiently reliable to use in recognizing a provision. Such an estimate would normally be derived from a range of possible outcomes.

Other salient features of provisions explained by the standard include the following:

1. For all estimated liabilities which are included within the definition of provisions, the amount to be recorded and presented on the balance sheet should be the best estimate as of the balance sheet date of the amount of expenditure which will be required to settle the obligation. This is often referred to as the "expected value" of the obligation, which is operationally defined as the amount the enterprise would pay, currently, to either settle the actual obligation or provide consideration to a third party to assume it. For estimated liabilities comprised of large numbers of relatively small, similar items, weighting by probability of occurrence can be used to compute the aggregate expected value; this is often used to compute accrued warranty reserves, for example. For those estimated liabilities comprised of only a few (or a single) discrete obligations, the most likely outcome may be used to measure the liability when there is a range of outcomes having roughly similar likelihoods; but, if possible outcomes include amounts much greater (and lesser) than the most likely, it may be necessary to accrue a larger amount if there is a significant chance that the larger obligation will have to be settled, even if that is not the most likely outcome as such.

2. The "risks and uncertainties" surrounding events and circumstances should be taken into account in arriving at the best estimate of a provision. However, as pointed out by the standard, uncertainty should not justify the creation of excessive provisions or a deliberate overstatement of liabilities.

3. The standard also addresses the use of present values or discounting (i.e., recording the estimated liability at present value, after taking into account the time value of money). While the entire subject of present value measurement in accounting has been widely debated, and in practice there is a notable lack of consistency (with some standards requiring it, others prohibiting it, and many others remaining silent on the issue), IAS 37 has stood

fast on the subject of present value measurement, despite some opposition voiced in response to the exposure draft and a plea for more guidance. The standard requires the use of discounting when the effect would be material. Thus, provisions estimated to be due farther into the future will have more need to be discounted than those due currently.

IAS 37 clarifies that the discount rate applied should be consistent with the estimation of cash flows (i.e., if cash flows are projected in nominal terms) that is, in the amount expected to be paid out, reflecting whatever price inflation occurs between the balance sheet date and the date of ultimate settlement of the estimated obligation, then a nominal discount rate should be used. If cash flows are projected in real terms, net of any price inflation, then a real interest rate should be applied. In either case, past experience must be used to ascertain likely timing of future cash flows, since discounting cannot otherwise be performed.

4. Future events that may affect the amount required to settle an obligation should be reflected in the provision amount where there is sufficient objective evidence that such future events will in fact occur. For example, if an enterprise believes that the cost of cleaning up a site at the end of its life will be reduced by future changes in technology, the amount recognized as a provision for cleanup costs should reflect a reasonable estimate of cost reduction resulting from any anticipated technological changes.

5. Gains from expected disposal of assets should not be taken into account in arriving at the amount of the provision (even if the expected disposal is closely linked to the event giving rise to the provision).

6. Reimbursements by other parties should be taken into account when computing the provision, only if it is virtually certain that the reimbursement will be received. The reimbursement should be treated as a separate asset on the balance sheet. However, in the income statement, the provision may be presented net of the amount recognized as a reimbursement.

7. Changes in provision should be reviewed at each balance sheet date and adjusted to reflect the current best estimate. If upon review it appears that it is no longer probable that an outflow of resources embodying economics will be required to settle the obligation, then the provision should be reversed.

8. Use of provision is to be restricted to the purpose for which it was recognized originally. If an expenditure is set against a provision that was originally recognized for another purpose, that would camouflage the impact of the two different events.

9. Provision for future operating losses should not be recognized. This is explicitly prescribed by the standard since future operating losses do not meet the definition of a liability (as defined in the standard) and the general recognition criteria laid down in the standard.

10. Present obligations under onerous contracts should be recognized and measured as a provision. The standard introduces the concept of onerous contracts which it defines as contracts under which unavoidable costs of meeting the obligations exceed the economic benefits expected under the contracts. Executory contracts that are not onerous do not fall within the purview of this standard. In other words, such contracts (executory contracts which are not onerous) need not be recognized as a provision.

The standard mandates that unavoidable costs under a contract represent the "least net costs of exiting from the contract." Such unavoidable costs should be measured at the **lower** of

- The cost of fulfilling the contract; **or**
- Any compensation or penalties arising from failure to fulfill the contract.

11. Provision for restructuring costs is recognized only when the general recognition criteria for provisions are met. A constructive obligation to restructure arises only when an enterprise has a **detailed formal plan** for the restructuring which identifies at least: the business or the part of the business concerned, principal locations affected, approximate number of employees that would need to be compensated for termination resulting from the restructuring (along with their function and location), expenditure that would be required to carry out the restructuring and information as to when the plan is to be implemented.

Further, the recognition criteria also requires that the enterprise should have raised a valid expectation in those affected by the restructuring that it will, in fact, carry out the restructuring by starting to implement that plan or announcing its main features to those affected by it. Thus, until both the conditions mentioned above are satisfied, a restructuring provision cannot be made based upon the concept of constructive obligation.

Only **direct** expenditure arising from restructuring should be provided for. Such direct expenditure should be both necessarily incurred for the restructuring **and** should not be associated with the ongoing activities of the enterprises. Thus, a provision for restructuring would not include costs like: cost of retraining or relocating the enterprise's current staff members or costs of marketing or investments in new systems and distribution networks (such expenditures are categorically disallowed by the standard as they are considered to be expenses relating to the future conduct of the business of the enterprise and thus are not liabilities relating to the restructuring program). Also, identifiable future operating losses up to the date of a restructuring are not to be included in the provision for a restructuring (unless they relate to an onerous contract). Furthermore, in keeping with the general measurement principles relating to provisions outlined in the standard, the specific guidance in the standard (IAS 37) relating to restructuring prohibits taking into account any gains on expected disposal of assets in measuring a restructuring provision, even if the sale of the assets is envisaged as part of the restructuring.

A management decision or a board resolution to restructure (an enterprise) taken before the balance sheet date does not automatically give rise to a constructive obligation at the balance sheet date unless the enterprise has, before the balance sheet date: either started to implement the restructuring plan, or announced the main features of the restructuring plan to those affected by it in a sufficiently specific manner such that a valid expectation is raised in them (that the enterprise will in fact carry out the restructuring).

Examples of events that may fall under the definition of restructuring are

- A fundamental reorganization of an enterprise that has a material effect on the nature and focus of the enterprise's operations;
- Drastic changes in the management structure, for example, making all functional units autonomous;
- Changing the focus of the business to a more strategic location or place by relocating the headquarters from one country or region to another; **and**
- The sale or termination of a line of business (if certain other conditions are satisfied, then a restructuring could be considered a discontinuing operation under IAS 35).

12. Disclosures mandated by the standard for provisions are the following:

- For each class of provision, the carrying amount at the beginning and the end of the period, additional provisions made in the period, amounts used during the period, unused amounts reversed during the period, and increase during the period in the discounted amount arising from the passage of time and the effect of change in discount rate (comparative information is **not** required).
- For each class of provision, a brief description of the nature of the obligation and the expected timing of any resulting outflows of economic benefits, an indication of the uncertainties regarding the amount or timing of those outflows (including, where necessary in order to provide adequate information, disclosure of major assumptions made concerning future events), and the amount of any expected reimbursement stating the amount of the asset that has been recognized for that expected reimbursement.
- In extremely rare circumstances, if the above disclosures as envisaged by the standard are expected to seriously prejudice the position of the enterprise in a dispute with third parties on the subject matter of the provision, then the standard takes a lenient view and allows the enterprise to disclose the general nature of the dispute together with the fact that, and reason why, the information has not been disclosed.

For the purposes of making the above disclosures, it may be essential to group or aggregate provisions. The standard also offers guidance on how to determine which provisions may be aggregated to form a class. As per the standard, in determining which provisions may be aggregated to report as a class, the nature of the items should be sufficiently similar for them to be aggregated together and reported as a class. For example, while it may be appropriate to aggregate into a single class all provisions relating to warranties of different products, it may not be appropriate to group and present, as a single class, amounts relating to normal warranties and amounts that are subject to legal proceedings.

The following section of the chapter provides examples of provisions that would need to be recognized based on the rules laid down by the standard. It also discusses common provisions and the accounting treatment which is often applied to these particular items.

Unlawful environmental damage. Cleanup costs and penalties resulting from unlawful environmental damage (e.g., an oil spill by a tanker ship which contaminates the water near the sea port) would need to be provided for in those countries which have laws requiring cleanup, since it would lead to an outflow of resources embodying economic benefits in settlement regardless of the future actions of the enterprise.

In case the enterprise which has caused the environmental damage operates in a country that has not yet enacted legislation requiring cleanup, in some cases a provision may still be required based on the principle of constructive obligation (as opposed to a legal obligation). This may be possible if the enterprise has a widely publicized environmental policy in which it undertakes to clean up all contamination that it causes and the enterprise has a clean track record of honoring its published environmental policy. The reason a provision would be needed under the second situation is because the recognition criteria have been met, that is, there is a present obligation resulting from a past obligating event (the oil spill) and the conduct of the enterprise has created a valid expectation on the part of those affected by it that the enterprise will clean up the contamination (a constructive obligation) and the outflow of resources embodying economic benefits is probable.

Provision for restructuring costs. An enterprise which publicly announces, before the balance sheet date, its plans to shut down a division in accordance with a board decision and a detailed formal plan, would need to recognize a provision for the best estimate of the costs of closing down the division. In this case the recognition criteria are met as follows: a present obligation has resulted from a past obligating event (public announcement of the decision to the public at large) which gives rise to a constructive obligation from that date, since it creates a valid expectation that the division will be shut down and an outflow of resources embodying economic benefits in settlement is probable.

However, in this case, if the enterprise had not publicly announced its plans to shut down the division before the balance sheet date, or did not start implementing its plan before the balance sheet date, no provision would need to be made since the board decision alone would not give rise to a constructive obligation at the balance sheet date (since no valid expectation has in fact been raised in those affected by the restructuring that the enterprise will start to implement that plan).

Onerous contract. An enterprise relocates its offices to a more prestigious office complex because the old office building which it was occupying (and has been there for the last 20 years), does not suit the new corporate image it wants to project. However, the lease of the old office premises cannot be canceled at the present time since it continues for the next 5 years. This is a case of an onerous contract wherein the unavoidable costs of meeting the obligations under the contract exceed the economic benefits under it. A provision is thus required to be made for the best estimate of unavoidable lease payments.

Decommissioning costs. An oil company installed an oil refinery on leased land. The installation was completed before the balance sheet date. On expiration of the lease contract, after a period of 7 years, the refinery would be relocated to another strategic location which would ensure uninterrupted supply of crude oil. The decommissioning costs of the oil refinery would need to be recognized at the balance sheet date. A provision should be recognized for the present value of the estimated decommissioning costs to take place after 7 years.

Taxes payable include federal or national, state or provincial, and local income taxes. Due to frequent changes in the tax laws, the amount of income taxes payable may have to be estimated. That portion deemed currently payable must be classified as a current liability. The remaining amount is classified as a long-term liability. Although estimated future taxes are broadly includable under the category "provisions," specific rules in IAS 12 (revised) prohibit discounting these amounts to present values.

Property taxes payable represent the unpaid portion of an entity's obligation to a state or other taxing authority that arises from ownership of real property. Often these taxes are levied in arrears, based on periodic reassessments of value and on governmental budgetary needs. Accordingly, the most acceptable method of accounting for property taxes is a monthly accrual of property tax expense during the fiscal period of the taxing authority for which the taxes are levied. The fiscal period of the taxing authority is the fiscal period that includes the assessment or lien date.

A liability for property taxes payable arises when the fiscal year of the taxing authority and the fiscal year of the entity do not coincide or when the assessment or lien date and the actual payment date do not fall within the same fiscal year. For example, XYZ Corporation is a calendar-year corporation that owns real estate in a state that operates on a June 30 fiscal year. In this state, property taxes are assessed and become a lien against property on July 1, although they are not payable until April 1 and August 1 of the next calendar year. XYZ Corporation would accrue an expense and a liability on a monthly basis beginning on July 1. At year end (December 31), the firm would have an expense for 6 months' property tax on their income statement and a current liability for the same amount.

Bonus payments may require estimation since the amount of the bonus payment may be affected by the amount of income taxes currently payable.

Compensated absences refer to paid vacation, paid holidays, and paid sick leave. IAS 19 (revised) addresses this issue and requires that an employer should accrue a liability for employee's compensation of future absences if the employee's right to receive compensation for future absence is attributable to employee services already rendered, the right vests or accumulates, ultimate payment of the compensation is probable, and the amount of the payment can reasonably be estimated.

If an employer is required to compensate an employee for unused vacation, holidays, or sick days, even if employment is terminated, the employee's right to this compensation is said to vest. Accrual of a liability for nonvesting rights depends on whether the unused rights expire at the end of the year in which earned or accumulated and are carried forward to succeeding years. If the rights expire, a liability for future absences should not be accrued at year end because the benefits to be paid in subsequent years would not be attributable to employee services rendered in prior years. If unused rights accumulate and increase the benefits otherwise available in subsequent years, a liability should be accrued at year end to the extent that it is probable that employees will be paid in subsequent years for the increased benefits attributable to the accumulated rights, and the amount can reasonably be estimated.

Pay for employee leaves of absence that represent time off for past services should be considered compensation subject to accrual. Pay for employee leaves of absence that will provide future benefits and that are not attributable to past services rendered would not be subject to accrual. Although in theory such accruals should be based on expected future rates of pay, as a practical matter these are often computed on current pay rates which may not materially differ and have the advantage of being known. Also, if the payments are to be made some time in the future, discounting of the accrual amounts would seemingly be appropriate, but again this may not often be done for practical considerations.

Similar arguments can be made to support the accrual of an obligation for postemployment benefits other than pensions if employees' rights accumulate or vest, payment is probable, and the amount can be reasonably estimated. If these benefits do not vest or accumulate, these would be deemed to be contingent liabilities. Contingent liabilities are discussed in IAS 37 and are considered later in this chapter.

Payee Unknown and the Amount May Have to Be Estimated

The following are further examples of estimated liabilities, which also will fall within the new definition of provisions under IAS 37. Accordingly, discounting should be applied to projected future cash flows to determine the amounts to be reported on the balance sheet if the effect of discounting is material, and if timing can be estimated with sufficient accuracy to accomplish this process.

Premiums are usually offered by an enterprise to increase product sales. They may require the purchaser to return a specified number of box tops, wrappers, or other proofs of purchase. They may or may not require the payment of a cash amount. If the premium offer terminates at the end of the current period but has not been accounted for completely if it extends into the next accounting period, a current liability for the estimated number of redemptions expected in the future period will have to be recorded. If the premium offer extends for more than one accounting period, the estimated liability must be divided into a current portion and a long-term portion.

Product warranties providing for repair or replacement of defective products may be sold separately or may be included in the sale price of the product. If the warranty extends into the next accounting period, a current liability for the estimated amount of warranty expense expected in the next period must be recorded. If the warranty spans more than the next period, the estimated liability must be partitioned into a current and long-term portion.

Contingent Liabilities

IAS 37 defines a contingent liability as an obligation which is either

- A possible obligation arising from past events, the outcome of which will be confirmed only on the occurrence or nonoccurrence of one or more uncertain future events which are not wholly within the control of the reporting enterprise; **or**
- A present obligation arising from past events, which is not recognized either because it is not probable that an outflow of resources will be required to settle an obligation or the amount of the obligation cannot be measured with sufficient reliability.

An enterprise should **not** recognize a contingent liability. Instead, it should disclose it in the notes to the financial statements (unless the possibility of an outflow of resources embodying economic benefits is remote, in which case even disclosure is not necessary).

Contingent liabilities may develop in a way not initially anticipated. Thus, it is imperative that they are assessed continually to determine whether an outflow of resources embodying economic benefits has become probable. If the outflow of future economic benefits becomes probable, then a provision is required to be recognized in the financial statements of the period in which the change in such a probability occurs (except in extremely rare cases, when no reliable estimate can be made of the amount needed to be recognized as a provision).

Contingent liabilities must be distinguished from estimated liabilities, although both involve an uncertainty that will be resolved by future events. However, an estimate exists because of uncertainty about the amount of an event requiring an acknowledged accounting recognition. The event is known and the effect is known, but the amount itself is uncertain. For example, depreciation is an estimate, but not a contingency, because the actual fact of physical depreciation is acknowledged, although the amount is obtained by an assumed accounting method.

In a contingency, whether there will be an impairment of an asset or the occurrence of a liability is the uncertainty that will be resolved in the future. The amount is also usually uncertain, although that is not an essential characteristic. Collectibility of receivables is a contingency because both the amount of loss and the identification of which customer will not pay in the future is unknown. Similar logic would hold for obligations related to product warranties. Both the amount and the customer are currently unknown.

Assessing the likelihood of contingent events. It is tempting to express quantitatively the likelihood of the occurrence of contingent events (e.g., an 80% probability), but this exaggerates the precision possible in the estimation process. For this reason, accounting standards have not been written to require quantification of the likelihood of contingent outcomes. Rather, qualitative descriptions, ranging along the continuum from remote to probable, have historically been prescribed.

IAS 37 sets the threshold for accrual at "more likely than not," which most experts have defined as being very slightly over a 50% likelihood. Thus, if there is even a hint that the obligation is more likely to exist than to not exist, it will need to be formally recognized if an amount can be reasonably estimated for it. The impact will be both to make it much less ambiguous when a contingency should be recorded, and to force recognition of far more of these obligations at earlier dates than they are being given recognition at present.

When a loss is probable and no estimate is possible, these facts should be disclosed in the current period. The accrual of the loss should be made in the period in which the amount of the loss can be estimated. This accrual of a loss in future periods is a change in estimate. It is **not** a prior period adjustment.

Remote contingent losses. With the exception of certain remote contingencies for which disclosures have traditionally been given, contingent losses that are deemed remote in terms of likelihood of occurrence are not accrued or disclosed in the financial statements. For example, every business risks loss by fire, explosion, government expropriation, or guarantees made in the ordinary course of business. These are all contingencies because of the uncertainty surrounding whether the future event confirming the loss will or will not take place. The risk of asset expropriation exists, but this has become less common an occurrence in recent decades and, in any event, would be limited to less developed or politically unstable nations. Unless there is specific information about the expectation of such occurrences, which would thus raise the item to the possible category in any event, thereby making it subject to disclosure, these are not normally discussed in the financial statements.

Litigation. The most difficult area of contingencies is litigation. In some developed nations there is a great deal of commercial and other litigation, some of which exposes reporting entities to risks of material losses. Accountants must generally rely on attorneys' assessments concerning the likelihood of such events. Unless the attorney indicates that the risk of loss is remote or slight, or that the impact of any loss that does occur would be immaterial to the company, the accountant will require that the entity add explanatory material to the financial statements regarding the contingency. In cases where judgments have been entered against the entity, or where the attorney gives a range of expected losses or other amounts, certain accruals of loss contingencies for at least the minimum point of the range must be made. Similarly, if the reporting entity has made an offer in settlement of unresolved litigation, that offer would normally be deemed the lower end of the range of possible loss and, thus, subject for accrual. In most cases, however, an estimate of the contingency is unknown and the contingency is reflected only in footnotes.

Contingent Assets

Per IAS 37, a contingent asset is a possible asset that arises from past events and whose existence will be confirmed only by the occurrence or nonoccurrence of one or more uncertain future events which are not wholly within the control of the reporting enterprise.

Contingent assets usually arise from unplanned or unexpected events that give rise to the possibility of an inflow of economic benefits to the enterprise. An example of a contingent asset is a claim against an insurance company which the enterprise is pursuing legally.

Contingent assets should not be recognized; instead, they should be disclosed if the inflow of the economic benefits is probable. As with contingent liabilities, contingent assets need to be continually assessed to ensure that developments are properly reflected in the financial statements. For instance, if it becomes virtually certain that the inflow of economic benefits will arise, the asset and the related income should be recognized in the financial statements of the period in which the change occurs. If, however, the inflow of economic benefits has become probable (instead of virtually certain), then it should be disclosed as a contingent asset.

Disclosures Prescribed by IAS 37 for Contingent Liabilities and Contingent Assets

An enterprise should disclose, for each class of contingent liability at the balance sheet date, a brief description of the nature of the contingent liability and, where practicable, an estimate of its financial effect measured in the same manner as provisions, an indication of the uncertainties relating to the amount or timing of any outflow, and the possibility of any reimbursement.

In aggregating contingent liabilities to form a class it is essential to consider whether the nature of the items is sufficiently similar to each other such that they could be presented as a single class.

In the case of contingent assets where an inflow of economic benefits is probable, an enterprise should disclose a brief description of the nature of the contingent assets at the balance sheet date and, where practicable, an estimate of their financial effect, measured using the same principles as provisions.

Where any of the above information is not disclosed because it is not practical to do so, that fact should be disclosed. In extremely rare circumstances, if the above disclosures as envisaged by the standard are expected to seriously prejudice the position of the enterprise in a dispute with third parties on the subject matter of the contingencies, then the standard takes a lenient view and allows the enterprise to disclose the general nature of the dispute, together with the fact that, and reason why, the information has not been disclosed.

Transitional Provisions

The effect of adopting IAS 37 should be reported as an adjustment to the opening balance of retained earnings. It is interesting to note that IAS 37 does not give the option of the allowed alternative treatment which was permitted by IAS 8. To that extent it is a departure from the accounting treatment prescribed under IAS.

Reporting Events Occurring After the Balance Sheet Date

Authorization date. The determination of the authorization date (i.e., the date when the financial statements could be considered legally authorized for issuance) is critical to the concept of events after the balance sheet date. It serves as the cutoff point after the balance sheet date, up to which the post-balance-sheet events are to be examined in order to ascertain whether such events qualify for the treatment prescribed by the revised standard IAS 10. This standard explains the concept through the use of illustrations.

The general principles that need to be considered in determining the authorization date of the financial statements are set out below.

- When an enterprise is required to submit its financial statements to its shareholders for approval after they have already been issued, the authorization date in this case would mean the date of original issuance and not the date when these are approved by the shareholders; and
- When an enterprise is required to issue its financial statements to a supervisory board made up wholly of nonexecutives, authorization date would mean the date on which management authorizes them for issue to the supervisory board.

Consider the following examples:

1. The preparation of the financial statements of Xanadu Corp. for the accounting period ended December 31, 2001, was completed by the

management on January 15, 2002. The draft financial statements were considered at the meeting of the board of directors held on January 18, 2002, on which date the Board approved them and authorized them for issuance. The annual general meeting (AGM) was held on February 10, 2002, after allowing the requisite notice period mandated by the corporate statute. At the AGM the shareholders approved the financial statements. The approved financial statements were filed by the corporation with the Company Law Board (the statutory body of the country that regulates corporations) on February 21, 2002.

Given these facts, the date of authorization of the financial statements of Xanadu Corp. for the year ended December 31, 2001 is January 18, 2002, the date when the board approved them and authorized them for issue (and not the date they were approved in the AGM by the shareholders). Thus, all post-balance-sheet events between December 31, 2001, and January 18, 2002, need to be considered by Xanadu Corp. for the purposes of evaluating whether or not they are to be accounted or reported under the revised IAS 10.

2. Suppose in the above cited case, the management of Xanadu Corp. was required to issue the financial statements to a supervisory board (consisting solely of nonexecutives including representatives of a trade union). The management of Xanadu Corp. had issued the draft financial statements to the supervisory board on January 16, 2002. The supervisory board approved them on January 17, 2002, and the shareholders approved them in the AGM held on February 10, 2002. The approved financial statements were filed with the Company Law Board on February 21, 2002.

In this case the date of authorization of financial statements would be January 16, 2002, the date the draft financial statements were issued to the supervisory board. Thus, all post-balance-sheet events between December 31, 2001, and January 16, 2002, need to be considered by Xanadu Corp. for the purposes of evaluating whether or not they are to be accounted or reported under the revised IAS 10.

Adjusting and nonadjusting events (after the balance sheet date). Two kinds of events after the balance sheet date are delineated by the standard. These are, respectively, "adjusting events after the balance sheet date" and "nonadjusting events after the balance sheet date." Adjusting events are those post-balance-sheet events that provide evidence of conditions that actually existed at the balance sheet date, albeit they were not known at the time. Financial statements should be adjusted to reflect adjusting events after the balance sheet date.

Examples of adjusting events, given by the standard, are the following:

1. Resolution after the balance sheet date of a court case which confirms a present obligation requiring either an adjustment to an existing provision or

recognition of a provision instead of mere disclosure of a contingent liability;

2. Receipt of information after the balance sheet date indicating that an asset was impaired or that a previous impairment loss needs to be adjusted. For instance, the bankruptcy of a customer subsequent to the balance sheet date usually confirms the existence of loss at the balance sheet date, and the disposal of inventories after the balance sheet date provides evidence (not always conclusive, however) about their net realizable value at the balance sheet date;

3. The determination after the balance sheet date of the cost of assets purchased, or the proceeds from assets disposed of, before the balance sheet date;

4. The determination subsequent to the balance sheet date of the amount of profit sharing or bonus payments, where there was a present legal or constructive obligation at the balance sheet date to make the payments as a result of events before that date; and

5. The discovery of frauds or errors, after the balance sheet date, that show that the financial statements were incorrect at year end before the adjustment.

Commonly encountered situations of adjusting events are illustrated below.

• During the year 2001 Taj Corp. was sued by a competitor for $10 million for infringement of a trademark. Based on the advice of the company's legal counsel, Taj accrued the sum of $5 million as a provision in its financial statements for the year ended December 31, 2001. Subsequent to the balance sheet date, on February 15, 2002, the Supreme Court decided in favor of the party alleging infringement of the trademark and ordered the defendant to pay the aggrieved party a sum of $7 million. The financial statements were prepared by the company's management on January 31, 2002, and approved by the Board on February 20, 2002. Taj Corp. should adjust the provision by $2 million to reflect the award decreed by the Supreme Court (assumed to be the final appellate authority on the matter in this example) to be paid by Taj Corp. to its competitor. Had the judgment of the Supreme Court been delivered on February 25, 2002, or later, this post-balance-sheet event would have occurred after the cutoff point (i.e., the date the financial statements were authorized for original issuance). If so, adjustment of financial statements would not have been required.

• Penn Corp. carries its inventory at the lower of cost and net realizable value. At December 31, 2001, the cost of inventory, determined under the first-in, first-out (FIFO) method, as reported in its financial statements for the year then ended, was $5 million. Due to severe recession and other negative economic trends in the market, the inventory could not be sold during the entire month of January 2002. On February 10, 2002, Penn Corp. entered into an agreement to sell the entire inventory to a competitor for $4 million. Presuming the financial statements were authorized for issuance on February 15, 2002, the company should recognize this loss of $1 million in the financial statements for the year ended December 31, 2001.

In contrast with the foregoing, nonadjusting events are those post-balance-sheet events that are indicative of conditions that arose after the balance sheet date. Financial statements should not be adjusted to reflect nonadjusting events after the balance sheet date. An example of a nonadjusting event is a decline in the market value of investments between the balance sheet date and the date when the financial statements are authorized for issue. Since the fall in the market value of investments after the balance sheet date is not indicative of their market value at the balance sheet date (instead it reflects circumstances that arose subsequent to the balance sheet date) the fall in market value need not, and should not, be recognized in the financial statements at the balance sheet date.

Not all nonadjusting events are significant enough to require disclosure, however. The revised standard gives examples of nonadjusting events that would impair the ability of the users of financial statements to make proper evaluations or decisions if not disclosed. Where nonadjusting events after the balance sheet date are of such significance, disclosure should be made for each such significant category of nonadjusting event, of the nature of the event and an estimate of its financial effect or a statement that such an estimate cannot be made. Examples given by the standard of such significant nonadjusting post-balance-sheet events are the following:

1. A major business combination or disposing of a major subsidiary;
2. Announcing a plan to discontinue an operation;
3. Major purchases and disposals of assets or expropriation of major assets by government;
4. The destruction of a major production plant by fire;
5. Announcing or commencing the implementation of a major restructuring;
6. Abnormally large changes in asset prices or foreign exchange rates;
7. Significant changes in tax rates and enacted tax laws;
8. Entering into significant commitments or contingent liabilities; and
9. Major litigation arising from events occurring after the balance sheet date.

Dividends proposed or declared after the balance sheet date. Dividends on equity shares proposed or declared after the balance sheet date should not be recognized as a liability at the balance sheet date. This is a significant change from the requirements under the predecessor standard, IAS 10. The earlier standard on this subject had permitted, as an allowed alternative to mere disclosure, formal balance sheet recognition of a proposed dividend as a liability. Under the revised standard, if dividends are proposed or declared subsequent to the balance sheet date, but before the financial statements are authorized for issue, these may not be recognized as a liability. Only disclosure is permitted in such circumstances. IAS 1 (revised 1997) permits an enterprise to make this disclosure either in the notes to the financial statements or on the face of the balance sheet as a separate component of equity; the revised IAS 10 reiterates this disclosure guidance.

Going concern considerations. Deterioration in an entity's financial position after the balance sheet date could cast substantial doubts about an enterprise's ability to continue as a going concern. Revised IAS 10 requires that an enterprise should not prepare its financial statements on a going concern basis if management determines after the balance sheet date either that it intends to liquidate the enterprise or cease trading, or that it has no realistic alternative but to do so. Revised IAS 10 notes that disclosures prescribed by IAS 1 (revised 1997) under such circumstances should also be complied with.

Disclosure requirements. The following disclosures are mandated by IAS 10 (revised 1999):

1. The date when the financial statements were authorized for issue and who gave that authorization. If the enterprise's owners have the power to amend the financial statements after issuance, this fact should be disclosed;
2. If information is received after the balance sheet date about conditions that existed at the balance sheet date, disclosures that relate to those conditions should be updated in the light of the new information; and
3. Where nonadjusting events after the balance sheet date are of such significance that nondisclosure would affect the ability of the users of financial statements to make proper evaluations and decisions, disclosure should be made for each such significant category of nonadjusting event, of the nature of the event and an estimate of its financial effect or a statement that such an estimate cannot be made.

Accounting for Financial Liabilities

IAS 39 has established new requirements for accounting for financial liabilities which are held for trading and those which are derivatives. These will now be accounted for at fair value. Other financial liabilities will continue to be reported at amortized historical cost, pending a possible later endorsement of the notion of employing fair value to account for all financial assets and liabilities. (The IASC considers IAS 39 to be only an interim standard, and in theory at least is committed to developing a comprehensive standard within the next 2 years. This is expected to endorse a pure fair value approach, although many problems and much opposition from various preparer and user constituencies will first have to be overcome.)

Initial measurement of financial liabilities. IAS 39 stipulates that all financial liabilities are to be initially measured at cost, which (assuming they are each incurred in an arm's-length transaction) would equal fair value. Any related transaction costs are included in this initial measurement. In rare instances when the fair value of the consideration received is not reliably determinable, resort is to be made to a computation of the present value of all future cash flows related to the liability. In such a case, the discount rate to apply would be the prevailing rate on similar instruments issued by a party having a similar credit rating.

Remeasurement of financial liabilities. While the adoption of a pure fair value reporting model for financial instruments was contemplated, and may yet come to fruition in the IASC's ongoing project on financial instruments, all major national standard setters, and the IASC, have concluded that at the present time such would not be a practical solution. IAS 39 provides that, subsequent to initial recognition, an enterprise should measure all financial liabilities, other than liabilities held for trading purposes and derivative contracts that are liabilities, at amortized cost. Where the initial recorded amount is not the contractual maturity value of the liability (e.g., as when transaction costs are added to the issuance price, or when there was a premium or discount upon issuance) periodic amortization should be recorded, using the constant effective yield method.

An exception to the general rule applies when the financial liability is held for trading or is a derivative. An example of the former would be a "short" position in a security, the market value of which will be reported as a liability on the balance sheet. By definition, a short position is held for trading, since it represents a gamble that the price of the underlying security which has been sold will fall in the near term. Derivatives could be any of a wide range of instruments, such as swaps, forwards, futures and options; these will be liabilities if the reporting entity will be obligated to perform (e.g., if it has sold a "naked" option, giving the counterparty the right to purchase a security, at a fixed price, which the reporting entity in fact does not own). All financial liabilities which are held for trading or are derivatives, with two exceptions, are to be reported at fair value.

The first exception to this general rule applies in the case of a derivative liability that is linked to and that must be settled by delivery of an unquoted equity instrument, the fair value of which cannot be reliably measured. Those derivatives are to be measured at cost rather than fair value.

Secondly, financial liabilities which have been designated as hedged items are to be accounted for under the special hedge accounting rules of IAS 39. These are explained in Chapter 5 and illustrated in Chapter 10.

The various issues which may arise in connection with obtaining fair value information are also set forth in Chapter 5 and will not be repeated here.

Gains or losses occurring upon remeasurement of financial liabilities held for trading are included in results of operations in the period in which the fair value change occurs.

13 LONG-TERM DEBT

PERSPECTIVE AND ISSUES

Long-term debt represents future sacrifices of economic benefits to be repaid over a period of more than 1 year or, if longer, the operating cycle. Long-term debt includes bonds payable, notes payable, lease obligations, pension and deferred compensation plan obligations, deferred income taxes, and unearned revenue. The accounting for bonds and long-term notes is covered in this chapter. Since at present, international accounting standards address only a few of these topics, the accounting recommendations herein are those of the authors, based on practices in many nations.

The proper valuation of long-term debt is the present value of future payments using the market rate of interest, either stated or implied in the transaction, at the date the debt was incurred. An exception to the use of the market rate of interest stated or implied in the transaction in valuing long-term notes occurs when it is necessary to use an imputed interest rate, if the debt is either noninterest-bearing or bears a clearly nonmarket rate of interest.

Sources of IAS
IAS 32

DEFINITIONS OF TERMS

Amortization. The process of allocating an amount to expense over the periods benefited.

Bond. A written agreement whereby a borrower agrees to pay a sum of money at a designated future date plus periodic interest payments at the stated rate.

Bond issue costs. Costs related to issuing a bond (i.e., legal, accounting, underwriting fees, and printing and registration costs).

Bonds outstanding method. The method of accounting for serial bonds that assumes the discount or premium applicable to each bond of the issue is the same dollar amount per bond per year.

Book value approach. The method of recording the stock issued from a bond conversion at the carrying value of the bonds converted.

Callable bond. A bond in that the issuer reserves the right to call and retire the bond prior to its maturity.

Carrying value. The face amount of a debt issue increased or decreased by the applicable unamortized premium or discount plus unamortized issue costs.

Collateral. Asset(s) pledged to settle the obligation to repay a loan, if not repaid.

Convertible debt. Debt that may be converted into common stock at the holder's option after specific criteria are met.

Covenant. A clause in a debt contract written for the protection of the lender that outlines the rights and actions of the parties involved when certain conditions occur (e.g., when the debtor's current ratio declines beyond a specified level).

Debenture. Long-term debt not secured by collateral.

Defeasance. Extinguishment of debt by creating a trust to service it.

Discount. Created when a debt instrument sells for less than face value and occurs when the stated rate on the instrument is less than the market rate at the time of issue.

Effective interest method. The method of amortizing the discount or premium to interest expense so as to result in a constant rate of interest when applied to the amount of debt outstanding at the beginning of any given period.

Effective rate. See market rate.

Face value. The stated amount or principal due on the maturity date.

Imputation. The process of interest rate approximation that is accomplished by examining the circumstances under which the note was issued.

Long-term debt. Probable future sacrifices of economic benefits arising from present obligations that are not currently payable within 1 year or the operating cycle of the business, whichever is longer.

Market rate. The current rate of interest available for obligations issued under the same terms and conditions.

Market value approach. The method of recording the stock issued from a bond conversion at the current market price of the bonds converted or the stock issued.

Maturity date. The date on which the face value (principal) of the bond or note becomes due.

Maturity value. See face value.

Premium. Created when a debt instrument sells for more than its face value and occurs when the stated rate on the instrument is greater than the market rate at the time of issue.

Principal. See face value.

Secured debt. Debt that has collateral to satisfy the obligation (i.e., a mortgage on specific property), if not repaid.

Serial bond. Debt whose face value matures in installments.

Stated rate. The interest rate written on the face of the debt instrument.

Straight-line method. The method of amortizing the premium or discount to interest expense such that there is an even allocation of interest expense over the life of the debt.

Take-or-pay contract. A contract in which a purchaser of goods agrees to pay specified fixed or minimum amounts periodically in return for products, even if delivery is not taken. It results from a project financing arrangement where the project produces the products.

Throughput agreement. An agreement similar to a take-or-pay contract except that a service is provided by the project under the financing arrangement.

Troubled debt restructure. Occurs when the creditor, for economic or legal reasons related to the debtor's financial difficulties, grants a concession to the debtor (deferment or reduction of interest or principal) that it would not otherwise consider.

Unconditional purchase obligation. An obligation to transfer a fixed or minimum amount of funds in the future or to transfer goods or services at fixed or minimum prices.

Yield rate. See market rate.

CONCEPTS, RULES, AND EXAMPLES

Notes and Bonds

Long-term debt generally takes one of two forms: notes or bonds. **Notes** represent debt issued to a single investor without intending for the debt to be broken up among many investors. Their maturity, usually lasting 1 to 7 years, tends to be shorter than that of a bond. **Bonds** also result from a single agreement. However, a bond is intended to be broken up into various subunits, typically $1,000 each, which can be issued to a variety of investors.

Notes and bonds share common characteristics: a written agreement stating the amount of the principal, the interest rate, when the interest and principal are to be paid, and the restrictive covenants, if any, that must be met. The interest rate is affected by many factors, including the cost of money, the business risk factors, and the inflationary expectations associated with the business.

Nominal vs. effective rates. The stated rate on a note or bond often differs from the market rate at the time of issuance. When this occurs, the present value of the interest and principal payments will differ from the maturity, or face value. If the market rate exceeds the stated rate, the cash proceeds will be less than the face value of the debt because the present value of the total interest and principal payments discounted back to the present yields an amount that is less than the face value. Because an investor is rarely willing to pay more than the present value, the bonds must be issued at a discount. The discount is the difference between the issuance price (present value) and the face, or stated value of the bonds. This discount is then amortized over the life of the bonds to increase the recognized interest expense so that the total amount of the expense represents the actual bond yield.

When the stated rate exceeds the market rate, the bond will sell for more than its face value (at a premium) to bring the effective rate to the market rate and will decrease the total interest expense. When the market and stated rates are equivalent at the time of issuance, no discount or premium exists and the instrument will sell at its face value. Changes in the market rate subsequent to issuance are irrelevant in determining the discount or premium or their amortization.

Notes are a common form of exchange in business transactions for cash, property, goods, and services. Most notes carry a stated rate of interest, but it is not uncommon for noninterest-bearing notes or notes bearing an unrealistic rate of interest to be exchanged. Notes such as these, which are long-term in nature, do not reflect the economic substance of the transaction since the face value of the note does not represent the present value of the consideration involved. Not recording the note at its present value will misstate the cost of the asset or services to the buyer as well as the selling price and profit to the seller. In subsequent periods, both the interest expense and revenue will be misstated.

While international accounting standards do not prescribe how to measure transactions such as described above, several different models are discussed. In describing one of the common methods of reporting the elements of financial statements in the IASC's *Framework for the Preparation and Presentation of Financial Statements,* it is stated that "liabilities are carried at the present discounted value of future net cash outflows…" In the authors' opinion, unless the obligations issued in nonmonetary transactions (e.g., acquisition of plant assets in exchange for long-term debt) are recorded at their discounted present values, using the borrowing entity's applicable marginal borrowing rate, the economic substance of the transaction will be misstated, possibly materially so.

Accordingly, it is suggested that all commitments to pay (and receive) money at a determinable future date be subjected to present value techniques and, if necessary, interest imputation, with the exceptions of the following:

1. Normal accounts payable due within 1 year
2. Amounts to be applied to purchase price of goods or services or that provide security to an agreement (e.g., advances, progress payments, security deposits, and retainages)
3. Transactions between parent and subsidiary
4. Obligations payable at some indeterminable future date (warranties)
5. Lending and depositor savings activities of financial institutions whose primary business is lending money
6. Transactions where interest rates are affected by prescriptions of a governmental agency (e.g., revenue bonds, tax exempt obligations, etc.)

Notes issued solely for cash. When a note is issued solely for cash, its present value is assumed to be equal to the cash proceeds. The interest rate is that rate which equates the cash proceeds to the amounts to be paid in the future (i.e., **no** interest rate is to be imputed). For example, a $1,000 note due in 3 years that sells for $889 has an implicit rate of 4% ($1,000 x .889, where .889 is the present value factor of a lump sum at 4% for 3 years). This rate is to be used when amortizing the discount.

Notes issued for cash and a right or privilege. Often when a note bearing an unrealistic rate of interest is issued in exchange for cash, an additional right or privilege is granted, such as the issuer agreeing to sell merchandise to the purchaser at a reduced rate. The difference between the present value of the receivable and the cash loaned should logically be regarded as an addition to the cost of the products purchased for the purchaser/lender and as unearned revenue to the issuer. This treatment stems from the desire to match revenue and expense in the proper periods and to differentiate between those factors that affect income from operations and income or expense from nonoperating sources. In the situation above, the discount (difference between the cash loaned and the present value of the note) will be amortized to interest revenue or expense, while the unearned revenue or contractual right is amortized to sales and inventory, respectively. The discount affects income from nonoperational sources, while the unearned revenue or contractual right affects the gross profit computation.   This differentiation is necessary because the amortization rates used differ for the two amounts.

Example of accounting for a note issued for both cash and a contractual right

1. Miller borrows $10,000 via a noninterest-bearing 3-year note from Krueger.
2. Miller agrees to sell $50,000 of merchandise to Krueger at less than the ordinary retail price for the duration of the note.
3. The fair rate of interest on a note such as this is 10%.

As set forth in the discussion above, the difference between the present value of the note and the face value of the loan is to be regarded as part of the cost of the products purchased under the agreement. The present value factor for an amount due in 3 years at 10% is .75132. Therefore, the present value of the note is $7,513 ($10,000 x .75132). The $2,487 ($10,000 – $7,513) difference between the face value and the present value is to be recorded as a discount on the note payable and as unearned revenue on the future purchases. The following entries would be made to record the transaction:

	Miller			*Krueger*	
Cash	10,000		Note receivable	10,000	
Discount on			Contract right with		
note payable	2,487		supplier	2,487	
Note payable		10,000	Cash		10,000
Unearned revenue		2,487	Discount on note		
			receivable		2,487

The discount on note payable (and note receivable) should be amortized using the effective interest (constant yield) method, while the unearned revenue account and contract right with supplier account are amortized on a pro rata basis as the right to purchase merchandise is used up. Thus, if Krueger purchased $20,000 of merchandise from Miller in the first year, the following entries would be necessary:

Miller			*Krueger*		
Unearned revenue	995*		Inventory (or cost of		
Sales		995	sales)	995	
			Contract right with		
Interest expense	751		supplier		995
Discount on			Discount on note receivable	751	
note payable		751**	Interest revenue		751

  * *$2,487 x (20,000/50,000)*
** *$7,513 x 10%*

The amortization of unearned revenue and contract right with supplier accounts will fluctuate with the amount of purchases made. If there is a balance remaining in the account at the end of the loan term, it is amortized to the appropriate account in that final year.

Noncash transactions. When a note is issued for consideration such as property, goods, or services, and the transaction is entered into at arm's length, the stated interest rate is presumed to be fair unless (1) no interest rate is stated, (2) the stated rate is unreasonable, or (3) the face value of the debt is materially different from the consideration involved or the current market value of the note at the date of the transaction. As discussed above, it is recommended that when the rate on the note is not considered fair, the note is to be recorded at the fair market value of the property, goods, or services received or at an amount that reasonably approximates the market value of the note, whichever is the more clearly determinable. When this amount differs from the face value of the note, the difference is to be recorded as a discount or premium and amortized to interest expense.

Example of accounting for a note exchanged for property

1. Alpha sells Beta a machine that has a fair market value of $7,510.
2. Alpha receives a 3-year noninterest-bearing note having a face value of $10,000.

In this situation, the fair market value of the consideration is readily determinable and thus represents the amount at which the note is to be recorded. The following entry is necessary:

Machine	7,510	
Discount on notes payable	2,490	
Notes payable		10,000

The discount will be amortized to interest expense over the 3-year period using the interest rate **implied** in the transaction.

If the fair market value of the consideration or note is not determinable, the present value of the note must be determined using an **imputed** interest rate. This rate will then be used to establish the present value of the note by discounting all future payments on the note at this rate. General guidelines for imputing the interest rate include the prevailing rates of similar instruments from creditors with similar credit ratings and the rate the debtor could obtain for similar financing from other sources. Other determining factors include any collateral or restrictive covenants involved, the current and expected prime rate, and other terms pertaining to the instrument. The objective is to approximate the rate of interest that would have resulted if an independent borrower and lender had negotiated a similar transaction under comparable terms and conditions. This determination is as of the issuance date, and any subsequent changes in interest rates would be irrelevant.

Bonds represent a promise to pay a sum of money at a designated maturity date plus periodic interest payments at a stated rate. Bonds are used primarily to borrow funds from the general public or institutional investors when a contract for a single amount (a note) is too large for one lender to supply. Dividing up the amount needed into $1,000 or $10,000 units makes it easier to sell the bonds.

In most situations, a bond is issued at a price other than its face value. The amount of the cash exchanged is equal to the total of the present value of the interest and principal payments. The difference between the cash proceeds and the face value is recorded as a premium if the cash proceeds are greater or a discount if they are less. The journal entry to record a bond issued at a premium follows:

Cash	(proceeds)
Premium on bonds payable	(difference)
Bonds payable	(face value)

The premium will be recognized over the life of the bond issue. If issued at a discount, "Discount on bonds payable" would be debited for the difference. As the premium is amortized, it will reduce interest expense on the books of the issuer (a discount will increase interest expense). The premium (discount) would be added to (deducted from) the related liability when a balance sheet is prepared.

The **effective interest method** is the preferred method of accounting for a discount or premium arising from a note or bond, although some other method may be used (e.g., straight-line) if the results are not materially different. Although the effective interest method is not prescribed under international accounting standards as such, the profession has made the use of the effective interest method the only acceptable one. Under the effective interest method, the discount or premium is to be amortized over the life of the debt in such a way as to result in a constant rate of interest when applied to the amount outstanding at the beginning of any given period. Therefore, interest expense is equal to the market rate of interest at the time of issuance multiplied by this beginning figure. The difference between the interest expense and the cash paid represents the amortization of the discount or premium.

Where use of the straight-line amortization method does not result in a material distortion as compared to the effective interest method, it would also be acceptable. Interest expense under the **straight-line method** is equal to the cash interest paid plus the amortized portion of the discount or minus the amortized portion of the premium. The amortized portion is equal to the total amount of the discount or premium divided by the life of the debt from issuance in months multiplied by the number of months the debt has been outstanding that year. Formerly, the straight-line method was used because it eliminated the complicated calculations required by the effective interest method; however, the prevalence of computers and of programs that compute the interest accrual under the more accurate effective interest method have largely eliminated this reason.

Amortization tables are often created at the time of the bond's issuance to provide figures when recording the necessary entries relating to the debt issue. They also provide a check of accuracy since the final values in the unamortized discount or premium and carrying value columns should be equal to zero and the bond's face value, respectively.

Example of applying the effective interest method

1. A 3-year, 12%, $10,000 bond is issued at 1/1/00, with interest payments semi-annually.
2. The market rate is 10%.

The amortization table would appear as follows:

Date	Credit cash	Debit int. exp.	Debit prem.	Unam. prem. bal.	Carrying value
1/1/00				$507.61	$10,507.61(a)
7/1/00	$ 600.00(b)	$ 525.38(c)	$ 74.62(d)	432.99(e)	10,432.99(f)
1/1/01	600.00	521.65	78.35	354.64	10,354.64
7/1/01	600.00	517.73	82.27	272.37	10,272.37
1/1/02	600.00	513.62	86.38	185.99	10,185.99
7/1/02	600.00	509.30	90.70	95.29	10,095.29
1/1/03	600.00	504.71(g)	95.29	--	$10,000.00
	$3,600.00	$3,092.39	$507.61		

(a)*PV of principal and interest payments*
    $10,000(.74622)   =   *$ 7,462.20*
    $ 600(5.07569)   =   *3,045.41*
                              $10,507.61

(b)*$10,000.00 x .06*

(c)*$10,507.61 x .05*
(d)*$600.00 – $525.38*
(e)*$507.61 – $74.62*
(f)*$10,507.61 – $74.62*
   (or $10,000 + $432.99)
(g)*Rounding error = $.05*

When the interest date does not coincide with the year end, an adjusting entry must be made. The proportional share of interest payable should be recognized along with the amortization of the discount or premium. Within the amortization period, the discount or premium can be amortized using the straight-line method, as a practical matter, or can be computed more precisely as described above.

If the bonds are issued between interest dates, discount or premium amortization must be computed for the period between the sale date and the next interest date. This is accomplished by "straight-lining" the period's amount calculated using the usual method of amortization. In addition, the purchaser prepays the seller the amount of interest that has accrued since the last interest date. This interest is recorded as a payable by the seller. At the next interest date, the buyer then receives the full amount of interest regardless of how long the bond has been held. This procedure results in interest being paid equivalent to the time the bond has been outstanding.

Costs may be incurred in connection with issuing bonds. Examples include legal, accounting, and underwriting fees; commissions; and engraving, printing, and registration costs. Although these costs should be classified as a deferred charge and amortized using the effective interest method, generally the amount involved is insignificant enough that use of the simpler straight-line method would not result in a material difference. These costs do not provide any future economic benefit and therefore should not be considered an asset. Since these costs reduce the amount of cash proceeds, they in effect increase the effective interest rate and probably should be accounted for the same as an unamortized discount. Short-term debt obligations that are expected to be refinanced on a long-term basis, and that accordingly are classified as long-term debt according to IAS 1 (revised 1997), are discussed in Chapter 12.

The following diagram illustrates the recommended accounting treatments for monetary assets (and liabilities).

Extinguishment of Debt

Early extinguishments. Management may reacquire or retire outstanding debt before its scheduled maturity. This decision is usually caused by changes in present or expected interest rates or in cash flows. One concern, however, is that in a period of rising rates, an entity can retire its debt early, at a discount (as rising rates cause a decline in the market value of fixed-rate debt instruments), that will be reported in the income statement as a gain, but then re-borrow at current market rates, thereby causing future periods to carry a heavier debt service burden. This is one example of "window dressing," which allows management to show favorable performance currently while affecting future results adversely.

Although accounting rules can prevent misleading reporting of certain forms of window dressing which are only sham transactions (such as nominal sales of investments under repurchase agreements, which in reality are only secured borrowings), other events are real transactions that must be given accounting recognition. The actual extinguishment of debt at a discount, giving rise to a gain, is one of the latter types of events; the only question is how best to make the users of the financial statements fully aware of the potential implications.

Although international standards have yet to address this, in the United States the accounting standard setters long ago mandated that gains or losses on debt extinguishment be given "extraordinary item" treatment in the statement of earnings.

ACCOUNTING FOR MONETARY ASSETS AND LIABILITIE

```
                    ┌─────────────────────────────────────┐
                    │  Monetary assets and liabilities      │
                    │  recorded at PV of future cash flows   │
                    └─────────────────────────────────────┘
```

Notes received or issued solely for cash	Notes received or issued for cash plus some right or privilege	Notes received or issued in a noncash exchange for property, goods, or services

Notes received or issued solely for cash:
- Cash exchanged = Present value of note
  - Face amount = Cash exchanged → No discount or premium recorded; Face rate = Yield rate
  - Face amount > Cash exchanged → Discount recorded; Face rate < Yield rate
  - Face amount < Cash exchanged → Premium recorded; Face rate > Yield rate

Notes received or issued for cash plus some right or privilege:
- Difference between PV of the note and the cash exchanged is the amount assigned to the right or privilege
- Discount or premium corresponds to the amount assigned to the right or privilege

Interest rate not assumed fair:
- No interest is stated
- Stated interest rate is unreasonable
- Stated face amount of the note is materially different from the current cash sales price for the same or similar items or from the FMV of the note at the date of the transaction

Interest rate assumed fair:
- Record note at face amount, which is assumed to be the FMV of the property, goods, or services

Recognize interest at other than stated rate:
- FMV of property, goods, or services exchanged is known or the FMV of the note is known
  - Use FMV of goods, property, or services. If there is no reliable FMV of the goods, property, or services, use FMV of note
  - Rate of interest equates future payments of the note with the FMV of the goods, property, or services or the FMV of the note
- FMV of property, goods, or services exchanged is not known and the FMV of note not known
  - Use imputed interest rate to calculate PV of the note and determine interest expense/income

The purpose was merely to highlight such transactions, not to preclude the transactions themselves or to defer or avoid recognition of the resultant gains or losses. Although gain or loss on debt extinguishment clearly does not meet the definition of an extraordinary item under US GAAP, a special rule established the requirement that such gains or losses be so accounted for.

International accounting standards establish (in IAS 8) a restrictive definition of extraordinary items. Clearly, this definition would not embrace such transactions as debt extinguishments, which are undertaken in the normal course of business by many entities. Therefore, the recommended, and only, recourse is to include adequate disclosure in the notes to the financial statements so that financial statement users are not mislead. This prescription is implied by IAS 1 (revised 1997), which stipulates that the statements should include "additional information . . . that is necessary for a fair presentation."

Defeasance of debt. Another phenomenon that borders on window dressing is the relatively recent practice of engaging in **in-substance defeasance** of debt. Under this practice, certain assets are set aside in an irrevocable trust arrangement, to be used solely for the servicing and ultimate retirement of specific debt obligations. The concept is that since the assets are unavailable for any other purpose, both the assets and the debt obligations can validly be removed from the enterprise's balance sheet. Although this accounting treatment does not change the entity's reported net worth, it does alter the relationship between its reported debt and its equity. Since this is often viewed as being a key indicator of an entity's financial strength and long-term viability, this could have a material impact on how the entity is evaluated by investors and lenders.

International accounting standards do not address the matter of defeasance of debt. In the United States, defeasance has been a permitted accounting practice for over 10 years, although it is possible that with the promised promulgation of a new standard on derecognition of financial instruments (subject of a recent exposure draft) this practice may again become prohibited. The authors agree that the currently permitted treatment can result in distorting implications being drawn from the financial statements and urge that in-substance defeasances not be accounted for as true debt extinguishments.

Computing the gain or loss on debt extinguishments. The difference between the net carrying value and the acquisition price is to be recorded as a gain or loss. If the acquisition price is greater than the carrying value, a loss exists. A gain is generated if the acquisition price is less than the carrying value. These gains or losses are to be recognized in the period in which the retirement took place. Since, under international standards, these cannot be defined as extraordinary, logic suggests that they be reported as "other" income or expense, which is the same category in which interest expense is normally reported. It would **not** be appropriate, however, to include any gain or loss in the interest pool from which capitalized interest is computed under IAS 23 (discussed in Chapter 8).

The unamortized premium or discount and issue costs should be amortized to the acquisition date and recorded prior to determination of the gain or loss. If the extinguishment of debt does not occur on the interest date, the interest payable accruing between the last interest date and the acquisition date must also be recorded.

Example of accounting for the extinguishment of debt

1. A 10%, 10-year, $200,000 bond is dated and issued on 1/1/00 at $98, with the interest payable semiannually.
2. Associated bond issue costs of $14,000 are incurred.
3. 4 years later, on 1/1/04, the entire bond issue is repurchased at $102 per $100 face value and is retired.
4. The straight-line method of amortization is used since the result is not materially different from that when the effective interest method is used.

The gain or loss on the repurchase is computed as follows:

Reacquisition price [(102/100) x $200,000]		$204,000
Net carrying amount:		
Face value	$200,000	
Unamortized discount [2% x 200,000 x (6/10)]	(2,400)	
Unamortized issue costs [14,000 x (6/10)]	(8,400)	189,200
Loss on bond repurchase		$ 14,800

The loss on bond repurchase (debt extinguishment) is treated as another nonoperating item, in the same manner as interest expense. It should not be capitalized under IAS 23 as part of cost of plant assets, however.

Troubled Debt Restructurings

Another issue related to long-term debt is that of troubled debt restructurings. These usually involve situations where the creditor, for economic or legal reasons related to the debtor's financial difficulties, grants the debtor a concession that would otherwise not be granted. For example, the creditor may accept debtor assets having a market value less than the outstanding amount owed as full settlement of the obligation, or may offer extensions of time to pay or a reduction of either interest rate or face value, or both. These steps are taken because the creditor perceives the situation as being risky and deems it better to take "half a loaf" than to gamble on the outcome of a bankruptcy filing or other drastic action by the debtor.

Although no particular international accounting standards address these occurrences, there are some interesting accounting issues to be dealt with. If the debt restructuring is a settlement of the debt at less than the carrying amount, whether for cash of by an exchange of an asset, the debtor will have realized a gain and the creditor will have incurred a loss. The amount of the gain and the loss will be measured by the difference between the fair value (**not** the book value) of the asset transferred to settle the debt. For example, if a debtor transfers an asset having a $4.5 million book value and a $5.0 million fair market value to settle debt and accrued interest due in the amount of $6.0 million, a gain of $1.0 million has been enjoyed on the settlement and an asset carried at $4.5 million has been converted to its market value of $5.0 million, for another gain of $500,000. The creditor, meanwhile, has incurred a loss of $1.0 million.

The restructuring of troubled debt by modification of terms is more likely to cause accounting confusion than is an exchange of assets. For example, if the creditor prospectively waives some or all of the interest on the debt, so that, for example, a $4 million, 10% loan becomes a $4 million 2% debt obligation, there are some who would argue that this does not give rise to loss recognition by the creditor or gain recognition by the debtor, since it is only a modification of future terms. That is, under this view the creditor would realize less income in future periods but would not reflect a loss on the **agreement** to accept lower yield in later periods. Similarly, if the due date of the debt is extended, some have argued that this also is not a recognizable economic event, but rather, is to be reported only in later periods.

Notwithstanding these perspectives, it should be clear that an economic event has occurred by the very fact of the restructuring. Since the goal of accounting is to report on economic events, a more rational response would be to measure these events when they occur and include the effect in the creditor's and debtor's respective income statements at that time. The only meaningful way to accomplish this is to measure the present value of future cash flows under the restructured loan agreement, discounted by the **effective** rate on the original borrowing. (Effective rate is used to denote that if there were deferred fees or other costs, or a premium or discount, being amortized over the term of the loan, these should be taken into account and used instead of the nominal interest rate on the original debt.) Thus, the difference between the present value of the newly defined future cash flows and the carrying amount of the debt immediately prior to the restructuring should be the measure of the gain or loss to be recognized.

Example of restructuring with gain/loss recognized

Assume that a debtor owes on a 5% interest-bearing note payable in 5 years a remaining principal balance of $90,000 plus accrued interest of $10,000. The lender agrees to a restructuring to assist the debtor, which is in financial straits and threatening to declare bankruptcy. The interest rate is reduced to 4% by the lender, the principal is reduced to $72,500, and the accrued interest is forgiven entirely.

Future cash flows (after restructuring):

Principal	$72,500
Interest (5 years x $72,500 x 4%)	14,500
Total cash to be received	$87,000

Note that it would **not** be meaningful simply to compare the new total expected cash flow from the loan, $87,000, to the carrying value of the loan ($100,000, including accrued interest), for an indicated loss of $13,000. This fails to consider the time value of money, since the $100,000 is owed to the creditor today, whereas the $87,000 will be collected over a 5-year period. Instead, it is necessary to compute the present value of future cash flows, using the effective rate of the original borrowing, 5%, as follows:

		5% 5 yrs. PV factor
Future cash flows (after restructuring):		
Principal	$56,806	($72,500 x 0.78353)
Interest	12,555	($ 2,900 x 4.32948)
Total present value	$69,361	

The difference between the amount owed immediately prior to the restructuring, $100,000, and the agreed-upon settlement, $69,361, is the measure of the economic loss, $30,639. The entries by the creditor would be as follows:

Beginning of Year 1

Bad debt expense	30,639	
Interest receivable		10,000
Valuation allowance		20,639

End of Year 1

Cash	2,900	
Valuation allowance	568	
Bad debt expense (or interest income)		3,468 (69,361 x .05)

End of Year 2

Cash	2,900	
Valuation allowance	596	
Bad debt expense (or interest income)		3,496 (69,929 x .05)

End of Year 3

Cash	2,900	
Valuation allowance	626	
Bad debt expense (or interest income)		3,526 (70,525 x .05)

End of Year 4

Cash	2,900	
Valuation allowance	658	
Bad debt expense (or interest income)		3,558 (71,151 x .05)

End of Year 5

Cash	2,900	
Valuation allowance	691	
Bad debt expense (or interest income)		3,591 (71,809 x .05)
Cash	72,500	
Valuation allowance	17,500	
Note receivable		90,000

Entries to be made by the debtor would largely mirror those shown above.

Convertible Debt

Bonds are frequently issued with the right to convert them into common stock of the company at the holder's option when certain terms and conditions are met (i.e., a target market price is reached). Convertible debt is used for two reasons. First, when a specific amount of funds is needed, convertible debt often allows fewer shares to be issued (assuming conversion) than if the funds were raised by directly issuing the shares. Thus, less dilution occurs. Second, the conversion feature allows debt to be issued at a lower interest rate and with fewer restrictive covenants than if the debt were issued without it.

This dual nature of debt and equity, however, creates a question as to whether the equity element should receive separate recognition. Support for separate treatment is based on the assumption that this equity element has economic value. Since the convertible feature tends to lower the rate of interest, it can easily be argued that a portion of the proceeds should be allocated to this equity feature. On the other hand, a case can be made that the debt and equity elements are inseparable, and thus that the instrument is either all debt or all equity. International accounting standards had not previously addressed this matter directly, although the focus of *Framework for Preparation and Presentation of Financial Statements* on "true and fair presentation" could be said to support the notion that the proceeds of a convertible debt offering be allocated between debt and equity accounts. Recently, however, IAS 32 has been promulgated, defining convertible bonds (among others) as compound financial instruments, the component parts of which must be classified according to their separate characteristics.

Features of convertible debt. Features of convertible debt typically include: (1) a conversion price 15 to 20% greater than the market value of the stock when the debt is issued; (2) conversion features (price and number of shares) that protect against dilution from stock dividends, splits, and so on; and (3) a callable feature at the issuer's option that is usually exercised once the conversion price is reached (thus forcing conversion or redemption).

Convertible debt also has its disadvantages. If the stock price increases significantly after the debt is issued, the issuer would have been better off simply by issuing the stock. Additionally, if the price of the stock does not reach the conversion price, the debt will never be converted (a condition known as overhanging debt).

Accounting for compound instruments. IAS 32 establishes the notion that component parts of compound instruments, such as convertible bonds, must be accounted for separately, consistent with their separate characteristics, but does not prescribe specific methodologies to accomplish this. However, several measurement strategies are noted in the standard, and these are illustrated in the following paragraphs.

Residual allocation method. One method of allocating proceeds from the issuance of convertible debt would be allocate to the less easily measured component (probably the conversion feature) the residual after first assigning the market value to the more directly measured component (the debt, absent the conversion feature). To illustrate this approach, consider the following fact situation.

Example of the residual allocation method

Istanbul Corp. sells convertible bonds having aggregate par (face) value of $25 million to the public at a price of $98 on January 2, 2000. The bonds are due December 31, 2007, but can be called at $102 anytime after January 2, 2003. The bonds carry a coupon of 6% and are convertible into Istanbul Corp. common stock at an exchange ratio of 25 shares per bond (each bond having a face value of $1,000). Taking the discount on the offering price into account, the bonds were priced to yield about 6.3% to maturity.

The company's investment bankers have advised it that without the conversion feature, Istanbul's bonds would have had to have carried an interest yield of 8% to have been sold in the current market environment. Thus, the market price of a pure bond with a 6% coupon at January 2, 2000, would have been about $883.48 (the present value of a stream of semiannual interest payments of $30 per bond, plus a terminal value of $1,000, discounted at a 4% semiannual rate).

This suggests that of the $980 being paid for each bond, $883.48 is being paid for the pure debt obligation, and another $96.52 is being offered for the conversion feature. Given this analysis, the entry to record the original issuance of the $25 million in debt securities on January 2, 2000, would be as follows:

Cash	24,500,000	
Discount on bonds payable	2,913,000	
Bonds payable		25,000,000
Paid-in-capital--conversion feature		2,413,000

The discount should be amortized to interest expense, ideally by the effective yield method (constant return on increasing base) over the 8 years to the maturity date. For purposes of this example, however, straight-line amortization ($2,913,000 ÷ 16 periods = $182,000 per semiannual period) will be used. Thus, the entry to record the June 30, 2000 interest payment would be as follows:

Interest expense	932,000	
Discount on bonds payable		182,000
Cash		750,000

The paid-in capital account arising from the foregoing transaction would form a permanent part of the capital of Istanbul Corp. If the bonds are later converted, this would be transferred to the common stock accounts, effectively forming part of the price paid for the shares ultimately issued. If the bondholders decline to convert and the bonds are eventually paid off at maturity, the paid-in capital from the conversion feature will form a type of "donated capital" to the enterprise; the bondholders effectively have forfeited this capital that they had contributed to the company.

If the bonds are not converted, the discount on the bonds payable will continue to be amortized until maturity. However, if they are converted, the remaining unamortized balance in this account, along with the face value of the bonds, will constitute the "price" being paid for the stock to be issued. To illustrate this, assume the following:

On July 1, 2003, all the bonds are tendered for conversion to common stock of Istanbul Corp. The remaining book value of the bonds will be converted into common stock, which does not carry any par or stated value. The first step is to compute the book value of the debt.

Bonds payable		$25,000,000
Discount on bonds payable		
Original discount	$ 2,913,000	
Less amortization to date (4.4 yrs.)	(1,638,000)	1,275,000
Net book value of obligation		$23,725,000

The entry to record the conversion, given the foregoing information, is as follows:

Bonds payable	25,000,000	
Paid-in-capital--conversion feature	2,413,000	
Discount on bonds payable		1,275,000
Common stock, no par value		26,138,000

Note that in the foregoing entry, the effective price recorded for the shares being issued is the book value of the remaining debt, adjusted by the price previously recorded to reflect the sale of the conversion feature. In the present instance, given the book value at the conversion date (a function of when the conversion privilege was exercised), and given the conversion ratio of 25 shares per bond, an effective price of $41.82 per share is being paid for the stock to be issued. This is determined without any reference to the market value at the date of the conversion. Presumably, the market price is higher, as it is unlikely that the bondholders would surrender an asset earning 6%, with a fixed maturity date, for another asset having a lower value and having an uncertain future worth (although if the dividend yield were somewhat higher than the equivalent bond interest, an unlikely event, this might happen).

Another approach to the conversion would be to reflect the stock issuance at the then-current market value, reporting a gain or loss for the difference between the market value per share and the amount computed on the book value basis, as shown above. However, this can be criticized because it is not normally acceptable to report income statement events (the gain or loss) arising from capital transactions. For this reason, the book value approach is recommended.

Relative market value approach. The alternative to the residual value allocation method described above for assigning the proceeds from the sale of convertible debt would be to measure directly the market value of each component of the compound financial instrument. This may be more easily accomplished in some circumstances than in others. For example, if options on Istanbul stock are currently being traded on the open market at the time the convertible debt is offered for sale, it would be possible to assess the value of the conversion feature, although some judgment might be involved to adjust for the different features and limitations of exchange traded options and the conversion feature. Consider the following example.

Example of the relative market value approach

As in the example above, Istanbul Corp. sells convertible bonds having aggregate par (face) value of $25 million to the public at a price of $98 on January 2, 2000. The bonds are due December 31, 2007, but can be called at $102 anytime after January 2, 2003. The bonds carry a coupon of 6% and are convertible into Istanbul Corp. common stock at an exchange ratio of 25 shares per bond (each bond having a face value of $1,000). Taking the discount on the offering price into account, the bonds were priced to yield about 6.3% to maturity.

The company's investment bankers again have advised it that without the conversion feature, Istanbul's bonds would have had to have carried an interest yield of 8% to have been sold in the current market environment. Thus, the market price of a "pure" bond with a 6% coupon at January 2, 2000, would have been about $883.48. Now, however, assume also that options on Istanbul stock are being traded on the open market. The common stock is presently selling for $32 per share; options to buy the stock at $42 are trading at $3.50 each.

Since 625,000 shares will be issued if all the bonds are converted, this suggests a gross value of $2,187,500 due to the conversion feature, or an equivalent of $87.50 per bond. However, the actual conversion feature is at a lower price than is attached to the market-traded options ($40 vs. $42), and these have a longer life (8 years vs. a typical 2 years on market-traded options), so the investment bankers advise Istanbul management that the value per stock right would be $6, or an indicated value of $150 per bond (since each is convertible into 25 shares), for a total value of $3,750,000. Since the total indicated value of the conversion privilege ($3,750,000) plus the pure bonds ($883.48 x 25,000 bonds = $22,087,000) is greater (at $25,837,000) than the actual selling price of the bonds ($24,500,000), the amounts to be allocated to the debt and to the equity conversion feature should be pro rated, as follows:

22,087,000/25,837,000	x	24,500,000	=	$20,944,050	($837.76 per bond)
3,750,000/25,837,000	x	24,500,000	=	$ 3,555,950	($142.24 per bond)

This suggests that of the $980 being paid for each bond, $837.76 is being paid for the pure debt obligation, and another $142.24 is being offered for the conversion feature. Given this analysis, the entry to record the original issuance of the $25 million in debt securities on January 2, 2000, would be as follows:

Cash	24,500,000	
Discount on bonds payable	4,055,950	
Bonds payable		25,000,000
Paid-in-capital--conversion feature		3,555,950

As with the earlier example, the indicated discount would be amortized over the term to maturity of the debt, 8 years in this case, by the effective yield method, or by the straight-line method if this would not make a material difference in reported financial position and results of operations.

It might be noted that under present US GAAP, when convertible debt is issued no value is apportioned to the conversion feature when recording the issue. However, it is likely that US standards will eventually follow the path set by IAS 32 in this regard, since the issue of accounting for compound financial instruments has been debated for over 5 years and the existence of the newly promulgated international standard will doubtless put added pressure on US standard setters.

Induced Conversion of Debt

A special situation may occur in that the conversion privileges of convertible debt are modified after issuance of the debt. These modifications may take the form of reduced conversion prices or additional consideration paid to the convertible debt holder. The debtor offers these modifications or "sweeteners" to induce prompt conversion of the outstanding debt. This is in addition to the normal strategy of calling the convertible debt to induce the holders to convert, assuming the underlying economic values make this attractive (debtors often do this when only a small fraction of the originally issued convertible debt remains outstanding).

Logically, there are two ways to account for these sweeteners. The first would be to treat this as a reduction in the proceeds of the stock offering, thereby reducing paid-in capital from the transaction. The second possible accounting treatment would be to record these payments as an expense in the period of conversion. The former position is based on the notion that costs associated with the raising of equity capital are netted against the proceeds so generated; if a sweetener is deemed needed to raise the equity capital in a given situation, this should be accounted for as any other costs, such as underwriting fees, would be. The latter position springs from a recognition that if it had been part of the original arrangement, a change in the exchange ratio or other adjustment would have affected the allocation of the original proceeds between debt and equity, and the discount or premium originally recognized would have been different in amount, and hence periodic amortization would have differed as well.

There are no specific international standards on this matter, and the arguments for both treatments are impressive. Accordingly, both are illustrated here. The example that follows illustrates the calculation and recording of the debt conversion expense if the cost of the sweetener is deemed to be a period cost.

Example of debt conversion expense

1. January 1, 2000, Imag Company issued ten 8% convertible bonds at $1,000 par value without a discount or premium, maturing December 31, 2010.
2. The bonds are initially convertible into no-par common stock of Imag at a conversion price of $25.
3. On July 1, 2004, the convertible bonds have a market value of $600 each.
4. To induce the convertible bondholders to convert their bonds quickly, Imag reduces the conversion price to $20 for bondholders who convert before July 21, 2004 (within 20 days).
5. The market price of Imag Company's common stock on the date of conversion is $15 per share.

The fair value of the incremental consideration paid by Imag upon conversion is calculated as follows for each bond converted before July 21, 2004:

Value of securities issued to debt holders:

Face amount	$1,000 per bond
÷ New conversion price	÷ $20 per share
Number of common shares issued upon conversion	50 shares
x Price per common share	x $15 per share
Value of securities issued	$ 750(a)

Value of securities issuable pursuant to the original conversion privileges:

Face amount	$1,000 per bond
÷ Original conversion price	÷ $25 per share
Number of common shares issuable pursuant to original conversion privilege	40 shares
x Price per share	x $15 per share
Value of securities issuable pursuant to original conversion privileges	$ 600 (b)
Value of securities issued	$ 750 (a)
Value of securities issuable pursuant to the original conversion privileges	600 (b)
Fair value of incremental consideration	$ 150

The entry to record the debt conversion for **each bond** is

Convertible debt	1,000	
Debt conversion expense	150	
Common stock--no par		1,150

If instead of the foregoing accounting treatment, it was decided to treat the sweetener as a cost of raising capital, in this fact situation the only change would be to credit common stock for $1,000 per bond rather than the market-determined $1,150. Depending on whether the stock carried a par or a stated value, it might have been necessary to make a slightly different entry, but the concept would be the same.

Debt Issued With Stock Warrants

Warrants are certificates enabling the holder to purchase a stated number of shares of stock at a certain price within a certain period. They are often issued with bonds to enhance the marketability of the bonds and to lower the bond's interest rate.

Detachable warrants are similar to other features, such as the conversion feature discussed earlier, which under IAS 32 make the debt a compound financial instrument and which necessitates that there be an allocation of the original proceeds among the constituent elements. Since warrants, which will often be traded in the market, are easier to value than are conversion features, the second method discussed above, pro rata allocation based on relative market values, is to be favored.

Example of accounting for a bond with a detachable warrant

1. A $1,000 bond with a detachable warrant to buy 10 shares of $10 par common stock at $50 per share is issued for $1,025.
2. Immediately after the issuance the bonds trade at $980 and the warrants at $60.
3. The market value of the stock is $54.

The relative market value of the bonds is 94% (980/1,040) and the warrant is 6% (60/1,040). Thus, $62 (6% x $1,025) of the issuance price is assigned to the warrants. The journal entry to record the issuance is

Cash	1,025	
Discount on bonds payable	37	
Bonds payable		1,000
Paid-in capital--warrants		
(or "Stock options outstanding")		62

The discount is the difference between the purchase price assigned to the bond, $963 (94% x $1,025), and its face value, $1,000. The debt itself is accounted for in the normal fashion.

The entry to record the subsequent future exercise of the warrant would be

Cash	500	
Paid-in capital--warrants	62	
Common stock		100
Paid-in capital		462 (difference)

Assuming the warrants are not exercised, the journal entry is

| Paid-in capital--warrants | 62 | |
| Paid-in capital--expired warrants | | 62 |

14 ACCOUNTING FOR LEASES

PERSPECTIVE AND ISSUES

Entrepreneurs who experiment with innovative means of financing have long used leasing as a vehicle to finance acquisitions of business assets. During the past few decades, however, the business of leasing has experienced staggering growth. The tremendous popularity of leasing is quite understandable, as it offers great flexibility coupled with a range of economic advantages over ownership in many situations. The lessee (borrower) is typically able to obtain 100% financing with leasing, whereas under a credit purchase arrangement the buyer would generally have to make an initial payment that would not be financed. In many cases the leasing arrangement offers tax benefits through larger tax deductions compared to the purchasing option. Also, during the term of the lease, the lessor receives from the lessee the equivalent of interest in the form of lease payments and, at the end of the lease term, usually some residual value. Finally, leasing often protects the lessee from the risk of obsolescence.

The lease transaction derives its accounting complexity from the number of alternatives available to the parties involved. Leases can be structured to allow manipulation of the tax benefits associated with the leased asset. They can be used to transfer ownership of the leased asset, and they can be used to transfer the risk of ownership. In any event, the economic substance of the transaction dictates the accounting treatment. The accounting for lease transactions is probably the best example of the accounting profession's substance over form principle, as set forth in the IASC's *Framework for the Preparation and Presentation of Financial Statements*. If the transaction effectively transfers ownership to the lessee, the substance of the transaction is that of a sale and should be recognized as such even though the transaction takes the form of a lease.

Until 1997, IAS 17, *Accounting for Leases*, was the only promulgated standard on lease accounting under International Accounting Standards. IAS 17 was approved in 1982 and became effective for years beginning on or after January 1, 1984. In 1997 the IASC issued an exposure draft, E56, as part of its "core set of standards" project, with the intention that only minor changes be made to IAS 17 at this time; a further, more comprehensive review of the entire set of lease accounting issues is expected at a later date. E56 was adopted in late 1997 as IAS 17 (revised), having as its major effect the elimination of the free choice permitted to lessors between two alternative income recognition methods. The international accounting standards, therefore, still do not address a range of important lease accounting issues, such as the accounting for leveraged leases.

Per the original IAS 17, lessors were required to recognize finance income based on a pattern reflecting a constant rate of return, but were permitted to compute that return on either the net investment outstanding (i.e., the book investment), or the net cash investment (which would be a different amount). The revised standard eliminates the second alternative and instead requires that the net (book) investment serve as the basis for the constant rate of return computation.

In general, almost any type of arrangement which satisfies the definition of a lease is covered by this standard. Both the original and the revised IAS 17 do exclude the following specialized types of lease agreements, however:

1. Lease agreements to explore for or use natural resources, such as oil, gas, timber, metals, and other mineral rights
2. Licensing agreements for such items as motion picture films, video recordings, plays, manuscripts, patents, and copyrights

While US GAAP also excludes the above noted items from coverage under its lease accounting standards, those excluded types of arrangements are addressed by other specific standards included under GAAP. Under IAS, by contrast, only those in the second excluded category (motion picture films, etc.) are addressed and these are dealt with in recently promulgated IAS 38, *Intangible Assets*. The accounting for rights to explore and develop natural resources has yet to be formally addressed by IAS.

Sources of IAS
IAS 4, 5, 17 (revised), 24, 36, 38
SIC 15

DEFINITIONS OF TERMS

Bargain purchase option (BPO). A provision in the lease agreement allowing the lessee the option of purchasing the leased property for an amount that is sufficiently lower than the fair value of the property at the date the option becomes exercisable. Exercise of the option must appear reasonably assured at the inception of the lease.

Contingent rentals. Those lease rentals that are not fixed in amount but are based on a factor other than simply the passage of time; for example, based on percentage of sales, price indices, market rates of interest, or use of the leased asset.

Economic life of leased property. IAS 17 (revised) defines economic life of a leased asset as either the period over which the asset is expected to be economically usable by one or more users or the number of production or similar units expected to be obtained from the leased asset by one or more users. (This was the definition of useful life under the original IAS 17.)

Executory costs. Those costs such as insurance, maintenance, and taxes incurred for leased property, whether paid by the lessor or lessee. If paid by the lessee, the lessee's obligation to pay such costs are excluded from the minimum lease payments.

Fair value of leased property (FMV). The amount for which an asset could be exchanged between a knowledgeable, willing buyer and a knowledgeable, willing seller in an arm's-length transaction. When the lessor is a manufacturer or dealer, the fair value of the property at the inception of the lease will ordinarily be its normal selling price net of volume or trade discounts. When the lessor is not a manufacturer or dealer, the fair value of the property at the inception of the lease will ordinarily be its cost to the lessor unless a significant amount of time has lapsed between the acquisition of the property by the lessor and the inception of the lease, in which case fair value should be determined in light of market conditions prevailing at the inception of the lease. Thus, fair value may be greater or less than the cost or carrying amount of the property.

Finance lease. A lease that transfers substantially all the risks and rewards associated with the ownership of an asset. The risks related to ownership of an asset include the possibilities of losses from idle capacity or technological obsolescence and of variations in return due to changing economic conditions; rewards incidental to ownership of an asset include expectation of profitable operations over the asset's economic life and expectation of gain from appreciation in value or the ultimate realization of the residual value. Title may or may not eventually be transferred to the lessee.

Gross investment in the lease. The sum total of (1) the minimum lease payments under a finance lease (from the standpoint of the lessor), plus (2) any unguaranteed residual value accruing to the lessor.

Inception of the lease. The date of the written lease agreement or, if earlier, the date of a commitment by the parties to the principal provisions of the lease.

Initial direct costs. Initial direct costs, such as commissions and legal fees, incurred by lessors in negotiating and arranging a lease. These generally include (1) costs to originate a lease incurred in transactions with independent third parties that (a) result directly from and are essential to acquire that lease and (b) would not have been incurred had that leasing transaction not occurred; and (2) certain costs directly related to specified activities performed by the lessor for that lease, such as evaluating the prospective lessee's financial condition; evaluating and recording guarantees, collateral, and other security arrangements; negotiating lease terms; preparing and processing lease documents; and closing the transaction.

Lease. An agreement whereby a lessor conveys to the lessee, in return for payment or series of payments, the right to use an asset (property, plant, equipment, or land) for an agreed-upon period of time. Other arrangements essentially similar to leases, such as hire-purchase contracts, bare-boat charters, and so on, are considered leases for purposes of the standard.

Lease term. The initial noncancelable period for which the lessee has contracted to lease the asset together with any further periods for which the lessee has the option to extend the lease of the asset, with or without further payment, which option it is reasonably certain (at the inception of the lease) that the lessee will exercise.

Lessee's incremental borrowing rate. The interest rate that the lessee would have to pay on a similar lease, or, if that is not determinable, the rate that at the inception of the lease the lessee would have incurred to borrow over a similar term (i.e., a loan term equal to the lease term), and with a similar security, the funds necessary to purchase the leased asset.

Minimum lease payments (MLP).

1. From the standpoint of the **lessee**. The payments over the lease term that the lessee is or can be required to make in connection with the leased property. The lessee's obligation to pay executory costs (e.g., insurance, maintenance, or taxes) and contingent rents are excluded from minimum lease payments. If the lease contains a bargain purchase option, the minimum rental payments over the lease term plus the payment called for in the bargain purchase option are included in minimum lease payments.

   If no such provision regarding a bargain purchase option is included in the lease contract, the minimum lease payments include the following:

   a. The minimum rental payments called for by the lease over the lease contract over the term of the lease (excluding any executory costs), plus

    b. Any guarantee of residual value, at the expiration of the lease term, to be paid by the lessee or a party related to the lessee.

2. From the standpoint of the **lessor**. The payments described above plus any guarantee of the residual value of the leased asset by a third party unrelated to either the lessee or lessor (provided that the third party is financially capable of discharging the guaranteed obligation).

Net cash investment in the lease. A term which was used by the original standard IAS 17 as a basis upon which to compute the return to the lessor; this method has been eliminated by IAS 17 (revised).

Net investment in the lease. The difference between the lessor's gross investment in the lease and the unearned finance income.

Noncancelable lease. A lease that is cancelable only

1. On occurrence of some remote contingency
2. With the concurrence (permission) of the lessor
3. If the lessee enters into a new lease for the same or an equivalent asset with the same lessor
4. On payment by the lessee of an additional amount such that at inception, continuation of the lease appears reasonably assured

Nonrecourse (debt) financing. Lending or borrowing activities in which the creditor does not have general recourse to the debtor but rather has recourse only to the property used for collateral in the transaction or other specific property.

Operating lease. A lease that does not meet the criteria prescribed for a finance lease.

Penalty. Any requirement that is imposed or can be imposed on the lessee by the lease agreement or by factors outside the lease agreement to pay cash, incur or assume a liability, perform services, surrender or transfer an asset or rights to an asset, or otherwise forego an economic benefit or suffer an economic detriment.

Rate implicit in the lease. The discount rate that at the inception of the lease, when applied to the minimum lease payments, and the unguaranteed residual value accruing to the benefit of the lessor, causes the aggregate present value to be equal to the fair value of the leased property to the lessor, net of any grants and tax credits receivable by the lessor.

Related parties in leasing transactions. Entities that are in a relationship where one party has the ability to control the other party or exercise significant influence over the operating and financial policies of the related party. Examples include the following:

1. A parent company and its subsidiaries
2. An owner company and its joint ventures and partnerships
3. An investor and its investees

Significant influence may be exercised in several ways, usually by representation on the board of directors but also by participation in the policy-making process, material intercompany transactions, interchange of managerial personnel, or dependence on technical information. The ability to exercise significant influence must be present before the parties can be considered related.

Renewal or extension of a lease. The continuation of a lease agreement beyond the original lease term, including a new lease where the lessee continues to use the same property.

Residual value of leased property. The fair value, estimated at the inception of the lease, that the enterprise expects to obtain from the leased property at the end of the lease term.

Sale and leaseback accounting. A method of accounting for a sale-leaseback transaction in which the seller-lessee records the sale, removes all property and related liabilities from its balance sheet, recognizes gain or loss from the sale, and classifies the leaseback in accordance with this section.

Unearned finance income. The excess of the lessor's gross investment in the lease over its present value.

Unguaranteed residual value. Part of the residual value of the leased asset (estimated at the inception of the lease) the realization of which by the lessor is not assured or is guaranteed by a party related to the lessor.

Useful life. Under IAS 17 (revised), this is defined as the estimated remaining period over which the economic benefits embodied by the asset are expected to be consumed, without being limited to the lease term. (The former definition of this term, as employed in the original standard IAS 17, has now been assigned to the term **economic life**.)

CONCEPTS, RULES, AND EXAMPLES

Classification of Leases--Lessee

For accounting and reporting purposes the lessee has two alternatives in classifying a lease.

1. Operating
2. Finance

It should be observed that finance leases are referred to as capital leases under US GAAP. Finance leases are those that essentially are alternative means of financing the acquisition of property or of substantially all the service potential represented by the property. The term **capital** is used because under accounting standards such leased property is treated as owned, and accordingly, capitalized on the balance sheet. Since, due to the relative paucity of guidance on lease accounting under IAS there will be many issues on which informal direction will be taken from

US GAAP, the terms **finance** and **capital** will be treated as synonymous in this chapter.

The proper classification of a lease is determined by the circumstances surrounding the leasing transaction. According to IAS 17 (both the original standard and the revised one), whether a lease is a finance lease or not will have to be judged based on the **substance** of the transaction, rather than the **form** of the contract. Further, if substantially all of the benefits and risks of ownership have been transferred to the lessee, the lease should be classified as a finance lease; such a lease is normally noncancelable and the lessor is assured of recovery of the capital invested plus a reasonable return on its investment. The original standard IAS 17 stipulated that substantially all of the risks or benefits of ownership are deemed to have been transferred if any one of the following four criteria has been met (these criteria continue under revised IAS 17 as well):

1. The lease transfers ownership to the lessee by the end of the lease term.
2. The lease contains a bargain purchase option (an option to purchase the leased asset at a price that is expected to be substantially lower than the fair value at the date the option becomes exercisable) and it is reasonably certain that the option will be exercisable.
3. The lease term is for the major part of the economic life of the leased asset. Title **may or may not** eventually pass to the lessee.
4. The present value (PV), at the inception of the lease, of the minimum lease payments is greater than, or equal to substantially all of, the fair value of the leased asset, net of grants and tax credits to the lessor at that time. Title **may or may not** eventually pass to the lessee.

The revised IAS 17 has expanded upon the foregoing list of criteria with an additional four criteria, which are summarized below.

5. The leased assets are of a specialized nature such that only the lessee can use them without major modifications being made.
6. If the lessee can cancel the lease, the lessor's losses associated with the cancellation are borne by the lessee.
7. Gains or losses resulting from the fluctuations in the fair value of the residual accrue to the lessee.
8. The lessee has the ability to continue the lease for a supplemental term at a rent which is substantially lower than market rent.

Thus, under the revised IAS 17, an evaluation of eight criteria (instead of four under the original standard) would be required to assess whether there is sufficient evidence to conclude that a given arrangement should be accounted for as a finance lease. Of the eight criteria set forth in the new standard, the first five are essentially determinative in nature, that is, meeting any one of these would normally result in concluding that a given arrangement is in fact a finance lease. The final three criteria, however, are more suggestive in nature, and the standard states that these "could" lead to classification as a finance lease.

The interest rate used to compute the present value should be the lessee's incremental borrowing rate unless it is practicable to determine the rate implicit in the lease, in which case that rate should be used. It is interesting to note that under US GAAP, in order to use the rate implicit in the lease to discount the minimum lease payments, this rate must be lower than the lessee's incremental borrowing rate. Logically, of course, if the lessee's incremental borrowing rate were lower than a rate offered implicitly in a lease, and the prospective lessee was aware of this fact, it would be more attractive to borrow and purchase, so the US rule may be somewhat superfluous. The IAS does not set this as a condition, however.

In general, if a lease agreement meets one of the eight criteria set forth above, it is to be classified as a finance lease in the financial statements of the lessee, under IAS 17 as revised. However, a further condition is imposed by both the original IAS 17 and the revised standard when the lease includes both land **and** buildings. In such cases, unless it is expected that title will pass to the lessee at the end of the lease term, those leases would not normally be considered finance leases, regardless of the other terms in the lease agreement. In other words, the first criterion must always be met in case of real estate leases in order for them to be classified as finance leases.

The language used in the third and fourth criteria, as set forth above, makes them rather subjective and somewhat difficult to apply in practice. Thus, given the same set of facts, it is possible for two enterprises to reach different conclusions regarding the classification of a given lease. The IAS 17 approach differs from that adopted by the corresponding US standard, SFAS 13, in that more subjective criteria are established by the international rule. In the US standard, a threshold of 75% or more of the useful life has been specified for classifying a lease as a finance lease, which thus creates a "bright line" test to be applied mechanically. The corresponding language under IAS 17 stipulates that capitalization results when the lease covers a "major part of the economic life" of the asset. Further, a threshold of "the present value of minimum lease payments equaling at least 90% of leased asset fair value" is set under the US standard, rather than the "substantially all of the fair value of the leased asset" employed under the international standard.

In the absence of interpretation or direction from the IASC, it may be argued that the expression "major part" implies 80% to 90%, instead of 75%, of the economic life of the asset, or that "substantially all" represents 95% or, for that matter, even 99% instead of 90% of fair value at the inception of the lease. Thus, some may hope that the IASC will address these issues when it revisits IAS 17, during its consideration of more fundamental reform of the standard, since these have been persistent problems in applying the standard.

While the original IAS 17 did not address the issue of change in lease classification resulting from alterations in lease terms, the revised IAS 17 provides for this contingency; it states that if the parties agree to alter the terms of the lease, other than by renewing the lease, in a manner that would have resulted in a different classification of the lease, had the changed terms been in effect at inception of the lease, then the revised lease agreement is to be considered a new lease agreement.

Classification of Leases--Lessor

The lessor has the following alternatives in classifying a lease:

1. Operating lease
2. Finance lease

    a. Plain or regular finance lease, hereinafter referred to as direct financing lease, which is the term used by US GAAP

    b. Finance lease by manufacturers or dealers, hereinafter referred to as sales-type lease, the term used by US GAAP

    c. Leveraged lease, wherein financing is through a third-party creditor instead of the lessor

Consistent accounting by lessee and lessor. Since the events or transactions that take place between the lessor and the lessee are based on an agreement (the lease) that is common to both the parties, it is normally appropriate that the lease be classified in a consistent manner by both parties. Thus, if any one of the eight criteria specified above for classification of a finance lease by the lessee is met, the lease should also be classified as a finance lease by the lessor. If the lease qualifies as a finance lease from the standpoint of the lessor, it would be classified either as a sales-type lease, a direct financing lease, or a leveraged lease, depending on the conditions present at the inception of the lease.

Notwithstanding this general observation, IAS 17 alludes to an exception to this general rule when it speaks about the "differing circumstances" sometimes leading to the same lease being classified differently by the lessor and lessee. The standard does not, unfortunately, expand on this matter, but once again it is possible to be informed by reference to US GAAP, which clearly sets forth the circumstances or factors which if not satisfied from the standpoint of the lessor would lead to different classifications by the lessor and the lessee. SFAS 13 stipulates that the following two conditions both need to be satisfied **in addition** to meeting any one of the criteria established for capitalization determination by the lessee, before a lease could be classified as a finance (capital) lease from the standpoint of a lessor:

1. Collectibility of the minimum lease payments is reasonably predictable.
2. No important uncertainties surround the amount of nonreimbursable costs yet to be incurred by the lessor under the lease.

Under US GAAP, therefore, if a lease transaction does not meet the criteria for classification as a sales-type lease, a direct financing lease, or a leveraged lease as specified above (by satisfying both of the above noted extra criteria), it is to be classified in the financial statements of the lessor as an operating lease. If the lessee has accounted for the lease as a capital lease, the asset being leased may appear on the balance sheets of both lessee and lessor.

Although guidance under IAS 17 does not establish additional conditions that must be fulfilled for the lessor to treat a lease as a financing transaction, as the US standard does, use of the "differing circumstances" language opens up the possibility that in any given situation, additional subjective considerations could be defined. This remains a matter for each enterprise to address on an individual basis, however.

Distinction Among Sales-Type, Direct Financing, and Leveraged Leases

A lease is classified as a sales-type lease when the criteria set forth above have been met and the lease transaction is structured such that the lessor (generally a manufacturer or dealer) recognizes a profit or loss on the transaction in addition to interest revenue. For this to occur, the fair value of the property, or if lower, the sum of the present values of the minimum lease payments and the estimated unguaranteed residual value, must differ from the cost (or carrying value, if different). The essential substance of this transaction is that of a sale, thus its name. Common examples of sales-type leases: (1) when an automobile dealership opts to lease a car to its customers in lieu of making an actual sale, and (2) the re-lease of equipment coming off an expiring lease.

A direct financing lease differs from a sales-type lease in that the lessor does not realize a profit or loss on the transaction other than interest revenue. In a direct financing lease, the fair value of the property at the inception of the lease is equal to the cost (or carrying value, if the property is not new). This type of lease transaction most often involves entities regularly engaged in financing operations. The lessor (a bank or other financial institution) purchases the asset and then leases the asset to the lessee. This transaction merely replaces the conventional lending transaction where the borrower uses the borrowed funds to purchase the asset.

There are many economic reasons why a lease transaction may be considered. These include

1. The lessee (borrower) is generally able to obtain 100% financing.
2. There may be tax benefits for the lessee.
3. The lessor receives the equivalent of interest as well as an asset with some remaining value at the end of the lease term (unless title transfers as a condition of the lease).
4. The lessee is protected from risk of obsolescence.

In summary, it may help to visualize the following chart when considering the classification of a lease:

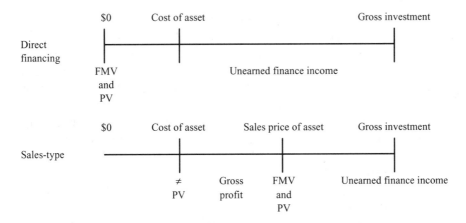

One specialized form of a direct financing lease is a **leveraged lease**. This type is mentioned separately both here and in the following section on how to account for leases because it is to receive a different accounting treatment by a lessor. A leveraged lease meets all the definitional criteria of a direct financing lease, but differs because it involves at least three parties: a lessee, a long-term creditor, and a lessor (commonly referred to as the **equity participant**). Other characteristics of a leveraged lease are as follows:

1. The financing provided by the long-term creditor must be without recourse as to the general credit of the lessor, although the creditor may hold recourse with respect to the leased property. The amount of the financing must provide the lessor with substantial leverage in the transaction.
2. The lessor's net investment declines during the early years and rises during the later years of the lease term before its elimination.

Accounting for Leases--Lessee

As discussed in the preceding section, there are two classifications that apply to a lease transaction in the financial statements of the lessee. They are as follows:

1. Operating
2. Finance

Operating leases. The accounting treatment accorded an operating lease is relatively simple; rental expense should be charged to income as the payments are made or become payable. IAS 17 stipulates that rental expense be "recognized on a systematic basis that is representative of the time pattern of the user's benefits, even if the payments are not on that basis." In case the lease payments are being made on a straight-line basis (i.e., equal payments per period over the lease term), recognition of the rental expense would normally be on a straight-line basis. However, if the lease agreement calls for either an alternative payment schedule or a scheduled rent increase over the lease term, the lease expense should still be recognized on a straight-line basis unless another systematic and rational basis is a better representation of actual physical use of the leased property. In such an instance it will be necessary to create either a prepaid asset or a liability, depending on the structure of the payment schedule. In SIC 15, it has been held that all incentives relating to a new or renewed operating lease are to be considered in determining the total cost of the lease, to be recognized on a straight-line basis over the term of the lease. Thus, for example, a rent holiday for 6 months as part of a 5-year lease would not result in only 6 months' rent expense being recorded during the first full year; rather, 4 and one half years' rent would be allocated over the full 5-year term. This would apply to both lessor and lessee.

Additionally, if the lease agreement provides for a scheduled increase(s) in contemplation of the lessee's increased (i.e., more intensive) physical use of the leased property, the total amount of rental payments, including the scheduled increase(s), should be charged to expense over the lease term on a straight-line basis. On the other hand, if the scheduled increase(s) is due to additional leased property, recognition should be proportional to the leased property with the increased rents recognized over the years that the lessee has control over the use of the additional leased property. (These suggestions, and many other recommendations made in this chapter, are based on guidance from US GAAP, since the IAS does not address these matters at the present time.)

Notice that in the case of an operating lease there is no balance sheet recognition of the leased asset because the substance of the lease is merely that of a rental. There is no reason to expect that the lessee will derive any future economic benefit from the leased asset beyond the lease term. There may, however, be a deferred charge or credit on the balance sheet if the payment schedule under terms of the lease does not correspond with the expense recognition, as suggested in the preceding paragraph.

Finance leases. The classification of a lease must be determined prior to consideration of the accounting treatment. Therefore, it is necessary first to evaluate the lease transaction against the eight criteria set forth in IAS 17 (revised 1997). Assuming that the lease agreement satisfies one of these (while recognizing that the last three of the eight are not absolutely determinative, but are instead persuasive), it must be accounted for as a finance lease.

According to IAS 17, the lessee shall record a finance lease as an asset and an obligation (liability) at an amount equal to the lesser of (1) the fair value of the leased property at the inception of the lease, net of grants and tax credits receivable by the lessors, or (2) the present value of the minimum lease payments. For purposes of this computation, the minimum lease payments are considered to be the payments that the lessee is obligated to make or can be required to make, excluding contingent rent and executory costs such as insurance, maintenance, and taxes. The minimum lease payments generally include the minimum rental payments, and any guarantee of the residual value made by the lessee or a party related to the lessee. If the lease includes a bargain purchase option (BPO), the amount required to be paid under the BPO is included in the minimum lease payments. The present value shall be computed using the incremental borrowing rate of the lessee unless it is practicable for the lessee to determine the implicit rate computed by the lessor.

(Under US GAAP, an important exception is made when the FMV of the leased asset is lower than the PV of the minimum lease payments, which exception has not yet been considered under IAS 17. In such a case an implicit rate is computed through a series of trial-and-error calculations. This rule is entirely logical, since it is well established in GAAP that assets are not to be recorded at amounts greater than fair value or net realizable value at acquisition. This exception has been illustrated in a numerical case study that follows.)

The lease term to be used in the present value computation is the fixed, noncancelable term of the lease, plus any further terms for which the lessee has the option to continue to lease the asset, with or without further payment, provided that it is reasonably certain, as of the beginning of the lease, that lessee will exercise such a renewal option.

Depreciation of leased assets. The depreciation of the leased asset will depend on how the lease qualified as a finance lease. If the lease transaction met the criteria as either transferring ownership or containing a bargain purchase option, the asset arising from the transaction is to be depreciated over the estimated useful life of the leased property. If the transaction qualifies as a finance lease because it met either the major part of economic life criteria, or because the present value of the minimum lease payments represented substantially all of the fair value of the underlying asset, then it must be depreciated over the shorter of the lease term or the useful life of the leased property. The conceptual rationale for this differentiated treatment arises because of the substance of the transaction. Under the first two criteria, the asset actually becomes the property of the lessee at the end of the lease term (or on exercise of the BPO). In the latter situations, title to the property remains with the lessor.

Thus, the leased asset is to be depreciated (amortized) over the shorter of the lease term or its useful life if title does not transfer to the lessee, but when it is reasonably certain that the lessee will obtain ownership by the end of the lease term, the leased asset is to be depreciated over the asset's useful life. The manner in which depreciation is computed should be consistent with the lessee's normal depreciation policy for other depreciable assets owned by the lessee, recognizing depreciation on the basis set out in IAS 4, *Depreciation Accounting*, and IAS 16, *Property, Plant, and Equipment*. Therefore, the accounting treatment and method used to depreciate (amortize) the leased asset is very similar to that used for an owned asset. The leased asset should not be depreciated (amortized) below the estimated residual value.

In some instances when the property is to revert back to the lessor, there may be a guaranteed residual value. This is an amount that the lessee guarantees to the lessor. If the fair value of the asset at the end of the lease term is greater than or equal to the guaranteed residual amount, the lessee incurs no additional obligation. On the other hand, if the fair value of the leased asset is less than the guaranteed residual value, the lessee must make up the difference, usually with a cash payment. The guaranteed residual value is often used as a device to reduce the periodic payments by substituting the lump-sum amount at the end of the term that results from the guarantee. In any event the depreciation (amortization) must still be based on the estimated residual value. This results in a rational and systematic allocation of the expense through the periods and avoids recognizing a large expense (or loss) in the last period as a result of the guarantee.

The annual (periodic) rent payments made during the lease term are to be apportioned between the reduction in the obligation and the finance charge (interest expense) in a manner such that the finance charge (interest expense) represents a constant periodic rate of interest on the remaining balance of the lease obligation. This is commonly referred to as the effective interest method. However, it is to be noted that IAS 17 also recognizes that an approximation of this pattern can be made, as an alternative.

At the inception of the lease the asset and liability (relating to future rental obligation) are recorded in the balance sheet of the lessee at the same amounts. However, since the depreciation charge for use of the leased asset and the finance expense during the lease term differ due to different policies being used to recognize them, as explained above, it is likely that the asset and related liability balances would not be equal in amount after inception of the lease.

The following examples illustrate the treatment described in the foregoing paragraphs:

Example of accounting for a finance lease--Asset returned to lessor

Assume the following:

1. The lease is initiated on 1/1/00 for equipment with an expected useful life of 3 years. The equipment reverts back to the lessor on expiration of the lease agreement.
2. The FMV of the equipment is $135,000.
3. Three payments are due to the lessor in the amount of $50,000 per year beginning 12/31/00. An additional sum of $1,000 is to be paid annually by the lessee for insurance.
4. Lessee guarantees a $10,000 residual value on 12/31/02 to the lessor.
5. Irrespective of the $10,000 residual value guarantee, the leased asset is expected to have only a $1,000 salvage value on 12/31/02.
6. The lessee's incremental borrowing rate is 10% (lessor's implicit rate is unknown).
7. The present value of the lease obligation is as follows:

PV of guaranteed residual value	=	$10,000 x 0.7513[*]	=	$ 7,513
PV of annual payments	=	$50,000 x 2.4869[**]	=	124,345
				$131,858

[*] *The present value of an amount of $1 due in three periods at 10% is 0.7513.*
[**] *The present value of an ordinary annuity of $1 for three periods at 10% is 2.4869.*

The first step in dealing with any lease transaction is to classify the lease. In this case, the lease term is for 3 years, which is equal to 100% of the expected useful life of the asset. Notice that the test of fair value versus present value is also fulfilled, as the PV of the minimum lease payments ($131,858) could easily be considered as being equal to substantially all the FMV ($135,000), being equal to 97.7% of the FMV. Thus, this lease should be accounted for as a finance lease.

In assumption 7 above the present value of the lease obligation is computed. Note that the executory costs (insurance) are not included in the minimum lease payments and that the incremental borrowing rate of the lessee was used to determine the present value. This rate was used because the implicit rate was not determinable.

NOTE: *To have used the implicit rate it would have to have been known to the lessee.*

The entry necessary to record the lease on 1/1/00 is

Leased equipment	131,858	
Lease obligation		131,858

Note that the lease is recorded at the present value of the minimum lease payments, which in this case is less than the FMV. If the present value of the minimum lease payments had exceeded the FMV, the lease would be recorded at FMV.

The next step is to determine the proper allocation between interest and a reduction in the lease obligation for each lease payment. This is done using the effective interest method as illustrated below.

Year	Cash payment	Interest expense	Reduction in lease obligation	Balance of lease obligation
Inception of lease				$131,858
1	$50,000	$13,186	$36,814	95,044
2	50,000	9,504	40,496	54,548
3	50,000	5,452	44,548	10,000

The interest is calculated at 10% (the incremental borrowing rate) of the balance of the lease obligation for each period, and the remainder of the $50,000 payment is allocated to a reduction in the lease obligation. The lessee is also required to pay $1,000 for insurance on an annual basis. The entries necessary to record all payments relative to the lease for each of the 3 years are shown below.

	12/31/00	12/31/01	12/31/02
Insurance expense	1,000	1,000	1,000
Interest expense	13,186	9,504	5,452
Lease obligation	36,814	40,496	44,548
Cash	51,000	51,000	51,000

The leased equipment recorded as an asset must also be amortized (depreciated). The balance of this account is $131,858; however, as with any other asset, it cannot be depreciated below the estimated residual value of $1,000 (note that it is depreciated down to the actual estimated residual value, **not** the guaranteed residual value). In this case, the straight-line depreciation method is applied over a period of 3 years. This 3-year period represents the lease term, **not** the life of the asset, because the asset reverts back to the lessor at the end of the lease term. Therefore, the following entry will be made at the end of each year:

| Depreciation expense | 43,619 | |
| Accumulated depreciation | | 43,619 [($131,858 – 1,000) ÷ 3] |

Finally, on 12/31/02 we must recognize the fact that ownership of the property has reverted back to the owner (lessor). The lessee made a guarantee that the residual value would be $10,000 on 12/31/02; as a result, the lessee must make up the difference between the guaranteed residual value and the actual residual value with a cash payment to the lessor. The following entry illustrates the removal of the leased asset and obligation from the books of the lessee:

Lease obligation	10,000	
Accumulated depreciation	130,858	
Cash		9,000
Leased equipment		131,858

The foregoing example illustrated a situation where the asset was to be returned to the lessor. Another situation exists (under BPO or transfer of title) where the asset is expected to remain with the lessee. Remember that leased assets are amortized over their useful life when title transfers or a bargain purchase option exists. At the end of the lease, the balance of the lease obligation should equal the guaranteed residual value, the bargain purchase option price, or a termination penalty.

Example of accounting for a finance lease--Asset ownership transferred to lessee *and* fair market value of leased asset lower than present value of minimum lease payments

Assume the following:

1. A 3-year lease is initiated on 1/1/00 for equipment with an expected useful life of 5 years.
2. Three annual lease payments of $52,000 are required beginning on 1/1/00 (note that the payment at the beginning of the year changes the PV computation). The lessor pays $2,000 per year for insurance on the equipment.
3. The lessee can exercise a bargain purchase option on 12/31/02 for $10,000. The expected residual value at 12/31/03 is $1,000.
4. The lessee's incremental borrowing rate is 10% (lessor's implicit rate is unknown).
5. The fair market value of the property leased is $140,000.

Once again, the classification of the lease must take place prior to the accounting for it. This lease is classified as a finance lease because it contains a bargain purchase option (BPO). Note that in this case, the PV versus FMV test is also clearly fulfilled.

The PV of the lease obligation is computed as follows:

PV of bargain purchase option	=	$10,000	x 0.7513[*]	=	$ 7,513
PV of annual payments	=	($52,000 – 2,000)	x 2.7355[**]	=	136,755
					$144,288

[*] *The present value of an amount of $1 due in three periods at 10% is 0.7513.*
[**] *The present value of an annuity due of $1 for three periods at 10% is 2.7355.*

Notice that in the example above, the present value of the lease obligation is greater than the FMV of the asset. Also notice that since the lessor pays $2,000 a year for insurance, this payment is treated as executory costs and hence excluded from calculation of the present value of annual payments. In conclusion, since the PV is greater than the FMV, the lease obligation (as well as the leased asset) must be recorded at the FMV of the asset leased (being the lower of the two). The entry on 1/1/00 is as follows:

Leased equipment	140,000	
Obligation under finance lease		140,000

According to IAS 17, the apportionment between interest and principal is to be such that interest recognized reflects the use of a constant periodic rate of interest applied to the remaining balance of the obligation. As noted above, a special rule applies under US GAAP (which are illustrated here) when the present value of the minimum lease payments exceeds the fair market value of the leased asset. When the PV exceeds the FMV of the leased asset, a new rate must be computed through a series of trial-and-error calculations. In this situation the interest rate was determined to be 13.265%. The amortization of the lease takes place as follows:

Year	Cash payment	Interest expense	Reduction in lease obligation	Balance of lease obligation
Inception of lease				$140,000
1/1/00	$50,000	$ --	$50,000	90,000
1/1/01	50,000	11,939	38,061	51,939
1/1/02	50,000	6,890	43,110	8,829
12/31/02	10,000	1,171	8,829	--

The following entries are required in years 2000 through 2002 to recognize the payment and depreciation (amortization).

		2000		2001		2002	
1/1	Operating expense	2,000		2,000		2,000	
	Obligation under finance lease	50,000		38,061		43,110	
	Accrued interest payable			11,939		6,890	
	Cash		52,000		52,000		52,000
12/31	Interest expense	11,939		6,890		1,171	
	Accrued interest payable		11,939		6,890		
	Obligation under finance lease						1,171
12/31	Depreciation expense	27,800		27,800		27,800	
	Accumulated depreciation		27,800		27,800		27,800
	($139,000, 5 years)						
12/31	Obligation under finance lease					10,000	
	Cash						10,000

Impairment of leased asset. The original IAS 17 did not address the issue of how impairments of leased assets are to be assessed or, if determined to have occurred, how they would need to be accounted for. The revised IAS 17 does note that the provisions of IAS 36 should be applied to leased assets in the same manner as they would be applied to owned assets. IAS 36 is discussed more fully in Chapter 8.

Accounting for Leases--Lessor

As illustrated above, there are four classifications of leases with which a lessor must be concerned.

1. Operating
2. Sales-type
3. Direct financing
4. Leveraged

Operating leases. As in the case of the lessee, the operating lease requires a less complex accounting treatment than does a finance lease. The payments received by the lessor are to be recorded as rent income in the period in which the payment is received or becomes receivable. As with the lessee, if either the rentals vary from a straight-line basis or the lease agreement contains a scheduled rent increase over the lease term, the revenue is to be recorded on a straight-line basis unless an alternative basis of systematic and rational allocation is more representative of the time pattern of earning process contained in the lease. Additionally, if the lease agreement provides for a scheduled increase(s) in contemplation of the lessee's increased physical use of the leased property, the total amount of rental payments, including the scheduled increase(s), is allocated to revenue over the lease term on a straight-line basis. However, if the scheduled increase(s) is due to additional leased property, recognition should be proportional to the leased property, with the increased rents recognized over the years that the lessee has control over use of the additional leased property.

The lessor must show the leased property on the balance sheet under the caption "Investment in leased property." This account should be shown with or near the property, plant, and equipment owned by the lessor, and depreciation should be determined in the same manner as for the rest of the lessor's owned property, plant, and equipment. IAS 17 stipulates that "when a significant portion of the lessor's business comprises operating leases, the lessor should disclose the amount of assets by each major class of asset together with the related accumulated depreciation at each balance sheet date." Further, "assets held for operating are usually included as property, plant, and equipment in the balance sheet."

In the case of operating leases, any initial direct (leasing) costs incurred by a lessor are either to be amortized over the lease term as the revenue is recognized (i.e., on a straight-line basis unless another method is more representative) or, alternatively, charged to expense as they are incurred.

Although there is no guidance on this matter under the international accounting standards, logically any incentives made by the lessor to the lessee are to be treated as reductions of rent and recognized on a straight-line basis over the term of the lease. This is also the position taken under US GAAP.

Depreciation of leased assets should be on a basis consistent with the lessor's normal depreciation policy for similar assets, and the depreciation expense should be computed on the basis set out in IAS 4, *Depreciation Accounting*, and IAS 16, *Property, Plant, and Equipment.*

Sales-type leases. In the accounting for a sales-type lease, it is necessary for the lessor to determine the following amounts:

1. Gross investment
2. Fair value of the leased asset
3. Cost

From these amounts, the remainder of the computations necessary to record and account for the lease transaction can be made. The first objective is to determine the numbers necessary to complete the following entry:

Lease receivable	xx	
Cost of goods sold	xx	
Sales		xx
Inventory		xx
Unearned finance income		xx

The gross investment (lease receivable) of the lessor is equal to the sum of the minimum lease payments (excluding contingent rent and executory costs) from the standpoint of the lessor, plus the nonguaranteed residual value accruing to the lessor. The difference between the gross investment and the present value of the two components of gross investment (i.e., minimum lease payments and nonguaranteed residual value) is recorded as "unearned finance income" (also referred to as "unearned interest revenue"). The present value is to be computed using the lease term and implicit interest rate (both of which were discussed earlier).

IAS 17 (revised) stipulates that the resulting unearned finance income is to be amortized and recognized into income using the effective interest method, which will result in a constant periodic rate of return on the "lessor's net investment" (which is the "lessor's gross investment" less the "unearned finance income"). The requirement that only a single computational approach be employed is the key change from the original IAS 17; that standard permitted a free choice of method in allocation of finance income by the lessor using the effective interest method based on either

1. The lessor's net investment outstanding in respect of the finance lease; or
2. The lessor's net cash investment outstanding in respect of the finance lease.

The available choice of computational methods permitted significantly different results to be reported by entities engaged in substantially identical transactions. The existence of this option has been eliminated by IAS 17 (revised).

Consideration of "prudence" is called for by IAS 17 in recognizing finance income, which is in any event a qualitative characteristic or attribute of financial statements prepared under the IAS. The IASC's *Framework for Preparation and Presentation of Financial Statements* makes it incumbent on financial statement preparers to exercise prudence; in other words, it requires caution in the exercise of judgment. IAS 17 clarifies this in the context of spreading income on a systematic basis, by giving the example of recognition of uncertainties relative to collectibility of lease rentals or to fluctuation of interest rates in the future. For instance, the uncertainties surrounding collectibility of lease rentals usually increase with the lease term (i.e., the longer the lease term, the greater are the risks involved), and thus in keeping with the principle of prudence, modification of the pattern of income recognition may be required to compensate.

For example, a lessor may decide to delay the recognition of finance income into the later years in the case of leases with terms spread over, say, 20 years and above, as opposed to short-term leases with terms of 3 to 5 years, since predicting with certainty long-term collectibility, which depends on a number of factors, such as the future financial position of the lessee, is a very difficult task. Effectively, more of the earlier collections might be seen as returns on investment, rather than income, until longer-term viability has been demonstrated.

Recall that the fair market value (FMV) of the leased property is, by definition, equal to the normal selling price of the asset adjusted by any residual amount retained (this amount retained can be exemplified by an unguaranteed residual value, investment credit, etc.). According to IAS 17, the selling price to be used for a sales-type lease is equal to the fair value of the leased asset, or, if lower, the sum of the present values of the MLP and the estimated unguaranteed residual value accruing to the lessor, discounted at a commercial rate of interest. In other words, the normal selling price less the present value of the unguaranteed residual value is equal to the present value of the MLP. (Note that this relationship is sometimes used while computing the MLP when the normal selling price and the residual value are known; this is illustrated in a case study that follows.)

The cost of goods sold to be charged against income in the period of the sale is computed as the historical cost or carrying value of the asset (most likely inventory) plus any initial direct costs. Initial direct costs should be recognized as an expense at the inception of the lease, since these costs are related to earning the manufacturer's or dealer's profit.

The estimated unguaranteed residual values used in computing the lessor's gross investment in a lease should be reviewed regularly. In case of a permanent reduction (impairment) in the estimated unguaranteed residual value, the income allocation over the lease term is revised and any reduction with respect to amounts already accrued is recognized immediately.

To attract customers, manufacturer or dealer lessors sometimes quote artificially low rates of interest. This has a direct impact on the recognition of built-in profit, which is an integral part of the deal and is inversely proportional to the finance income generated from the deal. Thus, if finance income is artificially low, this results in recognition of excessive profit from the transaction at the time of the sale. Under such circumstances, the standard requires that selling profit be restricted to that which would have resulted had a commercial rate of interest been used in the deal. Thus, the substance of the transaction should be reflected in the financial statements.

The difference between the selling price and the amount computed as the cost of goods sold is the gross profit recognized by the lessor on the inception of the lease (sale). Manufacturer or dealer lessors often give an option to their customers of either leasing the asset (with financing provided by them) or buying the asset outright. Thus, a finance lease by a manufacturer or dealer lessor, also referred to as a sales-type lease, generates two types of revenue for the lessor.

1. The gross profit (or loss) on the sale, which is the equivalent to the profit (or loss) that would have resulted from an outright sale at normal selling prices.
2. The finance income or interest earned on the lease receivable to be spread over the lease term based on a pattern reflecting a constant periodic rate of return on either the lessor's net investment outstanding or the net cash investment outstanding in respect of the finance lease.

The application of these points is illustrated in the example below.

Example of accounting for a sales-type lease

XYZ Inc. is a manufacturer of specialized equipment. Many of its customers do not have the necessary funds or financing available for outright purchase. Because of this, XYZ offers a leasing alternative. The data relative to a typical lease are as follows:

1. The noncancelable fixed portion of the lease term is 5 years. The lessor has the option to renew the lease for an additional 3 years at the same rental. The estimated useful life of the asset is 10 years.
2. The lessor is to receive equal annual payments over the term of the lease. The leased property reverts back to the lessor on termination of the lease.
3. The lease is initiated on 1/1/00. Payments are due on 12/31 for the duration of the lease term.
4. The cost of the equipment to XYZ Inc. is $100,000. The lessor incurs cost associated with the inception of the lease in the amount of $2,500.
5. The selling price of the equipment for an outright purchase is $150,000.
6. The equipment is expected to have a residual value of $15,000 at the end of 5 years and $10,000 at the end of 8 years.
7. The lessor desires a return of 12% (the implicit rate).

The first step is to calculate the annual payment due to the lessor. Recall that the present value (PV) of the minimum lease payments is equal to the selling price adjusted for the present value of the residual amount. The present value is to be computed using the implicit interest rate and the lease term. In this case, the implicit rate is given as 12% and the lease term is 8 years (the fixed noncancelable portion plus the renewal period). Thus, the structure of the computation would be as follows:

Normal selling price – PV of residual value = PV of minimum lease payment

Or, in this case,

$150,000 – (0.40388* x $10,000) = 4.96764** x Minimum lease payment
$145,961.20 ÷   4.96764   = Minimum lease payment
                $29,382.40   = Minimum lease payment

  * *0.40388 is the present value of an amount of $1 due in eight periods at a 12% interest rate.*
 ** *4.96764 is the present value of an annuity of $1 for eight periods at a 12% interest rate.*

Prior to examining the accounting implications of a lease, we must determine the lease classification. In this example, the lease term is 8 years (discussed above) while the estimated useful life of the asset is 10 years; thus this lease qualifies as something other than an operating lease. (Note that it also meets the FMV versus PV criterion because the PV of the minimum lease payments of $145,961.20, which is 97% of the FMV [$150,000], could be considered to be equal to substantially all of the fair value of the leased asset.) Now it must be determined if this is a sales-type, direct financing, or leveraged lease. To do this, examine the FMV or selling price of the asset and compare it to the cost. Because the two are not equal, we can determine this to be a sales-type lease.

Next, obtain the figures necessary to record the entry on the books of the lessor. The gross investment is the total minimum lease payments plus the unguaranteed residual value, or

$$($29,382.40 \times 8) + $10,000 = $245,059.20$$

The cost of goods sold is the historical cost of the inventory ($100,000) plus any initial direct costs ($2,500) less the PV of the unguaranteed residual value ($10,000 x 0.40388). Thus, the cost of goods sold amount is $98,461.20 ($100,000 + 2,500 – 4,038.80). Note that the initial direct costs will require a credit entry to some account, usually accounts payable or cash. The inventory account is credited for the carrying value of the asset, in this case $100,000.

The adjusted selling price is equal to the PV of the minimum payments, or $145,961.20. Finally, the unearned finance income is equal to the gross investment (i.e., lease receivable) less the present value of the components making up the gross investment (the minimum lease payment of $29,382.40 and the unguaranteed residual of $10,000). The present value of these items is $150,000 [($29,382.40 x 4.96764) + ($10,000 x 0.40388)]. Therefore, the entry necessary to record the lease is

Lease receivable	245,059.20	
Cost of goods sold	98,461.20	
Inventory		100,000.00
Sales		145,961.20
Unearned finance income		95,059.20
Accounts payable (initial direct costs)		2,500.00

The next step in accounting for a sales-type lease is to determine proper handling of the payment. Both principal and interest are included in each payment. According to IAS 17, interest is recognized on a basis such that a constant periodic rate of return is earned over the term of the lease. This will require setting up an amortization schedule as illustrated below.

Year	Cash payment	Interest	Reduction in principal	Balance of net investment
Inception of lease				$150,000.00
1	$ 29,382.40	$18,000.00	$ 11,382.40	138,617.00
2	29,382.40	16,634.11	12,748.29	125,869.31
3	29,382.40	15,104.32	14,278.08	111,591.23
4	29,382.40	13,390.95	15,991.45	95,599.78
5	29,382.40	11,471.97	17,910.43	77,689.35
6	29,382.40	9,322.72	20,059.68	57,629.67
7	29,382.40	6,915.56	22,466.84	35,162.83
8	29,382.40	4,219.57	25,162.83	$ 10,000.00
	$235,059.20	$95,059.20	$140,000.00	

A few of the columns need to be elaborated on. First, the net investment is the gross investment (lease receivable) less the unearned finance income. Notice that at the end of the lease term, the net investment is equal to the estimated residual value. Also note that the total interest earned over the lease term is equal to the unearned interest (unearned finance income) at the beginning of the lease term.

The entries below illustrate the proper treatment to record the receipt of the lease payment and the amortization of the unearned finance income in the first year.

Cash	29,382.40	
Lease receivable		29,382.40
Unearned finance income	18,000.00	
Interest revenue		18,000.00

Notice that there is no explicit entry to recognize the principal reduction. This is done automatically when the net investment is reduced by decreasing the lease receivable (gross investment) by $29,382.40 and the unearned finance income account by only $18,000. The $18,000 is 12% (implicit rate) of the net investment. These entries are to be made over the life of the lease.

At the end of the lease term the asset is returned to the lessor and the following entry is required:

Asset	10,000	
Leased receivable		10,000

If the estimated residual value has changed during the lease term, the accounting computations would have also changed to reflect this.

Direct financing leases. The accounting for a direct financing lease holds many similarities to that for a sales-type lease. Of particular importance is that the terminology used is much the same; however, the treatment accorded these items varies greatly. Again, it is best to preface our discussion by determining our objectives in the accounting for a direct financing lease. Once the lease has been classified, it must be recorded. To do this, the following amounts must be determined:

1. Gross investment
2. Cost
3. Residual value

As noted, a direct financing lease generally involves a leasing company or other financial institution and results in only interest revenue being earned by the lessor. This is because the FMV (selling price) and the cost are equal, and therefore no dealer profit is recognized on the actual lease transaction. Note how this is different from a sales-type lease, which involves both a profit on the transaction and interest revenue over the lease term. The reason for this difference is derived from the conceptual nature underlying the purpose of the lease transaction. In a sales-type lease, the manufacturer (distributor, dealer, etc.) is seeking an alternative means to finance the sale of his product, whereas a direct financing lease is a result of the consumer's need to finance an equipment purchase. Because the consumer is unable to obtain conventional financing, he or she turns to a leasing company that will purchase the desired asset and then lease it to the consumer. Here the profit on the transaction remains with the manufacturer while the interest revenue is earned by the leasing company.

Like a sales-type lease, the first objective is to determine the amounts necessary to complete the following entry:

Lease receivable	xxx	
Asset		xxx
Unearned finance income		xx

The gross investment is still defined as the minimum amount of lease payments (from the standpoint of a lessor) exclusive of any executory costs plus the unguaranteed residual value. The difference between the gross investment as determined above and the cost (carrying value) of the asset is to be recorded as the unearned finance income because there is no manufacturer's/dealer's profit earned on the transaction. The following entry would be made to record initial direct costs:

Initial direct costs	xx	
Cash		xx

Net investment in the lease is defined as the gross investment less the unearned income plus the unamortized initial direct costs related to the lease. Initial direct costs are defined in the same way that they were for purposes of the sales-type lease; however, the accounting treatment is different. Unlike under the sales-type lease, where these costs are required to be charged to expense immediately, under the direct finance lease there is an option available either

1. To amortize initial direct costs over the lease term, or
2. To charge them to expense immediately.

Thus, for a direct financing lease, when the first option is chosen, the unearned lease (i.e., interest) income and the initial direct costs will be amortized to income over the lease term so that a constant periodic rate is earned either on the lessor's net investment outstanding or on the net cash investment outstanding in the finance lease (i.e., the balance of the cash outflows and inflows in respect of the lease excluding executory costs chargeable to the lessee). Thus, the effect of the initial direct costs, in case the option to amortize is chosen, is to reduce the implicit interest rate, or yield, to the lessor over the life of the lease.

An example follows that illustrates the preceding principles.

Example of accounting for a direct financing lease

Emirates Refining needs new equipment to expand its manufacturing operation; however, it does not have sufficient capital to purchase the asset at this time. Because of this, Emirates Refining has employed Consolidated Leasing to purchase the asset. In turn, Emirates will lease the asset from Consolidated. The following information applies to the terms of the lease:

1. A 3-year lease is initiated on 1/1/00 for equipment costing $131,858, with an expected useful life of 5 years. FMV at 1/1/00 of equipment is $131,858.
2. Three annual payments are due to the lessor beginning 12/31/00. The property reverts back to the lessor on termination of the lease.
3. The unguaranteed residual value at the end of year 3 is estimated to be $10,000.
4. The annual payments are calculated to give the lessor a 10% return (the implicit rate).
5. The lease payments and unguaranteed residual value have a PV equal to $131,858 (FMV of asset) at the stipulated discount rate.
6. The annual payment to the lessor is computed as follows:

PV of residual value	=	$10,000 x .7513* = $7,513
PV of lease payments	=	Selling price – PV of residual value
	=	$131,858 – $7,513 = $124,345
Annual payment	=	$124,345 ÷ 2.4869** = $50,000

* *.7513 is the PV of an amount due in three periods at 10%.*
** *2.4869 is the PV of an ordinary annuity of $1 per period for three periods, at 10% interest.*

7. Initial direct costs of $7,500 are incurred by ABC in the lease transaction.

As with any lease transaction, the first step must be to classify the lease appropriately. In this case, the PV of the lease payments ($124,345) is equal to 94% of the FMV ($131,858), thus could be considered as equal to substantially all of the FMV of the leased asset. Next, determine the unearned interest and the net investment in lease.

Gross investment in lease	
[(3 x $50,000) + $10,000]	$160,000
Cost of leased property	131,858
Unearned finance income	$ 28,142

The unamortized initial direct costs are to be added to the gross investment in the lease, and the unearned finance income is to be deducted to arrive at the net investment in the lease. The net investment in the lease for this example is determined as follows:

Gross investment in lease	$160,000
Add:	
Unamortized initial direct costs	7,500
Less:	
Unearned finance income	28,142
Net investment in lease	$139,358

The net investment in the lease (Gross investment – Unearned finance income) has been increased by the amount of initial direct costs. Therefore, the implicit rate is no longer 10%. We must recompute the implicit rate, which is really the result of an internal rate of return calculation. We know that the lease payments are to be $50,000 per annum and that a residual value of $10,000 is available at the end of the lease term. In return for these payments (inflows) we are giving up equipment (outflow) and incurring initial direct costs (outflows), with a net investment of $139,358 ($131,858 + $7,500). The only way to obtain the new implicit rate is through a trial-and-error calculation as set up below.

$$\frac{50,000}{(1 + i)^1} + \frac{50,000}{(1 + i)^2} + \frac{50,000}{(1 + i)^3} + \frac{10,000}{(1 + i)^3} = \$139,358$$

Where: i = implicit rate of interest

In this case, the implicit rate is equal to 7.008%. Thus, the amortization table would be set up as follows:

	(a)	(b)	(c)	(d)	(e)	(f)
				Reduction in	Reduction in	
		Reduction in	PV x Implicit	initial direct	PVI net	PVI net investment
	Lease	unearned	rate	costs	investment	in lease
	payments	interest	(7.008%)	(b-c)	(a-b + d)	$(f)_{(n+1)} = (f)_n - (e)$
0						$139,358
1	$ 50,000	$13,186 (1)	$ 9,766	$3,420	$ 40,234	99,124
2	50,000	9,504 (2)	6,947	2,557	43,053	56,071
3	50,000	5,455 (3)	3,929	1,526	46,071	10,000
	$150,000	$28,145*	$20,642	$7,503	$129,358	

*Rounded

(b.1) $131,858 x 10% = $13,186
(b.2) [$131,858 – ($50,000 – 13,186)] x 10% = $9,504
(b.3) [$95,044 – ($50,000 – 9,504)] x 10% = $5,455

Here the interest is computed as 7.008% of the net investment. Note again that the net investment at the end of the lease term is equal to the estimated residual value.

The entry made initially to record the lease is as follows:

Lease receivable** [($50,000 x 3) + 10,000]	160,000	
Asset acquired for leasing		131,858
Unearned lease revenue		28,142

When the payment (or obligation to pay) of the initial direct costs occurs, the following entry must be made:

Initial direct costs	7,500	
Cash		7,500

Using the schedule above, the following entries would be made during each of the indicated years:

	Year 1		Year 2		Year 3	
Cash	50,000		50,000		50,000	
Lease receivable**		50,000		50,000		50,000
Unearned finance income	13,186		9,504		5,455	
Initial direct costs		3,420		2,557		1,526
Interest income		9,766		6,947		3,929

Finally, when the asset is returned to the lessor at the end of the lease term, it must be recorded on the books. The necessary entry is as follows:

Used asset	10,000	
Lease receivable**		10,000

    ***Also commonly referred to as the "gross investment in lease."*

Leveraged leases. Leveraged leases are discussed in detail in Appendix B of this chapter, because of the complexity involved in the accounting treatment based on guidance available under US GAAP, where this topic has been given extensive coverage. Under International Accounting Standards, this concept has been defined, but with only a very brief outline of the treatment to be accorded to this kind of lease. A leveraged lease is defined in IAS 17 as a finance lease which is structured such that there are at least three parties involved: the lessee, the lessor, and one or more long-term creditors who provide part of the acquisition finance for the leased asset, usually without any general recourse to the lessor. Succinctly, this type of a lease is given the following unique accounting treatment:

1. The lessor records his or her investment in the lease net of the nonrecourse debt and the related finance costs to the third-party creditor(s).
2. The recognition of the finance income is based on the lessor's net cash investment outstanding in respect of the lease.

Sale-Leaseback Transactions

Sale-leaseback describes a transaction where the owner of property (seller-lessee) sells the property and then immediately leases all or part of it back from the new owner (buyer-lessor). These transactions may occur when the seller-lessee is experiencing cash flow or financing problems or because there are tax advantages in such an arrangement in the lessee's tax jurisdiction. The important consideration in this type of transaction is recognition of two separate and distinct economic transactions. However, it is important to note that there is not a physical transfer of property. First, there is a sale of property, and second, there is a lease agreement for the same property in which the original seller is the lessee and the original buyer is the lessor. This is illustrated as follows:

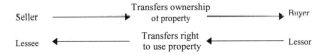

A sale-leaseback transaction is usually structured such that the sales price of the asset is greater than or equal to the current market value. The result of this higher sales price is a higher periodic rental payment over the lease term. The transaction is usually attractive because of the tax benefits associated with it, and because it provides financing to the lessee. The seller-lessee benefits from the higher price because of the increased gain on the sale of the property and the deductibility of the lease payments, which are usually larger than the depreciation that was previously being taken. The buyer-lessor benefits from both the higher rental payments and the larger depreciable basis.

Under IAS 17, the accounting treatment depends on whether the sale and lease-back results in a finance lease or an operating lease. If it results in a finance lease, any excess of sale proceeds need not immediately be recognized as income in the financial statements of the seller-lessee. If such an excess is recognized, it should be deferred and amortized over the lease term.

If a sale and leaseback transaction results in an operating lease

1. If it is evident that the transaction is established at fair value, any profit or loss should be recognized immediately.
2. If sale price is not established at fair value

   a. If sale price is below fair value, any profit or loss should be recognized immediately, except that when a loss is to be compensated by below fair market future rentals, the loss should be deferred and amortized in proportion to the rental payments over the period the asset is expected to be used.
   b. If the sale price is above fair value, the excess over fair value should be deferred and amortized over the period for which the asset is expected to be used.

IAS 17 stipulates that in case of operating leases, if at the time of the sale and leaseback transaction the fair value is less than the carrying amount of the leased asset, the difference between the fair value and the carrying amount should immediately be recognized.

However, in case the sale and leaseback result in a finance lease, no such adjustment is considered necessary unless there has been an impairment in value, in which case the carrying value should be reduced to the recoverable amount in accordance with the provisions of IAS 16, *Property, Plant, and Equipment.*

Additional guidance. Sale-leaseback transactions can be rather complex, and the guidance offered by IAS 17 is limited. Therefore, to provide further insight into this common type of financing arrangement, additional commentary is offered, based on the rules and interpretations under US GAAP.

The accounting treatment from the seller-lessee's perspective will depend on the degree of rights to use retained by the seller-lessee. The degree of rights to use retained may be categorized as follows:

1. Substantially all
2. Minor
3. More than minor but less than substantially all

The guideline for the determination substantially all is based on the classification criteria presented for the lease transaction. For example, a test based on the

90% recovery criterion seems appropriate. That is, if the present value of fair rental payments is equal to 90% or more of the fair value of the sold asset, the seller-lessee is presumed to have retained substantially all the rights to use the sold property. The test for retaining minor rights would be to substitute 10% or less for 90% or more in the preceding sentence.

If substantially all the rights to use the property are retained by the seller-lessee and the agreement meets at least one of the criteria for capital lease treatment, the seller-lessee should account for the leaseback as a capital lease, and any profit on the sale should be deferred and either amortized over the life of the property or treated as a reduction of depreciation expense. If the leaseback is classified as an operating lease, it should be accounted for as one, and any profit or loss on the sale should be deferred and amortized over the lease term. Any loss on the sale would also be deferred unless the loss were perceived to be a real economic loss, in which case the loss would be recognized immediately and not deferred.

If only a minor portion of the rights to use are retained by the seller-lessee, the sale and the leaseback should be accounted for separately. However, if the rental payments appear unreasonable based on the existing market conditions at the inception of the lease, the profit or loss should be adjusted so that the rentals are at a reasonable amount. The amount created by the adjustment should be deferred and amortized over the life of the property if a capital lease is involved or over the lease term if an operating lease is involved.

If the seller-lessee retains more than a minor portion but less than substantially all the rights to use the property, any excess profit on the sale should be recognized on the date of the sale. For purposes of this paragraph, excess profit is derived as follows:

1. If the leaseback is classified as an operating lease, the excess profit is the profit that exceeds the present value of the minimum lease payments over the lease term. The seller-lessee should use its incremental borrowing rate to compute the present value of the minimum lease payments. If the implicit rate of interest in the lease is known, it should be used to compute the present value of the minimum lease payments.
2. If the leaseback is classified as a capital (i.e., finance) lease, the excess profit is the amount greater than the recorded amount of the leased asset.

When the fair value of the property at the time of the leaseback is less than its undepreciated cost, the seller-lessee should immediately recognize a loss for the difference. In the example below, the sales price is less than the book value of the property. However, there is no economic loss because the FMV is greater than the book value.

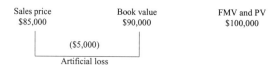

The artificial loss must be deferred and amortized as an addition to depreciation.

The following diagram summarizes the accounting for sale-leaseback transactions.

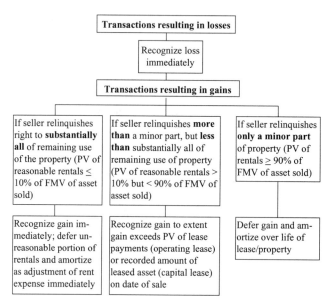

In the foregoing circumstances, when the leased asset is land only, any amortization should be on a straight-line basis over the lease term, regardless of whether the lease is classified as a capital or an operating lease.

Executory costs are not to be included in the calculation of profit to be deferred in a sale-leaseback transaction. The buyer-lessor should account for the transaction as a purchase and a direct financing lease if the agreement meets the criteria of **either** a direct financing lease **or** a sales-type lease. Otherwise, the agreement should be accounted for as a purchase and an operating lease.

Sale-leaseback involving real estate. Under US GAAP, three requirements are necessary for a sale-leaseback involving real estate (including real estate with equipment) to qualify for sale-leaseback accounting treatment. Those sale-leaseback transactions not meeting the three requirements should be accounted for as a deposit or as a financing. The three requirements are

1. The lease must be a normal leaseback.
2. Payment terms and provisions must adequately demonstrate the buyer-lessor's initial and continuing investment in the property.

3. Payment terms and provisions must transfer all the risks and rewards of ownership as demonstrated by a lack of continuing involvement by the seller-lessee.

A normal leaseback involves active use of the leased property in the seller-lessee's trade or business during the lease term.

The buyer-lessor's initial investment is adequate if it demonstrates the buyer-lessor's commitment to pay for the property and indicates a reasonable likelihood that the seller-lessee will collect any receivable related to the leased property. The buyer-lessor's continuing investment is adequate if the buyer is contractually obligated to pay an annual amount at least equal to the level of annual payment needed to pay that debt and interest over no more than (1) 20 years for land, and (2) the customary term of a first mortgage loan for other real estate.

Any continuing involvement by the seller-lessee other than normal leaseback disqualifies the lease from sale-leaseback accounting treatment. Some examples of continuing involvement other than normal leaseback include

1. The seller-lessee has an obligation or option (excluding the right of first refusal) to repurchase the property.
2. The seller-lessee (or party related to the seller-lessee) guarantees the buyer-lessor's investment or debt related to that investment or a return on that investment.
3. The seller-lessee is required to reimburse the buyer-lessor for a decline in the fair value of the property below estimated residual value at the end of the lease term based on other than excess wear and tear.
4. The seller-lessee remains liable for an existing debt related to the property.
5. The seller-lessee's rental payments are contingent on some predetermined level of future operations of the buyer-lessor.
6. The seller-lessee provides collateral on behalf of the buyer-lessor other than the property directly involved in the sale-leaseback.
7. The seller-lessee provides nonrecourse financing to the buyer-lessor for any portion of the sales proceeds or provides recourse financing in which the only recourse is the leased asset.
8. The seller-lessee enters into a sale-leaseback involving property improvements or integral equipment without leasing the underlying land to the buyer-lessor.
9. The buyer-lessor is obligated to share any portion of the appreciation of the property with the seller-lessee.
10. Any other provision or circumstance that allows the seller-lessee to participate in any future profits of the buyer-lessor or appreciation of the leased property.

Example of accounting for a sale-leaseback transaction

To illustrate the accounting treatment in a sale-leaseback transaction, suppose that Lessee Corporation sells equipment that has a book value of $80,000 and a fair value of $100,000 to Lessor Corporation, and then immediately leases it back under the following conditions:

1. The sale date is January 1, 2000, and the equipment has a fair value of $100,000 on that date and an estimated useful life of 15 years.
2. The lease term is 15 years, noncancelable, and requires equal rental payments of $13,109 at the beginning of each year.
3. Lessee Corp. has the option annually to renew the lease at the same rental payments on expiration of the original lease.
4. Lessee Corp. has the obligation to pay all executory costs.
5. The annual rental payments provide the lessor with a 12% return on investment.
6. The incremental borrowing rate of Lessee Corp. is 12%.
7. Lessee Corp. depreciates similar equipment on a straight-line basis.

Lessee Corp. should classify the agreement as a capital lease since the lease term exceeds 75% (which is deemed to be a major part) of the estimated economic life of the equipment, and because the present value of the lease payments is greater than 90% (deemed to be substantially all) of the fair value of the equipment. Assuming that collectibility of the lease payments is reasonably predictable and that no important uncertainties exist concerning the amount of nonreimbursable costs yet to be incurred by the lessor, Lessor Corp. should classify the transaction as a direct financing lease because the present value of the minimum lease payments is equal to the fair market value of $100,000 ($13,109 x 7.62817).

Lessee Corp. and Lessor Corp. would normally make the following journal entries during the first year:

Upon Sale of Equipment on January 1, 2000

Lessee Corp.			*Lessor Corp.*		
Cash	100,000		Equipment	100,000	
Equipment*		80,000	Cash		100,000
Unearned profit on					
sale-leaseback		20,000			
Leased equipment	100,000		Lease receivable		
Lease obligations		100,000	($13,109 x 15)	196,635	
			Equipment		100,000
			Unearned interest		96,635

Assumes new equipment

To Record First Payment on January 1, 2000

Lessee Corp.			*Lessor Corp.*		
Lease obligations	13,109		Cash	13,109	
Cash		13,109	Lease receivable		13,109

To Record Incurrence and Payment of Executory Costs

Lessee Corp.			*Lessor Corp.*
Insurance, taxes, etc.	xxx		(No entry)
Cash (accounts			
payable)		xxx	

To Record Depreciation Expense on the Equipment, December 31, 2000

Lessee Corp.		*Lessor Corp.*
Depreciation expense	6,667	(No entry)
Accum. depr.-- capital		
leases ($100,000 ÷ 15)	6,667	

To Amortize Profit on Sale-Leaseback by Lessee Corp., December 31, 2000

Lessee Corp.		*Lessor Corp.*
Unearned profit on sale-leaseback	1,333	(No entry)
Depr. expense ($20,000 ÷ 15)	1,333	

To Record Interest for 1999, December 31, 2000

Lessee Corp.		*Lessor Corp.*	
Interest expense	10,427	Unearned interest income	10,427
Accrued interest payable	10,427	Interest income	10,427

Partial Lease Amortization Schedule

Date	Cash payment	Interest expense	Reduction of obligation	Lease obligation
Inception of lease				$100,000
1/1/99	$13,109	$ --	$13,109	86,891
1/1/00	13,109	10,427	2,682	84,209

Leases Involving Land and Buildings--Guidance Under IAS 17

IAS 17 stipulates rules relating to leases of land and building. In general, the treatment of such leases is to be the same as for leases of other assets. However, since land has an indefinite useful life, if title is not expected to pass to the lessee at the end of the lease term, such leases are to be classified as operating leases. Were the lessee to capitalize such a lease arrangement, the fact that no periodic depreciation would be reported would inevitably result in a write-off of the asset at the termination of the lease, which clearly would not contribute to meaningful financial reporting.

Similarly, IAS recognizes the fact that buildings have useful lives that extend well beyond the lease terms, and often, long-term leases for buildings contain provisions whereby rents are regularly adjusted upward to market rates. Thus, if title is not expected to pass to the lessee at the end of the lease term or if rents are adjusted upward regularly to reflect market rates, the lessor retains a significant part of the risks and rewards incidental to ownership, and hence, such leases should **normally** be classified as operating leases. However, whether or not to capitalize the building in the financial statements of the lessee is a question of facts and circumstances, and to do so is not absolutely prohibited by the standard.

Leases Involving Real Estate--Guidance Under US GAAP

Again, the guidance under IAS 17 is limited, and the practice under US GAAP is instructive. Under those standards, leases involving real estate can be divided into the following four categories:

1. Leases involving land only
2. Leases involving land and building(s)
3. Leases involving real estate and equipment
4. Leases involving only part of a building

Leases Involving Land Only

Lessee accounting. If the lease agreement transfers ownership or contains a bargain purchase option, the lessee should account for the lease as a capital lease and record an asset and related liability in an amount equal to the present value of the minimum lease payments. If the lease agreement does not transfer ownership or contain a bargain purchase option, the lessee should account for the lease as an operating lease.

Lessor accounting. If the lease gives rise to dealer's profit (or loss) and transfers ownership (i.e., title), the standards require that the lease shall be classified as a sales-type lease and accounted for under the provisions of the US standard dealing with sales of real estate, in the same manner as would a seller of the same property. If the lease transfers ownership, both the collectibility and the no material uncertainties criteria are met, but if it does not give rise to dealer's profit (or loss), the lease should be accounted for as a direct financing or leveraged lease, as appropriate. If the lease contains a bargain purchase option and both the collectibility and no material uncertainties criteria are met, the lease should be accounted for as a direct financing, leveraged, or operating lease as appropriate. If the lease does not meet the collectibility and/or no material uncertainties criteria, the lease should be accounted for as an operating lease.

Leases Involving Land and Building

Lessee accounting. If the agreement transfers title or contains a bargain purchase option, the lessee should account for the agreement by separating the land and building components and capitalize each separately. The land and building elements should be allocated on the basis of their relative fair market values measured at the inception of the lease. The land and building components are accounted for separately because the lessee is expected to own the real estate by the end of the lease term. The building should be depreciated over its estimated useful life without regard to the lease term.

When the lease agreement neither transfers title nor contains a bargain purchase option, the fair value of the land must be determined in relation to the fair value of the aggregate properties included in the lease agreement. If the fair value of the land is less than 25% of the fair value of the leased properties in aggregate, the land is considered immaterial. Conversely, if the fair value of the land is 25% or greater of the fair value of the leased properties in aggregate, the land is considered material.

When the land component of the lease agreement is considered immaterial (FMV land < 25% total FMV), the lease should be accounted for as a single lease unit. The lessee should capitalize the lease if one of the following occurs:

1. The term of the lease is 75% or more of the economic useful life of the real estate
2. The present value of the minimum lease payments equals 90% or more of the fair market value of the leased real estate less any lessor tax credits

If neither of the two criteria above is met, the lessee should account for the lease agreement as a single operating lease.

When the land component of the lease agreement is considered material (FMV land ≥ 25% total FMV), the land and building components should be separated. By applying the lessee's incremental borrowing rate to the fair market value of the land, the annual minimum lease payment attributed to land is computed. The remaining payments are attributed to the building. The division of minimum lease payments between land and building is essential for both the lessee and lessor. The lease involving the land should **always** be accounted for as an operating lease. Under US GAAP, the lease involving the building(s) must meet either the 75% (of useful life) or 90% (of fair value) test to be treated as a capital lease. If neither of the two criteria is met, the building(s) will also be accounted for as an operating lease.

Lessor accounting.   The lessor's accounting depends on whether the lease transfers ownership, contains a bargain purchase option, or does neither of the two. If the lease transfers ownership and gives rise to dealer's profit (or loss), US GAAP requires that the lessor classify the lease as a sales-type lease and account for the lease as a single unit under the provisions of SFAS 66 in the same manner as a seller of the same property. If the lease transfers ownership, meets both the collectibility and no important uncertainties criteria, but does not give rise to dealer's profit (or loss), the lease should be accounted for as a direct financing or leveraged lease as appropriate.

If the lease contains a bargain purchase option and gives rise to dealer's profit (or loss), the lease should be classified as an operating lease. If the lease contains a bargain purchase option, meets both the collectibility and no material uncertainties criteria, but does not give rise to dealer's profit (or loss), the lease should be accounted for as a direct financing lease or a leveraged lease, as appropriate.

If the lease agreement neither transfers ownership nor contains a bargain purchase option, the lessor should follow the same rules as the lessee in accounting for real estate leases involving land and building(s).

However, the collectibility and the no material uncertainties criteria must be met before the lessor can account for the agreement as a direct financing lease, and in no such case may the lease be classified as a sales-type lease (i.e., ownership must be transferred).

The treatment of a lease involving both land and building can be illustrated in the following examples.

Example of accounting for land and building lease containing transfer of title

Assume the following:

1. The lessee enters into a 10-year noncancelable lease for a parcel of land and a building for use in its operations. The building has an estimated useful life of 12 years.
2. The FMV of the land is $75,000, while the FMV of the building is $310,000.
3. A payment of $50,000 is due to the lessor at the beginning of each of the 10 years of the lease.
4. The lessee's incremental borrowing rate is 10%. (Lessor's implicit rate is unknown.)
5. Ownership will transfer to the lessee at the end of the lease.

The present value of the minimum lease payments is $337,951 ($50,000 x 6.75902*). The portion of the present value of the minimum lease payments that should be capitalized for each of the two components of the lease is computed as follows:

FMV of land		$ 75,000	
FMV of building		310,000	
Total FMV of leased property		$385,000	
Portion of PV allocated to land	$337,951 x	$\frac{75,000}{385,000}$ =	$ 65,835
Portion of PV allocated to building	$337,951 x	$\frac{310,000}{385,000}$ =	272,116
Total PV to be capitalized			$337,951

The entry made to record the lease initially is as follows:

Leased land	65,835	
Leased building	272,116	
Lease obligation		337,951

6.75902 is the PV of an annuity due for 10 periods at 10%.

Subsequently, the obligation will be decreased in accordance with the effective interest method. The leased building will be amortized over its expected useful life.

Example of accounting for land and building lease without transfer of title or bargain purchase option

Assume the same facts as in the previous example except that title does not transfer at the end of the lease.

The lease is still a capital lease because the lease term is more than 75% of the useful life. Since the FMV of the land is less than 25% of the leased properties in aggregate, (75,000/385,000 = 19%), the land component is considered immaterial and the lease will be accounted for as a single lease. The entry to record the lease is as follows:

Leased property	337,951	
Lease obligation		337,951

Assume the same facts as in the previous example except that the FMV of the land is $110,000 and the FMV of the building is $275,000. Once again, title does not transfer.

Because the FMV of the land exceeds 25% of the leased properties in aggregate (110,000/385,000 = 28%), the land component is considered material and the lease would be separated into two components. The annual minimum lease payment attributed to the land is computed as follows:

$$\frac{\text{FMV of land}}{\text{PV factor}} \quad \frac{\$110,000}{6.75902^*} = \$16,275$$

The remaining portion of the annual payment is attributed to the building.

Annual payment	$ 50,000
Less amount attributed to land	(16,275)
Annual payment attributed to building	$33,725

The present value of the minimum annual lease payments attributed to the building is then computed as follows:

Minimum annual lease payment attributed to building	$ 33,725
PV factor	x 6.75902*
PV of minimum annual lease payments attributed to building	$227,948

The entry to record the capital portion of the lease is as follows:

Leased building	227,948	
Lease obligation		227,948

*6.75902 is the PV of an annuity due for 10 periods at 10%.

There would be no computation of the present value of the minimum annual lease payment attributed to the land since the land component of the lease will be treated as an operating lease. For this reason, each year, $16,275 of the $50,000 lease payment will be recorded as land rental expense. The remainder of the annual payment ($33,725) will be applied against the lease obligation using the effective interest method.

Leases involving real estate and equipment. When real estate leases also involve equipment or machinery, the equipment component should be separated and accounted for as a separate lease agreement by both lessees and lessors. According to US GAAP, "the portion of the minimum lease payments applicable to the equipment element of the lease shall be estimated by whatever means are appropriate in the circumstances." The lessee and lessor should apply the capitalization requirements to the equipment lease independently of accounting for the real estate lease(s). The real estate leases should be handled as discussed in the preceding two sections. In a sale-leaseback transaction involving real estate with equipment, the equipment and land are not separated.

Leases involving only part of a building. It is common to find lease agreements that involve only part of a building, as, for example, when a floor of an office building is leased or when a store in a shopping mall is leased. A difficulty that arises in this situation is that the cost and/or fair market value of the leased portion of the whole may not be determinable objectively.

Lessee accounting. If the fair value of the leased property is objectively determinable, the lessee should follow the rules and account for the lease as described in "leases involving land and building." If the fair value of the leased property cannot be determined objectively but the agreement satisfies the 75% test, the estimated economic life of the building in which the leased premises are located should be used. If this test is not met, the lessee should account for the agreement as an operating lease.

Lessor accounting. From the lessor's position, both the cost and fair value of the leased property must be objectively determinable before the procedures described under "leases involving land and building" will apply. If either the cost or the fair value cannot be determined objectively, the lessor should account for the agreement as an operating lease.

DISCLOSURE REQUIREMENTS UNDER IAS 17

Lessee Disclosures

1. **Finance Leases**

    IAS 17 (revised), paragraph 23, mandates the following disclosures for lessees under finance leases:

    a. For each class of asset, the net carrying amount at balance sheet date
    b. A reconciliation between the total of minimum lease payments at the balance sheet date, and their present value. In addition, an enterprise should disclose the total of the minimum lease payments at the balance sheet date, their present value, for each of the following periods:

    (1) Due in 1 year or less
    (2) Due in more than 1 but no more than 5 years
    (3) Due in more than 5 years

    c. Contingent rents included in profit or loss for the period
    d. The total of minimum sublease payments to be received in the future under noncancelable subleases as of the balance sheet date

    e. A general description of the lessee's significant leasing arrangements including, but not necessarily limited to the following:

       (1) The basis for determining contingent rentals

       (2) The existence and terms of renewal or purchase options and escalation clauses

       (3) Restrictions imposed by lease arrangements such as on dividends or assumptions of further debt or further leasing

Furthermore, the revised IAS 17, paragraph 23, clarifies that the requirements of IAS 32 (*Financial Instruments: Recognition and Measurement*) also are applicable to finance leases.

2. **Operating Leases**

    IAS 17 (revised), paragraph 26, sets forth in greater detail the disclosure requirements which will be applicable to lessees under operating leases. While some of these were suggested under original IAS 17 or are implicitly needed to provide adequate disclosure, the revised standard offers preparers more explicit guidance.

    Lessees should, in addition to the requirements of IAS 32, make the following disclosures for operating leases:

    a. Total of the future minimum lease payments under noncancelable operating leases for each of the following periods:

       (1) Due in 1 year or less

       (2) Due in more than 1 year but no more than 5 years

       (3) Due in more than 5 years

    b. The total of future minimum sublease payments expected to be received under noncancellable subleases at the balance sheet date

    c. Lease and sublease payments included in profit or loss for the period, with separate amounts of minimum lease payments, contingent rents, and sublease payments

    d. A general description of the lessee's significant leasing arrangements including, but not necessarily limited to the following:

       (1) The basis for determining contingent rentals

       (2) The existence and terms of renewal or purchase options escalation clauses

       (3) Restrictions imposed by lease arrangements such as on dividends or assumption of further debt or on further leasing

Lessor Disclosures

1. **Finance Leases**

    IAS 17 (revised), paragraph 39, requires enhanced disclosures compared to original IAS 17. Lessors under finance leases are required to disclose, in addition to disclosures under IAS 32, the following:

    a. A reconciliation between the total gross investment in the lease at the balance sheet date, and the present value of minimum lease payments receivable as of the balance sheet date, categorized into

        (1) Those due in 1 year or less
        (2) Those due in more than 1 year but not more than 5 years
        (3) Those due beyond 5 years

    b. Unearned finance income
    c. The accumulated allowance for uncollectible minimum lease payments receivable
    d. Total contingent rentals included in income
    e. A general description of the lessor's significant leasing arrangements

2. **Operating Leases**

    For lessors under operating leases, the revised IAS 17, paragraph 48, has prescribed the following expanded disclosures:

    a. For each class of asset, the gross carrying amount, the accumulated depreciation and accumulated impairment losses at the balance sheet date

        (1) Depreciation recognized in income for the period
        (2) Impairment losses recognized in income for the period
        (3) Impairment losses reversed in income for the period

    b. Depreciation recognized on assets held for operating lease use during the period
    c. The future minimum lease payments under noncancellable operating leases, in the aggregate and classified into

        (1) Those due in no more than 1 year
        (2) Those due in more than 1 but not more than 5 years
        (3) Those due in more than 5 years

    d. Total contingent rentals included in income for the period
    e. A general description of leasing arrangements to which it is a party

APPENDIX A

SPECIAL SITUATIONS NOT YET ADDRESSED BY IAS 17 BUT WHICH HAVE BEEN INTERPRETED UNDER US GAAP

In the following section, a number of interesting and common problem areas that have not been addressed by the international standards are briefly considered. The guidance found in US GAAP is referenced, as this is likely to represent the most comprehensive source of insight into these matters. However, it should be understood that this constitutes only possible approaches and is not authoritative guidance.

Termination of a Lease

The lessor shall remove the remaining net investment from his or her books and record the leased equipment as an asset at the lower of its original cost, present fair value, or current carrying value. The net adjustment is reflected in the income of the current period.

The lessee is also affected by the terminated agreement because he or she has been relieved of the obligation. If the lease is a capital lease, the lessee should remove both the obligation and the asset from his or her accounts and charge any adjustment to the current period income. If accounted for as an operating lease, no accounting adjustment is required.

Renewal or Extension of an Existing Lease

The renewal or extension of an existing lease agreement affects the accounting of both the lessee and the lessor. US GAAP specifies two basic situations in this regard: (1) the renewal occurs and makes a residual guarantee or penalty provision inoperative, or (2) the renewal agreement does not do the foregoing and the renewal is to be treated as a new agreement. The accounting treatment prescribed under the latter situation for a lessee is as follows:

1. If the renewal or extension is classified as a capital lease, the (present) current balances of the asset and related obligation should be adjusted by an amount equal to the difference between the present value of the future minimum lease payments under the revised agreement and the (present) current balance of the obligation. The present value of the minimum lease payments under the revised agreement should be computed using the interest rate that was in effect at the inception of the original lease.
2. If the renewal or extension is classified as an operating lease, the current balances in the asset and liability accounts are removed from the books and a gain (loss) recognized for the difference. The new lease agreement resulting from a renewal or extension is accounted for in the same manner as other operating leases.

TREATMENT OF SELECTED ITEMS IN ACCOUNTING FOR LEASES UNDER US GAAP

	Lessor — Operating	Lessor — Direct financing and sales-type	Lessee — Operating	Lessee — capital
Initial direct costs	Capitalize and amortize over lease term in proportion to rent revenue recognized (normally SL basis)	Direct financing: Record in separate account / Add to net investment in lease / Compute new effective rate that equates gross amt. of min. lease payments and unguar. residual value with net invest. / Amortize so as to produce constant rate of return over lease term / Sales-type: Expense in period incurred	N/A	N/A
Investment tax credit retained by lessor	N/A	Reduces FMV of leased asset for 90% test	N/A	Reduces FMV of leased asset for 90% test
Bargain purchase option	N/A	Include in: Minimum lease payments / 90% test	N/A	Include in: Minimum lease payments / 90% test
Guaranteed residual value	N/A	Include in: Minimum lease payments / 90% test / Sales-type: Include PV in sales revenues	N/A	Include in: Minimum lease payments / 90% test
Unguaranteed residual value	N/A	Include In: "Gross Investment in Lease" / Not included in: Minimum lease payments / 90% test / Sales-type: Exclude from sales revenue / Deduct PV from cost of sales	N/A	Include in: Minimum lease payments / 90% test
Contingent rentals	Revenue in period earned	Not part of minimum lease payments; revenue in period earned	Expense in period incurred	Not part of minimum lease payments; expense in period incurred
Amortization period	Amortize down to estimated residual value over estimated economic life of asset	N/A	N/A	Amortize down to estimated residual value over lease term or estimated economic life[c]
Revenue (expense)[a]	Rent revenue (normally SL basis) / Amortization depreciation expense)	Direct financing: Interest revenue on net investment in lease (gross investment less unearned interest income) / Sales-type: Dealer profit in period of sale (sales revenue less cost of leased asset) / Interest revenue on net investment in lease	Rent expense (normally SL basis)[b]	Interest expense and depreciation expense

[a] Elements of revenue (expense) listed for the items above are not repeated here (e.g., treatment of initial direct costs).

[b] If payments are not on a SL basis, recognize rent expense on a SL basis unless another systematic and rational method is more representative of use benefit obtained from the property, in which case, the other method should be used.

[c] If lease has automatic passage of title or bargain purchase option, use estimated economic life; otherwise, use the lease term.

Under the same circumstances, US GAAP prescribes the following treatment to be followed by the lessor:

1. If the renewal or extension is classified as a direct financing lease, then the existing balances of the lease receivable and the estimated residual value accounts should be adjusted for the changes resulting from the revised agreement.

   NOTE: Remember that an upward adjustment of the estimated residual value is not allowed.)

   The net adjustment should be charged or credited to an unearned income account.

2. If the renewal or extension is classified as an operating lease, the remaining net investment under the existing sales-type lease or direct financing lease is removed from the books and the leased asset recorded as an asset at the lower of its original cost, present fair value, or current carrying amount. The difference between the net investment and the amount recorded for the leased asset is charged to income of the period. The renewal or extension is then accounted for as for any other operating lease.

3. If the renewal or extension is classified as a sales-type lease **and** it occurs at or near the end of the existing lease term, the renewal or extension should be accounted for as a sales-type lease.

   NOTE: A renewal or extension that occurs in the last few months of an existing lease is considered to have occurred at or near the end of the existing lease term.

If the renewal or extension causes the guarantee or penalty provision to be inoperative, the lessee adjusts the current balance of the leased asset and the lease obligation to the present value of the future minimum lease payments (according to the relevant standard, "by an amount equal to the difference between the PV of future minimum lease payments under the revised agreement and the present balance of the obligation"). The PV of the future minimum lease payments is computed using the implicit rate used in the original lease agreement.

Given the same circumstances, the lessor adjusts the existing balance of the lease receivable and estimated residual value accounts to reflect the changes of the revised agreement (remember, no upward adjustments to the residual value). The net adjustment is charged (or credited) to unearned income.

Leases Between Related Parties

Leases between related parties are classified and accounted for as though the parties are unrelated, except in cases where it is clear that the terms and conditions of the agreement have been influenced significantly by the fact of the relationship.

When this is the case, the classification and/or accounting is modified to reflect the true economic substance of the transaction rather than the legal form.

If a subsidiary's principal business activity is leasing property to its parent or other affiliated companies, consolidated financial statements are presented. The US GAAP standard on related parties requires that the nature and extent of leasing activities between related parties be disclosed.

Accounting for Leases in a Business Combination

A business combination, in and of itself, has no effect on the classification of a lease. However, if, in connection with a business combination, the lease agreement is modified to change the original classification of the lease, it should be considered a new agreement and reclassified according to the revised provisions.

In most cases, a business combination that is accounted for by the pooling-of-interest method or by the purchase method will not affect the previous classification of a lease unless the provisions have been modified as indicated in the preceding paragraph.

The acquiring company should apply the following procedures to account for a leveraged lease in a business combination accounted for by the purchase method:

1. The classification of leveraged lease should be kept.
2. The net investment in the leveraged lease should be given a fair market value (present value, net of tax) based on the remaining future cash flows. Also, the estimated tax effects of the cash flows should be given recognition.
3. The net investment should be broken down into three components: net rentals receivable, estimated residual value, and unearned income.
4. Thereafter, the leveraged lease should be accounted for as described above in the section on leveraged leases.

Accounting for Changes in Lease Agreements Resulting From Refunding of Tax-Exempt Debt

If, during the lease term, a change in the lease results from a refunding by the lessor of tax-exempt debt (including an advance refunding) and (1) the lessee receives the economic advantages of the refunding and (2) the revised agreement can be classified as a capital lease by the lessee and a direct financing lease by the lessor, the change should be accounted for as follows:

1. If the change is accounted for as an extinguishment of debt

   a. **Lessee accounting**. The lessee should adjust the lease obligation to the present value of the future minimum lease payments under the revised agreement. The present value of the minimum lease payments should be computed by using the interest rate applicable to the revised agreement. Any gain or loss should be recognized currently as a gain or loss on the extinguishment of debt in accordance with the provisions of SFAS 4.

  b. **Lessor accounting**. The lessor should adjust the balance of the lease receivable and the estimated residual value, if affected, for the difference in present values between the old and revised agreements. Any resulting gain or loss should be recognized currently.

2. If the change is not accounted for as an extinguishment of debt

  a. **Lessee accounting**. The lessee should accrue any costs in connection with the debt refunding that is obligated to be refunded to the lessor. These costs should be amortized by the interest method over the period from the date of refunding to the call date of the debt to be refunded.

  b. **Lessor accounting**. The lessor should recognize any reimbursements to be received from the lessee, for costs paid in relation to the debt refunding, as revenue. This revenue should be recognized in a systematic manner over the period from the date of refunding to the call date of the debt to be refunded.

Sale or Assignment to Third Parties--Nonrecourse Financing

The sale or assignment of a lease or of property subject to a lease that was originally accounted for as a sales-type lease or a direct financing lease will not affect the original accounting treatment of the lease. Any profit or loss on the sale or assignment should be recognized at the time of transaction except under the following two circumstances:

1. When the sale or assignment is between related parties, apply the provisions presented above under "related parties."
2. When the sale or assignment is with recourse, it should be accounted for using the provisions of the US standard on sale of receivables with recourse.

The sale of property subject to an operating lease should not be treated as a sale if the seller (or any related party to the seller) retains "substantial risks of ownership" in the leased property. A seller may retain substantial risks of ownership by various arrangements. For example, if the lessee defaults on the lease agreement or if the lease terminates, the seller may arrange to do one of the following:

1. Acquire the property or the lease
2. Substitute an existing lease
3. Secure a replacement lessee or a buyer for the property under a remarketing agreement

A seller will not retain substantial risks of ownership by arrangements where one of the following occurs:

1. A remarketing agreement includes a reasonable fee to be paid to the seller
2. The seller is not required to give priority to the releasing or disposition of the property owned by the third party over similar property owned by the seller

When the sale of property subject to an operating lease is not accounted for as a sale because the substantial risk factor is present, it should be accounted for as a borrowing. The proceeds from the sale should be recorded as an obligation on the seller's books. Rental payments made by the lessee under the operating lease should be recorded as revenue by the seller even if the payments are paid to the third-party purchaser. The seller shall account for each rental payment by allocating a portion to interest expense (to be imputed in accordance with the provisions of APB 21), and the remainder will reduce the existing obligation. Other normal accounting procedures for operating leases should be applied except that the depreciation term for the leased asset is limited to the amortization period of the obligation.

The sale or assignment of lease payments under an operating lease by the lessor should be accounted for as a borrowing as described above.

Nonrecourse financing is a common occurrence in the leasing industry whereby the stream of lease payments on a lease is discounted on a nonrecourse basis at a financial institution with the lease payments collateralizing the debt. The proceeds are then used to finance future leasing transactions. Even though the discounting is on a nonrecourse basis, US GAAP prohibits the offsetting of the debt against the related lease receivable unless a legal right of offset exists or the lease qualified as a leveraged lease at its inception.

Money-Over-Money Lease Transactions

In cases where a lessor obtains nonrecourse financing in excess of the leased asset's cost, a technical bulletin states that the borrowing and leasing are separate transactions and should not be offset against each other unless a right of offset exists. Only dealer profit in sales-type leases may be recognized at the beginning of the lease term.

Acquisition of Interest in Residual Value

Recently, there has been an increase in the acquisition of interests in residual values of leased assets by companies whose primary business is other than leasing or financing. This generally occurs through the outright purchase of the right to own the leased asset or the right to receive the proceeds from the sale of a leased asset at the end of its lease term.

In instances such as these, the rights should be recorded by the purchaser at the fair value of the assets surrendered. Recognition of increases in the value of the interest in the residual (i.e., residual value accretion) to the end of the lease term are prohibited. However, a nontemporary write-down of the residual value interest should be recognized as a loss. This guidance also applies to lessors who sell the related minimum lease payments but retain the interest in the residual value. Guaranteed residual values also have no effect on this guidance.

Leases Involving Government Units

Leases that involve government units (i.e., airport facilities, bus terminal space, etc.) usually contain special provisions that prevent the agreements from being classified as anything but operating leases. These special provisions include the governmental body's authority to abandon a facility at any time during lease term, thus making its economic life indeterminable. These leases also do not contain a BPO or transfer ownership. The fair market value is generally indeterminable because neither the leased property nor similar property is available for sale.

However, leases involving government units are subject to the same classification criteria as those of nongovernment units, except when the following six criteria are met.

NOTE: If all six conditions are met, the agreement should be classified as an operating lease by both lessee and lessor.

1. A government unit or authority owns the leased property
2. The leased property is part of a larger facility operated by or on behalf of the lessor
3. The leased property is a permanent structure or part of a permanent structure that normally cannot be moved to another location
4. The lessor, or a higher governmental authority, has the right to terminate the lease at any time under the lease agreement or existing statutes or regulations
5. The lease neither transfers ownership nor allows the lessee to purchase or acquire the leased property
6. The leased property or similar property in the same area cannot be purchased or leased from anyone else

Accounting for a Sublease

A sublease is used to describe the situation where the original lessee re-leases the leased property to a third party (the sublessee), and the original lessee acts as a sublessor. Normally, the nature of a sublease agreement does not affect the original lease agreement, and the original lessee/sublessor retains primary liability.

The original lease remains in effect, and the original lessor continues to account for the lease as before. The original lessee/sublessor accounts for the lease as follows:

1. If the original lease agreement transfers ownership or contains a bargain purchase option and if the new lease meets any one of the four criteria

specified in US GAAP (i.e., transfers ownership, BPO, the 75% test, or the 90% test) and both the collectibility and uncertainties criteria, the sublessor should classify the new lease as a sales-type or direct financing lease; otherwise, as an operating lease. In either situation, the original lessee/ sublessor should continue accounting for the original lease obligation as before.

2. If the original lease agreement does not transfer ownership or contain a bargain purchase option, but it still qualified as a capital lease, the original lessee/sublessor should (with one exception) apply the usual criteria set by US GAAP in classifying the new agreement as a capital or operating lease. If the new lease qualifies for capital treatment, the original lessee/sublessor should account for it as a direct financing lease, with the unamortized balance of the asset under the original lease being treated as the cost of the leased property. The one exception arises when the circumstances surrounding the sublease suggest that the sublease agreement was an important part of a predetermined plan in which the original lessee played only an intermediate role between the original lessor and the sublessee. In this situation, the sublease should be classified by the 75% and 90% criteria as well as collectibility and uncertainties criteria. In applying the 90% criterion, the fair value for the leased property will be the fair value to the original lessor at the inception of the original lease. Under all circumstances, the original lessee should continue accounting for the original lease obligation as before. If the new lease agreement (sublease) does not meet the capitalization requirements imposed for subleases, the new lease should be accounted for as an operating lease.

3. If the original lease is an operating lease, the original lessee/sublessor should account for the new lease as an operating lease and account for the original operating lease as before.

APPENDIX B

LEVERAGED LEASES

One of the more complex accounting subjects regarding leases is the accounting for a leveraged lease. Once again, as with both sales-type and direct financing, the classification of the lease by the lessor has no effect on the accounting treatment accorded the lease by the lessee. The lessee simply treats it as any other lease and thus is interested only in whether the lease qualifies as an operating or a capital lease. The lessor's accounting problem is substantially more complex than that of the lessee.

To qualify as a leveraged lease, a lease agreement must meet the following requirements, and the lessor must account for the investment tax credit (when in effect) in the manner described below.

NOTE: Failure to do so will result in the lease being classified as a direct financing lease.

1. The lease must meet the definition of a direct financing lease. (The 90% of FMV criterion does not apply.)[*]
2. The lease must involve at least three parties.

    a. An owner-lessor (equity participant)
    b. A lessee
    c. A long-term creditor (debt participant)

3. The financing provided by the creditor is nonrecourse as to the general credit of the lessor and is sufficient to provide the lessor with substantial leverage.
4. The lessor's net investment (defined below) decreases in the early years and increases in the later years until it is eliminated.

The last characteristic (item 4) poses the accounting problem.

The leveraged lease arose as a result of an effort to maximize the tax benefits associated with a lease transaction. To accomplish this, it was necessary to involve a third party to the lease transaction (in addition to the lessor and lessee), a long-term creditor. The following diagram illustrates the existing relationships in a leveraged lease agreement:

---

[*] *A direct financing lease must have its cost or carrying value equal to the fair value of the asset at the inception of the lease. Thus, even if the amounts are not significantly different, leveraged lease accounting should not be used.*

The leveraged lease arrangement*

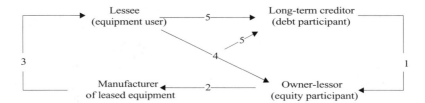

1. The owner-lessor secures long-term financing from the creditor, generally in excess of 50% of the purchase price. US GAAP indicates that the lessor must be provided with sufficient leverage in the transaction; thus the 50%.
2. The owner then uses this financing along with his or her own funds to purchase the asset from the manufacturer.
3. The manufacturer delivers the asset to the lessee.
4. The lessee remits the periodic rent to the lessor.
5. The debt is guaranteed by either using the equipment as collateral, the assignment of the lease payments, or both, depending on the demands established by the creditor.

The FASB concluded that the entire lease agreement be accounted for as a single transaction and not a direct financing lease plus a debt transaction. The feeling was that the latter did not readily convey the net investment in the lease to the user of the financial statements. Thus, the lessor is to record the investment as a net amount. The gross investment is calculated as a combination of the following amounts:

1. The rentals receivable from the lessee, net of the principal and interest payments due to the long-term creditor
2. A receivable for the amount of the investment tax credit (ITC) to be realized on the transaction (repealed in the United States but may yet exist in other jurisdictions)
3. The estimated residual value of the leased asset
4. The unearned and deferred income, consisting of

    a. The estimated pretax lease income (or loss), after deducting initial direct costs, remaining to be allocated to income
    b. The ITC remaining to be allocated to income over the remaining term of the lease

The first three amounts described above are readily obtainable; however, the last amount, the unearned and deferred income, requires additional computations. To derive this amount, it is necessary to create a cash flow (income) analysis by

---

*Adapted from "A Straightforward Approach to Leveraged Leasing" by Pierce R. Smith, **The Journal of Commercial Bank Lending**, July 1973, pp. 40-47.*

year for the entire lease term. As described in item 4 above, the unearned and deferred income consists of the pretax lease income (Gross lease rentals – Depreciation – Loan interest) and the unamortized investment tax credit. The total of these two amounts for all the periods in the lease term represents the unearned and deferred income at the inception of the lease.

The amount computed as the gross investment in the lease (foregoing paragraphs) less the deferred taxes relative to the difference between pretax lease income and taxable lease income is the net investment for purposes of computing the net income for the period. To compute the periodic net income, another schedule must be completed that uses the cash flows derived in the first schedule and allocates them between income and a reduction in the net investment.

The amount of income is first determined by applying a rate to the net investment. The rate to be used is the rate that will allocate the entire amount of cash flow (income) when applied in the years in which the net investment is positive. In other words, the rate is derived in much the same way as the implicit rate (trial and error), except that only the years in which there is a positive net investment are considered. Thus, income is recognized only in the years in which there is a positive net investment.

The income recognized is divided among the following three elements:

1. Pretax accounting income
2. Amortization of investment tax credit
3. The tax effect of the pretax accounting income

The first two are allocated in proportionate amounts from the unearned and deferred income included in calculation of the net investment. In other words, the unearned and deferred income consists of pretax lease accounting income and any investment tax credit. Each of these is recognized during the period in the proportion that the current period's allocated income is to the total income (cash flow). The last item, the tax effect, is recognized in the tax expense for the year. The tax effect of any difference between pretax lease accounting income and taxable lease income is charged (or credited) to deferred taxes.

When tax rates change, all components of a leveraged lease must be recalculated from the inception of the lease, using the revised after-tax cash flows arising from the revised tax rates.

If, in any case, the projected cash receipts (income) are less than the initial investment, the deficiency is to be recognized as a loss at the inception of the lease. Similarly, if at any time during the lease period the aforementioned method of recognizing income would result in a future period loss, the loss shall be recognized immediately.

This situation may arise as a result of the circumstances surrounding the lease changing. Therefore, any estimated residual value and other important assumptions must be reviewed on a periodic basis (at least annually). Any change is to be incorporated into the income computations; however, there is to be no upward revision of the estimated residual value.

The following example illustrates the application of these principles to a leveraged lease:

Example of simplified leveraged lease

Assume the following:

1. A lessor acquires an asset for $100,000 with an estimated useful life of 3 years in exchange for a $25,000 down payment and a $75,000 3-year note with equal payments due on 12/31 each year. The interest rate is 18%.
2. The asset has no residual value.
3. The PV of an ordinary annuity of $1 for 3 years at 18% is 2.17427.
4. The asset is leased for 3 years with annual payments due to the lessor on 12/31 in the amount of $45,000.
5. The lessor uses the ACRS method of depreciation for tax purposes and elects to reduce the ITC rate to 4%, as opposed to reducing the depreciable basis.
6. Assume a constant tax rate throughout the life of the lease of 40%.

Chart 1 analyzes the cash flows generated by the leveraged leasing activities. Chart 2 allocates the cash flows between the investment in leveraged leased assets and income from leveraged leasing activities. The allocation requires finding that rate of return which, when applied to the investment balance at the beginning of each year that the investment amount is positive, will allocate the net cash flow fully to net income over the term of the lease. This rate can be found only by a computer program or by an iterative trial-and-error process. The example that follows has a positive investment value in each of the 3 years, and thus the allocation takes place in each time period. Leveraged leases usually have periods where the investment account turns negative and is below zero.

Allocating principal and interest on the loan payments is as follows:

$$\$75,000 \div 2.17427 = \$34,494$$

Year	Payment	Interest 18%	Principal	Balance
Inception of lease	$ --	$ --	$ --	$75,000
1	34,494	13,500	20,994	54,006
2	34,494	9,721	24,773	29,233
3	34,494	5,261	29,233	--

Chart 1

	A	B	C	D	E	F	G	H	I
					Income tax payable (rcvbl.)	*Loan*		*Cash flow*	*Cumulative*
			Interest	*Taxable income*		*principal*		*(A+G-C*	*cash*
	Rent	*Depr.*	*on loan*	*(A-B-C)*	*Dx40%*	*payments*	*ITC*	*-E-F)*	*flow*
Initial	$ --	$ --	$ --	$ --	$ --	$ --	$ --	$(25,000)	$(25,000)
Year 1	45,000	25,000	13,500	6,500	2,600	20,994	4,000	11,906	(13,094)
Year 2	45,000	38,000	9,721	(2,721)	(1,088)	24,773	--	11,594	(1,500)
Year 3	45,000	37,000	5,261	2,739	1,096	29,233	--	9,410	7,910
Total	$135,000	$100,000	$28,482	$ 6,518	$ 2,608	$75,000	$4,000	$ 7,910	

The chart below allocates the cash flows determined above between the net investment in the lease and income. Recall that the income is then allocated between pretax accounting income and the amortization of the investment for credit. The income tax expense for the period is a result of applying the tax rate to the current periodic pretax accounting income.

The amount to be allocated in total in each period is the net cash flow determined in column H above. The investment at the beginning of year 1 is the initial down payment of $25,000. This investment is then reduced on an annual basis by the amount of the cash flow not allocated to income.

Chart 2

	1	2	3	4	5	6	7
		Cash Flow Assumption				*Income Analysis*	
	Investment		*Allocated*	*Allocated*		*Income*	*Investment*
	beginning	*Cash*	*to*	*to*	*Pretax*	*tax*	*tax*
	of year	*flow*	*investment*	*income*	*income*	*expense*	*credit*
Year 1	$25,000	$11,906	$ 7,964	$3,942	$3,248	$1,300	1,994
Year 2	17,036	11,594	8,908	2,686	2,213	885	1,358
Year 3	8,128	9,410	8,128	1,282	1,057	423	648
		$32,910	$25,000	$7,910	$6,518	$2,608	$4,000
			Rate of return = 15.77%				

1. Column 2 is the net cash flow after the initial investment, and columns 3 and 4 are the allocation based on the 15.77% rate of return. The total of column 4 is the same as the total of column H in Chart 1.

2. Column 5 allocates column D in Chart 1 based on the allocations in column 4. Column 6 allocates column E in Chart 1, and column 7 allocates column G in Chart 1 in the same basis.

The journal entries below illustrate the proper recording and accounting for the leveraged lease transaction. The initial entry represents the cash down payment, investment tax credit receivable, the unearned and deferred revenue, and the net cash to be received over the term of the lease.

The remaining journal entries recognize the annual transactions that include the net receipt of cash and the amortization of income.

	Year 1		*Year 2*		*Year 3*	
Rents receivable [Chart 1 (A-C-F)]	31,518					
Investment tax credit receivable	4,000					
Cash		25,000				
Unearned and deferred income		10,518				
[Initial investment, Chart 2 (5+7) totals]						
Cash	10,506		10,506		10,506	
Rent receivable		10,506		10,506		10,506
[Net for all cash transactions, Chart 1 (A-C-F) line by line for each year]						
Income tax receivable (cash)	4,000					
Investment tax credit receivable		4,000				
Unearned and deferred income	5,242		3,571		1,705	
Income from leveraged leases		5,242		3,571		1,705
[Amortization of unearned income, Chart 2 (5+7) line by line for each year]						

The following schedules illustrate the computation of deferred income tax amount. The annual amount is a result of the temporary difference created due to the difference in the timing of the recognition of income for book and tax purposes. The income for tax purposes can be found in column D in Chart 1, while the income for book purposes is found in column 5 of Chart 2. The actual amount of deferred tax is the difference between the tax computed with the temporary difference and the tax computed without the temporary difference. These amounts are represented by the income tax payable or receivable as shown in column E of Chart 1 and the income tax expense as shown in column 6 of Chart 2. A check of this figure is provided by multiplying the difference between book and tax income by the annual rate.

Year 1

Income tax payable	$ 2,600	
Income tax expense	(1,300)	
Deferred income tax (Dr)		$1,300
Taxable income	$ 6,500	
Pretax accounting income	(3,248)	
Difference	$ 3,252	
$3,252 x 40% = $1,300		

Year 2

Income tax receivable	$ 1,088	
Income tax expense	885	
Deferred income tax (Cr)		$1,973
Taxable loss	$ 2,721	
Pretax accounting income	2,213	
Difference	$ 4,934	
$4,934 x 40% = $1,973		

Year 3

Income tax payable	$ 1,096	
Income tax expense	(423)	
Deferred income tax (Dr)		$ 673
Taxable income	$ 2,739	
Pretax accounting income	(1,057)	
Difference	$ 1,682	
$1,682 x 40% = $673		

15 ACCOUNTING FOR INCOME TAXES

PERSPECTIVE AND ISSUES

The substitution of the liability method of computing deferred tax assets and liabilities for the venerable deferral method has been long foretold. As the balance sheet has reasserted primacy over the income statement over the past two decades, the accurate depiction of entities' financial positions has become the supreme goal of financial reporting, and ever-stricter compliance with definitions of assets and liabilities has been demanded. As a consequence, certain measurement concepts, particularly the matching principle which was so important in the era of income statement dominance, have faded in significance. Income tax accounting provides the most striking example of this change in philosophy.

The use of the deferral method had been required under the rules imposed by a number of national standard-setting bodies, most notably by the US Accounting

Principles Board (in Opinion 11, issued in 1967,) and was justified largely by the matching principle. The deferral method was optional under the earlier international accounting standard, IAS 12. However, the deferral method was often difficult to apply, and it had the unfortunate tendency of resulting in debits or credits on the balance sheet which bore little relationship to future tax benefits or obligations. The liability method, which was also permitted under IAS 12, is balance sheet oriented and is much more consistent with the conceptual definitions of assets and liabilities adopted by IASC, FASB, and others. In more recent years, the liability method has been mandated by the US Financial Accounting Standards Board (first in Statement 96, and then in its successor, 109) and other major standard-setting bodies.

The International Accounting Standards Committee in 1989 adopted the *Framework for the Preparation and Presentation of Financial Statements*, which offered definitions of assets and liabilities which served notice that the deferral method of accounting for interperiod tax allocation would no longer be conceptually tolerable. An initial proposal for a replacement for IAS 12 was exposed in 1989 as E33. This proposal, which was not enacted, prohibited the deferral method and mandated a version of the liability approach. A substantially revised exposure draft, E49, followed in 1994. The new international standard, IAS 12 (revised), adopted in late 1996 for application in 1998, embraces an approach which largely emulates SFAS 109, albeit with some distinctions.

Under the new standard, deferred assets and liabilities are to be presented at the amounts which are expected to flow to or from the reporting entity when the benefits are ultimately realized or the obligations are settled. Revised IAS 12 makes no significant distinction between operation losses and other types of deductible temporary differences, and requires that both be given recognition when realization is deemed to be probable. Discounting of these amounts to present values is not permitted. Both tax assets and liabilities are measured by reference to expected tax rates, which in general are the enacted, effective rates as of the balance sheet date. The new standard also alters the criteria for recordation of the tax effects of temporary differences arising from ownership interest in investees and subsidiaries, and for the accounting related to goodwill and negative goodwill arising from business acquisitions. Presentation of deferred tax assets or liabilities as current assets or liabilities is prohibited, and a somewhat lengthier list of additional disclosures has also been mandated by the new rules.

Sources of IAS

IAS 12 *(revised)*

DEFINITIONS OF TERMS

Accounting profit. Net profit or loss for the reporting period before deducting income tax expense.

Current tax expense. The amount of income taxes payable (recoverable) in respect of the taxable profit (tax loss) for a period.

Deductible temporary differences. Temporary differences that result in amounts that are deductible in determining taxable profit when the carrying amount of the asset or liability is recovered or settled.

Deferred tax asset. The amounts of income taxes recoverable in future periods in respect of deductible temporary differences, carryforwards of unused tax losses, and carryforwards of unused tax credits.

Deferred tax expense. The change during a reporting period in the deferred tax liabilities and deferred tax assets of an entity.

Deferred tax liability. The amounts of income taxes payable in future periods in respect of taxable temporary differences.

Gains and losses included in nonowner movements in equity but excluded from net income. Certain items which, under GAAP, are events occurring currently but which are reported directly in equity, such as changes in market values of noncurrent portfolios of marketable equity securities.

Interperiod tax allocation. The process of apportioning income tax expense among reporting periods without regard to the timing of the actual cash payments for taxes. The objective is to reflect fully the tax consequences of all economic events reported in current or prior financial statements and, in particular, to report the expected tax effects of the reversals of temporary differences existing at the reporting date.

Intraperiod tax allocation. The process of apportioning income tax expense applicable to a given period between income before extraordinary items and those items required to be shown net of tax such as extraordinary items and prior period adjustments.

Operating loss carryback or carryforward. The excess of tax deductions over taxable income. To the extent that this results in a carryforward, the tax effect thereof is included in the entity's deferred tax asset, unless not expected to be realized.

Permanent differences. Differences between accounting profit and taxable profit as a result of the treatment accorded certain transactions by the income tax regulations which differs from the accounting treatment. Permanent differences will not reverse in subsequent periods, and accordingly, do not create a need for deferred tax recognition.

Tax basis. The amount attributable (explicitly or implicitly) to an asset or liability by the taxation authorities in determining taxable profit.

Tax credits. Reductions in the tax liability as a result of certain expenditures accorded special treatment under the tax regulations.

Tax expense. The aggregate of current tax expense and deferred tax expense for a reporting period.

Tax planning strategy. A representation by management of a planned transaction or series of transactions that would affect the particular future years in which temporary differences will result in taxable or deductible amounts.

Taxable profit (loss). The profit (loss) for a taxable period, determined in accordance with the rules established by the taxation authorities, on which income taxes are payable (recoverable).

Taxable temporary differences. Temporary differences that result in taxable amounts in determining taxable profit of future periods when the carrying amount of the asset or liability is recovered or settled.

Temporary differences. The differences between tax and financial reporting bases of assets and liabilities that will result in taxable or deductible amounts in future periods. Temporary differences include "timing differences" as defined by prior GAAP as well as certain other differences, such as those arising from business combinations. Some temporary differences cannot be associated with particular assets or liabilities, but nonetheless, do result from events that received financial statement recognition and will have tax effects in future periods.

Unrecognized tax benefits. Deferred tax benefits that have not been recognized because they are not deemed probable of being realized.

CONCEPTS, RULES, AND EXAMPLES

Basic Concepts of Interperiod Income Tax Allocation

Over the years, a number of theories have been advanced regarding the computation of income tax expense when timing (or temporary--the distinction will be explained shortly) differences exist. The most popular of these have been the deferral method and the liability method. A third approach, the net of tax method (more accurately thought of as a variation on the other two methods, which focuses on the manner of displaying the tax debit or credit in the balance sheet), for a time received a moderate amount of academic support but was far less widely employed (or understood) by practitioners.

Although the deferral method was soundly based on the matching principle and was never promoted as being balance sheet oriented, in practice it suffered from some complexity and sometimes also resulted in material distortion of the balance sheet. This was considered acceptable during the late 1960s and 1970s, a time when most attention was being directed to the income statement, but as the focus in more recent years shifted again to the meaningful reporting of an entity's financial position, these issues have received renewed scrutiny. Following the adoption of the IASC's *Framework for the Preparation and Presentation of Financial State-*

ments, it was inevitable that substantial changes in accounting for income taxes would be made. The deferred charges and credits created by the application of the deferral method, permitted by the original IAS 12, were generally not true assets or liabilities as defined in the *Framework*, and accordingly do not belong on the balance sheet. The deferral method, as a consequence, could no longer be supported as being representative of generally accepted accounting principles.

Another longstanding debate relating to interperiod income tax allocation has been among proponents of no allocation (reporting only the amount of taxes currently payable as income tax expense), partial allocation (providing deferred taxes only for those timing differences whose ultimate reversal could be reasonably predicted), and comprehensive allocation. Taken together with the contest between the deferred and the liability methods, either of which could be applied in conjunction with the comprehensive or partial allocation approaches, the result was that a number of distinct measurement strategies could be applied to timing differences, yielding very different financial statement results.

IAS 12, adopted effective 1979, essentially favored comprehensive allocation, albeit with exceptions for certain items for which the tax effects were deemed not likely to reverse within 3 years. More significantly, however, IAS 12 permitted the application of either the deferral or the liability method, which are diametrically opposed theories regarding the determination of deferred taxes. Although that standard required full disclosure of whatever method was used, tax expense could be computed in very different manners for two otherwise identical entities, for which the standard was widely criticized. It is unlikely that many users of financial statements information would have been able to compute the adjustments necessary to make otherwise noncomparable reports comparable.

Under IAS 12, timing differences referred to items of income or expense that entered into the determination of taxable income in periods different than financial reporting income. Common examples of timing differences were depreciation, deferred compensation, prepaid income, bad debt reserves, and cash versus accrual accounting. These items are included in the broader concept of temporary differences as defined by revised IAS 12. However, the newer term is more inclusive than the one it replaces. It also connotes the effects of asset basis reductions for tax credits taken, asset basis increases resulting from inflation indexing, certain intercompany transfers among entities for which consolidated financial statements but not consolidated tax returns are prepared, and certain effects of accounting for purchase business combinations.

While the requirement for comprehensive interperiod tax allocation appears to be well understood in practice, the appropriate measurement of tax expense, including the tax effects of temporary differences, is less clear. This is addressed in the following section.

Measurement of Tax Expense

Current tax expense. Income tax expense for an entity is comprised of current tax expense and deferred tax expense. Either of these can be a benefit (that is, a credit), rather than an expense (a debit), depending on whether there is taxable profit or loss for the period. For convenience, the term "tax expense" will be used to denote either an expense or a benefit. Current tax expense is easily understood as the tax effect of the entity's reported taxable income or loss for the period, as determined by relevant rules of the various taxing authorities to which it is subject. Deferred tax expense, on the other hand, is more complicated: Depending on the theory being applied, it may be based on the current period difference between taxable and financial statement income, or it may be based on a projection of changes in the future implications of differences between certain tax and financial statement amounts.

Deferred tax expense under the deferral method. The deferral method permitted under original IAS 12 computed deferred tax expense by reference to the difference between taxable income and accounting income (referred to as accounting profit under revised IAS 12). Simply put, the deferral method determines the income tax expense for the period based on the accounting income, while the current liability is based on taxable income. The difference between the actual current liability and the income tax expense is treated as either a deferred charge or credit that is amortized ratably as the timing difference reverses. Timing differences that originate during the period are referred to as originating differences, while the reversal of tax effects arising from differences which originated in prior periods are referred to as reversing differences.

Thus, the deferral method was income statement oriented, since deferred tax expense was computed on income statement amounts. Once computed, with the offset to deferred tax expense being placed on the balance sheet as a deferred tax asset or liability, this amount was never revisited or revised, until ultimately it would be reversed when the underlying timing differences themselves were reversed. The fact that the amounts presented on the balance sheet might not truly represent future benefits to be received (i.e., tax savings) or obligations to be satisfied (i.e., tax liabilities) was not a concern.

When the deferral method was used, tax expense could be computed by a "shortcut" technique by applying the effective tax rate times pretax accounting income (accounting profit). The difference between the amount thus computed and current tax expense would then be the net change in the deferred tax asset or liability for the year.

Deferred tax expense under the liability method. Under the liability method the current period's total income tax expense cannot be computed directly. Rather, it must be calculated as the sum of the two components: current tax expense and deferred tax expense. This total will not, in general, equal the current tax rate times accounting profit. The reason is that deferred tax expense is defined as the change in the deferred tax asset and liability accounts in the current period, and this change may encompass more than the current tax rate times the net temporary differences occurring in the present reporting period.

It is generally agreed that IAS 12 permitted, and the aborted proposal E33 would have required, an income statement oriented version of this methodology, while revised IAS 12 has mandated a balance sheet oriented approach, much like that imposed by SFAS 109 under US GAAP. Depending on which variation on the liability method is employed, the precise amount of deferred tax assets and liabilities may vary somewhat. Nonetheless, either variant of the liability method would include in current period deferred tax expense the effects of changing tax rates on as-yet unreversed temporary differences. Thus, current period tax expense would include not merely the tax effects of currently reported revenue and expense items, but also certain tax effects of items reported previously.

Although the primary objective of income tax accounting under the liability method is no longer the proper matching of revenue and expense, the matching principle remains very important. Therefore, the tax effects of items excluded from the income statement, such as corrections of fundamental errors, are also excluded from the income statement.

Liability Method in Detail

Overview. The liability method is balance sheet oriented, in contrast to the deferral method, which is income statement oriented. (This is true for both the variant of the liability method advocated by IAS 12 and by the proposed, but not adopted, draft to replace IAS 12, E33, which computed deferred taxes by reference to the netchanges in timing differences, as well as for the method adopted by revised IAS 12, which computes deferred taxes by reference to the changes in temporary differences.) The primary goal of the liability method is to present the estimated actual taxes to be payable in future periods as the income tax liability on the balance sheet. To accomplish this goal it is necessary to consider the effect of certain enacted future changes in the tax rates when computing the current period's tax provision. The computation of the amount of deferred taxes is based on the rate expected to be in effect when the temporary differences reverse. The annual computation is considered a tentative estimate of the liability (or asset) that is subject to change as the statutory tax rate changes or as the taxpayer moves into other tax rate brackets.

The *Framework for the Preparation and Presentation of Financial Statements* defines liabilities as obligations resulting from past transactions and involving "giving up resources embodying economic benefits in order to satisfy the claim of [another] party." Assets are defined as "the potential to contribute, directly or indirectly, to the flow of cash . . . to the enterprise." As the background paper to revised IAS 12 made clear, the deferred debits and credits generated through the use of the deferral method do not meet the definitions of assets and liabilities prescribed by the *Framework*. This lack of consistency was one of the primary reasons for the

IASC's reconsideration of IAS 12, which culminated in the issuance of revised IAS 12 in 1996.

Application of the liability method is, in concept at least, relatively simple when compared to the deferral method. Unlike under the deferral method, there is no need to maintain a historical record of the timing of origination of the various un-reversed differences, since the effective rates at which the various components were established is not relevant. As the liability method is strictly a balance sheet approach, the primary concern is to state the obligation for taxes payable as accurately as possible, based on expected tax impact of future reversals. This is accomplished by multiplying the aggregate unreversed temporary differences, including those originating in the current period, by the tax rate expected to be in effect in the future to determine the expected future liability. This expected liability is the amount presented on the balance sheet at the end of the period. The difference between this amount and the amount on the books at the beginning of the period, simply put, is the deferred tax expense or benefit for the current reporting period.

An example of application of the liability method of deferred income tax accounting follows.

Simplified example of interperiod allocation using the liability method

Ghiza International has no permanent differences in either years 2000 or 2001. The company has only two temporary differences, depreciation and prepaid rent. No consideration is given to the nature of the deferred tax account (i.e., current or long-term) as it is not considered necessary for purposes of this example. Ghiza has a credit balance in its deferred tax account at the beginning of 1999 in the amount of $180,000. This balance consists of $228,000 ($475,000 depreciation temporary difference x 48% tax rate) of deferred taxable amounts and $48,000 ($100,000 prepaid rent temporary difference x 48% tax rate) of deferred deductible amounts.

For purposes of this example, it is assumed that there was a constant effective 48% tax rate in all periods prior to 2000. The pretax accounting income and the temporary differences originating and reversing in 2000 and 2001 are as follows:

Ghiza International

		2000		*2001*	
Pretax accounting income		$800,000		$1,200,000	
Timing differences:					
Depreciation:	originating	$(180,000)		$(160,000)	
	reversing	60,000	(120,000)	100,000	(60,000)
Prepaid					
rental income:	originating	75,000		80,000	
	reversing	(25,000)	50,000	(40,000)	40,000
Taxable income			$730,000		$1,180,000

The tax rates for years 2000 and 2001 are 46% and 38%, respectively. These rates are assumed to be independent of one another, and the 2001 change in the rate was not known until it took place in 2001.

Computation of tax provision--2000:

Balance of deferred tax account, 1/1/00		
Depreciation ($475,000 x 48%)		$228,000
Prepaid rental income ($100,000 x 48%)		(48,000)
		$180,000
Aggregate temporary differences, 12/31/00		
Depreciation ($475,000 + $120,000)	$ 595,000	
Prepaid rental income ($100,000 + $50,000)	(150,000)	
	$ 445,000	
Expected future rate (2000 rate)	x 46%	
Balance required in the deferred tax account, 12/31/00		204,700
Required addition to the deferred tax account		$ 24,700
Income taxes currently payable ($730,000 x 46%)		335,800
Total tax provision		$360,500

Computation of tax provision--2001:

Balance of deferred tax account, 1/1/01		
Depreciation ($595,000 x 46%)		$273,700
Prepaid rental income ($150,000 x 46%)		(69,000)
		$204,700
Aggregate timing differences, 12/31/01		
Depreciation ($595,000 + $60,000)	$ 655,000	
Prepaid rental income ($150,000 + $40,000)	(190,000)	
	$ 465,000	
Expected future rate (2001 rate)	x 38%	
Balance required in the deferred tax account, 12/31/00		176,700
Required reduction in the deferred tax account		$ (28,000)
Income taxes currently payable ($1,180,000 x 38%)		448,400
Total tax provision		$420,400

Liability Method Explained in Detail

While conceptually the liability method is rather straightforward, in practice there are a number of complexities to be addressed. In the following pages, the following measurement and reporting issues are discussed in greater detail.

1. Nature of temporary differences
2. Treatment of operating loss carryforwards
3. Measurement of deferred tax assets and liabilities
4. Valuation allowance for deferred tax assets that are not assured of realization
5. Effect of tax law changes on previously recorded deferred tax assets and liabilities
6. Effect of tax status changes on previously incurred deferred tax assets and liabilities
7. Tax effects of business combinations
8. Intercorporate income tax allocation
9. Exceptions to the general rules of revised IAS 12

Detailed examples of deferred income tax accounting under revised IAS 12 are presented throughout the following discussion of these issues.

Nature of Temporary Differences

The majority of the typical reporting entity's transactions are treated identically for tax and financial reporting purposes. Some transactions and events, however, will have different tax and accounting implications. In many of these cases, the difference relates to the period in which the income or expense will be recognized. Under IAS 12, the latter differences were referred to as "timing differences" and were said to **originate** in one period and to **reverse** in a later period. Common timing differences include those relating to depreciation methods, deferred compensation plans, percentage-of-completion accounting for long-term construction contracts, and cash vs. accrual accounting.

Revised IAS 12 introduces the concept of temporary differences, which is rather more comprehensive than that of timing differences. Temporary differences include all the categories of the earlier concept, plus a number of additional items as well. Temporary differences include all differences between the tax and financial reporting bases of assets and liabilities if those differences will result in taxable or deductible amounts in future years.

Examples of temporary differences that were also deemed to be timing differences under the original IAS 12 are the following:

1. **Revenue recognized for financial reporting purposes before being recognized for tax purposes.** Examples include revenue accounted for by the installment method for tax purposes, but reflected in income currently; certain construction-related revenue recognized on a completed-contract method for tax purposes, but on a percentage-of-completion basis for financial reporting; earnings from investees recognized by the equity method for accounting purposes but taxed only when later distributed as dividends to the investor. These are taxable temporary differences, which give rise to deferred tax liabilities.

2. **Revenue recognized for tax purposes prior to recognition in the financial statements.** These include certain types of revenue received in advance, such as prepaid rental income and service contract revenue. Referred to as deductible temporary differences, these items give rise to deferred tax assets.

3. **Expenses that are deductible for tax purposes prior to recognition in the financial statements.** This results when accelerated depreciation methods or shorter useful lives are used for tax purposes, while straight-line depreciation or longer useful economic lives are used for financial reporting; and when there are certain preoperating costs and certain capitalized interest costs that are deductible currently for tax purposes. These items are taxable temporary differences and give rise to deferred tax liabilities.

4. **Expenses that are reported in the financial statements prior to becoming deductible for tax purposes.** Certain estimated expenses, such as warranty costs, as well as such contingent losses as accruals of litigation expenses, are not tax deductible until the obligation becomes fixed. These are deductible temporary differences, and accordingly give rise to deferred tax assets.

In addition to these familiar and well understood timing differences, temporary differences include a number of other categories that also involve differences between the tax and financial reporting bases of assets or liabilities. These are

1. **Reductions in tax deductible asset bases arising in connection with tax credits.** Under tax provisions in certain jurisdictions, credits are available for certain qualifying investments in plant assets. In some cases, taxpayers are permitted a choice of either full accelerated depreciation coupled with a reduced investment tax credit, or a full investment tax credit coupled with reduced depreciation allowances. If the taxpayer chose the latter option, the asset basis is reduced for tax depreciation, but would still be fully depreciable for financial reporting purposes. Accordingly, this election would be accounted for as a taxable timing difference, and give rise to a deferred tax liability.

2. **Increases in the tax bases of assets resulting from the indexing of asset costs for the effects of inflation.** Occasionally, proposed and sometimes enacted by taxing jurisdictions, such a tax law provision allows taxpaying entities to finance the replacement of depreciable assets through depreciation based on current costs, as computed by the application of indices to the historical costs of the assets being remeasured. This reevaluation of asset costs gives rise to deductible temporary differences that would be associated with deferred tax benefits.

3. **Certain business combinations accounted for by the acquisition method.** Under certain circumstances, the costs assignable to assets or liabilities acquired in purchase business combinations will differ from their tax bases. The usual scenario under which this arises is when the acquirer must continue to report the predecessor's tax bases for tax purposes, although the price paid was more or less than book value. Such differences may be either taxable or deductible and, accordingly, may give rise to deferred tax liabilities or assets. These differences were in fact treated as timing differences under the original IAS 12, and will now be recognized as temporary differences by revised IAS 12.

4. **Assets which are revalued for financial reporting purposes although the tax bases are not affected.** This is analogous to the matter discussed in the preceding paragraph. Under certain international accounting standards (such as IAS 16, *Property, Plant, and Equipment*, and IAS 15, *Accounting*

for Investments), assets are written up to fair value although for tax purposes these adjustments are ignored until and unless the assets are disposed of. The discrepancies between the adjusted book carrying values and the tax bases are temporary differences under revised IAS 12, and deferred taxes are to be provided on these variations. This is required even if there is no intention to dispose of the assets in question, or if, under tax laws, exchanges for other, similar assets (or reinvestment of proceeds of sales in similar assets) would effect a postponement of the tax obligation.

Items that would not have been deemed timing differences under IAS 12 but are temporary differences under revised IAS 12 include the following:

1. **Assets and liabilities acquired in transactions that are not business combinations which are not deductible or taxable in determining taxable profit.** In some tax jurisdictions, certain assets are never deductible in computing taxable profit. Depending on jurisdiction, buildings, intangibles, and other assets may be nondeductible. Thus, the asset in question has a differing accounting basis than tax basis, which defines a temporary difference. Similarly, certain liabilities may not be recognized for tax purposes. While revised IAS 12 agrees that these represent temporary differences (since the tax basis of zero differs from the book basis in each instance) and that, under the principles of tax accounting using the liability method, this should result in the recognition of deferred tax liabilities or assets, the decision was made to not permit this. The reason given is that the new result would be to "gross up" the recorded amount of the asset or liability to offset the recorded deferred tax liability or benefit, and this would make the financial statements "less transparent." It could also be argued that, when as asset has as one of its attributes nondeductibility for tax purposes, the price paid for this asset has been affected accordingly, so that any such "gross-up" would cause the asset to be reported at an amount in excess of fair value.

2. **Assets and liabilities acquired in business combinations.** When assets and liabilities are valued at fair value, as required under IAS 22, but the tax basis is not adjusted (i.e., there is a carryforward basis for tax purposes), there will be differences between the tax and financial reporting bases of these assets and liabilities which constitute temporary differences. Deferred tax benefits and obligations need to be recognized for these differences.

3. **Goodwill that cannot be amortized (deducted) for tax purposes.** In some jurisdictions, goodwill cannot be deducted for tax purposes. Conceptually, when goodwill is carried on the balance sheet but cannot be amortized for tax purposes, the tax basis of this asset is zero, which thus differs from the financial reporting basis and which would therefore require that deferred taxes be assessed thereon. However, since goodwill or negative goodwill is a residual amount, any attempt to compute the deferred tax ef-

fect of the difference between tax and book bases would result in grossing up that very account (goodwill or negative goodwill, as the case may be). Although such a presentation could be rationalized, it would be of dubious usefulness to the readers of the financial statements. For this reason, revised IAS 12 has ruled that no deferred taxes be provided on the difference between the tax and book bases of nondeductible goodwill or nontaxable negative goodwill.

Measurement of Deferred Tax Assets and Liabilities

The procedure to compute the gross deferred tax provision (i.e., before addressing whether the deferred tax asset is probable of being realized and therefore should be recognized) is as follows:

1. Identify all temporary differences existing as of the reporting date.
2. Segregate the temporary differences into those that are taxable and those that are deductible. This step is necessary because under revised IAS 12 only those deferred tax benefits which are probable of being realized are recognized, whereas all deferred obligations are given full recognition.
3. Accumulate information about the deductible temporary differences, particularly the net operating loss and credit carryforwards that have expiration dates or other types of limitations.
4. Measure the tax effect of aggregate taxable temporary differences by applying the appropriate expected tax rates (federal plus any state, local, and foreign rates that are applicable under the circumstances).
5. Similarly, measure the tax effects of deductible temporary differences, including net operating loss carryforwards.

It should be emphasized that separate computations should be made for each tax jurisdiction, since in assessing the propriety of recording the tax effects of deductible temporary differences it is necessary to consider the entity's ability to absorb deferred tax benefits against tax liabilities. Inasmuch as benefits in one tax jurisdiction will not reduce taxes payable in another jurisdiction, separate calculations will be needed. Also, for purposes of balance sheet presentation (discussed below in detail), offsetting of deferred tax assets and liabilities is permissible only within jurisdictions, since there would never be a legal right to offset obligations due to, and from, different taxing authorities. Similarly, separate computations should be made for each taxpaying component of the business (i.e., if a parent company and its subsidiaries are consolidated for financial reporting purposes but file separate tax returns, the reporting entity comprises a number of components, and the tax benefits of any one will be unavailable to reduce the tax obligations of the others).

The principles set forth above are illustrated by the following examples.

Basic example of the computation of deferred tax liability and asset

Assume that Noori Company has pretax financial income of $250,000 in 1999, a total of $28,000 of taxable temporary differences, and a total of $8,000 of deductible temporary differences. There are no operating loss or tax credit carryforwards. The tax rate is a flat (i.e., not graduated) 40%. Also assume that there were no deferred tax liabilities or assets in prior years.

Taxable income is computed as follows:

Pretax financial income	$250,000
Taxable temporary differences	(28,000)
Deductible temporary differences	8,000
Taxable income	$230,000

The journal entry to record required amounts is

Current income tax expense	92,000	
Deferred tax asset	3,200	
Income tax expense--deferred	8,000	
Deferred tax liability		11,200
Income taxes currently payable		92,000

Current income tax expense and income taxes currently payable are each computed as taxable income times the current rate ($230,000 x 40%). The deferred tax asset of $3,200 represents 40% of deductible temporary differences of $8,000. The deferred tax liability of $11,200 is calculated as 40% of taxable temporary differences of $28,000. The deferred tax expense of $8,000 is the **net** of the deferred tax liability of $11,200 and the deferred tax asset of $3,200.

In 2001, Noori Company has pretax financial income of $450,000, aggregate taxable and deductible temporary differences are $75,000 and $36,000, respectively, and the tax rate remains a flat 40%. Taxable income is $411,000, computed as pretax financial income of $450,000 minus taxable differences of $75,000 plus deductible differences of $36,000. Current income tax expense and income taxes currently payable each are $164,400 ($411,000 x 40%).

Deferred amounts are calculated as follows:

	Deferred tax liability	*Deferred tax asset*	*Income tax expense--deferred*
Required balance at 12/31/01			
$75,000 x 40%	$30,000		--
$36,000 x 40%		$14,400	--
Balances at 12/31/00	11,200	3,200	--
Adjustment required	$18,800	$11,200	$7,600

The journal entry to record the deferred amounts is

Deferred tax asset	11,200	
Income tax expense--deferred	7,600	
Deferred tax liability		18,800

Because the **increase** in the liability in 2001 is larger (by $7,600) than the increase in the asset for that year, the result is a deferred tax **expense** for 2000.

Considerations for Recognition of Deferred Tax Assets

Although the case for presentation in the financial statements of any amount computed for deferred tax liabilities is clear, it can be argued that deferred tax assets should be included in the balance sheet only if they are, in fact, very likely to be realized in future periods. Since realization will almost certainly be dependent on the future profitability of the reporting entity, it may become necessary to ascertain the likelihood that the enterprise will be profitable. Absent convincing evidence of that, the concepts of conservatism and realization would suggest that the asset be treated as a contingent gain, and not accorded recognition until and unless ultimately realized.

In revised IAS 12, the IASC has adopted a posture which holds that deferred tax assets resulting from temporary differences and from tax loss carryforwards are to be given recognition only if realization is deemed to be **probable**. To operationalize this concept, the standard sets forth several criteria, which variously apply to deferred tax assets arising from temporary differences and from tax loss carryforwards. The standard establishes that

1. It is probable that future taxable profit will be available against which a deferred tax asset arising from a deductible temporary difference can be utilized when there are sufficient taxable temporary differences relating to the same taxation authority which will reverse either (a) in the same period as the reversal of the deductible temporary difference, or (b) in periods into which the deferred tax asset can be carried back or forward; or

2. If there are insufficient taxable temporary differences relating to the same taxation authority, it is probable that the enterprise will have taxable profits in the same period as the reversal of the deductible temporary difference or in periods to which the deferred tax can be carried back or forward, or there are tax planning opportunities available to the enterprise that will create taxable profit in appropriate periods.

Thus, there will be a modest element of judgment required in making an assessment about how probable the realization of the deferred tax asset is, in circumstances in which there is not a balance of deferred tax liability equal to or greater than the amount of the deferred tax asset. If it cannot be concluded that realization is probable, the deferred tax asset is not given recognition. The revised IAS 12 methodology is somewhat different than that which is applied under current US GAAP, which is prescribed by SFAS 109. In conformity with that standard, all deferred tax assets are first recorded, after which a valuation allowance or reserve is established to offset that portion which is not deemed to be "more likely than not" realizable. The net effect is similar under either approach, however, although the consensus opinion is that the US GAAP realization threshold, "more likely than not," represents a somewhat lower boundary than does IAS 12's "probable." While the former implies a probability of just slightly over 50%, the latter is thought to connote a likelihood in the range of 75-80% or even higher. Worded yet another way, it would be more challenging to support the existence of a valid deferred tax asset under the IAS standard than under US GAAP rules as they now exist.

Future temporary differences as a source for taxable profit to offset deductible differences. In some instances, an entity may have deferred tax assets that will be realizable when future tax deductions are taken, but it cannot be concluded that there will be sufficient taxable profits to absorb these future deductions. However, the enterprise can reasonably predict that, if it continues as a going concern, it will generate other temporary differences such that taxable profits will be created. It has often been argued that the going concern assumption underlying much of accounting theory is sufficient rationale for the recognition of deferred tax assets in such circumstances.

However, revised IAS 12 makes it clear that this is not valid reasoning. The reason is that the taxable temporary differences anticipated for future periods will themselves reverse in even later periods; these cannot do "double duty" by also being projected to be available to absorb currently existing deductible temporary differences. Thus, in evaluating whether realization of currently outstanding deferred tax benefits is probable, it is appropriate to consider the currently outstanding taxable temporary differences, but not taxable temporary differences which are projected to be created in later periods.

Tax planning opportunities that will help realize deferred tax assets. When an entity has deductible temporary differences and taxable temporary differences pertaining to the same tax jurisdiction, there is a presumption that realization of the relevant deferred tax assets is probable, since the relevant deferred tax liabilities should be available to offset these. However, before concluding on this it is necessary to consider further the **timing** of the two sets of reversals. If the deductible temporary differences will reverse, say, in the very near term, and the taxable differences will not reverse for many years, it is a concern that the tax benefits created by the former occurrence may expire unused prior to the latter event. Thus, when the availability of deferred tax obligations is the basis for recognition of deferred tax assets, it is also necessary to consider whether, under pertinent tax regulations, the benefit carryforward period is sufficient to assure that it will not be lost to the reporting enterprise.

For example, if the deductible temporary difference is projected to reverse in 2 years but the taxable temporary difference is not anticipated to occur for another 10 years, and the tax jurisdiction in question offers only a 5-year tax loss carryforward, then (absent other facts suggesting that the tax benefit is probable of realization) the deferred tax benefit could not be given recognition.

However, the entity might have certain tax planning opportunities available to it, such that the pattern of taxable profits could be altered to make the deferred tax benefit, which might otherwise be lost, probable of realization. For example, again depending on the rules of the salient tax jurisdiction, an election might be made to tax interest income on an accrual rather than a cash received basis, which might accelerate income recognition such that it would be available to offset or absorb the deductible temporary differences. Also, claimed tax deductions might be deferred to later periods, similarly boosting taxable profits in the short term.

More subtly, a reporting entity may have certain assets, such as buildings, which have appreciated in value. It is entirely feasible, in many situations, for an enterprise to take certain steps, such as selling the building to realize the taxable gain thereon and then either leasing back the premises or acquiring another suitable building, to salvage the tax deduction that would otherwise be lost to it due to the expiration of a loss carryforward period. If such a strategy is deemed to be reasonably available, even if the entity does not expect to have to implement it (for example, because it expects other taxable temporary differences to be originated in the interim), it may be used to justify recognition of the deferred tax benefits.

Consider the following example of how an available tax planning strategy might be used to support recognition of a deferred tax asset that otherwise might have to go unrecognized.

Example of the impact of a qualifying tax strategy

Assume that Kirloski Company has a $180,000 operating loss carryforward as of 12/31/00, scheduled to expire at the end of next year. Taxable temporary differences of $240,000 exist that are expected to reverse in approximately equal amounts of $80,000 in 2001, 2002, and 2003. Kirloski Company estimates that taxable income for 2001 (exclusive of the reversal of existing temporary differences and the operating loss carryforward) will be $20,000. Kirloski Company expects to implement a qualifying tax planning strategy that will accelerate the total of $240,000 of taxable temporary differences to 2001. Expenses to implement the strategy are estimated to approximate $30,000. The applicable expected tax rate is 40%.

In the absence of the tax planning strategy, $100,000 of the operating loss carryforward could be realized in 2001 based on estimated taxable income of $20,000 plus $80,000 of the reversal of taxable temporary differences. Thus, $80,000 would expire unused at the end of 2001 and the net amount of the deferred tax asset at 12/31/00 would be recognized at $40,000, computed as $72,000 ($180,000 x 40%) minus the valuation allowance of $32,000 ($80,000 x 40%).

However, by implementing the tax planning strategy, the deferred tax asset is calculated as follows:

Taxable income for 2001:	
Expected amount without reversal of	
taxable temporary differences	$ 20,000
Reversal of taxable temporary differences	
due to tax planning strategy, net of costs	<u>210,000</u>
	230,000
Operating loss to be carried forward	<u>(180,000)</u>
Operating loss expiring unused at 12/31/01	$ -0-

The deferred tax asset to be recorded at 12/31/00 is $54,000. This is computed as follows:

Full benefit of tax loss carryforward $180,000 x 40% =		$72,000
Less: Net-of-tax effect of anticipated expenses related to implementation of the strategy $30,000 – ($30,000 x 40%) =		18,000
Net		$54,000

Kirloski Company will also recognize a deferred tax liability of $96,000 at the end of 2000 (40% of the taxable temporary differences of $240,000).

Revised expectations that a deferred tax benefit is realizable. It may happen that in a reporting period a deferred asset is deemed not probable of being realized and accordingly is not recognized, but in a later reporting period the judgment is made that the amount in fact is realizable. If this change in expectation occurs, the deferred tax asset previously not recognized will now be recorded. This does not constitute a prior period adjustment, but instead is included in earnings, consistent with other changes in accounting estimates, in the current period. Thus, the tax provision in the period when the estimate is revised will be affected.

Similarly, if a deferred tax benefit provision is made in a given reporting period, but later events suggest that the amount is, in whole or in part, not probable of being realized, the provision should be partially or completely reversed. Again, this adjustment will be included in the tax provision in the period in which the estimate is altered. Under either scenario the footnotes to the financial statements will need to offer sufficient information to the users to permit meaningful interpretations to be made, since the amount of tax expense will bear an unusual relationship to the accounting profit for the period.

If the deferred tax provision in a given period is misstated due to a clerical error such as miscalculation of the effective expected tax rate, this would constitute a fundamental error, and the effect of the correction may be reflected in opening retained earnings. This should be distinguished from a change in an accounting estimate. Fundamental errors are discussed in Chapter 21.

Determining the extent to which the deferred tax asset is realizable. Assume that Zacharias Corporation has a deductible temporary difference of $60,000 at December 31, 2000. The applicable tax rate is a flat 40%. Based on available evidence, management of Zacharias Corporation concludes that it is probable that all sources will not result in future taxable income sufficient to realize more than $15,000 (i.e., 25%) of the deductible temporary difference. Also, assume that there were no deferred tax assets in previous years and that prior years' taxable income was inconsequential.

At 12/31/00 Zacharias Corporation records a deferred tax asset in the amount of $6,000 ($60,000 x 25% x 40%). The journal entry at 12/31/00 is

Deferred tax asset	6,000	
Income tax benefit--deferred		6,000

The deferred income tax benefit of $6,000 represents the tax effect of that portion of the deferred tax asset (25%) that is probable of being realized. In 2001 assume that Zacharias Corporation's results are

Pretax financial loss	$(32,000)
Reversing deductible differences from 2000	(10,000)
Loss carryforward for tax purposes	$(42,000)

The total of the loss carryforward ($42,000, as computed above) plus the amount of deductible temporary differences from 2000 not reversing in 2001 ($50,000) equals $92,000. Before considering how much of the benefit is probable of being realized, a deferred tax asset of $36,800 ($92,000 x 40%) is computed at the end of 2001. However, the management of Zacharias Corporation has to consider what portion of this deferred tax asset is probable of being realized. It concludes that it is probable that $25,000 of the tax loss carryforward will **not** be realized. Thus, the net tax loss carryforward that is **probable** of being realized is $92,000 − $25,000 = $67,000, which yields a tax benefit of $26,800 ($67,000 x 40%).

Since the balance in the deferred tax asset account had been $6,000, the adjustment needed is now as follows. The journal entry at 12/31/01 is

Deferred tax asset	20,800	
Income tax benefit--deferred		20,800

While the commonsense meaning of the **probable** criterion is clear enough, there can be a practical difficulty of assessing whether or not this threshold test is net in a given standard. Revised IAS 12 states that deferred tax assets can be recognized when there are sufficient taxable temporary differences relating to the same taxation authority and the same taxable entity which are expected to reverse in the same period as the expected reversal of the deductible temporary difference or in periods into which a tax loss arising from the deferred tax asset can be carried back or forward. The standard also suggests that, if there is an insufficiency of taxable temporary differences to absorb the deductible temporary differences, but it is deemed probable that sufficient taxable income will otherwise be earned, or that tax planning strategies are available to the entity, this can be used as a basis for concluding that it is probable that the benefits will be received.

As a practical matter, there are a number of positive and negative factors which may be evaluated in reaching a conclusion as to amount of the deferred tax asset to be recognized. Positive factors (those suggesting that the full amount of the deferred tax asset associated with the gross temporary difference should be recorded) might include

1. Evidence of sufficient future taxable income, exclusive of reversing temporary differences and carryforwards, to realize the benefit of the deferred tax asset

2. Evidence of sufficient future taxable income arising from the reversals of existing taxable temporary differences (deferred tax liabilities) to realize the benefit of the tax asset
3. Evidence of sufficient taxable income in prior year(s) available for realization of an operating loss carryback under existing statutory limitations
4. Evidence of the existence of prudent, feasible tax planning strategies under management control which, if implemented, would permit the realization of the tax asset. These are discussed in greater detail below.
5. An excess of appreciated asset values over their tax bases, in an amount sufficient to realize the deferred tax asset. This can be thought of as a subset of the tax strategies idea, since a sale or sale/leaseback of appreciated property is one rather obvious tax planning strategy to salvage a deferred tax benefit which might otherwise expire unused.
6. A strong earnings history exclusive of the loss that created the deferred tax asset. This would, under many circumstances, suggest that future profitability is likely and therefore that realization of deferred tax assets are probable.

Although the foregoing may suggest that the reporting entity will be able to realize the benefits of the deductible temporary differences outstanding as of the balance sheet date, certain negative factors should also be considered in determining whether realization of the full amount of the deferred tax benefit is probable under the circumstances. These factors could include

1. A cumulative recent history of accounting losses. Depending on extent and length of time over which losses were experienced, this could reduce the assessment of likelihood of realization below the important "probable" threshold.
2. A history of operating losses or of tax operating loss or credit carryforwards that have expired unused
3. Losses that are anticipated in the near future years, despite a history of profitable operations

Thus, the process of determining how much of the computed gross deferred tax benefit should be recognized involves the weighing of both positive and negative factors to determine whether, based on the preponderance of available evidence, it is probable that the deferred tax asset will be realized. Revised IAS 12 notes that a history of unused tax losses should be considered "strong evidence" that future taxable profits might prove elusive. In such cases, it would be expected that primary reliance would be placed on the existence of taxable temporary differences which, upon reversal, would provide taxable income to absorb the deferred tax benefits that are candidates for recognition in the financial statements. Absent those taxable temporary differences, recognition would be much more difficult.

To illustrate this computation in a more specific fact situation, assume the following facts:

1. Malpasa Corporation reports on a calendar year and adopted revised IAS 12 in 2000.
2. As of the December 31, 2000 balance sheet, Malpasa has taxable temporary differences of $85,000 relating to depreciation, deductible temporary differences of $12,000 relating to deferred compensation arrangements, a net operating loss carryforward (which arose in 1998) of $40,000, and a capital loss carryover of $10,000.
3. Malpasa's expected tax rate for future years is 40% for ordinary income, and 25% for net long-term capital gains. Capital losses cannot be offset against ordinary income.

The first steps are to compute the required balances of the deferred tax asset and liability accounts, without consideration of whether the tax asset would be probable of realization. The computations would proceed as follows:

Deferred tax liability:

Taxable temporary difference (depreciation)	$85,000
Effective tax rate	x____40%
Required balance	$34,000

Deferred tax asset:

Deductible temporary differences:	
Deferred compensation	$12,000
Net operating loss	40,000
	$52,000
Effective tax rate	x____40%
Required balance (a)	$20,800
Capital loss	$10,000
Effective tax rate	x____25%
Required balance (b)	$ 2,500

Total deferred tax asset:

Ordinary (a)	$20,800
Capital (b)	2,500
Total required balance	$23,300

The next step would be to consider whether realization of the deferred tax asset is probable. Malpasa management must evaluate both positive and negative evidence to determine this matter. Assume now that management identifies the following factors which may be relevant:

1. Before the net operating loss deduction, Malpasa reported taxable income of $5,000 in 2000. Management believes that taxable income in future years, apart from NOL deductions, should continue at about the same level experienced in 2000.
2. The taxable temporary differences are not expected to reverse in the foreseeable future.

3. The capital loss arose in connection with a transaction of a type that is unlikely to recur. The company does not generally engage in activities that have the potential to result in capital gains or losses.

4. Management estimates that certain productive assets have a fair value exceeding their respective tax bases by about $30,000. The entire gain, if realized for tax purposes, would be a recapture of depreciation previously taken. Since the current plans call for a substantial upgrading of the company's plant assets, management feels that it could easily accelerate those actions to realize taxable gains, should it be desirable to do so for tax planning purposes.

Based on the foregoing information, Malpasa Corporation management concludes that a $2,500 adjustment to deferred tax assets is required. The reasoning is as follows:

1. There will be some taxable operating income generated in future years ($5,000 annually, based on the earnings experienced in 2000), which will absorb a modest portion of the reversal of the deductible temporary difference ($12,000) and net operating loss carryforward ($40,000) existing at year end 2000.

2. More important, the feasible tax planning strategy of accelerating the taxable gain relating to appreciated assets ($30,000) would certainly be sufficient, in conjunction with operating income over several years, to permit Malpasa to realize the tax benefits of the deductible temporary difference and NOL carryover.

3. However, since capital loss carryovers are only usable to offset future capital gains and Malpasa management is unable to project future realization of capital gains, the associated tax benefit accrued ($2,500) will **probably** not be realized, and thus cannot be recognized.

Based on this analysis, deferred tax benefits in the amount of $20,800 should be recognized.

Effect of Tax Law Changes on Previously Recorded Deferred Tax Assets and Liabilities

The balance sheet oriented measurement approach of revised IAS 12 necessitates the reevaluation of the deferred tax asset and liability balances at each year end. Although revised IAS 12 does not directly address the question of changes to tax rates or other provisions of the tax law (e.g., deductibility of items) which may be enacted that will affect the realization of future deferred tax assets or liabilities, the effect of these changes should be reflected in the year-end deferred tax accounts in the period the changes are enacted. The offsetting adjustments should be made through the current period tax provision.

When revised tax rates are enacted, they may affect not only the unreversed effects of items which were originally reported in the continuing operations section of the income statement, but also the unreversed effects of items first presented as extraordinary items or in other income statement captions. Although it might be conceptually superior to report the effects of tax law changes on such unreversed temporary differences in these same income statement captions, as a practical matter the complexities of identifying the diverse treatments of these originating transactions or events would make such an approach unworkable. Accordingly, remeasurements of the effects of tax law changes should generally be reported in the tax provision associated with continuing operations.

Example of the computation of a deferred tax asset with a change in rates

Assume that the Fanuzzi Company has $80,000 of deductible temporary differences at the end of 2000, which are expected to result in tax deductions of approximately $40,000 each on tax returns for 2001-2002. Enacted tax rates are 50% for the years 1996-2000, and 40% for 2001 and thereafter.

The deferred tax asset is computed at 12/31/00 under each of the following independent assumptions:

1. If Fanuzzi Company expects to offset the deductible temporary differences against taxable income in the years 2001-2002, the deferred tax asset is $32,000 ($80,000 x 40%).
2. If Fanuzzi Company expects to realize a tax benefit for the deductible temporary differences by loss carryback refund, the deferred tax asset is $40,000 ($80,000 x 50%).

Assume that Fanuzzi Company expects to realize a tax asset of $32,000 at the end of 2000. Also assume that taxes payable in each of the years 1997-1999 were $8,000 (or 50% of taxable income). Realization of $24,000 of the $32,000 deferred tax asset is assured through carryback refunds even if no taxable income is earned in the years 2001-2002. Whether some or all of the remaining $8,000 will be recognized depends on Fanuzzi Company's assessment of the levels of future taxable earnings (i.e., whether the probable threshold is exceeded).

The foregoing estimate of the **certain** tax benefit, based on a loss carryback to periods of higher tax rates than are statutorily in effect for future periods, should be utilized only when future losses (for tax purposes) are expected. This restriction applies since the benefit thus recognized exceeds benefits that would be available in future periods, when tax rates will be lower.

Reporting the Effect of Tax Status Changes

Changes in the tax status of the reporting entity should be reported in a manner that is entirely analogous to the reporting of enacted tax changes. When the tax status change becomes effective, the consequent adjustments to deferred tax assets and liabilities are reported in current tax expense, as part of the tax provision relating to continuing operations.

The most commonly encountered changes in status are those attendant to an election, where permitted, to be taxed as a partnership or other "flow through" enterprise. (This means that the corporation will not be treated as a taxable entity but rather as an enterprise that "flows through" its taxable income to the owners on a current basis. This favorable tax treatment is available to encourage small businesses, and often will be limited to entities having sales revenue under a particular threshold level, or to entities having no more than a maximum number of shareholders.) Enterprises subject to such optional tax treatment may also request that a previous election be terminated. When a previously taxable corporation becomes a nontaxed corporation, the stockholders become personally liable for taxes on the company's earnings, whether the earnings are distributed to them or not (similar to the relationship among a partnership and its partners).

Although revised IAS 12 does not address the accounting for a change in tax status, given the balance sheet oriented determination of deferred tax assets and liabilities under this standard, a logical approach would be to eliminate deferred taxes by reversal through current period tax expense when a formerly taxable entity becomes nontaxable. For example, if an entity having a net deferred tax liability elects nontaxed corporation status, it will report a tax benefit in its current tax provision.

Similarly, if a previously nontaxed corporation becomes a taxable entity, the effect is to assume a net tax benefit or obligation for unreversed temporary differences existing at the date the change becomes effective. Accordingly, the financial statements for the period of such a change will report the effects of the event in the current tax provision. If the entity had at that date many taxable temporary differences as yet unreversed, it would report a large tax expense in that period. Conversely, if it had a large quantity of unreversed deductible temporary differences, a substantial deferred tax benefit (if probable of realization) would need to be recorded, with a concomitant credit to the current period's tax provision in the income statement. Whether eliminating an existing deferred tax balance or recording an initial deferred tax asset or liability, the income tax footnote to the financial statements will need to fully explain the nature of the events that transpired.

In some jurisdictions, nontaxed corporation elections are automatically effective when filed. In such a case, if a reporting entity makes an election before the end of the current fiscal year, it is logical that the effects be reported in current year income to become effective at the start of the following period. For example, an election filed in December 2000 would be reported in the 2000 financial statements to become effective at the beginning of the company's next fiscal year, January 1, 2001. No deferred tax assets or liabilities would appear on the December 31, 2000 balance sheet, and the tax provision for the year then ended would include the effects of any reversals that had previously been recorded. Practice varies, however, and in some instances the effect of the elimination of the deferred tax assets and liabilities would be reported in the year the election actually becomes effective.

Reporting the Effect of Accounting Changes Made for Tax Purposes

Occasionally, an entity will initiate or be required to adopt changes in accounting that affect income tax reporting but will not affect financial statement reporting. For example, in certain jurisdictions at varying times, the following changes have been mandated: use of the direct write-off method of bad debt recognition instead of providing an allowance for bad debts, while continuing to use the reserve method as required by GAAP for financial reporting; the "full costing" method of computing inventory valuations for tax purposes (adding some items that are administrative costs to overhead), while continuing to expense currently those costs not inventoriable under GAAP; and use of accelerated capital recovery (depreciation) methods for tax reporting while continuing to use normal methods for financial reporting. Often, these changes really involve two distinct temporary differences. The first of these is the one-time, catch-up adjustment which either immediately or over a prescribed time period affects the tax basis of the asset or liability in question (net receivables or inventory, in the examples above), and which then reverses as these assets or liabilities are later realized or settled and are eliminated from the balance sheet. The second change is the ongoing differential in the amount of newly acquired assets or incurred liabilities being recognized for tax and accounting purposes; these differences also eventually reverse. This second type of change is the normal temporary difference which has already been discussed. It is the first change that differs from those previously discussed earlier in the chapter.

As an example, consider that Leipzig Corporation has, at December 31, 2000, gross receivables of $12,000,000 and an allowance for bad debts in the amount of $600,000. Also assume that expected future taxes will be at a 40% rate. Effective January 1, 2001, the tax law is revised to eliminate deductions for accrued bad debts, with existing allowances required to be taken into income ratably over 3 years (a 3-year spread). A balance sheet of Leipzig Corporation prepared on January 1, 2001, would report a deferred tax benefit in the amount of $240,000 (i.e., $600,000 x 40%, which is the tax effect of future deductions to be taken when specific receivables are written off and bad debts are incurred for tax purposes); a current tax liability of $80,000 (one-third of the tax obligation); and a noncurrent tax liability of $160,000 (two-thirds of the tax obligation). Under the requirements of revised IAS 12, the deferred tax benefit must be entirely reported as noncurrent in classified balance sheets, inasmuch as no deferred tax benefits or obligations can be shown as current.

Implications of Changes in Tax Rates and Status Made in Interim Periods

Tax rate changes may occur during an interim reporting period, either because a tax law change mandated a mid-year effective date, or because tax law changes were effective at year end but the reporting entity has adopted a fiscal year end other than the natural year (December 31). The recently promulgated IAS on interim reporting, IAS 34 (addressed in detail in Chapter 19), has essentially embraced a mixed view on interim reporting--with many aspects conforming to a "discrete" approach (each interim period standing on its own) but others, including accounting for income taxes, conforming to the "integral" manner of reporting. Whatever the philosophical strengths and weaknesses of the discrete and integral approaches in general, the integral approach was clearly warranted in the matter of accounting for income taxes.

The fact that income taxes are assessed annually is the primary reason for reaching a conclusion that taxes are to be accrued based on an entity's estimated average annual effective tax rate for the full fiscal year. If rate changes have been enacted to take effect later in the fiscal year, the expected effective rate should take into account the rate changes as well as the anticipated pattern of earnings to be experienced over the course of the year. Thus, the rate to be applied to interim period earnings (or losses, as discussed further below) will take into account the expected level of earnings for the entire forthcoming year, as well as the effect of enacted (or substantially enacted) changes in the tax rates to become operative later in the fiscal year. In other words, as expressed by IAS 34, the estimated average annual rate would "reflect a blend of the progressive tax rate structure expected to be applicable to the full year's earnings enacted or substantially enacted changes in the income tax rates scheduled to take effect later in the financial year."

While the principle espoused by IAS 34 is both clear and logical, a number of practical issues arise in most situations. The standard does address in detail the various computational aspects of an effective interim period tax rate, some of which are summarized in the following paragraphs.

Many enterprises are subject to multiplicity of taxing jurisdictions, and in some instances the amount of income subject to tax will vary from one to the next, since the tax laws in different jurisdictions will include and exclude disparate items of income or expense from the tax base. For example, interest earned on government-issued bonds may be exempted from tax by the jurisdiction which issued them, but be defined as fully taxable by other tax jurisdictions the entity is subject to. To the extent feasible, the appropriate estimated average annual effective tax rate should be separately ascertained for each taxing jurisdiction and applied individually to the interim period pretax income of each jurisdiction, so that the most accurate estimate of income taxes can be developed at each interim reporting date. In general, an overall estimated effective tax rate will not be as satisfactory for this purpose as would a more carefully constructed set of estimated rates, since the pattern of taxable and deductible items will fluctuate from one period to the next.

Similarly, if the tax law prescribes different income tax rates for different categories of income, then, to the extent practicable, a separate tax rate should be applied to each category of interim period pretax income. IAS 34, while mandating such detailed rules of computing and applying tax rates across jurisdiction or across categories of income, nonetheless recognized that such a degree of precision may not be achievable in all cases. Thus, IAS 34 allows usage of a weighted-average of rates across jurisdictions or across categories of income provided it is a reasonable approximation of the effect of using more specific rates.

In computing an expected effective tax rate given for a tax jurisdiction, all relevant features of the tax regulations should be taken into account. Jurisdictions may provide for tax credits based on new investment in plant and machinery, relocation of facilities to backward or underdeveloped areas, research and development expenditures, levels of export sales, and so forth, and the expected credits against the tax for the full year should be given consideration in the determination of an expected effective tax rate. Thus, the tax effect of new investment in plant and machinery, when the local taxing body offers an investment credit for qualifying investment in tangible productive assets, will be reflected in those interim periods of the fiscal year in which the new investment occurs (assuming it can be forecast to occur later in a given fiscal year), and not merely in the period in which the new investment occurs. This is consistent with the underlying concept that taxes are strictly an annual phenomenon, but it is at variance with the purely discrete view of interim financial reporting.

IAS 34 notes that, although tax credits and similar modifying elements are to be taken into account in developing the expected effective tax rate to apply to interim earnings, tax benefits which will relate to onetime events are to be reflected from the interim period when those events take place. This is perhaps most likely to be encountered in the context of capital gains taxes incurred in connection with occasional dispositions of investments and other capital assets; since it is not feasible to project the rate at which such transactions will occur over the course of a year, the tax effects should be recognized only as the underlying events transpire.

While in most cases tax credits are to be handled as suggested in the foregoing paragraphs, in some jurisdictions tax credits, particularly those which relate to export revenue or capital expenditures, are in effect government grants. The account for government grants is set forth in IAS 20; in brief, grants are recognized in income over the period necessary to properly match them to the costs which the grants are intended to offset or defray. Thus, compliance with both IAS 20 and IAS 34 would necessitate that tax credits be carefully analyzed to identify those which are in substance grants, and then accounting for the credit consistent with its true nature.

When an interim period loss gives rise to a tax loss carryback, it should be fully reflected in that interim period. Similarly, if a loss in an interim period produces a tax loss carryforward, it should be recognized immediately, but only if the criteria set forth in revised IAS 12 are met. Specifically, it must be deemed probable that the benefits will be realizable before the loss benefits can be given formal recognition in the financial statements. In the case of interim period losses, it may be necessary to assess not only whether the enterprise will be profitable enough in future fiscal years to utilize the tax benefits associated with the loss, but furthermore, whether interim periods later in the same year will provide earnings of sufficient magnitude to absorb the losses of the current period.

Revised IAS 12 provides that changes in expectations regarding the realizability of benefits related to net operating loss carryforwards should be reflected currently in tax expense. Similarly, if a net operating loss carryforward benefit is not deemed probable of being realized until the interim (or annual) period when it in fact becomes realized, the tax effect will be included in tax expense of that period. Appropriate explanatory material must be included in the notes to the financial statements, even on an interim basis, to provide the user with an understanding of the unusual relationship between pretax accounting income and the provision for income taxes.

Accounting for Income Taxes in Business Combinations

One of the more complex aspects of interperiod income tax accounting occurs when business combinations, treated as acquisitions as defined by IAS 22, are consummated. The principal complexity relates to the recognition, at the date of the purchase, of the deferred tax effects of the differences between the tax and financial reporting bases of assets and liabilities acquired. Further difficulties arise in connection with the recognition of goodwill and negative goodwill. If the reporting entity expects that the ultimate tax allocation will differ from the initial one (such as when disallowance by the tax authorities of an allocation made to identifiable intangibles is anticipated by the taxpayer), yet another complex accounting matter must be dealt with.

Under the provisions of revised IAS 12, the tax effects of any differences in tax and financial reporting bases are to be reflected, from the date of the purchase, as deferred tax assets and liabilities. The same rules that apply to the recognition of deferred tax assets and liabilities arising under other circumstances (i.e., the origination of temporary differences by the reporting entity) are equally applicable to such instances, except for the initial recognition of an asset or liability in a transaction other than a business combination when, at the time of the transaction, neither accounting profit nor taxable profit is affected. Accordingly, if deferred tax assets are not deemed to be probable of ultimate realization, they are not recognized in any of these circumstances.

Depending on the tax jurisdiction in which they occur, acquisitions can be either taxable or nontaxable in nature. In a taxable acquisition, the total purchase price paid will be allocated to assets and liabilities for both tax and financial reporting purposes, although under some circumstances the specifics of these allocations may differ, and to the extent the allocation is made to nondeductible goodwill there will be differences in future periods' taxable and accounting profit. In a nontaxable acquisition, the predecessor entity's tax bases for the various assets and liabilities will be carried forward, while for financial reporting the purchase price will be allocated to the assets and liabilities acquired. Thus, in most cases, there will be significant differences between the tax and financial reporting bases. For this reason, both taxable and nontaxable acquisitions can involve the application of deferred income tax accounting.

Accounting for Purchase Business Combinations at Acquisition Date

Revised IAS 12 requires that the tax effects of the tax-book basis differences of all assets and liabilities generally be presented as deferred tax assets and liabilities as of the acquisition date. In general, this grossing-up of the balance sheet is a straightforward matter. An example, in the context of the business acquisition of Windlass Corp., follows:

1. The income tax rate is a flat 40%.
2. The acquisition of a business is effected at a cost of $500,000.

3. The fair values of assets acquired total $750,000.

4. The carryforward tax bases of assets acquired total $600,000.

5. The fair and carryforward tax bases of the liabilities assumed in the purchase are $250,000.

6. The difference between the tax and fair values of the assets acquired, $150,000, consists of taxable temporary differences of $200,000 and deductible temporary differences of $50,000.

7. There is no doubt as to the realizability of the deductible temporary differences in this case.

Based on the foregoing facts, allocation of the purchase price is as follows:

Gross purchase price	$ 500,000
Allocation to identifiable assets and (liabilities):	
Assets other than goodwill and deferred tax benefits	750,000
Deferred tax benefits	20,000
Liabilities, other than deferred tax obligations	(250,000)
Deferred tax obligations	(80,000)
Net of the above allocations	440,000
Allocation to goodwill	$ 60,000

Goodwill and negative goodwill. Goodwill arises when part of the price paid in a business combination accounted for as a purchase cannot be allocated to identifiable assets; negative goodwill results from bargain purchases. Goodwill may be tax deductible, depending on tax jurisdiction, or may be nondeductible. If it is deductible, the mandated amortization period may differ from that prescribed by IAS 22. Since under GAAP goodwill is to be amortized over its expected economic life (not to exceed 20 years, and generally not over 5 years), a temporary difference will often develop. Since negative goodwill is offset against all nonmonetary assets for financial reporting (if the benchmark treatment is employed), differences between tax and book depreciation will result in many situations.

If goodwill or negative goodwill is not deductible or taxable, respectively, in a given tax jurisdiction, in theory its tax basis is zero, and thus there is a difference between tax and financial reporting bases, to which one would logically expect deferred taxes would be attributed. However, given the residual nature of goodwill or negative goodwill, recognition of deferred taxes would in turn create yet more goodwill, and thus more deferred tax, etc. There would be little purpose achieved by loading up the balance sheet with more goodwill and related deferred tax in such circumstances, and the computation itself would be quite challenging. Accordingly, revised IAS 12 prohibits grossing up goodwill in such a fashion. Similarly, if there is negative goodwill which is not allocated to the cost of assets, but rather which is presented as a deferred credit items and which is not taxable, no deferred tax benefit will be computed and presented.

It is important to understand the slight inconsistency of the rules of revised IAS 12 as they relate to goodwill.

1. If positive goodwill is nondeductible for tax purposes, no deferred tax liability should be associated with it; but
2. No negative goodwill reported as a deferred revenue account in the financial statements should have a deferred tax benefit associated with it.

The accounting for a taxable purchase business combination is essentially similar to that for a nontaxable one. However, unlike the previous example, in which there were numerous assets with different tax and financial reporting bases, there are likely to be only a few differences in the case of taxable purchases. In jurisdictions in which goodwill is not deductible, attempts are often made for tax purposes to allocate excess purchase cost to tangible assets as well as to other intangibles, such as covenants not to compete. (Such attempts may or not survive review by the tax authorities, of course.) In jurisdictions where goodwill is deductible, presumably this is not a motivation, although because goodwill is often viewed as a suspect asset, entities will still be more comfortable if purchase cost can be attributed to "real" assets, even when goodwill can be amortized for tax purposes.

Accounting for Purchase Business Combinations After the Acquisition

Under the provisions of the original IAS 12, net deferred tax benefits were not to be carried forward as assets unless there was a reasonable expectation they would be realized. Under revised IAS 12 the criterion has evolved slightly; the new standard is that deferred tax assets must be probable of being realized. The assessment of this probability was discussed earlier in the chapter.

In the example above, it was specified that all deductible temporary differences were fully realizable, and therefore the deferred tax benefits associated with those temporary differences were recorded as of the acquisition date. In other situations, there may be substantial doubt concerning realizability; that is, it may not be **probable** that the benefits will be realized, and accordingly, the deferred tax asset would not be recognized, under revised IAS 12, at the date of the business acquisition. If so, the allocation of the purchase price would have to reflect that fact, and more of the purchase cost would be allocated to goodwill than would otherwise be the case. If at a later date it is decided that some or all of the deferred tax asset not recognized at the time of the acquisition is, in fact, probable of being ultimately realized, the effect of that reevaluation will be taken into tax expense (benefit) in the period in which the reevaluation is made. Furthermore, the portion of the extra goodwill recognized at the time of the business acquisition that remains unamortized at the date of the reevaluation must be written off to expense.

To illustrate this last concept, assume that a business acquisition is made on January 1, 2000, and the deferred tax assets of $100,000 are **not** recognized at that time, due to an assessment that realization is not probable. The unrecognized tax benefit is implicitly allocated to goodwill. Also assume that the goodwill is being amortized over 5 years. On January 1, 2002, the likelihood of ultimately realizing the tax benefit is reassessed as being probable, and all of these are projected for later years. The entries at that date are as follows:

Deferred tax benefits	100,000	
Income tax expense (benefit)		100,000
Amortization of goodwill	60,000	
Goodwill		60,000

Note that only the remaining **unamortized** balance of goodwill associated with the original nonrecognition of the deferred tax benefit is charged to expense at the date the deferred tax benefit is reassessed.

In some situations, the amount of deferred tax benefits upon reassessment will exceed the balance in the goodwill account, or there may have been no goodwill recognized in connection with the business acquisition at all. Revised IAS 12 stipulates that, as a result of this reassessment, negative goodwill cannot be recognized, nor can any existing negative goodwill be increased. The implication is that, while negative goodwill could have been first recognized at the time of a business acquisition which involved recognition of deferred assets, it would not be possible to later recognize deferred tax benefits under such circumstances.

A related issue arises when the acquirer, rather than the acquiree, had not previously recognized deferred tax benefits prior to the acquisition, due to imposition of the "probable" test. If as a result of the acquisition, this asset becomes probable of realization (e.g., if under relevant tax laws the earnings of the acquired entity will provide the acquirer with an opportunity to utilize the deductible temporary differences), it will be given recognition, with the result that the goodwill otherwise recorded in the transaction will be reduced, or negative goodwill will be increased or first given recognition.

Unitings of Interests

In unitings of interests, the combining entities generally do not adjust carrying values of assets and liabilities. Reissued or comparative financial statements of periods before the effective date of the combination are restated on a combined basis. Although revised IAS 12 does not address the question, one issue that may arise is if one of the combining entities had an unrecognized deferred tax benefit (i.e., the deferred tax benefit was not deemed to be probable of realization), the restated financials may or may not reflect the benefits. That is, the deferred tax benefits may be restored on a retrospective basis.

This treatment depends on whether the combined entity will be able, under provisions of the tax laws, to utilize the operating loss and tax credit carryforwards of the merged companies. If it can do so, the deferred tax benefits should be recognized in any restated prior-period financial statements. If, under the law, the benefits cannot be utilized in a consolidated tax return or if a consolidated return is not expected to be filed, the tax benefits would not be recognized in financial statements restated for the uniting of interests.

Under some circumstances, unitings of interests may be taxable, meaning that for tax purposes there will be a step-up of the net assets of one of the merged entities. The differences between the new, stepped-up tax bases and the carryforward book values utilized for financial reporting purposes are temporary differences giving rise to deferred tax benefits. Whether these benefits are given recognition depends on whether realization is deemed to be probable. If the deferred tax benefit is not recognized at inception, and it is later partially or fully recognized when it is determined that the likelihood of ultimate realization is probable, the effect of this accounting recognition should be reflected in tax expense for the current period.

Tax Allocation for Business Investments

As noted in Chapter 10, there are two basic methods of accounting for investments in the common stock of other corporations: (1) the cost method and (2) the equity method. The **cost method** requires that the investing corporation (investor) record the investment at its purchase price, and no additional entry is made to the account over the life of the asset (this does not include any valuation contra accounts). The cost method is used in instances where the investor is not considered to have significant influence over the investee. The ownership threshold generally used is 20% of ownership. This figure is not considered an absolute, but it will be used to identify the break between application of the cost and equity methods. Under the cost method, ordinary income is recognized as dividends are declared by the investee, and capital gains (losses) are recognized on disposal of the investment. For tax purposes, no provision is made during the holding period for the allocable undistributed earnings of the investee. Deferred tax computation is not necessary when using the cost method because there is no temporary difference.

The **equity method** is generally used whenever an investor owns more than 20% of an investee or has significant influence over its operations. The equity method calls for recording the investment at cost and then increasing this carrying amount by the allocable portion of the investee's earnings. The allocable portion of the investee's earnings is then included in the pretax accounting income of the investor. Dividend payments are no longer included in pretax accounting income but are considered to be a reduction in the carrying amount of the investment. However, for tax purposes, dividends are the only revenue realized. As a result, the investor needs to recognize deferred income tax expense on the undistributed earnings of the associate that will be taxed in the future.

IAS 28 distinguishes between an associate and a subsidiary and prescribes different accounting treatments for each. An associate is considered to be a corporation whose stock is owned by an investor who holds more than 20% but no greater than 50% of the outstanding stock. An association situation occurs when the investor has significant influence but not control over the corporation invested in. A subsidiary, on the other hand, exists when one enterprise exerts control over another, which is presumed when it holds more than 50% of the stock of the other entity.

Under revised IAS 12, two conditions must both be satisfied to justify **not** reflecting deferred taxes in connection with the earnings of a subsidiary (a control situation), branches and associates (significant influence), and joint ventures. These are (1) that the parent, investor or venturer is able to control the timing of the reversal of the temporary difference, and (2) it is probable that the difference will not reverse in the foreseeable future. Unless both conditions are met, the tax effects of these temporary differences must be given recognition.

When a parent company that has the ability to control the dividend and other policies of its subsidiary determines that dividends will not be declared, and thus that the undistributed profit of the subsidiary will not be taxed at the parent company level, no deferred tax liability is to be recognized. If this intention is later altered, the tax effect of this change in estimate would be reflected in the current period's tax provision.

On the other hand, an investor, even one having significant influence, cannot absolutely determine the associate's dividend policy. Accordingly, it has to be presumed that earnings will eventually be distributed and that these will create taxable income at the investor company level. Therefore, deferred tax liability must be provided for reporting entity's share of all undistributed earnings of its associates for which it is accounting by the equity method, unless there is binding agreement for the earnings of the investee to be not distributed within the foreseeable future.

In the case of the joint ventures, there are a wide range of possible relationships between the venturers, and in some cases the reporting entity has the ability to control the payment of dividends. As in the foregoing, if the reporting entity has the ability to exercise this level of control and it is probable that distributions will not be made within the foreseeable future, no deferred tax liability will be reported.

In all these various circumstances, it will be necessary to assess whether distributions within the foreseeable future are probable. The standard does not define "foreseeable future" and thus this will remain a matter of subjective judgment. The criteria of revised IAS 12, while subjective, are less ambiguous than under the original IAS 12, which permitted nonrecognition of deferred tax liability when it was "reasonable to assume that (the associates's) profits will not be distributed."

To illustrate the application of these concepts, assume that Parent Company owns 30% of the outstanding common stock of Investee Company and 70% of the outstanding common stock of Subsidiary Company. Additional data for the year 2000 are as follows:

	Investee Company	*Subsidiary Company*
Net income	$50,000	$100,000
Dividends paid	20,000	60,000

How the foregoing data are used to recognize the tax effects of the stated events is discussed below.

Income Tax Effects From Investee Company

The 2000 accounting profit of Parent Company will include equity in its associate's income equal to $15,000 ($50,000 x 30%). Parent's taxable income, however, will include dividend income of $6,000 ($20,000 x 30%), and, under applicable tax law, a credit of 80% of the $6,000, or $4,800, will also be allowed for the dividends received. This 80% dividends received deduction is a permanent difference between accounting and taxable profits.

The amount of the deferred tax credit in 2000 depends on the expectations of Parent Company as to the manner in which the $9,000 of undistributed income will be received. In many tax jurisdictions, the effective tax rate will differ based on method of realization; dividend income may be taxed at a different rate than capital gains (achieved on the sale of an investment in an associate, for example). If the expectation of receipt is via dividends, the temporary difference is 20% of $9,000, or $1,800, and the deferred tax credit for this originating temporary difference in 1999 is the current tax rate times $1,800. However, if the expectation is that receipt will be through future sale of the investment, the gain on which would be fully taxed, the temporary difference is $9,000 and the deferred tax credit is the current capital gains rate times the $9,000.

The entries below illustrate these alternatives. A tax rate of 34% is used for both ordinary income and for capital gains. Note that the amounts in the entries below relate only to Investee Company's incremental impact on Parent Company's tax accounts.

	Expectations for undistributed income	
	Dividends	*Capital gains*
Income tax expense	1,020	2,208
Deferred tax liability	612[b]	1,800[c]
Income taxes payable	408[a]	408[a]

[a]*Computation of income taxes payable:*

Dividend income--30% x ($20,000)	*$6,000*
Less 80% dividends received deduction	*(4,800)*
Amount included in Parent's taxable income	*$1,200*
Tax liability--34% x ($1,200)	*$ 408*

[b]*Computation of deferred tax liability (dividend assumption):*
Originating temporary difference:
Parent's share of undistributed income--

30% x ($30,000)	*$9,000*
Less 80% dividends received deduction	*(7,200)*
Originating temporary difference	*$1,800*
Deferred tax liability--34% x ($1,800)	*$ 612*

[c]*Computation of deferred tax liability (capital gain assumption):*
Originating temporary difference: Parent's share

of undistributed income--30% x ($30,000)	*$9,000*
Deferred tax liability--20% x ($9,000)	*$1,800*

Income Tax Effects From Subsidiary Company

The accounting profit of Parent Company will also include equity in Subsidiary income of $70,000 (70% x $100,000). This $70,000 will be included in pretax consolidated income if Parent and Subsidiary issue consolidated financial statements. Depending on the rules of the particular tax jurisdiction, it may be that for tax purposes, Parent and Subsidiary will not file a consolidated tax return (e.g., because the prescribed minimum level of control, that is, 80%, is not present). In the present example, assume that it will not be possible to file consolidated tax returns. Consequently, the taxable income of Parent will include dividend income of $42,000 (70% x $60,000). Assume further that there will be an 80% dividends received deduction, which will amount to $33,600. The originating temporary difference results from Parent's equity ($28,000) in Subsidiary's undistributed earnings of $40,000.

The amount of the deferred tax credit in 2000 depends on the expectations of Parent Company as to the manner in which this $28,000 of undistributed income will be received. The same expectations can exist as discussed previously, for Parent's equity in Investee's undistributed earnings (i.e., through future dividend distributions or capital gains).

The entries below illustrate these alternatives. A marginal tax rate of 34% is assumed. The amounts in the entries below relate only to Subsidiary Company's incremental impact on Parent Company's tax accounts.

	Expectations for undistributed income	
	Dividends	*Capital gains*
Income tax expense	4,760	12,376
Deferred tax liability	1,904[b]	9,520[c]
Income taxes payable	2,856[a]	2,856[a]

[a]*Computation of income taxes payable:*

Dividend income--70% x ($60,000)	$42,000
Less 80% dividends received deduction	(33,600)
Amount included in Parent's taxable income	$ 8,400
Tax liability--34% x ($8,400)	$ 2,856

[b]*Computation of deferred tax liability (dividend assumption):*
Originating temporary difference:

Parent's share of undistributed income-- 70% x ($40,000)	$28,000
Less 80% dividends received deduction	(22,400)
Originating temporary difference	$ 5,600
Deferred tax liability--34% x ($5,600)	$ 1,904

[c]*Computation of deferred tax liability (capital gain assumption):*

Originating temporary difference: Parent's share of undistributed income--70% x ($40,000)	$28,000
Deferred tax liability--34% x ($28,000)	$ 9,520

If a parent company owns a large enough percentage of the voting stock of a subsidiary and the parent, so that it may consolidate the subsidiary for both financial and tax reports, no temporary differences exist between pretax consolidated income and taxable income. Under the rules in some jurisdictions, it may be possible to submit separate tax returns even if consolidated returns could alternatively be filed; in such circumstances, there may be a tax rule that grants a 100% dividends received deduction, to avoid incurring double taxation. If, in the circumstances noted above, consolidated financial statements are prepared but a consolidated tax return is not, it would be the case that a dividends received deduction of 100% would be allowed. Accordingly, the temporary difference between pretax consolidated income and taxable income is zero if the parent assumes that the undistributed income will be realized in dividends.

Tax Effects of Compound Financial Instruments

IAS 32, *Financial Instruments: Disclosure and Presentation,* established the important notion that when financial instruments are compound, the separately identifiable components are to be accounted for according to their distinct natures. For example, when an enterprise sells convertible debt instruments, those instruments have characteristics of both debt and equity securities, and accordingly the issuance proceeds should be allocated among those components in the ratio which the fair values bear to the total proceeds. A problem arises, however, because the taxing authorities may not agree that a portion of the proceeds should be allocated to a secondary instrument. For example, when convertible bonds are sold, for tax reporting purposes the entire proceeds are considered to be the basis of the debt instrument in most jurisdictions, with no basis being allocated to the conversion feature. Accordingly this will create a temporary difference between the interest expense to be recognized for financial reporting purposes and interest to be recognized for income tax purposes, which in turn will have deferred tax implications.

Consider the following scenario. Tamara Corp. issues 6% convertible bonds due in 10 years with a face value of $3,000,000, with the bonds being convertible into Tamara common stock at the holders' option. Proceeds of the offering amount to $3,200,000, for an effective yield of approximately 5.13% at a time when "straight" debt with similar risks and time to maturity is yielding just under 6.95% in the market. Since the fair value of the debt component is thus $2.8 million out of the actual proceeds of $3.2 million, the convertibility feature is seemingly worth $400,000 in the financial marketplace. Thus the ratio of fair values is as follows:

Debt portion: $2,700,000 + $3,200,000 = .875 (i.e., 87.5%)
Equity portion: $400,000 + $3,200,000 = .125 (i.e., 12.5%)

If these ratios are then applied to the actual proceeds of the offering of the convertible debt, $3 million, the resulting computed amounts are used to record the transaction under the guidance of IAS 32, as follows:

Cash	3,000,000	
Unamortized net discount	375,000	
Debt payable		3,000,000
Equity--paid-in capital account		375,000

The unamortized debt discount will be amortized as additional interest cost over the life of the bonds (10 years, in this example) for financial reporting purposes, but for tax purposes the deductible interest cost will be limited, typically, to the actual interest paid in this instance. The "originating" phase of the temporary difference will be when the compound security is first sold; the "reversing" of this temporary difference will occur as the debt discount is amortized until the net carrying value of the debt equals the face value.

To illustrate, assume that the tax rate is 30%, and for simplicity, also assume that the debt discount will be amortized on a straight-line basis over the 10-year term ($375,000 ÷ 10 = $47,500 per year), although in practice amortization using the "effective yield" method is preferred. The entries to establish deferred tax liability accounting at inception, and to reflect interest accrual and reversal of the deferred tax account are as follows:

At inception (in addition to the entry shown above)

Equity--paid-in capital account	112,500	
Deferred tax payable		112,500

Each year thereafter

Interest expense	217,500	
Interest expense		180,000
Unamortized debt discount		37,500
Deferred tax payable	11,250	
Tax expense--deferred		11,250

Note that the offset to deferred tax liability at inception is a charge to equity, in effect reducing the credit to paid-in capital for the equity portion of the compound financial instrument to a net of tax basis, since allocating a portion of the proceeds to the equity component caused the creation of a nondeductible deferred charge, debt discount. When the deferred charge is later amortized, however, the reversing of the temporary difference leads to a reduction in tax expense to better "match" the higher interest expense reported in the financial statements than on the tax return.

Accounting for Income Taxes: Intraperiod Tax Allocation

While revised IAS 12 is concerned predominantly with the requirements of **interperiod** income tax allocation (deferred tax accounting), it also addresses the questions of **intraperiod** tax allocation. Intraperiod tax allocation relates to the matching in the income (or other financial) statement of various categories of comprehensive income or expense (continuing operations, extraordinary items, corrections of fundamental errors, etc.) with the tax effects of those items. The general principle is that tax effects should follow the items to which they relate. The computation of the tax effects of these items is, however, complicated by the fact that many, if not most, jurisdictions feature progressive tax rates. For that reason, a question arises as to whether overall "blended" rates should be apportioned across all the disparate elements (ordinary income, corrections of errors, etc.) or whether the marginal tax effects of items other than ordinary income should be reported instead.

Revised IAS 12 does not answer this question or, in fact, even address it. It might, however, be instructive to consider the two approaches, since this will affect the presentation of the income statement and, in the case of fundamental errors, the statement of retained earnings as well.

The blended rate approach would calculate the average, or effective, rate applicable to all an entity's taxable earnings for a given year (including the deferred tax effects of items that will be deductible or taxable in later periods, but that are being reported in the current year's financial statements). This effective rate is then used to compute income taxes on each of the individually reportable components. For example, if an entity has an effective blended rate of 46% in a given year, after considering the various tax brackets and any available credits against the gross amount of the tax computed, this rate is used to calculate the taxes on ordinary income, extraordinary income, the results of discontinued operations, the correction of fundamental errors, and the effects of changes in accounting principles, if any.

The alternative to the blended rate approach is what can be called the marginal tax effect approach. Using this computational technique, a series of "with-and-without" calculations will be made to identify the marginal, or incremental, effects of items other than those arising from ordinary, continuing operations. This is essentially the approach dictated under US GAAP (SFAS 109 and its various predecessors) and is the primary approach employed under UK GAAP as well. Since the prescription of this with-and-without method is detailed most extensively in current US GAAP, that explanation is referred to extensively in the following discussion.

Prior to the promulgation of current US GAAP, the with-and-without technique was applied under prior US standards in a step-by-step fashion proceeding down the face of the income statement. For example, an entity having continuing operations, discontinued operations, and extraordinary items would calculate tax expense as follows:

1. Tax would be computed for the aggregate results and for continuing operations. The difference between the two amounts would be allocated to the total of discontinued operations and extraordinary items.
2. Tax expense would be computed on discontinued operations. The residual amount (i.e., the difference between tax on the discontinued operations and the tax on the total of discontinued operations and extraordinary items) would then be allocated to extraordinary items.

Thus, the amount of tax expense allocated to any given classification in the statement of income (and the other financial statements, if relevant) was partially a function of the location in which the item was traditionally presented in the income and retained earnings statements.

Under current US GAAP, total income tax expense or benefit for the period is allocated among continuing operations, discontinued operations, extraordinary items, and stockholders' equity. The standard creates a few anomalies, however, since, as defined in current US GAAP, the tax provisions on income from continuing operations include not only taxes on the income earned from continuing operations, as expected, but also a number of other tax effects, including the following:

1. The impact of changes in tax laws and rates, which includes the effects of such changes on items that were previously reflected directly in stockholders' equity
2. The impact of changes in tax status
3. Changes in estimates about whether the tax benefits of deductible temporary differences or net operating loss or credit carryforwards are probable of realization.

   NOTE: Under current US GAAP the actual criterion is "more likely than not," which differs from IAS's "probable" criterion.

Under current US GAAP, stockholders' equity is charged or credited with the initial tax effects of items that are reported directly in stockholders' equity, including that related to corrections of the effects of accounting errors of previous periods, which under the international standards are known as fundamental errors. The effects of tax rate or other tax law changes on items for which the tax effects were originally reported directly in stockholders' equity are reported in continuing operations if they occur in any period after the original event. This approach was adopted by current US GAAP because of the presumed difficulty of identifying the original reporting location of items that are affected possibly years later by changing rates; the expedient solution was to require all such effects to be reported in the tax provision allocated to continuing operations.

Example of intraperiod allocation using the with-and-without approach

Assume that there were $50,000 in deductible temporary differences at 12/31/00; these remain unchanged during the current year, 2001.

Income from continuing operations	$400,000
Loss from discontinued operations	(120,000)
Extraordinary gain on involuntary conversion	60,000
Correction of fundamental error:	
understatement of depreciation in 2000	(20,000)
Tax credits	5,000

Tax rates are: 15% on first $100,000 of taxable income; 20% on next $100,000; 25% on next $100,000; 30% thereafter.

Expected future tax rates were 20% at December 31, 2000, but are judged to be 28% at December 31, 2001.

Retained earnings at December 31, 2000, totaled $650,000.

Intraperiod tax allocation proceeds as follows:

Step 1 --   Tax on total taxable income of $320,000 ($400,000 – $120,000 + $60,000 –
            $20,000) is **$61,000** ($66,000 based on rate structure, less tax credit of
            $5,000).

Step 2 --   Tax on income from continuing operations of $400,000 is **$85,000**, net of tax
            credit.

Step 3 --   The difference, $24,000, is allocated pro rata to discontinued operations,
            extraordinary gain, and correction of the error in prior year depreciation.

Step 4 --   Adjustment of the deferred tax asset, amounting to a $4,000 increase due to
            an effective tax rate estimate change [$50,000 x (.28 – .20)] is allocated to
            continuing operations, regardless of the source of the temporary difference.

A summary combined income and retained earnings statement is presented below.

Income from continuing operations,		
before income taxes		$400,000
Income taxes on income from continuing		
operations:		
Current	$90,000	
Deferred	(4,000)	
Tax credits	(5,000)	81,000
Income from continuing operations, net		319,000
Loss from discontinued operations,		
net of tax benefit of $36,000		(84,000)
Extraordinary gain, net of tax of $18,000		42,000
Net income		277,000
Retained earnings, January 1, 2000		650,000
Correction of fundamental error,		
net of tax effects of $6,000		(14,000)
Retained earnings, December 31, 2000		$913,000

Applicability to international accounting standards. Since revised IAS 12 is
silent on the method to be used to compute the tax effects of individual captions in
the statement of income and the statement of retained earnings, financial statement
preparers have the option of using essentially a with-and-without or blended rate
approach. Both can be rationalized from either practical or theoretical perspectives.
The blended rate method would clearly be easier to apply, since only one set of
computations using progressive tax rates would be needed. The blended rate
method also avoids the implication that items other than income from continuing
operations represented the "last dollars" earned, since the rates applicable to those
items would not be the highest marginal rates. On the other hand, the with-and-
without method averts the situation where the blended rate applied to income from
continuing operations is subject to wide variation due simply to the occasional existence of extraordinary and other unusual items.

On balance, and given the lack of a prescribed methodology in revised IAS 12,
the authors slightly favor the blended rate approach. Whichever methodology is
employed, however, it is vital that the notes to the financial statements clearly describe how the computation was made and disclose the tax effects of the various

components presented. Revised IAS 12 does, however, permit the tax effects of all extraordinary items to be presented in one amount, if computation of each extraordinary item is not readily accomplished.

Classification of Deferred Taxes

E49, which was the antecedent to revised IAS 12, stipulated that an enterprise that presents a classified balance sheet will categorize its deferred tax liabilities and assets as either current or noncurrent (1) consistent with the probable time of the recovery or settlement of the asset or liability with respect to assets and liabilities arising from current tax expense, and (2) based on the probable time of reversal of the underlying temporary differences with respect to deferred tax liabilities and assets arising from temporary differences. The final standard, however, has disavowed this approach.

Revised IAS 12 states that, when an enterprise prepares a classified balance sheet (separating current from noncurrent assets and liabilities), deferred tax assets and liabilities are never to be included in the current category. The standard does not explain the logic for this prohibition, but it may be that the prospect of requiring entities to assess the amount and pattern of temporary difference reversals proved daunting. In fact, the extent of this scheduling would have been rather limited, since the only concern would have been to assess whether the expected reversals would occur before or after the 1-year threshold. With an absolute rule, however, revised IAS 12 is undeniably easier to apply.

Deferred tax assets pertaining to certain tax jurisdictions may be fully or partially recognizable, while other such assets may not be recognized at all, based on application of the "probable" criterion to the expected timing and availability of taxable temporary differences and other items entering into the determination of taxable profit in each jurisdiction.

Tax assets and liabilities should not be offset in the balance sheet, except to the extent that they pertain to taxes levied by the same taxing authority and are similarly classified in the balance sheet (i.e., both being current or both being noncurrent).

Finally, when entities included in consolidated financial statements are taxed separately, a tax asset recognized by one member of the group should not be offset against a liability recognized by another member of the same group, unless a legal right of offset is enforceable. For example, in some jurisdictions the tax loss carryforward of an acquired affiliate entity cannot be used to reduce taxable profit of another member of the group, even if consolidated tax returns are being prepared. In such a case, the deferred tax asset recognized in connection with the tax loss carryforward cannot be offset against a deferred tax liability of another member of the consolidated group. Further, in evaluating whether realization of the tax asset is probable, the existence of the tax liability could not be considered.

Financial Statement Disclosures

Revised IAS 12 mandates a number of disclosures, including some which have not been required under earlier practice. The purpose of these disclosures, of course, is to provide the user with an understanding of the relationship between accounting profit and the related tax effects, as well as to aid in predicting future cash inflows or outflows related to tax effects of assets and liabilities already reflected in the balance sheet. Newly imposed disclosures are intended to provide greater insight into the relationship between deferred tax assets and liabilities recognized, the related tax expense or benefit recognized in earnings, and the underlying natures of the related temporary differences resulting in those items. There is also enhanced disclosure for discontinued operations under revised IAS 12. Finally, when deferred tax assets are given recognition under defined conditions, there will be disclosure of the nature of the evidence supporting recognition. The specific disclosures are presented in the following paragraphs in greater detail.

Balance sheet disclosures. A reporting entity is required to disclose the amount of a deferred tax asset and the nature of evidence supporting its recognition, when

1. Utilization of the deferred tax asset is dependent on future taxable profits in excess of the profits arising from the reversal of the existing taxable temporary differences; **and**
2. The enterprise has suffered a loss in the same tax jurisdiction to which the deferred tax assets relate in either the current or preceding period.

Income statement disclosures. Revised IAS 12 places primary emphasis on disclosure of the components of income tax expense or benefit. The following information must be disclosed about the components of tax expense for each year for which an income statement is presented.

The components of tax expense or benefit, which may include some or all of the following:

1. Current tax expense or benefit
2. Any adjustments recognized in the current period for taxes of prior periods
3. The amount of deferred tax expense or benefit relating to the origination and reversal of temporary differences
4. The amount of deferred tax expense or benefit relating to changes in tax rates or the imposition of new taxes
5. The amount of the tax benefit arising from a previously unrecognized tax loss, tax credit, or temporary difference of a prior period that is used to reduce current period tax expense
6. The amount of the tax benefit from a previously unrecognized tax loss, tax credit, or temporary difference of a prior period that is used to reduce deferred tax expense

7. Deferred tax expense arising from the write-down of a deferred tax asset because it is no longer deemed probable of realization

8. The amount of tax expense relating to changes in accounting policies and fundamental errors accounted for in accordance with the allowed alternative treatment stipulated by IAS 8 (i.e., by inclusion in income of the current period)

In addition to the foregoing, revised IAS 12 also requires that disclosures be made of the following items which are to be separately stated:

1. The aggregate current and deferred tax relating to items that are charged or credited to equity

2. Tax expense related to extraordinary items recognized during the period

3. The relationship between tax expense or benefit and accounting profit or loss either (or both) as

   a. A numerical reconciliation between tax expense or benefit and the product of accounting profit or loss times the applicable tax rate(s), with disclosure of how the rate(s) was determined; or

   b. A numerical reconciliation between the average effective tax rate and applicable rate, also with disclosure of how the applicable rate was determined

4. An explanation of changes in the applicable rate vs. the prior reporting period

5. The amount and date of expiration of unrecognized tax assets relating to deductible temporary differences, tax losses and tax credits

6. The aggregate amount of any temporary differences relating to investments in subsidiaries, branches, and associates and interests in joint ventures for which deferred liabilities have not been recognized

7. For each type of temporary difference, including unused tax losses and credits, disclosure of

   a. The amount of the deferred tax assets and liabilities included in each balance sheet presented; and

   b. The amount of deferred income or expense recognized in the income statement, if not otherwise apparent from changes in the balance sheets

8. Regarding discontinued operations, disclosure of the tax expense or benefit related to

   a. The gain or loss on discontinuance; and

   b. The profit or loss from the ordinary activities of the discontinued operation for the period and all prior periods presented.

Finally, in a new requirement, disclosure must be made of the amount of deferred tax asset and the evidence supporting its presentation in the balance sheet, when both these conditions exist: Utilization is dependent upon future profitability beyond that assured by the future reversal of taxable temporary differences, **and** the enterprise has suffered a loss in either the current period or the preceding period in the jurisdiction to which the deferred tax asset relates.

Examples of informative disclosures about income tax expense

The disclosure requirements imposed by revised IAS 12 are extensive and in some instances complicated. The following examples have been adapted from the standard itself, with some modifications.

Note: Income tax expense
Major components of the provisions for income taxes are as follows:

	2000	*2001*
Current tax expense	$75,500	$82,450
Deferred tax expense (benefit), relating to the origination and reversal of temporary differences	12,300	(16,275)
Effect on previously provided deferred tax assets and liabilities resulting from increase in statutory tax rates	--	7,600
Total tax provision for the period	$87,800	$73,775

The aggregate current and deferred income tax expense (benefit) which was charged (credited) to stockholder's equity for the periods

	2000	*2001*
Current tax, related to correction of fundamental error	$(5,200)	$ --
Deferred tax, related to revaluation of investments	--	45,000
Total	$(5,200)	$45,000

The relationship between tax expense and accounting profit is explained by the following reconciliations (*NOTE: Only one required*):

	2000	*2001*
Accounting profit	$167,907	$132,398
Tax at statutory rate (43% in 2000; 49% in 2001)	$ 72,200	$ 64,875
Tax effect of expenses which are not deductible:		
Charitable contributions	600	1,300
Civil fines imposed on the entity	15,000	
Effect on previously provided deferred tax assets and liabilities resulting from increase in statutory rates	--	7,600
Total tax provision for the period	$ 87,800	$ 73,775

	(%)	
	2000	*2001*
Statutory tax rate	43.0	49.0
Tax effect of expenses which are not deductible:		
Charitable contributions	0.4	1.0
Civil fines imposed on the entity	8.9	--
Effect on previously provided deferred tax assets and liabilities resulting from increase in statutory rates	--	5.7
Total tax provision for the period	52.3	55.7

In 2001, the federal government imposed a 14% surcharge on the income tax, which has affected 2001 current tax expense as well as the recorded amounts of deferred tax assets and liabilities, since when these benefits are ultimately received or settled, the new, higher tax rates will be applicable.

Deferred tax assets and liabilities included in the accompanying balance sheets as of December 31, 2000 and 2001 are as follows, as classified by categories of temporary differences:

	2000	*2001*
Accelerated depreciation for tax purposes	$ 26,890	$ 22,300
Liabilities for postretirement health care that are deductible only when paid	(15,675)	(19,420)
Product development costs deducted from taxable profits in prior years	2,500	--
Revaluation of fixed assets, net of accumulated depreciation	--	2,160
Deferred tax liability, net	$ 13,715	$ 5,040

APPENDIX

ACCOUNTING FOR INCOME TAXES IN INTERIM PERIODS

Interim Reporting

IAS 34, *Interim Financial Reporting*, established new requirements for interim reporting, while not making the reporting of interim results mandatory. While the DSOP preceding this standard's promulgation essentially endorsed a discrete approach (applying measurement principles to each interim period on a stand-alone basis), the final standard represents a judicious mix of integral and discrete viewpoints. As noted in the main body of this chapter, IAS 34 adopts an integral viewpoint with regard to income tax expense, as indeed was necessitated by the fact that taxing authorities almost universally apply their requirements to a full year, taken as a whole, with no attempt at interim measurement of results of operations.

In this appendix, supplementary guidance is offered, largely based on US GAAP, to assist in applying the principles of income tax accounting set forth in IAS 12 (revised) to interim periods when the enterprise elects (or is required by local law) to report on such as basis. This guidance should be understood as being illustrative rather than authoritative. Care should be taken in particular regarding areas of financial reporting which are guided by recently issued or revised international accounting standards (such as that for discontinuing operations).

The general consensus is that the appropriate perspective for interim period reporting is to view the interim period as an integral part of the year rather than as a discrete period. For purposes of computing income tax provisions, this objective is usually achieved by projecting income for the full annual period, computing the tax thereon, and applying the effective rate to the interim period income or loss, with quarterly (or monthly) revisions to the expected annual results and the tax effects thereof, as necessary.

Notwithstanding this general principle, however, there are certain complexities that arise only in the context of interim financial reporting. Included in this group of issues are (1) recognizing the tax benefits of losses based on expected earnings of later interim or annual periods, (2) reporting the benefits of net operating loss carryforwards in interim periods, and (3) reporting the effects of tax law changes in interim periods. Other matters requiring interpretation include the classification of deferred taxes on interim balance sheets and the allocation of interim period tax provisions between current and deferred expense.

Basic example of interim period accounting for income taxes

Andorra Woolens, Inc. estimates that accounting profit for the full fiscal year ending June 30, 2000, will be $400,000. The company expects amortization of goodwill for the year to be $30,000, the annual premium on an officer's life insurance policy is $12,000, and dividend income (from a less than 20% ownership interest) is expected to be $100,000. Under pertinent tax rules, goodwill is not amortizable and premiums paid on officer's life insurance is not an expense. Furthermore, there is a dividends received deduction of 70% for intercorporate investments of under 20%.

The company recognized income of $75,000 in the first quarter of the year. The deferred tax liability arises solely in connection with depreciation temporary differences; these differences totaled $150,000 at the beginning of the year and are projected to equal $280,000 at year end. The effective rate expected to apply to the reversal at both year beginning and year end is 34%. The change in the taxable temporary difference during the current interim period is $30,000.

Andorra Woolens must first calculate its estimated effective income tax rate for the year. This rate is computed using all the tax planning alternatives available to the company (e.g., tax credits, foreign rates, capital gains rates, etc.).

Estimated pretax accounting income		$ 400,000
Permanent differences:		
Add: Nondeductible officer's life		
insurance premium	$12,000	
Nondeductible amortization of		
organization costs	30,000	42,000
		442,000
Less: Dividends received deduction		
($100,000 x 70%)		(70,000)
Estimated "book" taxable income		372,000
Less: Change in taxable temporary difference		(130,000)
Estimated taxable income for the year		$ 242,000
Tax on estimated taxable income (see below)		$ 70,530
Effective tax rate for **current** tax provision		
[$70,530/(400,000 – 130,000)]		26.1%

Tax rate schedule			*Taxable*	
At least	*Not more than*	*Rate*	*income*	*Tax*
$ --	$50,000	15%	$ 50,000	$ 7,500
50,000	75,000	25%	25,000	6,250
75,000	--	34%	167,000	56,780
				$70,530

The deferred tax provision for the interim period should be based on the actual change in the temporary difference (depreciation, in this example) during the interim period. In this case the depreciation temporary difference grew by $30,000 during the period, and the expected tax rate that will apply to the reversal, in future years, is the marginal rate of 34%. Accordingly, the tax provision for the period is as follows:

"Ordinary" income for the interim period	$75,000
Less: Change in temporary difference	30,000
Net "ordinary" income	45,000
Applicable tax rate	26.1%
Current tax provision	$11,755
Tax effect of temporary difference ($30,000 x 34%)	10,200
Total provision	$21,955

Therefore, the entry necessary to record the income tax expense at the end of the first quarter is as follows:

Income tax expense	21,955	
Income taxes payable--current		11,755
Deferred tax liability		10,200

The financial statement presentation would remain the same as has been illustrated in prior examples.

In the second quarter, Andorra Woolens, Inc. revises its estimate of income for the full fiscal year. It now anticipates only $210,000 of book income, including only $75,000 of dividend income, because of dramatic changes in the national economy. Other permanent differences are still expected to total $42,000.

Estimated pretax accounting income		$ 210,000
Permanent differences:		
Add: Nondeductible officer's life insurance premium	$12,000	
Nondeductible amortization of organization		
costs	30,000	42,000
		252,000
Less: Dividends received deduction ($75,000 x 70%)		(52,500)
Estimated "book" taxable income		199,500
Less: Change in taxable temporary difference		(130,000)
Estimated taxable income for the year		$ 69,500
Tax on estimated taxable income (see below)		$ 12,375
Effective tax rate for **current** tax provision		
[$12,375/(210,000 – 130,000)]		15.5%

Tax rate schedule			Taxable	
At least	Not more than	Rate	income	Tax
$ --	$50,000	15%	$50,000	$ 7,500
50,000	75,000	25%	19,500	4,875
				$12,375

The actual earnings for the second quarter were $22,000, and the change in the temporary difference was only $10,000. The tax provision for the second quarter is computed as follows:

"Ordinary" income for the half year	$97,000
Less: Change in temporary difference	40,000
Net ordinary income	57,000
Applicable tax rate	15.5%
Current tax provision	$ 8,835
Tax effect of temporary difference ($40,000 x 34%)	13,600
Total provision	$22,435

Under the general principle that changes in estimate are reported prospectively, the results of prior quarters are not restated for changes in the estimated effective annual tax rate. Given the provision for current and deferred income taxes that was made in the first interim period, shown above, the following entry is required to record the income taxes as of the end of the second quarter:

Income tax expense	480	
Income taxes payable--current	2,920	
Deferred tax liability		3,400

The foregoing illustrates the basic problems encountered in applying the promulgated GAAP to interim reporting. In the following paragraphs, we discuss some items requiring modifications to the approach described above.

Net Operating Losses in Interim Periods

The tax effects of operating losses are treated no differently than any other temporary differences; if probable of being realized, the tax effects are reflected as deferred tax benefits in the period the loss is incurred. If not deemed probable, no tax effects are recognized; if the estimation of realizability changes in a later period, the deferred tax benefit is then recorded, with the offset being included in current period tax expense. However, given the desire to treat interim periods as integral parts of the annual period of which they are a component, the accounting treatment of net operating losses raises a number of issues. These include (1) calculation of the expected annual tax rate for purposes of interim period income tax provisions, and (2) recognition of an asset for the tax effects of a loss carryforward.

Carryforward from prior years. Loss carryforward benefits from prior years first given recognition (i.e., by recordation of a deferred tax benefit when none had been recognized in the period the loss was incurred) in interim periods are included in the ordinary tax provision. Common practice is to compute the expected annual effective tax rate on **ordinary** income at each interim reporting date, and use this rate to provide income taxes on ordinary income on a cumulative basis at each interim date. The tax effects of extraordinary items, discontinued operations, and other nonoperating categories were excluded from this computation; those tax effects are typically separately determined on a with-and-without basis, as explained later in this appendix.

Recognition of a previously unrecognized tax benefit should be included as a credit in the tax provision of the interim period when there is a reevaluation of the likelihood of future tax benefits being realized. Similarly, a reduction of the deferred tax benefit resulting from a revised judgment that the benefits are not probable of being realized would cause a catch-up adjustment to be included in the current interim period's ordinary tax provision. In either situation, the effect is **not** prorated to future interim periods by means of the effective tax rate estimate. To illustrate, consider the following example.

Example of carryforward from prior years

Dacca Corporation has a previously unrecognized $50,000 net operating loss carryforward; a flat 40% tax rate for current and future periods is assumed. Income for the full year (before NOL) is projected to be $80,000; in the first quarter a pretax loss of $10,000 will be reported.

Projected annual income	$80,000
x Tax rate	40%
Projected tax liability	$32,000

Accordingly, in the income statement for the first fiscal quarter, the pretax operating loss of $10,000 will give rise to a tax **benefit** of $10,000 x 40% = $4,000.

In addition, a tax benefit of $20,000 ($50,000 loss carryforward x 40%) is given recognition and is included in the current interim period tax provision relating to continuing operations. Thus, total tax benefit for the first fiscal quarter will be $24,000 (= $4,000 + $20,000).

If Dacca's second quarter results in a pretax operating income of $30,000, and the expectation for the full year remains unchanged (i.e., operating income of $80,000), the second quarter tax provision is $12,000 ($30,000 x 40%).

The tax provision for the fiscal first half-year will be a benefit of $12,000, as follows:

Cumulative pretax income through second quarter ($30,000 – $10,000)	$ 20,000
x Effective rate	40%
Tax provision before recognition of NOL carryforward benefit	$ 8,000
Benefit of NOL carryforward first recognized in first quarter	(20,000)
Total tax provision (benefit)	$(12,000)

The foregoing example assumes that during the first quarter, Dacca's judgment changed as to the full realizability of the previously unrecognized benefit of the $50,000 loss carryforward. Were this **not** the case, however, the benefit would have been recognized only as actual tax liabilities were incurred (through current period earnings) in amounts to offset the NOL benefit.

To illustrate the latter situation, assume the same facts about earnings for the first two quarters, and assume now that Dacca's judgment about realizability of prior period NOL does not change. Tax provisions for the first quarter and first half are as follows:

	First quarter	*First half-year*
Pretax income (loss)	$(10,000)	$20,000
x Effective rate	40%	40%
Tax provision before recognition of NOL carryforward benefit	$ (4,000)	$ 8,000
Benefit of NOL carryforward recognized	-0-	(8,000)
Tax provision (benefit)	$ (4,000)	$ -0-

Notice that recognition of a tax benefit of $4,000 in the first quarter is based on the expectation of at least a breakeven full year's results. That is, the benefit of the first quarter's loss was deemed probable of realization. Otherwise, no tax benefit would have been reported in the first quarter.

Estimated loss for the year. When the full year is expected to be profitable, it will be irrelevant that one or more interim periods results in a loss, and the expected effective rate for the full year should be used to record interim period tax benefits, as illustrated above. However, when the full year is expected to produce a loss, computation of the expected annual tax benefit rate must logically take into account the extent to which a deferred tax asset will be recordable at year end. For the first set of examples, below, assume that the realization of tax benefits related to operating loss carryforwards are not entirely probable. That is, only a portion of the benefits will be recognized.

For each of the following examples we assume that the L'avventura Corporation is anticipating a loss for the fiscal year of $150,000. A deferred tax liability of $30,000 is currently recorded on the company's books; all of the credits will reverse in the 15-year carryforward period permitted by applicable tax law. Assume that future taxes will be at a 40% rate.

Example 1

Assume that the company can carry back the entire $150,000 to the preceding 3 years. The tax potentially refundable by the carryback would (remember, this is only an estimate until year end) amount to $48,000 (an assumed amount). The effective rate is then 32% ($48,000/150,000).

	Ordinary income (loss)			*Tax (benefit) expense*	
				Less	
Reporting	*Reporting*	*Year-to-*	*Year-to-*	*previously*	*Reporting*
period	*period*	*date*	*date*	*provided*	*period*
1st qtr.	$ (50,000)	$ (50,000)	$(16,000)	$ --	$(16,000)
2nd qtr.	20,000	(30,000)	(9,600)	(16,000)	6,400
3rd qtr.	(70,000)	(100,000)	(32,000)	(9,600)	(22,400)
4th qtr.	(50,000)	(150,000)	(48,000)	(32,000)	(16,000)
Fiscal year	$(150,000)				$(48,000)

Note that both the income tax expense (2nd quarter) and benefit are computed using the estimated annual effective rate. This rate is applied to the year-to-date numbers just as in the previous examples, with any adjustment being made and realized in the current reporting period. This treatment is appropriate because the accrual of tax benefits in the first, third, and fourth quarters is consistent with the effective rate estimated at the beginning of the year; in contrast to those circumstances in which a change in estimate is made in a quarter relating to the realizability of tax benefits not provided previously (or provided for only partially).

Example 2

In this case assume that L'avventura Corporation can carry back only $50,000 of the loss and that the remainder must be carried forward. Realization of income to offset the loss is not deemed to be probable. The estimated carryback of $50,000 would generate a tax refund of $12,000 (again assumed). The company is assumed to be in the 40% tax bracket (a flat rate is used to simplify the example). The benefit of the operating loss carryforward is recognized only to the extent that it is deemed to be probable of realization. In this example, management has concluded that only one-fourth of the gross benefit will be realized in future years. Accordingly, only $10,000 of estimated tax benefit related to the carryforward of the projected loss is recordable. Considered in conjunction with the carryback of $12,000, the company will obtain a $22,000 tax benefit relating to the projected current year loss, for an effective tax benefit rate of 14.7%. The calculation of the estimated annual effective rate is as follows:

Expected net loss		$150,000
Tax benefit from carryback	$12,000	
Benefit of carryforward		
($100,000 x 40%)	$40,000	
Portion not deemed to be		
probable of realization	(30,000)	10,000
Total recognized benefit		$ 22,000
Estimated annual effective rate		
($22,000 ÷ 150,000)		14.7%

	Ordinary income (loss)			*Tax (benefit) expense*			
				Year-to-date		*Less*	
Reporting	*Reporting*	*Year-to-*			*Limited*	*previously*	*Reporting*
period	*period*	*date*	*Computed*		*to*	*provided*	*period*
1st qtr.	$ 10,000	$ 10,000	$ 1,470	$ --	$ --	$ 1,470
2nd qtr.	(80,000)	(70,000)	(11,733)	--	1,470	(10,263)
3rd qtr.	(100,000)	(170,000)	(14,667)	(22,000)	(10,263)	(4,404)
4th qtr.	20,000	(150,000)	(22,000)	--	(22,000)	--
Fiscal year	$(150,000)					$(22,000)

In the foregoing, the tax expense (benefit) is computed by multiplying the year-to-date income or loss by the estimated annual effective rate, and then subtracting the amount of tax liability or benefit provided in prior interim periods. It makes no difference if the current period indicates an income or a loss, assuming of course that the full-year estimated results are not being revised. However, if the cumulative loss for the interim periods to date exceeds the projected loss for the full year on which the effective tax benefit rate had been based, no further tax benefits can be recorded, as illustrated above in the provision for the third quarter.

Operating loss occurring during an interim period. An instance may occur in which the company expects net income for the year and incurs a net loss during one of the reporting periods. In this situation, the estimated annual effective rate, which was calculated based on the expected net income figure, is applied to the year-to-date income or loss to arrive at a total year-to-date tax provision. The amount previously provided is subtracted from the year-to-date figure to arrive at the provision for the current reporting period. If the current period operations resulted in a loss, the tax provision for the period will reflect a tax benefit.

Tax Provision Applicable to Discontinuing Operations or Extraordinary Items Occurring in Interim Periods

Extraordinary items. Extraordinary items and discontinuing operations are to be shown net of their related tax effects. The interim treatment accorded these items does not differ from the fiscal year-end reporting required by GAAP. However, common practice is not to include these items in computation of the estimated annual tax rate. These items are generally recognized in the interim period in which they occur; that is, they are not annualized. Recognition of the tax effects of a loss due to any of the aforementioned situations would be made if the benefits are expected to be realized during the year or if they will be recognizable as a deferred tax asset at year end under the provisions of revised IAS 12.

If a situation arises where realization is not probable in the period of occurrence but becomes assured in a subsequent period in the same fiscal year, the previously unrecognized tax benefit should be reported in income from continuing operations until it reduces the tax provision to zero, with any excess reported in other categories of income (e.g., discontinuing operations) that provided a means of realization for the tax benefit.

The following examples illustrate the treatment required for reporting extraordinary items. Again, these items are **not** to be used in calculating the estimated annual tax rate. For income statement presentation purposes, extraordinary items are shown net of their applicable tax provision.

The following data apply to the next two examples:

1. Dynamix Company expects fiscal year ending June 30, 2000, income to be $96,000 and net permanent differences to reduce taxable income by $25,500.
2. Dynamix Company also incurred a $30,000 extraordinary loss in the second quarter of the year.

Example 1

In this case, assume that the loss can be carried back to prior periods, and therefore the realization of any tax benefit is assured. Based on the information given earlier, the estimated annual effective tax rate can be calculated as follows:

Expected pretax accounting income	$96,000
Anticipated permanent differences	(25,500)
Expected taxable income	$70,500

Tax Calculation "Excluding" Extraordinary Item

$50,000	x	0.15	=	$ 7,500
20,500	x	0.25	=	5,125
$70,500				$12,625

Effective annual rate = 13.15% ($12,625 ÷ 96,000)

No adjustment in the estimated annual effective rate is required when the extraordinary, unusual, or infrequent item occurs. The tax (benefit) applicable to the item is computed using the estimated fiscal year ordinary income and an analysis of the incremental impact of the extraordinary item. The method illustrated below is applicable when the company anticipates operating income for the year. When a loss is anticipated but realization of benefits of loss carryforwards is not probable, the company computes its estimated annual effective rate based on the amount of tax to be refunded from prior years. The tax (benefit) applicable to the extraordinary item is then the decrease (increase) in the refund to be received.

Computation of the tax applicable to the extraordinary item is as follows:

Estimated pretax accounting income	$96,000
Permanent differences	(25,500)
Extraordinary item	(30,000)
Expected taxable income	$40,500

Tax Calculation "Including" Extraordinary Item

$$\underline{\$40,500} \ \times \ 0.15 \ = \ \underline{\$6,075}$$

Tax "excluding" extraordinary item	$12,625
Tax "including" extraordinary item	6,075
Tax benefit applicable to extraordinary item	$ 6,550

			Tax (benefit) applicable to				
			Ordinary income (loss)		*Extraordinary item*		
Reporting period	*Ordinary income (loss)*	*Extraordinary item*	*Reporting period*	*Year-to-date*	*Year-to-date*	*Previously provided*	*Reporting period*
1st qtr.	$10,000	$ --	$ 1,315	$ 1,315	$ --	$ --	$ --
2nd qtr.	(20,000)	(30,000)	(2,630)	(1,315)	(6,550)	--	(6,550)
3rd qtr.	40,000	--	5,260	3,945	(6,550)	(6,550)	--
4th qtr.	66,000	--	8,680	12,625	(6,550)	(6,550)	--
Fiscal year	$96,000	$(30,000)	$12,625				$(6,550)

Example 2

Again, assume that Dynamix Company estimates net income of $96,000 for the year with permanent differences of $25,500 that reduce taxable income. The extraordinary loss of $30,000 cannot be carried back and the ability to carry it forward is not probable. Because no deferred tax credits exist, the only way that the loss can be deemed to be realizable is to the extent that current year ordinary income offsets the effect of the loss. As a result, realization of the loss is assured only as, and to the extent that, there is ordinary income for the year.

			Tax (benefit) applicable to				
			Ordinary income (loss)		*Extraordinary item*		
Reporting period	*Ordinary income (loss)*	*Extraordinary item*	*Reporting period*	*Year-to-date*	*Year-to-date*	*Previously provided*	*Reporting period*
1st qtr.	$ 5,000	$ --	$ 658	$ 658	$ --	$ --	$ --
2nd qtr.	20,000	(30,000)	2,630	3,288	(3,288)[a]	--	(3,288)
3rd qtr.	(10,000)	--	(1,315)	1,973	(1,973)[a]	(3,288)	1,315
4th qtr.	81,000	--	10,652	12,625	(6,550)[a]	(1,973)	(4,577)
Fiscal year	$96,000	$(30,000)	$12,625				$(6,550)

[a]*The recognition of the tax benefit to be realized relative to the extraordinary item is limited to the lesser of the total tax benefit applicable to the item or the amount available to be realized. Because realization is based on the amount of tax applicable to ordinary income during the period, the year-to-date figures for the tax benefit fluctuate as the year-to-date tax expense relative to ordinary income fluctuates. Note that at no point does the amount of the tax benefit exceed what was calculated above as being applicable to the extraordinary item.*

Discontinuing operations in interim periods. The computations described for extraordinary items will also apply to the income (loss) from the discontinuing segment, including any provisions for operating gains (losses) subsequent to the measurement date.

If the decision to dispose of operations occurs in any interim period other than the first period, the operating income (loss) applicable to the discontinuing segment has already been used in computing the estimated annual effective tax rate. Therefore, a recomputation of the **total tax** is not required. However, the total tax is to be divided into two components.

1. That tax applicable to ordinary income (loss)
2. That tax applicable to the income (loss) from the discontinuing segment

This division is accomplished as follows: A revised estimated annual effective rate is calculated for the income (loss) from ordinary operations. This recomputation is then applied to the ordinary income (loss) from the preceding periods. The total tax applicable to the discontinuing segment is then composed of two items.

1. The difference between the total tax originally computed and the tax recomputed on remaining ordinary income
2. The tax computed on unusual, infrequent, or extraordinary items as described above

Example

Realtime Corporation anticipates net income of $150,000 during the fiscal year. The net permanent differences for the year will be $10,000. The company also anticipates tax credits of $10,000 during the fiscal year. For purposes of this example, we assume a flat statutory rate of 50%. The estimated annual effective rate is then calculated as follows:

Estimated pretax income	$150,000
Net permanent differences	(10,000)
Taxable income	140,000
Statutory rate	50%
Tax	70,000
Anticipated credits	(10,000)
Total estimated tax	$ 60,000
Estimated effective rate ($60,000 ÷ 150,000)	40%

The first two quarters of operations were as follows:

Reporting period	Ordinary income (loss) Reporting period	Year-to-date	Tax provision Year-to-date	Less previously provided	Reporting period
1st qtr.	$30,000	$30,000	$12,000	$ --	$12,000
2nd qtr.	25,000	55,000	22,000	12,000	10,000

In the third quarter, Realtime made the decision to dispose of Division X. During the third quarter, the company earned a total of $60,000. The company expects the disposal to result in a one-time charge to income of $50,000 and estimates that operating losses subsequent to the disposal will be $25,000. The company estimates revised ordinary income in the fourth quarter to be $35,000. The two components of pretax accounting income (discontinuing operations and revised ordinary income) are shown below.

| Reporting period | Revised ordinary income | Division X | |
		Loss from operations	Provision for loss on disposal
1st qtr.	$ 40,000	$(10,000)	$ --
2nd qtr.	40,000	(15,000)	--
3rd qtr.	80,000	(20,000)	(75,000)
4th qtr.	35,000	--	--
Fiscal year	$195,000	$(45,000)	$(75,000)

Realtime must now recompute the estimated annual tax rate. Assume that all the permanent differences are related to the revised continuing operations. However, $3,300 of the tax credits were applicable to machinery used in Division X. Because of the discontinuance of operations, the credit on this machinery would not be allowed. Any recapture of prior-period credits must be used as a reduction in the tax benefit from either operations or the loss on disposal. Assume that the company must recapture $2,000 of investment tax credit which is related to Division X.

The recomputed estimated annual rate for continuing operations is as follows:

Estimated (revised) ordinary income	$195,000
Less net permanent differences	(10,000)
	$185,000
Tax at statutory rate of 50%	$ 92,500
Less anticipated credits from continuing operations	(6,700)
Tax provision	$ 85,800
Estimated annual effective tax rate ($85,800 ÷ 195,000)	44%

The next step is then to apply the revised rate to the quarterly income from continuing operations as illustrated below.

| Reporting period | Ordinary income | | Estimated annual effective rate | Tax provision | | |
	Reporting period	Year-to-date		Year-to-date	Less previously provided	Reporting period
1st qtr.	$ 40,000	$ 40,000	44%	$17,600	$ --	$17,600
2nd qtr.	40,000	80,000	44%	35,200	17,600	17,600
3rd qtr.	80,000	160,000	44%	70,400	35,200	35,200
4th qtr.	35,000	195,000	44%	85,800	70,400	15,400
Fiscal year	$195,000					$85,800

The tax benefit applicable to the operating loss from discontinuing operations and the loss from the disposal must now be calculated. The first two quarters are calculated on a differential basis as shown below.

| Reporting period | Tax applicable to ordinary income | | Tax (benefit) expense applicable to Division X |
	Previously reported	Recomputed (above)	
1st qtr.	$12,000	$17,600	$ (5,600)
2nd qtr.	10,000	17,600	(7,600)
			$(13,200)

The only calculation remaining applies to the third quarter tax benefit pertaining to the operating loss and the loss on disposal of the discontinuing segment. The calculation of this amount is made based on the revised estimate of annual ordinary income, both including and excluding the effects of the Division X losses. This is shown below.

	Loss from operations of Division X	Provision for loss on disposal
Estimated annual income from continuing operations	$195,000	$195,000
Net permanent differences	(10,000)	(10,000)
Loss from Division X operations	(45,000)	--
Provision for loss on disposal of Division X	--	(75,000)
Total	$140,000	$110,000
Tax at the statutory rate of 50%	$ 70,000	$ 55,000
Anticipated credits (from continuing operations)	(6,700)	(6,700)
Recapture of previously recognized tax credits as a result of disposal	--	2,000
Taxes after effect of Division X losses	63,300	50,300
Taxes computed on estimated income before the effect of Division X losses	85,800	85,800
Tax benefit applicable to Division X	(22,500)	(35,500)
Amounts recognized in quarters one and two ($5,600 + $7,600)	(13,200)	--
Tax benefit to be recognized in the third quarter	$ (9,300)	$(35,500)

The quarterly tax provisions can be summarized as follows:

	Pretax income (loss)			Tax (benefit) applicable to		
Reporting period	Continuing operations	Operations of Division X	Provision for loss on disposal	Continuing operations	Operations of Division X	Provision for loss on disposal
1st qtr.	$ 40,000	$(10,000)	$ --	$17,600	$ (5,600)	$ --
2nd qtr.	40,000	(15,000)	--	17,600	(7,600)	--
3rd qtr.	80,000	(20,000)	(75,000)	35,200	(9,300)	(35,500)
4th qtr.	35,000	--	--	15,400	--	--
Fiscal year	$195,000	$(45,000)	$(75,000)	$85,800	$(22,500)	$(35,500)

The following income statement shows the proper financial statement presentation of these unusual and infrequent items. The notes to the statement indicate which items are to be included in the calculation of the annual estimated rate.

Income Statement

Net sales*		$xxxx
Other income*		<u>xxx</u>
		xxxx
Costs and expenses		
Cost of sales*	$xxxx	
Selling, general, and administrative expenses*	xxx	
Interest expense*	xx	
Other deductions*	xx	
Unusual items	xxx	
Infrequently occurring items	<u>xxx</u>	<u>xxxx</u>
Income (loss) from continuing operations before income		
taxes and other items listed below		xxxx
Provision for income taxes (benefit)**		<u>xxx</u>
Income (loss) from continuing operations before items listed below		xxxx
Discontinuing operations:		
Income (loss) from operations of discontinuing Division X		
(less applicable income taxes of $xxxx)	xxxx	
Income (loss) on disposal of Division X, including provision		
of $xxxx for operating losses during phase-out period (less		
applicable taxes of $xxxx)	<u>xxxx</u>	<u>xxxx</u>
Income (loss) before extraordinary items and cumulative effect		
of a change in accounting principle		xxxx
Extraordinary items (less applicable income taxes of $xxxx)		xxxx
Cumulative effect on prior years of a change in accounting		
principle (less applicable income taxes of $xxxx***)		<u>xxxx</u>
Net income (loss)		$<u>xxxx</u>

---

   * *Components of ordinary income (loss).*

  ** *Consists of total income taxes (benefit) applicable to ordinary income (loss), unusual items, and infrequent items.*

*** *This amount is shown net of income taxes. Although the income taxes are generally disclosed (as illustrated), this is not required.*

16 ACCOUNTING FOR EMPLOYEE BENEFITS

PERSPECTIVE AND ISSUES

With the release of the revised IAS 19 in early 1998, international accounting standards on postemployment benefit costs have completed three iterations. The new standard not only provides much broader coverage--it addresses not merely pensions, but all forms of employee benefits--it largely conforms with standards established by major national standard setters and eliminates alternatives, the existence of which were deemed to be impediments to the IASC's completion of its core set of standards project. IAS 19 (revised 1998) is effective for periods beginning after 1998, replacing the previous IAS 19 (revised 1993), which in turn superseded the original 1983 standard.

IAS 19 (revised 1998) significantly expands the requirements under IAS for accounting for the cost of not only pensions but of a range of other postemployment benefits commonly offered to employees or mandated by laws and regulations. It both narrows the range of acceptable alternatives available under prior IAS 19 and enlarges the set of informative disclosures. Among other important changes, the new standard eliminates all projected benefit valuation methods and permits only a single variant (usually known as the "projected unit credit" method) of the accrued benefit valuation method. It also creates a "corridor" approach to recognition of actuarial gains and losses, requires annual valuations vs. the earlier mandate for triennial valuations, and addresses past service cost recognition and other matters never dealt with by the earlier standards.

The former standard was stated to apply to all pension schemes, whether formal or informal, and also was to be utilized in developing the accounting for similar types of benefit programs. However, that standard was not very precise in defining the extent to which components of pension cost were to be disclosed in the financial statements, and also permitted a fair amount of latitude to preparers when it came to amortizing certain cost elements, such as those associated with plan amendments. The newly promulgated IAS 19 (revised 1998) represents a great improvement over its predecessor in regard to both of these matters.

IAS 19 (revised 1998) identifies and provides accounting direction for five categories of employee benefits: short-term benefits such as wages, bonuses, and emoluments such as medical care; postemployment benefits such as pensions and other postretirement benefits; other long-term benefits such as sabbatical leave; termination benefits; and equity compensation arrangements. The new standard departs from its predecessors by providing some guidance on all of these, whereas the earlier standards focused only on pensions. However, IAS 19 (revised 1998) provides its most explicitly detailed instructions with regard to defined benefit pension and other postretirement benefits plans, and relatively little as to the other types of employee benefits, particularly as to stock compensation arrangements.

Of the two major classes of pension plans, defined contribution and defined benefit, accounting for the latter is by far the more difficult. Given the central role that accounting estimates play in the accounting for defined benefit plans, some diversity will always be implicit in financial reporting, and full disclosure of key assumptions and methods is the best prescription to prevent misleading financial statement users. Due to the long-term nature of employee benefit plans, IAS 19 provides for delayed recognition of certain cost components, such as those resulting from changes in actuarial estimates (i.e., changes are not recognized immediately but are recognized subsequently in a gradual and systematic way). Estimates and averages may be used as long as material differences do not result. Explicit assumptions and estimates of future events should be used for each specified variable included in pension costs.

The principal emphasis of IAS 19 is on the calculation of the present value of the pension obligation, with somewhat less attention being directed toward determining the fair value of plan assets and on structuring the disclosure of the elements of periodic pension costs. The main accounting problems revolve around the amount to be expensed on the income statement and the amount to be accrued on the balance sheet.

IAS 19 also establishes requirements for disclosures to be made by employers when defined contribution or defined benefit pension plans are settled, curtailed, or terminated. Some previously unrecognized amounts are required to be recognized immediately under such circumstances.

IAS 19 (revised 1998) also devotes attention to the accounting for other postemployment benefit plans, which was at best implicit in the earlier standard and was not expressly dealt with. All postemployment benefits other than pensions are defined benefit plans and, thus, all the complications of defined benefit pension plans exist here as well; compounded, in the case of postretirement health care programs, by the need to project health care cost escalations over a lengthy time horizon.

Equity compensation plans, such as those inherent in stock option programs, pose particular problems, and attempts to deal with the accounting issues pertaining to these plans have been subject to much controversy. IAS 19 (revised 1998) establishes certain disclosure requirements but does not attempt to resolve recognition or measurement issues.

Sources of IAS
IAS 19 (revised 1998)

DEFINITIONS OF TERMS

Accrued benefit obligation. Actuarial present value of benefits (whether vested or nonvested) attributed by the pension benefit formula to employee service rendered before a specified date and based on employee service and compensation (if applicable) prior to that date. IAS 19 (revised 1998) requires that only the accrued benefit method be used to compute employee benefit obligations.

Accrued benefit valuation methods. Actuarial valuation methods that reflect retirement benefits based on service rendered by employees to the date of the valuation. Assumptions about projected salary levels to the date of retirement must be incorporated, but service to be rendered after the balance sheet date is not.

Accrued pension cost. Cumulative net pension cost accrued in excess of the employer's contributions.

Accrued postretirement benefit obligation. The actuarial present value of benefits attributed to employee service rendered to a particular date. Prior to an employee's full eligibility date, the accrued postretirement benefit obligation as of a particular date for an employee is the portion of the expected postretirement benefit obligation attributed to that employee's service rendered to that date. On and after the full eligibility date, the accrued and expected postretirement benefit obligations for an employee are the same.

Actuarial present value. Value, as of a specified date, of an amount or series of amounts payable or receivable thereafter, with each amount adjusted to reflect (1) the time value of money (through discounts for interest) and (2) the probability of payment (by means of decrements for events such as death, disability, withdrawal, or retirement) between the date specified and the expected date of payment.

Actuarial valuation. The process used by actuaries to estimate the present value of benefits to be paid under a retirement plan and the present values of plan assets and sometimes also of future contributions.

Amortization. Usually refers to the process of reducing a recognized liability systematically by recognizing revenues or reducing a recognized asset systematically by recognizing expenses or costs. In pension accounting, amortization is also used to refer to the systematic recognition in net pension cost over several periods of previously unrecognized amounts, including unrecognized prior service cost and unrecognized net gain or loss.

Attribution. Process of assigning pension benefits or cost to periods of employee service.

Career-average-pay formula (career-average-pay plan). Benefit formula that bases benefits on the employee's compensation over the entire period of service with the employer. A career-average-pay plan is a plan with such a formula.

Contributory plan. Pension plan under which employees contribute part of the cost. In some contributory plans, employees wishing to be covered must contribute; in other contributory plans, employee contributions result in increased benefits.

Current service cost. The cost to the employer under a retirement benefit plan for the services rendered by employees during the period, exclusive of cost elements identified as past service cost, experience adjustments, and the effects of changes in actuarial assumptions.

Curtailment. Event that significantly reduces the expected years of future service of present employees or eliminates, for a significant number of employees, the accrual of defined benefits for some or all of their future services. Curtailments include (1) termination of employee's services earlier than expected, which may or may not involve closing a facility or discontinuing a segment of a business, and (2) termination or suspension of a plan so that employees do not earn additional defined benefits for future services. In the latter situation, future service may be counted toward vesting of benefits accumulated based on past services.

Defined benefit pension plan. Defined by IAS 19 (revised 1998) as any postemployment benefit plan other than a defined contribution plan. These are generally retirement benefit plans under which amounts to be paid as retirement benefits are determinable, usually by reference to employees' earnings and/or years of service. The fund (and/or employer) is obligated, either legally or constructively, to pay the full amount of promised benefits whether or not sufficient assets are held in the fund.

Defined contribution pension plan. Benefit plans under which amounts to be paid as retirement benefits are determined by the contributions to a fund together with accumulated investment earnings thereon; the plan has no obligation to pay further sums if the amounts available cannot pay all benefits relating to employee services in the current and prior periods.

Employee benefits. All forms of consideration to employees in exchange for services rendered.

Equity compensation benefits. Benefits under which employees are entitled to receive employer's equity financial instruments, or which compensate employees based on the future value of such instruments.

Equity compensation plans. Formal or informal arrangements to provide equity compensation benefits.

Expected long-term rate of return on plan assets. Assumption as to the rate of return on plan assets reflecting the average rate of earnings expected on the funds invested, or to be invested, to provide for the benefits included in the projected benefit obligation.

Expected postretirement benefit obligation. The actuarial present value as of a particular date of the benefits expected to be paid to or for an employee, the employee's beneficiaries, and any covered dependents pursuant to the terms of the postretirement benefit plan.

Expected return on plan assets. Amount calculated as a basis for determining the extent of delayed recognition of the effects of changes in the fair value of assets. The expected return on plan assets is determined based on the expected long-term rate of return on plan assets and the market related value of plan assets.

Experience adjustments. Adjustments to benefit costs arising from the differences between the previous actuarial assumptions as to future events and what actually occurred.

Fair value. Amount that an asset could be exchanged for between willing, knowledgeable parties in an arm's-length transaction.

Final-pay plan. A defined benefit plan that promises benefits based on the employee's remuneration at or near the date of retirement. It may be the compensation of the final year, or of a specified number of years near the end of the employee's service period.

Flat-benefit formula (flat-benefit plan). Benefit formula that bases benefits on a fixed amount per year of service, such as $20 of monthly retirement income for each year of credited service. A flat-benefit plan is a plan with such a formula.

Fund. Used as a verb, to pay over to a funding agency (as to fund future pension benefits or to fund pension cost). Used as a noun, assets accumulated in the hands of a funding agency for the purpose of meeting pension benefits when they become due.

Funding. The irrevocable transfer of assets to an entity separate from the employer's enterprise, to meet future obligations for the payment of retirement benefits.

Gain or loss. Change in the value of either the projected benefit obligation or the plan assets resulting from experience different from that assumed or from a change in an actuarial assumption.

Interest cost component (of net periodic pension cost). Increase in the present value of the accrued benefit obligation due to the passage of time.

Measurement date. Date as of which plan assets and obligations are measured.

Mortality rate. Proportion of the number of deaths in a specified group to the number living at the beginning of the period in which the deaths occur. Actuaries use mortality tables, which show death rates for each age, in estimating the amount of pension benefits that will become payable.

Net periodic pension cost. Amount recognized in an employer's financial statements as the cost of a pension plan for a period. Components of net periodic pension cost are service cost, interest cost (which is implicitly presented as part of service cost), actual return on plan assets, gain or loss, amortization of unrecognized prior service cost, and amortization of the unrecognized net obligation or asset existing at the date of initial application of IAS 19.

Other long-term employee benefits. Benefits other than postemployment, termination and stock equity compensation benefits, which do not fall due wholly within 1 year of the end of the period in which service was rendered.

Past service cost. The actuarially determined cost arising on the introduction of a retirement benefit plan, on the making of improvements to such a plan, or on the completion of minimum service requirements for eligibility in such a plan, all of which give employees credit for benefits for service prior to the occurrence of one or more of these events.

Pay-as-you-go. A method of recognizing the cost of retirement benefits only at the time that cash payments are made to employees on or after retirement.

Plan assets. Assets held by an entity which is legally separate from the reporting enterprise, that are held for settlement of employee benefit obligations, are not available to reporting entity's creditors, and cannot be returned to the enterprise unless determined to be in excess of those needed for employee benefits payments.

Plan amendment. Change in terms of an existing plan or the initiation of a new plan. A plan amendment may increase benefits, including those attributed to years of service already rendered.

Postretirement benefits. All forms of benefits, other than retirement income, provided by an employer to retirees. Those benefits may be defined in terms of specified benefits, such as health care, tuition assistance, or legal services, that are provided to retirees as the need for those benefits arises, or they may be defined in terms of monetary amounts that become payable on the occurrence of a specified event, such as life insurance benefits.

Prepaid pension cost. Cumulative employer contributions in excess of accrued net pension cost.

Prior service cost. Cost of retroactive benefits granted in a plan amendment.

Projected benefit obligation. The actuarial present value as of a date of all benefits attributed by the pension benefit formula to employee service rendered prior to that date. The projected benefit obligation is measured using assumptions as to future compensation levels if the pension benefit formula is based on those future compensation levels (pay-related, final-pay, final-average-pay, or career-average-pay plans).

Projected benefit valuation methods. Actuarial valuation methods that reflect retirement benefits based on service both rendered and to be rendered by employees, as of the date of the valuation. Contrasted with accumulated benefit valuation methods, projected benefit valuation methods will result in a more level assignment of costs to the periods of employee service, although this will not necessarily be a straight-line allocation. Assumptions about projected salary levels must be incorporated. This was the allowed alternative method under IAS 19 (revised 1993), but is prohibited under newly promulgated IAS 19 (revised 1998).

Retirement benefit plans. Formal or informal arrangements whereby employers provide benefits for employees on or after termination of service, when such benefits can be determined or estimated in advance of retirement from the provisions of a document or from the employers' practices.

Retroactive benefits. Benefits granted in a plan amendment (or initiation) that are attributed by the pension benefit formula to employee services rendered in periods prior to the amendment. The cost of the retroactive benefits is referred to as prior service cost.

Return on plan assets. Interest, dividends and other revenues derived from plan assets, together with realized and unrealized gains or losses on the assets, less administrative costs including taxes payable by the plan.

Service. Employment taken into consideration under a pension plan. Years of employment before the inception of a plan constitute an employee's past service; years thereafter are classified in relation to the particular actuarial valuation being made or discussed. Years of employment (including past service) prior to the date of a particular valuation constitute prior service.

Settlement. Transaction that (1) is an irrevocable action, (2) relieves the employer (or the plan) of primary responsibility for a pension benefit obligation, and (3) eliminates significant risks related to the obligation and the assets used to effect the settlement. Examples include making lump-sum cash payments to plan participants in exchange for their rights to receive specified pension benefits and purchasing nonparticipating annuity contracts to cover vested benefits.

Short-term employee benefits. Benefits other than termination and equity compensation benefits which are due within 1 year after the end of the period in which the employees rendered the related service.

Terminal funding. A method of recognizing the projected cost of retirement benefits only at the time an employee retires.

Termination benefits. Employee benefits payable as a result of the entity's termination of employment before normal retirement or the employee's acceptance of early retirement inducements.

Unrecognized prior service cost. Portion of prior service cost that has not been recognized as a part of net periodic pension cost.

Vested benefits. Those benefits, the rights to which, under the conditions of a retirement benefit plan, are not conditional on continued employment.

CONCEPTS, RULES, AND EXAMPLES

Importance of Pension and Other Benefit Plan Accounting

For a variety of cultural, economic, and political reasons, the existence of private pension plans has increased tremendously over the past 30 years, and these arrangements are the most common "fringe benefit" offered by employers in many nations. For many employers, pension costs have become a very material component of compensation paid to employees and can represent an even bigger fraction of the reporting entity's net operating results. Unlike the case with wages, the timing of the payment of cash, to either the plan's administrators or its beneficiaries, can vary substantially from the underlying economic event. This creates the possibility of misleading financial statement presentation of the true costs of conducting business. For this reason, accounting for the cost of pension plans and similar schemes (postretirement benefits other than pensions, etc.) has received a great deal of attention from national and international standards setters.

Basic Objectives of Accounting for Pension and Other Benefit Plan Costs

Need for pension accounting rules. The principal objectives of pension accounting are to measure the compensation cost associated with employees' benefits and to recognize that cost over the employees' service period. The relevant international accounting standard, IAS 19 (revised 1998), is concerned only with the accounting aspects of pensions (and other benefit plans); the funding of pension benefits is considered to be a financial management matter and, accordingly, is not addressed by this pronouncement.

When an entity provides benefits, the amounts of which can be estimated in advance, to its retired employees and their beneficiaries, the arrangement is deemed to be a pension plan. The typical plan is written and the amount of benefits can be determined by reference to the plan documents. However, the plan and its provisions can also be implied from unwritten but established past practices. The accounting for most types of retirement plans is suggested by, if not heavily detailed in, IAS 19. Plans may be unfunded, insured, trust fund, defined contribution and defined benefit plans, and deferred compensation contracts, if equivalent. Independent (not employer sponsored) deferred profit sharing plans and pension payments made to selected employees on a case-by-case basis, are not considered pension plans.

The establishment of a pension plan represents a long-term commitment to employees. Although some entities manage their own plans, this commitment usually takes the form of contributions that are made to an independent trustee or, in some countries, to a governmental agency. These contributions are used by the trustee to acquire plan assets of various kinds, although the available types of investments may be restricted by governmental regulations in certain jurisdictions. Plan assets are used to generate a return, which typically consists of earned interest and/or appreciation in asset value.

The earnings from the plan assets (and occasionally, the proceeds from their liquidation) provide the trustee with cash to pay the benefits to which the employees become entitled. These benefits, in turn, are defined by the terms of the pension plan, which is known as the plan's benefit formula. In the case of defined benefit plans, the benefit formula incorporates many factors, including employee compensation, employee service longevity, employee age, and so on, and is considered to provide the best indication of pension obligations and costs. It is used as the basis for determining the pension cost recognized each fiscal year.

Income statement vs. balance sheet objectives. As the accounting requirements for pensions and other forms of postemployment benefits have evolved over the years, the primary objective has been to assign the periodic costs of such plans properly to the periods in which the related benefits are received by the employers incurring these costs. These benefits are obviously received when the workers are productively working on their jobs, not during the later years when they are enjoying their retirements. For that reason, accounting long ago recognized that the "pay-as-you-go" method of expense recognition, under which expense recognition would be deferred until the benefit payments to retirees were actually made, would cause an unacceptable mismatching of costs and benefits and a distortion of the income statement. The probable result of this mismatching would be the overstating of earlier years' results of operations and understating those of later years when large retirement payments are being made. As pensions and other fringe benefits expanded over the past generation to become a material and ever-increasing fraction of workers' compensation, this problem could no longer be ignored by accounting standards setters.

The reason that pay-as-you-go accounting was not eliminated completely long ago is that many pension plans and similar employee benefit plan arrangements are rather complex, and the accounting necessary to report on them properly is also difficult. Most significantly, in the case of defined benefit plans, actual costs may not be known for many years, even decades, since a variety of future events (employee turnover, performance of investments, salary increases, etc.) will affect the ultimate burden on the employer. Accordingly, the measurement of expense on a current basis demands that many complicated estimates be made, some involving actuarial computations, and accountants have often been reluctant to anchor the financial statements to estimates that are potentially very imprecise. Only when the impact of pay-as-you-go accounting became unacceptably distortive, due to the growing occurrence and magnitude of these benefit plans, were professional standards revised to prohibit continued use of that mode of accounting.

As pensions became an almost universal fixture of the employment landscape (in some nations, private pensions are mandated by law; in other countries, participation in government-sponsored plans is required), the failure to require such accounting became an impediment to meaningful financial reporting. Notwithstanding the limitations of actuarial and other estimates, financial statements incorporating the accrual of pension costs are vastly more accurate and useful than those based on a pay-as-you-go approach.

Evolution of international accounting standards on pension costs. About 30 years ago, major accounting standard-setting bodies began urging that pension costs be accrued properly in financial statements. At first, a wide range of actuarial methods were permitted, each of which could produce more meaningful results than the pay-as-you-go method, but over time the range of options permitted has been narrowed in major jurisdictions.

As presently constituted, pension accounting rules have tended to focus over-whelmingly on the income statement. That is, the dominant objective has been to match income and expense properly on a current basis, so that the periodic mea-surement of operating performance is within the bounds of material accuracy.

It has been less clear that the meaningful presentation of the balance sheet has been a priority, however. Thus, even when an employer has retained full responsi-bility for the ultimate payment of pension benefits (as with defined benefit plans), the employer's statement of financial position has usually excluded a complete rep-resentation of the assets and obligations of the pension scheme. This has been due partly to the fact that various "smoothing" approaches have been made to expense measurement, causing the balance sheet (given the rigors of double-entry book-keeping) to become the repository for the resulting deferred charges and credits and thus making the overall picture from the balance sheet side less meaningful. Fur-thermore, accountants have been genuinely ambivalent about the validity of pre-senting information about the assets and obligations of the pension plan on the face of the employer's balance sheet, believing that the pension plan constitutes a sepa-rate economic and reporting entity.

IAS 19 (revised 1998) is a substantial advance over its predecessor standards and is very similar in approach to the the corresponding US GAAP standards (SFAS 87, 88, and 106). In fact, it offers broader coverage than the US standards, touching on compensated absences and stock compensation arrangements (subjects of more extensive coverage in separate US GAAP standards, however) and short-term ar-rangements as well. IAS 19 (revised 1998) breaks with the past practice of permit-ting a range of methodologies resulting in potentially quite different financial state-ment results. Finally, IAS 19 (revised 1998) greatly expands the disclosures re-quired by employers having defined benefit plans, again largely mimicking the US requirements. By mandating one specific actuarial costing method, the new stan-dard effectively requires employers sponsoring defined benefit plans to engage in annual actuarial valuations, which will undoubtedly increase the cost of compliance for those with such plans. Overall, the effect of IAS 19 (revised 1998) will be to significantly increase the comparability of financial statements of entities with a wide range of employee benefit plans.

Basic Principles of IAS 19 (Revised 1998)

Applicability: pension plans. IAS 19 (revised 1998) is applicable to both de-fined contribution and defined benefit pension plans. The accounting for defined contribution plans is normally straightforward, with the objective of matching the cost of the program with the periods in which the employees earn their benefits. Since contributions are formula-driven, typically the payments to the plan will be made currently; if they do not occur by the balance sheet date, an accrual will be recognized for any unpaid current contribution liability. Once made or accrued, the employer has no further obligation for the value of the assets held by the plan or for the sufficiency of fund assets for payment of the benefits, absent any violation of the terms of the agreement by the employer.

IAS 19 (revised 1998) further provides that disclosure should be made of the amount of expense recognized in connection with the defined contribution pension plan. If not explicitly identified in the statement of income, this should therefore be disclosed in the notes to the financial statements.

Compared to defined contribution plans, the accounting for defined benefit plans is vastly more complex, because the employer (sponsor) is responsible not merely for the current contribution to be made to the plan on behalf of participants, but additionally for the sufficiency of the assets in the plan for the ultimate payments of benefits promised to the participants. Thus the current contribution is at best a partial satisfaction of its obligation, and the amount of actual cost incurred is not measured by this alone. The measurement of pension cost under a defined benefit plan necessarily involves the expertise of actuaries--persons who are qualified to estimate the numbers of employees who will survive (both as employees, in the case of vesting requirements which some of them may not yet have met; and as living persons who will be available to receive the promised retirement benefits), the salary levels at which they will retire (if these are incorporated into the benefit formula, as is commonly the case), their expected life expectancy (since benefits are typically payable for life), and other factors which will influence the amount of resources needed to satisfy the employer's promises. Actuarial determinations cannot be made by accountants, who lack the training and credentials, but the results of actuaries' efforts will be critical to the ability to properly account for defined benefit plan costs. Accounting for defined benefit plans is described at length in the following pages.

Applicability: other employee benefit plans. IAS 19 (revised 1998) explicitly addresses not merely pension plans (which were dealt with by earlier iterations of IAS 19 as well, although in rather less detail), but also four other categories of employee and postemployment benefits. These are

1. **Short-term employee benefits**, which include normal wages and salaries as well as compensated absences, profit sharing and bonuses, and such nonmonetary fringe benefits as health insurance, housing subsidies and employer-provided automobiles, to the extent these are granted to current (not retired) employees.
2. **Other long-term employee benefits**, such as long-term (sabbatical) leave, long-term disability benefits and, if payable after 12 months beyond the end of the reporting period, profit sharing and bonus arrangements and deferred compensation.
3. **Termination benefits.**

4. **Equity compensation benefits**, which are stock option plans, phantom stock plans, and similar compensation schemes which reward employees based upon the performance of the companies' share prices.

Each of the foregoing categories of employee benefits will be explained later in this chapter.

IAS 19 (revised 1998) also addresses postemployment benefits other than pensions, such as retiree medical plan coverage, as part of its requirements for pension plans, since these are essentially similar in nature. While the predecessor standard IAS 19 nominally covered these plans, the new standard explicitly addresses them as being variants of defined benefit arrangements. These are discussed further later in this chapter.

IAS 19 (revised 1998) considers all plans other than those explicitly structured as defined contribution plans to be defined benefit plans, with the accounting and reporting complexities that this implies. Unless the employer's obligation is strictly limited to the amount of contribution currently due, typically driven by a formula based on enterprise performance or by employee wages or salaries, the obligations to the employees (and the amount of recognizable expense) will have to be estimated in accordance with actuarial principles.

Cost recognition distinguished from funding practices. Although sound management practice may be to fund retirement benefit plans on a current basis, in some jurisdictions the requirement to do this is either limited or absent entirely. Furthermore, in some jurisdictions the currently available tax deduction for contributions to pension plans may be limited, reducing the incentive to make such contributions until such time as the funds are actually needed for making payouts to retirees. Since the objective of periodic financial reporting is to match costs and revenues properly on a current basis, the pattern of funding is obviously not a useful guide to proper accounting for pension costs.

"Pay-as-you-go," accrued benefit, and projected benefit methods of accounting for postretirement benefits. Before the establishment of strict accounting and financial reporting rules, it was not uncommon to account for pensions and other similar costs on the so-called "pay-as-you-go" basis. Briefly, this methodology recognized current period expense equal to only the amounts of benefits actually paid out to retirees and other beneficiaries in the reporting period. In support of this approach, the argument was usually made (1) it was very difficult, or expensive, to accurately measure (i.e., on an actuarial basis) the real cost of such plans, and (2) the effect on periodic earnings would not be much different in any event. However, pay-as-you-go obviously violates the concept of accrual basis accounting, and the presumption that periodic expense is not materially distorted is often not supported in fact. This method of accounting for pensions and other postretirement programs has accordingly not been acceptable since the first version of IAS 19 was promulgated in 1983.

While adherence to the accrual concept precluded pay-as-you-go accounting for the cost of employee benefit plans, for plans other than those which qualify as defined contribution arrangements there remained a range of acceptable, accrual-basis consistent methods. The first and second versions of IAS 19 granted wide discretion in selection of costing methods. The various techniques fall within two general groupings which are known as the "accrued benefit" and "projected benefit" methods. While IAS 19 (revised 1998) has ended the acceptability of the projected benefit methods, an understanding of the two approaches will be helpful to gaining a fuller comprehension of the intricacies of the financial reporting of pension plan-related costs in the financial statements of the sponsoring enterprise.

The accrued (or accumulated) benefit methods are based on services provided by employees through the date of valuation (the balance sheet date), without considering future services to be rendered by them. Periodic pension cost is a function, accordingly, of services that are provided in the current period. Since the obligation for future pension payments is computed as the discounted present value of the amounts to be paid in later years, accrued benefit methods will calculate increasing charges (even if wage levels are constant) as employees approach retirement, since the present values of future payments will increase as the time to retirement shortens. Periodic charges also increase, in most actual instances, because attrition rates (employees who leave, thereby forfeiting their rights to retirement payments) decline over time, since older employees show less inclination to change employment. While wages will typically increase over time as employees age, both due to compensation increases due to seniority and performance improvements, and as a result (if the past is any guide) of ongoing wage inflation, this should not be the cause of increasing pension costs as time to retirement grows shorter, since even accrued benefit valuation methods must be based on assumptions about future salary progression. Notwithstanding that over time these assumptions and expectations cannot be precisely accurate, the presumption should be that "estimation errors" will be randomly distributed, and that over the long run, good-faith estimates of salary progression and the resultant effects on periodic pension costs will be fairly accurate. Consequently, periodic pension costs should not drift upward as employees age because of wage increases.

The projected benefit valuation method, on the other hand, uses actuarial estimation techniques that consider both the services already rendered as well as those to be rendered by the employees. The goal is to allocate the entire retirement cost smoothly over each employee's respective working life. The pension obligation at any point in time is computed as the present value of the aggregate future payments earned to the balance sheet date. As with accrued benefit valuation methods, future salary progression must be taken into account in determining periodic pension costs over the working lives of employees. The difference, however, is that future costs are spread more evenly over the full period of employment (although this does not imply that straight-line allocation is an absolute requirement) as compared to the accrued benefit valuation methods, and, in particular, pension-related costs will not show the constantly increasing pattern exhibited by the alternative approach simply due to the shortening time horizon as retirement dates draw near.

Proponents of both accrued and projected benefit valuation approaches have claimed that the matching concept underlies their preferred method. For large employers having a work force comprised of individuals of all ages, and that typically replace older retiring workers with younger ones, pension costs will be similar under either method on an aggregate basis. While pension costs relative to older workers will be higher and costs relating to younger workers will be lower, if the accrued benefit valuation method is used vs. what would be reflected if the projected benefit valuation method were used, with a stable mix of ages of workers, this will not significantly vary. For smaller employers, or those with a work force skewed toward younger or older workers, then holding all other considerations constant, the periodic pattern of pension costs will diverge under these two methods.

Example of accrued and projected benefit methods

To understand the essential difference between accrued benefit and projected benefits methods, consider a simple case of a single employee hired today with no expectation of future salary increases, and promised a **total** retirement benefit of $10,000 if he retires after at least 10 years' service, or $14,000 if after 20 years' service. Ignoring present valuing (which does have to be taken into account in the actual accounting for employee benefit costs, however), the accrued benefit method would allocate 1/10 of the $10,000 = $1,000 in promised benefits to each of the first 10 years of service, and then 1/10 of the $4,000 increment = $400 to each of the next 10 years, since accrued benefit methods would not assume the employee would continue employment beyond the tenth year until after that threshold is surpassed. Projected benefit methods, on the other hand, would assign 1/20 of the $14,000 = $700 to each of the first 20 years' employment, being based on service rendered and to be rendered until expected retirement. This all presumes the employee is expected to work at least 20 years (based on experience, the employee's age, etc.). In actual practice, with multiple employees, statistical estimates are used such that full accrual of benefits is normally not made for all employees, given that a certain fraction will opt out before becoming vested, etc.

Net Periodic Pension Cost Under IAS 19 (Revised 1998)

General discussion. Absent specific information to the contrary, it is assumed that a company will continue to provide retirement benefits well into the future. The accounting for the plan's costs should be reflected in the financial statements and these amounts should not be discretionary. All pension costs should be charged against income. No amounts should be charged directly to retained earnings. The principal focus of IAS 19 (revised 1998) is on the allocation of cost to the periods being benefited, which are the periods in which the covered employees provide service to the reporting enterprise.

Periodic measurement of cost for defined contribution plans. Under the terms of a defined contribution plan (in some cases referred to as a "money purchase" plan), the employer will be obligated for fixed or determinable contributions in each period, often computed as a percentage of the wage and salary base paid to the covered employees during the period. For one example, contributions might be set at 4% of each employee's wages and salaries, up to $50,000 wages per annum. Generally, the contributions must actually be made by a specific date, such as 90 days after the end of the enterprise's fiscal year, consistent with local law. The expense must be accrued for accounting purposes in the year the cost is incurred, whether the contribution is made currently or not.

IAS 19 (revised 1998) requires that contributions payable to a defined contribution plan be accrued currently, even if not paid by year end. If the amount is due over a period extending more than 1 year from the balance sheet date, the long-term portion should be discounted at the rate applicable to long-term corporate bonds, if that information is known, or applicable to government bonds, in the alternative.

Employers may make further, discretionary contributions to benefit plans in certain periods. For example, if the entity enjoys a particularly profitable year, the board of directors may vote to grant another 2% of wages as a bonus contribution to the employees' benefit plan. The extent to which this is done will depend, among other factors, on the tax laws of the relevant jurisdiction. Normally, an enterprise making such a discretionary contribution does not do so simply to reward past performance by its workers. Rather, it does so in the belief that the gesture will cause its employees to be motivated to be more productive and loyal in the forthcoming years. IAS 19 (revised 1998) addresses profit sharing and bonus plans as a subset of its requirements concerning short-term compensation arrangements; it stipulates that such a payment should be recognized only when paid or when the entity has a legal or constructive obligation to make it, and it can be reliably estimated. There appears to be no basis for deferring recognition of the expense after that point, however, even though longer-term benefits to the entity might be hoped for.

Past service costs arise when a plan is amended retroactively, so that additional contributions are made with respect to services rendered in past years. For example, if a plan formerly required contributions of 5% of salaries and is amended retroactively to provide for contributions of 6%, an extra 1% of each employee's aggregate salary for all prior years will be transferred to the employee's pension account. When plans are amended in this fashion, it is generally management's belief that it will provide an incentive for greater efforts in the future. IAS 19 (revised 1998) does not explicitly address retroactive amendments to defined contribution plans, but by analogizing from the requirements concerning similar amendments to defined benefit plans, it is clear that, if fully vested immediately (as would almost inevitably be the case), these would have to be expensed currently.

Terminations of defined contribution plans generally provide no difficulties from an accounting perspective, since costs had been recognized currently in most instances. However, if certain costs, such as those associated with past services and with discretionary bonus contributions made in past years, have not yet been fully amortized, the remaining unrecognized portions of those costs must be expensed in the period when it becomes probable that the plan is to be terminated. This should be the period when the decision to terminate is made, which on occasion may precede the actual termination of the plan.

Periodic measurement of cost for defined benefit plans. Defined benefit plans present a far greater challenge to accountants than do defined contribution plans, since the amount of expense to be recognized currently will need to be determined on an actuarial basis. While under predecessor standard IAS 19 (revised 1993) both a benchmark treatment (using the accrued benefit valuation method) and an allowed alternative treatment (using the projected benefit valuation method) could be utilized, under IAS 19 (revised 1998) only the former is permitted. Furthermore, only a single variant of the accrued benefit method--the "projected unit credit" method--will be permitted. Only this method will be discussed in the following presentation.

Conceptually (and, for the first time, actually under IAS 19 [revised 1998]), net periodic pension cost will consist of the sum of the following six components:

1. Current (pure) service cost
2. Interest cost for the current period on the accrued benefit obligation
3. The expected return on plan assets
4. Actuarial gains and losses, to the extent recognized
5. Past service costs, to the extent recognized
6. The effects of any curtailments or settlements

While the former standard, IAS 19, did not separately address each of these elements, IAS 19 (revised 1998) does follow closely the model under US GAAP and separately present these. Disclosures required by the new standard effectively require that these cost components be displayed in the notes to the financial statements, while no such rule existed before under international accounting standards.

It is important to stress that current service cost, the core cost element of all defined benefit plans, must be determined by a qualified actuary. While the other items to be computed and presented are also developed by actuaries in most cases, they can be verified or even calculated directly by others, including the enterprise's internal or external accountants. The current service cost, however, is not an immediately apparent computation, as it relies upon a detailed census of employees (age, expected remaining working life, etc.) and the employer's experience (turnover, etc.), and is an intricate and elaborate computational exercise in many cases. Current service cost can only be developed by this careful, employee-by-employee analysis, and this is best left to those with the expertise to complete it.

Current service cost. Current service cost must be determined by an actuarial valuation and will be affected by assumptions such as expected turnover of staff, average retirement age, the plan's vesting schedule, and life expectancy after retirement. The probable progression of wages over the employees' remaining working lives will also have to be taken into consideration if retirement benefits will be affected by levels of compensation in later years, as will be true in the case of career average and final pay plans, among others.

Under the new standard, service cost is based on the present value of the defined benefit obligation, and is attributed to periods of service without regard to conditional requirements under the plan calling for further service. Thus, vesting is not taken into account in the sense that there is no justification for nonaccrual prior to vesting. However, in the actuarial determination of pension cost, the statistical probability of employees leaving employment prior to vesting must be taken into account, lest an over-accrual of costs be made.

Example of service cost attribution

To explain the concept of service cost, assume a single employee who is promised a pension of $1,000 per year for each year worked before retirement, for life, upon retirement at age 60 or thereafter. Further assume that this is the worker's first year on the job, and he is 30 years of age. The consulting actuary determines that if the worker, in fact, retires at age 60, he will have a life expectancy of 15 years, and at the present value of the required benefits ($1,000/yr x 15 years = $15,000) discounted at the long-term corporate bond rate, 8%, equals $8,560. In other words, based on the work performed thus far (1 year's worth), this employee has earned the right to a lump sum settlement of $8,560 at age 60. Since this is 30 years into the future, this amount must be reduced to present value, which at 8% is a mere $851, which is the pension cost to be recognized currently.

In year 2, this worker earns the right to yet another annuity stream of $1,000 per year upon retirement, which has, again, a present value of $8,560 at the projected retirement age of 60. However, since age 60 is now only 29 years hence, the present value of that promised benefit at the end of the current (second) year is $919, which represents the service cost in year 2. This pattern will continue: As the employee ages, the current cost of pension benefits grows apace, with (for example) the cost in the final working year being $8,560, before considering interest on the previously accumulated obligation--which would, however, add another $18,388 of expense, for a total cost for this one employee in his final working year of $26,948. It should be noted, however, that in "real life" situations, for employee groups in the aggregate, this may not hold, since new, younger employees will be added as older employees die or retire, which will tend to smooth out the annual cost of the plan.

It should be noted, parenthetically, that if the projected benefit approach (the allowed alternative under former IAS 19) were employed in the foregoing example, greater cost would be recognized in the early years of the employee's working life, since the actuarial determination would have been based on service provided and service to be provided. In this example, it would have been projected that the employee would remain on the job for 30 years, thereby earning an annual pension of $30,000, which will have a discounted present value at retirement of $256,800. This amount would be spread evenly over the employee's working life, for an annual cost of about $8,560. That is, the pension cost associated with this worker would be $8,560 in the first year of his working life and every year thereafter. (There are a number of actuarial valuation methods, and this simplified illustration is intended only to contrast the former benchmark treatment--now the mandatory one--with the previously allowed alternative.)

Interest on the accrued benefit obligation. As noted, since the actuarial determination of current period cost is the present value of the future pension benefits to be paid to retirees by virtue of their service in the current period, the longer the time until the expected retirement date, the lower will be the service cost recognized. However, over time this accrued cost must be further increased, until at the employees' respective retirement dates the full amounts of the promised payments have been accreted. In this regard, the accrued pension liability is much like a sinking fund that grows from contributions plus the earnings thereon.

Consider the example of service cost presented in the preceding section. The $851 obligation recorded in the first year of that example will have grown to $919 by the end of the second year. While former standard IAS 19 did not address this directly, IAS 19 (revised 1998) adopts the same approach as was established a decade earlier under US GAAP. This $68 increase in the obligation for future benefits, due to the passage of time, is under IAS 19 (revised 1998) reported as a component of pension cost, denoted as interest cost.

Other elements of benefit cost. While the former standard IAS 19 presented only a brief description of the elements of pension cost other than current service cost, this has dramatically changed under IAS 19 (revised 1998). The newly promulgated standard identifies the expected return on plan assets, actuarial gains and losses, past service costs, and the effects of any curtailments or settlements, as categories to be explicitly addressed in the disclosure of the details of annual pension cost for defined benefit plans. These will be discussed in the following sections, in turn.

The expected return on plan assets. IAS 19 (revised 1998) has adopted the approach of the corresponding US standard in accepting the notion that, since pension plan assets are intended as long-term investments, the random and perhaps sizable fluctuations from period to period should not be allowed to excessively distort the operating results reported by the sponsoring entity. The new standard identifies the expected return rather than the actual return on plan assets as a component of pension cost, with the difference between actual and expected return being an actuarial gain or loss to be dealt with as described below (deferred to future periods or, if significant, partially recognized). Expected return for a given period is determined at the start of that period, and is based on long-term rates of return for assets to be held over the term of the related pension obligation. Expected return is to incorporate anticipated dividends, interest, and changes in fair value, and is furthermore to be reduced in respect of expected plan administration costs.

For example, assume that at the start of 2000 the plan administrator expects, over the long term, and based on historical performance of plan assets, that the plan's assets will receive annual interest and dividends of 6%, net of any taxes due by the fund itself, and will enjoy a market value gain of another 2.5%. It is also noted that plan administration costs average .75% of plan assets, measured by fair value. With this data, an expected rate of return for 2000 would be computed as 6.00% + 2.50% − .75% = 7.75%. This rate would be used to calculate the return on assets, which would be used to offset service cost and other benefit plan cost components for the year 2000.

The difference between this assumed rate of return, 7.75% in this example, and the actual return enjoyed by the plan's assets would be added to or subtracted from the cumulative actuarial gains and losses. In theory, over the long run, these gains and losses will largely offset, inasmuch as they are the result of random fluctuations in market returns and of demographic and other changes in the group covered by the plan (such as unusual turnover, mortality, or changes in salaries). Since these are expected to largely offset, and given the very long time horizon over which pension benefit plan performance is to be judged, the notion of deferring these net gains or losses is appealing.

Actuarial gains and losses, to the extent recognized. Changes in the amount of the actuarially determined pension obligation and differences in the actual versus the expected yield on plan assets, as well as demographic changes (e.g., composition of the work force, changes in life expectancy, etc.) contribute to so-called actuarial (or "experience") gains and losses. While immediate recognition of these gains or losses could clearly be justified conceptually (because these are real and have already occurred), there are both theoretical arguments opposed to such immediate recognition (the distortive effects on the measure of current operating performance resulting from very long-term investments, much of which will reverse of their own accord over time) as well as great opposition by financial statement preparers and users. For this reason, IAS 19 does not require such immediate recognition, unless the fluctuations are so great that deferral is not deemed to be valid. IAS 19 (revised 1998) has essentially acceded to the US approach and defined a 10% corridor as representing the range of variation deemed to be "normal." While the use of a 10% threshold is arbitrary, it does have the advantage of apparent logic, since it has already been employed for over a decade in the US.

Thus, if the unrecognized actuarial gain or loss is no more than 10% of the larger of the present value of the defined benefit obligation or the fair value of plan assets, measured at the beginning of the reporting period, no recognition in the current period will be necessary (i.e., there will be continued deferral of the accumulated net actuarial gain or loss). On the other hand, if the accumulated net actuarial gain or loss exceeds this 10% corridor, the magnitude creates greater doubt that future losses or gains will offset these, and for that reason some recognition will be necessary. It is suggested by IAS 19 that this excess be amortized over the expected remaining working lives of the then-active employee participants, but the standard actually permits any reasonable method of amortization as long as (1) recognition is at no slower a pace than would result from amortization over the working lives of participants, and (2) that the same method is used for net gains and net losses. It would even be acceptable to fully recognize all actuarial gains or losses, without regard to the 10% corridor, immediately, if so desired, since such a practice would satisfy this criterion.

The corridor, and the amount of any excess beyond this corridor, must be computed anew each year, based on the present value of defined benefits and fair value of plan assets at the beginning of the year. Thus, there may have been, say, an unrecognized actuarial gain of $450,000 at the end of Year 1, which exceeds the 10% corridor boundary by, say, $210,000, and is therefore to be amortized over the average 21-year remaining working life of the plan participants, indicating a $10,000 reduction in pension cost in Year 2. If, at the end of Year 2, market losses or other actuarial losses reduce the accumulated actuarial gain below the threshold implied by the 10% corridor. Accordingly, in Year 3 there will be no further amortization of the net actuarial gain. This determination, therefore, must be made at the beginning of each period. Depending on the amount of unrecognized actuarial gain or loss at the end of Year 3, there may or may not be amortization in Year 4, and so on.

Past service costs, to the extent recognized. Past service costs refer to increases in the amount of a defined benefit liability which results from the initial adoption of a plan, or from a change or amendment to an existing plan which increases the benefits promised to the participants with respect to previous service rendered. Less commonly, a plan amendment could reduce the benefits for past services, if local laws permit this. Employers will amend plans for a variety of reasons, including competitive factors in the employment marketplace, but often it is done with the hope and expectation that it will engender goodwill among the workers and thus increase future productivity. For this reason, it is sometimes the case that these added benefits will not vest immediately, but rather must be earned over some defined time period.

IAS 19 (revised 1998) requires immediate recognition of past service cost as an expense when the added benefits vest immediately. However, when these are not immediately vested, recognition is to be on a straight-line basis over the period until vesting occurs. For example, if at January 1, 2000, the sponsoring entity grants an added $4,000 per employee in future benefits, and this computes, given the number of employees expected to receive these benefits, to a present value of $455,000, but vesting will not be until January 1, 2005, then a past service cost of ($455,000 ÷ 5 years =) $91,000 per year will be recognized. (To this amount, of course, must be added interest, as with service cost, as described above.)

The effects of any curtailments or settlements. Periodic defined benefit plan expense is also affected by any curtailments or settlements which have been incurred. The standard defines a curtailment as arising in connection with isolated events such as plant closings, discontinuations of operations, or termination or suspension of a benefit plan. Often, corporate restructurings will be accompanied by curtailments in benefit plans. Recognition can be given to the effect of a curtailment when the sponsor is demonstrably committed to make a material reduction in the number of covered employees, or it amends the terms of the plan such that a material element of future service by existing employees will no longer be covered or will receive reduced benefits. The curtailment must actually occur for it to be given recognition.

Settlements occur when the enterprise enters into a transaction which effectively transfers the obligation to another entity, such as an insurance company, such that the sponsor has no legal or constructive obligation to fund any benefit shortfall. Merely acquiring insurance which is intended to cover the benefit payments does not constitute a settlement, since a funding mechanism does not relieve the underlying obligation.

The effect of a curtailment or settlement is measured with reference to the change in present value of the defined benefits, any change in fair value of related assets (normally there is none), and any related actuarial gains or losses and past service cost which had not yet been recognized. The net amount of these elements will be charged or credited to pension expense in the period the curtailment or settlement actually occurs. For example, if a curtailment reduces the present value of future benefits by $40,000, or 5% of the precurtailment obligation ($800,000), and there was also an unrecognized actuarial gain of $60,000 and an unrecognized transition amount (past service cost) of $50,000, the income statement in the curtailment period would be $40,000 + (.05 x 60,000) – (.05 x 50,000) = $41,000 reduction in pension cost for the year.

Transition adjustment. The final element of periodic pension cost under IAS 19 relates to the effect of first adopting the accounting standard. The transition amount is the present value of the benefit obligation at the date the standard is adopted, less the fair value of plan assets at that date, less any past service cost to be deferred to later periods, if the criteria regarding vesting period are met. IAS 19 (revised 1998) continues to offer reporting entities two alternatives, similar to those set forth in the predecessor standard, albeit with a minor alteration. If the transitional liability is greater than the liability which would have been recognized under the entity's previous policy for accounting for pension costs, it must make an **irrevocable** choice to either

1. Recognize the increase in the pension obligation immediately, with the expense included in employee benefit cost for the period; or
2. Amortize the transition amount over no longer than a 5-year period, on the straight-line basis. (The earlier standard suggested amortization over the remaining working lives of employees working at the date of transition.) The unrecognized transition amount will not be formally included in the balance sheet, but must be disclosed.

If method (2) is elected, and the enterprise has a **negative** transitional liability (that is, an asset, resulting from an excess of pension assets over the related obligation), it is limited in the amount of such asset to present on its balance sheet to the total of any unrecognized actuarial losses plus past service cost, and the present value of economic benefits available as refunds from the plan or reductions in future contributions, with the present value determined by reference to the rate on high-quality corporate bonds. Furthermore, the amount of unrecognized transitional gain or loss as of each balance sheet date must be presented, as well as the amount recognized in the current period income statement.

Finally, if method (2) is employed, recognition of actuarial gains (which do not include negative past service cost) will be limited in two ways. If an actuarial gain is being recognized because it exceeds the 10% corridor or because the enterprise has elected a more rapid method of systematic recognition, then the actuarial gain should be recognized only to the extent the net cumulative gain exceeds the unrecognized transitional liability. And, in determining the gain or loss on any later settlement or curtailment, the related part of the unrecognized transitional liability must be incorporated.

IAS 19 also stipulates that, if the transitional liability is lower than the amount which would have been recognized under previous accounting rules, the adjustment should be taken into income immediately (i.e., amortization is not permitted).

Upon adoption of IAS 19 (revised 1998), the entity should not retrospectively compute the effect of the 10% corridor on actuarial gain or loss recognition. While the exposure draft preceding this standard (E54) did not address this, therefore leaving open the possibility that this would be necessary to accomplish, the standard itself makes it clear that retrospective application would be impracticable to accomplish and would not have generated useful information. It was therefore prohibited in the new IAS 19.

Employer's Liabilities and Assets

IAS 19 has as its primary, possibly sole, concern the measurement of periodic expense incurred in connection with pension plans of employers. One source of dissatisfaction with the standard is its failure to address the assets or liabilities that may be recognized on the employers' balance sheets as a consequence of expense recognition, which may include deferral of certain items (e.g., past service costs). In fact, the amounts that may find their way onto the balance sheet will often not meet the strict definition of assets or liabilities, but rather, will be "deferred charges or credits." This will consist of the cumulative difference between the amount funded and the amount expensed over the life of the plan.

IAS 19 has been criticized for not requiring, under appropriate circumstances, recognition of an additional, or minimum, liability when plans are materially underfunded. The point of comparison is the US GAAP standard, SFAS 87, which does demand that this minimum liability, which results when the accumulated (accrued) benefit obligation exceeds the fair value of plan assets and a liability in the amount of the difference is not already recorded as unfunded accrued pension cost. Under that standard, the additional minimum liability is recognized by an offset to an intangible asset up to the amount of unrecognized prior service cost. Any additional debit needed is considered a loss and is shown net of tax benefits as a separate component reducing equity. While E54 did propose that the balance sheet reflect the net debit or credit associated with the plan assets and obligations, ultimately the IASC Board concluded that additional measures of liability were potentially confusing and did not promise to provide relevant information. Accordingly, with the exception of any liability to be accrued under IAS 37 (regarding contingencies), the decision was made to dispense with this proposal.

Other Pension Considerations

Multiple and multiemployer plans. If an entity has more than one plan, IAS 19 provisions should be applied separately to each plan. Offsets or eliminations are not allowed unless there clearly is the right to use the assets in one plan to pay the benefits of another plan.

Participation in a multiemployer plan (to which two or more unrelated employers contribute) requires that the contribution for the period be recognized as net pension cost and that any contributions due and unpaid be recognized as a liability. Assets in this type of plan are usually commingled and are not segregated or restricted. A board of trustees usually administers these plans, and multiemployer plans are generally subject to a collective bargaining agreement. If there is a withdrawal from this type of plan and if an arising obligation is either probable or reasonably possible, the provisions of international accounting standards that address contingencies (IAS 10) apply.

Some plans are, in substance, a pooling or aggregation of single employer plans and are ordinarily without collective bargaining agreements. Contributions are usually based on a selected benefit formula. These plans are not considered multiemployer, and the accounting is based on the respective interest in the plan.

Business combinations. When an entity that sponsors a single employer-defined benefit plan is purchased in a manner that must be accounted for as an acquisition under the provisions of IAS 22, the purchaser should assign part of the purchase price to an asset if plan assets exceed the projected benefit obligation, or to a liability if the projected benefit obligation exceeds plan assets. The projected benefit obligation should include the effect of any expected plan curtailment or termination. This assignment eliminates any existing unrecognized components, and any future differences between contributions and net pension cost will affect the asset or liability recognized when the purchase took place.

Disclosure of Pension and Other Postemployment Benefit Costs

For defined contribution plans, IAS 19 (revised 1998) requires only that the amount of expense included in current period earnings be disclosed. If further required under IAS 24 (related parties), disclosures should be made about contributions made for key management personnel. Good practice would suggest, additionally, that there be disclosure of the general description of each plan, identifying the employee groups covered; and of any other significant matters related to retirement benefits that affect comparability with the previous period reported on,

For defined benefit plans, as would be expected, much more expansive disclosures are mandated. These include

1. A general description of each plan, identifying the employee groups covered
2. The accounting policy regarding recognition of actuarial gains or losses
3. A reconciliation of the plan-related assets and liabilities recognized in the balance sheet, showing at the minimum

    a. The present value of wholly unfunded defined benefit obligations
    b. The present value (gross, before deducting plan assets) of wholly or partly unfunded obligations
    c. The fair value of plan assets
    d. The net actuarial gain or loss not yet recognized in the balance sheet
    e. The past service cost not yet recognized in the balance sheet
    f. Any amount not recognized as an asset because of the limitation to the present value of economic benefits from refunds and future contribution reductions
    g. The amounts which are recognized in the balance sheet

4. The amount of plan assets represented by each category of the reporting entity's own financial instruments or by property which is occupied by, or other assets used by, the entity itself
5. A reconciliation of movements (i.e., changes) during the reporting period in the net asset or liability reported in the balance sheet
6. The amount of, and location in the income statement of, the reported amounts of current service cost, interest cost, expected return on plan assets, actuarial gain or loss, past service cost, and effect of any curtailment or settlement
7. The actual return earned on plan assets for the reporting period
8. The principal actuarial assumptions used, including (if relevant) the discount rates, expected rates of return on plan assets, expected rates of salary increases or other index or variable specified in the pension arrangement, medical cost trend rates, and any other material actuarial assumptions utilized in computing benefit costs for the period. The actuarial assumptions are to be explicitly stated in absolute terms, not merely as references to other indices.

Amounts presented in the sponsor's balance sheet cannot be offset (presented on a net basis) unless legal rights of offset exist. Furthermore, even with a legal right to offset (which itself would be a rarity), unless the intent is to settle on a net basis, such presentation would not be acceptable. Thus, a sponsor of two plans, one being in a net asset position, and another in a net liability position, cannot be netted in most instances.

Other Benefit Plans

Short-term employee benefits. Per IAS 19 (revised 1998), short-term benefits are those falling due within 12 months from the end of the period in which the employees render their services. These include wages and salaries, as well as short-term compensated absences (vacations, annual holiday, paid sick days, etc.), profit sharing and bonuses if due within 12 months after the end of the period in which these were earned, and such nonmonetary benefits as health insurance and housing or automobiles. The standard requires that these be reported as incurred. Since they are accrued currently, no actuarial assumptions or computations will be needed and, since due currently, discounting will not be employed.

Compensated absences may provide some accounting complexities, if these accumulate and vest with the employees. Under the terms of the new employee benefits standard, accumulating benefits can be carried forward to later periods when not fully consumed currently--for example, when employees are granted 2 weeks' leave per year, but can carry forward to later years an amount equal to, say, no more than 6 weeks, the compensated absence benefit can be said to be subject to limited accumulation. Depending on the program, accumulation rights may be limited or unlimited; and, furthermore, the usage of benefits may be defined to occur on a last-in, first-out (LIFO) basis, which, in conjunction with limited accumulation rights, further limits the amount of benefits which employees are likely to use, if not fully used in the period earned.

The cost of compensated absences should be accrued in the periods earned. In some cases (as when the plans subject employees to limitations on accumulation rights with or without the further restriction imposed by a LIFO pattern of usage), it will be understood that the amounts of compensated absences to which employees are contractually entitled will exceed the amount that they are likely to actually utilize. In such circumstances, the accrual should be based on the **expected** usage, based on past experience and, if relevant, changes in the plan's provisions since the last reporting period.

Example of compensated absences

Consider an entity with 500 workers, each of whom earns 2 weeks' annual leave, with a carryforward option limited to a maximum of 6 weeks, to be carried forward no longer than 4 years. Also, this employer imposes a LIFO basis on any usages of annual leave (e.g., a worker with 2 weeks' carryforward and 2 weeks earned currently, taking a 3-week leave, will be deemed to have consumed the 2 currently earned weeks plus 1 of the carryforward weeks, thereby increasing the risk of ultimately losing the older carried-forward compensated absence time). Based on past experience, 80% of the workers will take no more than 2 weeks' leave in any year, while the other 20% take an average of 4 extra days. At the end of the year, each worker has an average of 5 days' carryforward of compensated absences. The amount accrued should be the cost equivalent of ([.80 x 0 days] + [.20 x 4 days]) x 500 workers = 400 days' leave.

Other postretirement benefits. Other postretirement benefits include medical care and other benefits offered to retirees partially or entirely at the expense of the former employer. These are essentially defined benefit plans very much like defined benefit pension plans. Like the pension plans, these require the services of a qualified actuary in order to estimate the true cost of the promises made currently for benefits to be delivered in the future. As with pensions, a variety of determinants, including the age composition, life expectancies, and other demographic factors pertaining to the present and future retiree groups, and the course of future inflation of medical care (or other covered) costs (coupled with predicted utilization factors), need to be projected in order to compute current period costs. Developing these projections requires the skills and training of actuaries; the pattern of future medical costs has been particularly difficult to achieve with anything approaching accuracy. Unlike most defined benefit pension plans, other postretirement benefit plans are more commonly funded on a pay-as-you-go basis, which does not alter the accounting but does eliminate earnings on plan assets as a cost offset.

Other long-term employee benefits. These are defined by IAS 19 as including any benefits other than postemployment benefits (pensions, retiree medical care, etc.), termination benefits and equity compensation plans. Examples would include sabbatical leave, jubilee benefits, long-term profit sharing payments, and deferred compensation arrangements. Executive deferred compensation plans have become common in nations where these are tax-advantaged (i.e., not taxed to the employee until paid), and these give rise to deferred tax accounting issues as well as measurement and reporting questions as benefit plans, per se. In general, measurement will be less complex than for defined benefit pension or other postretirement benefits, although some actuarial measures may be needed.

Reportedly for simplicity, IAS 19 decided to not provide the "corridor" approach to nonrecognition of actuarial gains and losses for other long-term benefits. It also requires that past service cost (resulting from the granting of enhanced benefits to participants on a retroactive basis) and transition gain or loss to be reported in earnings in the period in which these are granted or occur. For liability measurement purposes, IAS 19 demands that the present value of the obligation be presented on the balance sheet, less the fair value of any assets which have been set aside for settlement thereof. The long-term corporate bond rate is used here, as with defined benefit pension obligations, to discount the expected future payments to present value. As to expense recognition, the same cost elements as are set forth for pension plan expense should be included, with the exceptions that actuarial gains and losses and past service cost must be recognized immediately, not amortized over a defined time horizon.

Termination benefits. Termination benefits are to be recognized only when the employer has demonstrated its commitment to **either** terminate the employee or group of employees before normal retirement date, or provide benefits as part of an inducement to encourage early retirements. Generally, a detailed, formal plan will be necessary to support a representation that such a commitment exists. According to IAS 19, the plan should, as a minimum, set forth locations, functions, and numbers of employees to be terminated; the benefits for each job class or other pertinent category; and the time when the plan is to be implemented, with inception to be as soon as possible and completion soon enough to largely eliminate the chance that any material changes to the plan will be necessary.

Since termination benefits do not confer any future economic benefits on the employing enterprise, these must be expensed immediately. If the payments are to fall due more than 12 months after the balance sheet date, however, discounting to present value is required (again, using the long-term corporate bond rate). Estimates, such as the number of employees likely to accept voluntary early retirement, may need to be made in many cases involving termination benefits. To the extent that accrual is based on such estimates, the possibility that greater numbers may accept, thereby triggering additional costs, further disclosure of loss contingencies may be necessary to comply with IAS 37.

Equity compensation benefits. Benefits based on stock option and similar plans have become extremely popular in certain nations; in some cases, in fact, the fraction of executive compensation represented by such plans overwhelms that payable currently in cash. However, the accounting for such plans (and for the compensation elements thereof, in particular) has been very controversial, largely because national accounting standards have long held these to be largely noncompensatory if certain conditions are met. For example, under US GAAP, the longstanding rule was that if the exercise price were no lower than fair value at grant date, no compensation was attributed to the options, notwithstanding that economic and finance theory clearly demonstrates that these are compensatory, and the huge demand by executives for such benefit plans strongly suggests that, in their eyes at least, these are obviously compensation arrangements.

An attempt to change US GAAP to require the attribution of compensation cost to option plans was met by unprecedented opposition, largely from corporations which have grown accustomed to having substantial amounts of executive compensation "off the income statement." Although a final rule requiring supplementary (footnote) disclosure of the effects of full compensation recognition was ultimately imposed (with the optional, almost never employed, ability to formally report this in the income statement), the experience probably left other standard setters, such as the IASC, with the impression that a strong stand on this issue would not be politically feasible at this time.

Accordingly, IAS 19 (revised 1998) does not include recognition and measurement standards regarding equity compensation benefit plans. It simply requires that additional disclosures be made such that users of the financial statements will be assisted in their efforts to assess the impact of such benefit programs on the respective reporting entity's financial position, performance and cash flows. Specifically, an enterprise's financial position may be affected if it is required to potentially issue equity financial instruments or convert other financial instruments, as when stock options vest and the employees are able to exercise these to acquire shares. Financial performance and cash flows, similarly, would be affected if exercise of options provides a source of cash to the enterprise, even as compensation costs are depressed (and profits are correspondingly elevated), because employees accept stock compensation in lieu of currently reportable salary and bonus.

To provide these limited insights, IAS 19 requires that an enterprise which provides equity compensation benefits must disclose the following:

1. The nature and terms of such plans, including any vesting provisions
2. The accounting policy regarding such plans
3. The amounts recognized in the financial statements for those plans
4. The number and terms of the reporting entity's shares or other equity instruments which are held by the plan and by employees at the beginning and end of the period, with explanation of dividend, voting and conversion rights, exercise dates and prices and expiration dates; and the changes in rights to shares which have vested during the reporting period
5. The number and terms of the reporting entity's shares or other equity instruments which were issued to the plan and to employees, or distributed by the plan to employees, during the period, with explanation of dividend, voting and conversion rights, exercise dates and prices and expiration dates; and the fair value of consideration received by the entity during the period
6. The number, exercise dates and exercise prices of share options exercised under the terms of the plan during the period
7. The number of share options held by the plan, or by employees under terms of the plan, that lapsed (expired without being exercised) during the period
8. The amount, and principal terms, of any loans or guarantees by the entity to or for the plan or participants therein

The standard furthermore requires disclosure, as of the beginning and end of the period, of the fair value of the entity's own equity financial instruments, apart from share options, which are held by equity compensation plans. Finally, disclosure is required of the fair value, at issuance, of the entity's equity financial instruments, apart from options, issued to the plan or to employees, or by the plan to employees, during the period. If it is not practicable to develop or obtain fair value data, that fact may be stated in lieu of actual disclosure.

When a reporting entity has a multitude of plans, disclosures under IAS 19 may be made by plan, in the aggregate, or in such groupings as are deemed to be most useful. The objective is to convey the enterprise's obligations to issue equity instruments under terms of these plans, as well as to communicate changes in the obligations during the period. While disclosure requirements are flexible, it is important that aggregation not conceal the essential characteristics of these equity compensation arrangements.

17 STOCKHOLDERS' EQUITY

PERSPECTIVE AND ISSUES

The IASC's *Framework for the Preparation and Presentation of Financial Statements* defines equity as the residual interest in the assets of an enterprise after deducting all its liabilities. Stockholders' equity is comprised of all capital contributed to the entity (including share premium, also referred to as capital paid-in in excess of par value) plus retained earnings (i.e., the entity's accumulated earnings less any distributions that have been made therefrom).

Stockholders' equity (referred to as equity in IAS 1 [revised]) also includes reserves, such as statutory or legal reserves, general reserves and contingency reserves, and revaluation surplus. IAS 1 (revised) categorizes stockholders' interests into three broad subdivisions: issued capital, reserves, and accumulated profits or losses. This newly revised standard also sets forth requirements for disclosures about the details of share capital for corporations and the various capital accounts of other types of enterprises.

Stockholders' equity represents an interest in the net assets (i.e., assets less liabilities) of the entity. It is not a claim on those assets in the sense that liabilities are. On liquidation of the business, an obligation arises for the entity to distribute any remaining assets to the shareholders after the creditors are paid.

Earnings are not generated by transactions in an entity's own equity (e.g., by the issuance, reacquisition, or reissuance of its common or preferred shares). Depending on the laws of the jurisdiction of incorporation, distributions to shareholders may be subject to various limitations, such as to the amount of retained (accounting basis) earnings.

A major objective of the accounting for stockholders' equity is the adequate disclosure of the sources from which the capital was derived. For this reason, a number of different paid-in capital accounts may be presented in the balance sheet. The rights of each class of shareholder must also be disclosed. Where shares are reserved for future issuance, such as under the terms of stock option plans, this fact must also be made known.

Sources of IAS

IAS 1 (revised), 8, 16, 25, 32   *SIC* 5, 16

CONCEPTS, RULES, AND EXAMPLES

The international accounting standards (IAS), including the statement of principles, deal only with presentation and disclosure requirements relating to stockholders' equity. IAS have yet to address the accounting for the various components of stockholders' equity. There are numerous complex accounting issues relating to the various components of stockholders' equity, some of which have been and others are still being tackled by standard-setting bodies worldwide. The absence of any international accounting standard dealing with the accounting treatment of equity transactions is an impediment to uniform and appropriate accounting by international conglomerates, multinational corporations and other companies that comply with IAS. Given the absence of any promulgated international GAAP on this highly complex and important area, this chapter makes extensive use of the guidance under US GAAP.

Presentation and Disclosure Requirements Under IAS

Stockholders' equity (referred to as equity in IAS 1 [revised]) also includes reserves such as statutory or legal reserves, general reserves and contingency reserves, and revaluation surplus. IAS 1 (revised) categorizes stockholders' interests in three broad subdivisions: issued capital, reserves, and accumulated profits or losses. This newly revised standard also sets forth requirements for disclosures about the details of share capital for corporations and the various capital accounts of other types of enterprises.

Disclosures relating to share capital.

1. **The number or amount of shares authorized, issued, and outstanding.**
   It is required that a company disclose information relating to the number of

shares authorized, issued, and outstanding. Each of these has a different connotation. Authorized share capital is the maximum number of shares that a company is permitted to issue, according to its articles of association or its charter or bylaws (these being given different names in different countries). The number of shares issued and outstanding could vary, based on the fact that a company could have acquired its own shares and is holding them as treasury stock (discussed below under reacquired shares).

2. **Capital not yet paid in.** In an initial public offering (IPO), subscribers may be asked initially to pay in only a portion of the par value, with the balance due in installments, which are known as **calls**. Thus, it is likely that on the date of the balance sheet, a certain portion of the share capital is not yet paid in. For instance, while the gross amount of the stock subscription increases capital, if the due date of the last and final call falls on February 7, 2001, following the accounting year end of December 31, 2000, the amount of capital not yet paid in should be shown as a deduction from stockholders' equity. In this manner, only the net amount (of capital) received up to the date of the balance sheet will be properly included in net stockholders' equity. IAS 1 (revised) requires that a distinction be made between shares which have been issued and fully paid, on the one hand, and those which have been issued but not fully paid, on the other hand. The number of shares outstanding at the beginning and at the end of each period presented must also be reconciled.

3. **Par value per share.** This is also generally referred to as legal value or face value per share. The par value of shares is specified in the corporate charter or bylaws and referred to in other documents, such as the share application and prospectus. Par value is the smallest unit of share capital that can be acquired unless the prospectus permits fractional shares (which is very unusual for commercial enterprises). In certain countries, including the United States, it is also permitted for corporations to issue no-par stock (i.e., stock that is not given any par value). In such cases, again depending on local corporation laws, sometimes a stated value is determined by the board of directors, which is then accorded effectively the same treatment as par value. IAS 1 (revised) requires disclosure of par values or of the fact that the shares were issued without par values.

Traditionally, companies often issued shares at par value in cases where shares are issued immediately on incorporation or soon thereafter. However, when a well-established company with a proven track record issues shares, it may issue new shares at a premium. As a practical matter, par values have had a much diminished importance as corporation laws have been modernized in many jurisdictions, and often the par values will be trivial, such as $1 or even $0.01 per share. In such cases, issuance prices even at inception of a new corporation will be substantially above par value.

4. **Movements in share capital accounts during the year.** This information is usually disclosed in the footnotes to the financial statements, generally in a statement format, although in some circumstances merely described in a narrative in the footnotes. This statement, referred to as the Statement of Changes in Stockholders' Equity, highlights the changes during the year in the various components of stockholders' equity. It also serves the purpose of reconciling the beginning and the ending balances of stockholders' equity, as shown in the balance sheet. Under the provisions of IAS 1 (revised), enterprises must now present either a statement showing the changes in all the equity accounts (including issued capital, reserves and accumulated profit or loss), or a statement reporting changes in equity other than those arising from transactions with, or distributions to, owners.

5. **Rights, preferences, and restrictions with respect to the distribution of dividends and to the repayment of capital.** When there is more than one class of share capital with varying rights, adequate disclosure of the rights, preferences, and restrictions attached to each such class of share capital will enhance understandability of the information provided by the financial statements.

6. **Cumulative preference dividends in arrears.** If a company does not pay dividends on the preference shares for a certain number of years, it is required by statute (corporate law worldwide requires this) to make up these arrears in later years, if the shares have a cumulative feature. These dividends have to be paid before any dividends are paid on other equity shares. Although practice varies, most preference shares are cumulative in nature; preference shares that do not have this feature are called **noncumulative preference shares**.

7. **Reacquired shares.** Shares that are reacquired by a company are referred to as **treasury stock**. In those jurisdictions where the corporate or company law of the country permits the repurchase of shares, such shares, on acquisition by the company or its consolidated subsidiary, become legally available for reissue or resale without further authorization. **Shares outstanding** refers to shares other than those held as treasury stock. Treasury stock does not reduce the number of shares issued but affects the number of shares outstanding. It is to be noted that certain countries prohibit companies from purchasing their own shares, since to do so is considered as a reduction of share capital that can be achieved only with the express consent of the shareholders in an extraordinary general meeting and then only under certain conditions.

In the United Kingdom, traditionally companies were prohibited from purchasing their own shares. However, the UK Companies Act of 1981 relaxed this prohibition by allowing this practice, subject of course to certain conditions. Even in the United States, for that matter, not all states recognize treasury stock, and in those states the reacquired shares are to be treated as having been retired. Normally, treasury stock is shown as a reduction of stockholders' equity. Under very rare circumstances it may be presented as an asset, and shown on the asset side of the balance sheet, provided that adequate disclosure is made of this. Accounting for treasury stock is discussed further, in detail, in the latter part of this chapter.

In SIC 16, the Standing Interpretations Committee has restated the principle that an entity's own shares, when reacquired, are to be reported as deductions from equity and not as assets in the consolidated balance sheet. The acquisition transaction should be reported in the statement of changes in equity. When later resold, any difference between acquisition cost and ultimate proceeds represents a change in equity, and is therefore not to be considered a gain or loss to be included in the income statement. According to the interpretation, the reductions in equity may be either shown explicitly in the balance sheet's equity section as a contra account, or reported in the notes thereto. These rules are entirely consistent with widespread practice and the requirements of other national accounting standards.

A proposed interpretation (SIC-D17) addresses the equally universal issue of how to account for costs incurred in connection either with share issuances or with share reacquisitions (i.e., treasury share transactions). Again consistent with common practice, this would require that such costs be associated with the related capital transaction, and thus accounted for as reductions of equity (if the corresponding transaction was a share issuance) or as increases in the contra equity account (in the case of share reacquisitions). Relevant costs are limited to incremental costs directly associated with the transactions. If the issuance involves a compound instrument as discussed by IAS 32, the issuance costs should be associated with the liability and equity components, respectively, using, in SIC-D17's terms, a "rational and consistent basis of allocation."

8. **Shares reserved for future issuance under options and sales contracts, including the terms and amounts.** Companies issue stock options that grant the holder of these options rights to a specified number of shares at a certain price. A good example of a stock option is an option granted under an employee stock ownership plan (ESOP). Stock options are an increasingly popular means of employee remuneration, and usually top management is offered such noncash perquisites as part of its remuneration package. If a company has shares reserved for future issuance under option plans or sales contracts, it is necessary to disclose the number of shares, including terms and amounts, so reserved.

An interpretation of the Standing Interpretations Committee (SIC 5) deals with situations in which enterprise obligations are to be settled in cash or in equity securities, depending on the outcome of contingencies not under the issuer's control. In general, these should be classed as liabilities, in accordance with the guidance in IAS 32, unless it is judged to be a remote possibility, at the time of issuance, that a settlement with cash or another financial asset will be required. In the latter case, classification as equity will be prescribed.

The accounting for stock options is dealt with later in this chapter and presents many intriguing and complex issues, most of which the accounting profession has already addressed. However, by looking at the number of technically complex issues in this area, the impression may be had that the profession is still unable to come to grips fully with this topic. Under US GAAP, for example, a number of pronouncements have been issued only in the area of ESOP, but the standard issued in 1993 is not mandatorily applicable to shares held as of that date; instead, employers may continue to use the prior accounting methods for shares purchased prior to that time. Significant changes in the authoritative literature have recently been promulgated on the matter of accounting for stock-based compensation (options, appreciation rights, etc.). These changes are also discussed later in this chapter.

Disclosures Relating to Other Equity

1. **Capital paid in excess of par value.** This is the amount received on the issuance of shares that is the excess over the par value. It is called additional paid-in capital in the United States, while in some other countries, including the United Kingdom, it is referred to as "share premium."

2. **Revaluation reserve.** When a company carries property, plant, and equipment at other than historical costs, as is permitted by IAS 16 (i.e., it does not follow the benchmark treatment but, instead, follows the allowed alternative treatment, and revalues property, plant, and equipment to fair value), the difference between the historical costs (net of accumulated depreciation) and the fair values is credited to the revaluation reserve. Under IAS 25, long-term investments could also be carried at revalued amounts. Thus, revaluation reserve could arise not only from revaluations of property, plant, and equipment but even from revaluations of long-term investments.

   The standard requires that movements of this reserve during the period (year) be disclosed, which is usually done in the footnotes. Also, restrictions as to any distributions of this reserve to shareholders should be disclosed.

3. **Reserves.** Reserves include capital as well as revenue reserves. Also, statutory reserves and voluntary reserves are included under this category. Finally, special reserves, including contingency reserves, are included herein.

   Statutory reserves (or legal reserves, as they are called in some jurisdictions) are created based on the requirements of the law or the statute under which the company is incorporated. For instance, most corporate statutes in

Middle Eastern countries require that companies set aside 10% of their net income for the year as a "statutory reserve," with such appropriations to continue until the balance in this reserve account equals 50% of the company's equity capital.

Sometimes a company's articles, charter, or bylaws may require that the company set aside each year a certain percentage of its net profit (income) by way of a contingency or general reserve. Unlike statutory or legal reserves, contingency reserves are based on the provisions of corporate bylaws. Apparently, the rationale behind creation of such reserves is to make the company strong by requiring that each year a stipulated percentage of profits be plowed back into equity instead of being distributed to shareholders.

The standard requires that movements during the period (year) in these reserves be disclosed, along with the nature and purpose of each reserve presented within owners' equity.

4. **Retained earnings.** By definition, retained earnings represents a corporation's accumulated profits (losses) less any distributions that have been made therefrom. However, based on provisions contained in the international accounting standards, other adjustments are also made to the amount of retained earnings. IAS 8 (revised 1993), *Net Profit or Loss for the Period, Fundamental Errors and Changes in Accounting Policies*, requires the following to be shown as adjustments to retained earnings:

   a. Under the benchmark treatment, correction of fundamental errors that relate to prior periods should be reported by adjusting the opening balance of retained earnings. Comparative information should be restated, unless it is impracticable to do so.

   b. Under the benchmark treatment, the resulting adjustment from a change in accounting policy which is to be applied retrospectively should be reported as an adjustment to the opening balance of retained earnings. Comparative information should be restated unless it is impracticable to do so.

When dividends have been proposed but not formally approved, and hence when such intended dividends have not yet become reportable as a liability of the enterprise, disclosure is required by IAS 1 (revised). Also, the amount of any cumulative preference dividends not recognized as charges against accumulated profits must be disclosed, whether parenthetically or in the footnotes.

Classification Between Liabilities and Equity

IAS 32 requires that the issuer of a financial instrument should classify the instrument, or its components, as a liability or as equity, according to the substance of the contractual arrangement on initial recognition. The crux of the issue is the differentiation between a financial liability and an equity instrument.

The standard defines a financial liability as a contractual obligation

1. To deliver cash or another financial asset to another enterprise, or
2. To exchange financial instruments with another enterprise under conditions that are potentially unfavorable.

An equity instrument, on the other hand, has been defined by the standard as any contract that evidences a residual interest in the assets of an enterprise after deducting all its liabilities.

Compound financial instruments. Increasingly, it is not uncommon for corporations to issue financial instruments that have attributes of both equity and liabilities. IAS 32 stipulates that an enterprise that issues such financial instruments, which are technically known as compound instruments, should classify the component parts of the financial instrument separately as equity or liability as appropriate. (For a detailed discussion on financial instruments, refer to Chapters 5 and 10.)

On a related topic, the IASC's Standing Interpretations Committee had reached preliminary consensus that instruments which give the issuer the option of settling in its own equity instruments or in cash should be classified as liabilities if the number of shares it would take to settle are contractually subject to adjustment based on fair value of the shares. Since the effect is to eliminate risks to the holder, it makes the obligation in essence a fixed one based on the cash option.

APPENDIX A

ILLUSTRATION OF FINANCIAL STATEMENT PRESENTATION UNDER US GAAP

This appendix provides an illustration of the various financial statements that **may** be required to be presented and are related to the stockholders' equity section of the balance sheet.

Stockholders' Equity Section of a Balance Sheet

Capital stock:		
Preferred stock, $100 par, 7% cumulative, 30,000 shares		
authorized, issued, and outstanding		$ 3,000,000
Common stock, no par, stated value $10 per share,		
500,000 shares authorized, 415,000 shares issued		4,150,000
Total capital stock		$ 7,150,000
Additional paid-in capital:		
Issued price in excess of par value--preferred	$ 150,000	
Issued price in excess of stated value--common	845,000	995,000
Total paid-in capital		$ 8,145,000
Donated capital		100,000
Retained earnings:		
Appropriated for plant expansion	$2,100,000	
Unappropriated	2,275,000	4,375,000
Total capital and retained earnings		$12,620,000
Less 10,000 common shares held in treasury, at cost		(120,000)
Total stockholders' equity		$12,500,000

Retained Earnings Statement

Balance at beginning of year, as reported	$ 3,800,000
Prior period adjustment--correction of an error in method	
of depreciation (less tax effect of $77,000)	115,000
Balance at beginning of year, restated	$ 3,915,000
Net income for the year	748,000
Cash dividends declared during the year	
Preferred stock	(210,000)
Common stock	(78,000)
Balance at end of year	$ 4,375,000

Statement of Changes in Stockholders' Equity (Including Retained Earnings Statement)

	Preferred stock Shares	Preferred stock Amount	Common stock Shares	Common stock Amount	Additional paid-in capital	Donated capital	Retained earnings	Treasury stock (common)	Total stockholders' equity
Balance, 12/31/99, as reported	--	--	400,000	$4,000,000	$840,000	$100,000	$3,800,000	$(120,000)	$ 8,620,000
Correction of an error in method of depr.	--	--	--	--	--	--	115,000	--	115,000
Balance, 12/31/00, restated	--	--	400,000	$4,000,000	$840,000	$100,000	$3,915,000	$(120,000)	$ 8,735,000
Preferred stock issued in public offering	30,000	$3,000,000	--	--	150,000	--	--	--	3,150,000
Stock options exercised	--	--	15,000	150,000	5,000	--	--	--	155,000
Net income	--	--	--	--	--	--	748,000	--	748,000
Cash dividends declared: Preferred, $7.00 per share	--	--	--	--	--	--	(210,000)	--	(210,000)
Common, $.20 per share	--	--	--	--	--	--	(78,000)	--	(78,000)
Balance, 12/31/01	30,000	$3,000,000	415,000	$4,150,000	$995,000	$100,000	$4,375,000	$(120,000)	$12,500,000

APPENDIX B

ADDITIONAL GUIDANCE UNDER US GAAP

As noted in the main portion of this chapter, international accounting standards have not addressed a number of complex and interesting issues that do arise in connection with financial reporting by enterprises in many countries. Although the material in this appendix is not authoritative, it is being provided with the intent that it be instructive as additional guidance. Since these are matters that are not addressed by IAS, the treatments illustrated herein are not prohibited for application to financial statements prepared in conformity with international accounting standards.

DEFINITIONS OF TERMS

Additional paid-in capital. Amounts received at issuance in excess of the par or stated value of capital stock and amounts received from other transactions involving the entity's stock and/or stockholders. It is classified by source.

Allocated shares. ESOP shares assigned to individual participants. These shares are usually based on length of service, compensation, or a combination of both.

Appropriation (of retained earnings). A segregation of retained earnings to communicate the unavailability of a portion for dividend distributions.

Authorized shares. The maximum number of shares permitted to be issued by a corporation's charter and bylaws.

Callable. An optional characteristic of preferred stock allowing the corporation to redeem the stock at specified future dates and at specific prices. The call price is usually at or above the original issuance price.

Cliff vesting. A condition of an option or other stock award plan which provides that the employee becomes fully vested at a single point in time.

Combination plans. Compensation plans under which employees receive two or more components, such as options and stock appreciation rights, all of which can be exercised. Thus, each component is actually a separate plan and is accounted for as such.

Committed-to-be-released shares. ESOP shares that will be allocated to employees for service performed currently. They are usually released by payment of debt service.

Compensatory plan. A stock option plan including elements of compensation that are recognized over the service period.

Compensatory stock option plans. Plans that do not meet the criteria for noncompensatory plans. Their main purpose is to provide additional compensation to officers and employees.

Constructive retirement method. Method of accounting for treasury shares that treats the shares as having been retired. The shares revert to authorized but unissued status. The stock and additional paid-in capital accounts are reduced, with a debit to retained earnings or a credit to a paid-in capital account for the excess or deficiency of the purchase cost over or under the original issuance proceeds.

Contributed capital. The amount of equity contributed by the corporation's shareholders. It consists of capital stock plus additional paid-in capital.

Convertible. An optional characteristic of preferred stock allowing the stockholders to exchange their preferred shares for common shares at a specified ratio.

Cost method. Method of accounting for treasury shares that presents aggregate cost of reacquired shares as a deduction from the total of paid-in capital and retained earnings.

Cumulative. An optional characteristic of preferred stock. Any dividends of prior years not paid to the preferred shareholders must be paid before any dividends can be distributed to the common shareholders.

Date of declaration. The date on which the board of directors votes that a dividend be paid. A legal liability (usually current) is created on this date in the case of cash, property, and scrip dividends.

Date of grant. The date on which the board of directors awards the stock to the employees in stock option plans.

Date of payment. The date on which the shareholders are paid the declared dividends.

Date of record. The date on which ownership of the shares is determined. Those owning stock on this date will be paid the declared dividends.

Deficit. A debit balance in the retained earnings account. Dividends may not generally be paid when this condition exists. Formally known as accumulated deficit.

Discount on capital stock. Occurs when the stock of a corporation is originally issued at a price below par value. The original purchasers become contingently liable to creditors for this difference.

Employee stock ownership plan (ESOP). A form of defined contribution employee benefit plan whereby the employer facilitates the purchase of shares of stock in the company for the benefit of the employees, generally by a trust established by the company. The plan may be leveraged by borrowings either from the employer-sponsor or from third-party lenders.

Fixed options. Options that grant the holder the rights to a specified number of shares at fixed prices. It is not dependent on achievement of performance targets.

Graded vesting. A vesting process whereby the employee becomes entitled to a stock-based award fractionally over a period of years.

Issued stock. The number of shares issued by the firm and owned by the shareholders and the corporation. It is the sum of outstanding shares plus treasury shares.

Junior stock. Shares with certain limitations, often as to voting rights, which are granted to employees pursuant to a performance compensation program. Such shares are generally convertible to ordinary shares on achievement of defined goals.

Legal capital. The aggregate par or stated value of stock. It represents the amount of owners' equity that cannot be distributed to shareholders. It serves to protect the claims of the creditors.

Liquidating dividend. A dividend distribution that is not based on earnings. It represents a return of contributed capital.

Measurement date. The date on which the price used to compute compensation under stock-based compensation plans is fixed.

Noncompensatory stock options. Options which, under current GAAP, do not include an element of compensation being paid to the participants. Under proposed GAAP all stock plans would include an element of compensation to be measured and allocated over the service periods of the employees.

Noncompensatory stock option plans. Plans whose primary purpose is widespread ownership of the firm among its employees and officers. They must meet four criteria (see APB 25, para 7, or the section on stock options).

No-par stock. Stock that has no par value. Sometimes a stated value is determined by the board of directors. In this case the stated value is accorded the same treatment as par value stock.

Outstanding stock. Stock issued by a corporation and held by shareholders (i.e., issued shares that are not held in the treasury).

Par value method. A method of accounting for treasury shares that charges the treasury stock account for the aggregate par or stated value of the shares acquired and charges the excess of the purchase cost over the par value to paid-in capital and/or retained earnings. A deficiency of purchase cost is credited to paid-in capital.

Participating. An optional characteristic of preferred stock whereby preferred shareholders may share ratably with the common shareholders in any profit distributions in excess of a predetermined rate. Participation may be limited to a maximum rate or may be unlimited (full).

Performance-based options. Options that are granted to employees conditional on the achievement of defined goals.

Phantom stock plan. A type of stock compensation arrangement that gives employees the right to participate in the increase in value of the company's shares (book value or market value, as stipulated in the plan) without actually being required to purchase the shares initially.

Quasi reorganization. A procedure that reclassifies amounts from contributed capital to retained earnings to eliminate a deficit in that account. All the assets and liabilities are first revalued to their current values. It represents an alternative to a legal reorganization in bankruptcy proceedings.

Retained earnings. The undistributed earnings of a firm.

Service period. The period over which a stock-based compensation award is earned by the recipient. If not otherwise defined in the plan, it is the vesting period.

Stock-based compensation. Any of a wide variety of compensation arrangements under which employees receive shares of stock, options to purchase shares, or other equity instruments, or under which the employer incurs obligations to the employees based on the price of the company's shares.

Stock options. Enables officers and employees of a corporation to purchase shares in the corporation.

Stock rights. Enables present shareholders to purchase additional shares of stock of the corporation. It is commonly used if a preemptive right is granted to common shareholders by some state corporation laws.

Suspense shares. ESOP shares that usually collateralize ESOP debt. They have not been allocated or committed to be released.

Tandem options. Compensation plans under which employees receive two or more components, such as options and stock appreciation rights, whereby the exercise of one component cancels the other(s). The accounting is based on the component that is more likely to be exercised.

Treasury stock. Shares of a corporation that have been repurchased by the corporation. This stock has no voting rights and receives no cash dividends. Some states do not recognize treasury stock. In such cases, reacquired shares are treated as having been retired.

Vesting. The process whereby the recipient of a stock-based compensation award earns the right to control or exercise the award.

CONCEPTS, RULES, AND EXAMPLES

Legal Capital and Capital Stock

Legal capital typically relates to that portion of the stockholders' investment in a corporation that is permanent in nature and represents assets that will continue to be available for the satisfaction of creditor's claims. Traditionally, legal capital was comprised of the aggregate par or stated value of common and preferred shares issued. In recent years, however, many states have eliminated the requirement that corporate shares have a designated par or stated value. Some states have adopted provisions of a model act that completely eliminated the distinction between par value and the amount contributed in excess of par.

Ownership interest in a corporation is made up of common and, optionally, preferred shares. The common shares represent the residual risk-taking ownership of the corporation after the satisfaction of all claims of creditors and senior classes of equity.

Preferred stock. Preferred shareholders are owners who have certain rights superior to those of common shareholders. These rights will pertain either to the earnings or the assets of the corporation. Preferences as to earnings exist when the preferred shareholders have a stipulated dividend rate (expressed either as a dollar amount or as a percentage of the preferred stock's par or stated value). Preferences as to assets exist when the preferred shares have a stipulated liquidation value. If a corporation were to liquidate, the preferred holders would be paid a specific amount before the common shareholders would have a right to participate in any of the proceeds.

In practice, preferred shares are more likely to have preferences as to earnings than as to assets. Some classes of preferred shares may have both preferential rights. Preferred shares may also have the following features: participation in earnings beyond the stipulated dividend rate; a cumulative feature, affording the preferred shareholders the protection that their dividends in arrears, if any, will be fully satisfied before the common shareholders participate in any earnings distribution; and convertibility or callability by the corporation. Whatever preferences exist must be disclosed adequately in the financial statements, either on the face of the balance sheet or in the notes.

In exchange for the preferences, the preferred shareholders' rights or privileges are limited. For instance, the right to vote may be restricted to common shareholders. The most important right denied to the preferred shareholders, however, is the right to participate without limitation in the earnings of the corporation. Thus, if the corporation has exceedingly large earnings for a particular period, these earnings would tend to accrue to the benefit of the common shareholders. This is true even if the preferred stock is participating (a fairly uncommon feature) because even participating preferred stock usually has some upper limitation placed on its degree of participation.

Occasionally, as discussed in the chapter, several classes of stock will be categorized as common (e.g., Class A common, Class B common, etc.). Since there can be only one class of shares that represents the true residual risk-taking investors in a corporation, it is clear that the other classes, even though described as common shareholders, must in fact have some preferential status. Typically, these preferences relate to voting rights. The rights and responsibilities of each class of shareholder, even if described as common, must be fully disclosed in the financial statements.

Issuance of shares. The accounting for the sale of shares by a corporation depends on whether the stock has a par or stated value. If there is a par or stated value, the amount of the proceeds representing the aggregate par or stated value is credited to the common or preferred stock account. The aggregate par or stated value is generally defined as legal capital not subject to distribution to shareholders. Proceeds in excess of par or stated value are credited to an additional paid-in capital account. The additional paid-in capital represents the amount in excess of the legal capital which may, under certain defined conditions, be distributed to shareholders. A corporation selling stock below par value credits the capital stock account for the par value and debits an offsetting discount account for the difference between par value and the amount actually received.

If there is a discount on original issue capital stock, it serves to notify the actual and potential creditors of the contingent liability of those investors. As a practical matter, corporations avoided this problem by reducing par values to an arbitrarily low amount. This reduction in par eliminated the chance that shares would be sold for amounts below par. Where corporation laws make no distinction between par value and amounts in excess of par, the entire proceeds from the sale of stock may be credited to the common stock account without distinction between the stock and the additional paid-in capital accounts. The following entries illustrate these concepts:

Facts: A corporation sells 100,000 shares of $5 par common stock for $8 per share cash.

Cash	800,000	
Common stock		500,000
Additional paid-in capital		300,000

Facts: A corporation sells 100,000 shares of no-par common stock for $8 per share cash.

Cash	800,000	
Common stock		800,000

Preferred stock will often be assigned a par value because in many cases the preferential dividend rate is defined as a percentage of par value (e.g., 10%, $25 par value preferred stock will have a required annual dividend of $2.50). However, the dividend can be stated as a dollar amount per year, thereby obviating the need for par values.

Stock issued for services. If the shares in a corporation are issued in exchange for services or property rather than for cash, the transaction should be reflected at the fair value of the property or services received. If this information is not readily available, the transaction should be recorded at the fair value of the shares that were issued. Where necessary, appraisals should be obtained to properly reflect the transaction. As a final resort, a valuation by the board of directors of the stock issued can be utilized. Stock issued to employees as compensation for services rendered should be accounted for at the fair value of the services performed, if determinable, or the value of the shares issued.

If shares are given by a major shareholder directly to an employee for services performed for the entity, this exchange should be accounted for as a capital contribution to the company by the major shareholder and as compensation expense incurred by the company. Only when accounted for in this manner will there be conformity with the general principle that all costs incurred by an entity, including compensation, should be reflected in its financial statements.

Issuance of stock units. In certain instances, common and preferred shares may be issued to investors as a unit (e.g., a unit of one share of preferred and two shares of common can be sold as a package). Where both of the classes of stock are publicly traded, the proceeds from a unit offering should be allocated in proportion to the relative market values of the securities. If only one of the securities is publicly traded, the proceeds should be allocated to the one that is publicly traded based on its known market value. Any excess is allocated to the other. Where the market value of neither security is known, appraisal information might be used. The imputed fair value of one class of security, particularly the preferred shares, can be based on the stipulated dividend rate. In this case, the amount of proceeds remaining after the imputing of a value of the preferred shares would be allocated to the common stock.

The foregoing procedures would also apply if a unit offering were made of an equity and a nonequity security such as convertible debentures.

Stock Subscriptions

Occasionally, particularly in the case of a newly organized corporation, a contract is entered into between the corporation and prospective investors, whereby the latter agree to purchase specified numbers of shares to be paid for over some installment period. These stock subscriptions are not the same as actual stock issuances, and the accounting differs.

The amount of stock subscriptions receivable by a corporation is sometimes treated as an asset on the balance sheet and is categorized as current or noncurrent in accordance with the terms of payment. However, most subscriptions receivable are shown as a reduction of stockholders' equity in the same manner as treasury stock. Since subscribed shares do not have the rights and responsibilities of actual outstanding stock, the credit is made to a stock subscribed account instead of to the capital stock accounts.

If the common stock has par or stated value, the common stock subscribed account is credited for the aggregate par or stated value of the shares subscribed. The excess over this amount is credited to additional paid-in capital. No distinction is made between additional paid-in capital relating to shares already issued and shares subscribed for. This treatment follows from the distinction between legal capital and additional paid-in capital. Where there is no par or stated value, the entire amount of the common stock subscribed is credited to the stock subscribed account.

As the amount due from the prospective shareholders is collected, the stock subscriptions receivable account is credited and the proceeds are debited to the cash account. Actual issuance of the shares, however, must await the complete payment of the stock subscription. Accordingly, the debit to common stock subscribed is not made until the subscribed shares are fully paid for and the stock is issued.

The following journal entries illustrate these concepts:

1. 10,000 shares of $50 par preferred are subscribed at a price of $65 each; a 10% down payment is received.

Cash	65,000	
Stock subscriptions receivable	585,000	
Preferred stock subscribed		500,000
Additional paid-in capital		150,000

2. 2,000 shares of no par common shares are subscribed at a price of $85 each, with one-half received in cash.

Cash	85,000	
Stock subscriptions receivable	85,000	
Common stock subscribed		170,000

3. All preferred subscriptions are paid, and one-half of the remaining common subscriptions are collected in full and subscribed shares are issued.

Cash [$585,000 + ($85,000 x 0.50)]	627,500	
Stock subscriptions receivable		627,500
Preferred stock subscribed	500,000	
Preferred stock		500,000
Common stock subscribed	127,500	
Common stock ($170,000 x 0.75)		127,500

When the company experiences a default by the subscriber, the accounting will follow the provisions of the state in which the corporation is chartered. In some jurisdictions, the subscriber is entitled to a proportionate number of shares based on the amount already paid on the subscriptions, sometimes reduced by the cost incurred by the corporation in selling the remaining defaulted shares to other stockholders. In other jurisdictions, the subscriber forfeits the entire investment on default. In this case the amount already received is credited to an additional paid-in capital account that describes its source.

Additional Paid-in Capital

Additional paid-in capital represents all capital contributed to a corporation other than that defined as par or stated value. Additional paid-in capital can arise from proceeds received from the sale of common and preferred shares in excess of their par or stated values. It can also arise from transactions relating to the following:

1. Sale of shares previously issued and subsequently reacquired by the corporation (treasury stock)
2. Retirement of previously outstanding shares
3. Payment of stock dividends in a manner that justifies the dividend being recorded at the market value of the shares distributed
4. Lapse of stock purchase warrants or the forfeiture of stock subscriptions, if these result in the retaining by the corporation of any partial proceeds received prior to forfeiture
5. Warrants that are detachable from bonds
6. Conversion of convertible bonds
7. Other gains on the company's own stock, such as that which results from certain stock option plans

When the amounts are material, the sources of additional paid-in capital should be described in the financial statements.

Donated Capital

Donated capital should also be adequately disclosed in the financial statements. Donated capital can result from an outright gift to the corporation (e.g., a major shareholder donates land or other assets to the company in a nonreciprocal transfer) or may result when services are provided to the corporation. Under current US GAAP, such nonreciprocal transactions will be recognized as revenue in the period the contribution is received.

In these situations, historical cost is not adequate to reflect properly the substance of the transaction, since the historical cost to the corporation would be zero. Accordingly, these events should be reflected at fair market value. If long-lived assets are donated to the corporation, they should be recorded at their fair value at the date of donation, and the amount so recorded should be depreciated over the normal useful economic life of such assets. If donations are conditional in nature, they should not be reflected formally in the accounts until the appropriate conditions have been satisfied. However, disclosure might still be required in the financial statements of both the assets donated and the conditions required to be met.

Retained Earnings

Legal capital, additional paid-in capital, and donated capital collectively represent the contributed capital of the corporation. The other major source of capital is retained earnings, which represents the accumulated amount of earnings of the corporation from the date of inception (or from the date of reorganization) less the cumulative amount of distributions made to shareholders and other charges to retained earnings (e.g., from treasury stock transactions). The distributions to shareholders generally take the form of dividend payments but may take other forms as well, such as the reacquisition of shares for amounts in excess of the original issuance proceeds.

Retained earnings are also affected by action taken by the corporation's board of directors. Appropriation serves disclosure purposes and serves to restrict dividend payments but does nothing to provide any resources for satisfaction of the contingent loss or other underlying purpose for which the appropriation has been made. Any appropriation made from retained earnings must eventually be returned to the retained earnings account. It is not permissible to charge losses against the appropriation account nor to credit any realized gain to that account. The use of appropriated retained earnings has diminished significantly over the years.

An important rule relating to retained earnings is that transactions in a corporation's own stock can result in a reduction of retained earnings (i.e., a deficiency on such transactions can be charged to retained earnings) but cannot result in an increase in retained earnings (any excesses on such transactions are credited to paid-in capital, never to retained earnings).

If a series of operating losses have been incurred or distributions to shareholders in excess of accumulated earnings have been made and if there is a debit balance in retained earnings, the account is generally referred to as accumulated deficit.

Dividends

Dividends are the pro rata distribution of earnings to the owners of the corporation. The amount and the allocation between the preferred and common shareholders is a function of the stipulated preferential dividend rate, the presence or absence of (1) a participation feature, (2) a cumulative feature, and (3) arrearages on the preferred stock, and the wishes of the board of directors. Dividends, even preferred stock dividends where a cumulative feature exists, do not accrue. Dividends become a liability of the corporation only when they are declared by the board of directors.

Traditionally, corporations were not allowed to declare dividends in excess of the amount of retained earnings. Alternatively, a corporation could pay dividends out of retained earnings and additional paid-in capital but could not exceed the total of these categories (i.e., they could not impair legal capital by the payment of dividends). States that have adopted the Model Business Corporation Act grant more latitude to the directors. Corporations can now, in certain jurisdictions, declare and pay dividends in excess of the book amount of retained earnings if the directors conclude that, after the payment of such dividends, the fair value of the corporation's net assets will still be a positive amount. Thus, directors can declare dividends out of unrealized appreciation, which, in certain industries, can be a significant source of dividends beyond the realized and recognized accumulated earnings of the corporation. This action, however, represents a major departure from traditional practice and demands both careful consideration and adequate disclosure.

Three important dividend dates are

1. The declaration date
2. The record date
3. The payment date

The declaration date governs the incurrence of a legal liability by the corporation. The record date refers to that point in time when a determination is made as to which specific registered stockholders will receive dividends and in what amounts. Finally, the payment date relates to the date when the distribution of the dividend takes place. These concepts are illustrated in the following example:

Example of payment of dividends

On May 1, 2000, the directors of River Corp. declare a $.75 per share quarterly dividend on River Corp.'s 650,000 outstanding common shares. The dividend is payable May 25 to holders of record May 15.

May 1	Retained earnings (or Dividends)	487,500	
	Dividends payable		487,500
May 15	No entry		
May 25	Dividends payable	487,500	
	Cash		487,500

If a dividends account is used, it is closed directly to retained earnings at year end.

Dividends may be made in the form of cash, property, or scrip, which is a form of short-term note payable. Cash dividends are either a given dollar amount per share or a percentage of par or stated value. Property dividends consist of the distribution of any assets other than cash (e.g., inventory or equipment). Finally, scrip dividends are promissory notes due at some time in the future, sometimes bearing interest until final payment is made.

Occasionally, what appear to be disproportionate dividend distributions are paid to some but not all of the owners of closely held corporations. Such transactions need to be analyzed carefully. In some cases these may actually represent compensation paid to the recipients. In other instances, these may be a true dividend paid to all shareholders on a pro rata basis, to which certain shareholders have waived their rights. If the former, the distribution should not be accounted for as a dividend but as compensation or some other expense category and included on the income statement. If the latter, the dividend should be grossed up to reflect payment on a proportional basis to all the shareholders, with an offsetting capital contribution to the company recognized as having been effectively made by those to whom payments were not made.

Property dividends. If property dividends are declared, the paying corporation may incur a gain or loss. Since the dividend should be reflected at the fair value of the assets distributed, the difference between fair value and book value is recorded at the time the dividend is declared and charged or credited to a loss or gain account.

Scrip dividends. If a corporation declares a dividend payable in scrip that is interest bearing, the interest is accrued over time as a periodic expense. The interest is not a part of the dividend itself.

Liquidating dividends. Liquidating dividends are not distributions of earnings, but rather, a return of capital to the investing shareholders. A liquidating dividend is normally recorded by the declarer through charging additional paid-in capital rather than retained earnings. The exact accounting for a liquidating dividend is affected by the laws where the business is incorporated, and these laws vary from state to state.

Stock dividends. Stock dividends represent neither an actual distribution of the assets of the corporation nor a promise to distribute those assets. For this reason, a stock dividend is not considered a legal liability or a taxable transaction.

Despite the recognition that a stock dividend is not a distribution of earnings, the accounting treatment of relatively insignificant stock dividends (defined as being less than 20 to 25% of the outstanding shares prior to declaration) is consistent with its being a real dividend. Accordingly, retained earnings are debited for the fair market value of the shares to be paid as a dividend, and the capital stock and additional paid-in capital accounts are credited for the appropriate amounts based on the par or stated value of the shares, if any. A stock dividend declared but not yet paid is classified as such in the stockholders' equity section of the balance sheet. Since such a dividend never reduces assets, it cannot be a liability.

The selection of 20 to 25% as the threshold for recognizing a stock dividend as an earnings distribution is arbitrary, but it is based somewhat on the empirical evidence that small stock dividends tend not to result in a reduced market price per share for outstanding shares. In theory, any stock dividend should result in a reduction of the market value of outstanding shares in an inverse relationship to the size of the stock dividend. The aggregate value of the outstanding shares should not change, but the greater number of shares outstanding after the stock dividend should necessitate a lower per share price. As noted, however, the declaration of small stock dividends tends not to have this impact, and this phenomenon supports the accounting treatment.

On the other hand, when stock dividends are larger in magnitude, it is observed that per share market value declines after declaration of the dividend. In such situations it would not be valid to treat the stock dividend as an earnings distribution. Rather, it should be accounted for as a split. The precise treatment depends on the legal requirements of the state of incorporation and on whether the existing par value or stated value is reduced concurrent with the stock split.

If the par value is not reduced for a large stock dividend and if state law requires that earnings be capitalized in an amount equal to the aggregate of the par value of the stock dividend declared, the event should be described as a stock split effected in the form of a dividend, with a charge to retained earnings and a credit to the common stock account for the aggregate par or stated value. When the par or stated value is reduced in recognition of the split and state laws do not require treatment as a dividend, there is no formal entry to record the split but merely a notation that the number of shares outstanding has increased and the per share par or stated value has decreased accordingly.

Treasury Stock

Treasury stock consists of a corporation's own stock that has been issued, subsequently reacquired by the firm, and not yet reissued or canceled. Treasury stock does not reduce the number of shares issued but does reduce the number of shares outstanding, as well as total stockholders' equity. These shares are not eligible to receive cash dividends. Treasury stock is not an asset, although in some circumstances, it may be presented as an asset if adequately disclosed. Reacquired stock that is awaiting delivery to satisfy a liability created by the firm's compensation plan or reacquired stock held in a profit sharing trust is still considered outstanding and would not be considered treasury stock. In each case, the stock would be presented as an asset with the accompanying footnote disclosure.

Three approaches exist for the treatment of treasury stock: the cost, par value, and constructive retirement methods.

Cost method. Under the cost method, the gross cost of the shares reacquired is charged to a contra equity account (treasury stock). The equity accounts that were credited for the original share issuance (common stock, paid-in capital in excess of par, etc.) remain intact. When the treasury shares are reissued, proceeds in excess of cost are credited to a paid-in capital account. Any deficiency is charged to retained earnings (unless paid-in capital from previous treasury share transactions exists, in which case the deficiency is charged to that account, with any excess charged to retained earnings). If many treasury stock purchases are made, a cost flow assumption (e.g., FIFO or specific identification) should be adopted to compute excesses and deficiencies on subsequent share reissuances. The advantage of the cost method is that it avoids identifying and accounting for amounts related to the original issuance of the shares and is, therefore, the simpler, more frequently used method. The cost method is most consistent with the one-transaction concept. This concept takes the view that the classification of stockholders' equity should not be affected simply because the corporation was the middle "person" in an exchange of shares from one stockholder to another. In substance, there is only a transfer of shares between two stockholders. Since the original balances in the equity accounts are left undisturbed, its use is most acceptable when the firm acquires its stock for reasons other than retirement, or when its ultimate disposition has not yet been decided.

Par value method. Under the second approach, the par value method, the treasury stock account is charged only for the aggregate par (or stated) value of the shares reacquired. Other paid-in capital accounts (excess over par value, etc.) are relieved in proportion to the amounts recognized on the original issuance of the shares. The treasury share acquisition is treated almost as a retirement. However, the common (or preferred) stock account continues at the original amount, thereby preserving the distinction between an actual retirement and a treasury share transaction.

When the treasury shares accounted for by the par value method are subsequently resold, the excess of the sale price over par value is credited to paid-in capital. A reissuance for a price below par value does not create a contingent liability for the purchaser. It is only the original purchaser who risks this obligation to the entity's creditors.

Constructive retirement method. The constructive retirement method is similar to the par value method except that the aggregate par (or stated) value of the reacquired shares is charged to the stock account rather than to the treasury stock account. This method is superior when (1) it is management's intention not to reissue the shares within a reasonable time period, or (2) the state of incorporation defines reacquired shares as having been retired.

The two-transaction concept is most consistent with the par value and constructive retirement methods. First, the reacquisition of the firm's shares is viewed as constituting a contraction of its capital structure. Second, the reissuance of the shares is the same as issuing new shares. There is little difference between the purchase and subsequent reissuance of treasury shares and the acquisition and retirement of previously issued shares and the issuance of new shares.

Treasury shares originally accounted for by the cost method can subsequently be restated to conform to the constructive retirement method. If shares were acquired with the intention that they would be reissued and it is later determined that such reissuance is unlikely (due for example, to the expiration of stock options without their exercise), it is proper to restate the transaction.

Example of accounting for treasury stock

1. 100 shares ($50 par value) that were sold originally for $60 per share are later reacquired for $70 each.
2. All 100 shares are subsequently resold for a total of $7,500.

To record the acquisition, the entry is

Cost method			*Par value method*			*Constructive retirement method*		
Treasury stock	7,000		Treasury stock	5,000		Common stock	5,000	
Cash		7,000	Additional paid-in			Additional paid-in		
			capital--common			capital--common		
			stock	1,000		stock	1,000	
			Retained earnings	1,000		Retained earnings	1,000	
			Cash		7,000	Cash		7,000

To record the resale, the entry is

Cost method			*Par value method*			*Constructive retirement method*		
Cash	7,500		Cash	7,500		Cash	7,500	
Treasury stock		7,000	Treasury stock		5,000	Common stock		5,000
Additional paid-			Additional paid-			Additional paid-		
in capital--			in capital--			in capital--		
treasury stock		500	common stock		2,500	common stock		2,500

If the shares had been resold for $6,500, the entry is

Cost method			*Par value method*			*Constructive retirement method*		
Cash	6,500		Cash	6,500		Cash	6,500	
*Retained earnings	500		Treasury stock		5,000	Common stock		5,000
Treasury stock		7,000	Additional paid-			Additional paid-		
			in capital--			in capital--		
			common stock		1,500	common stock		1,500

* *"Additional paid-in capital--treasury stock" or "Additional paid-in capital--retired stock" of that issue would be debited first to the extent it exists.*

Alternatively, under the par or constructive retirement methods, any portion of or the entire deficiency on the treasury stock acquisition may be debited to retained earnings without allocation to paid-in capital. Any excesses would always be credited to an "Additional paid-in capital--retired stock" account.

The laws of some states govern the circumstances under which a corporation may acquire treasury stock and they may prescribe the accounting for the stock. For example, a charge to retained earnings may be required in an amount equal to the treasury stock's total cost. In such cases, the accounting according to state law prevails. Also, some states define excess purchase cost of reacquired (i.e., treasury) shares as being "distributions" to shareholders which are no different in nature than dividends. In such cases, the financial statement presentation should adequately disclose the substance of these transactions (e.g., by presenting both dividends and excess reacquisition costs together in the retained earnings statement).

When a firm decides to retire the treasury stock formally, the journal entry is dependent on the method used to account for the stock. Using the original sale and reacquisition data from the illustration above, the following entry would be made:

Cost method			*Par value method*		
Common stock	5,000		Common stock	5,000	
Additional paid-in			Treasury stock		5,000
capital--common stock	1,000				
*Retained earnings	1,000				
Treasury stock		7,000			

* *"Additional paid-in capital--treasury stock" may be debited to the extent that it exists.*

If the constructive retirement method were used to record the treasury stock purchase, no additional entry would be necessary on formal retirement of the shares.

After the entry is made, the pro rata portion of all paid-in capital existing for that issue (i.e., capital stock and additional paid-in capital) will have been eliminated. If stock is purchased for immediate retirement (i.e., not put into the treasury) the entry to record the retirement is the same as that made under the constructive retirement method.

In the case of donated treasury stock, the intentions of management are important. If the shares are to be retired, the capital stock account is debited for the par or stated value of the shares, "Donated capital" is credited for the fair market value, and "Additional paid-in capital--retired stock" is debited or credited for the difference. If the intention of management is to reissue the shares, three methods of accounting are available. The first two methods, cost and par value, are analogous to the aforementioned treasury stock methods except that "Donated capital" is credited at the time of receipt and debited at the time of reissuance. Under the cost method, the current market value of the stock is recorded (an apparent contradiction), whereas under the par value method, the par or stated value is used. Under the last method, only a memorandum entry is made to indicate the number of shares received. No journal entry is made at the time of receipt. At the time of reissuance, the entire proceeds are credited to "Donated capital." The method actually used is generally dependent on the circumstances involving the donation and the preference of the firm.

Other Equity Accounts

There are other adjustments to balance sheet accounts that are accumulated and reflected as separate components of stockholders' equity. Under current US GAAP, these include unrealized gains or losses on available-for-sale portfolios of debt and marketable equity securities, accumulated gain or loss on translation of foreign currency-denominated financial statements, and the net loss not recognized as pension cost.

Stock Options

The subject of accounting for stock options has long been controversial in the United States. A rule made more than 20 years ago decreed that most stock options would not result in recognition of compensation expense if the option exercise price were at least equal to the market price at the date of the granting of the options. Although this defied logic (if such options were not valuable compensation, executives would not negotiate these as part of their total compensation programs) it had long been traditional that this accounting would be applied. However, as long as 10 years ago the profession's top standard setters concluded that most such plans should indeed give rise to the recognition of compensation cost, and then began a long, controversial project to develop the appropriate accounting procedures.

The standards-setting body ultimately did propose a new standard that would have required a fairly complicated measurement strategy for compensation cost for most such option arrangements. A great, orchestrated outcry arose from many sectors of industry, particularly from those enterprises, such as technology companies, which traditionally make great use of this technique of compensating executives. The ultimate result was that a final standard was promulgated which recommended, but did not require, use of this technique. Supplemental disclosures are required for entities that decline to adopt the suggested method, however, which effectively results in presentation of an alternative income amount as if the recommended technique had been employed.

Since this situation is still not fully resolved and is unique, at the present time, to the United States, detailed presentation of the very complex methodology is omitted here.

Stock Appreciation Rights

Another type of stock-based compensation program gives the employees the opportunity to participate in any increase in value of the company's stock without having to incur the cost of actually purchasing the shares themselves. Such plans are often referred to as phantom stock plans, stock appreciation rights, or variable stock award programs. A wide variety of such plans have been devised in practice. Some provide for the payment of cash to the employees, while others reward participants with shares of the sponsoring company's stock. Often such plans are granted together with compensatory stock option plans as either combination plans or as tandem plans: the former give the employees the rights to both the options and the phantom stock, while the latter require the employees to choose which they will exercise (simultaneously forfeiting the other).

Under US GAAP, compensation cost incurred in connection with stock appreciation rights or other variable awards is determined prospectively until full vesting is achieved, with future increases or decreases in market price resulting in charges or credits to periodic compensation expense. Total compensation cost is allocated ratably (if cliff vesting is provided by the plan) or proportionally (if graded vesting is provided). When an employee forfeits options or rights for which compensation had previously been accrued, the accrual is to be reversed against compensation expense in the period of the forfeiture.

Performance-based stock compensation plans often provide for payment in shares instead of cash. For example, a stock appreciation rights plan may contain a provision that the increase in value will be distributed to the participant in the form of sufficient shares of the sponsor's stock to have an aggregate fair market value equal to the amount of the award. If the plan provides only for payment in shares (a plan that most often is referred to as a phantom stock plan), the offset to the periodic charge for compensation cost should be to paid-in capital accounts. If the award is payable at the participant's choice in either cash or stock, a liability should be accrued, since the sponsor cannot control the means by which the obligation will be settled. If the payment will be made in cash or stock at the option of the company, the offset to compensation should be either to a liability account or to equity accounts, based on the best available information concerning the sponsor's intentions. As these intentions change from one period to another, the amounts should be reclassified as necessary.

Accounting for stock appreciation rights has been altered by the recent standard on stock-based compensation. Furthermore, there are many variations in these plans and thus the precise accounting cannot be stipulated in general terms. Further discussion of this topic is beyond the scope of this book.

Convertible Preferred Stock

The treatment of convertible preferred stock at its issuance is no different from that of nonconvertible preferred. When it is converted, the book value approach is used to account for the conversion. Use of the market value approach would entail a gain or loss for which there is no theoretical justification, since the total amount of contributed capital does not change when the stock is converted. When the preferred stock is converted, the "Preferred stock" and related "Additional paid-in capital--preferred stock" accounts are debited for their original values when purchased, and "Common stock" and "Additional paid-in capital--common stock" (if an excess over par or stated value exists) are credited. If the book value of the preferred stock is less than the total par value of the common stock being issued, retained earnings is charged for the difference. This charge is supported by the rationale that the preferred shareholders are offered an additional return to facilitate their conversion to common stock. Many states require that this excess instead reduce additional paid-in capital from other sources.

Preferred Stock With Mandatory Redemption

A mandatory redemption clause requires the preferred stock to be redeemed (retired) at a specified date(s). This feature is in contrast to callable preferred stock, which is redeemed at the issuing corporation's option. When combined with a cumulative dividend preference, the mandatory redemption feature causes the preferred stock to have the characteristics of debt, especially when the stock is to be redeemed in 5 to 10 years. The dividend payments represent interest, and redemption is the repayment of principal. However, there is one important difference. The dividend payments do not receive the same tax treatment as do interest payments. They are not deductible in determining taxable income.

Despite these debt-like characteristics, this class of preferred stock currently receives no special treatment under GAAP. It is treated as any other stock on issuance, and on redemption, the stock is treated as an ordinary retirement. (It should be noted that this conflicts with the requirements under the international standard, IAS 32, which does demand that a "substance over form" analysis be conducted and that items such as mandatorily redeemable stock be treated as debt. This is one instance, but not the only one, in which the international standards have progressed beyond the US standards.)

For disclosure purposes under US GAAP, the stock is treated as equity and is presented within the stockholders' equity portion of the balance sheet. Disclosure of the amounts and timing of any redemption payments for each of the 5 years following the balance sheet date is required as footnote disclosure, however.

Book Value Stock Plans

Another type of stock purchase plan, the book value plan, is intended also to be a compensation program for participating employees, although there are important secondary motives in many such plans, such as the desires to generate capital and to tie employees to the employer. Under the terms of typical book value plans, employees (or those attaining some defined level, such as manager) are given the opportunity or, in some cases, they are required to purchase shares in the company, which then must be sold back to the company on termination of employment.

Under US GAAP, if the employees participating in a nonpublic company's book value stock plan have substantive investments in the company that are at risk, the increases in book value during the period of ownership are not to be treated as compensation. However, if the employees are granted options to purchase shares at book value, compensation is to be recognized for value increases, presumably because under the latter scenario the employee has no investment at risk and is only being given an "upside" opportunity. This interpretation is also applicable to book value options granted to employees of publicly held companies.

For accounting purposes, shares issued at book value to employees are simply recorded as a normal stock sale. To the extent that book value exceeds par or stated value, additional paid-in capital accounts may also be credited.

For such plans in publicly owned companies, GAAP states that these plans are performance plans akin to stock appreciation rights, and accordingly, results in compensation expense recognition. This conclusion was reached at least in part due to pressure from the US securities regulators.

Junior Stock

Another category of stock-based compensation program involves junior stock. Typically, such shares are subordinate to normal shares of common stock with respect to voting rights, dividend rate, or other attributes, and are convertible into regular common shares if and when stipulated performance goals are achieved. Like stock appreciation rights, grants of junior stock represent a performance-based program, in contrast to fixed stock options.

An interpretation under US GAAP holds that compensation cost incurred in connection with grants of junior stock is generally to be accrued. However, compensation is to be recognized only when it is deemed to be probable (as that term is defined by the accounting literature dealing with contingencies) that the performance goals will be achieved. It may be that achievement is not deemed probable at the time the junior stock is issued, but it later becomes clear that such achievement is indeed likely. In other circumstances, the ability to convert junior stock to regular stock is dependent on the achievement of more than a single performance goal, and it is not probable that all such goals can be achieved, although some of them are deemed probable of achievement. In both scenarios, full accrual of compensation cost may be delayed until the estimated likelihood of achievement improves.

The rule specifies that the measure of compensation is derived from the comparison of the market price of ordinary common stock with the price to be paid, if any, for the junior stock. Since the junior stock will be convertible to ordinary common stock if the defined performance goals are achieved, the compensation to be received by the employees participating in the plan is linked to the value of unrestricted common shares.

Put Warrant

A detachable put warrant can either be put back to the debt issuer for cash or can be exercised to acquire common stock. US GAAP holds that these instruments should be accounted for in the same manner as mandatorily redeemable preferred stock. The proceeds applicable to the put warrant ordinarily are to be classified as equity. In the case of a warrant with a put price substantially higher than the value assigned to the warrant at issuance, however, the proceeds should be classified as a liability since it is likely that the warrant will be put back to the company.

The original classification should not be changed because of subsequent economic changes in the value of the put. The value assigned to the put warrant at issuance, however, should be adjusted to its highest redemption price, starting with the date of issuance until the earliest date of the warrants. Changes in the redemption price before the earliest put dates are changes in accounting estimates, and changes after the earliest put dates should be recognized in income. If the put is classified as equity, the adjustment should be reported as a charge to retained earnings, and if the put is classified as a liability, the adjustment is reported as interest expense.

Accounting for Stock Issued to Employee Stock Ownership Plans

Increasingly, US corporations have been availing themselves of favorable tax regulations that encourage the establishment of employee stock ownership plans. Employee stock ownership plans (ESOP) are defined contribution employee benefit plans in which shares of the sponsoring entity are given to employees as additional compensation.

In brief, ESOP are created by a sponsoring corporation that either funds the plan directly (unleveraged ESOP) or, as is more often the case, facilitates the borrowing of money either directly from an outside lender (directly leveraged ESOP) or from the employer, who in turn will borrow from an outside lender (indirectly leveraged ESOP). Borrowings from outside lenders may or may not be guaranteed by the sponsor. Since effectively the only source of funds for debt repayment are future contributions by the sponsor, US GAAP requires that the ESOP's debt be considered debt of the sponsor. Depending on the reasons underlying the creation of the ESOP (estate planning by the controlling shareholder, expanding the capital base of the entity, rewarding and motivating the workforce, etc.), the sponsor's shares may be contributed to the plan in annual installments, in a block of shares from the sponsor, or shares from an existing shareholder may be purchased by the plan.

Direct or indirect borrowings by the ESOP must be reported as debt in the sponsor's balance sheet. An offset to a contra equity account, not to an asset, is also reported since the plan represents a commitment (morally, if not always legally) to make future contributions to the plan and not a claim to resources. This results in a "double hit" to the sponsor's balance sheet (i.e., the recording of a liability and the reduction of net stockholders' equity), which is often an unanticipated and unpleasant surprise. This contra equity account was called "unearned compensation" under prior accounting rules but is now referred to as "unearned ESOP shares." If the sponsor lends funds to the ESOP without a "mirror" loan from an outside lender, this loan should not be reported in the employer's balance sheet as debt, although the debit should still be reported as a contra equity account.

As the ESOP services the debt (using contributions made by the sponsor and/or dividends received on sponsor shares held by the plan) the sponsor reflects the reduction of the obligation by reducing the debt and the contra equity account on its balance sheet. Simultaneously, income and thus retained earnings will be affected as the contributions to the plan are reported in the sponsor's current results of operations. Thus, the double hit is eliminated, but net worth continues to reflect the economic fact that compensation costs have been incurred. US GAAP requires that the interest cost component be separated from the remaining compensation expense, that is, that the sponsor's income statement should reflect the true character of the expenses being incurred rather than aggregating the entire amount into a category such as "ESOP contribution."

In a leveraged ESOP, shares held serve as collateral for the debt and are not allocated to employees until the debt is retired. In general, shares must be allocated by the end of the year in which the debt is repaid; however, to satisfy the tax laws, the allocation of shares may take place at a faster pace than retirement of the principal portion of the debt.

The cost of ESOP shares allocated is measured (for purposes of reporting compensation expense in the sponsor's income statements) based on the fair value on the release date, in contrast to the actual historical cost of the shares to the plan. Dividends paid on unallocated shares (i.e., shares held by the ESOP) are reported in the sponsor's income statement as compensation cost and/or as interest expense.

Example of accounting for ESOP transactions

Assume that Intrepid Corp. establishes an ESOP, which then borrows $500,000 from Second Interstate Bank. The ESOP then purchases 50,000 shares of Intrepid no-par shares from the company; none of these shares are allocated to individual participants. The entries would be

Cash	500,000	
Bank loan payable		500,000
Unearned ESOP shares (contra equity account)	500,000	
Common stock		500,000

The ESOP then borrows an additional $250,000 from the sponsor, Intrepid, and uses the cash to purchase a further 25,000 shares, all of which are allocated to participants.

Compensation	250,000	
Common stock		250,000

Intrepid Corp. contributes $50,000 to the plan, which the plan uses to service its bank debt, consisting of $40,000 principal reduction and $10,000 interest cost. The debt reduction causes 4,000 shares to be allocated to participants at a time when the average market value had been $12 per share.

Interest expense	10,000	
Bank loan payable	40,000	
Cash		50,000

Compensation	48,000	
Additional paid-in capital		8,000
Unearned ESOP shares		40,000

Dividends of $0.10 per share are declared (only the ESOP shares are represented in the following entry, but dividends are paid equally on all outstanding shares).

Retained earnings	2,900	
Compensation	4,600	
Dividends payable		7,500

Note that in all the foregoing illustrations the effect of income taxes is ignored. Since the difference between the cost and fair values of shares committed to be released is analogous to differences in the expense recognized for tax and accounting purposes with regard to stock options, the same treatment should be applied. That is, the tax effect should be reported directly in stockholders' equity rather than in earnings.

Corporate Bankruptcy and Reorganizations

Entities operating under and emerging from protection of the bankruptcy laws. The going concern assumption is one of the basic postulates underlying generally accepted accounting principles and is responsible for, among other things, the historical cost convention in financial reporting. For entities that have entered bankruptcy proceedings, however, the going concern assumption will no longer be of central importance.

Traditionally, the basic financial statements (balance sheet, income statement, and statement of cash flows) presented by going concerns were seen as less useful for entities undergoing reorganization. Instead, the statement of affairs, reporting assets at estimated realizable values and liabilities at estimated liquidation amounts, was recommended for use by such organizations. In more recent years, use of the statement of affairs has not frequently been encountered in practice. About 5 years ago, a new standard was promulgated, setting forth certain financial reporting standards for entities undergoing, and emerging from, reorganization under the bankruptcy laws.

Under GAAP, assets are presented at estimated realizable values. Liabilities are set forth at the estimated amounts to be allowed in the balance sheet and liabilities subject to compromise are to be distinguished from those that are not. Furthermore, US GAAP requires that in both statements of income and cash flows, normal transactions be differentiated from those that have occurred as a consequence of the entity's being in reorganization. While certain allocations to the latter category are rather obvious, such as legal and accounting fees incurred, others are less clear. For example, the standard suggests that if the entity in reorganization earns interest income on funds that would normally have been used to settle obligations owed to creditors, such income will be deemed to be income arising as a consequence of the bankruptcy action.

Another interesting aspect of this standard is the accounting to be made for the emergence from reorganization (known as "confirmation of the plan of reorganization"). GAAP now provides for "fresh start" financial reporting in such instances. This accounting is similar to that applied to purchase business combinations, with the total confirmed value of the entity on its emergence from reorganization being analogous to the purchase price in an acquisition. In both cases, this total value is to be allocated to the identifiable assets and liabilities of the entity, with any excess being allocated to goodwill. In the case of entities emerging from bankruptcy, goodwill ("reorganization value in excess of amounts allocable to identifiable assets") is measured as the excess of liabilities existing at the plan confirmation date, computed at present value of future amounts to be paid, over the "reorganization value" of assets. Reorganization value is calculated with reference to a number of factors, including forecasted operating results and cash flows of the new entity.

This standard applies only to entities undergoing formal reorganization under the bankruptcy code. Less formal procedures may still be accounted for under pre-existing quasi reorganization accounting procedures.

Quasi Reorganizations

Generally, this procedure is applicable during a period of declining price levels. It is termed "quasi" since the accumulated deficit is eliminated at a lower cost and with less difficulty than a legal reorganization. Under the provisions of US GAAP, the procedures in a quasi reorganization involve

1. Proper authorization from stockholders and creditors where required
2. Revaluation of assets to their current values. All losses are charged to retained earnings, thus increasing any deficit.
3. Elimination of any deficit by charging paid-in capital

   a. Additional paid-in capital to the extent it exists
   b. Capital stock when additional paid-in capital is insufficient. The par value of the stock is reduced, creating the extra additional paid-in capital to which the remaining deficit is charged.

No retained earnings may be created by a reorganization. Any excess created by the reduction of par value is credited to "Paid-in capital from quasi reorganization." Retained earnings must be dated for 10 years (less than 10 years may be justified under exceptional circumstances) after a quasi reorganization takes place. Disclosure similar to "since quasi reorganization of June 30, 2000" is appropriate.

18 EARNINGS PER SHARE

PERSPECTIVE AND ISSUES

Earnings per share (EPS) is a ratio (or index) that is widely used by both present and prospective investors to gauge the profitability of a corporation. Its purpose is to indicate, in an easily understood and readily comparable manner, how effective an enterprise has been in using the resources provided by the holders of its equity shares. At its simplest, EPS is computed by dividing net income (loss) by the number of shares of outstanding equity shares. The EPS computation becomes more complicated with the existence of potential ordinary shares; that is, securities which are not presently equity shares but which have the potential of causing additional equity shares to be issued in future. Examples of this class of instrument include convertible preference shares or convertible debt, and options or warrants. The accounting profession recognized many years ago that if earnings per share were to be calculated while ignoring these potentially dilutive securities, there would be a great possibility that the computed amount would be misleading. In addition, a lack of standardization in the precise manner in which these securities are included in the EPS computation would tend to make comparisons among corporations more difficult and potentially quite misleading as well. For these reasons, there have been attempts to prescribe the EPS computation by various standards setters over the past 40 years.

Possibly due to the ever-growing complexity of financial reporting (due, in turn, to the more complicated nature of business transactions and relationships), users of financial statements have long sought a concise, meaningful statistic which would capture succinctly the reporting enterprise's success or failure for the period being reported on. The concept of earnings per share evolved as an obvious candidate for this data element. The reaction of the accounting profession, first in the United States and later in the United Kingdom, was one of caution and concern, since it was feared that users would begin to use this summary statistic as a surrogate for the vastly more informative full set of financial statements; clearly, no summary element of data can convey even a small fraction of the information contained in a more expansive document, such as a balance sheet or an income statement.

Later, however, faced with an overwhelming clamor for such a statistic, the profession attempted to provide guidance on appropriate methods of computation and communication of earnings per share information, coupled with a prohibition against using other appealing but more misleading indexes, particularly cash flow per share. After a period of evolution, the long-standing US requirements (set forth in APB Opinion 15) were finally promulgated in the late 1960s. A similar UK standard followed a few years later. Both of these have been subject to much criticism on the basis of complexity and arbitrariness, but largely endured (with minor amendments) for 25 years. Most recently, the US standard has been superseded by SFAS 128, which essentially mirrors the new international accounting standard and which eliminates much of the complexity for which its venerable predecessor had been disparaged. The UK Accounting Standards Board (ASB) followed suit and also issued an exposure draft, FRED 16, in mid-1997. This closely follows IAS 33 and if adopted will make the new concept of basic earnings per share a virtually universal financial reporting requirement.

Rules governing the computation of earnings per share had never been a part of international accounting standards, but the need to develop an official position on this topic provided a welcome opportunity for joint research by national and international standard-setting bodies. The result is that the new international standard, IAS 33, is almost entirely replicated by the US standard, SFAS 128. This result should further the goals of internationalization of commerce and will probably also reinforce the emerging leadership role of international accounting standards.

The International Accounting Standards Committee issued IAS 33, *Earnings Per Share*, in early 1997, to become operative for financial statements covering periods beginning on or after January 1, 1998. The objective of IAS 33 is to prescribe the ground rules for the determination and presentation of earnings per share. It is interesting to note that the objectives of the standard were expanded from the time the Exposure Draft, E52, was issued until the final version of IAS 33 was promulgated. IAS 33 emphasizes the **denominator** of the earnings per share calculation and notes that even though EPS calculations have limitations, because different accounting policies typically can be used in the determination of earnings, which is in the **numerator** of the equation, **a consistently determined denominator enhances financial reporting**.

IAS 33 states that the standard should be applied to both enterprises whose ordinary shares or potential ordinary shares are publicly traded, and enterprises that are **in the process of issuing** ordinary shares or potential ordinary shares in public securities markets. The standard's antecedent, E52, did not mandate that the rules should be applied in this manner, by contrast. The standard's applicability to entities which have not yet issued shares but which are only in the process of doing so may introduce an element of subjectivity in attempting to apply IAS 33 in actual practice. Perhaps this will ultimately have to be clarified by the newly constituted Standing Interpretations Committee of the IASC.

In case of those enterprises whose shares are **not publicly traded** but which voluntarily choose to disclose EPS figures anyway, the IAS 33 makes it incumbent on these enterprises to calculate and disclose EPS in accordance with the provisions of this standard. Thus, while IAS 33 does not require presentation of EPS data by all enterprises, it does prescribe the computational methods to be used by all enterprises that choose to make such disclosures.

In situations when both parent company and consolidated financial statements are presented, IAS 33 requires that the information called for by this standard need only be presented based on the consolidated information. The reasoning given for this rule is that users of financial statements of a parent company are interested in the results of operations of the group as a whole as opposed to the parent company on a stand-alone basis. Of course, nothing prevents the enterprise from also presenting the parent-only information, including EPS, should it choose to do so.

Sources of IAS
IAS 33

DEFINITIONS OF TERMS

A number of terms used in a discussion of earnings per share have special meanings in that context. When used, they are intended to have the meanings given in the following definitions.

Antidilution. An increase in earnings per share or reduction in net loss per share, resulting from the inclusion of a potentially dilutive security, in EPS calculations.

Basic earnings per share. The amount of net profit or loss for the period that is attributable to each ordinary share that is outstanding during all or part of the period.

Call price. The amount at which a security may be redeemed by the issuer at the issuer's option.

Common stock. A stock that is subordinate to all other stocks of the issuer. Also known as ordinary shares.

Common stock equivalent. This expression is used under the US GAAP to denote a security which, because of its terms or the circumstances under which it was issued, is in substance equivalent to common stock. There is no equivalent concept under the proposed international accounting standards.

Contingent issuance. A possible issuance of ordinary (equity) shares that is dependent on the exercise of conversion rights, options, or warrants, the satisfaction of certain conditions, or similar arrangements.

Conversion price. The price that determines the number of ordinary (equity) shares into which a security is convertible. For example, $100 face value of debt convertible into five ordinary (equity) shares would be stated to have a conversion price of $20.

Conversion rate. The ratio of (1) the number of common shares issuable on conversion to (2) a unit of convertible security. For example, a preference share may be convertible at the rate of three ordinary shares for each preference share.

Conversion value. The current market value of the common shares obtainable on conversion of a convertible security, after deducting any cash payment required on conversion.

Diluted earnings per share. The amount of net profit for the period per share, reflecting the maximum dilutions that would have resulted from conversions, exercises, and other contingent issuances that individually would have decreased earnings per share and in the aggregate would have had a dilutive effect.

Dilution. A reduction in earnings per share or an increase in net loss per share, resulting from the assumption that convertible securities have been converted or that options and warrants have been exercised, or other contingent shares have been issued on the fulfillment of certain conditions. Securities that would cause such earnings dilution are referred to as dilutive securities.

Dual presentation. The presentation with equal prominence of two different earnings per share amounts on the face of the income statement: One is basic earnings per share; the other is diluted earnings per share.

Earnings per share. The amount of earnings for a period attributable to each ordinary (equity) share (common stock). For convenience, the term is used in IAS 33 to refer to either net income (earnings) per share or net loss per share. It should be used without qualifying language (e.g., diluted) only when no potentially dilutive convertible securities, options, warrants, or other agreements providing for contingent issuances of ordinary (equity) shares are outstanding.

Exercise price. The amount that must be paid for a ordinary (equity) share on exercise of a stock option or warrant.

If-converted method. A method of computing earnings per share data that assumes conversion of convertible securities as of the beginning of the earliest period reported (or at time of issuance, if later). This method was mandated under US GAAP.

Option. The right to purchase ordinary (equity) shares in accordance with an agreement upon payment of a specified amount, including but not limited to options granted to and stock purchase agreements entered into with employees.

Ordinary shares. Those shares that are subordinate to all other stocks of the issuer. Also known as common stock.

Redemption price. The amount at which a security is required to be redeemed at maturity or under a sinking-fund arrangement.

Senior security. This is an expression used under US GAAP and refers to a security having preferential rights and which is neither an ordinary (equity) share nor a common stock equivalent (as defined above). A nonconvertible preference share is an example of a senior security.

Time of issuance. The time of issuance generally is the date when agreement as to terms has been reached and announced, even though such agreement is subject to certain further actions, such as directors' or stockholders' approval.

Treasury stock method. A method of recognizing the use of proceeds that would be obtained on exercise of options and warrants in computing earnings per share. It assumes that any proceeds would be used to purchase ordinary (equity) shares at current market prices. The proposed international standard does not prescribe this method but uses a different calculation to achieve the same result.

Warrant. A security giving the holder the right to purchase shares of common stock in accordance with the terms of the instrument, usually on payment of a specified amount.

Weighted-average number of shares. The number of shares determined by relating (1) the portion of time within a reporting period that a particular number of shares of a certain security has been outstanding to (2) the total time in that period. For example, if 100 shares of a certain security were outstanding during the first quarter of a fiscal year and 300 shares were outstanding during the balance of the year, the weighted-average number of outstanding shares would be 250 [(100 x 1/4) + (300 x 3/4)].

CONCEPTS, RULES, AND EXAMPLES

Background

Investors and other interested parties have always sought a simple means of assessing a company's progress and performance. What on the surface looks like the ultimate distillation of an enterprise's financial data is the summary statistic known as earnings per share (EPS), which presents, in a single number, the net result of a period's operations from the perspective of the owner of its common or ordinary shares. Over the years, the accounting profession has attempted to discourage reliance on this measure or any other single condensed indicator which would omit much of the detail information that was deemed necessary to truly understand the entity's operations, but eventually, when the demand for such a criterion became irresistible, accountants attempted to develop guidelines that would at least ensure that any such benchmark measure would be valid and consistently applied.

In the United States, the profession's first attempt to provide guidance in this area was through Accounting Research Bulletin (ARB) 49 (1958). However, this pronouncement was generally ignored, and most enterprises still computed EPS simplistically, by dividing net income minus preferred stock dividends by a weighted-average of the number of common shares outstanding and ignoring the potential impact of other dilutive securities (which fortunately were typically not significant in those less complicated times). However, the distortion inherent in an EPS number computed without regard for potentially dilutive securities was exacerbated during the merger and acquisition activity of the 1960s. Many of these mergers, which resulted in higher reported earnings for the combined entity, were accomplished by the issuance of convertible securities, options, or warrants and by the retirement of the common stock of the merged company. Thus, an entity that disregarded outstanding dilutive securities when computing EPS could show an increase in EPS without a corresponding increase in profitability. The increase was due to larger combined earnings being divided by a smaller number of common shares.

In the US, the next official pronouncement on the subject was the Accounting Principles Board (APB) Opinion 9 (1966), which advised corporations with potentially dilutive securities (convertible preferred stock, convertible debt, or outstanding options or warrants) that if "potential dilution was material, supplementary pro forma computations of earnings per share should be furnished, showing what the earnings would be if conversions or contingent issuances took place." This standard suffered from some of the same weaknesses as its predecessor, and compliance, if marginally better than with ARB 49, was still not satisfactory.

The most significant development occurred when the APB published Opinion 15 (1969), which expanded the definition of those securities that have the potential to dilute EPS, and which provided much more specific guidance in computational matters, as well as clearly delineating the reporting and disclosure requirements. This pronouncement was not applicable to nonprofit corporations, government-owned corporations, registered investment companies, mutual companies without common stock or common stock equivalents, or (in a major change which occurred almost a decade after the original issuance of APB 15) nonpublic enterprises, as was later defined in SFAS 21. However, the standard required that if any of these exempted entities did voluntarily present EPS information, it had to have been prepared and displayed in conformity with the requirements of APB 15.

Although the standard established by APB 15 has been implemented universally over the past 25 years, it has been subject to severe criticism, most of which has focused on the complex and arbitrary nature by which potentially dilutive securities are treated. As a result, in mid-1993 the FASB began the process of looking for ways to revise APB 15 by inviting comment letters on the subject. A large majority of letters indicated a need to revise the denominator used in the EPS calculation. The board then initiated an earnings per share project and released an exposure draft of a new standard in mid-1996.

In the United Kingdom, the first accounting standard to be issued on the subject was SSAP 3, *Earnings Per Share*, which was issued in 1972 and prescribed not only minimum disclosure requirements relating to EPS but also dealt with the basis of calculating the ratio. Subsequently, the Accounting Standards Board (ASB) in the

United Kingdom came to realize that a great deal of emphasis was being placed on reported EPS figures, which led to the promulgation of a different interpretation in a later standard (FRS 3), which attempted to simplify EPS reporting and requires that EPS be calculated based on earnings after extraordinary items. It should be noted, however, that despite the ASB's stipulation in FRS 3 to present the EPS numbers in a standardized and simple manner, it also allows the companies in the United Kingdom to present additional EPS figures prepared on other bases as well, which have to be reconciled to the EPS number required by FRS 3. This, in the opinion of many authorities on the subject, has made the EPS reporting in the United Kingdom much more volatile and in reality only a starting point for further analyses.

Given the recent promulgation of virtually identical and essentially simplified standards by both the FASB and the IASC, there is reason to hope that, at least on this one rather narrow topic, it may be possible to develop a single solution for a financial reporting problem which all preparers can accept as being correct.

Simple Capital Structure

A simple capital structure may be said to exist either when the capital structure consists solely of ordinary (equity) shares or when it includes no potential ordinary shares, which could be in the form of options, warrants, or other rights, that on conversion or exercise could, in the aggregate, dilute earnings per share. Dilutive securities are essentially those that exhibit the rights of debt or other senior security holders (including warrants and options) and which have the potential on their issuance to reduce the earnings per share.

Computational guidelines. In its simplest form, the EPS calculation is net income divided by the weighted-average number of ordinary shares outstanding. The objective of the EPS calculation is to determine the amount of earnings available to each ordinary share. Complexities arise because net income does not necessarily represent the earnings available to the ordinary shareholder, and a simple weighted-average of ordinary shares outstanding does not necessarily reflect the true nature of the situation. Adjustments can take the form of manipulations of the numerator or of the denominator of the formula used to compute EPS, as discussed in the following paragraphs.

Numerator. The net income figure used as the numerator in any of the EPS computations must reflect any claims against it by holders of senior securities. The justification for this reduction is that the claims of the senior securities must be satisfied before any income is available to the common shareholder. These securities are usually in the form of preference shares, and the deduction from income is the amount of the dividend declared during the year on the preference shares. If the preference shares are cumulative, the dividend is to be deducted from income (or added to the loss), whether it is declared or not. If preference shares do not have a cumulative right to dividends and current period dividends have been omitted, such dividends should not be deducted in computing EPS. Cumulative dividends in arrears that are paid currently do not affect the calculation of EPS in the current period, since such dividends have already been considered in prior periods' EPS computations. However, the amount in arrears should be disclosed, as should all of the effects of the rights given to senior securities on the EPS calculation.

Denominator. The weighted-average number of ordinary shares outstanding is used so that the effect of increases or decreases in outstanding shares on EPS data is related to the portion of the period during which the related consideration affected operations. The difficulty in computing the weighted-average exists because of the effect that various transactions have on the computation of ordinary shares outstanding. Although it is impossible to analyze all the possibilities, the following discussion presents some of the more common transactions affecting the number of ordinary shares outstanding. The theoretical construct set forth in these relatively simple examples can be followed in all other situations.

If a company reacquires its own shares (referred to as treasury stock) in countries where it is legally permissible to do so, the number of shares reacquired should be excluded from EPS calculations as of the date of acquisition. The same theory holds for the issuance of ordinary shares during the period. The number of shares newly issued is included in the computation only for the period after their issuance date. The logic for this treatment is that the consideration for the shares was not available to generate earnings until the shares were issued. This same logic applies to the reacquired shares because the consideration relative to those shares was no longer available to generate earnings after the acquisition date.

A stock dividend (bonus issue) or a stock (share) split does not generate additional resources or consideration, but it does increase the number of shares outstanding. The increase in shares as a result of a stock split or dividend, or decrease in shares as a result of a reverse split, should be given retroactive recognition as an appropriate equivalent charge for all periods presented. Thus, even if a stock dividend or split occurs at the end of the period, it is considered outstanding for the entire period of each period presented. The reasoning is that a stock dividend or split has no effect on the ownership percentage of the common stockholder. As such, to show a dilution in the EPS reported would erroneously give the impression of a decline in profitability when in fact it was merely an increase in the shares outstanding due to the stock dividend or split.

IAS 33 carries this logic one step further by requiring the disclosure of pro forma (adjusted) amounts of basic and diluted earnings per share for the period in case of issue of shares with no corresponding change in resources (e.g., stock dividends or splits) occurring **after** the balance sheet date, but before the issuance of the financial statements. The reason given is that the nondisclosure of such transactions would affect the ability of the users of the financial statements to make proper evaluations and decisions. It is to be noted, however, that the EPS numbers as presented on the face of the income statement are not required by IAS 33 to be retroactively adjusted, as is the case under US GAAP, because such transactions do not reflect the amount of capital used to produce the net profit or loss for the period.

Complications also arise when a business combination occurs during the period. The treatment of the additional shares depends on the nature of the combination. If the business combination is recorded as a uniting of interests, the additional shares are assumed to have been issued at the beginning of the year regardless of when the combination occurred. Conversely, if the combination is accounted for as an acquisition, the shares are considered issued and outstanding as of the date of acquisition. The reason for this varied treatment lies in the income statement treatment accorded a uniting of interests vs. an acquisition. In a uniting of interests, the income of the acquired company is included in the statements for the entire year, whereas in an acquisition, the income is included only for the period after acquisition.

IAS 33 recognizes that in certain countries it is permissible for ordinary shares to be issued in partly paid form, and the standard accordingly stipulates that partly paid instruments should be included as ordinary share equivalents to the extent to which they carry rights (during the financial reporting year) to participate in dividends in the same manner as fully paid shares. Further, in the case of contingently issuable shares (i.e., ordinary shares issuable on fulfillment of certain conditions, say, on achieving a certain level of profits or sales), IAS 33 requires that such shares be considered outstanding and included in the computation of basic earnings per share only when all the required conditions have been satisfied.

IAS 33 gives examples of situations where ordinary shares may be issued, or the number of shares outstanding may be reduced, without causing corresponding changes in resources of the corporation. Such examples include bonus issues, a bonus element in other issues such as a rights issue (to existing shareholders), a share split, a reverse share split, and a capital reduction without a corresponding refund of capital. In all such cases the number of ordinary shares outstanding before the event is adjusted, as if the event had occurred at the beginning of the earliest period reported. For instance, in a 3-to-1 bonus issue the number of shares outstanding prior to the issue is multiplied by a factor of 4. These and other situations are summarized in the tabular list that follows.

In case of rights shares, the number of ordinary shares to be used in calculating basic EPS is the number of ordinary shares outstanding prior to the issue, multiplied by the following factor:

$$\frac{\text{Fair value immediately prior to the exercise of the rights}}{\text{Theoretical ex-rights fair value}}$$

There are several ways to compute the theoretical value of the shares on an ex-rights basis. IAS 33 suggests that this be derived by adding the aggregate fair value of the shares immediately prior to exercise of the rights to the proceeds from the exercise, and dividing the total by the number of shares outstanding after exercise. To illustrate, consider that the entity currently has 10,000 shares outstanding, with a market value of $15 per share, when it offers each holder rights to acquire one new share at $10 for each four shares held. The theoretical value ex-rights would be given as follows:

$$\frac{(10,000 \times \$15) + (2,500 \times \$10)}{12,500} = \frac{175,000}{12,500} = \$14$$

Thus, the ex-rights value of the ordinary shares is $14 each.

Weighted-Average (W/A) Computation	
Transaction	*Effect on W/A computation*
Common stock outstanding at the beginning of the period	Increase number of shares outstanding by the number of shares
Issuance of common stock during the period	Increase number of shares outstanding by the number of shares issued times the portion of the year outstanding
Conversion into common stock	Increase number of shares outstanding by the number of shares converted times the portion of the year outstanding
Company reacquires its stock	Decrease number of shares outstanding by number of shares reacquired times portion of the year outstanding
Stock dividend or split	Increase number of shares outstanding by number of shares issued or increased due to the split
Reverse split	Decrease number of shares outstanding by decrease in shares
Pooling of interest	Increase number of shares outstanding by number of shares issued
Purchase	Increase number of shares outstanding by number of shares issued times portion of year since acquisition

The foregoing do not characterize all possible complexities arising in the EPS computation; however, most of the others occur under a complex structure which is considered in the following section of this chapter. The illustration below applies the foregoing concepts to a simple capital structure.

Example of EPS computation--Simple capital structure

Assume the following information:

Numerator information			*Denominator information*	
a.	Income from ordinary activities before extraordinary items	$130,000	a. Common shares outstanding 1/1/00	100,000
b.	Extraordinary loss (net of tax)	30,000	b. Shares issued for cash 4/1/00	20,000
c.	Net income	100,000	c. Shares issued in 10% stock dividend declared in July 2000	12,000
d.	6% cumulative preference shares, $100 par, 1,000 shrs. issued and outstanding	100,000	d. Shares of treasury stock purchased 10/1/00	10,000

When calculating the numerator, the claims of senior securities (i.e., preference shares) should be deducted to arrive at the earnings attributable to ordinary (equity) shareholders. In this example the preference shares are cumulative. Thus, regardless of whether or not the board of directors declares a preference dividend, holders of the preference shares have a claim of $6,000 (1,000 shares x $100 x 6%) against 2000 earnings. Therefore, $6,000 must be deducted from the numerator to arrive at the net income attributable to the holders of ordinary shares. Note that any cumulative preference dividends in arrears are ignored in computing this period's EPS since they would have been incorporated into previous periods' EPS calculations. Also note that this $6,000 would have been deducted for noncumulative preferred only if a dividend of this amount had been declared during the period. The EPS calculations follow.

Earnings per common share

On income from continuing operations before extraordinary
items = ($130,000 – 6,000) ÷ Ordinary shares outstanding   = $1.00
On net income = ($100,000 – 6,000) ÷ Ordinary shares outstanding   = $0.76

The computation of the denominator is based on the weighted-average number of ordinary shares outstanding. Recall that a simple weighted-average is not considered appropriate because of the various complexities. The table below illustrates one way of computing the weighted-average number of shares outstanding.

Item	Number of shares actually outstanding	Fraction of the year outstanding	Shares times fraction of the year
Number of shares as of beginning of the year 1/1/00	110,000 [100,000 + 10%(100,000)]	12/12	110,000
Shares issued 4/1/00	22,000 [20,000 + 10%(20,000)]	9/12	16,500
Treasury shares purchased 10/1/00	(10,000)	3/12	(2,500)
Weighted-average number of common shares outstanding			124,000

Recall that the stock dividend declared in July is considered to be retroactive to the beginning of the year. Thus, for the period 1/1 through 4/1, 110,000 shares are considered to be outstanding. When shares are issued, they are included in the weighted-average beginning with the date of issuance. The stock dividend applicable to these newly issued shares is also assumed to have existed for the same period. Thus, we can see that of the 12,000 share dividend, 10,000 shares relate to the beginning balance and 2,000 shares to the new issuance (10% of 100,000 and 20,000, respectively). The purchase of the treasury stock requires that these shares be excluded from the calculation for the remainder of the period after their acquisition date. The figure is subtracted from the calculation because the shares were purchased from those outstanding prior to acquisition. To complete the example, we divided the previously derived numerator by the weighted-average number of common shares outstanding to arrive at EPS.

On income from continuing operations before extraordinary items =
($130,000 – 6,000) ÷ 124,000 common shares   = $1.00
On net income = ($100,000 – 6,000) ÷ 124,000 common shares   = $0.76

Reporting a $0.24 loss per share ($30,000 ÷ 124,000) due to the extraordinary item is optional. The numbers computed above for the EPS based on net income are the only presentation required on the face of the income statement.

Complex Capital Structure

The computation of EPS under a complex capital structure involves all of the complexities discussed under the simple structure and many more. By definition, a complex capital structure is one that has dilutive potential ordinary shares which have the potential to be exercised and reduce EPS. The effects of any antidilutive potential ordinary shares (those that increase EPS) is not to be included in the computation of diluted earnings per share.

Note that a complex structure requires dual presentation of both basic EPS and diluted EPS unless the basic earnings per share is a loss per share. In case the basic EPS is a loss per share, IAS 33 does not prohibit an enterprise from disclosing the figure for the diluted EPS (which was, however, the position taken by the Exposure Draft, E52).

For the purposes of calculating diluted EPS, the net profit attributable to ordinary shareholders and the weighted-average number of shares outstanding should be adjusted for the effects of all the dilutive potential ordinary shares.

According to IAS 33, the numerator, representing the net profit attributable to the ordinary shareholders for the period, should be adjusted by the after-tax effect, if any, of the following items:

1. Interest recognized in the period for the dilutive potential ordinary shares
2. Any dividends recognized in the period for the dilutive potential ordinary shares, where those dividends have been deducted in arriving at net profit attributable to ordinary shareholders
3. Any other changes in income or expenses that would result from the conversion of the dilutive potential ordinary shares

For instance, conversion of debentures into ordinary shares will reduce interest expense, which will cause an increase in the profit for the period. This will have a consequential effect on contributions based on the profit figure, say, employer's contribution to an employee profit sharing plan. The effect of such consequential changes on the bottom line should be considered in the computation of the numerator of the diluted EPS ratio.

The denominator, which has the weighted number of ordinary shares, should be adjusted (increased) by the weighted-average number of ordinary shares that would have been outstanding assuming the conversion of all dilutive potential ordinary shares.

Contingent Issuances of Ordinary Shares

As in the computation of the basic EPS, shares whose issuance is contingent on the occurrence of certain events are considered outstanding and included in the computation of diluted EPS only if the stipulated conditions have been met (the event has occurred). Issuances that are dependent on certain conditions being met can be illustrated through the following example. For instance, there may be a condition or requirement in a contract to increase earnings over a period of time to a certain stipulated level and that upon attainment of this level of earnings, the issuance of shares to take place; this is regarded as a contingent issuance of shares. These securities are included in the computation of diluted EPS.

There are basically two methods used to incorporate the effects of potential ordinary shares, popularly referred to as

1. The treasury stock method
2. The if-converted method

These terms were first popularized by the former US GAAP requirements set forth in APB 15. IAS 33 does not specifically refer to the methods it has prescribed by the foregoing names, but does mention, in the case of the method of accounting for share warrants and options that, in effect, the method prescribed by it produces the same results as the treasury stock method.

Treasury stock method. The treasury stock method, which is used to account for the hypothetical exercise of most warrants or options, requires that EPS be computed as if the options or warrants were exercised at the beginning of the period (or date of issuance, if later) and that the funds obtained from the exercise were used to purchase common stock at the average market price for the period.

For example, if a corporation has warrants outstanding for 1,000 shares of common stock exercisable at $10 per share and the average market price of the common stock is $16 per share, the following would hypothetically occur: The company would receive $10,000 (1,000 x $10) and issue 1,000 shares from the exercise of the warrants that would enable it to purchase 625 shares ($10,000 ÷ $16) in the open market. The net increase in the denominator (which effects a dilution in EPS) is 375 shares (1,000 issued less 625 repurchased). Under the terminology of IAS 33, those 375 shares are deemed to have been issued "for no consideration." In all cases where the exercise price is lower than the market price, assumed exercise will be dilutive and some portion of the shares will be deemed issued for no consideration. If the exercise price is greater than the average market price, the exercise should not be assumed since the result of this would be antidilutive.

Treasury Stock Method

Denominator must be increased by net dilution, as follows:

Net dilution = Shares issued − Shares repurchased

where

Shares issued = Proceeds received/Exercise price

Shares repurchased = Proceeds received/Average market price per share

---

If-converted method. The if-converted method is used for those securities that are currently sharing in the earnings of the company through the receipt of interest or dividends as senior securities but have the potential for sharing in the earnings as ordinary shares. The if-converted method logically recognizes that the convertible security can only share in the earnings of the company as one or the other, not as both. Thus, the dividends or interest less tax effects applicable to the convertible security as a senior security are not recognized in the net income figure used to compute EPS, and the weighted-average number of shares is adjusted to reflect the conversion as of the beginning of the year (or date of issuance, if later). See the example of the if-converted method for illustration of treatment of convertible securities when they are issued during the period and therefore were not outstanding for the entire year.

Example of the if-converted method

Assume a net income of $50,000 and a weighted-average number of common shares outstanding of 10,000. The following information is provided regarding the capital structure.

1. 7% convertible debt, 200 bonds each convertible into 40 ordinary shares. The bonds were outstanding the entire year. The income tax rate is 40%. The bonds were issued at par ($1,000 per bond). No bonds were converted during the year.

2. 4% convertible, cumulative preferred stock, par $100, 1,000 shares issued and outstanding. Each preferred share is convertible into 2 common shares. The preferred shares were issued at par and were outstanding the entire year. No shares were converted during the year.

The first step is to compute the basic EPS, that is, assuming only the issued and outstanding ordinary shares. This figure is simply computed as $4.60 ($50,000 – 4,000 preferred dividends) ÷ (10,000 ordinary shares outstanding). The diluted EPS must be less than this amount for the capital structure to be considered complex and for a dual presentation of EPS to be necessary.

To determine the dilutive effect of the preferred stock, an assumption (generally referred to as the if-converted method) is made that all of the preferred stock is converted at the earliest date that it could have been during the year. In this example, the date would be January 1. (If the preferred had been first issued during the year, the earliest date conversion could have occurred would have been the issuance date.) The effects of this assumption are twofold: (1) if the preferred is converted, there will be no preferred dividends of $4,000 for the year; and (2) there will be an additional 2,000 shares of common outstanding during the year (the conversion rate is 2 for 1 on 1,000 shares of preferred). Diluted EPS is computed, as follows, reflecting these two assumptions:

$$\frac{\text{Net income}}{\substack{\text{Weighted-average of common shares} \\ \text{outstanding } + \text{ Shares issued upon} \\ \text{conversion of preferred}}} = \frac{\$50,000}{12,000 \text{ shares}} = \$4.17$$

The convertible preferred is dilutive because it reduced EPS from $4.60 to $4.17. Accordingly, a dual presentation of EPS is required.

In the example, the convertible bonds are also assumed to have been converted at the beginning of the year. Again, the effects of the assumption are twofold: (1) if the bonds are converted, there will be no interest expense of $14,000 (7% x $200,000 face value), and (2) there will be an additional 8,000 shares (200 bonds x 40 shares) of common stock outstanding during the year. One note of caution, however, must be mentioned; namely, the effect of not having $14,000 of interest expense will increase income, but it will also increase tax expense. Consequently, the net effect of not having interest expense of $14,000 is $8,400 [(1 – 0.40) x $14,000]. Diluted EPS is computed as follows, reflecting the dilutive preferred and the effects noted above for the convertible bonds.

$$= \quad \frac{\text{Net income } + \text{ Interest expense (net of tax)}}{\substack{\text{Weighted-average of common shares} \\ \text{outstanding } + \text{ Shares issued upon} \\ \text{conversion of preferred and} \\ \text{conversion of bonds}}} \quad \frac{\$50,000 + 8,400}{20,000 \text{ shares}} = \$2.92$$

The convertible debt is also dilutive, as it reduces EPS from $4.17 to $2.92. Together the convertible bonds and preferred reduced EPS from $4.60 to $2.92. The following table summarizes the computations made for this example.

Computations of Basic and Diluted Earnings Per Share

Items	EPS on outstanding common stock (the "benchmark" EPS) Numerator	Denominator	Basic Numerator	Denominator	Diluted Numerator	Denominator
Net income	$50,000		$50,000		$50,000	
Preferred dividend	(4,000)					
Common shs. outstanding		10,000 shs.		10,000 shs.		10,000 shs.
Conversion of preferred				2,000		2,000
Conversion of bonds					8,400	8,000
Totals	$46,000	÷ 10,000 shs.	$50,000	÷ 12,000 shs.	$58,400	÷ 20,000 shs.
EPS		$4.60		$4.17		$2.92

The foregoing example was simplified to the extent that none of the convertible securities were, in fact, converted during the year. In most real situations, some or all of the securities may have been converted, and thus actual reported earnings (and basic EPS) would already have reflected the fact that preferred dividends were paid for only part of the year and/or that interest on convertible debt was accrued for only part of the year. These factors would need to be taken into consideration in developing a time-weighted numerator and denominator for the EPS equations.

Furthermore, the sequence followed in testing the dilution effects of each of several series of convertible securities may affect the outcome, although this is not always true. It is best to perform the sequential procedures illustrated above by computing the impact of each issue of potential ordinary shares from the most dilutive to the least dilutive. This rule also applies if convertible securities (for which the if-converted method will be applied) and options (for which the treasury stock approach will be applied) are outstanding simultaneously.

Finally, if some potential ordinary shares are only issuable on the occurrence of a contingency, conversion should be assumed for EPS computation purposes only to the extent that the conditions were met as of the balance sheet date. In effect, the end of the reporting period should be treated as if it were also the end of the contingency period.

No antidilution. No assumptions of conversion should be made if the effect would be antidilutive. As in the discussion above, it may be that the sequence in which the different issues or series of convertible or other instruments that are potentially ordinary shares are considered will affect the ultimate computation. The goal in computing diluted EPS is to calculate the maximum dilutive effect. The individual issues of convertible securities, options, and other items should be dealt with from the most dilutive to the least dilutive to effect this result.

Modified Treasury Stock Method

<u>Numerator</u>

Net income recomputed to reflect retirement
of debt or income from investments

- Add interest expense less tax effects
- Add income from investments less tax effects

- -

<u>Denominator</u>

Common stock outstanding + Number of shares not acquired
with proceeds from options and warrants

Disclosure Requirements Under IAS 33

1. Enterprises should present both basic EPS and diluted EPS on the face of the income statement for each class of ordinary shares that has a different right to share in the net profit for the period. Equal prominence should be given to both the basic EPS and diluted EPS figures for all periods presented.

2. Enterprises should present basic EPS and diluted EPS even if the amounts disclosed are negative. In other words, the standard mandates disclosure of not just **earnings per share** but even **loss per share** figures.

3. Enterprises should disclose amounts used as the numerator in calculating basic EPS and diluted EPS along with a reconciliation of those amounts to the net profit or loss for the period. Disclosure is also required of the weighted-average number of ordinary shares used as the denominator in calculating basic EPS and diluted EPS along with a reconciliation of these denominators to each other.

4. a. In addition to the disclosure of the figures for basic EPS and diluted EPS, as required above, if an enterprise chooses to disclose per share amounts using a reported component of net profit, other than net profit or loss for the period attributable to ordinary shareholders, such amounts should be calculated using the weighted-average number of

ordinary shares determined in accordance with the requirements of IAS 33; this will ensure comparability of the per share amounts disclosed;

b. In cases where an enterprise chooses to disclose the above per share amounts using a component of net profit not reported as a line item in the income statement, a reconciliation is mandated by the standard, which should reconcile the difference between the component of net income used with a line item reported in the income statement; and

c. When additional disclosure is made by an enterprise of the above per share amounts, basic and diluted per share amounts should be disclosed with equal prominence (just as basic EPS and diluted EPS figures are given equal prominence).

5. Enterprises are encouraged to disclose the terms and conditions of financial instruments or contracts generating potential ordinary shares since such terms and conditions may determine whether or not any potential ordinary shares are dilutive and, if so, the effect on the weighted-average number of shares outstanding and any consequent adjustments to the net profit attributable to the ordinary shareholders.

6. If changes (resulting from a bonus issue or share split, etc.) in the number of ordinary or potential ordinary shares occur, after the balance sheet date but before issuance of the financial statements, and the per share calculations reflect such changes in the number of shares, such a fact should be disclosed.

7. Enterprises are also encouraged to disclose a description of ordinary share transactions or potential ordinary share transactions, other than capitalization issues and share splits, occurring after the balance sheet date and which are of such importance that nondisclosure would affect the ability of the users of the financial statements to make proper evaluations and decisions.

19 INTERIM FINANCIAL REPORTING

PERSPECTIVE AND ISSUES

Interim financial reports are financial statements covering periods of less than a full financial year. Most commonly, such reports will be for a period of 3 months (which are referred to as quarterly [interim] financial reports), although in many jurisdictions tradition calls for semiannual or half-yearly (interim) financial reporting. The purpose of quarterly or other interim financial reports is to provide financial statement users with more timely information for investment and credit decisions, based on an ability to project full-year results from interim performance. Additionally, interim reports can yield significant information concerning trends affecting the business and seasonality effects, both of which could be buried in annual reports.

The basic objective of interim reporting is to provide frequent and timely assessments of enterprise performance. However, interim reporting has inherent limitations. As the reporting period is shortened, the effects of errors in estimation and allocation are magnified. The proper allocation of annual operating expenses is a significant concern. Because the progressive tax rates of most jurisdictions are applied to total annual income and various tax credits may arise, the determination of interim income tax expense is often difficult. Other annual operating expenses are often concentrated in one interim period yet benefit the entire year's operations. Examples include advertising expenses and major repairs or maintenance of equipment. The effects of seasonal fluctuations and temporary market conditions further limit the reliability, comparability, and predictive value of interim reports. Because of this reporting environment, the issue of independent auditor association with interim financial reports is subject to continuing controversy.

While some national standards had long existed regarding interim financial reporting, most notably in the United States where the pertinent requirements were established in 1973, international accounting standards on this topic had been totally absent until very recently. The first time the IASC addressed this issue was when it released a draft statement of principles (DSOP) in late 1996, after having solicited views on the topic by means of an issues paper earlier that year, which finally culminated in a standard on interim financial reporting in February 1998.

Two distinct views of interim reporting have been advocated, particularly by US and UK standard setters, but others believe that the distinction is less meaningful than it appears at first blush. The first view holds that the interim period is an integral part of the annual accounting period (the integral view), while the second views the interim period as a discrete accounting period of its own (the discrete view). Depending on which view is accepted, expenses would either be recognized as incurred or would be allocated to the interim periods based on forecasted annual activity levels such as sales volume. The integral approach would require more use of estimation, and forecasts of full-year performance would be necessary antecedents for the preparation of interim reports.

Sources of IAS

IAS 1 (revised 1997), 8, 20, 32, and 34

IASC's Framework for the Preparation and Presentation of Financial Statements

---

DEFINITIONS OF TERMS

Discrete view. An approach to measuring interim period income by viewing each interim period separately.

Estimated annual effective tax rate. An expected annual tax rate which reflects estimates of annual earnings, tax rates, tax credits, etc.

Integral view. An approach to measuring interim period income by viewing each interim period as an integral part of the annual period. Expenses are recognized in proportion to revenues earned through the use of special accruals and deferrals.

Interim financial report. An interim financial report refers to either a complete set of financial statements for an interim period (prepared in accordance with the requirements of IAS 1, revised 1997); or a set of condensed financial statements for an interim period (prepared in accordance with the requirements of IAS 34).

Interim period. A financial reporting period shorter than a full financial year (e.g., a period of 3 or 6 months).

Last-12-months reports. Financial reporting for the 12-month period which ends on a given interim date.

Liquidation of LIFO inventories. The situation which occurs when quarterly sales exceed purchases and base-period costs are released into cost of goods sold.

Seasonality. The normal, expected occurrence of a major portion of revenues or costs in one or two interim periods.

Year-to-date reports. Financial reporting for the period which begins on the first day of the fiscal year and ends on a given interim date.

CONCEPTS, RULES, AND EXAMPLES

Alternative Concepts of Interim Reporting

The argument is often made that interim reporting is generically different than financial reporting for a full fiscal year. Two distinct views of interim reporting have developed. Under the first view, the interim period is considered to be an integral part of the annual accounting period. Annual operating expenses are estimated and then allocated to the interim periods based on forecasted annual activity levels such as sales volume. When this approach is employed, the results of subsequent interim periods must be adjusted to reflect estimation errors.

Under the second view, the interim period is considered to be a discrete accounting period with status equal to a fiscal year. Thus, there are no estimations or allocations different from those used for annual reporting. The same expense recognition rules apply as under annual reporting, and no special interim accruals or deferrals are applied. Annual operating expenses are recognized in the interim period in which they are incurred, irrespective of the number of interim periods benefited.

Proponents of the integral view argue that the unique expense recognition procedures are necessary to avoid creating possibly misleading fluctuations in period-to-period results. Using the integral view results in interim earnings which are indicative of annual earnings and, thus, useful for predictive purposes. Proponents of the discrete view, on the other hand, argue that the smoothing of interim results for purposes of forecasting annual earnings has undesirable effects. For example, a turning point in an earnings trend which occurred during the year may be obscured.

Yet others have noted that the distinction between the integral and the discrete approaches is arbitrary and, in fact, rather meaningless. These critics note that interim periods bear the same relationship to full years as fiscal years do to longer intervals in the life cycle of a business, and that all periodic financial reporting necessitates the making of estimates and allocations. Direct costs and revenues are best accounted for as incurred and earned, respectively, which equates a discrete approach in most instances, while many indirect costs are more likely to require that an allocation process be applied, which is suggestive of an integral approach. In short, a mix of methods will be necessary as dictated by the nature of the cost or revenue item being reported upon, and neither a pure integral nor a pure discrete approach could be utilized in practice. The International Accounting Standard on interim financial reporting, IAS 34, does, in fact, adopt a mix of the discrete view and the integral view, as described more fully below.

Objectives of Interim Financial Reporting: The IASC Perspective

The purpose of interim financial reporting is to provide information which will be useful in making economic decisions (as, of course, is annual financial information). Furthermore, interim financial reporting is expected to provide information specifically about the financial position, performance, and change in financial position of an enterprise. The objective is general enough to embrace the preparation and presentation of either full financial statements or condensed information.

While accounting is often criticized for looking at an entity's performance through the rearview mirror, in fact it is well understood by standard setters that to be useful, such information must provide insights into future performance. As outlined in the objective of the IASC's standard on interim financial reporting, IAS 34, the primary, but not exclusive, purpose of timely interim period reporting is to provide interested parties (e.g., investors and creditors) with an understanding of the enterprise's earnings-generating capacity and its cash-flow-generating capacity, which are clearly future-oriented. Furthermore, the interim data is expected to give interested parties not only insights into such matters as seasonal volatility or irregularity, and provide timely notice about changes in patterns or trends, both as to income or cash generating behavior, but also into such balance-sheet-based phenomena as liquidity.

In reaching the positions set forth in the standard, the IASC had considered at the DSOP stage the importance of interim reporting in identifying the turning points in an enterprise's earnings or liquidity. In the Committee's opinion, the integral approach to interim reporting can mask these turning points and thereby prevent users of the financial statements from taking appropriate actions. If this observation is correct, this would be an important reason to endorse the discrete view. In fact, the extent to which application of an integral approach masks turning points is probably related to the extent of "smoothing" applied to revenue and expense data; it seems quite feasible that interim reporting in accordance with the integral view, if done sensitively, would reveal turning points as much as reports prepared under the contrary approach. As proof of this, one can consider national economic statistics, which are most commonly reported on seasonally adjusted bases, which is analogous to the consequence of utilizing an integral approach to interim reporting of enterprise financial information. Such economic data is often quite effective at highlighting so-called turning points and is employed far more typically than is unadjusted monthly data, for example.

While the objectives of interim reporting are highly consistent with those of annual financial reporting, there are, in the IASC's view, further concerns. These were identified in the DSOP on interim financial reporting as involving matters of cost and timeliness, as well as questions of materiality and measurement accuracy. In general, the conclusion is that to be truly useful, the information must be produced in a more timely fashion than is often the case with annual reports (although other research suggests that users' tolerance for delayed information is markedly declining in all arenas), and that some compromises in terms of accuracy may be warranted in order to achieve greater timeliness.

Basic Conclusions About Application of Accounting Principles to Interim Financial Reports

Although a cursory reading of the standard may give the impression that the IASC has favored a pure discrete view (as opposed to a pure integral view), some of the examples given in Appendix 2 to IAS 34 (e.g., the ones explaining the accounting treatment of income taxes and employer payroll taxes, or the example which explains the application of the standard to the treatment of contingent lease payments) lead one to believe that, in fact, the IASC has pursued an approach which is a combination of both the discrete view and the integral view.

Most noteworthy is the fact that this approach is very different from the position under certain leading national accounting standards, such as that imposed under US GAAP, which mandates the integral view. It is interesting to note, however, that neither position is pure in the sense that not all measures are consistent with the stated overall philosophy. Thus, the IASC's approach seems quite balanced. For example, while in IAS 34 the discrete view is endorsed in many situations, the method of accounting for income taxes prescribed is clearly compliant with an integral view, not a discrete view.

Further, IAS 34 states that interim financial data should be prepared in conformity with accounting policies used in the most recent annual financial statements. The only exception noted is when a change in accounting principle has been adopted since the last year-end financial report was issued. The standard also stipulates that the definitions of assets, liabilities, income, and expenses for the interim period are to be identical to those applied in annual reporting situations.

While IAS 34, in many instances, is quite forthright about declaring its allegiance to the discrete view of interim financial reporting, it does incorporate a number of important exceptions to the principle. These matters are discussed in greater detail below.

Statements and Disclosures to Be Presented in Interim Financial Reports

Content of an interim financial report. Instead of repeating or duplicating information previously presented in annual financial statements, interim financial reports should preferably focus on new activities, events, and circumstances that have occurred since the date of publication of the latest complete set of financial statements. IAS 34 has recognized the need to keep financial statement users abreast with the latest financial condition of an enterprise and has thus softened the presentation and disclosure requirements in the case of interim financial reports. Thus, in the interest of timeliness and cost considerations and to avoid repetition of information previously reported, the standard allows an enterprise, at its option, to provide information relating to its financial position in a condensed format, in lieu of comprehensive information provided in a complete set of financial statements, prepared in accordance with IAS 1 (revised 1997). The minimum requirements as to the components of the interim financial statements to be presented (under this option) and their content are discussed later.

IAS 34, paragraph 7, clarifies the following three important aspects of interim financial reporting.

- That the above concession extended by the standard to interim financial reports is in no way intended to either prohibit or discourage an enterprise from presenting a complete set of interim financial statements, as described in IAS 1 (revised 1997);
- That even in the case of condensed interim financial statements, if an enterprise chooses to add line items or additional explanatory notes to the condensed financial statements, over and above the minimum prescribed by this standard, the standard does not, in any way, prohibit or discourage the addition of such extra information to the prescribed minimum basic requirements; and
- That the recognition and measurement guidance in this standard apply to a complete set of interim financial statements as they apply to condensed interim financial statements. (Thus, a complete set of interim financial statements would include not only the disclosures specifically prescribed by this standard but also disclosures required by other IAS. For example, disclosures required by IAS 32, such as interest rate risk or credit risk would need to be incorporated in a complete set of interim financial statements in addition to the selected footnote disclosures prescribed by IAS 34.)

Minimum components of an interim financial report. IAS 34 sets forth minimum requirements in relation to condensed interim financial reports. The standard mandates that the following financial statements components be presented when an enterprise opts for the condensed format:

- A condensed balance sheet
- A condensed income statement
- A condensed statement showing **either** all changes in equity **or** changes in equity other than those arising from capital transactions with owners and distributions to owners
- A condensed cash flow statement
- Selected set of footnote disclosures

Form and content of interim financial statements.

1. IAS 34, paragraph 9, mandates that if an enterprise chooses the "complete set of (interim) financial statements" route instead of opting for the short-cut method of presenting only "condensed" interim financial statements,

then the form and content of the those statements should conform to the requirements of IAS 1 (revised 1997) for a complete set of financial statements.

2.   However, if an enterprise opts for the condensed format of interim financial reporting, then IAS 34, paragraph 10, requires that, at a minimum, those condensed financial statements should include each of the headings, and the subtotals, that were included in the enterprise's most recent annual financial statements, along with selected explanatory notes, as prescribed by the standard.

It is interesting to note that in paragraph 10, IAS 34 mandates circumspection in certain cases. The Standard notes that additional line items or notes may need to be added to the minimum disclosures prescribed above, if their omission would make the condensed interim financial statements misleading. This concept can be best explained through the following illustration:

> At December 31, 2000, an enterprise's comparative balance sheet had trade receivables which were considered doubtful and hence were fully reserved as of that date. Thus, on the face of the balance sheet as of December 31, 2000, the amount disclosed against trade receivables, net of provision, was a zero balance (and the comparative figure disclosed as of December 31, 1999, under the prior year column, was a positive amount since at that earlier point of time, that is, at end of the previous year, a small portion of the receivable was still considered collectible). At December 31, 2000, the fact that the receivable (net of the provision) ended up being presented as a zero balance on the face of the balance sheet was well explained in the notes to the annual financial statements (which clearly showed the provision being deducted from the gross amount of the receivable that caused the resulting figure to be a zero balance which was then carried forward to the balance sheet). If at the end of the first quarter of the following year the trade receivables were still doubtful of collection, thereby necessitating creation of a 100% provision against the entire balance of trade receivables as of March 31, 2001, and the enterprise opted to present a condensed balance sheet as part of the interim financial report, it would be misleading in this case to disclose the trade receivables as of March 31, 2001, as a zero balance, without adding a note to the condensed balance sheet explaining this phenomenon.

3.   IAS 34 requires disclosure of earnings per share (both basic EPS and diluted EPS) on the face of the interim income statement. This disclosure is mandated whether condensed or complete interim financial statements are presented.

4.   IAS 34, paragraph 13, mandates that an enterprise should follow the same format in its interim statement showing changes in equity as it did in its most recent annual financial statements.

5.   IAS 34, paragraph 14, requires that an interim financial report be prepared on a consolidated basis if the enterprise's most recent annual financial

statements were consolidated statements. Regarding presentation of separate interim financial statements of the parent company in addition to consolidated interim financial statements, if they were included in the most recent annual financial statements, this standard neither requires nor prohibits such inclusion in the interim financial report of the enterprise.

Selected explanatory notes. While a number of notes would potentially be required at an interim date, there should clearly be far less disclosure than is presently prescribed under other enacted IAS. IAS 34, paragraph 15, reiterates that it is superfluous to provide the same notes in the interim financial report that appeared in the most recent annual financial statements, since financial statement users have access to those statements in any case. On the contrary, at an interim date, it would be meaningful to provide an explanation of events and transactions that are significant to an understanding of the changes in financial position and performance of the enterprise, since the last annual reporting. In keeping with this line of thinking, IAS 34, paragraph 16, provides a list of **minimum** disclosures required to accompany the condensed interim financial statements, which are outlined below:

1. A statement that the same accounting policies and methods of computation are applied in the interim financial statements compared with the most recent annual financial statements or if those policies or methods have changed, a description of the nature and effect of the change
2. Explanatory comments about seasonality or cyclicality of interim operations
3. The nature and magnitude of significant items affecting interim results that are unusual because of nature, size, or incidence
4. Dividends paid, either in the aggregate or on a per share basis, presented separately for ordinary (common) shares and other classes of shares
5. Revenue and operating result for business segments or geographical segments, whichever has been the entity's primary mode of segment reporting
6. Any significant events occurring subsequent to the end of the interim period
7. Issuances, repurchases, and repayments of debt and equity securities
8. The nature and quantum of changes in estimates of amounts reported in prior interim periods of the current financial year or changes in estimates of amounts reported in prior financial years, if those changes have a material effect in the current interim period
9. The effect of changes in the composition of the enterprise during the interim period like business combinations, acquisitions or disposal of subsidiaries and long-term investments, restructuring, and discontinuing operations
10. The changes in contingent liabilities or contingent assets since the most recent annual financial statements

IAS 34, paragraph 17, provides examples of the kinds of disclosures that are required by paragraph 16 of the standard (discussed above). For instance, an example of unusual items might be (as given by IAS 34, Paragraph 17 [a]):

". . .the write-down of inventories to net realizable value and the reversal of such a write-down"

Finally, in case of complete set of interim financial statements, the standard allows additional disclosures mandated by other IASC standards. However, if the condensed format is used, then such additional disclosures required by other IAS standards are not required.

Comparative interim financial statements. The newly enacted standard endorses the concept of comparative reporting, which is generally acknowledged to be more useful than is the presentation of information about only a single period. This is consistent with the position which has been taken by the accounting profession around the globe for many decades (although comparative reports are not an absolute requirement in some jurisdictions, most notably in the US). The IASC furthermore mandates not only comparative (condensed or complete) interim income statements (e.g., the second quarter of 2000 together with the second quarter of 1999), but the inclusion of year-to-date columns as well (e.g., the first half of 2000 and also for the first half of 1999). Thus, an interim income statement would comprise four columns of data. On the other hand, in case of the remaining components of interim financial statements, the presentation of two columns of data would suffice, as mandated by IAS 34. For example, the other components of the interim financial statements should present data for the following two periods:

- The balance sheet as of the end of the current interim period and a comparative balance sheet as of the end of the immediately preceding financial year;
- The cash flow statement cumulatively for the current financial year to date, with a comparative statement for the comparable year-to-date period of the immediately preceding financial year; and
- The statement showing changes in equity cumulatively for the current financial year to date, with a comparative statement for the comparable year-to-date period of the immediately preceding financial year.

The following illustration should amply explain the above requirements of IAS 34.

XYZ Enterprise presents quarterly interim financial statements and its financial year ends on December 31 each year. For the second quarter of 2000, the XYZ Enterprise should present the following financial statements (condensed or complete) as of June 30, 2000:

1. An income statement with four columns presenting information for the 3-month periods ended June 30, 2000, and June 30, 1999; and for the 6-month periods ended June 30, 2000, and June 30, 1999

2. A balance sheet with two columns presenting information as of June 30, 2000 and as of December 31, 1999

3. A cash flow statement with two columns presenting information for the 6-month periods ended June 30, 2000, and June 30, 1999

4. A statement of changes in equity with two columns presenting information for the 6-month periods ended June 30, 2000, and June 30, 1999

Furthermore, IAS 34, paragraph 21, recommends that, for highly seasonal businesses, the inclusion of additional income statements columns for the 12 months ending on the date of the most recent interim report (also referred to as rolling 12-month statements) would be very useful. The objective of rolling 12-month statements is that seasonality concerns are eliminated, since by definition each rolling period contains all the seasons of the year. (Rolling statements cannot correct cyclicality that encompasses more than 1 year, such as business recessions.) Accordingly, the IASC encourages companies affected by seasonality to consider including these additional statements, which could result in an interim income statement comprising six or more columns of data.

Accounting Policies in Interim Periods

Consistency. The standard logically states that interim period financial statements should be prepared using the same accounting principles which had been employed in the most recent annual financial statements. This is consistent with the idea that the latest annual report provides the frame of reference which will be employed by users of the interim information. The fact that interim data is expected to be useful in making projections of the forthcoming full year's reported results of operations makes consistency of accounting principles between the interim period and prior year important, since the projected results for the current year will undoubtedly be evaluated in the context of year-earlier performance. Unless the accounting principles applied in both periods are consistent, any such comparison is likely to be less than fully valid.

The decision to require consistent application of accounting policies across interim periods and in comparison with the earlier fiscal year is not only an implication of the view of interim reporting as being largely a means of predicting the coming fiscal year results, it is also driven by the conclusion that interim reporting periods stand alone (rather than being merely an integral portion of the full year). To put it differently, when an interim period is seen as an integral part of the full year, it is easier to rationalize applying different accounting policies to the interim periods, if doing so will more meaningfully present the results of the portion of the full year within the boundaries of the annual reporting period. For example, deferral of certain costs at interim balance sheet dates, notwithstanding the fact that such costs could not validly be deferred at year end, might serve the theoretically legitimate purpose of providing a more accurate predictor of full-year results.

On the other hand, if each interim period is seen as a discrete unit to be reported upon without having to serve the higher goal of providing an accurate prediction of the full year's expected outcome, then a decision to depart from previously applied accounting principles is less easily justified. Given the IASC's stated clear preference for the discrete view of interim financial reporting, its proposed requirement regarding consistency of accounting principles is entirely logical.

Consolidated reporting requirement. The standard also requires that, if the enterprise's most recent annual financial statements were presented on a consolidated basis, then the interim financial reports in the immediate succeeding year should also be presented similarly. This is entirely in keeping with the notion of consistency of application of accounting policies. The rule does not, however, preclude or require publishing additional "parent company only" interim reports, even if the most recent annual financial statements did include such additional data.

Materiality as Applied to Interim Financial Statements

Materiality is, of course, one of the most fundamental concepts underlying financial reporting. At the same time, it has largely been resistant to attempts at definition. A number of international accounting standards do require that items be disclosed if material or significant or are of "such size" as would warrant separate disclosure; for example, IAS 8 requires that items of income and expense within profit or loss from ordinary activities which are of such size and nature or incidence that their disclosure is relevant to explain the performance of an enterprise are to be separately disclosed. However, guidelines for performing an arithmetical calculation of a threshold for materiality (in order to measure "such size") is not prescribed in IAS 8, or for that matter in any other IAS, but rather is left to the devices of each individual charged with responsibility for financial reporting to determine.

IAS 34 puts forward the notion that materiality for interim reporting purposes will differ from that defined in the context of an annual period. This follows from the decision to endorse the discrete view of interim financial reporting, generally. Thus, for example, discontinuing operations or extraordinary items would have to be evaluated for disclosure purposes against whatever benchmark, such as gross revenue, is deemed appropriate, as that item is being reported in the interim financial statements, and not in the prior year's financial statements or projected current full year's (period's) results. The effect would normally be to lower the threshold level for reporting such items: some items separately set forth in the interim financials might not be so presented in the full year's annual report which later includes that same interim period. The objective is not to mislead the user of the information by failing to include a disclosure which might appear to be material within the context of the interim report, since that is the user's immediate frame of reference. If later the threshold is raised and items previously presented are no longer deemed worthy of such attention, this is not thought to create a risk of misleading the user, in contrast to a failure to disclose an item in the interim financial statements which, measured against the performance parameters of the interim period, might appear significant.

To illustrate, assume that Xanadu Corp. has gross revenues of $2.8 million in the first fiscal quarter, and will in fact go on to earn revenues of $12 million for the full year. Traditionally, materiality is defined as 5% of revenues. If in the first quarter an extraordinary gain of $200,000 is incurred, this should be separately set forth in the quarterly financial statements, since it exceeds the defined 5% threshold for materiality. If there are no other extraordinary losses for the balance of the year, it might validly be concluded that disclosure in the year-end financials may be omitted, since a $200,000 loss is not material in the context of $12 million of revenues. Thus, Xanadu's first quarter report might include an item defined as extraordinary which is later redefined as not being extraordinary.

Recognition Issues

General concepts. The draft statement of principles holds that definitions of assets, liabilities, income, and expense should be the same for interim period reporting as at year end. These items are defined in the IASC's *Framework for the Preparation and Presentation of Financial Statements*. The effect of stipulating that the same definitions apply to interim reporting is to further underscore the concept of interim periods being discrete units of time upon which the statements report. For example, given the definition of assets as resources generating future economic benefits for the enterprise, expenditures which could not be capitalized at year end, because of a failure to meet this definition, could similarly not be given deferred recognition at interim dates. Thus, by applying the same definitions at interim dates, the IASC has mandated the same recognition rules as are applicable at the end of full annual reporting periods.

However, while the overall implication is that identical recognition and measurement rules are to be applied to interim financial statements, the draft statement does go on to set forth a number of modifications to the general rule. Some of these are in simple acknowledgment of the limitations of certain measurement techniques, and the recognition that applying those definitions at interim dates might necessitate interpretations different from those useful for annual reporting. In other cases, the standard clearly departs from the discrete view, since such departures are not only wise, but probably fully necessary. These specific recognition and measurement issues are addressed below.

Recognition of annual costs incurred unevenly during the year. It is frequently observed that certain types of costs are incurred in uneven patterns over the course of a fiscal year, while not being driven strictly by variations in volume of sales activity. For example, major expenditures on advertising may be prepaid at the inception of the campaign; tooling for new product production will obviously be heavily weighted to the preproduction and early production stages. Certain discretionary costs, such as research and development, will not bear any predictable pattern or necessary relationship with other costs or revenues.

If an integral view approach had been elected by the IASC, there would be potent arguments to be made in support of the accrual or deferral of certain costs. For instance, if a major expenditure for overhauling equipment is scheduled to occur during the final interim period, logic could well suggest that the expenditure should be anticipated in the earlier interim periods of the year. Under the discrete view adopted by the standard, however, such an accrual would be seen as an inappropriate attempt to smooth the operating results over all the interim periods constituting the full fiscal year. Accordingly, such anticipation of future expenses is prohibited, unless, of course, the future expenditure gives rise to a true liability in the current period or meets the test of being a contingency which is probable and the magnitude of which is reasonably estimable.

For example, many business enterprises grant bonuses to managers only after the annual results are known; even if the relationship between the bonuses and the earnings performance is fairly predictable from past behavior, these remain discretionary in nature and need not be given. Such a bonus arrangement would not give rise to a liability during earlier interim periods, inasmuch as the management has yet to declare that there is a commitment which will be honored. (Compare this with the situation where managers have contracts specifying a bonus plan, which clearly would give rise to a legal liability during the year, albeit one which might involve complicated estimation problems. Also, a bonus could be anticipated for interim reporting purposes if it could be considered a constructive obligation say, based upon past practice for which the enterprise has no realistic alternative and a realistic estimate of that obligation can be made).

Another example involves contingent lease arrangements. Often in operating leases the lessee will agree to a certain minimum or base rent, plus an amount which is tied to some variable such as sales revenue. This is typical, for instance, in retail rental contracts, such as for renting space in shopping malls, since it encourages the landlord to maintain the facilities in an appealing fashion such that tenants are successful in attracting customers. Only the base amount of the periodic rental is a true liability, unless the higher rent becomes payable as sales targets are achieved. If contingent rents are payable based on a sliding scale (e.g., 1% of sales volume up to $500,000, then 2% of amounts up to $1.5 million, etc.), the projected level of full-year sales should not be used to compute rental accruals in the early periods; rather, only the contingent rents payable on the actual sales levels already achieved should be so recorded.

While the foregoing examples were clearly categories of costs which, while often fairly predictable, would not constitute a legal obligation of the reporting enterprise until the associated conditions were fully met, there are other examples which are more ambiguous. Paid vacation time and holiday leave would often be enforceable as legal commitments, and if so, provision for these should be made in interim financial statements. In other cases, as when accrued vacation time is lost if not used by the end of a defined reporting year, such costs might not be subject to accrual under the discrete view. The facts of each such situation would have to be carefully analyzed to make such a determination.

Revenues received seasonally, cyclically, or occasionally. The standard is clear that revenues such as dividend income and interest earned cannot be anticipated or deferred at interim dates, unless such would be acceptable at year end. Thus, interest income is typically accrued for, since it is well established that this represents a contractual commitment. Dividend income, on the other hand, is not recognized until declared since even when highly predictable based on past experience, these are not obligations of the paying corporation until actually declared.

Furthermore, seasonality factors should not be smoothed out of the financial statements. For example, retail stores typically have a high percentage of annual revenues occurring in the holiday shopping period, and the quarterly or other interim financial statements should fully reflect such seasonality; thus, recognize it as it occurs.

Income taxes. The fact that income taxes are assessed annually by the taxing authorities is the primary reason for reaching the conclusion that taxes are to be accrued based on the estimated average annual effective tax rate for the full fiscal year. Further, if rate changes have been enacted to take effect later in the fiscal year (while some rate changes take effect in midyear, more likely this would be an issue if the enterprise reports on a fiscal year and the new tax rates become effective at the start of a calendar year), the expected effective rate should take into account the rate changes as well as the anticipated pattern of earnings to be experienced over the course of the year. Thus, the rate to be applied to interim period earnings (or losses, as discussed further below) will take into account the expected level of earnings for the entire forthcoming year, as well as the effect of enacted (or substantially enacted) changes in the tax rates to become operative later in the fiscal year. In other words, as the standard puts it, the estimated average annual rate would "reflect a blend of the progressive tax rate structure expected to be applicable to the full year's earnings including enacted or substantially enacted changes in the income tax rates scheduled to take effect later in the financial year."

IAS 34 addresses in detail the various computational aspects of an effective interim period tax rate which are summarized in the following paragraphs.

Multiplicity of taxing jurisdictions and different categories of income. Most enterprises are subject to a multiplicity of taxing jurisdictions, and in some instances the amount of income subject to tax will vary from one to the next, since different laws will include and exclude disparate items of income or expense from the tax base. For example, interest earned on government-issued bonds may be exempted from tax by the jurisdiction which issued them, but be defined as fully taxable by another tax jurisdictions the entity is subject to. To the extent feasible, the appropriate estimated average annual effective tax rate should be separately ascertained for each taxing jurisdiction and applied individually to the interim period pretax income of each jurisdiction, so that the most accurate estimate of income taxes can be developed at each interim reporting date. In general, an overall estimated effective tax rate will not be as satisfactory for this purpose as would a more carefully constructed set of estimated rates, since the pattern of taxable and deductible items will fluctuate from one period to the next.

Similarly, if the tax law prescribes different income tax rates for different categories of income (such as the tax rate on capital gains which usually differs from the tax rate applicable to business income in many countries), then, to the extent practicable, a separate tax rate should be applied to each category of interim period pretax income. The standard, while mandating such detailed rules of computing and applying tax rates across jurisdictions or across categories of income, recognizes that in practice such a degree of precision may not be achievable in all cases. Thus in all such cases, IAS 34 softens its stand and allows usage of a "weighted-average of rates across jurisdictions or across categories of income" provided "it is a reasonable approximation of the effect of using more specific rates."

Tax credits. In computing an expected effective tax rate for a given tax jurisdiction, all relevant features of the tax regulations should be taken into account. Jurisdictions may provide for tax credits based on new investment in plant and machinery, relocation of facilities to backward or underdeveloped areas, research and development expenditures, levels of export sales, and so forth, and the expected credits against the tax for the full year should be given consideration in the determination of an expected effective tax rate. Thus, the tax effect of new investment in plant and machinery, when the local taxing body offers an investment credit for qualifying investment in tangible productive assets, will be reflected in those interim periods of the fiscal year in which the new investment occurs (assuming it can be forecast to occur later in a given fiscal year), and not merely in the period in which the new investment occurs. This is consistent with the underlying concept that taxes are strictly an annual phenomenon, but it is at variance with the purely discrete view of interim financial reporting.

The interim reporting standard notes that, although tax credits and similar modifying elements are to be taken into account in developing the expected effective tax rate to apply to interim earnings, tax benefits which will relate to onetime events are to be reflected in the interim period when those events take place. This is perhaps most likely to be encountered in the context of capital gains taxes incurred in connection with occasional dispositions of investments and other capital assets; since it is not feasible to project the rate at which such transactions will occur over the course of a year, the tax effects should be recognized only as the underlying events transpire.

While in most cases tax credits are to be handled as suggested in the foregoing paragraphs, in some jurisdictions tax credits, particularly those which relate to export revenue or capital expenditures, are in effect government grants. The accounting for government grants is set forth in IAS 20; in brief, grants are recognized in income over the period necessary to properly match them to the costs which the grants are intended to offset or defray. Thus, compliance with both IAS 20 and IAS 34 would necessitate that tax credits be carefully analyzed to identify those which are in substance grants, and then accounting for the credit consistent with its true nature.

Tax loss tax credit carrybacks and carryforwards. When an interim period loss gives rise to a tax loss carryback, it should be fully reflected in that interim period. Similarly, if a loss in an interim period produces a tax loss carryforward, it should be recognized immediately, but only if the criteria set forth in revised IAS 12, are met. Specifically, it must be deemed probable that the benefits will be realizable before the loss benefits can be given formal recognition in the financial statements. In the case of interim period losses, it may be necessary to assess not only whether the enterprise will be profitable enough in future fiscal years to utilize the tax benefits associated with the loss, but, furthermore, whether interim periods later in the same year will provide earnings of sufficient magnitude to absorb the losses of the current period.

Revised IAS 12 provides that changes in expectations regarding the realizability of benefits related to net operating loss carryforwards should be reflected currently in tax expense. Similarly, if a net operating loss carryforward benefit is not deemed probable of being realized until the interim (or annual) period when it in fact becomes realized, the tax effect will be included in tax expense of that period. Appropriate explanatory material must be included in the notes to the financial statements, even on an interim basis, to provide the user with an understanding of the unusual relationship between pretax accounting income and the provision for income taxes.

Volume rebates or other anticipated price changes in interim reporting periods. IAS 34 prescribes that where volume rebates or other contractual changes in the prices of goods and services are anticipated to occur over the annual reporting period, these should be anticipated in the interim financial statements for periods within that year. The logic is that the effective cost of materials, labor, or other inputs will be altered later in the year as a consequence of the volume of activity during earlier interim periods, among others, and it would be a distortion of the reported results of those earlier periods if this were not taken into account. Clearly this must be based on estimates, since the volume of purchases, etc., in later portions of the year may not materialize as anticipated. As with other estimates, however, as more accurate information becomes available this will be adjusted on a prospective basis, meaning that the results of earlier periods should not be revised or corrected. This is consistent with the accounting prescribed for contingent rentals and is furthermore consistent with IAS 37's guidance on provisions.

The requirement to take volume rebates and similar adjustments into effect in interim period financial reporting applies equally to vendors or providers, as well as to customers or consumers of the goods and services. In both instances, however, it must be deemed probable that such adjustments have been earned or will occur, before giving recognition to them in the financials. This high a threshold has been set because the definitions of assets and liabilities in the IASC's *Framework for the Preparation and Presentation of Financial Statements* require that they be recognized only when it is probable that the benefits will flow into or out from the enterprise. Thus, accrual would only be appropriate for contractual price adjustments and related matters. Discretionary rebates and other price adjustments, even if typically experienced in earlier periods, would not be given formal recognition in the interim financials.

Depreciation and amortization in interim periods. The rule regarding depreciation and amortization in interim periods is more consistent with the discrete view of interim reporting. Charges to be recognized in the interim periods are to be related to only those assets actually employed during the period; planned acquisitions for later periods of the fiscal year are not to be taken into account.

While this rule seems entirely logical, it can give rise to a problem which is not encountered in the context of most other types of revenue or expense items. This occurs when the tax laws or financial reporting conventions permit or require that special allocation formulas be used during the year of acquisition (and often disposition) of an asset. In such cases, depreciation or amortization will be an amount other than the amount which would be computed purely based on the fraction of the year the asset was in service. For example, say that convention is that one-half year of depreciation is charged during the year the asset is acquired, irrespective of how many months it is in service. Further assume that a particular asset is acquired at the inception of the fourth quarter of the year. Under the requirements of IAS 34, the first three quarters would not be charged with any depreciation expense related to this asset (even if it was known in advance that the asset would be placed in service in the fourth quarter). However, this would then necessitate charging fourth quarter operations with one-half year's (i.e., two quarters') depreciation, which arguably would distort that final period's results of operations.

IAS 34 does address this problem area. It states that an adjustment should be made in the final interim period so that the sum of interim depreciation and amortization equals an independently computed annual charge for these items. However, since there is no requirement that financial statements be separately presented for a final interim period (and most enterprises, in fact, do not report for a final period), such an adjustment might be implicit in the annual financials, and presumably would be explained in the notes if material (the standard does not explicitly require this, however).

The alternative financial reporting strategy, that is, projecting annual depreciation, including the effect of asset dispositions and acquisitions planned for or reasonably anticipated to occur during the year, and then allocating this ratably to interim periods, has been rejected. Such an approach might have been rationalized in the same way that the use of the effective annual tax rate was in assigning tax expense or benefits to interim periods, but this has not been done.

Inventories. Inventories represent a major category for most manufacturing and merchandising enterprises, and some inventory costing methods pose unique problems for interim financial reporting. In general, however, the same inventory costing principles should be utilized for interim reporting as for annual reporting.

However, the use of estimates in determining quantities, costs and net realizable values at interim dates will be more pervasive.

Three particular difficulties are addressed in IAS 34. These are the matters of determining net realizable values at interim dates, the use of the LIFO costing method, and the allocation of manufacturing variances.

Regarding net realizable value determination, the standard expresses the belief that the determination of NRV at interim dates should be based on selling prices and costs to complete at those dates. Projections should not, therefore, be made regarding conditions which possibly might exist at the time of the fiscal year end. Furthermore, write-downs to NRV taken at interim reporting dates should be reversed in a subsequent interim reporting period only if it would be appropriate to do so at the end of the financial year.

LIFO inventory costing poses unique problems because it is almost solely driven by tax regulations (although in a few industries a case can be made that the physical flow of goods follows a last-in, first-out pattern) which provide an economic incentive to use the method. As a tax-driven accounting procedure, annual measurement is usually prescribed, and certain adjustments required at year end can potentially interfere with meaningful financial reporting if made at interim dates. The most commonly encountered issue is that of liquidation of lower cost LIFO layers at interim dates, only to have the physical quantity restored before year end.

To avoid distorting the operating results of the interim period in which the liquidation occurs (overstating interim profits by expensing lower cost inventory through cost of sales), as well as that of the later period when the inventory volume is restored (having the reverse effect), common practice has long been to provide a reserve for temporary liquidations of inventory, effectively charging current period cost of sales for the higher level of costs which, it is expected, will be incurred when the temporary liquidation is reversed. This is the method sanctioned under US GAAP as well.

The last of the special issues related to inventories which are addressed by IAS 34 concerns allocation of variances at interim dates. When standard costing methods are employed, the resulting variances are typically allocated to cost of sales and inventories in proportion to the dollar magnitude of those two captions, or according to some other rational system. IAS 34 requires that the price, efficiency, spending, and volume variances of a manufacturing enterprise are recognized in income at interim reporting dates to the extent those variances would be recognized at the end of the financial year. It should be noted that some standards have prescribed deferral of such variances to year end based on the premise that some of the variances will tend to offset over the course of a full fiscal year, particularly if the result of volume fluctuations due to seasonal factors. When variance allocation is thus deferred, the full balance of the variances are placed onto the balance sheet, typically as additions to or deductions from the inventory accounts. However, IAS 34 expresses a preference that these variances be disposed of at interim dates (instead of being deferred to year end) since to not do so could result in reporting inventory at interim dates at more or less than actual cost.

Foreign Currency Translation Adjustments at Interim Dates

Given the IASC's adoption of the discrete view regarding interim reporting, it is not surprising that the same approach to translation gains or losses as is mandated at year end would be adopted in IAS 34. IAS 21 prescribes rules for translating the financial statements for foreign operations into the reporting currency and also includes guidelines for using historical, average, or closing foreign exchange rates. It also lays down rules for either including the resulting adjustments in income or in equity. IAS 34 requires that consistent with IAS 21, the actual average and closing rates for the interim period be used in translating financial statements of foreign operations at interim dates. In other words, the future changes to exchanges rates (in the current financial year) are not allowed to be anticipated by IAS 34.

Where IAS 21 provides for translation adjustments to be recognized in the income statement in the period it arises, IAS 34 stipulates that the same approach be applied during each interim period. If the adjustments are expected to reverse before the end of the financial year, IAS 34 requires that enterprises not defer some foreign currency translation adjustments at an interim date.

Adjustments to Previously Reporting Interim Data

While year-to-date financial reporting is not required, although the standard does recommend it in addition to normal interim period reporting, the concept finds some expression in the standard's position that adjustments not be made to earlier interim periods' results. By measuring income and expense on a year-to-date basis, and then effectively backing into the most recent interim period's presentation by deducting that which was reported in earlier interim periods, the need for retrospective adjustment of information which was reported earlier is obviated. However, there may be the need for disclosure of the effects of such measurement strategies when this results effectively in including adjustments in the most current interim period's reported results.

Accounting Changes in Interim Periods

IAS 34, paragraph 43, requires that a change in accounting policy, other than one for which the transition is specified by a new IAS, should be reflected either

- By restating the financial statements of prior interim periods of the current year and the comparable interim periods of the prior financial year, if the enterprise follows the benchmark treatment under IAS 8, or
- By restating the financial statements of prior interim periods of the current financial year, without restating the comparable interim periods of the prior

financial years (i.e., when the enterprise follows the allowed alternative treatment under IAS 8).

The first option would be more informative because of the salutary effects on comparability of financial data for the current and preceding years. If the second option is adopted and the allowed alternative treatment is followed, then the entire cumulative adjustment is to be made prospectively in the determination of the profit or loss for the period in which the accounting policy is changed.

One of the objectives of the above requirement of IAS 34 is to ensure that a single accounting policy is applied to a particular class of transactions throughout the entire financial year. To allow differing accounting policies to be applied to the same class of transactions within a single financial year would be disastrous since it would, as pointed out by the standard, result in "interim allocation difficulties, obscured operating results, and complicated analysis and understandability of interim period information."

Use of estimates in interim periods. IAS 34, paragraph 41, recognizes that preparation of interim financial statements will require a greater use of estimates than annual financial statements. Appendix 3 to the standard provides examples of use of estimates to illustrate the application of this standard in this regard. The Appendix provides nine examples covering areas ranging from inventories to pensions. For instance, in the case of pensions, the Appendix states that for interim reporting purposes, reliable measurement is often obtainable by extrapolation of the latest actuarial valuation, as opposed to obtaining the same from a professionally qualified actuary, as would be expected at the end of a financial year. Readers are advised to read the other illustrations contained in Appendix 3 of IAS 34 for further guidance on the subject.

Impairment of assets in interim periods. IAS 34, paragraph 36, stipulates that an enterprise should apply the same impairment testing, recognition, and reversal criteria at an interim period as it would at the end of its financial year. However, this does not mean that a detailed impairment calculation as prescribed by IAS 36 would automatically need to be used at interim periods; instead, an enterprise would need to review for indications of significant impairments since the date of the most recent financial year to determine whether such a calculation is required.

Interim financial reporting in hyperinflationary economies. IAS 34, paragraph 32, requires that interim financial reports in hyperinflationary economies be prepared using the same principles as at the financial year end. Thus, the provisions of IAS 29 would need to be complied with in this regard. IAS 34 stipulates that in presenting interim data in the measuring unit, enterprises should report the resulting gain or loss on the net monetary position in the interim period's income statement. IAS 34 also requires that enterprises do not need to annualize the recognition of the gain or loss or use estimated annual inflation rates in preparing interim period financial statements in a hyperinflationary economy.

20 SEGMENT REPORTING

PERSPECTIVE AND ISSUES

Segment reporting, the disclosure of information about an enterprise's operations in different industries, its foreign operations and export sales, and its major customers, is a relatively recent development in the history of financial reporting.

Traditionally, businesses operated in a single industry segment, or within a very small number of such groupings, and thus the financial statements were relatively easy to understand, since they did not typically aggregate dissimilar operations. During the mid- to late-1960s, however, the trend toward conglomeration became noticeable, with a large number of business combinations that resulted in highly diversified corporations. Some of these companies voluntarily disclosed segment financial information in their annual reports, usually to emphasize the counter-cyclical natures of the various components, but the extent and nature of the disclosure varied widely. An official, but nonbinding, pronouncement from US accounting standard setters, issued in 1967, recommended that there be further voluntary disclosures. In addition, organizations representing preparers of financial statements sponsored research studies that generally supported the desirability and feasibility of segment reporting.

The regulator of the US securities markets (the Securities and Exchange Commission) began requiring line-of-business information in registrants' annual filings in 1970, but many diversified companies still failed to include segment information in the annual reports which they issued to stockholders. By 1974, the SEC required registrants to include some of this line-of-business information in their annual reports to stockholders. SFAS 14, issued in December 1976, established specific guidelines for the required disclosure of segment information on financial reports issued to stockholders under US GAAP. These requirements were later dropped for interim reports, and shortly thereafter were deleted entirely for non-publicly-held companies.

The first international standard, IAS 14, was issued in 1981 and largely followed the lead of the earlier US standard, and thus, the range of definitions of industry segments which were acceptable was fairly wide. Subsequently, the IASC significantly revised this standard, effective in mid-1998, by changing the method of determining reportable segments to conform more closely to how the business enterprise is internally managed. Later, standard setters in the US and elsewhere essentially conformed their standards to this new reporting philosophy, as well. Under this new approach, the challenge of preparing segment disclosures is relaxed when the segment data captured by the reporting entity's managerial reporting system corresponds with the standard's definitions of industry and/or geographical segments, while in other cases it will still be necessary to disaggregate and reaggregate data from the management information system to develop needed financial statement disclosures. Segment information, while recommended for all issuers of financial statements, is required only for those which have publicly traded debt or equity issues.

Sources of IAS
IAS 14 (revised)

DEFINITIONS OF TERMS

Accounting policies. Specific principles, bases, conventions, rules and practices adopted by an entity in preparing and presenting its financial statements.

Business segment. A distinguishable component of an enterprise that is engaged in providing a product or service or group of related products or services, and that is subject to risks and returns that are different from those of other business segments.

Cash flows. Inflows and outflows of cash and cash equivalents.

Common costs. Operating expenses incurred by the enterprise for the benefit of more than one industry segment.

Consolidated financial information. Aggregate (financial) information relating to an enterprise as a whole whether or not the enterprise has consolidated subsidiaries.

Corporate assets. Assets maintained for general corporate purposes and not used in the operations of any industry segment.

Discontinued operation. Resulting from the sale or abandonment of an operation that represents a separate, major line of business of an enterprise; the assets, net profit or loss, and activities can be distinguished physically, operationally, and for financial reporting purposes.

Extraordinary items. Income or expenses that arise from events or transactions that are clearly distinct from the ordinary activities of the enterprise and, therefore, are not expected to recur frequently or regularly.

General corporate expenses. Expenses incurred for the benefit of the corporation as a whole, which cannot be reasonably allocated to any segment.

Geographical segment. Distinguishable component of an enterprise engaged in operations in individual countries or groups of countries within particular geographic areas, as may be determined to be appropriate in the circumstances to reflect the nature of the enterprise's operations.

Identifiable assets. Those tangible and intangible assets used by an industry segment, including those the segment uses exclusively, and an allocated portion of assets used jointly by more than one segment.

Industry segment. A distinguishable component of an enterprise engaged in providing a different product or service or a different group of related products or services, primarily to unaffiliated customers. This term has been superseded by **business segment**.

Intersegment sales. Transfers of products or services, similar to those sold to unaffiliated customers, between industry segments or geographic areas of the enterprise.

Intrasegment sales. Transfers within an industry segment or geographic area.

Minority interest. That part of the net results of operations and of net assets of a subsidiary attributable to interests which are not owned, directly or indirectly through subsidiaries, by the parent.

Operating activities. The principal revenue producing activities of an enterprise and other activities that are not investing or financing activities.

Operating profit or loss. An industry segment's revenue minus all operating expenses, including an allocated portion of common costs.

Ordinary activities. Any activities which are undertaken by an enterprise as part of its business and such related activities in which the enterprise engages in furtherance of, incidental to or arising from, these activities.

Reportable segment. A business or geographical segment for which segment information is required to be disclosed.

Revenue. The gross inflow of economic benefits during a period arising in the ordinary course of business activities from sales to unaffiliated customers and from inter segment sales or transfers, excluding inflows from equity participants.

Segment accounting policies. The policies adopted for reporting the consolidated financial statements of the enterprise, as well as for segment reporting.

Segment assets. Operating assets employed by a segment in operating activities, whether directly attributable or reasonably allocable to the segment; these should exclude those generating revenues or expenses which are excluded from the definitions of segment revenue and segment expense.

Segment expense. Expense that is directly attributable to a segment, or the relevant portion of expense that can be allocated on a reasonable basis to a segment; it excludes extraordinary items, interest expense, losses on sales of investments or extinguishment of debt, equity method losses of associates and joint ventures, income taxes, and corporate expenses not identified with specific segments.

Segment revenue. Revenue that is directly attributable to a segment, or the relevant portion of revenue that can be allocated on a reasonable basis to a segment, and that is derived from transactions with parties outside the enterprise and from other segments of the same enterprise; it excludes extraordinary items, interest and dividend income, and gains on sales of investments or extinguishment of debt.

Transfer pricing. The pricing of products or services between industry segments or geographic areas.

CONCEPTS, RULES, AND EXAMPLES

Conceptual Basis for Segmental Reporting

As business organizations have become more complex over the years, and the conglomerate form of organization has become ever more popular, it has become necessary to concede that financial statements which present the full scope of an enterprise's operations have declined markedly in utility. While it is certainly possible to assess the overall financial health of the entity using such financial reports, it is much more difficult to evaluate management's operating and financial strategies, particularly with regard to its emphasis on specific lines of business. For example, the extent to which operating results for a period are the result of the development of new products with greater potential for future growth vs. mature product lines which nonetheless still account for a majority of the entity's total sales, would be largely masked in financial statements which did not present results by business segment.

The need for the inclusion of some type of disaggregated information in general purpose financial reports became critical by the late 1960s, and national accounting rule-making bodies accordingly began to address this topic around that time. In the US, for example, the need for segment information was one of the first agenda items identified upon the FASB's formation in 1973. The original, and long operative, US requirement, SFAS 14, was promulgated in 1976; while a revised standard, largely (but not entirely) embracing the same approach as does IAS 14 (revised), was recently adopted as SFAS 131, which was first effective in 1998. In the UK, the Companies Act of 1967 first mandated the disclosure of limited segment data; this requirement was expanded by later revisions of the Act, and disaggregated information was formally made part of the notes to the financial statements in 1981. A related professional accounting standard (SSAP 25) was adopted in 1990, with segments again defined either by class of business (similar to product or service areas) or by geographic location, with company management charged with the responsibility of determining which type of categorization would be most meaningful to financial statement users. As in the US, a threshold value of 10% is established for making a determination that a segment is material, and the criteria are virtually identical to those in the US under SFAS 14. Information to be disclosed is also modeled on the US requirement--sales, operating results, and identifiable assets (called net assets under the UK standard, but not actually defined there). It is not clear whether the UK standard will be subject to the same sort of revisions as have occurred in the US, Canada, and under the IAS.

On the international standard-setting scene, the relevant rules, which comprise original IAS 14, have been effective since 1983. The standard was reformatted, but not substantively altered, in 1995. In mid-1999 the IASC approved a successor to this standard, revised IAS 14, which will be used as the basis for the following discussion.

Applicability of IAS 14

In contrast to the new US standard on segment reporting (SFAS 131), which affects the financial reports (including interim ones) of only publicly held companies, the **original** international standard on segment reporting was intended to be applicable to both publicly held and "other economically significant entities." While this expression went undefined by that standard, presumably this implied that all business organizations, other than those which are small, locally-based, and nondiversified, were expected to apply the requirements of IAS 14.

Revised IAS 14, on the other hand, stipulates that the new standard will be applicable to those entities which have publicly traded equity or debt securities. This will essentially conform the international rules with those of the national standard-setting bodies, and limit this standard to publicly held entities. While the logic for presenting disaggregated information in the context of nonpublic enterprises is perhaps equally strong, the counter arguments--that owners and managers already have this information, and that general disclosure could place the entity in jeopardy from a competitive perspective--had been voiced so loudly for such a long time that it was not politically feasible to impose the requirement on privately owned entities.

In determining which segments of a given entity need to be separately presented, there was a contrast between the US approach and that of original IAS 14. This original standard asked that segment information be presented for business or geographic segments whose level of revenues, profits, assets, or employment are significant in the countries in which their major operations are conducted. However, the term significant was not defined, and in fact IAS 14 declined to quantify this threshold, while duly noting that other standard setters had chosen to establish such guidelines, thereby implying that those could be used to fill the vacuum. In the US, the FASB mandated a 10% boundary for recognition, but level of employment was not stipulated as one of the criteria (only assets, revenues, and profits were so identified).

Thus, the intent under original IAS 14 was for the segment data prescribed by that standard to be presented by any entity having substantial activities in more than one industry group or geographic region. It remained a matter of some judgment, however, as to where that threshold was to be placed.

Revised IAS 14 takes a very different approach to defining segments and to defining the threshold at which they become reportable segments. Under the new standard, the goal is to disaggregate business and geographical segments which have different risk and return profiles. The new standard sets forth a number of factors which can be used to determine whether the risks and returns are in fact at variance as between two or more segments. Furthermore, it is explicitly intended that the reporting entity's internal organization and financial reporting system should be used to help in making this determination. For example, the way in which the enterprise is organizationally structured should reveal whether geographical segments are defined in terms of location of productive operations or location of customers.

Not only is it necessary under revised IAS 14 to define which of the business and geographical segments are to be deemed reportable, it is also required that a determination be made about whether the business segments or the geographical segments will be the primary mode of segment reporting, with the alternative becoming the secondary mode. This depends, under the terms of the revised standard, upon whether the dominant source and nature of risk and return derives from the products and services it produces, or from operating in different countries or selling into different markets. The amount of information to be disclosed for the primary segments is much greater than for the secondary segments. The lack of quantitative thresholds is consistent with the decision to use the enterprise's internal organization and operation as the driver of the segment reporting model. In other words, a definable portion of the business will be a segment if management behaves as if it is.

Defining Industry and Geographic Segments

Understanding what is meant by industry segments has proven to be a difficult task for many preparers and users of financial statement information, and furthermore, some preparers have been inclined to define a segment in an overly broad fashion, to reduce the amount of disaggregated information which they present. However, there are very legitimate questions which can, and have, been raised on this matter. For one hypothetical example, consider a large manufacturer of a range of automobiles, which entity can convincingly argue that this represents a single segment, while other similar enterprises might hold that a number of segments exist, such as small cars, luxury cars, etc. Under the original IAS 14, the requirements for segment information appeared to tolerate using a liberal interpretation, so that in the foregoing example all automobile manufacturing could have been deemed to have been a single segment.

In IAS 14 (revised), the IASC has defined segments in terms more consistent with internal managerial decision making. Using the example above, if management makes distinct decisions about the production and marketing of small cars vs.

luxury cars, then those would be separate segments for disclosure purposes, regardless of brand names or other artificial distinctions among the product lines. According to the new standard, "an enterprise should look to its system of internal reporting to the board of directors and the chief executive officer for the purpose of identifying its business segments or geographical segments, for both its primary and secondary reporting formats...."

Characteristics of business and geographical segments. In the event that internally reported segments fail to satisfy the definitions of business and geographical segments, then the criteria in the standard are to be applied to ascertain the identities of the segments.

The standard stipulates the following factors to be considered in determining how to group products and services into business segments:

1. The nature of the products or services;
2. The nature and technology of the production processes;
3. The types of markets in which the products or services are sold;
4. Major classes of customers;
5. The distribution channels and methods for the products; and
6. A unique legislative or regulatory environment relating to part of the business, as might define banks, insurance companies, and utilities.

The following factors can be used to group geographical areas into geographical segments:

1. Proximity of operations;
2. Similarity of economic and political conditions;
3. Relationships between operations in different geographical areas;
4. Special risks associated with operations in a particular country; and
5. Underlying currency risks.

In the absence of internal organizational indicators which suffice to define business and geographical segments, the foregoing criteria should be applied in an attempt to identify primary and secondary segment formats. In that situation, the disclosure of segment data should include a statement to the effect that the externally reported segment data does not conform to that used internally, and the following three supplemental disclosures must be made for each segment which has revenue from sales to external customers amounting to 10% or more of total enterprise revenue from external customers:

1. Segment revenue from external customers;
2. The total carrying amount of segment assets; and
3. Capital expenditures.

Internal indications of segments are to be used whenever possible, however. The informational items to be disclosed for the segments, however they are defined, are discussed below.

Defining Reportable Segments

Reportable segments are business or geographical segments, whether identified either by internal organizational or financial reporting factors, or by application of the criteria set forth above, which meet the threshold test for becoming reportable. A segment will be reportable if a majority of its revenue is earned from sales to external customers, and furthermore

1. Its revenue from sales to external customers and from transactions with internal customers (other segments) is 10% or more of total revenue of all segments, **or**
2. Its segment result, whether profit or loss, is 10% or more of the combined result of all segments recording a profit or of all segments recording a loss, whichever is the greater in absolute monetary terms, **or**
3. Its assets are 10% or more of the total assets of all segments.

Thus, the revised IAS 14 essentially has embraced the quantitative criteria of the former US GAAP standard, SFAS 14, regarding the threshold criteria for reportability of individual segments. Note that the segment will be deemed reportable if any one of the three foregoing criteria are satisfied: The test is disjunctive, not conjunctive. However, since only those segments which earn a majority of revenues from external customers are subjected to this testing, those which are essentially vertically integrated will typically not be required to report as separate segments.

Comparative financial statements. IAS 14 (revised) also provides that if a segment were deemed to be reportable in the immediate preceding period (because one or more of the aforenoted 10% thresholds had been exceeded), then even failing each of these tests in the current year would not eliminate the need to present comparable segment data currently. However, this requirement is only applicable if management believes that the segment has continuing significance; absent this, such disclosure could be eliminated. The fact that continuing disclosure is dependent upon management attitudes introduces a subjective element. This may eventually be seen as permitting nondisclosure of important information, and more objective criteria may have to be imposed at some point in time.

Furthermore, if a segment is deemed to be reportable in the current reporting period because it satisfies a relevant threshold test for the first time, the comparative prior period disclosures should be restructured to include that segment as a reportable one, notwithstanding that it did not surpass the 10% thresholds in the prior year. In establishing these two requirements, comparability was obviously given a very substantial weighting.

Segment Reporting Under Revised IAS 14

For purposes of conforming with IAS 14, as it presently exists, segments should be defined in terms of groups of related products or services, or alternatively by types of customers to whom these are provided. It must remain a matter of judgment as to how this guideline is applied, and similar enterprises might reach different conclusions on this. For example, a manufacturer of electronic and mechanical components used in the automobile industry might market these to original equipment manufacturers (OEM) of automobiles and of heavy construction equipment, and also to after-market suppliers, in a number of different geographic markets (e.g., Western Europe, the former Eastern Bloc nations of Europe, and the Middle East). In presenting segment data, the entity might reach at least four distinct conclusions on how to define the segments, as follows:

1. It might argue that the entire business represents a single segment;
2. It could find that electronics and mechanical components are essentially different product lines and, thus, that there are two segments of the business;
3. It might conclude that the OEM market is generically different from the after market, thus defining two different segments in another way; or
4. It could reason that automobile OEM, construction equipment OEM, and after-market suppliers are each distinct, thus defining three segments of the business for which information is to be disclosed.

Thus, it is clear that management judgment will continue to play a large role in financial reporting of industry segments. In reaching its decisions, however, managements should weigh the similarities and differences among the products or services, the risk characteristics of the markets, the growth potential and the likely future importance of the segment to the entity as a whole. If some parts of the business are subject to particular or unusual regulatory oversight (such as banking typically is), this is a factor which suggests that it might constitute a separate segment for reporting purposes. The fact that a product or service line is produced in an organizationally separate unit, such as a division, may or may not be determinative; thus, internal accounting data might be usable for segment reporting, but might also need to be reclassified for that purpose.

The determination of geographic segments is likewise subject to the application of substantial amounts of judgment. Typically, however, it will be fairly obvious in any given circumstance how the breakdown among regions should be accomplished. The only real question, in most cases, will be how much detail to present. For example, if an enterprise has operations in western Europe and also in former Soviet Bloc nations such as Poland, some might conclude that these are separate segments since their economic systems were so different for so long, and the emerging nations of Eastern Europe represent materially different risks and growth opportunities. Others might conclude that Europe is a single region, based on transportation requirements and other criteria, especially when compared to North American, Latin American and Asian segments of the same business.

Disclosure Requirements Under Revised IAS 14

The draft which preceded the issuance of revised IAS 14 offered an expansive listing of mandatory disclosures to be made in both the primary and the secondary segment reporting formats. The comments received to the exposure draft, not surprisingly, indicated that many preparers of financial statements believed that these requirements would be excessive. While the final standard has eliminated a handful of the proposed disclosures, what remains is a wide-ranging set of data to be presented in the notes to the financial statements of any enterprise which operates in more than a single segment, and which is subject to the requirements.

All reporting entities will need to define whether business segments are to be the primary reporting format, in which case geographical segments will become the secondary reporting format, or whether the opposite is to be the case. This determination is made, as noted before, based on the dominant source of risk and return to the organization. Thus, if strategic decisions are made primarily in terms of geographical location of either operations (e.g., siting of manufacturing plants, sourcing materials, etc.) or customers, then geographical segments will be the primary reporting format. If decisions revolve around product or service offerings, then business segments will be the primary format. In either case, the format not chosen as primary will be used as secondary, which implies a substantial amount of informative disclosure, although somewhat less than in the primary format.

Primary reporting format disclosures. The following informative disclosures are mandated for each reportable segment:

1. Segment revenue, with separate disclosure of revenue derived from external customers and revenue derived from internal customers (i.e., from other segments). Also, the nature of the segment's revenue should be described, in the manner set forth in IAS 18 (i.e., separately disclosing revenues arising from sales of goods, rendering of services, interest, royalties, dividends, and from the exchange [bartering] of goods and services in each category).
2. Segment result.
3. Interest and dividend income and interest expense directly attributable to the segment or which can be reasonably allocated to the segment, separately--except that this need not be done for reportable segments the operations of which are primarily of a financial nature.
4. Total assets at carrying value.
5. Segment liabilities.
6. The contingencies or commitments which can be directly attributed to a reportable segment or allocated on a reasonable basis to segments.
7. Total expenditures to acquire segment assets during the reporting period (typically referred to as capital expenditures).
8. Total depreciation and amortization expense related to segment assets and included in segment results for the reporting period.

9. The nature of any item of revenue or expense which due to size, nature or incidence needs to be disclosed to explain performance of the segment for the period.

10. The nature and amount of extraordinary items which are directly attributable to a segment or reasonably allocable to it.

11. Significant noncash expenses, other than depreciation and amortization, that were deducted in arriving at segment results.

12. The segment's share of profit or loss of associates, joint ventures or other investments accounted for under the equity method, as well as the investment in that associate or joint venture.

13. A reconciliation of the information presented for reportable segments (the 12 categories above) to the amounts presented in the consolidated or enterprise-wide financial statements. In reconciling revenue, segment revenue from outsiders should be reconciled to total revenue from outside customers; segment results should be reconciled to a comparable measure of enterprise performance as well as to enterprise net income or loss; and segment liabilities should be reconciled to enterprise liabilities.

Secondary reporting format. The nature of the data presented in the secondary reporting format depends upon which of the two possible criteria determined the primary format, business or geography. If the primary disclosures were based on business segments, then the secondary, geographical, format must contain, for each segment which has sales to external customers **or** segment assets totaling 10% or more of the comparable enterprise-wide amounts

1. Segment revenue from external customers, determined by the geographical location of customer or market.

2. Total carrying amount of segment assets, determined by geographical location of the assets.

3. The total amount of capital expenditure for the period being reported on, by location of assets.

If the primary mode of reporting segment information is by geographical locations, on the other hand, then the secondary format information will be, for each business segment whose revenue from sales to external customers is 10% or more of total enterprise revenue from external customers, as follows:

1. Segment revenue from external customers.

2. Total carrying amount of segment assets.

3. The total amount of capital expenditures for the period.

Finally, if the entity defines primary segment format in terms of geographical area, based on the location of the production or service facilities, and if the markets in which the goods or services significantly differ from the location of the assets, then revenue from sales to external customers must also be reported by location of markets. The geographical markets to be identified are those whose sales to external customers is 10% or more of the corresponding enterprise total.

Other Disclosures Which May Be Necessary

Disclosures are necessary when a business or geographical segment is not deemed to be reportable because it earns a majority of its revenue from intersegment sales, yet 10% or more of enterprise sales to external customers is comprised of sales to external customers by this segment. This fact should be disclosed, as well as the sales revenue from external and intersegment sales generated by the segment.

The basis for determining prices for intersegment sales should be stated. This should be the same basis that the enterprise actually uses to recognize such transactions for internal reporting purposes. If the method has changed from the previous period, that fact should be adequately disclosed as well.

Segment disclosures are to be prepared using the same accounting principles that the enterprise uses for general external reporting in accordance with international accounting standards. If there have been changes in accounting principles employed at the enterprise level which also impact on segment informative disclosures, these should be dealt with in accordance with IAS 8. Under that standard's benchmark treatment, prior period information is restated to conform with the new principles, unless impracticable to do so. Under the allowed alternative treatment, the cumulative effect of the change in accounting principle is reported as a charge or credit in determining current period net income. If the alternative treatment is utilized, the cumulative effect should be included in segment operating performance, if reasonable allocations can be made, with sufficient disclosure to explain the performance of the segments for the period.

If there have been changes in accounting principles employed in determining segment disclosures, which have a material impact on the data provided to users of the financial statements, such as the method of allocating revenue and expenses to segments, then again consistent with the benchmark treatment stipulated by IAS 8, the comparative prior period information should be restated to conform with the new methods utilized. This is important even though aggregate enterprise amounts will not have been affected by the change, since the users' understanding of segment performance may be distorted unless efforts are made to provide them with insights into these matters.

Unless it is clear from other disclosures or from the body of the financial statements themselves, the segment information should include descriptions of the activities of each reportable business segment and should also indicate the composition of each geographical segment, both for primary and secondary reporting formats. A fair amount of judgment is required in deciding on what information should be provided, but in theory, to take the geographical segment disclosure as an example, such matters as stability of currencies, political risks, and market growth expectations are all potentially useful to recipients of the data and possibly necessary to interpret the financial disclosures most meaningfully. While these are technically voluntary disclosures, in ultimately reaching a judgment as to whether the financial statements are fairly presented, the adequacy of disclosures will have to be weighed.

If an enterprise operates in a single business or geographical segment and therefore is not required to, and does not, report either primary or secondary segment data, that fact should be disclosed and the nature of its business segment or geographical operations should be stated. In some cases an entity will operate within a single segment, but derive revenues from a number of diverse products or services; in such instances, the new standard requires that these be described and the amounts of revenues derived from any such group of products or services which constitute 10% or more of enterprise revenue should be set forth. This clearly will require the exercise of judgment, since there will be a thin line between such disclosures and the admission that the entity, in fact, is operating in more than a single segment and thus should have made the full set of informative disclosures required by revised IAS 14.

Finally, if the aggregate revenue from external customers from all reportable segments totals less than 75% of the revenue reported by the entity as a whole, the standard requires that there be a general description of the nature of the remaining sources of revenue. This would normally occur when the balance of revenues are derived from a range of individually minor activities which do not constitute a single or group of segments. In practice, this situation will not occur very often, as the defined and reportable segments will typically add to more than the 75% threshold level.

Revisions to Definitions of Segments

Over time, an entity may determine that the definition of industry or of geographic segments needs to be revised. The effect of making such a change could be to make information presented in earlier years no longer comparable to that currently presented in the financial statements. Accordingly, at a minimum, the fact of having made this change must be disclosed, with a sufficient description so that users can appreciate the general impact that change might have had. The reasons why the change was made, such as to better reflect the way management is currently making decisions about the segments of the business, should also be stated. If reasonably determinable, the actual effect of the change should be disclosed.

As an example, the manufacturer of electronic and mechanical automobile parts used in the example below might at some point conclude that its former manner of presentation of segment data as a dichotomy between electronic and mechanical products is no longer meaningful given the growing pervasiveness of electronic components in what had previously been entirely mechanical items. Thus, the entity might determine that a more useful categorization would be by type of customer, for example, original equipment manufacturers (OEM) vs. aftermarket, since the underlying economic forces differ substantially between these. In the year of the change in presentation, the fact of the change and the logic for it should be presented, and if possible the prior period's data, which had been presented earlier on the basis of product type, should be restated on the newly adopted basis of customer class. By doing this, the users of the financial statements would be able to understand the trends affecting the segments, as they are currently being defined.

Comprehensive example of segment reporting under revised IAS 14

To illustrate the expansion of reporting requirements under the new standard, revised IAS 14, a comprehensive illustration is given below. The facts assumed are as follows, as these would have been presented in conformity with the original IAS 14:

	(All amounts in $ millions)	
	Electronic components	*Mechanical components*
Net sales		
1999	345.0	228.6
2000	378.5	219.8
Operating profit		
1999	29.6	13.2
2000	36.0	8.5
Capital expenditures		
1999	12.1	3.5
2000	21.4	2.5
Identifiable assets		
1999	122.9	128.4
2000	140.2	118.5
Depreciation and amortization		
1999	13.7	15.9
2000	17.5	13.6

Unallocated (corporate) assets totaled $7.6 million in 1999 and $8.1 million in 2000. Unallocated corporate expenses equaled $3.4 million in 1999 and $4.5 million in 2000. Intersegment sales, which are made at cost, are not material in amount. Operating profit by segment is defined as third-party sales less operating expenses; corporate overhead and financing costs are excluded from segment expenses.

Revenue by geographic area is summarized below.

	(All amounts in $ millions)		
	Western Europe	*Eastern Europe*	*Middle East*
Net sales			
1999	348.8	113.4	111.7
2000	366.3	133.4	98.6
Operating profit			
1999	22.7	8.6	11.5
2000	20.6	13.9	10.0
Identifiable assets			
1999	178.4	63.2	9.7
2000	183.3	69.5	5.9

Western Europe includes primarily Germany and France, with a relatively small amount of activity in Belgium and the Netherlands. Eastern Europe includes Hungary, Poland, Slovakia and the Czech Republic. The Middle East is principally Lebanon and Syria, with a small level of activity in Egypt and Saudi Arabia. Sales in the Middle East are made almost entirely to after-market suppliers, whereas revenues derived from European markets are predominantly from original equipment manufacturers of automobiles and construction equipment. Approximately 12% and 14% of sales in Western Europe, for 1999 and 2000, respectively, were made to after-market suppliers; for Eastern European sales, the corresponding percentages were 19% and 23% for 1999 and 2000, respectively.

It is assumed that management has determined that the primary reporting format should be by business segment; the secondary reporting format, therefore, will by geographical segment. What follows is the set of required disclosures to conform with revised IAS 14:

Note 10: Segment information

Management has determined that the primary determinant of its decision making is the major products offered by the company, with lesser attention being based on geographical location of its customers. Accordingly, the primary disclosures, below, are based on business segment, alternatively, electronic or mechanical components, with the following secondary disclosures based on geographic location of customers.

	(All amounts in $ millions)	
	Electronic components	*Mechanical components*
Net sales		
1999--In total	345.0	228.6
1999--To external customers	336.3	228.6
1999--Intersegment sales	8.7	0.0
2000--In total	378.5	219.8
2000--To external customers	371.0	219.5
2000--Intersegment sales	7.5	.3
Operating profit		
1999	29.6	13.2
2000	36.0	8.5
Interest and dividend income		
1999--Interest income	1.2	.2
1999--Dividend income	.1	0
2000--Interest income	1.1	.3
2000--Dividend income	0	0
Interest expense		
1999	1.5	1.1
2000	1.2	1.0

	(All amounts in $ millions)	
	Electronic components	*Mechanical components*
Identifiable assets, at net carrying amounts		
1999	122.9	128.4
2000	140.2	118.5
Segment liabilities		
1999	62.3	43.4
2000	59.6	40.1
Contingent liabilities related to contractual disputes		
1999	2.5	1.0
2000	4.4	1.2
Capital expenditures		
1999	12.1	3.5
2000	21.4	2.5
Depreciation and amortization		
1999	13.7	15.9
2000	17.5	13.6
Nonrecurring items		
1999--Revenue from government contract	6.7	0
2000--Gain from settlement of patent suit	2.3	0
Equity in income of investee		
1999	2.2	0
2000	.5	0
Investment in equity method investee		
1999	5.6	0
2000	6.9	0

Segment information is reconciled to corresponding enterprise totals in the following section:

Net sales

1999--To external customers	
Electronic components	336.3
Mechanical components	228.6
Enterprise total sales	564.9

2000--To external customers	
Electronic components	371.0
Mechanical components	219.5
Enterprise total sales	590.5

Operating profit
 1999
    Electronic components   29.6
    Mechanical components   13.2
    Less: Unallocated corporate expenses   (3.4)
       Enterprise total operating profit   39.4

 2000
    Electronic components   36.0
    Mechanical components   8.5
    Less: Unallocated corporate expenses   (4.5)
       Enterprise total operating profit   40.0

Identifiable assets, at net carrying amounts
 1999
    Electronic components   122.9
    Mechanical components   128.4
    Unallocated corporate assets   7.6
       Enterprise total assets   258.9

 2000
    Electronic components   140.2
    Mechanical components   118.5
    Unallocated corporate assets   8.1
       Enterprise total assets   266.8

Segment liabilities
 1999
    Electronic components   62.3
    Mechanical components   43.4
       Enterprise total liabilities   105.7

 2000
    Electronic components   59.6
    Mechanical components   40.1
       Enterprise total liabilities   99.7

Revenue by geographic area is summarized below (based on location of customers).

	(All amounts in $ millions)		
	Western Europe	*Eastern Europe*	*Middle East*
Net sales			
1999	348.8	113.4	111.7
2000	366.3	133.4	98.6
Identifiable assets			
1999	178.4	63.2	9.7
2000	183.3	69.5	5.9
Capital expenditures			
1999	8.2	4.4	3.0
2000	12.5	5.5	5.9

Western Europe includes primarily Germany and France, with a relatively small amount of activity in Belgium and the Netherlands. Eastern Europe includes Hungary,

Poland, Slovakia and the Czech Republic. The Middle East is principally Lebanon and Syria, with a small level of activity in Egypt and Saudi Arabia. Sales in the Middle East are made almost entirely to aftermarket suppliers, whereas revenues derived from European markets are predominantly from original equipment manufacturers of automobiles and construction equipment. Approximately 12% and 14% of sales in Western Europe, for 1999 and 2000, respectively, were made to after-market suppliers; for Eastern European sales, the corresponding percentages were 19% and 23% for 1999 and 2000, respectively.

21 ACCOUNTING CHANGES AND CORRECTION OF FUNDAMENTAL ERRORS

PERSPECTIVE AND ISSUES

Information contained in an enterprise's financial statements over a period of time must be comparable if these are to be of value to users of those statements. Users of financial statements usually seek to identify trends in the enterprise's financial position, performance, and cash flows by studying and analyzing the information contained in those statements. Thus it is imperative that the same accounting policies be applied from year to year in the preparation of financial statements, and that any departures from this rule be clearly indicated.

Financial statements are the results of choices among different accounting principles and methodologies. Companies select those accounting principles and methods that they believe depict, in their financial statements, the economic reality of their financial position, results of operations, and changes in financial position. Changes take place because of changes in the assumptions and estimates underlying the application of these principles and methods, changes in the acceptable principles by a promulgating authority, such as an accounting standard-setting body, or other types of changes.

Accounting for and reporting of these changes is a problem that has faced the accounting profession for years. Much financial analysis is based on the consistency and comparability of annual financial statements. Any type of accounting change creates an inconsistency; thus, a primary focus of management in making the decision to change should be to consider its effect on financial statement comparability.

IAS 8 (revised 1993), which became operative for financial statements covering periods beginning on or after January 1, 1995, deals with accounting changes (i.e., changes in accounting estimates and changes in accounting principles) and addresses the correction of fundamental errors. IAS 8 also prescribes the classification, disclosure, and accounting treatment of certain items in the income statement, such as extraordinary items and discontinuing operations, which are the subject matter of Chapter 3. The objectives of this standard in prescribing such accounting treatment and disclosures is to enhance comparability both with an enterprise's financial statements of previous years and with the financial statements of other enterprises. Even though the correction of a fundamental error in financial statements issued previously is not considered an accounting change, it is discussed in this standard and therefore is covered in this chapter.

In the preparation of financial statements there is an underlying presumption that an accounting principle, once adopted, should not be changed in accounting for events and transactions of a similar type. This consistent use of accounting principles enhances the utility of the financial statements. The presumption that an entity should not change an accounting principle may be overcome only if the enterprise justifies the use of an alternative acceptable accounting principle on the basis that it is preferable.

Sources of IAS
IAS 8 (revised)   *SIC* 8

DEFINITIONS OF TERMS

Accounting policies. Specific principles, bases, conventions, rules, and practices adopted by an enterprise in preparing and presenting financial statements.

Change in accounting estimate. A revision of an accounting measurement based on new information, more experience, or subsequent developments. The use of reasonable estimates is an essential part of the financial statement preparation process and does not undermine their reliability. Since uncertainties are inherent in day-to-day business activities, revisions to such accounting estimates are an acceptable practice in the accounting process.

Change in accounting principle. A switch from one generally accepted accounting principle to another generally accepted accounting principle, including the methods of applying these principles.

Comparability. The quality of information that enables users to identify similarities in and differences between two sets of economic phenomena.

Consistency. Consistency refers to conformity from period to period with unchanging policies and procedures. It enhances the utility of financial statements to users by facilitating analysis and understanding of comparative accounting data.

Cumulative effect. The difference between the beginning retained earnings balance of the year in which the change is reported and the beginning retained earnings balance that would have been reported if the new principle had been applied retrospectively for all prior periods that would have been affected.

Error. The effect on the financial statements that results from mathematical mistakes, mistakes in applying accounting principles, misinterpretations of facts, fraud, or oversights.

Fundamental error. An error that has such a significant effect on the financial statements of one or more prior periods that those financial statements can no longer be considered to have been reliable at the date of their issue.

Pro forma information. Financial information that is prepared on an "as if" basis. The disclosure of required numbers computed on the assumption that certain events have transpired. Where allowed alternative treatments are followed in lieu of the benchmark treatments established by IAS 8, additional pro forma information is to be presented.

Restatement of comparative financial information. The recasting of a prior period's balance sheet or income statement information where there has been a change in accounting policy or correction of a fundamental error and the benchmark treatment is followed.

CONCEPTS, RULES, AND EXAMPLES

Importance of Comparability and Consistency in Financial Reporting

Generally accepted accounting principles have long held that an important objective of financial reporting is to encourage comparability among financial statements produced by essentially similar enterprises. This is necessary to facilitate informed economic decision making by investors, creditors, prospective employees, joint venturers, and others. While complete comparability will not be achieved as long as alternative principles of accounting and reporting remain acceptable for like transactions and events, a driving force in developing new accounting standards is to enhance comparability. The IASC's efforts in the early 1990s (the comparability project) did in fact narrow the range of acceptable alternative methods of accounting, and further narrowing will probably occur as the core set of standards undergoes development to comply with the historic agreement with IOSCO, as described in Chapter 1.

Comparability refers to the quality of information that enables users to identify similarities in and differences between two sets of economic phenomena. Normally, comparability is a quantitative assessment of a common characteristic.

An important implication of the qualitative characteristic of comparability is that users be informed of the accounting policies employed in the preparation of the financial statements, any changes in those policies, and the effects of such changes. Disclosure of accounting policies was discussed in Chapters 2, 3, and 4; this chapter addresses the appropriate communications of changes in accounting policies and related matters.

Compliance with IAS helps in achieving comparability, since the adoption of IAS by enterprises facilitates relative evaluation of financial data using a common accounting language. The need for comparability, however, should not be confused with mere uniformity and should not be allowed to become a barrier or an impediment to the adoption of improved accounting methods.

As contrasted with comparability, consistency refers to a given reporting entity's conformity from period to period with unchanging policies and procedures. The quality of consistency enhances the utility of financial statements to users by facilitating analysis and understanding of comparative accounting data.

According to IAS 1 (revised), "the presentation and classification of items in the financial statements should be retained from one period to the next unless a significant change in the nature of the operations of the enterprise or a review of its financial statement presentation demonstrates that more relevant information is provided in a different way." It is, however, inappropriate for an enterprise to continue accounting for transactions in the same manner if the policies adopted lack qualitative characteristics of relevance and reliability. Thus, if more reliable and relevant alternatives exist, it is better for the enterprise to change its methods of accounting for defined classes of transactions.

Reporting Accounting Changes

IAS 8 describes three ways of reporting accounting changes and the type of change for which each should be used. These are

1. Retrospectively
2. Currently
3. Prospectively

Retrospective treatment requires an adjustment to all current and prior period financial statements for the effect of the accounting change. Prior period financial statements presented currently are to be restated on a basis consistent with the newly adopted principle.

Current treatment requires reporting the cumulative effect of the accounting change in the current year's income statement as a special item. Prior period financial statements are not restated.

Prospective treatment of accounting changes requires **no** restatement of prior financial statements and **no** computing or reporting of the accounting change's cumulative effect in the current period's income statement. Only current and/or future periods' financial report data will reflect the accounting change.

Each type of accounting change and the proper treatment prescribed for them are discussed in detail in the following sections.

Change in Accounting Policy

A change in any accounting policy means that a reporting entity has switched from one generally accepted accounting principle to another. According to IAS 8, the term accounting policy includes the accounting principles, bases, conventions, rules and practices used. For example, a change in inventory costing from weighted-average to first-in, first-out would be a change in accounting policy, as would a change in accounting for borrowing costs from capitalization to immediate expensing.

An interpretation of a similar definition under US GAAP provides a meaningful framework by establishing that a change in the components used to cost a firm's inventory is a change in accounting principle. This FASB interpretation also clarified that the preferability assessment (relating to the selection of the appropriate accounting policy or principle in particular circumstances) must be made from the perspective of financial reporting basis and not from the income tax perspective.

Changes in accounting policy are permitted if

1. The change in accounting principle will result in a more appropriate presentation of events or transactions in the financial statements of the enterprise, or
2. The change in accounting principle is required by an accounting standard-setting body, or
3. The change in accounting principle is required by statute.

IAS 8 does not regard the following as changes in accounting policies:

1. The adoption of an accounting policy for events or transactions that differ in substance from previously occurring events or transactions; and
2. The adoption of a new accounting policy to account for events or transactions that did not occur previously or that were immaterial

The provisions of IAS 8 are not applicable to the initial adoption of a policy to carry assets at revalued amounts, although such adoption is a change in accounting policy. Rather, it is dealt with as a revaluation in accordance with IAS 16 or IAS 25, as appropriate under the circumstances.

Benchmark and Allowed Alternative Accounting Treatments

IAS 8 prescribes two methods of reporting a change in accounting policy, depending on whether the benchmark treatment or the allowed alternative method is used. If the benchmark treatment is used, a change in accounting policy is to be applied retrospectively (unless the amount of the resultant adjustment from the change relating to the prior period is not reasonably determinable). With application of the retrospective effect to the change in accounting policy, the following adjustments will have to be made:

1. The comparative information presented for the prior periods will be restated to reflect the effect of the change in accounting policy; the effect will be computed under the assumption that the new accounting policy had always been in use.

2. The cumulative effect of the change (resulting from the retrospective application of the accounting policy to prior periods) net of income taxes, if any, will be reported as an adjustment to the opening balance of the retained earnings.

3. Any other information with respect to prior periods, such as historical summaries of financial data, is also restated.

If the allowed alternative treatment is chosen by the enterprise instead of the benchmark treatment

1. The cumulative effect of the change (resulting from the retrospective application of the accounting policy) net of income taxes, if any, will have to be included in the determination of the current year's net profit or loss.

2. The comparative information for the prior period presented alongside the current year's figures need not be restated as in the case of the application of the benchmark treatment above. In other words, the comparative information will be presented as reported in the prior years' financial statements.

3. Additional pro forma comparative information (prepared based on the guidelines above for the application of the benchmark treatment) will also need to be presented.

The cumulative effect of a change in accounting principle is to appear as a single amount in the income statement between extraordinary items and net income if the allowed alternative treatment is used, and as a single amount shown as an adjustment to the opening retained earnings balance if the benchmark treatment is applied. This single amount should be the difference between

1. The amount of retained earnings at the beginning of the period, and

2. The amount of retained earnings that would have been reported at that date if the new accounting principle had been applied retroactively to all prior periods affected.

The cumulative effect is generally determined by first calculating income before taxes for both the new principle and the old principle for all prior periods affected. The difference between the two incomes for each prior period is then determined. Next, these differences are adjusted for tax effects. Finally, the net of tax differences for each prior period are totaled. This total represents the cumulative effect adjustment at the beginning of the current period. The cumulative effect will either be an addition to or a subtraction from current income, depending on how the change to the new principle affects income.

Generally, only the direct effects of the change and the related income tax effect should be included in the cumulative effect calculation (i.e., if the company changes its method of costing inventories, only the effects of the change in cost of goods sold, net of tax, are considered to be direct effects). Indirect effects, such as the effect on a profit-sharing contribution or bonus payments that would have occurred as a result of the change in net income, are not included in the cumulative effect computation unless these are to be recorded by the firm (i.e., the expense is actually incurred).

The computation of income on a pro forma basis must be made for each period currently presented. The objective is to present income before extraordinary items and net income as if the new principle were being applied. This is achieved by adjusting each period's income before extraordinary items as reported previously (i.e., applying the old principle). The adjustment is made by adding or subtracting the difference in income net of tax for the period to income before extraordinary items as reported previously. The difference, net of tax, is the change in income that occurs when the new principle is applied instead of the old principle. This results in a figure for income before extraordinary items that reflects the application of the new principle. Net income is then calculated as normally done from the adjusted income before extraordinary items. The per share amounts required are based on the pro forma income before extraordinary items and net income amounts.

The pro forma calculation differs from that of the cumulative effect. It is to include both the direct effects of the change and the nondiscretionary adjustments of items based on income before taxes or net income. Examples of nondiscretionary items are profit-sharing expense or certain royalties. Both of these expenses are in some way based on net income, generally as a specified percentage. The related tax effects should be recognized for **both** the direct and nondiscretionary adjustments.

The following example illustrates the computations and disclosures necessary when applying the cumulative effect method.

Example of benchmark and alternative treatments of changes in accounting policy under IAS 8

In 2000, the Zircon Company adopted the percentage-of-completion method of accounting for long-term construction contracts. The company had used the completed-contract method for all prior years.

The following sections present extracts from the statements of earnings and retained earnings of Zircon Company before adjusting for the effects of the change in accounting policy. Net profit for 2000 was determined under the percentage-of-completion method of accounting.

	2000	*1999*
Profit from ordinary activities		
before income taxes	$120,000	$130,000
Income taxes	(20,000)	(26,000)
Net profit	100,000	104,000
Retained earnings, beginning	134,000	30,000
Retained earnings, ending	$234,000	$134,000

The effects of the change in accounting policy are presented below.

	Difference in income under the percentage-of-completion method	*Effect of the change net of income taxes*
Prior to 1999	$20,000	$14,000
For 1999	15,000	10,500
Total as of the beginning		
of 2000	35,000	24,500
For 2000	$20,000	$14,000

The following pages provide an illustration of the accounting treatment and presentation of financial statements under the benchmark treatment and the allowed alternative treatment of the changes in accounting policies in accordance with IAS 8.

Changes in Accounting Policies: Benchmark Treatment

Zircon Company
Extracts from Income Statement

	2000	*1999 restated*
Profit from ordinary activities		
before income taxes	$120,000	$145,000
Income taxes	(20,000)	(30,500)
Net profit	$100,000	$114,500

Zircon Company
Statement of Retained Earnings

Retained earnings, beginning, as reported previously	$134,000	$ 30,000
Change in accounting policy, net of income taxes of		
$10,500 for 2000 and $6,000 for 1999 (see Note 1)	24,500	14,000
Retained earnings, beginning, as restated	158,500	44,000
Net profit	100,000	114,500
Retained earnings, ending	$258,500	$158,500

Zircon Company
Extracts From Notes to the
Financial Statements

Note 1: During 2000, Zircon Company changed the accounting policy for revenue and costs for a long-term construction contract from the completed-contract method to the percentage-of-completion method, to conform with the accounting treatment of contract revenue and contract costs under IAS 11, *Construction Contracts*. This change in accounting policy has been accounted for retrospectively. The comparative financial statements for 1999 have been revised to conform to the changed policy. The effect of this change is to increase income from contracts by $20,000 in 2000 and $15,000 in 1999. Opening retained earnings for 1999 has been increased by $14,000, which is the amount of the adjustment relating to periods prior to 1999, net of income tax effect of $6,000.

Explanation. Under the benchmark treatment, a change in accounting policy should be applied retrospectively unless the amount of any resulting adjustment that relates to prior periods is not reasonably determinable. Any resulting adjustment should be reported as an adjustment to the opening balance of retained earnings. Comparative information should be restated unless impracticable to do so. The steps in preparing the revised financial statements and related disclosures are as follows:

1. The 2000 income statement is not adjusted, since it already reflects application of the new policy.
2. The 1999 income statement is restated as follows:

Profit from ordinary activities before income	
taxes, as previously reported	$130,000
Effect of the change in accounting policy	15,000
As restated	145,000
Income taxes as previous reported	26,000
Income tax effect of the change in accounting	
policy ($15,000 – $10,500)	4,500
As restated	30,500
Net income as restated	$114,500

3. As presented in the statement of retained earnings, the opening retained earnings for 1999 was restated to reflect an increase of $14,000, which represents the amount of adjustment related to periods prior to 1999, net of income tax effect of $6,000. The opening balance of 2000 was adjusted by $24,500, which represented the effect of the change at the beginning of 2000, net of income taxes.

Changes in Accounting Policy: Allowed Alternative Treatment

Under the allowed alternative treatment set forth in IAS 8, the amount computed from the retroactive application of the new accounting policy is included in income of the current period. Additional pro forma presentations are also required under this approach. Using the same facts as in the preceding discussion, the alternative treatment is illustrated as follows:

Zircon Company
Extracts from Income Statement

	2000	1999	Pro forma (Restated) 2000	(Restated) 1999
Profit from ordinary activities, before income taxes and effect of change in accounting policy	$120,000	$130,000	$120,000	$145,000
Cumulative effect of change in accounting policy	35,000	--	--	--
Profit from ordinary activities, before income taxes	155,000	130,000	120,000	145,000
Income taxes (including effect of a change in accounting policy)	30,500	26,000	20,000	30,500
Net profit	$124,500	$104,000	$100,000	$114,500

Zircon Company
Statement of Retained Earnings

	2000	1999	Pro forma (Restated) 2000	(Restated) 1999
Retained earnings, beginning, as previously reported	$134,000	$ 30,000	$134,000	$ 30,000
Change in accounting policy for construction contracts, net of income taxes of $10,500 for 2000 and $6,000 for 1999 (Note 1)	--	--	24,500	14,000
Retained earnings, beginning, as restated	134,000	30,000	158,500	44,000
Net profit	124,000	104,000	100,000	114,500
Retained earnings, ending	$258,500	$134,000	$258,500	$158,000

Zircon Company
Extracts From Notes to the
Financial Statements

Note 1: An adjustment of $35,000 has been made in the income statement for 2000, representing the effect of a change in the accounting policy with respect to revenue and costs for long-term construction contracts. The company now uses the percentage-of-completion method instead of the completed-contract method, to conform to the accounting treatment of contract revenue and costs prescribed by IAS 11, *Construction Contracts*. This change in accounting policy has been accounted for retrospectively. Restated pro forma information, which assumes that the new policy had always been in use, is presented. Beginning retained earnings in the pro forma information for 1999 has been increased by $14,000, which is the amount of adjustment relating to periods prior to 1999, net of income tax effect of $6,000.

Explanation. Under the allowed alternative, a retroactive computation is still required, but instead of including the cumulative effect of the change in the restated balance of opening retained earnings, it is included in income of the current period. Furthermore, if the alternative treatment is elected, additional pro forma information must be presented (effectively, this means that the benchmark treatment must also be presented if the allowed alternative is used) unless it is impracticable to do so.

Adoption of International Accounting Standards

A special situation arises when an enterprise adopts international accounting standards for the first time. While it is possible to reason by analogy that this action represents a change in accounting principle (or more accurately, a simultaneous change in all accounting principles), it is more meaningful to view this event as a change in the basis of accounting, such as the change from the cash to the accrual basis of preparing financial statements would be. Just as it would be misleading, or at the least meaningless, to present comparative financial statements with 1 year on the cash basis and the next on the accrual basis, with the net adjustment to beginning balances in the second year's balance sheet either taken to second year income or shown as a charge or credit to beginning retained earnings, so it would be useless to present the first year under, say, US GAAP and the second year in accordance with IAS.

With more reporting entities embracing IAS, the question arises as to how the initial application should be reported (i.e., as a change in accounting principles or as a retroactive adjustment). The IASC's Standing Interpretations Committee has clarified the accounting for the adoption of IAS in the recently promulgated SIC 8. This interpretation finds that in the first period IAS are employed, the statements should be prepared as if IAS had always been utilized. Thus, retroactive application is required, except for those standards and interpretations which permit a different transitional treatment, or when the effects on prior periods cannot be determined. Comparative financial statements and information would be prepared in conformity with the IAS as well. Any net adjustment would be included in the opening balance of retained earnings of the earliest period reported upon.

Change in Amortization Method

Another special case in accounting for a change in principle takes place when a company chooses to change the systematic pattern of amortizing the costs of long-lived assets to expense. When a company adopts a new method of amortization for newly acquired identifiable long-lived assets and uses that method for all new assets of the same class without changing the method used previously for existing assets of the same class, there is a change in accounting principle. Obviously, there is no adjustment required to the financial statements or any cumulative type of adjustment. In these special cases, a description of the nature of the method changed and the effect on net income, income before extraordinary items, and related per share amounts should be disclosed in the period of the change.

If the new method is, instead, adopted for all assets, both old and new, the change would appear to be a change in accounting principle which should be accounted for as described above. However, under the provisions of IAS 16, *Prop-*

erty, Plant, and Equipment, this is not the case. That standard, discussed in greater detail in Chapter 8, establishes that a change in depreciation method should be made only if there has been a significant change in the expected pattern of economic benefits from the use of the assets; in such case, the change is to be accounted for as a change in accounting estimate, not a change in policy. (Change in accounting estimate is discussed in the following section.) It does not appear to be contemplated by international accounting standards that there could be a change in depreciation methods to a better method that would justify change in accounting policy treatment. Since such changes in depreciation method are fairly common under US GAAP, the international standard on this topic is certain to generate at least some controversy.

Change in Accounting Estimates

The preparation of financial statements requires frequent use of estimates for such items as asset service lives, salvage values, collectibility of accounts receivable, warranty costs, pension costs, and so on. These future conditions and events and their effects cannot be perceived with certainty; therefore, changes in estimates will be inevitable as new information and more experience is obtained. IAS 8 requires that changes in estimates be handled currently and prospectively. It states that "The effect of the change in accounting estimate should be accounted for in (a) the period of change if the change affects that period only or (b) the period of change and future periods if the change affects both." For example, on January 1, 1996, a machine purchased for $10,000 was originally estimated to have a 10-year life. On January 1, 2001 (5 years later), the asset is expected to last another 10 years. As a result, both the current period and the subsequent periods are affected by the change. The annual depreciation charge over the remaining life would be computed as follows:

$$\frac{\text{Book value of asset} - \text{Salvage value}}{\text{Remaining useful life}} = \frac{\$5,000 - 0}{10 \text{ years}} = \$500/\text{yr.}$$

A permanent impairment affecting the cost recovery of an asset should not be handled as a change in accounting estimate but should be treated as a loss of the period. (See the discussion in Chapter 8.)

In some situations it may be difficult to distinguish between changes in accounting policy and changes in accounting estimates. For example, a company may change from deferring and amortizing a cost to recording it as an expense when incurred because the future benefits of the cost have become doubtful. In this instance, the company is changing its accounting principle (from deferral to immediate recognition) because of its change in the estimate of the future value of a particular cost.

Although the international accounting standards do not address this matter per se, useful guidance is available by reference to the parallel standard under US GAAP, which is APB 20. In that standard, the board concluded that a change in accounting estimate that is in essence effected by a change in accounting principle should be reported as a change in accounting estimate, the rationale being that the effect of the change in accounting principle is inseparable from the effect of the change in estimate. In the example in the preceding paragraph, the company is changing its accounting principle (from deferral to immediate recognition) because of its change in the estimate of the future value of a particular cost. The amount of the cumulative effect would be the same as that attributable to the current or future periods.

Because the two changes are indistinguishable, changes of this type should logically be considered changes in estimates and accounted for in accordance with IAS 8. However, the change must be clearly indistinguishable to be combined. The ability to compute each element independently would preclude combining them as a single change. Also, for generally accepted auditing standards such a change is deemed a change in accounting principle for purposes of applying the consistency standard.

Correction of Fundamental Errors

Although good internal control and the exercise of due care will serve to minimize the number of errors made, these safeguards cannot be expected to completely eliminate errors in the financial statements. As a result, it was necessary for the accounting profession to promulgate standards that would ensure uniform treatment of accounting for error corrections.

IAS 8 is the promulgated international accounting standard dealing with the accounting for error corrections. It outlines the two methods of accounting for the correction of the fundamental errors, one of which is the preferred benchmark approach. IAS 8 indicates that fundamental errors are to be treated as prior period adjustments if the benchmark treatment is followed (i.e., the amount of the correction, net of the tax effect, if any, should be reported as an adjustment to the opening balance of the retained earnings). Comparative information should also be restated unless it is impracticable to do so.

If the allowed alternative treatment is opted by an enterprise, the amount of the correction of the fundamental error should be included in the determination of net profit or loss for the current period. The comparative information need not be restated under this method; instead, the comparative figures should be presented as reported in the financial statements of the prior period. In such a case, additional pro forma information (prepared in accordance with the foregoing guidelines for the application of the benchmark treatment) should also be presented (unless it is impracticable to do so).

IAS 8 identifies examples of fundamental errors as resulting from mathematical mistakes, mistakes in the application of accounting principles, or the oversight or misinterpretation of facts known to the accountant at the time the financial statements were prepared. A change from an unacceptable (or incorrect) accounting principle to a correct principle is considered a correction of an error, not a change in accounting principle. This should not be confused with the preferability dilemma discussed earlier, which involves two or more acceptable principles.

Although errors occur that affect both current and future periods, we are concerned primarily with the reporting of the correction of an error occurring in financial statements issued previously. Errors affecting current and future periods require correction but do not require disclosure, as they are presumed to be discovered prior to the issuance of financial statements. The correction of an error in the financial statements of a prior period discovered subsequent to their issuance should be reported as a prior period adjustment.

The essential distinction between a change in estimate and the correction of an error depends on the availability of information. An estimate requires correction because by its nature it is based on incomplete information. Later data will either confirm or contradict the estimate, and any contradiction will require correction. An error **misuses** existing information available at the time of the decision and is discovered at a later date. However, this discovery is not a result of additional information.

Under the benchmark treatment the required disclosures regarding the correction of a fundamental error include

1. The nature of the error
2. The amount of the correction for the current period and for each period presented
3. The amount of the correction relating to periods prior to those included in the comparative information
4. The fact that comparative information has been restated or that it is impracticable to do so

Under the allowed alternative treatment the disclosures differ since the accounting treatment differs. Under this method the clauses 2, 3, and 4 above will be replaced with

2. The amount of the correction recognized in the net profit or loss for the current period
3. The amount of the correction included in each period for which the pro forma information is presented and the amount of the correction relating to periods prior to those included in the pro forma information. If the pro forma information could not be presented due to impracticality, this fact should be disclosed, too.

The major criterion for determining whether or not to report the correction of the error is the materiality of the correction. There are many factors to be considered in determining the materiality of the error correction. Materiality should be considered for each correction individually as well as for all corrections in total. If the correction is determined to have a material effect on income before extraordinary items, net income, or the trend of earnings, it should be disclosed in accordance with the requirements set forth in the preceding paragraph.

Thus, under benchmark treatment, the prior period adjustment should be presented in the financial statements as follows:

Retained earnings, 1/1/00 as reported previously	xxx
Correction of error (description) in prior period(s) (net of $___ tax)	xxx
Adjusted balance of retained earnings at 1/1/00	xxx
Net income	xxx
Retained earnings, 12/31/00	xxx

In comparative statements, prior period adjustments should also be shown as adjustments to the beginning balances in the retained earnings statements. The amount of the adjustment on the earliest statement shall be the cumulative effect of the error on periods prior to the earliest period presented. The later retained earnings statements presented should also show a prior period adjustment for the cumulative amount as of the beginning of the period being reported on.

Example of accounting for fundamental errors under IAS 8

In 2000, the bookkeeper of Dhow Corp. discovered that in 1999 the company failed to record in the accounts depreciation expense in the amount of $20,000, relating to a newly constructed building. The following presents extracts from the statement of income and retained earnings for 2000 and 1999 before correction of the error:

	2000	*1999*
Gross profit	$200,000	$230,000
General and administrative expenses, including depreciation	(80,000)	(80,000)
Net income from ordinary activities, before income taxes	120,000	150,000
Income taxes	(20,000)	(30,000)
Net profit	100,000	120,000
Retained earnings, beginning	150,000	30,000
Retained earnings, ending	$250,000	$150,000

Dhow Corp.'s income tax rate was 20% for both years.

The following provides an illustration of the accounting treatment and presentation of financial statements under the benchmark treatment and the allowed alternative treatment, in accordance with IAS 8.

Correction of Fundamental Error: Benchmark Treatment

Dhow Corp.
Extracts From Income Statement

	2000	*1999* *restated*
Gross profit	$200,000	$230,000
General and administrative expenses, including depreciation	(80,000)	(100,000)
Net income from ordinary activities, before income taxes	120,000	130,000
Income taxes	(20,000)	(26,000)
Net profit	$100,000	$104,000

Dhow Corp.
Statement of Retained Earnings

	2000	1999 restated
Retained earnings, beginning, as reported previously	$150,000	$ 30,000
Correction of fundamental error, net of income taxes of $4,000 (see Note 1)	(16,000)	--
Retained earnings, beginning, as restated	134,000	30,000
Net profit	100,000	104,000
Retained earnings, ending	$234,000	$134,000

Dhow Corp.
Extracts From Notes to the
Financial Statements

Note 1: The company failed to record a depreciation charge in the amount of $20,000 in 1999. The financial statements for 1999 have been restated to correct this error.

Explanation. Under the benchmark treatment of fundamental errors, the amount of correction of a fundamental error that relates to prior periods should be reported by adjusting the opening balance of retained earnings. Comparative information should be restated unless it is impracticable to do so. The steps in preparing the revised financial statements and related disclosures are as follows:

1. As presented in the statement of retained earnings, the opening retained earnings was adjusted by $16,000, which represented the amount of error, $20,000, net of income tax effect of $4,000.
2. The comparative amounts in the income statement were restated as follows:

General and administrative expenses, including depreciation, before correction	$ 80,000
Amount of correction	20,000
As restated	$100,000
Income taxes before correction	$ 30,000
Amount of correction	4,000
As restated	$ 26,000

Correction of Fundamental Error: Allowed Alternative Treatment

Dhow Corp.
Extracts From Income Statement

	2000	1999	Pro forma (Restated) 2000	Pro forma (Restated) 1999
Gross profit	$200,000	$230,000	$200,000	$230,000
General and administrative expenses, including depreciation (see Note 1)	(80,000)	(80,000)	(80,000)	(100,000)
Correction of error (Note 1)	(20,000)	--	--	--
Profit from ordinary activities, before income taxes	100,000	150,000	120,000	130,000
Income taxes (including effect of a correction of a fundamental error)	16,000	30,000	20,000	26,000
Net profit	$ 84,000	$120,000	$100,000	$104,000

Dhow Corp.
Statement of Retained Earnings

	2000	1999	Pro forma (Restated) 2000	Pro forma (Restated) 1999
Retained earnings, beginning, as reported previously	$150,000	$ 30,000	$150,000	$ 30,000
Correction of fundamental error, net of income taxes of $4,000 (Note 1)	--	--	16,000	--
Retained earnings, beginning, as restated	150,000	30,000	134,000	30,000
Net profit	84,000	120,000	100,000	104,000
Retained earnings, ending	$234,000	$150,000	$234,000	$134,000

Dhow Corp.
Extracts From Notes to the
Financial Statements

Note 1: The company failed to record a depreciation charge in the amount of $20,000 in 1999. An adjustment has been made in the income statement for 1999, representing the correction of the fundamental error. Restated pro forma information for 2000 and 1999 is presented as if the error had been corrected in 1999.

Explanation. Under the allowed alternative treatment of fundamental errors, the amount of correction of a fundamental error that relates to prior periods should be included in the determination of net profit or loss for the current period. Comparative information should be presented as reported in the financial statements of the prior period. Additional pro forma information (effectively, the benchmark treatment) should be presented, unless impracticable to do so.

APPENDIX A

ACCOUNTING FOR CORRECTION OF ERRORS AND CHANGES IN ACCOUNTING POLICY UNDER US GAAP

The accounting for corrections of errors and changes in accounting policies differs markedly under US GAAP from that under the international standards. Under US GAAP, there is only the prescribed treatment; there are no allowed alternatives to the mandatory (benchmark) procedures, in contrast to IAS 8's benchmarks and alternatives. Since the requirements differ in each of these very important areas, and since many users and preparers of financial statements have previously been exposed to US GAAP, this appendix will summarize the corresponding requirements under the US standards.

Accounting for the Correction of Errors

Under international accounting standards, the preferred approach to reporting the effect of errors (called fundamental errors in IAS 8) is to present the cumulative effect of the error on all years prior to the earliest period being reported on as an adjustment of opening retained earnings, with the financial statements for all years presented being restated. This is identical to the required treatment under US GAAP. While IAS contemplates an allowed alternative treatment (including the cumulative effect of the error in current period earnings), the corresponding US standard, SFAS 16, does not offer this alternative.

Example of accounting for corrections of errors

Consider the following facts: Assume that ABC Company had overstated its depreciation expense by $50,000 in 1997 and $40,000 in 2000, both due to a mathematical mistake. The errors that affected both the income statement and the tax return in 1999 and 2000 are found in 2001.

The following prior period adjustment would be required in 2001 to correct the accounts (assuming a 40% tax rate):

Accumulated depreciation	90,000	
Income taxes payable		36,000
Retained earnings		54,000

Assuming that 2-year comparative statements are being presented, the resulting effects of the prior period adjustment should be included in each statement presented. The comparative statement of retained earnings would appear as follows (all figures other than corrections are assumed):

	2001	*2000*
Retained earnings, beginning of year (as reported previously)	$305,000	$250,000
Adjustments (see Note 1)	54,000	30,000
Restated, beginning of year	$359,000	$280,000
Net income	90,000	104,000
	$449,000	$384,000
Dividends	45,000	25,000
Retained earnings, end of year	$404,000	$359,000

Note 1: Correction of accounting error.

The balance of retained earnings at the end of 2000 has been restated from amounts reported previously to reflect a retroactive credit of $54,000 ($90,000 net of $36,000 tax) for overstatement of depreciation in the previous periods. Of this amount, $24,000 ($40,000 net of $16,000 tax) is applicable to 2000 and has been reflected as an increase in income for that year, and the balance (applicable to years prior to 2000) has been credited to 2000 beginning retained earnings.

The retained earnings as reported in 2000 and as they would have appeared in 2001 if no adjustments were made are as follows:

	2001	*2000*
Retained earnings, beginning of year	$305,000	$250,000
Net income	90,000	80,000
	$395,000	$330,000
Dividends	45,000	25,000
Retained earnings, end of year	$350,000	$305,000

Accounting for Changes in Accounting Policies

Under US GAAP, the cumulative effect of most changes in accounting policies must be included in income in the period of the change. Certain defined categories of accounting changes, however, must be handled by means of retroactive restatement. Furthermore, unlike under international standards, all changes in accounting policies (referred to under US GAAP as changes in accounting principles) are to be accounted for in the manner prescribed; under IAS, changes in depreciation methods, which in actuality are changes in accounting principle, are accounted for as changes in an estimate and handled prospectively.

Briefly, US GAAP requires all changes in accounting principle, except as specifically set forth (see the discussion below), to be accounted for by the cumulative effect method, whereby the net-of-tax effect of the change on beginning retained earnings is included as a separate item on the income statement of the year of change. The following example illustrates this approach.

Example of accounting for changes in accounting policies

ABC Co. decides in 2000 to adopt the straight-line method of depreciation for plant equipment. The straight-line method will be used for all new acquisitions as well as for plant equipment previously acquired, for which depreciation had been provided on an accelerated method. The following assumptions are being made:

1. The direct effect of the change is limited to the change in accumulated depreciation.
2. The tax rate is a constant 40%.
3. The executive incentive bonus is the only nondiscretionary item affected by the change. It is 10% of the pretax accounting income.
4. There are 1,000,000 shares of common stock outstanding throughout the entire period affected by the change.
5. An additional 100,000 shares would be issued if all the outstanding bonds, which are not common stock equivalents, were converted. Annual interest on this bond obligation is $25,000 (net of tax).
6. For 1999 and 2000 the income before extraordinary items is given as $1,100,000 and $1,200,000 respectively. There is an extraordinary item in each year amounting to $100,000 for 1999 and ($35,000) for 2000. The extraordinary items are included to illustrate the proper positioning of the cumulative effect adjustment on the income statement.

Year	Excess of accelerated depreciation over straight-line depreciation	Direct effects of change, net of tax	Nondiscre-tionary item, net of tax	Pro forma amounts
Prior to 1996	$ 20,000	$ 12,000	$ 1,200	$ 10,800
1996	80,000	48,000	4,800	43,200
1997	70,000	42,000	4,200	37,800
1998	50,000	30,000	3,000	27,000
1999	30,000	18,000	1,800	16,200
Total at beginning of 2000	$250,000	$150,000	$15,000	$135,000

The following narrative provides assistance in grasping the computational aspects of the information given above. The "excess of . . . depreciation" is given in this example. It is generally determined by recomputing the depreciation under the new method and obtaining the difference between the two methods. The "direct . . . tax" represents the effect of the actual change (i.e., depreciation) on income before extraordinary items adjusted for the tax effects. For example, in the years prior to 1996, the change in depreciation methods (from accelerated to straight-line) resulted in a $20,000 reduction in depreciation expense (or an increase in income). The net of tax number is $12,000 because the $20,000 increase in income is reduced by an $8,000 (40% x $20,000) increase in income tax expense.

The "nondiscretionary item, net of tax" represents the income statement items affected indirectly as a result of the change. In this case it was given that the executive incentive bonus equal to 10% of pretax accounting income was the only nondiscretionary item affected. Thus, in years prior to 1996, when pretax accounting income increased by $20,000, the bonus expense would have been $2,000 higher ($20,000 x 10%). It is generally agreed that this should also be computed net of tax, and because the expense would have increased by $2,000, the taxes would have decreased by $800 ($2,000 x 40%). The net of tax increase in expense is $1,200. The pro forma amounts are to include both the direct and indirect effects of the change. The computation for this example is as follows:

	Increase (decrease) in net income
Reduction in depreciation expense	$20,000
Increase in taxes (depreciation)	(8,000)
Increase in compensation expense	(2,000)
Reduction in taxes (compensation)	800
	$10,800

The pro forma amount is needed for disclosure purposes so that 1999 income can be shown on a comparative basis with 2000 net income (i.e., adding the 1999 income before the change). The pro forma increase or decrease will result in an income figure that reflects the same accounting principles as the 2000 income figure. Below are the necessary disclosures required by APB 20 for the aforementioned situation.

On the Face of the Income Statement

	2000	*1999*
Income before extraordinary item and cumulative effect of a change in accounting principle	$1,200,000	$1,100,000
Extraordinary item (description)	(35,000)	100,000
Cumulative effect on prior years (to December 31, 1999) of changing to a different depreciation method	150,000	--
Net income	$1,315,000	$1,200,000
Per share amounts:		
Earnings per common share--assuming no dilution:		
Income before extraordinary item and cumulative effect of a change in accounting principle	$1.20	$1.10
Extraordinary item	(0.04)	0.10
Cumulative effect on prior years (to December 31, 1999) of changing to a different depreciation method	0.15	--
Net income	$1.31	$1.20
Earnings per common share--assuming full dilution:		
Income before extraordinary item and cumulative effect of a change in accounting principle	$1.11	$1.02
Extraordinary item	(0.03)	0.09
Cumulative effect on prior years (to December 31, 1999) of changing to a different depreciation method	0.14	--
Net income	$1.22	$1.11

Pro forma amounts assuming the new depreciation method is applied retroactively:

Income before extraordinary item	$1,200,000	$1,116,200
Earnings per common share--assuming no dilution	$1.20	$1.12
Earnings per common share--assuming full dilution	$1.11	$1.01
Net income	$1,165,000	$1,216,200
Earnings per common share--assuming no dilution	$1.17	$1.22
Earnings per common share--assuming full dilution	$1.08	$1.11

In the Notes to the Financial Statements

Note A: Change in depreciation method for plant equipment.

During 2000 the company decided to change its method of computing depreciation on plant equipment from sum-of-the-years' digits (SYD) to the straight-line method. The company made the change because the straight-line method better matches revenues and cost amortization and therefore is a preferable accounting principle. The new method has been applied retroactively to equipment acquisitions of prior years. The effect of the change in 2000 was to increase income before extraordinary items by approximately $10,000 (or $0.01 per share). The adjustment of $150,000 (net of $100,000 in taxes) included in 2000 income is the cumulative effect of applying the new method retroactively. The pro forma amounts shown on the income statement have been adjusted for the effect of the retroactive application of the new depreciation method, the change in the provisions for incentive compensation that would have been made had the new method been used, and the related income taxes for both.

If the company elected to disclose the pro forma amounts in notes to the financial statements and not on the face of the income statement, the following disclosure would have been included as part of Note A. The following pro forma amounts show the effect of the retroactive application of the change from the SYD to straight-line method of depreciation.

	Actual	*Pro forma*
2000		
Income before extraordinary items	$1,200,000	$1,200,000
Primary earnings per share	$1.20	$1.20
Fully diluted earnings per share	$1.11	$1.11
Net income	$1,315,000	$1,165,000
Primary earnings per share	$1.31	$1.17
Fully diluted earnings per share	$1.22	$1.08
1999		
Income before extraordinary items	$1,100,000	$1,116,200
Primary earnings per share	$1.10	$1.12
Fully diluted earnings per share	$1.02	$1.01
Net income	$1,200,000	$1,216,200
Primary earnings per share	$1.20	$1.22
Fully diluted earnings per share	$1.11	$1.11

In the example above, notice how the four steps provided in APB 20 are followed.

1. No restatement takes place on the face of the income statements. The 1999 figures provided for comparative purposes are the same as those reported originally.
2. The cumulative effect of the change is included on the face of the income statement as a single amount. The $150,000 shown in 2000 represents the total direct effect net of tax for all years prior to 2000. The effect of the change in 2000 is included in the computation of ordinary income for 2000.
3. The required disclosure of the 2000 effects of the change, in both total and per share amounts, is usually done in the notes to the financial statements. This is assumed to be $10,000 in the example above, or $0.01 per share.
4. The pro forma amounts are used to make the statements from the 2 years comparable. The 1999 income before extraordinary items is increased by $16,200 to $1,116,200. This is the amount found in the original table across from 1999. Notice also how the 2000 net income figure no longer contains a cumulative ef-

fect adjustment. This is because 2000 and 1999 earnings, under the pro forma computations, are derived using the same accounting principles.

Under US GAAP there are five instances that require retroactive treatment. These are as follows:

1. Change from LIFO to another inventory method
2. A change in the method of accounting for long-term contracts
3. A change to or from the full cost method of accounting for exploration costs in the extractive industries
4. Any change made by a company first issuing financial statements for the purpose of obtaining additional equity capital, effecting a business combination, or registering securities
5. Any changes mandated by authoritative pronouncements (although this case is not specified by APB 20, the promulgating bodies have in most instances thus far required that the change be made retroactively). FASB Interpretation 20 has also indicated that AICPA SOP may mandate the treatment given the change.

The process of restating the financial statements in these situations was favored because it did not require that the cumulative effect of the change be included in net income. Rather, each of the years presented is adjusted to reflect the new accounting principle. The cumulative effect is calculated in the same manner as shown earlier for accounting changes receiving nonretroactive treatment. The cumulative effect of all periods prior to such period presented is treated as an adjustment to beginning retained earnings of the period. The net income of each period presented is recomputed applying the new principle. Thus, the adjustment to beginning retained earnings includes all income effects prior to each period presented, and the recomputed net income includes the effect of the new principle on income for each period presented. Together these two adjustments restate the retained earnings ending balance for the period presented to the amount it would have been had the new principle always been applied. This restatement process is followed consistently for all periods presented. According to APB 20, the nature of and justification for the change must be disclosed in the year the change is made. In addition, the effect of the change on income before extraordinary items, net income, and the related per share amounts should be disclosed for all periods presented. Again, subsequent financial statements do not need to repeat the disclosures.

The restatement need only reflect the direct effects of the change in accounting principle. The exception to this statement arises if the direct effect results in a change in a nondiscretionary item that will be recorded on the books. For example, assume that profit-sharing expense is based on net income. The company changes its method of accounting for long-term construction contracts, which results in an increase in income in all prior years. This increase in income would have changed the amount of the profit-sharing expense required during the applicable years.

However, the expense would be changed for the purpose of the restatement only if it is to be paid. If the profit-sharing agreement does not require an adjustment to the actual contribution, the increase in expense would not be recognized on the restated financial statements.

The following illustration (an adaption of Appendix B in APB 20) illustrates the proper restatement in a situation where the company changes its method of accounting for long-term construction contracts. As mentioned above, this is one of the five situations for which APB 20 requires retroactive treatment.

Example of retroactive treatment

During 2000, XYZ Company decided to adopt the percentage-of-completion method in accounting for all of its long-term construction contracts. The company had used the completed-contract method in previous years and had maintained records that were adequate to apply the percentage-of-completion method retroactively.

The following assumptions are made for this example:

1. A constant tax rate of 40%.
2. There are 1,000,000 common shares outstanding in all periods affected by the change.
3. An additional 100,000 shares would be issued if all of the outstanding bonds, which are not common stock equivalents, were converted. The annual interest on this bond obligation is $15,000 (net of tax).

	Pretax accounting income		Difference in income	
	Percentage-of-completion method	Completed-contract method		Net of tax effect
Year			Direct	
Prior to 1996	$1,800,000	$1,300,000	$500,000	$300,000
1996	900,000	800,000	100,000	60,000
1997	700,000	1,000,000	(300,000)	(180,000)
1998	800,000	600,000	200,000	120,000
1999	1,000,000	1,100,000	(100,000)	(60,000)
Total at beg. of 2000	$5,200,000	$4,800,000	$400,000	$240,000
2000	1,100,000	900,000	200,000	120,000
Total	$6,300,000	$5,700,000	$600,000	$360,000

Following is the proper method of disclosing this type of change as prescribed by APB 20.

On the Face of the Income Statement

	2000	As adjusted (see Note A) 1999
Income before extraordinary item	$660,000	$600,000
Extraordinary item (description)	--	(80,000)
Net income	$660,000	$520,000
Per share amounts:		
Earnings per common share--assuming no dilution:		
Income before extraordinary item	$0.66	$0.60
Extraordinary item	--	(.08)
Net income	$0.66	$0.52

Earnings per common share--assuming full dilution:

Income before extraordinary item	$0.61	$0.56
Extraordinary item	--	(.07)
Net income	$0.61	$0.49

On the Statement of Retained Earnings

	2000	As adjusted (see Note A) 1999
Balance at beginning of year, as previously reported	$17,910,000	$17,330,000
Add adjustment for the cumulative effect on prior years of applying retroactively the new method of accounting for long-term contracts (Note A)	240,000	300,000*
Balance at beginning of year	$18,150,000	$17,630,000
Net income	660,000	520,000
Balance at end of year	$18,810,000	$18,150,000

*This is the resultant amount of the change less the tax effect through 1999.

In the Notes to the Financial Statements

Note A: Change in method of accounting for long-term construction contracts.

In 2000 the company changed its method of accounting for long-term construction contracts from the completed-contract method to the percentage-of-completion method. The change was made because the company felt that the new method resulted in a more accurate recognition of revenue and a better matching of revenue and costs. The financial statements of prior periods have been restated to apply the new method retroactively. The company will continue to use the completed-contract method for income tax purposes. The effect of the accounting change in income of 2000 and on income previously reported for 1999 is as follows:

	Increase (decrease) 2000	1999
Effect on:		
Income before extraordinary item and net income	$120,000	$(60,000)
Earnings per common share--no dilution	0.12	(0.06)
Earnings per common share--full dilution	0.11	(0.05)

The balances of retained earnings for 1999 and 2000 have been adjusted for the effect (net of income taxes) of retroactively applying the new method of accounting.

Notice that the income statement does not highlight the change. This lack of disclosure has been the major argument surrounding the use of this method. Although both periods reflect the increase in income resulting from the change, it is assumed that the average user of the financial statements may not refer to the notes to understand the change.

The only change shown in the financial statements, per se, is the cumulative adjustment that is part of the statement of retained earnings. This amount is determined by totaling the effect of the change for all periods prior to the period presented in the financial statements. This amount is reflected as an adjustment to the beginning balance of retained earnings.

The notes to the financial statements must disclose the nature of and reason for the change. In addition, the effect of the change on income before extraordinary items and net income including the related per share amounts should be disclosed for all the years presented. In this case, the change for 2000 and 1999 is to increase (decrease) net income by $100,000 and ($50,000), respectively.

Cumulative effect not determinable. In promulgating APB Opinion 20, the APB realized that there would be certain circumstances in which the pro forma accounts or the cumulative effect amount would not be available. If the pro forma amounts cannot be determined or reasonably estimated for the individual prior periods, the cumulative effect should be shown on the income statement and the reason for not showing the pro forma amounts disclosed in the notes to the financial statements. In an instance where the cumulative effect cannot be determined, disclosure will be limited to showing the effect of the change on the results of operations for the period of the change (including per share data) and to explaining the reason for omitting accounting for the cumulative effect and disclosure of pro forma results. The board specified the change from the FIFO to LIFO method of inventory pricing as one circumstance under which it would be impossible to determine the cumulative effect.

Example of change from FIFO to LIFO

During 2000, Ramirez, Inc. decided to change the method used for pricing its inventories from FIFO to LIFO. The inventory values are as listed below for both FIFO and LIFO cost. Sales for the year amounted to $15,000,000 and the company's total purchases were $11,000,000. Other expenses amounted to $1,200,000 for the year. The company had 1,000,000 shares outstanding throughout the year.

Inventory values:

	FIFO	*LIFO*
12/31/99	$ 2,000,000	N/A
12/31/00	4,000,000	$ 1,800,000

The computations for net income would be as follows:

	FIFO	*LIFO*
Sales	$15,000,000	$15,000,000
Less: Cost of goods sold	9,000,000	11,200,000
Gross margin	$ 6,000,000	$ 3,800,000
Other expenses	1,200,000	1,200,000
Net income	$ 4,800,000	$ 2,600,000

The following footnote would be an example of the required disclosure in this circumstance:

Note A: Change in method of accounting for inventories.

During 2000, the company changed its method of accounting for all of its inventories from first-in, first-out (FIFO) to last-in, first-out (LIFO). The change was made because management believes that the LIFO method provides a better matching of costs and revenues. In addition, the adoption of LIFO conforms the company's inventory pricing policy to the one that is predominant in the industry. The change and its effect on net earnings ($000 omitted except for per share) and earnings per share for 2000 are as follows:

	Net earnings	Earnings per share
Net earnings before the change	$4,800	$4.80
Reduction of earnings by the change	2,200	2.20
Net earnings	$2,600	$2.60

There is no cumulative effect of the change on prior years because beginning inventory on January 1, 2000, at LIFO is the same as that which was reported on a FIFO basis at December 31, 1999. As a result of this change, the current period's financial statements are not comparable with those of any prior periods. The current cost of inventories valued at LIFO exceeds the carrying amount by $2,200,000 at December 31, 2000.

APPENDIX B

ACCOUNTING CHANGES IN INTERIM PERIODS

IAS 34, which addresses interim financial reporting, provides limited guidance on the topic of accounting changes made in interim periods (see discussion in Chapter 19). Since questions regarding the accounting for changes made in interim periods often arise in practice, this appendix will offer, for the readers' consideration, additional guidance on this important subject, drawn from standards promulgated under US GAAP. While this is not binding on enterprises reporting in conformity with IAS, and is intended only as illustrative material, it may prove to be a valuable reference in determining how to apply the principles of IAS 8 to interim period reporting.

APB 28 is the US GAAP standard concerned with interim reporting. APB 28 indicates that accounting changes are to be reported in interim periods in accordance with the provisions set forth in APB 20. The FASB then issued SFAS 3 to clarify the interim treatment of an accounting change and to provide examples. Of particular concern in SFAS 3 was the treatment to be accorded cumulative effect accounting changes (including a change to LIFO for which no cumulative effect can be determined) and accounting changes made in the fourth quarter by publicly traded companies.

The treatment of a cumulative effect change in an interim period depends on the quarter in which the change is made. If the cumulative effect accounting change is made in the first quarter, the cumulative effect on the beginning balance of retained earnings should be included in the net income of the first quarter. Again, the income for the first quarter of the current period is computed using the newly adopted method, and the cumulative effect of the change shall be shown on the income statement after extraordinary items and before net income. In accordance with APB 20, the comparative periods are not to be restated.

If the cumulative effect accounting change is made in a period other than the first quarter, no cumulative effect of the accounting change should be included in the net income of the period. Rather, the prechange interim periods of the year in which the change is made should be restated to reflect the newly adopted accounting principle. The cumulative effect on the beginning balance of retained earnings is then shown in the first interim period of the year in which the change is made. This includes any year-to-date or other financial statements that include the first interim period.

SFAS 3 requires that the following disclosures be made regarding a cumulative effect accounting change in an interim period in addition to the treatment described above for the actual amount of the cumulative effect:

1. In the financial statements for the period in which the change is made, the nature and justification of the change.

2. Disclosure of the effect of the change on income from continuing operations, net income, and related per share amounts for the interim period in which the change is made. If the change is made in other than the first interim period, they should also disclose the effect of the change on income from continuing operations, net income, and related per share amounts for each prechange interim period, and income from continuing operations, net income, and related per share amounts for each prechange interim period restated.

3. In the period in which the change is made, the pro forma amounts for income from continuing operations, net income, and the related per share amounts should be disclosed for

    a. The interim period in which the change is made
    b. Any interim periods of prior years for which financial information is presented

    If no prior year fiscal information is presented, disclosure should be made, in the period of the change, of the actual and pro forma amounts of income from continuing operations, net income, and related per share amounts for the interim period of the immediately preceding fiscal year that corresponds to the interim period in which the change is made. The pro forma amounts are to be calculated in accordance with APB 20 (discussed earlier).

4. The same disclosures described in items 1 and 2 above should be made regarding any year-to-date or last-twelve-months financial statements that include the period of the change.

5. For a postchange interim period (same fiscal year), disclosure should be made of the effect of the change on income from continuing operations, net income, and the related per share amounts for the postchange period.

As mentioned earlier, a change to the LIFO method of pricing inventories generally results in a situation where the cumulative effect is not determinable. If such a change occurs in the first interim period, then the same disclosures described above for the cumulative effect accounting change should be made with the exception of the pro forma amounts. If the change is made in a period other than the first interim period, the disclosures should include those mentioned above **and** restatement of the financial information presented for prechange interim periods of that year reflecting the adoption of the new accounting principle.

The following examples illustrate the foregoing principles relative to a cumulative effect accounting change made both in the first interim period and in other than the first period. We use the same facts and assumptions for both examples.

Example of accounting change in first interim period

In 2000, ABC Company decided to adopt the straight-line method of depreciation for plant equipment. The new method was to be used for both new acquisitions and previously acquired plant equipment. In prior periods, the company had used an accelerated method of computing depreciation on plant equipment. The following assumptions are made:

1. The effects of the change are limited to the direct effect on depreciation and the indirect effect on the incentive compensation, as well as the related tax effects.
2. The incentive compensation is 10% of pretax accounting income.
3. There is a constant tax rate of 50%.
4. There were 1,000,000 shares issued and outstanding throughout the periods covered, with no potential for dilution.
5. The company presents comparative interim statements.
6. Assume that the following information is given for years 1999 and 2000716

Period	Net income on the basis of old accounting principle (accelerated depreciation)	Gross effect of change to straight-line depreciation	Gross effect less income taxes	Net effect after incentive compensation and related income taxes
Prior to first qtr. 1999		$ 20,000	$ 10,000	$ 9,000
First quarter 1999	$1,000,000	30,000	15,000	13,500
Second quarter 1999	1,200,000	70,000	35,000	31,500
Third quarter 1999	1,100,000	50,000	25,000	22,500
Fourth quarter 1999	1,100,000	80,000	40,000	36,000
Total at beg. of 2000	$4,400,000	$250,000	$125,000	$112,500
First quarter 2000	$1,059,500*	$ 90,000	$ 45,000	$ 40,500*
Second quarter 2000	1,255,000	100,000	50,000	45,000
Third quarter 2000	1,150,500	110,000	55,000	49,500
Fourth quarter 2000	1,146,000	120,000	60,000	54,000
	$4,611,000	$420,000	$210,000	$189,000

The net income for 2000 has been broken down into income based on the old accounting principle and the effect of the change. These numbers are unrealistic in the sense that the 2000 income figure would be computed based on the new principle (e.g., the first quarter net income is $1,100,000, which is $1,059,500 + $40,500).

In the first example we apply the SFAS 3 criteria applicable to a change made in the first quarter. Notice that in interim reporting the same principles are followed as were set for annual financial reporting. The cumulative effect is considered to be a change in the beginning balance of retained earnings and, therefore, effective at the beginning of the year. To include the cumulative effect in any interim period other than the first, or year-to-date including the first, would be misleading. In this case we are dealing with the first period, and the $125,000, representing the direct effects net of tax, is presented on the face of the income statement. Also, as with the annual reporting, the pro forma amounts reflecting the direct and indirect effects of the change are also presented. In this case the 2000 number already reflects the change, and from the information given we can see that the total effect on the first quarter of 1999 was to increase net income by $13,500.

As required, the notes state the nature and justification of the change. Also included in the notes are the total cumulative effect, the effect on the earnings of the first quarter of the year in which the change is made (this disclosure makes allowable a comparison between statements), and the nature of the pro forma amounts. Essentially, if the change is made in the first quarter, the reporting and disclosure requirements are very similar to those in the annual financial statements.

The following quarterly financial statements and note illustrate the foregoing principles:

| | Three months ended March 31, | |
	2000	1999
Income before cumulative effect of a change in accounting principle	$1,100,000	$1,000,000
Cumulative effect on prior years (to December 31, 1999) of changing to a different depreciation method (Note A)	125,000	--
Net income	$1,225,000	$1,000,000
Amounts per common share:		
Income before cumulative effect of a change in accounting principle	$1.10	$1.00
Cumulative effect on prior years (to December 31, 1999) of changing to a different depreciation method (Note A)	0.13	--
Net income	$1.23	$1.00
Pro forma amounts assuming the new depreciation method is applied retroactively (Note A):		
Net income	$1,100,000	$1,013,500
Net income per common share	$1.10	$1.01

Note A: Change in depreciation method for plant equipment.

During the first quarter of 2000, the company decided to change the method of computing depreciation on plant assets from the accelerated method used in previous periods to the straight-line method. The change was made to better match the amortized cost of the asset to the revenue produced by it. The retroactive application of the new method resulted in a cumulative effect of $125,000 (net of $125,000 in income taxes), which is included in the income for the first quarter of 2000. The effect of the change on the first quarter of 2000 was to increase income before cumulative effect of a change in accounting principle by $40,500 ($0.04 per share) and net income by $165,500 ($0.17 per share). The pro forma amounts reflect the effect of retroactive application on depreciation, the change in provisions for incentive compensation that would have been made in 1999 had the new method been in effect, and the related income taxes.

Example of accounting change in other than first interim period

In this case we assume that the change is made in the third quarter of the year and that the company is presenting comparative financial information for both the current quarter and year-to-date. As mentioned above, the cumulative effect is not necessarily to be presented in the period of the change because it relates to the beginning of the year. Thus, in the illustration below, the 3 months ended September 30 do not include an amount for the cumulative effect; however, the 9-month statements do. The presentation of the 3-month statements reflects the effect of the accounting change for 2000 and does not reflect this change for 1999. The 1999 statement is the same as it was presented in the prior year. The pro forma amounts and the disclosure in the notes provide the information necessary to make these two interim periods comparable.

The 9-month statement for 2000 reflects the effect of the change for the entire 9-month period. Thus, the results of the 6-month period for 2000 added to the 3-month results would not equal the amounts shown in the 9-month statement. This is because the prior statement for the 6-month period would not have reflected the new principle that the 3-month and 9-month figures do. Again, the 1999 numbers are presented as they were in the preceding year. The remainder of the example is really no different from the disclosure required by another accounting change, with one exception. The exception is that the effect of the change on the preceding interim periods must also be disclosed. Note that the cumulative effect is included in the first period. The total of the three individual quarters will now equal the total income shown in the 9-month statement.

	3 months ended September 30,		9 months ended September 30,	
	2000	*1999*	*2000*	*1999*
Income before cumulative effect of a change in accounting principle	$1,200,000	$1,100,000	$3,600,000	$3,300,000
Cumulative effect on prior years (to December 31, 1999) of changing to a different depreciation method (Note A)	--	--	125,000	--
Net income	$1,200,000	$1,100,000	$3,725,000	$3,300,000
Amounts per common share:				
Income before cumulative effect of a change in accounting principle	$1.20	$1.10	$3.60	$3.30
Cumulative effect on prior years (to December 31, 1999) of changing to a different depreciation method (Note A)	--	--	0.13	--
Net income	$1.20	$1.10	$3.73	$3.30
Pro forma amounts assuming the new depreciation method is applied retroactively (Note A):				
Net income	$1,200,000	$1,122,500	$3,600,000	$3,367,500
Net income per common share	$1.20	$1.12	$3.60	$3.37

Note A: Change in depreciation method for plant equipment.

During the third quarter of 2000, the company decided to change the method of computing depreciation on plant assets from the accelerated method used in previous periods to the straight-line method. The change was made to better match the amortized cost of the asset to the revenue produced by it. The retroactive application of the new method resulted in a cumulative effect of $125,000 (net of $125,000 in income taxes), which is included in the income for the 9 months ended September 30, 2000. The effect of the change on the 3 months ended September 30, 2000, was to increase net income by $49,500 ($0.05 per share); the effect of the change on the 9 months ended September 30, 2000, was to increase income before cumulative effect of a change in accounting principle by $135,000 ($0.14 per share) and net income by $260,000 ($0.26 per share). The pro forma amounts reflect the effect of retroactive application on depreciation, the change in the provisions for incentive pay that would have been made in 1999 had the new method been in effect, and the related income taxes.

The effect of the change on the first and second quarters of 2000 is as follows:

	Three months ended	
	March 31, 2000	*June 30, 2000*
Net income as originally reported	$1,059,500	$1,255,000
Effect of change in depreciation method	40,500	45,000
Income before cumulative effect of a change in accounting principle	1,100,000	1,300,000
Cumulative effect on prior years (to December 31, 1999) of changing to a different depreciation method	125,000	--
Net income as restated	$1,255,000	$1,300,000
Per share amounts:		
Net income as originally reported	$1.06	$1.26
Effect of change in depreciation method	0.04	0.04
Income before cumulative effect of a change in accounting principle	1.10	1.30
Cumulative effect on prior years (to December 31, 1999) of changing to a different depreciation method	0.13	--
Net income as restated	$1.23	$1.30

22 FOREIGN CURRENCY

PERSPECTIVE AND ISSUES

At the turn of the century, globalization seems to have become the keyword. Most domestic corporations worldwide are reaching out beyond national boundaries and engaging in international trade. Global economic restructuring is rampant: signing of trade pacts such as GATT, NAFTA, and the recent setting up of the World Trade Organization (WTO) has lent further impetus to the process of internationalization. International activity by most domestic corporations has increased significantly, which means that transactions are consummated not only with independent foreign entities but also with foreign subsidiaries.

It is well known that foreign subsidiaries, associates, and branches handle their accounts and prepare financial statements in the respective currencies of the countries in which they are located. Thus, it is more than likely that a multinational company (MNC) ends up receiving, at year end, financial statements from various foreign subsidiaries expressed in a number of foreign currencies, such as francs, pounds, lira, dinars, dirhams, riyals, and yen. However, for users of these financial statements to analyze the MNC's foreign involvement properly, these foreign currency financial statements must first be expressed in terms that the users can understand. This means that the foreign currency financial statements of the various subsidiaries will have to be translated into the currency of the country where the MNC is registered.

The international GAAP governing the translation of foreign currency financial statements and foreign currency transactions is found primarily in IAS 21 (revised 1993), *The Effects of Changes in Foreign Exchange Rates*. This standard supersedes International Accounting Standard IAS 21, *Accounting for the Effects of Changes in Foreign Exchange Rates*, approved in 1983. IAS 21 applies to

1. Accounting for foreign currency transactions (e.g., exports, imports, and loans) which are denominated in other than an enterprise's functional currency
2. Translation of foreign currency financial statements of branches, divisions, subsidiaries, and other investees that are incorporated in the financial statements of an enterprise by consolidation, proportionate consolidation, or by the equity method

As stated in IAS 21, this standard does not deal with hedge accounting for foreign currency items other than the classification of exchange differences arising on a foreign currency liability accounted for as a hedge of a net investment in a foreign entity. The IASC is currently working on the second phase of the financial instruments project, and the second standard on financial instruments (the first being IAS 32) will address other aspects of hedging, including criteria for the use of hedge accounting.

Sources of IAS
IAS 21   *SIC* 7, 11

DEFINITIONS OF TERMS

Closing rate. This refers to the spot rate (defined below) at the balance sheet date.

Conversion. The exchange of one currency for another.

Exchange difference. The difference resulting from reporting the same number of units of a foreign currency in the reporting currency at different exchange rates.

Exchange rate. This refers to the ratio for exchange of two currencies.

Fair value. The amount for which an asset could be exchanged, or a liability could be settled, between knowledgeable, willing parties in an arm's-length transaction.

Foreign currency. A currency other than the reporting currency of the entity being referred to (e.g., the yen is a foreign currency for a US reporting entity). (Under the US GAAP composites of currencies, such as the Special Drawing Rights on the International Monetary Fund (SDR), used to set prices or denominate amounts of loans, and so on, have the characteristics of foreign currency for purposes of applying SFAS 52. No such clarification or interpretation is found in the IAS.)

Foreign currency financial statements. Financial statements that employ as the unit of measure a foreign currency that is not the reporting currency of the enterprise.

Foreign currency transactions. Transactions whose terms are denominated in a foreign currency or require settlement in a foreign currency. Foreign currency transactions arise when an enterprise (1) buys or sells on credit goods or services whose prices are denominated in foreign currency, (2) borrows or lends funds and the amounts payable or receivable are denominated in foreign currency, (3) is a party to an unperformed foreign exchange contract, or (4) for other reasons acquires or disposes of assets or incurs or settles liabilities denominated in foreign currency.

Foreign currency translation. The process of expressing in the reporting currency of the enterprise amounts that are denominated or measured in a different currency.

Foreign entity. When the activities of a foreign operation are not an integral part of those of the reporting entity, such a foreign operation is referred to as a foreign entity.

Foreign operation. A foreign subsidiary, associate, joint venture, or branch of the reporting enterprise whose activities are based or conducted in a country other than the country where the reporting enterprise is domiciled.

Functional currency. A term used under the US GAAP in relation to foreign currency translations wherein it is defined as the currency of the primary economic environment in which the entity operates; normally, that is the currency of the environment in which an entity primarily generates and expends cash.

Monetary items. Money held and assets and liabilities to be received or paid in fixed or determinable amounts of money. Stated differently, monetary items refer to cash, claims to receive a fixed amount of cash, and obligations to pay a fixed amount of cash.

Net investment in a foreign entity. This refers to the reporting enterprise's share in the net assets of that entity.

Nonmonetary items. All balance sheet items other than cash, claims to cash, and cash obligations.

Reporting currency. The currency in which an enterprise presents its financial statements.

Reporting enterprise. An entity or group whose financial statements are being referred to. Under this standard, those financial statements reflect (1) the financial statements of one or more foreign operations by consolidation, proportionate consolidation, or equity accounting; (2) foreign currency transactions; or (3) both of the foregoing.

Spot rate. The exchange rate for immediate delivery of currencies exchanged.

Transaction date. In the context of recognition of exchange differences from settlement of monetary items arising from foreign currency transactions, transaction date refers to the date at which a foreign currency transaction (e.g., a sale or purchase of merchandise or services the settlement for which will be in a foreign currency) occurs and is recorded in the accounting records.

CONCEPTS, RULES, AND EXAMPLES

Classification of Foreign Operations

Under IAS 21, the way in which the foreign operations are financed and operate (i.e., in relation to the reporting entity) determines the method that would be used to translate their financial statements. Stated differently, the classification accorded to a foreign operation will determine the methodology to be used in translating their financial statements. According to IAS 21, a foreign operation may be classified into either one of two categories: (1) a foreign operation that is integral to the operations of the reporting entity, or (2) a foreign operation that is not integral to the operations of the reporting entity (referred to as a foreign entity).

The following factors, if present, indicate that a foreign operation is a foreign entity (i.e., the foreign operation is not integral to the operations of the reporting entity):

1. Its activities are carried out with significant autonomy.
2. Transactions with the reporting entity are not a high proportion of the foreign enterprise's operations.
3. Its activities are financed principally from its own resources or through local borrowings in lieu of the reporting entity's funds.
4. Cost of labor, material, and other components of the foreign operation's products or services are paid or settled primarily in the local currency rather than the currency of the reporting entity.
5. Its sales are principally made in currencies other than the reporting currency.
6. Cash flows of the reporting enterprise are insulated from the day-to-day activities of the foreign operation rather than being affected directly by the activities of the foreign operation.

The classification of a foreign operation is to be based on the facts surrounding each case, and sometimes this could be quite subjective and unclear. Thus, a degree of caution is to be exercised in judgments relating to classification of borderline cases, since on such a classification will depend the method that will ultimately be used to translate the foreign operation's financial statements into the reporting currency.

Translation of Foreign Operations That Are Integral to the Operations of the Reporting Enterprise

The financial statements of foreign operations that are integral to the operations of the reporting enterprise should be translated based on the premise that these are, in substance, the transactions of the reporting enterprise itself. Thus, the rules contained within IAS 21, dealing with reporting of foreign currency items of an enterprise's own transactions, will generally apply to such a foreign operation with the exception of any rules that specifically override the foregoing provisions and stipulate otherwise. These requirements or rules for translating the financial statements of such a foreign operation are the following:

1. Foreign currency monetary items should be reported using the closing rate.
2. Foreign currency nonmonetary items when carried at historical costs should be reported using the exchange rate at the date of the transaction.
3. Foreign currency nonmonetary items when carried at fair values (e.g., revalued property, plant, and equipment under the allowed alternative treatment prescribed by IAS 16) should be reported using exchange rates that existed when the fair values were determined.
4. Generally, all income and expense items should be translated using exchange rates at the dates of the transactions. In practice, a rate that approximates the actual rate at the date of the transaction is used. For instance, an average rate based on month-end exchange rates might be used for translation of the annual expense and income figures on the financial statement of the foreign operation into the reporting currency. However, as specifically provided by the standard, depreciation expense should be translated either using the exchange rate at the date of purchase of the asset, or if the asset is carried at fair value (i.e., revalued under the allowed alternative treatment prescribed by IAS 16), the rate that existed on the date of such valuation.
5. Generally, exchange differences arising from reporting an entity's monetary items at rates different from those in which they were initially reported in previous financial statements should be recognized as income or expense in the period in which they arise. Note, however, that an exception is made, in the case of exchange differences relating to monetary items which are, in substance, part of the enterprise's net investment in a foreign entity. In such a case they should be classified as a separate component of equity in the reporting enterprise's financial statements until disposal of the net investment at which time they should be recognized as income or expense (of the same period the gain or loss on disposal is recognized). Similarly, exchange differences which arise from a foreign liability accounted as a hedge of an enterprise's net investment in a foreign entity should be classified as a separate component of equity on the balance sheet until the disposal of the net

investment (at which time they should be recognized as income or expense in the same period as the gain or loss on disposal is recognized).

IAS 21 further elaborates the translation methodology for two items and stipulates as follows:

1. The translation of the cost and depreciation of property, plant, and equipment is to be done based on rates in effect at the date(s) of acquisition, and if revalued (i.e., carried at fair value), then at the exchange rate(s) at the date(s) of such revaluation.
2. Inventories should be translated at the rates in effect at the dates of acquisition; however, if carried at a lower realizable value (or recoverable amount), then the exchange rate prevailing on the date when such lower realizable value (or recoverable amount) was determined (the rate in which case will be the closing rate, since determination of lower of cost or net realizable value is usually undertaken at the balance sheet date).

Sometimes an adjustment may be required to reduce the carrying amount of an asset in the financial statements of the reporting enterprise even though such an adjustment was not necessary in the financial statements of the foreign operation. This stipulation of IAS 21 can best be illustrated by the following case study.

Example

Inventory of merchandise owned by a foreign operation (which is integral to the operations of the reporting enterprise) is being carried by the foreign operation at 3,750,000 SR (Saudi riyals) on its balance sheet. Suppose that the exchange rate fluctuated from 3.75 SR = 1 US dollar at September 15, 2000, when the merchandise was bought, to 4.25 SR = 1 US dollar at December 31, 2000 (i.e., the balance sheet date). The translation of this item (appearing on the balance sheet of the foreign operation) into the reporting currency will necessitate an adjustment to reduce the carrying amount of the inventory to its net realizable value if this value when translated into the reporting currency is lower than the carrying amount translated at the rate prevailing on the date of purchase of the merchandise.

Although the net realizable value, which in terms of Saudi riyals is 4,000,000 (SR), is higher than the carrying amount in Saudi riyals (i.e., 3,750,000 SR) when translated into the reporting currency (i.e., US dollars) at the balance sheet date, the net realizable value is lower than the carrying amount (translated into the reporting currency at the exchange rate prevailing on the date of acquisition of the merchandise). Thus, on the financial statements of the foreign operation the inventory would not have to be adjusted. However, when the net realizable value is translated at the closing rate (which is 4.25 SR = 1 US dollar) into the reporting currency, it will require the following adjustment:

1. Carrying amount translated at the exchange rate on September 15, 2000 (i.e., the date of acquisition) = SR 3,750,000 @ 3.75 SR to 1 US dollar = $1,000,000.
2. Net realizable value translated at the closing rate = SR 4,000,000 @ 4.25 SR to 1 US dollar = $941,176.

3.   Adjustment needed = $1,000,000 − $941,176 = $58,824.

Conversely, IAS 21 further stipulates that an adjustment that already exists on the financial statements of the foreign operation may need to be reversed in the financial statements of the reporting enterprise. To illustrate this point let us consider the facts of the example above with some variation as below.

Example

All other factual details remaining the same as above, let's assume that the inventory above, which is carried on the books of the foreign operation at Saudi riyals (SR) 3,750,000, instead has a net realizable value of SR 3,250,000 on the closing date. Also assume that the exchange rate fluctuated from SR 3.75 = 1 US dollar at the date of acquisition of the merchandise to SR 3.00 = 1 US dollar on the balance sheet date.

Since in terms of Saudi riyals, the net realizable value on the balance sheet date was lower than the carrying value of the inventory, an adjustment must have been made on the balance sheet of the foreign operation (in Saudi riyals) to reduce the carrying amount to the lower of cost or net realizable value. In other words, a contra asset account (e.g., allowance for obsolete inventory) representing the difference between the carrying amount (SR 3,750,000) and the net realizable value (SR 3,250,000) must have been created on the books of the foreign operation.

On translating the financial statements of the foreign operation into the reporting currency, however, it is noted that due to the fluctuation of the exchange rates the net realizable value when converted to the reporting currency [SR 3,250,000 (@ 3.00 SR = 1 US dollar) = $1,083,333] is no longer lower than the translated carrying value which is to be converted at the exchange rate prevailing on the date of acquisition of the merchandise [SR 3,750,000 (@ SR 3.75 = 1 US dollar) = $1,000,000].

Thus, as required by IAS 21, para 28, a reversal of the adjustment (for obsolescence) is required on the financial statements of the reporting enterprise, on translation of the financial statements of the foreign operation.

Translation Methods Commonly Used in Translating Financial Statements of Foreign Operations

In practice, one encounters four methods that could be used to translate assets and liabilities of a company's foreign operations. The primary distinction among the methods is the classification of assets and liabilities that would be translated at either the current or historical rate. Although the IAS recognizes the current rate method to translate the financial statements of a foreign entity, all four methods have been explained briefly below since internationally these methods are used in certain countries.

The first method is known as the **temporal method**. This method translates cash, receivables, payables, and assets and liabilities carried at present or future values at the current rate, with the remaining assets and liabilities carried at historical costs translated at the applicable historical rates. In essence, the accounting principles used to measure the assets and liabilities in the foreign statements are retained. However, the foreign exchange gains or losses that arise from this method do so because of this method and not because the economic events that affect the foreign entity's operations are reflected.

It is worth noting that the temporal method was the mandated method in the United States under SFAS 8 until it was superseded by SFAS 52, which requires the current rate method to be used under US GAAP. In most cases the temporal method produces the same results as the second approach, the monetary/ nonmonetary method.

The remeasurement technique, required by US GAAP (when the books and records are not maintained in the functional currency), is essentially the same as the **monetary/nonmonetary method**. This method translates nonmonetary assets and liabilities at the proper historical rates. Under this method, it is the characteristics of assets and liabilities that are used as the basis for classification rather than the method of accounting, as under the first approach. It is by mere coincidence that assets and liabilities are measured on bases that coincide approximately with the monetary/nonmonetary classification, which produces the aforementioned similar results. A problem with this method is that not all items may be classified as monetary or nonmonetary, and some arbitrary decisions must be made.

The third method is the **current/noncurrent method**, which, as implied, stresses balance sheet classification as the basis for translation. Current assets and liabilities are translated at the current rate and noncurrent assets and liabilities at the applicable historical rates. A major weakness under this approach is the treatment of inventory and long-term debt. Inventory, a current asset, would be translated at its current cost, a major departure from traditional GAAP. The translation of foreign-denominated long-term debt under this approach would be misleading to users, as it would be translated at its historical value.

For instance, from the perspective of a US reporting entity, if the dollar weakens internationally, it will take more dollars to repay this obligation, a fact that would not be apparent from the reporting entity's financial statements. Furthermore, some balance sheets are not classified and variations between current and noncurrent classifications of classified balance sheets may be based arbitrarily on management's intentions.

The last approach is known as the **current rate method** and is the approach mandated by IAS for translation of financial statements of a foreign entity. This is also the prescribed method under certain other accounting standards, for instance the US GAAP, when the functional currency is the foreign currency. A distinguishing feature of this method is that all assets and liabilities, both monetary and nonmonetary, are translated at the closing rate. The basis of this method is the "net investment concept," wherein the foreign entity is viewed as a separate entity that the parent invested into, rather than being considered as part of the parent's operations.

Standard setters in countries such as the United States have expressed a preference for this method. The reason for preferring this method over others was that users could benefit most when the information provided about the foreign entity retains the relationships and results created in the environment (economics, legal, and political) in which the entity operates. Under this approach, the reasoning follows that foreign-denominated debt is used to purchase assets that create foreign-denominated revenues. These assets act as a hedge against the debt from changes in the exchange rate. The excess (net) assets will, however, be affected by this foreign exchange risk, and this is the effect that is recognized by the parent.

Note that under the US GAAP, if the foreign entity's local currency is the functional currency, it requires the current rate method when translating the foreign entity's financial statements. On the other hand, if the US dollar is the functional currency, US GAAP requires the remeasurement method when translating the foreign entity's financial statements. (Both of these methods are illustrated through numerical case studies later in this chapter.)

Translation of Financial Statements of a Foreign Operation That Is Not Integral to the Operations of the Reporting Enterprise (i.e., Foreign Entity)

The following rules should be used in translating the financial statements of a foreign entity:

1. All assets and liabilities, whether monetary or nonmonetary, should be translated at the closing rate.
2. Income and expense items should be translated at the exchange rates at the dates of the transactions, except when the foreign entity reports in a currency of a hyperinflationary economy (as defined in IAS 29), in which case they should be translated at the closing rates.
3. All resulting exchange differences should be classified as a separate component of equity of the reporting enterprise until disposal of the net investment in a foreign entity.

Guidance Under IAS 21 in Special Situations

Minority interests. When a foreign entity is consolidated but is not wholly owned by the reporting enterprise, there will be minority interest reported in the consolidated balance sheet. IAS 21 requires that the accumulated exchange differences resulting from translation and attributable to the minority interest be allocated to and reported as minority interest instead of as a separate component of equity.

Goodwill arising on acquisition of a foreign entity. Any goodwill (which in the authors' opinion includes negative goodwill) arising on the acquisition of a foreign entity should be treated as either

1. An asset (or a liability in case of negative goodwill) of the foreign entity and translated at the closing rate, or
2. An asset (or a liability in case of negative goodwill) of the reporting entity which is either already expressed in the reporting currency or is converted to the reporting currency, such as nonmonetary items that are carried at

historical costs and translated at the exchange rate on the date of the transaction in accordance with IAS 21.

Fair value adjustments to carrying amount of assets and liabilities arising on acquisition of a foreign entity. IAS 21 prescribes the same treatment for this as well as for goodwill arising on acquisition of a foreign entity (discussed above).

Exchange differences on elimination of intragroup balances. While incorporating the financial statements of a foreign entity into those of the reporting enterprise, normal consolidation procedures, such as elimination of intragroup balances and transactions, are undertaken as required by IAS 27 and IAS 31. However, IAS 21 requires that exchange differences arising from intragroup monetary items should not be eliminated against corresponding amounts arising on other intragroup balances. This is because monetary items represent commitments to convert one currency into another and expose the reporting enterprise to a gain or loss through currency fluctuations. Thus, on consolidation, such exchange differences would continue to be recognized either as income or expense, or if they arise from exceptional circumstances described in IAS 21, they should be classified as equity until the disposal of the net investment.

Different reporting dates. When reporting dates up to which the financial statements of a foreign entity and those of the reporting enterprise differ, the foreign entity normally switches and prepares financial statements with reporting dates coinciding with those of the reporting enterprise. However, sometimes this may not be practicable to do. In such circumstances IAS 27 allows the use of financial statements drawn up to different dates, provided that the difference is no more than 3 months. In such a case, the assets and liabilities of the foreign entity should be translated at the exchange rates prevailing on the balance sheet date of the foreign entity. Adjustments should be made for any significant movements in exchange rates between the balance sheet date of the foreign entity and that of the reporting entity in accordance with the provisions of IAS 27 and IAS 28 relating to this matter.

Disposal of a foreign entity. Any cumulative exchange differences are to be carried as a separate component of equity until the disposal of the foreign entity in terms of the specific stipulation in IAS 21. The standard prescribes the treatment of the cumulative exchange differences account, on the disposal of the foreign entity. This balance, which has in a way been deferred, should be recognized as income or expense in the same period in which the gain or loss on disposal is recognized.

Disposal has been defined to include a sale, liquidation, repayment of share capital, or abandonment of all or part of the entity. Normally, payment of dividend would not constitute a repayment of capital. However, in rare circumstances, it does; for instance, when an enterprise pays dividends out of capital instead of divisible profits, as defined in the companies' acts of certain countries where this expression is used, such as the United Kingdom, this would constitute repayment of capital. In such circumstances, obviously, dividends paid would constitute a disposal for the purposes of this standard.

IAS 21 further stipulates that in the case of a partial disposal of an interest in a foreign entity, only a proportionate share of the related accumulated exchange differences is recognized as a gain or a loss. However, the standard clarifies that a write-down of the carrying amount of the foreign entity does not constitute a partial disposal, and thus the deferred exchange differences carried forward as part of equity would not be affected by such a write-down.

Change in classification of a foreign operation. Since the classification of a foreign operation either as a foreign entity or otherwise depends on the way the foreign operation operates in relation to the reporting enterprise or is financed, a subsequent change in these circumstances could sometimes lead to a change of the initial classification. In such circumstances the translation procedures applicable to the revised classification should be applied from the date of change in the classification.

Comprehensive example of the practical application of the current rate method

Assume that a US company has a 100%-owned subsidiary in Germany that began operations in 2000. The subsidiary's operations consist of leasing space in an office building. This building, which cost 500 deutsche marks (DM), was financed primarily by German banks. All revenues and cash expenses are received and paid in deutsche marks. The subsidiary also maintains its books and records in DM.

As a result, management of the US company has decided that the financial statements of the German subsidiary be translated for incorporation into its financials as if it were a foreign operation that was not integral to the operations of the reporting entity, in other words, as if it were a foreign entity. The subsidiary's balance sheet at December 31, 2000, and its combined statement of income and retained earnings for the year ended December 31, 2000, are presented below in DM.

German Company
Balance Sheet
At December 31, 2000

Assets			*Liabilities and stockholders' equity*		
Cash	DM	50	Accounts payable	DM	30
Note receivable		20	Unearned rent		10
Land		100	Mortgage payable		400
Building		500	Common stock		40
Accumulated depreciation		(10)	Additional paid-in capital		160
			Retained earnings		20
			Total liabilities and		
Total assets	DM	660	stockholders' equity	DM	660

German Company
Combined Statement of Income and Retained Earnings
For the Year Ended December 31, 2000

Revenues	DM	200
Operating expenses (including depreciation expense of DM 10)		170
Net income	DM	30
Add retained earnings, January 1, 2000		--
Deduct dividends		(10)
Retained earnings, December 31, 2000	DM	20

Various exchange rates for 2000 are as follows:

1 DM = $0.40 at the beginning of 2000 (when the common stock was issued and the land
        and building were financed through the mortgage)
1 DM = $0.43 weighted-average for 2000
1 DM = $0.42 at the date the dividends were declared and the unearned rent was re-
        ceived
1 DM = $0.45 at the end of 2000

Since the German subsidiary is a foreign entity (as per IAS 21), the German company's financial statements must be translated into US dollars in terms of the provisions of IAS 21 (i.e., by the current rate method). This translation process is illustrated below.

German Company
Balance Sheet Translation
At December 31, 2000

Assets	*DM*		*Exchange rates*	*US dollars*
Cash	DM	50	0.45	$ 22.50
Accounts receivable		20	0.45	9.00
Land		100	0.45	45.00
Building (net)		490	0.45	220.50
Total assets	DM	660		$297.00
Liabilities and stockholders' equity				
Accounts payable	DM	30	0.45	$ 13.50
Unearned rent		10	0.45	4.50
Mortgage payable		400	0.45	180.00
Common stock		40	0.40	16.00
Additional paid-in capital		160	0.40	64.00
Retained earnings		20	(see income statement)	8.70
Cumulative exchange difference (translation adjustments)		--	--	10.30
Total liabilities and stockholders' equity	DM	660		$297.00

German Company
Combined Income and Retained Earnings Statement Translation
For the Year Ended December 31, 2000

	DM	*Exchange rates*	*US dollars*
Revenues	DM 200	0.43	$86.00
Expenses (including DM 10 depreciation expense)	170	0.43	73.10
Net income	DM 30		$12.90
Add retained earnings, January 1	--	--	--
Deduct dividends	(10)	0.42	(4.20)
Retained earnings, December 31	DM 20		$ 8.70

German Company
Statement of Cash Flows
For the Year Ended December 31, 1999

	DM	*Exchange rates*	*US dollars*
Operating activities			
Net income	DM 30	0.43	$ 12.90
Adjustments to reconcile net income to net cash provided by operating activities:			
Depreciation	10	0.43	4.30
Increase in accounts receivable	(20)	0.43	(8.60)
Increase in accounts payable	30	0.43	12.90
Increase in unearned rent	10	0.42	4.20
Net cash provided by operating activities	DM 60		$ 25.70
Investing activities			
Purchase of land	(100)	0.40	(40.00)
Purchase of building	(500)	0.40	(200.00)
Net cash used by investing activities	(600)		(240.00)
Financing activities			
Common stock issue	200	0.40	80.00
Mortgage payable	400	0.40	160.00
Dividends paid	(10)	0.42	(4.20)
Net cash provided by financing	590		235.80
Effect on exchange rate changes on cash	N/A		1.00
Increase in cash and equivalents	DM 50		$ 22.50
Cash at beginning of year	-0-		-0-
Cash at end of year	DM 50	0.45	$ 22.50

The following points should be noted concerning the current rate method:

1. All assets and liabilities are translated using the current exchange rate at the balance sheet date (1 DM = $0.45). All revenues and expenses should be translated at the rates in effect when these items are recognized during the period. Due to practical considerations, however, weighted-average rates can be used to translate revenues and expenses (1 DM = $0.43).

2. Stockholders' equity accounts are translated by using historical exchange rates. Common stock was issued at the beginning of 2000 when the exchange rate was 1

DM = $0.40. The translated balance of retained earnings is the result of the weighted-average rate applied to revenues and expenses and the specific rate in effect when the dividends were declared (1 DM = $0.42).

3. Cumulative exchange differences (translation adjustments) result from translating all assets and liabilities at the current rate, while stockholders' equity is translated by using historical and weighted-average rates. The adjustments have no direct effect on cash flows; however, changes in exchange rate will have an indirect effect on sale or liquidation. Prior to this time, the effect is uncertain and remote. Also, the effect is due to the net investment rather than the subsidiary's operations. For these reasons the translation adjustments balance is reported as a separate component in the stockholders' equity section of the US company's consolidated balance sheet. This balance essentially equates the total debits of the subsidiary (now expressed in US dollars) with the total credits (also in dollars). It may also be determined directly, as shown next, to verify the translation process.

4. The cumulative exchange differences (translation adjustments) credit of $10.30 is calculated as follows:

Net assets at the beginning of 2000 (after common stock was issued and the land and building were acquired through mortgage financing)	200 DM (0.45 – 0.40)	=	$10.00 credit
Net income	30 DM (0.45 – 0.43)	=	.60 credit
Dividends	10 DM (0.45 – 0.42)	=	.30 debit
Exchange difference (translation adjustment)			$10.30 credit

5. Since the translation adjustments balance that appears as a separate component of stockholders' equity is cumulative in nature, the change in this balance during the year should be disclosed in the financial statements. In the illustration, this balance went from zero to $10.30 at the end of 2000. The analysis of this change was presented previously. In addition, assume that the following occurred during 2001:

German Company
Balance Sheet
December 31

Assets		2001		2000		Increase/(decrease)
Cash	DM	100	DM	50	DM	50
Accounts receivable		-0-		20		(20)
Land		150		100		50
Building (net)		480		490		(10)
Total assets	DM	730	DM	660	DM	70
Liabilities and stockholders' equity						
Accounts payable	DM	50	DM	30	DM	20
Unearned rent		-0-		10		(10)
Mortgage payable		450		400		50
Common stock		40		40		-0-
Additional paid-in capital		160		160		-0-
Retained earnings		30		20		10
Total liabilities and stockholders' equity	DM	730	DM	660	DM	70

German Company
Combined Statement of Income and Retained Earnings
For the Year Ended December 31, 2001

Revenues	DM	220
Operating expenses (including depreciation expense of DM 10)		170
Net income	DM	50
Add: Retained earnings, Jan. 1, 2001		20
Deduct dividends		(40)
Retained earnings, Dec. 31, 2001	DM	30

Exchange rates were:
1 DM = $0.45 at the beginning of 2001
1 DM = $0.48 weighted-average for 2001
1 DM = $0.50 at the end of 2001
1 DM = $0.49 when dividends were paid in 2001 and land bought by incurring mortgage

The translation process for 2001 is illustrated below.

German Company
Balance Sheet Translation
At December 31, 2001

Assets	*DM*		*Exchange rates*	*US dollars*
Cash	DM	100	0.50	$ 50.00
Land		150	0.50	75.00
Building		480	0.50	240.00
Total asets	DM	730		$365.00
Liabilities and stockholders' equity				
Accounts payable	DM	50	0.50	$ 25.00
Mortgage payable		450	0.50	225.00
Common stock		40	0.40	16.00
Addl. paid-in capital		160	0.40	64.00
Retained earnings		30	(see income statement)	13.10
Cumulative exchange difference (translation adjustments)		--		21.90
Total liabilities and stockholders' equity	DM	730		$365.00

German Company
Combined Income and Retained Earnings Statement Translation
For the Year Ended December 31, 2001

	DM		*Exchange rates*	*US dollars*
Revenues	DM	220	0.48	$105.60
Operating expenses (including depreciation of DM 10)		170	0.48	81.60
Net income	DM	50	0.48	$ 24.00
Add: Retained earnings 1/1/01		20	--	8.70
Less: Dividends		(40)	0.49	(19.60)
Retained earnings 12/31/01	DM	30		$ 13.10

German Company
Statement of Cash Flows
For the Year Ended December 31, 2001

	DM	*Exchange rates*	*US dollars*
Operating activities			
Net income	DM 50	.48	$24.00
Adjustments to reconcile net income to net cash provided by operating activities:			
Depreciation	10	.48	4.80
Decrease in accounts receivable	20	.48	9.60
Increase in accounts payable	20	.48	9.60
Decrease in unearned rent	(10)	.48	(4.80)
Net cash provided by operating activities	DM 90		$43.20
Investing activities			
Purchase of land	(50)	.49	(24.50)
Net cash used by investing activities	(50)		(24.50)
Financing activities			
Mortgage payable	50	.49	24.50
Dividends	(40)	.49	(19.60)
Net cash provided by financing activities	10		4.90
Effect of exchange rate changes on cash	NA		3.90
Increase in cash and equivalents	DM 50		$27.50
Cash at beginning of year	50		22.50
Cash at end of year	DM 100	.50	$50.00

Using the analysis that was presented before, the total exchange differences (translation adjustment) attributable to 2001 would be computed as follows:

Net assets at January 1, 2001	220 DM	(0.50 – 0.45) =	$11.00 credit
Net income for 2001	50 DM	(0.50 – 0.48) =	1.00 credit
Dividends for 2001	40 DM	(0.50 – 0.49) =	0.40 debit
Total			$11.60 credit

The balance in the cumulative exchange differences (translation adjustment) account at the end of 2001 would be $21.90 ($10.30 from 2000 and $11.60 from 2001).

6. Use of the equity method by the US company in accounting for the subsidiary would result in the following journal entries based on the information presented above:

	2000		*2001*	
Original investment				
Investment in German subsidiary	80*		--	
Cash		80		--
*[$0.40 x common stock of 40 DM plus additional paid-in capital of 160 DM]				
Earnings pickup				
Investment in German subsidiary	12.90		24**	
Equity in subsidiary income		12.90		24
**[$0.48 x net income of 50 DM]				

Dividends received

Cash	4.20		19.60
Investment in German subsidiary		4.20	19.60

Exchange difference (translation adjustments)

Investment in German subsidiary	10.30		11.60
Translation adjustments		10.30	11.60

Note that the stockholders' equity of the US company should be the same whether or not the German subsidiary is consolidated (IAS 28). Since the subsidiary does not report the translation adjustments on its financial statements, care should be exercised so that it is not forgotten in application of the equity method.

7. If the US company disposes of its investment in the German subsidiary, the translation adjustments balance becomes part of the gain or loss that results from the transaction and must be eliminated. For example, assume that on January 2, 2002, the US company sells its entire investment for 300 DM. The exchange rate at this date is 1 DM = $0.50. The balance in the investment account at December 31, 2001, is $115 as a result of the entries made previously.

	Investment in German Subsidiary	
1/1/00	80.00	
	12.90	4.20
	10.30	
1/1/01	99.00	
	24.00	
	11.60	19.60
12/31/01	115.00	

The following entries would be made to reflect the sale of the investment:

Cash (300 DM x $0.50)	150	
Investment in German subsidiary		115
Gain from sale of subsidiary		35
Translation adjustments	21.90	
Gain from sale of subsidiary		21.90

If the US company had sold a portion of its investment in the German subsidiary, only a proportionate share of the translation adjustments balance (cumulative amount of exchange differences) would have become part of the gain or loss from the transaction. To illustrate, if 80% of the German subsidiary was sold for 250 DM on January 2, 2002, the following journal entries would be made:

Cash	125	
Investment in German subsidiary (0.8 x $115)		92
Gain from sale of subsidiary		33
Cumulative exchange difference (translation adjustments)		
(0.8 x $21.90)	17.52	
Gain from sale of subsidiary		17.52

For an illustration of the remeasurement method under US GAAP, refer to Appendix B of this chapter.

Translation of Foreign Currency Transactions

According to IAS 21, a foreign currency transaction is a transaction "denominated in or requires settlement in a foreign currency." Denominated means that the amount to be received or paid is fixed in terms of the number of units of a particular foreign currency, regardless of changes in the exchange rate.

From the viewpoint of a US company, for instance, a foreign currency transaction results when it imports or exports goods or services to a foreign entity or makes a loan involving a foreign entity and agrees to settle the transaction in currency other than the US dollar (the reporting currency of the US company). In these situations, the US company has "crossed currencies" and directly assumes the risk of fluctuating exchange rates of the foreign currency in which the transaction is denominated. This risk may lead to recognition of foreign exchange differences in the income statement of the US company. Note that exchange differences can result only when the foreign currency transactions are denominated in a foreign currency.

When a US company imports or exports goods or services and the transaction is to be settled in US dollars, the US company will incur neither gain nor loss because it bears no risk due to exchange rate fluctuations. The following example illustrates the terminology and procedures applicable to the translation of foreign currency transactions.

Assume that a US company, an exporter, sells merchandise to a customer in Germany on December 1, 2000, for 10,000 DM. Receipt is due on January 31, 2001, and the US company prepares financial statements on December 31, 2000. At the transaction date (December 1, 2000), the spot rate for immediate exchange of foreign currencies indicates that 1 DM is equivalent to $0.50.

To find the US dollar equivalent of this transaction, the foreign currency amount, 10,000 DM, is multiplied by $0.50 to get $5,000. At December 1, 2000, the foreign currency transaction should be recorded by the US company in the following manner: Accounts receivable--Germany 5,000; sales 5,000. The accounts receivable and sales are measured in US dollars at the transaction date using the spot rate at the time of the transaction. While the accounts receivable is measured and reported in US dollars, the receivable is denominated or fixed in DM.

This characteristic may result in foreign exchange differences if the spot rate for DM changes between the transaction date and the date of settlement (January 31, 2001). If financial statements are prepared between the transaction date and the settlement date, all receivables and liabilities that are denominated in a foreign currency (the US dollar) must be restated to reflect the spot rates in existence at the balance sheet date.

Assume that on December 31, 2000, the spot rate for DM is 1 DM = $0.52. This means that the 10,000 DM are now worth $5,200 and that the accounts receivable denominated in DM should be increased by $200. The following journal entry would be recorded as of December 31, 2000:

Accounts receivable--Germany	200	
Foreign currency exchange difference		200

Note that the sales account, which was credited on the transaction date for $5,000, is not affected by changes in the spot rate. This treatment exemplifies the two-transaction viewpoint (which is a US GAAP expression). In other words, making the sale is the result of an operating decision, while bearing the risk of fluctuating spot rates is the result of a financing decision. Therefore, the amount determined as sales revenue at the transaction date should not be altered because of a financing decision to wait until January 31, 2001, for payment of the account.

The risk of a foreign exchange transaction loss can be avoided either by demanding immediate payment on December 1 or by entering into a forward exchange contract to hedge the exposed asset (accounts receivable). The fact that the US company in the example did not act in either of these two ways is reflected by requiring the recognition of foreign currency exchange differences (transaction gains or losses) in its income statement (reported as financial or nonoperating items) in the period during which the exchange rates changed.

This treatment has been criticized, however, because both the unrealized gain and/or loss are recognized in the financial statements, a practice that is at variance with traditional GAAP. Furthermore, earnings will fluctuate because of changes in exchange rates and not because of changes in the economic activities of the enterprise.

On the settlement date (January 31, 2001), assume that the spot rate is 1 DM = $0.51. The receipt of 10,000 DM and their conversion into US dollars would be journalized in the following manner:

Foreign currency	5,100	
Foreign currency transaction loss	100	
Accounts receivable--Germany		5,200
Cash	5,100	
Foreign currency		5,100

The net effect of this foreign currency transaction was to receive $5,100 from a sale that was measured originally at $5,000. This realized net foreign currency transaction gain of $100 is reported on two income statements: a $200 gain in 2000 and a $100 loss in 2001. The reporting of the gain in two income statements causes a temporary difference between pretax accounting and taxable income. This results because the transaction gain of $100 is not taxable until 2001, the year the transaction was completed or settled. Accordingly, interperiod tax allocation is required for foreign currency transaction gains or losses.

Benchmark vs. Allowed Alternative Treatment

The benchmark treatment for exchange difference requires that they be recognized as income or expenses in the period in which they arise. However, in the case of exchange differences that arise from (1) a severe devaluation or depreciation of a currency against which there is no practical means of hedging and that affects liabilities which cannot be settled, and (2) the recent acquisition of an asset invoiced in a foreign currency, the standard permits (under an allowed alternative treatment) such exchange differences to be added to the carrying value of the related asset provided that such adjusted carrying value does not exceed the lower of the replacement cost and the amount recoverable.

Accounting for the Introduction of the Euro (European Currency Unit)

With many of the nations of Europe poised to adopt the unified currency known as the Euro in 1999, with other countries promising to join within a few more years, the question arises of how to account for this event in the financial statements of entities first reporting on this basis. The Standing Interpretations Committee has ruled, in SIC 7, that the requirements of IAS 21 should be strictly applied to the changeover to the Euro. Thus, foreign currency monetary assets and liabilities arising in transactions will be translated into the reporting currency at closing (balance sheet date) rates, with immediate income or loss recognition. The cumulative differences from financial statement translation will be categorized in equity and taken into income only as the net foreign investment is disposed of. Exchange differences from liability translation are not to be incorporated into the carrying value of related assets.

Capitalization of Losses Resulting From Severe Currency Devaluations

Another recent pronouncement by the Standing Interpretations Committee has addressed one of the complications arising from severe currency devaluations. SIC 11 has held that foreign exchange losses on liabilities can be included in the carrying value of related assets only if the liabilities could not have been settled, and it was impracticable to hedge the exposure. (The carrying value of the assets would be limited to their recoverable amounts, in any case.) It would be necessary to demonstrate that foreign currency sufficient to settle the obligation was not available to the reporting entity, and that currency forwards or other hedges were not available. This is considered to be unlikely, but not impossible, to demonstrate. Furthermore, per SIC 11, this would apply only to acquisitions of assets within 12 months of the severe devaluation.

Disclosure Requirements

A number of disclosure requirements have been prescribed by IAS 21. Primarily, disclosure is required of the amounts of exchange differences included in net income or loss for the period, exchange differences that are included in the carrying amount of an asset, and those that are classified as equity along with a reconciliation of the beginning and ending balance in the cumulative exchange difference account carried as part of the equity.

When there is a change in classification of a foreign operation, disclosure is required as to the nature of the change, reason for the change, and the impact of the change on the current and each of the prior years presented. When the reporting currency is different from the currency of the country of domicile, the reason for this should be disclosed, and in case of any subsequent change in the reporting currency, the reason thereof should also be disclosed. An enterprise should also disclose the method selected to translate goodwill and fair value adjustments arising on the acquisition of a foreign entity. Disclosure is encouraged of an enterprise's foreign currency risk management policy.

APPENDIX A

HEDGING

As explained earlier, IAS 21 (revised 1993) does not address hedge accounting for foreign currency items other than classification of exchange differences arising on a foreign currency liability accounted for as a hedge of a net investment in a foreign entity. IAS 21 categorically states that other aspects of hedging will be dealt with in a forthcoming IAS on financial instruments. In the absence of comprehensive guidance presently available in the IAS, the treatment under US GAAP has been included herein as a source of guidance and reference only.

Relevant Provisions on Hedging Under US GAAP

Foreign currency transaction gains or losses on assets and liabilities which are denominated in a currency other than the functional currency can be hedged if the US company enters into a forward exchange contract. Hedges and other futures contracts that are not entered into with respect to a foreign currency transaction are accounted for in accordance with SFAS 80, *Accounting for Futures Contracts.*

In the previous example, which illustrated the accounting for foreign currency transactions, the US company could have entered into a forward exchange contract on December 1 to sell 10,000 DM for a negotiated amount to a foreign exchange broker for future delivery on January 31, 2001. This forward contract is a hedge against the exposed asset position created by having an account receivable denominated in DM. The negotiated rate referred to above is called a futures or forward rate.

In most cases, this futures rate is not identical to the spot rate at the date of the forward contract. The difference between the futures rate and the spot rate at the date of the forward contract is referred to as a discount or premium. Any discount or premium must be amortized over the term of the forward contract, generally on a straight-line basis. The amortization of discount or premium is reflected in a separate revenue or expense account, not as an addition or subtraction to the foreign currency transaction gain or loss amount. It is important to observe that under this treatment, no net foreign currency transaction gains or losses result if assets and liabilities denominated in foreign currency are completely hedged at the transaction date.

To illustrate a hedge of an exposed asset, consider the following additional information for the German transaction.

On December 1, 2000, the US company entered into a forward exchange contract to sell 10,000 DM on January 31, 2001, at $0.505 per DM. The spot rate on December 1 is $0.50 per DM. The journal entries that reflect the sale of goods and the forward exchange contract appear as follows:

Sale transaction entries			Forward exchange contract entries *(futures rate 1 DM = $0.505)*		
12/1/99 (spot rate 1 DM = $0.50)			Due from exchange broker	5,050	
Accounts receivable--			Due to exchange broker		5,000
Germany	5,000		Premium on forward contract		50
Sales		5,000			
			Foreign currency transaction loss	200	
12/31/99 (spot rate 1 DM = $0.52)			Due to exchange broker		200
Accounts receivable--			Premium on forward contract	25	
Germany	200		Financial revenue		
Foreign currency transaction			($25 = $50/2 months)		25
gain		200			
			Due to exchange broker	5,200	
1/31/00 (spot rate 1 DM = $0.51)			Foreign currency		5,100
Foreign currency	5,100		Foreign currency transaction gain		100
Foreign currency transaction loss	100		Cash	5,050	
Accounts receivable--			Due from exchange broker		5,050
Germany		5,200	Premium on forward contract	25	
			Financial revenue		25

The following points should be noted from the entries above:

1. The net foreign currency transaction gain or loss is zero. The account "Due from exchange broker" is fixed in terms of US dollars, and this amount is not affected by changes in spot rates between the transaction and settlement dates. The account "Due to exchange broker" is fixed or denominated in DM. The US company owes the exchange broker 10,000 DM, and these must be delivered on January 31, 2001. Because this liability is denominated in DM, its amount is determined by spot rates. Since spot rates change, this liability changes in amount equal to the changes in accounts receivable because both of the amounts are based on the same spot rates. These changes are reflected as foreign currency transaction gains and losses which net out to zero.

2. The premium on forward contract is fixed in terms of US dollars. This amount is amortized to a financial revenue account over the life of the forward contract on a straight-line basis.

3. The net effect of this transaction is that $5,050 was received on January 31, 2001, for a sale originally recorded at $5,000. The $50 difference was taken into income via amortization. SFAS 52 does not require a forward exchange contract for a hedge to take place.

For example, it is possible for a foreign currency transaction to act as an economic hedge against a parent's net investment in a foreign entity if

1. The transaction is designated as a hedge.
2. It is effective as a hedge.

To illustrate, assume that a US parent has a wholly owned British subsidiary which has net assets of £2 million. The US parent can borrow £2 million to hedge its net investment in the British subsidiary. Assume further that the British pound is the functional currency and that the £2 million liability is denominated in pounds. Fluctuations in the exchange rate for pounds will have no net effect on the parent company's consolidated balance sheet because increases (decreases) in the translation adjustments balance due to the translation of the net investment will be offset by decreases (increases) in this balance due to the adjustment of the liability denominated in pounds.

APPENDIX B

ADDITIONAL GUIDANCE FROM US GAAP

Application of the Remeasurement Method

In the example presented in the earlier part of this chapter, the DM was the functional currency because the German subsidiary's cash flows were primarily in DM. Assume, however, that the financing of the land and building was in US dollars instead of DM and that the mortgage payable is denominated in US dollars (i.e., must be paid in US dollars). Although the rents collected and the majority of the cash flows for expenses are in DM, management has decided that, due to the manner of financing, the US dollar is the functional currency. The books and records, however, are maintained in DM. The translation of the German financial statements is accomplished by use of the remeasurement method (also known as the monetary/nonmonetary method). This method is illustrated below using the same information that was presented before for the German subsidiary.

German Company
Balance Sheet Translation (Remeasurement Method)
(US dollar is the functional currency)

Assets	*DM*		*Exchange rates*	*US dollars*
Cash	DM	50	0.45	$ 22.50
Note receivable		20	0.45	9.00
Land		100	0.40	40.00
Building (net)		490	0.40	196.00
Total assets	DM	660		$267.50
Liabilities and stockholders' equity				
Accounts payable	DM	30	0.45	$ 13.50
Unearned rent		10	0.42	4.20
Mortgage payable		400	0.45	180.00
Common stock		40	0.40	16.00
Additional paid-in capital		160	0.40	64.00
Retained earnings		20	(see income statement)	(10.20)
Total liabilities and stockholders' equity	DM	660		$267.50

German Company
Combined Income and Retained Earnings Statement Translation
(Remeasurement Method)
(US dollar is the functional currency)
For the Year Ended December 31, 2000

	DM	*Exchange rates*	*US dollars*
Revenues	DM 200	0.43	$ 86.00
Expenses (excluding depreciation)	(160)	0.43	(68.80)
Depreciation expense	(10)	0.40	(4.00)
Translation loss	--	(see analysis below)	(19.20)
Net income (loss)	DM 30	--	$ (6.00)
Retained earnings, January 1	--	--	--
Dividends paid	(10)	0.42	(4.20)
Retained earnings, December 31	DM 20		$(10.20)

German Company
Translation (Remeasurement Method) Loss
For the Year Ended December 31, 2000

	DM		*Exchange rate*	*US dollars*	
	Debit	*Credit*		*Debit*	*Credit*
Cash	DM 50		0.45	$22.50	
Note receivable	20		0.45	9.00	
Land	100		0.40	40.00	
Building (net)	490		0.40	196.00	
Accounts payable		DM 30	0.45		$ 13.50
Unearned rent		10	0.42		4.20
Mortgage payable		400	0.45		180.00
Common stock		40	0.40		16.00
Additional paid-in capital		160	0.40		64.00
Retained earnings		--	--		--
Dividends declared	10		0.42	4.20	
Revenues		200	0.43		86.00
Operating expenses	160		0.43	68.80	
Depreciation expenses	10		0.40	4.00	
Totals	DM 840	DM 840		$344.50	$363.70
Loss from remeasurement				19.20	
Totals				$363.70	$363.70

The following observations should be noted about the remeasurement method:

1. Assets and liabilities that have historical cost balances (nonmonetary assets and liabilities) are translated by using historical exchange rates (i.e., the rates in effect when the transactions occurred). Monetary assets and monetary liabilities, on the other hand, are translated by using the current exchange rate at the balance sheet date.

2. Revenues and expenses that occur frequently during a period are translated, for practical purposes, by using the weighted-average exchange rate for the period. Revenues and expenses that represent allocations of historical balances (e.g., depreciation) are translated by using historical exchange rates.

Note that this is a different treatment as compared to the current rate method. Note also that in 2001, the unearned rent from 2000 of 10 DM would be translated at the rate of 1 DM = $0.42. The unearned rent at the end of 2000 is not considered a monetary liability. Therefore, the $0.42 historical exchange rate should be used for all applicable future years.

3. If the functional currency is the US dollar rather than the local foreign currency, the amounts of specific line items presented in the reconciliation of net income to net cash flow from operating activities will be different for nonmonetary items (e.g., depreciation). Note, however, that the net cash flow from operating activities will be the same in the reporting currency regardless of the applicable functional currency.

4. In a purely mechanical sense, calculation of the translation gain (loss) is the amount needed to make the dollar debits equal to the dollar credits in the German company's trial balance.

5. The translation loss of $19.20 is reported on the US company's consolidated income statement because the US dollar is the functional currency. When the reporting currency is the functional currency, as it is in this example, it is assumed that all of the foreign entity's transactions occurred in US dollars. Accordingly, translation gains and losses are taken immediately to the income statement in the year in which they occur as they can be expected to have direct cash flow effects. They are not deferred in a translation adjustments account as they were when the functional currency was the DM (current rate method).

6. The use of the equity method of accounting for the subsidiary would result in the following entries by the US company during 2000:

Original investment

Investment in German subsidiary	80	
Cash		80

Earnings (loss) pickup

Equity in subsidiary loss	6	
Investment in German subsidiary		6

Dividends received

Cash	4.20	
Investment in German subsidiary		4.20

Note that translation gains and losses are included in the subsidiary's net income (net loss) as determined in US dollars before the equity pickup is made by the US company.

7. In highly inflationary economies, those in which cumulative inflation is greater than 100% over a 3-year period, the functional currency is the reporting currency (i.e., the US dollar; SFAS 52, para 11). The remeasurement method must be used in this situation even though the factors indicate the local currency is the functional currency. The board made this decision

to prevent the evaporation of the foreign entity's fixed assets, a result that would occur if the local currency were the functional currency.

Summary of Current Rate and Remeasurement Methods

1. Before foreign currency financial statements can be translated into US dollars, management of the US entity must select the functional currency for the foreign entity whose financial statements will be incorporated into theirs by consolidation, combination, or the equity method. As the example illustrated, this decision is crucial because it may have a material effect on the financial statements of the US company.

2. If the functional currency is the local currency of the foreign entity, the current rate method is used to translate foreign currency financial statements into US dollars. All assets and liabilities are translated by using the current exchange rate at the balance sheet date. This method ensures that all financial relationships remain the same in both local currency and US dollars. Owners' equity is translated by using historical rates, while revenues (gains) and expenses (losses) are translated at the rates in existence during the period when the transactions occurred. A weighted-average rate can be used for items occurring numerous times throughout the period. The translation adjustments (debit or credit) that result from the application of these rules are reported as a separate component in owners' equity of the US company's consolidated balance sheet (or parent-only balance sheet if consolidation was not deemed appropriate).

3. If the functional currency is the reporting currency (the US dollar), the foreign currency financial statements are remeasured into US dollars. All foreign currency balances are restated to US dollars using both historical and current exchange rates. Foreign currency balances that reflect prices from past transactions are translated by using historical rates, while foreign currency balances that reflect prices from current transactions are translated by using the current exchange rate. Translation gains/losses that result from the remeasurement process are reported on the US company's consolidated income statement.

A summary of the provisions of the US GAAP relating to foreign currency translation is presented below in tabular form.

Functional currency	Functional currency determinants	Translation method	Reporting
Local currency of foreign company*	a. Operations not integrated with parent's operations b. Buying and selling activities primarily in local currency c. Cash flows not immediately available for remittance to parent d. Financing denominated in local currency	Current rate (all assets/ liabilities translated use current exchange rate; revenues/ expenses use weighted-average rate; equity accounts use historical rates)	Translation adjustments are reported in equity section of the US company's consolidated balance sheet Analysis of changes in accumulated transaction adjustments disclosed via footnote or separate schedule
US dollar	a. Operations integrated with parent's operations b. Buying and selling activities primarily in the United States and/or US dollars c. Cash flows immediately available for remittance to parent d. Financing denominated in US dollars	Remeasurement (monetary assets/ liabilities use current exchange rate; historical cost balances use historical rates; revenues/expenses use weighted-average rates and historical rates, the latter for allocations such as depreciation expense)	Translation gain/loss is reported on the US company's consolidated income statement

*The functional currency could be a foreign currency other than the local currency. If this is the case, the foreign currency statements are first remeasured in the functional currency before the current rate method is applied.

23 RELATED-PARTY DISCLOSURES

PERSPECTIVE AND ISSUES

Transactions between enterprises that are considered "related parties" (as defined) are required to be adequately disclosed in financial statements of the reporting enterprise. Most accounting standard-setting bodies around the world, including the IASC, have made such financial statement disclosures compulsory. The rationale for mandating such disclosures stems from the possibility that enterprises which are related to each other, either by virtue of their ability to "control" or exercise "significant influence" (both as defined) usually have leverage in the determination or setting of prices to be charged for such related-party transactions. Thus, in order to ensure transparency in financial statement disclosures, a reporting enterprise is required to disclose the nature, type, and elements of the transactions with related parties.

International Accounting Standard (IAS) 24 addresses the related-party issue and prescribes extensive disclosures. This standard became effective for periods beginning on or after January 1, 1986. No substantive changes or revisions have been made to this standard since its initial adoption, except for the reformatting of the standard in 1994, which was undertaken by the IASC with the intention to bring all IAS in line with the presentation adopted for IAS from 1991 onwards.

Although IAS 24 categorically states that "related-party relationships are a normal feature of commerce and business," it nevertheless recognizes that a related-party relationship could have an effect on the financial position and operating results of the reporting enterprise, due to the possibility that transactions between **related** parties may not be effected at the same amounts as between **unrelated** parties and thus, requires that related-party transactions be disclosed by the reporting enterprise.

This standard has been operative for over a decade now, yet one notices that in certain countries, related-party transactions are still not being disclosed properly in financial statements prepared in accordance with IAS 24. This is probably due to the sensitive nature of such disclosures. Even though one does find footnotes to financial statements that are captioned "related-party transactions," it is fairly evident that the full gamut of disclosures as required by IAS 24 is often missing. For instance, there seems to be a great deal of resistance on the part of corporate entities (unless they are closely held) to report certain types of related-party transactions, such as loans to directors or key management personnel or to close members of their family. It appears that in certain countries, especially developing countries, where certain aggressive business tactics or extensive employment of family members are commonplace, disclosure of such related-party transactions in footnotes to the financial statements would be looked at askance by financial statement users. Thus, disclosure of related-party transactions is usually one of the contentious issues in statutory audits in such countries. Public accounting firms in such countries are usually faced with the dilemma of either qualifying their audit reports as a consequence of inadequate related-party disclosure (which could result in their termination by the audit client) or issuing a clean (unqualified) opinion based upon a liberal interpretation of the standard, which in other words means that they would be taking an aggressive stand on such a contentious issue. Now that IAS 1 (revised 1997) mandates full compliance with all IAS as a prerequisite to making a claim that financial reporting has been prepared under IAS, it would be rather difficult to adopt such a soft approach; therefore public accounting firms in such countries will face a tougher choice, at least in the case of some clients.

Related-party disclosures are prescribed by most accounting standards around the globe, including US GAAP and UK GAAP. The US GAAP counterpart of IAS 24 is SFAS 57, *Related-Party Disclosures*, which was issued in March 1982. On the other hand, the UK standard, FRS 8, *Related-Party Disclosures*, which is comparatively a recent promulgation on the subject, was issued in October 1995. There are some significant differences between both the US and UK standards with IAS 24; however, in general, these three standards could be considered similar to each other.

Sources of IAS
IAS 1 (revised 1997), 5, 8, 24, 27, 28, 30

DEFINITIONS OF TERMS

Close members of the family of an individual. For the purpose of IAS 24, close members of the family of an individual are defined as "those that may be expected to influence, or be influenced by, that person in their dealings with the enterprise."

Control. An enterprise is considered to have the ability to control another enterprise if either of the two conditions is met: (1) it owns, directly or indirectly, through subsidiaries, more than one-half of the voting power of the other enterprise; or (2) it owns a substantial interest in the voting power along with the power to direct, by statute or agreement, the financial and operating policies of the management of that other enterprise.

Key management personnel. For the purpose of IAS 24, key management personnel are defined as "those persons having authority and responsibility for planning, directing, and controlling the activities of the reporting enterprise, including directors and officers of companies and close members of the families of such individuals."

Related party. Entities are considered to be related parties when one of them has either the ability to control the other, or can exercise significant influence over the other in making financial and operating decisions.

Related-party transactions. Related-party transactions are dealings between related parties involving transfer of resources or obligations between them, regardless of whether a price is charged for the transactions.

Significant influence. For the purposes of this standard, an enterprise is considered to possess the ability to exercise significant influence over another enterprise if it participates in, as opposed to controls, the financial and operating policy decisions of that other enterprise.

CONCEPTS, RULES, AND EXAMPLES

The Need for Related-Party Disclosures

For strategic reasons, enterprises sometimes carry out certain aspects of their business activity through associates or subsidiaries. For example, in order to ensure guaranteed supply of raw materials, an enterprise may decide to purchase a major portion of its requirements (of raw materials) through a subsidiary, which could be accomplished by the popular vehicle of vertical integration. Another example of this phenomenon could be the following: an enterprise whose subsidiaries are in diverse businesses, which are quite dissimilar to the business of the parent, may decide to make a substantial trade investment in the business of its major supplier. In this way, it could control or exercise significant influence over the financial and operating decisions of its major supplier (the investee). Such related-party relationships and transactions are a normal feature of commerce and business. However, related-party relationships and transactions may not, in all cases, be entered into because of commercial propriety or expedience. Further, a related-party relationship could have an impact on the financial position and operating results of the reporting enterprise because of any of the following reasons:

1. Related parties may enter into certain transactions with each other which unrelated parties may not normally want to enter into.
2. Amounts charged for transactions between related parties may not be comparable to amounts charged for similar transactions between unrelated parties.

3. The mere existence of the relationship may sometimes be sufficient to affect the dealings of the reporting enterprise with other (unrelated) parties. (For instance, an enterprise may stop purchasing from its major supplier on acquiring a subsidiary which is a competitor of its [erstwhile] major supplier).

4. Transactions between enterprises would not have taken place if the related-party relationship had not existed. (This situation could be best explained through an illustration. For example, a company sells its entire output to an associate at cost. It would not have survived but for these related-party sales to the associate, since it does not have any takers for the kind of goods it deals in. In other words, the only reason it is still in business is because it is able to sell its total output to an associate that is committed to purchase its total production. Also, the reason it sells its product to the associate, at cost, is because, this way at least, it would break even and by doing so be able to recoup its costs, which is better than trying to sell small portions of its output to outsiders at a profit and ending up with significant unsold inventory.)

Because of peculiarities, such as the above, that distinguish related-party transactions from transactions with unrelated parties, accounting standards (including IAS) have almost universally mandated financial statement disclosure of such transactions. Disclosures of related-party transactions in financial statements, in a way, is a means of conveying a message to users of financial statements that certain related-party relationships exist as of the date of the financial statements, or certain transactions were consummated with related parties during the period which the financial statements cover, and the results of these related-party transactions have been incorporated in the financial statements being presented. Since related-party transactions could have an effect on the financial position and operating results of the reporting enterprise, disclosure of such transactions would be prudent based on the much-acclaimed principle of transparency (in financial statements). In this way, the users of financial statements could make informed decisions while using the information presented to them in the financial statements.

Scope of the Standard

IAS 24, *Related-Party Disclosures*, is to be applied in dealing with related parties and transactions between a reporting enterprise and its related parties. The requirements of this standard apply to the financial statements of each reporting enterprise.

Applicability

The requirements of the standard should be applied only to the related-party relationships described in IAS 24, paragraph 3, which are summarized below.

a. Enterprises that control (directly or indirectly through intermediaries) or are controlled by, or are under common control with the reporting enterprise. Examples: parent company, subsidiaries, and fellow subsidiaries;

b. Associates, as defined in IAS 28;

c. Individuals owning, directly or indirectly, an interest in the voting power of the reporting enterprise that gives them significant influence over the enterprise, and close members of the family of any such individual;

d. Key management personnel and close members of the families of such individuals; and

e. Enterprises in which a substantial interest in the voting power is owned, directly or indirectly, by any person described in c. or d. above, or over which such a person is able to exercise significant influence. This includes enterprises owned by

- Directors of the reporting enterprise;
- Major shareholders of the reporting enterprise; and
- Enterprises that have a member of key management in common with the reporting enterprise.

Substance Over Form

The standard clarifies that in applying the deeming provisions of IAS 24 to each possible related-party relationship, consideration should be given to the substance of the relationship and not merely the legal form.

Exclusions

IAS 24, paragraph 6, does not consider the following as being related parties for the purposes of the standard. In other words, the standard specifically excludes the following:

a. Two companies having only a common director, notwithstanding the specific requirements of IAS 24, paragraphs 3(d) and 3(e) summarized above. However, if the common director is in fact able to affect the policies of both companies in their mutual dealing, then such a possibility has to be evaluated on its own merits;

b. Certain agencies, entities or departments which have a major role to play in the enterprises day-to-day business. For example

- Providers of finance (banks and creditors)
- Trade unions
- Public utilities
- Government departments and agencies

e. Entities upon which the enterprise may be economically dependent, due to the volume of business the enterprise transacts with them. For example:

- A single customer;
- A major supplier;
- A franchisor;
- A distributor; or
- A general agent.

Exemptions

IAS 24, paragraph 4, exempts disclosure of related-party transactions in the following cases:

1. In consolidated financial statements, in respect of intragroup transactions;
2. In parent company's financial statements, when they are published or made available, say, by being attached to the consolidated financial statements;
3. In financial statements of wholly owned subsidiary, if its parent, which is incorporated in the same country, provides consolidated financial statements in that country; and
4. In financial statements of state-controlled enterprises, with respect to transactions with other state-controlled enterprises.

The standard does not require that any indication be given in the financial statements that transactions occurred that fell within these exemptions.

Significant Influence

The existence of the ability to exercise significant influence is an important concept in relation to this standard. It is one of the two criteria mentioned in the definition of a related party, which when present would, for the purposes of this standard, make one party related to another. In other words, for the purposes of this standard, if one party is considered to have the ability to exercise significant influence over another, then by virtue of this requirement of the standard, the two parties are considered to be related.

The existence of the ability to exercise significant influence may be evidenced in one or more of the following ways:

- By representation on the board of directors of the other enterprise;
- By participation in the policy-making process of the other enterprise;
- By having material intercompany transactions between two enterprises;
- By interchange of managerial personnel between two enterprises; or
- By dependence on another enterprise for technical information.

Significant influence may be gained through agreement or statute or share ownership. Under the provisions of IAS 24, similar to the presumption of significant influence under IAS 28, *Accounting for Investments in Associates*, an enterprise is deemed to possess the ability to exercise significant influence if it directly or indirectly, through subsidiaries, holds 20% or more of the voting power of another enterprise (unless it can be clearly demonstrated that despite holding such voting power the investor does not have the ability to exercise significant influence over the investee). Conversely, if an enterprise, directly or indirectly through subsidiaries, owns less than 20% of the voting power of another enterprise it is presumed that the investor does not possess the ability to exercise significant influence (unless it can be clearly demonstrated that the investor does have such an ability despite holding less than 20% of the voting power). Further, while explaining the concept of significant influence, IAS 28 also clarifies that "a substantial or majority ownership by **another investor** does not necessarily preclude an investor from having significant influence" (emphasis added).

In the authors' opinion, by defining the term "related party" to include the concepts of control and significant influence, and by further broadening the definition to cover not just direct related-party relationships, but even indirect ones like those with "close members of the family of an individual," the IASC has cast a wide net to cover related-party transactions which would normally not be considered otherwise. This makes disclosures under this standard subjective, and the related-party issue itself a more contentious one, since it lends itself to aggressive interpretations by the reporting enterprise. This obviously could have a significant bearing on the related-party disclosures emanating from these interpretations. On the one hand, based on a strict interpretation of the provisions of the standard, certain hitherto unreported related-party transactions may now have to be disclosed, but on the other hand reporting enterprises may not do so, based on an aggressive stand taken by them. However, in taking such an aggressive stand, the reporting enterprises are well advised to get ready with good strong reasoning to support any nondisclosure of related-party transactions, lest they cross the thin line of not fully complying with IAS under the revised IAS 1 (revised 1997), which may have serious repercussions in terms of financial statement reporting under IAS.

Methods of Pricing Related-Party Transactions

The transfer of resources between business entities is given accounting recognition based on the prices charged for transactions between them. Normally, prices charged in unrelated-party transactions are arm's-length prices. However, a related party may have some degree of flexibility in setting prices for related-party transactions by virtue of either the existence of control or the ability to exercise significant influence over the other party.

Pricing of transactions between related parties can be accomplished in a variety of ways. The following methods are some of the ways that related-party transactions may be priced:

1. Comparable uncontrolled price method

    When merchandise supplied in a related-party transaction and the conditions relating thereto are similar to normal trading conditions, this method is used. Under this method, prices are set by reference to similar (comparable) goods sold in economically similar (comparable) market to a buyer unrelated to the seller.

2.   Resale price method

When the sale of the merchandise is routed through a related party, or, the goods are first transferred to a related party before their actual sale to an independent third party, this method is often used. Under the resale price method, the "resale price" to be charged by the ultimate seller, in this case the intermediary related party, is reduced by a margin in order to arrive at a transfer price to be charged to the intermediary related party, the reseller. The margin, represents an amount from which the reseller would seek to cover his costs and make an appropriate profit.

3.   Cost-plus method

When the parties intend to add a certain markup to the cost of the merchandise, this method is used. Under this method, a certain percentage is added as a markup to the supplier's cost. The percentage of markup is normally based on comparable returns in similar businesses or industries based on either capital employed or turnover.

Besides the foregoing three pricing methods, the standard also recognizes these two special situations

- Where "no price" is charged between related parties; for instance, in the case of sharing of common services (e.g., secretarial services at the group corporate headquarters) by related companies free of cost, or free provision of management services to certain companies in the group, or the extension of free credit to an associate resulting in intercorporate debt at no interest; and
- Where transactions are priced at cost; otherwise transactions would not have taken place if such a related-party relationship would not have existed.

To illustrate this, let us consider the following example of a vertical integration:

Subsidiary A sells most of its production to fellow Subsidiary B, at cost, because Subsidiary A was specially established by the parent company in order to ensure the timely supply of raw materials to Subsidiary B, which has traditionally experienced stoppages in work due to erratic supply of essential raw materials. Thus, a major portion of the production of Subsidiary A is sold to Subsidiary B. Also, the product that Subsidiary A produces has no demand in the market it operates in, thus it sells most of its production to its fellow subsidiary at cost (since it would be unable to break even otherwise).

Financial Statement Disclosures

IAS 24 recognizes that in many countries certain related-party disclosures are prescribed by law. Particularly, transactions with directors, because of the fiduciary nature of their relationship with the enterprise, are mandated financial statement disclosures in those countries. In fact, the corporate legislations in some countries go a step further and require certain disclosures which are even more stringent than the disclosure requirements under IAS 24, or for that matter, disclosure requirements under most leading accounting standards.

For example, under the Companies Act of a certain country, besides the usual disclosures pertaining to related-party transactions, under the corporate law, companies are required to disclose not just year-end balances that are due to or due from directors or certain other related parties, but are required to disclose even the highest balances for the period (for which financial statements are presented) which were due to or due from them to the corporate entity. In the authors' opinion, the IASC might consider specifically adding such a requirement to the current list of disclosures under IAS 24, since the present requirement to disclose only outstanding balances with related parties as of the balance sheet date lends itself to manipulations by the reporting enterprises.

For example, an enterprise which has advanced large sums of money to its directors could make arrangements with the directors to get them to repay the loans to the enterprise a few days before the last day of the reporting period, and agree to loan back to those directors these amounts right after first day of the next reporting period. Under the present disclosure requirements in IAS 24 (discussed below), it does not appear that such amounts of loans to directors (despite being material) would need to be disclosed, since none of them were actually outstanding at the end of the reporting period. However, if the requirements of IAS 24 were extended to include disclosure of not just outstanding balances at the end of the reporting period, but also the highest balance(s) due to or due from related parties during the period for which the financial statements are presented, then such manipulations, like the above-mentioned artifice, would be caught under such broad disclosure requirements.

In the authors' further opinion, such additional disclosures appear to be within the spirit of the standard and would go a long way in improving or rather enhancing transparency in financial reporting. It should be noted that under IAS 30, paragraph 58(a), banks and similar financial institutions are specifically required to make this additional disclosure (for a detailed discussion of disclosures of related-party transactions in the case of banks and similar financial institutions, please refer to the relevant chapter of this book).

IAS 24, paragraph 19, provides examples of situations where related-party transactions may lead to disclosures by a reporting enterprise in the period that they affect.

- Purchases or sales of goods (finished or unfinished, meaning work in progress)
- Purchases or sales of property and other assets
- Rendering or receiving of services
- Agency arrangements
- Leasing arrangement
- Transfer of research and development
- License agreements
- Finance (including loans and equity participation in cash or in kind)
- Guarantees and collaterals
- Management contracts

The foregoing should not be considered an exhaustive list of situations requiring disclosure, and as very clearly stated in the standard, these are only "examples of situations . . . which may lead to disclosures." In practice, many other situations are encountered which would warrant disclosure. For example, a maintenance contract for maintaining and servicing computers, entered into with a subsidiary company, would need to be disclosed by the reporting enterprise.

IAS 24, paragraphs 20 and 21, require disclosure of a related-party relationship where control exists, irrespective of whether there have been transactions between the related parties. In the authors' opinion, it is worth noting that an important aspect of this requirement which may not be very obvious to the reader is that disclosure is only necessary under this requirement of the standard in the case of a related-party relationship that arises only through control. Thus, by inference, one would conclude that in the case of a related-party relationship by virtue of significant influence, there is no need to disclose a related-party relationship under this requirement of the standard, unless there have been actual transactions based on this relationship.

To illustrate this point, let us consider the following example:

Company A owns 25% of Company B, and by virtue of share ownership of more than 20% of the voting power, would be considered to possess the ability to exercise significant influence over Company B. During the year, Company A entered into an agency agreement with Company B; however, no transactions took place during the year between the two companies based on the agency contract. Since Company A is considered a related party to Company B by virtue of the ability to exercise significant influence, no disclosure of this related-party relationship would be needed under IAS 24, paragraphs 20 and 21. In case, however, Company A owned 51% or more of the voting power of Company B and thereby would be considered related to Company B on the basis of control instead, disclosure of this relationship would be needed, irrespective of whether any transactions actually took place between them.

Per IAS 24, paragraph 22, if there have been transactions between related parties, the reporting enterprise should disclose

- The nature of the related-party transaction
- The type of transactions
- The elements of the transactions necessary for an understanding of the financial statements

The elements necessary for an understanding of the financial statements, as per IAS 24, paragraph 23, would normally include

- An indication of the volume of the transactions, either as an amount or an appropriate proportion
- Amounts or appropriate proportions of outstanding items
- Pricing policies

Thus, for example, when an enterprise purchases raw materials amounting to $5 million from an associated company, and these purchases account for 75% of its total purchases for the year, the following disclosures under the above requirement would seem appropriate:

> During the year, purchases amounting to $5 million (alternative wording: 75% of purchases for the year) were made from an associated company. These purchases were made at normal commercial terms. At December 31, 1999, the balance remaining outstanding from this associated company amounted to $ 2.3 million.

IAS 24, paragraph 24, requires that items of a similar nature may be disclosed in aggregate. However, when separate disclosure is necessary for an understanding of the effects of the related-party transactions on the financial statements of the reporting enterprise, aggregation is not proper.

A good example of an aggregated disclosure is total sales made during the year to a number of associated companies, instead of separately disclosing sales made to each associated company. Further, an example of a separate disclosure (as opposed to aggregated disclosure) is the disclosure of year-end balances from various related parties disclosed separately by category (e.g., directors, associated companies, etc.) In the latter case, it makes sense to disclose separately by categories of related parties, instead of aggregating all balances from various related parties together and disclosing, say, the total amount due from all related parties as one amount. In fact, separate disclosure in this case seems necessary for an understanding of the effects of related-party transactions on the financial statements of the reporting enterprise.

IAS 24, paragraph 24, reiterates one of the exemptions from disclosure mandated earlier in the standard, (i.e., in paragraph 4[a]). which was discussed earlier in this chapter. Per IAS 24, paragraph 24, disclosure of transactions between members of a group is unnecessary in consolidated financial statements, since the consolidated financial statements present information about the parent and subsidiaries as a single reporting enterprise. However, in the case of associated companies, since they are not presented as a single reporting enterprise, and intracompany transactions are not eliminated (due to use of the equity method of accounting), separate disclosure of related-party transactions is warranted.

IAS 24, paragraph 18, specifically mentions other IAS, wherein disclosures of related-party transactions have been prescribed as well. The following IAS have been cited by IAS 24:

- IAS 5, which calls for disclosure of significant intercompany transactions and investments in, and balances with, group and associated companies

    NOTE: This standard has been repealed and replaced by IAS 1 (revised 1997) which contains similar disclosure requirements in paragraphs 72 and 73 of the standard.

- IAS 27, which requires disclosure of a list of significant subsidiaries
- IAS 28, which requires disclosure of a list of significant associates
- IAS 8, which requires disclosure of extraordinary items and exceptional items (i.e., those that are of such size, nature, or incidence that their disclosure is relevant to explain the performance of the enterprise) that arise in transactions with related parties

24 SPECIALIZED INDUSTRY ACCOUNTING

BANKS AND SIMILAR FINANCIAL INSTITUTIONS

PERSPECTIVE AND ISSUES

Disclosure requirements relating to financial statements of banks and similar financial institutions are contained in IAS 30. A broad definition of the term "bank" has been given by IAS 30 and covers all those enterprises (whether the word bank is included in their name or not)

1. Which are financial institutions
2. Whose principal activities are to accept deposits and borrow money with the intention of lending and investing
3. Which are within the scope of banking and similar legislations

Since banks' operations differ in many material respects from other commercial enterprises and liquidity and solvency is of paramount importance, their financial reporting inevitably will be somewhat specialized in nature. In recognition of their special needs, IAS 30 lays down a number of disclosure requirements. Some of these disclosures may seem unusual from the standpoint of other commercial enterprises and may be perceived by users of the banks' financial statements as excessive or superfluous; however, these disclosures have been made mandatory for banks, keeping in view the special characteristics of banks' operations and the role they play in maintaining public confidence in the monetary system of the country through their close relationship with regulatory authorities (such as the country's central bank) and the government. Further, a bank is exposed not only to liquidity risks but even risks arising from currency fluctuations, interest rate movements, changes in market prices, and counterparty failure. These risks are associated not only with assets and liabilities, which are recognized on a bank's balance sheet, but also with off-balance-sheet items. Thus, certain disclosure requirements as outlined by IAS 30 relate to off-balance-sheet items as well.

It is a well-known fact that, compared to the other international accounting standards, IAS 30 took an inordinate amount of time before issuance in its final form. Although the standard became operative for financial statements of banks covering periods beginning on or after January 1, 1991, after having finally been approved in 1990, it is worth noting that the due process was, in fact, initiated by the IASC through the publication of a discussion paper in 1980. This was followed by two exposure drafts: E29 and E34. It should be noted, however, that even though the promulgation of IAS 30 spanned a number of years, it encompassed numerous deliberations and consultations with regulatory authorities and users of banks' financial statements. Also, representatives of bankers from around the world (including the United States and Europe) were consulted extensively. Thus, it is not surprising that this standard has such extensive disclosure requirements.

Although IAS 30 applies exclusively to financial statements of banks and similar financial institutions, it should be borne in mind that disclosure requirements according to other international accounting standards, such as IAS 24, *Related-Party Disclosures*, IAS 16, *Property, Plant, and Equipment*, and so on, also need to be considered while preparing a bank's financial statements. Further, IAS 7, *Cash Flow Statements*, stipulates special provisions that are applicable to financial institutions, and the appendix to IAS 7 illustrates the "direct method" for the preparation of cash flow statements by financial institutions.

Sources of IAS
IAS 1 (revised), 7, 10, 16, 18, 24, 25, 30, 37

CONCEPTS, RULES, AND EXAMPLES

Accounting Policies

International Accounting Standard (IAS) 1, which applies to financial statements of all commercial, industrial, and business enterprises in general (which includes banks and similar financial institutions as well), requires that disclosure be made of all significant accounting policies that were adopted in the preparation and presentation of an entity's financial statements. To comply with the standard above and also since different banks use diverse methods for recognition and measurement of items on their financial statements, disclosure of accounting policies relating to certain important items has been prescribed by IAS 30. This will enable users of the bank's financial statements to better understand the basis of preparation of those financial statements. Specifically, disclosure of the following accounting policies is prescribed by the standard:

1. The accounting policy setting forth the recognition of the principal types of income. An example of this disclosure follows:

   a. "Interest income and loan commitment fees are recognized on a time proportion basis* taking into account the principal outstanding and the rate applicable. Other fee income is recognized when due."

   b. "Accrual of interest ceases on loans placed in the non accrual status if in the opinion of the management the loans are unlikely to be repaid as per the terms of agreement or when the principal or interest is past due 90 days or more."**

      * *IAS 18 specifically requires that interest income be recognized on a time proportion basis.*
      ** *In some countries this is referred to as "interest in suspense" or "reserved interest."*

2. Accounting policies relating to the valuation of investments and dealing securities. An illustration follows:

   Note 1: Valuation of Investments. Long-term investments are stated at cost with provision being made for any decline other than temporary in value. Trading investments are stated at the lower of cost or market, the carrying amount being determined on an aggregate portfolio basis.

3. Accounting policy explaining the distinction between transactions and events that result in the recognition of assets and liabilities on the balance sheet vs. those that give rise to contingencies and commitments, including off-balance-sheet items. An example follows:

   Note 1: Contingent Obligations. Loans and advances to customers result from and include facilities granted to customers and are utilized before year end; however, undrawn facilities, such as lines of credit, extended to customers, that are irrevocable according to agreements with customers (and cannot be withdrawn at the discretion of the bank), are disclosed as commitments.

4. Accounting policy that outlines the basis for the determination of

   a. The provision for possible losses on loans and advances
   b. Write-off of uncollectable loans and advances

   > **Note 1: Provision for Loan Losses.** Provision is made for possible losses in relation to loans and advances to customers that have been individually reviewed and specifically identified as doubtful and is referred to as specific provision. A general provision based on experience is also made based on the risks that are likely to be present in any portfolio of bank advances that have not yet been identified specifically. Loans and advances on which all legal and other possible courses of action for recovery have been exhausted are written off as bad debts.

5. Accounting policy explaining the basis for determining and setting aside amounts toward general banking risks and the accounting treatment accorded to this reserve.

   Regulatory bodies, such as the central bank of the country in which the bank is incorporated or the local legislation, may require or allow a bank to set aside amounts for general banking risks, including future losses or other unforeseeable risks or even reserves for contingencies over and above accruals required by IAS 37, *Provisions, Contingent Liabilities, and Contingent Assets,* which is effective from mid-1999, or by IAS 10 for earlier periods. It would not be proper to allow banks to charge these additional reserves to the income statement, as this would distort the true financial position of the bank. Thus, IAS 30 requires that the above mentioned reserves be appropriated out of the retained earnings and be separately disclosed as such. An example is

   > **Note 1: Statutory Reserves.** In accordance with the bank's articles of association, 10% of the net income for the year is to be set aside as a contingency reserve each year. Such appropriations of net income are to continue until the balance in the contingency reserve equals 50% of the bank's issued capital.

Preparation and Presentation of Banks' Financial Statements

The following ground rules have been established by IAS 30 for the preparation and presentation of the financial statements of banks:

1. The income statement of a bank should be presented in a manner that groups income and expenses by nature and discloses the amounts of the principal types of income and expenses. This principle has been further elucidated by the standard as follows:

a. Disclosures in the income statement or in the footnotes should include, but are not limited to, the following items:

   (1) Interest and similar income
   (2) Interest expense and similar charges
   (3) Dividend income
   (4) Fee and commission income
   (5) Fee and commission expense
   (6) Gains less losses arising from dealing securities
   (7) Gains less losses arising from investment securities
   (8) Gains less losses arising from dealing in foreign currencies
   (9) Other operating income
  (10) Losses on loans and advances
  (11) General and administrative expenses
  (12) Other operating expenses

These disclosures, to be incorporated into the bank's income statement, are of course in addition to disclosure requirements of other international accounting standards.

b. Separate disclosure of the principal types of income and expenses as above is essential in order that users of the bank's financial statements can assess the performance of the bank.

c. To enhance financial statement transparency, IAS 30 prohibits the offsetting of income and expense items, except those relating to hedges and to assets or liabilities wherein the legal right of setoff exists and the offsetting represents the expectation as to the realization or settlement of the asset or liability. In case income and expense items were allowed to be offset, it would prevent users from assessing the return on particular classes of assets; this, in a way, would restrict users of financial statements in their assessment of the performance of the bank.

d. The following income statement items are, however, allowed to be presented on a net basis:

   (1) Gains or losses from dealings in foreign currencies
   (2) Gains or losses from disposals of investment securities
   (3) Gains or losses from disposals and changes in the carrying amount of dealing securities

Example of bank financial reporting

ABC Banking Corporation
Statement of Income
For the Years Ended December 31, 2000 and 1999

	2000	*1999*
Income from banking activities:		
Interest income	$400,000	$380,000
Fees and commissions	50,000	40,000
Net gain from disposal of investment securities	20,000	13,000
Net income from dealing securities	2,000	2,000
Net gain from dealings in foreign currencies	14,000	10,000
Dividend income	1,000	2,000
Other operating income	7,000	6,000
	$494,000	$453,000
Expenses relating to banking activities:		
Interest expense	$205,000	$200,000
Provision for losses on loans and advances	70,000	50,000
Provision for diminution in value of investments	1,000	1,000
	$276,000	$251,000
Net income from banking activities	$218,000	$202,000
Other income	9,000	8,000
	$227,000	$210,000
General and administration expenses	$ 80,000	$ 75,000
Depreciation on fixed assets	11,000	10,000
Provision for taxation	6,000	6,000
Net income for the year	$130,000	$119,000

2. The balance sheet of a bank should group assets and liabilities by nature and list them in the order of their respective liquidity. This is explained further by the standard as follows:

    a. Disclosure of the grouping of assets and liabilities by their nature and listing them by their respective liquidity is illustrated by the standard. These are to be made either on the face of the balance sheet or in the footnotes. The following disclosures are prescribed with a proviso that disclosures should include but are not limited to:

Assets	*Liabilities*
Cash and balances with the central bank	Deposits from other banks
	Other money market deposits
Treasury bills and other bills eligible for rediscounting with the central bank	Amounts owed to other depositors
	Certificates of deposits
Government and other securities held for dealing purposes	Promissory notes and other liabilities evidenced by paper
Placements with, and loans and advances to, other banks	Other borrowed funds
Other money market placements	
Loans and advances to customers	
Investment securities	

These disclosures, to be incorporated into the bank's income statement, are of course in addition to disclosure requirements of other international accounting standards.

b. Grouping the assets and liabilities by nature does not pose a problem and, in fact, is probably the most logical way of combining financial statement items for presentation on the bank's balance sheet. For instance, deposits with other banks and loans/advances to other banks are combined and presented as a separate line item on the asset side of a bank's balance sheet and referred to as placements with other banks. These items would, however, be presented differently on financial statements of other commercial enterprises since deposits with banks in those instances would be combined with other cash and bank balances, and loans to banks would probably be classified as investments. On the other hand, balances with other banks are not combined with balances with other parts of the money market, even though by nature they are placements with other financial institutions, since this gives a better understanding of the bank's relations with and dependency on other banks vs. other constituents of the money market.

c. Listing of assets by liquidity could be considered synonymous with listing of liabilities by maturity, since maturity is a measure of liquidity in case of liabilities. For instance, certificates of deposits are liabilities of banks and have contractual maturities of perhaps, 1 month, 3 months, 6 months, and 1 year. Similarly, there are other bank liabilities, such as promissory notes, that may not be due, perhaps, for another 3 years from the balance sheet date. Thus, a relative maturity analysis would suggest that the certificates of deposit be listed on the bank's balance sheet before or above the promissory notes since they would mature earlier. Similarly, assets of a bank could be analyzed based on their relative liquidity, and those assets that are more liquid than others (i.e., will convert into cash faster than others) should be listed on the balance sheet above the others. Thus, cash balances and balances with the central bank are usually listed above other assets on the balance sheets of all banks, being relatively more liquid than other assets.

d   Offsetting of assets against liabilities, or vice versa, is generally not allowed unless a legal right of setoff exists and the offsetting represents the expectation as to the realization or settlement of the asset or liability. This is true even in the case of other enterprises; IAS 1 (revised 1997), which applies to all enterprises reporting in accordance with IAS, including banks, contains similar provisions.

e. IAS 25 provides that enterprises that do not distinguish between current and long-term investments in their balance sheets nevertheless make a distinction for measurement purposes and determine the carrying amount for investments in accordance with the provisions of IAS 25 (which prescribes different treatments for the determination of the carrying values of short-term investments vis-à-vis long-term investments).

IAS 30 specifically requires that a bank disclose the market value of investments in dealing securities and marketable investment securities if these values are different from the carrying amounts in the financial statements. It is important to note that investments in dealing securities are considered as short-term investments, since they are acquired and held with the intention of reselling. On the other hand, even though they are marketable, marketable investment securities are considered long-term investments since they are acquired and held for yield or capital growth purposes and are usually held to maturity (this is required not only by IAS 25 but even by IAS 30).

Example

ABC Banking Corporation
Balance Sheet
As at December 31, 2000 and 1999

	2000	*1999*
Assets		
Cash and balances with central bank	$ 480,000	$ 370,000
Trading investments	364,000	26,000
Funds under management	40,000	28,000
Deposits with banks	3,685,000	2,990,000
Loans and advances, net	8,286,000	6,786,000
Long-term investments	358,000	283,000
Property and equipment, net	90,000	89,000
Other assets	55,000	44,000
Total assets	$13,358,000	$10,616,000
Liabilities and Shareholders' Equity		
Liabilities:		
Due to banks	$ 2,187,000	$ 998,000
Customer deposits	8,040,000	6,536,000
Long-term loan from government	1,300,000	1,380,000
Other liabilities	108,000	96,000
Total liabilities	$11,635,000	$ 8,930,000
Shareholders' Equity:		
Share capital	$ 1,250,000	$ 1,250,000
Statutory reserve	73,000	60,000
Contingency reserve	29,000	12,000
General reserve	325,000	325,000
Retained earnings	46,000	39,000
Total shareholders' equity	$ 1,723,000	$ 1,686,000
Total liabilities and shareholders' equity	$13,358,000	$10,616,000
Commitments and contingent liabilities	$15,300,000	$12,100,000

Cash Flow Statement for a Financial Institution (Including a Bank)

Cash flow statements are an integral part of financial statements. Every enterprise is required to present a cash flow statement in accordance with the provisions of IAS 7 for financial statements covering periods beginning on or after January 1, 1994.

Although the general requirements of IAS 7 are common to all enterprises, the standard does contain special provisions that are applicable only to financial institutions. These specific provisions deal with reporting of certain cash flows on a "net basis." The following cash flows are to be reported on a net basis:

1. Cash receipts and payments on behalf of customers when the cash flows reflect the activities of the customer rather than those of the enterprise; the standard refers to "the accepting and repayment of demand deposits of a bank"
2. Cash receipts and payments for the acceptance and repayment of deposits with a fixed maturity date
3. The placement of deposits with and withdrawal of deposits from other financial institutions
4. Cash advances and loans made to customers and the repayment of those advances and loans

The appendix to IAS 7 (see the discussion below) illustrates the application of the standard to financial institutions preparing cash flow statements under the direct method (for a more detailed discussion of cash flow statements, see Chapter 4).

Example of cash flow statement for banks

Neighborhood Bank
Statement of Cash Flows
For the Year Ended December 31, 2000

Cash flows from operating activities:

Interest and commission receipts	$28,447
Interest payments	(23,463)
Recoveries on loans previously written off	237
Cash payments to employees and suppliers	(997)
Operating profit before changes in operating assets	4,224

(Increase) decrease in operating assets:

Short-term funds	(650)
Deposits held for regulatory or monetary control purposes	234
Funds advanced to customers	(288)
Net increase in credit card receivables	(360)
Other short-term negotiable securities	(120)

Increase (decrease) in operating liabilities:

Deposits from customers	600	
Negotiable certificates of deposit	(200)	
Net cash from operating activities before income tax	3,440	
Income taxes paid	(100)	
Net cash from operating activities		$3,340

Cash flows from investing activities:

Disposal of subsidiary Y	50	
Dividends received	200	
Interest received	300	
Proceeds from sales of nondealing securities	1,200	
Purchase of nondealing securities	(600)	
Purchase of property, plant, and equipment	(500)	
Net cash from investing activities		650

Cash flows from financing activities:

Issue of loan capital	1,000	
Issue of preference shares by subsidiary undertaking	800	
Repayment of long-term borrowings	(200)	
Net decrease in other borrowings	(1,000)	
Dividends paid	(400)	
Net cash from financing activities		200
Effects of exchange rate changes on cash and cash equivalents		600
Net increase in cash and cash equivalents		4,790
Cash and cash equivalents at beginning of period		4,050
Cash and cash equivalents at end of period		$8,840

Disclosure Requirements for Banks and Similar Institutions

Contingencies and commitments including off-balance-sheet items. Contingencies represent conditions or situations, the ultimate outcome of which will be determined by future events which themselves may or may not occur. Accounting for and disclosure of provisions and contingencies has been addressed by IAS 37 (effective from mid-1999) and earlier, by IAS 10. Liabilities of life insurance companies arising from insurance policies issued by them and other entities, such as retirement benefit plans, have been specifically excluded from the scope of both IAS 10 and IAS 37. However, contingencies and events occurring after the balance sheet date relating to the banking industry are required to be disclosed in accordance with the provisions of this standard since it has not specifically been excluded from the purview of the standard. This is further reinforced by IAS 30, which makes it mandatory for banks to disclose certain contingencies and commitments dealt with by IAS 10. The disclosures required in this regard are the following:

1. The nature and amount of commitments to extend credit that are irrevocable because they cannot be withdrawn at the discretion of the bank without incurring significant penalty or expenses

2. The nature and amount of contingencies and commitments arising from off-balance-sheet items, including those relating to

   a. Direct credit substitutes, which include general guarantees of indebtedness, bank acceptances, and standby letters of credit, which serve as financial backup for loans and securities

b. Transaction-related contingencies, which include performance bonds, bid bonds, warranties, and standby letters of credit related to particular transactions

c. Trade-related contingencies, which are self-liquidating and short-term trade-related contingencies arising from the movement of goods, such as documentary credit wherein the underlying goods are used as security for the bank credit; sometimes referred to as trust receipts, or simply as TR

d. Sales and repurchase agreements that are not reflected or recognized on the bank's balance sheet

e. Interest and foreign exchange rate related items, which include items such as options, futures, and swaps

f. Other commitments, including other off-balance-sheet items such as revolving underwriting facilities and note issuance facilities

It is important for the users of the bank's financial statements to be cognizant about the contingencies and irrevocable commitments because these may have an effect in the future on the liquidity and solvency of the bank. For instance, undrawn facilities, to which the bank is irrevocably committed, could serve as a good example of what could happen to a bank's liquidity position if a majority of the customers utilize them at the same time, for example, when there is a sudden shortage of funds in the market, due to economic reasons or otherwise. Thus, disclosing such irrevocable commitments and contingencies, in the footnotes or elsewhere, is of paramount importance to the user of the bank's financial statements.

Also, off-balance-sheet items, such as letters of credit (LC), guarantees, acceptances, and so on, constitute an important part of the bank's business and thus should be disclosed in the financial statements, since without knowing about the magnitude of such items, a fair evaluation of the bank's financial position is not possible (mostly because it adds significantly to the level of business risk the bank is exposed to at any given point of time).

Certain items which are typically not included in the balance sheet are commonly referred to as memoranda accounts, and less frequently are called contra items. These are often interrelated items which are both contingent assets and contingent liabilities, such as bills held for collection for customers, which if and when collected will in turn be remitted to the customer and not retained by the bank. The logic is that since the asset and liability both have contingent aspects, and since the bank is effectively only acting as an agent on behalf of a customer, it is valid to exclude both elements from the statement of financial condition. The existence of such items, however, generally must be disclosed even if not formally recognized.

Example of disclosure of contingencies and commitments

	2000	*1999*
At December 31, 2000 and 1999, the contingent liabilities and commitments were the following (in 000s of US dollars):		
Letters of credit	$10,000	$ 9,000
Guarantees	11,000	8,000
Acceptances	12,000	11,000
Forward foreign exchange commitments	13,000	12,000
Commitments under undrawn lines of credit	15,000	12,000
	$61,000	$52,000

Maturities of Assets and Liabilities

Information about maturities of assets and liabilities is the most important disclosures required of banks, since it gives users a concise picture of the bank's liquidity. Well managed banks typically exhibit closely aligned maturities of assets, such as loans and investments, and liabilities, such as time deposits. To the extent these are mismatched, it not only raises a liquidity (or even solvency) question, but also in periods of changing interest rates it places the bank at risk of having its normal "spread" (the difference between interest earned and interest paid) become diminished or turn negative. Since even an otherwise healthy institution, having positive net worth, can have mismatches in some of the maturities, potential problems are identified through the schedule of asset and liability maturities which would not otherwise be apparent from the financial statements.

Maturity groupings applied to assets and liabilities differ from bank to bank, and IAS 30 does not prescribe the periods but only gives examples of periods that are used in practice, as follows:

1. Up to 1 month
2. From 1 month to 3 months
3. From 3 months to 1 year
4. From 1 year to 5 years
5. From 5 years and above

It is imperative that the maturity periods adopted by a bank should be the same for assets and liabilities. This ensures that the maturities are matched and brings to light dependency, if any, on other sources of liquidity.

Maturities could be expressed in more than one way, for instance, by remaining period to the repayment date or by the original period to the repayment date. IAS 30 recommends that the maturity analysis of assets and liabilities be presented by the remaining period to the repayment date, as this provides the best basis to evaluate the liquidity of the bank.

In some countries time deposits could be withdrawn even on demand, and advances given by the bank may be repayable on demand, in which case, maturities according to the contractual dates should be used for the purposes of this analysis since it reflects the liquidity risks attaching to the bank's assets and liabilities.

Certain assets do not have a contractual maturity date. In all such cases the period in which these assets are assumed to mature is usually taken to be the expected date on which the assets will be realized. For instance, in the case of fixed assets that have no maturity date as such, as in the case of a certificate of deposit, the authors are of the opinion that their remaining useful lives as of the balance sheet date could be used as a measure of the maturity profile of these assets.

Example of disclosure of maturities of assets and liabilities

The maturity profile of assets and liabilities at December 31, 2000, was as follows:

	Up to 3 months	3 months to 1 year	1 year to 5 years	Over 5 years
	($ in thousands)			
Assets				
Cash and short-term funds	$ 10,157	$ --	$ --	$ --
Deposits with banks	298,771	--	--	--
Marketable securities	101,013	--	--	--
Accounts receivable	113,109	76,173	--	--
Trading investments	121,243	148,456	14,582	--
Accrued interest and other assets	9,919	18,681	2,150	--
Investments	--	66,160	300,099	--
Fixed assets	--	--	--	57,997
Total assets	$654,212	$309,470	$316,831	$57,997
Liabilities				
Deposits from banks	$105,492	$18,400	$ --	$ --
Other deposits	36,062	1,033	130,127	--
Proposed dividend	15,000	--	--	--
Accrued interest and other payable	38,882	9,952	30,865	--
Medium-term facilities	--	250,000	330,000	--
Total liabilities	$195,436	$279,385	$490,992	$ --

Concentration of Assets, Liabilities and Off-Balance-Sheet Items

Banks are required to disclose any significant concentrations of its assets, liabilities, and off-balance-sheet items. Such disclosures are a means of identification of potential risks, if any, that are inherent in the realization of the assets and liabilities (the funds available) to the bank.

Concentration of assets, liabilities, and off-balance-sheet items could be disclosed in the following ways:

1. By geographical areas such as individual countries, group of countries, or regions within a country
2. By customer groups such as governments, public authorities, and commercial enterprises
3. By industry sectors such as real estate, manufacturing, retail, and financial

4. Other concentrations of risk that are appropriate in the circumstances of the
    bank

**Example of disclosure of concentration of assets, liabilities, and off-balance-sheet
items**

($ in thousands)

| | 2000 | | | 1999 | | |
	Assets	*Liabilities*	*Off-balance-sheet*	*Assets*	*Liabilities*	*Off-balance-sheet*
Geographical region						
North America	$ 679,829	$ 26,103	$ 57,479	$ 681,958	$ 86,267	$ 146,099
Europe	662,259	778,470	621,316	574,699	662,690	1,117,110
Middle East	93,003	184,485	114,984	71,328	216,486	98,236
Other	279	--	--	10,525	370	198,138
Total	$1,395,370	$989,058	$793,779	$1,338,510	$965,813	$1,559,583
Industry sector						
Banking and fi-nance	$ 314,563	$866,483	$715,141	$ 482,874	$846,513	$1,484,248
Food processing	40,535	--	--	40,777	--	--
Luxury merchandise	336,966	3,797	11,811	224,829	--	1,649
Retail	356,879	--	--	315,554	--	--
Real estate	96,743	--	63,871	68,744	--	72,947
Manufacturing and services	153,151	--	--	124,366	--	--
Other	96,533	118,779	2,956	81,366	119,300	739
Total	$1,395,370	$989,058	$793,779	$1,338,510	$965,813	$1,559,583

Losses on Loans and Advances

Loans and advances to customers may sometimes become uncollectable, and in
those circumstances the bank would have to suffer losses on loans, advances, and
other credit facilities. The amount of losses that are specifically identified and the
potential losses not specifically identified should both be recognized as expenses
and deducted from the carrying amount of the loans and advances. The assessment
of these losses is dependent on management judgment and it is essential that it
should be applied consistently from one period to another. Any amounts set aside in
excess of the foregoing provision for losses on loans and advances, say, if required
by local circumstances or legislation, should be treated as an appropriation of
retained earnings and is not to be included in the determination of net profit or loss
for the period. Similarly, any credits resulting in the reduction of such amounts are
to be credited to retained earnings.

A number of disclosure requirements are prescribed by IAS 30 in this regard, as
summarized below.

1. The accounting policy describing the basis on which uncollectable loans
    and advances are recognized as an expense and written off.
2. Details of movements in the provision for losses on loans and advances
    during the period: These details should include the amount recognized as
    an expense in the period on account of losses on loans and advances, the

amount charged in the period for loans and advances written off, and the amount credited in the period resulting from the recovery of the amounts previously written off.

3. The aggregate amount of the provision for losses on loans and advances at the balance sheet date.

4. The aggregate amount included in the balance sheet as loans and advances on which no interest has been accrued (referred to in some countries as "interest in suspense" or "reserved interest") and the basis used to determine the carrying amount of such loans and advances.

Example of disclosure of loans and advances

	2000	*1999*
Balance, beginning of the year	$500,000	$400,000
Provision during the year--against specific advances	50,000	50,000
Provision during the year--against potential losses	20,000	70,000
Written off during the year	(10,000)	(20,000)
Balance, end of the year	$560,000	$500,000

Example of disclosure of interest in suspense

	2000	*1999*
Loans and advances on which interest is not taken to income	$2,000,000	$1,500,000
Movements in interest in suspense:		
Balance, beginning of year	$ 500,000	$ 490,000
Reserved during the year	50,000	30,000
Released during the year	(10,000)	(20,000)
Balance, end of year	$ 540,000	$ 500,000

Related-Party Transactions

Parties are considered to be related if one has the ability to control the other or exercise significant influence over the other in making financial and operating decisions. IAS 24 requires that related-party transactions be disclosed. When a bank has entered into transactions with related parties, the nature of the relationship (e.g., director, shareholder, etc.), the type of transaction (loans and advances or off-balance-sheet financing, etc.), and the elements of the transaction should be disclosed. The elements that are to be disclosed include the bank's lending policy to related parties and, in respect of related-party transactions, the amount included in or the proportion of

1. Each of loans and advances, deposits and acceptances, and promissory notes; disclosures may include the aggregate amounts outstanding at the beginning and end of the year as well as changes in these accounts during the year

2. Each of the principal types of income, interest expense, and commissions paid

3. The amount of the expense recognized in the period for the losses on loans and advances and the amount of the provision at the balance sheet date
4. Irrevocable commitments and contingencies and commitments from off-balance-sheet items

Example of related-party disclosures

Note 5: Related-Party Transactions. The bank has entered into transactions in the ordinary course of business with certain related parties, such as shareholders holding more than 20% equity interest in the bank and with certain directors of the bank.

At December 31, 2000 and 1999, the following balances were outstanding in the aggregate in relation to those related-party transactions:

	2000	1999
Loans and advances	2,000,000	1,800,000
Customer deposits	750,000	600,000
Guarantees	3,000,000	1,500,000

For the years ended December 31, 2000 and 1999, the following income and expense items are included in the aggregate amounts arising from the above-related transactions:

	2000	1999
Interest income	300,000	270,000
Interest expense	40,000	35,000
Commissions	60,000	30,000

Disclosure of General Banking Risks

Based on local legislation or circumstances, a bank may need to set aside a certain amount each year for general banking risks, including future losses or other unforeseeable risks, in addition to the provision for losses on loans and advances explained earlier. The bank may also be required to earmark a certain amount each year as a contingency reserve, over and above the amounts accrued under IAS 10. All such amounts set aside should be treated as appropriations of retained earnings, and any credits resulting from the reduction of such amounts should be returned directly to retained earnings and not included in determination of net income or loss for the year.

Disclosure of Assets Pledged as Security

If the bank is required by law or national custom to pledge assets as security to support certain deposits or other liabilities, the bank should then disclose the aggregate amount of secured liabilities and the nature and carrying amount of the assets pledged as security.

Disclosure of Trust Activities

If a bank is holding in trust, or in any other fiduciary capacity, assets belonging to others, those assets should not be included on the bank's financial statements since they are being held on behalf of third parties such as trusts and retirement funds. If a bank is engaged in significant trust activities, this deserves disclosure of the fact and an indication of the extent of those trust activities. Such disclosure will take care of any potential liability in case the bank fails in its fiduciary capacity. The safe custody services that banks offer are not part of these trust activities.

Comprehensive example of bank financial statements[*]

ABC Banking Corporation
Balance Sheet
As at 31 December 2000

Assets	Note	2000 (US $000s)	1999 (US $000s)
Cash and balances with central banks		$ 106,792	$ 97,706
Treasury bills	3	487,424	954,030
Deposits and due from banks		749,049	615,790
Loans, advances and overdrafts	4	2,057,230	1,836,814
Investments	5	607,068	402,129
Investment in associated companies	6	96,320	93,219
Interest receivable and other assets	7	48,818	53,480
Government bonds		375,375	389,004
Premises and equipment		83,244	82,929
Total assets		$4,611,320	$4,525,101
Liabilities and shareholders' equity			
Liabilities			
Deposits and due to banks and other financial instructions		$ 690,837	$ 595,616
Customers' current savings and other deposits		3,267,663	3,305,946
Interest payable and other liabilities	8	98,070	79,443
Proposed dividend		39,830	39,830
Total liabilities		$4,096,400	$4,020,835
Shareholders' equity			
Share capital	9	$ 398,342	$ 398,342
Statutory reserve	10	48,958	43,708
General reserve	10	42,070	36,820
Retained earnings		25,550	25,396
Total shareholders' equity		514,920	504,266
Total liabilities and shareholders' equity		$4,611,320	$4,525,101

Notes 1 to 19 form an integral part of these financial statements.

---

[*] *In order to fully comply with all International Accounting Standards certain other disclosures may need to be added to these financial statements. This example is meant to illustrate certain common disclosures seen in published financial statements of banks. For full compliance with IAS, refer to earlier parts of this chapter and other chapters where applicable.*

ABC Banking Corporation
Statement of Income and Retained Earnings
For the Year Ended 31 December 2000

	Note	2000 (US $000s)	1999 (US $000s)
Operating income			
Interest income		$ 250,579	$ 238,350
Interest expense		182,266	163,940
Net interest income		$ 68,313	$ 74,410
Other operating income	12	38,003	43,316
Income from associated companies		7,000	6,510
Total operating income		$ 113,316	$ 124,236
Operating expenses			
Staff costs		$ 43,071	$ 39,830
Other operating expenses		33,369	32,970
Total operating expenses		$ 76,440	$ 72,800
		$ 36,876	$ 51,436
Profit before provisions and recoveries			
Net (provisions) and recoveries:			
Relating to loans, advances, and overdrafts		$ 25,200	$ 22,183
Relating to the value of investments	5	(1,232)	1,407
Relating to other contingencies		(2,723)	(175)
Profit before taxation		$ 58,121	$ 74,851
Taxation--foreign branch		(5,579)	(4,249)
Profit for the year		$ 52,542	$ 70,602
Retained earnings at beginning of the year		$ 25,396	$ 34,440
Translation adjustment	11	(553)	602
		$ 77,385	$ 105,644
Appropriations:			
Transfer to statutory reserve	10	(5,250)	(7,063)
Transfer to general reserve	10	(5,250)	(31,500)
Proposed dividend		(39,830)	(39,830)
Directors' remuneration		(455)	(455)
Donations		(1,050)	(1,400)
Retained earnings at end of the year		$ 25,550	$ 25,396

Notes 1 to 19 form an integral part of these financial statements.

ABC Banking Corporation
Statement of Cash Flows
For the Year Ended December 31, 2000

	Note	2000 (US $000s)	1999 (US $000s)
Cash flows from operating activities			
Profit before taxation		$ 58,121	$ 74,851
Adjustment for:			
Dividend income		(6,608)	(5,684)

	Note	2000 (US $000s)	1999 (US $000s)
Net (provisions) recoveries:			
Relating to loans, advances, and overdrafts		(25,200)	(22,183)
Relating to the value of investments		1,232	(1,407)
Relating to other contingencies		2,723	175
Income from associated companies		(7,000)	(6,510)
Depreciation		10,010	9,905
Net gains on investments		(7,112)	(16,884)
(Increase) decrease in operating assets:			
Treasury bills		460,201	(56,021)
Deposits and due from banks		106,358	(167,979)
Loans, advances, and overdrafts		(192,668)	(282,086)
Government bonds		16,709	--
Interest receivable and other assets		4,662	14,210
Increase (decrease) in operating liabilities:			
Deposits and due to banks and other financial institutions		95,221	(8,806)
Customers' current savings and other deposits		(38,283)	470,512
Interest payable and other liabilities		8,771	(917)
Taxation of foreign branch		(5,579)	(4,249)
Net cash flow from operating activities		$ 481,558	$ (3,073)
Cash flows from investing activities			
Guarantee fund bonds redeemed		$ --	$ 262,857
Purchase of investments		(401,366)	(65,198)
Maturities and redemptions of investments		202,307	139,566
Purchase of shares in associated companies		(896)	(28,595)
Dividends from associated companies		4,795	3,374
Purchase of premises and equipment		(12,208)	(6,615)
Sale proceeds from disposal of premises and equipment		1,883	--
Dividend received		6,608	5,684
Net cash flow from investing activities		$ (198,877)	$ 311,073
Cash flows from financing activities			
Dividends paid		(39,830)	--
Effect of exchange rate changes		(553)	602
Net increase in cash and cash equivalents		242,298	308,602
Cash and cash equipments at beginning of the year	18	1,022,476	713,874
Cash and cash equivalents at end of the year	19	$1,264,774	$1,022,476

Notes 1 to 19 form an integral part of these financial statements.

ABC Banking Corporation
Notes to the Financial Statements
For the Year Ended December 31, 2000

Note 1: Activities. The ABC Banking Corporation, a public share holding company, was incorporated in XXX by a government decree. The bank operates under a banking license issued by the Central Bank of XXX. The overseas branches operate under the laws of their respective countries.

Note 2: Summary of Significant Accounting Policies. The financial statements have been prepared in accordance with international accounting standards.* The significant accounting policies adopted are as follows:

a. **Accounting convention.** The financial statements are prepared under the historical cost convention.

b. **Foreign currencies.** Assets and liabilities in foreign currency at the date of the balance sheet are translated at market rates of exchange prevailing at the year end. Foreign exchange gains and losses arising from the translation of the net investment in foreign branches and the foreign associate of the bank are taken directly to shareholders' funds. Other translation gains or losses are credited to or charged against income. Gains and losses arising from the difference between spot and forward rates on forward foreign exchange contracts which are entered into in connection with loans and deposits are credited to or charged against income over the periods of the related contracts. Other forward foreign exchange contracts are translated at rates of exchange prevailing at year end, and the resultant gains and losses are taken to income.

c. **Revenue recognition.** Interest receivable and payable are recognized on a time proportion basis taking account of the principal outstanding and the rate applicable. Loan interest that is 90 days or more overdue is excluded from income until received in cash. Fees receivable and payable are recognized when earned. Premiums and discounts on dated bonds, bills and other securities are amortized on a straight-line basis to the dates of maturity.

d. **Investments.** Investments acquired with the intention of being held for trading purposes are stated at market value. Unrealized gains and losses are taken to the statement of income. Investments held with the intention of being retained until maturity are stated at cost, adjusted for any premium or discount amortized from date of purchase to date of maturity on a straight-line basis. Long-term investments are stated at cost with reduction for any decline other than temporary in their value.

e. **Investment in associated companies.** Associated companies are companies in which the bank has a long-term investment comprising an interest of not less than 20% in the voting capital and over which it exerts significant influence. Investment in associated companies is accounted for using the equity method.

f. **Provision for loans, advances, and overdrafts.** Specific and general provisions for loans, advances, and overdrafts are made on the basis of a continuing appraisal of the lending portfolio with regard to the bank's previous experience and current economic conditions. The specific element relates to identified risk advances, whereas the general element relates to risks that are likely to be present in any portfolio of bank advances but which have not yet been specifically identified. Loans and advances are stated net of provisions.

g. **Government bonds.** Government bonds are stated at cost.

h. **Depreciation.** Freehold land is not depreciated. Leasehold premises are depreciated by equal annual installments over the remaining periods of the re-

---

* *In the authors' opinion, in order to fully comply with IAS, certain other disclosures may need to be added to these financial statements. (Please refer to the authors' comments at the beginning of this example.)*

spective leases. All other fixed assets are depreciated over their estimated useful lives on a straight-line basis.

i. **Employees' end-of-service benefits.** Provision is made for amounts payable under the relevant labor laws applicable to employees' accumulated periods of service at the date of the statement of condition.

j. **Fiduciary assets.** Assets held in trust or in a fiduciary capacity are not included in these financial statements.

Note 3: Treasury bills. These are short-term treasury bills issued by the governments of XXX.

Note 4: Loans, Advances, and Overdrafts.

a. The composition of the loans, advances, and overdrafts portfolio, net of provisions, is as follows:

	2000	1999
	(US $000s)	*(US $000s)*
Banks and other financial institutions	$ 428,330	$ 345,345
Others	1,628,900	1,491,329
	$2,057,230	$1,836,674

b. Provisions against loans, advances, and overdrafts, calculated in accordance with the basis set out in Note 2f., are as follows:

	2000	1999
	(US $000s)	*(US $000s)*
Balance at beginning of the year	$ 566,552	$ 669,151
Recoveries credited to income	(44,345)	(61,089)
Charge against income	19,145	38,906
Amounts written off	(33,915)	(81,158)
Relating to debt relief scheme	30,695	--
Amount ceded to central bank	(6,573)	--
Other movements	3,927	742
Balance at end of year	$ 535,486	$ 566,552

Other movements include exchange adjustments relating to loans, advances, and overdrafts denominated in foreign currencies and transfers from interest suspense account.

c. Loans, advances, and overdrafts (net of provisions against principal and interest) on which interest is not being accrued amount to $16,384,000 (1999: $16,700,000).

Note 5: Investments.

	2000	1999
	(US $000s)	*(US $000s)*
Quoted securities	$ 121,345	$ 116,403
Quoted bonds	178,073	127,043
Unquoted securities	56,966	77,518
Treasury bonds	154,042	--
Managed funds	108,738	92,029
Other investments	2,163	2,163
	$ 621,327	$ 415,156
Less: Provision for reduction in value	14,259	13,027
	$ 607,068	$ 402,129

The market value of quoted securities and bonds as of December 31, 2000, amounted to $48,290,000 (1999: $42,095,000).

Note 6: Investment in Associated Companies.

	2000		1999	
	% of interest		*% of interest*	
	held	*(US $000s)*	*held*	*(US $000s)*
XXX Inc.	49.00	$70,042	49.00	$67,956
National Commercial				
Facilities Co. PSC	20.25	25,382	20.25	25,263
Other		896		--
		$96,320		$93,219

Note 7: Interest Receivable and Other Assets.

	2000	1999
	(US $000s)	*(US $000s)*
Interest receivable	$ 28,105	$ 28,889
Acquired assets pending sale	7,595	14,826
Other	13,118	9,765
	$ 48,818	$ 53,480

Note 8: Interest Payable and Other Liabilities.

	2000	1999
	(US $000s)	*(US $000s)*
Interest payable	$ 26,446	$ 33,327
Accrued expenses	3,514	2,618
Other	68,110	43,498
	$ 98,070	$ 79,443

Note 9: Share Capital.

Authorized:		
700,000,000 shares of $1 each	700,000	700,000
Issued and fully paid:		
398,341,750 shares of $1 each	398,342	398,342

Note 10: Reserves.

		Statutory	*General*
		reserve	*reserve*
	Note	*(US $000s)*	*(US $000s)*
a. Balance at beginning of the year	10b.	$ 43,708	$ 36,820
Transfers for the year		5,250	5,250
Balance at end of the year		$ 48,958	$ 42,070
b. Transfers for the year			

(1) **Statutory reserve.** As required by the Commercial Companies Law, 10% of the profit for the year has been transferred to statutory reserve. The bank may resolve to discontinue such annual transfers when the reserve is equal to 25% of the issued share capital. The reserve cannot be utilized for the purpose of distribution except in such circumstances as stipulated in the Commercial Companies Law.

(2) **General reserve.** The transfer to general reserve has been made in accordance with the provisions of the bank's articles of association and

underlines the shareholders' commitment to enhance the strong equity base of the bank.

Note 11: Translation Adjustment. These arise from foreign exchange gains and losses relating to the investment in foreign branches and the foreign associate of the bank. Retained earnings are stated net of accumulated foreign currency translation losses of US $1,140,000 (1999: US $1,061,000).

Note 12: Other Operating Income.

	2000 (US $000s)	1999 (US $000s)
Dividend income	$ 6,608	$ 5,684
Fees and commissions	16,604	11,431
(Losses) gains on managed funds	(1,876)	15,526
Net gains on trading investments	8,988	1,358
Profit on foreign exchange	3,647	6,013
Other income	4,032	3,304
	$38,003	$43,316

Note 13: Related-Party Transactions. Certain related parties (principally associated companies and directors of the bank, their families, and companies of which they are principal owners) were customers of the bank in the ordinary course of business. Facilities in the personal names of the directors are fully collateralized. The transactions with these parties were made on substantially the same terms, including interest rates, as those prevailing at the same time for comparable transactions with unrelated parties and did not involve more than a normal amount of risk.

	2000		1999	
	Associated companies (US $000s)	Other (US $000s)	Associated companies (US $000s)	Other (US $000s)
Loan, advances, and overdrafts	23,982	48,468	21,350	49,182
Direct credit substitutes	48,811	8,183	18,305	10,535
Deposits	399	4,284	91	1,239

Note 14: Maturities of Assets and Liabilities. The maturity profile of the assets and liabilities as of December 31 was as follows:

	2000		1999	
	Assets (US $000s)	Liabilities (US $000s)	Assets (US $000s)	Liabilities (US $000s)
Call and maturing within 1 year	$2,590,434	$3,952,515	$2,772,644	$3,853,829
From 1 year to 3 years	738,199	86,954	488,285	150,185
Over 3 years	1,282,687	56,931	1,264,172	16,821
	$4,611,320	$4,096,400	$4,525,101	$4,020,835

Note 15: Concentration of Assets, Liabilities, and Off-Balance-Sheet Items.

	2000		
	Assets *(US $000s)*	*Liabilities* *(US $000s)*	*Off-balance- sheet items* *(US $000s)*
Geographic region			
South America	$3,376,331	$3,868,487	$ 458,136
Asia	99,967	2,093	37,982
Africa	293,524	93,205	80,409
Australia	747,159	112,994	133,238
Others	94,339	19,621	26,040
	$4,611,320	$4,096,400	$ 735,805
Industry sector			
Trading and manufacturing	$ 539,224	$ 410,032	$ 180,936
Banks and financial institutions	1,550,787	506,905	313,152
Construction and real estate	128,380	22,967	117,649
Others	2,392,929	3,156,496	124,068
	$4,611,320	$4,096,400	$ 735,805

	1999		
	Assets *(US $000s)*	*Liabilities* *(US $000s)*	*Off-balance- sheet items* *(US $000s)*
Geographic region			
South America	$3,482,913	$3,698,800	$ 380,716
Asia	124,873	31,423	91,378
Africa	221,732	66,983	95,242
Australia	597,016	222,516	35,938
Others	98,567	1,113	7,091
	$4,525,101	$4,020,835	$ 610,365
Industry sector			
Trading and manufacturing	$ 523,614	$ 121,926	$ 99,960
Banks and financial institutions	1,317,421	800,828	233,275
Construction and real estate	116,494	10,899	136,059
Others	2,567,572	3,087,182	141,071
	$4,525,101	$4,020,835	$ 610,365

Note 16: Segmental Information. The bank's operating results arise primarily from the activities of commercial and retail banking from its operations based in South America.

Note 17: Contingent Liabilities and Commitments. The bank has exposure in the normal course of business arising from transactions in interest rate swaps and forward rate agreements. In addition, the bank has the following contingent liabilities and commitments:

	2000	1999
	(US $000s)	*(US $000s)*
Contingent liabilities		
Letters of credit	$ 68,404	$ 100,583
Guarantees	184,331	188,783
Acceptances	27,909	18,781
	$ 280,644	$ 308,147
Commitments		
Undrawn loan commitments	$ 72,555	$ 60,795
Forward foreign exchange contracts	382,431	241,087
Other commitments	175	336
	$ 455,161	$ 302,218
	$ 735,805	$ 610,365

The bank has irrevocably guaranteed to the holders of units in a guaranteed fund, on the maturity date, the return of either US $1,000 per unit or the highest net asset value per unit as of the end of three annual dates.

A counter guarantee in favor of the bank has been issued by Bank International, South America.

Note 18: Cash Flow Reconciliation. Reconciliation of net increase in cash and cash equivalents.

	2000	1999	Change
	(US $000s)	*(US $000s)*	*(US $000s)*
Cash and balance with central banks	$ 106,792	$ 97,706	$ 9,086
Deposits and due from banks	687,428	447,811	239,617
Treasury bills	470,554	476,959	(6,405)
Cash and cash equivalents	$1,264,774	$1,022,476	$ 242,298

Note 19: Components of Cash and Cash Equivalents. Cash and cash equivalents include cash on hand, amounts held by other banks and financial institutions, and treasury bills with maturities of 3 months or less.

ACCOUNTING AND REPORTING BY RETIREMENT BENEFIT PLANS

PERSPECTIVE AND ISSUES

IAS 26 sets out the form and content of the general-purpose financial reports of retirement benefit plans. This standard deals with accounting and reporting to all participants of a plan as a group, and not with reports which might be made to individuals about their particular retirement benefits. The standard applies to

- Defined contribution plans where benefits are determined by contributions to the plan together with investment earnings thereon; and
- Defined benefit plans where benefits are determined by a formula based on employees' earnings and/or years of service.

IAS 26 may be compared to IAS 19. The former addresses the financial reporting considerations for the benefit plan itself, as the reporting entity, while the latter deals with employers' accounting for the cost of such benefits as they are earned by the employees. While these standards are thus somewhat related, there will not be any direct interrelationship between amounts reported in benefit plan financial statements and amounts reported under IAS 19 by employers.

IAS 26 was approved by the IASC in June 1986 and became operative for financial statements of retirement benefit plans covering periods beginning on or after January 1, 1988. While IAS 19 has been revised twice, IAS 26 was never revised by the IASC. It was, however, reformatted in 1994 to bring it in line with the current IASC practice.

Sources of IAS
IAS 26

DEFINITIONS OF TERMS

Actuarial present value of promised retirement benefits. The present value of the expected future payments by a retirement benefit plan to existing and past employees, attributable to the service already rendered.

Defined benefit plans. Retirement benefit plans whereby retirement benefits to be paid to plan participants are determined by reference to a formula usually based on employees' earnings and/or years of service.

Defined contribution plans. Retirement benefit plans whereby retirement benefits to be paid to plan participants are determined by contributions to a fund together with investment earnings thereon.

Funding. The transfer of assets to a separate entity (distinct from the employer's enterprise), the "fund," to meet future obligations for the payment of retirement benefits.

Net assets available for benefits. The assets of a retirement benefit plan less its liabilities other than the actuarial present value of promised retirement benefits.

Participants. The members of a retirement benefit plan and others who are entitled to benefits under the plan.

Retirement benefit plans. Formal or informal arrangements based upon which an enterprise provides benefits for its employees on or after termination of service, which are usually referred to as "termination benefits." These could take the form of annual pension payments or lump-sum payments. Such benefits, or the employer's contributions towards them, should however be determinable or possible of estimation in advance of retirement, from the provisions of a document (i.e., based on a formal arrangement) or from the enterprise's practices (which is referred to as an informal arrangement).

Vested benefits. Entitlements, the rights to which, under the terms of a retirement benefit plan, are not conditional on continued employment.

CONCEPTS, RULES AND EXAMPLES

Scope

IAS 26 should be applied in accounting and reporting by retirement benefit plans. The terms of a retirement plan may require that the plan present an annual report; in some jurisdictions this may be a statutory requirement. IAS 26 does not establish a mandate for the publication of such reports by retirement plans. However, if such reports are prepared by a retirement plan, then the requirements of this standard should be applied to them.

IAS 26 categorically states that to the extent other IAS are not superseded by this standard they apply to the reports of retirement benefit plans as well. To illustrate this, consider the treatment prescribed by IAS 26 in valuing retirement benefit plan assets. According to IAS 26, para 32, retirement benefit plan investments should be carried at fair value. This requirement may be considered as superseding the provisions of IAS 25 which, while not restricting the choice only to fair value, allow a free choice of treatments depending on whether investments are current or long-term. (Note that IAS 25 is being superseded by IAS 39, but the latter has a delayed effective date and in 2000 many enterprises will continue to apply IAS 25. IAS 39 adopts a fair value approach for most financial assets and thus can be said to conform to IAS 26.)

IAS 26 regards a retirement benefit plan as a separate entity, distinct from the employer of the plan's participants. It is noteworthy that this standard also applies to retirement benefit plans that have sponsors other than employer (e.g., trade associations or groups of employers). Furthermore, this standard deals with accounting and reporting by retirement benefit plans to all participants as a group; it does not deal with reports to individual participants with respect to their retirement benefit entitlements.

The standard applies the same basis of accounting and reporting to informal retirement benefit arrangements as it applies to formal retirement benefit plans. It is also worthy of mention that this standard applies whether or not a separate fund is created and regardless of whether there are trustees. The requirements of this standard also apply to retirement benefit plans with assets invested with an insurance company, unless the contract with the insurance company is in the name of a specified participant or a group of participants and the responsibility is solely of the insurance company.

Defined Contribution Plans

Retirement benefit plans are usually described as being either defined contribution or defined benefit plans. When the quantum of the future benefits payable to the retirement benefit plan participants is determined by the contributions paid by the participants' employer, the participants, or both, together with investment earnings thereon, such plans are defined contribution plans. Defined benefit plans, by contrast, promise certain benefits, often determined by formulae which involve factors such as years of service and salary level at the time of retirement, without regard to whether the plan has sufficient assets; thus the ultimate responsibility for payment (which may be guaranteed by an insurance company, the government or some other entity, depending on local law and custom) remains with the employer. In rare circumstances, a retirement benefit plan may contain characteristics of both defined contribution and defined benefit plans; such a hybrid plan is deemed to be a defined benefit plan for the purposes of this standard.

IAS 26, para 13, requires that the report of a defined contribution plan contain a statement of the net assets available for benefits and a description of the funding policy. In preparing the statement of the net assets available for benefits, the guidance contained in IAS 26, para 32 (i.e., that plan investments should be carried at fair value, which for marketable securities would be market value) should be followed. In case an estimate of fair value is not possible, disclosure is required of the reason as to why fair value has not been used. As a practical matter, most plan assets will have determinable market values, since the plans' trustees' discharge of their fiduciary responsibilities will generally mandate that only marketable investments be held.

An example of a statement of net assets available for plan benefits, for a defined contribution plan, is set forth below.

XYZ Defined Contribution Plan
Statement of Net Assets Available for Benefits
December 31, 20X1
(in thousands of US dollars)

Assets
Investments at fair value

US government securities	5,000
US municipal bonds	3,000
US equity securities	3,000
Non-US equity securities	3,000
US debt securities	2,000
Non-US corporate bonds	2,000
Others	1,000
Total investments	19,000

Receivables

Amounts due from stockbrokers on sale of securities	15,000
Accrued interest	5,000
Dividends receivable	2,000
Total receivables	22,000

Cash	5,000
Total assets	46,000

Liabilities
Accounts payable

Amounts due to stockbrokers on purchase of securities	10,000
Benefits payable to participants--due and unpaid	11,000
Total accounts payable	21,000

Accrued expenses	11,000
Total liabilities	32,000
Net assets available for benefits	14,000

Defined benefit plans. When amounts to be paid as retirement benefits are determined by reference to a formula, usually based on employees' earnings and/or years of service, such retirement benefit plans are defined benefit plans. The key factor is that the benefits are fixed or determinable, without regard to the adequacy of assets which may have been set aside for payment of the benefits. This contrasts to the defined contribution plans approach, which is to provide the workers, upon retirement, with the amounts which have been set aside, plus or minus investment earnings or losses which have been accumulated thereon, however great or small that amount may be.

IAS 26, para 17, requires that the report of a defined benefit plan should contain **either**

1. A statement that shows

    a. The net assets available for benefits;

b. The actuarial present value of promised retirement benefits, distinguishing between vested and nonvested benefits; and

c. The resulting excess or deficit;

or

2. A statement of net assets available for benefits including **either**

a. A note disclosing the actuarial present value of promised retirement benefits, distinguishing between vested and nonvested benefits; or

b. A reference to this information in an accompanying actuarial report.

IAS 26, para 28, recommends, but does not mandate, that in each of the three formats described above, a trustees' report in the nature of a management or directors' report and an investment report may also accompany the statements.

The standard does not make it incumbent upon the plan to obtain annual actuarial valuations. If an actuarial valuation has not been prepared on the date of the report, the most recent valuation should be used as the basis for preparing the financial statement. The date of the valuation used should be disclosed. Actuarial present values of promised benefits should be based either on current or projected salary levels; whichever basis is used should be disclosed. The effect of any changes in actuarial assumptions that had a material impact on the actuarial present value of promised retirement benefits should also be disclosed. The report should explain the relationship between actuarial present values of promised benefits, the net assets available for benefits and the policy for funding the promised benefits.

As in the case of defined contribution plans, investments of a defined benefit plan should be carried at fair value, which for marketable securities, would be market value (IAS 26, para 32).

The following are examples of the alternative types of reports prescribed for a defined benefit plan:

ABC Defined Benefit Plan
Statement of Net Assets Available for Benefits, Actuarial Present Value of Accumulated Retirement Benefits and Plan Excess or Deficit
December 31, 20X1
(in thousands of US dollars)

1. Statement of Net Assets Available for Benefits

Assets	
Investments at fair value	
US government securities	50,000
US municipal bonds	30,000
US equity securities	30,000
Non-US equity securities	30,000
US debt securities	20,000
Non-US corporate bonds	20,000
Others	10,000
Total investments	190,000

Receivables

Amounts due from stockbrokers on sale of securities	150,000
Accrued interest	50,000
Dividends receivable	20,000
Total receivables	220,000
Cash	50,000
Total assets	460,000

Liabilities

Accounts payable

Amounts due to stockbrokers on purchase of securities	100,000
Benefits payable to participants –due and unpaid	110,000
Total accounts payable	210,000
Accrued expenses	110,000
Total liabilities	320,000
Net assets available for benefits	140,000

2. Actuarial present value of accumulated plan benefits

Vested benefits	100,000
Nonvested benefits	20,000
Total	120,000

3. Excess of net assets available for benefits over actuarial present value of accumulated plan benefits — 20,000

ABC Defined Benefit Plan
Statement of Changes in Net Assets Available for Benefits
December 31, 20X1
(in thousands of US dollars)

Investment income

Interest income	40,000
Dividend income	10,000
Net appreciation (unrealized gain) in fair value of investments	10,000
Total investment income	60,000

Plan contributions

Employer contributions	50,000
Employee contributions	50,000
Total plan contributions	100,000
Total additions to net asset value	160,000

Plan benefit payments

Pensions (annual)	30,000
Lump sum payments on retirement	30,000
Severance pay	10,000
Commutation of superannuation benefits	15,000
Total plan benefit payments	85,000
Total deductions from net asset value	85,000

Net increase in asset value	<u>75,000</u>
Net assets available for benefits	
Beginning of year	65,000
End of year	140,000

Additional Disclosures

IAS 26, para 34, requires that the reports of a retirement benefit plans, both defined benefit plans and defined contribution plans, should also contain the following information:

1. A statement of changes in net assets available for benefits;
2. A summary of significant accounting policies; and
3. A description of the plan and the effect of any changes in the plan during the period.

In accordance with IAS 26, para 35, reports provided by retirement benefits plans may include the following, if applicable:

1. A statement of net assets available for benefits disclosing

   a. Assets at the end of the period suitably classified;
   b. The basis of valuation of assets;
   c. Details of any single investment exceeding either 5% of the net assets available for benefits or 5% of any class or type of security;
   d. Details of any investment in the employer; and
   e. Liabilities other than the actuarial present value of promised retirement benefits;

2. A statement of changes in net assets available for benefits showing the following:

   a. Employer contributions;
   b. Employee contributions;
   c. Investment income such as interest and dividends;
   d. Other income;
   e. Benefits paid or payable (analyzed, for example, as retirement, death and disability benefits, and lump-sum payments);
   f. Administrative expenses;
   g. Other expenses;
   h. Taxes on income;
   i. Profits and losses on disposal of investments and changes in value of investments; and
   j. Transfers from and to other plans;

3. A description of the funding policy;
4. For defined benefit plans, the actuarial present value of promised retirement benefits (which may distinguish between vested benefits and nonvested

benefits) based on the benefits promised under the terms of the plan, on service rendered to date and using either current salary levels or projected salary levels. This information may be included in an accompanying actuarial report to be read in conjunction with the related information; and

5. For defined benefit plans, a description of the significant actuarial assumptions made and the method used to calculate the actuarial present value of promised retirement benefits.

According to IAS 26, para 36, since the report of a retirement benefit plan contains a description of the plan, either as part of the financial information or in a separate report, it may contain the following:

1. The names of the employers and the employee groups covered;
2. The number of participants receiving benefits and the number of other participants, classified as appropriate;
3. The type of plan--defined contribution or defined benefit;
4. A note as to whether participants contribute to the plan;
5. A description of the retirement benefits promised to participants;
6. A description of any plan termination terms; and
7. Changes in items 1. through 6. during the period covered by the report.

Furthermore, it is not uncommon to refer to other documents that are readily available to users and in which the plan is described, and to include only information on subsequent changes in the report.

AGRICULTURE

PERSPECTIVE AND ISSUES

Over the course of its over-25-year existence, the IASC has been primarily focused on the task of developing financial reporting standards which are relevant to general-purpose financial reporting, without regard to the nature of the reporting entity's particular business operations. In the more recent of these years, completion of the core set of standards, which too was oriented toward general-purpose financial statement needs, has been of paramount importance. Having essentially completed that task (although IOSCO's verdict has yet to be delivered), the IASC is now turning to a number of specialized industry reporting concerns. Apart from banking (addressed earlier in this chapter, and subject to expanded disclosure rules for several years already), specialized industry needs have received virtually no attention from the IASC, but now projects on agriculture, insurance and the extractive industries, and perhaps others, will be given due consideration.

Agriculture is the first of these to be addressed (a draft statement of position was issued almost 3 years ago) and will perhaps be the most controversial, if not most significant, of these projects. Interestingly, the standard which will be promulgated by the IASC, probably in 2000, will be the first major declaration on this subject from any of the world's accounting standard setters. The lack of attention, notwithstanding the fact that agriculture is prominent as an economic activity in most nations and in many of them, particularly in the lesser industrialized nations of the world, it may even dominate the economy, is due to the fact that in general agriculture is carried on by private, small, often family-run enterprises, for which external financial reporting is a low priority.

The forthcoming standard on agriculture, set forth in exposure draft E65, *Agriculture*, will govern the financial reporting for so-called biological assets up to the point of harvest, after which the existing standard on inventory costing (IAS 2) will become determinative. Fair value accounting will be embraced by the new standard, such that biological assets will be measured as of each balance sheet date at fair value, with the change from the prior period (other than that accounted for by acquisitions or dispositions of biological assets) being included in operating earnings. While it will be encouraged that the changes in fair value be analyzed into its two component elements (that due to changes in prices, and that due to growth during the reporting period) either on the face of the income statement itself or in the notes thereto, this will not be a requirement.

Sources of IAS
E65

DEFINITIONS OF TERMS

Active market. Market for which all these conditions exist: the items traded within the market are homogeneous; willing buyers and sellers can normally be found at any time; and prices are available to the public.

Agricultural activity. Managed biological transformation of biological assets into agricultural produce for sale, consumption, further processing, or into other biological assets.

Agricultural land. Land used directly to support and sustain biological assets in agricultural activity; the land itself is not a biological asset, however.

Agricultural produce. The harvested product of the enterprise's biological assets awaiting sale, processing, or consumption.

Bearer biological assets. Those which bear agricultural produce for harvest. The biological assets themselves are not the primary agricultural produce, but rather are self-regenerating (such as sheep raised for wool production; fruit trees).

Biological assets. Living plants and animals controlled by the enterprise as a result of past events. Control may be through ownership or through another type of legal arrangement.

Biological transformation. The processes of growth, degeneration, production and procreation, which cause qualitative and quantitative changes in living organisms and the generation of new assets in the form of agricultural produce or additional biological assets of the same class.

Carrying amount. Amount at which an asset is recognized in the balance sheet after deducting any accumulated depreciation or amortization and accumulated impairment losses thereon.

Consumable biological assets. Those which are to be harvested as the primary agricultural produce, such as livestock intended for meat production, annual crops, and trees to be felled for pulp.

Fair value. The amount for which an asset could be exchanged or a liability settled between knowledgeable, willing parties in an arm's-length transaction.

Group of biological assets. A herd, flock, etc., that is managed jointly to ensure that the group is sustainable on an ongoing basis, and is homogeneous as to both type of animal or plant and activity for which the group is deployed.

Harvest. The detachment of agricultural produce from the biological asset, the removal of a living plant from agricultural land for sale and replanting, or the cessation of a biological asset's life processes.

Immature biological assets. Those that are not yet harvestable or able to sustain regular harvests.

Mature biological assets. Those which are harvestable or able to sustain regular harvest. Consumable biological assets are mature when they have attained harvestable specifications; bearer biological assets are mature when they are able to sustain regular harvests.

Net realizable value.   Estimated selling price in the ordinary course of business, less the estimated costs of completion and the estimated costs necessary to make the sale.

CONCEPTS, RULES AND EXAMPLES

Background

Agricultural activities have received scant attention, if any, from accounting standard setters; this may be a function of the fact that the major national and international accounting standard setters are those of the US and the UK, the economies of which are far less dependent upon agriculture than are many of the less developed nations of the world. The IASC, while seeking to become the world's standard setter, has to date however been most influential in the developing nations, many of which have adopted IAS in total, and many more of which have based national standards on the IAS with only minor changes. Perhaps because of its sensitivity to this constituency, the agriculture project has received a good deal of serious attention. When issued, it will be by far the most comprehensive addressing of this financial reporting topic.

The exclusion of agriculture from most established accounting and financial reporting rules can be understood in the context of the unique features of the industry: biological transformations (growth, procreation, production, degeneration) which alter the very substance of the biological assets; the wide variety of characteristics of the living assets which challenge traditional classification schemes; the nature of management functions in the industry; and the predominance of small, closely held ownership. On the other hand, in many nations agriculture is a major industry, ranging up to 50% of gross national product of some nations (as much as 58% in New Zealand, in fact), and logic would suggest that comprehensive systems of financial reporting for business enterprises cannot be deemed complete while excluding so large a segment of the economy.

Heretofore, the general lack of a sense of urgency in dealing with this subject has been abetted by the fact that much of agriculture is controlled by closely held or family held businesses, with few if any outside owners who might have demanded formal financial statements prepared in accordance with agreed-upon accounting principles. Also, grantors of farm credit have historically looked to the character of the borrower, usually a long-time resident with deep roots in the community, rather than to financial statements. While some of these factors continue to be valid, the IASC has concluded that meaningful financial reporting concerns had to be given due attention.

Of course, a stand-alone standard on agriculture would not have been the only possible means of imposing financial reporting requirements on biological assets.

However, in the realm of international accounting standards, most of the existing standards which logically could have addressed agricultural issues (IAS 2 on inventories; IAS 4 on depreciation; IAS 16 on plant, property, and equipment; and IAS 18 on revenue recognition) have deliberately excluded most or all agriculture-related applications. A review of published financial statements for agriculture-related enterprises reveals the consequences of this neglect. A wide range of methods and principles are applied to such businesses as forest products, livestock and grain production. For example, some companies account for timberlands at original cost, charging depreciation only to the extent of net harvesting, with reforestation costs charged to expense as incurred; others capitalize reforestation costs and even carrying costs, and charge depletion on a units of production basis; and yet others value forest lands at net present value of expected future cash flows.

Thus, the IASC has concluded that excluding agriculture from the scope of IAS is not appropriate, but also accepts the need for a relatively simple, uniform and coherent set of principles applicable to this industry grouping. It believes that extending certain modifications to the historical cost model, which have already been applied by existing IAS (e.g., to plant and equipment and to investments), offers the best solution to this problem. Finally, the new standard will apply only to biological assets, as those are the aspects of agriculture which have unique characteristics; the accounting for assets such as inventories and plant and equipment will be guided by existing standards such as IAS 2 and IAS 16. In other words, once the biological transformation process is complete (e.g., when grain is harvested, animals are slaughtered, or trees are cut down), the specialized accounting principles to be imposed on agriculture will cease to apply.

Defining Agriculture

Agriculture will be defined as essentially the management of the biological transformation of plants and animals to yield produce for consumption or further processing. The term agriculture will encompass livestock, forestry, annual and perennial cropping, orchards, plantations, and aquiculture. However, agriculture will be distinguished from so-called "pure exploitation," where resources are simply removed from the environment (e.g., by fishing or deforestation) without management initiatives such as operation of hatcheries or reforestation or other attempts to manage their regeneration. The forthcoming standard will not apply to pure exploitation activities, nor will it apply to agricultural produce, which is harvested and thus a nonliving product of the biological assets; and agriculture produce incorporated in further processing in integrated agribusiness enterprises that involve activities which are not unique to agriculture.

E65 sets forth a three-part test or set of criteria for agricultural activities. First, the plants or animals which are the object of the activities must be alive and capable of transformation. Second, the change must be managed, by which a range of activities is being implied (e.g., fertilizing the soil and weeding in the case of crop growing, feeding and providing health care in the instance of animal husbandry, etc.). Third, there must be basis for the measurement of change, such as the ripeness of vegetables, the weight of animals, circumference of trees, and so forth. If these three criteria are satisfied, the activity will be impacted by the financial reporting requirements to be imposed by E65's resulting standard.

Biological assets are the principal assets of agricultural activities, and they are held for their transformative potential. This results in two major types of outcomes: the first may involve asset changes as through growth or quality improvement; degeneration; or procreation. The second involves the creation of separable products initially qualifying as agricultural produce. The management of the biological transformation process is the distinguishing characteristic of agricultural activities.

Biological assets often are managed in groups, such as herds of animals, groves of trees, fields of crops. To be considered a group, however, the components must be homogeneous in nature and must further be homogeneous in the activity for which the group is deployed. For example, trees maintained for production of fruit are not in the same group as the same type of tree (e.g., cherry) grown for lumber.

The forthcoming standard will apply to forests and similar regenerative resources excluded from IAS 16; producers' inventories of livestock, agriculture, and forest products, including those excluded from IAS 2, to the extent they are to be measured at net realizable value; and natural increases in herds and agricultural and forest products excluded from IAS 18. It will also address financial statement presentation and disclosure (the primary province of IAS 1 revised). Furthermore, it will establish that, unless explicit exclusions are provided, all international accounting standards are meant to apply equally to agriculture.

Basic Principles Set Forth in E65: Fair Value Accounting Is Necessary

The forthcoming standard will apply to all enterprises which undertake agricultural activities. Animals or plants will be recognized as assets when it is probable that the future economic benefits associated with the asset will flow to the reporting entity, and when the cost or value to the enterprise can be measured reliably. There will be a strong presumption that any enterprise entering into agricultural activities on a for-profit basis will have an ability to measure cost and/or fair value. The standard will also govern the initial measurement of agricultural produce, which is the end product of the biological transformation process; and will furthermore guide the accounting for government grants pertaining to agricultural assets.

The most important feature of the new standard will be the requirement that biological assets are to be measured at each balance sheet date at their respective fair values. This departure from historical cost is the most significant facet of the IASC proposal, and one which has generated a good deal of debate. The imperative to deploy fair value accounting springs from the long production periods for many crops (an extreme being forests under management for as long as 30 years before being harvested) and, even more typically, for livestock. In the absence of fair value accounting with changes in value being reported in operating results, the entire earnings of a long-term production process might only be reported at lengthy intervals, which would not faithfully represent the underlying economic activities being carried out.

Over the long run, of course, such as over the lifetimes of the assets in question, total income being recognized would not differ. It would, however, be a gross distortion to report no earnings, or even losses from having incurred various costs with no corresponding realized revenues, for many years, with substantial profits being reported only when the crop is ultimately harvested. Accordingly, the use of historical costs based on completed transactions is not deemed meaningful in the case of agricultural activities.

Furthermore, each stage of the biological transformation process is considered to be significant, as each stage (growth, degeneration, procreation, and production) contributes to the amount of expected economic benefits to be derived from the biological assets. Unless a fair value model were used, there would be no explicit recognition (in effect, no matching) of the benefits associated with each of these discrete events. Furthermore, this recognition underlines the need to apply the same measurement concept to each stage in the life cycle of the biological assets; for example, with live weight change, fleece weight change, aging, deaths, lambs born, and wool shorn, in the case of a flock of sheep.

The obvious argument in favor of historical cost-based measures derives from the superior reliability of that mode of measurement. With completed transactions, there is no imprecision due to the inherently subjective process of making or obtaining fair value assessments. By contrast, superior relevance is the strongest argument for current value measurement schemes. The IASC evaluated various measures, including current cost and net realizable value as well as market value, as alternatives to historical cost, but ultimately identified fair value (ironically, the one approach not addressed in the IASC's seminal document, the *Framework for the Preparation and Presentation of Financial Statements)* as having the best combination of attributes for the determination of agriculture-related earnings. The IASC was particularly influenced by the market context in which agriculture takes place and the transformative characteristics of biological assets and concluded that fair value would offer the best balance of relevance, reliability, comparability, and understandability.

The IASC also concluded that annual determinations of fair value would be necessary to properly portray the combined impact of nature and financial transactions for any given reporting period. Less frequent measurements were rejected because of the continuous nature of biological transformations, the lack of direct correlation between financial transactions and the different outcomes arising from biological transformation (thus, the former could not serve as surrogate indicators of the latter during off periods), the volatilities which often characterize natural and market environments affecting agriculture, and the fact that market-based measures are in fact readily available. The idea of maintaining historical cost as an allowed alternative was similarly rejected, essentially because historical cost is not viewed as meaningful in this context, coupled with concerns about the extreme lack of comparability that would result from the acceptability of two so disparate methodologies.

Determining Fair Values

The primary determinant of fair value would be market value, just as it is for financial instruments having active markets (as set forth in IAS 32, discussed at length in Chapter 5). The use of so-called "farm gate" market prices would reflect both the "as is" and "where is" attributes of the biological assets. Where these so-called "farm gate" prices are not available, market values would have to be reduced by transaction costs, including transport, to arrive at net market values which would equate to fair values.

In the case of products for which market values might not be readily available, other approaches to fair value determination would have to be employed. This is most likely to be an issue where market values exist but, due to market imperfections, are not deemed to be useful. For example, when access to markets is restricted or unduly influenced by temporary monopoly or monopsony conditions, or when no market actually exists as of the balance sheet date, alternative measures will be called for. In such circumstances, it might be necessary to refer to such indicators as the most recent market prices for the class of asset at issue, market prices for similar assets (e.g., different varieties of the same crop), sector benchmarks (e.g., relating value of a dairy farm to the kilograms of milk solids or fat produced), net present value of expected future cash flows discounted at a risk-class rate, or net realizable values for short-cycle products for which most growth has already occurred. Last and probably least useful would be historical costs, which might be particularly suited to biological assets which have thus far experienced little transformation.

A practical problem arises when the indirect method of valuation implicitly values both the crop and the land itself. The proposed standard indicates that such valuations should be allocated to the different assets to give a better indication of the future economic benefits each will confer. If a combined market price, for example, can be obtained for the land plus the immature growing crops situated thereon, and a quotation for the land alone can also be obtained, this will permit a fair value assessment of the immature growing crops (while the land itself will generally be presented on the balance sheet at cost, not fair value). Another technique would involve the subdivision of the assets into classes based on age, quality, or other traits, and the valuation of each subgroup by reference to market prices. While these methods may involve added effort, the draft concludes that the usefulness of the resulting financial statements will be materially enhanced if this is done.

Increases in fair value due to the growth of the biological asset is only one-half of the accounting equation, of course, since there will normally have been cost inputs incurred to foster the growth (e.g., applications of fertilizer to the fields, etc.). Under the provisions of E65, costs of producing and harvesting biological assets are to be charged to expense as incurred. This is necessary, since if costs were added to the assets' carrying value (analogous to interest on borrowings in connection with long-term construction projects) and the assets were also adjusted to fair value, there would be risk of double-counting cost or value increases. As mandated, however, value increases due to either price changes or growth, or both, will be taken into current income, where costs of production will be appropriately matched against them, resulting in a meaningful measure of the net result of periodic operations.

Recognition of Changes in Biological Assets

The 1996 DSOP proposed that the change in carrying amounts for a group of biological assets was to be allocated between changes due to differences in fair value and physical changes due to growth and other natural phenomena. The intent was to have the former, which corresponds to revaluations of plant and equipment assets under the alternative treatment permitted by IAS 16, reported directly in equity, while the latter would be included in current period operating results. However, even if this were conceptually sound, the practical difficulties of allocating such value changes has more recently been appreciated by the IASC. In Exposure Draft E65, therefore, the IASC instead calls for both of these value changes to be included in current operations. While separate disclosure of the fair value changes and the effects of growth, either on the face of the income statement or in the notes thereto, is urged by the proposal, this is not going to be an actual requirement, again because of the possibility that these might not be separately measurable.

The DSOP also stipulates that the economic effects of extraordinary items should be separately presented in the income statement (as with other enterprises). The exposure draft states that events which, as a result of their size, nature or incidence, are relevant to an understanding of the enterprise's financial statements should be discussed in the notes. Examples include the proverbial 100-year flood and outbreaks of extremely virulent crop diseases. However, distinguishing the normal events which inevitably affect agriculture (storms, drought, etc.) from extraordinary ones (severe or extended storms and droughts, etc.) may present a unique challenge in practice.

Agricultural Produce

Agricultural produce is distinguished from biological assets and is not to be measured at fair value other than at the point of harvest, which is the point where biological assets become agricultural produce. For example, when crops are harvested they become agricultural produce and are initially valued at the fair value as of the date of harvest, at the location of harvest (i.e., the value of harvested crops at a remote point of delivery would not be pertinent measure). If there has been a time interval between the last valuation and the harvest, the value as of the harvest date should be determined or estimated; any increase or decrease since the last valuation would be taken into earnings.

Financial Statement Presentation

Balance sheet. The draft statement of principles suggested that biological assets should be classified as a distinct class of assets, being part of neither current nor noncurrent assets. The exposure draft, in contrast, stipulates that biological assets should be included in current and noncurrent assets, as appropriate, either in the aggregate or by major groups of biological assets.

The draft encourages that biological assets be further categorized according to class of animal or plant, nature of activities (e.g., being maintained for harvesting or as breeding stock), and the maturity or immaturity for the intended purpose. If the plant or animal is being maintained for consumption (to be harvested, etc.), maturity is gauged by attainment of harvestable specifications. If the plant or animal is for bearing purposes, the maturity criterion will be the attainment of sufficient maturity to sustain economic harvests.

In any event, the nature and stage of production of each group of biological assets should be described in narrative format in the notes to the financial statements. Consumable biological assets should be differentiated from bearer assets, with further subdivisions into mature and immature subgroups for each of these. The purpose of these disclosures is to give the users of the financial statements some insight into the timing of future cash flows, since the mature subgroups will presumably be realized through market transactions in the near future, and the pattern of cash flows resulting from bearer assets differs from those deriving from consumables.

Income statement. The changes in fair value should be presented on the face of the income statement, ideally broken down between groups of biological assets. However, group level detail may be reserved to the notes to the financial statements.

Also, while separate disclosure of the components of fair value change (i.e., that due to growth and that due to price changes) is encouraged, the IASC retreated from the position in the DSOP, which would have made this mandatory. Clearly, the change in fair value which is a consequence of price changes (whether general inflation or specific changes in the market prices of given commodities, such as wheat, due to factors such as the expectations regarding the harvest) is generically distinct from the growth which has occurred during the period being reported on. Distinguishing between these two factors would be important in making the financial reporting process more meaningful, and should be strongly encouraged. The draft does include several examples of how this dichotomizing of fair value changes can be accomplished and presented in the financial statements.

IAS 1 permits the presentation of expenses in accordance with either a natural classification (e.g., materials purchases, depreciation, etc.) or a functional basis (cost of sales, administrative, selling, etc.). E65 urges that the natural classification of income and expenses be adopted for the income statement. Sufficient detail is to be included in the face of the income statement to support an analysis of operating performance. However, these are recommendations, not strict requirements.

Disclosures. The major imposition of new disclosures by the standard which will evolve from E65 will likely be the reconciliation of carrying amount changes for the latest year being reported on (comparative data not being required). This reconciliation will be structured so as to highlight the following elements:

1. Changes in fair value attributable to physical changes and those due to changes in the per unit fair values (i.e., price changes), if the preparer adheres to the recommendation of the standard;
2. Increases due to purchases of biological assets and decreases due to sales thereof;
3. Decreases due to harvest;
4. The effects of net exchange differences arising on the translation of the financial statements of a foreign entity; and
5. Any other changes in the carrying amount of the biological assets.

Complying with IAS 1, regarding disclosure of the nature of operations, would, in the context of enterprises engaged in agricultural activities, result in disclosures (in narrative form or as quantified terms) of groups of biological assets, the nature of activities regarding each of these groups, the maturity or immaturity for intended purposes of each group, the relative significance of different groups by reference to nonmonetary amounts (e.g., numbers of animals, acres of trees) dedicated to each, and nonfinancial measures or estimates of the physical quantities of each group of assets at the balance sheet date and the output of agricultural produce during the period just ended.

Finally, a number of additional disclosures are mandated by the agriculture exposure draft, including the measurement bases used to derive fair values; whether an independent appraiser was utilized; for assets valued by net present value (rather than market prices), the discount rate employed and the number of years' future cash flows assumed; further details about the changes in fair value from the prior period; any restrictions on title and any pledging of biological assets as security for liabilities; commitments for further development or acquisitions of biological assets; specifics about risk management strategies employed by the entity (the use of hedging is widespread; the futures market, now heavily employed to control financial risks, was developed originally for agricultural commodities); and activities which are unsustainable, along with estimated dates of cessation of those activities. Other disclosures are of the carrying amount of agricultural land (historical cost or revalued amount) and of agricultural produce (governed by IAS 2, and subject to separate classification in the balance sheet).

Agricultural Land

Agricultural land will not be considered a biological asset and, thus, the principles espoused in the exposure draft for such assets would not apply to land. The requirements of IAS 16, which are applicable to other categories of plant, property, and equipment, would apply equally to agricultural land. The proposal encourages the use of the allowed alternative method (that is, revaluation), particularly for land-based systems such as orchards, plantations, and forests, where the fair value of the biological asset was determined from net realizable values which included the underlying land. It is also suggested that land be further classified in the balance sheet according to specific uses; alternatively, this information can be conveyed in the notes to the financial statements.

Intangible Assets Related to Agriculture

Under IAS 38, intangible assets may be carried at cost (the benchmark treatment) or at revalued amounts (the allowed alternative treatment), but only to the extent that active markets for the intangible exists, which is not expected to be commonly the case. Agricultural activities are expected to frequently involve intangibles such as water rights, production quotas, and pollution rights, and these might have active markets.

The IASC has recommended that, for the sake of consistency with the primary conclusions expressed in E65, if intangibles which pertain to the entity's agricultural activities have active markets, these should be presented in the balance sheet at their fair values. While E65 urges the use of the alternative method in IAS 38, however, it does not make this a requirement.

Government Grants

IAS 20 addresses the accounting for government grants, whether received with conditions attached or not, and whether received in cash or otherwise. E65 further states that if an unconditional grant is received in connection with biological assets that are measured at fair value, it should be recognized as income when it becomes receivable. For grants which are conditional, on the other hand, recognition in income will occur when there is reasonable assurance that the conditions have been met. If conditional grants are received before the conditions have been met, the item should be recognized as a liability, not revenue. For grants received in the form of nonmonetary assets, fair value is assessed as a means of accounting for the grant.

Transition to the New Standard

When the final standard is issued, which is likely to be in 2000, enterprises will have to apply the measurement criteria as of the beginning of the fiscal (financial reporting) year. The adjustment to previously reported carrying amounts will be taken into income in the year of the adoption as the effect of a change in accounting policies, so that this impact is not to be confused with fair value changes occurring in the current period. Given the likelihood of adoption of this new standard, it might be useful for agricultural enterprises to begin to direct some attention to fair value measurement strategies and the specific values of the biological assets employed by them.

As a result of the adoption of the new standard on agriculture, there will also be several consequential changes to be made to a number of other international standards. IAS 2 will be amended to explicitly recognize that the cost of agricultural produce harvested by the reporting enterprise will be the fair value thereof as of the date of harvest, at the place of harvest. Other less noteworthy changes will be made to IAS 16, 17, 20, and 36.

25 ACCOUNTING FOR INFLATION AND HYPERINFLATION

PERSPECTIVE AND ISSUES

The historical cost-based accounting model, employed almost universally for at least the past 60 years, resulted largely from the profession's embracing of the concepts of conservatism (or prudence), realization, and the stable measuring unit following the crash of 1929. Despite the obvious attractiveness of historical cost, especially its susceptibility to objective measurement, periodically there have been movements to adopt an accounting model that would be more consistent with economic reality. These efforts usually have coincided with periods of price instability. The most recent one occurred in the mid-1970s through the early 1980s in many developed nations.

Popular interest in inflation accounting (as all the various methods are referred to collectively) has diminished markedly since price stability has been largely restored over the past decade, and most of the financial reporting standards adopted (including the US, UK, and international standards) have been dropped or have fallen into disuse during this time. However, the ultimate return of inflation is a likelihood borne out by historical experience, and it would be unfortunate if the development of reporting models would have to begin again with a clean slate. Therefore, the financial reporting approaches to addressing both general and specific price changes are reviewed in this chapter.

The objectives of general price level (constant dollar or inflation) accounting, on the one hand, and specific price (current value, replacement cost, or current cost) accounting, on the other, are quite distinct, although often confused. The former attempts to address the measurement unit problem, which results from accounting's assumption that the unit of measurement of economic transactions (the US dollar, British pound, Swiss franc, etc.) remains immutable over time. For example, the results of transactions at different times, made with dollars of different purchasing power, are simply added together in the financial statements. As a consequence, statement users are given no insight into such matters as purchasing power gains or losses incurred by the entity.

Current cost accounting, in contrast, addresses the issue of valuation and the timing of earnings recognition. The realization principle generally precludes earnings recognition until all steps in the earnings process have been completed. (Losses, on the other hand, are often recognized earlier.) Many have argued, however, that when specific prices are rapidly rising, the failure to give these recognition until assets are sold causes significant economic events to be concealed from both outside parties (stockholders, employees, etc.) and from management, to the detriment of all concerned.

In the United States and the United Kingdom, general price level accounting or disclosures related thereto had been favored by professional standards setters. This was largely due to the greater ease with which these adjustments could be made, as well as to a conceptual opposition to breaching the realization principle. However, in both nations governmental agencies or commissions, as well as most academicians thinking about the issues, favored instead an accounting model that would address specific price changes, believing that such an approach would provide more useful information to decision makers. Once the momentum toward price level accounting was halted, standards were developed in the United States, the United Kingdom, and by the international standard setter, IASC, to require some disclosures on the current cost basis of accounting.

As noted, constant dollar and current value accounting are responses to different measurement issues and should not have been seen as true alternatives. However, the ability of statement users to comprehend a variety of different income measures presented to them simultaneously is limited. Accordingly, if historical costing is to remain as the primary measurement method for general purpose financial reporting, perhaps only one other measure will be required as a supplement. If so, some variant of current costing will undoubtedly be preferred. The current cost/constant dollar method first imposed by the US standard and later largely duplicated by the international standard (later made optional, however) is likely to be chosen for this mission.

IAS 29 addresses financial reporting in hyperinflationary economies. In general, this applies the same principles as general price level accounting, although the precise mechanism varies depending on whether the basic financial reporting model is one of historical costing or of current costing. Although IAS 15 has been made voluntary, IAS 29 remains mandatory where applicable.

Sources of IAS
IAS 15, 29

DEFINITIONS OF TERMS

Common dollar reporting. Synonymous with general price level or constant dollar financial reporting.

Constant dollar accounting. An accounting model that treats dollars of varying degrees of purchasing power essentially in the manner that foreign currencies are treated; dollars are translated into current purchasing power units and presented in restated financial statements. Constant dollar accounting converts all nonmonetary assets and equities from historical to current dollars by applying an index of general purchasing power. Specific value changes are ignored, and thus there are no holding gains or losses recognized. Monetary items are brought forward without adjustment, and these accounts (cash, claims to fixed amounts of cash, and obligations to pay fixed amounts of cash) therefore do give rise to purchasing power gains or losses. Constant dollar accounting does not attempt to address value changes.

Current cost accounting. An accounting model that attempts to measure economic values and changes therein, whether or not realized in the traditional accounting sense. In current cost accounting financial statements, nonmonetary items are reflected at current value amounts, measured variously by replacement cost, exit value, fair market value, net present value, or by other methodologies. Current cost-based statements of earnings will report as operating income the amount of resources that are available for distribution (to shareholders and others) without impairing the entity's ability to replace assets as they are sold or consumed in the operation of the business. Holding gains may or may not also be reportable as a component of income, although these are never deemed to be distributable unless the entity is liquidating itself. In a pure current cost accounting system, no purchasing power gains or losses are given recognition, but hybrid models have been proposed under US GAAP and IAS, which do recognize these as well as specific price changes.

Distributable (replicatable) earnings. The amount of resources that could be distributed (e.g., by dividends to shareholders) from the current period's earnings without impairing the entity's operating capacity vs. its level at the beginning of the period. This parallels the classic definition of economic income. It is generally conceded that current cost would provide the best measure of distributable earnings. Traditional historical cost-based financial reporting, on the other hand, does not attempt to measure economic income, but rather, seeks to match actual costs incurred against revenues generated; the result in many cases is that this measure of income will exceed real economic earnings.

Economic value. The ideal measure of current value/current cost; also known as deprival value. In practice, surrogate measures are often used instead.

Excess of specific price changes over general price level increase. A measure first introduced by the US GAAP standard on inflation accounting (SFAS 33) and usable under IAS 15 as well. This is the amount of increase in current cost of inventories and plant assets, in excess of the increase that would have occurred during the period had the change in values been at the rate of change of a broad-based market basket of goods and services.

Exit value. Also known as net realizable value, this is the measure of the resources that could be obtained by disposing of a specified asset, often for scrap or salvage value. Valuing assets at exit value is not generally valid as a measure of current cost, since value in use usually exceeds exit value, and most assets held by the enterprise will not be disposed of; however, for assets that are not to be replaced in the normal course of business, exit value may be a meaningful measure.

Fair value. Fair market value, or market value. For certain specialized properties, such as natural resources, this may be the most meaningful measure of current cost.

Fair value accounting. A now obsolete term which implies current cost or current value financial reporting.

Gains/losses on net monetary items. Synonymous with general purchasing power gains and losses.

Gearing adjustment. A term used in the proposed British inflation accounting standard, which reflects the conclusion that if an entity is financed externally (i.e., by debt), it may not need to retain resources in an amount equal to the replacement cost of goods sold and of depreciation in order to maintain existing productive capacity; sufficient borrowed funds must, however, continue to be available so that the existing degree of financial leverage (gearing) can be maintained in the future. This adjustment is not addressed by IAS 15.

Holding gains/losses. In general, the increase or decrease in the current cost of nonmonetary assets (plant assets and inventories, for the most part) during a period. Notwithstanding the gain/loss terminology, such items are not generally recognized as part of income but rather as part of stockholders' equity, although practice varies. Holding gains are not distributable to shareholders without impairing operating capacity. In some models, only the excess of specific price changes over general price level changes are deemed to be holding gains/losses.

Hyperinflation. The condition in an economy in which there is such extreme inflation that historical cost financial statements become meaningless; characterized by a general aversion of the population to holding monetary assets, the conducting of business in ways that provide some protection against inflation, such as denominating transactions in a stable foreign currency or indexing to compensate for price changes, and a cumulative inflation rate over 3 years approaching 100%.

Inventory profits. The overstatement of income resulting from charging cost of sales at historical levels instead of at replacement costs; during periods of rapid inflation, historical cost based income will exceed real, economic earnings (distributable or replicatable earnings); this is partly the result of inventory profits. Not all entities are affected similarly. Those using LIFO costing will be less severely affected, and entities having faster inventory turnover will also have less inventory profits.

Monetary items. Claims to, or obligations to pay, fixed sums of cash or its equivalent. Examples are accounts receivable and accounts payable. If constant dollar accounting is employed, net monetary assets or liabilities will create purchasing power gains or losses in periods of changing general prices, since such fixed claims to cash or obligations to pay cash gain or lose value as the general purchasing power of the currency grows or shrinks.

Net present value. The future cash flows that will be generated by operation of an asset, discounted by a relevant factor such as the opportunity cost of capital, to an equivalent present value amount. This is a surrogate measure for economic value (deprival value) that is useful in certain circumstances (e.g., determining the future net cash flow of income producing real estate). For other assets, such as machinery, this is difficult to compute because future cash flows are difficult to forecast and because the assets are part of integrated processes generating cash flows that cannot be attributed to each component.

Net realizable value. Generally used in accounting to denote the amount that could be realized from an immediate disposition of an asset. Also known as exit value. Net realizable value is sometimes used for current costing purposes if the asset in question is not intended to be held beyond a brief period.

Nonmonetary items. Items that are not claims to, or obligations to pay fixed sums of cash or its equivalent. Examples are inventories and plant assets. When constant dollar accounting is employed, all nonmonetary items are adjusted to current dollar equivalents by application of a general measure of purchasing power changes. If current cost accounting is employed, nonmonetary items are recorded at current economic values (measured by replacement cost, deprival value, etc.); nonmonetary equity accounts may be explicitly adjusted or the necessary balancing amounts can be imputed. Holding gains and losses result from applying current cost measures to nonmonetary items.

Price level accounting. See constant dollar accounting.

Purchasing power accounting. See constant dollar accounting.

Purchasing power gains/losses. The economic benefit or detriment that results when an entity has claims to fixed amounts of cash (monetary assets) or has obligations to pay fixed sums (monetary liabilities) during periods when the general purchasing power of the monetary unit is changing. An excess of monetary assets over monetary liabilities coupled with rising prices results in a purchasing power loss; an excess of monetary liabilities results in a gain. These are reversed if prices are declining.

Realized holding gains/losses. Holding gains/losses can be realized or unrealized. If an appreciated item of inventory is sold, the holding gain is realized; if unsold at period end, it is unrealized. Historical cost based accounting does not recognize unrealized holding gains/losses (with some exceptions), and realized holding gains/losses are merged with other operating income and not given separate recognition. Use of the term holding gain/loss was prohibited by the inflation accounting standard under US GAAP and is not addressed by IAS 15.

Recoverable amount. The amount that could be obtained either from the continued use of an asset (the net present value of future cash flows) or from its disposal (exit or net realizable value).

Replacement cost. The lowest cost that would be incurred to replace the service potential of an asset in the normal course of the business.

Replicatable earnings. See distributable earnings.

Reproduction cost. The cost of acquiring an asset identical to the one presently in use. The distinction between reproduction cost and replacement cost is that operating efficiencies and technological changes may have occurred and the nominally identical asset would have a different productive capacity. Typically, replacement costs are lower than reproduction costs, and use of the latter would tend to overstate the effects of inflation.

Unrealized holding gains/losses. Holding gains or losses that have yet to be realized through an arm's-length transaction.

Value in use. Also known as value to the business, this is defined as the lesser of current cost or net recoverable amount.

INFLATION ADJUSTED FINANCIAL REPORTING

CONCEPTS, RULES, AND EXAMPLES

Historical Review of Inflation Accounting

Accounting practice today, on virtually a worldwide basis, relies heavily on the historical cost measurement strategy, whereby resources and obligations are given recognition as assets and liabilities, respectively, at the original (dollar, yen, etc.) amount of the transaction from which they arose. Once recorded, these amounts are not altered to reflect changes in value, except to the limited extent that GAAP requires recognition of impairments (e.g., lower of cost or fair value for inventories, etc.). Most long-lived assets such as buildings are amortized against earnings on a rational basis over their estimated useful lives, while short-lived assets are expensed as physically consumed. Liabilities are maintained at cost until paid off or otherwise discharged.

It is useful to recall that before the historical cost model of financial reporting achieved nearly universal adoption, various alternative recognition and measurement approaches were experimented with. Fair value accounting was in fact widely employed in the nineteenth and early twentieth centuries, and for some regulatory purposes (especially in setting utility service prices, where regulated by governmental agencies) remained in vogue until 25 years ago. The retreat from fair value accounting was, in fact, due less to any inherent attractiveness of the historical cost model than to negative reaction to abuses in fair value reporting. This came to a climax during the 1920s in much of the industrialized world, when prosperity and inflation encouraged overly optimistic reflections of values, much of which were reversed after the onset of the worldwide Great Depression.

Most of what are known as generally accepted accounting principles (GAAP) were developed after the crash of 1929. The more important of the basic postulates, which underlie most of the historical cost accounting principles, include the realization concept, the stable currency assumption, the matching concept, conservatism (or prudence), and historical costing. Realization means that earnings are not recognized until a definitive event, involving an arm's-length transaction in most instances, has occurred. Stable currency refers to the presumption that a $1,000 machine purchased today is about the same as a $1,000 machine purchased 20 years ago, in terms of real productive capacity. The matching concept has come to suggest a quasi-mechanical relationship between costs incurred in prior periods and the revenues generated currently as a result; the net of these is deemed to define earnings. Conservatism, among other things, implies that all losses be provided for but that gains not be anticipated, and is often used as an argument against fair value accounting. Finally, the historical costing convention was adopted as the most objectively verifiable means of reporting economic events.

The confluence of these underlying postulates has served to make historical cost based accounting, as it has been practiced for the past 60 years, widely supported. Even periods of rampant inflation, as the Western industrialized nations experienced during the 1970s, has not seriously diminished enthusiasm for this model, despite much academic research and the fairly sophisticated and complete alternative financial reporting approaches proposed in the United Kingdom and the United States and a later international accounting standard that built on those two recommendations. All of these failed to generate wide support and have largely been abandoned, being relegated to suggested supplementary information status, with which very few reporting enterprises comply.

What should accounting measure? Accounting was invented to measure economic activity in order to facilitate it. It is an information system, the product of which is used by one or more groups of decision makers: managers, lenders, investors, even current and prospective employees. In common with other types of decision-relevant data, financial statements can be evaluated along a number of dimensions, of which relevance and objectivity are frequently noted as being the most valuable. Information measured or reported by accounting systems should be, on the one hand, objective in the sense that independent observers will closely agree that the information is correct, and on the other hand, the information should be computed and reported in such as way that its utility for decision makers is enhanced.

Objectivity has become what one critic called an occupational distortion of the accounting profession. While objectivity connotes a basic attitude of unprejudiced fairness that should be highly prized, it has also come to denote an excessive reliance on completed cash transactions as a basis for recording economic phenomena. However, objectivity at the cost of diminished relevance may not be a valid goal. It has been noted that "relevance is the more basic of the virtues; while a relevant valuation may sometimes be wrong, an irrelevant one can never be of use, no matter how objectively it is reached." Both the FASB in the United States and the IASC in the international arena have published conceptual framework documents which support the notion that more relevant information, even if necessitating a departure from the historical costing tradition, could be more valuable to users of financial statements.

Why inflation undermines historical cost financial reporting. Actual and would-be investors and creditors, as well as entity managers and others, desire accounting information to support their decision-making needs. Financial statements that ignore the effects of general price level changes as well as changes in specific prices are inadequate for several reasons.

1. Reported profits often exceed the earnings that could be distributed to shareholders without impairing the entity's ability to maintain the present level of operations, because so-called inventory profits are included in earnings and because depreciation charges are not adequate to provide for asset replacements.

2. Balance sheets fail to reflect the economic value of the business, because plant assets and inventories, especially, are recorded at historical values which may be lower than current fair values or replacement costs.

3. Future earnings prospects are not easily projected from historical cost-based earnings reports.

4. The impact of changes in the general price level on monetary assets and liabilities is not revealed, yet can be severe.

5. Because of the foregoing deficiencies, future capital needs are difficult to forecast, and in fact may contribute to the growing leveraging (borrowing) by many enterprises, which adds to their riskiness.

6. Distortions of real economic performance leads to social and political consequences ranging from suboptimal capital allocations to ill-conceived tax policies and public perceptions of corporate behavior.

Example

A business starts with one unit of inventory, which cost $2 and which at the end of the period is sold for $10 at a time when it would cost $7 to replace that very same unit on the display shelf. Traditional accounting would measure the earnings of the entity at $10 − $2 = $8, although clearly the business is only $3 "better off" at the end of the period than at the beginning, since real economic resources have only grown by $3 (after replacing the unit sold there is only that amount of extra resource available). The illusion that there was profit of $8 could readily destroy the entity if, for example, dividends of more than $3 were withdrawn or if fiscal policy led to taxes of more than $3 on the $8 profit.

On the other hand, if the financial report showed only $3 profit for the period, there could be several salutary effects. Owners' expectations for dividends would be tempered, the entity's real capital would more likely be preserved, and projections of future performance would be more accurate, although projections must always be fine-tuned since the past will never be replicated precisely.

The failure of the historical cost balance sheet to reflect values is yet another major deficiency of traditional financial reporting. True, accounting was never intended to report values per se, but the excess of assets over liabilities has always been denoted as net worth, and to many that clearly connotes value. Similarly, the alternative titles for the balance sheet, statement of financial position and statement of financial condition, strongly suggest value to the lay reader. The confusion largely stems from a failure to distinguish **realized** from **unrealized** value changes; if this distinction were carefully maintained, the balance sheet could be made more useful while remaining true to its traditions.

Evolving use of the financial statements. The traditional balance sheet was the primary, even the only, financial statement presented during much of accounting's history. However, beginning during the 1960s, the income statement achieved greater importance, partly because users came to realize that the balance sheet had become the repository for unmatched costs, deferred debits and credits, and other items that bore no relationship to real economic assets and obligations. In the aggressive and high-growth 1960s and early 1970s, the focus was largely on summary measures of enterprise performance, such as earnings per share, which derived from the income statement. During this era, the matching concept became the key underlying postulate that drove new accounting rules.

As a result of a series of unpleasant economic events, including numerous credit crunches and recessions in the 1970s and 1980s, the focus substantially shifted back to the balance sheet. Partly in response, the major accounting standard-setting bodies developed conceptual standards that urged the elimination of some of the items previously found on balance sheets that were not really either assets or liabilities. Some of these were the leftovers from double entry bookkeeping, which was oriented toward achieving income statement goals; an example is the interperiod tax allocations that resulted in the reporting of ever-growing deferred tax liabilities that were never going to be paid. While the tension between achieving a meaningful balance sheet and an accurate income statement is inherent in the accounting model in use for almost 500 years, accountants are learning that improvements in both can be achieved. Inflation adjusted accounting can contribute to this effort, as will be demonstrated.

General vs. specific price changes. An important distinction to be understood is that between general and specific price changes, and how the effects of each can be meaningfully reported on in financial statements. Changes in specific prices, as with the inventory example above, should not be confused with changes in the general level of prices, which give rise to what are often referred to as purchasing power gains or losses, and result from holding net monetary assets or liabilities during periods of changing general prices. As most consumers are well aware, during periods of general price inflation, holding net monetary assets typically results in experiencing a loss in purchasing power, while a net liability position leads to a gain, as obligations are repaid with "cheaper" dollars. Among other effects, prolonged periods of general price inflation motivates entities to become more leveraged (more indebted to others) because of these purchasing power gains, although in reality creditors are aware of this and adjust interest rates to compensate.

Specific prices may change in ways that are notably different from the trend in overall prices, and they may even move in opposite directions. This is particularly true of basic commodities such as agricultural products and minerals, but may also be true of manufactured goods, especially if technological changes have great influence. For example, even during the years of rampant inflation during the 1970s some commodities, such as copper, were dropping in price, and certain goods, such as computer memory chips, were also declining even in nominal prices. For entities dealing in either of these items, holding inventories of these **nonmonetary** goods (usually a hedge against price inflation) would have produced large economic losses during this time. Thus, not only the changes in general prices, but also the changes in specific prices, and very important, the interactions between these can have major effects on an enterprise's real wealth. Measurement of these phenomena should be within the province of accounting.

Experiments and proposals for inflation accounting. Over the past 50 years there have been a number of proposals for pure price level accounting, financial reporting that would be sensitive to changes in specific prices, and combinations of these. There have been proposals (academic proposals) for comprehensive financial statements that would be adjusted for inflation, as well as for supplemental disclosures that would isolate the major inflation effects without abandoning primary historical cost based statements (generally, the professional proposals and regulatory requirements were of this type). To place the requirements of IAS 15 in context, a number of its more prominent predecessors will be reviewed in brief.

Price level accounting concepts and proposals. At its simplest, price level accounting views any given currency at different points in time as being analogous to different currencies at the same point in time. That is, 1955 US dollars have the same relationship to 1996 dollars as 1996 Swiss francs have to 1996 dollars. They are "apples and oranges" and cannot be added or subtracted without first being converted to a common measuring unit. Thus, "pure" price level accounting is held to be within the mainstream historical cost tradition and is merely a translation of one currency into another for comparative purposes. A broadly based measure of all prices in the economy should be used in accomplishing this (often, a consumer price index of some sort is employed).

Consider a simple example. Assume that the index of general prices was as follows:

January 1, 1979	65
January 1, 1991	100
January 1, 2000	182
December 31, 2000	188

Also assume the following items selected from the December 31, 2000 balance sheet:

	Historical cost	Price level adjusted cost
Cash	$ 50,000	$ 50,000
Inventories (purchased 1/1/00)	350,000	
x 188/182		361,538
Land (acquired 1/1/79)	500,000	
x 188/65		1,446,154
Machinery (purchased 1/1/91)	300,000	
x 188/100		564,000
Accumulated depreciation	(200,000)	
x 188/100		(376,000)
Book value of assets	$1,000,000	$2,045,692
Less monetary liabilities	(500,000)	(500,000)
Net assets	$ 500,000	$1,545,692

In the foregoing, all nonmonetary items were adjusted to "current dollars" using the same index of general prices. This is not based on the notion that items such as inventory and machinery actually experienced price changes of that magnitude, but on the idea that converting these to current dollars is a process akin to converting foreign currency denominated financial statements. The implication is that the historical cost balance sheet, showing net assets of $500,000, is equivalent to a balance sheet that reports some items in German marks, some in French francs, some in Italian lira, and so on. The price level adjusted balance sheet, by contrast, is deemed to be equivalent to a balance sheet in which all items have been translated into dollars.

This analogy is a weak one, however. Not only are such statements essentially meaningless, they can also be misleading from a policy viewpoint. For example, during a period of rising prices, an entity holding more monetary assets than monetary liabilities will report an economic loss due to the decline in the purchasing power of its net monetary assets. Nonmonetary assets, of course, are adjusted for price changes and thus appear to be "immune" from purchasing power gains or losses. The implication is that holding nonmonetary assets is somehow preferable to holding monetary assets.

In the foregoing example, the net monetary liabilities at year end are $500,000 – $50,000 = $450,000. Assuming the same net monetary liability position at the beginning of 2000, the gain experienced by the entity (due to owning monetary debt during a period of depreciating currency) would be given as

$$(\$450,000 \times 188/182) - \$450,000 = \$14,835$$

This suggests that the entity has experienced a gain, at the obvious expense of its creditors, which have incurred a corresponding loss, in the amount of $14,835. This fails entirely to recognize that creditors may have demanded an inflation adjusted rate of return based on actual past and anticipated future inflationary behavior of the economy; if this were addressed in tandem with the computed purchasing power gain, a truer picture would be given of the real wisdom of the entity's financial strategy.

Furthermore, the actual price level protection afforded by holding investments in nonmonetary assets is a function of the changes in their specific values. If the replacement value of the inventory had declined, for example, during 1995, having held this inventory during the year would have been an economically unwise maneuver. Land that cost $500,000 might, due to its strategic location, now be worth $2.5 million, not the indicated $1.4 million, and the machinery might be obsolete due to technological changes, and not worth the approximately $190,000 suggested by the price level adjusted book value. In fairness, of course, the advocates of price level accounting do not claim that these adjusted amounts represent **values**, per se. However, the utility of these adjusted balance sheet captions for decision makers is difficult to fathom and the potential for misunderstanding is great.

US and UK proposals. A number of proposals have been offered over the years for either replacing traditional financial statements with price level adjusted statements, or for including supplementary price level statements in the annual report to shareholders. In the United States, the predecessor of the current accounting standard setter, the Accounting Principles Board, proposed supplementary reporting in 1969; no major publicly held corporation complied with this request, however. The FASB made a similar proposal in 1974 and might have succeeded in imposing this standard had not the US securities market watchdog, the SEC, suggested instead that a current value approach be developed. (Later the SEC did impose a replacement costing requirement on large companies, and the FASB followed with its own version a few years thereafter.)

In the United Kingdom a similar course of events occurred. After an early postwar recommendation (not implemented) that there be earnings set aside for asset replacements, a late-1960s proposal for supplementary price level adjusted reporting was made, followed a few years later by a more comprehensive constant dollar recommendation. As happened in the United States at about the same time, what appeared to be a private sector juggernaut favoring price level adjustments was derailed by governmental intervention. A Royal Commission, established in 1973, eventually produced the so-called Sandilands report, supporting current value accounting and not addressing the reporting of purchasing power gains or losses at all. This marked the end of British enthusiasm for general price level adjusted financial statements. Even a fairly complex later proposal (ED 18) made in 1977 did not incorporate any measure of purchasing power gains or losses, although it did add some novel embellishments to what basically was a current value model.

Other European nations have never been disposed favorably toward general price level accounting, with the exception of France. However, Latin American nations, having dealt with virtually runaway inflation for decades, have generally welcomed this type of financial reporting and in some cases have required it, even for some tax purposes. While price level adjustments are no more logical in Brazil, for example, than in the United States, since specific prices are changing, often at widely disparate rates, the role of accounting in those nations, serving as much more of an adjunct to the countries' respective tax collection and macroeconomic policy efforts than in European or other Western nations, has tended to encourage support for this approach to accounting for changing prices.

Current value models and proposals. By whatever name it is referred to, current value (replacement cost, current cost) accounting is really based on a wholly different concept than is price level (constant dollar) accounting. Current value financial reporting is far more closely tied to the original intent of the accounting model, which is to measure enterprise economic wealth and the changes therein from period to period. This suggests essentially a "balance sheet orientation" to income measurement, with the difference between net worth (as measured by current values) at year beginning and year end being, after adjustment for capital transactions, the measure of income or loss for the intervening period. How this is further analyzed and presented in the income statement (as realized and unrealized gains and losses) or even whether some of these changes even belong in the income statement (or instead, are reported in a separate statement of movements in equity, or are taken directly into equity) is a rather minor bookkeeping concern.

Although the proliferation of terminology of the many competing proposals can be confusing, four candidates as measures of current value can readily be identified: economic value, net present value, net realizable value (also known as exit value), and replacement cost (which is a measure of entry value). A brief explanation will facilitate the discussion of the IAS requirements later in this chapter.

Economic value is usually understood to mean the equilibrium fair market value of an asset. However, apart from items traded in auction markets, typically only securities and raw commodities, direct observation of economic value is not possible.

Net present value is often suggested as the ideal surrogate for economic value, since in a perfect market values are driven by the present value of future cash flows to be generated by the assets. Certain types of assets, such as rental properties, have predictable cash flows and in fact are often priced in this manner. On the other hand, for assets such as machinery, particularly those that are part of a complex integrated production process, determining cash flows is difficult.

Net realizable values (NRV) are more familiar to most accountants, since even under existing US, UK, and international accounting standards, there are numerous instances when references to NRV must be made to ascertain whether asset write-downs are to be required. NRV is a measure of "exit values" since these are the amounts that the organization would realize on asset disposition, net of all costs; from this perspective, this is a conservative measure (exit values are lower than entry values in almost all cases, since transactions are not costless), but also is subject to criticism since under the going concern assumption it is not anticipated that the enterprise will dispose of all its productive assets at current market prices, indeed, not at any prices, since these assets will be retained for use in the business.

The biggest failing of this measure, however, is that it does not assist in measuring economic income, since that metric is intended to reveal how much income an entity can distribute to its owners, and so on, while retaining the ability to replace its productive capacity as needed. In general, an income measure based on exit values would overstate earnings (since depreciation and cost of sales would be based on lower exit values for plant assets and inventory) when compared with an income measure based on entry values. Thus, while NRV is a familiar concept to many accountants, this is not the ideal candidate for a current value model.

Replacement cost is intended as a measure of entry value and hence of the earnings reinvestment needed to maintain real economic productive capacity. Actually, competing proposals have engaged in much hairsplitting over alternative concepts of entry value, and this deserves some attention here. The simplest concept of replacement value is the cost of replacing a specific machine, building, and so on, and in some industries it is indeed possible to determine these prices, at least in the short run, before technology changes occur. However, in many more instances (and in the long run, in all cases) exact physical replacements are not available, and even nominally identical replacements offer varying levels of productivity enhancements that make simplistic comparisons distortive.

As a very basic example, consider a machine with a cost of $40,000 that can produce 100 widgets per hour. The current price of the replacement machine is $50,000, that superficially suggests a specific price increase of 25% has occurred. However, on closer examination, it is determined that while nominally the same machine, some manufacturing enhancements have been made (e.g., the machine will require less maintenance, will require fewer labor inputs, runs at a higher speed, etc.) which have altered its effective capacity (considering reduced downtime, etc.) to 110 widgets per hour. Clearly, a naive adjustment for what is sometimes called "reproduction cost" would overstate the machine's value on the balance sheet and overstate periodic depreciation charges, thereby understating earnings. A truer measure of the replacement cost of the service potential of the asset, not the physical asset itself, would be given as

$$\$40,000 \times (50,000/40,000) \times 100/110 = \$45,454$$

That is, the service potential represented by the asset in use has a current replacement cost of $45,454, considering that a new machine costs 25% more but is 10% more productive.

Consider another example: An integrated production process uses machines A and B, which have reproduction costs today of $40,000 and $45,000, respectively.

However, management plans to acquire a new type of machine, C, which at a cost of $78,000 will replace both machines A and B and will produce the same output as its predecessors. The combined reproduction cost of $85,000 clearly overstates the replacement cost of the service potential of the existing machines in this case, even if there had been no technological changes affecting machines A and B.

Some, but not all, proposals that have been made in academia over the past 60 years, and by standards setters and regulatory authorities over the past 20 years, have understood the foregoing distinctions. For example, the US SEC requirements of the mid-1970s called for measures of the replacement cost of productive capacity, which clearly implied that productivity changes had to be factored in. The subsequent private sector rules issued by FASB seemed to redefine what the SEC had mandated to highlight its own current cost requirement; in essence, the FASB's current costs were nothing other than the SEC's replacement costs. Other proposals have been more ambiguous, however. Furthermore, measuring the impact of technological change adds vastly to the complexity of applying replacement cost measures, since raw replacement costs (known as reproduction costs) are often easily obtained (from catalog prices, etc.), but productivity adjustments must be ascertained by carefully evaluating advertising claims, engineering studies, and other sources of information, which can be a complex and costly process.

Limitations on replacement cost. While entry value is clearly the most logical of the alternative measures discussed thus far, under certain circumstances one of the other candidates would be preferable as a measure to use in current cost financial reporting. For example, consider a situation in which the value in use (economic value or net present value of future cash flows) is lower than replacement cost, due to changing market conditions affecting pricing of the entity's output. In such a circumstance, although the enterprise may continue to use the machines on hand and to sell the output profitably, it would not contemplate replacement of the asset, instead viewing it as a cash cow. If current cost financial statements were to be developed that incorporated depreciation based on the replacement cost of the machine, earnings would be understated, since actual replacement is not to be provided for. A number of other hypothetical circumstances could also be presented; the end result is that a series of decision rules can be developed to guide the selection of the best measure of current cost. These are summarized in the following table, where NRC stands for net replacement cost, which is synonymous with current cost; NRV is net realizable value or exit value; and EV is the same as net present value.

Conditions	Value to the business
EV > NRC > NRV	NRC
NRC > EV > NRV	EV
NRC > NRV > EV	NRV
EV > NRV > NRC	NRC
NRV > EV > NRC	NRC
NRV > NRC > EV	NRC

Measuring Income Under the Replacement Cost Approach

There are two reasons to employ replacement cost accounting: (1) to compute a measure of earnings that can probably be replicated on an ongoing basis by the enterprise and approximates real economic wealth creation, and (2) to present a balance sheet that presents the economic condition of the entity at a point in time. Of these, the first is by far the more important objective, since decision makers' use of financial statements is largely oriented toward the future operations of the business, in which they are lenders, owners, managers, or employees.

Given the foregoing, the principal use of replacement cost information will be to assist in computing current period earnings on a true economic basis. The income statement items which on the historical cost basis are most distortive, in most cases, are depreciation and cost of sales. Historical cost depreciation can be based on asset prices that are 10 to 40 years old, during which time even modest price changes can compound to very sizable misrepresentations. Cost of sales will not typically suffer from compounding over such a long period, since turnover for most businesses will be in a matter of months (although this can be greatly distorted if low LIFO inventory costs are released into cost of sales), but since cost of sales will account for a much larger part of the entity's total costs than does depreciation, it can still have a major impact.

Thus, current cost/replacement cost/current value earnings are typically computed by adjusting historical cost income by an allowance for replacement cost depreciation and cost of sales. Typically, these two adjustments will effectively derive a modified earnings amount that closely approximates economic earnings. This modified amount can be paid out as dividends or otherwise disbursed, while leaving the enterprise with the ability to replace its productive capacity and continue to operate at the same level as it had been. (This does not, however, address the matter of purchasing power that may have been gained or lost by holding net monetary assets or liabilities during the period, which requires yet another computation.)

Determining current costs. In practice, replacement costs are developed by applying one or more of four principal techniques: indexation, direct pricing, unit pricing, and functional pricing. Each has advantages and disadvantages, and no single technique will be applicable to all fact situations and all types of assets. The following are useful in determining current costs of plant assets.

Indexation is accomplished by applying appropriate indices to the historical cost of the assets. Assuming that the assets in use were acquired in the usual manner (bargain purchases and other such means of acquisition will thwart this effort, since any index when applied to a nonstandard base will result in a meaningless adjusted number) and that an appropriate index can be obtained or developed (which incorporates productivity changes as well as price variations), this will be the most efficient approach to employ. For many categories of manufactured goods, such as machinery and equipment, this technique has been widely used with excellent results. One concern is that many published indices actually address only reproduction costs, and if not adjusted further, the likely outcome will be that costs are overstated and adjusted earnings will be artificially depressed.

Direct pricing, as the name suggests, relies on information provided by vendors and others having data about the selling prices of replacement assets. To the extent that these are list prices that do not reflect actual market transactions, these must be adjusted, and the same concern with productivity enhancements mentioned with reference to indexation must also be addressed. Since many enterprises are in constant, close contact with their vendors, obtaining such information is often straightforward, particularly with regard to machinery and other equipment.

Unit pricing is the least commonly employed method but can be useful when estimating the replacement cost of buildings. This is the bricks-and-mortar approach, which relies on statistical data about the per unit cost of constructing various types of buildings and other assets. For example, construction cost data may suggest that single-story light industrial buildings in cold climates (e.g., Europe) with certain other defined attributes may have a current cost of $47 per square foot, or that a first-class high-rise urban hotel in England has a construction cost of $125,000 per room. By expanding these per unit costs to the scale of the enterprise's facilities, a fairly accurate replacement cost can be derived. There are complications: for example, costs are not linearly related to size of facility due to the presence of fixed costs, but these are widely understood and readily dealt with. Unit pricing is typically not meaningful for machinery or equipment, however.

Functional pricing is the most difficult of the four principal techniques and is best reserved for highly integrated production processes, such as refineries and chemical plants, where attempts to price individual components would be exceptionally difficult. For example, a plant capable of producing 400,000 tons of polyethylene annually could be priced as a unit by having an engineering estimate made of the cost to construct similar capacity in the current environment. Clearly, this is not a merely mechanical effort, as indexation in particular is likely to be, but demands the services of a skilled estimator. Technological issues are neatly avoided since the focus is on creating a new plant with defined output capacity, using whatever mix of components would be most cost-effective. This technique has been widely employed in actual practice.

Inventory costing problems. For a merchandising concern, direct pricing is likely to be an effective technique to assist in developing cost of sales on a current cost basis. Manufacturing firms, on the other hand, will need to build up replacement cost basis cost of goods manufactured and sold by separately analyzing the cost behavior of each major cost element (e.g., labor contracts, overhead expenses, and raw materials prices). It is unlikely that these will have experienced the same price movements, and therefore an averaging approach would not be sufficiently accurate. Also, as product mix changes over time, the entity may be subject to varying influences from one period to the next. Finally, the inventory costing method used (e.g., LIFO vs. FIFO) will affect the extent of adjustment to be made, with (assuming that costs trend upward over time) relatively greater adjustments made to cost of sales determined on the FIFO basis, since relatively older costs are included in the GAAP income statement.

Whatever assortment of methods is used, the end product is a restated inventory of plant assets, depreciation on which must then be computed. For the current cost earnings data to be comparable with the historical cost financial statements, it is usually recommended that no other decisions be superimposed. For example, no changes in asset useful lives should be made, for to do so would exacerbate or ameliorate the impact of the replacement cost depreciation and make interpretation very difficult for anyone not intimately familiar with the company. Some ancillary costs may need to be adjusted in computing cost of sales and depreciation on the revised basis. For example, if the only replacement machines available will reduce the need for skilled labor, the (higher) replacement cost depreciation should be reduced by related cost savings, if accurately predictable. There are literally scores of similar issues to be addressed, and indeed entire volumes have been written providing detailed guidance on how to apply current cost measures.

Examples of current costing adjustments to depreciation and cost of sales

Example 1

Hapsburg Corp. is a wholesale distributor for a single product. For 2000, the company reports sales of $35,000,000, representing sales of 600,000 units of its single product. The traditional income statement reports cost of sales as follows:

	($000 omitted)
Beginning inventory	$ 8.8
Purchases, net	25.7
Ending inventory	(6.5)
Cost of goods sold	$28.0

Reference to purchase orders reveals the fact that product cost early in 2000 was $42 per unit and was $55 per unit late in December of that year. The company employs FIFO accounting.

Since there is no evidence presented to the effect that net realizable value of the product is below current replacement cost, current cost can be used without modification.

Beginning current cost	$42.0
Ending current cost	$55.0
Average	$48.5

Total cost of sales for the period, on a replacement cost basis, is therefore $48.5 x 600,000 units = $29,100,000.

Example 2

In the following example, deprival value is, for one product line, better measured by net realizable value than by replacement cost. The company, St. Ignatz Mfg. Co., manufactures and sells two products, A and B. Product A has been a declining item for several years, and management now believes that it must close this line due to the shrinking market share, which will not support higher costs. St. Ignatz will continue to produce Product B and may possibly expand into new products in the future.

Company records show the following results in 2000:

		($000,000 omitted)	
	Product A	*Product B*	*Total*
Sales	$19.5	$40.5	$60.0
Cost of sales			
Beginning inventory	12.5	6.8	
Purchases	8.7	20.0	
Ending inventory	(3.0)	(5.4)	
Cost of sales	18.2	21.4	39.6
Gross profit	$ 1.3	$19.1	20.4
All other expenses			(18.8)
Net income			$ 1.6

The company's manufacturing records show the following data:

Current costs, beginning of year	$52.0	$75.0
Current costs, ending of year	$63.0	$79.0
Current costs, average	$57.5	$77.0

Sales in 2000 comprised 390,000 units of Product A and 540,000 units of Product B. Management believes that the market for Product A cannot support further price increases, and thus the remaining inventory will probably be sold at a loss. Selling expenses are estimated at $6 per unit.

Product A has a recoverable value lower than current manufacturing costs. The net recoverable amount is given by the selling price per unit less selling expenses: $50 – $6 = $44 per unit. Current cost of sales is $44 x $390,000 = $17,160,000. Note that recoverable amount, not replacement cost, is used.

Product B has an average current cost of $77 per unit, so 2000 cost of sales on a current cost basis is $77 x $540,000 = $41,580,000.

Total cost of sales on the current cost basis is therefore $17,160,000 + $41,580,000 = $58,740,000.

Example 3

Jacquet Corp. reports depreciation of $16,510 for 2000 in its historical cost based financial statements prepared on the basis of GAAP. A summary of plant assets reveals the following:

Asset class	*Total depreciable cost**	*Useful life (yr)*	*Depreciation rate (%)***
A	$24,000	8	12 1/2
B	50,000	10	10
C	45,000	12	8 1/3
D	60,000	15	6 2/3
E	19,000	25	4

* *Depreciable cost is historical cost less salvage value.*
** *Depreciation rate is 1/useful life.*

Management employs appraisals and other methods, including information from vendors and indices, to develop current cost data as shown below.

Asset class	*1/1/00*	Current costs *12/31/00*	*Average*
A	$28,000	$31,000	$29,500
B	56,000	60,000	58,000
C	55,000	60,000	57,500
D	62,000	68,000	65,000
E	30,000	33,000	31,500

From this information, the current cost depreciation for the year 2000 can be computed as follows:

Asset class	Depreciation rate (%)	Average current cost	Depreciation
A	12 1/2	$29,500	$ 3,687.5
B	10	58,000	5,800.0
C	8 1/3	57,500	4,792.0
D	6 2/3	65,000	4,333.0
E	4	31,500	1,260.0
			$19,872.5

Note that the replacement cost basis depreciation for the year is $3,362.50 greater than was the historical cost depreciation.

Purchasing power gains or losses in the context of current cost accounting. Thus far, general price level (or purchasing power or constant dollar) accounting has been viewed as a reporting concept totally separate from current value (or current cost or replacement cost) accounting. As noted, advocates of price level adjustments have argued that these are not attempts to measure value, as current cost accounting is, but merely to "translate" old dollars into current dollars. For their part, advocates of current value accounting have generally been more focused on deriving a measure of the "replicatable" economic earnings of the enterprise, usually with no mention of the fact that changing specific prices of productive assets exist against a backdrop of changing general price levels.

In fact, the FASB requirements imposed in the late 1970s (and dropped in the 1980s for lack of interest) attempted to measure both general and specific price changes. That standard included a requirement for reporting purchasing power gains or losses, as well as for stating the amount of adjustment for current cost depreciation and cost of sales. The IASC has imposed a somewhat similar requirement in IAS 15 (compliance with which is now wholly voluntary), albeit with less specificity. The guidance in the now dormant FASB standard can be used by those attempting to report under IAS 15 without limitation, as there are no conflicts between these sets of rules.

Requirements Under IAS 15

The experience of the international accounting standard that was designed to reveal the effects of inflation is very similar to the experiences in the United States and the United Kingdom. That is, while there was a great clamor, primarily from the financial analyst community, in favor of this supplementary financial reporting model, once it was mandated there was a noticeable decline in interest. It would appear that analysts much prefer to develop their own estimates of the impact of inflation on the companies they follow and may have an inherent distrust of management-supplied data. As for management, it generally argued that such information was useless before the standard was imposed, which at the time seemed to be self-serving posturing in the hope that an expensive new mandate could be averted.

As in the United States, after a few years of demanding the supplementary information (IAS 15 was imposed in 1981), the IASC announced in 1989 that due to lack of worldwide support for this noble experiment, it would no longer be required to comply with the standard, although still encouraged. In the event that inflation again becomes a concern, which eventually it will as such cycles are almost inevitable, this standard can be reactivated.

Alternative approaches permitted. The standard was intended to require certain supplementary current value and constant dollar information. A great deal of latitude was given to entities, which could choose from among a range of supportable methods to accomplish this directive. As the standard notes, the two main methods are intended to (1) recognize income after the general purchasing power of shareholders' equity has been maintained (price level accounting), and (2) recognize income after the operating capacity of the enterprise is maintained (current value accounting, which may or may not also include adjustments related to the general price level).

General purchasing power approach. IAS 15 does not stipulate what index should be used to measure the change in the general level of prices but does identify depreciation and cost of sales as being subject to adjustment, as well as a need to measure the effect of changing prices on net monetary items held.

Current cost approach. IAS 15 acknowledges the existence of various methods, with replacement cost being identified as the principal measurement strategy, subject to the caveat that if replacement cost is higher than both net realizable value and present value, replacement value is not to be used. Instead, the higher of net realizable value and present value would denote current value, as explained earlier in this chapter. Replacement costs are said to be found in information about current acquisitions of new or used assets of similar productive capacities or service potentials. Specific price indices are also favorably noted as sources of current cost data. Net realizable value is generally a representation of net current selling price (i.e., exit value), while present value is the discounted amount of future receipts attributable to the asset.

The standard discusses at some length the need to determine an adjustment for the effects of changing prices on net monetary items, including long-term debt, but suggests that some current cost methods (which it does not name) may not need to address this separately. In particular, the discussion in IAS 15 alludes to the argument (made explicitly in the British proposal of the 1970s but not otherwise enacted in any standards) that since depreciable assets in particular are often acquired at least in part in exchange for monetary debt, the gross replacement cost adjustment exaggerates the negative effect on earnings and that this is moderated to the extent leveraging is used.

In fact, one can make this argument, but as noted earlier in the chapter, to do so assumes that added borrowing in periods of rising prices is "costless" in the sense that no premium is added by lenders to compensate for either (1) the borrowers' greater riskiness as they become more leveraged, or (2) for the loss to be incurred on repayment of the debt in devalued currency. It is not likely that in the long run lenders will go uncompensated for either of these, and therefore to offset the higher charges for depreciation and cost of sales by the fraction to be borne by the lenders may be imprudent.

Minimum disclosures required by IAS 15. The disclosures required (now made optional) include the following:

1. The amount of adjustment to, or the adjusted amount of, depreciation of property plant and equipment
2. The amount of adjustment to, or the adjusted amount of, cost of sales
3. The adjustments relating to monetary items, the effect of borrowing, or equity interests when such adjustments have been taken into account in determining income under the (inflation) accounting method adopted
4. The overall effect on results of the adjustments described above, as well as any other items reflecting the effects of changing prices.
5. If a current cost method is used, the current cost of property, plant, and equipment and of inventories should be disclosed.
6. There should be a description of the methods used to compute the foregoing items.

Example of disclosure consistent with IAS 15

DeKalb Thermodynamics Inc.
Statements of Income From Continuing Operations
Year Ended December 31, 2000

	As reported in primary statements	*Adjusted for general inflation*	*Adjusted for changes in specific prices (current costs)*
Net sales and other revenue	$253,000	$253,000	$253,000
Cost of goods sold	$197,000	$204,384	$205,408
Depreciation and amortization	10,000	14,130	19,500
Other operating expense	20,835	20,835	20,835
Interest expense	7,165	7,165	7,165
Provision for income taxes	9,000	9,000	9,000
	$244,000	$255,514	$261,908
Income (loss) from continuing operations	$ 9,000	$ (2,514)	$ (8,908)
Gain from decline in purchasing power of net amounts owed		$ 7,729	$ 7,729
Increase in specific prices (current costs) of inventories and property, plant, and equipment held during the year			$ 24,608
Effect of general price level increase			18,959
Excess of increase in specific prices over increase in general price level			$ 5,649

Note: Current costs are determined by consulting current prices posted for plant assets, net of applicable discounts, and by reference to indexed or replacement costs adjusted for productivity increases. The gain on purchasing power change is determined by reference to the consumer price index for all urban consumers.

FINANCIAL REPORTING IN HYPERINFLATIONARY ECONOMIES

CONCEPTS, RULES, AND EXAMPLES

Hyperinflation and Financial Reporting

Hyperinflation is a condition that is difficult to define precisely, as there is not a clear demarcation between merely rampant inflation and true hyperinflation. However, in any given economic system, when the general population has so lost faith in the stability of the local economy that business transactions are commonly either denominated in a stable reference currency of another country, or are structured to incorporate an indexing feature intended to compensate for the distortive effects of inflation, this condition may be present. As a benchmark, when cumulative inflation over 3 years approaches or exceeds 100%, it must be conceded that the economy is suffering from hyperinflation.

Hyperinflation is obviously a major problem for any economy, as it creates severe distortions and, left unaddressed, results in uncontrolled acceleration of the rate of price changes, ending in inevitable collapse as was witnessed in post-World War I Germany. From a financial reporting perspective, there are also major problems, since even over a brief interval, such as a year or even a quarter, the income statement will contain transactions with such a variety of purchasing power units that aggregation becomes meaningless, as would adding dollars, francs, and marks. This is precisely the problem discussed earlier in this chapter, but raised to an exponential level.

In a truly hyperinflationary economy, users of financial statements are unable to make meaningful use of such statements unless they have been recast into currency units having purchasing power defined by prices at or near the date of the statements. Unless this common denominator is employed, the financial statements are too difficult to interpret for purposes of making management, investing, and credit decisions. Although some sophisticated users, particularly in those countries where hyperinflation has been endemic, such as some of the South American nations, including Brazil and Argentina, and for certain periods nations such as Israel, are able to apply rules of thumb to cope with this problem, in general modifications must be made to general-purpose financial statements if they are to have any value.

Under international accounting standards, if hyperinflation is deemed to characterize the economy, a form of price level accounting must be applied to the financial statements to conform with generally accepted accounting principles. IAS 29 requires that all the financial statements be adjusted to reflect year-end general price levels, which entails applying a broad-based index to all nonmonetary items on the balance sheet and to all transactions reported in the income statement and the cash flow statement.

Restating Historical Cost Financial Statements Under Hyperinflation Conditions

The precise adjustments to be made depend on whether the financial reporting system is based on historical costs or on current costs, as described in IAS 15 and explained earlier in this chapter. Although in both cases the goal is to restate the financial statements into the measuring unit that exists at the balance sheet date, the mechanics will vary to some extent.

If the financial reporting system is based on historical costing, the process used to adjust the balance sheet can be summarized as follows:

1. Monetary assets and liabilities are already presented in units of year-end purchasing power and receive no further adjustment. (See the appendix for a categorization of different assets and liabilities as to their status as monetary or nonmonetary.)

2. Monetary assets and liabilities that are linked to price changes, such as indexed debt securities, are adjusted according to the terms of the contractual arrangement. This does not change the characterization of these items as monetary, but it does serve to reduce or even eliminate the purchasing power gain or loss that would have otherwise been experienced as a result of holding these items during periods of changing general prices.

3. Nonmonetary items are adjusted by applying a ratio of indices, the numerator of which is the general price level index at the balance sheet date and the denominator of which is the index as of the acquisition or inception date of the item in question. For some items, such as plant assets, this is a straightforward process, while for others, such as work in process inventories, this can be more complex.

4. Certain assets cannot be adjusted as described above, because even in nominally historical cost financial statements these items have been revised to some other basis, such as fair value or net realizable amounts. For example, under the allowed alternative method of IAS 16, plant, property, and equipment can be adjusted to fair value. In such a case, no further adjustment would be warranted, assuming that the adjustment to fair value was made as of the latest balance sheet date (although IAS 16 only demands that this be done at least every 3 years). If the latest revaluation was as of an earlier date, the carrying amounts should be further adjusted to compensate for changes in the general price level from that date to the balance sheet date, using the indexing technique noted above.

5. Consistent with the established principles of historical cost accounting, if the restated amounts of nonmonetary assets exceed the recoverable amounts, these must be reduced appropriately. This can easily occur, since (as discussed earlier in this chapter) specific prices of goods will vary by differing amounts, even in a hyperinflationary environment, and in fact some may decline in terms of current cost even in such cases, particularly when technological change occurs rapidly. Since the application of price level accounting, whether for ordinary inflation or for hyperinflation, does not imply an abandonment of historical costing, being a mere translation into more timely and relevant purchasing power units, the rules of that mode of financial reporting still apply. Generally accepted accounting principles require that assets not be stated at amounts in excess of realizable amounts, and this constraint applies even when price level adjustments are reflected.

6. Equity accounts must also be restated to compensate for changing prices. Paid-in capital accounts are indexed by reference to the dates when the capital was contributed, which are usually a discrete number of identifiable transactions over the life of the enterprise. Revaluation accounts, if any, are eliminated entirely, as these will be subsumed in restated retained earnings. The retained earnings account itself is the most complex to analyze and in

practice is often treated as a balancing figure after all other balance sheet accounts have been restated. However, it is possible to compute the adjustment to this account directly, and that is the recommended course of action, lest other errors go undetected. To adjust retained earnings, each year's earnings should be adjusted by a ratio of indices, the numerator being the general price level as of the balance sheet date, and the denominator being the price level as of the end of the year for which the earnings were reported. Reductions of retained earnings for dividends paid should be adjusted similarly.

7. IAS 29 addresses a few other special problem areas. For example, the standard notes that borrowing costs typically already reflect the impact of inflation (more accurately, interest rates reflect inflationary expectations), and thus it would represent a form of double counting to fully index capital asset costs for price level changes when part of the cost of the asset was capitalized interest, as defined in IAS 23 as an allowed alternative method. As a practical matter, interest costs are often not a material component of recorded asset amounts, and the inflation-related component would only be a fraction of interest costs capitalized. However, the general rule is to delete that fraction of the capitalized borrowing costs which represents inflationary compensation, since the entire cost of the asset will be indexed to current purchasing units.

To restate the current period's income statement, a reasonably accurate result can be obtained if revenue and expense accounts are multiplied by the ratio of end-of-period prices to average prices for the period. Where price changes were not relatively constant throughout the period, or when transactions did not occur ratably, as when there was a distinct seasonal pattern to sales activity, a more precise measurement effort might be needed. This can be particularly important when a devaluation of the currency took place during the year.

While IAS 29 addresses the cash flow statement only perfunctorily (its issuance was prior to the revision of IAS 7), this financial statement must also be modified to report all items in terms of year-end purchasing power units. For example, changes in working capital accounts, used to convert net income into cash flow from operating activities, will be altered to reflect the real (i.e., inflation adjusted) changes. To illustrate, if beginning accounts receivable were $500,000 and ending receivables were $650,000, but prices rose by 40% during the year, the apparent $150,000 increase in receivables (which would be a use of cash) is really a $50,000 decrease [($500,000 x 1.4 = $700,000) – $650,000], which in cash flow terms is a source of cash. Other items must be handled similarly. Investing and financing activities should be adjusted on an item-by-item basis, since these are normally discrete events that do not occur ratably throughout the year.

In addition to the foregoing, the adjusted income statement will report a gain or loss on net monetary items held. As an approximation, this will be computed by applying the change in general prices for the year to the average net monetary assets (or liabilities) outstanding during the year. If net monetary items changed materially at one or more times during the year, a more detailed computation would be warranted. In the income statement, the gain or loss on net monetary items should be associated with the adjustment relating to items that are linked to price level changes (indexed debt, etc.) as well as with interest income and expense and foreign exchange adjustments, since theoretically at least, all these items contain a component that reflects inflationary behavior.

Restating Current Cost Financial Statements Under Hyperinflation Conditions

If the financial reporting system is based on current costing (as described earlier in the chapter), the process used to adjust the balance sheet can be summarized as follows:

1. Monetary assets and liabilities are already presented in units of year-end purchasing power and receive no further adjustment. (See the appendix for a categorization of different assets and liabilities as to their status as monetary or nonmonetary.)
2. Monetary assets and liabilities that are linked to price changes, such as indexed debt securities, are adjusted according to the terms of the contractual arrangement. This does not change the characterization of these items as monetary, but it does serve to reduce or even eliminate the purchasing power gain or loss that would have otherwise been experienced as a result of holding these items during periods of changing general prices.
3. Nonmonetary items are already stated at year-end current values or replacement costs and need no further adjustments. Issues related to recoverable amounts and other complications associated with price level adjusted historical costs should not normally arise.
4. Equity accounts must also be restated to compensate for changing prices. Paid-in capital accounts are indexed by reference to the dates when the capital was contributed, which are usually a discrete number of identifiable transactions over the life of the enterprise. Revaluation accounts are eliminated entirely, as these will be subsumed in restated retained earnings. The retained earnings account itself will typically be a "balancing account" under this scenario, since detailed analysis would be very difficult, although certainly not impossible, to accomplish.

The current cost income statement, absent the price level component, will reflect transactions at current costs as of the transaction dates. For example, cost of sales will be comprised of the costs as of each transaction date (usually approximated on an average basis). To report these as of the balance sheet date, these costs will have to be further inflated to year-end purchasing power units, by means of the ratio of general price level indices, as suggested above.

In addition to the foregoing, the adjusted income statement will report a gain or loss on net monetary items held. This will be similar to that discussed under the historical cost reporting above. However, consistent with IAS 15, current cost income statements already will include the net gain or loss on monetary items held, which need not be computed again.

To the extent that restated earnings differ from earnings on which income taxes are computed, there will be a need to provide more or less tax accrual, which will be a deferred tax obligation or asset, depending on the circumstances.

Comparative Financial Statements

Consistent with the underlying concept of reporting in hyperinflationary economies, all prior-year financial statement amounts must be updated to purchasing power units as of the most recent balance sheet date. This will be a relatively simple process of applying a ratio of indices of the current year-end price level to the year earlier price level.

Other Disclosure Issues

IAS 29 requires that when the standard is applied, the fact that hyperinflation adjustments have been made be noted. Furthermore, the underlying basis of accounting--historical cost or current cost--should be stipulated, as should the price level index that was utilized in making the adjustments.

Economies Which Cease Being Hyperinflationary

When application of IAS 29 is discontinued, the amounts reported in the last balance sheet that had been adjusted become, effectively, the new cost basis. That is, previously applied adjustments are not reversed, since an end to a period of hyperinflation generally means only that prices have plateaued, not that they have deflated to earlier levels.

APPENDIX

MONETARY VS. NONMONETARY ITEMS

Item	*Monetary*	*Nonmonetary*	*Requires analysis*
Cash on hand, demand deposits, and time deposits	x		
Foreign currency and claims to foreign currency	x		
Securities			
Common stock (passive investment)		x	
Preferred stock (convertible or participating) and convertible bonds			x
Other preferred stock or bonds	x		
Accounts and notes receivable and allowance for doubtful accounts	x		
Mortgage loan receivables	x		
Inventories		x	
Loans made to employees	x		
Prepaid expenses			x
Long-term receivables	x		
Refundable deposits	x		
Advances to unconsolidated subsidiaries	x		
Equity in unconsolidated subsidiaries		x	
Pension and other funds			x
Property, plant, and equipment and accumulated depreciation		x	
Cash surrender value of life insurance	x		
Purchase commitments (portion paid on fixed-price contracts)		x	
Advances to suppliers (not on fixed-price contracts)	x		
Deferred income tax charges	x		
Patents, trademarks, goodwill, and other intangible assets		x	
Deferred life insurance policy acquisition costs	x		
Deferred property and casualty insurance policy acquisition costs		x	
Accounts payable and accrued expenses	x		
Accrued vacation pay			x
Cash dividends payable	x		
Obligations payable in foreign currency	x		
Sales commitments (portion collected on fixed-price contracts)		x	
Advances from customers (not on fixed-price contracts)	x		
Accrued losses on purchase commitments	x		
Deferred revenue			x
Refundable deposits	x		
Bonds payable, other long-term debt, and related discount or premium	x		
Accrued pension obligations			x
Obligations under product warranties		x	
Deferred income tax obligations	x		
Deferred investment tax credits		x	
Life or property and casualty insurance policy reserves	x		
Unearned insurance premiums		x	
Deposit liabilities of financial institutions	x		

26 GOVERNMENT GRANTS

PERSPECTIVE AND ISSUES

Government grants or other types of government assistance are usually provided to enterprises to encourage them to embark on activities that they would not, presumably, have undertaken in the absence of such assistance. Government assistance is action by the government aimed at providing economic benefits to an enterprise or a class of enterprises that fulfill certain criteria. A government grant, on the other hand, is government assistance that entails the transfer of resources in return for compliance, either past or future, with certain conditions relating to the enterprise's operating activities.

International Accounting Standard (IAS) 20, which is the standard relating to accounting for government grants and disclosure of government assistance, was approved in November 1982. The standard was reformatted in 1994, but there were no substantive changes made to the originally approved text of the standard. However, certain terminology was changed and a revised format was adopted in order to conform it to current IASC practice. Since IOSCO advised the IASC in June 1994 that IAS 20 was acceptable to it for the purposes of the core set of standards, IAS 20 was not reviewed as part of the IASC/IOSCO core set of standards work program. Currently, the IASC has no plans to review IAS 20, although it realizes that the choice of treatments with respect to grants related to assets allowed under the standard may technically not be consistent with the IASC's *Framework* (IASC Insight, June 1998).

The receipt of government assistance could be important to the presentation of financial statements of an enterprise; thus the method of accounting used to recognize such government assistance must be appropriate. IAS 20 deals with the accounting treatment and disclosure of government grants and the disclosure requirements of government assistance. Depending on the nature of the assistance given and the conditions attached to it, government assistance could be of many types. Government assistance can take the form of a grant, a forgivable loan and other forms of assistance, such as technical advice.

Sources of IAS
IAS 20, *SIC* 10

DEFINITIONS OF TERMS

Fair value. The amount for which an asset could be exchanged between a knowledgeable, willing buyer and a knowledgeable, willing seller in an arm's-length transaction.

Forgivable loans. Those loans which the lender undertakes to waive repayment of under certain prescribed conditions.

Government. For the purposes of IAS 20, the term government refers not only to a government (of a country), as is generally understood, but also to government agencies and similar bodies whether local, national, or international.

Government assistance. Government assistance is action by government aimed at providing an economic benefit to an enterprise or group of enterprises qualifying under certain criteria. It includes a government grant and also includes other kinds of nonmonetary government assistance such as providing, at no cost, legal advice to an entrepreneur for setting up a business in a free trade zone. It **excludes** benefits provided indirectly through action affecting trading conditions in general; for example, laying roads that connect the industrial area in which an enterprise operates to the nearest city or imposing trade constraints on foreign companies in order to protect domestic entrepreneurs in general.

Government grants. A government grant is a form of a government assistance that involves the transfer of resources to an enterprise in return for past or future compliance (by the enterprise) of certain conditions relating to its operating activities. It excludes

- Those forms of government assistance that cannot reasonably be valued, and
- Transactions with governments that cannot be distinguished from the normal trading transactions of the enterprise.

Grants related to assets. Those government grants whose primary condition is that an enterprise qualifying for them should acquire (either purchase or construct) a long-term asset or assets are referred to as "grants related to assets." Subsidiary conditions may also be attached to such a grant. Examples of subsidiary conditions include specifying the type of long-term assets, location of long-term assets, or periods during which the long-term assets are to be acquired or held.

Grants related to income. Government grants, other than those related to assets, are grants related to income.

CONCEPTS, RULES AND EXAMPLES

Scope

This standard deals with the accounting treatment and disclosure requirements of grants received by enterprises from a government. It also mandates disclosure requirements of other forms of government assistance.

The standard specifies certain exclusions. In addition to the **three exclusions** contained within the definitions of the terms "government grant" and "government assistance," IAS 20, para 2, excludes the following from the purview of the standard:

1. Special problems arising in reflecting the effects of changing prices on financial statements or similar supplementary information;
2. Government assistance provided in the form of tax benefits (including income tax holidays, investment tax credits, accelerated depreciation allowances and concessions in tax rates); and
3. Government participation in the ownership of the enterprise.

The rationale behind excluding clauses 1. and 2. above seems fairly obvious (they are covered by other international accounting standards); IAS 15 addresses the effects of changing prices on financial statements, while tax benefits are dealt with by IAS 12. The reason for excluding clause 3. above, however, has been the subject of much controversy and conjecture. Authorities on the subject have offered different opinions as plausible reasons for specifically excluding "government participation in the ownership of the enterprise" from the scope of IAS 20. According to one school of thought, participation in ownership of an enterprise is normally in anticipation of a return on the investment while government assistance is provided with an economic cause in mind, for example, the public interest or public policy. Furthermore, government assistance is provided "to encourage an enterprise to embark on a course of action which it would not have taken if the assistance was not provided" (IAS 20, para 4). Thus, supporters of this school of thought argue that because the rationale behind the two government actions is vastly different, such exclusion seems proper.

According to another group of experts, the nonexclusion of government ownership from the scope of the standard would have caused great difficulty in implementing the standard in certain cases. For instance, distinguishing economic benefits provided by the government to a government corporation based on ownership criteria vis-à-vis economic benefits provided by the government to a government corporation under a normal government assistance program (under which program other enterprises also receive government grants) would be practically impossible. Thus, according to the proponents of the above line of thinking, government participation in the ownership of an enterprise is specifically excluded from the scope of IAS 20. Whatever the intent may be, with such exclusion contained in IAS 20, government participation in ownership of an enterprise would automatically be excluded from the scope of this standard. Thus, when the government invests in the equity of an enterprise (with the intention of encouraging the enterprise to undertake a line of business that it would normally not have embarked on), such government participation in ownership of the enterprise would **not qualify** as a government grant under this standard.

Government Grants

Government grants are assistance provided by government by transfer of resources (either monetary or nonmonetary) to enterprises. In order to qualify as a government grant, in strict technical terms, it is a prerequisite that the grant should be provided by the government to an enterprise in return for past or future compliance with conditions relating to the operating activities of the enterprise.

For quite some time now, it has been unclear whether the provisions of IAS 20 would apply even to government assistance aimed at encouraging or supporting business activities in certain regions or industry sectors, since related conditions may not specifically relate to the operating activities of the enterprise. Examples of such grants are: government grants which involve transfer of resources to enterprises to operate in a particular area (i.e., an economically backward area) or a particular industry (i.e., an agriculture-based industry which due to its low profitability may not be a popular choice of entrepreneurs). The Standing Interpretations Committee's interpretation, SIC 10, has clarified that "the general requirement to operate in certain regions or industry sectors in order to qualify for the government assistance constitutes such a condition in accordance with IAS 20.03." This has set at rest the confusion as to whether or not such government assistance do fall within the definition of government grants and thus the requirements of IAS 20 apply to them as well.

Recognition of Government Grants

Criteria for recognition. Government grants are provided in return for past or future compliance of certain conditions. Thus grants should not be recognized until there is **reasonable assurance** that both

1. The enterprise will comply with the conditions attaching to the grant; and
2. The grant(s) will be received.

Some interesting issues relating to recognition and treatment of government grants are considered below.

Firstly, the receipt of the grant does not provide any assurance that in fact the conditions attaching to the grant have or will be complied with by the enterprise. Thus, both conditions are equally important and the enterprise should have reasonable assurance with respect to the two conditions before a grant could be recognized.

Secondly, the term "reasonable assurance" has not been defined in this standard. However, one of the recognition criteria for income under the IASC's *Framework* is existence of "sufficient degree of certainty." Furthermore, under IAS 18, revenue is recognized only when it is probable that economic benefits will flow to the enterprise. Thus, the criterion of reasonable assurance could possibly be interpreted as probable. Comparing this with the criterion for the recognition of "contingent gains" under IAS 37, it appears that there the criterion has been made more stringent than the above criterion for recognition of a government grant. In case of recognition of a government grant, it seems the criterion has been relaxed to a degree lower than virtually certain--it has been pegged at the reasonable assurance level. However, under IAS 37 and for that matter even under the former IAS 10, which dealt with contingencies before the standard was revised in 1999, contingent gains could only be recognized if, and only if, realization was virtually certain. In the authors' opinion, this issue needs to be considered by the IASC in case a revision of the standard is undertaken at a later point in time.

Thirdly, under IAS 20, para 10, a forgivable loan from government is treated as a government grant when there is reasonable assurance that the enterprise will meet the terms of forgiveness of the loan. Thus, on receiving a forgivable loan from a government and on fulfilling the criterion of reasonable assurance with respect to meeting the terms of forgiveness of the loan, an enterprise would normally recognize the government grant. Some authorities on the subject have suggested that the grant would be recognized when the loan is forgiven and not when the forgivable loan is received. Under IAS 20, para 10, it is fairly obvious that "a forgivable loan from the government is treated as a grant when there is reasonable assurance that the enterprise will meet the terms for forgiveness of the loan"(emphasis added). In the authors' opinion, this implies that the recognition of the grant is to be made at the point of time when the forgivable loan is granted, as opposed to the point of time when it is actually forgiven.

Finally, IAS 20, para 11, clarifies that once a grant has been recognized, any related contingency would be treated in accordance with IAS 10, *Contingencies and Events Occurring After the Balance Sheet Date*. This would imply that for periods beginning on or after July 1, 1999, any related contingency should be treated in accordance with IAS 37 which supersedes the former IAS 10 with respect to contingencies.

Recognition period. Two broad approaches with respect to the accounting treatment of government grants have been discussed by the standard: the "capital approach" and the "income approach." The standard clearly does **not** support the capital approach, which advocates crediting a grant directly to the shareholders' equity. Endorsing the income approach, the standard lays down the rule for recognition of government grants as follows: Government grants should be recognized as income, on a systematic and rational basis, over the periods necessary to match them with the related costs. As a corollary, and by way of abundant precaution, the standard reiterates that government grants should **not** be credited directly to shareholders' interests.

The standard lays down rules for recognition of grants under different conditions. These are explained through numerical examples as follows:

1. *"Grants in recognition of specific costs are recognized as income over the same period as the relevant expense."* (IAS 20, para 17).

To illustrate this rule, let us consider the following example: An enterprise receives a grant of $ 30 million to defray environmental costs over a period of 5 years. Environmental costs will be incurred by the enterprise as follows:

Year	Costs
1	$1 million
2	$2 million
3	$3 million
4	$4 million
5	$5 million

Total environment costs will equal $15 million, whereas the grant received is $30 million.

Applying the principle outlined in the standard for recognition of the grant, that is, recognizing the grant as income "over the period which matches the costs" and using a "systematic and rational basis," the total grant would be recognized as follows:

Year	Grant recognized
1	$ 30 * (1/15) = $ 2 million
2	$ 30 * (2/15) = $ 4 million
3	$ 30 * (3/15) = $ 6 million
4	$ 30 * (4/15) = $ 8 million
5	$ 30 * (5/15) = $ 10 million

2. *"Grants related to depreciable assets are usually recognized as income over the periods and in the proportions in which depreciation on those assets is charged."* (IAS 20, para 17)

The following example will illustrate the above rule:

An enterprise receives a grant of $100 million to purchase a refinery in an economically backward area. The enterprise has estimated that such a refinery would cost $200 million. The secondary condition attached to the grant is that the enterprise should hire laborers locally (i.e., from the economically backward area where the refinery is located) instead of employing laborers from other parts of the country. It should maintain a ratio of 1:1 (local laborers : laborers from outside) in its labor force for the next 5 years. The refinery is to be depreciated using the straight-line method over a period of 10 years.

The grant will be recognized over a period of 10 years. In each of the 10 years, the grant will be recognized in proportion to the annual depreciation on the refinery. Thus, $10 million will be recognized as income in each of the 10 years. With regard to the secondary condition of maintenance of the ratio of 1:1 in the labor force, this contingency would need to be disclosed in the footnotes to the financial statements for the next 5 years (during which period the condition is in force) in accordance with disclosure requirements of IAS 37.

3. *"Grants related to nondepreciable assets may also require the fulfillment of certain obligations and would then be recognized as income over periods which bear the cost of meeting the obligations."* (IAS 20, para 19)

To understand this rule, let us consider the following case study:

ABN Inc. was granted 1000 acres of land, on the outskirts of the city, by a local government authority. The condition attached to this grant was that ABN Inc. should clean up this land and lay roads by employing laborers from the village in which the land is located. The government has fixed the minimum wage payable to the workers. The entire operation will take 3 years and is estimated to cost $60 million. This amount will be spent as follows: $10 million each in the first and second years and $40 million in the third year. The fair value of this land is presently $120 million.

ABN Inc. would need to recognize the fair value of the grant over the period of 3 years in proportion to the cost of meeting the obligation. Thus, $120 million will be recognized as follows:

Year	Grant recognized
1	$ 120 * (10/60) = $ 20 million
2	$ 120 * (10/60) = $ 20 million
3	$ 120 * (40/60) = $ 80 million

4. *"Grants are sometimes received as part of a package of financial or fiscal aids to which a number of conditions are attached."* (IAS 20, para 19)

When different conditions attach to different components of the grant, the terms of the grant would have to be evaluated in order to determine how the various elements of the grant would be earned by the enterprise. Based on that assessment, the total grant amount would then be apportioned.

For example, an enterprise receives a consolidated grant of $120 million. Two-thirds of the grant is to be utilized to purchase a college building for students from third-world or developing countries. The balance of the grant is for subsidizing the tuition costs of those students for 4 years from the date of the grant.

The grant would first be apportioned as follows:

Grant related to assets   (2/3) = $ 80 million, and
Grant related to income (1/3) = $ 40 million

The grant related to assets would be recognized in income over the useful life of the college building, for example, 10 years, using a systematic and rational basis. Assuming the college building is depreciated using the straight-line method, this portion of the grant (i.e., $80 million) would be recognized as income over a period of 10 years at $8 million per year.

The grant related to income would be recognized over a period of 4 years. Assuming that the tuition subsidy will be offered evenly over the period of 4 years, this portion of the grant (i.e., $40 million) would be taken to income over a period of 4 years at $10 million per year.

5. *"A government grant that becomes receivable as compensation for expenses or losses already incurred or for the purpose of giving immediate financial support to the enterprise with no future related costs should be recognized as income of the period in which it becomes receivable, as an extraordinary item, if appropriate."* (IAS 20, para 20)

Sometimes grants are awarded for the purposes of giving immediate financial support to an enterprise, for example, to revive a commercial insolvent business (referred to as "sick unit" in third-world countries). Such grants are not given as incentives to invest funds in specified areas or for a specified purpose from which the benefits will be derived over a period of time in the future. Instead such grants are awarded to compensate an enterprise for losses incurred in the past. Thus, they should be recognized as income in the period in which the enterprise becomes eligible to receive such grants.

A grant may be awarded to an enterprise to compensate it for losses incurred in the past for operating out of an economically backward area that has been hit by an earthquake recently. During the period the enterprise operated in that area, the area experienced an earthquake and thus the enterprise incurred massive losses. Such a grant received by the enterprise should be recognized as income in the year in which the grant becomes receivable. Also, since the losses suffered are extraordinary in nature, the grant may need to be presented as an extraordinary item in the financial statements.

Nonmonetary Grants

A government grant may not always be given in cash or cash equivalents. Sometimes a government grant may take the form of a transfer of a nonmonetary asset, such as grant of a plot of land or a building in a remote area. In these circumstances the standard prescribes the following optional accounting treatments:

1. To account for both the grant and the asset at the fair value of the nonmonetary asset, or
2. To record both the asset and the grant at a "nominal amount."

Presentation of Grants Related to Assets

Presentation on the balance sheet. Government grants related to assets, including nonmonetary grants at fair value, should be presented in the balance sheet in either of the two ways

1. By setting up the grant as deferred income, or
2. By deducting the grant in arriving at the carrying amount of the asset.

To understand this better, let us consider the following case study:

> Natraj Corp. received a grant related to a factory building which it bought in 1997. The total amount of the grant was $3 million. Natraj Corp. purchased the building from an industrialist identified by the government. The factory building was located in the slums of the city and was to be repossessed by a government agency from the industrialist, in case Natraj Corp. had not purchased it from him. The factory building was purchased for $9 million by Natraj Corp. The useful life of the building is not considered to be more than 3 years mainly because it was not properly maintained by the industrialist.

Under Option 1: Set up the grant as deferred income.

- The grant of $3 million would be set up initially as deferred income in 1997.
- At the end of 1997, $1 million would be recognized as income and the balance of $2 million would be carried forward in the balance sheet.
- At the end of 1998, $1 million would be taken to income and the balance of $1 million would be carried forward in the balance sheet.
- At the end of 1999, $1 million would be taken to income.

Under Option 2: The grant will be deducted from carrying value.

The grant of $3 million is deducted from the gross book value of the asset to arrive at the carrying value of $6 million. The useful life being 3 years, annual depreciation of $2 million per year is charged to the income statement for the years 1997, 1998, and 1999.

The effect on the operating results is the same whether the first or the second option is chosen.

Under the second option, the grant is indirectly recognized in income through the reduced depreciation charge of $1 million per year, whereas under the first option, it is taken to income directly.

Presentation in the cash flow statement. When grants related to assets are received in cash, there is an inflow of cash to be shown under the investing activities section of the cash flow statement. Furthermore, there would also be an outflow resulting from the purchase of the asset. IAS 20, para 28, specifically requires that both these movements should be shown separately and not be netted. The standard further clarifies that such movements should be shown separately regardless of whether or not the grant is deducted from the related asset for the purposes of the balance sheet presentation.

Presentation of Grants Related to Income

The standard allows a free choice between two presentations:

Option 1: Grant presented as a credit in the income statement, either separately or under a general heading other income

Option 2: Grant deducted in reporting the related expense

The standard does not show any bias towards any one option. It acknowledges the reasoning given in support of each approach by its supporters. The standard considers both methods as acceptable. However, it does recommend disclosure of the grant for a proper understanding of the financial statements. The standard recognizes that the disclosure of the effect of the grants on any item of income or expense may be appropriate.

Repayment of Government Grants

When a government grant becomes repayable, for example, due to nonfulfillment of a condition attaching to it, it should be treated as a change in estimate, under IAS 8, and accounted for prospectively (as opposed to retrospectively).

Repayment of a grant related to income should

1. First be applied against any unamortized deferred income (credit) set up in respect of the grant, and
2. To the extent the repayment exceeds any such deferred income (credit), or in case no deferred credit exists, the repayment should be recognized immediately as an expense.

Repayment of a grant related to an asset should be

1. Recorded by increasing the carrying amount of the asset or reducing the deferred income balance by the amount repayable, and
2. The cumulative additional depreciation that would have been recognized to date as an expense in the absence of the grant should be recognized immediately as an expense.

When a grant related to an asset becomes repayable, it would become incumbent upon the enterprise to assess whether any impairment in value of the asset (to which the repayable grant relates) has resulted. For example, a bridge is being constructed through funding from a government grant and during the construction period, because of nonfulfillment of the terms of the grant, the grant became repayable. Since the grant was provided to assist in the construction, it is possible that the enterprise may not be in a position to arrange funds to complete the project. In such a circumstance, the asset is impaired and may need to be written down to its recoverable value, in accordance with IAS 36.

Government Assistance

Government assistance includes government grants. IAS 20 deals with both accounting and disclosure of government grants and disclosure of government assistance. Thus government assistance comprises government grants and other forms of government assistance (i.e. those not involving transfer of resources).

Excluded from the government assistance are certain forms of government benefits that cannot reasonably have a value placed on them, such as free technical or other professional advice. Also excluded from government assistance are government benefits that cannot be distinguished from the normal trading transactions of the enterprise. The reason for the second exclusion is obvious: although the benefit cannot be disputed, any attempt to segregate it would necessarily be arbitrary.

Loans at zero or low interest are a form of government assistance. They should not have a value attributed to them in the financial statements, since the benefit could only be quantified by imputing interest costs, which is arbitrary. Thus, an enterprise that is currently benefiting from such assistance (e.g., in the form of low interest), but is likely to borrow funds in the near future at commercial rates of interest, would need to disclose when the full interest is going to commence.

Disclosures

IAS 20, para 39 prescribes the following disclosures:

1. The accounting policy adopted for government grants, including the methods of presentation adopted in the financial statements;
2. The nature and extent of government grants recognized in the financial statements and an indication of other forms of government assistance from which the enterprise has directly benefited; and
3. Unfulfilled conditions and other contingencies attaching to government assistance that has been recognized.

APPENDIX

DISCLOSURE CHECKLIST

This checklist provides a reference to the disclosures common to the financial statements of enterprises which are complying with International Accounting Standards (IAS). Disclosures required by all standards which are effective as of January 1, 2000, are set forth in this checklist. However, to minimize confusion, those IAS which are not effective until later dates are excluded. Thus, IAS 39, *Financial Instruments: Recognition and Measurement*, which is effective for periods beginning on or after July 1, 2001, is not considered herein (but IAS 39 Disclosures are set forth in Chapter 10). Similarly, changes to IAS which have been proposed but which have not been promulgated, are not addressed in this checklist.

DISCLOSURE CHECKLIST INDEX

General

A. Basis of Reporting
B. Compliance With International Accounting Standards
C. Accounting Changes
D. Related-Party Disclosures
E. Contingent Liabilities and Contingent Assets
F. Events After Balance Sheet Date
G. Comparative Information
H. Going Concern
I. Current/Noncurrent Distinction

Balance Sheet

A. Minimum Disclosures on the Face of the Balance Sheet
B. Additional Line Items on the Face of the Balance Sheet
C. Further Subclassifications of Line Items Presented
D. Inventories
E. Property, Plant, and Equipment
F. Intangible Assets
G. Other Long-Term Assets
H. Financial Instruments
I. Provisions
J. Deferred Tax Liabilities and Assets
K. Pensions
L. Employers' Accounting for Postretirement Benefits Other Than Pensions
M. Leases--From the Standpoint of Lessees

   N.   Leases--From the Standpoint of Lessors
   O.   Stockholders' Equity

Income Statement

   A.   Minimum Disclosures on the Face of the Income Statement
   B.   Investments
   C.   Income Taxes
   D.   Extraordinary Items
   E.   Discontinuing Operations
   F.   Segment Data
   G.   Construction Contracts
   H.   Foreign Currency Translation
   I.   Business Combinations and Consolidations
   J.   Earnings per Share
   K.   Dividends per Share
   L.   Impairments of Assets

Statement of Cash Flows

   A.   Basis of Presentation
   B.   Format
   C.   Additional Recommended Disclosures

Statement of Changes in Equity

   A.   Statement of Changes in Equity
   B.   Statement of Recognized Gains and Losses

Notes to the Financial Statements

   A.   Structure of the Notes to the Financial Statements
   B.   Accounting Policies

Interim Financial Statements

   A.   Minimum Components of an Interim Financial Report
   B.   Form and Content of Interim Financial Statements
   C.   Selected Explanatory Notes

Disclosures for Banks and Similar Financial Institutions (IAS 30)

   A.   Income Statement
   B.   Balance Sheet
   C.   Contingencies and Commitments Including Off-Balance-Sheet Items
   D.   Maturities of Assets and Liabilities

E. Concentrations of Assets and Liabilities
F. Losses on Loans and Advances
G. General Banking Risks
H. Assets Pledged as Security
I. Related-Party Transactions
J. Trust Activities

GENERAL

A. Basis of Reporting

1. Name of the enterprise whose financial statements are being presented, or other means of identification;
2. Enterprise's country of incorporation, domicile and legal form;
3. Address of its registered office or principal place of business if different from the registered office;
4. Disclosure whether the financial statements cover the individual enterprise or a group of enterprises;
5. Name of the reporting enterprise's parent and the ultimate parent enterprise of the group;
6. Number of employees either as of the year end or the average for the period;
7. Currency in terms of which financial statements are expressed;
8. Level of precision used in the presentation of the figures in the financial statements;
9. Description of the nature of the enterprise's operations and its principal activities;
10. Balance sheet date and the period covered by the financial statements.

(IAS 1 [revised 1997], Paras 46 and 102)

B. Compliance With International Accounting Standards

1. An enterprise whose financial statements comply with International Accounting Standards should disclose that fact. Unless financial statements comply with all the requirements of each applicable IAS and each applicable interpretation of the Standing Interpretations Committee (SIC), they should not be described as complying with IAS.

(IAS 1 [revised 1997], Para 11)

2. In extremely rare cases, when management has concluded that compliance with a requirement of an IAS would be misleading, and thus departure from a requirement is necessary to achieve a fair presentation, an enterprise should disclose

a. That the management has concluded that the financial statement fairly present the enterprise's financial position, financial performance and cash flows;

b. That it has complied in all material respects with the applicable IAS except that it departed from a Standard in order to achieve a fair presentation;

c. The IAS from which the enterprise has departed, the nature of the departure, including the treatment that the Standard would require, the reason why that treatment would be misleading in the circumstances, and the treatment actually adopted; and

d. The financial impact of the departure on the enterprise's net profit or loss, assets, liabilities, equity, and cash flows for each period presented.

(IAS 1 [revised 1997], Para 13)

3. When an International Accounting Standard is applied before it becomes operative (i.e., before its effective date as mandated by the specific standard) that fact should be disclosed.

(IAS 1 [revised 1997], Para 19)

C. Accounting Changes

1. Change in accounting policy (alternative disclosures rules apply based on election of benchmark or allowed alternative treatment).

   a. If benchmark treatment is elected

      (1) Reason(s) for the change;

      (2) Amount of adjustment on current period and for each period presented;

      (3) Amount of adjustment relating to periods prior to those included in the comparative information; and

      (4) (a) If comparative information has been restated, the fact that it has been restated, or

      (b) If comparative information is not restated because it is not practicable to do so, then disclosure of this fact.

(IAS 8, Para 53)

   b. If allowed alternative treatment is elected

      (1) Reason(s) for the change;

      (2) The amount of adjustment recognized in the net profit or loss for the current period;

      (3) The amount of the adjustment included in each period for which pro forma information is presented and the amount of adjustment

relating to periods prior to those included in the financial statements; and

(4) If it is not practicable to present pro forma information, this fact should be disclosed.

(IAS 8, Para 57)

2. Change in accounting estimate

a. Nature and amount of change in an accounting estimate, if material.
b. If it is not practicable to quantify the amount, this fact should be disclosed.

(IAS 8, Para 30)

3. Correction of fundamental errors

a. If benchmark treatment is elected

(1) The nature of the fundamental error;
(2) The amount of the correction for the current period and for each period presented;
(3) The amount of the correction which relates to periods prior to those included in the comparative information; and
(4) (a) If comparative information has been restated, this fact should be made explicit, or
(b) If comparative information is not restated because it is not practicable to do so, then this fact must be disclosed.

(IAS 8, Para 37)

b. If allowed alternative treatment is elected

(1) The nature of fundamental error;
(2) The amount of the correction of the fundamental error which is recognized in the net profit or loss for the current period;
(3) The amount of the correction of the fundamental error which is included in each period for which pro forma information is presented and the amount of correction relating to periods prior to those included in the pro forma information; and
(4) If it is not practicable to present pro forma information, this fact should be disclosed.

(IAS 8, Para 40)

D. Related-Party Disclosures

1. Those related-party relationships where "control" exists should be disclosed--**whether or not there have been transactions between the related parties**.

    (IAS 24, Para 20)

2. Where transactions have taken place between related parties, the following disclosures are required to be made by the reporting enterprise:

    a. The nature of the related-party relationship;
    b. The types of related-party transactions; and
    c. The elements of the transactions necessary for an understanding of the financial statements, including

        (1) An indication of the volume of the transactions either as an amount or as an appropriate proportion;
        (2) Amounts or appropriate proportions of outstanding items; and
        (3) Pricing policies.

    (IAS 24, Paras 22 & 23)

3. Aggregation of items of similar nature is permitted, unless separate disclosure is needed for an understanding of the effects of the related-party transactions on the financial statements of the reporting enterprise.

    (IAS 24, Para 24)

E. Contingent Liabilities and Contingent Assets

1. An enterprise should disclose for each class of contingent liability, unless the possibility of any outflow in settlement is remote, a brief description of the nature of the contingent liability. If practicable, an enterprise should also disclose an estimate of its financial effect, an indication of the uncertainties relating to the amount or timing of the outflow, and the possibility of any reimbursement.

    (IAS 37, Para 86)

2. An enterprise should disclose a brief description of the nature of the contingent assets at the balance sheet date, where an inflow of economic benefits is probable. Where practical, an estimate of their financial effect should be disclosed.

    (IAS 37, Para 89)

3. Where an enterprise does not disclose any information required by IAS 37, para 86, and IAS 37, para 89, because it is not practical to do so, that fact should be disclosed.

    (IAS 37, Para 91)

4. In **extremely rare circumstances,** if disclosure of some or all of the information required by IAS 37, para 86, and IAS 37, para 89, would prejudice seriously the position of the enterprise in a dispute with other parties, on the subject matter of the contingent liability or contingent asset, an enterprise **need not disclose such information.** Instead, in such cases it should disclose the general nature of the dispute, along with the fact that, and reason why, the information has not been disclosed by the enterprise.

(IAS 37, Para 92)

F. Events After the Balance Sheet Date

1. When nonadjusting events after the balance sheet date are so significant that nondisclosure would affect the ability of the users of the financial statements to make proper evaluations and decisions, an enterprise should disclose the nature of the event and an estimate of its financial effect. Such disclosure is required for each significant category of nonadjusting post balance sheet event. If such an estimate is not possible, a statement to that effect should be made.

(IAS 10 [revised 1999], Para 20)

2. The date when the financial statements were authorized for issue and who gave the authorization should be disclosed by an enterprise. If the enterprise's owners or others have the power to amend the financial statements after issuance, the enterprise should disclose that fact.

(IAS 10 [revised 1999], Para 16)

3. If an enterprise receives information after the balance sheet date about the conditions that existed at the balance sheet date, the enterprise should update disclosures that relate to these conditions, based on the new information received.

(IAS 10 [revised 1999], Para 18)

G. Comparative Information

1. Financial statements should disclose comparative information in respect of the preceding period for all numerical information presented.

(IAS 1 [revised 1997], Para 38)

2. In the case of property, plant, and equipment, comparative information is **not required** for reconciliation of carrying amount at the beginning and end of the period.

(IAS 16 [revised 1998], Para 60)

3. In the case of intangible assets, comparative information is **not required** for reconciliation of carrying amount at the beginning and end of the period.

(IAS 38, Para 107)

4. In the case of provisions, comparative information is **not required** for the reconciliation of carrying amount at the beginning and end of the period.

(IAS 37, Para 84)

H. Going Concern

When management is aware in making its assessment of material uncertainties related to events or conditions which may cast significant doubt upon the enterprise's ability to continue as a going concern, those uncertainties should be disclosed. When the financial statements are not prepared on a going concern basis, that fact should be disclosed, together with the basis on which the financial statements are prepared and the reason why the enterprise is not considered to be a going concern.

(IAS 1 [revised 1997], Para 23)

I. Current/Noncurrent Distinction

Whether an enterprise chooses a classified presentation of the balance sheet with current/noncurrent distinction, or it presents an unclassified balance sheet, it should disclose, for each asset and liability item that combines amounts expected to be recovered or settled both before and after 12 months from the balance sheet date, the amount expected to be recovered or settled after more than 12.

(IAS 1 [revised 1997], Para 54)

BALANCE SHEET

A. Minimum Disclosures on the Face of the Balance Sheet

The face of the balance sheet should include, as a minimum, the following categories:

1. Property, plant, and equipment;
2. Intangible assets;
3. Financial assets (excluding amounts shown [d], [f], and [g] below);
4. Investments accounted for using the equity method;
5. Inventories;
6. Trade and other receivables;
7. Cash and cash equivalents;

8. Trade and other payables;
9. Tax liabilities and assets as required by IAS 12;
10. Provisions;
11. Noncurrent interest-bearing liabilities;
12. Minority interest; and
13. Issued capital and reserves.

(IAS 1 [revised 1997], Para 66)

B. Additional Line Items on the Face of the Balance Sheet

Additional line items, headings and subtotals should be presented on the face of the balance sheet when an IAS requires it, or when such presentation is necessary to present fairly the enterprise's financial position.

(IAS 1 [revised 1997], Para 67)

C. Further Subclassifications of Line Items Presented

Further subclassifications of the line items (presented on the face of the balance sheet), classified in a manner appropriate to the enterprise's operations, should be disclosed either on the face of the balance sheet or in the notes to the financial statements. Subclassification of line items should, when appropriate, be done based on the nature of the item and, amounts payable to and receivable from the parent enterprise, fellow subsidiaries and associates and other related parties should be disclosed separately.

(IAS 1 [revised 1997], Para 72)

D. Inventories

1. The accounting policies and the cost formula used in inventory valuation.

(IAS 2, Para 34[a])

2. Total carrying amount and the breakdown of the carrying amount by appropriate subclassifications, such as merchandise, production supplies, work in progress, and finished goods.

(IAS 2, Paras 34[b] & 35)

3. Carrying amount of inventories carrying at net realizable value.

(IAS 2, Para 34[c])

4. Carrying amount of inventories pledged as security for liabilities.

(IAS 2, Para 34[f])

5. The amount of any reversal of write-down that is recognized as income, along with disclosure of circumstances or events that led to the reversal.

(IAS 2, Paras 34 [d] & [e])

6. When the cost of inventories is determined using the last-in, first-out (LIFO) formula (under the "allowed alternative treatment"), disclose the difference between the amount of inventories as shown in the balance sheet and either

    a. The lower of amount arrived at using the "benchmark treatment" and the net realizable value; or
    b. The lower of current cost at the balance sheet date and net realizable value.

    (IAS 2, Para 36)

7. Disclose either of the following:

    a. Cost of inventories reported in expense for the period; or
    b. Operating costs, applicable to revenues, recognized as expenses for the period, classified by their nature (e.g., raw materials consumed).

    (IAS 2, Para 37)

E. Property, Plant, and Equipment (PP&E)

1. In respect of each class (i.e., groupings of assets of a similar nature and use) of PP&E, the following disclosures are required:

    a. Measurement basis/bases used for the determination of the gross carrying amount; if more than one basis has been employed, then also the gross carrying amount determined in accordance with that basis in each category;
    b. The depreciation method(s) used;
    c. Either the useful lives or the depreciation rates used;
    d. The gross carrying amount and the accumulated depreciation at the beginning and the end of the period;
    e. A reconciliation of the carrying amount at the beginning and the end of the period disclosing

        (1) Additions;
        (2) Disposals;
        (3) Acquisitions by means of business combinations;
        (4) Increases/decreases resulting from revaluations and from impairment losses recognized or reversed directly in equity (if any);
        (5) Impairment losses recognized in the income statement (if any);
        (6) Impairment losses reversed in the income statement (if any);
        (7) Depreciation;
        (8) Net exchange differences arising from translation of financial statements of a foreign entity (in accordance with IAS 21); and

(9) Other changes, if any.

(Comparative information is not required for the reconciliation in e. above.)

(IAS 16 [revised 1998], Para 66)

2. Additional disclosure to be made include the following:

    a. The existence and amounts of restrictions on title, and PP&E pledged as security for liabilities;
    b. The accounting policy for restoration costs relating to items of PP&E;
    c. The amount of expenditures in respect of PP&E in the course of construction; and
    d. The amount of outstanding commitments for acquisition of PP&E.

    (IAS 16 [revised 1998], Para 67)

3. In case items of PP&E are stated at revalued amounts, disclose the following information:

    a. The basis used to revalue the items of PP&E;
    b. The effective date of revaluation;
    c. Whether an independent party prepared the valuation;
    d. The nature of the indices used to determine replacement costs;
    e. The carrying amount of each class of PP&E that would have been included in the financial statements had the assets been carried under the benchmark treatment; and
    f. The revaluation surplus, including the movements for the period in that account and disclosure of any restrictions on the distribution of the balance in the revaluation surplus account to shareholders.

    (IAS 16 [revised 1998], Para 70)

4. An enterprise should disclose information on impaired property, plant, and equipment under IAS 36 in addition to information required under IAS 16, para 60. [Refer E.1.e. (4) to (6) above.]

    (IAS 16 [revised 1998], Para 65)

5. Other recommended disclosures

    a. The carrying amount of temporarily idle PP&E;
    b. The gross carrying amount of fully depreciated PP&E still in use;
    c. The carrying amount of PP&E retired from active use and held for sale; and
    d. In cases where items of PP&E are carried at cost less accumulated depreciation (in accordance with the "benchmark treatment") the fair value of PP&E if it is materially different from the carrying amount.

    (IAS 16 [revised 1998], Para 71)

F. Intangible Assets

1. In case of each class of intangible assets, distinguishing between internally generated intangible assets and other intangible assets, the financial statements should disclose

   a. The useful lives or the amortization rates used;
   b. The amortization methods used;
   c. The gross carrying amount and the accumulated amortization (aggregated with accumulated impairment) at the beginning and at the end
   d. The line item(s) of the income statement in which the amortization of intangible assets is included;
   e. A reconciliation of the carrying amount at the beginning and the end of the period showing:

      (1) Additions, indicating separately those from internal development and through business combinations;
      (2) Retirements and disposals;
      (3) Increases or decreases resulting from revaluations and from impairment losses recognized or reversed directly in equity (if any);
      (4) Impairment losses recognized in income statement (if any);
      (5) Impairment losses reversed in the income statement (if any);
      (6) Amortization recognized;
      (7) Net exchange differences arising on translation of financial statements of a foreign entity; and
      (8) Other changes in carrying amount.

      (Comparative information is not required.)

                                                      (IAS 38, Para 107)

2. Additional disclosures with respect to intangibles are the following:

   a. If the amortization period of more than 20 years is used to amortize an intangible asset, the reasons why the presumption that the useful life will not exceed 20 years will is rebutted. The enterprise should describe the factors that were instrumental in determining the useful life of more than 20 years);
   b. In case of an individual intangible asset that is material to the financial statements as a whole, a description, the carrying amount, and the remaining amortization period;
   c. In case of intangible assets acquired by way of a government grant and initially recognized at fair value: the fair value initially recognized for these assets, their carrying amounts, and whether they are carried under the benchmark treatment or the allowed alternative treatment for subsequent measurements;

    d. The existence and the carrying amount of intangible assets pledged as security for liabilities; and

    e. The amount of commitments for the acquisition of intangible assets.

(IAS 38, Para 111)

3. In the case of intangible assets carried under the allowed alternative method (i.e., at revalued amounts), the following disclosures are prescribed:

    a. By class of intangible assets: the effective date of the revaluation, the carrying amount of revalued intangible assets, and the carrying amount that would have been included had the revalued intangible assets been carried under the benchmark treatment (i.e., at cost less accumulated amortization); and

    b. The quantum of revaluation surplus that relates to intangible assets at the beginning and the end of the period, indicating the changes during the period and any restrictions on the distributions of the balance to shareholders.

(IAS 38, Para 113)

4. The financial statements should disclose the aggregate amount of research and development expenditure recognized as an expense during the period.

(IAS 38, Para 115)

G. Other Long-Term Assets

The following items should be disclosed separately:

1. Long-term investments

    a. Disclosures about investments in subsidiaries include the following:

        (1) (a) When certain subsidiaries have not been consolidated (i.e., where control is intended to be temporary or where the subsidiary operates under severe long-term restrictions), and these instead have been accounted for as if they were passive investments, the reason(s) for not consolidating the subsidiary.

(IAS 27, Para 32 [h(i)])

        (b) The names of any enterprises in which more than one half of the voting power is owned, directly or indirectly through subsidiaries, but which, because of the absence of control, are not subsidiaries.

(IAS 27, Para 32 [b(iii)])

        (2) A parent company, which is itself a wholly (or virtually wholly) owned subsidiary, and which is not presenting consolidated finan-

cial statements, should disclose the reasons why consolidated financial statements have not been presented, together with the bases on which subsidiaries are accounted for in its separate financial statements, as well as the name and registered office of its parent that publishes consolidated financial statements.

(IAS 27, Para 8)

(3) In separate financial statements of a parent company, investments in subsidiaries that would otherwise be included in the consolidated financial statements should be either

(a) Accounted for using the equity method; or
(b) Carried at cost or revalued amounts under the parent's accounting policy for long-term investments.

A description of the method used to account for these subsidiaries should be disclosed.

(IAS 27, Para 32 [c])

(4) The following disclosures are required in consolidated financial statements (in addition to disclosures outlined above):

(a) A listing of significant subsidiaries, including the name, country of incorporation or residence, proportion of ownership interest and, if different, proportion of voting power held;

(IAS 27, Para 32 [a])

(b) The nature of relationship between the parent and a subsidiary of which the parent does not own, directly or indirectly through subsidiaries, more than one half of the voting power, but which is being accounted for as a subsidiary due to the existence of effective control;

(IAS 27, Para 32[b(ii)])

(c) The effect of the acquisition and disposal of subsidiaries on the financial position at the reporting date, and the results for the period and the corresponding amounts for the preceding period; and

(IAS 27, Para 32[b(iv)])

(d) The fact that uniform accounting policies were not used for like transactions and other events affecting the parent and the subsidiaries, together with the proportion of the items in the consolidated financial statements to which the different accounting policies have been applied, if applicable.

(IAS 27, Para 21)

b. Investments in associates

   (1) If an investment in an associate is carried at cost or revalued amounts, when the equity method would be the appropriate accounting method for the associate if the investor issued consolidated financial statements, the investor is required to disclose what would have been the effect had the equity method been applied.

(IAS 28, Para 14[b])

   (2) Investments in associates accounted for using the equity method should be classified as long-term assets and separately set forth in the balance sheet. The investor's share of profits or losses of such investments should be disclosed as a separate item in the income statement and the investor's share of any extraordinary item or prior period items should be separately disclosed as well.

(IAS 28, Para 28)

   (3) The following disclosures are also required:

   (a) An appropriate listing and description of significant associates, including the proportion of ownership interest and, if different, the proportion of voting power; and

   (b) The method(s) used to account for such investments.

(IAS 28, Para 27)

c. Other long-term investments

   (1) Mandatory disclosures

   (a) The accounting policies for

   1] The determination of the carrying amounts of investments; and

   2] The treatment of revaluation surplus upon the sale of a revalued investment.

   (b) The market value of marketable securities, if they are not carried at market values;

   (c) The fair values of investment properties, if they are accounted for as long-term investments and not carried at fair value;

   (d) Significant restrictions on the realizability of investments or the remittance of income and the proceeds of disposal;

   (e) In the case of long-term investments carried at revalued amounts

   1] The policy regarding the frequency of revaluations;

   2] The date of the latest revaluation; and

       3] The basis of revaluation and whether an external appraisal was obtained.

    (f) The changes in the revaluation surplus for the period and the nature of such changes; and

    (g) In the case of those entities whose principal business is the holding of investments, an analysis of the portfolio of investments.

(IAS 25, Para 49)

  (2) Recommended disclosures

    (a) An analysis of long-term investments by category;

    (b) The directors' assessment of the fair value of investments that are not marketable;

    (c) In the case of investments that are not marketable, the method of assessing value used for comparison with cost, where applicable;

    (d) Amount of any previous "revaluation surplus" which related to investments disposed of during the year and which had been previously distributed or converted into share capital; and

    (e) Details of any single investment which represents a significant fraction of the reporting entity's assets.

(IAS 25, Para 50)

H. Financial Instruments

  1. Mandatory disclosures

    a. For each class of either financial asset, financial liability or equity instrument, whether recognized in the balance sheet or not, disclose the following:

      (1) Information concerning the extent and nature of the instrument, including significant terms and conditions which may affect the amount, timing, or certainty of future cash flows; and

      (2) The accounting policies and methods used to account for the instruments, including relevant criteria for recognition and the basis of measurement employed.

(IAS 32, Para 47)

    b. For each class of either financial asset or financial liability, whether recognized in the balance sheet or not, disclose the following information about exposure to interest rate risk:

(1) The dates of contractual repricing or maturity, whichever comes first; and

(2) The effective interest rates, if applicable.

(IAS 32, Para 56)

c. For each class of financial asset, whether recognized in the balance sheet or not, disclose the following information about exposure to credit risk:

(1) The amount which represents the maximum credit risk exposure as of the balance sheet date, without regard to any collateral held, should the other party fail to perform under the terms of the instrument; and

(2) Any significant concentrations of credit risk.

(IAS 32, Para 66)

d. For each class of financial asset or financial liability, whether or not recognized in the balance sheet, disclose fair value information, unless this cannot be developed on a timely basis with sufficient reliability, in which case that fact must be stated, together with relevant information about the principal characteristics which would be determinative of the fair values of the instruments.

(IAS 32, Para 77)

e. When financial assets are carried at amounts in excess of fair values, disclose the following:

(1) The carrying amounts and fair values of individual assets or appropriately grouped assets; and

(2) The reasons for not presenting the assets at fair values, including the nature of any evidence supporting management's belief that the carrying amounts will be recovered.

(IAS 32, Para 88)

f. For instruments accounted for as hedges of anticipated transactions, disclose the following information:

(1) A description of the anticipated transactions, including the timing of expected occurrence;

(2) A description of the hedging instruments used; and

(3) The amount of any deferred (unrecognized) gains or losses, as well as the expected timing of recognition.

(IAS 32, Para 91)

2. Recommended disclosures

a. The total amount of change in the fair values of financial assets and liabilities which has been recognized in income or expense for the year being reported on.

b. The total amount of deferred (unrecognized) gain or loss on hedging instruments, other than those associated with anticipated transactions.

c. The average aggregate carrying amount during the year of recognized financial assets and liabilities; the average aggregate principal, stated or notional amounts of unrecognized financial assets and liabilities; and the average aggregate fair value of all financial assets and liabilities, particularly when the amounts as of the balance sheet date may not be indicative of the level of activity during the year then ended.

d. Any other information which would enhance users' understanding of the financial instruments.

(IAS 32, Para 94)

I. Provisions

1. For each class of provision:

a. The carrying amount at the beginning and end of the period;

b. Additional provisions made during the current period, including increases to existing provisions;

c. Amounts utilized (i.e., incurred and charged against the provision) during the period;

d. Unused amounts reversed during the period; and

e. The increase during the period in the discounted amount resulting from the passage of time and the effect of any change in discount rate.

(Comparative information is not required.)

(IAS 37, Para 84)

2. For each class of provision an enterprise should disclose the following:

a. A brief description of the nature of the obligation and the expected timing of resulting outflows of economic benefits;

b. An indication of any uncertainties about the amount or timing of those outflows. Where necessary, disclosure of major assumptions made concerning future events; and

c. The amount of any expected reimbursement, disclosing any asset that has been recognized for that expected reimbursement.

(IAS 37, Para 85)

3. In **extremely rare circumstances**, if some or all disclosures as outlined in IAS 37, Para 84 and 85, are expected to prejudice seriously the position of the enterprise in a dispute with other parties, an enterprise need not disclose

such information. Instead, it should disclose the general nature of the dispute, along with the fact that, and reason why, the information has not been disclosed.

(IAS 37, Para 92)

J. Deferred Tax Liabilities and Assets

1. Tax assets and tax liabilities should be presented separately from other assets and liabilities; deferred tax assets and liabilities should be distinguished from those arising from current tax expense.

(Revised IAS 12, Para 69)

2. If a classified balance sheet is presented, deferred tax assets and liabilities should not be included in current assets and liabilities.

(Revised IAS 12, Para 70)

3. Current tax assets and tax liabilities should not be offset unless there is a legally enforceable right of offset and the enterprise intends to settle on a net basis, or to realize the asset and settle the liability simultaneously.

(Revised IAS 12, Para 71)

4. Deferred tax assets and tax liabilities relating to different jurisdictions should be presented separately.

(Revised IAS 12, Para 74)

5. Deferred tax assets and tax liabilities relating to different enterprises in a group which are taxed separately by the taxation authorities should not be offset unless there is a legally enforceable right of offset.

(Revised IAS 12, Para 74)

6. When utilization of deferred tax assets is dependent upon future profitability in excess of amounts from the reversals of taxable temporary differences, and the entity has incurred losses in either the current or preceding period, the amount of deferred tax asset should be disclosed together with the nature of any evidence of its realizability.

(Revised IAS 12, Para 82)

K. Employee Benefits--Defined Benefit Pension and Other Postretirement Benefit Programs

1. The enterprise's accounting policy for recognizing actuarial gains and losses.
2. A general description of the types of plans in use.

3. A reconciliation of the assets and liabilities recognized in the balance sheet, at a minimum presenting

    a. The present values, as of the balance sheet dates, of wholly unfunded defined benefit obligations;

    b. The present values, as of the balance sheet dates, before any deduction for fair value of plan assets, of defined benefit obligations that are wholly or partially funded;

    c. The fair value of plan assets as of the balance sheet dates;

    d. Net actuarial gains or losses excluded from the balance sheets;

    e. Past service costs not yet recognized in the balance sheets;

    f. Any amounts not recognized as assets due to application of IAS 19, para 58(b); and

    g. The amounts recognized in the balance sheets.

4. The amounts included in the fair value of plan assets for

    a. Each category of the reporting enterprise's own financial instruments; and

    b. Any property occupied by, or other assets used by, the reporting enterprise.

5. A reconciliation showing changes during the period in the net liability (or asset) recognized in the balance sheets.

6. The total expense recognized in the income statements, for each of the following cost components, identifying the line item(s) of the income statement in which these are included:

    a. Current service cost;

    b. Interest cost;

    c. Expected return on plan assets;

    d. Actuarial gains or losses;

    e. Past service cost; and

    f. The effects of any curtailments or settlements.

7. The actual return on plan assets; and

8. The principal actuarial assumptions used as of the balance sheet dates, including, where applicable (to be disclosed in absolute, not relative, terms)

    a. The discount rates;

    b. The expected rates of return on any plan assets for the periods presented in the financial statements;

    c. The expected rates of salary increases (and/or changes in an index or other variable specified in the formal or constructive terms of a plan as the basis for future benefit increases);

    d. Medical cost trend rates; and

e.   Any other material actuarial assumptions used.

(Revised IAS 19, Para 120)

L.   Employee Benefits--Other Benefit Plans

1.   For defined contribution pension plans and similar arrangements, the amount recognized as expense for the period being reported upon must be disclosed.

(Revised IAS 19, Para 46)

2.   For long-term compensated absences, long-term disability plans, profit sharing or bonus arrangements or deferred compensation plans payable more than 12 months after the end of the period in which benefits are earned, and similar types of benefit plans, any disclosures which would be mandated by other international standards, such as IAS 8 and IAS 24 (there being no specific disclosures required by IAS 19).

(Revised IAS 19, Para 131)

3.   For termination benefits, disclosures mandated for contingencies by IAS 10, as well as other disclosures which may be required under other international accounting standards such as IAS 8 and IAS 24.

(Revised IAS 19, Paras 141-143)

4.   For equity compensation benefits (e.g., those relating to stock option plans and other such arrangements)

a.   The nature and terms, including vesting provisions, of the plans;
b.   The enterprise's accounting policy for such plans;
c.   The amounts recognized in the financial statements for such plans;
d.   The number and terms (including, if applicable, dividend and voting rights, conversion rights, exercise dates, exercise prices, and expiration dates) of the enterprise's own equity financial instruments which are held by equity compensation plans (and, in the event of share options, by employees) as of the beginning and end of the period being reported upon, together with indications of the extents to which vesting has occurred;
e.   The number and terms (including, if applicable, dividend and voting rights, conversion rights, exercise dates, exercise prices and expiration dates) of equity financial instruments issued by the enterprise to equity compensation plans or to employees (or of the enterprise's own equity financial instruments distributed by equity compensation plans to employees) during the period being reported upon, together with the fair value of any consideration received from the equity compensation plans or employees;

f. The number, exercise dates, and exercise prices of share options exercised under equity compensation plans during the period;

g. The number of share options held by equity compensation plans, or held by employees under such plans, that lapsed during the period; and

h. The amount and principal terms of any loans or guarantees granted by the reporting enterprise to, or on behalf of, equity compensation plans.

i. The fair values, at beginning and end of the period being reported upon, of the enterprise's own equity financial instruments, other than share options, held by equity compensation plans; and

j. The fair value, at the date of issue, of the enterprise's own equity financial instruments, other than share options, issued by the enterprise to equity compensation plans or to employees, or by the equity compensation plan to employees, during the period.

k. Whenever it is impracticable to determine the fair value of the equity financial instruments, other than share options, that fact must be disclosed.

(Revised IAS 19, Paras 147-148)

5. For short-term employee benefits, such as short-term compensated absences and profit sharing or bonus arrangements to be paid within 12 months after the end of the period in which the employees render the related services, any disclosures which would be required by other international accounting standards, such as IAS 24, must be made.

(Revised IAS 19, Para 23)

M. Leases--From the Standpoint of a Lessee

1. For finance leases

In addition to requirements of IAS 32, the revised IAS 17, Paragraph 23, mandates the following disclosures for lessees under finance leases:

a. For each class of asset, the net carrying amount at balance sheet date;

b. A reconciliation between the total of minimum lease payments at the balance sheet date, and their present value. In addition, an enterprise should disclose the total of the minimum lease payments at the balance sheet date, their present value, for each of the following periods:

(1) Due in 1 year or less,
(2) Due in more than 1 but no more than 5 years, and
(3) Due in more than 5 years.

c. Contingent rents included in profit or loss for the period.

    d. The total of minimum sublease payments to be received in the future under noncancelable subleases as of the balance sheet date.

    e. A general description of the lessee's significant leasing arrangements including, but not necessarily limited to the following:

        (1) The basis for determining contingent rentals;

        (2) The existence and terms of renewal or purchase options and escalation clauses; and

        (3) Restrictions imposed by lease arrangements such as on dividends or assumptions of further debt or further leasing.

(IAS 17 [revised 1997], Para 23)

2. For operating leases

    Lessees should, in addition to the requirements of IAS 32, make the following disclosures for operating leases:

    a. Total of the future minimum lease payments under noncancelable operating leases for each of the following periods:

        (1) Due in 1 year or less;

        (2) Due in more than 1 year but no more than 5 years; and

        (3) Due in more than 5 years.

    b. The total of future minimum sublease payments expected to be received under noncancelable subleases at the balance sheet date;

    c. Lease and sublease payments included in profit or loss for the period, with separate amounts of minimum lease payments, contingent rents, and sublease payments;

    d. A general description of the lessee's significant leasing arrangements including, but not necessarily limited to the following:

        (1) The basis for determining contingent rentals,

        (2) The existence and terms of renewal or purchase options and escalation clauses, and

        (3) Restrictions imposed by lease arrangements such as on dividends or assumption of further debt or on further leasing.

(IAS 17 [revised 1997], Para 26)

N. Leases--From the Standpoint of Lessor

1. For finance leases

    Lessors under finance leases are required to disclose, in addition to disclosures under IAS 32, the following:

a. A reconciliation between the total gross investment in the lease at the balance sheet date, and the present value of minimum lease payments receivable as of the balance sheet date, categorized into

(1) Those due in 1 year or less;
(2) Those due in more than 1 year but not more than 5 years; and
(3) Those due beyond 5 years.

b. Unearned finance income.
c. The accumulated allowance for uncollectible minimum lease payments receivable.
d. Total contingent rentals included in income.
e. A general description of the lessor's significant leasing arrangements.

(IAS 17 [revised 1997], Para 39)

2. For operating leases
    For lessors under operating leases the following expanded disclosures are prescribed:

a. For each class of asset, the gross carrying amount, the accumulated depreciation and accumulated impairment losses at the balance sheet date, including

(1) Depreciation recognized in income for the period;
(2) Impairment losses recognized in income for the period;
(3) Impairment losses reversed in income for the period.

b. Depreciation recognized on assets held for operating lease use during the period.
c. Future minimum lease payments under noncancellable operating leases, in the aggregate and classified into

(1) Those due in no more than 1 year;
(2) Those due in more than 1 but not more than 5 years; and
(3) Those due in more than 5 years.

d. Total contingent rentals included in income for the period.
e. A general description of leasing arrangements to which it is a party.

(IAS 17 [revised 1997], Para 48)

O. Stockholders' Equity

The following disclosures should be made by an enterprise either on the face of the balance sheet or in the notes:

1. For each class of share capital

a. The number of shares authorized;

    b.   The number of shares issued and fully paid, and issued but not fully paid;

    c.   Par value per share, or the fact that the shares have no par value;

    d.   A reconciliation of the number of shares outstanding at the beginning of the year to the number of shares outstanding at the end of the year;

    e.   The rights, preferences and restrictions attaching to each class of shares, including restrictions on the distribution of dividends and the repayment of capital;

    f.   Shares reserved for future issuance under options and sales contracts, including terms and amounts; and

    g.   Shares held by the enterprise itself or by subsidiaries or associates of the enterprise;

2.   For reserves within the owners' equity, a description, nature, and purpose of each reserve;

3.   For proposed dividends (i.e., those that have not formally been approved for payment) the amount included (or not included) in liabilities; and

4.   For cumulative preference dividends, the amount not recognized.

(An enterprise without share capital, such as a partnership, should disclose information equivalent to that required above, showing movements during the year in each category of equity interest and the rights, preferences, and restrictions attaching to each category of equity interest.)

(IAS 1 [Revised 1997], Para 74)

INCOME STATEMENT

A. Disclosures on the Face of the Income Statement

1.   Minimum disclosures on the face of the income statement should include the following:

    a.   Revenue;

    b.   Results of operating activities;

    c.   Finance costs;

    d.   Share of profits and losses of associates and joint ventures accounted for using the equity method;

    e.   Tax expense;

    f.   Profit or loss from ordinary activities;

    g.   Extraordinary items;

    h.   Minority interests; and

    i.   Net profit or loss for the period.

2.   Additional line items on the face of the income statement

Additional line items, headings and subtotals should be presented on the face of the income statement when required by an IAS or when such a presentation is necessary in order to fairly present the enterprise's financial performance.

(IAS 1 [revised 1997], Para 75)

B. Investments

1. Disclosure is required of the following significant amounts included in income:

   a. Interest, royalties, dividends, and rentals on long-term and current investments;
   b. Profits and losses on disposal of current investments; and
   c. Changes in value of such investments.

   (IAS 25, Para 49[b])

2. The following should be included in income:

   a. Investment income from

      (1) Interest, royalties, dividends, and rentals on long-term and current investments;
      (2) Profits and losses on disposal of current investments;
      (3) Unrealized gains and losses on current investments carried at market value, where such a policy has been adopted under IAS 25, para 31; and
      (4) Reductions in market value and reversals of such reductions needed to carry current investments at the lower of cost and market.

   b. In relation to long-term investments, reductions of the carrying amount for other than a temporary decline in value and reversals of such reductions; and
   c. Profits and losses on disposals of long-term investments, computed in accordance with the provisions of IAS 25, para 33.

   (IAS 25, Para 41)

C. Income Taxes

1. Tax expense related to profit or loss from ordinary activities should be presented on the face of the income statement.

   (Revised IAS 12, Para 77)

2. The major components of tax expense should be presented separately. These commonly would include the following:

a. Current tax expense;
b. Any adjustments recognized in the period for current tax of prior periods;
c. The amount of deferred tax expense relating to the origination and the reversal of timing differences;
d. The amount of deferred tax expense relating to changes in tax rates or the imposition of new taxes;
e. The amount of deferred tax expense or benefit relating to changes in tax rates or the imposition of new taxes;
f. The amount of the benefit arising from a previously unrecognized tax loss, tax credit, or temporary difference of a prior period that is used to reduce current taxes;
g. The amount of a benefit from a previously unrecognized tax loss, tax credit, or temporary difference of a prior period that is used to reduce deferred taxes;
h. Deferred tax expense related to a write-down of a deferred tax asset or the reversal of a write-down; and
i. The amount of tax expense relating to changes in accounting policies and correction of fundamental errors, accounted for consistent with the allowed alternative method under IAS 8.

(Revised IAS 12, Paras 79 and 80)

3. The following items also require separate disclosure:

   a. Tax expense relating to items which are charged or credited to equity;
   b. Tax expense relating to extraordinary items;
   c. An explanation of the relationship between tax expense or benefit and accounting profit or loss either (or both) as

      (1) A numerical reconciliation between tax expense or benefit and the product of accounting profit or loss times the applicable tax rate(s), with disclosure of how the rate(s) was determined; or
      (2) A numerical reconciliation between the average effective tax rate and the applicable rate, also with disclosure of how the applicable rate was determined.

   d. An explanation of changes in the applicable tax rates vs. the prior period;
   e. The amount and expiration date of deductible temporary differences, and unused tax losses and tax credits for which no deferred tax asset has been recognized;
   f. Aggregate temporary differences associated with investments in subsidiaries, branches, and associates, and interests in joint ventures, for which deferred tax liabilities have not been recognized;

g. For each type of temporary difference, and for each type of unused tax loss or unused credit, the amount of deferred tax asset and liability recognized in the balance sheet and the amount of deferred tax expense or benefit recognized in the income statement, unless otherwise apparent from changes in the balance sheet accounts; and

h. With regard to discontinued operations, the tax expense relating to the gain or loss on discontinuance and the tax expense on the profit or loss from ordinary activities of the discontinued operation.

(Revised IAS 12, Para 81)

D. Extraordinary Items

1. The net profit or loss for the period should be comprised of

a. Profit or loss from ordinary activities; and
b. Extraordinary items.

2. Each of the above components should be disclosed on the on the face of the income statement.

(IAS 8, Para 10)

3. The nature and the amount of each extraordinary item should be separately disclosed.

(IAS 8, Para 11)

E. Discontinuing Operations

1. Initial disclosure event

a. The financial statements beginning with period in which the "initial disclosure event" (as defined in IAS 35, para 16) occurs, should include the following information relating to a "discontinuing operation:"

(1) A description of the discontinuing operation;
(2) The business or geographical segment(s) in which it is reported;
(3) The date and the nature of the initial disclosure event;
(4) The date or period in which the discontinuance is expected to be completed if known or determinable;
(5) The carrying amounts, as of the balance sheet date, of the total assets and the total liabilities to be disposed of;
(6) The amounts of revenue, expenses, and pretax profit or loss from ordinary activities attributable to the discontinuing operation during the current financial reporting period, and the income tax expense relating thereto; and

(7) The amounts of net cash flows attributable to the operating, investing, and financing activities of the discontinuing operation during the current financial reporting period.

(IAS 35, Para 27)

b. If the initial disclosure event occurs after the end of an enterprise's financial reporting period but before the financial statements for that period are approved by the board of directors (or similar governing body), those financial statements should include the above disclosures as well.

(IAS 35, Para 29)

2. Disposal of assets and settlement of liabilities

On disposing of assets or settling liabilities attributable to a discontinuing operation or when an enterprise enters into binding agreements for the sale of such assets or the settlement of such liabilities, the enterprise's financial statements should include the following information on the occurrence of the event:

a. The amount of pretax gain or loss and the income tax expense relating to the gain or loss; and
b. The net selling price or range of prices, net of expected disposal costs, of the net assets for which the enterprise has entered into one or more binding sale agreements, the expected timing of the receipt of cash flows, and the carrying amount of those net assets.

(IAS 35, Para 31)

3. Updating disclosures

In addition to the disclosures required by IAS 34, paras 27 and 31 (outlined above), an enterprise should include in its financial statements for periods subsequent to the one in which the "initial disclosure event" occurs, a description of any significant changes in the amount or timing of cash flows relating to assets and liabilities to be disposed of or settled and the events causing those changes.

(IAS 35, Para 33)

4. Continuance of disclosures

The above disclosures should continue in financial statements for the periods up to and including the period in which the discontinuance is completed. If an enterprise abandons or withdraws from a plan that was previously reported as a discontinuing operation, that fact and its effect should be disclosed.

(IAS 35, Paras 35 and 36)

5. Separate disclosure for each discontinuing operation

All disclosures required by IAS 35 should be presented separately for each discontinuing operation.

(IAS 35, Para 38)

6. Presentation of disclosures
   The disclosures required by IAS 35, paras 27 to 37, may be presented either in the notes to the financial statements or on the face of the financial statements except the disclosure of the amount of the pretax gain or loss recognized on the disposal of assets or settlement of liabilities attributable to the discontinuing operations (as required by IAS 35, Para 31[a]) should be shown on the face of the income statement.

(IAS 35, Para 39)

7. Not an extraordinary item
   A discontinuing operation should be not be presented as an extraordinary item.

(IAS 35, Para 41)

8. Restatement of prior periods
   Comparative information for prior periods that is presented in financial statements prepared after the initial disclosure event should be restated to segregate continuing and discontinuing assets, liabilities, income, expenses, and cash flows in a manner similar to that required by IAS 35, Paras 27 to 43.

(IAS 35, Para 45)

9. Disclosure in interim financials
   The notes to an interim financial report should describe any significant activities or events since the end of the most recent annual reporting period relating to discontinuing operation and any significant changes in the amount or timing of cash flows relating to the assets and liabilities to be disposed of or settled.

(IAS 35, Para 47)

F. Segment Data

1. For each reportable segment based on the enterprise's primary reporting format

   a. Segment revenue, with revenue from external customers distinguished from revenue from transactions with other segments;

(IAS 14 [Revised 1997], Para 51)

b. Segment results (net profit or loss if this is computable without making arbitrary allocations; an other measure, such as gross margin, in other instances), with an indication if accounting policies other than those adopted for consolidated financial reporting have been employed;

(IAS 14 [Revised 1997], Para 52)

c. Total carrying values for segment assets;

(IAS 14 [Revised 1997], Para 55)

d. Total liabilities;

(IAS 14 [Revised 1997], Para 56)

e. Total cost incurred during the period being reported upon for acquisitions of segment assets expected to be used for greater than one period (i.e., plant assets and intangibles), determined on an accrual (not cash) basis;

(IAS 14 [Revised 1997], Para 57)

f. Total depreciation and amortization expense of segment assets during the period;

(IAS 14 [Revised 1997], Para 58)

g. (Optional but recommended) The nature and amounts of any items of segment revenue or expense that are of such size, nature, or incidence as to be relevant to explain performance;

(IAS 14 [Revised 1997], Para 59)

h. Total amounts of significant noncash expenses other than depreciation and amortization (this may be omitted if the segment cash flow data encouraged by IAS 7 is provided, however);

(IAS 14 [Revised 1997], Para 61)

i. The aggregate of the enterprise's share of the net profit or loss of associates, joint ventures, or other equity method investments, if substantially all the associates' operations are within the single segment, and, if so, the aggregate amount of the investments in those associates; and

(IAS 14 [Revised 1997], Paras 64 and 66)

j. A reconciliation between the information provided by segment and the aggregated information presented in the consolidated or enterprise financial statements (e.g., segment revenues from external customers reconciled to total revenues; segment results to the same measurement item on an enterprise-wide basis, etc.).

(IAS 14 [Revised 1997], Para 67)

2. For each reportable segment based on the enterprise's secondary reporting format

    a. If the primary reporting format is business segments, then the following should be presented:

        (1) Segment revenue from external customers by geographical area based on location of customers, for each geographical segment whose revenues from external customers is 10% or greater of total enterprise revenues from external customers;

        (2) Total carrying amount of segment assets by geographical location of assets, for each geographical segment whose segment assets are 10% or greater of total assets; and

        (3) The total cost incurred during the period to acquire segment assets expected to be used for more than one period, by geographical location of assets, for each geographical segment whose segment assets are 10% or greater of total assets.

        (IAS 14 [Revised 1997], Para 69)

    b. If the primary reporting format is geographical segments (whether based on location of assets or of customers), the following should be reported for each business segment whose revenue from external customers is 10% or greater of total enterprise revenue from external customers, **or** whose segment assets are 10% or greater of total assets of all segments:

        (1) Segment revenues from external customers;
        (2) Total carrying amounts of segment assets; and
        (3) Total cost incurred during the period to acquire segment assets expected to be used for more than one period.

        (IAS 14 [Revised 1997], Para 70)

    c. If the primary reporting format is geographical segments based on location of assets, and if location of customers differs from location of assets, then the enterprise should also report revenues from external customers for each customer-based geographical segment whose revenue from external customers is 10% or greater of total enterprise revenue from external customers.

        (IAS 14 [Revised 1997], Para 71)

    d. If the primary reporting format is geographical segments based on location of customers, and if location of customers differs from location of assets, then the enterprise should also report the following for each asset-based geographical segment whose revenue from external customers or segment assets are 10% or greater of total enterprise revenue from external customers or consolidated assets, respectively:

(1) Total carrying amount of segment assets by geographical location; and

(2) Total cost incurred during the period to acquire segment assets expected to be used for more than one period.

(IAS 14 [Revised 1997], Para 72)

3. If a business or geographical segment is not reportable because a majority of revenues are from sales to other segments, but nevertheless revenues from external customers is 10% or greater of total enterprise revenues, this fact should be disclosed and the amounts of revenues from external customers and from other segments must be stated.

(IAS 14 [Revised 1997], Para 74)

4. The bases of pricing intersegment transfers, and changes therein, should be disclosed.

(IAS 14 [Revised 1997], Para 75)

5. Changes in accounting policies for segment reporting having material effects on segment information should be disclosed, and prior period segment presented as comparative data should be restated, unless impracticable to do so. Disclosures should include description and nature of change, reasons for making the change, whether comparative data has been restated or the fact that it was impracticable to do so, and the financial effect of the change, if reasonably determinable. If segment definitions have changed and prior period data has not been restated, then the current period data should be prepared and presented under both the old and the new classification schemes, so that comparability will be preserved.

(IAS 14 [Revised 1997], Para 76)

6. The types of products and services included in each reportable business segment, and the composition of each reported geographical segment, both primary and secondary, should be disclosed unless otherwise reported in the financial statements.

(IAS 14 [Revised 1997], Para 81)

G. Construction Contracts

1. An enterprise which accounts for construction contracts in accordance with IAS 11 should disclose the following in its financial statements:

    a. The amount of contract revenue recognized as revenue in the period;

    b. The methods used to determine the contract revenue recognized in the period; and

   c.   The methods used to determine the stage of completion for contracts in progress.

(IAS 11, Para 39)

2.   Each of the following should be disclosed for the contracts in progress:

   a.   The aggregate amount of costs incurred and recognized profits (net of any recognized losses) to date;

   b.   The amount of advances received; and

   c.   The amount of retentions.

H. Foreign Currency Translation

1.   Disclosure is required of the following:

   a.   The amount of exchange differences included in net profit or loss for the period;

   b.   Net exchange differences classified as a separate component of equity, and a reconciliation of the amount of such exchange differences at the beginning and the end of the period; and

   c.   Amount of exchange differences that arose during the period and which is included in the carrying value of an asset in accordance with IAS 21, para 21 under the "allowed alternative treatment."

(IAS 21, Para 42)

2.   If the reporting currency is different from the currency of the country in which the enterprise is domiciled, disclosure is required of the following:

   a.   The reason for using a different currency; and

   b.   The reason for any change in the reporting currency.

(IAS 21, Para 43)

3.   When there is a change in classification of a significant foreign operation, the following disclosures are required:

   a.   The nature of the change;

   b.   The reason for the change;

   c.   The impact of the change in classification on the shareholders' equity; and

   d.   The impact on the net profit or loss for each period presented as if the change had occurred at the beginning of the period presented.

(IAS 21, Para 44)

4.   Disclosure is required of the method selected to translate

   a.   Goodwill arising on the acquisition of a foreign entity; and

b. Fair value adjustments to the carrying amounts of assets and liabilities arising on the acquisition of that foreign entity.

(IAS 21, Para 45)

5. A change in exchange rates occurring after the balance sheet date which is of such importance that nondisclosure would affect the ability of users of the financial statements to make proper evaluations and decisions should be disclosed.

(IAS 21, Para 46)

6. (Recommended additional disclosure) An enterprise is encouraged to disclose its foreign currency risk management policy.

(IAS 21, Para 47)

I. Business Combinations and Consolidations

1. For all business combinations, the following disclosures are required in the period in which a business combination takes place:

   a. The names and descriptions of the combining enterprises;
   b. The method of accounting for the combination;
   c. The effective date of the combination for accounting purposes; and
   d. A description of any operations of the combining entities which are to be disposed of.

(IAS 22, Para 70)

2. For business combinations accounted for as acquisitions, the following disclosures are also required:

   a. The percentage of voting shares acquired;
   b. The cost of the acquisition and the nature of the consideration paid or payable; and
   c. The nature and amount of any restructuring, plant closure, or similar costs provided for in connection with the acquisition and recognized at that time.

(IAS 22, Para 71)

3. The following disclosures are required in the financial statements:

   a. The treatment being used to account for goodwill or negative goodwill, including the amortization period;
   b. Justification of an estimated life for goodwill longer than 5 years, if applicable;
   c. Justification for an amortization method other than straight-line, if applicable, including identification of the method used; and

    d. A reconciliation of goodwill and negative goodwill at the beginning and end of the reporting period, showing

      (1) The gross amount and the accumulated amortization at the beginning of the period;

      (2) Any additional goodwill or negative goodwill recorded during the period;

      (3) Amortization charged during the period;

      (4) Any other write-offs during the period; and

      (5) The gross amount and the accumulated amortization at the end of the period.

(IAS 22, Para 72)

4. If in an acquisition the fair values of assets and liabilities obtained or of consideration paid can only be provisionally determined at the end of the period in which it occurred, this must be stated and explained. Subsequent adjustments to the provisional fair values should be disclosed and explained in the financial statements of the period in which they occur.

(IAS 22, Para 73)

5. For unitings of interests, the following disclosures are also required:

    a. A description and amount of shares issued, together with the percentage of each entity's voting shares exchanged to effect the uniting;

    b. The amounts of assets and liabilities contributed by each entity; and

    c. Sales revenue, other operating revenues, extraordinary items and net profit or loss of each enterprise prior to the date of the combination that are included in the net profit or loss of the combined entity as reported in the financial statements.

(IAS 22, Para 74)

6. If a business combination occurs after the date of the financial statements, the disclosures set forth above should nonetheless be made, unless impractical to do so, in which case that fact should be stated.

(IAS 22, Para 76)

J. Earnings per Share

1. Enterprises should present both basic EPS and diluted EPS on the face of the income statement for each class of ordinary shares that has a different right to share in the net profit for the period. Equal prominence should be given to both the basic EPS and diluted EPS figures for all periods presented.

(IAS 33, Para 47)

2. Enterprises should present basic EPS and diluted EPS even if the amounts disclosed are negative. In other words, the standard mandates disclosure of not just **earnings per share** but even **loss per share** figures.

(IAS 33, Para 48)

3. Enterprises should disclose amounts used as the numerator in calculating basic EPS and diluted EPS along with a reconciliation of those amounts to the net profit or loss for the period. Disclosure is also required of the weighted-average number of ordinary shares used as the denominator in calculating basic EPS and diluted EPS along with a reconciliation of these denominators to each other.

(IAS 33, Para 49)

4. a. In addition to the disclosure of the figures for basic EPS and diluted EPS, as required above, if an enterprise **chooses to disclose** per share amounts using a reported component of net profit, other than net profit or loss for the period attributable to ordinary shareholders, such amounts should be calculated using weighted-average number of ordinary shares determined in accordance with the requirements of IAS 33; this will ensure comparability of the per share amounts disclosed;

    b. In cases where an enterprise chooses to disclose the above per share amounts using a component of net profit not reported as a line item in the income statement, a reconciliation is mandated by the standard, which should reconcile the difference between the component of net income used with a line item reported in the income statement; and

    c. When additional disclosure is made by an enterprise of the above per share amounts, basic and diluted per share amounts should be disclosed with equal prominence (just as basic EPS and diluted EPS figures are given equal prominence).

(IAS 33, Para 51)

5. Enterprises are encouraged to disclose the terms and conditions of financial instruments or contracts generating potential ordinary shares, since such terms and conditions may determine whether or not any potential ordinary shares are dilutive and, if so, the effect on the weighted-average number of shares outstanding and any consequent adjustments to the net profit attributable to the ordinary shareholders.

(IAS 33, Para 50)

6. If changes (resulting from bonus issue or share split etc.) in the number of ordinary or potential ordinary shares occur, after the balance sheet date but before issuance of the financial statements, and the per share calculations

reflect such changes in the number of shares, such a fact should be disclosed.

(IAS 33, Para 43)

7. Enterprises are also encouraged to disclose a description of ordinary share transactions or potential ordinary share transactions, **other than capitalization issues** and **share splits**, occurring after the balance sheet date and which are of such importance that nondisclosure would affect the ability of the users of the financial statements to make proper evaluations and decisions.

(IAS 33, Para 45)

K. Dividends per Share

An enterprise should disclose, either on the face of the income statement or in the notes, the amount of dividends per share, declared or proposed, for the period covered by the financial statements.

(IAS 1 [Revised 1997], Para 85)

L. Impairments of Assets

1. For each class of assets, the financial statements should disclose:

    a. The amount of impairment losses recognized in the income statement during the period and the line item(s) of the income statements in which those impairment losses are included;
    b. The amount of reversals of impairment losses recognized in the income statement during the period and the line item(s) of the income statement in which those impairment losses are reversed;
    c. The amount of impairment losses recognized directly in equity during the period; and
    d. The amount of reversals of impairment losses recognized directly in equity during the period.

(IAS 36, Para 113)

2. If impairment loss for an asset or a cash-generating unit is recognized or reversed during the period and is **material** to the financial statements as a whole, an enterprise should disclose:

    a. Events and circumstances that led to the recognition or reversal of the impairment loss;
    b. Amount of the impairment loss recognized or reversed;
    c. For an individual asset, its nature and the primary reportable segment to which it belongs, based on the enterprise's primary format (as defined in IAS 14, if that IAS applies to the enterprise);

d. For a cash-generating unit, a description of the cash-generating unit, the amount of the impairment loss recognized or reversed by the class of assets and by the reportable segment based on the enterprise's primary format (as defined by IAS 14, if that IAS applies to the enterprise) and if the aggregation of assets for identifying the cash-generating unit has changed since the previous estimate of the cash-generating unit's recoverable amount (if any), the enterprise should describe the current and former manner of aggregating assets and the reasons for the change;

e. Whether the recoverable amount of the asset (cash-generating unit) is its net selling price or its value in use;

f. The basis used to determine net selling price (such as with reference to an active market or any other manner) in case the recoverable amount is net selling price; and

g. If recoverable amount is value in use, the discount rate(s) used in the current estimate and previous estimate (if any) of value in use.

(IAS 36, Para 117)

3. If impairment losses recognized (reversed) during the period are **material** in aggregate to the financial statements of the enterprise as a whole, an enterprise should disclose a brief description of the following:

a. The main classes of assets affected by impairment losses (reversals of impairment losses) for which no information is disclosed under IAS 36, para 117); and

b. The main events and circumstances that led to the recognition (reversal) of these impairment losses for which no information is disclosed under IAS 36, para 117).

(IAS 36, Para 118)

CASH FLOW STATEMENT

A. Basis of Presentation

1. A cash flow statement (CFS) should be prepared in accordance with IAS 7 and presented as an integral part of an enterprise's financial statements for each period for which the financial statements are presented.

(IAS 7, Para 1)

2. The CFS should report cash flows during the period, classified by

a. Operating activities;
b. Investing activities; and
c. Financing activities.

(IAS 7, Para 10)

B. Format

1. Cash flows from operating activities should be reported using either

   a. The direct method, under which major classes of gross cash receipts and gross cash payments are disclosed; **or**

   b. The indirect method, wherein net profit or loss for the period is adjusted for the following:

      (1) The effects of noncash transactions;

      (2) Any deferrals or accruals of past or future operating cash receipts or payments; and

      (3) Items of income or expense related to investing or financing cash flows.

   (IAS 7, Para 18)

2. An enterprise should generally report (separately) major gross cash receipts and payments from investing and financing activities.

   (IAS 7, Para 21)

3. Under the following circumstances, however, an enterprise's* cash flows arising from operating, investing, or financing activities may be reported on a net basis:

   a. Cash receipts and payments on behalf of customers when the cash flows reflect the activities of the customer rather than those of the enterprise; and

   b. Cash receipts and payments for items in which the turnover is quick, the amounts are large, and maturities are short.

   (IAS 7, Para 22)

4. Cash flows arising from extraordinary items should be classified as either

   a. Operating activities;

   b. Investing activities; or

---

* *Cash flows of financial institutions may be reported on a net basis under the following cases:*

   1. *Cash flows from the acceptance and repayment of deposits with fixed maturity dates;*

   2. *Placement of deposits with and withdrawal of deposits from other financial institutions; and*

   3. *Cash advances and loans made to customers and the repayment of those advances and loans.*

   (IAS 7, Para 24)

c.   Financing activities.

Each of these items should be disclosed separately.

(IAS 7, Para 29)

5.   Cash flows from interest received and dividends received and dividends paid should be classified consistently (from period to period) as either

a.   Operating activities;
b.   Investing activities; or
c.   Financing activities.

Each of these items should be disclosed separately.

(IAS 7, Para 31)

6.   In relation to cash and cash equivalents, a cash flow statement should

a.   Disclose the policy which it adopts in determining the components;
b.   Disclose the components; and
c.   Present a reconciliation of the amounts in its CFS with similar items reported in the balance sheet.

(IAS 7, Paras 45 & 46)

7.   The effect of exchange rate changes on cash and cash equivalents held or due in foreign currency should be presented separately from cash flows from operating, investing and financing activities.

(IAS 7, Para 28)

8.   Noncash transactions arising from investing and financing activities should be excluded from the CFS. Such transactions do not require the use of cash and cash equivalents and thus should be disclosed elsewhere in the financial statements by way of a note that provides all the relevant information about these activities.

(IAS 7, Para 43)

9.   Cash payments and receipts relating to taxes on income should be separately disclosed and classified as cash flows from operating activities unless they could specifically be identified with financing and/or investing activities.

(IAS 7, Para 35)

10.   In relation to acquisitions or disposals of subsidiaries or other business units which should be presented separately and classified as investing activities, an enterprise should disclose the following:

a.   The total purchase or sale price;

b.   Portion of the consideration discharged by cash and cash equivalents;
c.   Amount of cash and cash equivalents acquired or disposed; and
d.   Amount of assets and liabilities (other than cash or cash equivalents) summarized by major category.

(IAS 7, Para 40)

11.   Significant cash and cash equivalent balances held by the enterprise which are not available for use by the group should be disclosed by the enterprise along with a commentary by management.

(IAS 7, Para 48)

C.   Additional Recommended Disclosures

Additional disclosures which may be relevant to financial statement users in understanding an enterprise's financial position and liquidity have been encouraged by IAS 7 and include the following:

1.   The amount of undrawn borrowing facilities including disclosure of restrictions, if any, as to their use;
2.   The aggregate amount of cash flows related to interests in joint ventures reported using the proportionate consolidation;
3.   The aggregate amount of cash flows that represent increases in operating capacity separately from those cash flows that are required to maintain the operating capacity; and
4.   Disclosure of segmental cash flow information in order to provide financial statement users better information about the relationship of cash flows of the business as a whole vis-à-vis cash flows from its segments.

(IAS 7, Para 50)

STATEMENT OF CHANGES IN EQUITY

A.   Statement of Changes in Equity

As a separate component of its financial statements, an enterprise should present a statement showing the following six items:

1.   The net profit or loss for the period;
2.   Each item of income and expense, gain or loss which, as prescribed by other Standards, is recognized directly in equity, and the total of these items;
3.   The cumulative effect of changes in accounting policy and the correction of fundamental errors dealt with under the Benchmark Treatment in IAS 8;
4.   Capital transactions with owners and distributions to owners;
5.   The balance of retained earnings (referred to as "accumulated profit or loss") at the beginning of the period and at the balance sheet date, and the movements for the period; and

6. A reconciliation between the carrying amount of each class of equity capital, share premium and each reserve at the beginning and the end of the period, separately disclosing each movement.

(IAS 1 [Revised 1997], Para 86)

B. Statement of Recognized Gains and Losses

1. As an alternative to the "Statement of Changes in Equity," an enterprise may present as a separate component of its financial statements, a "Statement of Recognized Gains and Losses" showing the following three items:

   a. The net profit or loss for the period;
   b. Each item of income and expense, gain or loss which, as prescribed by other Standards, is recognized directly in equity, and the total of these items; and
   c. The cumulative effect of changes in accounting policy and the correction of fundamental errors dealt with under the benchmark treatment in IAS 8.

2. When a "Statement of Recognized Gains and Losses" is presented (as an alternative to the "Statement of Changes in Equity") the following three items are presented in the notes to the financial statements:

   a. Capital transactions with owners and distributions to owners;
   b. The balance of retained earnings (referred to as "accumulated profit or loss") at the beginning of the period and at the balance sheet date, and the movements for the period; and
   c. A reconciliation between the carrying amount of each class of equity capital, share premium and each reserve at the beginning and the end of the period, separately disclosing each movement.

(IAS 1 [Revised 1997], Para 86)

NOTES TO THE FINANCIAL STATEMENTS

A. Structure of the Notes

1. The notes to the financial statements should

   a. Present information regarding the basis of preparation of the financial statements and the specific accounting policies selected and applied for significant transactions and events;
   b. Disclose information required by IAS which is not presented elsewhere in the financial statements; and

   c. Provide additional information which is not presented on the face of the financial statements but which is necessary for a fair presentation.

(IAS 1 [Revised 1997], Para 91)

2. The notes to the financial statements should be presented in a systematic manner. Each item on the face of the balance sheet, income statement and cash flow statement should be cross-referenced to any related information in the notes to the financial statements.

(IAS 1 [Revised 1997], Para 92)

3. The following order of presentation of the notes is normally adopted which assists users of financial statements in understanding them and comparing them with those of other enterprises:

   a. Statement of compliance with IAS;
   b. Statement of the measurement basis/bases and accounting policies applied;
   c. Supporting information for items presented on the face of each financial statement in the order in which each line item and each financial statement is presented; and
   d. Other disclosures, including

      (1) Contingencies and commitments and other financial disclosures; and
      (2) Nonfinancial disclosures.

(IAS 1 [Revised 1997], Para 94)

B. Accounting Policies

1. The accounting policies section of the notes to the financial statements should describe the following:

   a. The measurement basis (bases) used in preparing the financial statements; and
   b. Each specific accounting policy that is necessary for a proper understanding of the financial statements.

(IAS 1 [Revised 1997], Para 97)

2. Examples of accounting policies that an enterprise may consider presenting include, but are not restricted to, the following:

   a. Revenue recognition;
   b. Basis of consolidation of subsidiaries and method of accounting for investments in associates;
   c. Business combinations;

    d. Joint ventures;

    e. Recognition and depreciation/amortization of tangible and intangible assets;

    f. Capitalization of borrowing costs and other expenditures;

    g. Construction contracts;

    h. Investment properties;

    i. Financial instruments and investments;

    j. Leases;

    k. Research and development costs;

    l. Inventories;

    m. Taxes, including deferred taxes;

    n. Provisions;

    o. Employee benefit costs;

    p. Foreign currency translation and hedging;

    q. Definition of business and geographical segments and the basis for allocation of costs between segments;

    r. Definition of cash and cash equivalents;

    s. Inflation accounting; and

    t. Government grants.

(IAS 1 [Revised 1997], Para 99)

INTERIM FINANCIAL STATEMENTS

A. Minimum Components of an Interim Financial Report

An interim financial report should include, at a minimum, the following components:

1. A condensed balance sheet;

2. A condensed income statement;

3. A condensed statement showing **either** all changes in equity **or** changes in equity other than those arising from capital transactions with owners and distributions to owners;

4. A condensed cash flow statement; and

5. Selected set of footnote disclosures.

(IAS 34, Para 8)

B. Form and Content of Interim Financial Statements

1. If an enterprise chooses the "complete set of (interim) financial statements" route, instead of opting for the shortcut method of presenting only "condensed" interim financial statements, then the form and content of

those statements should conform to the requirements of IAS 1 (revised 1997) for a complete set of financial statements.

(IAS 34, Para 9)

2. However, if an enterprise opts for the condensed format of interim financial reporting, then IAS 34, paragraph 10, requires that, at a minimum, those condensed financial statements should include

    a. Each of the headings, and
    b. Subtotals that were included in the enterprise's most recent annual financial statements, along with selected explanatory notes, prescribed by the standard.

    (Additional line items or notes should be included if their omission would make the condensed interim financial statements misleading.)

(IAS 34, Para 10)

3. Basic and diluted earnings per share should be presented on the face of an income statement, complete or condensed, for an interim period.

(IAS 34, Para 11)

4. An interim financial report should be prepared on a consolidated basis if the enterprise's most recent annual financial statements were consolidated statements. As regards presentation of separate interim financial statements of the parent company in addition to consolidated interim financial statements, if they were included in the most recent annual financial statements, this standard neither requires nor prohibits such inclusion in the interim financial report of the enterprise.

(IAS 34, Para 14)

C. Selected Explanatory Notes

The minimum disclosures required to accompany the condensed interim financial statements are the following:

1. A statement that the same accounting policies and methods of computation are applied in the interim financial statements compared with the most recent annual financial statements or if those policies or methods have changed, a description of the nature and effect of the change;
2. Explanatory comments about seasonality or cyclicality of interim operations;
3. The nature and magnitude of significant items affecting interim results that are unusual because of nature, size, or incidence;
4. Dividends paid, either in the aggregate or on a per share basis, presented separately for ordinary (common) shares and other classes of shares;

5. Revenue and operating result for business segments or geographical segments, whichever has been the entity's primary mode of segment reporting;

6. Any significant events occurring subsequent to the end of the interim period;

7. Issuances, repurchases, and repayments of debt and equity securities;

8. The nature and quantum of changes in estimates of amounts reported in prior interim periods of the current financial year or changes in estimates of amounts reported in prior financial years, if those changes have a material effect in the current interim period;

9. The effect of changes in the composition of the enterprise during the interim period like business combinations, acquisitions or disposal of subsidiaries and long-term investments, restructuring, and discontinuing operations; and

10. The changes in contingent liabilities or contingent assets since the most recent annual report.

(IAS 34, Para 16)

DISCLOSURES FOR BANKS AND SIMILAR FINANCIAL INSTITUTIONS (IAS 30)

A. Income Statement

1. The income statement of a bank should be presented in a manner that groups income and expenses by nature and discloses the amounts of the principal types of income and expenses.

2. Disclosures in the income statement or in the footnotes should include, but are not limited to, the following items:

   a. Interest and similar income
   b. Interest expense and similar charges
   c. Dividend income
   d. Fee and commission income
   e. Fee and commission expense
   f. Gains less losses arising from dealing securities
   g. Gains less losses arising from investment securities
   h. Gains less losses arising from dealing in foreign currencies
   i. Other operating income
   j. Losses on loans and advances
   k. General and administrative expenses
   l. Other operating expenses

(IAS 30, Paras 9 and 10)

B. Balance Sheet

1. The balance sheet of a bank should group assets and liabilities by nature and list them in the order of their respective liquidity. These are to be made either on the face of the balance sheet or in footnotes.

2. The disclosures should include, but are not limited to

   a. Assets

      (1) Cash and balances with the central bank.
      (2) Treasury bills and other bills eligible for rediscounting with the central bank.
      (3) Government and other securities held for dealing purposes.
      (4) Placements with, and loans and advances to, other banks.
      (5) Other money market placements.
      (6) Loans and advances to customers.
      (7) Investment securities.

   b. Liabilities

      (1) Deposits from other banks.
      (2) Other money market deposits.
      (3) Amounts owed to other depositors.
      (4) Certificates of deposits.
      (5) Promissory notes and other liabilities evidenced by paper.
      (6) Other borrowed funds.

3. These disclosures, to be incorporated into the bank's income statement, are in addition to disclosure requirements of other international accounting standards.

(IAS 30, Paras 18 and 19)

4. The market value of dealing securities and marketable investment securities should be disclosed if these values are different from the carrying amounts in the financial statements.

(IAS 30, Para 24)

C. Contingencies and Commitments Including Off-Balance-Sheet Items
The disclosures required in this regard are the following:

1. The nature and amount of commitments to extend credit that are irrevocable because they cannot be withdrawn at the discretion of the bank without incurring significant penalty or expenses

2. The nature and amount of contingencies and commitments arising from off-balance-sheet items, including those relating to

a. Direct credit substitutes, which include general guarantees of indebtedness, bank acceptances, and standby letters of credit, which serve as financial backup for loans and securities;

b. Transaction-related contingencies, which include performance bonds, bid bonds, warranties, and standby letters of credit related to particular transactions;

c. Trade-related contingencies, which are self-liquidating and short-term trade-related contingencies arising from the movement of goods, such as documentary credit wherein the underlying goods are used as security for the bank credit; sometimes referred to as trust receipts, or simply as "TR";

d. Sales and repurchase agreements that are not reflected or recognized on the bank's balance sheet;

e. Interest and foreign exchange rate related items, which include items such as options, futures, and swaps; and

f. Other commitments, including other off-balance-sheet items such as revolving underwriting facilities and note issuance facilities.

(IAS 30, Para 26)

D. Maturities of Assets and Liabilities

An analysis of assets and liabilities into relevant maturity groupings based on the remaining period at the balance sheet date to the contractual maturity date should be disclosed.

(IAS 30, Para 30)

E. Concentrations of Assets and Liabilities

1. Any significant concentration of assets, liabilities, and off-balance-sheet items should be disclosed. Such disclosures should be made in terms of geographical areas, customer or industry groups, or other concentrations of risk.

2. The amount of significant net foreign currency exposures should be disclosed.

(IAS 30, Para 40)

F. Losses on Loans and Advances

1. The following disclosures are prescribed with respect to "losses on loans and advances":

a. The accounting policy describing the basis on which uncollectible loans and advances are recognized as an expense and written off;

b. Details of the movements in the provision for losses on loans and advances during the period, disclosing separately the amount charged to income in the period for losses on uncollectible loans and advances, the amount charged in the period for loans and advances written off and the amount credited in the period for loans and advances previously written off that have been recovered;

c. The aggregate amount of the provision for losses on loans and advances at the balance sheet date; and

d. The aggregate amount included in the balance sheet for loans and advances on which interest is not being accrued and the basis used to determine the carrying amount of such loans and advances.

(IAS 30, Para 43)

2. Any amounts set aside in respect of losses on loans and advances in addition to those losses that have been specifically identified, or potential losses which experience indicates are present in the portfolio of loans and advances, should be accounted for as appropriations of retained earnings. Any credits resulting from the reduction of such amounts should be treated as increases in retained earnings and not included in the determination of net income.

(IAS 30, Para 44)

G. General Banking Risks

Any amounts set aside in respect of general banking risks, including future losses and other unforeseeable risks or contingencies in addition to those for which accrual must be made under IAS 10, should be separately disclosed as appropriations of retained earnings. Any credits resulting from the reduction of such amounts result in an increase in retained earnings and are not included in the determination of net income.

(IAS 30, Para 50)

H. Assets Pledged as Security

The aggregate amount of secured liabilities and the nature and carrying amount of the assets pledged as security should be disclosed.

(IAS 30, Para 53)

I. Related-Party Transactions

When a bank has entered into transactions with related parties, the nature of the relationship, the type of transaction, and the elements of the transaction should be disclosed. The elements that are to be disclosed include the bank's lending policy to related parties and, in respect of related-party transactions, the amount included in or the proportion of

1. Each of loans and advances, deposits and acceptances, and promissory notes--disclosures may include the aggregate amounts outstanding at the beginning and end of the year as well as changes in these accounts during the year;
2. Each of the principal types of income, interest expense, and commissions paid;
3. The amount of the expense recognized in the period for the losses on loans and advances and the amount of the provision at the balance sheet date; and
4. Irrevocable commitments and contingencies and commitments from off-balance-sheet items.

(IAS 30, Para 58)

J. Trust Activities

If a bank is engaged in significant trust activities--wherein banks commonly act as trustees and in other fiduciary capacities that result in the holding or placing of assets on behalf of individuals, trusts, retirement benefit plans and other institutions, and such relationships are legally supported--disclosure of that fact and an indication of the extent of those activities should be made.

(IAS 30, Para 55)